Mergers, Acquisitions, and Buyouts

A Transactional Analysis of the Governing Tax, Legal, and Accounting Considerations

June 2003 Edition

Martin D. Ginsburg
Georgetown University Law Center

Jack S. Levin
Kirkland & Ellis

Volume 3
Chapters 12–17

Volume Co-authors
Donald E. Rocap
William R. Welke
Patrick C. Gallagher
James D. Sonda
Theodore L. Freedman

This volume is current through June 30, 2003

PUBLISHERS

1185 Avenue of the Americas, New York, NY 10036
www.aspenpublishers.com

Copyright © 2003 by Jack S. Levin and The Chicago Classical Recording Foundation

Printed in the United States of America

Library of Congress Catolog No. 94-74474

ISBN 0-7355-3854-9 Volume 3
ISBN 0-7355-3851-4 Set

About Aspen Publishers

Aspen Publishers, headquartered in New York City, is a leading information provider for attorneys, business professionals, and law students. Written by preeminent authorities, our products consist of analytical and practical information covering both U.S. and international topics. We publish in the full range of formats, including updated manuals, books, periodicals, CDs, and online products.

Our proprietary content is complemented by 2,500 legal databases, containing over 11 million documents available through our Loislaw division. Aspen Publishers also offers a wide range of topical legal and business databases linked to Loislaw's primary material. Our mission is to provide accurate, timely, and authoritative content in easily accessible formats, supported by unmatched customer care.

Other Aspen Publishers products treating tax issues include:

Structuring Venture Capital, Private Equity, and Entrepreneurial Transactions

Multistate Corporate Tax Guide

Corporate Tax Planning: Takeovers, Leveraged Buyouts, and Restructuring

Venture Capital and Public Offering Negotiation

Corporate Finance and Securities Laws

Tax Planning for Troubled Corporations

Financial Products: Taxation, Regulation, and Design

To order any Aspen Publishers title, go to *www.aspenpublishers.com* or call 1-800-638-8437.

For more information on Loislaw products, go to *www.loislaw.com* or call 1-800-364-2512.

For Customer Care issues, e-mail *CustomerCare@aspenpublishers.com*; call 1-800-234-1660; or fax 1-800-901-9075.

Aspen Publishers
A Wolters Kluwer Company

SUBSCRIPTION NOTICE

This Aspen Publishers product is revised twice a year to reflect important changes in the subject matter. If you purchased this product directly from Aspen Publishers, we have already recorded your subscription for the update service.

If, however, you purchased this product from a bookstore and wish to receive future updates and revised or related volumes billed separately with a 30-day examination review, please contact our Customer Service Department at 1-800-234-1660 or send your name, company name (if applicable), address, and the title of the product to:

Aspen Publishers
7201 McKinney Circle
Frederick, MD 21704

About the Authors

Martin D. Ginsburg is Professor of Law at Georgetown University Law Center in Washington, D.C. His professional corporation is of counsel to the firm of Fried, Frank, Harris, Shriver & Jacobson.

Professor Ginsburg attended Cornell University, stood very low in his class, and played on the golf team. He graduated magna cum laude from Harvard Law School which, in those years, did not field a golf team.

Professor Ginsburg entered private practice in New York City in 1958. Although beloved by partners, clients, and opposing counsel, including Mr. Levin, he withdrew from full-time practice when appointed the Beekman Professor of Law at Columbia Law School. He moved to Georgetown University in 1980 when his wife obtained a good job in Washington.

In the interim, Professor Ginsburg served as Chairman of the Tax Section of the New York State Bar Association, Chairman of the Committee on Taxation of the Association of the Bar of the City of New York, Chairman of the Committee on Simplification of the Section of Taxation of the American Bar Association, Member of the Advisory Group to the Commissioner of Internal Revenue, and Member of the Advisory Group to the Tax Division of the Department of Justice. Since 1974 Professor Ginsburg has acted as Consultant to the American Law Institute's Federal Income Tax Project on the revision of the corporate and partnership tax laws; from 1984 to 1987 he was a member of the ABA Tax Section Council where he performed no useful service at all.

In addition to Columbia and Georgetown, he has taught at New York University School of Law (Adjunct Professor 1967-79 and Visiting Professor 1993), Stanford Law School (Visiting Professor 1978), the University of Leiden in Holland (1982), the Salzburg Seminar in Austria (1984), Harvard Law School (Visiting Professor 1986), and the University of Chicago Law School (Visiting Professor 1990).

In 1986, someone who probably prefers never to be identified endowed a Chair in Taxation in his name at Georgetown; no one appears willing to occupy the Ginsburg Chair, and it remains vacant. In 1993 the National Women's Political Caucus gave Professor Ginsburg its "Good Guy" award; history reveals no prior instance of a tax lawyer held to be a "Good Guy," or even a "Decent Sort."

Professor Ginsburg is a Fellow of the American College of Tax Counsel, a frequent speaker at tax seminars, mainly in warm climates, and the author of a ghastly number of articles on corporate and partnership taxation, business acquisitions, and other stimulating things. Professor Ginsburg's spouse was a lawyer before she found better work. Their older child was a lawyer before she became a schoolteacher. The younger child, when he feels grumpy, threatens to become a lawyer.

Jack S. Levin, through his professional corporation, is a senior partner in the law firm of Kirkland & Ellis, where it is widely rumored that the professional corporation does more of the work than does Mr. Levin. In person he has also long been a lecturer at the University of Chicago Law School and the Harvard Law School, teaching a course on *Structuring Venture Capital, Private Equity, and Entrepreneurial Transactions.*

Mr. Levin graduated summa cum laude from the Northwestern University School of Business in 1958, where unlike Professor Ginsburg he was not on the golf team. In May 1958 Mr. Levin won the Illinois Gold Medal on the CPA examination, an accomplishment secretly admired by Professor Ginsburg.

In 1961 Mr. Levin graduated summa cum laude from the Harvard Law School, ranking first in a class of 500, and served as Recent Case Editor of the Harvard Law Review, accomplishments that required no athletic prowess at all.

After graduation Mr. Levin served as law clerk to Chief Judge J. Edward Lumbard of the United States Court of Appeals for the Second Circuit and later as Assistant to the Solicitor General of the United States for tax matters under Archibald Cox and Thurgood Marshall, where he argued numerous cases to the U.S. Supreme Court and the Federal Courts of Appeals and slowly began to develop the modest tennis game in which he still takes immodest pride.

Mr. Levin is author of an exciting 1000 page book *Structuring Venture Capital, Private Equity, and Entrepreneurial Transactions,* which he has updated and republished each year since 1994 (Aspen Publishers) with the invaluable assistance of Professor Ginsburg who serves as a special editor, allowing Professor Ginsburg to claim credit for the many creative and few well written portions.

Mr. Levin is a frequent speaker at major tax institutes, Practising Law Institute programs, and ALI-ABA seminars, mainly in warm climates, and venture capital/private equity conferences, mainly at ski resorts, and has also authored numerous articles and chapters of books on a variety of interesting tax and venture capital topics, although, to the best of anyone's knowledge, no one has ever read any of them.

Mr. Levin is a member of the American College of Tax Counsel and the Tax Advisory Group to the American Law Institute's Federal Income Tax Project on the Revision of the Corporate Tax Laws.

Over past times Mr. Levin has also served as a member of the Harvard Board of Overseers Committee for visiting the Harvard Law School, Chairman of the ABA Subcommittee on Corporate Distributions, Chairman of the Chicago Federal Tax Forum, Chairman of the Harvard Law School Fund Raising Drives in 1986, 1991, 1996, and 2001, a member of the Little, Brown & Company and the CCH Tax Advisory Boards, an Executive Committee member of the Chicago Bar Association's Taxation Committee, Chairman of the Lawyers Division of the Chicago Jewish United Fund, president of the Birchwood Club, board member of The Mid-America Club, and, more important, for 13 years as Parliamentarian of the Winnetka Town Meeting (Winnetka, Illinois, being for the very few who do not know, the nation's model for honest and efficient government as described further below).

Through many patient years of practice and the selection of an extraordinary partner, Mr. Levin won the Kirkland & Ellis doubles tennis tournament four successive times during the summers of 1987 through 1991, and it has been downhill ever since.

Overcoming a lifetime of fear, Mr. Levin some years ago at age 45 (through his professional corporation, in case of debilitating injury) took up downhill skiing, a sport he enthusiastically pursues shoulder-to-shoulder with a number of his venture capital clients, who (unlike Mr. Levin) are professional risk takers.

In May 2000 the American Jewish Committee presented Mr. Levin the Learned Hand Award for contributions to his profession and the community. Although disagreeing with AJC's selection, Professor Ginsburg nevertheless delivered a warm keynote address entitled A Salute To Imperfection, while Justice Ruth Bader Ginsburg, the family's better part, presented the award.

In December 2002 the Illinois Venture Capital Association presented Mr. Levin with a lifetime achievement award for service to the venture capital industry, an honor Professor Ginsburg questioned, only in small part because not asked to speak at the awards dinner.

While neither Mr. Levin nor Professor Ginsburg has ever achieved election to any public office, Mr. Levin's wife Sandy (the family's socially useful member) has at various times been elected President of the Winnetka Public School Board and a Trustee of the Winnetka Village Council. As Winnetka elected officials serve without monetary compensation, Mr. Levin devotes most of his time to the remunerative practice of law, less to teaching, none to the professional tennis or skiing circuits. Jack and Sandy have four daughters, two with law degrees and three with MBAs, four sons-in-law, one with a law degree and three with MBAs, and ten grandchildren, none of whom have yet graduated from anything.

Donald E. Rocap is a partner in the Chicago office of Kirkland & Ellis, where he specializes in the tax aspects of complex transactions. He is a lecturer at the University of Chicago Law School. Mr. Rocap received his undergraduate degree from Duke University and his J.D. from the University of Virginia Law School, where he was a member of the Order of the Coif and, more noteworthy, a member of the Law School's championship soccer team. Prior to joining Kirkland & Ellis, Mr. Rocap was Deputy Tax Legislative Counsel (Regulatory Affairs) at the U.S. Treasury Department's Office of Tax Policy. Since joining Kirkland & Ellis, he has studiously avoided playing competitive tennis with Mr. Levin.

William R. Welke is a partner in the Chicago office of Kirkland & Ellis. He received his undergraduate degree from the Massachusetts Institute of Technology and graduated magna cum laude from the University of Michigan Law School. He is a frequent writer and speaker on tax issues.

Patrick C. Gallagher is a partner with the New York office of Kirkland & Ellis. He received his J.D. from Harvard Law School with honors, an M.A. degree from the University of Chicago, and a B.A. degree from Pomona College. Since 1993, Mr. Gallagher has been a member of the Executive Committee of the New York State Bar Association Tax Section, and has co-chaired from time to time the NYSBA Tax Section's committees on consolidated returns, reorganizations, corporations, and partnerships. He has co-authored numerous articles and bar association reports.

James D. Sonda is a partner in the Chicago office of Kirkland & Ellis. He received a B.A. in Economics from the University of Michigan and also has attended Columbia University. He graduated magna cum laude from the University of Michigan Law School. Following graduation, he was named a Humphrey Fellow in Law and Economics. Mr. Sonda has received a Ph.D. in Economics. Mr. Sonda has broad litigation experience in a wide range of commercial matters and is an expert in the application of economics to legal issues.

Theodore L. Freedman is a partner in the New York office of Kirkland & Ellis, where he specializes in business insolvency, bankruptcy, and workouts (with an emphasis on Chapter 11 reorganizations and creditors' rights laws). Mr. Freedman is a graduate of Lawrence University and Northwestern University Law School, where he graduated with honors and served as Executive Editor of the Northwestern University Law Review. He has lectured and served on panels discussing bankruptcy and creditors' rights matters and is the author/managing editor of Collier International Business Insolvency Guide (Lexis Publishing 2002).

Acknowledgments

The authors wish to thank Jeffrey T. Sheffield, George B. Javaras, Todd F. Maynes, Keith E. Villmow, H. Kurt von Moltke, Steven E. Clemens, Thomas L. Evans, Daneen Jachino, Kevin J. Coenen, Olga A. Loy, Lee E. Allison, Gregory W. Gallagher, Michael J. Hauswirth, Natalie H. Keller, David C. Kung, and Pratibha J. Shenoy, of Kirkland & Ellis; Richard A. Wolfe of Fried, Frank, Harris, Shriver & Jacobson; Stephen S. Bowen, Christian E. Kimball, Douglas C. Barnard, Philip A. Stoffregen, Daniel P. Meehan, Herwig J. Schlunk, Richard E. Aderman, John R. Garrett, Robert E. Musgraves, Jonathan C. Lipson, Thomas M. Zollo, Michael R. Gervasio, Amy Fisher Chase, and Jeffrey T. Soukup, formerly of Kirkland & Ellis; B. Peter Rose, Mark V. Sever, James F. Somers, and others, of Ernst & Young LLP; and Sean S. Sullivan, formerly of Ernst & Young LLP, for their invaluable assistance in the preparation of this volume.

The authors are grateful to Gary R. Wendorf, Susan P. Gadzala, and Elaine C. Crowley, Legal Assistants at Kirkland & Ellis, without whose tireless efforts in organizing these volumes and moving from scribbled notes to polished product they would not have seen the light of day and without whose Herculean efforts the thousands of updates to these volumes would be so much waste paper.

This publication is designed to provide accurate and authoritative information in regard to the subject matter covered. It is sold with the understanding that the publisher is not engaged in rendering legal, accounting, or other professional service and that the authors are not offering such advice in this publication. If legal advice or other expert assistance is required, the services of a competent professional person should be sought.

Summary of Contents

Volume 4

Detailed Table of Contents

Volume 1

Chapter 1

Introduction

Chapter 2

Taxable Purchase of T's Stock and Taxable Reverse Subsidiary Merger

Contents

Contents

Contents

Contents

Contents

Contents

Chapter 3

Taxable Purchase of T's Assets and Taxable Forward Merger

Contents

Chapter 4

Taxable Acquisitions: Acquisition Expenses, Allocation of Stepped-Up Basis, Amortization of Intangibles, Covenants Not to Compete, Etc.

Contents

Contents

Contents

Chapter 5

Unwanted Assets

Volume 2

Chapter 6

Basic Principles of Tax-Free Reorganizations

Contents

Contents

Contents

Chapter 7

Reorganizations Under "Solely for Voting Stock" Rule

Contents

Chapter 8

Reorganizations Not Under "Solely for Voting Stock" Rule

Contents

Chapter 9

Acquisitions and Dispositions Using Code §351

Chapter 10

Tax-Free Spin-Offs

Contents

Chapter 11

Special Considerations in Taxable and Tax-Free Acquisitions Involving S Corporation

Contents

Contents

Contents

Volume 3

Chapter 12

Net Operating Losses, Net Capital Losses and Excess Credits in Taxable and Tax-Free Acquisitions

Contents

Contents

Contents

Chapter 13

Tax Aspects of Financing LBOs—Debt and Preferred Stock

Contents

Contents

Contents

Chapter 14

Tax Aspects of Structuring LBOs

Contents

Chapter 15

Management Compensation

Contents

Contents

Contents

Contents

Chapter 16

Evolving Acquisition Techniques Using Partnership or LLC

Contents

Chapter 17

Corporate and Securities Law, Accounting, Fraudulent
Conveyance, Antitrust Reporting, and Other Non-Tax
Considerations in Taxable and Tax-Free Acquisitions

Contents

Contents

Contents

Contents

Contents

The detailed table of contents for Volume 4, *Sample Acquisition Agreements*, is set forth at the beginning of Volume 4.

Mergers, Acquisitions, and Buyouts

CHAPTER 12

Net Operating Losses, Net Capital Losses and Excess Credits in Taxable and Tax-Free Acquisitions

Chapter 12. NOL (and Other Tax Attribute) Carryovers

¶1201 NOL CARRYFORWARDS AND CARRYBACKS GENERALLY

¶1201.1 Post-'97 Losses

A corporation incurring a net operating loss ("NOL") in a taxable year beginning after 8/5/97 normally carries the NOL back to each of the two preceding taxable years (or to each of the five preceding taxable years for an NOL incurred in a tax year ending in 2001 or 2002, as further described below) and then forward to each of the 20 following taxable years.[1] An NOL must be carried to the earliest available taxable year; to the extent the NOL is not fully absorbed by taxable income from that year, it is carried forward to the next available year.[2]

EXAMPLE 1

T, a calendar year taxpayer, is formed in 1998. It has the following net income and loss:

1998	($100)
1999	(200)
2000	200

¶1201 [1] Code §172(b)(1), as amended by the 1997 and 2002 Acts. Under an exception, an "eligible loss" generally may be carried back three (rather than two) years. An "eligible loss" is (1) in the case of an individual, a loss of property arising from casualty or theft and (2) in the case of a small business (generally a corporation or partnership with average annual gross receipts of $5 million or less) or a taxpayer engaged in the farming business, an NOL attributable to a Presidentially declared disaster. Code §172(b)(1)(F) (added by the 1997 Act).

In addition, an NOL to the extent attributable to product liabilities and certain liabilities under environmental or workers compensation laws (collectively, "specified liability losses") may be carried back ten years. Code §172(b)(1)(C), (f). In Host Marriott Corporation v. United States, 267 F.3d 363, 2001-2 U.S.T.C. ¶50,580 (4th Cir. 2001), the Fourth Circuit held, under the pre-1998 version of Code §172(f), that specified liability losses included certain interest on corporate income tax deficiencies. However, effective for tax years ending after 10/21/98, Congress changed this unintended result by narrowing the definition of specified liability losses to exclude tax deficiency interest. See Code §172(f)(1)(B).

[2] Code §172(b)(2).

T carries forward its 1998 $100 NOL plus $100 of its 1999 NOL to offset fully its $200 taxable income for 2000. T's remaining $100 1999 NOL is carried forward annually until it is fully absorbed by T's income. Any portion of the 1999 NOL remaining after 2019 (i.e., 20 years after the year the NOL was incurred) will expire unused.

EXAMPLE 2

Same as Example 1, except T has the following net income and loss:

1998	$100
1999	(75)
2000	100

T carries back its 1999 $75 NOL to 1998 and receives a refund of part of its 1998 tax paid.

Subject to the limitations discussed in this Chapter 12, generally the NOL of an affiliated group of corporations filing consolidated returns (1) is calculated on a "single entity" basis by netting the income and losses of all members of the group and (2) may be carried back or forward to offset the consolidated taxable income of the entire group.[3]

An NOL corporation may irrevocably elect to relinquish the entire two-year carryback period with respect to an NOL incurred in a particular year, in which case the NOL is first carried forward to the year following the year it was incurred.[4]

---

[3] See Reg. §1.1502-21(e) (defining consolidated NOL) and §1.1502-21(a) (determining consolidated NOL deduction). See also United Dominion Industries, Inc. v. U.S., 532 U.S. 822, 2001-1 U.S.T.C. ¶50,340 (2001), where the Supreme Court held, in determining how a consolidated group calculates its "specified liability loss" for a year (which is eligible for a 10-year carryback under Section 172(b)(1)(C)) Code §172(f)'s limitation of the carryback amount to the taxpayer's "net operating loss" for the year refers to the consolidated NOL of the group, not the NOL of the separate member that generated the specified liability, stressing that "the Code and regulations governing affiliated groups of corporations filing consolidated returns provide only one definition of NOL: 'consolidated' NOL," citing Reg. §1.1502-21(e)'s predecessor.

[4] Code §172(b)(3).

EXAMPLE 3

Same as Example 2, except that T elects to forgo the carryback period. Thus, T does not receive a refund of any of its 1998 tax paid. Instead, T's 1999 NOL is carried forward to offset $75 of T's 2000 income.

An election to relinquish the carryback period with respect to the NOL of a consolidated group may not be made separately for any member, with one exception.[5]

Effective for a post-6/25/99 acquisition, if T is a member of a consolidated group before P's acquisition of T (whether or not T is the common parent) and T becomes a member of P's consolidated group, the P group may irrevocably elect to relinquish, with respect to all post-acquisition NOLs of the P group attributable to T, the portion of the carryback period for which T was a member of the prior group (the "split election rule").[6] The split election rule is available only if every other corporation joining P's group that was affiliated with T immediately before it joined P's group (e.g., any T subsidiary) is also included in the waiver. Unlike the normal NOL carryback waiver, the split election rule is not an annual election, but rather applies to all post-acquisition NOLs of the P group that could otherwise be carried back to T's former group.

The split election rule was created because of the computational and disclosure difficulties associated with negotiating who obtains the benefit of post-acquisition NOLs carried back into T's prior group (which, for example, may require T's prior group to disclose to P confidential tax information regarding the prior group's ability to use the carryback). By permitting the P group to waive the portion of its post-acquisition NOLs attributable only to T and T's former affiliates, the split election rule permits the parties to avoid these difficulties without the punitive effect of requiring the P group to waive the carryback of its remaining post-acquisition NOLs.[7] The split election rule by its terms applies only if T belonged to a consolidated group before P acquired T (even if T was the parent of that group); hence it does not apply if T was a stand-alone corporation or if T was a parent or subsidiary of an affiliated group not filing consolidated returns.

A corporation incurring an NOL in a tax year ending in 2001 or 2002 normally carries the NOL back to each of the five (rather than only two) preceding taxable years and then forward to each of the 20 following taxable years.[8] The corporation

---

[5] Reg. §1.1502-21(b)(3)(i).

[6] Reg. §1.1502-21(b)(3)(ii)(B), -21(h)(5) (effective date).

[7] See T.D. 8823 (1999 SRLY NOL regulations), Preamble ¶¶66-68.

[8] Code §172(b)(1)(H), added by the 2002 Act. This special five-year carryback rule also applies to "eligible losses" that otherwise would be carried back three years under Code §172(b)(1)(F), but does not affect the ten-year carryback of "specified liability losses" under Code §172(b)(1)(C), each as discussed earlier in this section. The unenacted House version (H.R. 108-94) of the 2003 Act, would have extended the five-year carryback to NOLs incurred in tax years ending in 2003, 2004, and 2005, but this provision was not included in the legislation as enacted.

may make an irrevocable election to waive the five-year carryback rule for any loss year and instead to apply the basic carryback rules described above.[9] Thus, if a corporation incurs an NOL in a tax year ending in 2001 or 2002, the corporation may either (1) carry the NOL back five years, (2) irrevocably elect to waive the five-year carryback rule for the loss year and to carry the NOL back two years, or (3) irrevocably elect to waive both the five-year and two-year carryback rules and to carry the NOL forward only.

Rev. Proc. 2002-40 issued 5/02[10] grants relief to a corporation incurring an NOL in a tax year ending in 2001 or 2002 which previously filed its tax return without regard to the 2002 Act's five-year NOL carryback rule. Specifically, if a corporation incurred an NOL in a tax year ending in 2001 or 2002, but on a previously filed tax return either carried back the NOL two years or waived the two-year carryback (without waiving the five-year carryback), the corporation may still elect to apply the five-year loss carryback rule by filing before 11/1/02 either a normal refund claim (amending its prior tax return) or an application for a tentative carryback adjustment (see ¶1206.8) in accordance with Rev. Proc. 2002-40. If the corporation previously either carried back such an NOL two years or waived the two-year carryback period and does nothing further, the five-year carryback rule does not apply. If the corporation neither applied nor waived the two-year carryback period in its original return (e.g., the corporation incurred an NOL for 2001 but did not carry it back under the two-year rule because it had no income in either 1999 or 2000), the five-year carryback period applies automatically unless the corporation makes an appropriate filing before 11/1/02 relinquishing the five-year carryback.

Temporary regulations issued in 5/02[11] provide similar relief for a P consolidated group that (1) acquires T, (2) incurs an NOL for a tax year ending during 2001 or 2002 that is attributable to T, and (3) does not at any time apply the split election rule described above to waive, with respect to such 2001 or 2002 T NOL, the portion of the carryback period for which T was a member of a prior group. Under these circumstances, two elections are available. *First*, if the P group could have applied the split election rule (i.e., P acquired T after 6/25/99) but did not, P may irrevocably elect, with respect to such 2001 or 2002 T NOL, to relinquish the portion of the five-year carryback period for which T was a member of the prior group. If the P group at any time applied or applies the split election rule, the P group is automatically treated as having made such election to relinquish the portion of the five-year carryback period for which T was a member of the prior group. *Second*, regardless of when P acquires T, P may irrevocably elect, with respect to such 2001 or 2002 T NOL, to relinquish the portion of the five-year carryback period other than the non-extended carryback period (i.e., the two tax years immediately before the tax year in which the loss was incurred) for which T was a member of a prior group. Thus, unlike the first election, the second election only applies to the third, fourth, and fifth carryback years of the five-year carryback period.

[9] Code §172(j).
[10] 2002-1 C.B. 1096.
[11] Temp. Reg. §1.1502-21T(b)(3)(ii)(C), T.D. 8997 (5/30/02).

Each of these two elections is available only if (1) every other P group member that was a T affiliate immediately before joining P's group (e.g., any T subsidiary) is also included in the election and (2) none of such 2001 or 2002 T NOL has been carried back to a tax year of any prior T group to the extent such tax year would be covered by the carryback waiver. These elections are made year-by-year, so that a different election may be made for 2001 than for 2002. The elections must be filed with the P group's timely filed (including extensions) original or amended return for (1) in the case of a 2001 T NOL, the P group's tax year ending in 2001, but not later than 10/31/02, and (2) in the case of a 2002 T NOL, the P group's tax year ending in 2002, but not later than 9/15/03.

¶1201.2   Pre-'98 Losses

A corporation incurring an NOL in a taxable year beginning before 8/6/97 normally may carry the NOL back to each of the three preceding taxable years and forward to each of the 15 following taxable years.[12] Otherwise the principles described in ¶1201.1 above apply.

¶1201.3   AMT Losses

A corporation's federal income tax liability for a taxable year is the greater of its regular tax or its alternative minimum tax ("AMT") for the year.[13] Corporate AMT is generally equal to 20% of a corporation's alternative minimum taxable income ("AMTI"), and a corporation's AMTI is equal to its regular taxable income with an add-back of so-called "tax preference items" and other modifications.[14]

For AMT purposes, the basic NOL carryback and carryforward rules described above generally apply, except that (subject to the next paragraph) a taxpayer's NOL deduction for any tax year is limited to 90% of AMTI, determined without regard to the NOL deduction.[15] Thus a corporation with an NOL in excess of its regular taxable income for the year to which the NOL is carried back or forward incurs no regular income tax, but generally incurs AMT equal to 2% of the corporation's AMTI for the year (determined without regard to the NOL)—i.e., 10% of AMTI x 20% corporate AMT rate.

The 2002 Act temporarily suspended the 90% AMT NOL deduction limitation (so that 100% of AMTI could be offset by NOLs) for deductions attributable to (1) the carryback of an NOL arising in a tax year ending in 2001 or 2002 and (2) the carryforward of an NOL to a tax year ending in 2001 or 2002.[16]

[12] Code §172(b)(1), before amendment by the 1997 Act.
[13] Code §55(a).
[14] Code §55(b), §56, §57, §58.
[15] Code §56(d).
[16] Code §56(d)(1) (as amended by the 2002 Act).

¶1202   GENERAL DESCRIPTION OF TAX ATTRIBUTE LIMITATIONS IN ACQUISITIONS

Numerous statutory provisions limit the use of a corporation's NOL carryforwards (notably Code §§269, 381, 382, 384, and the consolidated return regulations) and carrybacks (notably Code §§381, 172(b)(1)(E), and the consolidated return regulations) after the corporation has been acquired or in certain circumstances after it has made an acquisition. Code §382 is one of the more complex provisions applicable to NOL carryforwards (and through Code §383 to the carrying forward of other tax attributes) because of its extreme length and intricacy.

Limitations similar to the NOL carryforward and carryback limitations also apply in carrying forward and carrying back T's unused tax credits and unused net CLs, as discussed at ¶1207.

This chapter covers the following topics:

- The effect on T's NOL when T is acquired in a taxable acquisition (¶1203 below) or tax-free acquisition (¶1204) and the stock basis consequences to P, T's new owner, of T's NOL expiration (¶1203.3).
- The effect on P's NOL when P acquires T in a taxable or tax-free acquisition (¶1205).
- The ability to carry back P's and T's post-acquisition NOLs and obtain a refund of T's or P's taxes paid before P acquired T (¶1206).
- The effect on T's and P's other tax attributes (in particular, unused tax credits and unused net CLs) when P acquires T in a taxable or tax-free acquisition (¶1207).
- A closer look at the intricacies of Code §382 than is given in the ¶1203 through ¶1205 transactional discussion (¶1208).

¶1203   T NOL WHEN P OR S ACQUIRES T IN TAXABLE ACQUISITION

If P or S acquires T's assets in a taxable acquisition, T's NOLs do not carry over to P or S (see ¶1203.1). If P or S acquires T's stock in a taxable acquisition, T's NOLs continue to be usable by T, subject to the limitations discussed in ¶1203.2. If P purchases T's stock and T's NOL thereafter expires, P's basis in T's stock may be reduced by the amount of the expired NOL, as discussed in ¶1203.3.

¶1203.1   T Sells Assets to P or S

T's NOLs will not carry over to P or S when P or S acquires T's assets in a taxable transaction (e.g., by direct purchase or by a taxable merger of T into P or S).[1] T's NOLs can, however, be used by T to offset (1) income recognized by T

¶1203   [1] See Code §381.

as a result of the asset sale, (2) T's subsequent income if T's assets are acquired by direct purchase and T does not liquidate, and (3) any gain recognized by T as a result of T's subsequent liquidation. In addition, if T liquidates into an 80% parent corporation ("Parent") under Code §332, T's remaining NOL will carry over to Parent under Code §381 and thus generally will be available to offset Parent's future income. T's liquidation will qualify under Code §332 only if Parent owns 80% of T's stock by vote and by value and T transfers "property" (which includes money, such as the proceeds from T's asset sale) to Parent in the liquidation.[2] If T's liquidation does not qualify under Code §332 (i.e., T is not 80% owned by a corporation or T has no assets at the time of the liquidation), T's NOL remaining after the application of clauses (1) through (3) above will expire unused.

EXAMPLE

T, a calendar year taxpayer, is formed in 1997 and incurs a $100 NOL in that year. On 1/1/98 T sells assets to P at a gain of $40. T's $40 gain on the asset sale may be fully offset by $40 of T's NOL. However, T's NOL will not transfer to P. If corporation X owns 80% of T and T liquidates under Code §332, T's remaining $60 NOL will be available to offset X's future income. If T liquidates and the liquidation does not qualify under Code §332. T's remaining $60 NOL is applied against gain that T recognizes in the liquidation and otherwise expires unused.

¶1203.2   T's Shareholders Sell T Stock to P or S

Except for the specific statutory limitations discussed below, when T's shareholders sell their T stock to P or S in a taxable transaction, T's pre-acquisition NOLs continue to be usable by T.

In addition, if T is later liquidated or merged tax free into P or a P affiliate, T's NOLs will be available to the successor corporation, subject to the limitations discussed at T ¶1203.2.5. Otherwise, however, T's NOLs are permitted to offset the future income of P and P's other affiliates only if (1) P or S acquires sufficient T stock to file a consolidated return with T and (2) P's or S's acquisition of T's stock does not attract the restrictive impact of the SRLY rules (see ¶1203.2.4).

If P acquires T in a reverse subsidiary cash merger (i.e., P's transitory subsidiary S merges into T in a taxable transaction, with T's old shareholders receiving cash, notes, and/or other consideration and P receiving newly issued T stock in exchange for its S stock—see ¶202), T's NOLs are treated in the same manner as if P had purchased T's stock directly.

---

[2] Code §332(a), (b)(1); Rev. Rul. 69-379, 1969-2 C.B. 48.

¶1203.2.1   Code §338 Election

If P or S makes a Code §338 election (but not a Code §338(h)(10) election) with respect to its purchase of T stock, the transaction is treated as a sale of assets by old T to new T. Old T's NOL can be used to offset income T recognizes as a result of its Code §338 deemed asset sale, but any remaining T NOL expires unused. Making the Code §338 election in connection with an ownership change under Code §382 (as typically will be the case) does not alter this result, subject to limitations discussed in ¶1208.2.4.

If T's NOL exceeds T's gain on its Code §338 deemed asset sale, the excess NOL survives if the parties make a Code §338(h)(10) election. In that case, T is treated as having sold its assets to P and liquidated tax free into Bigco under Code §332 so that Bigco inherits T's remaining NOL.

EXAMPLE

T is formed in 1996 and incurs a $100 NOL in that year. On 2/1/97 T's shareholders sell all of T's stock to P for $50. At the time of the sale, T has a $10 basis in its assets, which are worth $50. P makes a Code §338 election with respect to T. Under the ADSP formula of the final Code §338 regulations (see ¶205.5), old T recognizes a $40 gain from its deemed asset sale, which is fully offset by $40 of its NOL.

However, Old T's remaining $60 NOL expires unused unless a Code §338(h)(10) election was permitted and made, in which case T's old parent Bigco would inherit the unused T NOL.

¶1203.2.2   Code §269(a) Change of Control with Tax Avoidance Principal Purpose

T's NOLs will be eliminated and thus will not continue to be usable by T if (1) P or S (or a group) acquires 50% or more of T's stock (by value or by vote—counting all stock, including non-voting, non-convertible, limited preferred) or P or S acquires T's assets in a COB transaction (when T is not controlled (i.e., 50% or more by value or by vote) by P or its shareholders immediately before the acquisition) and (2) "the principal purpose" of the acquisition is to avoid tax by securing tax benefits that P or S would not otherwise enjoy (e.g., T's NOL).

The following are some of the factors taken into account in determining whether P's or S's "principal purpose" was to avoid tax by securing the benefit of T's NOL:

(1)   *Whether the evidence indicates that P's or S's principal goal in purchasing T's stock was to acquire T's business, assets, and operations or to obtain T's NOL.* In this regard, memos, letters, notes, and oral testimony play a role. The actual events also play an important role. For example, if P or S quickly

closed or abandoned T's business (or quickly contracted its operations), this is powerful evidence that P or S was not after T's business. Similarly, it is a bad fact if T's NOL is very large and the expected future profits from T's business operations (even after the changes in the business planned by P or S) are very small in relation to the price P or S paid for T.

On the other hand, it is a good fact if P or S spends substantial amounts to improve T's business, expects to generate substantial profits (in relation to the purchase price for T) from T's business, and does in fact continue T's business for a substantial period and generate substantial profits.

(2) *Whether P or S drops unrelated income-producing assets into T.* Because of the SRLY rules (discussed below), T's pre-acquisition NOL can be used to offset only T's profits, not P's or S's profits. Hence, P or S may want to contribute income-producing assets to T so that the income from such assets can be offset by T's NOL. If P or S quickly contributes assets unrelated to T's business, this will be evidence that P's or S's acquisition of T's stock was for a tax avoidance purpose.[3]

(3) *The fact that Code §382 limits the future use of T's NOL* (or that Code §383 limits the future use of T's excess tax credits and net CLs) is "relevant" in determining whether the principal purpose of an acquisition is to evade or avoid federal income tax.[4] This is sensible since the application of Code §382 often will substantially impair the value of T's NOL for P. As a practical matter, any post-1986 acquisition by P of 100% of the stock of unrelated T generally will trigger Code §§382 and 383. These regulations apply generally to any ownership change (as defined in Code §382) occurring after 12/31/86. See ¶¶1203.2.3, 1207 (discussion of Code §383), and 1208 (detailed discussion of Code §382).

Legislative Update

The unenacted Senate version of the 2003 Act (S. 1054) would have amended Code §269(a) to apply to any acquisition of corporate stock or corporate assets in a COB transaction, effectively eliminating the "control" requirement in current Code §269(a).

An identical provision was reintroduced in the Senate on 6/2/03 as part of the Working Taxpayer Fairness Restoration Act (S. 1162) to be effective for stock and property acquired after 2/13/03. An identical provision also appears in the Abusive Tax Shelter Shutdown and Taxpayer Accountability Act of 2003 (H.R. 1555), introduced 4/2/03, to be effective for transactions after enactment.

[3] Reg. §1.269-3(b)(1).
[4] Reg. §1.269-7.

EXAMPLE 1

P purchases all of T's stock in a taxable transaction for $1,000 at a time when T is operating a chain of retail drug stores at a loss and has a $3,000 NOL. Shortly after the acquisition, P causes T to abandon or curtail its operating business (the drug stores). Contemporaneous memos and correspondence as well as oral testimony indicate that, when negotiating the acquisition, P did not believe T's business and assets were very desirable, but rather that P's principal motivation for the acquisition was to obtain T's NOL. In addition, shortly after the acquisition, P contributes to T an unrelated manufacturing business operated by P. Based on these facts, a judge or jury is likely to conclude that tax avoidance was P's principal purpose for acquiring T and hence that Code §269 applies to eliminate T's NOL.

However, in reaching this result, the judge or jury is entitled to take into account the fact that, even if Code §269 were not applicable, Code §382 (discussed below) would permit post-acquisition T to use its $3,000 NOL in only modulated amounts, e.g., $50 per year if the long-term tax-exempt rate were 5% (i.e., 5% of the $1,000 purchase price). Hence, post-acquisition T's tax savings from using the NOL should not exceed $17.50 per year (35% × $50).

Whether a judge or jury would conclude that this application of Code §382 vitiates the evidence of tax avoidance of course implicates a factual issue.

In any event, even if P anticipated that it could avoid Code §269 on the factual grounds described above, then it is highly unlikely that P would pay $1,000 for T's stock unless T's assets and business have substantial value.

EXAMPLE 2

Same as Example 1, except that shortly after P acquires T's stock, P does not abandon or curtail T's business but contributes substantial cash to T (rather than a manufacturing business), which T uses to expand its retail drug store business. Contemporaneous memos and correspondence as well as oral testimony indicate that, when negotiating the acquisition, P believed that T's business and assets were desirable, that P intended to expand the business and improve management, and that P expected to make substantial profits (in relation to the $1,000 purchase price) from the business. Based on these facts, a judge or jury is likely to conclude that tax avoidance was not P's principal purpose for the T acquisition and thus that Code §269 does not apply to T's NOL.

EXAMPLE 3

Same as Example 1, except that shortly after P acquires T's stock, P contributes to T several profitable retail drug stores owned by P (the "P stores") rather than a manufacturing business. Contemporaneous memos and correspondence as well as oral testimony indicate that P expected the P stores to be integrated operationally with T's old stores, expected economies of scale from joint buying and advertising, and expected the management of the P stores to help the operation of T's old stores. Based on these facts, a judge or jury is likely to conclude that P's contribution of the P stores to T was motivated by business, not tax avoidance, considerations and hence that the contribution did not tend to prove that P's purchase of T's stock had tax avoidance as the principal purpose.

EXAMPLE 4

Same facts as Examples 2 and 3 except that, despite P's optimistic expectations at the time of the acquisition and P's best efforts after the acquisition, T's chain of retail drug stores continued to operate at an ever-increasing loss and hence, 18 months after the acquisition, P closed the retail drug store business. Thereafter, P contributed another business to T in hopes that the new business's profits could use the leftover T NOL. Based on these facts, a judge or jury would weigh the actual result (abandonment of T's business 18 months after the acquisition) against P's memos, correspondence, oral testimony, expenditures, and efforts in order to determine whether P's genuine purpose at the time of the acquisition was principally business motivated or principally tax-avoidance motivated. In this regard, the trier of fact is likely to be favorably impressed if (1) P's plans at the time it acquired T were realistic, (2) a reasonable person would have believed (and P's executives actually believed) that T's business could be saved and made sufficiently profitable to justify the $1,000 purchase price, (3) P spent considerable sums and substantial effort to carry out the plans, and (4) P's realistic plans were ultimately frustrated by supervening unanticipated events (rather than expected or predictable events).

The 1986 Act Conference Report states that the 1986 Act amendments to Code §§382 and 383 "do not alter the continuing application of section 269 to acquisitions made for the principal purpose of evasion or avoidance of Federal income tax."[5] Consistent with this legislative history, Reg. §1.269-7 provides that if the principal

---

[5] H.R. Conf. Rep. No. 841, 99th Cong., 2d Sess. II, at 194 (1986).

purpose of an acquisition is the evasion or avoidance of federal income tax, the IRS can apply Code §269 to disallow the use of an NOL, credit, etc., notwithstanding that the NOL, credit, etc. may be subject to an annual use limitation under Code §382 or §383. As noted above, however, the regulation also sensibly provides that in determining whether the principal purpose of an acquisition is the evasion or avoidance of federal income tax, it is "relevant" whether the NOL, credit, etc. is subject to a use limitation under Code §382 or §383.

When T is bankrupt or insolvent, three important Code §269 rules apply, all adverse to bankrupt or insolvent T. *First*, if P or S is acquiring T pursuant to a reorganization plan in a title 11 case, a bankruptcy court determination that tax avoidance is not the principal purpose of the plan "is not controlling" for Code §269 purposes because the government, rather than the taxpayer, has the burden of proof on the tax avoidance issue in the title 11 case while the taxpayer has the burden of proof on this issue in a Code §269 tax case.[6]

Second, creditor interests are not treated as stock ownership for Code §269 purposes, despite the rule in *Helvering v. Alabama Asphaltic Limestone Co.*,[7] that creditor interests in a troubled company may take on an equity-like character sufficient to satisfy the continuity of shareholder interest requirement applicable to corporate reorganizations (see ¶610). Rather, creditors of a bankrupt T are treated as acquiring beneficial ownership of T's stock for Code §269 purposes "no earlier than the time a bankruptcy court confirms a plan of reorganization."[8] As a result, whether T's creditors in bankruptcy acquire control of T with the principal purpose of tax avoidance is determined by reference to a date no earlier than such confirmation date, and the creditors' intentions on earlier dates (such as when their interests took on an equity-like character sufficient to satisfy the *Alabama Asphaltic* standard) are not relevant according to the regulation.[9]

Third, if P or S acquires T in connection with a title 11 or similar case and the acquisition qualifies for the benefits of Code §382(*l*)(5) (which exempts each qualifying acquisition from the customary Code §382 NOL limitations—see ¶1208.2.1.5), the acquisition nevertheless will be considered to have a principal purpose of tax avoidance for Code §269 ("absent strong evidence to the contrary"), and hence will generally extinguish T's NOL altogether, unless T "carries on more than an insignificant amount of an active trade or business during and subsequent

---

[6] Reg. §1.269-3(e).

[7] 315 U.S. 179, 42-1 U.S.T.C. ¶9245 (1942).

[8] Reg. §1.269-5(b).

[9] Under Code §269(b), Code §269 will apply if (1) P or S acquires T's stock in a "qualified stock purchase" under Code §338, (2) no Code §338 election is made, (3) T is liquidated pursuant to a plan of liquidation "adopted not more than 2 years after the acquisition date," and (4) the principal purpose of the liquidation is tax avoidance or evasion. See ¶¶1203.2.5, 1204.2.4, and 1204.3.4. Prior to the Code §269 regulations, there was strong argument that, when P is a creditor of bankrupt T and acquires T stock pursuant to a bankruptcy reorganization plan, the "acquisition date" of the T stock for purposes of Code §269(b)'s two-year rule could be a preconfirmation date under *Alabama Asphaltic* principles. However, Reg. §1.269-5(b) states that "for purposes of section 269," creditors are considered to acquire stock of bankrupt T no earlier than the time a bankruptcy court confirms a reorganization plan. Therefore, it appears that this regulation could delay the commencement of the two-year period during which certain liquidations may be subject to Code §269(b).

to the title 11 or similar case."[10] See ¶1208.3 for further discussion of this require-ment, including (1) a comparison with the two-year Code §382(c) continuity of business enterprise requirement and (2) an argument that this requirement is misguided.

These Code §269 regulations apply generally to any ownership change (as defined in Code §382) occurring after 12/31/86. The presumption that the acquisi-tion of T in connection with a title 11 or similar case has the principal purpose of tax avoidance for Code §269 applies only to acquisitions effected pursuant to a plan of reorganization confirmed after 8/14/90.[11]

¶1203.2.3 Code §382 Ownership Change

If, as a result of P's or S's purchase of T's stock, the percentage of T's stock (by FV, not counting certain non-voting, non-convertible, limited preferred stock) owned (directly or by attribution) by P and S is more than 50 percentage points above the lowest percentage of T's stock P and S owned at any time during the preceding three-year period (an "ownership change"), then Code §382 generally will limit the use of T's pre-acquisition NOLs as follows:[12]

(1) T's pre-acquisition NOLs will be wholly eliminated unless T meets the "continuity of business enterprise" test of Code §382 at all times during the two-year period beginning on the date of the ownership change, i.e., T continues a significant historic line of business or continues to use a significant portion of its historic business assets. As discussed at ¶1208.3 below, this is the same "continuity of business enterprise" test that applies in tax-free reorganizations under Code §368.

(2) If T meets the continuity of business enterprise test (so that its NOLs are not eliminated under (1) above), and assuming Code §269 has not elimi-nated T's NOLs, T's NOLs will continue, subject to an annual limitation equal to the "long-term tax-exempt rate" at the time of the ownership change times the FV of all of T's stock, valued immediately before the ownership change but disregarding any T shares redeemed in connection with the ownership change.

For purposes of Code §382, any T stock owned or acquired by P or S is treated as owned proportionately by P's shareholders.[13] Hence, an ownership change

---

[10] Reg. §1.269-3(d).

[11] T.D. 8388, 1992-1 C.B. 137. The regulations do not specify their effective date in the case of a Code §269 acquisition that does not also constitute a Code §382 ownership change. Presumably, the regulations apply to Code §269 acquisitions made after 12/31/86.

[12] If the purchase by P and S is not sufficiently substantial to constitute an "ownership change" (i.e., is equal to or less than 50 percentage points), then increases in ownership of T stock by other persons during the preceding three-year period (as well as increases in ownership of T stock by P, S, and other persons during the succeeding three-year period) must be considered and, if sufficiently substantial, will cause an "ownership change."

[13] Code §382(*l*)(3)(A).

technically is measured not at the P (or S) level but rather at the level of P's shareholders.

Code §382, which is discussed in detail at ¶1208 below, generally applies to an ownership change occurring after 12/31/86. See ¶1208.7.

EXAMPLE 1

Individual A has long owned 100% of T's stock. P is owned by persons unrelated to A and T. On 1/1/97, when T has a $100 NOL, P buys 50% of T's stock from A. Because P has not acquired more than 50% of T's stock, there has not been an "ownership change" under Code §382. Therefore, Code §382 will not limit T's ability to carry forward its NOL to offset T's future income so long as there is no further change in T's stock ownership before 1/1/00.

EXAMPLE 2

Same as Example 1 except that on 1/1/99 A sells one of his remaining shares to B, an unrelated person. A's stock sale to B causes an ownership change on 1/1/99 because more than 50% of T's stock has changed hands within a three-year period. Therefore, assuming T continues its historic business, T may carry forward its pre-1/2/99 NOL to offset its post-1/1/99 income subject to an annual limitation equal to the FV of T's stock immediately before B's purchase times the long-term tax-exempt bond rate then in effect.

EXAMPLE 3

Same as Example 2, except that on 1/1/00 (one year after B's stock purchase) T sells all of its assets and business, and enters a new business. T may not carry forward any portion of its pre-1/2/99 NOL to offset its post-1/1/99 income, except perhaps the gain T recognizes on the sale of its historic assets (pursuant to the BIG rules discussed at ¶1208.2.3 below).

EXAMPLE 4

Individual A has long owned 100% of T's stock. In addition, A has long owned 10% of P's stock. The remaining 90% of P's stock is owned by persons unrelated to A. On 1/1/97 P buys 55% of T's stock from A. Code §382 looks through P to its individual shareholders in determining stock ownership. Therefore, only 49.5% of T's stock has changed hands because A, who previously owned 100% of T, continues to own 50.5% (45% directly plus 5.5% indirectly through P). Accordingly, there has not been a Code §382 ownership change with respect to T.

¶1203.2.4 Consolidated Return Regulations

If P's or S's purchase of T's stock causes T to become a member of P's consolidated group (see ¶1205.2.1), and if there is no Code §382 ownership change of T at the time of or within 6 months before or after P's or S's purchase of T, then any of T's pre-acquisition NOLs that continue to be usable by T (under the rules discussed above) will become "separate return limitation year" NOLs (i.e., "SRLY NOLs"), usable only against T's profits, not against the profits of other members of the P consolidated group.[14]

In contrast, if there is a Code §382 ownership change of T at the time of, or within 6 months before or after, P's or S's purchase of T's stock (which often will be the case), then for tax years of the P group for which the due date (without extensions) of P's consolidated return is after 6/25/99 (even if P or S acquired T in an earlier tax year), T's pre-acquisition NOLs generally will not be SRLY NOLs (the "§382 Overlap Rule").[15] Therefore, for those years, subject to any applicable Code §382 limitation, T's NOLs may be carried forward to offset the future income of T, P and any other member of P's consolidated group. However, for prior years of the P group T's pre-acquisition NOLs are SRLY NOLs.

EXAMPLE 1

Individual A has long owned 100% of T's stock. P, an unrelated corporation, purchases all of T's stock on 1/1/00, when T has a $100 NOL. P and T file consolidated returns after the purchase, using a calendar taxable year. Because P's purchase results in a Code §382 ownership change of T, under the §382 Overlap Rule the purchase does not cause T's NOL to be a SRLY NOL. Therefore, T's NOL (assuming it is not eliminated by Code §§338, 269 or 382, and subject to any applicable Code §382 limitation) may be carried forward to offset the future income of T, P and any other member of P's consolidated group.

---

[14] Reg. §1.1502-21(c); Temp. Reg. §1.1502-21T(c); Reg. §1.1502-21A(c).
[15] Reg. §1.1502-21(g), (h). For further discussion of the §382 Overlap Rule, see ¶1205.2.4.2(4).

EXAMPLE 2

Same as Example 1, except that P purchases T on 1/1/97. Under the pre-1999 SRLY rules, for the P group's 1997 and 1998 tax years T's NOL (assuming it is not eliminated by Code §§338, 269, or 382) may be carried forward to offset only T's future income, not the future income of P or any other member of P's consolidated group. (In addition, T's NOL will be subject to the annual limitation of Code §382.) However, because P's 1997 purchase resulted in a Code §382 ownership change for T, under the §382 Overlap Rule T's NOL ceases to be a SRLY NOL for the P group's 1999 and later tax years. Therefore, subject to any applicable Code §382 limitation, T's NOL may be carried forward to 1999 and later years to offset income of T, P and any other member of P's consolidated group.

If, at the time P or S acquired T's stock, T had subsidiaries that were included in T's (and, after the acquisition, P's) consolidated return, then for taxable years of the P consolidated group ending before 1/29/91, the portion of T's consolidated SRLY NOL attributable to each member of T's former consolidated group is generally usable only against the future income of that member, not against the future income of any other corporation. In contrast, for taxable years ending after 1/28/91, T's consolidated SRLY NOL might be usable against the future income of T's entire former group (but not against the future income of P, S, or their other affiliates), under the principles discussed in ¶1205.2.4.2.

¶1203.2.5   T's Later Liquidation into P (or into S If S Purchased T's Stock)

If T is liquidated into P tax free under Code §332, T's basis in its assets will carry over to P, and T's NOLs (assuming they were not eliminated for any of the reasons discussed above) will also carry over to and be usable by P.[16] However, if T's NOLs became SRLY NOLs as a result of T's entry into P's consolidated group, T's losses will retain their SRLY taint in P's hands, meaning that T's losses

---

[16] Code §§381(a)(1), 334(b)(1).

A provision included in the version of the 2003 Act adopted by the Senate 5/15/03 (S. 1054), but not included in the Act as enacted, would have amended Code §334(b)(1) so that where Bigco is a domestic corporation and the liquidating subsidiary is a foreign corporation, Bigco would take a FV basis in BIL property if gain or loss on such property (1) is not subject to U.S. income tax in the liquidating corporation's hands immediately prior to the transfer and (2) is subject to U.S. income tax in Bigco's hands immediately after the transfer. An identical provision was reintroduced in the Senate on 6/2/03 as part of the Working Taxpayer Fairness Restoration Act (S. 1162) to be effective for transactions after 2/13/03. The provision also appears in the Abusive Tax Shelter Shutdown and Taxpayer Accountability Act of 2003 (H.R. 1555), introduced 4/2/03 and effective for transactions after enactment.

will be usable only against the profits of T's successor P (and, for taxable years ending after 1/28/91, possibly against the post-acquisition income of one or more T subsidiaries, as discussed in ¶1205.2.4.2), but not against the profits of other members of the P group.

If Code §382's annual limitation applies to T's NOLs as a result of P's original purchase, it will continue to apply after T's liquidation into P.[17] However, the liquidation itself will not trigger Code §382 because it does not alter T's beneficial ownership.

Code §269 applies to the liquidation of T if it is pursuant to a plan adopted within two years after P acquired at least 80% of T's stock by vote and by value by purchase within a 12-month period without making a Code §338 election. Accordingly, T's NOLs will be eliminated if the principal purpose for the liquidation is to avoid tax by shifting the benefit of T's NOLs to P.[18]

EXAMPLE 1

Individual A has long owned 100% of T's stock. P, a corporation unrelated to A and T, purchases 60% of T's stock from A on 1/1/99 (resulting in a Code §382 ownership change of T) and the remaining 40% on 12/31/99 (resulting in a SRLY event for T). T has a $100 NOL carryover into the taxable year 2000. No Code §338 election is made, and following the 12/31/99 purchase P and T file consolidated returns. P expects that T's business, which is unrelated to P's, will continue to generate losses in 2000 and beyond and that P will have significant taxable income. If P does not liquidate T, T's post-12/31/99 NOLs will be available to offset the profits of the entire P group. However, because the 1/1/99 Code §382 ownership of T and the 12/31/99 SRLY event did not occur within a six-month period, the §382 Overlap Rule does not apply. Therefore, T's $100 pre-1/1/00 NOL is a SRLY NOL usable only against T's future profits, not the future profits of other members of the P group. In addition, the portion of the NOL that accrued before 1/1/99 is subject to a Code §382 limitation. In an effort to obtain access to T's pre-1/1/00 NOL (subject to any Code §382 limitation on the pre-1/1/99 portion), P liquidates T on 1/2/00. Code §269(b) may apply to eliminate all of T's NOL.

EXAMPLE 2

Same as Example 1, except that P can demonstrate that its primary purpose in buying T's stock and liquidating T was to obtain T's historic business assets for use in P's own similar business. Code §269(b) should not apply

---

[17] Reg. §1.382-2(a)(1).
[18] Code §269(b). See Bowen & Sheffield, Section 269 Revisited, 61 Taxes 881 (1983).

in this case, and P should be able to use T's $100 pre-1/1/00 NOL to shelter its own future income (but, under the SRLY rules, not the income of any P affiliate) up to any annual limitation imposed by Code §382 on the pre-1/1/99 portion.

Under Code §269(c), IRS has the power to allow "part" of an NOL deduction disallowed by Code §269 or to "apportion" or "allocate" such deduction "among the corporations, or properties, or parts thereof, [but] only to such extent as [the IRS] determines will not result in the evasion or avoidance of Federal income tax." Query whether, in the case of a liquidation of T into P that had a prohibited Code §269(b) tax avoidance motive, IRS would be willing to exercise its Code §269(c) power to allow T's pre-acquisition SRLY NOL (which otherwise would be eliminated by Code §269(b)) to continue to be used only against the profits from T's old business in P's hands.

The two-year continuity of business enterprise requirement of Code §382 applies in tax-free reorganizations as well as in other acquisitions. See ¶¶1204 and 1208.3. Thus, Code §382 contemplates that P can acquire T's assets in an "A" or "C" reorganization without terminating T's business. By analogy, if P (or S) purchases T's stock in a transaction subject to Code §382, the mere transfer of T's business to P (or S) through a liquidation of T occurring within two years after the purchase should not violate the continuity of business enterprise requirement of Code §382.

¶1203.2.6 T's Later Merger into S

If P has purchased T's stock and thereafter P merges T into S, another P subsidiary, in a tax-free merger (see Code §368(a)(1)(A) and (D)), the applicable rules are similar to those discussed at ¶1203.2.5:

(1) T's NOLs (assuming they survived P's purchase of T's stock as described above) will carry over and be usable by S (the surviving corporation) under Code §381(a)(2); and

(2) T's losses will retain any SRLY taint and/or Code §382 taint in S's hands, i.e., T's SRLY NOLs will be usable only against S's profits (and, for taxable years ending after 1/28/91, possibly against the profits of one or more S subsidiaries, but not against the profits of other members of the P group), and T's Code §382-tainted NOLs will be usable only to the extent of T's Code §382 limitation.

¶1203.2.7 T Part of Bigco Consolidated Group Prior to P's Pre-3/7/02 Acquisition of T's Stock

When T was part of Bigco's consolidated group and P acquired T's stock from Bigco before 3/7/02, Bigco could under some circumstances elect to retain all or a portion of T's NOLs and CL carryforwards. When Bigco had a loss on the sale of T's stock that was disallowed by Reg. §1.1502-20(a) (see ¶212.4.4.1), Reg. §1.1502-20(g) allowed Bigco to keep for its own use all or a portion of any T NOLs and CL carryforwards (including T NOLs and CL carryforwards that other members of the Bigco group were not entitled to use under the SRLY limitation) up to the amount of the disallowed loss on T's stock. Bigco could specifically designate the T loss carryforwards that were reattributed. Any T NOLs and CL carryforwards retained by Bigco were not available to T after the acquisition. For further discussion of Bigco's reattribution of T's losses in connection with its pre-3/7/02 sale of T, see ¶212.4.4.4. For retroactive adjustments to the amount of previously reattributed losses that may be permitted or required in connection with certain post-3/6/02 elections affecting P's pre-3/7/02 acquisition of T, see ¶212.4.3.2.

¶1203.3   Potential Reduction of P's Outside Basis in T's Stock When T's NOL Expires While P and T File Consolidated Return

¶1203.3.1   General Rule

If P purchases T's stock or acquires T by a taxable reverse subsidiary merger (in each case without a Code §338 or §338(h)(10) election) in a taxable year beginning after 12/31/94, and if any part of T's NOL thereafter expires unused while P and T are filing a consolidated return, P's basis in T's stock will be reduced by the amount of the expired NOL unless P and T timely elected to waive T's NOL (generally by an attachment to P's consolidated return for the year of the P-T acquisition), as described in ¶1203.3.2.[19]

EXAMPLE 1

On 1/1/95 P, a calendar year taxpayer filing consolidated federal income tax returns with its subsidiaries, purchases all of T's stock (without a Code §338 or §338(h)(10) election) for $100. T becomes a member of P's consolidated tax group on 1/2/95 as a result of the acquisition. At that time T has a $1,000 NOL, which is scheduled to expire in the year 2001. The future use of T's NOL after the P-T acquisition is severely limited by Code §382 and the SRLY rules. To no one's surprise, T's $1,000 NOL expires unused in 2001 while P and T are still filing a consolidated return.

Unless P and T elected on their 1995 consolidated tax return (i.e., their return for the year of the P-T acquisition) to forfeit T's NOL, the 2001 expiration of T's NOL will cause a $1,000 reduction in P's basis in T's stock. Thus, if P's basis in T's stock in 2001 but before the reduction is still $100

---

[19] See Reg. §1.1502-32(b)(3)(iii)(A), (b)(4).

(i.e., P's 1995 cost for the T stock), P's basis in T's stock is reduced in 2001 to negative $900, reflected as a $900 "excess loss account." If T operates at break-even and P thereafter (e.g., in 2002) sells T's stock for $100 (i.e., an amount equal to P's 1995 cost), P will have $1,000 of taxable gain from the sale (i.e., $100 proceeds less negative $900 stock basis) even though P has derived no economic profit from the sale.

If P in turn is a consolidated subsidiary of another corporation ("Parent"), any negative adjustment to P's basis in T's stock also "tiers up" and reduces Parent's basis in P's stock by the amount of the expired NOL.

EXAMPLE 2

Same as Example 1 except that P's stock is 100% owned by Parent, which has a $1,500 basis in P's stock immediately before T's NOL expires in 2001. In the absence of the election described below, the 2001 expiration of T's $1,000 NOL while Parent, P, and T are filing a consolidated return, in addition to reducing by $1,000 P's basis in T's stock, will reduce by $1,000 (i.e., to $500) Parent's basis in P's stock. Thus, if Parent subsequently (e.g., in 2002) sells P's stock, Parent's gain will be $1,000 higher (or its loss will be $1,000 smaller) than if T's NOL had not expired.

The principles discussed in this section also apply if, in a taxable year beginning after 1994, (1) P acquires T's stock in a "B" or reverse subsidiary "A" reorganization (see ¶1204.3) and any part of T's NOL thereafter expires, in which case P's basis in T's stock will be reduced by the amount of the expired NOL unless P and T timely elected to waive T's NOL, or (2) P's subsidiary S acquires T's assets in a subsidiary "A" or subsidiary "C" reorganization in exchange for P stock (see ¶1204.2) and any part of T's NOL (acquired by S in the reorganization) thereafter expires, in which case P's basis in S's stock will be reduced by the amount of the expired NOL unless P and S timely elected to waive T's NOL. See ¶1204.4.

¶1203.3.2   Exceptions and Strategies

In any purchase of a loss corporation's stock after 1994, it is critical to try to avoid the strange and, as illustrated above, potentially catastrophic consequences of this misguided new tax regulation. The problem may be addressed in one of three ways:

First, P and T may irrevocably elect to treat all or a designated portion of T's NOL as expiring for all federal income tax purposes immediately before T becomes a member of the P group (an "NOL waiver election").[20] The election must be

---

[20] Reg. §1.1502-32(b)(4)(i).

made jointly by P and T on the P group's consolidated federal income tax return for the year T becomes a member of the P group, which return (taking into account a normal six-month extension) must be filed no later than the 15th day of the ninth month after the end of P's taxable year in which P acquires T. If P purchases T from Bigco's consolidated group, the expiration is treated as occurring immediately after T ceases to be a member of Bigco's consolidated group so that Bigco's pre-acquisition basis in T's stock is not reduced by T's deemed NOL expiration. If P and T file an NOL waiver election, the consequences vary depending on whether P acquired at least 80% of T's stock by taxable purchase in a single 12-month period.

If, within a 12-month period, P acquires T stock by taxable purchase, i.e., an acquisition (including a taxable reverse subsidiary merger) in which P takes a Code §1012 cost basis—enough T stock to consolidate (generally 80% by vote and by value—see ¶1205.2.1) (a "qualifying cost basis transaction"), the NOL waiver election and resulting deemed expiration of T's NOL avoid any stock basis reduction.

EXAMPLE 3

Same as Example 1 except that P and T make an NOL waiver election with respect to T's entire $1,000 NOL on the P group's 1995 consolidated income tax return, which is filed on 9/15/96 (i.e., 3/15/96 initial due date plus normal six-month extension).

As a result of the election, (1) neither P nor T may use T's NOL after P acquires T, (2) the expiration of T's NOL does not reduce P's basis in T's stock, in contrast to Example 1, and (3) if P is owned by Parent, the expiration of T's NOL does not reduce Parent's basis in P's stock, in contrast to Example 2. Therefore, on the later sale of T's stock for $100, P sensibly does not recognize a huge "phantom" gain.

If P acquires T's stock in any way other than a "qualifying cost basis transaction" (e.g., by a tax-free acquisition of T's stock *or* a series of taxable purchases with no purchase of 80% in any one 12-month period *or* a purchase of 79% of T's stock with the remaining 21% acquired by P in a Code §351 transaction) and P and T file a timely NOL waiver election, P's basis in T's stock is reduced at the time of the P-T acquisition by the *lesser* of (1) the waived portion of T's NOL or (2) the amount necessary to cause P's basis in T's stock to equal T's inside "net asset basis." For this purpose, T's "net asset basis" is the adjusted tax basis of T's assets, plus the amount of any T NOL not waived, less T's liabilities. In addition, if P's stock is owned by Parent, the waived portion of T's NOL does not reduce Parent's basis in P's stock (i.e., for this purpose, the reduction of P's basis in T's stock described immediately above is treated as occurring before T entered the Parent group).

EXAMPLE 4

Same as Example 1 except that P acquires all of T's stock in a tax-free "B" reorganization in which T's shareholders receive P voting stock with an FV of $100. Immediately before the P-T acquisition, T's shareholders had an aggregate basis in their T stock of $50.

P's initial basis in T's stock under Code §362(b) (before taking into account any NOL waiver election) is $50 (the prior T shareholders' basis in T's stock immediately before the transaction), and T has a $1,000 NOL that will expire in 2001.

Unless P and T made an NOL waiver election for T on their 1995 consolidated tax return, the 2001 expiration of T's NOL while P and T are filing a consolidated return will reduce P's basis in T's stock by $1,000. Thus, if P's basis in T's stock immediately before the 2001 NOL expiration is still $50, P's basis in T's stock is reduced by $1,000, creating an excess loss account (negative basis) of $950. If P then sells T's stock for $100 (i.e., P's 1995 economic cost), P will have $1,050 of taxable gain from the sale (i.e., $100 proceeds less $950 negative basis) even though P has derived no economic profit from the sale.

In contrast, if P and T elect to waive T's $1,000 NOL on their 1995 tax return, P's basis in T's stock is reduced at the time of the 1995 acquisition, but not below T's inside net asset basis at that time. Hence, if at that time the adjusted tax basis of T's assets exceeds T's liabilities by $40 and the NOL waiver covers all of T's NOL, then P's basis in T's stock is reduced from $50 to $40 so that P would recognize $60 gain if it then sold T's stock for $100.

Every taxable or tax-free acquisition of a loss corporation after 1994 in which T's NOL survives must be analyzed closely to determine whether an NOL waiver election should be made. Generally it will be desirable to waive T's NOL except to the extent that (1) P is confident the NOL will be used to shelter future income or (2) any potential negative stock basis adjustments resulting from T's NOL expiration can be addressed through one or more of the strategies described in *Second* or *Third* below. As the above discussion of this new trap for the unwary illustrates, inaction is not likely to prove wise.

Second, in some cases it may be possible to avoid a reduction in T's outside basis (or avoid at least the adverse consequences thereof) by (1) liquidating T into P tax-free under Code §332 or (2) selling P's stock rather than T's or (3) selling T's assets rather than T's stock.

EXAMPLE 5

Same as Example 1 except that P, the common parent corporation of the P-T consolidated group, was newly formed in 1995 to acquire T, P owns no assets other than the T stock, and P's shareholders have a $50 basis in their P stock. After T's $1,000 NOL expires in 2001 (so that P has a $900 excess loss account in T's stock), P's shareholders sell P's stock (rather than T's stock) to a third party for $100.

Since P's outside stock basis was not affected by the NOL expiration, the P shareholders recognize $50 gain on the sale of their P stock.

EXAMPLE 6

Same as Example 1 except that after T's NOL expires in 2001 (so that P has a $900 excess loss account in T's stock) P liquidates T (perhaps by an upstream merger) into P.

P's excess loss account in T's stock is eliminated by P's tax-free liquidation into T under Code §332, without adverse consequences to P or T.

EXAMPLE 7

Same as Example 6 except that P liquidates T under Code §332 before T's NOL expires.

When T's NOL expires in 2001, there is no reduction in the basis at which P's shareholders hold their P stock, even if P is filing a consolidated return with other subsidiaries in 2001. This is the case because the NOL-basis-reduction rule applies only to reduce the outside basis of stock of a subsidiary in a consolidated group, and P is the common parent.

EXAMPLE 8

Same as Example 1 except that, instead of selling T's stock after T's NOL expires in 2001, P sells T's assets and then liquidates T tax free under Code §332.

The P group reports taxable gain on the asset sale (which T's NOL may wholly or partly shelter), but the liquidation of T extinguishes whatever remains of T's excess loss account, with no adverse effect on T or P.

It may be more difficult to escape the adverse basis reduction consequences of T's expired NOL if (1) P is owned by Parent, in which case T's NOL expiration also will reduce Parent's outside basis in P's stock (as shown in Example 2 above), (2) P is an historic operating company with a business independent of T's, in which case the approach described in Example 8 (sale of T's assets) may work, but the approach described in Example 5 (sale of P's stock rather than T's stock) will work only if it is desirable and feasible to sell P's business in addition to T's, or (3) the net inside basis of T's assets is materially less than T's outside stock basis, in which case an asset sale as described in Example 8, depending on the size and availability of T's NOL, could be costly to the P group.

Third, the basis reduction rule can be avoided entirely if T is not filing a consolidated return with P (or any other parent corporation) when its NOL expires in 2001. P can thus avoid the basis reduction rule by (1) electing not to file a consolidated return prior to the 2001 NOL expiration, which requires IRS's approval if P has been filing consolidated returns, or (2) deconsolidating T from P's consolidated group prior to the 2001 NOL expiration, e.g., by transferring 21% of T's voting stock to a third party.

¶1204   T NOL WHEN P OR S ACQUIRES T IN TAX-FREE ACQUISITION

If P or S acquires T's stock or assets in a tax-free reorganization, T's NOLs continue to be available subject to numerous limitations. These limitations are discussed below in the context of three categories of transactions: P acquires T's assets in an "A" or "C" reorganization (¶1204.1), S acquires T's assets in a forward subsidiary "A" or subsidiary "C" reorganization (¶1204.2), and P acquires T's stock in a "B" or reverse subsidiary "A" reorganization (¶1204.3). If T's NOL expires unused, P's basis in T's (or S's) stock may be reduced by the amount of the expired NOL (¶1204.4).

¶1204.1   *T Transfers Assets to P in "A" or "C" Reorganization*

When P acquires T's assets in an "A" or "C" reorganization, P inherits T's NOL under Code §381,[1] subject to the limitations discussed below.

¶1204.1.1   Code §269(a) Acquisition of Assets with Tax Avoidance Principal Purpose

T's NOLs will be eliminated and thus will not carry over to P at all if P acquires T's assets in a COB transaction and the principal purpose of the acquisition is to avoid tax by securing the benefit of T's NOL. See generally ¶1203.2.2.

¶1204   [1] See Code §381(c)(1)(B) prorating, in P's first taxable year ending after the T-P reorganization, T's NOL deduction inherited by P; Technical Advice Memorandum 200044003 (6/22/00) (application to AMT NOL carryover).

¶1204.1.2 Code §382

Generally the Code §382 limitation will apply if, after the reorganization, T's shareholders own less than 50% of P's stock (measured by FV, not counting certain non-voting, non-convertible, limited preferred stock). In making this measurement, generally only T shareholders who owned their T stock for at least three years before the reorganization are counted. For example, if T's shareholders received 60% of P's stock in the reorganization but individual A purchased 20% of T's stock within three years before the reorganization (but after Code §382's effective date), T's shareholders would be treated as owning only 48% of P (80% of 60%), and the Code §382 limitation would apply. When the limitation applies, it limits T's NOL carryforwards as follows:

(1) T's NOLs will be wholly eliminated unless T's business enterprise is continued at all times during the two-year period beginning on the date of the reorganization, i.e., P continues a significant historic line of T's business or continues to use a significant portion of T's historic business assets.

(2) If T's business enterprise is continued, P's use of T's NOLs will be subject to an annual limitation equal to the long-term tax-exempt bond rate times the FV of T's stock immediately before the reorganization (but disregarding any T shares redeemed in connection with the ownership change).

Code §382 generally applies to an ownership change resulting from an "A" or "C" reorganization pursuant to a plan of reorganization "adopted" (as discussed at ¶1208.7) after 12/31/86. See ¶1208 for further discussion of Code §382.

EXAMPLE 1

Individual A has long owned 100% of T's stock. P is owned by persons unrelated to A and T. On 1/1/00, when T has a $100 NOL, T merges into P in an "A" reorganization. Pursuant to the merger, A acquires 50% of P's outstanding stock. Because A owns at least 50% of P's stock after the merger, there has not been an ownership change under Code §382. Therefore, Code §382 will not limit P's ability to carry forward T's NOL to shelter P's post-merger income so long as there is no further change in T's ownership before 1/1/03 (i.e., within the three-year look-forward period). However, under the SRLY rules discussed below, T's NOL may not offset the post-merger income of any other member of P's consolidated group.

EXAMPLE 2

Same as Example 1, except that A receives only 49% of P's outstanding stock in the merger. Because A owns less than 50% of P's stock after the merger, there has been a Code §382 ownership change. Therefore, assuming P continues T's historic business, P may carry forward T's NOL to offset the P group's post-merger income, subject to an annual limitation equal to the FV of T's stock immediately before the merger times the long-term tax-exempt bond rate then in effect. Because there is a Code §382 ownership change, under the §382 Overlap Rule (see ¶1205.2.4.2(4)) T's NOL does not become a SRLY NOL.

EXAMPLE 3

Same as Example 2 except that on 1/1/01 (one year after the merger) P sells all of T's historic business and assets. P may not carry forward any portion of T's pre-acquisition NOL to offset P's post-1/1/00 income, except perhaps for gain P recognizes on the sale of T's historic assets (pursuant to the "BIG" rules discussed at ¶1208.2.3).

¶1204.1.3 Consolidated Return Regulations

If P is a member of an affiliated group filing consolidated returns (see ¶1205.2.1), and if there is no Code §382 ownership change with respect to T's NOL at the time of or within six months before or after the reorganization, any of T's NOLs that carry over to P will be SRLY and hence will be usable only against P's separate profits, not against the profits of other members of P's consolidated group. In contrast, if there is a Code §382 ownership change with respect to T's NOL at the time of, or within six months before or after, the reorganization, then under the §382 Overlap Rule (see ¶1205.2.4.2(4)), for tax years of the P group for which the due date (without extensions) of P's consolidated return is after 6/25/99 (even if P acquired T's assets in an earlier tax year), T's pre-acquisition NOLs generally will not be SRLY NOLs. Therefore, for those years, subject to any applicable Code §382 limitation, T's NOLs may be carried forward to offset the future income of P and any other member of P's consolidated group. However, for prior years of the P group T's pre-acquisition NOLs are SRLY NOLs.

EXAMPLE 1

Individual A has long owned 100% of T's stock. P is a calendar year corporation owned by persons unrelated to A and T. On 1/1/00, when T has a $100 NOL, T merges into P in an "A" reorganization in which A receives less than 50% of P's stock. Because the merger results in a Code §382 ownership change of T, under the §382 Overlap Rule the merger does not cause T's NOL to be a SRLY NOL. Therefore, T's NOL (assuming it is not eliminated by Code §269 or §382, and subject to any applicable Code §382 limitation) may be carried forward to offset the future income of P and any other member of P's consolidated group.

EXAMPLE 2

Same as Example 1, except that T's merger into P occurs on 1/1/97. Under the pre-1999 SRLY rules, for the P group's 1997 and 1998 tax years T's NOL (assuming it is not completely eliminated by Code §269 or Code §382) may be carried forward to offset only P's post-merger income, not the future income of any other member of P's affiliated group. However, because the 1997 merger resulted in a Code §382 ownership change of T, under the §382 Overlap Rule T's NOL ceases to be a SRLY NOL for the P group's 1999 and later tax years. Therefore, subject to any applicable Code §382 limitation, T's NOL may be carried forward to those years to offset future income of P and any other member of P's consolidated group.

If, at the time of the reorganization, T had subsidiaries that were included in T's (and, after the acquisition, P's) consolidated return, then for taxable years of the P consolidated group ending before 1/29/91, the portion of T's consolidated SRLY NOL attributable to T itself is generally usable only against P's future income, not against the future income of any other corporation, and the portion of T's consolidated SRLY NOL attributable to each T subsidiary is generally usable only against the future income of that subsidiary, not against the future income of any other corporation. In contrast, for taxable years ending after 1/28/91, T's consolidated SRLY NOL might be usable against the future income of T's entire former group as well as the future income of P (but not against the future income of P's other affiliates), under the principles discussed in ¶1205.2.4.2.

If T's pre-reorganization shareholders receive more than 50% of P's common and preferred stock (by FV) in the reorganization as a result of owning T stock, the transaction is a "reverse acquisition" under Reg. §§1.1502-75(d)(3) and 1.1502-1(f)(3). Hence, the T group is treated as remaining in existence (with P as the new parent) and the P group is treated as terminating for purposes of the consolidated return regulations. In such case, T's NOL would not be a SRLY NOL. Often a reverse acquisition results in a Code §382 ownership change of P, causing the §382 Overlap Rule to apply to any pre-acquisition NOLs of P. If this is not the case (and in any event for tax years for which the due date (without extensions) of the consolidated return is before 6/26/99), any NOLs of P or its subsidiaries would be SRLY NOLs and hence usable only against the post-acquisition profits of the corporation that holds the NOL (and, for taxable years ending after 1/28/91, possibly against the post-acquisition income of other members of the former P group under the principles discussed in ¶1205.2.4.2).

¶1204.2   T Transfers Assets to S in Subsidiary "A" or Subsidiary "C" Reorganization in Exchange for P Stock

When S acquires T's assets in a subsidiary "A" or subsidiary "C" reorganization, S inherits T's NOL under Code §381, subject to the limitations discussed below.

¶1204.2.1   Code §269(a) Acquisition of Assets with Tax Avoidance Principal Purpose

T's NOLs are eliminated, and thus do not carry over to S at all, if S acquires T's assets in a COB transaction and the principal purpose of the acquisition is to avoid tax by securing the benefit of T's NOL. See generally ¶1203.2.2.

¶1204.2.2   Code §382

Generally the Code §382 limitation will apply if, after the reorganization, T's shareholders own less than 50% of P's stock (and hence own less than 50% of S's stock through P) measured by FV, not counting certain non-voting, non-convertible, limited preferred stock. In making this measurement, generally only T shareholders who owned their T stock for at least three years before the reorganization are counted. For example, if T's shareholders received 60% of P's stock in the reorganization but individual A purchased 20% of T's stock within three years before the reorganization (but after Code §382's effective date), T's shareholders would be treated as owning only 48% of P (80% of 60%), and hence 48% of S, and the Code §382 limitation would apply. When the limitation applies, it limits T's NOL carryforwards as follows:

(1)   T's NOLs will be wholly eliminated unless T's business enterprise is continued at all times during the two-year period beginning on the date of the reorganization, i.e., S continues a significant historic line of T's business or continues to use a significant portion of T's historic business assets.

(2)   If T's business enterprise is continued, S's use of T's NOLs will be subject to an annual limitation equal to the long-term tax-exempt bond rate times the FV of T's stock immediately before the reorganization (but after any redemption connected with the ownership change).

For purposes of Code §382, the S stock owned by P is treated as owned proportionately by P's shareholders.[2]

Code §382 generally applies to an ownership change resulting from a subsidiary "A" or subsidiary "C" reorganization pursuant to a plan of reorganization

---

[2] Code §382(*l*)(3)(A).

"adopted" (as discussed at ¶1208.7) after 12/31/86. See ¶1208 below for a detailed discussion of Code §382.

EXAMPLE 1

Individual A has long owned 100% of T's stock. P is owned by persons unrelated to A and T. On 1/1/00, when T has a $100 NOL, T transfers all of its assets to S in a subsidiary "C" reorganization in exchange for 49% of P's outstanding stock. T liquidates, distributing its P stock to A. P and S file consolidated returns. Because A owns less than 50% of P's stock after the reorganization, and hence less than 50% of S's stock, there has been an ownership change under Code §382. Therefore, assuming S continues T's historic business, S may carry forward T's NOL to offset the P group's postreorganization income, subject to an annual limitation equal to the FV of T's stock immediately before the reorganization times the long-term tax-exempt bond rate then in effect.

EXAMPLE 2

Same as Example 1, except that on 1/1/01 (one year after the reorganization) S sells all of T's historic business and assets. S may not carry forward any portion of T's pre-acquisition NOL to offset the P group's post-1/1/00 income, except perhaps for gain the P group recognizes on the sale of T's historic assets (pursuant to the BIG rules discussed at ¶1208.2.3 below).

¶1204.2.3   Consolidated Return Regulations

If S is a member of an affiliated group filing consolidated returns (see ¶1205.2.1), and if there is no Code §382 ownership change with respect to T's NOL at the time of or within 6 months before or after the reorganization, any of T's pre-acquisition NOLs that carry over to S will be SRLY and hence will be usable only against S's profits, not against the profits of other members of the P-S consolidated group. In contrast, if there is a Code §382 ownership change with respect to T's NOL at the time of, or within 6 months before or after, the reorganization, then under the §382 Overlap Rule (see ¶1205.2.4.2(4)), for tax years of the P group for which the due date (without extensions) of P's consolidated return is after 6/25/99 (even if S acquired T's assets in an earlier tax year), T's pre-acquisition NOLs generally will not be SRLY NOLs. Therefore, for those years, subject to any applicable Code §382 limitation, T's NOLs may be carried forward to offset the future income of P, S and any other member of P's consolidated group. However, for prior years of the P group T's pre-acquisition NOLs are SRLY NOLs.

EXAMPLE 1

Individual A has long owned 100% of T's stock. P is a calendar year corporation owned by persons unrelated to A and T. On 1/1/00, when T has a $100 NOL, T merges into S in a forward subsidiary "A" reorganization under Code §368(a)(2)(D) in which A receives less than 50% of P's stock. P and S file consolidated returns after the reorganization. Because the merger results in a Code §382 ownership change of T, under the §382 Overlap Rule the merger does not cause T's NOL to be a SRLY NOL. Therefore, T's NOL (assuming it is not eliminated by Code §269 or §382, and subject to any applicable Code §382 limitation) may be carried forward to offset the future income of P, S and any other member of P's consolidated group.

EXAMPLE 2

Same as Example 1, except that T's merger into S occurs on 1/1/97. Under the pre-1999 SRLY rules, for the P group's 1997 and 1998 tax years, T's NOL (assuming it is not completely eliminated by Code §269 or §382) may be carried forward only to offset S's post-merger income, not the future income of P or any other affiliate of S. However, because the 1997 merger resulted in a Code §382 ownership change of T, under the §382 Overlap Rule T's NOL ceases to be a SRLY NOL for the P group's 1999 and later tax years. Therefore, subject to any applicable Code §382 limitation, T's NOL may be carried forward to those years to offset future income of P, S and any other member of P's consolidated group.

If, at the time of the reorganization, T had subsidiaries that were included in T's (and, after the acquisition, P's) consolidated return, then for taxable years of the P consolidated group ending before 1/29/91, the portion of T's consolidated SRLY NOL attributable to T itself is generally usable only against S's future income, not against the future income of any other corporation, and the portion of T's consolidated SRLY NOL attributable to each T subsidiary is generally usable only against the future income of that subsidiary, not against the future income of any other corporation. In contrast, for taxable years ending after 1/28/91, T's consolidated SRLY NOL might be usable against the future income of T's entire former group as well as the future income of S (but not against the future income of P or P's other affiliates), under the principles discussed in ¶1205.2.4.2.

If T's pre-reorganization shareholders receive more than 50% of P's common and preferred stock (by FV) in the reorganization as a result of owning T stock, the transaction is a "reverse acquisition" under Reg. §§1.1502-75(d)(3) and 1.1502-1(f)(3). Hence the T group is treated as remaining in existence (with P as the new parent) and the P group is treated as terminating for purposes of the consolidated return regulations. In such case, T's NOL would not be a SRLY NOL. Often a reverse acquisition results in a Code §382 ownership change of P, causing the §382 Overlap Rule to apply to any pre-acquisition NOLs of P. If this is not the case (and in any event for tax years for which the due date (without extensions) of the consolidated return is before 6/26/99), any NOLs of P or its subsidiaries would be SRLY and hence usable only against the post-acquisition profits of the corporation that holds the NOL (and, for taxable years ending after 1/28/91, possibly against the post-acquisition income of other members of the former P group, under the principles discussed in ¶1205.2.4.2).

¶1204.2.4 S's Later Liquidation into P

Assume that, in a later transaction separate from the initial reorganization, S (having acquired T's assets in a tax-free reorganization) liquidates into P. Code §269(b) (regarding certain liquidations the principal purpose of which is to avoid taxes) will not apply to the liquidation standing alone because S did not originally "purchase" T's stock. Compare ¶1203.2.5 above. However, if the S-into-P liquidation occurs so soon after the reorganization that the reorganization and liquidation are treated as a step transaction in which P acquired T's assets in a "C" reorganization, then Code §269 will apply to the transaction as described at ¶1204.1.1. If so, T's NOLs will be eliminated (and therefore not carry over to P) if the principal purpose of the overall transaction is to avoid tax by securing the benefit of T's NOL.[3]

If the annual limitation of Code §382 applied to T's NOL as a result of the original T-S subsidiary reorganization, it will continue to apply after S's liquidation into P.[4] However, the liquidation alone will not alter the beneficial ownership of S and therefore will not itself trigger Code §382.

Regardless of when S is liquidated into P, if P is a member of a consolidated group, and if T's NOL became a SRLY NOL as a result of the original T-S subsidiary reorganization, then after the liquidation T's pre-acquisition SRLY NOLs will be usable only against the profits of P (S's successor in liquidation) and (for taxable years ending after 1/28/91), possibly against the post-acquisition income of one or more T subsidiaries, but not against the profits of other members of P's consolidated group, under the principles discussed in ¶1205.2.4.2.

---

[3] Code §269(a).
[4] See Reg. §1.382-2(a)(1).

¶1204.3   T's Shareholders Transfer T Stock to P in "B" or Reverse Subsidiary "A" Reorganization

When P acquires T's stock in a "B" reorganization or in a tax-free reverse subsidiary merger (i.e., a reverse subsidiary "A" reorganization, with S merging into T), T's NOL continues to be usable by T, subject to the limitations discussed below.

¶1204.3.1   Code §269(a) Acquisition of Assets with Tax Avoidance Principal Purpose

T's NOLs will be eliminated and hence will not continue to be usable by T if P acquires T's stock in a "B" reorganization or reverse subsidiary "A" reorganization and the principal purpose of the acquisition is to avoid tax by securing the benefit of T's NOL. See generally ¶1203.2.2.

¶1204.3.2   Code §382

Generally, the Code §382 limitation will apply if, after the reorganization, T's shareholders own less than 50% of P's stock (and hence own less than 50% of T's stock through P) measured by FV, not counting certain non-voting, non-convertible, limited preferred stock. In making this measurement, generally only T shareholders who owned their T stock for at least three years before the reorganization are counted. For example, if T's shareholders received 60% of P's stock in the reorganization but individual A purchased 20% of T's stock within three years before the reorganization (but after Code §382's effective date), T's shareholders would be treated as owning only 48% of P (80% of 60%), and hence 48% of T, and the Code §382 limitation would apply. When the limitation applies, it limits T's NOL carryforwards as follows:

(1)   T's NOLs will be wholly eliminated unless T's business enterprise is continued at all times during the two-year period beginning on the date of the reorganization, i.e., T continues a significant historic line of business or continues to use a significant portion of its historic business assets.

(2)   If T's business enterprise is continued, T's NOLs will be subject to an annual limitation equal to the long-term tax-exempt bond rate times the FV of T's stock immediately before the reorganization (but disregarding any T shares redeemed in connection with the ownership change).

For purposes of Code §382, the T stock owned or acquired by P is treated as owned proportionately by P's shareholders.[5]

---

[5] Code §382(*l*)(3)(A).

Code §382 generally applies to an ownership change resulting from a "B" reorganization or reverse subsidiary "A" reorganization pursuant to a plan of reorganization "adopted" (as discussed at ¶1208.7) after 12/31/86. See ¶1208 below for a detailed discussion of Code §382.

EXAMPLE 1

Individual A has long owned 100% of T's stock. P is owned by persons unrelated to A and T. On 1/1/00, when T has a $100 NOL, P acquires all of T's stock from A in a "B" reorganization in exchange for 49% of P's outstanding stock. P and T file consolidated returns. Because A owns less than 50% of P's stock after the reorganization, and hence less than 50% of T's stock, there has been an ownership change under Code §382. Therefore, assuming T continues its historic business, T may carry forward its NOL to offset the P group's postreorganization income, subject to an annual limitation equal to the FV of T's stock immediately before the reorganization times the long-term tax-exempt bond rate then in effect.

EXAMPLE 2

Same as Example 1 except that on 1/1/01 (one year after the reorganization) T sells all of its historic business and assets and enters a new business. T may not carry forward any portion of its pre-acquisition NOL to offset the P group's post-1/1/00 income, except perhaps for gain T recognizes on the sale of its historic assets (pursuant to the BIG rules discussed at ¶1208.2.3).

¶1204.3.3   Consolidated Return Regulations

If P files a consolidated return with T (see ¶1205.2.1), and if there is no Code §382 ownership change of T at the time of or within 6 months before or after P's acquisition of T, any of T's pre-acquisition NOLs that continue to be usable by T will be SRLY and hence will be usable only against T's profits, not against P's profits or the profits of other members of the P-T consolidated group. In contrast, if there is a Code §382 ownership change of T at the time of, or within 6 months before or after, P's acquisition of T, then under the §382 Overlap Rule (see ¶1205.2.4.2(4)), for tax years of the P group for which the due date (without extensions) of P's consolidated return is after 6/25/99 (even if P acquired T in an earlier tax year), T's pre-acquisition NOLs generally will not be SRLY NOLs. Therefore, for those years, subject to any applicable Code §382 limitation, T's NOLs may be carried forward to offset the future income of T, P and any other member of P's consolidated group. However, for prior years of the P group T's pre-acquisition NOLs are SRLY NOLs.

EXAMPLE 1

Individual A has long owned 100% of T's stock. P is a calendar year corporation owned by persons unrelated to A and T. On 1/1/00, when T has a $100 NOL, S merges into T in a reverse subsidiary "A" reorganization, with A exchanging all of his or her T stock for 20% of P's stock and P's S stock being cancelled in exchange for newly issued T stock, so T becomes a 100% P subsidiary. P and T file consolidated returns after the reorganization. Because the merger results in a Code §382 ownership change of T, under the §382 Overlap Rule the merger does not cause T's NOL to be a SRLY NOL. Therefore, T's NOL (assuming it is not eliminated by Code §269 or §382, and subject to any applicable Code §382 limitation) may be carried forward to offset the future income of T, P and any other member of P's consolidated group.

EXAMPLE 2

Same as Example 1, except that S's merger into T occurs on 1/1/97. Under the pre-1999 SRLY rules, for the P group's 1997 and 1998 tax years T's NOL (assuming it is not completely eliminated by Code §269 or §382) may be carried forward only to offset T's post-acquisition income, not the future income of P or any other member of P's affiliated group. However, because the 1997 merger resulted in a Code §382 ownership change of T, under the §382 Overlap Rule T's NOL ceases to be a SRLY NOL for the P group's 1999 and later tax years. Therefore, subject to any applicable Code §382 limitation, T's NOL may be carried forward to those years to offset future income of T, P and any other member of P's consolidated group.

If, at the time of the reorganization, T had subsidiaries that were included in T's (and, after the acquisition, P's) consolidated return, then for taxable years of the P consolidated group ending before 1/29/91, the portion of T's consolidated SRLY NOL attributable to each member of T's former consolidated group is generally usable only against the future income of that member, not against the future income of any other corporation. In contrast, for taxable years ending after 1/28/91, T's consolidated SRLY NOL might be usable against the future income of T's entire former group (but not against the future income of P or P's other affiliates) under the principles discussed below in ¶1205.2.4.2.

If T's pre-reorganization shareholders receive more than 50% of P's common and preferred stock (by FV) in the reorganization as a result of owning T stock, the transaction is a "reverse acquisition" under Reg. §§1.1502-75(d)(3) and 1.1502-1(f)(3). Hence, the T group is treated as remaining in existence (with P as the new parent) and the P group is treated as terminating for purposes of the consolidated return regulations. In such case, T's NOL would not be a SRLY NOL. Often a reverse acquisition results in a Code §382 ownership change of P, causing the §382 Overlap Rule to apply to any pre-acquisition NOLs of P. If this is not the case (and in any event for tax years for which the due date (without extensions) of the consolidated return is before 6/26/99), any NOLs of P or its subsidiaries would be SRLY NOLs and hence usable only against the post-acquisition profits of the corporation that holds the NOL (and, for taxable years ending after 1/28/91, possibly against the post-acquisition income of other members of the former P group, under the principles discussed in ¶1205.2.4.2).

¶1204.3.4   T's Later Liquidation into P

If T is liquidated into P so soon after P acquires T's stock that the reorganization and liquidation are treated as a step transaction in which P acquired T's assets directly in a "C" reorganization (see Rev. Rul. 67-274, 1967-2 C.B. 141), then Code §269 will apply to the transaction as described at ¶¶1204.2.4 and 1204.1.1 above.

If the annual limitation of Code §382 applied to T's NOL as a result of the original stock acquisition, it will continue to apply after T's liquidation into P.[6] However, the liquidation alone will not alter the beneficial ownership of T and therefore will not itself trigger Code §382.

Regardless of when T is liquidated into P, if P is T's successor in liquidation and P is a member of a consolidated group, and if T's NOL became a SRLY NOL as a result of P's original acquisition of T, then after the liquidation T's pre-acquisition SRLY NOLs will be usable only against P's profits, and (for taxable years ending after 1/28/91, possibly against the post-acquisition income of one or more T subsidiaries), but not against the profits of other members of P's consolidated group, under the principles discussed in ¶1205.2.4.2.

¶1204.4   Potential Reduction of P's Outside Basis in T's Stock When T's NOL Expires While P and T File Consolidated Return

If P acquires T's stock in a "B" or reverse subsidiary "A" reorganization (see ¶1204.3) in a taxable year beginning after 1994, and if any part of T's NOL ultimately expires unused, P's outside basis in T's stock will be reduced at the time of expiration by the amount of the expired NOL unless P and T timely elected to waive T's NOL (generally by an attachment to P's consolidated return for the year of the P-T acquisition), as further discussed in ¶1203.3.

---

[6] See Reg. §1.382-2(a)(1).

Similarly, if S acquires T's assets in a subsidiary "A" or subsidiary "C" reorganization in exchange for P stock (see ¶1204.2) in a taxable year beginning after 1994, and if any part of T's NOL (inherited by S in the reorganization) ultimately expires unused, P's outside basis in S's stock will be reduced at the time of the expiration by the amount of the expired NOL unless P and S timely elected to waive the NOL (generally by an attachment to P's consolidated return for the year of the P-T acquisition), as further discussed in ¶1203.3.

¶1205   P NOL WHEN P ACQUIRES T

P's ability to use its own NOLs to offset T's future income after P's taxable or tax-free acquisition of T is subject to numerous limitations, as discussed below in connection with asset acquisitions (¶1205.1) and stock acquisitions (¶1205.2). Among these limitations is Code §384 (limiting the use of P's pre-acquisition losses to offset T's BIGs at the time P acquired T), which was enacted in 1987 and is discussed in detail at ¶1205.2.5. Operating T as a partnership with P, VC, and Mgmt as partners may allow the use of P's NOLs against part of T's taxable income (¶1205.3).

¶1205.1   P Acquires T's Assets

P's ability to use its own NOLs after acquiring T's assets in a taxable or tax-free transaction is discussed below.

¶1205.1.1   P Acquires T's Assets in Taxable Purchase

Generally there is no limitation on P's ability to purchase T's assets for cash and/or notes (or to acquire them in a taxable merger of T into P) and use its own NOL to offset future income generated by such assets. Neither Code §269 nor Code §384 (discussed below) applies because the acquisition is not a COB transaction. Code §382 does not apply because there is no change in P's beneficial ownership. Finally, the consolidated return regulations are not implicated because P has neither acquired nor become a subsidiary.

¶1205.1.2   P Acquires T's Assets in "A" or "C" Reorganization

When P acquires T's assets in an "A" or "C" reorganization, P's pre-acquisition NOL (and the non-SRLY NOL of any other member of P's consolidated group) may be used to offset the future taxable income generated by T's assets subject to the limitations discussed below.

(1) Code §269(a) acquisition of assets with tax avoidance principal purpose.
P will not be able to use its NOL to offset income from T's assets if P (or other
P group members) acquires T's assets in a COB transaction and the principal
purpose of the acquisition is to avoid tax by securing tax benefits P would not
otherwise enjoy (e.g., applying P's NOL against the future income generated by
T's assets). See generally ¶1203.2.2.

(2) Code §382. If T or T's shareholders receive a significant amount of P stock
in connection with P's acquisition of T's assets, Code §382 could apply. Specifically,
if, as a result of the reorganization and/or other transactions, the percentage of
P stock owned (directly or by attribution) by T's pre-reorganization shareholders
or other persons is more than 50 percentage points above the lowest percentage
of P stock owned by them during the preceding three-year period (an "ownership
change"), then Code §382 generally will limit P's NOL carryforwards as follows:[1]

  (a) P's NOLs will be wholly eliminated unless P meets the continuity of
       business enterprise test of Code §382 at all times during the two-year
       period beginning on the ownership change date.
  (b) If P meets the continuity of business enterprise test, P's NOLs will be
       subject to an annual limitation equal to the long-term tax-exempt bond
       rate times the FV of P's stock immediately before the ownership change
       (but disregarding any P shares redeemed in connection with the owner-
       ship change).

Code §382 generally applies to an ownership change pursuant to a plan of
reorganization "adopted" (as discussed at ¶1208.7) after 12/31/86. See ¶1208
below for a detailed discussion of Code §382.

(3) Consolidated return regulations. If P is a member of an affiliated group
filing consolidated returns (see ¶1205.2.1), and if T's pre-reorganization shareholders receive more than 50% of P's common and preferred stock (by FV) in the
reorganization as a result of owning T stock, the transaction is a "reverse acquisition" under Reg. §§1.1502-75(d)(3) and 1.1502-1(f)(3). Hence, the T group is treated
as remaining in existence (with P as the new parent) and the P group is treated
as terminating for purposes of the consolidated return regulations. Often a reverse
acquisition results in a Code §382 ownership change of P, causing the §382 Overlap
Rule to apply to any pre-acquisition NOLs of P. If this is not the case (and in any
event for tax years for which the due date (without extensions) of the consolidated
return is before 6/26/99), any NOLs of P or its subsidiaries would be SRLY and
hence usable only against the postreorganization income of the corporation that
holds the NOL (and, for taxable years ending after 1/28/91, possibly against the
post-acquisition income of other members of the former P group, as discussed

¶1205 [1] If no ownership change has yet occurred (i.e., there has not yet been a more-than-50-
percentage-point change in the ownership of P's stock), then increases in ownership of P stock during
the succeeding three-year period must be considered along with the prior changes and, if sufficiently
substantial, will cause an ownership change.

below at ¶1205.2.4.2). P, as transferee of T's assets, nevertheless could use its NOL to offset future income generated by such assets.

(4)   Code §384 limitation on P's ability to offset T's built-in gain. Code §384 (enacted by the 1987 Act and substantially amended retroactively by the 1988 Act) generally limits the use of P's (and its affiliated group's) NOLs to offset the BIG in T's assets at the time P (or other members of its affiliated group) acquires T's assets in an "A," "C," or acquisitive "D" reorganization. In such a case, Code §384 generally prohibits P from using its pre-acquisition NOL (or the pre-acquisition NOL of any member of P's affiliated group) to offset any BIG recognized on the disposition of any asset owned by T at the time P acquired T if the disposition occurs within five years after the date P acquired T (the "acquisition date"). "Built-in gain" with respect to a T asset is generally the excess of the asset's FV on the acquisition date over its adjusted basis on that date, but also includes any item of income recognized after the acquisition date that is attributable to periods before the acquisition date.

However, Code §384 generally is not applicable if

(a)   T's aggregate BIG is not more than the lesser of (i) 15% of the aggregate FV of T's assets (other than cash, receivables, other cash items, and certain marketable securities) immediately before the acquisition or (ii) $10 million (generally effective for ownership changes after 10/2/89 under the 1989 Act),[2] or

(b)   P and T have belonged to the same "controlled group" (i.e., P and its affiliates, or certain P shareholders, have owned more than 50% of T's stock by vote and by value, not counting non-voting limited preferred stock and certain other stock) throughout the lesser of the five-year period ending on the acquisition date or the period of T's (or, if shorter, P's) existence, or

(c)   the acquisition date is before 12/16/87 or pursuant to a binding written contract, letter of intent, or merger agreement in effect before 12/16/87.

For a detailed discussion of Code §384, including its application to asset acquisitions, see ¶1205.2.5 below.

¶1205.2   P Acquires Sufficient T Stock to File Consolidated Return with T

If P and T are members of the same "affiliated group" and file a consolidated return, P's pre-acquisition NOL (and the non-SRLY NOL of any other member

[2] For pre-10/3/89 ownership changes, and for later ownership changes pursuant to a written binding contract in effect on 10/2/89 and at all times thereafter before the ownership change, the percentage threshold described in text is 25% rather than 15%, and the $10 million threshold does not apply.

of P's group) may be used to offset T's taxable income, subject to the limitations discussed at ¶¶1205.2.2 through 1205.2.5. This is true even if T has other shareholders (e.g., VC and Mgmt) so long as they do not own enough T stock to prevent T from being a member of P's affiliated group.

Except as otherwise noted, the following discussion applies whether P acquires T's stock in a taxable acquisition (e.g., by direct purchase or reverse subsidiary cash merger) or in a tax-free reorganization (e.g., a "B" reorganization or a reverse subsidiary "A" reorganization).

¶1205.2.1   "Affiliated Group" Definition

T can file a consolidated return as part of P's "affiliated group" only if P (or other members of its affiliated group) owns:

(1)   T stock possessing at least 80% of T's total combined voting power and
(2)   T stock with an FV of at least 80% of the FV of all T's outstanding stock.[3]

However, in applying (2), a class of preferred stock will be ignored if it meets all of the following conditions:

(1)   it is not entitled to vote,
(2)   it is limited and preferred as to dividends and does not significantly participate in corporate growth,
(3)   its redemption and liquidation rights do not exceed its issue price plus a reasonable redemption or liquidation premium, and
(4)   it is not convertible into another class of stock.[4]

For further discussion of these and other requirements for including T in P's affiliated group, see ¶211.1.

In some circumstances Reg. §1.1504-4 treats options, warrants, convertible obligations, and similar interests as exercised under the 80-80 test of Code §1504. See ¶211.2 for an extensive discussion of the regulation.

¶1205.2.2   Code §269(a) Change of Control with Tax Avoidance Principal Purpose

P will not be able to use its NOL to offset T's income if P (or other P group members) acquires 50% or more of T's stock (by value or by vote) and "the principal purpose" of the acquisition is to avoid tax by securing tax benefits P would not otherwise enjoy (e.g., applying P's NOL against T's future income stream). In *Briarcliff Candy Corporation and Subsidiaries*,[5] for example, the court

---

[3] Code §1504(a)(2).
[4] Code §1504(a)(4).
[5] 54 T.C.M. 667, T.C. Mem. 1987-487 (1987).

applied Code §269(a) when a loss corporation (P) acquired the stock of a profitable consolidated group for the principal purpose of "securing the deduction of net operating losses that [P] would have otherwise been unable to use." See generally ¶1203.2.2.

Legislative Update

The unenacted Senate version of the 2003 Act (S. 1054) would have amended Code §269(a) to apply to any acquisition of corporate stock or corporate assets in a COB transaction, effectively eliminating the "control" requirement in current Code §269(a).

An identical provision was reintroduced in the Senate on 6/2/03 as part of the Working Taxpayer Fairness Restoration Act (S. 1162) to be effective for stock and property acquired after 2/13/03. An identical provision also appears in the Abusive Tax Shelter Shutdown and Taxpayer Accountability Act of 2003 (H.R. 1555), introduced 4/2/03, to be effective for transactions after enactment.

¶1205.2.3   Code §382

If a significant amount of P stock changes hands as a result of P's acquisition of T's stock (e.g., if P issues its stock to T's old shareholders in the transaction), Code §382 could apply. Specifically, if, as a result of the acquisition and/or other transactions, the percentage of P stock owned (directly or by attribution) by T's pre-acquisition shareholders or other persons is more than 50 percentage points above the lowest percentage of P stock owned by them during the preceding three-year period (an "ownership change"), then Code §382 generally will limit P's NOL carryforwards as follows:[6]

(1) P's NOLs will be wholly eliminated unless P meets the continuity of business enterprise test of Code §382 at all times during the two-year period beginning on the ownership change date.

(2) If P meets the continuity of business enterprise test, P's NOLs will be subject to an annual limitation equal to the long-term tax-exempt bond rate times the FV of P's stock immediately before the ownership change (but disregarding any P shares redeemed in connection with the ownership change).

---

[6] If no ownership change has yet occurred (i.e., there has not yet been a more-than-50-percentage-point change in the ownership of P's stock), then increases in ownership of P stock during the succeeding three-year period must be considered along with the prior changes and, if sufficiently substantial, will cause an ownership change.

Code §382 generally applies to ownership changes occurring after 12/31/86, but under some circumstances takes account of stock transfers after 5/5/86. See ¶1208.7. See also ¶1208 for a detailed discussion of Code §382.

¶1205.2.4 Consolidated Return Regulations

The following regulations governing the filing of consolidated returns by affiliated groups of corporations also may limit the use of P's NOLs.

¶1205.2.4.1 *Consolidated Return Change of Ownership Freeze Rules*

Temporary regulations published in 6/96 provide that the rules described below do not apply to a "consolidated return change of ownership" ("CRCO") occurring after 12/31/96 (or after 1/28/91 if the taxpayer elects to apply retroactively all of the 6/96 temporary regulations as described in ¶1205.2.4.2(2)).[7] The basis for repeal of the CRCO rules is that "[t]he policies underlying the CRCO rules have been subsumed by the single entity approach to the application of section 382 to consolidated groups" (see ¶1208.6).[8] Therefore, the following discussion is relevant only for CRCOs occurring before 1/1/97 (before 1/29/91 for electing taxpayers).

If P undergoes a CRCO before or during the taxable year in which P acquires T's stock, P's pre-acquisition NOL cannot be used to offset T's post-acquisition income, even if P and T file consolidated returns.[9] Specifically, if P suffers a CRCO, the NOL of P and its pre-CRCO group members can be used to offset the future income of only those corporations that were members of P's group immediately before the first day of the taxable year in which the CRCO occurred ("old members"). Such a CRCO "freeze" generally occurs whenever:

(1) any one or more of P's ten largest shareholders (measured by stock FV and including both direct stock ownership and ownership by attribution) owns a percentage of P's outstanding stock that is more than 50 percentage points greater than such person or persons owned at the beginning of the taxable year or the beginning of the preceding taxable year, and

(2) the increase is attributable to purchase or to a decrease in the amount of P stock outstanding (e.g., a non-pro-rata redemption).[10]

The CRCO definition recited above comes from old Code §382, which is incorporated by reference into Reg. §1.1502-1(g). Old Code §382 was repealed by the 1986 Act, generally effective 12/31/86. Hence, it is surprising that CRCO (1) continued from 1986 to 1996 to be defined in the regulations by reference to old Code §382

---

[7] See Temp. Reg. §§1.1502-21T(d) and 1.1502-21T(g)(3).
[8] IRS Notice of Proposed Rulemaking CO-78-90, Preamble at E., 1990-1 C.B. 757.
[9] See Reg. §§1.1502-1(g) and 1.1502-21A(d).
[10] Reg. §1.1502-1(g).

and (2) so continues for any CRCO occurring through 12/31/96 (which may have significance for many years after 1996) unless a taxpayer elects to apply the 6/96 temporary regulations retroactively.

EXAMPLE 1

Unrelated individuals A, B, and C each owned one-third of P's stock since P's formation in 1980. P is the parent of an affiliated group that has long filed consolidated returns on a calendar year basis. On 1/1/84 (before the 1986 effective date of new Code §382), when the P group had a $300 NOL, B and C sold all their P stock to A. This resulted in a CRCO because A's ownership of P stock increased by more than 50 percentage points (from 33.3% to 100%) by purchase. The P group continued to generate NOLs. On 1/1/90, when the P group has a $500 NOL, P purchases all the stock of unrelated T and includes T in P's consolidated returns. Under the CRCO rules, the P group's pre-1984 NOL ($300) may not be carried forward to offset any of T's future income, and can be used only against income generated by P and the old members of P's group, i.e., those that were P affiliates on 12/31/83.

EXAMPLE 2

Same as Example 1 except that B and C sold their P stock to A on 12/31/96 (after the 1986 effective date of new Code §382) rather than on 1/1/84. Unless P elects retroactive application of the 6/96 temporary regulations (see ¶1205.2.4.2(2)), the CRCO result described above would be the same, and P's NOL would also be subject to new Code §382's annual limitation.

EXAMPLE 3

Same as Example 2 except that on 1/1/84 B and C sold all their P stock to corporation X instead of to individual A. The analysis is the same (i.e., the CRCO rules apply) because X's ownership of P stock increased by more than 50 percentage points (from 0% to 66.6%) by purchase. Note that corporation X's purchase of 66.6% of P's stock was not a SRLY event because corporation X acquired less than 80% of P's stock.

P can avoid the CRCO limitation with respect to T by liquidating T (under Code §332) or merging it (tax free) into a pre-CRCO old member of the P group. Thus, if in the above examples P liquidates T, the CRCO rules will no longer prevent the P group from using its pre-CRCO NOL to shelter income generated by T's assets. However, such a liquidation or merger will not necessarily prevent the application of Code §384. See ¶1205.2.5.

If a CRCO occurs with respect to P before the end of the taxable year in which P acquires T's stock (e.g., because P shares are transferred by purchase, whether or not in connection with P's acquisition of T, so that such purchase along or in conjunction with prior stock transfers causes P to suffer a CRCO), the CRCO will prevent P from using its NOLs to offset T's income (unless P liquidates T). This is because T was not a member of P's group immediately before the first day of the taxable year in which the CRCO occurred and hence is not an "old member" of P's group. If P issues more than 50% of its stock to T's old shareholders in connection with its acquisition of T's stock in a tax-free reorganization (e.g., a "B" reorganization or a reverse subsidiary "A" reorganization), the transaction will be a reverse acquisition (discussed below) and not a CRCO (which requires a transfer of P stock by purchase).

If a CRCO occurs after the end of the taxable year in which P acquires T, it will not impair P's ability to use its NOL to offset T's income because T is now an old member of P's group.

EXAMPLE 4

Same as Example 1 except that B and C sold their P stock to A on 1/1/91 (i.e., after the end of the taxable year in which P's 1/1/90 purchase of T's stock occurred) rather than on 1/1/84. The CRCO rules will not impair P's continued use of its NOL against T's income. Under the CRCO rules, P's NOL is unavailable only with respect to the income of corporations that join P's group after 12/31/90. (However, P's pre-1/2/91 NOL will be subject to Code §382's annual limitation.)

¶1205.2.4.2   *Separate Return Limitation Year Rules*

Taking a significant and laudable step towards simplifying the NOL limitation rules, regulations published in 1999 (the "1999 Regulations") substantially limit the circumstances in which the "separate return limitation year" ("SRLY") rules described below apply. In general, the 1999 Regulations provide that if (1) corporation X is the parent of a consolidated group which succeeds to P's NOL by reason of an acquisition of P's assets (e.g., in an "A" or "C" reorganization) or stock (without a Code §338 or §338(h)(10) election), and (2) an ownership change results in the application of a Code §382 limitation to P's NOL at the time of, or within six months before or after, X's acquisition of P (which often will be the case), then for tax years of the X group for which the due date (without extensions) of X's consolidated return is after 6/25/99 (e.g., 1999 and thereafter if X is a calendar year corporation), P's pre-acquisition NOLs do not become (or, if X acquired P in an earlier tax year, will cease to be) SRLY NOLs as a result of the acquisition (the "§382 Overlap Rule").

For further discussion of the 1999 Regulations and the circumstances in which the SRLY rules continue to apply, see ¶1205.2.4.2(4) below.

(1)   Taxable years ending before 2/91. For taxable years of the P consolidated group ending before 1/29/91, the portion of the P group's SRLY NOL attributable to each member of P's consolidated group is usable only against the post-SRLY income of that member, not against the future income of other P group members, T, or any other corporation.[11] This "SRLY fragmentation" rule applies to P's SRLY NOL whether the SRLY transaction occurs before, in connection with, or any time after P acquires T. P's NOL generally will become a SRLY NOL whenever another corporation ("X") acquires sufficient P stock for affiliation (i.e., 80% by vote and by value) so that P is included in X's (i.e., the new parent corporation's) consolidated return.[12]

EXAMPLE 5

P's stock has always been owned by individual A. On 1/1/89, when P has a $200 NOL, P purchases all of T's stock from persons unrelated to P. P and T file consolidated returns. T is a profitable corporation, and its income is offset by P's NOL (assuming T's income does not derive from BIGs subject to Code §384, as discussed in ¶1205.2.5). On 1/1/90, when P's NOL has been reduced to $100, X, a calendar-year corporation unrelated to the P group, purchases all of P's stock from A, and P and T are included in X's consolidated return. SRLY fragmentation of P's NOL results because P joined X's consolidated group in a taxable year that ended before 1/29/91. Hence, P's pre-1990 SRLY NOL ($100) is available to offset only P's future income (subject to the limitation of Code §382), not the future income of T (except to the extent provided in (2) below) or any other member of X's group until taxable years of the X group beginning after 12/31/96, for which the rules described in (3) and (4) below will apply.

---

(2)   Taxable years ending after 1/91 and beginning before 1/97. For taxable years ending after 1/28/91 and beginning before 1/1/97, temporary regulations published in 6/96 (the "1996 Temporary Regulations")[13] provide that the P group may either:

---

[11] Reg. §1.1502-21A.

[12] Reg. §1.1502-1.

[13] Temp. Reg. §1.1502-21T (limitation on SRLY NOLs), -15T (limitation on SRLY BILs) (T.D. 8677), each in effect prior to 6/25/99; Reg. §1.1502-21(h)(6), -15(h)(2).

(a) apply the SRLY rules described immediately above applicable to a taxable year ending before 1/29/91 (the "Old Regulations"), or

(b) apply the SRLY rules described in (3) (NOLs) and (5) (BILs) below applicable to a post-1996 taxable year, provided all of the following conditions are satisfied: (i) all of the 1996 temporary consolidated loss regulations (including under Code §382—see ¶1208.6) are consistently applied on the P group's final return (original or amended) for each taxable year within the transition period for which the statute of limitations does not preclude the filing of an amended return on 1/1/97, (ii) the 1996 Temporary Regulations concerning SRLY NOLs and built-in deductions are applied only with respect to the losses and deductions of those corporations that became members of P's group, and to acquisitions occurring, after 1/28/91 (and only with respect to such losses and deductions), and (iii) appropriate adjustments are made in the earliest subsequent open year to reflect any inconsistency in a year for which the statute of limitations precludes P from filing an amended return on 1/1/97.[14]

Thus, whichever approach is chosen, until a consolidated return year beginning after 12/31/96, the rules of the Old Regulations relating to the treatment of SRLY NOLs and built-in deductions continue to apply to corporations that became members of P's group before, and to acquisitions occurring before, 1/29/91.

(3) NOL carryovers to taxable years beginning after 1996 through and including taxable years for which consolidated return due before 6/99. Under the 1996 Temporary Regulations and the 1999 Regulations, if P and its subsidiaries undergo a SRLY transaction (e.g., become members of X's consolidated group) at any time, then to the extent P's consolidated pre-acquisition NOL is carried forward to taxable years of the X group beginning after 12/31/96 through and including taxable years for which the due date (without extensions) of the X group's consolidated return is before 6/26/99, P's consolidated NOL is a SRLY NOL. To the extent P and its subsidiaries are a "SRLY subgroup" with respect to the NOL carryforward, P's SRLY NOL may offset not only the income for such years of the former P group member that generated the NOL, but also the income of all other former P group members included in the SRLY subgroup (though not the income of X or X's other affiliates).[15] To the extent P's consolidated NOL is carried forward to tax years for which the due date (without extensions) of the X group's consolidated return is after 6/25/99, the rules described in (4) below apply.

Upon X's acquisition of P, P and its subsidiaries generally are a SRLY subgroup with respect to the P group's NOL carryforward (a) if the P group members that incurred the NOL incurred it after they joined P's consolidated group and (b) if a member incurred the NOL less than five years after joining P's consolidated

---

[14] Temp. Reg. §1.1502-21T(g)(3).
[15] Temp. Reg. §1.1502-21T (in effect prior to 6/25/99); Reg. §1.1502-21(h)(6).

group, the NOL did not arise from a net unrealized built-in loss ("NUBIL") that existed when that member joined P's consolidated group.[16]

EXAMPLE 6

Same as Example 5. P incurred its NOL while it was the parent of the P group, and P's NOL did not arise from a NUBIL that arose outside of the P group. Therefore, P and T are a SRLY subgroup with respect to the NOL. Accordingly, for taxable years of the X group beginning after 12/31/96 through and including taxable years for which the due date (without extensions) of the X group's consolidated return is before 6/26/99, P's $100 SRLY NOL may be used against the future income of both P and T (rather than merely P's future income for pre-1991 taxable years as in Example 5), but not against the future income of X or any other member of X's group.

If a P group member fails to qualify for inclusion in P's SRLY subgroup (e.g., the member already has an NOL when it joins P's consolidated group, or, within five years after joining P's group, the member incurs an NOL attributable to a NUBIL that existed when the member joined P's group), then unless the member is combined with other similarly situated members as described below, a SRLY transaction for the P group generally will result in SRLY fragmentation of the NOL attributable to that member.[17]

EXAMPLE 7

P acquires T on 12/31/97, at which time T has an NOL that T is entitled to carry forward to 1998. Thereafter, T is included with P's other subsidiaries in P's consolidated return. Corporation X purchases P's stock on 7/1/98. Because T incurred its 12/31/97 SRLY NOL before joining P's group, for taxable years of the X group through and including taxable years for which the due date (without extensions) of the X group's consolidated return is before 6/26/99, T's SRLY NOL is usable only against the future income of T (subject to Code §382), not against the future income of P, X, or any other member of the X consolidated group.

If two or more but not all members of P's group are a SRLY subgroup with respect to an NOL, then there is partial SRLY fragmentation. That is, after a SRLY

---

[16] See Temp. Reg. §1.1502-21T(c)(2). P and its subsidiaries have a NUBIL, if the aggregate adjusted basis of the P group's assets exceeds their aggregate FV by more than the lesser of (1) 15% of their aggregate FV or (2) $10 million as described in ¶1208.4(3)(d) and adjusted by the 1996 Temporary Regulations and the 1999 Regulations.

[17] See Temp. Reg. §1.1502-21T(c)(1); Reg. §1.1502-21(c)(1).

transaction, the portion of the P group's NOL attributable to a SRLY subgroup is usable only against the future income of that subgroup's members, not against the future income of any other P group member.

The members of a SRLY subgroup include any "successor" or "predecessor" to a member.[18] The following rules apply for determining successors and predecessors:

Rule 1: "Successor" is (particularly for pre-6/25/99 transactions) narrowly defined to include only a corporation receiving assets from a "predecessor" in (i) a tax-free liquidation, (ii) a tax-free reorganization, (iii) any COB transaction (e.g., a Code §351 transfer of assets) on or after 6/25/99, or (iv) a COB transaction after 12/31/96 but before 6/25/99 in which "the amount by which basis differs from value, in the aggregate, is material."[19]

Rule 2: For a transaction that occurs before 6/25/99, only one member may be a predecessor or successor of one other member.[20]

Rule 3: For taxable years for which the due date (without extensions) of the consolidated return is before 6/26/99, unless IRS otherwise determines, any increase in the consolidated taxable income of a SRLY subgroup attributable to a successor is disregarded unless "the successor acquires substantially all the assets and liabilities of its predecessor and the predecessor ceases to exist."[21] For taxable years for which the due date (without extensions) of the consolidated return is after 6/25/99, a more liberal rule applies: A successor's net income is excluded from the consolidated taxable income of a SRLY subgroup unless *any* of the following applies: (i) the successor acquires substantially all the assets and liabilities of its predecessor, and the predecessor ceases to exist (i.e., the pre-1999 exception); (ii) the successor was a member of the SRLY subgroup when the subgroup's members joined the new consolidated group; (iii) all of the successor's stock is owned directly by corporations that were members of the subgroup when the subgroup members joined the new consolidated group; or (iv) IRS otherwise determines.[22]

EXAMPLE 8

IRS applied the above rules to the following pre-1999 transaction in IRS Letter Ruling 9715035 (4/11/97). P owned all the stock of S1, which in turn owned all the stock of S2. P acquired the stock of unrelated T, a loss corporation, by a tax-free reverse subsidiary merger of S1 into T in which

[18] Temp. Reg. §1.1502-21T(f)(1); Reg. §1.1502-21(f)(1).
[19] Reg. §1.1502-1(f)(4) (as amended in 1999).
[20] Id.
[21] Temp. Reg. §1.1502-21T(f)(2).
[22] Reg. §1.1502-21(f)(2). See also Preamble (¶¶58-59) of the 1999 Regulations.

T became a 100% P subsidiary. Following the S1-T merger, (1) T contributed to S2 (which was a first tier T subsidiary after the merger) the stock of T's historic subsidiaries, the FV of which "materially exceeded" basis and represented over 90% of the precontribution FV of all T's historic assets, (2) T contributed some of the remaining 10% of T's historic assets to a newly formed T subsidiary (S3), and (3) T retained the balance of its historic assets. IRS ruled (under the pre-1999 successor rules) that, after the above steps, (1) S2 is a "successor" to T and hence is included in T's SRLY subgroup (because S2 received substantially all of T's assets in a COB transaction and the built-in gain in the transferred assets was "material"—see rule 1 above), (2) S3 is not a "successor" to T and hence is not part of T's SRLY subgroup (because S2 is T's successor and T can have no more than one successor—see rule 2 above), and (3) any increase in the T SRLY subgroup's future income, to the extent attributable to T's successor S2, "may" be disregarded for SRLY purposes (because T did not "cease to exist" after transferring substantially all its assets to S2—see rule 3 above).

However, for taxable years of the P group for which the due date of P's consolidated return is after 6/25/99, under new exception (iii) to rule 3 above, S2's net income should not be disregarded in calculating the T-S2 subgroup's income for SRLY purposes, because all of S2's stock is owned directly by T, which became a member of the SRLY subgroup when it joined P's group.

EXAMPLE 9

Same as Example 8, except the T-S1 merger occurs on 1/1/00. In contrast to Example 8, S3 (as well as S2) is a "successor" to T, because rule 1(iii) (COB successor) applies, and rule 2 (the one successor rule) does not apply, to post-6/24/99 transactions. In addition, both S2's and S3's income should be included in the T-S2-S3 subgroup's income for SRLY purposes under exception (iii) to rule 3.

(4)   NOL carryovers to taxable years for which consolidated return due after 6/99: §382 Overlap Rule. The 1999 Regulations[23] generally follow the 1996 Temporary Regulations with one major departure: they simplify the consolidated NOL limitation rules by frequently eliminating the SRLY limitation on an NOL if it would overlap with the application of Code §382. For this purpose, an overlap with Code §382 occurs with respect to an NOL if the loss corporation becomes a member of a consolidated group (the SRLY event) within six months before or after an ownership change giving rise to a Code §382 limitation with respect to that NOL (the §382 event). If such an overlap occurs, the SRLY event will not

---

[23] Reg. §1502-21 (NOLs), -15 (BILs) (T.D. 8823).

result in application of the SRLY limitation to that NOL (or to an NOL arising after the §382 event and before the SRLY event), effective for taxable years for which the due date (without extensions) of the consolidated return is after 6/25/99 (the "§382 Overlap Rule") subject to a limited transition rule described below.[24]

Under the limited transition rule, according to Notice 2000- 53,[25] future regulations will provide that if loss corporation T ceased to be a member of a consolidated group (the "Bigco group") as a result of P's QSP of T that occurred (a) during a Bigco tax year to which the 1999 Regulations applied but (b) before 6/26/99 (the "Interim Period"), then T (or P) may elect to calculate T's NOL carryovers to post-acquisition periods as though the §382 Overlap Rule did not apply to T while it was a member of the Bigco group.[26] For example, the Interim Period for a corporation with a calendar tax year end is the period 1/1/99 through 6/25/99. The rationale for the transition rule is that the §382 Overlap Rule, by eliminating retroactively (to 1/1/99 for a calendar year group) the SRLY limitation applicable to T's pre-acquisition NOL while T belonged to the Bigco group, could increase the Bigco group's absorption of T's NOL and thus reduce the amount of T's available post-acquisition NOL resulting in unexpected adverse consequences to P. The election is made solely for T (by T or by P if P is T's new consolidated return parent) on T's original or amended tax return for its first (separate or consolidated) tax year after T leaves the Bigco group. The election requires no action by Bigco, and has no effect on any Bigco consolidated return for which the due date is after 6/25/99.

Since the transition rule does not affect Bigco's tax returns (i.e., Bigco can take advantage of the §382 Overlap Rule during the Interim Period), under the transition rule T's NOL might be used twice: once by the Bigco group during the Interim Period (during which the §382 Overlap Rule permits Bigco to use T's NOL to absorb income generated by other Bigco group members without regard to any SRLY limitation that might otherwise apply to T's NOL) and again by T after the acquisition (since T will have calculated its NOL carryover as though the §382 Overlap Rule did not apply to T's NOL while T was a member of Bigco's group). There should be no double benefit to the parties, however, because Bigco's absorption of T's NOL will reduce Bigco's tax basis in T's shares (see Reg. §1.1502-32(b)(3)(i)) and thus increase Bigco's gain (or decrease Bigco's loss) on the sale of T.

The §382 Overlap Rule applies even if the SRLY event and/or the §382 event occurred before the effective date of the 1999 Regulations. In such cases, any affected NOL is a SRLY NOL for tax years for which the due date of the consolidated return (without extensions) is on or before 6/25/99, but ceases to be a SRLY NOL in later tax years. See the examples in ¶¶1203.2.4 (stock purchase), 1204.1.3 ("A" or "C" reorganization), 1204.2.3 (subsidiary "A" or subsidiary "C" reorganization), and 1204.3.3 ("B" or reverse subsidiary "A" reorganization).

Thus, under the §382 Overlap Rule, if (1) corporation X is the parent of a consolidated group which succeeds to P's NOL by reason of an acquisition of P's

---

[24] Reg. §1502-21(g) (NOLs); -15(g) (BILs).

[25] 2000-2 C.B. 293.

[26] A similar election will be available for calculating T's BILs and net capital losses.

assets (e.g., in an "A" or "C" reorganization) or P's stock (without a Code §338 or §338(h)(10) election), and (2) an ownership change results in the application of a Code §382 limitation to P's NOL at the time of, or within six months before or after, X's acquisition of P, then for tax years of the X group for which the due date (without extensions) of X's consolidated return is after 6/25/99 (e.g., 1999 and thereafter if X is a calendar year corporation), P's pre-acquisition NOLs do not become (or, if X acquired P in an earlier tax year, will cease to be) SRLY NOLs as a result of the acquisition.

IRS's sound rationale for creating the §382 Overlap Rule is that "the simultaneous or proximate imposition of a [Code §382] limitation reasonably approximates a corresponding SRLY limitation," so that, particularly when weighed against the complexity of applying both SRLY and Code §382 limitations to an NOL, the SRLY limitation is not necessary for transactions that trigger a Code §382 limitation.[27]

In Notice 98-38, 1998-2 C.B. 222, IRS noted the complexity of the pre-1999 SRLY rules and stated that it was considering amending the SRLY limitation along the lines of the stock-value-based mechanism of Code §382. Instead of adopting this approach, the 1999 Regulations (1) through the §382 Overlap Rule, eliminate the SRLY limitation altogether in many instances where Code §382 applies, and (2) where the §382 Overlap Rule does not apply, generally retain the SRLY limitation in the form in which it appears in the 1996 Temporary Regulations (as described in (3) above).

The §382 Overlap Rule substantially reduces the circumstances in which the SRLY NOL limitation applies, because transactions that result in a SRLY event typically also result in a §382 event. In many such cases (e.g., P purchases all the stock of unrelated loss corporation T), the SRLY event and the §382 event occur simultaneously, as illustrated in the examples in ¶¶1203.2.4 (stock purchase), 1204.1.3 ("A" or "C" reorganization), 1204.2.3 (subsidiary "A" or subsidiary "C" reorganization), and 1204.3.3 ("B" or reverse subsidiary "A" reorganization).

If the SRLY event and the §382 event occur within a six month period but not on the same day, the §382 Overlap Rule applies in the following manner:

(1) *§382 event precedes SRLY event.* If the SRLY event occurs during the six-month period beginning with the date of the §382 event, the §382 Overlap Rule applies beginning with the tax year that includes the SRLY event.[28] As a result, no SRLY limitation is triggered at any time, including with respect to an NOL incurred between the time of the §382 event and the SRLY event, even though no Code §382 limitation applies to such NOL.[29]

EXAMPLE 10

P, a calendar year corporation, purchases 60% of T's stock on 1/1/00 (resulting in a §382 event) and the remaining 40% on 4/30/00 (a SRLY

---

[27] 1999 Regulations, Preamble ¶38.
[28] Reg. §1.1502-21(g)(3)(i).
[29] Reg. §1.1502-21(g)(2)(ii)(B).

event). P and T thereafter file consolidated returns. T has a $100 NOL on 1/1/00 and a $150 NOL on 4/30/00. As a result of the §382 event, T's $100 pre-1/1/00 NOL is subject to a Code §382 limitation. The SRLY event occurs after but within six months of the §382 event, so that the Overlap Rule applies for P's 2000 tax year. Therefore, no SRLY limitation applies to T's pre-4/30/00 NOL, including the $50 NOL that accrued between 1/1/00 and 4/30/00, even though this interim $50 NOL is not subject to a Code §382 limitation. Hence, (i) T $100 pre-1/1/00 NOL may be used against post-1/1/00 income of T and against post-4/30/00 income of P, T and any other member of P's consolidated group, in each case subject to the Code §382 limitation, and (ii) T's $50 NOL accrued between 1/1/00 and 4/30/00 may be used against the post 4/30/00 income of P, T and any other member of P's group, without limitation under Code §382.

(2) *§382 event follows SRLY event.* If the §382 event occurs during the period beginning the day after the SRLY event and ending six months after the SRLY event, the §382 Overlap Rule applies from the beginning of the tax year following the §382 event.[30] As a result, a SRLY limitation applies from the time of the SRLY event through the end of the tax year in which the §382 event occurs. This rule is intended to ensure that at least one loss limitation regime (SRLY or Code §382) applies to T's losses for all periods following T's entry into P's consolidated group.[31] Unfortunately there is a bit of overkill, because this rule subjects any pre-SRLY-event NOL to both SRLY and Code §382 limitations from the Code §382 ownership change date through the end of the tax year in which the §382 event occurs.

EXAMPLE 11

P, a calendar year corporation, has always owned 40% of T's only class of stock, and the remaining 60% has always been owned by unrelated individual A. On 12/31/99, P purchases an additional 40% of T's stock from A, resulting in a SRLY event. At that time T has a $100 NOL. Thereafter P includes T in its consolidated return. P purchases the remaining 20% of T's stock on 5/1/00. At that time T has a $150 NOL. P's 5/1/00 purchase is a §382 event, because P has purchased more than 50% of T's stock during a 3-year period. Therefore, T's $150 pre-5/1/00 NOL is subject to a Code §382 limitation. The §382 event occurs after but within six months of the SRLY event. Therefore the §382 Overlap Rule applies as follows: T's $100 12/31/99 NOL is subject to a SRLY limitation from the day after the SRLY event (1/1/00) through the end of P's tax year in which the Code §382 ownership

---

[30] Reg. §1.1502-21(g)(3)(ii).
[31] 1999 Regulations, Preamble ¶47.

change occurs (12/31/00). In addition, T's pre-5/1/00 NOL is subject to a Code §382 limitation commencing 5/1/00. Thus, T's NOL may be used as follows:

(i)   From 1/1/00 through 12/31/00, T's $100 pre-1/1/00 NOL is subject to a SRLY limitation and therefore can be used only against the income of T, not against the income of P or any other member of P's group.

(ii)   From 5/1/00, T's entire $150 pre-5/1/00 NOL is subject to a Code §382 limitation based on the FV of T's stock on 5/1/00.

(iii) From and after 1/1/01, the SRLY limitation in (a) above ceases to apply, but the Code §382 limitation in (b) above continues to apply, so that T's $150 pre-5/1/00 NOL may be used against post-12/31/00 income of P, T and any other member of P's group, subject to the Code §382 limitation.[32]

If there is no §382 event within six months before or after the SRLY event, the §382 Overlap Rule does not apply, so that any pre-SRLY-event NOLs become SRLY NOLs. This result can occur when the acquisition of the loss corporation occurs in stages over a period exceeding six months. The 1999 Regulations provide no exceptions to the six-month rule, even if the §382 event and the SRLY event occur pursuant to a plan or binding commitment.

EXAMPLE 12.   No Overlap

Individual A has always owned all of T's stock. On 1/1/00 unrelated corporation P purchases 60% of T's stock. At that time T has a $100 NOL. Under the purchase agreement, P is required to purchase, and A is required to sell, the remaining 40% of T's stock as soon as certain regulatory approvals are obtained. The approvals are obtained eight months later, and on 9/30/00 P purchases the remaining 40% of T's stock. At that time T has a $150 NOL. Thereafter T is included in P's consolidated return.

P's 1/1/00 purchase of 60% of T's stock is a §382 event resulting in the application of a Code §382 limitation to T's $100 pre-1/1/00 NOL. P's purchase of the remaining 40% of T's stock on 9/30/00 is a SRLY event, because it results in P's ownership of at least 80% of T's stock by vote and value.[33] The §382 Overlap Rule does not apply, because the §382 event and the SRLY event did not occur within a six month period. Therefore, T's $150

---

[32] See Reg. §1.1502-21(g)(5) example (4).

[33] P's and A's binding agreement to complete the transfer of the remaining 40% of T's stock from A to P would not by itself result in a SRLY event prior to the actual closing, because Reg. §1.1504-4(d)(2)(iii) disregards, for purposes of determining whether the 80% stock ownership test for tax consolidation is satisfied, stock purchase agreements subject only to "reasonable closing conditions" (see ¶211.2.2(7)).

pre-10/1/00 NOL is a SRLY NOL which may (subject to the Code §382 limitation on T's $100 NOL attributable to the pre-1/1/00 period) be used against post-9/30/00 income of T, but not income of P or any other member of P's group.

In contrast, if in this example P had purchased 40% (rather than 60%) of T's stock on 1/1/00 and the remaining 60% (rather than 40%) on 9/30/00, (1) there would be no Code §382 ownership change of T on 1/1/00, and (2) on 9/30/00, there would be both a Code §382 ownership change and a SRLY event. Therefore the §382 Overlap Rule would apply. In that case, subject to the Code §382 limitation, T's $150 pre-10/1/00 NOL could be used to offset post-9/30/00 income of P, T and any other member of P's consolidated group.

The §382 Overlap Rule also does not apply when a loss corporation (P) acquires T's stock or assets in a tax-free "A", "B" or "C" reorganization that constitutes a "reverse acquisition" of P and is therefore a SRLY event with respect to P's NOL (see ¶¶1204.1.3, 1204.2.3 and 1204.3.3), but does not result in a Code §382 ownership change of P. This can occur, for example, where T's shareholders receive common stock and Straight Preferred (as described in ¶1208.1.1) of P which represents more than 50% (by FV) of P's outstanding common and preferred stock (thus causing a reverse acquisition), but they do not receive more than 50% of P's common stock (since a Code §382 ownership change is determined without regard to Straight Preferred (see ¶1208.1.1).

The §382 Overlap Rule requires not merely a Code §382 ownership change, but also that the "ownership change giv[es] rise to a section 382(a) limitation."[34] Therefore, apparently the §382 Overlap Rule does not apply, and a SRLY limitation is imposed, when bankrupt T undergoes a Code §382 ownership change but, under Code §382(l)(5), no Code §382 limitation is imposed (see ¶1208.2.1.5). Depriving the taxpayer of the benefit of the §382 Overlap Rule in this case seems harsh. Code §382(l)(5) is designed to provide tax relief to troubled companies, whereas the 1999 Regulations undermine this policy by creating a punitive result vis-a-vis other taxpayers when Code §382(l)(5) is invoked. In addition, Code §382(l)(5) already contains its own punitive measures that are intended to compensate for relief from the Code §382 limitation. See Code §382(l)(5)(B) (reduction of NOL by prior interest payments) and §382(l)(5)(D) (imposing a zero Code §382 limitation upon a second ownership change within two years).

If the acquisition involves an NOL for which there is a SRLY subgroup and/or a Code §382 subgroup (as described in ¶1208.6), the §382 Overlap Rule applies to the SRLY subgroup, not separately to its members. The subgroup provisions are very complex. In general, however, the 1999 Regulations impose a strict requirement that the §382 Overlap Rule applies with respect to an NOL *only* if its SRLY subgroup is coextensive with (i.e., identical to) its Code §382 subgroup.[35]

---

[34] Reg. §1.1502-21(g)(2)(ii).
[35] Reg. §1.1502-21(g)(4).

The rationale for retaining the SRLY limitation where the SRLY subgroup is smaller than the Code §382 subgroup is clear and reasonable: a Code §382 limitation based on the stock value of the larger Code §382 subgroup is an overly generous substitute for the actual income of the smaller SRLY subgroup.[36]

> ### EXAMPLE 13. No Overlap: SRLY Subgroup Smaller than §382 Subgroup
>
> Individual A has always owned all the stock of P and its sister company T, which are calendar year corporations. On 12/31/99, P purchases all the stock of T and includes T in its consolidated group. At that time T has a $100 NOL carryover to 2000. The purchase results in a SRLY event, but not a §382 event (since A continues to own T through P). Hence the §382 Overlap Rule does not apply, and T's $100 pre-1/1/00 NOL becomes a SRLY NOL usable only against the post-12/31/99 income of T but not future income of P or other members of P's group. In 2000, the P-T group incurs an additional $50 NOL. On 6/1/05, X, an unrelated calendar year corporation, purchases all of P's stock from A, and P and T join X's consolidated group, resulting in both a §382 event and a SRLY event.
>
> With respect to T's $100 pre-1/1/00 NOL, P and T are a Code §382 subgroup because of Reg. §1.1502-96(a), which treats T's pre-1/1/00 NOL as a non-SRLY NOL as of the end of 2004 (see ¶1208.6.3.4). Therefore, after X's purchase of P, T's pre-1/1/00 NOL is subject to a Code §382 subgroup limitation based on the FV of P's stock immediately before X acquires P. In contrast, P and T and are not a SRLY subgroup with respect to the T NOL, because Reg. §1.1502-96(a) applies only for determining Code §382 subgroups, not SRLY subgroups.[37] Therefore, although both a SRLY event and a §382 event occur on 6/1/05 with respect to T's $100 NOL, the NOL's SRLY subgroup and its §382 subgroup are not coextensive, so that the §382 Overlap Rule does not apply. As a result, T's $100 pre-1/1/00 NOL continues to be usable only against the future income of T, not the future income of X, P or any other member of X's consolidated group.
>
> With respect to the $50 P-T NOL incurred during 2000, X's 6/1/05 purchase of P's stock also is both a SRLY event and a §382 event. Moreover, P and T are both a SRLY subgroup and a Code §382 subgroup with respect to that NOL. Therefore, the §382 Overlap Rule applies, so this NOL does not become a SRLY NOL and is usable against the post-6/1/05 income of T, P, X and any other member of X's consolidated group, subject to a §382 limitation based on the FV of P's stock immediately before X's 6/1/05 purchase of P.[38]

---

[36] See 1999 Regulations, Preamble ¶43.
[37] Reg. §1.1502-96(a)(5).
[38] See Reg. §1.1502-21(g)(5) example (7).

Regrettably, the §382 Overlap Rule also does not apply with respect to an NOL whose SRLY subgroup is larger than its Code §382 subgroup. As a policy matter this makes little sense, because in such a case the NOL is subject to a more stringent Code §382 limitation than would apply if the Code §382 subgroup included all SRLY subgroup members. Fortunately, this problem seems limited primarily to cases where there is a failure to make the Code §382 deemed subgroup parent election described in ¶1208.6.2.2.

EXAMPLE 14. No Overlap: SRLY Subgroup Larger than §382 Subgroup

Bigco owns all the stock of T1 and T2. On 12/31/99, unrelated corporation P purchases from Bigco all the stock of T1 and T2, which join P's consolidated group. At that time, Bigco has a $200 consolidated NOL carryover to 2000, of which $100 is attributable to each of T1 and T2. P does not make an election under Reg. §1.1502-91(d)(4) to treat the Code §382 subgroup parent requirement as having been satisfied (the "deemed subgroup parent election") (see ¶1208.6.2.2).

P's purchase is a SRLY event for both T1 and T2, which are a SRLY subgroup with respect to their combined $200 pre-1/1/00 NOL. However, because they do not bear an 80-80 Code §1504(a)(1) relationship to each other immediately after joining P's group, in the absence of the deemed subgroup parent election they are not a Code §382 subgroup. Accordingly, P's purchase results in the application of separate Code §382 limitations to T1's $100 NOL and T2's $100 NOL based on the FV (immediately before the acquisition) of T1's and T2's stock, respectively.

P's 12/31/99 purchase causes both a SRLY event and a §382 event to occur with respect to T1's and T2's NOLs. However, the SRLY subgroup and the §382 subgroup are not coextensive with respect to either NOL, so the §382 Overlap Rule does not apply for either NOL. As a result, T1's $100 NOL may be used (subject to the Code §382 limitation) against post-12/31/99 income of the T1-T2 SRLY subgroup, but not against the future income of P or any other member of P's group. A similar rule applies to T2's $100 NOL.[39]

The 1999 Regulations liberalize the "successor" and "predecessor" rules for determining SRLY subgroups, as discussed in ¶1205.2.4.2(3) above.

The §382 Overlap Rule also applies to built-in losses, as discussed immediately below.

(5) BILs recognized in tax years beginning after 1996. The 1996 Temporary Regulations and the 1999 Regulations also limit the deductibility, after a SRLY event, of BILs recognized in tax years beginning after 12/31/96 to the extent the

---

[39] See Reg. §1.1502-21(g)(5) example (6).

loss is attributable to a NUBIL that existed at the time of a SRLY event, subject to relief under the §382 Overlap Rule for tax years for which the due date (without extensions) of the consolidated return is after 6/25/99.[40] Specifically, if P has a NUBIL at the time of a SRLY event (e.g., at the time P joins X's consolidated group), then any BILs recognized during the next five years, to the extent attributable to the NUBIL, generally are treated as a SRLY NOL subject to the rules described in (3) above, except to the extent the §382 Overlap Rule described in (4) above applies for 1999 and later years. If a recognized BIL is treated as a SRLY NOL, SRLY fragmentation generally applies, so BILs attributable to each member of the P group generally are deductible only against the future income of that member.[41] However, this SRLY BIL limitation generally is applied on a subgroup (i.e., aggregate) basis to members of the P group that were continuously affiliated for the five-year period preceding their joining the consolidated group in which the loss is recognized.[42]

EXAMPLE 15

Individual A has always owned all of P's stock, and P has owned all of T's stock since 1/1/94. X is an unrelated, stand-alone, calendar year corporation that has no NOL or NUBIL. X purchases all of P's stock on 1/1/98. X, P, and T file consolidated returns thereafter. At the time of the 1/1/98 acquisition, P and T have a NUBIL. The NUBIL is attributable solely to T and accrued while P and T were affiliated. X's acquisition of P was a SRLY event with respect to the NUBIL. Therefore, except to the extent the §382 Overlap Rule applies for 1999 and later years, if the X group recognizes a loss attributable to T's NUBIL within five years after the 1/1/98 acquisition, it will be treated as a SRLY NOL. Moreover, since P and T were affiliated for less than five years before X's 1/1/98 purchase of P, SRLY fragmentation applies. Hence any such SRLY NOLs will be deductible (subject to Code §382) only against the future income of T (the entity to which the NUBIL is attributable), not the future income of X, P, or any other corporation.

X's 1/1/98 acquisition of P was also a §382 event with respect to T's NUBIL. For the same reason P and T are not a SRLY subgroup, they are not a Code §382 subgroup with respect to T's NUBIL.[43] Therefore, if the X group recognizes a loss attributable to T's NUBIL within five years after the 1/1/98 acquisition, it will be subject to an annual Code §382 limitation based on

[40] Reg. §1.1502-15; Temp. Reg. §1.1502-15T (in effect before 6/25/99).
[41] Reg. §1.1502-15(b); Temp. Reg. §1.1502-15T(b).
[42] See Reg. §1.1502-15(c); Temp. Reg. §1.1502-15T(c). For purposes of this 5-year affiliation requirement for NUBIL subgroups, if P has a NUBIL and joins X's group in a transaction in which the §382 Overlap Rule applies with respect to P's NUBIL, P (and any other members of the P group that are included in the determination of P's NUBIL) are deemed to have been affiliated with X for five years. Reg. §1.1502-15(c)(3). The SRLY BIL rules of Temp. Reg. §1.1502-15T replaced, generally for taxable years beginning after 12/31/96, the quite different SRLY BIL rules appearing in Reg. §1.1502-15A. For pre-1997 transition rules, see Temp. Reg. §1.1502-15T(f)(2). See also IRS Notice 91-27, 1991-2 C.B. 629.
[43] See Reg. §1.1502-91(c), (d); ¶1208.6.5.

the 1/1/98 FV of T's (not P's) stock on 1/1/98. Since T's NUBIL was subject to a simultaneous SRLY event and §382 event, the §382 Overlap Rule applies. Therefore, for tax years of the X group for which the due date (without extensions) of the consolidated return is after 6/25/99 (i.e., X's 1999 and later tax years), any recognized BILs attributable to T's 1/1/98 NUBIL (even if recognized before 1999) are not (or cease to be) SRLY NOLs. Hence they may be applied against post-1998 income of T, X, P and any other member of X's consolidated group, subject to the Code §382 limitation.

EXAMPLE 16

Same as Example 15 except that P has owned all of T's stock since 1/1/92, six years before X acquires P. Since P and T were affiliated for more than five years before X acquired P, the SRLY rules and the Code §382 rules apply to the NUBIL by reference to the P-T subgroup, rather than T alone. Since the SRLY subgroup and the Code §382 subgroup are co-extensive (i.e., each includes P and T), the §382 Overlap Rule applies. Therefore, if the X group recognizes a loss within five years after the 1/1/98 acquisition that is attributable to the P-T subgroup's 1/1/98 NUBIL, (1) the loss is subject to a Code §382 limitation based on the 1/1/98 FV of P's stock (not merely T's stock), (2) for the X group's 1998 tax year, the loss may be applied (subject to the Code §382 limitation) against the income of P and T, but not against the income of X or any other member of X's group, and (3) for the X group's 1999 and later tax years, under the §382 Overlap Rule the loss may be applied (subject to the Code §382 limitation) against the income of X, P, T and any other members of X's group.

As the above examples suggest, the §382 Overlap Rule applies to recognized BILs in a manner similar to its application to NOLs (described in 4. above).[44] One difference is that, if the SRLY event and the §382 event occur within a six month period but not simultaneously, the §382 Overlap Rule does not apply in certain cases where BIL assets are transferred in a COB transaction between the times of the two events.[45] In addition, notwithstanding application of the §382 Overlap Rule to a corporation's NUBIL, the SRLY rules apply to BIL assets acquired by the corporation in a COB transaction after the later of the SRLY event and the §382 event.[46]

(6) P's later liquidation of T—regardless of date. P can avoid or eliminate SRLY fragmentation of P and T by liquidating T (under Code §332) or merging T (tax free) into P. Thus, in Examples 12 and 13 above (where the §382 Overlap

---

[44] Compare Reg. §1.1502-15(g) (BILs) with §1.1502-21(g) (NOLs).
[45] See Reg. §1.1502-15(g)(3).
[46] Reg. §1.1502-15(g)(5), -15(b)(2)(ii), -15(g)(6) example (2).

Rule does not apply, so that a SRLY limitation is imposed even for post-1998 tax years), if, after the SRLY event, T is liquidated into P, the SRLY rules will no longer prevent T's NOL from sheltering income generated by P's assets, subject to the Code §382 limitation. In those examples T's NOL still may not be used to offset the income of any other corporation in P's (or, in Example 13, X's) group. In addition, such a liquidation or merger will not necessarily prevent the application of Code §384 with respect to any BIG of P. See ¶1205.2.5.

¶1205.2.4.3   *Reverse Acquisition Rules*

If P is a member of an affiliated group filing consolidated returns, and if T's pre-acquisition shareholders receive more than 50% of P's common and preferred stock (by FV) in exchange for their T stock in connection with P's acquisition of T's stock (e.g., in a "B" reorganization or reverse subsidiary "A" reorganization), then the transaction is a "reverse acquisition" under Reg. §§1.1502-75(d)(3) and 1.1502-1(f)(3). Hence, the T group is treated as remaining in existence (with P as the new parent) and the P group is treated as terminating for purposes of the consolidated return regulations. Often a reverse acquisition results in a Code §382 ownership change of P, causing the §382 Overlap Rule to apply to any pre-acquisition NOLs of P. If this is not the case (and in any event for tax years for which the due date (without extensions) of the consolidated return is before 6/26/99), any NOLs of P or its subsidiaries would be SRLY and hence usable only against the post-acquisition income of the corporation that holds the NOL (and, for taxable years ending after 1/28/91, possibly against the post-acquisition income of other members of the former P group), as discussed in ¶1205.2.4.2.

¶1205.2.5   Code §384 Limitation on P's Ability to Offset T's Built-in Gain

The 1987 Act enacted a new limitation on the use of P's (and its affiliated group's) NOLs to offset the BIG in T's assets at the time P acquires T's stock or assets. The 1988 Act corrected a number of significant technical flaws in Code §384 generally retroactive to the effective date of the 1987 Act.

Code §384 generally prohibits P from using its pre-acquisition NOL (or the pre-acquisition NOL of any member of P's affiliated group other than T) to offset any BIG recognized on the disposition of any asset owned by T at the time P acquired T if the disposition occurs within five years after the date P acquired T (the "acquisition date"). BIG with respect to a T asset is generally the excess of the asset's FV on the acquisition date over its adjusted basis on that date, but also includes any item of income recognized after the acquisition date that is attributable to periods before the acquisition date.

However, as further discussed under "Code §384 exceptions" below, Code §384 generally is not applicable in any of the following circumstances:

(1)   T's aggregate BIG is not more than the lesser of (a) 15% of the aggregate FV of T's assets (other than cash, receivables, other cash items, and certain marketable securities) immediately before the acquisition or (b) $10 million (generally effective for ownership changes after 10/2/89 under the 1989 Act).[47]

(2)   P and T have belonged to the same "controlled group" (i.e., P and its affiliates, or certain P shareholders, have owned more than 50% of T's stock by vote and by value, not counting non-voting limited preferred stock and certain other stock) throughout the lesser of the five-year period ending on the acquisition date or the period of T's (or, if shorter, of P's) existence.

(3)   The acquisition date is before 12/16/87 or pursuant to a binding written contract, letter of intent, or merger agreement in effect before 12/16/87.

A more detailed discussion of Code §384 follows.

¶1205.2.5.1   Taxable or Tax-Free Stock Acquisition

Code §384 applies when P (or other members of P's affiliated group) acquires sufficient T stock for affiliation under Code §1504 (i.e., 80% of T's stock by vote and by value), whether the acquisition is taxable (e.g., a direct stock purchase or a reverse subsidiary cash merger of S into T) or tax free (e.g., a "B" reorganization or a reverse subsidiary "A" reorganization).[48]

In this case, if T's BIG at the time of the acquisition exceeds the lesser of 15% of its asset FV (not counting cash, receivables, other cash items, and certain marketable securities) or $10 million, any BIG recognized during the five-year period beginning on the stock acquisition date (i.e., the day P and its group acquired sufficient T stock for affiliation) cannot be offset by the pre-acquisition NOL (i.e., any NOL accruing before the stock acquisition date) of any member of the P group other than T.

Code §384 literally applies whether or not P and T file consolidated returns. However, if P and T do not file consolidated returns, then even without Code §384 P cannot use its NOL to offset T's income. Therefore, in the case of a stock acquisition, Code §384 appears to have practical significance only if P and T file consolidated returns (or if, as discussed below, P and T are combined in a tax-free merger or liquidation within five years after P's acquisition of T).

---

[47] For pre-10/3/89 ownership changes, and for later ownership changes pursuant to a written binding contract in effect on 10/2/89 and at all times thereafter before the ownership change, the percentage threshold described in text is 25% rather than 15%, and the $10 million threshold does not apply.

[48] See Code §384(a)(1)(A), as amended by the 1988 Act.

EXAMPLE 1

Individual A has long owned 100% of P's stock. On 1/1/90, when P has a $500 NOL, P purchases 100% of T's outstanding stock from persons unrelated to A and P. Immediately before the stock acquisition, the aggregate FV of T's assets (other than cash items and certain marketable securities) is $1,000, and their aggregate tax basis is $600, so T has a $400 BIG, i.e., more than 15% of its asset FV. Code §384 applies as of 1/1/90 because T became a member of P's affiliated group on that date. Hence, P's NOL cannot be used to offset any of T's 1/1/90 BIG that is recognized before 1/1/95 (i.e., within five years after the stock acquisition date).

EXAMPLE 2

Assume in Example 1 that T and P file consolidated returns after the stock acquisition and that on 1/1/90 T owns a building with a $200 FV and a $50 basis, representing a $150 BIG ($200 − $50). Assume that the building appreciates an additional $50 during 1990 and that T sells the building on 12/31/90 for $250, when its basis is still $50. If Code §384 did not apply, T's $200 gain on the sale could be offset by P's NOL under the consolidated return rules. However, under Code §384 $150 (the BIG on the stock acquisition date) of T's $200 gain may not be offset by P's NOL (although the remaining $50 of gain attributable to post-acquisition appreciation may be offset).

EXAMPLE 3

Same as Example 2 except that P and T do not file consolidated returns. Because P and T file separate returns, P's NOL may not be used to absorb any of T's gain on the sale of the building, whether or not Code §384 applies. Hence, Code §384 (which does apply) would appear superfluous in this case.

EXAMPLE 4

Same as Example 1 except that P acquires 80% of T's stock (by vote and by value) in a "B" reorganization, with T's old shareholders receiving 40% of P's stock in exchange. Code §384 applies in the same fashion as in Example 1. (Note that there is no Code §382 ownership change with respect to P because less than 50% of P's stock has changed hands.)

Code §384 (as amended by the 1988 Act) applies to any successor of T (or P) to the same extent that it applied to T (or P).[49] Thus, P cannot escape the application of Code §384 by first acquiring T's stock and then liquidating T or merging downstream into T. The legislative history is explicit on this point:

[A]ssume that [P], which has net operating loss carryovers, acquires control of [T], which has net unrealized built-in gain in excess of the de minimis threshold. The two corporations subsequently file a consolidated return. Under the stock acquisition rule, income attributable to [T]'s recognized built-in gains may not be offset by [P]'s pre-acquisition losses during the subsequent five-year recognition period. If [T] is liquidated into [P] under section 332 within five years after the acquisition, income attributable to [T]'s recognized built-in gains may not be offset by [P]'s pre-acquisition losses during the remainder of the five-year period. The same result would occur if [P] merged downstream into [T].[50]

Except as provided in future regulations, stock transfers between members of an affiliated group do not trigger Code §384 (as amended by the 1988 Act).[51]

EXAMPLE 5

Same as Example 1 except that on 1/1/92 (two years after acquiring T's stock) P transfers the T stock to another P subsidiary. The 1/1/92 transfer does not itself trigger Code §384. However, the Code §384 taint resulting from P's original acquisition of T will continue for the remainder of the five-year period commencing on the date of the original acquisition.

EXAMPLE 6

Same as Example 2, i.e., P purchases 100% of T's stock in a taxable transaction, except that immediately afterwards P liquidates T under Code §332. The liquidation itself neither triggers Code §384 nor nullifies its prior application. Thus, the result is the same as in Example 2, i.e., even though P holds T's appreciated assets and sells the building, P cannot use its NOL to offset $150 of the $200 gain P recognizes on the building sale because there was $150 of BIG with respect to the building when P acquired T's assets in a Code §332 tax-free liquidation. The result would be the same even if (as in Example 3) P and T were not filing consolidated returns.

[49] Code §384(c)(7), as added by the 1988 Act.
[50] H.R. Rep. No. 795, 100th Cong., 2d Sess. 411-412 (1988) (hereinafter "1988 House Report"); S. Rep. No. 445, 100th Cong., 2d Sess. 435 (1988) (hereinafter "1988 Senate Report"); Joint Comm. on Taxation, Description of the Technical Corrections Act of 1988 (H.R. 4333 and S. 2238), JCS-10-88, 100th Cong., 2d Sess. 421 (1988).
[51] See Code §384(c)(6), as added by the 1988 Act.

¶1205.2.5.2 Tax-Free Asset Acquisition

Code §384 applies when P (or members of its affiliated group) acquires T's assets in an "A," "C," or acquisitive "D" reorganization, or when T acquires S's assets in a reverse subsidiary "A" reorganization.[52]

Code §384 does not apply when P (or members of its affiliated group) acquires T's assets in a taxable purchase, and of course there is no need for Code §384 to apply to such a transaction because P takes a cost basis in the purchased assets, and hence there should be no BIG.

If T's BIG at the time of the tax-free asset reorganization exceeds the lesser of 15% of its asset FV (not counting cash, receivables, other cash items, and certain marketable securities) or $10 million, any BIG recognized during the five-year period beginning on the asset acquisition date (i.e., the day of the tax-free asset reorganization) cannot be offset by the pre-acquisition NOL (i.e., any NOL accruing before the asset acquisition date) of any corporation other than T.

EXAMPLE 7

Same as Example 2 except that, instead of purchasing T's stock, P acquires T's assets in exchange for P stock in an "A" or "C" reorganization. Same result as Example 2, i.e., even though P holds T's appreciated assets and P sells the building, P cannot use its NOL to offset $150 of the $200 gain P recognizes on the building sale because there was $150 of BIG with respect to the building when P acquired T's assets from T in a tax-free reorganization.

¶1205.2.5.3 Code §384 Exceptions

There are four basic exceptions to Code §384:

(1) Code §384 does not apply if P and T have been members of the same "controlled group" throughout the lesser of the five-year period ending on the stock or asset acquisition date or, if T and/or P did not exist throughout this five-year period, the period of T's or P's existence (whichever is shorter). P and T generally will belong to the same controlled group if either (a) P and other members of P's group owned more than 50% of T's stock by vote and by value (not counting stock described in Code §1563(c), i.e., non-voting, limited, preferred stock, and certain other types of stock), or (b) five or fewer individuals, estates, or trusts owned more than 50% of both P's and T's stock (as described in (a) above) by vote and by value.[53] The legislative history to the 1988 Act amendment states that "[i]t is intended that this rule will be interpreted together with the successor rule [of Code §384(c)(7), described earlier] to prevent the avoidance of

---

[52] See Code §384(a)(1)(B), as amended by the 1988 Act.
[53] See Code §384(b), as retroactively amended by the 1988 Act.

the purpose of the rule through the use of a newly formed company to acquire or otherwise combine its assets with assets of a corporation that would be subject to the limitations."[54]

EXAMPLE 8

P's affiliated group owns exactly 50% of T's only outstanding class of stock during the period 1/1/80 through 1/1/90 and purchases the remaining 50% of T's stock on 1/2/90. On 1/2/90 P has an NOL and T has a substantial BIG. Code §384 applies commencing 1/2/90 because P's group did not own more than 50% of T's stock during the five years preceding the acquisition date.

EXAMPLE 9

Same as Example 8 except that on 1/2/90 P acquired all of T's assets in an "A" or "C" reorganization. Same result as Example 8.

EXAMPLE 10

Same as Examples 8 and Example 9 except that P's affiliated group owned 51% of T's stock during the period 1/1/80 through 1/1/90. Code §384 is not applicable.

EXAMPLE 11

On 1/1/90 P, which has a substantial NOL, forms T (a new 100% subsidiary) to which P contributes assets with a 1/1/90 FV of $1 million and a basis in P's hands of $300,000. Two years later, on 1/1/92, T sells the contributed assets for $1.3 million, a $1 million gain. Although P "acquired" T's stock on 1/1/90 (when it formed T), and at that time T had a $700,000 BIG (as a result of P's contribution of appreciated assets), P's formation of T will not trigger Code §384 because P's ownership of more than 50% of T's stock during the entire period of T's existence (even though less than five years) satisfies the safe harbor. Therefore, Code §384 will not limit P's ability to use its NOL to offset T's income from the 1/1/92 asset sale.

---

[54] 1988 House Report at 413; 1988 Senate Report at 515.

(2) Code §384 does not apply unless, immediately before the stock or asset acquisition, the FV of T's assets exceeds their aggregate basis by more than the lesser of (a) 15% of their aggregate FV (not taking into account cash, receivables, other cash items, or certain marketable securities, except as otherwise provided in regulations[55]) or (b) $10 million (generally effective for ownership changes after 10/2/89 under the 1989 Act).[56]

EXAMPLE 12

On 1/1/90 P, which has a $1,000 NOL, acquires T's assets in a reorganization covered by Code §384. Immediately before the acquisition, T has the following assets:

Asset	FV	Basis
Cash	$ 50	$ 50
Land and building	375	200
Machinery and equipment	325	250
Inventory	250	100
Total	$1,000	$600

Hence, the FV of T's assets (excluding cash) ($950) exceeds their aggregate basis ($550) by 42% of their aggregate FV ($400 (i.e., $950 FV – $550 basis) ÷ $950 FV = 42%). Because 42% exceeds the 15% threshold, T's BIGs are subject to the Code §384 limitation. For example, if P sells the land and building for $375 or more on 2/1/90, thus recognizing a $175 BIG, no part of this BIG may be offset by P's NOL (although any gain in excess of $175 may be offset by P's NOL).

[55] Code §§384(a), 384(c)(1)(C), 384(c)(8), and 382(h)(3)(B)(ii), all as retroactively amended by TAMRA. According to H.R. Conf. Rep. No. 1104, 100th Cong., 2d Sess. 10 (1988), such regulations would apply prospectively only.

[56] For ownership changes occurring on or before 10/2/89, and for later ownership changes made pursuant to a written binding contract in effect on 10/2/89 and at all times thereafter before the ownership change, the percentage threshold described in text is 25% rather than 13%, and the $10 million threshold does not apply.

EXAMPLE 13

Same as Example 12 except that T's assets immediately before the reorganization are as follows:

Asset	FV	Basis
Cash	$ 50	$ 50
Land and building	275	200
Machinery and equipment	250	250
Inventory	100	100
Total	$675	$600

Code §384 does not apply because the FV of T's assets (other than cash) immediately before the ownership change ($625) does not exceed their aggregate basis ($550) by more than 15% of their aggregate FV ($75 ÷ $625 = 12%) or by more than $10 million. Hence, in contrast to Example 12, if P sells the land and building for $275 or more on 2/1/90, P's $75 recognized BIG (as well as any gain in excess of $75) may be fully offset by P's NOL.

(3) Code §384 does not apply to gain recognized by T more than five years after P acquired T's stock or assets in a COB transaction. However, IRS Notice 90-27[57] creates an unfortunate exception for taxpayers with respect to installment sales. According to the notice, future regulations will provide that if T sells (on the installment method) a BIG asset before P acquired T or during the five-year period after P acquired T, Code §384 will apply to any installment gain recognized by T after the five-year recognition period has expired. That is, solely for purposes of such installment sale gain, the five-year recognition period will be extended through the date of the last installment payment (or the date of disposition of the installment obligation). Absent this special rule, gain from installments received by T after the five-year recognition period has expired would not be subject to Code §384. These future regulations will be effective for installment sales after 3/25/90 (unless pursuant to a binding written contract entered into on or before such date and continuously in effect until the sale).

This special rule for installment sales seems unreasonably harsh and one-sided. *First*, Code §384(c)(1)(B) provides that "[a]ny item of income which is properly taken into account for any recognition period taxable year but which is attributable to periods before the acquisition date shall be treated as recognized built-in gain for the taxable year in which it is properly taken into account. . . ." Under this statutory rule, if T sold an asset (on the installment method) before P acquired T

[57] 1990-1 C.B. 336.

(a prerecognition period sale) and T receives an installment payment after P acquired T, and during the five-year recognition period (a recognition period payment) T's installment gain from the recognition period payment is subject to Code §384, i.e., when the installment method defers gain into the five-year recognition period, such gain is covered by Code §384. As a corollary, however, it would appear that gain deferred by the installment method beyond the five-year recognition period should not be subject to Code §384 (whether resulting from a prerecognition period asset sale or an asset sale during the recognition period). However, under Notice 90-27 such gain is subject to Code §384; in this respect, the notice is inconsistent with Code §384(c)(1)(B).

Second, Notice 90-27 observes that the reason for installment method deferral is merely to alleviate the seller's potential liquidity problems associated with having to report full gain before the receipt of cash with which to pay the resulting tax. The implication seems to be that, to the extent Code §384 would have applied to a sale if the sale had not been reported on the installment method, it should also apply if the sale is reported on the installment method. However, the notice seeks to go further and to apply Code §384 to prerecognition period installment sales where the payment is made (a) during the five-year recognition period or (b) after the five-year recognition period. It is possible to read Code §384(c)(1)(B) as mandating this result with respect to such payments received during the five-year recognition period but not to such payments received thereafter. It is unclear as a policy matter why bona fide installment sales made before P acquired T should be subject in perpetuity to Code §384 merely because the seller did not collect the full sale price at the time of the sale.

(4) Code §384 does not apply if the stock or asset acquisition date is before 12/16/87 or if the acquisition is pursuant to either "a binding written contract in effect" before 12/16/87 or "a letter of intent or agreement of merger signed" before 12/16/87.[58]

¶1205.3   *T Operated as Partnership with P, VC, and Mgmt as Partners*

P's share of T Partnership's taxable income can be offset by P's NOLs, but the share of T Partnership's taxable income allocated to persons other than P cannot be offset by P's NOLs.[59]

EXAMPLE

P (an NOL company), VC, and Mgmt acquire T's assets for cash and contribute the assets to a newly formed partnership. Each of P, VC, and Mgmt provides one-third of the cash used to acquire T's assets, and under

---

[58] §10226(c) of the 1987 Act.
[59] See, e.g., Code §702.

> the partnership agreement each has a one-third interest in partnership capital, tax items, and distributions. P may carry forward its NOL to offset its allocable share of partnership income. However, P's NOL cannot offset the two-thirds of partnership income allocable to VC and Mgmt.

Before the 1986 Act, it was generally permissible for T Partnership to allocate a larger share of its taxable income to P in the early years and a smaller portion in the later years (the so-called Goldome technique) so long as the allocation had "substantial economic effect" within the meaning of Code §704(b) and the regulations promulgated thereunder.[60]

However, Code §382 requires Treasury to issue regulations necessary or appropriate "to prevent the avoidance of the purposes of [Code §382] through the use of related persons, pass-through entities, or other intermediaries."[61] The 1986 Conference Report,[62] addressing Goldome-type transactions, states that "a special allocation of income to a loss partner should not be permitted to result in a greater utilization of losses than would occur if the principles of section 382 were applicable," even if the allocation has substantial economic effect. The Conference Report suggests the following as possible regulatory measures to limit such allocations:

(1) a "general rule" that (a) applies the limitations of Code §382 (and Code §383, regarding excess credits and net CLs) to a loss corporation partner's distributive share of each item of partnership income and (b) taxes any portion of such distributive share not absorbed by the partner's NOLs at the highest marginal tax rate; and

(2) reallocating partnership income away from the loss corporation to the extent other partners "have not been reasonably compensated for their services to the partnership."

The Conference Report contemplated that such regulations, as they apply to partnerships, would be effective for transactions after 10/22/86.[63]

Partnership anti-abuse regulations (Reg. §1.701-2) promulgated in 12/94 implement Congress's directive to a limited extent, effective for partnership transactions after 5/11/94.[64] These regulations state that it is implicit in the intent of subchapter K (i.e., the partnership provisions of the Code) that each partnership transaction (1) must be entered into for a "substantial business purpose," (2) must be respected under substance over form principles, and (3) except as subchapter K otherwise clearly contemplates, must "accurately reflect the partners' economic agreement"

---

[60] See, e.g., Reg. §1.704-1(b)(5) example (8).

[61] Code §382(m)(3).

[62] H.R. Conf. Rep. No. 841, 99th Cong., 2d Sess. II, at 194 (1986) (hereinafter "1986 Conference Report II").

[63] See 1986 Conference Report II, at 194-195.

[64] See ¶1604.1 for further discussion of these partnership anti-abuse regulations.

and "clearly reflect" each partner's income.[65] "[I]f a partnership is formed or availed of in connection with a transaction a principal purpose of which is to reduce substantially the present value of the partners' aggregate federal tax liability" in a manner "inconsistent" with the intent of subchapter K, IRS may recast the transaction to achieve tax results consistent with such intent.[66] Whether a partnership arrangement is consistent with the intent of subchapter K is based on all facts and circumstances. Among the non-exclusive factors the regulations identify as relevant are whether partnership items are allocated in compliance with the literal requirements of Code §704(b) and the regulations thereunder but "with results that are inconsistent with the purpose of section 704(b) and those regulations."[67] In this connection, "particular scrutiny will be paid to partnerships in which income or gain is specially allocated to one or more partners that are legally or effectively exempt from federal taxation," such as a partner that is (1) a tax-exempt organization or (2) a corporation with an NOL.[68]

More illuminating than the above generalities is a taxpayer-favorable example contained in the regulations concerning a real estate partnership.[69] Under the partnership arrangement, depreciation deductions and tax credits are specially allocated to partners other than a corporate partner unable to use the deductions and credits because of an NOL. The example concludes that the arrangement is consistent with the intent of subchapter K and hence will be respected, because, under the facts of the example, (1) the allocations have substantial economic effect under Code §704 and the regulations thereunder (or are considered to be consistent with the partners' interests in the partnership under Reg. §1.704-2(e)), and (2) the partners to whom the depreciation deductions and credits are specially allocated "would bear the economic burden of any decline in the value of the building (to the extent of the partnership's investment in the building), notwithstanding that [those partners] believe it is unlikely that the building will decline in value (and, accordingly, ... anticipate significant timing benefits through the special allocation)."

This example indicates that special allocations of income to an NOL partner should continue to be respected under current law if (1) the allocations comply with the technical requirements of Code §704 and the regulations thereunder and (2) the partnership arrangement has a substantial business purpose, is consistent with the partners' economic agreement, and otherwise passes muster under the partnership anti-abuse regulation.

[65] Reg. §1.701-2(a).
[66] Reg. §1.701-2(b).
[67] Reg. §1.701-2(c)(5).
[68] Id.
[69] Reg. §1.701-2(d) example (6).

¶1206   CARRYBACK OF POST-ACQUISITION NOL TO RECOVER T OR P PRE-ACQUISITION TAXES

Assume that T is a profitable company and that P either (1) acquires T's stock, and thereafter includes T in P's consolidated group, or (2) acquires T's assets.[1] Because of a downturn in business or because the P group has substantial deductions for interest paid on the acquisition debt, or both, the P group may incur NOLs during its first few taxable years following the acquisition.

An NOL generally may be carried *back* two years (five years in the case of an NOL incurred in a tax year ending in 2001 or 2002, and three years in the case of an NOL incurred in a taxable year beginning before 8/6/97) and *forward* twenty years (fifteen years in the case of an NOL incurred in a taxable year beginning before 8/6/97).[2] If P group post-acquisition NOLs can be carried *back* into P's or T's pre-acquisition taxable years to produce a refund, the NOLs will produce an earlier cash flow benefit for the P group than if such NOLs are usable only as carryforwards to later years. See ¶1201.1 for rules concerning waiver of NOL carrybacks.

This section discusses the circumstances under which post-acquisition NOLs of P group (including T) can be carried back to obtain a refund of taxes paid by P or T in P or T taxable years preceding the acquisition. This discussion applies whether T's stock or assets are acquired (1) by P in a conventionally financed acquisition, (2) by P or P's newly formed subsidiary S in a tax-free reorganization, or (3) by Newco in an LBO. Indeed, the issue of carrybacks often arises in a LBO, because the Newco group typically has no taxable income other than from T's business and an LBO generally creates substantial interest expense in post-acquisition periods.

The rules concerning NOL carrybacks differ significantly depending on whether P acquires T's stock or assets. If P acquires T's stock, whether (1) in a taxable purchase or taxable reverse subsidiary merger without a Code §338 election, or (2) in a tax-free "B" reorganization or reverse subsidiary "A" reorganization, post-acquisition NOLs incurred by the P group that are attributable to T can, subject to the limitations and other rules discussed in ¶¶1206.1 through 1206.6 below, be carried back to pre-acquisition tax years of T (or of T's former consolidated group), but not to pre-acquisition tax years of the P group.[3] ¶¶1206.1 through 1206.6 discuss the NOL carryback rules applicable to stock acquisitions without a Code §338 election. Specifically, ¶1206.1 considers the "CERT" limitation enacted by the 1989 Act. The five subsequent sections (¶¶1206.2 through 1206.6) consider other rules regarding NOL carrybacks where P acquires T's stock without a Code §338 election in three different factual patterns:

¶1206   [1] P will often be a newly formed corporation, "Newco," which acquires T in an LBO.

[2] Code §172(b), as amended by the 1997 and 2002 Acts. See generally ¶1201.

[3] See Reg. §1.1502-21(b)(2)(i) (generally prohibiting a carryback into the P group's pre-acquisition tax years of a post-acquisition NOL attributable to T that may be carried back to T's prior tax years).

(1) before P acquires T's stock, T is a free standing corporation, i.e., T is not a member of an affiliated group filing a consolidated return;

(2) before P acquires T's stock, T is the common parent of an affiliated group (the "old T group") filing a consolidated return; and

(3) before P acquires T's stock, T is a member of an affiliated group filing a consolidated return (the "Bigco group"), but T is not the common parent of the group.

In contrast, if the P group acquires (or is treated as acquiring) T's assets, whether (1) by P's taxable purchase of T's assets, (2) by P's taxable purchase of T's stock with a Code §338 or §338 (h)(10) election, (3) by P's tax-free acquisition of T's assets in an "A" or "C" reorganization, or (4) by P's subsidiary S's tax-free acquisition of T's assets in a subsidiary "A" or subsidiary "C" reorganization, then P group post-acquisition NOLs attributable to T's former assets generally can be carried back to P group pre-acquisition tax years, but not to pre-acquisition tax years of T or of T's former consolidated group, as further discussed in ¶1206.7.

For a discussion of the filing procedures available to carry back a post-acquisition NOL or capital loss to pre-acquisition years to obtain a refund of taxes previously paid, see ¶1206.8.

¶1206.1 Corporate Equity Reduction Transaction Limitation on NOL Carryback

As an expression of unhappiness over the 1980s' rapid increase of corporate indebtedness generated by highly leveraged buyouts and recapitalizations, Congress in the 1989 Tax Act enacted Code §§172(b)(1)(E) and 172(h).[4] These provisions limit the ability of a C corporation involved in a "corporate equity reduction transaction" (a "CERT") to carry back an NOL incurred (1) in the taxable year in which the CERT occurs or (2) in either of the two succeeding taxable years to a taxable year prior to the taxable year in which the CERT occurs. In general, a CERT occurs when one corporation ("P") acquires 50% or more by vote or by value of the stock of another corporation ("T") without a Code §338 or §338(h)(10) election (a "major-stock-acquisition CERT") or when a corporation ("T") makes an extraordinarily large distribution (including a redemption distribution) to its shareholders (an "excess-distribution CERT").[5]

---

[4] See H.R. Rep. No. 247, 101st Cong., 1st Sess. at 108 (1989) (as reprinted in CCH Stand. Fed. Tax Rep. no. 40 (9/20/89)) (hereinafter "1989 House Report"); S. Rep. No. 56, 101st Cong., 1st Sess. at 99 (1989) (as reprinted in CCH Stand. Fed. Tax Rep. no. 43 (10/16/89)) (hereinafter "1989 Senate Report"); H.R. Conf. Rep. No. 386, 101st Cong., 1st Sess. at 71 (1989) (as reprinted in CCH Stand. Fed. Tax Rep. no. 50 (11/22/89)) (hereinafter "1989 Conference Report"). Subsequent citation by page number to the legislative history of the CERT provisions will be to the CCH version of each report as reprinted in Standard Federal Tax Reports.

[5] The CERT provisions are generally effective for a CERT occurring after 8/2/89.

¶1206.1.1   General CERT Rule

If a C corporation[6] generates an NOL (1) in the taxable year in which it is involved in a CERT or (2) in either of the two succeeding taxable years, the portion of the NOL, if any, attributable to interest deductions allocable to the CERT may not be carried back to taxable years prior to the taxable year in which the CERT occurred.[7] Any portion of a corporation's NOL that cannot be carried back to pre-CERT taxable years under the CERT limitation may be carried forward under the normal NOL carryforward rules of Code §172 (or carried back to the taxable year of the CERT or any year thereafter).[8]

EXAMPLE 1

On 1/1 year 1, T, a calendar year corporation, is involved in a CERT. T had $5 of taxable income in each of its preceding taxable years. In year 1 T has a $5 NOL, $4 of which is attributable to interest deductions allocable (under the rules discussed below) to the CERT.

T may carry back only $1 of its year 1 NOL (i.e., the portion of the NOL not attributable to CERT interest deductions) under the carryback rules described in ¶1206.1. The remaining $4 of T's NOL (i.e., the portion of the NOL attributable to CERT interest deductions) can only be carried forward.

EXAMPLE 2

Same as Example 1, except that in year 1 (the year of the CERT) T has $2 of taxable income and in year 2 T has a $5 NOL, of which $4 is attributable to interest deductions allocable to the CERT.

T may carry back $1 of the year 2 NOL (i.e., the portion of the NOL not attributable to CERT interest deductions) to years preceding year 1 under the normal carryback rules, and $2 of the year 2 NOL to year 1 (i.e., to offset the full amount of T's year 1 taxable income because year 1 is the CERT year). T can carry only the remaining $2 of year 2 NOL forward.

The major-stock-acquisition CERT rules (as discussed below) apply to the acquiring corporation (P), a target corporation (T), or both.[9] The excess-distribution

---

[6] The CERT provisions apply only to a C corporation, not to an S corporation. Code §172(b)(1)(E)(iii).
[7] Code §172(b)(1)(E)(i).
[8] Code §172(b)(1)(E)(i) (flush language).
[9] Code §172(b)(1)(E)(iii) (defining each of P and T as an "applicable corporation" to which the carryback restriction is applied).

CERT rules apply to a corporation that makes an unusually large distribution to its shareholders.[10]

In applying the CERT rules, except as provided in regulations, all members of an affiliated group filing a consolidated return are treated as one corporation.[11] Accordingly, for a consolidated group, (1) whether a transaction constitutes a CERT is determined on a consolidated group basis, and (2) if, through the actions of one of its members, the group becomes involved in a CERT, the CERT rules apply to post-CERT NOLs of each member of the group. See ¶¶1206.1.2.4 and 1206.1.4 for examples illustrating the application of the CERT rules to a consolidated group.

In determining the portion of a corporation's NOL that is tainted (i.e., attributable to interest deductions allocable to the CERT), the CERT rules adopt an anti-taxpayer approach by requiring the corporation to take the interest deductions allocable to the CERT into account last, after all other deductions.[12]

EXAMPLE 3

In year 1 T is involved in a CERT. During that year, T's taxable income is as follows:

Gross taxable income	$20
Tax deductions other than interest	(18)
Interest deductions not allocable to CERT	(2)
Interest deductions allocable to CERT	(5)
Taxable income	$ (5)

Thus, in year 1 T had a $5 NOL.

To compute the portion of the $5 NOL that is subject to the CERT limitations, T must compute its taxable income by taking into account the interest deductions allocable to the CERT after all other deductions, i.e., T reduces its $20 of gross taxable income first by its $20 of non-CERT deductions and then by the $5 of CERT-related interest deductions. As a result, the entire amount of T's $5 NOL is subject to the CERT limitations.

Thus, in Example 3, for instance, T cannot "stack" its CERT-related interest first and claim that none of its $5 NOL is attributable to the CERT-related interest. Likewise, T cannot take the position that because CERT-related interest constitutes

---

[10] Code §172(b)(1)(E)(iii). The CERT rules also apply to any successor of a corporation involved in a CERT.

[11] Code §172(h)(4)(C).

[12] Code §172(h)(4)(A).

only 20% of T's total deductions in year 1, only 20% of T's $5 NOL is attributable to the CERT-related interest.

Unless otherwise stated, each of the examples below assumes the following:

(1) Each of the entities involved is a C corporation.

(2) Each of the entities uses a calendar year.

(3) Each of the entities is widely held, i.e., is not a member of an affiliated group, unless the example states, e.g., that T was part of Bigco's group before the transaction or becomes part of P's group after it.

(4) No entity makes a Code §338 or §338(h)(10) election.

¶1206.1.2   Definition of CERT and Application of CERT Rules

The term "corporate equity reduction transaction" (i.e., CERT) means either a "major stock acquisition" or an "excess distribution."[13]

¶1206.1.2.1   Major Stock Acquisition

A "major stock acquisition" occurs if P, or P and any group of persons acting in concert with P, acquires 50% or more by vote or by value of T's stock (including Code §1504(a)(4) preferred stock).[14] For this purpose, all stock purchases during any 24-month period are aggregated, and stock purchases separated by more than 24 months are aggregated if made pursuant to a plan.[15] If this type of CERT occurs, both P and T are considered to have undergone a CERT.[16]

There is one exception to the definition of a "major stock acquisition." If P purchases 80% or more of T's stock and makes a Code §338 or Code §338(h)(10) election with respect to T,[17] the purchase is not a major stock acquisition.[18]

---

[13] Code §172(h)(3)(A).

[14] Code §172(h)(3)(B) and (D).

[15] Id.

[16] Code §172(b)(1)(E)(iii)(I).

[17] See ¶205 for a discussion of Code §§338 and 338(h)(10).

[18] Code §172(h)(3)(B)(ii). A Code §338 election eliminates T's prior tax history (or, in the case of a Code §338(h)(10) election, leaves T's tax history with the seller ("Bigco")) and thus eliminates any ability to carry back a post-acquisition NOL to a pre-acquisition tax year of T. Thus, this exception will be of value only when P is an existing corporation that has paid taxes in prior years so that P can recover its own previously paid taxes through an NOL carryback. When a newly formed corporation ("Newco") acquires T in an LBO and makes a Code §338 or Code §338(h)(10) election, this exception will be of no value since Newco would have paid no prior taxes that can be recovered through an NOL carryback. Under a second exception in effect only for acquisitions before 10/10/90, if P acquired T stock and, immediately before the acquisition, T was a member (other than a common parent) of a Code §1504 affiliated group, the stock acquisition was not a major stock acquisition. However, the 1990 Act eliminated this second exception. See old Code §172(h)(3)(B)(ii)(II) (prior to repeal by the 1990 Act).

EXAMPLE 4

P purchases for cash common and/or preferred stock of T representing at least 50% of T's outstanding stock by vote or by value. Immediately prior to the purchase T is not a member of an affiliated group. P's purchase of the T stock is a major stock acquisition.[19]

EXAMPLE 5

Same as Example 4 except that immediately prior to the transaction T was a member of Bigco's affiliated group as defined in Code §1504(a) (i.e., Bigco or other members of Bigco's group owned at least 80% by vote and 80% by value of T's stock) and the transaction occurred after to 10/9/90. P's purchase of T's stock is a major stock acquisition.

Read literally, the definition of a major stock acquisition includes a transaction whereby P acquires 50% or more of T's stock directly from T. It is, however, inappropriate for the CERT rules to apply to such an acquisition since P's transfer of cash or other assets to T for T stock does not reduce overall corporate equity. Nonetheless, given Congress' stated reasons for eliminating the affiliated group exception to the definition of "major stock acquisition,"[20] IRS might take the position that such a transaction is a major-stock-acquisition CERT. It is to be hoped, however, that IRS will reach the sensible conclusion and will not treat the new issue transaction as a major-stock-acquisition CERT.

EXAMPLE 6

P transfers $10 of borrowed funds (or other assets) to T in return for 50% of T's outstanding stock. It is not appropriate for this transfer to constitute

[19] P's acquisition of T stock in a tax-free transaction in exchange for P stock also constitutes a CERT. However, as discussed in ¶1206.1.3, in such case there should be no interest expense allocable to the CERT under the avoided cost rule unless P issued boot in addition to P stock.

[20] See footnote 18 above. The relevant legislative history gives two reasons for this elimination: (1) the rationale for enacting the original CERT rules—i.e., that "the leveraging involved in the CERT substantially alters the nature of the corporation and is not related to a natural business cycle or an unexpected financial reversal"—applies to all debt-financed CERTs, including P's debt-financed purchase of T from the Bigco group, and (2) if P purchases T from the Bigco group, the proceeds that the Bigco group receives might not remain in the Bigco group, but rather Bigco might distribute the proceeds to its shareholders, thereby reducing aggregate corporate equity. H.R. Rep. No. 881, 101st Cong., 2d Sess. at 101 (1990) (as reprinted in CCH Stand. Fed. Tax Rep. no. 46-1 (10/17/90)); S. 3209, 101st Cong., 2d Sess. at 172 (1990) (as reprinted in CCH Stand. Fed. Tax Rep. No. 46-2 (10/18/90)). Neither argument seems convincing. Reason (1) is overbroad in that it could apply to any extraordinary

a major-stock-acquisition CERT because the transaction does not reduce overall corporate equity.[21]

EXAMPLE 7

P transfers $10 of borrowed funds (or other assets) to a newly formed P subsidiary, S, in exchange for all of S's stock. It is not appropriate for this transfer to constitute a major-stock-acquisition CERT because the transaction does not reduce overall corporate equity.

¶1206.1.2.2   Excess Distribution

An "excess distribution" occurs if a corporation's distributions (including redemptions) with respect to its stock (other than Code §1504(a)(4) preferred stock) during a single taxable year exceed the greater of:

(1)   150% of the average of such distributions made by the corporation during the preceding three taxable years or

(2)   10% of the FV of the stock of the corporation (excluding Code §1504(a)(4) preferred stock) at the beginning of the taxable year.[22]

For this purpose, a corporation's distributions during the current taxable year, as well as its distributions described in (1) above for the previous three taxable years, are reduced by the amount of money or other property (other than its own stock) the corporation receives during the respective periods in exchange for issuing its own stock (other than Code §1504(a)(4) stock).[23]

---

debt-financed purchase made by P, including one in which P purchases all of T's outstanding stock and makes a Code §338 election with respect to T; Congress had already addressed reason (2) in the excess distribution provisions of the CERT rules.

[21] If T later uses the $10 million to redeem the T stock not owned by P, the integrity of the CERT provisions is preserved by the excess distribution rules discussed below.

[22] Code §172(h)(3)(C) and (E). Excess distributions were included in the definition of CERT, at least in part, to cover the leveraged recapitalization of a single corporation or group. Thus, an excess distribution need not occur as part of an acquisition transaction in order to be a CERT.

[23] Code §172(h)(3)(E)(ii). The statute may be a bit ambiguous in two respects: First, the provision is not completely clear that consideration the corporation receives in exchange for Code §1504(a)(4) preferred stock is ignored as stated in the text. However, because redemptions of Code §1504(a)(4) preferred stock are ignored, it would make no sense to count consideration received by the corporation in issuances of such stock. Moreover, the legislative history indicates that such consideration is ignored. 1989 House Report at 109; 1989 Senate Report at 100; 1989 Conference Report at 71.

Second, it appears that in testing for an excess-distribution CERT, the distribution in the year being tested is reduced by money or other property received by the corporation for its stock in only that year, but that in calculating the prior year distributions described in (1) above, the distributions in the previous three years are reduced by the money or other property received by the corporation for its stock during the previous three years.

Once it has been ascertained that a corporation has undergone an excess-distribution CERT, the amount treated as an excess distribution is the excess of the current year's distributions (reduced as discussed in the preceding sentence) over the greater of the amount described in (1) above (reduced as discussed in the preceding sentence) or the amount described in (2) above.

EXAMPLE 8

During years 1, 2, and 3 T's average distributions with respect to its common stock (including redemptions) were $6. On 1/1 year 4 the FV of T's common stock is $100. On 6/1 year 4 T redeems $25 of its common stock (either pro rata from all shareholders or non-pro-rata). Fifteen dollars of the 6/1 year 4 redemption is an excess distribution and hence a CERT (i.e., the excess of $25 over the greater of $10 (10% of $100 FV) and $9 (150% of $6 average distributions)).

Although the CERT provisions are silent on this point, presumably if T makes a tax-free distribution to its shareholders of stock or securities of another corporation as part of a tax-free reorganization or tax-free Code §355 transaction, the distributed stock or securities should not count in determining whether T made an excess distribution during the taxable year. This type of tax-free distribution by T does not reduce overall corporate equity, and the requisites for a tax-free reorganization or Code §355 transaction in effect ensure that T cannot use a transaction of this type to circumvent the underlying intent of the excess-distribution CERT rules. It is hoped that regulations will clarify this point.

EXAMPLE 9

On 1/1 year 5 T's outstanding stock has an FV of $100, which includes the $20 FV of T's wholly owned subsidiary, S. T made only nominal distributions during years 2-4. On 2/1 year 5 T distributes to its shareholders all the stock of S in a wholly tax-free Code §355 transaction. T makes no other distributions in year 5.

T's distribution of the S stock presumably should be ignored in determining whether T made an excess-distribution CERT in year 5, in which case T did not make an excess distribution in year 5.

EXAMPLE 10

On 1/1 year 5 T's outstanding stock has an FV of $100. T made only nominal distributions during years 2-4. On 2/1 year 5 P acquires T through a Code §368(a)(1)(A) tax-free merger of T into P, with the T shareholders receiving solely $100 of P stock in exchange for their T stock.

For tax purposes, the merger of T into P presumably will be treated as though T transferred all its assets to P for $100 of P stock and then liquidated, distributing the P stock to the T shareholders.[24] T's deemed distribution of $100 of P stock to T's shareholders presumably should be ignored in determining whether T made an excess distribution in year 5.

Trying to apply the excess distribution rules to situations more complicated than the relatively simple fact patterns in Examples 9 and 10 turns the mind to mush. For instance, it is not at all clear how the excess distribution rules apply if T makes a taxable distribution of another corporation's stock to the T shareholders, or if T makes a tax-free Code §355 distribution of S stock to the T shareholders and, within the same taxable year, S pays a dividend to its shareholders (i.e., the T shareholders). Likewise, if P acquires T's stock in a tax-free reorganization for P stock and boot, it is unclear how the excess distribution rules apply to the boot (i.e., in applying the 10% of FV limitation, is the boot treated as a T distribution or a P distribution). Finally, if T purchases stock of another corporation in a major-stock-acquisition CERT and then T later makes a fully taxable distribution of that stock to the T shareholders (constituting an excess distribution), it is unclear whether double counting under the CERT rules is avoidable.

EXAMPLE 11

The FV of T's stock (and thus its equity value) is $100. The FV of unrelated X's stock (and thus its equity value) is $50. On 1/1 year 5 T purchases from individuals for $10 of borrowed cash 20% of the outstanding X stock (and T owns no other X stock). On 2/1 year 5 T distributes the X stock to T's shareholders as a dividend.

T's debt-financed purchase of the $10 of X stock and T's distribution of the X stock to T's shareholders reduced overall corporate equity by $10. That is, prior to these transactions, the combined equity value of T and X was $150 (i.e., $100 T equity and $50 X equity), and after these transactions, the combined equity value of T and X is only $140 (i.e., $90 T equity and $50 X equity).[25] Accordingly, the X stock distributed by T to its shareholders arguably should count in determining whether T made an excess distribution in year 5.

---

[24] See Rev. Rul. 67-326, 1967-2 C.B. 143; cf. Rev. Rul. 69-6, 1969-1 C.B. 104.

[25] T's $100 equity value remained $100 after T borrowed $10 and purchased the X stock, but was reduced by $10 as a result of T's distribution of the X stock to the T shareholders (i.e., T had incurred a $10 liability and had no corresponding asset).

EXAMPLE 12

Same as Example 11 except that T purchases the $10 of X stock directly from X (thereby increasing X's equity value to $60). In this case, T's purchase and distribution of X stock did not reduce overall corporate equity. That is, although the transactions reduced T's corporate equity from $100 to $90, X's corporate equity increased from $50 to $60. Thus, overall corporate equity remained at $150, and it appears that T's distribution of the X stock should not count in determining whether T made an excess distribution in year 5.

EXAMPLE 13

Same as Example 11 except that T purchases the $10 of X stock from another corporation or corporations (rather than from individuals). Arguably, the X stock should not count in determining whether T made an excess distribution in year 5 because the purchase and distribution of the X stock did not reduce overall corporate equity by replacing non-corporate shareholders with debt.

EXAMPLE 14

Same as Example 11 except that T purchases the X stock on 1/1 year 5 but does not distribute the X stock to its shareholders until 1/1 year 10 (i.e., five years after the purchase). In this case, because T held the X stock for five years, any debt T has outstanding in year 10 should arguably not be associated with the purchase of the X stock (i.e., should not be treated as replacing corporate equity). That is, the regulations might exclude from an excess distribution X stock that T held for a specified period of time.

EXAMPLE 15

Same as Example 9 (i.e., on 2/1 year 5 T, with an FV of $100, distributes to its shareholders in a tax-free Code §355 transaction all the stock of S, with an FV of $20) except that on 7/1 year 5 T makes a $10 cash distribution to its shareholders, and on 10/1 year 5 S (which T had spun off 8 months earlier) makes a $2 cash distribution to its shareholders.

As discussed in Example 9, the S stock that T distributed to its shareholders presumably should not count in determining whether T made an excess distribution in year 5. In such case, T's $10 cash distribution did not exceed 10% of the 1/1 year 5 $100 FV of the T stock, and S's $2 cash distribution did not exceed 10% of the 1/1 year 5 $20 FV of the S stock. Thus, it can be argued that neither T nor S made an excess distribution in year 5.

However, under this view, T's Code §355 distribution increases the amount of cash that can be distributed to the T shareholders (by T and S) in a taxable year without triggering an excess-distribution CERT (i.e., if T had not distributed the S stock to the T shareholders, and T had distributed $12 in cash, T would have had a $2 excess-distribution CERT). The solution in the case of a spin-off appears to be a required allocation of T's $10 limitation (between T and S) in some fashion for purposes of computing whether T and/or S made an excess distribution in year 5.

EXAMPLE 16

Same as Example 10 (i.e., T merges into P in a tax-free "A" reorganization) except that P acquires T in return for $50 P stock and $50 cash boot.

As noted in Example 10, the merger presumably will be treated for tax purposes as though T transferred its assets to P for $50 P stock and $50 cash and then T liquidated, distributing the P stock and cash to the T shareholders. Hence, T arguably made an excess distribution to its shareholders of $40, i.e., the amount by which the $50 cash exceeded 10% of the $100 FV of T's stock on 1/1 year 5 (as noted earlier, the P stock distributed by T to its shareholders should presumably be ignored).[26]

On the other hand, under the Supreme Court's 1989 decision in *Clark v. Commissioner*,[27] the merger of T into P might be treated as though T received $100 of P stock and then P redeemed $50 of such stock for $50 cash. If this were the case, P (rather than T) might have made an excess distribution.

EXAMPLE 17

The FV of T's stock is $100 on 1/1 year 5 and on 1/1 year 6. T made only nominal distributions during years 2-4. On 1/1 year 5 T purchases 50% of the stock of unrelated X for $20. Thus, T was involved in a major-stock-acquisition CERT. On 1/1 year 6 T distributes the X stock (FV $20) to T's shareholders as a dividend. The distribution apparently constitutes an excess-distribution CERT to the extent of $10, i.e., the excess of $20 over 10% of the $100 FV of T's stock.

---

[26] See ¶1206.1.7 for a discussion of the potential consequences to P, as successor to T, if T in fact is treated as having made an excess distribution.

[27] 489 U.S. 726, 89-1 U.S.T.C. ¶9230 (1989). For a discussion of *Clark*, see ¶801.4.3.

Arguably, the maximum amount of T debt allocated to its two CERTs should be $20. However, under the current CERT rules $30 might be allocated to T's two CERTs.

¶1206.1.2.3   *Transaction Constituting Both Major Stock Acquisition and Excess Distribution*

Apparently, a transaction may result in both a major stock acquisition and an excess distribution. For example, assume P acquires T's stock by forming a transitory subsidiary that merges into T, paying cash to T's old shareholders. To the extent that P contributes equity money to the transitory subsidiary, P has purchased stock of T (a major stock acquisition). To the extent that the transitory subsidiary borrows money and T becomes liable on the acquisition debt as a result of the merger, T has redeemed its own stock (potentially an excess distribution, depending on the size of the redemption).[28] This issue is discussed in greater detail in ¶1206.1.6.

¶1206.1.2.4   *Application to Consolidated Group*

As noted earlier, all members of an affiliated group filing a consolidated return are treated as a single taxpayer in applying the CERT rules. Accordingly, the determination of whether a major stock acquisition or excess distribution has occurred is made on a consolidated group basis. Moreover, if one member of a consolidated group is involved in a CERT, the CERT rules apply to NOLs generated by all members of the group.

EXAMPLE 18

P, S, and other corporations are members of an affiliated group filing a consolidated return, with P as the common parent. P owns 80% of the outstanding S stock (FV $80), and the remaining 20% of S's stock (FV $20) is owned by outside investors. The FV of the P group as a whole is (on 1/1 year 4) $500. S has made only nominal distributions during the prior three years.

In year 4 S redeems the 20% of its stock held by the outside investors for $20. P and the other members of the group make no distributions (other than intragroup distributions). The $20 distribution by S in redemption of its stock exceeds both (1) 150% of the average distributions made by S during years 1-3 and (2) 10% of the FV of the outstanding S stock at the beginning of the year. The distribution is not an excess-distribution CERT, however,

---

[28] See Rev. Rul. 79-273, 1979-2 C.B. 125; Rev. Rul. 78-250, 1978-1 C.B. 83. See also ¶202.

because the P consolidated group is treated as a single taxpayer and the $20 distribution by S does not exceed 10% of the FV of the aggregate stock of the P group.

EXAMPLE 19

Same as Example 18 except that the P affiliated group does not file a consolidated return. The $20 distribution by S in redemption of its stock is an excess-distribution CERT to the extent of $10 (i.e., the amount by which the $20 distribution exceeds 10% of the FV of the S stock on 1/1 year 4). However, the CERT would have been avoided if P, rather than S, had purchased the 20% of S's stock.

EXAMPLE 20

In year 1 P, the common parent of an affiliated group filing a consolidated return, acquires all the stock of T with funds P borrowed from an unrelated lender. As a result, P was involved in a major-stock-acquisition CERT. In year 2, the P group generates an NOL, 100% of which is attributable to losses incurred by S, a long-time member of the P group. To the extent the P group NOL is attributable to interest deductions allocable (under the rules discussed below) to the CERT, the NOL cannot be carried back to pre-year 1 taxable years of the P group, even though the member that generated the NOL (i.e., S) was not involved in the CERT. See also Example 38 below.

If P acquires Bigco's subsidiary T and T makes a distribution to Bigco as part of P's acquisition of T, the excess-distribution CERT rules could apply. However, if Bigco and T filed a consolidated return immediately before the transaction, a distribution by T to Bigco should not constitute an excess distribution, in the absence of contrary regulations, because the CERT rules treat T and Bigco as a single taxpayer.

EXAMPLE 21

Bigco owns all of the stock of T, which has an FV of $100. Bigco and T do not file a consolidated return. T has paid no dividends in the prior three years. P wishes to acquire T's stock.

If the acquisition is structured so that part of the consideration received by Bigco is in the form of a redemption or dividend from T, a portion of the transaction may be an excess distribution. For instance, if T redeems $40 of its stock from Bigco and P purchases T's remaining stock for $60, $30 of the $40 redemption will be an excess distribution (i.e., the excess of $40 over 10% of the $100 FV of the T stock).

EXAMPLE 22

Same as Example 21 except that Bigco and T file a consolidated return. Even if the acquisition is structured so that $40 of the $100 consideration to Bigco is a redemption by T, T's distribution to Bigco apparently does not constitute an excess distribution because T and Bigco are treated as a single corporation.[29] However, P's acquistion of T is a major-stock-acquisition CERT (if the acquisition occurs after 10/9/90).

EXAMPLE 23

Same as Example 21 except that P purchases all T's stock from Bigco for $100 borrowed cash and the day after the acquisition, T borrows $40 and distributes the cash to P. P uses the cash to repay $40 of P's acquisition debt.

P's purchase of the T stock is a major-stock-acquisition CERT. However, the distribution from T to P is not an excess distribution because P and T are members of a consolidated group.

¶1206.1.3   Interest Deduction Allocable to CERT

Except as provided in regulations, the avoided-cost method is used to allocate interest deductions to a CERT.[30] Thus, "the amount of debt that is treated as incurred or continued to finance [the CERT] is based on the amount of interest

---

[29] If P's purchase of T stock would deconsolidate T from the Bigco group, it is important that T redeem its stock before P's purchase so that the redemption occurs while T is a member of the Bigco group. However, the IRS could attempt to argue that, because the redemption was part of a transaction that resulted in T leaving the Bigco group, Bigco and T should not be treated as a single corporation (cf. Rev. Rul. 82-20, 1982-1 C.B. 7).

In addition, if the redemption occurs pursuant to a reverse subsidiary merger of a transitory P subsidiary into T, and the amount of T stock deemed purchased by P (through P's equity contribution to the transitory subsidiary) is sufficient to deconsolidate T, there may be an issue as to whether the redemption occurred while T was part of the Bigco consolidated group. Query whether the precedent dealing with the time that T leaves the Bigco group and enters the P group is relevant. Compare IRS TAM 7904002 (12/16/77) *with* IRS TAM 7914004 (12/13/78). See ¶211.3.

[30] Code §172(h)(2)(B) adopts Code §263A(f)(2)(A)(ii) (the avoided-cost method) and rejects Code §263A(f)(2)(A)(i) (specific tracing). 1989 House Report at 110. See Code §263A(f)(2)(A); Reg. §1.263A-9(a)(1) (discussing avoided-cost method and specific tracing under the uniform capitalization rules).

expense that would have been avoided if [the CERT] had not been made and the amount of such expenditures [for the CERT] were used to repay the indebtedness of the taxpayer."[31]

EXAMPLE 24

P borrows $80 and uses those funds, along with $20 of its own cash, to acquire the stock of T for $100. P and T have no other debt. All interest on the $80 debt is allocated to the CERT because the debt could have been avoided if P had not acquired T.

Compared to other alternatives, the avoided-cost rule is generally taxpayer-hostile because it allocates a taxpayer's new and existing debt to the CERT before allocating the debt to any other uses.[32]

EXAMPLE 25

On 1/1 year 1 P purchases a new plant for $100, financed with a $100 mortgage loan. P has no other debt.

On 12/1/ year 1 P purchases all the stock of T for $100 cash, none of which is borrowed (on a tracing basis). T has no debt outstanding.

After P's acquisition of T, all the interest incurred on the prior $100 mortgage debt will be allocated to the CERT (because P could have paid off or avoided the mortgage debt had P not used $100 cash to purchase T) and the CERT limitation will prevent any NOL arising from this interest expense from being carried back to P's pre-year 1 taxable years. This is true even if P purchased the plant at a time when it had no plan or intention subsequently to acquire T.[33]

---

[31] Reg. §1.263A-9(a)(1), dealing with the uniform capitalization rules. The debt that could have been repaid or avoided had there been no CERT is treated as bearing an average interest rate based on all the interest paid by P and T. 1989 House Report at 110; 1989 Senate Report at 100-101; Reg. §1.263A-9(c)(1)(ii); IRS Notice 88-99, 1988-2 C.B. 422.

[32] The CERT rules could have adopted a more taxpayer-friendly approach of allocating interest deductions to a CERT either by tracing the use of borrowed funds or by allocating debt among all of the P group's assets proportionately. IRS has regulatory authority to modify the statutory method of allocation of interest to CERTs. Code §172(h)(2)(B).

P is apparently entitled to count non-interest-bearing trade payables in this calculation. See IRS Notice 88-99, 1988-2 C.B. 422, 426; Evans, The Evolution of Federal Income Tax Accounting—A Growing Trend Towards Mark-to-Market, 67 Taxes 824, 828 (1989). Presumably, intragroup debt is ignored in the case of a consolidated group.

[33] Query whether this result would hold true if the mortgage debt was incurred before P had any plan or intention to acquire T and the terms of the mortgage debt prohibit prepayment or permit prepayment only at a substantial penalty. IRS has taken the position under the uniform capitalization rules that debt is treated as hypothetically repaid in applying the avoided-cost method despite prepayment penalties making it unlikely that a taxpayer would actually prepay the loan. IRS Notice 88-99, 1988-2 C.B. 422, 425. It is not entirely obvious that this IRS position represents a reasonable

EXAMPLE 26

On 1/1 year 1 P purchases all the stock of T for $100 cash, none of which is borrowed (on a tracing basis). P and T have no debt outstanding.

One year later, on 1/1 year 2, P purchases a new plant for $100, financed with a $100 mortgage debt bearing 10% interest. P and T have no other debt outstanding.

All the interest incurred on the subsequent $100 mortgage debt apparently will be allocated to the CERT (because P could have avoided the mortgage debt if it had not used $100 of cash to purchase T), and the CERT limitation will prevent any NOL arising from this interest expense in years 2 and 3 from being carried back to P's pre-year 1 taxable years. This is apparently true even if, when P acquired T, P had no plan or intention subsequently to purchase the plant.[34]

EXAMPLE 27

On 1/1 year 1 P buys a plant for $100 cash, financed with a $100 mortgage debt, and acquires the stock of T in a tax-free transaction solely in exchange for $100 of P stock. P and T have no other debt.

Because P did not spend any cash (or any consideration other than P stock) in acquiring T's stock, none of P's $100 mortgage debt should be attributable to the CERT.[35] (Moreover, P's acquisition of the T stock for P stock does not reduce overall corporate equity.)

EXAMPLE 28

Same as Example 27 except that P acquires T's stock in a reorganization with boot, i.e., for $80 of P stock and $20 of cash. Interest deductions on $20 of the mortgage debt will be allocated to the CERT under the avoided-cost method.

---

reading of the Code §263A(f)(2)(A)(ii) statutory language. See generally Evans, The Evolution of Federal Income Tax Accounting—A Growing Trend Towards Mark-to-Market, 67 Taxes 824, 830 (1989).

[34] If P purchased the new plant because its old plant was destroyed in a fire, P probably could exclude interest on the mortgage debt from the CERT rules on the ground that the debt was incurred because of an "unforeseeable extraordinary adverse event." See the discussion below.

[35] In this example, the avoided-cost method may be more favorable than a method that allocates debt pro rata to all the group's assets.

¶1206.1.3.1   Limitation on Interest Deduction

Code §172(h)(2)(C) provides a cap on the amount of interest deductions allocated to a CERT. Specifically, the amount of interest deductions allocated to a CERT may not *exceed* the amount, if any, by which a corporation's aggregate interest deductions for the NOL year *exceed* the corporation's average interest deductions for the three years prior to the CERT. This cap, in some cases, mitigates the results of the avoided-cost method of allocation.[36]

EXAMPLE 29

On 1/1 year 1 P purchases a new plant for $100, financed with a $100 mortgage loan bearing 10% interest. P has no other debt.

On 1/1 year 4 P purchased the stock of T for $100 in cash, none of which is borrowed (on a tracing basis). T has no debt outstanding.

Under the avoided-cost method, all the interest incurred on the $100 mortgage debt after P's acquisition of T would be allocated to the CERT because P could have paid off the mortgage debt if it had not used $100 of cash to purchase T's stock. However, P's interest deduction for year 4 allocated to the CERT under the avoided-cost method ($10) does not exceed P's average interest deduction for years 1-3 ($10). Therefore, none of P's interest expense is allocated to the CERT.[37]

¶1206.1.3.2   Additional Limitations

There are two additional limitations on the application of the CERT rules. First, if the amount of a corporation's interest deductions allocated to a CERT (taking into account the cap discussed above) is less than $1 million, the corporation is treated as having no interest deductions allocable to the CERT.[38]

Second, if a corporation suffers an "unforeseeable extraordinary adverse event" after a CERT, indebtedness is allocated (using the same avoided-cost method) to any unreimbursed costs paid or incurred in connection with the event before

[36] If P acquires the stock of unrelated T, and as a result T becomes a member of the P consolidated group, it appears that, notwithstanding that P and T were not members of the same consolidated group immediately prior to the CERT, both P's and T's pre-CERT interest expense should be considered in the calculation of the cap because after the CERT, P and T are treated as one taxpayer.

[37] The cap is based on P's average interest deductions in the three taxable years before the CERT. If P has floating rate debt, P's interest deductions after a CERT could exceed the interest deductions on the same debt in the three years prior to the CERT. However, the legislative history of the CERT rules states that Congress expects IRS to adopt regulations providing that increases in interest expense attributable solely to fluctuating interest rates are to be ignored for purposes of applying the cap. 1989 House Report at 110; 1989 Senate Report at 101.

[38] Code §172(h)(2)(D). See 1989 House Report at 110; 1989 Senate Report at 100.

being allocated to the CERT.[39] Moreover, in applying the cap discussed earlier, interest on the indebtedness allocated to such unreimbursed costs is not taken into account in determining whether the corporation's interest expense during its current taxable year exceeds the prior three-year average.[40]

Neither the statute nor its legislative history indicates what type of event constitutes an "unforeseeable extraordinary adverse event." Presumably, a major casualty loss, e.g., from a fire or earthquake, would qualify (to the extent not reimbursed by insurance), but small cyclical fluctuations in business profitability would not. Between these extremes, it is difficult to predict what is both "unforeseeable" and "extraordinary."

It is also unclear why the unforeseeable events exception applies only to an event occurring after the CERT. The logic behind the exception seems no less applicable to debt-financed costs arising out of an extraordinary event occurring before the CERT.

EXAMPLE 30

P signs a contract on 1/1 year 2 to purchase for $100 on 2/1 year 2 all the stock of T. P has no debt. P also has on hand $100 of cash to pay for T's stock. On 2/1 year 2 P uses the $100 of cash on hand to purchase the T stock.

On 2/2 year 2 (i.e., the next day) an earthquake destroys P's plant and P immediately borrows $100 of cash to replace the plant.

The $100 of debt is not allocated to P's acquisition of T's stock in a CERT because the debt is allocated to an unforeseeable extraordinary event (i.e., the earthquake) that occurred after the CERT.

EXAMPLE 31

Same as Example 30 except that the earthquake occurred on 1/15 year 2 (i.e., after P signed the contract to acquire T's stock but before closing). Immediately after the earthquake P borrows $100 of cash to replace the plant, and P then closes the acquisition of T's stock on 2/1 year 2 with the $100 of cash on hand.

The result appears to be the opposite of Example 30 because the earthquake occurred before the CERT. Hence, it appears that the $100 of debt arising out of the earthquake will be allocated to P's acquisition of the T stock in a CERT and that any NOL attributable to interest deductions on such debt will be subject to the CERT limitations, notwithstanding that P

---

[39] Code §172(h)(2)(E). The rule apparently applies to debt existing at the time of the "unforeseeable extraordinary adverse event" even if no new debt is incurred because of the "unforeseeable extraordinary adverse event."

[40] Code §172(h)(2)(E).

incurred the $100 debt because of an unforeseeable extraordinary adverse event.

EXAMPLE 32

Same as Example 31 except that the earthquake occurred on 12/31 year 1, i.e., while P was negotiating to acquire T but shortly before P signed the contract to acquire T. The result is apparently the same as Example 31.

¶1206.1.4   Consolidated Group Caveats

As noted earlier, in applying the CERT rules, except as provided in regulations, all corporations that are members of an affiliated group filing a consolidated return are treated as one taxpayer. As the examples below illustrate in part, the application of the CERT rules to consolidated groups produces potentially surprising results in some cases and results that are far from clear in other cases.[41]

EXAMPLE 33

P is the common parent of a consolidated group consisting of P and S. P has no outstanding debt, but S has outstanding a $100 loan incurred by S on 12/1 year 1 to purchase a new plant. Prior to 12/1 year 1 S incurred only nominal interest expense. On 1/1 year 2 P purchases all the stock of T, a widely held corporation, for $100 of unborrowed P cash. T has no outstanding debt.

The T stock purchase constitutes a major stock acquisition and thus a CERT. Moreover, because the CERT rules treat the members of the P group as a single taxpayer, the interest expense S incurs on its $100 loan apparently will be allocated to the CERT under the avoided cost allocation method (i.e., had P not purchased T's stock, the $100 used to purchase the stock could have been used to pay off S's $100 loan).

EXAMPLE 34

On 2/1 year 1 P, the common parent of a consolidated group, purchased for $100 of unborrowed P cash all the outstanding stock of T, a widely held

---

[41] Code §§172(h)(4)(C) and 172(h)(5)(A) and (C) grant IRS authority to issue regulations addressing at least some of the issues raised in the following examples.

corporation. At the time of the purchase, no member of the P group had any outstanding debt, and T had outstanding a $100 loan incurred by T to purchase a new plant on 1/1 year 1. T had nominal interest expense in the years prior to year 1.

The stock purchase constitutes a major stock acquisition and thus a CERT. However, although the members of the P group, including T, are treated as one taxpayer under the CERT rules, arguably none of the interest on T's $100 debt should be allocated to the CERT under the avoided cost method. T gains access to P's cash only after its acquisition by P; it makes no sense to assume that P would have used its $100 of cash to repay T's debt had P not acquired T.

EXAMPLE 35

Same as Example 34 except that T borrows the $100 to acquire the plant on 3/1 year 1, after P has acquired T's stock. It is unclear whether interest on T's debt will be allocated to P's major-stock-acquisition CERT. An argument similar to that of Example 34 can be made here as well (i.e., if P had not acquired T, P's cash would not have been available to purchase T's plant and T's borrowing would still have been necessary). However, the argument has less force after the acquisition when it is more difficult to distinguish T from P's other subsidiaries.

EXAMPLE 36

On 1/1 year 1 P, the common parent of a consolidated group, purchases for $100 borrowed cash all the outstanding stock of T, which has no outstanding debt. Prior to 1/1 year 1 P had incurred only nominal interest expense. The stock purchase constitutes a major stock acquisition and thus a CERT.

In year 1 P breaks even (taking into account its interest deductions) on a separate-company basis, but T has a $10 NOL from business operations. P would like T to carry back the $10 NOL to pre-year 1 T taxable years.

Because P and T file a consolidated return, they are treated as a single taxpayer for purposes of applying the CERT rules. As discussed in ¶1206.1.1, under Code §172(h)(4)(A) interest deductions allocable to a CERT are treated as the last deductions taken in determining the portion of a corporation's NOL that is attributable to interest deductions allocable to a CERT. Consequently, even though P itself generated income at least equal to its CERT-related interest deductions, the CERT limitation apparently will apply to T's $10 NOL. See also Example 38 below.

EXAMPLE 37

On 1/1 year 4 T borrowed $10 and distributed the funds to its shareholders. The FV of the outstanding T stock on 1/1 year 4 prior to the distribution was $40, T had made only nominal distributions to its shareholders during years 1-3, and T had incurred only nominal interest expense during years 1-3. As a result, $6 of the $10 distribution constituted an excess-distribution CERT (i.e., the excess of $10 over 10% of $40).

During year 4, the Code §172(h)(2)(C) cap does not help T because T's average interest expense in years 1-3 was nominal (and assume T's CERT-related interest exceeds the $1 million floor of Code §172(h)(2)(D)). Thus, all T's interest on $6 of debt in year 4 is allocable to the excess-distribution CERT, and any T NOL generated in year 4 attributable to such interest deduction is subject to the CERT limitation.

On 1/1 year 5 P, the common parent of a consolidated group, purchases for $30 of unborrowed P cash all the stock of T. On that date, P has no outstanding debt, although P had incurred significant interest expense during years 2-4 on debt P repaid in year 4.

P's purchase of the T stock causes both P and T to be involved in a major-stock-acquisition CERT. Moreover, the CERT rules treat P and T (and the other members of the P group) as a single taxpayer. Thus, with respect to the major-stock-acquisition CERT, P and T will have a significant Code §172(h)(2)(C) cap because of P's interest deductions in years 2-4 (although, as noted in Example 36 there is apparently no debt allocable to the major-stock-acquisition CERT under the avoided-cost method). It is unclear, however, whether T's Code §172(h)(2)(C) cap for the year 4 excess-distribution CERT can be recomputed in year 5 to take into account P's interest deductions during years 2 and 3 or whether T's cap from the year 4 excess-distribution CERT is frozen based solely on T's nominal interest expense in years 1-3.

In IRS Chief Counsel Advice 200305019,[42] IRS considered how the CERT taint should be applied to the different portions of the P group's consolidated NOL where P acquires T in a CERT and the P group incurs a post-acquisition NOL, part of which is generated by historic members of the P group (and thus, subject to the CERT rules, available for carryback to prior years of the P group) and part of which is generated by T (and thus, subject to the CERT rules, available for carryback only to prior separate return years of T—see ¶1206.2). The facts of CCA 200305019 are along the lines of the following example.

---

[42] 12/31/02, issued 1/31/03.

EXAMPLE 38

P is the common parent of a consolidated group that includes wholly-owned S. On 1/1 year 1, S purchases all of T's stock using the proceeds of a loan obtained by S on the purchase date. No election for T is made under Code §338 or §338(h)(10). S's purchase of T's stock is a major stock acquisition and thus a CERT. In year 1, the P group incurs a $30 consolidated NOL, arising from (1) P's stand-alone $40 NOL, (2) S's stand alone taxable income of $20, and (3) T's stand-alone $10 NOL. S has $5 of year 1 interest deductions attributable to the CERT and therefore $5 of the P group's consolidated NOL is CERT-tainted. The P-S group (excluding T) and T each have taxable income for their respective carryback years.

CCA 200305019 apportions the $5 CERT limitation in two steps. *First*, the P group's $30 consolidated NOL is allocated between P and T in proportion to their respective stand-alone NOLs under the normal consolidated NOL apportionment rule of Reg. §1.1502-21(b)(2)(iv). Thus, $24 (40/50) of the $30 consolidated NOL is apportioned to P and available for carryback to the P-S group's prior years, and the remaining $6 NOL (10/50 x $30) is apportioned to T and available for carryback to T's separate return years, in each case subject to any applicable CERT limitation. *Second*, the portion of the consolidated NOL so allocated to each of P and T is multiplied by the CERT-tainted fraction of the consolidated NOL (i.e., $5/$30, or 1/6) to determine how much of P's and T's respective NOLs is CERT-tainted. Thus, $4 (1/6) of P's $24 NOL is CERT-tainted, and $1 (1/6) of T's $6 NOL is CERT-tainted, and in each case may not be carried back to years preceding year 1. P's remaining $20 non-CERT-tainted NOL may be carried back to consolidated P-S years preceding year 1, and T's remaining $5 non-CERT-tainted NOL may be carried back to separate return years of T preceding year 1. IRS reasonably observes that that the foregoing methodology is consistent with the treatment under the CERT rules of all members of a consolidated group (here, P, S, and T) as one taxpayer.[43]

¶1206.1.5 Structuring CERT Timing

A corporation that contemplates involvement in a CERT may find it advantageous to structure the timing of the CERT to occur as close to the end of a taxable year as practicable.

---

[43] See Code §172(h)(4)(C). For this reason, IRS in CCA 200305019 expressly rejects an approach that would apply the CERT taint only to that part of the consolidated NOL apportioned to the specific group member that incurred the interest expense related to the CERT (here S, which had positive income on a stand-alone basis and therefore is allocated none of the P group's consolidated NOL).

EXAMPLE 39

On 1/1 year 2 P purchases all the outstanding stock of T for $100 of borrowed cash. Both P and T use the calendar year, and P had no other debt outstanding before year 2. P had $15 of income in year 1.

P's stock purchase constitutes a CERT and, under the avoided-cost method, all the interest on P's $100 debt in years 2-4 will be allocated to the CERT.

P generates a $5 NOL for each of the years 2-4, all of which is attributable to interest expense allocable to the CERT. Because the CERT occurs in year 2, years preceding year 2 are pre-CERT years and none of the year 2 or later NOLs may be carried back to obtain a refund of pre-year 2 P taxes.[44]

EXAMPLE 40

Same as Example 39 except that P purchases the T stock one day earlier, i.e., on 12/31 year 1 rather than on 1/1 year 2.

Interest accrued on the $100 debt in years 1-3 is allocable to the CERT. However, this is only two years and one day of interest, rather than three years as in Example 39.

Moreover, because year 1 is the year in which the CERT occurred, P can carry back $5 of NOL from each of years 2 and 3 ($10 total) to year 1.[45] That is, year 1 is not a pre-CERT year; hence, post-CERT NOLs can be carried back to year 1.

In addition, the $5 year 4 NOL is not subject to the CERT limitation in this Example 40 because the year 4 NOL is incurred in the third taxable year following the CERT. However, the year 4 NOL cannot be carried back to any year earlier than year 2 under the general two-year carryback rule of Code §172 applicable to NOLs incurred in taxable years beginning after 2002 (see ¶1201).

Moreover, the timing of distributions may affect whether an excess-distribution CERT occurs.

---

[44] If P and T file a consolidated return, the result in Example 39 apparently would be the same even if T, rather than P, generates the $5 NOL, i.e., the NOL could not be carried back to pre-year 2 T taxable years. See Example 36 above. If, however, P and T file separate returns, T's NOL could be carried back to prior T taxable years because (1) P and T are not treated as a single corporation and (2) even if T has outstanding debt, no T funds were expended with respect to the CERT.

[45] P's income in year 1 is still $15 less one day's worth of interest on the $100 loan.

EXAMPLE 41

T's stock has an FV of $100. T has made only nominal distributions and redemptions in years 1-3. On 1/1 year 4 T distributes $18 as a dividend to its shareholders. The distribution is an excess-distribution CERT to the extent of $8 (i.e., the excess of $18 over 10% of $100).

EXAMPLE 42

Same as Example 41 except that T distributes $9 on 12/31 year 3 and $9 on 1/1 year 4. No excess-distribution CERT occurs. The $9 distribution on 12/31 year 3 is less than $10 (10% of T's $100 FV). The $9 distribution on 1/1 year 4 is less than $9.10 (10% of T's $91 FV after the 12/31 year 3 distribution).

¶1206.1.6   Bootstrap Acquisition

If P acquires the stock of T in a "bootstrap" acquisition—e.g., P purchases part of the T stock and T redeems its remaining stock—the acquisition could constitute both an excess-distribution CERT and a major-stock-acquisition CERT.

EXAMPLE 43

P transfers $30 to its newly formed subsidiary, S, and S borrows $70. On 1/1 year 1 P merges S into T in a reverse subsidiary cash merger, with T's shareholders receiving $100. As a result of the merger, T became liable for the $70 borrowed by S. T made only nominal distributions during the previous three taxable years.

Because T became liable for the $70 borrowed by S, T is treated as having redeemed $70 of its stock.[46] Accordingly, T made an excess distribution of $60 (i.e., the excess of $70 over 10% of the $100 FV of the T stock).

Additionally, P is treated as having purchased $30 of the outstanding S stock (100% of the S stock after the redemption).[47] Thus, P and T are involved in a major stock acquisition.

[46] See Rev. Rul. 78-250, 1978-1 C.B. 83; Rev. Rul. 79-273, 1979-2 C.B. 125; IRS Letter Ruling 8912049 (12/28/88); IRS Letter Ruling 8905060 (11/10/88). See also ¶202.

[47] Any argument that P purchased only 30% of the outstanding T stock, rather than 100%, likely would not prevail. Cf. Reg. §1.338-3(b)(5).

Because of differences between the treatment of major stock acquisitions and excess distributions, P (and perhaps T) may obtain an NOL carryback advantage by structuring the acquisition of T as a bootstrap acquisition (i.e., by having T redeem, or be treated as redeeming, a portion of its stock).

EXAMPLE 44

On 1/1 year 4 P purchases all the outstanding stock of T for $100, $80 of which P borrowed from an unrelated lender. P and T have no other outstanding debt, and during years 1-3 P made only nominal interest payments. T's average annual distributions with respect to its stock (other than Code §1504(a)(4) stock) during years 1-3 were $8 per year.

P's purchase of the T stock is a major-stock-acquisition CERT and all the interest on the $80 debt is allocated to the CERT. Accordingly, any NOL attributable to the interest on the $80 debt cannot be carried back to pre-year 4 taxable years.

EXAMPLE 45

Same as Example 44 except that P acquires T by transferring $20 of unborrowed P cash to a newly formed P subsidiary, S, and S borrows $80 and merges into T, with T becoming liable on the $80 debt.

Because T became liable on the $80 debt, T is treated as having redeemed $80 of its stock. Accordingly, T made an excess distribution of $68 (i.e., the excess of $80 over the greater of (1) 10% of the FV of the outstanding T stock ($10) or (2) 150% of T's average distributions during years 1-3 (150% of $8)). Thus, $68 of the $80 debt is allocated to the CERT and any NOL attributable to the interest on the $68 debt cannot be carried back to pre-year 4 taxable years.

In contrast to Example 44, in which the entire $80 debt was allocated to the CERT, in Example 45 only $68 of the debt is allocated to the CERT.

Code §172(h)(3)(B)(i) defines a major stock acquisition as an acquisition by P, or P and any group of persons acting in concert with P, of at least 50% of the stock of "another corporation." Arguably, under this literal language, redemptions by T of its own stock after P purchases some T stock do not count in determining whether P (or P and a group of persons acting in concert with P) acquired at least 50% of T's stock because T's redemption of its own stock is not an acquisition of stock of "another corporation." Hence, if P purchases less than 50% of T's stock and sometime thereafter becomes a more-than-50% T shareholder as a result of a redemption by T, arguably P has not effected a major stock acquisition.

EXAMPLE 46

On 1/1 year 3 P purchases for $49 of borrowed funds 49 of T's 100 outstanding shares. On 1/1 year 4 T redeems with $15 of borrowed funds 15 of its outstanding shares (thereby increasing P's interest in T to 57.6%). T made only nominal distributions during years 1-3.

The redemption by T of 15% of its stock constitutes an excess distribution equal to $5 (i.e., the excess of $15 over the greater of (1) 10% of the FV of the outstanding T stock ($10) or (2) the average annual distributions by T during the prior three years). However, under the literal language of Code §172(h)(3)(B)(i) the redemption arguably does not convert P's 49% stock purchase into a major-stock-acquisition CERT. If this is so, any NOL P generates as a result of interest on payments on its $49 debt is not subject to the CERT limitations.

EXAMPLE 47

Same as in Example 46 except that on 2/1 year 3 (i.e., one month after P purchased 49 T shares), T redeemed the 51 shares of its stock not owned by P for $51 of borrowed funds (thereby causing T to be wholly owned by P). Arguably, although the redemption by T constitutes an excess distribution equal to $41, the redemption does not convert P's purchase of T stock into a major-stock-acquisition CERT.

IRS is likely to dispute the conclusions reached in Examples 46 and 47, particularly if P's purchase and T's redemption are part of a plan.[48] In fact, IRS might use its regulatory authority under Code §172(h)(5) to aggregate P's purchase of T stock and T's redemption in determining whether P acquired at least 50% of T's stock. Accordingly, it is unclear whether and in what circumstances P can avoid a major-stock-acquisition CERT by purchasing less than 50% of T's stock and later backing into a 50%-or-more interest in T through T redemptions.[49]

---

[48] Under Code §172(h)(3)(D)(ii), all acquisitions made during any 24-month period are treated as having been made pursuant to a plan.

[49] If IRS takes the position that a subsequent redemption by T can convert an earlier purchase by P into a major stock acquisition, presumably the major-stock-acquisition CERT will be deemed to occur on the date P's interest in T equals or exceeds 50%. Cf. Temp. Reg. §1.338-3T(b)(5)(iv) example (2), and Reg. §1.338-2(b)(5)(iv) example (2) as in effect prior to 1/6/00.

¶1206.1.7   Application to Successor Corporation

The CERT rules apply to any corporation involved in a CERT and to any "successor corporation" of a corporation involved in a CERT.[50] The CERT rules, however, do not define the term "successor corporation" or indicate how the CERT rules are to apply to successor corporations. Instead, Code §172(h)(5)(A) grants IRS the authority to issue regulations applying the CERT rules to successor corporations. Until a regulation (or other guidance) is issued, there will be some uncertainty regarding the application of the CERT rules to successor corporations.

EXAMPLE 48

T is a wholly owned subsidiary of Bigco, but T and Bigco do not file a consolidated return. The FV of T's outstanding stock is $100, T has made only nominal distributions in the past three years, and T has no outstanding debt.

On 1/1 year 4 T distributes $50 of unborrowed T cash to Bigco. The distribution constitutes an excess distribution equal to $40 (i.e., the excess of $50 over the greater of (1) 10% of the FV of the T stock ($10) or (2) the average distributions made by T during years 1-3).

On 1/1 year 5 P purchases all of T's stock from Bigco for $50 of borrowed cash, and immediately thereafter T merges upstream into P in a Code §332 liquidation. The stock purchase is a major stock acquisition.

P, as successor to T, arguably is a "successor corporation" and arguably inherits T's $40 excess-distribution CERT. It is unclear, however, whether and how the CERT rules apply to P in this situation. Conceivably, $40 of P's debt might be allocated to T's CERT, notwithstanding that T gained access to P's cash only after its acquisition by P. Compare Example 34.

EXAMPLE 49

On 1/1 year 4 P acquired T by the merger of T into P in a tax-free reorganization under Code §368(a)(1)(A), in which T's shareholders received $50 of P stock and $50 of borrowed P cash in exchange for their T stock. In years 1-3, T made only nominal distributions to its shareholders and P made only nominal interest payments.

The merger of T into P presumably is treated for tax purposes as though T transferred its assets to P for $50 of P stock and $50 cash and T then distributed the P stock and cash to the T shareholders.[51] Hence, it could be argued that, as discussed in ¶1206.1.2.2 and illustrated in Example 18, the deemed distribution by T to its shareholders constituted a CERT to the extent

---

[50] Code §172(b)(1)(E)(iii)(III).
[51] See Rev. Rul. 67-326, 1967-2 C.B. 143; cf. Rev. Rul. 69-6, 1969-1 C.B. 104.

of $40, i.e., the amount by which the $50 cash exceeded 10% of the $100 FV of the T stock (as noted in ¶1206.1.2.2, the P stock distributed by T to its shareholders presumably should be ignored).

As successor to T, P arguably inherits T's $40 excess-distribution CERT and arguably $40 of P's debt must be allocated to the CERT. (As also discussed in ¶1206.1.2.2 under the Supreme Court's recent decision in *Clark v. Commissioner*, the merger of T into P might be treated as though T received all P stock and P then redeemed $50 of that stock for $50 cash, in which case P might have made an excess distribution.)

¶1206.1.8   Conclusion

The CERT provisions may prove the beginning of a process whereby Congress will seek to reduce or eliminate the income tax advantages of replacing corporate equity with debt.

Unfortunately, the CERT provisions were not completely thought out. As drafted, the provisions produce a number of surprising results and are in many respects ambiguous. As a result, the provisions are a trap for the unwary taxpayer that consciously or inadvertently enters their domain.

Congress delegated to IRS significant authority to issue regulations interpreting the CERT provisions. Until IRS provides long awaited guidance it is often unclear whether and to what extent a corporation involved in a leveraged buyout, whether as the acquiror or target, or in a leveraged recapitalization, is subject to the CERT limitations.

¶1206.2   *T Freestanding Corporation Before P Acquires T's Stock*

If T is a freestanding corporation and P acquires T's stock in either (1) a taxable purchase or a taxable reverse subsidiary merger without a Code §338 or §338(h)(10) election, or (2) a tax-free "B" reorganization or a reverse subsidiary "A" reorganization, then post-acquisition NOLs of the P group that are attributable to T (other than an NOL produced by interest deductions allocable to a CERT) may be carried back into T's pre-acquisition taxable years. Post-acquisition NOLs that are attributable to P or to any other member of P's group may not be carried back into T's pre-acquisition taxable years.[52]

[52] See Reg. §1.1502-21(b); Temp. Reg. §1.1502-21T(b) (generally applicable to tax years for which the due date, without extensions, of the consolidated return is before 6/26/99); Reg. §1.1502-79A(a)(1) (generally applicable to NOLs arising in consolidated return years beginning before 1/1/97). For this purpose, a group's consolidated NOL is generally allocated among the members of the group in proportion to each member's separate NOL. See Reg. §1.1502-21(b)(2)(iv); Temp. Reg. §1.1502-21T(b)(2)(iv) (generally applicable to tax years for which the due date, without extensions, of the consolidated return is before 6/26/99); Reg. §1.1502-79A(a)(3) (generally applicable to NOLs arising in consolidated return years beginning before 1/1/97). The effective dates of some of the

EXAMPLE

P, a calendar year taxpayer, purchases all of T's stock on 1/1 year 3 for cash (none of which is borrowed). During year 3 (1) P's business produces a net taxable loss of $90, (2) T's business produces a net taxable loss of $5, (3) none of the losses are attributable to interest deductions allocable to a CERT, and (4) P and T file a consolidated return showing a $95 NOL.

T's $5 NOL may be carried back against T's pre-acquisition (i.e., year 1 and year 2) taxable income to obtain a refund of federal income tax paid by T in such earlier years (and not against P's or the P group's pre-acquisition income). P's $90 NOL may be carried back only against its pre-acquisition income (and income of the P group to the extent in existence in those years).

¶1206.3   T Common Parent of Old T Group Before P Acquires T's Stock

If T is the common parent of the old T group before P acquires T's stock in either (1) a taxable purchase or a taxable reverse subsidiary merger without a Code §338 election, or (2) a tax-free "B" reorganization or a reverse subsidiary "A" reorganization, then P's acquisition of T's stock terminates the existence of the old T group.[53] If, after the acquisition, members of the P group that formerly were members of the old T group generate NOLs that are not used by the new group, such NOLs (to the extent that they are not produced by interest deductions allocable to a CERT) may be carried back to the old T group's pre-acquisition taxable years, subject to the separate return limitation year ("SRLY") rules.[54]

¶1206.3.1   P Acquires T and Carries Back Post-acquisition T NOL to T Taxable Year Ending Before 1/91

If P acquires T's stock and a post-acquisition NOL generated by a member of the old T group (other than T, the common parent of the old T group) after it

---

pre-1999 rules are not entirely clear, because there appears to be an inconsistency between, on the one hand, the effective date rules of 1.1502-79A(f) and 1.1502-79 (which are based on the year in which the loss arises) and, on the other hand, the general effective date rules of Temp. Reg. §1.1502-21T (which are based on the taxpayer's consolidated return year, regardless of the year in which the loss arises).

[53] Reg. §1.1502-75(d)(1).

[54] Reg. §1.1502-1(f); Reg. §1.1502-21(c); Temp. Reg. §1.1502-21T(c) (generally applicable to tax years for which the due date, without extensions, of the consolidated return is before 6/26/99); Reg. §1.1502-21A(c) (generally applicable to tax years beginning before 1/1/97, or in some cases only to tax years ending before 1/29/91).

leaves the old T group (by becoming a member of the P group) is carried back to a taxable year ending before 1/29/91, then such post-acquisition NOL generally may be carried back into years for which the old T group filed consolidated returns, but only to the extent of the member's taxable income in the carryback year (the "SRLY fragmentation" rule).[55] On the other hand, any post-acquisition NOL generated by T itself may be carried back against the pre-acquisition consolidated income of the entire old T group, i.e., without regard to T's separate taxable income in the carryback year because T was the common parent of the old T group for the carryback year.[56]

The P group's NOL for any post-acquisition year is generally allocated among the members of the P group (including T and the other former members of the old T group) in proportion to the separate NOL of each member for such year.[57]

EXAMPLE 1

Assume the following facts:

(a) P, a calendar year corporation, acquires all of T's stock on 1/1/91.

(b) At the time of the acquisition and for some years in the past, T, a common parent corporation filing (before 1/1/91) a consolidated return on a calendar year basis, has had two wholly owned subsidiaries, S1 and S2.

(c) During 1991, the P group incurs a $100 aggregate taxable loss (none of which is produced by interest deductions allocable to a CERT):

	1991 NOL
P	$ (10)
T	(55)
S1	(10)
S2	(25)
Total NOL	$(100)

(d) In the prior taxable year of the old T group to which the P group's NOL would be carried back, the old T group had $100 of aggregate taxable income:

---

[55] Reg. §1.1502-21A(c); Reg. §1.1502-21A(h) (effective date); Temp. Reg. §1.1502-21T(g) (effective date).

[56] See Reg. §1.1502-1(f)(2)(i).

[57] Reg. §1.1502-79A(a)(3); Temp. Reg. §1.1502-21T(b)(2)(iv).

	Prior Year Income
T	$ 50
S1	40
S2	10
Total income	$100

The P group's $100 post-acquisition NOL may be carried back under the SRLY rules to the old T group's carryback year only to the extent of $75:

(a) T's $55 post-acquisition NOL can be carried back to the extent of the pre-acquisition taxable income of the entire T consolidated group, i.e., it is not limited by T's $50 of taxable income in the carryback year because T was the common parent of the old T group.

(b) S1's $10 post-acquisition NOL can be carried back because S1 had at least $10 of taxable income in the carryback year.

(c) Only $10 of S2's $25 post-acquisition NOL can be carried back because S2 had only $10 of taxable income in the carryback year.

(d) None of P's $10 post-acquisition NOL can be carried back into the T consolidated return because P was not a member of the old T group. It may, however, be carried back against P's pre-acquisition taxable income (as well as the income of other members of the P group, to the extent that the P group was in existence in such years).

¶1206.3.2   Carryback of T Post-acquisition NOL to T Taxable Year Ending After 1990 and Beginning Before 1997

If P acquires T and an NOL generated by a member of the old T group after the acquisition is carried back to a taxable year of the old T group ending after 1/28/91 and beginning before 1/1/97, the P group may either (1) apply the rules described immediately above in connection with carrybacks to T group taxable years ending before 1/29/91 or (2) apply the rules described immediately below in connection with carrybacks to T group taxable years beginning after 12/31/96 if the taxpayer elects to apply retroactively the 6/96 temporary consolidated loss regulations in their entirety, as further described in ¶1205.2.4.2(2).

¶1206.3.3   Carryback of T Post-acquisition NOL to T Taxable Year Beginning After 1996

If P acquires T and an NOL generated by a member (a "loss member") of the old T group (other than T, the common parent of the old T group) after the acquisition is carried back to a taxable year beginning after 12/31/96, then such post-acquisition NOL generally may be carried back into years for which the old T group filed consolidated returns to the extent of the consolidated taxable income for the carryback year of those old T group members that constitute a "SRLY subgroup" with respect to the NOL carryback (rather than merely to the extent of the loss member's separate taxable income for the carryback year).[58] A SRLY subgroup with respect to an NOL carryback from the P group into the former T group generally consists of the member carrying back the NOL (the loss member) and each other member of the former T group that has been continuously affiliated with the loss member from the year to which the NOL is carried through the P consolidated return year in which the NOL arises.[59] If there is no SRLY subgroup with respect to an NOL carryback (i.e., no member of the old T group qualifies for inclusion in a SRLY subgroup with the loss member), the SRLY fragmentation rule described in ¶1206.3.1 generally applies (i.e., a post-acquisition NOL generated by a loss member other than T may be carried back to prior T group years, but only to the extent of the loss member's taxable income in the carryback year).[60] Whether or not all or part of the old T group qualifies as a SRLY subgroup, any post-acquisition NOL generated by T itself may be carried back against the pre-acquisition consolidated income of the entire old T group, because T was the common parent of the old T group for the carryback year.[61]

As in the case of a carryback of a post-acquisition NOL of a member of the old T group to a T group taxable year ending before 1/29/91, the P group's NOL for any post-acquisition year is generally allocated among P's group members (including T and the other former T group members) in proportion to the separate NOL of each member for such year.[62]

EXAMPLE 2

Same as Example 1 except that P acquires all of T's stock on 1/1/00 rather than on 1/1/91, the P group incurs its $100 NOL in 2000 rather than in 1991, and the NOL is carried back to the 1998 year of the old T group. Because the carryback year begins after 12/31/96, $90 of the P group's $100 post-acquisition NOL may be carried back to the old T group's 1998 tax year.

---

[58] Reg. §1.1502-21(c)(2); Temp. Reg. §1.1502-21T(c)(2) (generally applicable to tax years for which the due date, without extensions, of the consolidated return is before 6/26/99), §1.1502-21T(g) (effective date for pre-1999 rules). See also Notice 91-27, 1991-2 C.B. 629 (prior law effective date).

[59] Reg. §1.1502-21(c)(2)(ii); Temp. Reg. §1.1502-21T(c)(2)(ii).

[60] Reg. §1.1502-21(c)(1); Temp. Reg. §1.1502-21T(c)(1) (generally applicable to tax years for which the due date, without extensions, of the consolidated return is before 6/26/99).

[61] See Reg. §1.1502-1(f)(2)(i). For a discussion of the SRLY rules as they apply to NOL carryovers, see ¶1205.2.4.2. The §382 Overlap Rule discussed in ¶1205.2.4.2(4), which provides that the SRLY rules do not apply to an NOL carryover in post-1998 tax years in certain cases where the NOL is subject to a Code §382 limitation, is not relevant to NOL carrybacks, because Code §382 does not limit the use of NOL carrybacks.

[62] Reg. §1.1502-21(b)(2)(iv); Temp. Reg. §1.1502-21T(b)(2)(iv).

(a) As in Example 1, T's $55 post-acquisition NOL can be carried back to the extent of the pre-acquisition taxable income of the entire T consolidated group because T was the common parent of the old T group.

(b) In contrast to Example 1, the $35 combined NOL attributable to S1 and S2 may be carried back to the extent of the pre-acquisition taxable income of the entire T consolidated group even though S2's share of the NOL ($25) exceeds S2's taxable income for the carryback year ($10). This is the case because T, S1, and S2 have been continuously affiliated with each other from the carryback year (when they constituted T's consolidated group) through the P consolidated return year in which the NOL arises (i.e., 2000). Hence T, S1, and S2 are a SRLY subgroup with respect to the carryback.

(c) As in Example 1, none of P's $10 post-acquisition NOL can be carried back into the T consolidated return because P was not a member of the old T group. It may, however, be carried back against the pre-acquisition taxable income of P (and other P group members to the extent that the P group existed in such years).

Subject to the transition rules discussed in ¶1206.3.2 above, the pre-subgroup SRLY fragmentation rules described in ¶1206.3.1 apply to the extent T's post-acquisition NOL is carried back to a T consolidated return year beginning before 1/1/97.

EXAMPLE 3

Same as Example 1 except that P acquires all of T's stock on 1/1/98 rather than on 1/1/91, and the P group incurs its $100 NOL in 1998 rather than in 1991. Assume that for T's taxable year ended 12/31/96, the first year to which the $100 NOL is carried back, the old T group had $100 of aggregate taxable income:

	T Group's 1996 Income
T	$ 50
S1	40
S2	10
Total	$100

T's 1996 taxable year begins before 1/1/97. Therefore, under the 6/96 temporary regulations, unless the taxpayer elects to apply retroactively all of the 6/96 temporary regulations as described in ¶1206.3.2, the rules described in

¶1206.3.1 (i.e., SRLY fragmentation) will apply to the carryback to 1996, even though P acquired T in a taxable year beginning after 12/31/96. As a result, only $75 of the P group's $100 post-acquisition NOL may be carried back to the old T group's 1996 taxable year, as computed in the ¶1206.3.1 example.

Of the remaining $25 post-acquisition NOL, $15 (i.e., the remaining NOL reduced by the $10 attributable to P, which may not be carried back to T group years under either the old or the new SRLY rules) may be carried back to the T group's taxable year ending 12/31/97. Since that taxable year begins after 12/31/96, the new SRLY regulations described in this ¶1206.3.3 (including the SRLY subgroup concept) will apply in determining the extent to which the remaining $15 NOL is available to reduce the T group's 1997 income.

As Example 3 illustrates, different sets of SRLY rules may apply to the same NOL in different carryback years, depending on whether the carryback year begins before 1/1/97 or after 12/31/96.

¶1206.4 T Member of Bigco Group Before P Acquires T's Stock

If T is a member (but is not the parent) of another affiliated group (the Bigco group) before P acquires T's stock in either (1) a taxable purchase or a taxable reverse subsidiary merger without a Code §338 or §338(h)(10) election, or (2) a tax-free "B" reorganization or a reverse subsidiary "A" reorganization, then the P group's post-acquisition NOLs that are attributable to T or a T subsidiary (and not attributable to interest deductions allocable to a CERT) can be carried back into the taxable years of the Bigco group subject to the SRLY rules described above at ¶1206.3.[63] Thus, a post-acquisition NOL generated by T or a T subsidiary (a "loss member") generally may be carried back (1) if to a taxable year of the Bigco group ending before 1/29/91, only to the extent of the loss member's separate taxable income in the carryback year, (2) if to a taxable year of the Bigco group ending after 1/28/91 and beginning before 1/1/97, either as described in (1) above or (if the taxpayer elects to apply retroactively the 1996 temporary consolidated loss regulations in their entirety—see ¶1205.2.4.2(2)), as described in (3) below, and (3) if to a taxable year of the Bigco group beginning after 12/31/96, to the extent of the aggregate taxable income of the relevant "SRLY subgroup" (if any) in the carryback year (generally consisting of the loss member and all other members of the old T group that have been continuously affiliated with the loss member from the carryback year through the P consolidated return year in which the NOL arises, which necessarily will exclude Bigco and Bigco affiliates that were not acquired by P).

[63] When T is a member of Bigco's consolidated group, it may be possible to structure P's acquisition of T's stock in a way that reduces the impact of the CERT rules. See Example 22 in ¶1206.1.2.4.

However, there is a procedural problem relating to whether Bigco rather than P is entitled to the federal income tax refund, and hence P must take special precautions in the purchase agreement to ensure that P (rather than Bigco) will receive the benefits of any carryback of T's post-acquisition NOL to a pre-acquisition year. When T's NOL is carried back to a year in which T was a member of Bigco's consolidated group, only Bigco, the common parent of the Bigco group, can claim the carryback on a consolidated return or in a claim for a refund. Similarly, Bigco, the common parent of the Bigco group, will receive any resulting tax refund without any obligation under the tax laws to pay the refund to Newco and T.[64]

Hence, it is highly desirable from P's standpoint to cover this issue in the contract pursuant to which P is acquiring T's stock from Bigco. P should thus insist on provisions in the stock purchase agreement (1) requiring the Bigco group to cooperate with P and T in claiming the benefit of any post-acquisition T NOL carryback and (2) obligating Bigco to pay the resulting tax benefit to Newco or T.

If P cannot obtain such contractual provisions, P should consider electing to forgo the carryback of its (including T's) NOLs.[65]

¶1206.5 Structuring LBO Acquisition Debt in T Rather Than in Newco

As described above, when Newco purchases T's stock in an LBO, post-acquisition NOLs of the Newco group may be carried back into pre-acquisition years of T and its pre-acquisition subsidiaries only if those post-acquisition NOLs are attributable to T or its subsidiaries. Thus, prior to the 1989 adoption of the CERT rules, it was often desirable to structure Newco's acquisition of T and its old subsidiaries so that all or a portion of the acquisition debt was housed in T or in T's old subsidiaries that were profitable before the acquisition. If the interest expense generated a loss in Newco, the NOL could not be carried back to pre-acquisition years of T and its old subsidiaries; in contrast, if the interest expense generated a loss in T or in one of its old subsidiaries, it was often possible (as described in ¶¶1206.2 to 1206.4) to carry the NOL back into the old T group's pre-acquisition taxable years and claim a refund.

EXAMPLE 1

Newco, capitalized with $100 of equity and $900 of debt bearing 10% interest, purchased all of T's stock for $1,000 on 1/1/89. During 1989 (1) Newco had $90 of interest expenses and no other taxable income or loss,

---

[64] Reg. §1.1502-77(a). Cf. Reg. §1.1502-78; Prop. Reg. §1.1502-78(a) (1984) (T may file an application for a tentative carryback adjustment for its post-acquisition NOLs; any adjustment, however, will be paid to the common parent of the Bigco group).

[65] See Code §172(b)(3). See ¶1201.1 for rules concerning the waiver of NOL carrybacks, including the "split election rule" available for acquisitions occurring after 6/25/99.

(2) T's business produced a net taxable loss of $5, and (3) Newco and T filed a consolidated return showing a $95 NOL.

Only the $5 NOL attributable to T may be carried back against T's pre-acquisition (i.e., 1986-1988) taxable income to obtain a refund of federal income tax paid by T in such earlier years. The $90 of NOL attributable to Newco cannot be carried back against T's pre-acquisition income but can be carried forward against the consolidated taxable income of the entire Newco group (including T).

EXAMPLE 2

Same as Example 1 except that Newco was capitalized with $100 of equity and formed a wholly owned subsidiary, Merger Sub, to which it contributed the $100. Merger Sub borrowed $900 at 10% interest and merged into T on 1/1/89, with T's shareholders receiving $1,000. As a result of the merger, T became liable for the $900 borrowed by Merger Sub. During 1989 (1) Newco had no interest expense and no other taxable income or loss, (2) T had a $95 net taxable loss (of which $90 was attributable to interest on the $900 debt), and (3) Newco and T filed a consolidated return showing a $95 NOL. The entire $95 NOL is attributable to T and may be carried back against T's pre-acquisition (i.e., 1986-1988) income to obtain a refund of federal income tax paid by T in such earlier years. The CERT rules are not applicable because Newco's acquisition of T occurred on 1/1/89, before the effective date for the CERT rules.

The NOL carryback benefit from this technique—structuring the LBO acquisition debt in T and its subsidiaries rather than in Newco—has been limited in many cases by the CERT limits adopted in the 1989 Act. See ¶1206.1.

EXAMPLE 3

Same as Example 2 except that Newco acquires T's stock on 1/1 year 1 (a post-1990 year); T made no distributions (including redemptions) with respect to its stock in prior years; and Newco and T have no debt other than the acquisition debt. Because T becomes liable for the $900 borrowed by Merger Sub, T is treated as if it had redeemed $900 of its stock, causing an excess distribution equal to $800 (the excess of the redemption over the greater of 10% of the FV of the T stock (i.e., $100) or 150% of T's average distributions in the prior three years). In addition, P is treated as purchasing $100 of T stock with its equity contribution (100% of T's stock after the redemption), causing a major stock acquisition. All of T's $900 acquisition debt is apparently allocable to the CERT ($800 to the excess distribution and

$100 to P's major stock acquisition). Thus, the $90 interest expense on the acquisition debt is allocable to the CERT and produces $90 of the $95 NOL.[66] T may therefore carry back only $5 of NOL (the portion not produced by interest allocable to the CERT) to years prior to year 1. The remaining $90 of NOL must be carried forward.

There may be other advantages to structuring the LBO to place the LBO debt in T and its subsidiaries. See e.g., ¶¶1402.3.1 and 1402.1.3. In addition, under some circumstances (due to differences between the treatment of major stock acquisitions and excess distributions), there may be an NOL carryback advantage to placing debt in T even when the CERT rules apply, if T will be treated as if it had redeemed a portion of its stock.

EXAMPLE 4

T is a freestanding company. In a post-1989 tax year, Newco borrows $95 million and purchases T's stock in an LBO for $100 million in cash. P and T have no other debt. During the applicable carryback period, T's average annual distributions with respect to its stock (including redemptions) were $8 million a year. P's purchase is a major stock acquisition, and all the interest on the debt is allocable to the CERT. Thus, any loss incurred in the tax year in which the CERT occurred or in either of the two succeeding tax years to the extent attributable to interest deduction on the $95 million debt may not be carried back (although any NOL in excess of this amount could be carried back).

EXAMPLE 5

Same as Example 4 except that P forms a transitory subsidiary, Merger Sub, that borrows the $95 million and merges into T. Because T becomes liable for the $95 million borrowed by Merger Sub, T is treated as if it had redeemed $95 million of its stock, causing an excess distribution equal to $83 million (the excess of the $95 million redemption over the greater of (1) 10% of the FV of the T stock ($10 million) or (2) 150% of T's average distributions in the prior three years ($12 million = 150% × $8 million)). In addition, P is treated as purchasing $5 million of T stock (100% of T's stock after the redemption), causing a major stock acquisition. Thus, $88 million of the $95 million of debt will be allocated to the excess distribution of $83 million and the $5 million major stock acquisition. Apparently, $7 million of debt will not be allocable to a CERT. If T's NOL exceeds the interest deductions on

---

[66] The de minimis rule is ignored for purposes of the example.

$88 million of debt, the NOL may be carried back. In contrast, in Example 4 T's NOL could be carried back only if it exceeded the interest deductions on $95 million of debt.

¶1206.6   Merger or Liquidation of T Following P's Acquisition of T's Stock

If, after acquiring T's stock, P liquidates T under Code §332 or merges it into P or a P subsidiary (with T ceasing to exist), the ability to carry back T's post-acquisition NOLs into T's pre-acquisition years may be lost. (The same principles apply to an old T subsidiary.)

Under Code §381(b)(3), where a corporation receives the assets of another corporation in a transaction to which Code §381(a) applies (such as a Code §332 liquidation or a tax-free merger), the surviving entity may not carry back post-acquisition NOLs into the transferor's pre-acquisition taxable year unless the transfer is an "F" reorganization.[67] If the surviving entity cannot carry back NOLs to pre-acquisition years of the transferor, then it cannot carry back NOLs to pre-acquisition years of the transferor's old consolidated group.

The Code §332 liquidation of T into P or a P subsidiary conceivably could qualify as an "F" reorganization. Although in 1982 Congress amended Code §368(a)(1)(F) to limit "F" reorganizations to mere changes in identity, form, or place of organization "of one corporation," the Conference Report states that "[t]his limitation does not preclude the use of more than one entity to consummate the transaction provided only one *operating* company is involved."[68] Thus, the liquidation of T into P or a P subsidiary might qualify as an "F" reorganization if the transferee is a passive entity (e.g., a Newco formed to acquire T in an LBO) rather than an operating corporation.[69] However, in amending Code §368(a)(1)(F) in 1982, Congress arguably was concerned about permitting the amalgamation of two sets of tax attributes to qualify as an "F" reorganization. Therefore, if the transferee is not a completely passive entity (e.g., the transferee is a holding company that has been in existence for more than one taxable year and has borrowed money and incurred an NOL), the liquidation of T into the transferee might not qualify as an "F" reorganization.

If the liquidation or merger is not an "F" reorganization (but is merely a tax-free Code §332 liquidation or other Code §368 reorganization), the literal language of

---

[67] Code §381(b)(3) does not limit the ability of the surviving entity to carry back NOLs into its own pre-acquisition tax years. However, in an LBO, Newco will typically have no pre-acquisition years to which post-acquisition NOLs can be carried back for a refund. See ¶1206.7.

[68] H.R. Conf. Rep. No. 760, Pub. L. No. 248, 97th Cong., 2d Sess. 541 (1982) (emphasis added).

[69] In Eastern Color Printing Co. v. Commissioner, 63 T.C. 27 (1974), *acq.*, 1975-2 C.B. 1, the Tax Court held under pre-1982 law that, although an "F" reorganization could not involve two operating companies, the merger of a subsidiary into its 100% parent, a passive holding company whose only assets were cash, its corporate name, and the subsidiary's stock, was a valid "F" reorganization.

Code §381(b)(3) appears to preclude NOL carrybacks from the surviving entity to pre-acquisition years of the transferor.

Some precedent suggests that Code §381(b)(3) should not be applied literally in all cases. In *Bercy Industries, Inc.*[70] the Ninth Circuit held that when T was acquired in a Code §368(a)(2)(D) forward subsidiary merger into a shell corporation, the surviving entity could carry back post-acquisition NOLs to T's pre-acquisition years despite Code §381(b)(3). The forward subsidiary merger was not an "F" reorganization because of the change in T's ownership. The court found, however, that the purpose of Code §381(b)(3) was to avoid the need for a complicated tracing of the source of post-acquisition losses (under an approach similar to that of *Libson Shops, Inc. v. Koehler*,[71]) to either the transferor's business or the transferee's business; because the transferee in *Bercy* was a shell corporation with no business that could produce losses, the court found no need to apply Code §381(b)(3).

Bercy may thus imply that, when P or the P subsidiary into which T is liquidated or merged does not have a business so that no need arises to allocate post-acquisition losses between P's or the P subsidiary's business and T's business, Code §381(b)(3) does not apply, even if the transaction does not constitute an "F" reorganization. However, because *Bercy* requires the transferee to be a shell corporation, it is not likely to extend the "F" reorganization exception to any significant extent. Moreover, IRS has formally rejected the *Bercy* decision as unsound.[72]

¶1206.7   P (or S) Acquires T's Assets in Taxable or Tax-Free Acquisition or Purchases T's Stock with Code §338 or §338(h)(10) Election

In contrast to the NOL carryback rules described in ¶¶1206.1 through 1206.6 above, which apply where P acquires T's stock without a Code §338 or §338(h)(10) election, if the P group acquires (or is treated as acquiring) T's assets, whether (1) by P's taxable purchase of T's assets, (2) by P's taxable purchase of T's stock with a Code §338(or §338(h)(10) election, or (3) by P's tax-free acquisition of T's assets in an "A" or "C" reorganization, then post-acquisition NOLs of the P group attributable to the acquired T assets (like NOLs of the P group generally) may be carried back to pre-acquisition tax years of the P group, but not to pre-acquisition tax years of T or of T's former consolidated group.[73]

---

[70] Bercy Indus., Inc. v. Commissioner, 640 F.2d 1058, 81-1 U.S.T.C. ¶9303 (9th Cir. 1981), *rev'g* 70 T.C. 29 (1978).

[71] 353 U.S. 382, 57-1 U.S.T.C. ¶9691 (1957).

[72] See Action on Decision CC-1984-002.

[73] See Code §172 (generally permitting a taxpayer (here P) to carryback post-acquisition NOLs into its own pre-acquisition tax years); §338(a)(2) (in the case of a taxable stock purchase of T with a Code §338 or §338(h)(10) election, T is treated as a "new corporation" after the acquisition, including for purposes of Code §172 and §1502, and therefore is precluded from carrying back NOLs from the P group's post-acquisition years to T's pre-acquisition years); §381(b)(3) (the transferee of assets (here P) in an "A" or "C" reorganization may not carry back post-acquisition NOLs to pre-acquisition tax

Similarly, if P's newly-formed subsidiary S acquires T's assets in a tax-free subsidiary "A" or subsidiary "C" reorganization, post-reorganization NOLs of the P group attributable to T's successor S arising in tax years ending on or after 6/25/99 also may be carried back to pre-acquisition tax years of the P group, but not to pre-acquisition tax years of T or T's former group.[74] However, because of a flaw in the 1996 temporary SRLY regulations, it is not entirely clear whether post-acquisition NOLs attributable to S that arise in years ending before 6/25/99 may be carried back into pre-acquisition tax years of the P group—an irrational result that would deprive the parties of any carryback whatsoever, since no carryback would be permitted to T's pre-acquisition years either.[75]

If P is newly formed to acquire T and therefore has no taxable income for pre-acquisition tax years, the ability, after the P group acquires T's assets, to carry back post-acquisition NOLs attributable to T's operations of course will not be useful. However, if P is an historic operating company, carrying back post-acquisition NOLs attributable to the acquired T assets may produce substantial tax benefits, particularly given the non-applicability of the CERT rules to asset acquisitions (see ¶1206.1).

¶1206.8   Loss Carryback Filing Procedures

Two alternative filing procedures are available to carry back a post-acquisition NOL or net capital loss to pre-acquisition years to obtain a refund of (or credit for) taxes paid for those prior years.

¶1206.8.1   Claim for Refund

The taxpayer eligible for the refund or credit (T, Bigco or P, as the case may be—see ¶1206.2 through ¶1206.7) can file a normal refund claim by amending its tax return(s) for the year(s) to which the NOL or capital loss is carried back. Generally a corporation can carry back an NOL two years (five years for an NOL

---

years of the transferor (here T)—see also ¶1206.6). See also Reg. §1.1502-21(b)(2)(i) (prohibiting the carryback of a post-acquisition NOL into the P group's pre-acquisition tax years only to the extent the NOL may be carried back to T's prior tax years).

[74] Reg. §§1.1502-21(b)(2)(ii)(B), 1.1502-21(h)(4) (effective date); Code §381(b)(3) (prohibiting carryback into T's pre-acquisition years).

[75] Temp. Reg. §1.1502-21T(b)(2)(ii)(B) provided that the P group could carry back post-acquisition NOLs generated by S provided S "has been a member [of the P group] continuously since [S's] organization." However, this 1996 regulation also referred to the "successor" rule of Temp. Reg. §1.1502-21T(f). Under the successor rule, S is the successor to T in a Code §381(a) transfer of T's assets to S (e.g., in a subsidiary "A" or subsidiary "C" reorganization). These two rules, applied together, might be interpreted to mean that S, as T's successor, has not been continuously affiliated with P, which would preclude a carryback to P's pre-acquisition years of post-acquisition NOLs generated by S. Reg. §1.1502-21(b)(2)(ii)(B) (1999) eliminates this ambiguity by providing that the successor rule is disregarded for this purpose. See also T.D. 8823 (the 1999 SRLY NOL regulations), Preamble ¶¶54–56.

incurred in a tax year ending in 2001 or 2002) and a capital loss three years.[76] The refund claim generally must be filed with IRS (1) within three years after the due date (including extensions) for filing the return for the tax year in which the NOL or capital loss to be carried back arose (the "loss year")[77] or (2) within two years after the time the tax was paid, whichever is later.[78]

¶1206.8.2 Tentative Carryback Adjustment

Alternatively, the taxpayer eligible for the refund or credit may take advantage of a simplified and expedited procedure called a "tentative carryback adjustment," which is specifically designed for carrying back NOLs, net capital losses, and excess credits.[79] An application for a tentative carryback adjustment (IRS Form 1139) generally must be filed with IRS (1) on or after the filing date for the return for the loss year and (2) within 12 months after the end of the loss year. In making the determination under clause (2), effective for loss years beginning after 12/31/2000, where P acquires T and, immediately before the acquisition, T was either a stand-alone corporation or the parent of a consolidated group, T's separate return year ending on the acquisition date is deemed to end on the same day as P's tax year that includes the acquisition.[80]

EXAMPLE

On 4/30 year 1 (which is 2001 or later), P purchases 100% of stand-alone corporation T's stock. Both P and T are calendar year taxpayers. After the P-T acquisition, T is included in P's consolidated return. During T's short year 1/1 through 4/30 year 1 (the "April short year"), T incurs an NOL. Because P includes T in P's consolidated return, the filing due date (including extensions) for T's separate return for its April short year is 9/15 year 2 (i.e., 3/15 year 2, which is the due date for filing P's year 1 return, plus a normal six-month extension).[81]

---

[76] Code §172 and §1212(a). See ¶1201 and ¶1207.

[77] Normally the due date for filing a corporate income tax return is the 15th day of the third month after the end of the tax year, with a customary six-month extension (e.g., 9/15 year 2 for a calendar year corporation's tax year ending 12/31 year 1). Code §6072(b); Reg. §1.6081-3.

[78] Code §6511(a) and (d)(2).

[79] See Code §6411.

[80] Reg. §1.1502-78(e) (published in 6/01, and finalizing Temp. Reg. §1.1502-78T(g) which had been published in 1/01 in T.D. 8919).

[81] See Reg. §1.1502-76(c) (where P acquires T and includes T in P's consolidated return, the due date for T's return for the short year ending on the acquisition date is extended to the due date for the filing of P's consolidated return for the acquisition year). In the absence of this regulation, the due date (plus extensions) for T's April short year return in the above example would be 1/15 year 2 (i.e., 7/15 year 1 plus a normal six-month extension). The extension provided by this regulation is designed to give the P-T group time to determine T's taxable income for the acquisition year and properly allocate that income between T's short year and the balance of P's tax year.

To obtain a tentative carryback adjustment, T must file an application to carry back its April short year NOL by 12/31 year 2 (i.e., 12 months after the end of P's tax year that includes the acquisition). To file a regular refund claim with respect to T's NOL carryback (see ¶1206.8.1 above), T generally must file the claim by 9/15 year 5 (i.e, 3 years after the due date, including a normal six-month extension, of T's tax return for its April short year) or, if later, within two years after T paid its tax for the year to which the NOL is being carried back.[82]

The advantage of the tentative carryback adjustment procedure is that IRS is obligated to act on the filing within 90 days. Specifically, within 90 days after an application for a tentative carryback adjustment is filed, IRS conducts a limited review of the application and, except to the extent IRS finds errors or omissions, IRS first credits any resulting decrease in tax against taxes otherwise owed by the taxpayer, and then refunds the balance to the taxpayer.[83]

The disadvantage of this procedure is that, if IRS disallows the adjustment, the taxpayer does not have the normal procedural rights (e.g., the ability to file a lawsuit) associated with tax refund claims.[84] These rights can be preserved by filing, in addition to the tentative carryback adjustment, a normal refund claim with respect to the carryback, either in connection with filing the tentative carryback adjustment or (subject to the statute of limitations remaining open) if and when the tentative carryback adjustment is disallowed.

¶1207   NET CAPITAL LOSS AND EXCESS TAX CREDIT

In addition to NOLs, the following credits and losses of T or P generally may be carried back or forward to the extent they are not used in the year they arise:

- If a corporation incurs capital losses in excess of capital gains for any taxable year, the resulting "net capital loss" ("net CL") is treated as a short-term CL and generally may be carried back to each of the three preceding taxable years and forward to each of the five following taxable years.[1] If an individ-

---

[82] Before the 2001 regulatory modification, the filing deadline for tentative carryback adjustments sometimes impeded using this procedure at all. For example, assume the facts of the above example except that year 1 was a pre-2001 year, so that the regulatory amendment deeming T's April short year to end concurrently with P's acquisition year was not in effect. Under prior law, T was required to apply for the tentative carryback adjustment by 4/30 year 2 (i.e., 12 months after the end of T's April short year), even though the due date (including a normal six-month extension) for T's separate return for the April short year was not until 9/15 year 2. This problem under prior law did not arise where, before P acquired T, T was a member (but not the parent) of another consolidated group, because in that case P's acquisition of T does not accelerate the close of the selling group's tax year.

[83] Code §6411(b).

[84] See Code §6411(a); Reg. §1.6411-1(b)(2).

¶1207   [1] Code §1212(a).

ual or other non-corporate taxpayer incurs a net CL: (1) the first $3,000 may be deducted currently;[2] and (2) any remaining net CL may be carried forward indefinitely (but may not be carried back), retains its character as net long-term CL or net short-term CL as the case may be, and may be deducted to the extent of the sum of the individual's net CG for the year to which the net CL is carried plus $3,000.[3] See ¶107.2.1 for a discussion of (1) 1997 Act amendments to the tax rates applicable to certain CGs incurred by individuals and (2) the ordering rules for netting CLs against different baskets of CGs after these amendments.

- Any excess "general business credit" (including investment tax credit and research credit) arising in a taxable year (1) beginning after 12/31/97 generally may be carried back one year and carried forward 20 years and (2) beginning before 1/1/98 generally may be carried back three years and carried forward 15 years.[4]
- Any excess "foreign tax credit" of a taxpayer, i.e., the amount by which certain taxes paid or deemed paid to a foreign country for a taxable year exceed the U.S. taxes against which such foreign taxes are currently creditable, generally may be carried back two years and carried forward five years.[5]
- Any alternative minimum tax ("AMT") incurred by a corporate or non-corporate taxpayer, reduced by certain items, may be carried forward indefinitely as a credit against regular income tax (but not AMT) until it is fully absorbed.[6] The AMT credit for a particular carryover year is limited to the amount by which the taxpayer's regular tax liability for the year exceeds the taxpayer's tentative minimum tax for the year. The AMT credit may not be carried back.

Limitations analogous to those discussed at ¶¶1202 through 1206 in connection with NOLs generally apply to these tax attributes as well.[7] Some of the principal limitations on the continued availability of excess credits and net CLs are summarized below. Many of the following concepts are discussed in greater detail in the context of NOLs at ¶¶1202 through 1206.

¶1207.1   T Excess Credit or Net Capital Loss

The limitations on the continued use of T's excess credits or net CL when P or S acquires T's assets or stock in a taxable or tax-free acquisition are similar to those applicable to T's NOLs discussed at ¶¶1203 and 1204.

[2] Code §1211.
[3] Code §1212(b).
[4] Code §39(a), as amended by the 1997 Act.
[5] Code §904(c).
[6] Code §53.
[7] See Code §§383, 381, 269, and 384(d) and the consolidated return regulations.

¶1207.1.1   Taxable Acquisition of T's Assets

T's excess credits and net CL (like T's NOLs) will not carry over to P or S if P or S acquires T's assets in a taxable transaction.[8] See ¶1203.1.

¶1207.1.2   Taxable Acquisition of T's Stock Plus Code §338 or §338(h)(10) Election

If P or S purchases T's stock and makes a Code §338 election with respect to the purchase, T's excess credits and net CL (like T's NOLs) will automatically be eliminated unless T, before the acquisition, was a member (other than the parent) of a consolidated group or an 80-80 non-consolidated Bigco subsidiary and a Code §338(h)(10) election was made with respect to the purchase. See ¶1203.2.1.

¶1207.1.3   Code §269(a) Change of Control and Tax Avoidance Principal Purpose

If P (or S) acquires T's assets in a COB transaction (i.e., an "A" or "C" reorganization or a subsidiary "A" or subsidiary "C" reorganization) or more than 50% of T's stock (by value or by vote) in a taxable or tax-free acquisition, and if "the principal purpose" of the acquisition is tax avoidance (e.g., securing the use of T's excess credits and net CL), then T's excess credits and net CL will be eliminated. See generally ¶1203.2.2.

Legislative Update

The unenacted Senate version of the 2003 Act (S. 1054) would have amended Code §269(a) to apply to any acquisition of corporate stock or corporate assets in a COB transaction, effectively eliminating the "control" requirement in current Code §269(a).

An identical provision was reintroduced in the Senate on 6/2/03 as part of the Working Taxpayer Fairness Restoration Act (S. 1162) to be effective for stock and property acquired after 2/13/03. An identical provision also appears in the Abusive Tax Shelter Shutdown and Taxpayer Accountability Act of 2003 (H.R. 1555), introduced 4/2/03, to be effective for transactions after enactment.

---

[8] Code §381.

¶1207.1.4   Code §383 Ownership Change

Code §383 (as amended by the 1986 Act) applies by reference the NOL limitation rules of Code §382 to T's excess credits and net CL. Hence, if there is an "ownership change" with respect to T (within the meaning of Code §382), Code §383 generally will limit the use of T's excess credits and net CL as follows:

(1)   They will be wholly eliminated (along with T's NOLs) unless T (or the transferee of its assets) meets the continuity of business enterprise test of Code §382 at all times during the two-year period beginning on the date of the ownership change.

(2)   If the continuity of business enterprise test is satisfied, the aggregate amount of T's prechange losses (capital and ordinary) and prechange credits that can be carried forward to a postchange year is subject to the Code §382 limitation for the year, converting the portion of the limitation not absorbed by loss carryovers into an equivalent amount of taxes for purposes of limiting credit carryovers.

Loss carryovers and credit carryovers are treated separately and are subject to ordering rules, as follows:[9] The amount of T's taxable income for any postchange year that can be offset by T's prechange capital and ordinary losses cannot exceed the Code §382 limitation for the postchange year. For this purpose, T's Code §382 limitation is reduced first by net CL carryovers and then by ordinary loss carryovers, in the following order:

(1)   Prechange CLs that are "recognized BILs" (i.e., CLs attributable to prechange periods but recognized after the ownership change date) and are subject to the Code §382 limitation, as described in ¶1208.4(3).

(2)   All other prechange CLs.

(3)   Prechange ordinary losses that are "recognized BILs" subject to the Code §382 limitation, as described in ¶1208.4(3).

(4)   All other prechange ordinary losses.

For an illustration of how the ordering rules apply to prechange ordinary losses, see ¶1208.4 (Example 2 and accompanying text).

If the Code §382 limitation for the year is not completely absorbed by the loss carryovers described above, T's prechange credits, if any, are carried forward as follows: The amount of T's tax liability for the postchange year (computed without regard to any minimum tax liability) that can be offset by prechange credits cannot exceed a separately computed credit limitation for the year. This credit limitation is the credit equivalent of any Code §382 limitation remaining after carrying forward prechange capital and ordinary losses. Specifically, the credit limitation is the excess of (a) T's tax liability for the year over (b) T's tax liability computed after deducting any Code §382 limitation not absorbed by the losses described in

[9] See generally Reg. §1.383-1(d)(2).

(1) through (4) above. The credit limitation is absorbed by T's prechange credits in the following order:

(5)   T's excess foreign tax credits attributable to prechange periods.
(6)   T's excess general business credit attributable to prechange periods.
(7)   T's excess minimum tax credit attributable to prechange periods.

Where T has subsidiaries, the subgroup and other principles described in ¶1208.6 apply for purposes of Code §383, with appropriate adjustments to reflect that Code §383 applies to credits and net CLs.[10]

¶1207.1.5   Consolidated Return Regulations

The consolidated return regulations also may limit the post-acquisition use of T's excess pre-acquisition general business credits, minimum tax credits and net CLs, as discussed below.[11]

(1)   T transfers assets to P in "A" or "C" reorganization (or to S in subsidiary "A" or subsidiary "C" reorganization). If (a) T transfers its assets to P (or S) in a COB transaction that does not constitute a "reverse acquisition" (see ¶¶1204.1.3 and 1204.2.3), (b) there is no Code §382 ownership change with respect to T's excess credits and net CLs at the time of or within six months before or after the COB transaction, and (c) P (or S) is a member of an affiliated group filing consolidated returns, then any of T's unused pre-acquisition general business credits, minimum tax credits and net CL that carry over to P (or S) will become "separate return limitation year" ("SRLY") credits or losses. SRLY credits and losses generally are usable only against the acquiring corporation's (P or S, as the case may be) share of the P group's taxes (in the case of unused credits) or CGs (in the case of unused net CL), not against the taxes or CGs attributable to other members of the P consolidated group. See ¶¶1204.1.3 and 1204.2.3 for special rules applicable when the T assets transferred to P or S in the reorganization include T subsidiaries.

In contrast, if there is a Code §382 ownership change with respect to T's excess credits and net CLs at the time of, or within six months before or after, the COB transaction, then under the §382 Overlap Rule (see ¶1205.2.4.2(4)), for tax years of the P group for which the due date (without extensions) of P's consolidated return is after 6/25/99 (for net CL) or 5/25/00 (for excess credits) (even if P acquired T's assets in an earlier tax year), the carryover of T's pre-acquisition

---

[10] Reg. §1.1502-98 and -99 (effective date); Reg. §1.1502-98A (effective for Code §382 testing dates before 6/25/99) and §1.1502-99A(e) (prior law effective date).

[11] Reg. §§1.1502-1 (definition of SRLY); 1.1502-3(c) and (d) (general business credit); 1.1502-22 (net capital loss) and -22T (prior law); 1.1502-55 (alternative minimum tax credit). See generally ¶1205.2.4. For consolidated return years for which the due date of the income tax return (without extensions) is after 3/13/98, the SRLY rules described in ¶1207.1.5 generally do *not* apply to excess foreign tax credits (see Reg. §1.1502-4(f)) or to overall foreign losses (see Reg. §1.1502-9 and Reg. §1.1502-9A(prior law)), subject to elective effective date exceptions contained in the regulations.

excess credits and net CL generally will not be SRLY-limited. Therefore, for those years, subject to any applicable Code §383 limitation, T's excess credits and net CLs may be carried forward to offset the future taxes and CG of P and any other member of P's consolidated group. However, for prior years of the P group T's pre-acquisition excess general business credits, minimum tax credits and net CL are subject to the SRLY limitation described above.

(2)   P (or S) acquires T's stock by purchase or in "B" or reverse subsidiary "A" reorganization. If (a) P (or S) acquires T's stock by purchase or in a "B" or reverse subsidiary "A" reorganization that does not constitute a reverse acquisition (see ¶1204.3.3), (b) there is no Code §382 ownership change of T at the time of or within six months before or after the reorganization, and (c) P (and S) and T file a consolidated return, T's excess pre-acquisition general business credits, minimum tax credits and net CLs that continue to be usable by T will become SRLY credits or losses. Hence, they generally will be usable only against T's share of the P group's taxes and CGs, not against the taxes or CGs attributable to other members of the P consolidated group. See ¶1204.3.3 for special rules applicable when T has subsidiaries at the time of the reorganization.

In contrast, if there is a Code §382 ownership change of T at the time of, or within six months before or after, the reorganization, then under the §382 Overlap Rule (see ¶1205.2.4.2(4)), for tax years of the P group for which the due date (without extensions) of P's consolidated return is after 6/25/99 (for net CL) or 5/25/00 (for excess credits) (even if P acquired T in an earlier tax year), the carryover of T's pre-acquisition excess credits and net CL generally will not be SRLY-limited. Therefore, for those years, subject to any applicable Code §383 limitation, T's excess credits and net CLs may be carried forward to offset the future taxes and CG of T, P and any other member of P's consolidated group. However, for prior years of the P group T's pre-acquisition excess general business credits, minimum tax credits and net CL are subject to the SRLY limitation described above.

¶1207.2   P Excess Credit or Net Capital Loss

The limitations on the continued use of P's excess credits and net CL after a taxable or tax-free acquisition of T's assets or stock are similar to the limitations on the use of P's NOLs discussed at ¶1205.

¶1207.2.1   Code §269(a) Change of Control and Tax Avoidance Principal Purpose

If P (or S) acquires T's assets in a COB transaction (i.e., an "A" or "C" reorganization or a subsidiary "A" or subsidiary "C" reorganization) and "the principal purpose" of the acquisition is tax avoidance (e.g., applying P's excess credits or net CL against future taxes and CGs generated by T's assets), P will not be able to use its excess credits or net CL against future taxes and CGs generated by T's assets.

Similarly, if P (or S) acquires 50% or more of T's stock (by value or by vote) in a taxable or tax-free transaction and "the principal purpose" of the acquisition is tax avoidance (e.g., applying P's excess credits or net CL against future taxes and CGs generated by T), P will not be able to use its excess credits or net CL against future taxes and CGs generated by T, even if P (and S) and T file consolidated returns.

See generally ¶1203.2.2.

Legislative Update

The unenacted Senate version of the 2003 Act (S. 1054) would have amended Code §269(a) to apply to any acquisition of corporate stock or corporate assets in a COB transaction, effectively eliminating the "control" requirement in current Code §269(a).

An identical provision was reintroduced in the Senate on 6/2/03 as part of the Working Taxpayer Fairness Restoration Act (S. 1162) to be effective for stock and property acquired after 2/13/03. An identical provision also appears in the Abusive Tax Shelter Shutdown and Taxpayer Accountability Act of 2003 (H.R. 1555), introduced 4/2/03, to be effective for transactions after enactment.

¶1207.2.2 Code §383 Ownership Change

If there is a Code §382 ownership change with respect to P (e.g., if P issues sufficient P stock to T's old shareholders in connection with P's (or S's) acquisition of T's stock or assets), Code §383 generally limits the future use of P's excess credits and net CL as follows:

(1) They are wholly eliminated (along with P's NOLs) unless P meets the Code §382 continuity of business enterprise test at all times during the two-year period beginning on the ownership change date.

(2) If P meets the continuity of business enterprise test, the aggregate amount of P's prechange losses (capital and ordinary) and prechange credits that can be carried forward to a postchange year is subject to the Code §382 limitation for the year, converting the portion of the limitation not absorbed by capital and ordinary loss carryovers into an equivalent amount of taxes for purposes of limiting credit carryovers. See ¶1207.1.4 for details on the unitary limitation.

When P has subsidiaries, the subgroup and other principles described in ¶1208.6 apply for purposes of Code §383, with appropriate adjustments to reflect that Code §383 applies to credits and net CLs.[12]

¶1207.2.3 Consolidated Return Regulations

The consolidated return regulations limit P's ability to use its own excess credits and net CLs (like P's own NOLs) in connection with certain acquisitions of T's assets or stock, as discussed below.[13]

(1) P acquires T's assets in "A" or "C" reorganization. If P is a member of an affiliated group filing consolidated returns, and if T's pre-reorganization shareholders receive more than 50% of P's common and preferred stock (by FV) in the reorganization as a result of owning T stock, the transaction is a "reverse acquisition," as discussed at ¶1205.1.2. Often a reverse acquisition of P results in a Code §382 ownership change of P, causing the SRLY rules not to apply to the carryover of P's excess credits and net CL by reason of the §382 Overlap Rule (see ¶1205.2.4.2(4)). If the §382 Overlap Rule does not apply (and in any event for tax years for which the due date (without extensions) of P's consolidated return is before 6/26/99 (for net CL) or 5/26/00 (for excess credits)), any excess pre-reorganization general business credits, minimum tax credits and net CL of P (or any P subsidiary) become SRLY and thus usable only against the postreorganization taxes and CGs of the corporation that holds the credit or net CL (and, for taxable years ending after 1/28/91, possibly against the post-acquisition income of other members of the former P group, under the principles discussed at ¶1205.2.4.2). P, as transferee of T's assets, nevertheless could use its own excess credits and net CL to offset future taxes and CGs generated by such assets (subject to the limitations of Code §§383 and 384).

(2) P acquires T's stock in taxable or tax-free acquisition. Effective only for "consolidated return changes of ownership" ("CRCOs") occurring before 1/1/97 (or before 1/29/91 if the taxpayer elected to apply retroactively all of the 1996 temporary consolidated loss regulations as described in ¶1205.2.4.2(2), if P underwent a CRCO before or during the taxable year in which P acquired T's stock, P's excess pre-CRCO credits and net CL cannot offset T's future taxes and CGs, but rather can offset the future taxes and CGs only of those corporations that were members of P's group immediately before the first day of the taxable year in which the CRCO occurred (a "CRCO freeze"). As discussed at ¶1205.2.4.1, a

---

[12] Reg. §1.1502-98 and -99; Reg. §1.1502-98A and -99A(e) (prior law).

[13] See Reg. §§1.1502-1 (definition of SRLY); 1.1502-3(c) and (d) (general business credit); 1.1502-22 (net capital loss) and -22T (prior law); 1.1502-55 (alternative minimum tax credit). For consolidated return years for which the due date of the income tax return (without extensions) is after 3/13/98, the SRLY and CRCO rules described in ¶1207.2.3 generally do *not* apply to excess foreign tax credits (see Reg. §1.1502-4(f)) or to overall foreign losses (see Reg. §1.1502-9 and Reg. §1.1502-9A), subject to elective effective date exceptions contained in the regulations.

CRCO generally occurs whenever the percentage of P's stock owned by any one or more of P's 10 largest shareholders has increased by more than 50 percentage points within a specified period and the increase is attributable to purchase or to a decrease in the amount of P stock outstanding.

If P undergoes a SRLY transaction before, in connection with, or any time after its acquisition of T's stock, and if there is no Code §382 ownership change of P at the time of or within six months before or after the SRLY transaction, the pre-SRLY general business credits, minimum tax credits and net CL of P or any P subsidiary generally can be used only against the future taxes and CGs of (1) the corporation to which the credit or net CL is attributable and (2) for taxable years ending after 1/28/91, possibly other members of the P group (including T and its subsidiaries if the SRLY transaction occurs *after* P acquired T). A SRLY transaction is generally one in which another *corporation* comes to own 80% or more of P's stock by vote and by value and includes P in its consolidated return. In contrast, if there is a Code §382 ownership change of P at the time of, or within six months before or after, the SRLY transaction, then under the §382 Overlap Rule (see ¶1205.2.4.2(4)), for tax years of the P group for which the due date (without extensions) of P's consolidated return is after 6/25/99 (for net CL) or 5/25/00 (for excess credits) (even if P acquired T in an earlier tax year), the carryover of the P group's pre-SRLY excess credits and net CL generally will not be SRLY-limited. Therefore, for those years, subject to any applicable Code §383 limitation, the P group's excess credits and net CLs may be carried forward to offset the future taxes and CG of P, T and any other member of P's consolidated group. However, for prior years the P group's pre-acquisition excess general business credits, minimum tax credits and net CL are subject to the SRLY limitation described above. See ¶1205.2.4.2.

If P is a member of an affiliated group filing consolidated returns, and if T's pre-acquisition shareholders receive more than 50% of P's common and preferred stock (by FV) in exchange for their T stock in connection with P's acquisition of T's stock (e.g., in a "B" reorganization or reverse subsidiary "A" reorganization), then the transaction is a "reverse acquisition," as discussed at ¶1205.2.4.3. Often a reverse acquisition of P results in a Code §382 ownership change of P, causing the SRLY rules not to apply to the carryover of P's excess credits and net CL by reason of the §382 Overlap Rule (see ¶1205.2.4.2(4)). If the §382 Overlap Rule does not apply (and in any event for tax years for which the due date (without extensions) of P's consolidated return is before 6/26/99 (for net CL) and 5/26/00 (for excess credits)), any excess pre-acquisition general business credits, minimum tax credits and net CL of P (or any P subsidiary) will be subject to the SRLY rules, as discussed in connection with "A" and "C" reorganizations above.

¶1207.2.4   Code §384 Limitation on P's Ability to Offset T's Built-in Gain

Code §384(d) states that "rules similar to" the BIG rules of Code §384 "shall apply in the case of any [excess general business credit or excess minimum tax credit] or net capital loss." Thus, Code §384 may limit P's ability to use its own (or its affiliated group members') pre-acquisition credits and net CLs to offset future taxes and CGs attributable to the disposition of T's BIG assets within five years after the date P acquires T's stock or assets. For a discussion of Code §384, see ¶1205.2.5.

¶1208 MORE DETAILED LOOK AT CODE §382

The preceding portion of this chapter summarizes the application of Code §382 and other limitations on the carryforward and carryback of tax attributes in a transactional context. The following discussion analyzes Code §382 in more detail. The 1986 Act replaced the prior version of Code §382 with a new and more intricate set of rules. The 1988 Act made numerous amendments to the 1986 Act that generally are effective retroactively as though enacted in 1986 as part of the new version of Code §382.

In general, Code §382 imposes an annual limitation on the use of T's NOL carryforwards after certain more-than-50% changes in T's ownership (such as P's or S's acquisition of T) within a three-year period.[1] The annual limit is equal to the long-term tax-exempt bond rate times the FV of T's stock immediately before the ownership change (but after any redemption connected with the ownership change). Moreover, if T's business enterprise is not continued for two years after the ownership change, T's NOLs are disallowed altogether. The same set of rules applies to ownership changes resulting from both stock purchases and tax-free reorganizations. Code §382 applies to ownership changes occurring after 12/31/86 except that, as discussed at ¶1208.7, stock transfers on and after 5/6/86 are taken into account in certain circumstances.

This section discusses the following aspects of Code §382: definition of "ownership change" (taking into account the elaborate temporary regulations on this subject) (¶1208.1), computation of the annual Code §382 limitation (¶1208.2), continuity of business enterprise requirement (¶1208.3), losses subject to the annual limitation (¶1208.4), certain anti-abuse rules (¶1208.5), proposed regulations regarding the application of Code §382 where T has subsidiaries (¶1208.6), and effective date provisions (¶1208.7).

¶1208.1 *Transactions Invoking Code §382 Taint: Ownership Changes*

The annual Code §382 limitation takes effect (i.e., T's NOLs become "tainted") when T undergoes an "ownership change." In 1987, IRS issued detailed temporary

---

¶1208 [1] This discussion of Code §382 assumes that T (rather than P or S) has NOLs. If P or S has NOLs and there is a change in P's ownership (and hence indirectly a change in S's ownership) arising from P's or S's acquisition of T or otherwise, then an analysis similar to that applied to T in the text would apply to P or S. See ¶¶1205.1.2 and 1205.2.3.

regulations defining "ownership change" that have since been amended and supplemented frequently.[2] An ownership change occurs whenever, immediately after the close of any "testing date," the percentage of T's stock (or, if T no longer exists, the stock of its successors) owned by any one or more "5% shareholders" is more than 50 percentage points higher than the lowest percentage of T's stock that such shareholders owned at any time during a specified "testing period" (generally, the three-year period preceding the testing date—see ¶1208.1.4).[3]

A "testing date" is a day on which any of the following occurs:

(1)   an "owner shift" (see ¶1208.1.2),
(2)   for testing dates before 11/5/92, an "equity structure shift" (see ¶1208.1.3), or
(3)   the issuance or transfer of an option if on such date the option would be treated as exercised under Reg. §1.382-4(d).[4]

The concept of "5% shareholder" is highly complex, particularly when entities directly or indirectly own T stock. See ¶1208.1.7. In general, a 5% shareholder is any individual or entity that directly or indirectly owns 5% or more of T's "stock" (as defined at ¶1208.1.1) either as a result of one of the above transactions or at any other time during the testing period.[5] Except as discussed at ¶1208.1.7, all T stock owned by persons who are *not* 5% shareholders of T is treated as stock owned by *one* 5% shareholder of T.[6]

All increases in the percentage ownership of T's stock are computed as of the close of the testing date.[7] As a result, an individual who buys and sells T stock on the same day is treated as never having owned that stock. For example, IRS has ruled privately that the purchase and sale of T common stock by underwriters on the same day pursuant to a public offering was "disregarded for all purposes of section 382," so the stock was treated as directly sold by T to the ultimate purchasers.[8]

---

[2] See Temp. Reg. §1.382-2T. For an excellent critical commentary on the 1987 regulations, see N.Y. St. Bar Assn., Tax Sec. Comm. on Net Operating Losses, Supplemental Report on Section 382 (Including Temporary Regulations) (2/22/88), *reprinted in* Tax Analysts' Highlights and Documents 1726 (2/25/88).

[3] Code §382(g)(1); Temp. Reg. §1.382-2T(a)(1). However, IRS has concluded in several private letter rulings that, under the facts of each ruling, a merger of Code §501(c)(3) tax-exempt organizations that owned taxable subsidiaries with NOLs did not result in a Code §382 ownership change with respect to the subsidiary NOLs. See IRS Letter Ruling 200028005 (4/14/00), 9643012 (7/19/00), and 9001063 (10/13/89). While the rulings do not give a rationale for their conclusion, presumably one factor is that a Code §501(c)(3) organization does not have "shareholders"; instead their organizational documents typically state that upon liquidation any residual assets are directed to another tax-exempt organization.

[4] Reg. §1.382-2(a)(4); Temp. Reg. §1.382-2T(a)(2) (pre-11/5/92 testing dates). For pre-11/5/92 testing dates, the requirement under clause (3) that the option be treated as exercised does not apply since under the pre-11/5/92 option regulations, all options are treated as exercised if such exercise would cause an ownership change. See Temp. Reg. §1.382-2T(a)(2); ¶1208.1.6.7 below.

[5] Code §382(k)(7); Temp. Reg. §1.382-2T(g).

[6] Code §382(g)(4)(A).

[7] Reg. §1.382-2(a)(4)(i); Temp. Reg. §1.382-2T(a)(2)(i) (pre-11/5/92 testing dates).

[8] IRS Letter Ruling 8809081 (12/9/87).

Changes in ownership by death, gift, divorce, or separation are disregarded.[9] All other changes in ownership (whether or not by purchase) are counted. For special ownership change rules applicable when T has subsidiaries, see ¶1208.6.

¶1208.1.1   Definition of Stock

In determining whether an ownership change has occurred, changes in the holdings of all T "stock" are taken into account, except that preferred stock is generally disregarded (regardless of whether such classification helps IRS or the taxpayer) if:

(1)   it is non-voting (or is entitled to vote solely as a result of dividend arrearages),

(2)   it is limited and preferred as to dividends and does not participate significantly in corporate growth,

(3)   it has redemption and liquidation rights that do not exceed the stock's issue price (except for a reasonable redemption or liquidation premium), and

(4)   it is not convertible into another class of stock.[10]

Preferred stock that meets all four of these requirements (or is otherwise disregarded under exception (1) below) and hence is non-stock for purposes of Code §382's ownership change test is herein referred to as "Straight Preferred."

There are several additional exceptions to the above definition of stock, each of which functions as an anti-abuse rule (i.e., the following are intended to help IRS, not the taxpayer):

(1)   An ownership interest that otherwise would be treated as stock under the above rule will be disregarded if:

    (a)   at the time of its issuance or transfer, "the likely participation of such interest in future corporate growth is disproportionately small when compared to the value of such stock as a proportion of the total value of [T's] outstanding stock,"

    (b)   treating the interest as not constituting stock would result in an ownership change, and

    (c)   T's NOL (including T's net unrealized BIL, if any—see ¶1208.4) exceeds a specified de minimis amount, i.e., twice the FV of T's stock (*including* stock disregarded under this exception) times the long-term tax-exempt rate described at ¶1208.2.1.[11]

(2)   An ownership interest that otherwise would not be treated as stock and is *not* an "option" (as described in exception (3) below) *will* be treated as stock if:

---

[9] Code §382(*l*)(3)(B); Reg. §1.382-2(a)(4)(ii)(A).

[10] Code §382(k)(6)(A); Reg. §1.382-2(a)(3)(i).

[11] Temp. Reg. §1.382-2T(f)(18)(ii); Code §382(k)(6)(B)(ii); H.R. Conf. Rep. No. 841, 99th Cong., 2d Sess. II, at 173 (hereinafter "1986 Conference Report II").

   (a)   at the time of its issuance or transfer, "such interest offers a potential significant participation in the growth of the corporation,"

   (b)   treating the interest as stock would result in an ownership change, and

   (c)   T's NOL (including T's net unrealized BIL, if any—see ¶1208.4) exceeds a specified de minimis amount, i.e., twice the FV of T's stock (*including* ownership interests treated as stock under this exception) times the long-term tax-exempt rate described at ¶1208.2.1.[12]

(3) In general, any T stock subject to an "option" (defined to include any option, contingent purchase, warrant, convertible debt instrument, put, stock subject to a risk of forfeiture, contract to acquire stock, or similar interest, whether or not it is contingent or otherwise currently exercisable) is treated as acquired, by the holder's exercise of the option, on the date of issuance or transfer of the option (and generally on any subsequent testing date until an ownership change occurs) if the option is issued, transferred, or structured with "a principal purpose" of avoiding or ameliorating the impact of an ownership change and certain other conditions are met.[13]

Exception (2) above applies to an "ownership interest" that is not otherwise stock and is not an option. The regulations do not explain what types of instruments are intended to be covered by the rule. The rule clearly was not written to cover convertible preferred, which, as discussed below, is either stock under the basic rule (i.e., it is not Straight Preferred and hence is not excluded) *or* an option. Nor was the rule written to cover a convertible debenture, which is an option and hence covered by exception (3), not (2). Perhaps the rule is intended to cover such instruments as (a) a debenture with contingent interest measured by profits (which "offers [the holder] a potential significant participation in the growth of the corporation") and (b) a stock appreciation right (SAR) or phantom stock interest. Query, however, whether an SAR or a phantom stock interest is an "ownership interest" and hence within the scope of exception (2) at all.

EXAMPLE 1

On 1/1/90 T issues to A a long-term, fixed-rate debt instrument that is convertible at the holder's option into T common stock. The conversion price is substantially less than the FV of T's common stock at the time of the conversion. The definition of "option" in Exception 3 includes convertible debt. Therefore, although this debt might otherwise be treated as "stock" (apparently in an amount equal to the value of the convertible debt) under exception (2), it will instead be subject to the option rules (and hence will be stock apparently in an amount equal to the value of the underlying stock).

---

[12] Temp. Reg. §1.382-2T(f)(18)(iii); Reg. §1.382-4(d)(12).

[13] Reg. §§1.382-4(d)(2) through (6). See ¶1208.1.6. For the harsher option rules applicable for pre-11/5/92 testing dates, see ¶1208.1.6.7.

Whether an instrument is treated as "stock" (either under the basic definition or under exception (2)) or as an "option" (under exception (3)) is important for several reasons. First, the option rule can trigger an ownership change (by the option's deemed exercise) on any testing date during the option's life, however long that may be. In contrast, a "stock" transaction is disregarded after the end of the three-year testing period. Second, as Example 1 illustrates, an option's FV for purposes of the ownership change rules apparently is the value of the stock into which it is convertible, whereas the FV of an instrument treated as stock under the basic definition or exception (2) is the value of the instrument itself. Third, exceptions (1) and (2) apply only to stock that is either issued after 9/3/87 or transferred to (or by) a 5% shareholder after 9/3/87.[14] In contrast, the option rule of exception (3) (or its predecessor rule) applies to options issued as early as 5/6/86. See ¶1208.1.6.

Regulations finalized in 3/94 (generally applicable to convertible stock issued after 11/92 and, as discussed below, in some cases earlier) provide that convertible stock whether preferred or common will always be treated as "stock" and may simultaneously be treated as an "option" for purposes of the ownership change rules. Specifically:

(1) convertible stock is treated as both stock and an option "if the terms of the conversion feature permit or require the tender of consideration other than the stock being converted [e.g., cash or debt]"[15] and

(2) all other convertible stock is treated solely as stock and not as an option.[16]

EXAMPLE 2

On 1/1/94 T has 150 shares of common stock outstanding with an FV of $400. On such date T issues preferred stock that has a $300 FV and is convertible into 100 shares of T common stock until 1/1/99. The preferred is convertible solely by tender of the preferred stock and for no other consideration. Therefore, under exception (2) above, it is treated solely as "stock" for ownership change purposes. Whether the preferred causes an ownership change is determined by reference to the FV of the preferred itself. No ownership change results from the preferred's issuance standing alone, because the preferred represents less than 50% of T's total stock by FV ($300 ÷ $700 = 43%). Furthermore, the preferred issuance will be disregarded after 12/31/96 (i.e., the end of the three-year testing period after its issuance).

---

[14] Temp. Reg. §1.382-2T(m)(4)(iv).

[15] For an example of such a conversion feature, see Rev. Rul. 62-140, 1962-2 C.B. 181 (holding period of stock following exercise of conversion right).

[16] Reg. §§1.382-2(a)(3)(ii) and 1.382-4(d)(9)(ii).

EXAMPLE 3

Same as Example 2 except that the preferred's FV at issuance on 1/1/94 is $500. The preferred's issuance causes an ownership change, because the preferred represents more than 50% of T's equity ($500 ÷ $900 = 56%).

EXAMPLE 4

Same as Example 2 except that the preferred may be converted at the holder's option by tendering cash rather than solely the preferred stock. Under exception (1) above, the preferred is treated as both stock and an option. Analyzed as stock, the preferred by itself does not cause an ownership change, as discussed in Example 2. Analyzed as an option, and assuming the preferred was deemed converted under the option rules discussed in ¶1208.1.6, whether the preferred causes an ownership change is determined by reference to the common stock into which the preferred is convertible. Therefore, the issuance standing alone does not cause an ownership change, because the preferred is equivalent to only a 40% interest in T's common (i.e., 100 ÷ 250 shares). In contrast to Example 2, however, when viewed as an option the preferred (in combination with other stock issuances or transfers) might cause an ownership change on a testing date after 12/31/96 because the deemed exercise rule for options generally applies indefinitely.

These rules generally apply to all convertible stock issued after 11/4/92 and to certain convertible stock issued before that date.[17]

---

[17] Under the regulations, for purposes of the ownership change rules, convertible stock issued before 11/5/92 but after 7/19/88:

(1)   is treated solely as an "option" and not as "stock" if, when issued, it would have qualified as Straight Preferred except for its conversion feature (i.e., it was non-voting, non-participating, etc.) ("Pure Convertible Preferred");

(2)   is treated as both stock and an option if the terms of the conversion feature permit or require the tender of consideration other than the stock being converted (e.g., cash or debt);

(3)   otherwise is treated solely as stock and not as an option.

Reg. §§1.382-2(b)(2)(ii)(A) and 1.382-4(h)(2)(iv).

Under the regulations, for purposes of the ownership change rules, convertible stock issued before 7/20/88:

(1)   is treated solely as an "option" and not as "stock" if (a) when issued, it qualified as Pure Convertible Preferred and (b) T made the election described in IRS Notice 88-67 on or before the earlier of the date prescribed in the notice or 12/7/92;

For acquisitions before 7/13/89, the acquisition of certain T stock by an employee stock ownership plan ("ESOP") is not taken into account in determining whether an ownership change has occurred, provided that, immediately after the acquisition, the ESOP owns at least 50% of (1) each class of T's outstanding stock (excluding Straight Preferred) or (2) the total value of all of T's outstanding stock (excluding Straight Preferred), and subject to certain other requirements.[18] Regarding acquisitions of T stock by an ESOP generally, see ¶1406.

¶1208.1.2   Owner Shift

An "owner shift" is any change in the ownership of T's stock that affects the percentage of such stock owned by any 5% shareholder.[19] The regulations identify the following transactions as owner shifts:[20]

(1)   Purchase or disposition of T stock by 5% shareholder.

EXAMPLE 1

T is publicly traded and has more than 10,000 shareholders. No T shareholder has ever owned 5% or more of T's stock. No owner shift (or ownership change) will result from market activity in T's stock so long as no 5% shareholder exists (other than the single 5% shareholder consisting of all of T's less-than-5% shareholders as a group).

EXAMPLE 2

On 1/1/90 P purchases 51% of T's stock from T's old shareholders. Neither P nor its shareholders have previously owned any T stock. The transaction

---

(2)   is treated as both stock and an option if (a) the terms of the conversion feature permit or require the tender of consideration other than the stock being converted (e.g., cash or debt) and (b) T made the election described in IRS Notice 88-67 on or before the date prescribed in the notice; and

(3)   otherwise is treated solely as stock and not as an option. Reg. §§1.382-2(b)(2)(ii)(B) and 1.382-4(h)(2)(iii).

In contrast to the treatment of convertible stock issued before 11/5/92, the rule described in text treats all convertible stock as stock and only some convertible stock also as an option. According to the preamble to the proposed version of the 3/94 regulations (CO-18-90), the reason for this reclassification was the perceived leniency of the 1994 Code §382 option regulations in comparison to the predecessor regulations. See ¶1208.1.6.

[18] Former Code §382(*l*)(3)(C). The 1989 Act repealed this special ESOP rule, generally effective for acquisitions of T stock after 7/12/89.

[19] Code §382(g)(2); Temp. Reg. §1.382-2T(e)(1)(i).

[20] Temp. Reg. §1.382-2T(e)(1); 1986 Conference Report II, at 174.

is an owner shift, because P has become a 5% shareholder by virtue of the stock purchase. The owner shift results in an ownership change, because P's percentage interest in T immediately after the owner shift (51%) is more than 50 percentage points higher than the lowest percentage of T stock P owned at any time during the preceding three years.

(2) Code §351 exchange affecting percentage of T's stock owned by 5% shareholder.

EXAMPLE 3

Individual A has long owned 100% of T's stock. Individual B owns certain other assets. A and B form Newco. A contributes his T stock to Newco in exchange for 49% of Newco's common stock, and B contributes the other assets to Newco in exchange for 51% of Newco's common stock. The transaction is an owner shift, because B has become a 5% shareholder of T by virtue of the exchange. The owner shift results in an ownership change, because B's percentage interest in T immediately after the owner shift (51%) is more than 50 percentage points higher than the lowest percentage of T stock B owned at any time during the preceding three years.

(3) Redemption affecting percentage of T's stock owned by 5% shareholder.

EXAMPLE 4

Individual A owns 51% of T's common stock, and unrelated individual B owns 49% of T's common stock. On 1/1/90 T redeems all of A's common. The redemption is an owner shift because it has increased B's percentage interest in T. The redemption results in an ownership change because it has increased B's percentage interest in T from 49% to 100%, i.e., more than 50 percentage points.

(4) Recapitalization affecting percentage of T's stock owned by 5% shareholder (e.g., an issuance of new common stock in exchange for old long-term debt or Straight Preferred, i.e., preferred that is not treated as stock under any of the ownership change rules discussed at ¶1208.1.1).

EXAMPLE 5

Individual A has long owned 100% of T's common stock. B owns 100% of a class of T's non-voting, limited, non-convertible preferred stock, which is not treated as stock under the Code §382 ownership change rules. On 1/1/90, pursuant to a tax-free recapitalization, B exchanges all the Straight Preferred for T common stock representing 6% of T's outstanding common stock after the recapitalization.

The transaction is an owner shift because B (by virtue of the recapitalization) became a 5% shareholder and the recapitalization increased B's "stock" interest in T from 0% to 6%. This owner shift does *not* result in an ownership change, because B's percentage interest in T after the owner shift is only 6 percentage points higher than the lowest percentage of T stock that B owned at any time during the preceding three years. However, subsequent owner shifts over the next three years, when aggregated with this 6 percentage point owner shift, may cause an ownership change.

EXAMPLE 6

Same as Example 5 except that in the recapitalization B surrenders long-term, fixed rate, non-convertible debt of T rather than Straight Preferred. The conclusion is the same.

EXAMPLE 7

Same as Example 5 except that in the recapitalization B surrenders voting convertible preferred stock of T (which has been treated as "stock" under the basic definition of stock at ¶1208.1.1) rather than Straight Preferred. The old convertible preferred and the new common stock have the same FV. This is not an owner shift because B's percentage interest in T's stock has not changed.

(5) T stock issuance affecting percentage of stock owned by 5% shareholder.

EXAMPLE 8

Individual A has long owned 100% of T's stock. On 1/1/90 T issues new stock in a public or private offering. A acquires no stock in the offering, and

none of the buyers in the public or private offering acquires 5% or more of
T's stock. As a result of the offering, A's ownership of T common stock
declines to 20%, and the less-than-5% shareholders who purchased in the
offering own 80% of T's outstanding stock. Under new Code §382, the
offering is an owner shift because it affects (i.e., reduces) the percentage of
T stock owned by A, a 5% shareholder. T's new less-than-5% shareholders
are treated as a single 5% shareholder for purposes of determining whether
an ownership change has occurred. Their 80% stock ownership after the
owner shift is more than 50 percentage points higher than the lowest percentage of T stock they owned at any time during the preceding three years
(0%). Thus, an ownership change has occurred.[21]

**(6)   "Equity structure shift" affecting percentage of stock owned by 5%
shareholder.**

¶1208.1.3   Equity Structure Shift: Tax-Free Reorganization

As noted in ¶1208.1, testing dates before 11/5/92 included the date of any
"equity structure shift," which means (1) any tax-free reorganization (other than
an "F" reorganization or a divisive "D" or "G" reorganization) and (2) to the
extent provided in future regulations, "taxable reorganization-type transactions
[e.g., a taxable merger], public offerings, and similar transactions."[22] However,
because all transactions described in (2) already constitute owner shifts, and
because of the operation of the regulations' "segregation rules" (see ¶1208.1.7.3),
IRS has for the moment concluded that such regulations are unnecessary.[23] Indeed,
apart from some effective date provisions (see ¶1208.1.7.3), it appears irrelevant
under the temporary regulations whether a transaction that qualifies as an owner
shift also constitutes an equity structure shift.
   In determining whether an ownership change results from an equity structure
shift, the less-than-5% shareholders of each corporation that was a party to the
reorganization are segregated and treated as a single, separate 5% shareholder
unless the parties can demonstrate overlapping ownership.[24] See ¶1208.1.7.3.

EXAMPLE 1

   On 1/1/90 T is merged into P in an "A" reorganization, with P surviving.
Both T and P are publicly traded, and no shareholder owns 5% of P or T at

[21] 1986 Conference Report II, at 175 example (4); see also Temp. Reg. §1.382-2T(j)(2)(iii)(B)(2) example (3).
[22] Code §382(g)(3); 1986 Conference Report II, at 178.
[23] See T.D. 8149, at II(D), 1987-2 C.B. 85.
[24] Code §382(g)(4)(B).

any time. In the merger, T's shareholders receive 40% of P's stock and P's shareholders retain 60%. An "A" reorganization is an equity structure shift. Furthermore, there has been an ownership change with respect to T, because P is T's successor and the percentage (60%) of P's stock owned by P's pre-merger shareholders (who, as less-than-5% shareholders, are collectively treated as a separate, single 5% shareholder) after the reorganization is more than 50 percentage points higher than the lowest percentage of T's stock that was owned by them during the preceding three years (0%). In contrast to the above result, if former T shareholders (who had held T stock for over three years) had received at least 50% of P's stock in the merger, there would not have been an ownership change of T.[25]

EXAMPLE 2

Same as Example 1 except that P has actual knowledge that each of ten individuals has owned both 2% of P's stock and 2% of T's stock for more than three years ending on the merger date. In this case, there would be no ownership change. In the merger, P's old shareholders, in addition to retaining 60% of P's stock in their capacity as P shareholders, would receive an additional 8% of P's stock in their capacity as T shareholders (i.e., 20% of the 40% of P's stock distributed to T's shareholders). Therefore, the percentage of P's (i.e., T's successor's) stock owned by P's old shareholders after the reorganization (68%) would be only 48 (rather than 60) percentage points higher than the lowest percentage of T's stock that they owned during the preceding three years (20%).[26] Obviously, difficult factual questions can abound in demonstrating who actually owns the stock of a widely held company.

¶1208.1.4 Three-Year Testing Period

In general, the relevant period for determining whether an ownership change has occurred (the "testing period") is the three-year period ending on the testing date (i.e., the day of any owner shift or option transfer or issuance).[27]

In determining the amount by which 5% shareholders of T have increased their percentage interest in T, the percentage interest of each 5% shareholder on the testing date is compared to the lowest percentage interest of such shareholder at any time during the testing period.

[25] 1986 Conference Report II, at 177 example (8). See also Temp. Reg. §1.382-2T(j)(2)(iii)(B)(2) example (5) ("B" reorganization involving two public companies, in which the acquiror is the loss company).
[26] See Temp. Reg. §1.382-2T(j)(2)(iii)(A) and (B)(2) example (2).
[27] Code §382(i); Temp. Reg. §1.382-2T(d)(1).

EXAMPLE 1

T's only class of stock has long been owned 40 shares by individual A, 40 shares by individual B, and 20 shares by individual C. On 1/1/90 A sells his 40 shares to individual D. On 7/1/90 C sells her 20 shares to A. Hence T's stock ownership has been as follows:

Stockholder	Pre-1/1/90	1/1/90	7/1/90
A	40	0	20
B	40	40	40
C	20	20	0
D	0	40	40

Even though only 40% of T's stock has changed hands as of 7/1/90 when compared to T's pre-1/1/90 stock ownership (i.e., D's interest has increased by 40 percentage points, whereas each of A's and C's interest has declined by 20 percentage points), an ownership change has occurred on 7/1/90. In addition to D's 40 percentage point increase, A's ownership interest has increased by 20 percentage points from the lowest percentage of T's stock that A owned at any time during the preceding three years (0% from 1/1/90 to 6/30/90).[28]

There are three exceptions to the three-year rule:

(1) The earliest testing period does not begin before 5/6/86 (i.e., stock and option transactions before 5/6/86 are disregarded). See ¶1208.7.

(2) If an ownership change occurs any time after 5/5/86 (even if it occurs before 1/1/87 and therefore does not trigger new Code §382—see ¶1208.7), the testing period for determining whether a subsequent new Code §382 ownership change occurs does not begin until the day after the earlier ownership change.[29]

EXAMPLE 2

A owns 100% of T's stock. On 1/1/90 A sells 51% of T's stock to B and 29% to C (i.e., both sales occur on the same day).

---

[28] See Temp. Reg. §1.382-2T(c)(4).
[29] Code §382(i)(2); Temp. Reg. §1.382-2T(d)(2).

EXAMPLE 3

A owns 100% of T's stock. On 1/1/90 A sells 51% of T's stock to B. The next day, 1/2/90, A sells 29% of T's stock to C.

Although these are essentially the same transactions, the results are different. Each is an ownership change. However, in Example 3 it appears that T has also undergone 29 points of a second ownership change. Hence, in Example 3, if more than an additional 21 percentage points of T's stock changes hands before 1/2/93 (e.g., if A and B sell in the aggregate 22 percentage points of T's stock), there will apparently be a second ownership change. In Example 2, both sales occur on the same day, so both are part of the first ownership change and neither counts toward a second ownership change. New Code §382 does not expressly provide for a "step transaction" analysis that would treat Examples 2 and 3 alike.

(3) The testing period will not begin before the earlier of:
   (a) the first day of the first taxable year from which a loss or excess credit is carried forward to the first taxable year ending after the testing date on which the ownership change occurs or
   (b) the first day of the taxable year in which the transaction being tested occurs (thus taking account of the case where T's loss first arises in the taxable year of the ownership change).[30]

EXAMPLE 4

P purchases 40% of T's stock on 12/1/87 and another 40% on 1/1/90. Both P and T are calendar year taxpayers. T incurs its first NOL in 1989, which results in NOL carrybacks to pre-1989 years and also an NOL carryover to 1990. The testing period with respect to T's NOL will not begin before 1/1/89 (the first day of T's first year from which an NOL is carried forward to 1990). Therefore, P's 12/1/87 purchase is disregarded in determining whether there has been an ownership change. Hence, although P has purchased 80% of T's stock within a three-year period, there has been no ownership change under new Code §382.

Exception (3) generally does not apply if T has a "net unrealized BIL" on the testing date, i.e., if the aggregate adjusted basis of T's assets exceeds their aggregate FV by the lesser of 15% of their aggregate FV or $10 million (not taking into

---

[30] Code §382(i)(3), as retroactively amended by the 1988 Act; Temp. Reg. §1.382-2T(d)(3)(i).

account cash, receivables, other cash items, or marketable securities that have not changed substantially in value).[31] However, if the taxpayer can establish the taxable year in which the net unrealized BIL first accrued, the testing period will not begin before the earlier of the first day of such year or the date specified in exception (3).[32]

EXAMPLE 5

Same as Example 4 except that T has had a net unrealized BIL for many years. Exception 3 will not apply. Therefore, P's 40% purchase of T's stock on 12/1/87 is taken into account, and T will suffer an ownership change on 1/1/90.

EXAMPLE 6

Same as Example 4 except that T, which has a net unrealized BIL on 1/1/90, establishes that such loss did not accrue until sometime in 1988. In contrast to Examples 4 and 5, the testing period will begin 1/1/88 (i.e., the first day of the first taxable year in which the net unrealized BIL first accrued). Accordingly, the testing period will not include 12/1/87 (the date of the first 40% stock purchase), so an ownership change will not occur on 1/1/90.

For the implications of exception (3) when T options are outstanding, see ¶¶1208.1.6.2 and 1208.1.6.4.

¶1208.1.5 Ownership Attribution Rules

To determine who owns stock for purposes of the ownership change rules, the following attribution rules apply:

(1) An individual and such individual's spouse, children, grandchildren, and parents are all treated as one person for purposes of new Code §382.[33]
(2) Stock owned by a corporation, partnership, estate, or trust is treated as owned proportionately by such entity's shareholders, partners, or benefici-

---

[31] Code §382(i)(3); Temp. Reg. §1.382-2T(d)(3)(ii). For ownership changes occurring on or before 10/2/89, and for later ownership changes made pursuant to a written binding contract in effect on 10/2/89 and at all times thereafter before the ownership change, the percentage threshold described in text is 25% rather than 15%, and the $10 million threshold does not apply.

[32] Temp Reg. §1.382-2T(d)(3)(ii).

[33] Code §382(l)(3)(A)(i).

aries.[34] Stock that is attributed from an entity under this rule is not treated as held by that entity, except as provided in regulations.[35] As discussed at ¶1208.1.7, however, the regulations generally provide that if an entity directly or indirectly owns 5% of T, the entity's shareholders are treated as a separate 5% shareholder.

(3) Except as provided in regulations, there is no attribution from shareholders, partners, and beneficiaries to the corporations, partnerships, trusts, and estates they own.[36]

For the treatment of options, convertible securities, contracts to buy or sell stock and similar interests, see ¶1208.1.6. For attribution of stock ownership among persons making a "coordinated acquisition" of T shares, see ¶1208.1.7.2.

¶1208.1.6   Deemed Exercise of Options and Similar Instruments

¶1208.1.6.1   In General

T may have many options outstanding, as well as other instruments and contracts covered by Code §382's sweeping definition of "option." Each must be taken into account in analyzing the application of Code §382.

For Code §382 purposes, "option" is defined to include "[a]ny contingent purchase, warrant, convertible debt, put, stock subject to a risk of forfeiture, contract to acquire stock, or similar interest . . . regardless of whether it is contingent or otherwise not currently exercisable."[37] As further discussed in ¶1208.1.1, convertible stock issued on or after 11/5/92 is treated as an option "only if the terms of the conversion feature permit or require the tender of consideration other than the stock being converted [e.g., cash or debt]."[38]

Code §382 provides that, except to the extent provided in regulations, any T stock subject to an "option" is treated as acquired on any testing date, by the

---

[34] Code §382(*l*)(3)(A) (applying modified Code §318 attribution rules). Taxpayer friendly attribution rules in 6/03 temporary regulations apply to distributions from a qualified trust described in Code §401(a), to which the attribution rules of Code §318 do not apply. More specifically, the 6/03 temporary regulations were promulgated in response to a concern that a qualified trust's distribution of an ownership interest in a loss corporation might cause an ownership change even though the distribution did not change beneficial ownership of the loss corporation. The 6/03 temporary regulations alleviate that concern by (1) treating distributees as if they had acquired the ownership interest at the time and in the manner acquired by the qualified trust and (2) not treating the distribution as causing the day of the distribution to be a testing date. Temp. Reg. §1.382-10T is effective for distributions after 3/27/03 or earlier at the taxpayer's election.

[35] Code §382(*l*)(3)(A)(ii). Under Temp. Reg. §1.382-2T(h)(2)(iii), an entity that does not own, directly or indirectly, at least 5% of the loss corporation generally is treated as an individual shareholder who is unrelated to any other shareholder.

[36] Code §382(*l*)(3)(A)(iii).

[37] Reg. §1.382-4(d)(9)(i). See Temp. Reg. §1.382-2T(h)(4)(v) (generally for testing dates before 11/5/92).

[38] Reg. §1.382-4(d)(9)(ii).

owner's deemed exercise of the option, if such deemed exercise would result in an ownership change.[39]

For any testing date after 11/4/92 (subject to the election described below), regulations finalized in 3/94 (the "new option rules") treat an option as exercised for Code §382 ownership change purposes only if the option is issued or transferred with a "principal purpose of avoiding or ameliorating an ownership change" and satisfies certain other requirements.[40] The new option rules are described in ¶¶1208.1.6.2 through 1208.1.6.6.

For any testing date after 5/5/86 and before 11/5/92 (subject to the election described below), prior regulations (the "old option rules") declined Congress's invitation to ameliorate the statutory rule quoted above and generally treated any combination of outstanding T options as exercised on any testing date if to do so would cause an ownership change of T.[41] The old option rules were particularly harsh and unreasonable given their application throughout the life of an option and to options issued before the three-year testing period began. The old option rules are discussed in ¶1208.1.6.7. Pre-5/6/86 options are discussed in ¶1208.1.6.9.

T may elect to apply the old option rules for purposes of determining whether an ownership change occurs (1) on any testing date on or before 5/17/94, or (2) if T is under court jurisdiction in a title 11 or similar case filed on or before 5/17/94, on any testing date at or before the time the plan of reorganization becomes effective.[42]

¶1208.1.6.2 Basic Deemed Exercise Rule

In determining whether an ownership change results on any testing date after 11/4/92,[43] any T stock subject to an "option" is treated as acquired on the date of the option's issuance or transfer if the option satisfies on that date any one of three tests: the ownership test, the control test, or the income test, each of which is further described below. An option is not treated as exercised in any other circumstance.[44]

Certain options (see ¶1208.1.6.3) and transfers (see ¶1208.1.6.4) are exempt or partly exempt from this deemed exercised rule.

(1) Ownership test. An option satisfies the ownership test if it is issued, transferred, or structured (alone or in combination with other arrangements) with

---

[39] Code §382(l)(3)(A)(iv), as retroactively amended by the 1988 Act; Code §382(k)(6)(B)(i).

[40] Reg. §1.382-4(h)(2)(i).

[41] Temp. Reg. §1.382-2T(m)(4)(vi).

[42] Reg. §1.382-4(h)(2)(vi)(A). This election generally must be made on T's income tax return for the first taxable year ending after 11/4/92 in which a testing date occurs. See Reg. §1.382-4(h)(2)(vi)(C). See also Reg. §1.382-4(h)(2)(vi)(B) (impact of election on convertible stock and on applying the "control test" described in ¶1208.1.6.2).

[43] The old option rules described in ¶1208.1.6.7 (rather than the rules described in ¶¶1208.1.6.2 through 1208.1.6.6) apply to testing dates as late as 5/17/94 (and in some cases later if T is bankrupt) to the extent T has elected their application as described in ¶1208.1.6.1.

[44] Reg. §1.382-4(d)(1).

"a principal purpose" of avoiding or ameliorating the impact of an ownership change of T by providing the holder of the option, before its exercise or transfer, with "a substantial portion" of the attributes of ownership of the underlying stock.[45]

Relevant factors taken into account in applying the ownership test include (but are not limited to):

(a) the relationship (at the time of issuance or transfer) between the exercise price and the value of the underlying stock,

(b) whether the option provides the holder or a related person with the right to participate in management or other "stockholder" rights,

(c) the existence of reciprocal options (e.g., corresponding put and call options), and

(d) the ability of the holder of an option with a fixed exercise price to share in future appreciation of the underlying stock (although neither this ability to share in future appreciation, nor any protection from risk of loss, taken alone, will control whether an option satisfies the ownership test).[46]

(2) **Control test.** An option satisfies the control test if:

(a) it is issued, transferred, or structured (alone or in combination with other arrangements) with "a principal purpose" of avoiding or ameliorating the impact of an ownership change of T, and

(b) the option holder and any "related persons" have, in the aggregate, a more-than-50% "direct and indirect" ownership interest in T (determined as though the increased percentage interest that would result from the exercise of the option in question and any other options held by such persons, and "any other intended increases" in such persons' percentage ownership interest, actually occurred on the date of the option's issuance or transfer).[47]

In applying clause (b), persons are "related" if they (i) bear a relationship specified in Code §267(b) or §707(b) (which generally require more than 50% common ownership) or (ii) have "a formal or informal understanding among

---

[45] Reg. §1.382-4(d)(3).

[46] Reg. §1.382-4(d)(6)(ii).

[47] Reg. §1.382-4(d)(4)(i). Unfortunately, the regulations do not elaborate on the phrase "any other intended increase," though presumably it is linked to the "principal purpose" prong of the test, which provides that the entire transaction involved in the structuring, issuance, or transfer of an option is to be considered.

themselves to make a coordinated acquisition" of T's stock (as described in ¶1208.1.7.2).[48]

Relevant factors taken into account in applying the control test include (but are not limited to) the economic interests of the option holder or related persons in T and their influence over T's management (in either case, through the option, a related arrangement, or rights in stock).[49]

(3)   Income test. An option satisfies the income test if it is issued, transferred, or structured (alone or in combination with other arrangements) with "a principal purpose" of avoiding or ameliorating the impact of an ownership change of T by facilitating the creation of income (including accelerating income or deferring deductions) or value (including unrealized BIGs) prior to the exercise or transfer of the option.[50]

Relevant factors in applying the income test include (but are not limited to) whether, in connection with the option issuance or transfer, (1) T engages in any income acceleration transaction (e.g., a transaction outside the ordinary course of T's business that accelerates income or gain into the period prior to the option's exercise (or defers deductions to the period after exercise)) or (2) the option holder or a related person purchases stock (including Straight Preferred) from, or makes a capital contribution or loan to, T. A stock purchase, capital contribution, or loan (1) grows "more probative" of an option satisfying the income test the larger the amount received by T, and (2) "generally" is not taken into account in applying the income test if it is made to enable T to continue basic business operations (e.g., meet monthly payroll or fund other operating expenses).[51]

Whether an option satisfies the ownership, control, or income test depends on all relevant fact and circumstances. In addition to the specific factors described above in connection with each test, factors relevant in applying all three tests include (but are not limited to) (1) any business purposes for the issuance, transfer, or structure of the option, (2) the likelihood that the option will be exercised (taking into account contingencies), (3) any related transactions, and (4) the consequences of treating the option as exercised.

However, the presence or absence of a factor does not create a presumption under any of the three tests; an option will *not* be treated as exercised if a principal purpose of its issuance, transfer, or structuring is to avoid an ownership change by having it treated as exercised.[52]

---

[48] Reg. §1.382-4(d)(4)(ii)(A). "Indirect" ownership is determined by applying the constructive ownership rules of Temp. Reg. §1.382-2T(h), other than Temp. Reg. §1.382-2T(h)(2)(i)(A) (which treats stock attributed under Code §318(a)(2) as no longer owned by the entity from which it is attributed) and Temp. Reg. §1.382-2T(h)(4) (which generally treats options as exercised in the case or pre-11/5/92 testing dates—see ¶1208.1.6.7). Reg. §1.382-4(d)(4)(ii)(B).

An option issued on or before 3/17/94, or an option issued before 5/17/94 pursuant to a plan in existence before 3/17/94, is not treated as exercised under the control test on any testing date prior to a transfer of the option after 3/17/94, which transfer would itself cause the option to satisfy the control test. Reg. §1.382-4(h)(2)(ii).

[49] Reg. §1.382-4(d)(6)(iii).
[50] Reg. §1.382-4(d)(5).
[51] Reg. §1.382-4(d)(6)(iv).
[52] Reg. §1.382-4(d)(6)(i).

¶1208.1.6.3   Exempt and Partly Exempt Options

The following options are exempt from the deemed exercised rule and hence are disregarded in determining whether T has an ownership change (except to the extent provided in (1) below):[53]

(1) *A stock purchase agreement or "similar arrangement"* (presumably including a reverse subsidiary merger agreement) if (a) the terms are "commercially reasonable," (b) the parties' obligations to close are subject only to "reasonable closing conditions," and (c) the transaction closes on a change date within one year after the agreement is entered into. However, a contract satisfying these conditions is *not* exempt from the "income test" described in ¶1208.1.6.2.

EXAMPLE 1

On 7/1/94 P enters into a typical contract to acquire 100% of T's stock. The terms of the contract are commercially reasonable and the closing conditions are reasonable. The contract is not entered into with "a principal purpose" of avoiding or reducing the impact of an ownership change by facilitating the creation of income or value before the closing date. The acquisition closes on 1/1/95. The contract satisfies the above safe harbor and therefore is ignored for ownership change purposes. An ownership change will occur on 1/1/95, when P actually purchases 100% of T's stock.[54]

EXAMPLE 2

Same as Example 1 except that the contract is entered into with "a principal purpose" of avoiding or reducing the impact of an ownership change by facilitating the creation of income or value before the closing date. Because the contract satisfies the "income test," P will be deemed to acquire 100% of T's stock on 7/1/94 (despite the contract's compliance with the other safe harbor requirements), resulting in an ownership change on that date.

EXAMPLE 3

Individual A has long owned 100% of T's stock. On 7/1/94 P1 purchases 40% of T's stock from A. On 1/1/97 P2 enters into a contract to acquire 30% of T's stock from A. The terms of the contract are commercially reasonable

---

[53] See Reg. §1.382-4(d)(7).

[54] In contrast to this result, the option regulations in effect for testing dates before 11/5/92 would have caused an ownership change on 7/1/94, the contract date, rather than on the closing date. See ¶1208.1.6.7.

and the closing conditions are reasonable. The acquisition by P2 closes on 12/31/97.

The date of the closing, 12/31/97, is not a change date because (a) P2 acquires only 30% of T's stock on that date and (b) P1's purchase of 40% of T's stock on 7/1/94 is not within the three-year testing period for determining whether 12/31/97 is a change date (i.e., that three-year testing period begins on 1/1/95). Since the P2 acquisition did not close on a change date, P2's 1/1/97 purchase agreement is not an exempt option. Therefore, if the 1/1/97 purchase agreement satisfies either the ownership, control, or income test, P2 will be deemed to have acquired 30% of T's stock on 1/1/97. In that case, an ownership change would result on 1/1/97, because the three-year testing period for determining whether 1/1/97 is a change date includes not only P2's deemed 30% purchase but also P1's 7/1/94 purchase of 40% of T's stock.

(2) *An option that is part of a security arrangement* (including an agreement to hold stock in escrow or under a pledge or other security agreement, or an option to acquire stock upon a loan default) in a typical lending transaction, if the arrangement is subject to customary commercial conditions.

(3) *An option with "customary terms and conditions"* provided to an employee, director, or independent contractor in connection with the performance of services for T or a related person, if the option (a) is not excessive in relation to the services performed, (b) is non-transferable, and (c) does not have a "readily ascertainable" FV (as defined in Reg. §1.83-7(b)) on the date of issuance.

EXAMPLE 4

Individual A has always owned 100% of T's stock. There have never been any outstanding options with respect to T's stock. On 1/1/93 P, an unrelated corporation, buys 45% of T's stock from A. On 7/1/93 T adopts an employee stock option plan with customary terms and conditions and, pursuant to the plan, issues to its employees, as reasonable compensation, options to acquire 6% of T's stock. The exercise price of the options is the FV of T's stock on the option grant date. The options are non-transferable except upon an employee's death and do not have a readily ascertainable FV.

Under the safe harbor, the options will not be deemed exercised. In contrast, under the prior option rules described in ¶1208.1.6.7, the employee options would be deemed exercised upon issuance, resulting in an ownership change on 7/1/93. This is the case because the deemed exercise of the employee options, when combined with P's recent stock purchase, would result in a transfer within three years of more than 50% of T's outstanding stock.

(4) *An option entered into between stockholders, or between a stockholder and a corporation,* to acquire stock of a stockholder solely upon the stockholder's death, disability, mental incompetency, or, in the case of stock acquired in connection with the performance of services to the corporation or a related person, the stockholder's retirement.

(5) *A bona fide right of first refusal* with customary terms between T's stockholders (or between T and a T stockholder) and regarding T's stock.

(6) *Any other option designated by IRS as exempt.*

¶1208.1.6.4   *Exempt Transfer*

The transfer of an option will not result in the deemed exercise of the option under the above rules if:

(1)   neither the transferor nor the transferee is a "5% shareholder" (as described in ¶1208.1.7) and neither person would be a 5% shareholder if all the options to acquire stock held by that person were treated as exercised;

(2)   the transfer is between members of separate public groups resulting from the application of the segregation rules described in ¶1208.1.7.3; or

(3)   the transfer occurs by reason of death, gift, divorce, or separation.[55]

¶1208.1.6.5   *Subsequent Treatment of Option Deemed Exercised*

If an option is treated as exercised on the date of its issuance or transfer under the above rules, the subsequent treatment of the option is as follows.

If an ownership change *does not* result on such issue or transfer date, the option is deemed exercised on each subsequent testing date for determining whether there is an ownership change.[56]

If an ownership change *does* result on the issue or transfer date (or, if not at that time, on a subsequent testing date), the following rules apply.[57]

(1) Subject to rule (3) below, the option is not again treated as exercised unless and until it is transferred in a transaction that, taken by itself, has a principal purpose of avoiding or ameliorating the impact of an ownership change and otherwise satisfies the ownership, control, or income test.

EXAMPLE 1

T has 40 shares of stock outstanding, which individual A has always owned. There have never been any outstanding options with respect to T's stock. On 1/1/93, T issues to unrelated individual B an option to acquire

---

[55] Reg. §1.382-4(d)(11).
[56] Reg. §1.382-4(d)(2)(ii).
[57] Reg. §1.382-4(d)(10).

60 shares of T stock. The option satisfies the ownership, control, or income test, resulting in deemed exercise of the option and an ownership change of T (since B is treated as acquiring 60% of T's stock on 1/1/93). On 1/1/94 A sells A's 40 shares to unrelated individual C.

A's 1/1/94 sale apparently causes a second ownership change. This occurs because, under the rule described above, B's optioned shares are not treated as outstanding for determining whether A's 1/1/94 stock sale triggers a second ownership change. Therefore, the 1/1/94 stock sale is treated as a sale of 100% of T's stock.

This result, while it may be ameliorated in the circumstances described in rules (2) and (3) below, seems harsh and inconsistent with the 1/1/93 deemed exercise of B's option. In contrast, under Temp. Reg. §1.382-2T(h)(4)(vii)(A), which is generally applicable for testing dates before 11/5/92, A's 1/1/94 stock sale sensibly would have been treated as a sale of only 40% of T's stock, not 100% (see ¶1208.1.6.7(4)).

(2) Subject to rule (3) below, the actual exercise of the option by the person who owned the option immediately after the ownership change (or by a person who acquired the option in an exempt transfer described in ¶1208.1.6.4) does not contribute to another ownership change on any testing date on or after the exercise date.

EXAMPLE 2

Same as Example 1 except that on 7/1/93 B exercises the option to acquire 60 newly issued shares from T. Under rule (2), B's exercise of the option does not cause an ownership change. In addition, in contrast to Example 1, presumably A's 1/1/94 sale will not trigger an ownership change because the actual issuance of 60 T shares to B causes B to become a 60% shareholder on 7/1/93, so that A's 1/1/94 sale is a sale of only 40% of T's stock.

(3) If T on its original tax return properly treated the option as exercised on the ownership change date, and if the option actually is exercised within three years of the change date, then, in lieu of rules (1) and (2) above, T may treat the option as having been exercised on the change date for determining whether an ownership change occurs on all testing dates after such change date (filing amended tax returns as needed). In addition, if T so treats the option, a postchange date transfer of the option is treated as a transfer of the underlying stock, and the actual exercise of the option is disregarded.

EXAMPLE 3

Same as Example 1 except that on 12/1/95 (i.e., within three years of the option's 1/1/93 issuance) B exercises the option to acquire 60 newly issued shares from T. Assuming T properly treated the 1/1/93 option issuance to B as causing an ownership change on 1/1/93, T may treat B's option as having been exercised on 1/1/93 for determining subsequent ownership changes. In contrast to Example 1, if B's option had been exercised on 1/1/93, A's sale of 40 shares on 1/1/94 would not have resulted in an ownership change, because it would have been a sale of only 40% of T's stock. Therefore, T may file an amended return for 1994 reporting that A's sale of 40 shares on 1/1/94 did not result in an ownership change.

(4) Except as provided in ¶1208.1.6.6, if the option ultimately lapses unexercised or is forfeited without payment, T may not disregard the ownership change triggered by the original deemed exercise of the option. This harsh rule is in contrast to the sensible result under the prior regulations, described in ¶1208.1.6.7(3).

¶1208.1.6.6 Transition Rules

Several special rules apply to options that (1) were deemed exercised under the rules described in ¶1208.1.6.7 (generally concerning pre-11/5/92 testing dates) (the "old option rules") and (2) continue to be outstanding after the effective date of the rules described in ¶¶1208.1.6.2 through 1208.1.6.5 (generally concerning post-11/4/92 testing dates) (the "new option rules").

If an option exists immediately before and after an ownership change occurring when the old option rules applied, then:

(1)   the option will not be treated as exercised under the new option rules unless and until it is transferred in a transaction that meets one of the tests for deemed exercise; and

(2)   subject to the 120-day rule described in ¶1208.1.6.7(5), the actual exercise of the option by the person who owned the option immediately after the ownership change (or by a person who acquired the option in an exempt transfer described in ¶1208.1.6.4) will not contribute to another ownership change.[58]

In contrast to the general rule of ¶1208.1.6.5(4), if an option that is treated as exercised under the old (rather than the new) option rules lapses or is forfeited

---

[58] Reg. §1.382-4(h)(2)(v).

without payment, the option is treated for Code §382 purposes as though it had never been issued.[59]

If an option is treated as exercised under the old option rules and is actually exercised within 120 days after the deemed exercise date, T may elect to treat the ownership change as having occurred on the actual option exercise date rather than on the deemed exercise date.[60]

¶1208.1.6.7   *Testing Dates After 4/86 and Before 11/92*

(1)   In general. In determining whether an ownership change resulted on any testing date after 5/5/86 and before 11/5/92,[61] any T stock subject to an "option" was treated as acquired on any testing date, by the owner's deemed exercise of the option, if such deemed exercise would have resulted in an ownership change.[62] This rule applied throughout the life of the option, even if the option was issued before the three-year testing period began.[63] Thus, under these rules an outstanding option or similar instrument was an "evergreen time bomb" ready to explode in combination with other changes in stock ownership to cause an ownership change.

These former option rules, as discussed further below, were extremely harsh and unreasonable.

EXAMPLE 1

T, a privately held corporation, issues after 5/5/86 a 10-year option on 10% of its stock to A, and the option remains outstanding for 10 years.

If at any time before 11/5/92 (or possibly a later date if T made an election as described in ¶1208.1.6.1) there are owner shifts during a three-year period accumulating to over 40%, A's option is treated as exercised at the time the other owner shifts first accumulate to over 40%, thus causing an ownership change when considered in conjunction with the other owner shifts.

If instead T's stock were publicly traded and A's option was not "in the money" at the time of issuance, however, the option rule would not apply so long as A continued to own the option, as discussed in ¶1208.1.6.7(2)(b).

---

[59] Temp. Reg. §1.382-2T(m)(4)(vi). See also ¶1208.1.6.7(3).

[60] Temp. Reg. §1.382-2T(m)(4)(vi). See also ¶1208.1.6.7(5).

[61] The rules described here also applied to testing dates as late as 5/17/94 (and in some cases later if T is bankrupt) to the extent T elected their application as described in ¶1208.1.6.1.

[62] Temp. Reg. §1.382-2T(h)(4).

[63] Thus, these regulations declined the invitation of the 1986 Blue Book, which stated: "It is expected that the Treasury Department may consider whether there are circumstances in which it may be appropriate to limit the operation of this rule to transactions occurring during any three-year testing period that includes the date the option or other interest is issued or transferred." Staff of the Joint Comm. on Taxation, 100th Cong., 1st Sess., General Explanation of the Tax Reform Act of 1986, at 311 n.32 (comm. print 1987).

The option rule applied selectively (i.e., on a worst-case basis for the taxpayer) to options which, if treated as exercised, would cause an ownership change, not to all options (even if on the same terms) outstanding at any particular time. This rule was overly broad and excessively taxpayer-hostile.

EXAMPLE 2

A owns (and has for many years owned) 100 shares of T stock, the only outstanding shares. On 1/1/90 (a date before 11/5/92 or possibly a later date if T made an election as described in ¶1208.1.6.1) T issues two 10-year options: one for 101 shares to A and one for 101 shares to B.

There has been an ownership change because B is treated as having gone from no prior T ownership to owning 101 shares out of 201 (50.2%) on 1/1/90. B's option is treated as exercised because such deemed exercise results in an ownership change.[64] A's option (although identical to B's) is not treated as exercised because a deemed exercise would defeat the ownership change.

EXAMPLE 3

T's only outstanding stock consists of 100 shares of common stock. For many years, individuals A and B have owned 95 and 5 common shares, respectively. On 1/1/90 (a date before 11/5/92 or possibly a later date if T made an election as described in ¶1208.1.6.1) T issues to A and B rights to acquire for 60 days, for a price equal to the stock's current FV or for a lower price, 25 newly issued shares for each share of common they own. A and B each fully exercises his rights on 3/1/90, i.e., A buys 2,375 common shares (95 × 25) and B buys 125 common shares (5 × 25), so their percentage ownership of T is still 95% and 5%, respectively.

An ownership change occurred on 1/1/90: B's stock rights (but not A's) were treated as exercised on 1/1/90, so B is treated as owning 130 shares (5 old shares plus 125 new shares) on that date compared to A's 95. Thus, B's ownership interest increased on 1/1/90 from 5% to 57.8% (130 ÷ 225), or 52.8%, resulting in an ownership change. A's and B's actual exercise of the rights is irrelevant for purposes of determining whether an ownership change has occurred: B is treated as having exercised the rights on 1/1/90 despite B's actual exercise on a later date, whereas A's actual exercise does not relate back to the date of B's deemed exercise.[65] Temp. Reg.

---

[64] But see the special rule, discussed below, treating an option as never having been issued and allowing T to make a claim for refund, subject to the statute of limitations for refunds, if the deemed exercise of the option causes an ownership change and the option ultimately lapses unexercised or is forfeited.

[65] Cf. supra note 63.

> §1.382-2T(h)(4)(vi)(B) states that T may elect to treat the ownership change as having occurred on the date of B's actual exercise (rather than on 1/1/90), but this rule determines only the date of the ownership change, not whether an ownership change occurred.

The above examples demonstrate that the option rule was overly broad. In particular, Example 3 indicates that it was apparently impossible to issue stock rights in a manner that avoided the option rule's fatal consequences (except by issuing stock rights exercisable only before the end of the day on which they were issued). In Example 3, assuming A and B fully exercise their stock rights, it simply defies economic reality to conclude (as the option rule did) that there was a change in A's and B's respective percentage interests in T.

For purposes of the option rule, the extent to which an option was contingent, called for a high exercise price, or was otherwise not currently exercisable was disregarded.[66]

Classic buy-sell agreements between shareholders of a closely held corporation apparently were covered by the option rule, unless one of the narrow exceptions discussed in ¶1208.1.6.7(2) applied.[67]

EXAMPLE 4

Individual A has long owned 100% of T's stock. T has a substantial NOL from its calendar 1989 taxable year. On 1/1/90 (a date before 11/5/92 or possibly a later date if T made an election as described in ¶1208.1.6.1) A sells 20% of the stock to individual B. As part of the transaction, A and B also enter into a buy-sell agreement whereby, should either wish to sell T stock in the future, the other is first entitled to purchase the stock at FV.

Unless one of the narrow exceptions discussed in ¶1208.1.6.7(2) (such as exception (d) therein) applies, the buy-sell agreement apparently will result in an ownership change since by virtue of this "option" B is deemed to own 100% of T as of 1/1/90.

Moreover, IRS concluded in a 1991 letter ruling that a tender offer was an option for Code §382 purposes, even though the tender offer was subject to the following substantial conditions (among others): (1) valid tender of at least 90% of T's shares, (2) waivers from various T creditors, and (3) approval of the offer and the related short-form merger by T's board of directors and a special committee consisting of unaffiliated directors.[68] This ruling seems particularly aggressive given that neither T nor T's public shareholders were party to any agreement whatsoever until T's board approved the transaction or T's shareholders accepted

---

[66] Temp. Reg. §1.382-2T(h)(4)(iii).
[67] See IRS Letter Ruling 8929018 (4/19/89).
[68] IRS Letter Ruling 9211028 (12/13/91).

the offer. Nevertheless, IRS held that the moment the tender offer commenced, it "was made public and became non-withdrawable as a practical or legal matter" and hence constituted an option for Code §382 purposes.[69]

(2) Exempt options. The regulations exempted certain options from the deemed exercise rule, including the following:[70]

(a) *Generally any option if, on the testing date, T's NOL (including T's net unrealized BIL—see ¶1208.4) was less than a specified de minimis amount* (i.e., twice the FV of T's stock times the long-term tax-exempt rate, as described in ¶1208.2.1).

(b) *If T's stock was actively traded on an established securities market, any option that was continuously owned by the same 5% shareholder for at least three years,* provided the option was not "in the money" on the testing date.

(c) *Any right to receive or obligation to issue a fixed dollar amount of stock pursuant to the terms of a convertible debt instrument* if the conversion price was based on the stock's FV on or about the conversion date.

(d) *Any option entered into between T's shareholders (or between T and one of its direct shareholders) with respect to the shareholder's ownership interest in T that was exercisable only upon the shareholder's "death, complete disability, or mental incompetency."* See ¶1208.1.6.7(1), Example 4.

(e) *Options to acquire or sell T stock owned by certain non-corporate shareholders upon their retirement,* so long as the option was issued when T is not a loss corporation and the owner "actively participate[d] in the management of the entity's trade or business." Query whether "retirement" means that the shareholder must have reached a specified age or merely that he must have left the company's employ. Would this rule, for example, cover a buy-sell agreement under which the continuing shareholders had an option to buy the stock of a shareholder-employee when his employment terminated for any reason (including by resignation or firing)?

(f) *Poison pill rights.* Under the authority of Temp. Reg. §1.382-2T(h)(4)(x), IRS in Rev. Rul. 90-11, 1991-1 C.B. 10, announced that poison pill "rights" of the reasonably standard sort described in the ruling—see the discussion of Rev. Rul. 90-11 in ¶¶604.1 and 703.1.6—were excepted from the operation of the option rule of Temp. Reg. §1.382-2T(h)(4)(i) until the poison pill rights "can no longer be redeemed for a nominal amount by the issuing corporation [T] without shareholder approval." Rev. Rul. 90-11 stresses that poison pill rights are considered to fall within the ambit of this welcome pronouncement "only if the principal purpose for the adoption of the plan providing for such rights is to establish a mechanism by which a publicly held corporation can, in the future, provide shareholders with rights to purchase stock at substantially less than fair market value as a means of responding to unsolicited offers to acquire the corporation." The poison pill pronouncement was effective for rights provided for by plans adopted before, on, or after publication of Rev. Rul. 90-11.

---

[69] The tender offer and merger were consummated. It should be noted that, had they not been, the tender offer "option" would have been disregarded for Code §382 purposes under the option lapse rule described in ¶1208.1.6.7(3).

[70] See generally Temp. Reg. §1.382-2T(h)(4)(ix) and (h)(4)(x).

Exceptions (a) and (e) were both based on the status of T's NOL (and net unrealized BIL) at a specified time. If either exception might apply, a third rule, also based on the amount of T's NOL (and net unrealized BIL), often was relevant as well. As discussed in ¶1208.1.4, Code §382(i)(3) provides that the three-year Code §382 testing period does not begin before the earliest of (1) the first day of the first taxable year from which a loss or excess credit is carried forward to the first taxable year ending after the testing date, (2) if T has a net unrealized BIL on the testing date (meaning a net BIL greater than the applicable threshold amount—see ¶1208.4(3)(d)), the first day of the first taxable year in which the net unrealized BIL first accrued, or (3) the first day of the taxable year in which the transaction being tested occurs.

EXAMPLE 1

Individual A has long owned all of the stock of T, a calendar year corporation. On 1/1/91 unrelated corporation P acquires from A an unrestricted option to buy 40% of T's stock. On 6/1/92 A sells 15% of T's stock to an unrelated buyer. T incurs its first NOL in 1992 and has no net unrealized BIL.

Under exception (a), the option held by P is not deemed exercised before 6/1/92 because T has no NOL and no net unrealized BIL on 1/1/91 (the only testing date before 6/1/92). (Exception (d) does not apply to the P option because the option is not restricted to A's death, disability, or incompetency, and exception (e) does not apply because P is not an individual.)

Under Code §382(i)(3), the testing period with respect to the 6/1/92 stock sale begins on 1/1/92 (i.e., the first day of the taxable year in which the transaction being tested occurs). Although the P option arose before the relevant testing period commences, options are subject to the deemed exercise rule as long as they remain outstanding, unless an express exception applies. As of 6/1/92, exception (a) above no longer applies to the P option, assuming that T's NOL on that date exceeds the de minimis threshold. If P actually exercised its option on 6/1/92, such exercise, when combined with A's 15% stock sale on that date, would result in a more-than-50% ownership change. Hence, under the deemed exercise rule, the P option is treated as exercised on 6/1/92, resulting in an ownership change on that date.

EXAMPLE 2

Same as Example 1 except that on 1/1/91 A sells to P 40% of T's outstanding stock rather than merely an option to acquire such stock.

In contrast to the result in Example 1, there is no ownership change on 6/1/92. This is the case because the 1/1/91 stock sale precedes the testing period relevant for the 6/1/92 testing date (which testing period begins on 1/1/92), and therefore the 1/1/91 stock sale is not counted in determining whether there is an ownership change on 6/1/92.

See also ¶1208.1.6.7(4).

(3)   Effect of option lapse or forfeiture. If an option was treated as exercised under the deemed exercise rule and the option later "lapses unexercised or the owner of such option irrevocably forfeits his right to acquire stock pursuant to the option," the option will be treated for Code §382 purposes as if it had never been issued.[71] In that case, T can file an amended return for prior years (subject to any applicable statute of limitations) if the Code §382 limitation is thus made inapplicable.

EXAMPLE 1

On 1/1/88 T, a calendar year taxpayer, issues a 10-year option on 10% of its stock to A. The option remains outstanding for 10 years, at which time it lapses unexercised. During 1988 other owner shifts occurred, accumulating to more than 40% (after taking into account the deemed exercise of A's option).[72] Therefore, A's option was treated as exercised in 1988, causing an ownership change in that year.

When the 10-year option expires on 12/31/97, T may file amended returns with respect to its open years (normally 1994-1996 under the usual three-years-from-filing-the-return rule) but not with respect to its closed years (normally 1988-1993). Hence, T should consider taking steps before the lapse of the limitations period for the taxable years 1988-1993.

If A irrevocably forfeits the option before 12/31/97, T can file refund claims for whatever earlier years are still open at the time of the revocation.

EXAMPLE 2

Same as Example 1 except that on 1/1/92 (four years after the option was issued) T makes a cash payment to A in cancellation of A's option. The payment is equal to the FM of the underlying stock on 1/1/92 in excess of the option price.

It could be argued that this literally constitutes A's "irrevocable forfeiture" of the right to acquire stock pursuant to the option, and that T therefore can file a claim for refund for 1988 and subsequent years. The IRS, however,

[71] Temp. Reg. §1.382-2T(h)(4)(viii).

[72] In determining whether the deemed exercise of A's option will trigger an ownership change, the dilution of the existing T shareholders that would result from the deemed exercise of A's option must be taken into account. For example, if individual B had purchased 41 of T's 100 outstanding shares in 1988 (thereby causing a 41% owner shift), the deemed exercise of A's option would not trigger an ownership change (assuming no additional owner shift occurred during the testing period) because B would be diluted from 41% to 36.9% (i.e., 41 ÷ 111.1), and 36.9% plus 10% does not exceed the 50% ownership change threshold. Had B purchased 45 of T's 100 outstanding shares in 1988, the deemed exercise of A's option would trigger an ownership change to 40.5% (i.e., 45 ÷ 111.1).

apparently takes the position that A's acceptance of such a cash payment is in effect an exercise of the option and a resale to T of the underlying stock rather than a "forfeiture."[73]

(4) Effect of ownership change on outstanding option. If an option was outstanding immediately before and after an ownership change (the "first ownership change"), then in determining whether there is a future ownership change (the "second ownership change"):

(a) The option's actual exercise is disregarded if the option is exercised by the 5% shareholder who owned the option immediately before and after the first ownership change. This rule applies whether or not the option was treated as exercised in connection with the first ownership change, i.e., whether or not it was necessary to treat the option as exercised on the date of the first ownership change in order for that ownership change to occur.[74] The rule appears to apply even if the first ownership change caused a bankrupt T no harm under Code §382(a) because of Code §382(l)(5) (see ¶1208.1.6.8).

(b) The option is not treated as exercised after the first ownership change so long as it continues to be owned by the 5% shareholder who owned the option immediately before and after the first ownership change. As in the case of (a) above, this rule applies whether or not the option was treated as exercised in connection with the first ownership change.[75]

---

[73] See, e.g., IRS Letter Ruling 9244017 (7/30/92); IRS Letter Ruling 9203014 (10/17/91); IRS Letter Ruling 9109035 (11/30/90); IRS Letter Ruling 8930034 (5/1/89). The analysis could depend on the size of the payment (i.e., the option's FV on the settlement date). See, e.g., Rev. Rul. 88-31, 1988-1 C.B. 302 (when an instrument ("Right") entitles the holder to receive a cash payment equal to $11 less the FV of the issuer's common stock on the settlement date, subject to a specified ceiling and a $0.10 floor, and the actual settlement price is $0.10, "[t]he return of this de minimis amount in all events does not detract from the fact that, in substance, the Right has lapsed").

[74] Temp. Reg. §1.382-2T(h)(4)(vi)(A). The language of this regulation could be read to suggest that, with respect to an option to acquire new stock from T, stock issued on actual exercise of such option is disregarded for purposes of determining the number of T shares outstanding in calculating a future ownership change. However, such a reading of the regulations makes no economic sense and would be inconsistent with the principles of Temp. Reg. §1.382-2T(h)(4)(vii)(A) (essentially treating options that are deemed exercised in connection with an ownership change as outstanding stock for this purpose).

See ¶1208.1.6.8 for a discussion of the modified option rules applicable to a bankrupt T.

[75] Temp. Reg. §1.382-2T(h)(4)(x)(F)(1). With respect to an option to acquire new stock from T, it appears that after an ownership change in which such option was deemed to be exercised (but not after an ownership change in which such option was not deemed to be exercised), stock covered by such unexercised option is treated as outstanding T stock for purposes of determining whether T has a future ownership change. Temp. Reg. §1.382-2T(h)(4)(vii)(A).

Except as discussed in (a) above, if an option was not treated as exercised under the deemed exercise rule, the option's actual exercise was taken into account under the ownership change rules.[76]

An "ownership change" can occur only with respect to a "loss corporation," i.e., a corporation that either is "entitled to use" an NOL carryover or has an NOL (or net unrealized BIL) for the year of the ownership change.[77] Therefore, it appears that T's options can be "purged" under rules (a) and (b) above only in a year when T is a loss corporation.

These pre-11/92 rules are illustrated by the following examples:

EXAMPLE 1

Individual A has long owned all of T's stock. In 1989, T issues to corporation P an unrestricted 10-year option to acquire 51% of T's stock on a fully diluted basis. On 1/1/91 A sells all of T's outstanding stock to unrelated individual B. The option held by P remains outstanding. T is not a loss corporation (i.e., has no NOL and no net unrealized BIL) at any time during 1989, 1990, or 1991.

P's option is not treated as exercised under the deemed exercise rule in 1989, 1990, or 1991 because T has no NOL or net unrealized BIL during that period (see exception (a) described in ¶1208.1.6.7(2). Moreover, because T is not a loss corporation in 1991, B's purchase of all of T's stock on 1/1/91 is not an ownership change. Therefore, rules (a) and (b) above do not apply to P's option, which continues to be subject to the deemed exercise rule after 1/1/91. For example, if T first incurs an NOL or accrues a net unrealized BIL in 1992 and there is a testing date on 10/1/92, P's option will be deemed exercised on the testing date, resulting in an ownership change (assuming T's NOL or net unrealized BIL exceeds the de minimis amount described in exception (a) at ¶1208.1.6.7(2).

EXAMPLE 2

Same as Example 1 except that T has a $1 NOL in 1991.

Because T is a loss corporation in 1991, in contrast to Example 1, the 1/1/91 stock sale causes an ownership change. Therefore, under rules (a) and (b) above, so long as P continues to own the 51% option, the option will never be treated as exercised under the deemed exercise rule, nor will P's actual exercise of the option be taken into account for Code §382 purposes. The analysis is the same whether or not T's $1 1991 NOL exceeds the de

---

[76] Temp. Reg. §1.382-2T(h)(4)(xii).

[77] See Code §§382(g)(1) (defining ownership change as a specified shift with respect to "stock of the loss corporation"), 382(k)(1); Temp. Reg. §1.382-2T(a)(1) ("An ownership change occurs with respect to a corporation if it is a loss corporation on a testing date").

minimis threshold of exception (a) described at ¶1208.1.6.7(2) because the result depends solely on the occurrence of an ownership change on 1/1/91, which does not require the deemed exercise of P's option.

(5)   Actual exercise within 120 days of deemed exercise. If an option is treated as exercised under the deemed exercise rule and the option actually was exercised within the period ending 120 days after the deemed exercise date, T could elect to treat the ownership change as having occurred on the actual option exercise date rather than on the deemed exercise date.[78] This rule determined only the date of the ownership change, not whether an ownership change occurred. The desirability of this election depended, among other things, on (a) whether T's NOL (including any BILs required to be added to T's NOL—see ¶1208.4) increased or decreased between the deemed exercise date and the actual exercise date and (b) whether T's Code §382 limitation (including any BIGs permitted to be added to T's Code §382 limitation—see ¶1208.2) increased or decreased between the deemed exercise date and the actual exercise date. For example, the election generally was favorable for T if T's NOL decreased and the FV of T's stock increased between the time of the deemed option exercise date and the actual option exercise date. If the option was actually exercised after the 120-day period elapsed, the election was unavailable, and the deemed exercise date was the date of the ownership change.

These pre-11/92 rules are illustrated by the following examples:

EXAMPLE 1

On 4/15/91 P enters into a binding written contract with T's shareholders to acquire all of T's stock. Such a contract is treated as an option for purposes of the deemed exercise rule, so that under the general rule an ownership change would result on 4/15/91.

On 8/10/91 P acquires all of T's stock pursuant to the 4/15/91 contract.

Because 8/10/91 is within 120 days of the 4/15/91 contract date, T may elect to treat the ownership change as having occurred on 8/10/91 rather than on 4/15/91.

EXAMPLE 2

Same as Example 1 except that the acquisition closes on 8/20/91 rather than on 8/10/91. Since 8/20/91 is not within 120 days of the 4/15/91 contract date, T may not elect to treat the 8/20/91 closing date as the Code

---

[78] Temp. Reg. §1.382-2T(h)(4)(vi)(B).

§382 ownership change date. Therefore, the ownership change date will be the 4/15/91 contract date.

¶1208.1.6.8   Bankrupt T

If T is bankrupt and is reorganized pursuant to a plan of reorganization confirmed in a "title 11 or similar case" (as defined in ¶1208.2.1.5), then any option created (1) by the solicitation or receipt of acceptances to the plan, (2) by the confirmation of the plan, or (3) under the plan, will not be treated as exercised under the deemed exercise rule until the plan becomes effective.[79] However, this rule does not apply if, in connection with the plan and before the effective date, T issues stock or otherwise receives a capital contribution for a principal purpose of using before the effective date losses and credits that would be limited or eliminated under Code §382 but for this rule.[80]

As discussed in ¶1208.2.1.5, a bankrupt T that undergoes an ownership change while under the jurisdiction of a court in a title 11 or similar case is exempt from the Code §382 annual use limitation provided that, immediately after the ownership change, its pre-ownership change shareholders and certain of its creditors (the "good shareholder/creditor group") own at least 50% of its stock (or 50% of the stock of its parent, if also bankrupt).[81] Treasury was concerned that a bankrupt T could use the before/after rule described in ¶1208.1.6.7(4) to circumvent the Code §382(l)(5) requirement that the good shareholder/creditor group own at least 50%, by issuing options, rather than stock, to new investors, who would exercise the options shortly after the ownership change and thereby reduce the equity interest of the good shareholder/creditor group to less than 50%.[82] Treasury has published regulations addressing this concern, which generally apply to ownership changes occurring on or after 9/5/90.[83] The regulations provide that, in determining whether a bankrupt T satisfies the 50% ownership test of Code §382(l)(5), options to acquire T stock (or stock of its parent, if also bankrupt) that are outstanding at the time of its ownership change and that, if exercised, would cause the resulting stock to be held by persons who were not in the good shareholder/creditor group will be treated as exercised at that time if to do so would cause T to fail the 50% ownership test of Code §382(l)(5).

---

[79] Reg. §1.382-9(o)(1). This rule generally applies to any testing date on or after 9/5/90, although T could have elected either to have the rule apply to pre-9/5/90 testing dates or not to have the rule apply to testing dates between 9/5/90 and 4/8/92. Reg. §1.382-9(o)(2). See ¶1208.1.6.1 for the general application of the old and new option rules to bankrupt companies.

[80] Reg. §1.382-9(o)(2), effective for any testing date on or after 4/8/92.

[81] Code §382(l)(5).

[82] See CO-62-89, 1990-2 C.B. 680.

[83] Reg. §1.382-9(e) and (o).

EXAMPLE 1

As part of its court-approved plan of reorganization, a bankrupt T agrees to cancel its existing stock, issue 100 shares of new T stock to qualified T creditors, and issue to a new investor ("A") an option to acquire 110 shares of T stock from T for cash at any time during the next three years. Because deeming the 110-share option as having been exercised as part of the reorganization will cause the good shareholder/creditor group to fail the 50% ownership test, the option held by A will be deemed to have been exercised. As a result, §382 will apply to T's ownership change.[84]

An option held by a person in the good shareholder/creditor group is not subject to the deemed exercise rule.[85] However, if a good shareholder/creditor (1) acquires an option under the reorganization plan as a result of being a good shareholder/creditor and (2) exercises the option within three years of the ownership change, then T can take into account the actual exercise of the option in determining whether the good shareholder/creditor group satisfied the 50% ownership test with respect to the ownership change.[86]

EXAMPLE 2

Same as Example 1 except that, as part of the court-approved plan of reorganization, T issues to qualified creditors not only 100 shares of new T stock but also an option to acquire an additional 110 shares of T stock from T on exactly the same terms as the identical 110-share option issued simultaneously to A, the new investor. The qualified creditors do not exercise any of their options within three years of the ownership change. Same result as Example 1, i.e., Code §382 applies, because the option held by the qualified creditors is not treated as exercised, but the identical option held by A is treated as exercised.

EXAMPLE 3

Same as Example 2 except that, within three years of the ownership change, the qualified creditors exercise enough of their options to purchase an additional 20 shares of T stock. T may take such stock into account in determining whether the good shareholder/creditor group satisfied the 50%

---

[84] See Reg. §1.382-9(e)(3) example (2).
[85] Reg. §1.382-9(e)(1).
[86] Reg. §1.382-9(e)(2)(ii).

ownership test at the time of the ownership change. The qualified creditors own 120 out of the 230 shares that would be outstanding if the option held by A were deemed exercised, and therefore satisfy the 50% ownership test. Hence, if T chooses this approach, A's options will not be deemed exercised, and §382(a) will not apply to T's ownership change.[87]

If an option that is treated as exercised under the above rule later lapses unexercised or is forfeited, the rule discussed in ¶1208.1.6.7(3) will apply to treat the option as though it had never been issued (unless the option holder acquires additional stock or options after the ownership change and before such lapse or forfeiture).[88] In such case, and also in the case where the exercise of options by the good shareholder/creditor group results in a later determination that Code §382(l)(5) was satisfied (as illustrated in Example 3), T may appropriately amend its prior tax returns, subject to any applicable statute of limitations.[89]

¶1208.1.6.9 Option Issued Before 5/86

An option issued before 5/6/86 will not be treated as exercised under the option rules unless it is transferred after 5/6/86 by or to a 5% shareholder (or a person who would be a 5% shareholder if the option were exercised).[90] However, if a pre-5/6/86 option is so disregarded, the acquisition of stock pursuant to the option's actual exercise will be taken into account for purposes of Code §382.[91]

EXAMPLE 1

On 1/1/86 T grants individual A a five-year option to purchase 10% of T's stock. On 1/1/90 P purchases 45% of T's stock. Because the deemed exercise rule does not apply to A's pre-5/6/86 option, no ownership change occurs on 1/1/90. On 12/31/90 A exercises the pre-5/6/86 option. This will cause an ownership change on 12/31/90 because more than 50% of T's stock has changed hands within three years.

EXAMPLE 2

Same as Example 1 except that A's option was granted on 7/1/86. Because A's option was issued after 5/5/86, P's 1/1/90 purchase of 45% of T's stock,

---

[87] See Reg. §1.382-9(e)(3) example (3).
[88] Reg. §1.382-9(e)(2)(i).
[89] Reg. §1.382-9(e)(2)(iii).
[90] Temp. Reg. §1.382-2T(m)(8)(i).
[91] See also Temp. Reg. §1.382-2T(m)(8)(iii) (disregarding certain options issued or transferred between 9/18/86 and 12/31/86).

together with the deemed exercise of A's option, will cause an ownership change under Code §382 on 1/1/90. A's subsequent exercise of the post-5/5/86 option on 12/31/90 is disregarded.

¶1208.1.7   Identifying 5% Shareholder—Aggregation and Segregation Rules

The regulations contain elaborate rules for identifying T's 5% shareholders. Such identification is necessary because, in determining whether an ownership change has occurred, only changes in the stock ownership of T's 5% shareholders are taken into account. The rules discussed below include: (1) reporting requirements, whereby T periodically must identify and report to IRS the percentage interests of certain persons in T; (2) "aggregation rules," which combine certain less-than-5% shareholders of T and treat them as a single 5% shareholder; (3) "segregation rules," which, in the case of certain transactions, treat as two or more 5% shareholders persons who otherwise would be combined and treated as a single 5% shareholder under the aggregation rules; and (4) certain presumptions regarding stock ownership and exceptions to their application.

¶1208.1.7.1   General Principles and Reporting Requirements

T (or its successor) must file a statement with its federal income tax return identifying, with respect to four testing dates each year (specifically, the testing date, if any, in each calendar quarter which is closest to the end of such quarter), each 5% shareholder and such shareholder's percentage stock ownership.[92] For every testing date, T must determine (but need not report to IRS, except as provided above) the stock ownership (and the changes in stock ownership during the testing period) of all of the following:[93]

(1) any individual who directly owns 5% or more of T's stock;
(2) any entity that directly owns 5% or more of T's stock (a "first-tier entity");
(3) any "higher-tier entity" that indirectly owns 5% or more of T's stock (a "higher-tier entity" is any entity that directly owns 5% or more of the stock of a first-tier entity or any other higher-tier entity);
(4) any individual who indirectly owns 5% or more of T's stock as a result of directly owning 5% or more of a first-tier entity or higher-tier entity.

Each individual described in (1) or (4) above is a 5% shareholder.[94] All other persons with a direct or indirect ownership interest in T are treated as one or more 5% shareholders of T under the so-called aggregation and segregation rules

---

[92] Temp. Reg. §1.382-2T(a)(2)(ii).
[93] Temp. Reg. §1.382-2T(k)(3), (f)(9), (f)(10), (f)(14).
[94] Temp. Reg. §1.382-2T(g)(1)(i).

contained in the regulations, which are discussed below. For purposes of all these rules, the regulations expand the definition of "entity" to include "a group of persons who have a formal or informal understanding among themselves to make a coordinated acquisition of stock," generally effective for testing dates after 11/19/90.[95]

EXAMPLE

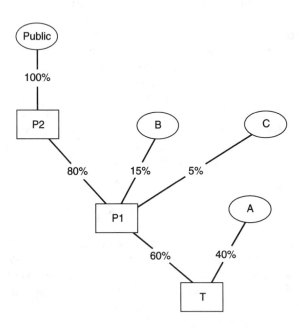

T is a loss corporation owned 60% by P1 and 40% by individual A. P1 is owned 80% by P2, 15% by individual B, and 5% by individual C. P2 is widely held, with no shareholder ever having owned 5% of its stock. Applying the above principles:

- A is a 5% shareholder of T because A directly owns 40% of T's stock (see rule (1) above).
- P1 is a first-tier entity because it owns 60% of T's stock (see rule (2) above).
- B, by virtue of directly owning 5% or more of the stock of a first-tier entity (P1), indirectly owns 9% (15% of 60%) of T's stock. Therefore, B is a 5% shareholder under rule (4) above.
- P2 is a higher-tier entity that indirectly owns 5% or more (80% of 60%, or 48%) of T's stock (see rule (3) above). T need not separately identify

---

[95] Temp. Reg. §1.382-2T(f)(7); Reg. §1.382-3(a). See ¶1208.1.7.2 for further discussion and examples.

P2's shareholders because none of them owns 5% or more of P2's stock (see rules (3) and (4) above).

- C is not a 5% shareholder under rules (1) or (4), because C does not directly or indirectly own 5% or more of T's stock (i.e., C owns 5% of 60%, or only 3%, of T's stock indirectly). If C were an entity (rather than an individual), it would be a higher-tier entity, but not a reportable higher-tier entity indirectly owning 5% or more of T's stock (see rule (3) above), because it indirectly would own only 3%.

Therefore, A and B are 5% shareholders, and T's other beneficial owners (C and P2's shareholders) will constitute one or more 5% shareholders of T under the aggregation and segregation rules discussed below.

¶1208.1.7.2 Aggregation Rules

As indicated above, T is required to identify for each testing date every first-tier entity and every higher-tier entity that indirectly owns 5% or more of T's stock. Proposed regulations expand the definition of "entity" to include "a group of persons who have a formal or informal understanding among themselves to make a coordinated acquisition of stock," generally effective for testing dates after 11/19/90.[96] Once all such entities are identified, the aggregation rules of Temp. Reg. §1.382-2T(j)(1) generally operate as follows:

(1) If a shareholder of such an entity either (a) directly owns less than 5% of the entity or (b) directly owns 5% or more of the entity but directly or indirectly owns less than 5% of T, then the shareholder generally is disregarded and combined with all other such shareholders of the entity into the entity's "public group."[97]

(2) If a public group so identified indirectly owns 5% or more of T's stock, that public group is a 5% shareholder.

(3) If the public group of a higher-tier entity indirectly owns less than 5% of T's stock, the public group is not a 5% shareholder but instead is treated as part of the public group of the next lower-tier entity.

(4) Similarly, if the public group of any first-tier entity indirectly owns less than 5% of T's stock, that public group is not a 5% shareholder but instead is treated as part of T's public group (which also includes all other less-than-5% shareholders of T).

(5) T's public group, even if it owns less than 5% of T's stock, is treated as a separate 5% shareholder.

Thus, each public group described in (2) or (5) above is a 5% shareholder.[98]

---

[96] Temp. Reg. §1.382-2T(f)(7); Reg. §1.382-3(a).
[97] See Temp. Reg. §1.382-2T(f)(13).
[98] Temp. Reg. §1.382-2T(g)(1)(ii) and (iii).

EXAMPLE 1

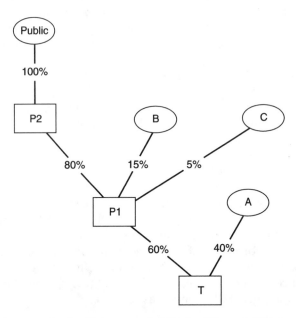

Same as previous example: T is owned 60% by P1 and 40% by individual A. P1 is owned 80% by P2, 15% by individual B, and 5% by individual C. P2 is widely held, with no shareholder ever having owned 5% of its stock.

- Because each of P2's shareholders owns less than 5% of P2's stock, all of P2's shareholders are treated as one public group under rule (1) above. P2's public group indirectly owns 48% (80% of 60%) of T's stock. Therefore, P2's public group is a 5% shareholder under rule (2) (i.e., it is not treated as part of P1's public group under rule (3)).
- P1's public group consists of C alone because each of P1's other shareholders (P2 and B) directly owns 5% or more of P1 and (indirectly) 5% or more of T (rule (1)). Because C indirectly owns only 3% of T's stock (5% of 60%), C is treated as part of T's public group under rule (4). T does not otherwise have a public group because each of T's direct shareholders, P1 and A, owns 5% or more of T. Hence T's public group, after application of the aggregation rules, consists of C alone, who therefore is a 5% shareholder despite owning only 3% of T's stock (rule (5)).

Thus, T has four 5% shareholders: A, B, C, and the public group consisting of P2's shareholders.

EXAMPLE 2

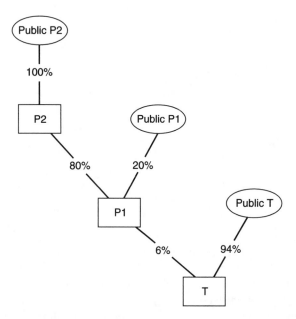

P1 owns 6% of T's stock, and P2 owns 80% of P1's stock. All of P2's stock and the rest of T's and P1's stock is widely held, with no shareholder ever having owned 5% of any entity. P2 owns (indirectly) only 4.8% of T's stock (80% of 6%). Therefore, although P2 owns well over 5% of P1, P2 (or, technically, P2's shareholders, Public P2) is treated as a member of P1's public group, along with all of P1's other shareholders (rule (1)). P1's public group (as defined to include P2) is a 5% shareholder, because it indirectly owns the entire 6% of T's stock owned by P1 (rule (2)). All of T's shareholders other than P1 constitute T's public group, because no one of them owns 5% of T's stock (rule (4)). T's public group is a 5% shareholder (rule (5)). Therefore, under the aggregation rules T has two 5% shareholders: P1's public group (6%) and T's public group (94%).

EXAMPLE 3

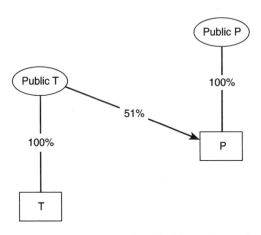

T and unrelated P have long been widely held, with no shareholder ever having owned 5% of either corporation's stock. P purchases 51% of T's stock on 1/1/90. After the purchase, P's public group, consisting of all of P's shareholders ("Public P"), is a 5% shareholder of T, because it indirectly owns 51% of T's stock (see rule (2) above). Therefore, P's purchase causes an ownership change, because a 5% shareholder (Public P) has increased its interest in T by 51 percentage points within three years.

EXAMPLE 4

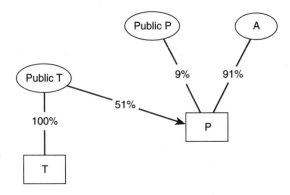

Same as Example 3 except that P, at the time it acquires 51% of T's stock, is 91% owned by individual A and 9% owned by the public ("Public P").

After the purchase, A indirectly owns 46.4% of T by virtue of owning 91% of P (91% of 51% equals 46.4%), and therefore A is a 5% shareholder. Public P, although it owns 9% of P, is not a 5% shareholder of T because it indirectly owns only 4.6% (9% of 51%) of T's stock. Instead, Public P is treated as part of T's public group (see rule (4) above). Therefore, after P's purchase of T's stock, T has two 5% shareholders: T's public group (which includes Public P), owning 53.6% of T's stock (49% directly owned by T's old public group plus 4.6% indirectly owned by Public P), and A, who indirectly owns 46.4% of T's stock. Thus, in contrast to Example 3, there is no ownership change because the only 5% shareholder whose interest in T has increased as a result of P's stock purchase is A, and A's interest in T has increased by only 46.4 percentage points.

This result is odd given that an ownership change would have resulted if P had been 100% owned by Public P, as Example 3 illustrates. Although one would expect the "segregation rules" discussed below to treat Public P and T's old public shareholders as separate 5% shareholders, the segregation rules do not apply to this transaction. Therefore, until the regulations are amended, the Example 3 suggests a reliable tax planning approach.

The aggregation rules generally "presume" that the members of each public group that the aggregation rules identify neither belong to any other public group nor are related to any other direct or indirect shareholder.[99] However, these presumptions may not apply to the extent T has actual knowledge of contrary facts or in cases of tax avoidance. See ¶1208.1.7.4.

As noted above, regulations expand the definition "entity" to include "a group of persons who have a formal or informal understanding among themselves to make a coordinated acquisition of stock, "generally effective for testing dates after 11/19/90.[100] The regulations specify that "a principal element" in this determination is "whether the investment decision of each member of a group is based on the investment decision of one or more other members."

EXAMPLE 5

T has long been widely held, with no shareholder ever having owned 5% of T's stock. During 1991 a group of 20 unrelated individuals (the "Purchasers"), none of whom previously owned any T stock, purchases 60% of T's stock from T's historic shareholders. No Purchaser is acquainted with any other Purchaser, and no Purchaser is aware that other Purchasers are

---

[99] Temp. Reg. §1.382-2T(j)(1)(iii).

[100] Temp. Reg. §1.382-2T(f)(7); Reg. §1.382-3(a)(1). For any group of persons that, pursuant to such an understanding, makes a coordinated stock acquisition before 11/20/90, the expanded definition generally applies only if, after 11/19/90, the group increases or reduces its interest in T by at least five percentage points relative to the group's percentage interest on 11/19/90.

buying or planning to buy T stock. No Purchaser acquires 5% or more of T's stock.

Before the 1991 acquisitions, no individual or entity directly or indirectly owned 5% of T's stock. Therefore, T had one 5% shareholder, consisting of the public group that included all of T's shareholders (rules (1) and (2)). The Purchasers, although they collectively acquired 60% of T's stock, did not act pursuant to a formal or informal understanding among themselves. Therefore, they are not treated as a single "entity." Because no Purchaser individually acquired 5% or more of T's stock, the stock purchases by the Purchasers are disregarded for Code §382 purposes. Under the aggregation rules, the Purchasers are included in the historic public group consisting of all of T's shareholders.

EXAMPLE 6

T has long been widely held, with no shareholder ever having owned 5% of T's stock. A group of 20 unrelated individuals (the "Group"), none of whom owns any T stock, agree among themselves to acquire 60% of T's stock. In accordance with this agreement, on 1/1/91, each member of the group directly purchases 3% of T's stock from the historic shareholders.

Because the Group acquired T's stock pursuant to an understanding among its members, under the proposed regulations the Group is treated as an "entity" for Code §382 purposes. Therefore, although each Group member acquired less than 5% of T's stock, the Group is treated as a single new 5% shareholder that increased its ownership of T stock from 0% to 60% on 1/1/91, resulting in an ownership change on that date. After the ownership change, T has two 5% shareholders: the public group consisting of T's historic shareholders (owning 40%), and the Group (owning 60%).[101]

EXAMPLE 7

Same as Example 6 except that, rather than agreeing among themselves to acquire T's stock, each member of the Group is contacted independently by T's management, who convinces each investor to purchase T stock based on an understanding that T will assemble a group that in the aggregate will acquire more than 50% of T's stock. Same result as Example 6 since the Group members made a coordinated acquisition of T stock pursuant to a formal or informal understanding among themselves.[102]

[101] See Reg. §1.382-3(a)(1)(ii) example (1).
[102] See Reg. §1.382-3(a)(1)(ii) example (2).

EXAMPLE 8

Same as Example 6 except that, rather than agreeing among themselves to acquire T's stock, each member of the Group is told by the same investment advisor that T's stock is undervalued and is a good investment. Each Group member purchases 3% of T's stock based on the investment advisor's recommendation, not on the investment decisions of the other Group members. Because there is no formal or informal understanding among the Group members to make a coordinated stock acquisition, the Group is not treated as an entity. Hence, the result is the same as in Example 5 (i.e., the stock purchases are disregarded for Code §382 purposes).[103]

The regulations provide, as an exception to the expanded entity definition, that creditor participation in formulating an insolvency workout or bankruptcy reorganization plan (whether as members of a creditors' committee or otherwise) and the receipt of stock by creditors in satisfaction of debt pursuant to the workout or reorganization do not cause the creditors to be considered an entity.[104] In addition, in IRS Letter Ruling 9533024 (8/19/95), IRS concluded that, where stock of a public T is controlled by an investment advisor (IA) for the accounts of its clients, and the clients (rather than the IA) possess economic ownership of the T shares (i.e., the right to receive dividends and sale proceeds), then (1) the clients (not the IA) will be treated as owning the shares for Code §382 purposes and (2) two or more clients will not constitute an "entity" merely because (a) one or more of the IA's directors or employees are also directors and/or employees of the clients, (b) the IA has the authority to vote the shares, acquire or sell the shares, file with the SEC Schedules 13D or 13G with respect to the shares (unless such schedule states that the clients are "acting in concert or otherwise are engaged in a coordinated acquisition" of the shares), or communicate with T's management, (c) the IA adheres to its general policies for voting securities and/or (d) the IA communicates with the clients regarding the investment. Similarly, in IRS Letter Ruling 9610012 (12/5/95), IRS ruled that investment funds sharing a common IA (apparently a family of mutual funds) will not constitute an entity merely because (1) the funds share a common IA, (2) the IA votes the securities purchased on behalf of each fund, (3) each of the funds has the same board of directors, and (4) the funds limit their aggregate investment in a particular corporation's stock to a set percentage of the corporation's outstanding stock.

In determining whether an ownership change occurred before 9/4/87, the aggregation rules apply only to T stock acquired after 5/5/86 by any first- or

---

[103] See Reg. §1.382-3(a)(1)(ii) example (3). See also IRS Letter Ruling 9533024 (8/19/95) (discussed in text below).

[104] Reg. §1.382-3(a)(1).

higher-tier entity, unless T elects to apply all of the aggregation and segregation rules without regard to when T's stock was acquired.[105]

¶1208.1.7.3   *Segregation Rules*

The aggregation rules essentially combine T's less-than-5% shareholders into public groups and treat each group as a 5% shareholder. The temporary regulations also contain "segregation rules," which have the opposite effect.[106] These segregation rules provide that certain types of transactions will cause T's less-than-5% shareholders, who otherwise would be grouped together and treated as a single 5% shareholder under the aggregation rules, to become segregated into two or more public groups, each of which is treated as a separate 5% shareholder.[107]

If a particular transaction triggers the segregation rules, these rules apply only in determining whether an ownership change occurs within a testing period that includes the transaction date.[108] Hence, once an ownership change occurs and a new testing period begins, any prior application of the segregation rules is disregarded (see Examples 1 and 2 below).

Some of the principal types of transactions that trigger the segregation rules are discussed in (1) through (4) below. In addition, regulations adopted in 10/93 granting certain exemptions from the existing segregation rules are discussed in (5) below.

(1)   Reorganizations and stock issuances by T. The segregation rules apply in an "A," "C," or non-divisive "D" or "G" reorganization to which T is a party, or in a transfer of the stock of T (or its successor) by T (or its successor) in any other transaction to which Code §1032 applies (e.g., a purchase by any person of newly issued T stock).[109] In any such case, the less-than-5% shareholders of T immediately before the transaction are segregated from those that acquire stock of T (or T's successor) as a result of the transaction. For this purpose, the less-than-5% shareholders of T who receive stock in the transaction are presumed not to include any 5% shareholders existing before the transaction, except to the extent T has actual knowledge of contrary facts or in cases of tax avoidance (as discussed in ¶1208.1.7.4).

EXAMPLE 1

T has one million shares of common stock outstanding, and no shareholder has ever owned 5% of T's stock. On 1/1/90 T issues three million new shares for cash in a public offering. No person owns 5% of T's stock after the

---

[105] Temp. Reg. §1.382-2T(m)(4)(i).
[106] Temp. Reg. §1.382-2T(j)(2), (3).
[107] Temp. Reg. §1.382-2T(g)(1)(iv).
[108] Temp. Reg. §1.382-2T(j)(2)(i).
[109] Temp. Reg. §1.382-2T(j)(2)(iii)(B).

offering. If the aggregation rules alone applied, 100% of T's stock would be owned by the same 5% shareholder (i.e., the public group consisting of all of T's less-than-5% shareholders) both before and after the offering. Hence, no ownership change would result because the offering would not have increased the percentage interest of such 5% T shareholder. However, under the segregation rules, T's shareholders before the offering (Public #1) and those who received shares in the offering (Public #2) are treated as two separate 5% shareholders. Public #2 owns 75% of T's stock (i.e., three million of four million shares) after the offering and is presumed not to have owned any T stock before the offering (except as discussed in ¶1208.1.7.4). Therefore, the public offering results in an ownership change on 1/1/90 since Public #2's percentage interest in T increased by more than 50 percentage points (from 0% to 75%) on that date. For purposes of subsequent transactions, Public #1 and Public #2 will not be segregated because the ownership change causes a new testing period to begin on 1/2/90.[110]

EXAMPLE 2

T has long had 1,000 shares of stock outstanding. Individual A has always owned 490 of the shares, and less-than-5% shareholders (Public #1) have always owned the remaining 510 shares. On 1/1/89 individual B purchases all 490 of A's shares. Over the next two years, T issues 30 new shares to its executives, who never previously owned any T stock. Even though the executives have not acquired (either individually or as a group) 5% or more of T's stock (30 ÷ 1,030 = only 2.9%), they are treated as one or more 5% shareholders separate from Public #1 because they acquired their T stock in a Code §1032 issuance. Therefore, an ownership change has occurred because 5% shareholders (B and the executives) have acquired 50.5% of T's stock (520 shares ÷ 1,030 shares) within three years. For purposes of subsequent transactions, Public #1 and the executives will be treated as a single 5% shareholder rather than segregated into two 5% shareholders because a new testing period begins after the ownership change.

See the examples at ¶1208.1.3 ("A" reorganization of T into P).

(2) Redemptions. When T acquires (redeems) its stock in exchange for property, T's less-than-5% shareholders immediately before the transaction are segregated into two groups, so the stock redeemed is treated as though it was owned by one 5% shareholder (Public #1), and the stock not redeemed is treated as though it was owned by a separate 5% shareholder (Public #2).[111] For this purpose,

---

[110] See Temp. Reg. §1.382-2T(j)(2)(iii)(B)(2) example (3).
[111] Temp. Reg. §1.382-2T(j)(2)(iii)(C).

Public #1 is presumed not to include any members of Public #2 (i.e., the less-than-5% shareholders of T who owned the redeemed stock are presumed not to own any stock after the redemption), except to the extent T has actual knowledge of contrary facts (e.g., T can demonstrate that the redemption was pro rata among all its stockholders) or in cases of tax avoidance (as discussed in ¶1208.1.7.4).

EXAMPLE 3

T has one million shares of common stock outstanding, and no shareholder has ever owned 5% or more of its stock. On 1/1/90 T redeems 510,000 shares of its stock for cash. Under the segregation rules, the shareholders of T before the offering are treated as two separate 5% shareholders: the redeemed interests (Public #1) and the interests that were not redeemed (Public #2). As a result of the redemption, Public #2's ownership interest in T has increased 51 percentage points, from 49% (490,000 ÷ 1,000,000) to 100% (490,000 ÷ 490,000). Therefore, unless T can demonstrate overlapping ownership between Public #1 and Public #2 (e.g., the redemption was pro rata among all T's shareholders), an ownership change results.[112]

EXAMPLE 4

Same as Example 3 except that T redeems 400,000 rather than 510,000 shares. No ownership change results because Public #2's ownership interest in T has increased by only 40 percentage points, from 60% (600,000 ÷ 1,000,000) to 100% (600,000 ÷ 600,000). However, in determining whether an ownership change occurs during the next three years, Public #2 is treated as a 5% shareholder whose interest in T increased 40 percentage points on 1/1/90 as a result of the redemption.

In Example 4, it appears at first blush that an ownership change will result if an additional 11 percentage points of T's stock changes hands. However, as a practical matter, shareholders other than Public #2 generally must acquire more than 50% of T's stock (rather than merely over 10%) before an ownership change results, so in many circumstances it seems that the redemption will not have harmed T. This point is illustrated in Examples 5 through 7 below, each of which assumes the same facts as Example 4: On 1/1/90 T redeemed 400,000 of its one million outstanding shares so that immediately after the redemption, all of T's 600,000 outstanding shares are owned by Public #2, whose interest in T increased 40 percentage points as a result of the redemption.

---

[112] Temp. Reg. §1.382-2T(j)(2)(iii)(C)(2) example (1).

EXAMPLE 5

On 1/1/91 individual A buys 100,000 shares of T's stock on the open market (i.e., from Public #2). A's stock interest has increased by 17 percentage points, from 0% to 17% (100,000 ÷ 600,000). However, Public #2's percentage interest has declined by a like amount, from 100% to 83% (500,000 ÷ 600,000), thus eroding 17 points of Public #2's 40 percentage point increase which resulted from the redemption. No ownership change results from A's purchase because only 40% of T's stock has changed hands during the testing period (17 points for A and 23 points for Public #2). In other words, because of the tandem effect of A's percentage increase and Public #2's percentage decrease, A's stock purchase has not contributed at all to bringing about an ownership change.

EXAMPLE 6

On 1/1/91 individual A buys 600,000 shares of T stock directly from T. Thus A's percentage interest in T has increased by 50 percentage points, from 0% to 50% (600,000 ÷ 1,200,000). As in Example 5, however, Public #2's percentage interest has declined by a like amount (i.e., from 100% to 50%). This eliminates altogether Public #2's 40 percentage point increase that resulted from the redemption. No ownership change results because the only 5% shareholder whose interest in T has increased during the past three years is A, and A's interest has increased by only 50 percentage points. As in Example 5, in this case the application of the segregation rules to the redemption has not contributed at all to bringing about an ownership change.

EXAMPLE 7

On 1/1/91 T merges into P in an "A" reorganization, with T's shareholders receiving 51% of P's stock in the merger. P's old shareholders (who are treated as one or more separate 5% shareholders under the segregation rules discussed at (1) above) have increased their percentage interest in T's successor (P) by 49%. However, the stock interest of T's old shareholders (Public #2) has declined by 49% (from 100% to 51%). As in Example 11, this eliminates entirely Public #2's 40 percentage point increase that resulted from the redemption. Thus, there is no ownership change because only 49% of T's stock has changed hands during the past three years.

(3) Deemed acquisition of T stock resulting from deemed option exercise. When an option is deemed exercised under the rules discussed at ¶1208.1.6, T's less-than-5% shareholders immediately before the transaction are segregated from those deemed to acquire T stock upon exercise of the option, in a manner similar to the segregation rules applicable to new issuances of T stock (discussed at (1) above).[113]

(4) Dispositions by certain 5% shareholders. If an entity or individual directly owns 5% of T's stock and transfers T stock to less-than-5% shareholders, the less-than-5% shareholders that receive such T stock are segregated from the less-than-5% shareholders of T that existed immediately before the transaction.[114]

T (or its successor) may combine any public groups first identified during the same taxable year as a result of the application of the segregation rules to the transactions described in (1) and (3) above (i.e., tax-free reorganizations, stock issuances, and deemed stock issuances pursuant to the deemed exercise of options), provided each public group so combined owns less than 5% of T's (or its successor's) stock.[115]

EXAMPLE 8

T is a calendar year taxpayer. During 1990 T issues 0.5% of its stock on each of four dates in satisfaction of its interest obligation with respect to two classes of outstanding debentures. Each issuance of T stock normally results in the identification of an additional, separate public group under the rule described in (1) above. However, because each public group identified under the above facts owns less than 5% of T's stock, each such T public group may be combined with the other such groups into a single public group.[116]

As the above discussion and examples illustrate, the segregation rules are complex and can produce unexpected results. Accordingly, loss corporations contemplating any transactions that may alter their stock ownership need to examine the rules closely.

Unless T elects to apply all the aggregation and segregation rules without limitation, the regulations limit the application of the segregation rules in the case of transactions occurring before 9/4/87.[117] For example, for testing dates before 9/4/87 the segregation rules generally apply to tax-free reorganizations but not to public offerings or redemptions.

---

[113] Temp. Reg. §1.382-2T(j)(2)(iii)(D).
[114] See Temp. Reg. 1.382-2T(j)(3).
[115] Temp. Reg. §1.382-2T(j)(2)(iv).
[116] See Temp. Reg. §1.382-2T(j)(2)(iv)(B) example.
[117] Temp. Reg. §1.382-2T(m)(4).

(5)   10/93 regulations: small issuance exception and cash issuance exemption. To alleviate the adverse impact of the segregation rules on loss corporations, IRS issued regulations in 10/93 that provide two limitations on the application of the segregation rules: the "small issuance exception" and the "cash issuance exemption."[118]

Small issuance exception. The regulations generally provide that the segregation rules do not apply to a "small issuance," except to the extent the value of T stock issued in that issuance and all other small issuances previously made during the taxable year exceeds the "small issuance limitation." A "small issuance" is an issuance by T of stock not exceeding the small issuance limitation. For each taxable year, T generally may, at its option, apply the small issuance exception (a) on a corporation-wide basis, in which case the small issuance limitation is 10% of the total value of T's stock outstanding at the beginning of the year (excluding the value of Straight Preferred, i.e., non-voting, non-convertible, non-participating preferred stock) or (b) on a class-by-class basis, in which case the small issuance limitation is 10% of the number of shares of the class outstanding at the beginning of the taxable year. If more than one class of stock is issued in a single issuance (or in certain related issuances), the small issuance limitation must be determined under (a) above.

EXAMPLE 9

T, a calendar year taxpayer, has 1,000 shares of common stock outstanding (and no other outstanding stock or options), and no shareholder has ever owned 5% or more of T's stock. Hence, all of T's shares are treated as held by a single public group (Public #1). On 10/1/93 T issues 30 shares of common stock to its employees as compensation. On 12/1/93 T issues another 120 shares of common stock to its employees as compensation. The stock issued to T's employees is not subject to a substantial risk of forfeiture. At all times throughout the year, the fair market value ("FV") of T's stock is $100 per share.

The 10/1/93 issuance is a small issuance because the number of shares issued (30) does not exceed the small issuance limitation of 100 shares (i.e., 10% of the number of common shares outstanding on 1/1/93, the beginning of the year of the issuance). Therefore, the segregation rules do not apply to the 10/1/93 issuance, and the 30 employee shares will be treated as acquired by Public #1 so that the issuance would not contribute to an ownership change of T.

The 12/1/93 issuance of 120 shares is not a small issuance under the regulations because it exceeds the small issuance limitation of 100 shares (i.e., 10% of the number of common shares outstanding on 1/1/93, the

---

[118] Reg. §1.382-3(j) (T.D. 8490, 1993-2 C.B. 120), *superseding* proposed regulations issued in 11/92 (CO-99-91).

beginning of the year of the issuance). Therefore, unless the 12/1/93 shares qualify for the "cash issuance exemption" discussed below, the segregation rules will apply to the entire 12/1/93 issuance so that those 120 employee shares will be considered acquired by a new 5% shareholder (Public #2). Under this analysis, after the 12/1/93 issuance, Public #2's percentage ownership has increased from 0% to 10% (i.e., 120 ÷ 1,150 shares).

In the absence of the small issuance and cash issuance exemptions, both the 10/1/93 and 12/1/93 issuances would have triggered the segregation rules so that, after the 12/1/93 issuance, one new 5% shareholder (Public #2) would have been treated as owning 3% of T's stock (i.e., 30 ÷ 1,150 shares) and another new 5% shareholder (Public #3) would have been treated as owning 10% of T's stock (i.e., 120 ÷ 1,150).

EXAMPLE 10

Same as Example 9 except that on 12/1/93 T issues 90 rather than 120 shares to its employees.

Under the regulations, the 10/1/93 issuance is exempt from the segregation rules, using the analysis in Example 9.

Unlike that example, here the 12/1/93 issuance is a small issuance because the number of shares issued (90) does not exceed the small issuance limitation of 100 shares. However, the 12/1/93 issuance, when combined with all prior issuances during T's taxable year (i.e., the 10/1/93 issuance of 30 shares), exceeds by 20 shares T's small issuance limitation of 100 (i.e., 120 shares issued during the year less 100-share small issuance exemption equals 20 shares). Therefore, the small issuance exception applies only to 70 of the shares issued on 12/1/93; the remaining 20 shares are subject to the segregation rules, unless they qualify for the "cash issuance exemption" discussed below. As a result, after 12/1/93 a new 5% shareholder (Public #2) would be considered to own 20/1,120 of T's stock, so Public #2's percentage ownership has increased from 0% to 2%.

In the absence of the small issuance and cash issuance exemptions, both the 10/1/93 and 12/1/93 issuances would have triggered the segregation rules so that, after the 12/1/93 issuance, one new 5% shareholder (Public #2) would have been treated as owning 3% of T's stock (i.e., 30/1,120 shares) and another new 5% shareholder (Public #3) would have been treated as owning 8% of T's stock (i.e., 90/1,120).

EXAMPLE 11

Same as Example 9 except that the FV of T's stock declines from $100 per share on 1/1/93 to $60 per share on 10/1/93 and 12/1/93.

In contrast to Example 9, apparently the 12/1/93 issuance is a small issuance fully exempt from the segregation rules. This is the case because the regulations permit T to elect to compute the small issuance limitation as 10% of T's aggregate stock "value" on 1/1/93 (the beginning of the taxable year of issuance), rather than based on the number of outstanding T shares. Since T's aggregate stock FV on 1/1/93 is $100,000 (i.e., $100 per share FV times 1,000 shares outstanding), the small issuance limitation under this approach is $10,000. The FV of the 120 shares issued on 12/1/93, after share FV has declined to $60, is $7,200. Since this amount is less than the small issuance exemption of $10,000, the 12/1/93 issuance is a small issuance. Moreover, the combined value (determined at the time of issuance) of the 12/1/93 and 10/1/93 issuances is $9,000 (i.e., $60 per share FV times 150 shares issued). Since this aggregate FV does not exceed the $10,000 small issuance exemption, apparently the entire 120-share issuance on 12/1/93 is exempt from the segregation rules. In sum, the regulations apparently would exempt all 150 T shares issued during the year, even through they represent 15% of T's previously outstanding shares.

We suspect that the value rule was included in the regulations merely to facilitate calculation of the small issuance limitation when T has multiple classes of stock. However, as Example 11 illustrates, the regulations literally permit application of the rule even when only one class of stock is outstanding.

The amount of stock exempted under the small issuance exception is limited to the stock issued less the stock acquired by 5% shareholders (other than direct public groups). In addition, the small issuance exception does not apply to an issuance of stock in any tax-free reorganization other than a tax-free recapitalization under Code §368(a)(1)(E).

Cash issuance exemption. If T issues stock "solely for cash" (other than in a tax-free reorganization), the regulations provide that the segregation rules do not apply to the lesser of (1) the stock issued equal to one-half of the aggregate percentage of stock owned by direct public groups immediately before the issuance or (2) the amount of stock issued less the amount of stock acquired by 5-percent shareholders (other than direct public groups).[119] The cash issuance exemption does not apply to a small issuance exempted under the rules described immediately above. For purposes of the cash issuance exemption, a share of stock is not issued "solely for cash" if (1) the acquiror, as a condition of acquiring that share for cash, is required to purchase other stock for non-cash consideration or (2) the share is acquired upon the exercise of an option that was neither issued solely for cash nor distributed with respect to stock.[120]

---

[119] Reg. §1.382-3(j)(3), (4), (6).
[120] Reg. §1.382-3(j)(3)(ii).

EXAMPLE 12

Same facts as in Example 1 except that the public offering occurs in 1993. Since 100% of T's stock immediately before the issuance is owned by direct public groups (i.e., Public #1), under the cash issuance exemption, 50% of the stock issued in the offering, or 1.5 million shares, is exempt from the segregation rules. Those 1.5 million exempt shares are considered acquired by Public #1 (i.e., T's historic shareholders) rather than by Public #2. Hence, Public #2 is considered to acquire only 1.5 million shares rather than 3 million as in Example 1. Accordingly, Public #2's percentage ownership has increased from 0% to only 37.5% (i.e., 1.5 million out of 4 million shares outstanding immediately after the offering), so no ownership change results.

EXAMPLE 13

Same as Example 9. As discussed in Example 9 the 120-share issuance on 12/1/93 does not qualify for the small issuance exception because it exceeds the 100-share small issuance limitation.

In addition, it appears that the 12/1/93 issuance would not qualify for the cash issuance exemption because the shares were issued directly to T's employees as compensation rather than "solely for cash," as required by the regulations. However, disqualifying this issuance from the cash issuance exemption elevates form over substance: T, rather than directly issuing the 120 shares to its employees as compensation, instead could have paid them $12,000 of cash bonuses, and the employees promptly could have used the cash to purchase the 120 shares. While the federal income tax consequences would otherwise be identical to T and the employees, the 12/1/93 issuance, as modified, clearly would qualify as a cash issuance. As a result, 50% (i.e., one-half of the percentage of stock owned by direct public groups immediately before the 12/1/93 issuance), or 60, of the 12/1/93 shares, would be exempt from the segregation rules. Accordingly, only the remaining 60 of the shares issued on 12/1/93 would be subject to the segregation rules so that, after the 12/1/93 issuance, a new Public group (Public #2) would be considered to own 60 shares and to have increased its percentage ownership from 0% to 5% (i.e., 60 ÷ 1,150 shares).

The irrational distinction illustrated by Example 13 would be avoided if the regulations were amended to provide that any shares issued either as compensation for services or in exchange for property in a fully taxable exchange will be considered issued for cash for purposes of the cash issuance exemption.

The regulations generally apply to issuances of stock in taxable years beginning after 11/3/92. However, taxpayers may elect to have the regulations apply retroactively to all stock issuances in taxable years beginning before 11/4/92.[121]

¶1208.1.7.4 *Presumptions*

As discussed above, both the aggregation and segregation rules generally "presume" that the members of each public group that they identify neither belong to any other public group nor are related to any other direct or indirect shareholder of T.[122] These and other presumptions contained in the regulations make possible the application of the ownership change rules when the determination of actual stock ownership would involve insuperable difficulties (e.g., public companies).[123]

However, the presumptions may not apply to the extent T has actual knowledge of facts to the contrary, and they will not apply in certain cases of tax avoidance.[124]

In particular, for purposes of determining whether an ownership change occurs on a particular testing date to the extent T "has actual knowledge" of stock ownership by an individual (or entity) who in fact owns 5% of T's stock but is treated as owning less as a result of the presumptions, T generally must take such actual stock ownership into account.

EXAMPLE 1

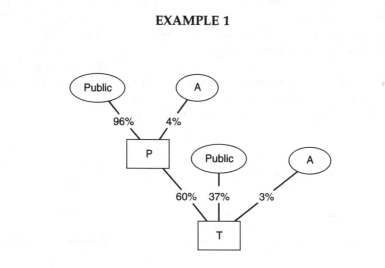

---

[121] Reg. §1.382-3(j)(14).

[122] See, e.g., Temp. Reg. §1.382-2T(j)(1)(iii), (j)(2)(iii)(B), and (j)(2)(iii)(C).

[123] For example, Temp. Reg. §1.382-2T(k)(1) generally provides that, if T's stock (or the stock of a T shareholder) is publicly traded, T may rely on the existence and absence of filings of Schedules 13D and 13G to identify its (or such shareholder's) 5% shareholders, unless T has actual knowledge of facts to the contrary. See also IRS Letter Ruling 9533024 (8/18/95) (elaborating the scope of permitted reliance on Schedule 13D and 13G filings in the context of an investment advisor's ownership of T shares on behalf of multiple beneficial owners).

[124] See Temp. Reg. §1.382-2T(j)(1)(iii), (j)(2)(iii)(A), (k)(2), and (k)(4).

P has long owned 60% of T's stock. The remaining 40% of T's stock and all of P's stock is widely held, with no shareholder ever having owned 5%. Individual A owns 4% of P's stock and 3% of T's stock. Both P and T are aware of such ownership.

If the normal presumptions applied, the aggregation rules would treat T as having two 5% shareholders: the public group consisting of all of P's shareholders (owning 60% of T) and the public group consisting of all of T's shareholders other than P (owning 40% of T). A would not be a 5% shareholder because (1) A does not directly own 5% or more of T's stock (A owns only 3% directly), and (2) A does not indirectly own 5% or more of T's stock as a result of directly owning 5% or more of a first- or higher-tier entity (A owns only 4% of P). See ¶1208.1.7.1.

However, P and T are aware that A's aggregate direct and indirect ownership of T stock is in fact 5.4% (3% directly and 2.4% through P). Therefore, the aggregation rules do not apply to A, so T has the following 5% shareholders: A (5.4%), the public group consisting of P's shareholders other than A (57.6%), and the public group consisting of T's shareholders other than P and A (37%).

In addition, except as provided above, to the extent T "has actual knowledge" of cross ownership by members of different public groups, T may take such ownership into account. See Example 3 at ¶1208.1.7.3 and Example 2 at ¶1208.1.3.

Finally, "if the ownership interests in [T] are structured by a [direct or indirect T shareholder] to avoid treating a person as a 5-percent shareholder ... for a principal purpose of circumventing the section 382 limitation," then T's actual stock ownership generally will be taken into account. In contrast to the two rules discussed above, "[t]his anti-abuse rule applies even if [T] does not have actual knowledge regarding the ownership interests involved."[125]

EXAMPLE 2

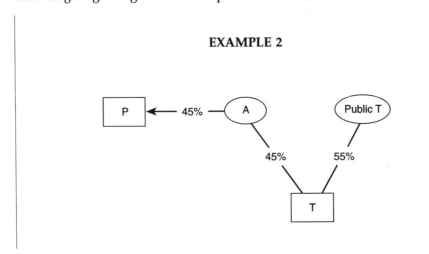

[125] T.D. 8149, at II(N), 1987-2 C.B. 85.

Individual A has always owned 45% of T's stock. The remaining 55% of T's stock is publicly traded. No shareholder other than A has ever owned 5% of T's stock. On 1/1/90 P purchases all 45% of A's T stock. P is unrelated to A or T and is widely held, with no shareholder owning 5% of its stock. Individual B (who has never owned any P or T stock) wishes to purchase 10% of T's stock on the open market without causing an ownership change. Accordingly, B forms five corporations, each wholly owned by B. Each corporation acquires 2% of T's stock in a series of small purchases during 1991. Neither T nor P nor A is aware of B's actions.

After B's indirect stock purchases, no individual or entity other than P directly owns 5% of T's stock. In addition, no individual or entity indirectly owns 5% of T's stock by virtue of directly owning 5% of a single first-tier entity or a single higher-tier entity (i.e., each of B's five corporations gives B only a 2% interest in T). Therefore, T is not required to separately identify any of its shareholders other than P (see ¶1208.1.7.1), and all of T's shareholders other than P would be treated as a single 5% shareholder under the aggregation rules if the normal presumptions applied. Accordingly, B would not be a separate 5% shareholder, so B's indirect stock purchases would not cause an ownership change.

However, under the anti-abuse rule, B's indirect acquisition of 10% of T's stock "for a principal purpose of circumventing the section 382 limitation" is taken into account. Therefore, B is a 5% shareholder whose increase in percentage ownership during the testing period (10%), when combined with P's increase (45%), causes an ownership change in 1991.[126]

¶1208.1.8   Multiple Transactions

Because Code §382 scrutinizes stock transactions occurring over a period of up to three years (and possibly longer when options are involved), an ownership change can result from a series of related or unrelated transactions, none of which alone constitutes an ownership change.

EXAMPLE 1

T's stock has long been owned by several individuals. On 1/1/90 T merges into P in an "A" reorganization, with T's shareholders receiving 60% of P's stock and P's old shareholders retaining 40%. P's stock is widely held, and no single shareholder has ever owned 5% of P's stock. There is no ownership change with respect to T because P's shareholders own only 40% of the stock of T's successor (P) as a result of the merger. However, within three years after the merger, one of T's former shareholders sells 11% of P's stock

---

[126] Temp. Reg. §1.382-2T(k)(5) (similar example).

to individual A, who has never owned any T or P stock. This sale results in an ownership change because the percentage of P's (T's successor's) stock owned by P's old shareholders (who are treated as a single 5% shareholder under the segregation rules) (40%) and by A (11%) is more than 50 percentage points higher than the lowest percentage of the loss corporation's stock that such shareholders owned during the prior three years (0% before 1/1/90).[127]

EXAMPLE 2

Individual A has long owned 10% of T's stock. The remaining 90% of T's stock and all of P's stock have long been widely held, with no single shareholder owning 5% of T's or P's stock. On 1/1/90 A sells his 10% of T's stock to individual B, who has never owned any T or P stock. Within three years P acquires all of T's stock in a "B" reorganization, with T's shareholders receiving 55% of P's stock. Hence, B will receive 5.5% of P's stock (10% of 55%) and T's old shareholders (other than B) will receive 49.5% (90% of 55%). The reorganization causes an ownership change because the percentage of T stock owned (by attribution through P—see ¶1208.1.5) by P's old shareholders (who are treated as a single 5% shareholder under the segregation rules) (45%) and B (5.5%) is more than 50 percentage points higher than the lowest percentage of T stock those shareholders owned during the preceding three years (0% before 1/1/90).

A special rule applies in determining the consequences of a stock transaction that occurs after a transaction to which the segregation rules applied. In determining whether the later transaction causes an ownership change:

Unless a different proportion is established by either the loss corporation or the Internal Revenue Service, the acquisition of [T's or its successor's] stock ... on any date on which more than one public group ... exists by virtue of the application of the [segregation rules] shall be treated as being made proportionately from each public group existing immediately before such acquisition.[128]

EXAMPLE 3

T and P are both publicly traded, with no single shareholder ever having owned 5% or more of T's or P's stock. P merges into T in an "A" reorganization on 1/1/90, with P's shareholders receiving 40% of T's stock and T's old shareholders retaining 60%. Within three years individual B, who has never owned T or P stock, buys 20% of T's stock on a public stock exchange.

[127] See Temp. Reg. §1.382-2T(m)(9) example (2)(i) (similar analysis when P merges into T).
[128] Temp. Reg. §1.382-2T(j)(2)(vi). See Code §382(g)(4); Temp. Reg. §1.382-2T(j)(3)(v).

Under the proportionality rule, unless a different proportion is established, B will be treated as having purchased 12% of T's stock (20% of 60%) from T's old shareholders and 8% (20% of 40%) from P's old shareholders. Therefore, B's purchase results in an ownership change since the percentage of T stock owned by P's old shareholders (32%: 40% acquired in the merger less 8% treated as sold to B) and B (20%) is more than 50 percentage points higher than the lowest percentage of T stock those shareholders owned during the prior three years (0% before 1/1/90).[129]

For other examples of multiple transactions, see ¶¶1208.1.4, 1208.1.6.1 Example 5, 1208.1.6.2 through 1208.1.6.6, and 1208.1.7.3 and 1208.1.7.4.

¶1208.1.9   Stock Ownership Determinations Based on FV

In determining whether an ownership change has occurred, the percentage of stock held by any person is based on FV.[130] Reg. §1.382-2(a)(3)(i) provides that, solely for determining the percentage of stock owned by any person, "each share of all the outstanding shares of stock that have the same material terms is treated as having the same value" so that a control premium or blockage discount is not taken into account. This regulatory valuation rule (1) applies for any testing date after 1/28/91, (2) apparently is limited to determining whether an ownership change has occurred, and (3) does not apply to computing T's Code §382 limitation, which involves measuring T's aggregate stock FV, not the percentage of stock owned by particular T shareholders.[131]

However, except as provided in future regulations, "any change in proportionate ownership which is attributable solely to fluctuations in the relative fair market values of different classes of stock shall not be taken into account."[132]

EXAMPLE 1

On 1/1/90 T's aggregate stock has an FV of $1,000. Individual A owns 100% of T's common with a $100 FV and individual B owns 100% of T's preferred stock with a $900 FV. Assume that the preferred has sufficient participation rights in future growth and/or sufficient conversion features that it counts as "stock" under the ownership change rules (see ¶1208.1.1). However, its rights are substantially less than the common's, so that the common appreciates far more rapidly than the preferred. Because of T's spectacular earnings performance, its aggregate stock appreciates in value during 1993 from $1,000 to $3,000; i.e., by 1/1/94 its common has appreciated

---

[129] See 1986 Conference Report II, at 179-180 example (13).
[130] Code §382(k)(6)(C), (k)(5).
[131] See Code §382(e)(1) and the discussion of IRS TAM 9332004 (8/13/93) in ¶1208.2.1.3 below.
[132] Code §382(l)(3)(C).

in value from $100 to $2,000 while the preferred has appreciated in value from $900 to $1,000. Thus A's percentage interest in T (by virtue of owning the common) on 1/1/90 was 10% ($100 ÷ $1,000) but on 1/1/94 was 67% ($2,000 ÷ $3,000). Because this 57% increase in A's interest (from 10% to 67%) was attributable "solely to fluctuations in the relative fair market values of different classes of [T] stock" and there were no purchases or other changes in the ownership of T stock during the prior three-year period, the statutory exception should apply and no ownership change should result.

Without further guidance, the application of this rule is unclear when P purchases 50% or less of T's stock by value and, after such purchase, the class of stock purchased by P appreciates more rapidly in value than the remaining stock so that, within three years, the stock purchased by P (because of such post-purchase appreciation) has become more than 50% of T's stock by value.

EXAMPLE 2

On 1/1/90 T's aggregate stock has an FV of $1,000, and individual A owns (and has for more than three years owned) 100% of T's two classes of outstanding stock: common stock with a $100 FV and preferred stock with a $900 FV. Assume that the preferred has sufficient participation rights in future growth and/or sufficient conversion features that it counts as "stock" under the ownership change rules (see ¶1208.1.1). However, its rights are substantially less than the common, so the common appreciates far more rapidly than the preferred. A sells all of the common stock to P on 1/1/90. No ownership change results because only 10% of T's outstanding stock by value has changed hands (i.e., the common stock is worth $100, or 10% of the $1,000 total value of T's outstanding stock). By 1/1/92 T's aggregate stock has increased in value to $2,100, i.e., the common stock has increased in value from $100 to $1,150, while the preferred has increased in value to $950. Thus, the percentage of T's outstanding stock (by FV) represented by the common has increased from 10% to 55% ($1,150 ÷ $2,100). Under the above rule, it appears that no ownership change results because P's purchase gave P only 10% of T's stock by value; P's percentage interest in T increased from 10% to 55% only as a result of the fluctuating relative values of T's classes of stock.

However, an especially hostile regulatory interpretation of the statutory language might take the position that the increase in P's percentage interest by value from 0% on 1/1/90 to 55% on 1/1/92 was not "attributable *solely* to fluctuations in the relative fair market values of different classes of stock" (emphasis added), but rather was attributable partly to P's purchase of common stock on 1/1/90 and partly to the value fluctuation.

On the other hand, a taxpayer-friendly reading of the statute would exclude from the Code §382 test the value fluctuations occurring after P purchased T's common stock. Until regulations are promulgated, it is not possible to predict whether IRS will adopt such a taxpayer-friendly reading of the exception or (as it did in the option area) a taxpayer-hostile interpretation.

EXAMPLE 3

Same facts as in Example 2 except that (in addition to purchasing 100% of T's common stock from A on 1/1/90 for $100) P also purchases from A on 1/1/92 one-ninth of T's preferred stock, worth $105 ($950 preferred FV on 1/1/92 ÷ 9). Therefore, on 1/1/92 P owns $1,255, or 60%, of T's outstanding stock by value:

	Measured by 1/1/92 Value		Measured by 1/1/90 Value	
Total common	$1,150	(55%)	$100	(10%)
Total preferred	950	(45%)	900	(90%)
Total stock value	$2,100	(100%)	$1,000	(100%)
Common held by P on 1/1/92	$1,150	(55%)	$100	(10%)
Preferred held by P on 1/1/92	105	(5%)	100	(10%)
Total stock held by P on 1/1/92	$1,255	(60%)	$200	(20%)

Does P's purchase of the T preferred on 1/1/92 cause an ownership change? The taxpayer-friendly answer is no because the 100% of T's common purchased by P on 1/1/90 was only 10% of T's aggregate stock by value when purchased (i.e., $100 1/1/90 FV of common ÷ $1,000 1/1/90 FV of common and preferred), and the one-ninth of T's preferred stock purchased by P on 1/1/92 was only 5% of T's aggregate stock by value on 1/1/92 (i.e., $105 1/1/92 FV of purchased preferred ÷ $2,100 1/1/92 FV of all common and preferred). Therefore, ignoring value fluctuations, P has purchased substantially less than 50% of T's stock by value. Only by taking into account the $1,050 increase in the value of T's common after it was purchased by P would there be an ownership change. Unfortunately, until regulations are promulgated, the result is unclear.

¶1208.2   Computation of Annual Code §382 Limitation

In general, for any taxable year ending after the date of an ownership change, the amount of taxable income (computed without regard to any NOL deductions or any of T's "recognized BILs," as described in ¶1208.4(3))[133] that can be offset by T's pre-acquisition NOLs and recognized BILs is the sum of the following amounts (the "Code §382 limitation"):

(1)   the FV of T's stock (including all preferred stock) immediately before the ownership change times the "long-term tax exempt rate" in effect at that time;

(2)   T's (or its successor's) unused Code §382 limitation, if any, from the preceding taxable year;

(3)   T's (or its successor's) "recognized BIGs" for the year; and

(4)   subject to limitations, the excess of T's Code §338 gain, if any, over the portion of such gain taken into account in computing recognized BIGs for the year.

Each of these elements is discussed below. This annual limitation and the continuity of business enterprise rule (violation of which can eliminate T's NOL altogether, as discussed at ¶1208.3) are the principal operative provisions of Code §382.

For special rules in determining the applicable Code §382 limitation(s) when T has subsidiaries, see ¶1208.6.

¶1208.2.1   FV of T Stock Multiplied by Long-Term Tax-Exempt Rate

Except for certain gain inherent in T's assets at the time of the ownership change (see ¶¶1208.2.3 and 1208.2.4 below), the amount of T's (or its successor's) taxable income that can be offset by T's pre-acquisition NOLs (and "recognized BILs," as discussed in ¶1208.4) is limited annually to the FV of T's stock (including all preferred stock) immediately before the ownership change, multiplied by the "long-term tax-exempt rate" (defined below).[134]

In the case of a postchange year that is shorter than 365 days, temporary regulations provide that the preceding annual limitation amount is multiplied by a fraction, equal to the number of days in such taxable year divided by 365, in determining T's Code §382 limitation for such year.[135]

---

[133] See Code §§382(k)(4) and 382(h)(1)(B)(i).

[134] Code §382(b)(1).

[135] Temp. Reg. §1.382-5T (T.D. 8679), published in 1996 (and superseding 1991 Prop. Reg. §1.382-4), although it is effective retroactive to the 1986 enactment of new Code §382.

¶1208.2.1.1   Definition of Stock

The FV of T's stock includes the FV of all T's stock, including Straight Preferred (i.e., preferred which was excluded in determining whether the ownership change occurred).[136] The IRS has statutory authority to issue future regulations treating warrants, options, convertible debt interests, and other similar interests as stock, and treating stock as not stock, for this purpose.[137] Despite the absence of such regulations, IRS has concluded in a letter ruling that, in the case of warrants to acquire unissued or treasury stock (as opposed to options on outstanding shares, which are already counted in T's stock value), "it generally is appropriate to count the value of such warrants" in computing T's Code §382 limitation.[138] The deemed exercise of an option under the ownership change rules (see ¶1208.1.6) does not apply for purposes of determining the FV of T's stock and computing the Code §382 limitation.[139]

EXAMPLE 1

Individual A has long owned 100% of T's two outstanding classes of stock: common stock and a class of Straight Preferred. On 1/1/90 P purchases 100% of T's common stock from A for $500 (its FV at that time). The preferred has a 1/1/90 FV of $1,000. P's purchase causes an ownership change because the T Straight Preferred is not counted as "stock" in determining whether an ownership change has occurred. However, in the absence of regulations to the contrary, the Straight Preferred is counted as "stock" in computing the Code §382 limitation. Thus, the FV of T's stock for this purpose is $1,500.

¶1208.2.1.2   Redemptions and Other Corporate Contractions

If a "redemption" occurs "in connection with" an ownership change—either before or after the change—the FV of T's stock is determined after taking the redemption into account.[140] This rule thus covers traditional *Zenz*-type transactions, in which T sells some of its shares to P and redeems the rest as part of the same plan.[141]

---

[136] Code §382(e)(1).
[137] Code §382(k)(6).
[138] IRS TAM 9332004 (8/13/93).
[139] See Temp. Reg. §1.382-2T(h)(4)(i).
[140] Code §382(e)(2).
[141] See Zenz v. Quinlivan, 213 F.2d 914, 54-2 U.S.T.C. ¶9445 (6th Cir. 1954); B. Bittker & J. Eustice, Federal Income Taxation of Corporations and Shareholders ¶9.06 (7th ed. 2000).

EXAMPLE 2

Same as Example 1 except that T redeems its preferred stock for $1,000 immediately after the ownership change. The FV of T's stock for purposes of computing the Code §382 limitation is only $500.

EXAMPLE 3

Individual A has long owned 100% of T's common stock, its only class of stock outstanding. On 1/1/90 P purchases 70% of A's T stock for $700 (its FV at that time), and T redeems A's remaining common for $300. P's purchase causes an ownership change. The total FV of T's stock "immediately before" the ownership change is $1,000. However, the FV of T's stock for purposes of computing the Code §382 limitation is only $700 as a result of the redemption.

The redemption rule also appears to cover transactions that are not "redemptions" for corporate law purposes but are treated as redemptions under the tax law. For example, assume that P acquires T by reverse subsidiary cash merger (with P's transitory subsidiary S being merged into T) in which part of the purchase price comes from T (including T's cash on hand, money borrowed by T, debt instruments issued by T to its former shareholders, and money borrowed by S which becomes a T obligation as a result of the merger) and part of the purchase price comes from P (i.e., P stock, P debt, and P cash). Such a transaction is treated for tax purposes (but not necessarily for corporate law purposes) as though T had redeemed its stock to the extent that T's shareholders receive cash and debt instruments from T. See ¶202. Therefore, it appears that this would constitute a "redemption" for Code §382 purposes.

EXAMPLE 4

Individual A has long owned 100% of T's common stock, its only class of stock outstanding. On 1/1/90 P forms S, contributing $200 to S in exchange for 100% of S's stock. On the same date S borrows an additional $1,000 from Bank and merges into T in a reverse subsidiary cash merger, with T surviving. Pursuant to the merger, T's old shareholders receive the $1,200 cash held by S immediately before the merger, and their T stock is cancelled. P's S stock is converted into T stock. In addition, pursuant to the merger the $1,000 Bank debt becomes an obligation of T secured by T's assets. The merger causes a Code §382 ownership change because P's shareholders, who owned no T stock before the merger, now own (indirectly through P) 100% of T's stock. Although T's old shareholders received $1,200 for their T stock, $1,000 is treated as redemption proceeds for tax (but not necessarily corporate) purposes. Therefore, the FV of T's stock for purposes of computing the Code §382 limitation presumably is only $200 (i.e., the FV of T's stock immediately before the merger ($1,200) reduced by the Bank debt which encumbers T's assets as a result of the merger ($1,000)).

What about money borrowed by P in order to acquire T? To the extent T's old shareholders receive in exchange for their stock money borrowed by P, the transaction ordinarily is treated as a sale rather than as a redemption for tax purposes. See ¶202. Therefore, the redemption rule of Code §382(e)(2), read literally, should not cause T's FV to be reduced by P's borrowings.

However, the 1988 Act expanded the statutory rule regarding redemptions to cover "other corporate contractions" (effective retroactively to ownership changes after 6/10/87).[142] The legislative history of the corporate contraction rule states that "[t]he rule for redemptions was intended to apply to transactions that effect similar economic results," even if such transactions do not constitute "redemptions" for other tax purposes.[143] An IRS 2001 Field Service Advice concluded that T's dividend distribution (not in redemption of T shares) to P of surplus T cash was such a contraction.[144]

With respect to "bootstrap" acquisitions, the 1988 legislative history states:

a "bootstrap" acquisition, in which [T's] aggregate corporate value is directly or indirectly reduced or burdened by debt to provide funds to the old shareholders, could generally be subject to the provision. This may include cases in which debt used to pay the old shareholders remains an obligation of an acquisition corporation or an affiliate, *where [T] is directly or indirectly the source of funds for repayment of the obligation.*

Thus, according to the legislative history, in certain instances P debt could be treated as a "corporate contraction."

EXAMPLE 5

Same as Example 4 except that P borrowed from Bank #2 the $200 it contributed to S. The receipt by T's old shareholders of the $200 cash from P in exchange for their T stock is treated as a sale rather than a redemption under conventional tax principles. Therefore, the redemption rule alone,

---

[142] Code §382(e)(2), as amended by the 1988 Act.

[143] H.R. Rep. No. 795, 100th Cong., 2d Sess. 43 (1988) (hereinafter "1988 House Report"); S. Rep. No. 445, 100th Cong., 2d Sess. 52 (1988) (hereinafter "1988 Senate Report"); Joint Comm. on Taxation, Description of the Technical Corrections Act of 1988 (H.R. 4333 and S. 2238), JCS-10-88, 100th Cong., 2d Sess. 44 (1988) (emphasis added).

[144] See IRS Field Service Advice 200140049 (10/5/01).

taken literally, would not apply to that portion of the exchange. However, a taxpayer-hostile reading of the corporate contraction rule might treat P's borrowing as a "corporate contraction," because, although P has acquired stock with a pre-merger FV of $1,200, the stock value is entirely offset by the $1,200 increase in the aggregate T-level and P-level debt resulting from the merger. Under such an analysis, T's FV for purposes of computing the Code §382 limitation would be further reduced by P's $200 debt (i.e., from $200 to $0).

The corporate contraction rule raises difficult questions. *First,* for ownership changes before 6/11/87 (i.e., the effective date of the new corporate contraction rule), may taxpayers rely on traditional tax law principles in determining which transactions will be treated as "redemptions" for purposes of computing the Code §382 limitation? For example, if in connection with a pre-6/11/87 ownership change P or Newco borrows money in order to purchase T's stock in an LBO, might T's value for purposes of computing the Code §382 limitation be reduced by the amount of P's or Newco's borrowing, as illustrated in Examples 4 and 5 above? Code §382(m)(4), before its amendment by the 1988 Act, granted IRS the regulatory authority to treat "corporate contractions" as redemptions for Code §382 purposes. The 1988 Act, when it codified the corporate contraction rule, eliminated this regulatory authority, but did so only with respect to post-6/10/87 ownership changes. This leaves the possibility of regulations effective retroactively to pre-6/11/87 ownership changes.

Second, what is the scope of the "corporate contraction" principle? The legislative history quoted earlier states that it *"may include* [P] debt ... where [T] is directly or indirectly the source of funds for repayment of the obligation" (emphasis added). Is the rule limited to cases in which T is the expected source of funds to repay the P debt? Or might it apply when P expects to repay the debt out of P's own earnings (not T's)? If only T's earnings are covered, why does the rule say "include"? If the rule is limited to cases in which T is to be the source of funds to repay the debt, how is this determined before the debt is repaid (perhaps many years later)? Does it turn on P's expectations? How are these determined when P intends to repay its own debt, repay the debt incurred to buy T, pay for capital expenditures and acquisitions, pay dividends, etc., and to do so out of many sources, including P's earnings, T's earnings, additional borrowings, etc.? Suppose P "expects" to pay the debt incurred to buy T partly from each source?

There are at least three possible interpretations of the ambiguous corporate contraction principle and its legislative history:

(1)   A *narrow interpretation* might limit the application of the "contraction" concept to an LBO or bootstrap acquisition in which (a) the corporation acquiring T's stock or assets (Newco) is a shell corporation with no other business or cash flow, or (b) the corporation acquiring T's stock or assets (old P) has other businesses and/or cash flow but segregates the acquisition debt in a new shell subsidiary (S), which makes the acquisition, so

that only T and its cash flow are liable for and will be the source for repaying the acquisition debt. See Example 4.

(2)   An *intermediate interpretation* might use a tracing approach so that (in addition to the situations described in (1) above) the "contraction" concept would apply when P, a large purchasing corporation that is fully liable for the acquisition debt's repayment, incurs debt to acquire T, i.e., the debt proceeds can be traced to the payment of the purchase price, unless P can clearly demonstrate that it did not (or does not intend to) repay the indebtedness out of T's cash flow. See Example 5.

(3)   An *expansive interpretation* might apply the "contraction" concept (in addition to the situations described in (1) and (2) above) even when the purchase price for T is paid from large P's cash on hand (i.e., working capital), which, had the cash not been so used to acquire T, could have paid down old P debt. That is, a corporate contraction would result if P's old debt was "continued," i.e., allowed to remain outstanding, to finance the acquisition. The mechanics of this interpretation might resemble the draconian "avoided cost" rules announced in 1988 with respect to the interest capitalization rules of Code §263A.[145]

Until regulations are promulgated, which may not occur for years, it is impossible to predict the approach Treasury and IRS will take.

In *Berry Petroleum Co. v. Commissioner*,[146] the Tax Court applied a tracing approach variation of the expansive interpretation of the "corporate contraction" principle. In *Berry*, P used cash on hand to purchase T's stock for $6.5 million. Between 7 and 10 months after the P-T acquisition, T made loans to P totalling $3.6 million. 13 months after the acquisition, T forgave the loans by declaring a $3.6 million dividend to P. The court concluded that (1) at the time the loans were made P did not intend to repay them, (2) T's distribution of $3.6 million to P (through the loans and subsequent loan forgiveness) was a "corporate contraction" because it reduced T's equity capital and value, and (3) the contraction occurred "in connection with" T's ownership change because "[P's] need for cash and its ability to borrow from [T] had their origins in, and were connected causally with, [P's] acquisition of [T] and [T's] sale of [certain assets following the ownership change]."

¶1208.2.1.3   Value of Stock

Stock value is measured immediately before the ownership change. "[T]he price at which [T's] stock changes hands in an arm's-length transaction would be evidence, but not conclusive evidence, of the value of the stock."[147] For example,

---

[145] See IRS Notice 88-99, 1988-2 C.B. 422.

[146] 104 T.C. 584 (1995), *aff'd per unpublished order*, 142 F.3d 442, 98-1 U.S.T.C. ¶50,398 (9th Cir. 1998). For a fuller discussion of *Berry Petroleum*, see Henderson & Goldring, *Tax Planning for Troubled Corporations* §508.4.1.1 (Aspen Publishers 2001).

[147] 1986 Conference Report II, at 187.

IRS has concluded in a letter ruling that, when T's stock is publicly traded, (1) the trading price of T's shares is not the exclusive measure of T's aggregate stock value if the facts and circumstances support a different value, and (2) in particular, the per-share value of a controlling block of stock may be greater than the per-share trading price of that stock on the exchange.[148]

¶1208.2.1.4   *Certain Capital Contributions Disregarded*

"Any capital contribution" that T receives "as part of a plan a principal purpose of which is to avoid or increase any limitation" under Code §382 is not taken into account (thus potentially reducing the Code §382 limitation amount).[149] Except as provided by regulations, any capital contribution made during the two-year period ending on the ownership change date is treated as part of such a plan. Section II of the 1986 Conference Report (at 189) states that regulations "generally" will except from this rule:

(1)   capital contributions received by T on T's formation, unless the aggregate basis of the incorporated assets exceeds by more than 25% their FV (disregarding cash, cash equivalents, and certain marketable securities);

(2)   capital contributions received by T before the first year from which there is an NOL or excess credit carryforward (or in which a BIL described in (1) arose); and

(3)   capital contributions made "to continue basic operations of [T's] business (e.g., to meet the monthly payroll or fund other operating expenses . . .)."

Regarding the above exceptions, IRS has indicated in letter rulings that the absence of enabling regulations will not preclude it from applying appropriate exceptions to the two-year rule. Specifically, TAM 9332004 (8/13/93) concluded that a capital contribution qualified under Exception 3 to the extent the proceeds were used to meet "operating expenses of [T] arising proximate in time to the time the contribution was made." Thus, proceeds used to pay off the balance due on a lawsuit settlement and for working capital qualified for the exception, but proceeds used to repay outstanding debt incurred 21 months earlier lacked "sufficient proximity in time to the borrowing" and hence were not used to "continue basic operations." IRS subsequently took a more liberal view of "proximate in time." In IRS Letter Ruling 9630038 (5/1/96), IRS ruled that Exception 3 applied where capital contributions received in a public offering were intended, at the time of the offering, to be used by T for research and development costs and working capital purposes over a 24-month period, even though T later used the offering proceeds at a much slower rate than originally anticipated and, at the time of the ownership change date, estimated that it would not exhaust the offering

---

[148] IRS TAM 9332004 (8/13/93). This ruling is appropriately limited to computation of T's Code §382 limitation and does not apply to determinations of whether an ownership change has occurred. See Reg. §1.382-2(a)(3)(i), discussed in ¶1208.1.9 above.

[149] Code §382(*l*)(1).

proceeds for another 16 months (or a total of 40 months after the offering). T merely represented that "part or all of the proceeds of the offering were used to pay operational expenses . . . [which] arose shortly before, and after, the day of the offering and were reasonable in amount."

Similarly, in IRS Letter Ruling 9541019 (7/10/95), IRS concluded that capital contributions made pursuant to two public stock offerings that were part of a bank's plan to improve its deteriorating financial position and avoid regulatory sanctions qualified under Exception 3. The ruling stressed T's representation that "100 percent of the net proceeds of the offerings will be used as partial collateral for . . . reverse repurchase agreements" that were part of its overall financial improvement plan.[150]

The statute covers "any capital contribution." This clearly includes a contribution of cash and/or property by a shareholder to T. Section II of the 1986 Conference Report (at 189) also states that for this purpose a capital contribution "includ[es] a Code §351 transfer," hence (if this statement in the legislative history is a valid interpretation of the statute) covering a transfer of cash and/or property by new or existing shareholders in exchange for T stock if the transferors own (immediately after the transfer) at least 80% of T's stock. Suppose, however, the transferors do not own the requisite 80% control of T after the transfer? Is the transfer nonetheless a capital contribution? If so, why did the legislative history refer to a Code §351 transfer? Compare Code §118 with Code §1032.

EXAMPLE 6

T was formed many years ago and has had a substantial NOL since 1988. On 1/1/89 P, a corporation unrelated to T, contributes $1,000 to T in exchange for 100% of a newly issued class of Straight Preferred (i.e., preferred that is disregarded in determining whether an ownership change occurs). On 7/1/90 P purchases 100% of T's common stock (T's only other stock outstanding for $500 (its FV) from T's shareholders, who are unrelated to P. This results in an ownership change. P's 1/1/89 purchase of T preferred stock was not a Code §351 contribution. In the absence of regulations, it is unclear whether P's purchase of the preferred was a "capital contribution" and hence is disregarded in computing T's Code §382 limitation. Therefore, it is unclear whether the FV of T's stock for this purpose is $500 or $1,500.

Even if a capital contribution can be taken into account in determining the value of T's stock as a result of the exceptions described above, the value of T's stock may still be reduced under Code §382(*l*)(4) if T has substantial non-business assets. In IRS Letter Ruling 9630038 (5/1/96), described above, IRS ruled that

---

[150] In a more recent bank ruling, IRS Letter Ruling 9835027 (8/28/98), P made two capital contributions to its bank subsidiary S to "achieve the statutory minimum capital ratio levels required by [bank] Regulators." The ruling concludes that the capital contributions were made "to continue basic corporate operations" of S and hence were covered by Exception 3 above.

public offering proceeds intended to be used for research and development and working capital qualified for Exception 3. IRS nonetheless concluded, however, that the value of T's stock must be reduced under Code §382(l)(4) because T's cash on hand, apparently including a portion of the offering proceeds, constituted more than one-third of T's total assets. See, to similar effect, IRS Field Service Advice 200140049 (10/5/01), and generally ¶1208.2.1.6.

¶1208.2.1.5   Title 11 Bankruptcy and Similar Cases

(1) Ownership changes not subject to Code §382 limitation. If T is under court jurisdiction "in a title 11 or similar case" (as defined below), and if T's old shareholders and its creditors own, after an ownership change and as a result of their former shareholder or creditor status, 50% or more of the stock of T (or of a controlling corporation, if also in bankruptcy) by vote and by value, then Code §382(l)(5) (as retroactively amended by the 1988 Act) provides that the Code §382 limitation will not apply. In making this 50% determination, stock transferred to a creditor is counted only if transferred in full or partial satisfaction of the debt (including accrued interest thereon) and only if the debt either (a) was held by the same creditor for at least 18 months before the filing date of the title 11 or similar case or (b) both arose in the ordinary course of T's business and has always been held by the same person.[151]

Regulations issued in 3/94[152] give examples of ordinary course indebtedness and relax somewhat the holding period requirements of the 50% test by:

(a)   generally permitting T to treat debt as always having been owned by the beneficial owner of the debt immediately before the ownership change if the beneficial owner is not, immediately after the change, either a 5% shareholder or an entity through which a 5% shareholder owns an indirect ownership interest in T;

(b)   generally permitting holding period "tacking" (treating the transferee as having owned debt for the period it was held by the transferor) in certain "qualified transfers" of the debt, including a transfer (i) between certain 80%-or-more related persons, (ii) within 90 days after the loan's origination pursuant to a customary syndication, (iii) by an underwriter pursuant to an underwriting, (iv) at death, by gift, or pursuant to a divorce or separation instrument, (v) by reason of a subrogation in which the transferee acquires a claim against T because of a payment to the claimant under an insurance policy or a guarantee, letter of credit or similar security arrangement, or (vi) of an account receivable in a customary commercial factoring transaction made within 30 days after the account arose, provided in each case that the transferee does not acquire the debt for "a principal purpose" of benefitting from T's losses; and

---

[151] Code §382(l)(5)(E); Reg. §1.382-9(d)(1).
[152] Reg. §1.382-9(d) (T.D. 8529, 1994-1 C.B. 131).

(c)   providing that in a Code §1001 debt exchange or modification, the owner of the new debt is treated as having owned the new debt for the period that it owned the old debt, and the new debt is treated as having arisen in the ordinary course of T's trade or business if the old debt so arose.[153]

For purposes of making this 50% determination, special option attribution rules described in ¶1208.1.6.8 apply.

If T's ownership change qualifies under Code §382(*l*)(5), although T's NOLs and recognized BILs (described in ¶1208.4(3)) will not be subject to the Code §382 limitation, (a) T's NOLs nevertheless will be reduced by any interest paid or accrued by T during a specified period on any debt converted into stock (i.e., the period from the beginning of the third complete taxable year preceding the ownership change through the ownership change date) and (b) for ownership changes before 1/1/95, T's NOLs and other tax attributes will be reduced by 50% of the amount that, but for the application of the now-repealed common law stock-for-debt exception permitted by former Code §108(e)(10)(B), would have reduced such NOLs and other tax attributes as cancellation of indebtedness income.[154] In addition, T's NOLs may be extinguished (and, presumably, its recognized BILs disallowed) altogether unless T satisfies certain active business requirements during and after the title 11 or similar case, as discussed in ¶1208.3.

T (or its successor) may elect not to have Code §382(*l*)(5) apply.[155] If Code §382(*l*)(5) applies to an ownership change and if a second ownership change occurs within two years after an ownership change to which Code §382(*l*)(5) applies, Code §382(*l*)(5) cannot apply to the second ownership change, and the Code §382 limitation with respect to the second ownership change will be zero.[156] This rule does not apply if T elects out of Code §382(*l*)(5) with respect to the first ownership change. In that case the Code §382 limitation for both the first and the second ownership change are computed under the basic rules described in ¶1208.2 or the rules discussed immediately below, as applicable).

Special rules under Code §382(*l*)(5) apply to qualified transactions by certain troubled financial institutions occurring before 1/1/90.[157]

(2)   Ownership changes subject to Code §382 limitation. If T has undergone a "G" reorganization or an exchange of debt for stock in a title 11 or similar case, and if (by reason of T's election out or otherwise) Code §382(*l*)(5) does not apply, then T's pre-acquisition losses will be subject to the Code §382 limitation. In that

---

[153] These regulations are generally effective for ownership changes occurring after 3/16/94, although T may elect to apply them retroactively to ownership changes that occurred after 12/31/86. Reg. §1.382-9(d)(6).

[154] Code §382(*l*)(5)(B), (C).

[155] Code §382(*l*)(5)(H). This election is irrevocable and generally must be made by the due date (including any extensions) of T's tax return for the taxable year that includes the ownership change. However, in the case of an ownership change occurring before 3/17/94 (provided T elects to apply retroactively the Code §382(*l*)(6) regulations described below), T may elect not to have Code §382(*l*)(5) apply by the date T files its first tax return after 5/16/94. Reg. §1.382-9(i) and (p).

[156] Code §382(*l*)(5)(D); Reg. §1.382-9(n)(1).

[157] See, e.g., Code §§382(*l*)(5)(F) and 597, both as amended by the 1988 Act.

event, Code §382(*l*)(6) provides that T's stock value for purposes of computing the annual Code §382 limitation "shall reflect the increase (if any) in value of [T] resulting from any surrender or cancellation of creditors' claims in the transaction."[158]

Regulations under Code §382(*l*)(6) interpret this provision in a manner that takes into account an increase in T's stock value attributable to (a) a direct conversion of T debt into T stock, (b) an indirect conversion of T debt into T stock (e.g., by way of a cash or property contribution to T's capital or an issuance of T stock for cash or property when such cash or property is used to pay T debt), and (c) within limitations, an infusion of fresh capital (e.g., a cash or property contribution to T's capital or an issuance of T's stock for cash or property when such cash or property is retained by T). Specifically, the proposed regulations provide that, in a title 11 or similar case in which Code §382(*l*)(5) does not apply, T's stock value for purposes of computing the annual Code §382 limitation is the lesser of the values determined under the following tests:

(a)   The *stock value test*: T's stock FV immediately after the ownership change, valuing any stock issued in connection with the ownership change at an amount not exceeding the cash and the value of any property (including T debt) received by T in consideration for the issuance of such stock, and

(b)   The *asset value test*: T's asset FV (determined without regard to liabilities) immediately before the ownership change.[159]

The effect of the asset value test is essentially to ensure that T's value for Code §382 limitation purposes will not under any circumstance exceed the amount T's stock value would have been if all of T's prechange creditors had converted all their prechange debt into T stock.

Legislative Update

The unenacted Senate version (S. 1054) of the 2003 Act, effective for ownership changes after 12/31/02, would have doubled the annual Code §382 limitation for any post-change year beginning in 2004 or 2005 if T were an old loss corporation under court jurisdiction in a title 11 or similar case.

---

[158] Code §382(*l*)(6), as retroactively amended by the 1988 Act.
[159] Reg. §1.382-9(j), (k)(7).

EXAMPLE 7

T has an ownership change in a title 11 case. Immediately before the ownership change, T's asset FV and liabilities are as follows:

$100	Gross asset FV
(110)	Liabilities
$ (10)	Shareholder FV deficit

In connection with the ownership change, the following transactions occur:

(1)   a T creditor exchanges $20 of outstanding T debt for newly issued T stock,

(2)   individual B purchases newly issued T stock for $20 cash, and T immediately uses such cash to pay T creditors, and

(3)   individual C purchases newly issued T stock for $20 cash, and T retains such cash.

Therefore, immediately after the ownership change, T's stock FV is $50, computed as follows:

$120	Gross asset FV (i.e., $100 original asset FV plus $20 retained cash from individual C)
(70)	Liabilities (i.e., $110 original liabilities less $40 liability reduction from steps (1) and (2) above)
$ 50	Postchange stock FV

Code §382(*l*)(5) does not apply to the ownership change (either because T is ineligible or because T elects out). T therefore must compute its annual Code §382 limitation. Subject to the anti-abuse rules described below, T's value (in computing the annual Code §382 limitation) is $50, because $50 is the lesser of the amount determined under the stock value test (i.e., $50, T's stock FV immediately after the ownership change) and the amount determined under the asset value test (i.e., $100, T's gross asset FV immediately before the ownership change).

EXAMPLE 8

Same as Example 7 except that individual C purchases newly issued T stock for $120 rather than $20. Therefore, immediately after the ownership change, T's stock FV is $150, computed as follows:

$220	Gross asset FV (i.e., $100 original asset FV plus $120 retained cash from individual C)
(70)	Liabilities (i.e., $100 original liabilities less $40 liability reduction from steps (1) and (2) in Example 7)
$150	Postchange stock FV

In contrast to Example 7, and again subject to the anti-abuse rules discussed below, here T's value for purposes of computing T's Code §382 limitation is $100 because $100 is the lesser of the amounts determined under the stock value test (i.e., $150, T's stock FV immediately after the ownership change) and the asset value test (i.e., $100, T's gross asset FV immediately before the ownership change).

The Code §382(*l*)(6) regulations coordinate the asset value and stock value tests with other valuation rules of Code §382 as follows:[160]

(a) The amount of any postchange redemption or contraction to which the rules described in ¶1208.2.1.2 would apply reduces the amount determined under the stock value test (but not the asset value test).
(b) If T receives a capital contribution (including, for this purpose, cash or property in exchange for newly issued debt) as part of a plan "one of the principal purposes" of which is to avoid or increase the Code §382 limitation, such capital contribution is disregarded in applying the asset value test (but not the stock value test). See ¶1208.2.1.4.
(c) If T has substantial non-business assets (as described in ¶1208.2.1.6, but taking into account only assets held by T immediately before the ownership change), (i) the amount determined under the stock value test is reduced by the excess of the non-business assets' FV over the non-business assets' share of T's postchange debt, and (ii) the amount determined under the asset value test is reduced by the non-business assets' FV.

In addition, the regulations reduce the amount determined under the stock value test by the value of stock that is issued as part of a plan, one of the principal

---

[160] Reg. §1.382-9(k), (*l*).

purposes of which is increasing the Code §382 limitation "without subjecting the investment to the entrepreneurial risks of corporate business operations."[161] The regulations unfortunately do not elaborate on this murky principle.

The Code §382(*l*)(6) regulations generally apply to any ownership change occurring after 3/16/94. However, T may elect to apply the regulations in their entirety to any ownership change occurring on or before that date.[162]

(3)   Title 11 or similar case. As noted above, the benefits of Code §§382(*l*)(5) and 382(*l*)(6) are available only if T is under court jurisdiction "in a title 11 *or similar* case" (emphasis added). "Title 11 or similar case" is defined as "(i) a case under title 11 of the United State Code [i.e., the federal bankruptcy laws], or (ii) a receivership, foreclosure, or similar proceeding in a Federal or State court."[163] Depending on the nature of the claims against T and the composition of T's creditors and shareholders, certain state court proceedings may achieve the benefits of Code §382(*l*)(5) or §382(*l*)(6) in a more economical and expeditious manner than the costly and protracted federal court proceedings under title 11 of the United States Code.

In particular, under a somewhat obscure and little-used provision of Delaware law, the Delaware Court of Chancery is authorized to approve a compromise or settlement of the claims of T's creditors (or a class of T's creditors) and/or stockholders (or a class of stockholders) if the compromise or settlement is agreed to by (a) more than 50% in number and at least 75% in value of T's creditors, or a class thereof, to be bound by the compromise, and/or (b) more than 50% in number and at least 75% in value of T's shareholders, or a class thereof, to be bound by the compromise.[164] If all of T's creditors and shareholders to be bound by the compromise consent to it, the procedure is straightforward and can be completed at a relatively low cost within a week after filing in Delaware court. To bind any non-consenting T creditors or shareholders, however, T's certificate of incorporation must contain, at the time they became creditors or shareholders of T, the provisions of Delaware law authorizing the compromise procedure described above.[165] Because of this limitation on the ability to bind T's non-consenting creditors and shareholders, investors in T (particularly those that will hold both debt and equity of T) should consider including this Delaware provision in T's articles of incorporation in connection with forming or acquiring T. However, even when this provision is included in T's articles, there may be significant due process and federal preemption obstacles to impairing non-consenting creditors, and perhaps non-consenting shareholders, in such a state court proceeding.

Although a state court proceeding of the above type should qualify as a "title 11 or similar case" for purposes of Code §§382(*l*)(5) and 382(*l*)(6) and for purposes of the "G" reorganization rules (see ¶804), a state court proceeding (in contrast to a federal bankruptcy proceeding) will not qualify as a "title 11 case" for purposes

---

[161] Reg. §1.382-9(k)(6).
[162] Reg. §1.382-9(p).
[163] Code §§382(*l*)(5)(G), 368(a)(3)(A).
[164] Del. Gen. Corp. Law §§102(b)(2), 302(b).
[165] Del. Gen. Corp. Law §302(a).

of Code §108 (concerning cancellation of debt income, or "CODI"). In general, if a T debt is cancelled under Code §108, T will have taxable CODI (in the amount of the cancelled debt) except to the extent that T is in a title 11 bankruptcy case or is insolvent. Therefore, if a state court proceeding is used to extinguish creditor claims against T, T will have taxable CODI except to the extent it can demonstrate it was insolvent at the time of the debt cancellation.[166] See ¶605.

¶1208.2.1.6   *Reduction in T's FV When T or Successor Has Substantial Non-Business Assets*

If, immediately after an ownership change, at least one-third of the FV of T's total assets consists of "non-business assets" (i.e., assets held for investment, including cash and marketable stock or securities),[167] then T's FV for purposes of computing the Code §382 limitation is reduced by the excess of the pre-acquisition FV of T's non-business assets over "the non-business asset share of indebtedness for which [T] is liable."[168]

In *Berry Petroleum Co. v. Commissioner,*[169] P agreed to purchase T's stock and, prior to closing the stock purchase, P agreed to sell approximately one-half of T's assets to a third party (Bigco). The Tax Court characterized the assets P had contracted to sell to Bigco as business assets "immediately before" T's ownership change, but as non-business assets "immediately after" the ownership change. Interpreting ambiguous statutory language, the court held that the one-third-of-FV threshold is measured "immediately after" the ownership change, and hence required T's FV to be reduced for purposes of computing the Code §382 limitation. However, in determining the amount of the reduction in T's value, the court held that only non-business assets held "immediately before" the ownership change are taken into account. Accordingly, T's value was *not* reduced by the value of assets P had agreed to sell to Bigco. Rather, T's value was reduced only by the

[166] Similarly, the "stock for debt" exception of former Code §108(e)(10)(B) (as in effect for stock transferred before 1/1/95 or pursuant to a "title 11 or similar case" filed before 1/1/94) applied only to stock transferred in satisfaction of debt in a "title 11 case" or to the extent T was insolvent. See ¶605.

[167] IRS concluded in IRS Letter Ruling 9630038 (5/1/96) that cash and cash equivalents were non-business assets for this purpose even where such assets were held to meet T's anticipated research and development costs and other working capital needs over the 18-month period following the ownership change date.

[168] Code §382(l)(4); 1986 Conference Report II at 190. In the case of a merger, when the ownership change combines the assets of T and P in a single corporation, Code §382(l)(4) read literally applies the test to all the assets of the surviving entity rather than only to T's former assets. However, this appears to be a drafting error for several reasons: (1) it contradicts another part of the statute (compare Code §382(l)(4)(A), which applies the test to the assets of the surviving entity, with Code §382(l)(4)(B)(i), which assumes that the test applies only to T's assets); (2) it is inconsistent with the original (and otherwise virtually identical) provision appearing in the 1985 House Bill; and (3) it makes no sense to apply the test to P's assets since the value of P's assets is not part of the basic formula for determining the pre-acquisition FV of T's assets and therefore is not a source of potential abuse.

[169] 104 T.C. 584 (1995), *aff'd per unpublished order,* 142 F.3d 442, 98-1 U.S.T.C. ¶50,398 (9th Cir. 1998). For a fuller discussion of *Berry Petroleum,* see Henderson & Goldring, *Tax Planning for Troubled Corporations* §508.4.1.1 (Panel Publishers 2001).

value of a note receivable that represented less than 10% of the value of T's assets immediately before the ownership change.

If T owns at least 50% of the stock (by voting power and value) of a subsidiary, then stock and securities of the subsidiary are not treated as assets held for investment, and instead T is deemed to own its ratable share of the subsidiary's assets.[170]

EXAMPLE 9

On 1/1/90, when the FV of T's stock is $1,500, T undergoes an ownership change as a result of a sale of T stock by T's shareholders. T has no subsidiaries. Immediately before and after the ownership change, T has liabilities of $500 and the following assets:

Asset	FV
Cash	$ 500
Marketable securities	300
Land and buildings	600
Machinery and equipment	300
Inventory	300
Total	$2,000

T's cash and marketable securities constitute 40% ($800 ÷ $2,000) of T's total assets. Because at least one-third of the FV of T's total assets immediately after the ownership change consists of non-business assets, the above rule applies. Therefore, the FV of T's stock for purposes of computing T's Code §382 limitation is reduced by $600, i.e., the excess of T's pre-acquisition non-business assets ($800) over the portion of T's indebtedness attributable thereto (40% of $500 equals $200). Hence, the FV of T's stock for computing its annual Code §382 limitation is $900 ($1,500 − $600).

¶1208.2.1.7   Foreign Corporation

If T is a foreign corporation, its stock FV is determined taking into account only items treated as connected with the conduct of a U.S. trade or business, unless otherwise provided in regulations.[171]

---

[170] Code §382(l)(4)(E).
[171] Code §382(e)(3).

¶1208.2.1.8   Long-Term Tax-Exempt Rate

The "long-term tax-exempt rate" is the highest of the federal long-term rates determined under Code §1274(d) (adjusted to reflect differences between rates on long-term taxable and tax-exempt obligations) in effect for the month in which the ownership change occurs or for the two preceding months.[172] The rate is published monthly by IRS. For example, for 3/99 the rate (adjusted as described above) was 4.68%, and the highest of the three adjusted federal rates for 3/99 and the preceding two months was 4.71%.

¶1208.2.2   Unused Limitation Carryover

If for any year T (or its successor) does not have sufficient taxable income to use up its full Code §382 limitation, its unused limitation is carried forward on a cumulative basis.[173]

¶1208.2.3   Built-in Gain

T's (or its successor's) Code §382 limitation is increased by the amount of T's (or its successor's) "recognized BIGs" for the year.[174] A recognized BIG includes any gain T (or its successor) recognizes during the year on the disposition of any asset to the extent that all of the following conditions are satisfied:

(1)   T (or its successor) establishes that T held the asset immediately before the ownership change date.

(2)   T (or its successor) establishes that the amount being added to the Code §382 limitation does not exceed the asset's FV on the ownership change date less its adjusted basis on that date.

(3)   T (or its successor) recognizes the gain during the five-year period beginning on the ownership change date.

(4)   Immediately before the ownership change, T had a "net unrealized BIG," i.e., the aggregate FV of T's assets exceeded their aggregate basis by more than the lesser of (a) 15% of their aggregate FV or (b) $10 million (generally effective for ownership changes after 10/2/89 under the 1989 Act).[175] In making this determination, cash, cash items (including receivables) and any marketable security that has not changed substantially in value are disregarded, except as provided in future regulations (which, according

---

[172] Code §382(f).
[173] Code §382(b)(2).
[174] Code §382(h).
[175] For ownership changes occurring on or before 10/2/89, and for later ownership changes made pursuant to a written binding contract in effect on 10/2/89 and at all times thereafter before the ownership change, the percentage threshold described in text is 25% rather than 15%, and the $10 million threshold does not apply.

to the 1988 Conference Report, would apply prospectively only).[176] In addition, if a "redemption" or (for ownership changes after 6/10/87) any other "corporate contraction" occurs in connection with an ownership change (as discussed at ¶1208.2.1), then to the extent provided in future regulations, T's net unrealized BIG is computed after taking the redemption or other corporate contraction into account.[177]

EXAMPLE 1

On 1/1/99, when T has a $500 NOL, T undergoes an ownership change as a result of P purchasing all of T's stock from T's shareholders on that date. Immediately before the ownership change, the FV of T's stock is $400, its liabilities are $600, and its assets are as follows:

Asset	FV	Basis
Cash	$ 50	$ 50
Land and building	375	200
Machinery and equipment	325	250
Inventory	250	100
Total	$1,000	$600

Assume that the long-term tax-exempt rate then in effect is 5%, so T's annual Code §382 limitation (without regard to the BIG rule) is $20 (5% of $400 stock value). Immediately before the ownership change, the FV of T's assets (excluding cash) ($950) exceeds their aggregate basis ($550) by 42% of their aggregate FV (i.e., ($950 FV − $550 basis) ÷ $950 FV = 42%). Because 42% exceeds the 15% threshold described in (4) above, T's recognized BIGs for the next five years will increase its annual Code §382 limitation.

Assume that T sells its land and building on 2/1/99 for $375 or more, hence recognizing a $175 BIG. Under the BIG rule, T may carry forward $175 of its NOL to offset the gain. In addition, $20 of T's NOL (i.e., T's basic Code §382 limitation) is still available to absorb other income T earns during the taxable year following the ownership change. Hence, if T's 1999 taxable income, computed before NOL offset, equals or exceeds $195 ($175 BIG recognized in 1999 plus $20 Code §382 annual limitation), $195 of NOL will offset 1999 income. If 1999 taxable income, computed before NOL offset, is less than $195 (e.g., $100), all of that 1999 income will be offset by NOL and the unused limitation (e.g., $95, equal to $195 total 1999 limitation minus

---

[176] Code §382(h)(3)(B)(ii), as amended by the 1988 Act; 1988 House Report at 47; 1988 Senate Report at 57; H.R. Conf. Rep. No. 1104, 100th Cong., 2d Sess. 10 (1988).

[177] Code §382(h)(3)(A), as amended by the 1988 Act. For ownership changes before 6/2/88, redemptions and other corporate contractions are taken into account for this purpose whether or not regulations so provide. See 1988 Act §1006(d)(28).

$100 1999 income before NOL) will be carried forward on a cumulative basis. See ¶1208.2.2.

EXAMPLE 2

Same as Example 1, except that immediately before the ownership change T's liabilities are $275 and T's assets are as follows:

Asset	FV	Basis
Cash	$ 50	$ 50
Land and building	275	200
Machinery and equipment	250	250
Inventory	100	100
Total	$675	$600

T's Code §382 limitation will not be increased by any BIG recognized by T on the sale of its assets because the FV of T's assets (other than cash) immediately before the ownership change ($625) does not exceed their aggregate basis ($550) by more than 15% of their aggregate FV ($75 ÷ $625 = 12.0%) or by more than $10 million. Hence, in contrast to Example 1, if T sells its land and building for $275 or more on 2/1/99, recognizing a $75 BIG, only $20 of T's NOL (i.e., T's basic Code §382 limitation) may be deducted against the gain and any other income T earns during the taxable year following the ownership change.

The total recognized BIG included in the Code §382 limitation for any taxable year is limited to T's net unrealized BIG described in (4) above (before reduction by the 15%/$10 million threshold amount), reduced by the recognized BIGs for prior years that ended within the five-year period beginning on the ownership change date.

EXAMPLE 3

Same as Example 1, except that immediately before the ownership change T's assets are as follows:

Asset	FV	Basis
Cash	$ 50	$ 50
Land and building	425	200
Machinery and equipment	50	250
Inventory	475	100
Total	$1,000	$600

As in Example 1 immediately before the ownership change, the FV of T's assets (excluding cash) ($950) exceeds their aggregate basis ($550) by 42% of their aggregate FV. This exceeds the 15%/$10 million threshold, so T has a net unrealized BIG of $400. Therefore, T's recognized BIGs for the next five years will increase T's annual Code §382 limitation, but only to the extent of T's $400 net unrealized BIG.

Assume that T sells its inventory in 2000 for $500 and its land and building in 2001 for $600. T's recognized BIG on the 2000 inventory sale is $375 (i.e., $475 FV on 1/1/99 less $100 basis on 1/1/99). This amount does not exceed T's $400 net unrealized BIG. Hence, T's Code §382 limitation for 2000 is increased by the full $375 BIG recognized in 2000, so T's aggregate Code §382 limitation for 2000 is $395 (i.e., $20 basic limitation plus $375).

T's recognized BIG on the 2001 land and building sale is $225 (i.e., $425 FV on 1/1/99 less $200 basis on 1/1/99). However, the excess of T's $400 net unrealized BIG over T's recognized BIGs from prior years ($375 from the 2000 inventory sale) is only $25. Therefore T's Code §382 limitation for 2001 is increased by only $25 of the BIG recognized in 2001, to $45 (i.e., $20 basic limitation plus $25).

In computing T's recognized BIGs, "[a]ny item of income which is properly taken into account during the [five-year] recognition period but which is attributable to periods before the [ownership] change date shall be treated as a recognized built-in gain for the taxable year in which it is properly taken into account," and T's net unrealized BIG is adjusted accordingly.[178] According to the legislative history, such income items would include (1) cash basis receivables that arose before but are collected after the ownership change date and (2) income attributable to prechange periods but recognized after the ownership change pursuant to Code §481 adjustments arising from changes in accounting method.[179] However, in IRS Technical Advice Memorandum 199942003 (10/22/99), IRS concluded that where (before a change in ownership) accrual method T receives a pre-payment for services to be rendered after the change in ownership, but T elects to defer the income to the post-change period when it performs the services (as permitted by Rev. Proc. 71-21, 1971-2 C.B. 549), such amount is not included in net unrealized BIG or recognized BIG.

---

[178] Code §382(h)(6), as retroactively amended by TAMRA and the 1989 Act.
[179] 1988 House Report at 46; 1988 Senate Report at 56.

In a 1993 Field Service Advisory,[180] IRS concluded that "a reasonable argument" could be made that income earned after the ownership change from licensing zero-basis software, where the income represents a return of expenses (incurred in creating the software) that had been deducted before the ownership change, is recognized BIG under Code §382(h). IRS reasoned: "Under. . .§382(h)(2), post-change depreciation that is attributable to pre-change built-in loss is treated as recognized built-in loss. The flip side . . . is that post-change income attributable to pre-change depreciation, which generated the built-in gain, should be treated as recognized built-in gain." The FSA finds it "likely" that a court would support the taxpayer's position for BIG treatment and advised against litigating that position, although commenting that the National Office is studying the issue.

In contrast, a Technical Advice Memorandum nine years later[181] concludes that post-change operating income attributable to another low-basis wasting asset, in this case an existing patient base (i.e., patients for whom the taxpayer was supplying home health products and services as of the change date), is not included in net unrealized BIG or recognized BIG under Code §382(h)(6), for three reasons:

First, although post-change *deductions* attributable to net unrealized BIL inherent in a wasting asset on the change date (i.e., depreciation, amortization, and depletion) are taken into account as recognized BIL under Code §382(h)(2)(B), there is no evidence Congress intended to mirror such treatment on the income side (except in the case of BIG recognized on disposition of the asset). To the contrary, post-change operating income attributable to a wasting asset's BIG is distinguishable from the examples of Code §382(h)(6) income items noted above from the legislative history, all of which concern specific items of income that have "accrued" as of the change date (i.e., the right to the income has become fixed), but because of the taxpayer's accounting method or a statutory deferral provision, the income is taken into account in a later period.

Second, to conclude otherwise would raise significant administration issues, because (in contrast to taking into account scheduled depreciation and amortization deductions from a wasting asset for BIL purposes), in the case of a zero-basis wasting asset with no depreciation schedule, an alternative methodology would need to be developed for determining the rate of BIG consumption.

Third, the 2002 TAM distinguishes the 1993 FSA, where the software generating the post-change licensing income was fully expensed before the change date and there was "an undeniable close relationship between the software development costs that created the NOLs and the licensing income flowing from that software." In contrast, in the TAM the taxpayer's post-change activities (i.e., services provided for which post-change expenses were incurred) rather than pre-change activities essentially generated the [post-change] revenue for which BIG treatment was claimed.

IRS Notice 90-27[182] applies the Code §382 BIG rules to installment sales in a manner favorable to taxpayers. According to the notice, future regulations will provide that if T sells a BIG asset before or during the five-year recognition period

---

[180] IRS Field Service Advisory TL-N-5525-93.
[181] IRS Technical Advice Memorandum 200217009 (4/26/02).
[182] 1990-1 C.B. 336.

in a sale reported on the installment method, the BIG rules will continue to apply to any installment gain recognized after the five-year recognition period has expired. That is, solely for purposes of such installment sale gain, the five-year recognition period is extended through the date of the last installment payment (or the date of disposition of the installment obligation). Apart from this modification, the installment gain is subject to the regular BIG rules. This special rule favors taxpayers in a Code §382 context because otherwise gain from installments paid after the five-year recognition period has expired would not increase the Code §382 limitation and thus would be subject to the regular Code §382 limitation. (In contrast, the rule's application is decidedly unfavorable to taxpayers in a Code §384 context, as discussed in ¶1205.2.5.) These future regulations will be effective for installment sales after 3/25/90 (unless pursuant to a binding written contract entered into on or before such date and continuously in effect until the sale).

If P or any P affiliate has an NOL or a net unrealized BIL (i.e., a BIL exceeding the applicable threshold—see ¶1208.4(3)(d)) when P acquires T, then any BIG of T could be subject not only to the BIG rule of Code §382 but also to new Code §384 (discussed at ¶1205.2.5 above). As the following examples illustrate, the relationship between Code §382, Code §384, and the 15%/$10 million de minimis rule of both provisions must be considered closely in such circumstances.

EXAMPLE 4

T has long been owned by individual A, and P has long been owned by unrelated shareholders. Both P and T are calendar year taxpayers. On 1/1/99 T has a $100 NOL and a $500 unrealized BIG (which exceed the 15%/$10 million de minimis amount), and P has a $200 NOL. On 1/2/99 P purchases 100% of T's stock from A, and thereafter P and T file consolidated returns. Assume that during 1999, T recognizes $150 of BIG and has $25 of other income.

Because of T's ownership change, T's NOL will be subject to the annual Code §382 limitation. However, under Code §382's BIG exception, T's entire $100 NOL will be available to offset T's recognized BIGs as incurred. Thus T's NOL will be reduced to $0 in 1999, leaving T with 1999 net recognized BIG of $50 and 1999 net other income of $25.

P's $200 NOL is available to offset T's $25 of other income. However, under Code §384, T's remaining $50 of BIG for 1999 cannot be offset by P's remaining ($175) NOL or the NOL of any P affiliate, not even to the extent of T's annual Code §382 limitation. Similarly, any BIG T recognizes for five years after the acquisition cannot be offset by any pre-acquisition NOLs of P's old group. In contrast, P's post-acquisition losses can offset T's BIGs (and T's other income) without limitation, and P's pre-acquisition NOL can offset T's post-acquisition income other than BIG without limitation.

EXAMPLE 5

Same as Example 4, except that T's $500 BIG does not exceed the 15%/$10 million de minimis amount. Assume that T's annual Code §382 limitation is $10. Code §382's BIG rule will not apply. Therefore, only $10 of T's 1999 income (including T's $150 BIG) can be offset by T's NOL, leaving $165 of T income and a $90 T NOL. Thus, the Code §382 result is worse than in Example 4, in which the BIG rule permitted T's entire NOL to be applied against T's 1999 BIG.

However, because of Code §384's 15%/$10 million de minimis BIG rule, Code §384 will not apply either. Therefore, all of T's remaining 1999 income of $165, including its BIG, will be offset by P's $200 NOL, leaving T with no 1999 net income (in contrast to $50 of net income in Example 4). The result is that, on 1/1/00, T has a $90 NOL (rather than a $0 NOL, as in Example 4) that can offset T's taxable income (including T's future recognized BIGs) only at the rate of $10 per year; and T has a remaining BIG of $350 ($500 − $150) that can be used freely against P's remaining NOL (in contrast to Example 4, in which T has a remaining BIG of $400 to which Code §384 applies). In addition, T's remaining $90 NOL will be a SRLY NOL that may be used only to offset income generated by T, not income generated by P or any of T's other affiliates. In short, because T's BIG does not exceed the 15%/$10 million de minimis thresholds of Code §§382 and 384, the tax result here is radically different from that in Example 4.

¶1208.2.4 Code §338 Election Gain

If P completes a Code §338 "qualified stock purchase" ("QSP") of T (i.e., P acquires by purchase within a 12-month period 80% or more of T's stock by vote and by value, excluding Straight Preferred) on the same day that P acquires sufficient T stock to cause an ownership change, and if P makes a Code §338 election with respect to T, T's Code §338 gain apparently is not within the ambit of Code §382 because it is not income recognized in a postchange year but rather is income reported on "old T's" final tax return.[183] In that case, T's Code §338 gain is reduced by T's NOL without limitation.

EXAMPLE 1

Same as Example 2 at ¶1208.2.3, except that P makes a Code §338 election with respect to the T stock so that T immediately recognizes its $75 Code §338 gain.

---

[183] Code §382(a) and (d)(2).

T may carry forward $75 of its NOL to offset fully the $75 gain T recognizes as a result of the Code §338 election. However, the remainder of T's $500 NOL ($425) is automatically eliminated because the transaction is treated as a sale of assets by Old T to New T.

In contrast, as discussed in ¶1208.2.3 Example 2, if T did not make the Code §338 election, only $28 of T's NOL (i.e., T's basic Code §382 limitation) would be available annually to offset T's income (including any gain T recognized as it actually disposed of its BIG assets), although T's entire $500 NOL would survive (subject to the 20-year limit on NOL carryforwards—see ¶1201).

However, if P's purchase of T stock results in an ownership change on a day preceding the QSP (e.g., P buys 60% of T's stock on day 1 and the other 40% on day 2), T's Code §338 gain will be subject to the BIG rules of Code §382, with a favorable exception noted below. Specifically, T's Code §382 limitation for the year of the QSP is increased by the lesser of (1) the BIG inherent in T's assets at the time of the ownership change (i.e., the 60-percent purchase on day 1), to the extent such gain is recognized as a result of the Code §338 election with respect to the day 2 QSP, or (2) T's net unrealized BIG at the time of the ownership change on day 1. Note that either or both of these amounts might be substantially less than T's actual Code §338 gain.

EXAMPLE 2

On 1/1/91, when T has a $500 NOL, P acquires 60% of T's stock, resulting in a Code §382 ownership change. Immediately before the ownership change, T's assets are as follows:

Asset	FV	Basis
Cash	$ 50	$ 50
Machinery and equipment	50	250
Inventory	900	300
Total	$1,000	$600

T's only BIG asset is its inventory, which has a BIG of $600 (i.e., $900 FV less $300 basis on 1/1/91). T's net unrealized BIG is $400 (i.e., $1,000 aggregate asset FV less $600 aggregate basis on 1/1/91), which exceeds the 15%/$10 million threshold (as shown in ¶1208.2.3 Example 3).

P acquires the remaining 40% of T's stock 11 months later, on 12/1/91, and makes a Code §338 election with respect to the QSP of T's stock completed on 12/1/91. Between 1/1/91 and 12/1/91, T's inventory appreciated in value from $900 to $1,150, and T neither sold nor acquired any assets:

Asset	FV	Basis
Cash	$ 50	$ 50
Machinery and equipment	50	250
Inventory	1,150	300
Total	$1,250	$600

Thus T's assets appreciated $250 from the ownership change date to the QSP date, so on 12/1/90 their FV exceeds their basis by $650 rather than by $400. T's Code §338 gain is $650, equal to T's $1,250 asset FV less T's $600 asset basis on 12/1/91.

Under the basic BIG rules discussed in ¶1208.2.3(4), T's Code §382 limitation for 1991 is increased by only $400, which is the lesser of (1) the amount of T's 1/1/91 BIGs recognized by reason of the Code §338 election as of 12/1/91 (i.e., $600, equal to the portion of T's $850 Code §338 gain on T's inventory (T's only BIG asset) attributable to BIG on 1/1/91), or (2) T's net unrealized BIG on 1/1/91 (i.e., $400).

The additional $250 of Code §338 gain for 1991 (i.e., the excess of T's $650 Code §338 gain over the $400 increase in T's Code §382 limitation) is subject to T's annual Code §382 limitation. In addition, the Code §338 election terminates T's remaining NOL as of 12/1/91.

In contrast to other circumstances in which BIG is recognized, the above treatment of Code §338 gain, in which a delay occurs between the ownership change and the QSP, applies whether or not T's net unrealized BIG on the ownership change date exceeds the 15%/$10 million de minimis threshold described at ¶1208.2.3(4). That is, under the regular BIG rules, if T's net unrealized BIG on the ownership change date did not exceed the 15%/$10 million de minimis threshold, BIG triggered by a subsequent QSP and Code §338 election would not increase T's Code §382 limitation at all. However, a special rule (Code §382(h)(1)(C)) provides that, if P makes a Code §338 election "in connection with an ownership change" of T and T's net unrealized BIG at the time of the ownership change does not exceed the 15%/$10 million de minimis threshold, T's Code §382 limitation for the year of the QSP is increased by the lesser of (1) "the recognized BIGs by reason of such election" with respect to the day 2 QSP, or (2) T's net unrealized BIG (determined without regard to the de minimis threshold) at the time of the ownership change on day 1.[184]

---

[184] Code §382(h)(1)(C), as retroactively amended by the 1988 Act.

EXAMPLE 3

Same as Example 2 except that T's $400 net unrealized BIG on 1/1/91 does not exceed the de minimis threshold (e.g., because T has sufficient other non-cash assets, each with an FV equal to basis, that T's $400 net unrealized BIG no longer exceeds 15% of T's asset FV and, of course, is also less than $10 million). Code §382(h)(1)(C) will apply. Accordingly, T's Code §382 limitation for 1991 will be increased by $400 which represents the lesser of T's "recognized BIGs by reason of [the Code §338] election" as of 12/2/91 (i.e., $600, equal to the portion of T's $850 Code §338 gain on T's inventory attributable to BIG on 1/1/91) or T's $400 net unrealized BIG on the 1/1/91 ownership change date, just as in Example 2. Without the special rule of Code §382(h)(1)(C), T's Code §382 limitation would not be increased at all as a result of the Code §338 election, which simply would terminate T's "unused" NOL as of 12/1/90.

As the above discussion indicates, in contrast to the regular BIG rules, and whether a QSP of T's stock occurs on the Code §382 ownership change date or later, there is no de minimis threshold that T must overcome in order to increase its Code §382 limitation by BIGs recognized pursuant to a Code §338 election. Thus, a Code §338 election should be considered when T's BIG is sufficient to absorb a substantial portion of T's NOL but T's net unrealized BIG does not exceed the de minimis threshold. In considering whether a Code §338 election is appropriate, it must also be kept in mind that a Code §338 election will eliminate the portion of T's NOL exceeding the amount permitted to be applied against T's Code §338 gain. See Example 1.

¶1208.2.5   Limitation Not Applicable to Pre-acquisition Income

In general, the Code §382 limitation does not apply to taxable income allocable (on a daily pro rata basis, except as provided in regulations) to the portion of T's taxable year through and including the ownership change date, and T's NOL thus can be used in full against such income.[185] Effective for ownership changes on or after 6/22/94, regulations permit taxpayers to elect (subject to certain conditions and adjustments) to allocate T's taxable income for the ownership change year between the portion of the year through and including the ownership change date and the portion of the year beginning after the ownership change date, based on a closing of the books as of the change date rather than ratably.[186]

---

[185] Code §382(b)(3) and (m)(2).
[186] See Reg. §1.382-6(b) (T.D. 8546, 1994-2 C.B. 43).

For ownership changes prior to 6/22/94, taxpayers were required to allocate ratable unless they obtained a letter ruling.[187]

¶1208.3 Continuity of Business Enterprise Requirement

¶1208.3.1 In General

T's NOL carryforwards (including any recognized BILs, described in ¶1208.4) are disallowed completely (except to the extent of recognized BIGs or Code §338 gains, as described above), unless T's "business enterprise" is continued at all times during the two-year period beginning on the ownership change date.[188] The 1986 Conference Report states this is the same requirement that must be satisfied under current law before a transaction can qualify as a tax-free reorganization under Code §368. See ¶611. Thus, it is a "facts and circumstances" test requiring T or its successor to do either of the following:[189]

(1) Continue T's "historic business." If T has more than one line of business, T or its successor need only "continue a significant line of business."
(2) Use "a significant portion" of T's historic business assets in a business.

The new rule is more lenient than the business continuation rule of old Code §382(a), which required T to continue to conduct a trade or business "substantially the same" as its historic business.[190] For example, according to the old Code §382 regulations, T violates the business continuation rule of old Code §382 if it:

(1) "discontinues more than a minor portion" of its historic business;
(2) "changes the location of a major portion of its activities," if as a result T's business is "substantially altered"; or
(3) was "primarily engaged" in providing "services by a particular individual or individuals" and, after its change in ownership, is engaged primarily in providing "services by different individuals."[191]

In contrast, Section II of the 1986 Conference Report (at 189) states that the continuity of business enterprise requirement of new Code §382 may be satisfied even though T (or its successor) "discontinues more than a minor portion of [T's] historic business" and that "[c]hanges in the location of [T's] business or [T's] key employees" will not violate the provision.

For the application of the Code §382 continuity of business enterprise requirement when T has subsidiaries, see ¶1208.6.

---

[187] See IRS Notice 87-79, 1987-2 C.B. 387.
[188] Code §382(c).
[189] See Reg. §1.368-1(d); 1986 Conference Report II, at 189.
[190] Old Code §382(a)(1)(C).
[191] Reg. §1.382(a)-1(h) (obsolete).

¶1208.3.2   Exception for Bankrupt T Subject to Code §382(*l*)(5)

If T is under court jurisdiction in a "title 11 or similar case" (as defined in ¶1208.2.1.5) and Code §382(*l*)(5) applies to the ownership change (because T meets the other requirements of Code §382(*l*)(5) and does not elect out of that provision), then in addition to the benefits described in ¶1208.2.1.5, the continuity of business enterprise requirement of Code §382(c) will not apply.[192] However, concerned that the Code §382(*l*)(5) exemption could permit trafficking in shell bankrupt Ts, Treasury reached the protective conclusion that, in exempting bankrupt Ts from Code §382, Congress did not intend to exempt them from Code §269 as well.[193] Reg. §1.269-3(d) adds flesh to the bones by inserting into Code §269 a continuity of business enterprise requirement that is similar in many respects to the Code §382(c) requirement:

> Absent strong evidence to the contrary, a requisite Code §269 acquisition of control or property [see ¶1203.2.2] in connection with an ownership change to which section 382(*l*)(5) applies [i.e., an ownership change of a qualifying bankrupt T] is considered to be made for the principal purpose of evasion or avoidance of Federal income tax unless the corporation carries on more than an insignificant amount of an active trade or business during and subsequent to the title 11 or similar case. . . . The determination of whether the corporation carries on more than an insignificant amount of an active trade or business is made without regard to the continuity of business enterprise requirement set forth in [Reg.] §1.368-1(d).[194] The determination is based on all the facts and circumstances [such as] the amount of business assets that continue to be used, or the number of employees in the work force who continue employment, in an active trade or business (although not necessarily the historic trade or business). Where the corporation continues to utilize a significant amount of its business assets or work force, the requirement of carrying on more than an insignificant amount of an active trade or business may be met even though all trade or business activities temporarily cease for a period of time in order to address business exigencies.

This regulation applies to any ownership change effected pursuant to a plan of reorganization confirmed by a court in a title 11 or similar case after 8/14/90.

The Code §269 business continuation test appears to be more lenient than the Code §382(c) business continuation test in several respects. First, the regulations require carrying on "more than an insignificant amount of an active trade or business," but such trade or business need not be an "historic" business of T nor must it rise to the level of "a significant line of business," in contrast to the Code §382(c)/368 requirement. Second, the regulations are satisfied if "a significant amount of [T's] . . . work force" is used, even if such use does not satisfy either

---

[192] See Reg. §1.382-9(m). This conclusion also follows from the statute because even though non-compliance with the continuity of business enterprise requirement reduces the Code §382 limitation to zero (Code §382(c)(1)), such reduction will limit the future use of T's NOLs only by operation of Code §382(a), from which Code §382(*l*)(5) exempts qualifying transactions.

[193] T.D. 8388, 1992-1 C.B. 137.

[194] See ¶611.

the historic business or the historic assets prong of the Code §382(c)/368 test. Third, the regulations expressly permit a "temporary" cessation of "all trade or business activities" in some circumstances.

On the other hand, in at least two respects the Code §269 regulations may be harsher than the Code §382(c)/§368 business continuation test. First, in contrast to the two-year required business continuation period of Code §382(c), the Code §269 regulations merely refer to the period "during and subsequent to the title 11 or similar case," which could be longer or shorter than two years but in any event is vague. Second, while NOL disallowance under Code §382(c) does not apply to the extent of T's BIGs or Code §338 gain, the Code §269 regulations apparently would extinguish T's NOL entirely (unless IRS, in its discretion, mitigates this result by virtue of its authority under Code §269(c)). Thus, ironically, the Code §269 regulations, which apply only when Code §382(*l*)(5) also applies, could put P and T in a worse position (because Code §382(*l*)(5) preempts Code §382(c)) than if T had elected out of Code §382(*l*)(5), although Code §382(*l*)(5) was enacted as a relief measure.

Not surprisingly, when proposed, Code §269 regulations were roundly criticized by practitioners as essentially reintroducing (in a revised, flawed, ambiguous, and difficult-to-apply form) a subjective statutory requirement from which Code §382(*l*)(5) expressly exempts qualifying transactions. IRS takes the position that these regulations are consistent with the statement in Section II of the 1986 Conference Report (at 194) that the enactment of new Code §382 does "not alter the continuing application of section 269."[195] While this may be an acceptable proposition as applied to Code §382 ownership changes generally, it is questionable whether this legislative history justifies regulations overturning Congress's express and narrow purpose in enacting Code §382(*l*)(5) to exempt qualifying transactions from both the Code §382(a) NOL limitation and the Code §382(c) continuity of business enterprise requirement. Moreover, as indicated, the regulations could have the perverse effect of producing a harsher result where Code §382(*l*)(5) does apply than where it does not. If Code §382(*l*)(5) is considered too permissive, any limitation on its scope arguably should be implemented by statutory amendment, not by "legislative" regulations that vitiate the statute.

¶1208.4 Losses Subject to Limitation

Losses subject to the Code §382 limitation ("prechange losses") include the following amounts:

(1) Any NOL of T carried forward to the taxable year that includes the ownership change date. Code §382(d)(1)(A).

(2) T's NOL for the taxable year in which the ownership change occurs, to the extent the NOL is allocable (on a daily pro rata basis, except as provided in regulations) to the portion of the year through and including the owner-

---

[195] T.D. 8388, 1992-1 C.B. 137.

ship change date.[196] Effective for ownership changes on or after 6/22/94, regulations permit taxpayers to elect (subject to certain conditions and adjustments) to allocate T's NOL for the ownership change year between the portion of the year through and including the ownership change date and the portion of the year beginning after the ownership change date, based on a closing of the books as of the change date rather than ratably.[197] For ownership changes prior to 6/22/94, taxpayers were required to allocate ratably unless they obtained a letter ruling.[198]

(3)   T's "recognized BIL" is essentially treated like an NOL for Code §382 purposes.[199] This includes any loss T (or its successor) recognizes on the disposition of any asset to the extent that all of the following conditions are satisfied:

(a)   T (or its successor) fails to establish that T acquired the asset after the ownership change date.

(b)   T (or its successor) fails to establish that the loss exceeds the asset's adjusted basis on the ownership change date less its FV on that date.

(c)   T (or its successor) recognizes the loss during the five-year period beginning on the ownership change date.

(d)   Immediately before the ownership change, T had a "net unrealized BIL," i.e., the aggregate adjusted basis of T's assets exceeded their aggregate FV by more than the lesser of (i) 15% of their aggregate FV or (ii) $10 million (generally effective for ownership changes after 10/2/89, under the 1989 Act).[200] In making this determination, cash, cash items (including receivables), and any marketable security that has not changed substantially in value are disregarded, except as provided in future regulations (which, according to the 1988 Conference Report, would apply prospectively only), in the same manner as discussed in connection with BIGs at ¶1208.2.3. In addition, if a "redemption" or (for ownership changes after 6/10/87) any other "corporate contraction" occurs in connection with an ownership change, then to the extent provided in future regulations, T's net unrealized BIL is computed after taking the redemption or other corporate contraction into account, as further discussed in connection with BIGs at ¶1208.2.3.

EXAMPLE 1

On 1/1/99 T has a $200 NOL (determined without regard to any BIL). T undergoes an ownership change on that date as a result of P's purchase

---

[196] Code §382(d)(1) and (m)(2).

[197] See Reg. §1.382-6(b) (T.D. 8546, 1994-2 C.B. 43).

[198] See IRS Notice 87-79, 1987-2 C.B. 387.

[199] See Code §382(h).

[200] For ownership changes occurring on or before 10/2/89, and for later ownership changes made pursuant to a written binding contract in effect on 10/2/89 and at all times thereafter before the

of 55% of T's stock from T's shareholders. Both P and T are calendar year taxpayers. Immediately before the ownership change, the FV of T's stock is $300, T has $750 of liabilities, and T holds the following assets:

Asset	FV	Basis
Cash	$ 50	$ 50
Land and buildings	500	450
Machinery and equipment	250	300
Inventory	250	400
Total	$1,050	$1,200

Assume that the long-term tax-exempt rate then in effect is 5%, so the annual Code §382 limitation applicable to T's prechange losses is $15 (5% of $300). Immediately before the ownership change, the aggregate adjusted basis of T's assets excluding cash ($1,150) exceeds their aggregate FV ($1,000) by exactly 15% (($1,150 – $1,000) ÷ $1,000 = 15%). Because T's BIL does not exceed the lesser of the 15% threshold or the $10 million threshold specified in paragraph (3)(d) above, any BIL T recognizes during the next five years will not be treated as a prechange loss and hence will not be subject to T's Code §382 limitation.

Thus, assume that for its taxable year ended 12/31/99 T incurs a $150 BIL from the sale (for $250 or less) of all the inventory it held on 1/1/99 and that T otherwise has $300 of taxable income. T may use its recognized BIL to fully offset its income for the year. Thus, T's 1999 taxable income will be $135:

$300	Net income before recognized BIL and NOL carryforward
(150)	Recognized BIL on sale of inventory
(15)	Prechange losses deductible in 1999 under Code §382
$135	Taxable income

$185 of T's NOL (i.e., $200 NOL – $15 NOL deducted in 1999) will be deductible after 1999, subject to T's Code §382 limitation.

---

ownership change, the percentage threshold described in text is 25% rather than 15%, and the $10 million threshold does not apply.

EXAMPLE 2

Same as Example 1, except that T's basis in its land and buildings on 1/1/99 is $500 instead of $450. Now the aggregate adjusted basis of T's assets immediately before the ownership change is $1,250 so that the aggregate adjusted basis of T's assets (other than cash) immediately before the ownership change ($1,200) exceeds their aggregate FV ($1,000) by more than 15% (i.e., $200 ÷ $1,000 = 20%). Therefore the BIL rule applies, so any BIL T recognizes during the next five years will be treated as a prechange loss subject to T's Code §382 limitation. Hence, in contrast to Example 1, T may not use the $150 BIL it recognizes in 1999 from the sale of inventory to offset its other income for that year, except to the extent of its Code §382 limitation. Thus, T's 1999 taxable income will be $285, $150 more than in Example 1:

$300	Net income before recognized BIL and NOL carryforward
(15)	Portion of $15 recognized BIL deductible in 1999 under Code §382
$285	T's 1999 taxable income

$335 of T's prechange losses (i.e., $200 NOL + $150 BIL − $15 recognized BIL deducted in 1999) will be deductible after 1999, subject to T's Code §382 limitation.

As Example 2 indicates, when T's BIL exceeds the de minimis threshold and therefore is subject to the Code §382 limitation, Reg. §1.383-1(d)(2) reduces T's postchange income (to the extent of the Code §382 limitation) first by T's recognized BILs and then by carrying forward NOLs recognized before the ownership change. This seems a harsh rule, as it requires deducting later-recognized losses first, thus increasing the likelihood that T's older NOLs will expire unused. For further discussion of the loss ordering rules, see ¶1207.1.4.

The total recognized BIL subject to the Code §382 limitation for any taxable year is limited to T's net unrealized BIL described in paragraph (3)(d) above (including the 15%/$10 million threshold amount), reduced by the recognized BILs for prior taxable years that ended within the five-year period beginning on the ownership change date.

Effective for ownership changes occurring after 12/15/87 depreciation or amortization otherwise allowable with respect to an asset during the five-year BIL recognition period generally is treated as a recognized BIL to the extent attributable to the asset's adjusted basis in excess of its FV on the date of the ownership change.[201] Furthermore, "[a]ny amount which is allowable as a deduction during the [five-year] recognition period (determined without regard to any carryover) but which is attributable to periods before the [ownership] change date shall be treated as a recognized BIL for the taxable year for which it is allowable as a deduction," and T's net unrealized BIL is adjusted accordingly.[202]

¶1208.5 Anti-Abuse Rules

Section II of the 1986 Conference Report (at 194) states that new Code §382 "does not alter the continuing application of section 269, relating to acquisitions made to evade or avoid taxes, as under present law. Similarly, the SRLY and CRCO principles under the [consolidated return] regulations . . . will continue to apply." In addition, Code §382(m) requires Treasury to "prescribe such regulations as may be necessary or appropriate to carry out the purposes" of Code §§382 and 383. Previously discussed examples of such regulations include possible future regulations addressing Goldome-type transactions (see ¶1205.3) and regulations concerning transactions structured to avoid having a person treated as a 5% shareholder "for a principal purpose of circumventing the section 382 limitation" (see ¶1208.1.7.4).

¶1208.6 Code §382 Application When T Has Subsidiaries or Is Acquired from Bigco

In 1999 IRS published final regulations addressing the application of Code §382 to consolidated groups and to "controlled" (i.e., at least 50% related) but non-consolidated subsidiaries (the "1999 Regulations").[203] The 1999 Regulations, which finalize, with modifications, temporary regulations published in 1996, are generally effective for Code §382 testing dates that occur on or after 6/25/99.

After a brief discussion of background and prior law (¶1208.6.1), ¶¶1208.6.2 through 1208.6.6 summarize the long and complex 1999 Regulations, and how they differ from the 1996 regulations. The 1999 Regulations generally apply Code §382 on a consolidated basis to the extent T and its subsidiaries are a "loss group" or a "loss subgroup" with respect to an NOL or NUBIL (see ¶1208.6.2). The 1999 Regulations are relevant whenever there is a Code §382 ownership change of T and, immediately before the ownership change, either (i) T is the parent of a consolidated group that has an NOL or BIL (see ¶1208.6.3), or (ii) T is a consolidated subsidiary of Bigco and T (or a T subsidiary, if any) has an NOL or BIL (see ¶1208.6.4). This section also discusses the application of the 1999 Regulations to net unrealized built-in losses ("NUBILs") (¶1208.6.5), the application of the

---

[201] Code §382(h)(2)(B), as amended by the 1987 Act.

[202] Code §382(h)(6), as retroactively amended by the 1988 Act and the 1989 Act.

[203] Reg. §§1.1502-90 through -99 (T.D. 8824) (consolidated groups); Reg. §§1.382-5 and -8 (T.D. 8825) (controlled groups).

1999 Regulations to controlled, non-consolidated subsidiaries (¶1208.6.6), and certain effective date provisions (¶1208.6.7).

For a discussion of the related 1999 SRLY loss regulations (including the §382 Overlap Rule, which eliminates the application of the SRLY loss limitation in certain circumstances where there is a Code §382 ownership change within six months before or after the SRLY event), see ¶1205.2.4.2(4).

¶1208.6.1   Background and Prior Law

Though Code §382 was enacted in 1986, before 1991 there was virtually no statutory, regulatory, or other guidance concerning the application of Code §382 when T had subsidiaries. In particular, apart from a statement in the 1986 Act legislative history that the SRLY and CRCO rules continued to apply,[204] there was little if any authority on the relationship between Code §382 and the consolidated return regulations. Numerous problems arose in attempting to apply Code §382 when T had subsidiaries, because the rules could have significantly different consequences depending on whether they were applied to T and its subsidiaries on a consolidated basis (i.e., treating T and its subsidiaries as a single entity), on an entity-by-entity basis, or using a hybrid approach.

In 1991 IRS published proposed regulations (CO-132-87 and CO-077-90) addressing the application of Code §382 to consolidated and controlled groups. The proposed regulations, if adopted, generally would have been effective 1/29/91. To eliminate uncertainty regarding whether the final regulations existing at that time or the 1991 proposed regulations (if adopted) applied after 1/29/91, in 1996 IRS replaced the 1991 proposed regulations with substantially identical temporary regulations (the "1996 Temporary Regulations").[205] The 1996 Temporary Regulations were generally effective for Code §382 testing dates occurring on or after 1/1/97 but before 6/25/99 (the effective date of the 1999 Regulations). For transition rules applicable to pre-1/1/97 periods, see ¶1208.6.6.

¶1208.6.2   Consolidated Approach for Loss Group or Loss Subgroup

¶1208.6.2.1   In General

In connection with a Code §382 ownership change of T, to the extent that T and/or one or more of its subsidiaries compose a Code §382 "loss group" (a "Loss Group") or "loss subgroup" (a "Loss Subgroup") with respect to a pre-change NOL or NUBIL, Code §382 applies to the NOL or NUBIL on a consolidated basis, by reference to the applicable Loss Group or Loss Subgroup. Specifically:

---

[204] See ¶1208.5. As discussed in ¶1205.2.4, however, the CRCO rules were generally eliminated in 1996, and the SRLY loss limitation rules were substantially revised in 1996 and scaled back in 1999.

[205] See Reg. §§1.1502-90A through 1.1502-99A, 1.382-5, and 1.382-8 (as the 1999 Regulations redesignated the 1996 Temporary Regulations).

(1)   an ownership change of T (or of the Loss Subgroup's parent, if a T subsidiary), under the rules described in ¶1208.6.3.1, results in an ownership change for the entire Loss Group or Loss Subgroup;

(2)   the Code §382 limitation generally is computed and applied to the applicable NOL or NUBIL on a consolidated basis for the Loss Group or Loss Subgroup as a whole (i.e., by treating the Loss Group or Loss Subgroup as a single corporation for this purpose), rather than on a member-by-member basis (see ¶1208.6.3.2), and

(3)   the continuity of business enterprise requirement applies to the Loss Group or Loss Subgroup on a consolidated basis (see ¶1208.6.3.3).

If a T group member to which an NOL or NUBIL is attributable is not included in a Loss Group or Loss Subgroup with respect to the NOL or NUBIL (a "Separate Loss Member"), Code §382 applies to the NOL or NUBIL on a separate company basis, solely by reference to the Separate Loss Member.

¶1208.6.2.2   *Identifying Loss Groups, Loss Subgroups, and Separate Loss Members*

If T is the common parent of a consolidated group and is subject to an ownership change in which T remains the parent of the group (e.g., P acquires more than 50% but less than 80% of T's stock, or T is acquired by a non-corporate purchaser), T and all of its subsidiaries are generally a Loss Group with respect to a pre-change NOL if the T group member (or members) that incurred the NOL either (i) incurred the NOL at least five years after joining T's group, or (ii) incurred the NOL within such five year period provided the NOL did not arise from a NUBIL that existed when the member(s) joined T's group.[206]

If T and its subsidiaries are subject to an ownership change in which T becomes a member of a different consolidated group (e.g., T is acquired from and thus ceases to be consolidated with Bigco, and/or T is acquired by and becomes a member of P's consolidated group), two or more members of T's former consolidated group are generally a Loss Subgroup with respect to a pre-change NOL if both of the following requirements are satisfied:

(1)   The member (or members) that incurred the NOL either (i) incurred it at least five years after joining T's group (or Bigco's, as the case may be) or (ii) incurred it within such five year period but the NOL did not arise from a NUBIL that existed when the member(s) joined T's (or Bigco's) group.

(2)   After they become members of the new (P) group, either (i) they bear an 80-80 relationship to each other through the Loss Subgroup's parent (the "subgroup parent requirement"), or (ii) if P acquires T in a taxable year

---

[206] Reg. §1.1502-91(c)(1). See Reg. §1.1502-91(d)(1). T and its subsidiaries have a "net unrealized built-in loss," or NUBIL, if the aggregate adjusted basis of the T group's assets exceeds their aggregate FV by more than the lesser of (1) 15% of their aggregate FV or (2) $10 million (generally effective for ownership changes after 10/2/89 as described in ¶1208.4(3)(d) and adjusted by the 1999 Regulations.

for which the due date of the consolidated return (without extensions) is after 6/25/99, P elects to treat the subgroup parent requirement as satisfied (the "deemed subgroup parent election").[207]

EXAMPLE 1

Bigco owns all of the stock of T1 and 60% of the stock of T2. T1 owns the remaining 40% of the stock of T2. On 1/1/99, Bigco sells all of its T1 stock and its 60% direct stock interest in T2 to P. Both the P group and the Bigco group have calendar taxable years.

After P acquires T1 and T2, neither T1 nor T2 is an 80-80 subsidiary of the other (i.e., T1 owns only 40% of T2's stock, and T2 owns none of T1's stock). Therefore, they are not a Loss Subgroup under clause (2)(i) above. However, because P acquired T in a tax year (1999) for which the original due date of the return (3/15/00) is after 6/25/99, P can elect to treat T1 and T2 as satisfying the subgroup parent requirement and hence as a Loss Subgroup. This election was added by the 1999 Regulations and not available under the 1996 Temporary Regulations.[208] Accordingly, if the above transaction occurred under prior law (or if P failed to make the deemed subgroup parent election), T1 and T2 would not be a Loss Subgroup.

For the determination of Loss Groups and Loss Subgroups with respect to NUBILs, see ¶1208.6.5.

A Separate Loss Member is a T subsidiary to which an NOL or NUBIL is attributable that is not included in a Loss Group or Loss Subgroup with respect to the NOL or NUBIL. This can occur when a member already has an NOL upon joining T's (or Bigco's) consolidated group, or when a member has a NUBIL and has been affiliated with T's (or Bigco's) group less than five years before P acquires T. Generally the ownership change rules, the Code §382 limitation rules, and the continuity of business enterprise requirement apply on a stand-alone basis to a Separate Loss Member with respect to its separate NOL or NUBIL, as further discussed in ¶¶1208.6.3 and 1208.6.5.[209] However, under the so-called "fold-in" rule, a Separate Loss Member might later become included in a Loss Group or Loss Subgroup by reason of the passage of time or an ownership change (see ¶1208.6.3.4).

T and its subsidiaries will not be treated as a Loss Group or Loss Subgroup if any one of them is "formed, acquired, or availed of with a principal purpose" of tax avoidance under Code §382.[210] This is a harsher standard than Code §269, which can deny tax benefits only when "the principal purpose" of an acquisition is tax avoidance (see ¶1203.2.2).

---

[207] Reg. §§1.1502-91(d)(1), 1.1502-91(d)(4), 1.1502-99(b)(1) (effective date). See ¶1205.2.4.2(4).
[208] Compare Reg. §1.1502-91(d) with Reg. §1.1502-91A(d).
[209] See Reg. §1.1502-94.
[210] Reg. §1.1502-91(d)(5).

¶1208.6.3   P Acquires T When T Is Consolidated Group Parent

This section reviews the application of Code §382 when, immediately before P acquires T, T is the parent of a consolidated group that has an NOL or NUBIL. The manner in which Code §382 applies depends on the extent to which T and/or any T subsidiaries constitute a Loss Group, a Loss Subgroup or a Separate Loss Member with respect to the T group's pre-change NOL or NUBIL or any portion thereof (see generally ¶1208.6.2). For special NUBIL considerations, see ¶1208.6.5.

¶1208.6.3.1   Determining Ownership Change

If T and all of its consolidated subsidiaries are a Loss Group or Loss Subgroup with respect to an NOL or NUBIL, the T group will have an ownership change if either of two methods for determining ownership changes signals an ownership change of T. The two methods are the "parent change method" and the "supplemental method."

Under the "parent change method," the T consolidated group has an ownership change if T itself has an ownership change under the basic rules described in ¶1208.1.[211]

EXAMPLE 1

Individual A has always owned 100% of T's stock. S has always been a 100% subsidiary of T and has always been included in T's consolidated return, and the T-S group has an NOL. Unrelated corporation P purchases from A 51% of T's stock, resulting in an ownership change of T. The T-S group is a Loss Subgroup with respect to the pre-change NOL (see ¶1208.6.2.2). Therefore, under the parent change method there has been an ownership change of the T-S Loss Subgroup.

Under the "supplemental method," if a 5% shareholder of T increases its percentage of stock ownership both in T and in any T subsidiary ("S"), the parent change method is applied by treating T as having issued to such 5% shareholder new T stock equal in FV to the FV of the S stock represented by the percentage increase in the 5% shareholder's ownership of S (determined on a separate entity basis).[212] For this purpose, effective for Code §382 testing dates on or after 6/25/99, a 5% shareholder of T (e.g., P) is treated as increasing its ownership interest in S's stock to the extent that another person ("B") increases its percentage ownership of S's stock "pursuant to a plan or arrangement under which the 5% shareholder

---

[211] Reg. §1.1502-92(b).
[212] Reg. §1.1502-92(c).

increases its percentage ownership interest in [T]."[213] However, also effective for Code §382 testing dates on or after 6/25/99, a 5% shareholder's (or B's) increase in S stock ownership is taken into account under the supplemental method only if either (i) T has actual knowledge of the increase in the 5% shareholder's ownership interest in S (or has actual knowledge of the plan or arrangement under which B increases its interest in S) before the date T's tax return is filed for the year that includes the date of the increase, or (ii) at any time during the testing period the 5% shareholder of T is also a 5% shareholder of S.[214] Thus, under the supplemental method, an ownership change of the T consolidated group can result even though less than 50% of the stock of T itself has changed hands during the three-year testing period.

EXAMPLE 2

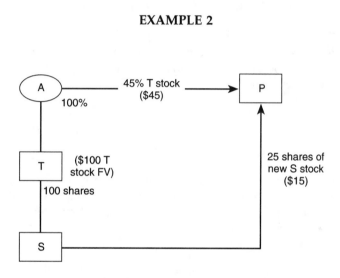

Individual A has always owned 100% of T's stock. S has always been a 100% subsidiary of T and has always been included in T's consolidated return. The T-S group has an NOL. On a date when the FV of T's stock is $100 and T owns 100 S common shares, unrelated corporation P purchases (1) 45% of T's stock from A for $45 and (2) 25 newly issued S common shares (i.e., 20% of the total S stock now outstanding (25 shares ÷ 125 shares)) for $15.

Only 45% of T's stock has been transferred, so under the basic ownership change rules T has no ownership change. Therefore, in contrast to Example

---

[213] Reg. §1.1502-92(c)(3). This rule covers a plan under which P purchases less than 50% of T's stock and then causes a public offering of S. See Reg. §1.1502-92(c)(5) example (2). For testing dates before 6/25/99, the 1996 Temporary Regulations impose a harsher rule that takes into account under the supplemental method any increase in S stock ownership by any other person acting "pursuant to a plan or arrangement" with any 5% shareholder of T (even if not the 5% shareholder increasing its interest in T). See Reg. §1.1502-92A(c)(1).

[214] Reg. §1.1502-92(c)(2)(iii). For pre-6/25/99 testing dates, there is no similar exception to the "plan or arrangement" rule under the 1996 Temporary Regulations (described in the preceding footnote).

1, under the parent change method there is no ownership change of the T-S group. Under the supplemental method, however, the parent change method is reapplied by assuming that, in addition to purchasing actual T stock from A, P purchased newly issued T stock with a $15 FV (i.e., the FV of the S stock that P purchased). Hence, P is deemed to have acquired 52.1% of T's stock, determined as follows (assuming that T is deemed to have outstanding after the ownership change $100 FV of actual stock plus $15 FV of stock deemed newly issued under the supplemental method):

% of T stock actually purchased by P ($45/$115)	39.1%
% of T stock deemed purchased by P ($15/$115)	13.0%
Total T stock deemed purchased by P	52.1%

Since P is deemed to have acquired more than 50% of T's stock, an ownership change of the T-S group (not merely an ownership change of S) results under the supplemental method.

EXAMPLE 3

Same as Example 2, except that (1) P purchases 45% of T's stock from A for $45, and (2) unrelated individual B purchases for $15 25 shares of newly issued S stock representing 20% of the total S stock thereafter outstanding (i.e., 25 shares ÷ 125 shares).

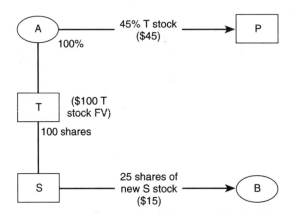

If B purchased the S stock "pursuant to a plan or arrangement" with P and (if the purchase is on or after 6/25/99) T has actual knowledge of the plan or arrangement before filing its tax return for the year that includes the issuance of S stock to B, the result is the same as in Example 2 (i.e., an ownership change of the T-S group under the supplemental method) because the S stock acquired by B is treated as a deemed issuance of new T stock to P as described in Example 2. If B was not acting pursuant to a plan or arrangement with P, no ownership change of the T-S group results because (1) there is no ownership change of T under the parent change method and (2) the supplemental method does not apply.

If two or more (but fewer than all) members of T's consolidated group are a Loss Subgroup with respect to all or part of T's pre-change NOL or NUBIL (determined as described in ¶1208.6.2), the ownership change rules described above apply separately to each Loss Subgroup. For each Loss Subgroup, an ownership change of the subgroup's parent (under either the parent change method or the supplemental method) results in an ownership change of the entire subgroup.[215]

If a T group member is a Separate Loss Member with respect to a pre-change NOL or NUBIL (see ¶1208.6.2), the ownership change rules apply separately to that entity.[216] The "supplemental method" described above does not apply in determining whether a Separate Loss Member has an ownership change, because the supplemental method applies only in connection with an NOL or NUBIL for which there is a Loss Group or a Loss Subgroup.[217]

There are special rules for testing dates, testing period, and information statements required to be filed by T.[218]

¶1208.6.3.2 Computing Annual Code §382 Limitation

If T and all of its consolidated subsidiaries are a Loss Group or Loss Subgroup with respect to an NOL or NUBIL at the time of an ownership change, the Code §382 limitation with respect to the NOL or NUBIL is computed on an aggregate basis rather than on a member-by-member basis. Specifically, the consolidated Code §382 limitation is generally equal to the aggregate value of the T consolidated group multiplied by the applicable long-term tax-exempt rate, subject to the adjustments described in ¶1208.2 (i.e., (1) reduction of stock FV by the amount of certain redemptions, other corporate contractions, capital contributions, and non-business assets, and (2) increase of Code §382 limitation by any unused limitation carryover, recognized BIG, and Code §338 election gain).[219] For this purpose, the value of the T consolidated group is equal to the sum of (1) the FV of T's stock (including any Code §1504(a)(4) Straight Preferred stock not taken

---

[215] Reg. §1.1502-92.

[216] Reg. §1.1502-94(b).

[217] See Reg. §1.1502-92(c)(2)(i), -92(c)(3)(iii).

[218] See Reg. §1.1502-92 (generally effective for testing dates on or after 6/25/99); Reg. §1.1502-92A (prior law).

[219] Reg. §1.1502-93(a).

into account in determining whether there is an ownership change—see ¶1208.1.1) plus (2) the FV of any T group member's stock (including any Straight Preferred stock) not directly or indirectly owned by other T group members.[220]

Subject to the consolidated Code §382 limitation, future income of the entire T Loss Group or Loss Subgroup may be offset by the applicable NOL or recognized BILs, even if the NOL or NUBIL is attributable to members of T's group other than those generating such income. Moreover, subject to the consolidated Code §382 limitation, if the transaction results in T and its subsidiaries joining P's consolidated group, both the 1999 Regulations and the 1996 Temporary Regulations facially permit T's consolidated NOL or recognized BILs to offset future income of P's entire consolidated group, even though the Code §382 limitation is computed solely by reference to T's Loss Group or Loss Subgroup and the NOL or NUBIL is attributable solely to T and its subsidiaries.[221] However, at least in the case of pre-1999 tax years, because the T group's NOL or NUBIL arose before T joined P's consolidated group, as a practical matter the SRLY rules generally will prohibit the use of the T group's NOL or BILs to offset the future income of P or any other corporation not included in T's Loss Group or Loss Subgroup (see ¶1205.2.4.2). More specifically, if corporation P acquires T in a transaction that results in T and its subsidiaries joining P's consolidated group and also causes a Code §382 ownership change of T, then:

(1)   For tax years of the P group for which the due date (without extensions) of P's consolidated return is after 6/25/99 (i.e., 1999 and thereafter if P is a calendar year corporation), the pre-acquisition NOLs and NUBILs of the former T group generally do not become (or, if P acquired T in an earlier tax year, generally will cease to be) SRLY NOLs and SRLY NUBILs as a result of the acquisition (under the "§382 Overlap Rule" discussed in ¶1205.2.4.2(4)). To the extent the §382 Overlap Rule applies, the former T group's NOLs and recognized BILs are usable (subject to the applicable Code §382 limitation) against the future income of all P group members.

(2)   If the acquisition occurs on or after 1/1/97 (or after 1/28/91, if P elected to apply retroactively the 1996 SRLY regulations as described in ¶1205.2.4.2(2)), subject to the possible application of the §382 Overlap Rule in 1999 and thereafter as described in (1) above, the combined effect of

---

[220] Reg. §1.1502-93(b). A T group member is considered to "indirectly" own stock of another member through a non-member only if the member owns 5% or more of the non-member's stock.

[221] See Reg. §1.1502-91(a) and Reg. §1.1502-91A(a) ("Following an ownership change of a loss group (or a loss subgroup) . . . , the amount of *consolidated taxable income* for any post-change year which may be offset by pre-change consolidated attributes (or pre-change subgroup attributes) shall not exceed the consolidated section 382 limitation (or subgroup section 382 limitation) for such year") (emphasis added). Cf. United Dominion Industries, Inc. v. United States, 532 U.S. 822, 2001-1 U.S.T.C. ¶50,340 (2001), (in determining how a consolidated group calculates its "specified liability loss" for a year (which is eligible for a 10-year carryback under Section 172(b)(1)(C)) Code §172(f)'s limitation of the carryback amount to the taxpayer's "net operating loss" for the year refers to the consolidated NOL of the group, not the NOL of the separate member that generated the specified liability, stressing that "the Code and regulations governing affiliated groups of corporations filing consolidated returns provide only one definition of NOL: 'consolidated' NOL," citing Reg. §1.1502-21(e)'s predecessor.

the Code §382 and SRLY regulations is generally that, subject to the Code §382 limitation, the T group's consolidated NOL and recognized BILs are usable against the future income of all of the T group's members but not of P or P's other affiliates.

(3) If the acquisition occurred before 1/1/97 (or before 1/29/91, if P elected to apply retroactively the 1996 SRLY regulations as described in ¶1205.2.4.2(2)), subject to the possible application of the §382 Overlap Rule in 1999 and thereafter, generally SRLY "fragmentation" applies (i.e., the portion of the NOL or recognized BILs attributable to each member of T's Loss Group or Loss Subgroup are usable, subject to the Code §382 limitation, only against the future income of that member, not against the future income of other T group members, P, or any other corporation).

EXAMPLE 4

Individual A has always owned all of T's stock. T formed S in 1997 and has always filed consolidated returns with S. In 1999 the T-S group incurs a $40 NOL, which is attributable solely to S and is carried forward to 2000. P purchases all of T's stock on 1/1/00, resulting in an ownership change for the T-S group. Assume that on 1/1/00 the long-term tax-exempt rate is 5% and the FVs of T's and S's stock are as follows:

	T Consolidated	T Without S	S
Pre-acquisition NOL	$ 40	$ 0	$ 40
Stock FV	500	400	100

T and S are a Loss Subgroup with respect to the $40 NOL because the NOL did not arise from a NUBIL that existed when S joined T's group (see ¶1208.6.2.2). Therefore, the Code §382 limitation with respect to the NOL is computed on an aggregate basis for T and S. Specifically, the Code §382 limitation is $25 (i.e., T's $500 stock FV on 1/1/00 multiplied by the 5% long-term tax-exempt rate in effect on that date). Therefore, after the ownership change, the amount of future income that may be offset by the T group's $40 NOL is limited to $25 per year. Subject to this limitation, the NOL may offset future income of both T and S, even though the NOL is attributable solely to S. In addition, because there is a Code §382 ownership change when T and S join P's consolidated group on 1/1/00, the §382 Overlap Rule applies, so that the T-S NOL does not become a SRLY NOL (see ¶1205.2.4.2(4)). Therefore, subject to the Code §382 limitation, the NOL may also offset future income of P and P's other affiliates.

For additional examples of the relationship between Code §382 and the SRLY NOL limitation rules, see ¶1205.2.4.2.

EXAMPLE 5

Individual A has always owned 100% of T's stock. T has always owned 90% of S's outstanding common stock and included S in its consolidated return. The remaining 10% of S's common stock and a class of Code §1504(a)(4) Straight Preferred stock of S (which is disregarded in determining whether an ownership change has occurred) are owned by unrelated individual B. P purchases from A all of T's stock, resulting in an ownership change of the T-S group. At that time, T's and S's stock FVs are as follows:

		S stock		
Stock	*T stock*	*Owned by T*	*Owned by B*	*Total*
T common	$100			$100
S common		$36	$ 4	40
S preferred	___	___	$50	50
Total	$100	$36	$54	$190

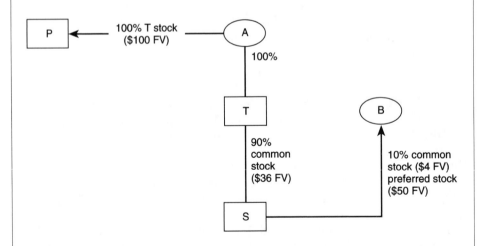

The FV of the T group for purposes of computing the Code §382 limitation is $154, equal to the sum of (1) the FV of T's stock ($100) plus (2) the FV of all S stock (including Straight Preferred stock) not owned by T (i.e., the S common stock ($4) and S preferred stock ($50) owned by B).

If two or more (but fewer than all) members of T's consolidated group compose a Loss Subgroup with respect to all or part of T's pre-change NOL or NUBIL (determined as described in ¶1208.6.2), a separate Code §382 limitation is computed and applied for each subgroup with respect to the applicable NOL or NUBIL, based on the above principles. Within each Loss Subgroup, the limitation is computed and applied on an aggregate basis for the subgroup as a whole, rather than on member-by-member basis.[222]

If a T group member is a Separate Loss Member with respect to an NOL or NUBIL attributable to it, the Code §382 limitation is computed on a separate entity basis for that member, taking into account its stock FV alone and otherwise based on the rules described above. The amount of income for a post-change year that may be offset by the Separate Loss Member's NOL or recognized BIL may not exceed the Code §382 limitation as separately determined.[223]

In the case of an ownership change of a Loss Subgroup or Separate Loss Member, subject to the resulting Code §382 limitation, both the 1999 Regulations and the 1996 Temporary Regulations facially permit the Loss Subgroup's (or Separate Loss Member's) NOL or recognized BIL to offset post-change income of the entire consolidated group (T's or P's, as the case may be), even though the Code §382 limitation is computed solely by reference to the Loss Subgroup (or Separate Loss Member) and the NOL or NUBIL is attributable to that subgroup (or member).[224] However, the Loss Subgroup's (or Separate Loss Member's) NOL or NUBIL will have arisen before the subgroup (or member) joined T's consolidated group. Therefore, except to the extent the §382 Overlap Rule applies, under the SRLY rules a Loss Subgroup's (or Separate Loss Member's) NOL or recognized BILs generally will be available to offset only that subgroup's (or member's) future income, not the future income of other consolidated group members (see ¶1205.2.4.2).

EXAMPLE 6

This example is based on Example 4 except that S incurred the $40 NOL before becoming a member of T's consolidated group. Specifically, individual A has always owned 100% of T's stock. S's stock has always been owned 60% by T and 40% by unrelated individual B. On 1/1/99, when S has a $40 NOL, T purchases B's 40% interest in S, so S becomes a 100% T subsidiary. The T-S group files a consolidated return thereafter, reporting no income or loss for 1999 and carrying forward the NOL to 1999 and 2000. P purchases

---

[222] Reg. §1.1502-93.

[223] Reg. §1.1502-94.

[224] See Reg. §§1.1502-91(a) and 1.1502-91A(a) (Loss Subgroups); Reg. §1.1502-94(b) (in the case of a Separate Loss Member, the separately applied Code §382 limitation limits "the amount of *consolidated taxable income*" by the Separate Loss Member's NOL and recognized BILs) (emphasis added).

all of T's stock 1/1/00. Assume that on 1/1/00 the long-term tax-exempt rate is 5% and the FVs of T's and S's stock are as follows:

	T (Consolidated)	T (Without S)	S
Pre-1/1/00 NOL	$ 40	$ 0	$ 40
Stock FV	500	400	100

S is a Separate Loss Member with respect to its $40 NOL because S incurred the NOL before joining T's group (and because separate tracking of the NOL has not ceased—see ¶1208.6.3.4). Therefore, the ownership change and Code §382 limitation rules apply separately to S upon P's 1/1/00 purchase of T's stock. The purchase results in an ownership change of S, as in Example 4. However, in contrast to that example, the Code §382 limitation for the NOL is based on S's stock FV alone ($100), not T's stock FV, so the annual Code §382 limitation is only $5 (5% of $100). Subject to this limitation, the Code §382 regulations facially permit S's NOL to offset post-1/1/00 income of P's entire consolidated group. However, S incurred its NOL before joining T's group, and there was not a Code §382 ownership change of S at the time, or within six months before or after, S joined T's consolidated group on 1/1/99. Therefore, the §382 Overlap Rule does not apply to T's 1/1/99 acquisition of S, and as a result S's pre-1/1/99 $40 NOL is a SRLY NOL which is available to offset only S's post-1/1/99 income, not the future income of any other corporation.

The composition of the T group's NOL and NUBIL may be such that different Loss Subgroups and/or Separate Loss Members exist with respect to different components of the NOL or NUBIL.

EXAMPLE 7

Same as Example 6, except that in addition to the $40 NOL incurred by S before joining T's group, the T-S group incurs a $50 NOL during 1999 and carries forward both the 1998 and 1999 NOLs to 2000.

	T (Consolidated)	T (Without S)	S
Pre-1/1/00 NOL	$ 90	$ 50	$ 40
Stock FV	500	400	100

As in Example 6, S is a Separate Loss Member with respect to its $40 1998 NOL because S incurred the NOL before joining T's group. Therefore, upon P's 1/1/00 purchase of T's stock, the ownership change and Code §382 limitation rules apply separately to S with respect to this $40 NOL. Thus, as in Example 6, the purchase results in an ownership change of S, and the Code §382 limitation for this $40 NOL is based on S's stock FV alone ($100), not T's stock FV, and results in an annual Code §382 limitation of $5 (5% of $100). Moreover, since S incurred its NOL before joining T's group and the §382 Overlap Rule did not apply, under the SRLY rules S's NOL is available to offset only S's future income, not the future income of any other corporation.

In contrast, T and S are a Loss Subgroup with respect to T's $50 1999 NOL, since the NOL was incurred after T and S began filing consolidated returns. Therefore, the Code §382 limitation with respect to T's 1999 NOL is computed on an aggregate basis for T and S. The Code §382 limitation is $25 (i.e., T's $500 stock FV on 1/1/00 multiplied by the 5% long-term tax-exempt bond rate in effect on that date). Therefore, after the ownership change, the amount of future income that may be offset by T's $50 1999 NOL is $25 per year. Subject to this limitation, the NOL may offset future income of both T and S even though the NOL is attributable solely to S. In addition, because there is a Code §382 ownership change when T and S join P's consolidated group on 1/1/00, the §382 Overlap Rule applies, so that the $50 1999 T-S NOL does not become a SRLY NOL (see ¶1205.2.4.2(4)). Therefore, subject to the Code §382 limitation, this $50 NOL may also offset future income of P and P's other affiliates.

For additional examples of the relationship between Code §382 and the SRLY NOL limitation rules, see ¶1205.2.4.2.

¶1208.6.3.3   *Continuity of Business Enterprise Requirement*

A Loss Group or a Loss Subgroup "is treated as a single entity" in determining whether it satisfies the two-year Code §382 continuity of business enterprise requirement (i.e., the requirement that, if not satisfied, will result in termination of the relevant NOL—see ¶1208.3).[225] This is illustrated by the following regulatory example:[226]

EXAMPLE 8

T owns all the stock of two subsidiaries, S1 and S2. The T group has an ownership change at a time when it has a consolidated NOL attributable

---

[225] Reg. §1.1502-93(d)(1).
[226] See Reg. §1.1502-93(d)(2).

solely to S2. Assume that T, S1 and S2 are a Loss Group with respect to the NOL. Each of T, S1 and S2 has conducted historically a separate line of business, each "approximately equal" in value to the others. One year after the ownership change, T discontinues its own separate business and the business of S2. The separate business of S1 is continued for the remainder of the required two-year continuity period. The continuity of business enterprise requirement is met even though the separate businesses of T and S2 are discontinued.

Presumably the continuity of business enterprise requirement is applied on a stand-alone basis in the case of a Separate Loss Member.

EXAMPLE 9

Individual A has always owned 100% of T's stock. S1 has always been a 100% subsidiary of T and has always been included in T's consolidated return. S2 has always been owned 75% by T and 25% by unrelated individual B. On 1/1 year 1, when S2 had an NOL, T purchased B's 25% minority interest in S2, so S2 became a 100% subsidiary of T and joined T's consolidated group. On 1/1 year 2, when S2 still has its unused 7/1 year 1 NOL, unrelated P purchases all of T's stock from A. S2 incurred its NOL before joining the T-S1 group, and the NOL is still being "separately tracked" on 1/1 year 2 (see ¶1208.6.3.4). Therefore, S2 is a Separate Loss Member with respect to this NOL.

Each of T, S1, and S2 has conducted historically a separate line of business, and the three businesses are approximately equal in value. On 1/1 year 3, one year after the ownership change, T discontinues its own separate business and the separate business of S2. The separate business of S1 continues during the remainder of the required two-year continuity period. Since S2 is a Separate Loss Member with respect to its NOL, presumably the continuity of business enterprise requirement with respect to that NOL is applied to S2 on a stand-alone basis. Hence, in contrast to the result in Example 8, it appears that the termination of S2's separate business violates the business continuity requirement in this example, resulting in extinguishment of S2's NOL.[227]

EXAMPLE 10

Same as Example 9 except that in addition to S2's NOL, at the time of the 1/1 year 2 ownership change the T group has a consolidated NOL

---

[227] The example given in the 1999 Regulations (which also appears in the 1996 Temporary Regulations), upon which Example 8 is based, does not specify that the T-S1-S2 group in Example 8

attributable to T, with respect to which T, S1, and S2 are a Loss Group. The termination of T's and S2's separate businesses apparently terminates the pre-affiliation NOL solely attributable to S2, for the reasons given in Example 9. However, since T, S1, and S2 are a Loss Group with respect to the NOL attributable to T, continuing S1's business should satisfy the business continuity requirement with respect to that NOL, as in Example 8.

¶1208.6.3.4   *Fold-In Rule: End of Separate Tracking of NOL or NUBIL*

If a T group member is a Separate Loss Member (or if two or more, but not all, T group members are a Loss Subgroup) with respect to an NOL or NUBIL, and if the Separate Loss Member (or Loss Subgroup) either (1) has a Code §382 ownership change within six months before, on, or at any time after becoming a member of T's (or Bigco's) group or (2) has no ownership change for a period of five consecutive years after joining T's (or Bigco's) group, then "separate tracking" of the relevant NOL or NUBIL ceases.[228] That is, after the ownership change date or the end of the five-consecutive-year period, whichever first occurs, the rules concerning Code §382 ownership change, annual limitation, and business continuity generally will apply to the relevant NOL or NUBIL by reference to T's (or Bigco's) Loss Group rather than by reference to the Separate Loss Member (or the Loss Subgroup) to which the NOL or NUBIL is attributable.[229]

Cessation of separate tracking does not eradicate the effect of prior ownership changes (or SRLY events) with respect to the relevant NOL or NUBIL.[230] For example, if separate tracking of S's NOL ceases because S has an ownership change upon joining T's consolidated group, the annual Code §382 limitation (and any SRLY limitation) arising from that ownership change generally continues to apply after a subsequent ownership change, as illustrated in Example 11 below.

EXAMPLE 11

Same as Example 6, except that T purchased B's 40% minority interest in S on 12/1/94 (i.e., five years and one month before P acquires T on 1/1/00), at which time S had the $40 NOL. S's NOL ceases to be separately tracked on 12/1/99 because that day is the end of a five-year period after S joined T's group during which S did not have an ownership change. Therefore,

---

is a Loss Group or Loss Subgroup with respect to the NOL. See Reg. §1.1502-93(d)(2). This would appear a necessary assumption, however, given the rule that in determining business continuity a Loss Group or Loss Subgroup is treated as one corporation.

[228] Reg. §1.1502-96(a). The test described in clause (1) generally applies to any testing date on or after 6/25/99. Reg. §1.1502-99(a). The 1996 Temporary Regulations had a somewhat different test based on "an ownership change . . . in connection with, or after," joining T's (or Bigco's) group. Reg. §1.1502-96A(a).

[229] See Reg. §1.1502-96(a).

[230] See Reg. §1.1502-96(c).

when P acquires T on 1/1/00, T and S will be a Loss Subgroup with respect to the $40 NOL, so that the Code §382 limitation with respect to the NOL is computed on an aggregate basis for T and S rather than solely by reference to S's stock FV. The resulting annual limitation is $25 (i.e., T's $500 stock FV on 1/1/00 multiplied by the 5% long-term tax-exempt rate, as in Example 4) rather than only $5 (as in Example 6).

However, S's NOL is a SRLY NOL as a result of the 12/1/94 transaction. In contrast to Example 4 (in which the NOL may offset post-1/1/00 income of both T and S), under the SRLY rules S's $40 NOL may offset only post-12/1/94 income of S, not income of P, T, or any other corporation. In addition, any other pre-1/1/00 NOLs of the T-S group will be subject to the Code §382 limitation calculated above and also will become SRLY NOLs by reason of P's 1/1/00 purchase of T. This is because the §382 Overlap Rule does not apply to P's 1/1/00 purchase, since T and S are a Loss Subgroup for Code §382 purposes but are not a SRLY subgroup (see ¶1205.2.4.2(4), Example 13).

EXAMPLE 12

Same as Example 6, except that on 1/1/99, when S has a $40 NOL, T purchases from unrelated individual B 100% (rather than only 40%) of S's stock. Assume that on 1/1/99 S's stock FV is $200 and that the long-term tax-exempt rate is 5%. As in the earlier example, P purchases all of T's stock on 1/1/00, when the long-term tax-exempt rate is also 5%.

	T (Consolidated)	T (Without S)	S
Pre-1/1/00 NOL	$ 40	$ 0	$ 40
1/1/00 stock FV	500	400	100
1/1/99 stock FV	—	—	200

In contrast to Example 6, here there is an ownership change of S on 1/1/99 because T purchases 100%, rather than only 40%, of S's stock. As a result, S's $40 1/1/99 NOL is subject to an annual Code §382 limitation of $10 (i.e., S's $200 1/1/99 stock FV multiplied by the 5% long-term tax-exempt rate) with respect to post-1/1/99 income. However, under the §382 Overlap Rule, T's 1/1/99 purchase of S generally does not cause S's NOL to become a SRLY NOL (see ¶1205.2.4.2(4)).

Because S had an ownership change upon joining T's group, for purposes of future ownership changes separate tracking of S's NOL ceases. Thus, when P purchases T's stock on 1/1/00, the rules concerning ownership change, Code §382 limitation, and continuity of business enterprise apply on a consolidated basis by treating T and S as a Loss Subgroup with respect to the $40 NOL. (This is in contrast to Example 6, in which S, as a Separate Loss Member on 1/1/00, is treated on a stand-alone basis with respect to the 1/1/00 ownership change.) Therefore, the Code §382 limitation with respect to the 1/1/00 ownership change is $25 (i.e., T's $500 stock FV multiplied by the 5% long-term tax-exempt rate), as in Example 4.

However, S's $40 NOL has already been subject to a lesser ($10) Code §382 limitation as a result of its 1/1/99 ownership change, and this limitation remains in effect after 1/1/00.

The net result under these facts is that the Code §382 limitation applicable to S's $40 NOL after 1/1/00 ($10) is higher than in Example 6 (in which the 1/1/00 limitation is only $5 because it is computed on a stand-alone basis for S on 1/1/00, after S's stock FV has declined from $200 to $100) but lower than in Example 4 (in which the annual limitation after 1/1/00 is $25 because there was no prior ownership change of S and S was never a Separate Loss Member).

¶1208.6.4 P Acquires T (with or without Subsidiaries) from Bigco

This section concerns the application of Code §382 when, immediately before P acquires T, T is a 100% subsidiary of Bigco. The rules described in ¶¶1208.6.4.2 through 1208.6.4.4 below are relevant whether or not T has subsidiaries.

¶1208.6.4.1   In General

The same Code §382 principles generally apply to P's acquisition of T whether T is the parent of a consolidated group (as in ¶1208.6.3 above) or a subsidiary of Bigco. In particular, the rules previously discussed in connection with an ownership change of the T consolidated group, concerning ownership change determinations (¶1208.6.3.1), the Code §382 limitation amount (¶1208.6.3.2) and the continuity of business enterprise requirement (¶1208.6.3.3), apply in a comparable manner when P acquires T and its subsidiaries from Bigco, as do the NUBIL considerations discussed in ¶1208.6.5.

Whether or not T has subsidiaries, however, several new issues arise when P purchases T's stock from Bigco and an ownership change of T results. These concern the mandatory or elective apportionment to departing T and its subsidiaries (if any) of all or a portion of the Bigco group's (1) consolidated NOL and NUBIL (see ¶1208.6.4.2), (2) consolidated Code §382 limitation arising from a prior ownership change of the Bigco group (see ¶1208.6.4.3), and (3) consolidated NUBIG (see ¶1208.6.4.4).

¶1208.6.4.2   *Mandatory Apportionment of Bigco NOL and NUBIL*

When P acquires T (with or without subsidiaries) from the Bigco group, the Bigco group's consolidated NOL must be apportioned, for Code §382 and other purposes, between T and its subsidiaries, on the one hand, and Bigco and its retained subsidiaries, on the other, based on a regulatory formula.[231]

Similarly, effective for Code §382 testing dates (or if T ceases to be a member of the Bigco group) on or after 6/25/99, any consolidated NUBIL of the Bigco group must be apportioned, for Code §382 and other purposes, between T and its subsidiaries, on the one hand, and Bigco and its retained subsidiaries, on the other, based on a regulatory formula.[232] Under prior law, no portion of Bigco's NUBIL was allocated to departing group members.

¶1208.6.4.3   *Elective Apportionment of Code §382 Limitation from T*
                   Prior Ownership Change

Assume that P acquires T (with or without subsidiaries) from the Bigco consolidated group and that the Bigco group had a Code §382 ownership change before P acquired T (the "prior ownership change"). Upon T's departure from the Bigco group, Bigco and T may jointly elect to apportion to T and its subsidiaries part or all of Bigco's consolidated Code §382 limitation arising from the prior ownership change.[233] If no elective apportionment is made, T's share of the Code §382 limitation with respect to the prior ownership change is zero.[234]

EXAMPLE 1

Bigco owns all of T's stock. The Bigco group has a $200 consolidated NOL arising in year 1 that is carried over to year 2. On 1/1 year 2 the Bigco group has an ownership change. Assume that the 1/1 year 2 ownership change results in a $10 consolidated Code §382 limitation applicable to Bigco's $200 pre-1/1 year 2 NOL. During year 2 the Bigco group has no net income or loss. On 1/1 year 3 P buys all of T's stock from Bigco. Assume that, under applicable apportionment rules, T is allocated $90 of Bigco's consolidated NOL as of 1/1 year 3.[235] Upon P's 1/1 year 3 acquisition of T, Bigco and T do not elect to allocate to T any portion of the Bigco group's $10 Code §382 limitation arising from the 1/1 year 2 ownership change.

---

[231] See Reg. §1.1502-21(b).

[232] Reg. §1.1502-95(e), -99(a). The mandatory NUBIL allocation rule also applies if (i) T ceases to be a member of the Bigco group before 6/25/99 in a tax year for which the due date of the tax return (without extensions) is after 6/25/99, and (ii) Bigco and T timely elect to allocate some or all of the Bigco group's NUBIG to T and its subsidiaries (as described in ¶1208.6.3.4). Reg. §1.1502-99(b)(5).

[233] Reg. §1.1502-95(c).

[234] *Id.*

[235] See Reg. §1.1502-21(b).

Because the parties did not allocate to T any part of Bigco's 1/1 year 2 consolidated Code §382 limitation, T's Code §382 limitation with respect to its $90 NOL on 1/1 year 3 essentially will be zero, regardless of T's FV on 1/1 year 3. The reason is that T's $90 NOL has been subject to two ownership changes. Therefore, it is subject to two Code §382 limitations—one computed on 1/1 year 3 (based on T's FV at that time), and one equal to T's allocable share ($0) of the Bigco group's $10 Code §382 limitation computed on 1/1 year 2. T's NOL can offset annual post-1/1 year 3 T income only to the extent of the lesser of those two limitations (i.e., $0).[236] Bigco retains full use of the 1/1 year 2 $10 Code §382 limitation with respect to the $110 portion of the 1/1 year 2 NOL not allocated to T (i.e., $200 1/1 year 2 consolidated Bigco NOL less $90 allocated to T).

The election to apportion part or all of a prior Code §382 limitation to T and its subsidiaries upon their departure from Bigco's group must be agreed upon by Bigco and T and filed by Bigco.[237] Thus, if P is acquiring T from Bigco and Bigco had a prior ownership change, Bigco need not apportion any of its prior Code §382 limitation to T (in which case $0 would be apportioned to T) unless P and Bigco agree in advance on the manner of apportioning the prior limitation. The apportionment election must be filed with Bigco's income tax return for the taxable year in which T leaves the Bigco group.[238] Thus, Bigco and P, if they choose to negotiate an efficient allocation of Bigco's prior Code §382 limitation, may have some opportunity to base apportionment on observation of Bigco's and T's relative post-acquisition taxable income/loss positions.

EXAMPLE 2

P acquires T and its subsidiaries from Bigco's consolidated group on 2/1 year 1. Bigco and T had a prior ownership change, resulting in a Code §382 limitation still in effect on 2/1 year 1. Bigco has a calendar taxable year. Bigco and P agree to mutually decide on apportionment of the Bigco group's prior Code §382 limitation shortly before Bigco is required to report the apportionment on its applicable tax return. Bigco's tax return for calendar year 1 generally will be due on 9/15 year 2 (i.e., 3/15 year 1 original due date plus normal six-month extension). Thus, Bigco and P have 19 1/2 months after the acquisition to consider how to apportion the limitation. (Regardless of the apportionment of the Bigco group's prior Code §382 limitation, the T group's NOL on 2/1 year 1 will be subject to a new Code §382 limitation resulting from P's acquisition of T.)

---

[236] See Reg. §1.1502-96(c).
[237] Reg. §1.1502-95(f)(3).
[238] Reg. §1.1502-95(f)(3).

For retroactive adjustments to the amount of Bigco's Code §382 limitation previously apportioned to T that may be permitted in connection with certain post-3/6/02 elections affecting Bigco's pre-3/7/02 disposition of T's stock, see ¶212.4.3.2(2).

¶1208.6.4.4 Elective Apportionment of Bigco NUBIG

Effective for Code §382 testing dates (or if T ceases to be a member of the Bigco group) on or after 6/25/99, Bigco and T may jointly elect to apportion part or all of Bigco's consolidated NUBIG, if any, to T and its subsidiaries upon their departure from Bigco's group.[239] The election must be signed jointly by Bigco and T and filed by Bigco. If no elective apportionment is made, under a zero default rule no portion of Bigco's NUBIG is allocated to departing T and its subsidiaries.[240] Under prior law, no mechanism was available for allocating any of Bigco's NUBIG to departing group members.

¶1208.6.5 Net Unrealized Built-in Loss

When P acquires T, T and all its subsidiaries generally will be a Loss Subgroup with respect to a NUBIL (i.e., a net BIL exceeding the threshold amount described in ¶1208.4(3)(d), subject to regulatory adjustments) to the extent that (1) they were continuously affiliated for the five-year period preceding their becoming members of P's consolidated group (or, if shorter, the period from 1/1/87 to the time they become members of P's consolidated group)[241] and (2) they have a NUBIL (determined on an aggregate basis for the relevant group or subgroup) when they join P's group.[242] Any T group member that has a NUBIL but is not included in a Loss Subgroup with respect to the NUBIL will be a Separate Loss Member with respect to the NUBIL and hence treated on a stand-alone basis.[243] Separate tracking of a NUBIL attributable to a Separate Loss Member or a Loss Subgroup may cease in the event of an ownership change or the passage of time, as described in ¶1208.6.3.4.

EXAMPLE 1 Five-Year Affiliation

Individual A has always owned all of T's stock, and T has continuously owned all of S's stock for more than five years. P, a stand-alone entity that

---

[239] Reg. §1.1502-95(c), -99(a). The elective NUBIG allocation rule also applies if T ceases to be a member of the Bigco group before 6/25/99 in a tax year for which the due date of the tax return (without extensions) is after 6/25/99, provided the NUBIG allocation election is timely made. Reg. §1.1502-99(b)(5).

[240] Reg. §1.1502-95(c).

[241] See Reg. §1.1502-99A(c)(2)(i). See also IRS Notice 91-27, 1991-2 C.B. 629.

[242] See Reg. §1.1502-91(d)(2).

[243] See Reg. §1.1502-94(a)(1)(ii).

has no NOL or NUBIL, purchases all of T's stock after 12/31/96, and P, T, and S file consolidated returns thereafter. At the time of the purchase, T and S have a NUBIL (determined on an aggregate basis for T and S). The NUBIL is attributable solely to S and accrued while T and S were affiliated. T and S are a Loss Subgroup with respect to the NUBIL, because they were continuously affiliated for five years before joining P's consolidated group and have a NUBIL (determined on an aggregate basis) when they become members of P's group. Therefore, upon P's purchase of T's stock, (1) there is an ownership change of the T-S Loss Subgroup with respect to the NUBIL, (2) any BILs recognized during the five-year period following P's acquisition of T, if attributable to the T-S NUBIL, are subject to a Code §382 limitation computed based on T's (not merely S's) stock FV, and (3) the two-year business continuity requirement is applied, taking into account the combined businesses of T and S (but not P).

For the application of the SRLY rules (including the §382 Overlap Rule) to analogous facts, see ¶1205.2.4.2(5), Example 16.

EXAMPLE 2   No Five-Year Affiliation

Same as Example 1 except that T and S did not become affiliated with each other until four years before P acquires T. As in Example 1, the T-S NUBIL existing when P acquires T is attributable solely to S and accrued while T and S were affiliated.

T and S are not a Loss Subgroup with respect to the NUBIL because they were not continuously affiliated for the five-year period preceding their acquisition by P. This is the result even though the T-S NUBIL accrued solely during the four-year period of T's and S's affiliation. Therefore, upon P's purchase of T's stock, T and S are Separate Loss Members with respect to any NUBIL, so Code §382 applies on a stand-alone basis (see ¶1208.6.2). For example, T and S are analyzed separately, without regard to each other, to determine whether either has a NUBIL. Since the NUBIL is attributable to S, (1) P's purchase of T's stock causes an ownership change of S, (2) any BILs recognized during the five-year period following P's acquisition of T, if attributable to S's NUBIL, are subject to a Code §382 limitation computed based on S's (not T's or P's) stock FV (presumably resulting in a lower Code §382 limitation than in Example 1), and (3) the two-year business continuity requirement is applied taking into account only S's business, not T's or P's (i.e., the requirement is more stringent than in Example 1).

For the application of the SRLY rules (including the §382 Overlap Rule) to analogous facts, see ¶1205.2.4.2(5), Example 15.

EXAMPLE 3   "Successor" Rule

Same as Example 1 except that, three years before P purchased T's stock, T created S as a 100% subsidiary by transferring T assets to S in exchange for S's stock.

If T's transfer of assets to S occurred on or after 6/25/99, T and S are a Loss Subgroup with respect to the NUBIL, despite not having been affiliated for the five-year period preceding their acquisition by P. This is because S is treated as a "successor" to T under the 1999 Regulations, and therefore T and S are treated as a single corporation with respect to the NUBIL.[244]

In contrast, if T's transfer of assets to S occurred after 12/31/96 but before 6/25/99, under the pre-1999 definition of "successor" S is not a successor to T unless, at the time of the transfer, "the amount by which basis [of the transferred assets] differs from value, in the aggregate, is material."[245] If S is not T's successor, T and S are not a Loss Subgroup with respect to the NUBIL, because they were not continuously affiliated for the five-year period preceding their acquisition by P. This is the result even though S was affiliated with T during S's entire existence and even though the NUBIL accrued while T and S were affiliated. Under this scenario, upon P's acquisition of T, the analysis would be the same as in Example 2.

For additional discussion of "successors" and "predecessors" in connection with SRLY subgroups, see ¶1205.2.4.2(3).

As Examples 2 and 3 illustrate, the five-year prior affiliation requirement for NUBIL Loss Group (or Subgroup) status can produce harsh results by requiring separate entity treatment of each NUBIL entity (generally resulting in a lower Code §382 limitation, for example) even when (1) the NUBIL accrued while T and S were affiliated or (2) S was formed by T (before 6/25/99) and therefore should be regarded merely as T's alter ego. The five-year prior affiliation rule was adopted on administrative grounds, because of concern over the complexity of a "tracing" approach that would require composing NUBIL subgroups based on the year in which NUBILs actually accrued: "Because an accurate method of determining economic accrual (e.g., tracing) [of NUBILs among group members] would present significant problems for tax administration and for compliance by taxpayers, the IRS and Treasury believe that the five-year affiliation requirement is the best available proxy for determining when built-in attributes arise."[246] This rationale does not support the flawed pre-1999 result in Example 3, where the

---

[244] Reg. §1.1502-91(j); Reg. §1.1502-1(f)(4) (as amended in 1999).

[245] Reg. §1.1502-1(f)(4) (prior to 1999 amendment). See also IRS Notice 91-27, 1991-2 C.B. 629.

[246] 1999 Regulations (T.D. 8824), Preamble ¶48. See also IRS Notice of Proposed Rulemaking, CO-78-90, Preamble B2 (stating a comparable rationale for the analogous BIL subgroup principle contained in the 1991 proposed SRLY regulations), 1991-1 C.B. 757.

facts present no abuse potential or tracing difficulties; as illustrated in Example 3, this defect fortunately has been corrected for post-6/25/99 COB asset transfers.

Possibly through an oversight in the 1996 Temporary Regulations, for Code §382 testing dates before 6/25/99 and after 1/1/97 (or earlier if the taxpayer elected to apply the 1996 Temporary Regulations retroactively—see ¶1208.6.8), the rules for qualifying as a Loss Group (or Subgroup) with respect to a NUBIL appear to be different (and in some respects more lenient) if T's consolidated group is acquired by an individual or non-corporate entity rather than by a corporation. For example, if, immediately before individual A acquires T, the T consolidated group has a NUBIL, it appears that T and all of its subsidiaries will be a Loss Group with respect to the NUBIL if the members that accrued the NUBIL accrued it after they joined T's group, even if they joined T's group less than five years before A acquires T.[247]

EXAMPLES 4 AND 5

Same as Examples 2 and 3, respectively, except that T is acquired by individual A rather than by corporation P. If the acquisition occurred before 6/25/99 and after 1/1/97, apparently T and its subsidiaries are a Loss Group with respect to the NUBIL, so Code §382 applies on a consolidated basis to T and its subsidiaries, as in Example 1. In addition, the SRLY rules do not apply since the T consolidated group remains intact.

The inconsistency under the 1996 Temporary Regulations between the NUBIL subgroup rules applicable when the T consolidated group was acquired by different types of taxpayers made little sense, inasmuch as Code §382 is essentially concerned with beneficial ownership of T, not the legal form of ownership. The 1999 Regulations (effective for Code §382 testing dates on or after 6/25/99) eliminate this inconsistency by expanding the five-year affiliation requirement for NUBIL subgroups to cover ownership changes of T (like those in Examples 4 and 5) that do not terminate T's consolidated group.[248]

For the application of the SRLY rules (including the §382 Overlap Rule) to NUBILs, see generally ¶1205.2.4.2(5).

---

[247] Specifically, if the members of T's consolidated group that accrued the NUBIL accrued it after joining T's consolidated group, under the 1996 Temporary Regulations they should be neither "new loss members" (i.e., Separate Loss Members) nor Loss Subgroup members for purposes of Reg. §1.1502-91A(g)(2), and hence T and all its subsidiaries should be a Loss Group under Reg. §1.1502-91A(c)(1)(iii).

[248] See Reg. §1.1502-91(g)(2) and -91(c)(1)(iii); Reg. §1.1502-99(a) (effective date). See also 1999 Regulations (T.D. 8824), Preamble ¶¶55-57.

In contrast to the treatment when individual A acquires T's consolidated group, under the 1996 Temporary Regulations, if individual A acquires T and its subsidiaries from Bigco, then the basic five-year prior affiliation rule described above applies with respect to the T group's NUBIL. This is the case because T and its subsidiaries do not qualify as a "loss group" under Reg. §1.1502-91A(c)(1) if T and its subsidiaries either join or leave a consolidated group as a result of the ownership change. See, e.g., Reg. §1.1502-92A(b)(2) examples (3) and (4).

¶1208.6.6   50%-or-More T Subsidiaries Not Included in T's Consolidated Return

¶1208.6.6.1   Regulatory Authority Generally

Code §382(m)(5), as retroactively amended by the 1988 Act, grants IRS the authority to issue regulations providing, in the case of multiple corporations subject to at least 50% common control, "appropriate adjustments to value, built-in gain or loss, and other items so that items are not omitted or taken into account more than once." The regulations discussed immediately below (which generally reduce T's stock FV, for Code §382 limitation purposes, by T's interest in a controlled but non-consolidated subsidiary) were issued under the authority of this provision.

¶1208.6.6.2   Adjusting Code §382 Limitation

If a T consolidated group member owns stock of a "controlled" subsidiary that is not included in T's consolidated return, the 1999 Regulations (and the 1996 Temporary Regulations) essentially require the FV of such stock to be allocated for Code §382 limitation purposes between the T consolidated group member and the controlled subsidiary.[249] For this purpose, a controlled subsidiary, very generally, is a corporation under 50% or more common control (measured by stock FV or stock voting power) with the applicable T group member but that is not included in T's consolidated group. The apparent principle behind this rule is that, unless the controlled subsidiary is included in T's consolidated group, it is improper to count the subsidiary's FV more than once in computing T's and the non-consolidated subsidiary's respective Code §382 limitations.

The 1999 Regulations (and the 1996 Temporary Regulations) contain two basic operative rules:

(1)   For Code §382 limitation purposes, a T consolidated group member's FV is generally reduced by the FV of the stock of each non-consolidated controlled subsidiary that the T group member directly owns immediately after the ownership change.

(2)   The non-consolidated controlled subsidiary may irrevocably elect to re-store to the relevant T group member some or all of the previously reduced FV, subject to various adjustments. The election must be filed with the loss corporation's tax return for the taxable year in which the ownership change occurs.

---

[249] See Reg. §1.382-8.

EXAMPLE 1

T, a loss corporation, owns 60%, and unrelated individual A owns 40%, of the stock of S, also a loss corporation. Since S is not an 80-80 subsidiary of T, S is not included in T's consolidated group. P purchases all of T's stock. At that time T's and S's stock FV's are as follows:

T stock FV:	
Excluding 60% interest in S	$140
Equity interest in S	60
Including 60% interest in S	$200
S stock FV:	
Stock held by T	$ 60
Stock held by A	40
Total stock FV	$100

P's purchase of T's stock results in an ownership change for both T and S. Without the value adjustment provision of rule (1) above, for purposes of computing T's and S's Code §382 limitation, T's FV would be $200, and S's FV would be $100. This would double count the $60 FV of the S stock owned by T. Under rule (1) above, T's stock FV for purposes of computing T's Code §382 limitation is reduced by the FV of T's S stock, to $140 (i.e., $200 T stock FV less $60 FV of S stock held by T). S's FV for purposes of its Code §382 limitation remains $100. In contrast, if S irrevocably elects under rule (2) above to restore to T the $60 FV reduction, T's FV will be $200 for Code §382 limitation purposes, and S's FV will be reduced to $40 (i.e., $100 S stock FV less $60 FV of S stock held by T).

Surprisingly, any 50%-or-more owned foreign corporation is treated as a controlled subsidiary for purposes of the above rule, even if the subsidiary is not engaged in a U.S. trade or business and hence could not use any portion of the T group's Code §382 limitation that might be allocated to it. The breadth of this rule creates an unfortunate trap for the unwary.

EXAMPLE 2

T is either a stand-alone corporation or the parent of a consolidated group. T owns 100% of the stock of FC, a profitable foreign corporation. P purchases all of T's stock. At that time T's and FC's stock FVs are $100 and $40, respectively.

P's purchase of T's stock results in an ownership change of T. FC is not included in T's consolidated group, because FC is not a U.S. corporation.[250] Therefore, FC is a non-consolidated controlled subsidiary for purposes of the Code §382 limitation adjustment rule. Hence in computing the Code §382 limitation applicable to T's NOL after the ownership change, the FV of T's stock is reduced from $100 to $60 (i.e., by the $40 FV of the FC shares owned by T) unless FC timely elects to restore such value to T. This reduction would occur even though FC has no losses, and even if FC is not engaged in a U.S. trade or business. Particularly if FC is not engaged in a U.S. trade or business, this result makes no sense, because (1) FC is not a U.S. taxpayer and hence cannot use any Code §382 limitation allocated to it and (2) T (not FC) will be subject to U.S. tax on FC's income when such income is distributed to T.

¶1208.6.7   Effective Dates

¶1208.6.7.1   1999 Regulations

The 1999 Regulations discussed in ¶¶1208.6.2 through 1208.6.6 above generally apply for any Code §382 testing date on or after 6/25/99, with exceptions noted in the text above.[251]

¶1208.6.7.2   1996 Temporary Regulations

The 1996 Temporary Regulations generally applied to any Code §382 testing date on or after 1/1/97 but before 6/25/99.[252]

The 1996 Temporary Regulations provide that, for the period preceding 1/1/97, a consolidated group could use any one of three methods, described below, provided the chosen method is consistently applied, to determine whether any ownership change occurred during such period, and if so, the amount of the corresponding Code §382 limitation for all taxable years (including those ending after 1/1/97):

(1) generally a method that does not differ "materially" from the 1996 Temporary Regulations (other than the apportionment rule described in ¶1208.6.4.3), or

(2) a "reasonable application" of the prior Code §382 rules and regulations applied to each T group member on a separate entity basis (allocating to each member its share of the consolidated NOL under the SRLY rule and

---

[250] See Code §1504(b)(3).
[251] Reg. §1.1502-99.
[252] Reg. §1.1502-99A(a).

applying rules similar to those described in ¶1208.6.6.2 to avoid duplicating value in computing the Code §382 limitation), or

(3) a method approved by IRS upon application by the group's common parent.[253]

If a permitted method was not used with respect to a pre-1/1/97 ownership change, the Code §382 limitation had to be reduced, for postchange years for which an income tax return is filed after 1/1/97, to recapture, as quickly as possible, any previously claimed Code §382 limitation exceeding the amount that the Temporary Regulations (other than the effective date rules) would have allowed.[254] Similarly, a consolidated group (e.g., P's or T's) could amend prior tax returns with respect to pre-1/1/97 ownership changes, but only if the amended returns (1) were filed before 3/26/97[255] and (2) modified the amount of the Code §382 limitation in strict compliance with the Temporary Regulations (other than the effective date rules).[256] In other words, if P or T filed a consolidated return with respect to a pre-1/1/97 ownership change and the return did not adopt one of the three permitted methods described above, the effective date provisions appear to force P or T, by the recapture rule or by the amended return rule, into belated but strict compliance with the substantive provisions of the Temporary Regulations.[257]

¶1208.6.8   Conclusion

In determining whether T and its subsidiaries are a Loss Group or include Loss Subgroups and/or Separate Loss Members, the T group's consolidated NOL and NUBIL must be broken down into component parts based generally on the time the NOL was incurred (or the NUBIL accrued) and the specific entity that incurred the NOL (or accrued the NUBIL). The existence of a Loss Group, Loss Subgroup, or Separate Loss Member must be determined as of the time of P's acquisition of T (or other ownership change of T) with respect to each such component part of the T group's NOL and NUBIL. Therefore, depending on the origin and composition of T's consolidated NOL and NUBIL, multiple and/or overlapping Loss Groups, Loss Subgroups, and Separate Loss Members may result (as illustrated in Examples 7 and 10).

Much of the complexity of the Code §382 consolidated loss regulations lies in (1) identifying the applicable Loss Group, Loss Subgroup, or Separate Loss Member with respect to each component part of the T group's consolidated NOL and

---

[253] Reg. §1.1502-99A(c)(2).

[254] Reg. §1.1502-99A(c)(1)(ii).

[255] See IRS Announcement 96-117, 1996-46 I.R.B. 12 (correcting erroneous date of 9/24/96 contained in the version of Temp. Reg. §1.1502-99T(d)(4) (now §1.1502-99A(d)(4)) which appeared in the Internal Revenue Bulletin, 1996-31 I.R.B. at 28).

[256] Reg. §1.1502-99A(d).

[257] A special transition rule applies to the regulations regarding non-consolidated subsidiaries described in ¶1208.6.6.2. See Reg. §1.382-8(j).

NUBIL, (2) applying the rules concerning ownership change, Code §382 limitation, and business continuity with respect to each such component part, and (3) when relevant, applying any concurrent SRLY limitation (though the 1999 SRLY regulations substantially reduce the circumstances where a Code §382 limitation and a SRLY loss limitation will both apply—see ¶1205.2.4.2(4)).

In contrast, the application of the Temporary Regulations can be fairly straightforward where the T group is a Loss Group with respect to its consolidated NOL and NUBIL.

¶1208.7 *Effective Dates*

Code §382 generally applies to an ownership change resulting from any of the following transactions:[258]

(1) An owner shift (other than a reorganization described in (2) below) occurring after 12/31/86.

(2) A tax-free reorganization (other than a divisive reorganization or an "F" reorganization) occurring pursuant to a plan of reorganization "adopted" after 12/31/86. "[A] plan of reorganization shall be treated as adopted on the earlier of (i) the first date that the boards of directors of all the parties to the reorganization have adopted the plan or have recommended adoption to their shareholders, or (ii) the date the shareholders approve such reorganization."[259]

(3) Any transfer of an option to or by a 5% shareholder after 12/31/86 or any issuance of an option after 12/31/86.

As discussed at ¶1208.1.4, in determining whether an ownership change occurs under Code §382 on a particular testing date, the testing period (normally a three-year lookback) does not begin before the later of (1) 5/6/86 or (2) the day after the most recent ownership change preceding the testing date.[260] Because Code §382 disregards any changes in T stock ownership occurring before 5/6/86 (including any option transfers or issuances), ownership changes under Code §382 cannot occur before 5/6/86.[261]

Furthermore, as indicated above, if an ownership change under Code §382 occurs between 5/6/86 and 12/31/86, it does not invoke the 1986 Act version of Code §382; rather, it starts a new testing period beginning the next day and hence limits the lookback of Code §382.

---

[258] Temp. Reg. §1.382-2T(m)(1).
[259] Temp. Reg. §1.382-2T(m)(2).
[260] Code §382(i)(2); Temp. Reg. §1.382-2T(d)(2) and (m)(3).
[261] See Temp. Reg. §1.382-2T(m)(3); 1986 Act §621(f)(3), as amended by 1988 Act §1006(d)(14).

A change of ownership of T occurring wholly or partly before the effective date of Code §382 may be subject to the pre-1986 Act version of Code §382.[262]

For other transitional rules applicable in determining whether an ownership change has occurred, see ¶1208.1.1 (definition of stock), ¶1208.1.6 (stock options issued before 5/6/86 or issued or transferred between 9/18/86 and 12/31/86), and ¶1208.1.7 (application of aggregation and segregation rules to pre-9/4/87 transactions).

For the effective date of the provisions described in ¶1208.6, applicable when T has subsidiaries, see ¶1208.6.7.

---

[262] For rules concerning the interaction between the old and new versions of Code §382, see generally Temp. Reg. §1.382-2T(m)(7). See also 1988 Act §1006(d)(11) (stating that the pre-1986 Act version of Code §382 does not apply to "any increase in percentage points" occurring after 12/31/88 or to any reorganization plans "adopted" after 12/31/86).

CHAPTER 13

Tax Aspects of Financing LBOs—Debt and Preferred Stock

¶1301 INTRODUCTION

This chapter discusses a number of tax concerns that arise where P, in financing its acquisition of T (or Newco formed to effectuate a leveraged buyout (an "LBO") of T), issues new debt or equity securities to third parties to obtain funds with which to acquire T, to T's shareholders in exchange for T's stock, or to T in exchange for T's assets. These financing-related tax concerns include:

(1) Possible recharacterization of P debt instruments as equity (¶1302.2).
(2) Possible additional statutory limitations on P's (or Newco's) ability to deduct interest on its debt financing, including:
   - Possible Code §163(e)(5) deferral and/or disallowance of OID deductions on high yield OID and payment-in-kind ("PIK") debt instruments (¶1303).
   - Possible Code §279 disallowance of interest deductions on subordinated acquisition debt that is convertible into equity or issued as part of an investment unit which includes an option to acquire stock (¶1304).
   - Possible Code §163(j) deferral of interest deductions on debt that is held or guaranteed by a tax-exempt organization or foreign person related to the issuer (¶1305).
   - Possible Code §163(*l*) disallowance of interest deductions on debt that is convertible into, or payable by reference to the value of, equity of the issuer or a related party (¶1306).
(3) Possible Code §163(d) disallowance of interest deductions to individual investors who borrow money to buy P stock (¶1308).
(4) Possible original issue discount ("OID") or Code §483 imputed interest on debt issued by P, and possible imputed dividends on preferred stock issued by P (¶1309).
(5) Possible dividend characterization where P (or Newco) later redeems some or all of the preferred stock issued to finance an LBO (¶1310).

As indicated above, where the acquisition is an LBO the acquiring corporation is generally referred to as "Newco" (because it is newly formed for purposes of the LBO) rather than "P," although the operative tax rules are essentially the same. Because many of the following topics are particularly relevant to acquisitions in which substantial debt is incurred, as will be the case in an LBO, the terms "Newco" and "P" generally are used interchangeably herein.

¶1302   P (OR NEWCO) DEBT: OVERVIEW OF LIMITATIONS ON INTEREST DEDUCTIBILITY; BASIC TAX DIFFERENCES BETWEEN DEBT AND PREFERRED STOCK; CODE §385 EQUITY CHARACTERIZATION

¶1302.1   *Overview of Limitations on Interest Deductibility*

In an LBO, P (or Newco) finances its acquisition of T in part by issuing new debt securities (1) to third parties (to obtain funds with which to acquire T), (2) to T (in exchange for T's assets), or (3) to T's shareholders (in exchange for T's stock).

Interest paid or accrued by a corporation is generally deductible under Code §163. Accordingly, debt financing can offer a significant advantage over equity (preferred or common stock) financing by reducing a corporate issuer's future income taxes through interest deductions. However, a corporation's ability to deduct interest on its debt is subject to the following, primarily statutory, limitations:

(1) Possible recharacterization of the debt as equity under Code §385 or case law principles (see ¶1302.2).
(2) Possible Code §163(e)(5) deferral and/or disallowance of OID deductions on high yield OID and PIK debt instruments (see ¶1303).
(3) Possible Code §279 disallowance of interest deductions on subordinated acquisition debt that is convertible into equity or issued as part of an investment unit which includes an option to acquire stock (see ¶1304).
(4) Possible Code §163(j) deferral of interest deductions on debt that is held or guaranteed by a tax-exempt organization or foreign person related to the issuer (see ¶1305).
(5) Possible Code §163(*l*) disallowance of interest deductions on debt that is payable in, or by reference to the value of, issuer equity (see ¶1306).

¶1302.2   Basic Tax Differences Between Debt and Preferred Stock

The distinction between debt and preferred (or common) stock is important to both the issuer and the recipient for the following tax reasons:

First, if Newco (or P) issues debt, it can deduct interest expense (including OID),[1] subject to the statutory limitations described in ¶1302.1, but if Newco issues preferred stock, it cannot deduct dividend payments or preferred OID.

Second, dividends received by a corporate holder of preferred stock attract the 70%, 80% or 100% DRD,[2] but interest received by a corporate holder of a debt instrument is fully taxable. A tax-exempt institutional investor generally will be indifferent (from a tax standpoint) as to the receipt of dividends or interest.

Third, because different tax accounting rules apply, the timing and character of income to a holder from accrued but unpaid yield on the instrument may differ depending on whether the instrument is treated as debt or equity for tax purposes. Both cash and accrual method debt holders generally are subject to constant-yield-to-maturity accrual of interest income under the OID rules, as discussed in ¶¶1309.1 and 1309.2. In contrast, subject to Code §305(c) (see ¶1309.3), accumulated but unpaid and undeclared dividends on preferred stock generally are not

---

¶**1302** [1] Code §163.
[2] Code §243.

included currently in either a cash or accrual method holder's income.[3] Moreover, to the extent accumulated but undeclared preferred dividends have not previously been included in the holder's income, any resulting gain on a sale or redemption of the preferred stock is treated as CG (assuming the disposition qualifies for Code §302 exchange treatment—see ¶1310).[4]

Fourth, repayment of debt principal is tax free to the payee (to the extent of the payee's basis in the debt), but redemption of preferred stock may give rise to dividend treatment.[5] See ¶1310.

Fifth, if debt principal or interest is forgiven, the issuer generally has taxable income or is subject to tax attribute reduction under Reg. §1.61-12 or Code §108. These consequences do not apply when stock becomes worthless or is canceled.

Sixth, a corporation may amortize the cost of issuing debt but may amortize only certain "organizational expenses" of issuing stock.[6] See ¶¶402.1, 402.2, 402.7.

¶1302.3   *Characterizing P's (or Newco's) Debt Instruments as Equity—Code §385*

Code §385 authorizes Treasury to issue regulations to determine whether an interest in a corporation should be treated as stock or debt for tax purposes. It also provides a non-exclusive list of factors that future regulations may take into account in making this determination:

(1)   "whether there is a written unconditional promise to pay on demand or on a specified date a sum certain in money in return for adequate consideration. . . , and to pay a fixed rate of interest,"

(2)   "whether there is subordination to or preference over any indebtedness of the corporation,"

---

[3] A dividend generally is includible in shareholder income only when it is "unqualifiedly made subject to" the shareholder's demand. Reg. §1.301-1(b). This rule applies to both cash and accrual method shareholders. See Comm'r v. Tar Products Corp., 130 F.2d 866 (3d Cir. 1942); Comm'r v. American Light & Traction Co., 156 F.2d 398 (7th Cir. 1946); Dynamics Corp. of America v. U.S., 392 F.2d 241 (Ct. Cl. 1968).

[4] See Rev. Rul. 69-131, 1969-1 C.B. 94; Cummins Diesel Sales Corp. v. United States, 323 F. Supp. 1114 (S.D. Ind. 1971), *aff'd*, 459 F.2d 668 (7th Cir. 1972). In contrast, when a corporation redeems preferred stock of a shareholder who has a legal right to an unpaid preferred dividend because the dividend was previously declared, the dividend amount is includible in shareholder income as a dividend distribution under Code §301(a). Rev. Rul. 69-130, 1969-1 C.B. 93. In addition, if the preferred stock terms entitle the holder to be paid accumulated dividends before any dividend is paid on the issuer's common stock, a dividend on the common triggers a legal obligation to pay accumulated preferred dividends (even though undeclared), so that subsequent redemption of the preferred results in ordinary income to the holder to the extent of accumulated preferred dividends. See Rev. Rul. 75-320, 1975-2 C.B. 105; Crown v. Commissioner, 58 T.C. 825 (1972), *aff'd*, 487 F.2d 1404 (7th Cir. 1973).

[5] Code §302(d).

[6] Compare Helvering v. Union Pacific R.R. Co., 293 U.S. 282, 1935-1 U.S.T.C. ¶9011 (1934), with Code §248.

(3) the issuer's debt-to-equity ratio,
(4) whether there is convertibility into stock, and
(5) the relationship between holdings of the issuer's stock and holdings of the interest in question.

In 1980 Treasury released the first of three drafts of the Code §385 regulations distinguishing debt from equity.[7] These legislative regulations were extremely complex, and finally, in light of Treasury's embarrassment regarding adjustable rate convertible notes ("ARCNs"), Treasury withdrew the Code §385 regulations in 1983 before they ever took effect.[8] Treasury may yet publish another set of more narrowly drawn regulations.

With the withdrawal of the Code §385 regulations, there has been a return to the general guidelines and factors of existing case law and IRS rulings.[9] In general, among the principal factors that weigh in favor of purported debt being treated as debt for tax purposes are that:

(1)   The debt has a fixed maturity date not too far removed.
(2)   The debt is an unconditional obligation to pay.
(3)   The debt has a fixed interest rate.
(4)   The creditor has reasonable rights upon default (e.g., acceleration).
(5)   The debt is non-convertible, non-participating, non-voting and has no other equity features.
(6)   The debtor has sufficient anticipated cash flow to meet debt service.
(7)   There is a substantial disparity between debt holdings and stock holdings in terms of the identity of the holders and their proportionate interests.
(8)   The debtor's debt-equity ratio ("DER") is not excessive.
(9)   The debt grants the holder no management voice.
(10) The debt is not subordinated to other creditors.
(11) After issuance of the debt, the holder acts like a reasonable creditor, taking reasonable steps to enforce its rights.
(12) The debt was not issued in the acquisition of basic business assets.

See also the discussion of equity-flavored debt instruments at ¶203.6.7.

EXAMPLE 1

VC forms Newco, capitalizing it with $1 million of cash. In return VC receives a $999,000, 50-year Newco debenture bearing stated interest of 3%

---

[7] See T.D. 7747, 1981-1 C.B. 141.

[8] See T.D. 7920, 1983-2 C.B. 69 (withdrawing Code §385 regulations); Rev. Rul. 83-98, 1983-2 C.B. 40 (treating ARCNs as equity); Treasury Department Release (6/24/83), CCH Stand. Fed. Tax Rep. Vol. 10, ¶6623 (1983) (concluding that ARCNs were not "grandfathered" by Code §385 regulations, which would have treated ARCNs as debt).

[9] See, e.g., Rev. Rul. 68-54, 1968-1 C.B. 69; Rev. Rul. 73-122, 1973-1 C.B. 66. See generally Plumb, The Federal Income Tax Significance of Corporate Debt: A Critical Analysis and a Proposal, 26 Tax L. Rev. 369 (1971).

(substantially below market and the AFR), payable quarterly, and all 100 shares of Newco common stock.

Newco uses the $1 million to acquire T's assets. VC and Newco reasonably believe that, after the acquisition, there is a substantial risk Newco will *not* have adequate cash flow to service the debt. In fact, Newco does not make any interest payments on the debenture. Moreover, VC takes no action in response to Newco's repeated interest defaults, although a reasonable creditor would have done so.

It is very likely that the $999,000 debenture will be treated for tax purposes as equity, in light of such factors as:

(1) The 50-year maturity date.
(2) The 999:1 DER ($999,000 of debt to $1,000 of equity).
(3) The 100% overlap in ownership between Newco's common stock and the debenture.
(4) The substantially below market interest rate on the debenture.
(5) Newco's failure to pay the interest timely.
(6) VC's failure to act like a reasonable creditor, including taking reasonable steps to enforce its rights when the interest was not timely paid.
(7) Newco's use of the debt proceeds to acquire basic assets coupled with substantial doubt whether, after the acquisition, Newco would have sufficient cash flow to service the debt.

EXAMPLE 2

VC and Mgmt form Newco, capitalizing it with $1 million of cash as follows: Mgmt pays $50,000 for 50 shares of Newco's common stock (50%). VC pays $50,000 for the other 50 shares of Newco's common stock (50%). VC also pays (a) $200,000 for Newco preferred stock with a $200,000 face amount and (b) $700,000 for a Newco debenture with a $700,000 face amount, due in 7 years, bearing 10% interest (a market rate) payable quarterly.

Newco uses the $1 million to acquire T's assets. The parties reasonably believe that, after the acquisition, Newco will have sufficient cash flow to service the debt. In fact, Newco does make all the interest payments on the debenture timely, except for the second quarterly interest payment. However, when Newco was late on the second quarterly interest payment, VC immediately took reasonable steps to enforce its rights, obtaining certain additional contractual covenants from Newco and an agreement from Newco (with reasonable penalties for breach) to pay off the interest arrearage within 60 days. Throughout the arrearage period VC continued to press for payment of the interest arrearage, and Newco did indeed pay off the interest arrearage within the 60 day extension period.

It is very likely that the $700,000 debenture will be treated for tax purposes as debt, in light of such factors as:

(1) The 7 year maturity date (as compared to 50 years in Example 1).
(2) The 2.3:1 DER ($700,000 of debt to $300,000 of preferred and common equity) (as compared to 999:1 in Example 1).
(3) The 50% overlap in ownership between Newco's common stock and the debenture (as compared to 100% in Example 1).
(4) The market rate of interest on the debenture (as compared to the unreasonably low rate in Example 1).
(5) Newco's timely interest payments, except for the 60-day delay on one quarterly payment (as compared to consistent default on interest payments in Example 1).
(6) VC acting like a reasonable creditor in the face of the one quarterly interest arrearage (as compared to VC's consistent inaction in Example 1).
(7) The parties' reasonable belief that, although the debt proceeds were used to acquire basic assets, Newco would, after the acquisition, have sufficient cash flow to service the debenture (as compared to the substantial doubt in Example 1).

The 1989 Act amended Code §385 to permit future regulations treating an interest in a corporation as partly stock and partly debt for tax purposes. The 1989 Conference Report observes that "[g]enerally, there has been a tendency by the courts to characterize an instrument entirely as debt or entirely as equity."[10] Such regulations would apply only to instruments issued after the date "public guidance" is provided ("whether by regulation, ruling, or otherwise").[11]

Additionally, effective 10/25/92 Code §385(c) directs that the issuer's characterization (at time of issue) of an interest in a corporation, as stock or as indebtedness, binds the issuer although not, of course, IRS. The initial characterization generally will bind all holders; however (except as may be provided in regulations) a holder is not bound if, on his tax return, the holder discloses that he is treating the corporate interest in a manner inconsistent with the issuer's characterization of it. Query how this will work if the issuer says "debt" and the shareholders say "stock" (1) in a Code §351 transfer of appreciated property to Newco, or (2) if Newco is an S corporation, or (3) the combination of (1) and (2).

---

[10] See H.R. Conf. Rep. No. 386, 101st Cong., 1st Sess. at 59 (1989) (as reprinted in CCH Stand. Fed. Tax Rep. no. 50 (11/22/89)). For some exceptions to this rule, see Farley Realty Corp. v. Commissioner, 279 F.2d 701, 60-2 U.S.T.C. ¶9525 (2d Cir. 1960) (as discussed in ¶203.6.7, bifurcating a debt instrument with fixed interest and continent interest) and the following cases bifurcating debt instruments with only fixed interest: Bihlmaier v. Commissioner, 17 T.C. 620 (1951), acq., 1952-1 C.B. 1; United Engineers & Constructors, Inc. v. Smith, 59-1 U.S.T.C. ¶9322 (E.D. Pa. 1959); Funk v. Commissioner, 35 T.C. 42 (1960), acq., 1961-2 C.B. 4; Scotland Mills, Inc. v. Commissioner, 24 T.C.M. 265, T.C. Mem. 1965-48 (1965); C.M. Gooch Lumber Sales Co. v. Commissioner, 49 T.C. 649 (1968).

[11] 1989 Act §7208(a)(2).

EXAMPLE 3

A's sole proprietorship has an FV of $1 million. The FV of the proprietorship assets is $600,000 above their tax basis. B is an executive of the proprietorship. A and B incorporate the business in newly organized Newco, with A contributing $7,500 for 75 Newco common shares and B contributing $2,500 for 25 Newco common shares. Simultaneously, A transfers to Newco proprietorship business, assets, and liabilities and Newco issues to A in exchange an instrument, denominated on its face a "debenture" with a $1 million principal payable 10 years hence, and interest at a fair rate equal to 2% above the prime rate payable annually. Newco's "debenture" is subordinated to all creditors, present and future, but is not convertible (directly or indirectly) into Newco stock.

As obliged (or permitted) by Code §385(c):

- Newco will treat the debenture as debt for tax purposes.
- Sensitive to Newco's extremely "thin" capitalization, A reasonably determines to treat the Newco debenture as stock and not as debt for tax purposes, and A so discloses in all relevant federal tax returns she files.
- Consistent with her treatment of Newco's debenture as stock, A reports the exchange as a Code §351(a) transaction, resulting in no recognized gain on her exchange with Newco. A claims a substituted basis of $400,000 in the Newco debenture under Code §358(a).
- Newco claims a basis in the proprietorship assets equal to the basis at which A held those assets; Newco's view is that whether its debenture is debt or stock, under Code §362(a) A's basis carries over to Newco, without any increase since A on the transfer did not recognize gain (according to the reporting on her tax return).

EXAMPLE 4

Same as Example 3. In addition, Newco is a C corporation for its initial taxable year, but timely elects to become an S corporation for its second year.

Whether properly treated as debt or stock for other tax purposes, the Newco debenture for purposes of Code §1361(b)(1)(D) (defining an S corporation) is "straight debt" which under Code §1361(c)(5) will not be treated as a second class of stock. Accordingly, without regard to the way in which A has characterized Newco's debenture on her tax return, commencing year 2 Newco will qualify as an S corporation. Because Newco was a C corporation for its first taxable year, Code §1374 (imposing corporate-level tax on BIGs in Newco's assets) will apply to Newco, during its first 10 years as an S corporation, even though the BIGs accrued while the assets were owned by A in proprietorship format and did not accrue while Newco was a C corporation.

EXAMPLE 5

Same as Examples 3 and 4 except that, sensitive to the Code §1374 penalty exposed in Example 4, Newco files a Code §1362 election to be an S corporation at the outset, effective for Newco's first taxable year.

Because Newco could, as in Example 4, validly elect S status commencing year 2, we conceive no good reason why Newco should not be permitted to elect S status for year 1. The signal advantage of the S election for year 1 is avoidance of the Code §1374 10-year tax, but that is an entirely sensible result since the target of that provision—asset appreciation built up while the enterprise was a C corporation—is wholly absent here.

In this example the concern, if there is one, stems from what might be termed the unprovided for case:

- Although Code §1361(c)(5) treats "straight debt" as debt only for purposes of determining S eligibility (i.e., straight debt is not a second class of stock), regulations promulgated in 1992 went further and announced that straight debt "even if it is considered equity under general principles" of federal tax law, "is generally treated as debt and when so treated is subject to the applicable rules governing indebtedness for other purposes of the Code."[12] If Newco is an S corporation in its initial year, treating the debenture as "indebtedness for other purposes of the Code" clashes with A's characterization of the debenture as stock for purposes of Code §351(a).
- When Newco commences as a C corporation and converts to S status for year 2, recharacterizing as debt the Newco debenture that properly was seen by A as equity for year 1 raises an obvious tax concern. Has A in year 2 exchanged old Newco stock for new Newco debt, a "redemption" certain to occasion unpleasant tax consequences? Perceiving the C to S problem, the 1992 regulation flatly announced that "the conversion from C corporation status to S corporation status is not treated as an exchange of debt for stock with respect to such an instrument."[13]
- Unfortunately, IRS has not to this time reacted to the problem focused in this example, in which the characterization issue is presented, not in the context of conversion from C to S status, but in the initial

---

[12] Reg. §1.1361-1(*l*)(5)(iv).
[13] Reg. §1.1361-1(*l*)(5)(v).

> incorporation of a proprietorship or partnership in which the desired conversion is from non-corporate operation to S corporation status.
>
> Sensibly, we believe, IRS should reach a favorable conclusion—i.e., non-recognition of gain by A and valid S election by Newco—in Example 5. We are of this belief because those favorable results without doubt obtain in Example 4. The penalty imposed on the taxpayers in Example 4—10 year corporate level taxation of BIG under Code §1374—is aberrational because the gain in question did not accrue during C corporation ownership of the assets. Thus it would be senseless to assert that a Code §1374 double tax penalty was intended to be or ought to be the price of achieving the desired tax results of non-recognition by A and a valid S election by Newco.

Although IRS often has successfully taken the position that a purported debt instrument should be treated as equity for tax purposes, it has very rarely argued that purported stock should be treated as debt.[14] One reason for IRS's one-sided litigating position is that equity characterization (and the resulting denial of interest deductions for the issuer and potential dividend taxation of the holder on principal repayment) is in the vast majority of cases more revenue-productive for IRS, which therefore has had little interest in establishing contrary precedent. Moreover, the stock as debt argument appears weak on the merits. While a noteholder's claim may be reduced in substance to that of an equity holder by excessive subordination, a high DER, high proportionality, acting like a stockholder, and other means, it is not possible to overcome inherent state law limitations on the rights of a shareholder (including very limited rights vis-a-vis creditors with respect to the payment of dividends, redemptions and liquidating distributions, rights on default, and rights in bankruptcy).

¶1303   CODE §163(e)(5) DEFERRING AND/OR PERMANENTLY DISALLOWING OID AND PIK INTEREST DEDUCTIONS

¶1303.1   *Introduction*

(1)   1989 LBO Hearings. In early 1989 the House Ways and Means Committee held extensive hearings on LBOs. At those hearings substantial criticism was voiced regarding the tax treatment of debt instruments that (a) do not pay interest currently but rather are issued with substantial OID, such as zero-coupon deben-

---

[14] Two well-known cases in which IRS argued that purported stock should be treated as debt are Ragland Investment Co. v. Commissioner, 52 T.C. 867 (1969), *aff'd per curiam*, 435 F.2d 118, 71-1 U.S.T.C. ¶9102 (6th Cir. 1970), and Zilkha & Sons, Inc. v. Commissioner, 52 T.C. 607 (1969). IRS lost both cases (i.e., the courts treated the purported stock as equity), and IRS acquiesced in *Zilkha*. See 1970-1 C.B. xvi.

tures ("OID debentures"), *or* (b) require or permit the issuer to pay interest in the form of additional debt instruments ("bunny debentures") of the issuer (i.e., "PIK debentures" or pay-in-kind debentures).

(2)   PIK debentures—payment of interest in debentures versus stock. A debenture that requires or permits the issuer to pay interest in the form of issuer *stock* has not traditionally been considered a PIK debenture. (See ¶1309.2.) However, as discussed below, Code §163(e)(5) and (i), enacted by the 1989 Act[1] in response to the above described LBO hearings, treats a debenture as a PIK debenture subject to the new provision if it requires or permits the issuer to pay interest in the form of *either* bunny debentures *or* stock of the issuer or a related person.

(3)   Regular OID rules. As discussed in ¶¶1309.1 and 1309.2, under the OID rules of Code §§1271-1275 and the regulations thereunder (the "regular OID rules"), the holder of an OID debenture or a debenture that pays interest in the form of bunny debentures normally includes OID in income, and the issuer normally deducts OID, as interest on the debenture accrues on a constant yield basis. In contrast, if a debenture pays interest in *stock* (common or preferred) rather than in bunny debentures, the regular OID rules treat such interest as currently paid, so that the holder has interest income and (subject to Code §163(*l*)[2]) the issuer deducts interest, equal to the FV of the stock issued, and the regular OID rules do not apply at all.

(4)   1989 House Bill. The House version of the 1989 Act, passed in 10/89, included a proposed Code §386 (the "1989 House Bill"),[3] which would have treated a corporate debt instrument as preferred stock for all federal income tax purposes (so that, among other things, the interest thereon would be non-deductible) where the debt instrument (1) contains significant OID or PIK features and (2) has certain other statutorily defined characteristics described below.

(5)   1989 Senate Bill. The Senate version of the 1989 Act, passed in 10/89 (the "1989 Senate Bill"),[4] defined in the same manner as the 1989 House Bill the OID and PIK debentures covered, but would have respected covered debenture as debt while deferring the corporate issuer's interest deductions (though not the holder's OID income inclusion) until the interest was actually paid (other than in bunny debentures or stock of the issuer or a related person).

¶1303   [1] The Revenue Reconciliation Act of 1989, Pub. L. No. 101-239 (hereinafter "1989 Act").

[2] Code §163(*l*), enacted in 1997, permanently disallows any deduction for interest paid or accrued (including OID) on debt issued by a corporation if "a substantial amount of the principal or interest" on the debt is payable in, or by reference to the value of, equity of the issuer or a related party (including by reason of a conversion right or similar option exercisable by the issuer or holder). For this purpose, a conversion right or similar option exercisable by the holder is taken into account only if "there is a substantial certainty the option will be exercised." Code §163(*l*) generally applies to debt issued after 6/8/97. See ¶1306.

[3] H.R. 3299, §11202.

[4] S. 1750, §6202.

(6)   1989 Act. As finally enacted on 12/19/89, Code §163(e)(5) and (i) defines in the same manner as the 1989 House and Senate Bills the OID and PIK debentures covered.[5] However, unlike the 1989 House Bill, the 1989 Act does not treat such debentures as preferred stock for any purpose. Nor does it merely adopt the 1989 Senate Bill's relatively simple deferral approach.

Instead, the 1989 Act bifurcates the OID on such a debenture into (a) *a deferred-deduction interest portion* as to which the issuer's deduction is deferred until the issuer actually pays the interest (other than in bunny debentures or stock of the issuer or a related person), but which is nevertheless reported by the holder as income as it accrues under the regular OID rules, and (b) for a debenture whose yield exceeds a specified threshold, *a permanently non-deductible portion* which is never deductible by the issuer but is nevertheless reported by the holder as income as it accrues under the regular OID rules and may qualify for the dividends-received deduction ("DRD") if the holder is a corporation.

The resulting legislation effectively adopts a pattern familiar in much of the other tax legislation enacted since 1989. It eschews simplicity and clear statement, adopting instead a dazzling array of complex rules, definitions, and exceptions, creating a wondrous mosaic of confusion and bewilderment, far more intricate than necessary to address the issue at hand. The proliferation of provisions exemplified by Code §163(e)(5) and (i) has turned the Code into an unadministrable morass.

This ¶1303 first summarizes the operation of Code §163(e)(5) and (i) (¶1303.2) and then discusses some of the many practical issues and problems that the statute raises (¶1303.3).

¶1303.2   Summary of Statutory Mechanics

The statute contains a definitional provision (Code §163(i), discussed in ¶1303.2.1) and three operative provisions (Code §163(e)(5), discussed in ¶1303.2.2). At the heart of the statutory labyrinth lies the definition of an "applicable high yield discount obligation," or an "AHYDO." If a debenture is an AHYDO, the provision (a) defers the issuer's deductions for OID until actually paid, (b) in some cases permanently disallows a portion of the issuer's OID deductions, and (c) if the holder of the debenture is a corporation and the issuer has sufficient earnings and profits ("E&P"), permits the holder a DRD with respect to the amount of OID deductions permanently disallowed to the issuer.

The provision is generally effective for a debenture issued (or assumed) after 7/10/89, with the exceptions discussed in ¶1303.3.4.

---

[5] 1989 Act §7202.

¶1303.2.1 Definition of Applicable High Yield Discount Obligation

¶1303.2.1.1 Four-Factor Test

Code §163(e)(5) applies to any "applicable high yield discount obligation" (AHYDO). Code §163(i) defines an AHYDO as any debenture that has *all four* of the following characteristics:[6]

(1) The debenture is issued by a corporation[7] (e.g., Newco,[8] the acquiring corporation in an LBO).
(2) The debenture has a "maturity date . . . more than 5 years from the date of issue."
(3) The debenture's "yield to maturity" equals or exceeds five percentage points over the applicable federal rate (the "AFR") in effect for the month in which the debenture is issued.[9]
(4) The debenture is issued with "significant OID" (as defined below).

¶1303.2.1.2 PIK Feature Treated as OID

Code §163(i) generally treats PIK interest in the same fashion as OID. In determining whether a debenture is an AHYDO, "any payment to be made in the form of another obligation of the issuer (or a related person within the meaning of Code §453(f)(1)) shall be assumed to be made when such obligation is required to be paid in cash or in property other than such obligation."[10] Thus, if Newco's PIK debenture pays interest in the form of Newco bunny debentures (or the debentures of a related person), such interest is treated for all AHYDO purposes as paid at the maturity date of such bunny debentures, hence giving rise to OID.

---

[6] Throughout this ¶1303, "debenture" means any debt instrument (whether secured or unsecured) as broadly defined in Code §1275(a). See Code §163(i)(4).

The "AHYDO" definition in Code §163(i) as enacted is the same as the definition of the debt instruments to which the 1989 House Bill's preferred stock characterization rule and the 1989 Senate Bill's interest deferral rule would have applied.

[7] Code §163(e)(5)(A). Technically, the requirement that the issuer be a corporation is not contained in Code §163(i)'s definition of an AHYDO but rather is set forth in Code §163(e)(5) as a prerequisite for invoking Code §163(e)(5)'s operative rules. However, for ease of presentation, it is described herein as a fourth AHYDO requirement.

[8] For simplicity, this ¶1303.2.1 refers to the issuing corporation as "Newco," but the tax rules are the same if the debenture is issued by a long-standing corporation. However, Code §163(e)(5) does not apply during any period when the issuer is an S corporation. See ¶1303.3.1.9.

[9] For this purpose, the AFR is determined without regard to the lowest-three-month provision of Code §1274(d)(2). See H.R. Budget Comm. Rep. on H.R. 3299, H.R. Rep. No. 247, 101st Cong., 1st Sess. at 73 n.21 (1989) (as reprinted in CCH Stand. Fed. Tax Rep. no. 40 (9/21/89)) (hereinafter "1989 House Report"); Senate Finance Committee Print on S. 1750, S. Print No. 56, 101st Cong., 1st Sess. at 71 n.2 (1989) (as reprinted in CCH Stand. Fed. Tax Rep. no. 42 (10/11/89)) (hereinafter "1989 Senate Report").

[10] Code §163(i)(3)(B), as amended by the 1990 Act retroactive to the effective date of Code §163(e)(5).

If Newco's PIK debenture pays interest in the form of Newco preferred or common stock (or the stock of a related person), somewhat different rules apply. In determining whether such a debenture has more than a five-year term or has significant OID, such stock is treated in the same manner as a bunny debenture.[11] That is, it is subject to the rule quoted above, so that such interest paid in stock is deemed paid when the issuer is required to redeem the stock (other than by issuance of a debt or equity instrument of Newco or a related person). In contrast, in determining whether such a debenture's yield to maturity equals or exceeds the AFR plus five percentage points, interest to be paid in Newco's (or a related person's) stock is deemed paid when such stock is scheduled to be *issued* (rather than when it is required to be redeemed), as further discussed in ¶1303.3.1.3.

In addition, "any payment under the instrument shall be assumed to be made on the last day permitted under the instrument."[12] Thus, if Newco has the *option* to pay the interest on its debenture in cash or by issuing Newco's (or a related person's) bunny debentures (or stock), the original debenture is treated as issued with OID by assuming that Newco will exercise the option to pay interest in bunny debentures (or stock) and that the bunny debentures will be paid in cash or other property at their maturity date (or the stock will be paid in cash or other property when the issuer is required to redeem it), other than by issuance of a debt or equity instrument of Newco or a related person.

Code §163(*l*), enacted in 1997, permanently disallows any deduction for interest paid or accrued (including OID) on debt issued by a corporation if "a substantial amount of the principal or interest" on the debt is payable in, or by reference to the value of, equity of the issuer or a related party (including by reason of a conversion right or similar option exercisable by the issuer or holder). For this purpose, a conversion right or similar option exercisable by the holder is taken into account only if "there is a substantial certainty the option will be exercised." Code §163(*l*) generally applies to debt issued after 6/8/97. To the extent Code §163(*l*) permanently disallows any deduction for interest paid or accrued on debt that pays interest in the form of issuer stock, it is of course irrelevant to the issuer whether Code §163(e)(5) applies. See ¶1306.

¶1303.2.1.3   *Meaning of "Significant OID"*

The statutory definition of "significant OID" borders on the incomprehensible. We first discuss below the unnecessarily complex statutory language and then attempt a simplified explanation of the language's general purport.

Under Code §163(i), a debenture has "significant OID" if, according to the debenture's terms:

(1)   the aggregate amount includible in the holder's gross income with respect to the debenture (including OID amortization under the regular OID rules)

---

[11] Code §163(i)(3)(B), as amended by the 1990 Act retroactive to the effective date of Code §163(e)(5).
[12] Code §163(i)(3)(A).

during *either* (a) the period from the debenture's issuance to the close of the first "accrual period" ending after the fifth anniversary of the debenture's issuance (i.e., a period of between five and six years after the debenture's issuance) *or* (b) the period from the debenture's issuance to the close of any "accrual period" ending after the period described in (a) *exceeds*

(2) the sum of (a) "the aggregate amount of interest to be paid" under the debenture during such period (assuming that any payments will be made on the last date permitted by the debenture) and (b) "the product of the [debenture's] issue price . . . (as defined in §§1273(b) and 1274(a)) and its yield to maturity" (i.e., an amount generally equal to the first 12 months' yield on the debenture).[13]

Accrual period. Code §163(i)(2)(A) refers to Code §1272(a)(5) for the definition of "accrual period." For debt instruments issued after 4/3/94, Reg. §1.1272-1(b)(1)(ii) defines "accrual period" as follows:

An accrual period is an interval of time over which the accrual of OID is measured. Accrual periods may be of any length and may vary in length over the term of the debt instrument, provided that [i] each accrual period is no longer than one year and [ii] each scheduled payment of principal or interest occurs either on the final day of an accrual period or on the first day of an accrual period.[14]

The final OID regulations allow each debt holder and the issuer to select any permitted accrual periods (including accrual periods that vary in length over the debt term) that satisfy the above criteria, even if they are inconsistent with the accrual periods selected by other parties.[15]

---

[13] Code §163(i)(2) and (3). See ¶1303.3.1.5 for a discussion whether the first 12 months' yield is computed as compound or simple interest.

[14] By contrast, 1986 Prop. Reg. §1.1272-1(d), which generally is authority for debt instrument issued before 12/22/92, generally defined "accrual period" as (a) the *regular* intervals of one year or less during which a debenture either *pays or compounds* interest, (b) the short period (if any) from issuance to the beginning of the first regular accrual period, and (c) the short period (if any) from the end of the last regular accrual period to maturity. Hence, the 1986 proposed OID regulation differs from the final regulation (and the nearly identical proposed regulation issued in 1992) in two significant respects: (i) the 1986 regulation generally required accrual periods of fixed length, in contrast to the variable intervals permitted by the final regulation, and (ii) under the 1986 regulation, accrual period lengths are determined by the payment and compounding terms stated in the debenture, and are not discretionary with the holder and issuer.

In contrast to the final and 1986 proposed regulations, Code §1272(a)(5) defines "accrual period" quite differently as each one of the series of six-month periods ending with the debenture's maturity date and also as the short period (if any) from the debenture's issuance to the beginning of the first such full six-month accrual period, "[e]xcept as otherwise provided in regulations." Because the final OID regulations described above substantially alter the general rule of Code §1272(a)(5), the Code definition is now obsolete. Since Code §1272(a)(5) explicitly permits regulatory exceptions, we assume that the reference in Code §163(i)(2)(A) to "accrual period (as defined in section 1272(a)(5))" incorporates these and any future regulatory modifications to the 6-month statutory rule.

[15] See, e.g., Reg. §1.1272-1(j) (examples computing the holder's OID income by reference to the accrual periods selected by the holder, without reference to the accrual periods selected by the issuer or by other holders; e.g., example (1) states that, in the case of a debenture providing for a single

EXAMPLE 1

On 12/1/93 Newco issues a debenture which is scheduled to mature on 1/1/04 (i.e., 10 years and one month after issuance). The debenture pays interest on 1/1/94 and semiannually thereafter on 7/1 and 1/1 of each year.

As discussed above, each debt holder and the issuer may elect accrual periods of any length (or of varying lengths), as long as (i) each accrual period is no longer than one year and (ii) each scheduled payment of principal or interest occurs at the end or the beginning of an accrual period. Assume a person elects to use the longest possible accrual periods. These consist of the periods between the scheduled semiannual interest payment dates. In such case, the debenture has a front-end one-month short accrual period ending on 1/1/94, which is the first payment date and 20 full six-month accrual periods ending each 7/1 and 1/1 thereafter through 1/1/04.

EXAMPLE 2

Same as Example 1 except the debenture is scheduled to mature on 2/1/04 (rather than on 1/1/04) and the interest for the month of 1/2004 will be paid at maturity. Just as in Example 1, assuming a person elects to use the longest possible accrual periods, the debenture has 20 full six-month accrual periods plus a front-end short accrual period ending 1/1/94.

In addition, the debenture in Example 2 has a back-end short accrual period ending on 2/1/04, the debenture's maturity date.

EXAMPLE 3

Same as Example 1 except the debenture *pays* no interest throughout its life. Instead, interest *accrues* throughout its life and *compounds* semiannually on each 1/1 and 7/1, with all compounded interest and principal paid at maturity on 1/1/04. Since there are no payments prior to maturity, each debt holder and the issuer generally may elect accrual periods of any length up to one year. If a person elects to use accrual periods corresponding to the semiannual compounding period provided for by the terms of the debenture, the accrual periods will be the same as in Example 1, i.e., the debenture has a short one-month accrual period ending 1/1/94 and then 20 six-month accrual periods.

---

payment at maturity, the holder "decides" to compute OID using semiannual accrual periods); Reg. §1.163-7(d) (providing that issuer's choice of accrual periods control for purposes of Code §163(i)(2)).

EXAMPLE 4

Same as Example 3 except the debenture *accrues and compounds* interest throughout its life each calendar *quarter* (rather than semiannually, as in Example 3). Since there are no payments prior to maturity, each debt holder and the issuer generally may elect accrual periods of any length up to one year. If a person elects to use accrual periods corresponding to the quarterly compounding period provided for by the terms of the debenture, the debenture will have a short one-month accrual period ending 1/1/94 and then 40 three-month accrual periods.

The OID regulations permit the issuer and/or each holder in the above examples to elect to use accrual periods shorter than those specified in the examples (or longer periods of up to one year), as long as each scheduled principal or interest payment occurs at the end or the beginning of an accrual period. To the extent they elect to use inconsistent accrual periods, the issuer's accrual period election will control, for purposes of computing "significant OID" under Code §163(i), as further discussed in ¶1303.3.1.5.[16]

EXAMPLE 5

Same as Example 3 except that the issuer and all holders elect to use monthly rather than semiannual accrual periods. The debenture will have 121 monthly accrual periods from issuance to maturity.

EXAMPLE 6

Same as Example 3 except that the holders elect monthly accrual periods, while the issuer elects six-month accrual periods corresponding to the scheduled payment dates. The issuer's accrual periods control for computing significant OID.

In the unusual situation in which a debenture provides for a single payment at maturity and for no other payment or compounding dates, the issuer and/or holders are free to elect (consistent or inconsistent) accrual periods of any fixed or variable intervals as long as each accrual period is no longer than one year and each scheduled payment of principal or interest occurs at the end or the

---

[16] Reg. §1.163-7(d).

beginning of an accrual period. In such cases, for Code §163(e)(5) purposes, the applicable accrual periods for instruments issued after 12/21/92 are those elected by the issuer.[17]

Measuring for significant OID. Under the significant OID test described above, the measurement to determine if a debenture has significant OID is made several times, and the debenture is treated as having significant OID if it fails any *one* such measurement.

The first measurement is made by reference to the five to six years from the debenture's issuance to the close of the first accrual period that ends *after* the fifth anniversary of issuance. The debenture is treated as having significant OID if Newco is not required by the debenture's terms to pay by the end of such five-to-six-year period all interest (including OID) accrued on the debenture, except an amount equal to the first 12 months' yield accrued after issuance.[18]

Moreover, a *series of additional measurements* is made by reference to the period from the debenture's issuance to the end of *each* accrual period ending after the first measurement period, and the debenture is treated as issued with significant OID (even if it survived the first five-to-six-year measurement) if Newco is not required by the debenture's terms to have paid by the end of each such period all interest (including OID) accrued on the debenture, except an amount equal to the first 12 months' yield accrued after issuance.

EXAMPLE 7

On 12/1/93 Newco issues a debenture which is scheduled to mature on 1/1/04 (i.e., 10 years and one month after issuance). The debenture pays interest (or accrues and compounds interest) semiannually on 1/1 and 7/1 of each year. (These facts are the same as Example 1 for a debenture *paying* interest on 1/1 and 7/1 and the same as Example 3 for a debenture *accruing and compounding* interest on 1/1 and 7/1.)

Assuming the issuer elects to use accrual periods corresponding to the six-month intervals between payment dates, the *first measurement* covers the one-month front-end short accrual period plus the next 10 full six-month accrual periods (i.e., 12/1/93 through 1/1/99). The *second measurement* covers the initial five-year and one-month period covered by the first measurement plus the next six-month accrual period (i.e., 12/1/93 through 7/1/99). The *third measurement* covers the five-year and seven-month period covered by the second measurement plus the next six-month accrual period (i.e., 12/1/93

---

[17] See Reg. §1.163-7(e). For debt instruments that were issued before 12/22/92 and provided for a single payment at maturity and for no other payment or compounding dates. Prop. Reg. §1.1272-1(d)(1)(iii) (consistent with the general rule of Code §1272(a)(5)) generally mandated a series of six-month accrual periods ending with the debenture's maturity date plus a short front-end accrual period (if any).

[18] See ¶1303.3.1.5 for a discussion of whether the first 12 months' yield is computed as compound or simple interest.

through 1/1/00). Each *subsequent measurement* covers the prior measurement period plus an additional six-month accrual period.

EXAMPLE 8

Same as Example 7 except that the issuer elects to use daily accrual periods rather than semiannual accrual periods. The *first measurement* covers the first five years and one day of the debenture's term (i.e., 12/1/93 through 12/2/98). The *second measurement* covers the initial five-year and one-day covered by the first measurement plus the next daily accrual period (i.e., 12/1/93 through 12/3/98). Each *subsequent measurement* covers the prior measurement period plus an additional daily accrual period.

Measurement when debenture issued. All of these measurements are made at the time the debenture is issued based on the terms of the debenture and assuming that "any payment under the instrument shall be ... made on the last day permitted under the instrument."[19] Thus, the determination whether a debenture has significant OID turns on the debenture's terms at issuance, not on whether the interest is actually paid. For the application of this principle to debentures paying variable rate or contingent interest, see ¶¶1303.3.1.7 and 1303.3.1.8. For a discussion of the extent to which post-issuance conduct or the possibility of post-issuance conduct may affect the debenture's characterization, see ¶1303.3.3.

Practical interpretation of significant OID language. In general, a debenture escapes significant OID (and hence will *not* be an AHYDO) even if:

(1)   Newco pays no interest (i.e., all interest merely accrues or is paid in bunny debentures or stock) until immediately prior to the end of the initial measurement period (between five and six years after issuance), and then at the end of such initial measurement period, Newco is required by the debenture's terms to pay in cash all interest accrued or paid by bunny debentures (or Newco is contractually required to redeem all interest paid in stock) through the end of such initial measurement period, except an amount equal to the first 12 months' yield accrued after issuance,[20] *and*

(2)   each accrual period thereafter Newco is required by the debenture's terms to pay the interest accrued during such accrual period, leaving unpaid only an aggregate amount equal to the first 12 months' yield accrued after issuance.

---

[19] Code §163(i)(3)(A).

[20] See ¶1303.3.1.5 for a discussion of whether the first 12 months' yield is computed as compound or simple interest.

On the other hand, the statute can be a trap for the unwary, in that minor variations in a debenture's terms may mean the difference between full application of Code §163(e)(5)'s interest deferral and disallowance rules and complete exemption from such rules.

EXAMPLE 9

On 6/1/93 Newco issues privately, for $100 cash, a six-year zero-coupon debenture (maturing on 6/1/99) with a redemption price of $250. The debenture provides for a single payment at maturity and for no other payment or compounding dates. The issuer elects to use six-month accrual periods under Reg. §1.1272-1(b). Therefore, the debenture's first measurement period for significant OID purposes is the 5 ½ years ending 12/1/98.[21]

The debenture in Example 9 is an AHYDO, because it satisfies all four requirements:

(1) The debenture is issued by a corporation.
(2) The debenture has a term exceeding five years.
(3) The debenture has a yield to maturity of 15.87% (i.e., the annual rate of interest, compounded semiannually, at which $100 will grow to $250 over a six-year period is 15.87%), which exceeds the AFR (5.26% compounded semiannually for midterm instruments issued in 6/93) by more than five percentage points.
(4) The debenture has significant OID, because the aggregate amount that the holder would include in income during the first 5 ½ years of the debenture's term, i.e., $131.62 of OID (based on a 15.87% yield to maturity, compounded semiannually, on $100 of principal for 5 ½ years), exceeds the sum of (a) the aggregate interest actually payable during such period ($0) plus (b) an amount equal to the first 12 months' yield accrued after issuance (presumably $16.50, i.e., 15.87% of 100, compounded semiannually).[22]

Since the debenture in Example 9 is an AHYDO, it is subject to Code §163(e)(5)'s interest deferral and disallowance rules unless it qualifies under the grandfather rules described in ¶1303.3.4.

By contrast, a minor change in a debenture's terms can exempt the debenture from the AHYDO definition and hence from Code §163(e)(5)'s operative rules.

---

[21] The result also would be the same if the debenture had been issued before 12/22/92 because 1986 Prop. Reg. §1.1272-1(d)(1)(iii) would have mandated six-month accrual periods for a debenture with these terms.

[22] See ¶1303.3.1.5 for a discussion whether the first 12 months' yield is computed as compound interest (i.e., $16.50), as assumed in text above, or as simple interest (i.e., $15.87).

EXAMPLE 10

Same as Example 9 except that on 12/1/98 (i.e., the last day of the first 5 ½ year measurement period) Newco is required by the terms of the debenture to pay all interest accruing through such date ($131.62), except for an amount equal to the first 12 months' yield accrued after issuance (presumably $16.50),[23] i.e., Newco is required to pay $115.12 of interest on 12/1/98. In addition, Newco is required by the debenture to pay an amount equal to the first 12 months' yield ($16.50) and the last six months' yield ($18.38) at maturity of the debenture on 6/1/99.

The debenture is not an AHYDO, because it does not have significant OID, and thus Code §163(e)(5) does not apply.

EXAMPLE 11

Same as Example 10 except that the debenture requires Newco to pay only $115.00 of interest on 2/28/95 rather than $115.12. The debenture now has significant OID and hence is an AHYDO, despite terms that are substantially identical to those in Example 10. Thus, Code §163(e)(5) does apply.

EXAMPLE 12

Same as Example 9 except the debenture provides for *annual* compounding, and neither the issuer nor the holder elects to use a shorter accrual period, so that the Example 12 debenture's accrual period is one year under Reg. §1.1272-1(b) (in contrast to the six month accrual period in Example 9).

The debenture does not have significant OID, because it is scheduled to pay all interest, as well as all principal, by the close of the first accrual period ending after the fifth anniversary of the debenture's issuance (i.e., by the

---

[23] See ¶1303.3.1.5 for a discussion whether the first 12 months' yield is computed as compound interest (i.e., $16.50), as assumed in text above, or as simple interest (i.e., $15.87).

debenture's maturity date on 6/1/99).[24] Therefore, the debenture is not an AHYDO, and Code §163(e)(5) does not apply.[25]

It is strange indeed that the debenture in Example 9 should be fully covered by Code §163(e)(5)'s operative rules while the debenture in Example 12 should escape them altogether, merely because the Example 9 debenture has a six-month accrual period while the Example 12 debenture has a one-year accrual period.

¶1303.2.2   Treatment of Interest on Applicable High Yield Discount Obligations

¶1303.2.2.1   Treatment of Issuer

Code §163(e)(5) bifurcates the OID on an AHYDO into (a) a deferred-deduction interest element, the deduction for which is deferred until the interest is actually paid (other than in bunny debentures or stock of the issuer or a related person), and (b) for an AHYDO whose total yield exceeds the AFR plus *six* percentage points (i.e., one percentage point higher than the minimum yield necessary for a debenture to constitute an AHYDO), a permanently non-deductible element (the "disqualified portion" of the AHYDO's OID). Stated differently, only the disqualified portion of an AHYDO's OID is permanently disallowed; all other interest on the AHYDO is deductible when paid.

¶1303.2.2.2   Treatment of Holder

Code §163(e)(5) does *not* affect the operation of the regular OID rules. Therefore, the holder of an AHYDO, whether or not the issuer's deductions are deferred or

---

[24] In electing to use an annual accrual period, the issuer should be careful to elect an annual accrual period which ends *on* the 6/1/99 maturity date of the debenture (as opposed to an annual accrual period which ends on the day before the 6/1/99 maturity date). Cf. Reg. §1.1272-1(j) (examples generally assume use of a final accrual period which ends on the day before the stated maturity date).

If the issuer in Example 12 elects to use annual accrual periods which begin on the issue date and each anniversary thereafter and end on the day *before* each anniversary (including the day before the 6/1/99 maturity date), a literal reading of Code §163(i) would suggest that the debenture has significant OID, since the accrued interest on the debenture is not paid until the actual maturity date (i.e., the day after the close of the first accrual period ending after the fifth anniversary of the debenture's issuance). The issuer may, however, be able to argue that it should be deemed to pay the interest before the close of the first accrual period ending after the fifth anniversary of the debenture's issuance. See, e.g., Reg. §§1.1272-1(f)(1), 1.1274-4(c)(3) (for purposes of determining the term of an instrument "the term of the debt instrument includes either the issue date or the maturity date, but not both dates"); Reg. §1.1272-1(j) (assumption in the examples that the "final" accrual period ends on the day before the stated maturity date implies that the debenture is deemed to be repaid at the close of the day before the stated maturity date).

[25] The result in Example 12 would be the same if the debenture had been issued before 12/22/92, because the debenture's accrual period would have been one year under 1986 Prop. Reg. §1.1272-1(d)(1)(i).

disallowed, reports all OID as interest income as it accrues under the regular OID rules. Code §163(e)(5) contains a special rule, however, under which a corporate holder of an AHYDO is entitled to a DRD with respect to the disqualified portion (i.e., the permanently non-deductible portion) of the AHYDO's OID.

¶1303.2.2.3   Determining OID "Disqualified Portion"

Although the statutory language is a bit murky,[26] it appears that the "disqualified portion" of an AHYDO's OID for a year (i.e., the portion which is permanently non-deductible to the issuer and eligible for the DRD if held by a corporation) is the *lesser of* (a) the debenture's total yield for the year, whether or not paid (the debenture's "total return"), multiplied by a fraction, the *numerator* of which is the debenture's "disqualified yield" (i.e., the excess of its yield to maturity over the sum of the AFR for the month of issuance plus six percentage points) and the *denominator* of which is the debenture's "yield to maturity," or (b) the debenture's accrued OID for the year.[27] Thus, none of the AHYDO's OID is subject to Code §163(e)(5)'s interest disallowance rule unless the debenture's yield exceeds the AFR plus six percentage points, and the interest disallowance rule phases in as the debenture's yield increase above the AFR plus six percentage points.

For purposes of this calculation, all interest on an AHYDO is treated as OID except for qualified stated interest ("QSI"), as defined for purposes of the regular OID rules by Code §1273(a)(2) and the OID regulations.[28] Reg. §1.1273-1(c) narrowly defines QSI as stated interest payments that are unconditionally payable in cash or in property (other than debt instruments of the issuer) at least annually at a single fixed rate (or at a variable rate if certain other requirements are satisfied). Interest unconditionally payable *in stock* at a fixed rate at least annually is not considered QSI for purposes of Code §163(i) and is included in OID for purposes of Code §163(e)(5).[29] Interest is "unconditionally payable" only if (1) "late payment (other than a late payment that occurs within a reasonable grace period) or non-payment is expected to be penalized or reasonable remedies exist to compel payment," (2) either the lending transaction reflects arm's-length dealing or the issuer intends to enforce such remedies, and (3) the interest is not payable on the occurrence of a contingency such as the existence of profits (for this purpose, the possibility of non-payment due to default, insolvency, or similar circumstances, or due to the exercise of a conversion right, is ignored). See ¶1303.3.2.1 for a discussion of the narrowness of the QSI concept.[30]

---

[26] See ¶1303.3.2.1.

[27] Code §163(e)(5)(C); H.R. Conf. Rep. No. 386, 101st Cong., 1st Sess. at 47-48 (1989) (as reprinted in CCH Stand. Fed. Tax Rep. no. 50 (11/22/89)) (hereinafter "1989 Conference Report").

[28] Code §163(e)(5)(C)(ii); 1989 Conference Report at 47.

[29] Code §§163(e)(5)(A), 163(i)(3)(B). See also ¶1303.3.2.3.

[30] For debentures issued before 12/22/92, the portion of interest that was excluded from OID was called qualified periodic interest payments ("QPIP"), which was similar to QSI. 1986 Prop. Reg. §1.1273-1(b)(1)(ii)(A) narrowly defined QPIP as a series of interest payments based on a fixed interest rate (or a variable rate tied to a single objective index of market interest rates) which is unconditionally payable at fixed periodic intervals of one year or less throughout the debenture's life. 1986 Prop. Reg.

Non-qualified stated interest debentures. For an AHYDO that does not provide for any QSI, the "disqualified portion" of its OID is the product of the total yield for the year (whether or not paid) multiplied by a fraction, the *numerator* of which is the debenture's "disqualified yield" (i.e., the excess of its yield to maturity over the sum of the AFR plus six percentage points) and the *denominator* of which is the debenture's "yield to maturity."

EXAMPLE 13

At a time when the AFR is 9%, compounded annually, Newco issues for $100 cash a 10-year debenture paying no interest currently, i.e., all interest accrues until maturity (or paying interest only in the form of bunny debentures which mature on the same date as the original debenture), with a yield to maturity of 20%, compounded annually.

The debenture's yield to maturity is 20%. The AFR (9%) plus six percentage points is 15%. Thus, the debenture's "disqualified yield" is 5% (20% less 15%). The 5% disqualified yield is 25% of the total yield (5% ÷ 20%).

Hence, 25% of the debenture's interest accruing each year (e.g., $5 of the $20 interest accruing in the first year and $6 of the $24 interest accruing in the second year) is non-deductible to Newco (but is includible in the holder's income as it accrues and is eligible for the DRD if the debenture is held by a corporation). The remaining 75% of the interest accruing each year (e.g., $15 of the first year's interest and $18 of the second year's interest) is deductible only when paid at maturity (but is includible in the holder's income as it accrues).[31]

Payments of original issue discount before maturity. If any part of the OID on an AHYDO (i.e, any interest that does not qualify as QSI) is actually paid before maturity, it must be determined how much of the amount paid represents the "disqualified portion" of the AHYDO's OID (and thus, is permanently disallowed) and how much of the payment is deductible when paid. While the statute is silent on this question, the 1989 Conference Report (at 47) states: "The allocation of payments of OID made . . . before maturity between the disqualified portion and the remainder [i.e, the portion which is deductible when actually paid] is to be made pursuant to Treasury regulations. The conferees expect such

---

§1.1273-1(b)(1)(iii) provided that interest is "unconditionally payable" if (1) the failure to pay such interest must result in consequences to the issuer that are typical in normal lending transactions, e.g., acceleration of all amounts due or compounding at a penalty rate significantly higher than the debenture's normal rate, and (2) the interest generally may not be payable on the occurrence of a stated contingency (such as the existence of profits).

Unless otherwise noted, the discussion of QSI in this ¶1303 generally applies as well to QPIP on debentures issued before 12/22/92.

[31] See 1989 Conference Report at 47 (Example 1).

regulations to provide that such payments will be allocated on a pro rata basis between accrued but unpaid OID treated as [deferred-deduction] interest, and the accrued but unpaid disqualified portion of the OID."

EXAMPLE 14

Same as Example 13 except that during the second year Newco pays $16 cash interest on the AHYDO. According to the 1989 Conference Report, $4 (25% of $16) is treated as a payment of the previously accrued disqualified portion, and $12 (75% of $16) is treated as a payment of the previously accrued deferred portion. Hence Newco may deduct the $12 when paid.[32] The cash payment does not, however, affect the holder's reporting of the transaction, which is the same as in Example 13.

Qualified stated interest debentures. As indicated earlier, for an AHYDO on which part of the interest is QSI (a "QSI debenture"), the "disqualified portion" of its OID for a year is the *lesser of* (1) the debenture's OID accrued for the year *or* (2) the product of the debenture's "total return" times a fraction, the *numerator* of which is the debenture's "disqualified yield" (i.e., the yield in excess of the AFR plus six percentage points) and the *denominator* of which is the debenture's "yield to maturity." "Total return" is defined by Code §163(e)(5)(C)(ii) as the OID that would have resulted had all QSI been included in the debenture's stated redemption price at maturity. Thus, total return for the debenture's lifetime is the sum of all payments required by the debenture less the debenture's issue price, and total return for a year appears to be the sum of a debenture's accrued OID for the year and its QSI for the year.[33] The effect of this elaborate rule is that "deductions will not be disallowed for amounts that qualify as [QSI]," because they are not OID.[34]

EXAMPLE 15

At a time when the AFR is 9%, compounded annually, Newco issues for $100 cash a 10-year debenture with a yield to maturity of 20%, consisting of $16 (i.e., 16% on the debenture's original face amount) payable annually in cash and $4 (i.e., 4% of the debenture's original face amount) that accrues and compounds annually at a 20% rate until maturity.

[32] See 1989 Conference Report at 47-48 (Example 2).
[33] See ¶1303.3.2.1 for a discussion whether "total return" is an annual or a lifetime-of-the-debenture concept.
[34] See 1989 Conference Report at 47, which refers to "qualified periodic interest payments" as defined in 1986 Prop. Reg. §1.1273-2(b)(1)(ii)(A), but should apply equally to QSI.

Just as in Example 13, the AHYDO's "disqualified yield" is 5%, because the debenture's yield to maturity (20%) exceeds by five percentage points the sum of the AFR (9%) plus six percentage points. Just as in Example 13, the disqualified yield is 25% of the yield to maturity (5% ÷ 20%).

Because a portion of the interest on this AHYDO is QSI, the amount permanently disallowed as a Newco deduction each year (and thus eligible for the DRD in a corporate holder's hands) is the *lesser of* (a) the OID for the year *or* (b) 25% of the debenture's "total return" for the year (i.e., the debenture's total accrued OID and QSI for the year). Thus no part of the 16% QSI will be disallowed or deferred in any year.

In the first year, the debenture's OID is $4, while 25% of the debenture's total return of $20 is $5 (25% × ($4 OID + $16 QSI) = $5). Thus the amount of first year interest permanently disallowed (and eligible for the DRD in a corporate holder's hands) is $4 (the *lesser of* $4 of OID *or* $5 fractional share of the total interest), in contrast to the permanent disallowance of $5 of first year interest in Example 13.

In the second year, the debenture's OID is $4.80, while 25% of the debenture's total return of $20.80 is $5.20 (25% × ($4.80 OID + $16 QSI) = $5.20). Thus the amount of second year interest permanently disallowed (and eligible for the DRD in a corporate holder's hands) is $4.80 (the *lesser of* $4.80 of OID *or* $5.20 fractional share of the total interest).

¶1303.2.2.4   Dividends-Received Deduction for Corporate Holder

Solely for purposes of the DRD provisions of Code §§243, 245, 246 and 246A, a corporate holder of an AHYDO treats as a dividend from the issuer (the "dividend equivalent portion") that portion of the OID includible in the holder's income (under the regular OID rules) which (a) "is attributable to the disqualified portion" of the AHYDO's OID and (b) "would have been treated as a dividend" had it been distributed with respect to the issuer's stock.[35] The corporate holder thus reports as interest income the full amount of the accrued OID calculated under the regular OID rules of Code §1272 and may be entitled to a partially offsetting DRD under this special Code §163(e)(5) rule.

EXAMPLE 16

When the AFR is 9%, compounded annually, Newco issues for $100 cash a 10-year debenture paying no interest currently and bearing a yield to maturity of 20%, compounded annually. A corporation ("C") owns the debenture.

As discussed in Example 13, the debenture's OID for the first year is $20, of which $5 (25%) is the disqualified portion. Thus, C reports $20 of OID as interest income in the first year. Because C is a corporation, and assuming

---

[35] Code §163(e)(5)(B).

Newco has sufficient current or accumulated E&P, $5 of C's $20 interest income (i.e., the portion attributable to the disqualified portion of OID) is treated, solely for purposes of the DRD rules, as a dividend from Newco. Thus, C is entitled to a $3.50 DRD (70% of $5) under Code §243, so that C has net taxable income of $16.50 ($20 interest income less $3.50 DRD).[36] If Newco has no E&P to support the dividend, C reports the $20 of OID as interest income, without any offsetting DRD.

¶1303.2.2.5 Effect on E&P

Code §163(e)(5) generally does not apply for purposes of determining the issuer's E&P.[37] Thus, the issuer's E&P is reduced currently by accrued OID expense, whether or not Code §163(e)(5) defers or disallows the issuer's OID deduction.

There is one exception to this rule: Solely for purposes of determining the amount of the corporate holder's DRD, "no reduction [to the issuer's E&P] shall be made for any amount attributable to the disqualified portion of any OID on such obligation."[38] Thus, a corporate holder is not denied the DRD solely because the issuer's E&P was reduced currently by the disqualified portion of the OID.

The 1989 Conference Report (at 48) clarifies that this special rule does *not* apply in determining the issuer's E&P "in subsequent years." Thus, the issuer's E&P for a year is reduced by all OID accrued in *prior years*, whether such OID was deducted or deferred or disallowed under Code §163(e)(5).

EXAMPLE 17

Same as Example 16 except that in the first year Newco has $22 of E&P (current and accumulated) before taking into account the $20 of accrued OID for such year on the debenture held by C.

If Newco's E&P were reduced currently by all of the accrued OID, only $2 of E&P would remain in determining whether C could claim the DRD with respect to the $5 disqualified portion of OID. In that case, only $2 rather

---

[36] However, if C satisfies the 20% DRD stock ownership test with respect to Newco, the DRD would be 80% rather than 70%. See Code §243(c). Also, if C is an SBIC, the DRD would be 100% (Code §243(a)(2)); if C owns 80% of Newco and meets certain other requirements, the DRD would be 100% (Code §243(a)(3) and (b)); and if C has debt-financed its Newco debenture, the amount of the 70% or 80% DRD would be reduced proportionately (Code §246A). If Newco is a foreign corporation, the DRD is generally not available at all. Code §§243(a) and 245. Finally, additional limitations on C's DRD would apply if C's taxable income for the year is less than the amount of its dividend income plus its dividend equivalent income (Code §246(b)), if C fails to satisfy certain holding period requirements with respect to the Newco debenture (Code §246(c)), or if Newco is a specialized type of entity (Code §246(a)). For further discussion of several of these issues, see ¶1303.3.2.4.

[37] Code §163(e)(5)(E).

[38] Code §163(e)(5)(E).

than $5 of C's OID would be treated as a dividend for DRD purposes, despite the non-deductibility to Newco of the entire $5 disqualified portion.

Under the special rule described above, Newco's E&P for this purpose is reduced currently only by the $15 deferred portion of the first year's OID, not by the $5 disqualified portion. Thus, in determining whether the $5 disqualified portion of the OID gives rise to a dividend for DRD purposes, Newco's E&P is $7 ($22 – $15). For all other purposes, Newco's E&P is $2.

This special rule ceases to apply at the beginning of the next year, at which time Newco's E&P becomes $2 for all purposes.[39]

¶1303.3 Issues and Problems

The following discussion considers some of the practical issues and problems raised by the AHYDO rules and, if not already clear from ¶1303.2, demonstrates as well the rules' excessive complexity and serious inequities.

¶1303.3.1 Definition of Applicable High Yield Discount Obligation

¶1303.3.1.1 Not Limited to LBOs and Subordinated Debentures

Although it arises out of the House's 1989 LBO hearings, Code §163(i) (unlike Code §279) is not limited to debentures issued in connection with an acquisition. Rather, it also applies to OID or PIK debentures (a) issued by Newco for cash to raise working capital or (b) issued to a long-standing corporation's shareholders in a leveraged restructuring.

Moreover, although much of the focus of the 1989 LBO hearings was on junk bonds (i.e., *subordinated* debentures), Code §163(i) (unlike Code §279) is not limited to *subordinated* debentures. Rather, it also applies to OID or PIK debentures issued by Newco that are *pari passu* with Newco's other unsecured creditors and even debt instruments which are secured (i.e., senior to Newco's unsecured creditors). Nevertheless, the AHYDO prerequisite of a yield not less than five percentage points above the AFR necessarily means that a debenture will be covered only if it is substantially less than investment grade.

¶1303.3.1.2 More Than Five-Year Term

An OID or PIK debenture will not be an AHYDO unless it has a "maturity date . . . more than 5 years from the date of issue." Thus, any debenture with a term exceeding five years is covered, even if the OID or PIK feature lasts less

---

[39] See 1989 Conference Report at 48 (Example 3).

than five years, e.g., a 10-year debenture that pays interest in bunny debentures or stock for the first four years and then pays interest in cash periodically for the remaining six years. However, if the duration of the OID or PIK feature is brief, the amount of OID may be too small to constitute "significant" OID (as defined in ¶1303.2.1.3), in which case the debenture will not be an AHYDO.

Although a debenture that matures on or before the fifth anniversary of its issuance will not normally be an AHYDO, there are at least two possible exceptions. *First*, Code §163(i)(5) grants IRS authority to promulgate "regulations to prevent avoidance of the purposes of this [provision] through the use of . . . agreements to borrow amounts due under the debt instrument." Hence, regulations may well treat Newco's debenture as having a more than five-year maturity if, on its face, it matures in five years or less but the debenture holder has agreed at the time the debenture is issued to loan Newco additional funds in the future—in effect, to refinance the debenture.[40] Presumably such regulations will not seek to go further and so treat a third party's agreement to make a future loan to Newco (i.e., a loan agreement between Newco and a person not related to the debenture holder).[41]

Second, suppose a Newco debenture (the "junior debenture") is due in five years or less but is subordinated in right of payment to other Newco debt (the "senior indebtedness") and the senior indebtedness has the right to prevent the junior debenture from being paid in accordance with its terms if the senior indebtedness has not previously been paid. IRS might (perhaps in regulations) take the position that in some such circumstances the junior debenture does not really have a maturity date of five years or less (e.g., where the senior debt is not due until after the fifth anniversary of the junior debenture's issuance).[42]

¶1303.3.1.3   Yield Exceeding AFR Plus Five (or Six) Percentage Points

The following considerations are relevant in determining whether a debenture's yield to maturity equals or exceeds five (or six) percentage points over the AFR.

Applicable federal rate. The appropriate AFR (midterm or long-term) turns on the debenture's scheduled weighted average maturity.[43] Moreover, as discussed

---

[40] See ¶1303.3.3.2 for additional tracing and allocation issues raised by multiple borrowing agreements.

[41] In a related context, interest paid with money borrowed from the same person to whom the interest is due is often treated as having been paid with a note and hence is not deductible by a cash method borrower; however, interest paid with money borrowed from a third party (i.e., a person not related to the person to whom the interest is due) is treated as paid in cash and hence is deductible by a cash method borrower. See Battelstein v. Commissioner, 631 F.2d 1182, 80-2 U.S.T.C. ¶9840 (5th Cir. 1980), *cert. denied*, 451 U.S. 938 (1981).

[42] For the effect of such subordination on whether interest is unconditionally payable for QSI (or, generally for debentures issued before 12/22/92, QPIP) purposes, see ¶1303.3.2.1. For the effect of a conversion feature on a debenture's maturity date, see ¶1303.3.1.4.

[43] Reg. §1.1274-4(c).

in ¶1303.2.1.1, the controlling rate is the AFR for the month in which the debenture is issued.

Code §163(i)(1) authorizes regulations permitting a rate *higher* than the AFR if the taxpayer establishes that the higher rate is based on the same principles as the AFR and is appropriate for the debenture's term. In the case of foreign currency debentures, a surrogate for the AFR should be developed by regulations or otherwise, perhaps in the manner prescribed in Reg. §1.1274-4(d).

"Yield to maturity" not defined. Neither Code §163(i) nor the 1989 committee reports define "yield to maturity" (although they refer to the regular OID rules for definitions of "accrual period," "issue price," and "qualified periodic interest payments").[44] Without further guidance, presumably the definition of yield to maturity appearing in the regular OID rules is intended to apply.[45]

Fees paid by Newco to the lender. It is not altogether clear whether a commitment fee and/or a closing fee paid by Newco to the lender increases the debenture's yield or is treated as a payment for services. It is likely that points which Newco pays to the lender at the front-end increase the debenture's yield. It is not clear whether Newco's reimbursement of the lender's expenses (e.g., attorneys' fees) increases the debenture's yield.[46]

Non-traded debenture issued in exchange for non-traded property. Under the regular OID rules, the yield to maturity of a debenture whose issue price is determined under Code §1274 (i.e., a non-traded debenture issued in exchange for non-traded property, such as stock of a private company) is either the AFR or, if the debenture bears a stated interest rate that exceeds the AFR and is paid or compounded at least annually throughout the debenture's term, such stated interest rate.[47] Therefore, it appears that such a debenture will not have a yield in excess of the AFR plus five percentage points (and hence, will not be an AHYDO) unless the debenture bears stated interest in excess of that sum, even

---

[44] The failure of Code §163(i) to cross-refer to the regular OID rules for the definition of yield to maturity may be explained by the absence of a *statutory* definition in Code §1272; yield to maturity is defined only in Reg. §1.1272-1(b)(1)(i) (or, generally for debentures issued before 12/22/92, 1986 Prop. Reg. §1.1272-1(f)).

[45] But see ¶1303.3.1.5 for a discussion of one situation when there should be a difference.

[46] Reg. §1.1273-2(g) generally provides that, in the case of a private lending transaction: (i) payments from the borrower to the lender for the lender's services (such as "commitment fees" or "loan processing costs") are treated as payment for services and therefore are not taken into account for OID purposes; (ii) any other payments from the borrower to the lender (including points, other than points that are paid in connection with a residential mortgage and deductible currently under Code §461(g)(2)) constitute a return (by the borrower to the lender) of part of the loan proceeds, thus decreasing the issue price and increasing OID and yield to maturity; and (iii) any payment from the lender to the borrower is treated as an additional amount loaned. (1986 Prop. Reg. §1.1273-2(f) provided similarly for debentures issued before 12/22/92.) This Code §1273 regulation should apply for purposes of Code §§163(e)(5) and (i).

[47] See Code §1274; Reg. §1.1274-2(c)(1). For debentures issued before 12/22/92, 1986 Prop. Reg. §1.1274-3(b) generally required, in addition, that the stated interest rate (rather than the AFR) will apply only if payment or compounding occurs at regular intervals throughout the debenture's term.

though a market interest rate on similar debentures may substantially exceed the AFR plus five points.

Consider the following three examples, in each of which the parties have agreed to exchange non-traded property for a non-traded zero-coupon debenture that pays $1,000 after 10 years.

EXAMPLE 18

At a time when the AFR is 9%, compounded annually, Newco's sole shareholder ("A") sells all of Newco's stock to an unrelated purchasing corporation ("P") in exchange for P's 10-year debenture. Neither P's debenture nor Newco's stock is traded. The P debenture pays no stated interest and has a stated principal amount of $1,000 due in 10 years.

The parties believe that Newco's stock is worth $150 at the time of the sale, which would imply an issue price for the debenture of $150 and a yield to maturity of 21%, compounded annually—well in excess of the AFR plus five percentage points.

However, since the P debenture bears no stated interest and was issued in exchange for non-traded property, Code §1274 determines the debenture's issue price based on a discount rate equal to the AFR (9% compounded annually). Hence under Code §1274 the debenture has a yield to maturity of only 9%, compounded annually, and an issue price of $422 ($1,000 discounted at a 9% annual rate for 10 years).

Thus, the debenture is *not* an AHYDO.

EXAMPLE 19

Same as Example 18 except that P's 10-year debenture has a stated principal amount of $352, a stated interest rate of 11% accrued and compounded annually and payable at maturity (a rate well below market), and a stated amount payable at maturity of $1,000 ($352 principal and $648 accrued interest).

Since the debenture bears stated interest in excess of the AFR, its yield to maturity under Code §1274 is the stated rate of 11%, which is less than the AFR (9%) plus five percentage points. Thus, the debenture is *not* an AHYDO.

EXAMPLE 20

Same as Example 18 except that P's 10-year debenture has a stated principal amount of $150, a stated interest rate of 21% accrued and compounded annually and payable at maturity (a market rate of interest), and a stated amount payable at maturity of $1,000 ($150 principal and $850 accrued interest).

Since the debenture's stated interest rate exceeds the AFR (9%) plus five percentage points (and the debenture meets the other tests), the debenture *is* an AHYDO.

Code §163(i)(2)(B) as finally enacted (in contrast to the 1989 House Bill) expressly refers to Code §1274 for the determination of a debenture's issue price for one purpose (Code §163(i)(2)(A)), thus supporting the conclusion that Code §1274 is to be applied in making determinations (with respect to a non-traded debenture issued for non-traded property) throughout Code §163(i). Moreover, the transaction described above is not among the "potentially abusive situations" described in Reg. §1.1274-3(a) (or in 1986 Prop. Reg. §1.1274-4(g)). It might be addressed, however, in regulations under Code §163(i)(5), which authorizes "regulations to prevent avoidance of the purposes of this [provision] through the use of . . . other arrangements."[48]

Interest paid in stock. The 1990 Act retroactively amended Code §163(i)(3) in effect to provide that, in computing whether a debenture's yield to maturity exceeds the AFR plus five percentage points (and the extent to which a debenture's yield to maturity exceeds the AFR plus six percentage points), but not for other purposes, interest to be paid in Newco's (or a related person's) stock is deemed

---

[48] If the parties to a sale of non-traded property reduce a debenture's yield in the manner stated above—i.e., by stating an initial principal amount greater than FV and an interest rate less than market (or no interest rate at all)—in order to avoid classification as an AHYDO, there will be a tax cost to the issuer, since reducing the yield reduces the issuer's interest deductions. However, the issuer should ultimately recover the lost interest deductions when it disposes of (or depreciates) the purchased non-traded property, which should then have a correspondingly higher tax basis. Under Reg. §1.1012-1(g), the issuer's tax basis in the property is equal to the issue price of the debenture, which in turn is based on the debenture (if the debenture has no stated interest rate) or the stated interest rate (if the debenture has a stated interest rate not less than the AFR).

Thus, in Examples 18 through 20, P's basis in the Newco stock purchased is the present value of the debenture's $1,000 redemption price discounted at a rate equal to the debenture's Code §1274 yield, resulting in a tax basis of $422 in Example 18 (based on a 9% yield), $352 in Example 19 (based on an 11% yield), and $150 in Example 20 (based on a 21% yield). Hence, whereas Code §163(e)(5) permanently disallows a portion of the interest deduction where a debenture bears a rate greater than the AFR plus six percentage points, a lower yield on a debenture issued in Code §1274 transaction defers but does not permanently disallow the issuer's tax benefit.

The issue discussed above also affects the seller's tax ramifications in a Code §1274 transaction, since Reg. §1.1001-1(g) provides that the seller's amount realized on the sale is generally the issue price of the debenture. Moreover, for purposes of the Code §453 installment sale rules, the selling price is computed net of OID and any other interest. See Temp. Reg. §15A.453-1(b)(2)(ii). Thus, the lower the yield, the higher the selling price and the greater the amount of gain recognition that is tax deferred under the installment method of reporting. This can produce a taxpayer-adverse result under Code §453A, since the higher installment gain recognition produces a greater penalty interest charge under Code §453A.

In short, the tax costs and benefits to both sides should be weighed carefully before using Code §1274 as a creative solution to the Code §163(e)(5) problem in a sale of non-traded property for a non-traded debenture.

paid when such stock is scheduled to be issued. This is in contrast to the general rule (applicable to interest payable in bunny debentures or stock) that PIK interest is deemed paid for AHYDO purposes when it is required to be paid in cash or other property (e.g., when the bunny debenture or stock is scheduled to be redeemed). Without this exception to the general deemed payment rule, stock without a mandatory redemption feature presumably would not contribute to yield at all, since it would never be required to be paid in cash or other property. See ¶1303.3.1.6.

Regarding the application of this special yield-to-maturity computation rule to interest paid in *preferred* stock, the 1990 Conference Report (at 165) states:

> The conferees understand that, in the case of a debt instrument that makes payments in the form of stock which provides for an annual dividend rate and a stated redemption amount by a fixed date [i.e., certain preferred stock], the amount of stock to be taken into account [in computing yield to maturity] should generally be determined by discounting such payments. The discount rate for such purpose shall be the yield on the debt instrument determined assuming the payments under the stock are made as provided.

¶1303.3.1.4   *Warrants and Conversion Privileges*

(1)   Allocation of consideration to a warrant or common stock. Under the regular OID rules, where a debenture is issued as part of an investment unit along with warrants and/or common stock in exchange for cash or publicly traded property (or when the investment unit is publicly traded), the purchase price for the investment unit is allocated between the debenture and the warrants and/or common stock,[49] thus often increasing yield and creating or increasing the debenture's OID. Because Code §163(i)(2)(B) refers to the regular OID rules for the definition of "issue price," this investment unit rule should extend to the new OID/PIK provision.

Where a debenture is issued as part of an investment unit along with common shares or warrants, but neither the debenture nor the common shares or warrants have a readily ascertainable FV (e.g., because they are not publicly traded), there can be a difficult factual valuation issue. Depending on the valuation of the investment unit's components, the debenture may or may not have significant OID and may or may not have a yield five (or six) percentage points above the AFR. For similar valuation difficulties in the case of debentures that provide for future contingent payments, see ¶1303.3.1.8.

(2)   No allocation to conversion privilege. Under the regular OID rules, no part of the purchase price for a debenture is separately allocated to a right to convert the debenture into stock or another debt instrument of the issuer or a

---

[49] Code §1273(c)(2); Reg. §1.1273-2(h).

related person (a "conversion privilege").[50] Hence, a convertible debenture issued at face value would have no OID even if the conversion privilege were quite valuable, unless regulations to the contrary are promulgated pursuant to Code §163(i)(5), which authorizes "such regulations as may be appropriate to carry out the purposes of this [provision], including . . . modifications to [this provision] in the case of . . . conversion rights. . . ." If regulations are promulgated to the contrary, the amount of OID for purposes of the new OID/PIK provision would often be greater than the amount of OID for purposes of the regular OID rules, thus adding to the already plentiful confusion.

(3) **Effect of conversion privilege on maturity.** Apart from the allocation issue discussed above, the existence of a conversion privilege raises a second issue: Does the conversion privilege cause the debenture's stated maturity date to be disregarded for purposes of the new provision? In determining whether a debenture has more than a five-year term or has significant OID (but not in determining the debenture's yield to maturity—see ¶1303.3.1.3), "any payment under the instrument shall be assumed to be made on the last day permitted under the instrument" and "any payment to be made in the form of [stock] of the issuer (or a related person . . .) shall be assumed to be made when such [stock] is required to be paid in cash or in property. . . ."[51]

Thus, in the unusual circumstance where the *issuer* has the option to require a debenture holder to accept stock in payment of the debenture principal at or before the stated maturity date, the stated maturity date is apparently disregarded for purposes of determining under the new provision whether the debenture has more than five-year maturity and whether the debenture has significant OID, so that the date (if any) when the issuer is required to redeem such stock is treated as the maturity date.

However, in the more typical circumstance where only the *holder* (not the issuer) has the option to require the issuer to pay the debenture principal with stock, so that the issuer is unconditionally obligated to pay the debenture in cash at its stated maturity unless the holder waives such requirement by electing to convert, the holder's conversion option should have no effect on the debenture's maturity date for purposes of the new provision.

Nevertheless, a thoroughly mystifying sentence in the 1989 Conference Report (at 48) implies the opposite: "The conferees expect that for purposes of determining the maturity of an obligation, . . . regulations would provide that the right to convert an applicable instrument into the stock of the issuer may be disregarded if such right is solely in the hands of the holder and the exercise price is the fair

---

[50] See Reg. §1.1232-3(b)(2); Reg. §1.1273-2(j). But cf. Rev. Rul. 70-108, 1970-1 C.B. 78, concluding that where a convertible preferred holder had the right (but not the obligation) to pay an additional cash amount and receive additional shares of the issuer on conversion, the right to purchase the additional shares constitutes in effect a separate warrant.

If the conversion were into stock of another corporation (or into any other property), the law is more complicated. See, e.g., Rev. Rul. 69-135, 1969-1 C.B. 198 (debenture convertible into stock of an unrelated corporation).

[51] Code §163(i)(3)(A) and (B), as retroactively amended by the 1990 Act.

market value, at the date of conversion, of the amount of stock received." The convertible debenture described in the quoted sentence is typical in that it is convertible at the *holder's* option, but is atypical with respect to the conversion price. A typical convertible debenture is convertible into a *fixed* number of common shares, regardless of the price at which the issuer's common shares are trading when the holder elects to convert (e.g., a $1,000 debenture convertible at the holder's option into 50 common shares (i.e., at a fixed conversion price of $20 per share), subject to formula antidilution). However, the quoted sentence contemplates a debenture with a *variable* conversion price equal to the stock's FV at the time of conversion.

By stating that the holder's option to convert "may be disregarded" by the regulations "for purposes of determining the maturity of an obligation" where conversion is *both* at the *holder's* option and at a *variable* price equal to the stock's FV at conversion, the quoted sentence suggests that where conversion is at the holder's option *but at a fixed price*, the regulations should be drafted so that the holder's conversion privilege will somehow affect the debenture's maturity date for purposes of the new provision.

Where a debenture is convertible only at the holder's option, the issuer is unconditionally obligated to pay it at its stated maturity unless the holder elects to convert. For this reason, we believe that the IRS, in drafting regulations under Code §163(i), should treat such a debenture as maturing on its scheduled maturity date, rather than on a later date as suggested by the 1989 Conference Report.[52]

¶1303.3.1.5   Significant Original Issue Discount Determination

The following issues specifically concern the "significant" OID determination discussed in ¶1303.2.1.3.

(1)   Calculation of first 12 months' yield for purposes of computing significant OID. As discussed above, a debenture will not have significant OID so long as by the end of the first measurement period (i.e., the period from issuance to the close of the first accrual period ending after the fifth anniversary of issuance) and by the end of each subsequent accrual period, all interest accrued through such date has been paid, except for "the product of the issue price of such instrument . . . and its yield to maturity." Unfortunately, the quoted statutory exception from Code §163(i)(2)(B)(ii) is ambiguous.

EXAMPLE 21

Newco plans to issue a debenture with a $100 face amount for $100 of cash. The debenture will bear interest at a 20% rate, compounded semiannu-

---

[52] We do not believe the result should be any different for a debenture (convertible only by the holder) with an in-the-money conversion privilege. If the conversion privilege is sufficiently deep in the money, the debenture will be treated as stock under traditional debt/equity principles. See, e.g.,

ally. Newco elects to use semiannual accrual periods for OID purposes. Newco plans to structure the debenture so that (a) all interest accrues until the end of the first measurement period, i.e., the last day of the 11th semiannual accrual period, (b) Newco is required to pay on the last day of such 11th semiannual accrual period all interest accrued, except the amount permitted to remain unpaid by Code §163(i)(2)(B)(ii), and (c) Newco is required to pay on the last day of each semiannual accrual period thereafter all interest accrued, except the amount permitted to remain unpaid by Code §163(i)(2)(B)(ii).

The question in Example 21 is whether the amount that Code §163(i)(2)(B)(ii) permits to remain unpaid is $20 or $21. Because the debenture compounds interest semiannually, it will actually accrue $21 of interest during the first 12 months, i.e., 10% of $100 during the first six months *plus* 10% of $110 during the second six months. Stated differently, 20% compounded semiannually is 21% per year. Hence, one would suppose that the amount of interest Newco can leave accrued and unpaid at the end of each measurement period is $21.

On the other hand, the statutory words "the product of the [debenture's] issue price . . . and its yield to maturity" could mean $20, the product of the $100 original issue price and the 20% annual interest rate stated in the debenture (i.e., without adjustment for compounding within the year), in which case Newco could leave no more than $20 of interest accrued and unpaid at the end of each measurement period. The regular OID rules adopt this latter meaning of "yield to maturity," i.e., the annual interest rate on the debenture, without adjustment for compounding within the year, for purposes of the regular OID rules.[53]

However, a strong argument can be made that this unadjusted annual interest rate definition from the regular OID rules should not control in the substantially different context of Code §163(i). The regular OID rules certainly use compounding: Code §1272(a)(3)(A)(ii) refers to "yield to maturity (determined on the basis of compounding at the close of each accrual period . . .)." Thus, for purposes of the regular OID rules, "yield to maturity" is a simple rate for each accrual period, and Code §1272(a)(3) achieves compounding by applying the simple rate each accrual period to the debenture's adjusted issue price, i.e., its enhanced principal amount (including the interest accrued in prior accrual periods). In contrast, because Code §163(i)(2)(B)(ii) does not contain the period-to-period compounding feature of Code §1272(a)(3), "yield to maturity" for purposes of Code §163(i)(2)(B)(ii) should be the debenture's actual annualized yield.

In short, for purposes of Code §163(i)(2)(B)(ii), "the product of the issue price . . . and its yield to maturity" should mean all yield accruing on the debenture during the first 12 months. Moreover, as discussed in ¶1303.3.1.3, neither Code §163(i) nor the 1989 committee reports refer to the regular OID rules for the

---

Rev. Rul. 82-150, 1982-2 C.B. 110 (where an option, purchased for $70,000, entitled the holder to acquire, for an exercise price of $30,000, stock worth $100,000 at the time the option was issued, the holder was treated as the actual owner of the optioned stock).

[53] See Reg. §1.1272-1(b)(1)(i).

definition of "yield to maturity" (although they do for several other definitions), suggesting that the definition of "yield to maturity" appearing in the regular OID rules is not necessarily intended to apply for this purpose.[54]

Nonetheless, until the meaning of "yield to maturity" for purposes of Code §163(i)(2)(B)(ii) is clarified, it is doubtless safer to structure a debenture designed to avoid significant OID based on the conservative assumption that "yield to maturity" has the simple interest meaning specified in the regular OID rules, resulting in a slightly smaller first-year OID cushion for instruments with an initial accrual period of less than one year.

(2) Payment of principal versus payment of interest. As discussed above, the determination of whether a debt instrument has significant OID is made by comparing the aggregate amount of interest accrued on the instrument through the end of certain accrual periods to the "aggregate amount of interest [required] to be paid on the debt instrument" by the close of such accrual periods. As a result of this formulation, whether a debt instrument has significant OID may depend on whether scheduled payments on the debt are characterized as payments of interest or principal.

Fortunately, the OID regulations generally provide that all payments on a debt instrument are characterized for income tax purposes as a payment of interest to the extent of all previously accrued and unpaid interest and OID.[55] Consequently, all scheduled payments on the debt instrument, whether characterized in the instrument as payments of interest or principal, should be treated for purposes of Code §163(e)(5) as reducing any unpaid OID outstanding on the date of the scheduled payment.

EXAMPLE 22

On 1/1 year 1 Newco issues a 10-year PIK debenture. For the first five years the debenture is outstanding, it is scheduled to pay PIK interest (i.e., by issuing bunny debentures). On 1/1 year 7 (the end of the first annual compounding period after the debenture's five-year anniversary), Newco is required to pay in cash all interest accrued since 1/1 year 6 and to redeem a portion of the outstanding debentures equal to the amount of all bunny debentures issued on the debenture. Newco is required to pay all interest accruing thereafter in cash on a current basis.

---

[54] The 1989 committee reports do not resolve the question. All the examples in the 1989 House and Senate Reports involve debentures that provide for *annual* compounding of interest, and Examples 1 and 2 of the 1989 Conference Report are ambiguous on the issue.

[55] Reg. §1.446-2(e)(1); Reg. §1.1275-2(a). The regulations contain one exception under which a "pro rata repayment" on a debt instrument may be allocated in part to unpaid principal rather than to accrued but unpaid interest/OID. Reg. §1.446-2(e)(4); Reg. §1.1275-2(a)(2)(iii). A pro rata repayment is defined, in part, as a payment that "is not made pursuant to the instrument's payment schedule." Reg. §1.1275-2(f)(2). Because the Code §163(e)(5) rules are applied at the time a debt instrument is issued, and by taking into account only scheduled payments on the instrument, unscheduled payments which may be treated as "pro rata repayments" should not affect the Code §163(e)(5) calculation.

Assuming Newco elects to use an annual accrual period, the debenture's first measurement period ends 1/1 year 7 (the end of the first accrual period ending more than five years after issuance). On 1/1 year 7, all interest accrued through such date is required by the debenture's terms to be paid in cash. This is because the scheduled redemption of debentures is treated as a payment of the accrued but unpaid interest/OID on the debentures. The result will be the same regardless of whether the debentures which are actually redeemed are the bunny debentures or a portion of the originally issued debentures.

(3)   Payment of interest on or before last day of accrual period. A key question in applying the significant OID test is whether, under the debenture's terms, all interest accrued through the close of the accrual period is required to be paid by the end of each measurement period (except an amount equal to the first 12 months' yield accrued after issuance). Therefore, unless the regulations adopt a leeway period, it appears that a debenture which leaves the first 12 months' yield unpaid must require all other interest accrued through each accrual period ending after the fifth anniversary of issuance to be paid on or before the last day of such accrual period, not on the day after the end of each accrual period or a few days after the end of each accrual period.[56]

(4)   Accrual periods. As discussed in ¶1303.2.1.3, the OID regulations (in contrast to the 1986 proposed regulation) permit the issuer and holder each to elect accrual periods of any length (which may vary over the term of the debt instrument), as long as each accrual period is no longer than one year and each scheduled principal or interest payment occurs at the end of an accrual period. Apparently the issuer and holder may even elect inconsistent accrual periods, and one holder may elect accrual periods inconsistent with those elected by another holder of the same class of debt, as long as the accrual periods satisfy the above criteria. If the issuer and holder (or different holders) elect inconsistent accrual periods, the issuer's accrual periods will control for purposes of computing significant OID.

In contrast to the 1986 proposed OID regulation (which determined the applicable accrual period based on the stated terms of the debt instrument), the final regulation generally places the burden on each party to choose an accrual period. For example, apparently an instrument that provides for quarterly compounding does not foreclose a party from adopting daily accrual periods. Because the presence of significant OID must be determined at issuance, it may be important for the issuer to document its choice of the proper accrual period(s) at that time.

---

[56] See ¶1303.2.1.3 note 23 for a further discussion of this issue. The 1989 House Report (at 74) and 1989 Senate Report (at 71) clarify that "amounts required to be paid on the last day of the accrual period are treated as required to be paid before the close of the accrual period."

¶1303.3.1.6   Interest Paid in Stock as a Payment-in-Kind Feature

As discussed in ¶1303.2.1.2, where Newco is required or permitted to pay interest on a debenture in the form of stock (either common or preferred), then in determining whether the debenture has more than a five-year term or has significant OID, Code §163(i)(3), as retroactively amended by the 1990 Act, treats such interest as paid when the stock is required to be "paid [e.g., by redemption] in cash or in property other than [stock or debt of the issuer or a related person]" (the "mandatory redemption rule"). In the case of preferred stock with a mandatory redemption date, it appears that the redemption date specified in the instrument will control. In the case of common stock where the original debenture contractually obligates Newco to redeem such common stock at a specified date, such specified date should similarly control.

However, in the case of preferred stock with no mandatory redemption date or common stock not subject to a contractual obligation to redeem on a specified date, the interest payment date for Code §163(i) purposes appears to be indefinite under the mandatory redemption rule. This raises an issue in determining whether such a debenture has significant OID. Under Code §163(i)(2), significant OID results if a specified statutory amount exceeds the product of the debenture's "issue price" (as defined in Code §§1273 and 1274) and its "yield to maturity." Since the mandatory redemption rule literally applies in making this determination, interest paid in stock without a mandatory redemption feature apparently does not add to a debenture's "yield to maturity," thus enhancing the risk that the debenture has significant OID.

EXAMPLE 23

When the AFR is 9%, compounded annually, Newco issues, for $100 cash, a $100 face amount debenture with a term of six years and one month. The debenture bears interest at a 20% rate, compounded annually. Seventeen percent interest is unconditionally payable annually in cash. Newco has the option to pay the remaining 3% interest annually in cash or in Newco common stock, valued for this purpose at the stock's FV at the time the stock is issued in payment of the interest. There is no contractual obligation for Newco to redeem any common stock issued as interest payments. Both the issuer and the holder elect to use an annual accrual period.

Interest paid in stock is treated as currently paid for purposes of the regular OID rules (see ¶1309.2). Therefore, as of the end of year six, the debenture holder will have included $120 of interest in gross income (i.e., $20 annual interest for six years), whether Newco actually pays the interest in cash or in common stock. Hence, the debenture has significant OID if $120 exceeds the sum of (i) the aggregate amount of interest to be "paid" during such period and (ii) the product of the debenture's $100 issue price and its "yield to maturity." Under the mandatory redemption rule, Newco is deemed to pay only $102 of interest during the six-year period (i.e., $17 annual cash interest for six years).

> If the mandatory redemption rule *does not* apply in computing issue price times yield to maturity (i.e., Newco's stock is deemed to be a payment of interest when issued, consistent with other yield to maturity computations under Code §§163(e)(5) and (i)), yield to maturity will be 20% (reflecting both the cash and stock portions of the interest). Hence the debenture will not have significant OID, because the $120 of interest reported in the holder's gross income will not exceed the sum of clauses (i) and (ii) above (i.e., $102 + ($100 × 20%) = $122).
>
> In contrast, if the mandatory redemption rule *does* apply in computing issue price times yield to maturity (as it literally appears to), yield to maturity for this purpose will be only 17% (reflecting the cash interest only). Hence the debenture will have significant OID, because the $120 of interest reported in the holder's gross income exceeds the sum of clauses (i) and (ii) (i.e., $102 + ($100 × 17%) = $119).

Regulations or other guidance should clarify that yield to maturity is to be computed for significant OID purposes by treating interest paid in stock as paid when such stock is scheduled to be issued. Since this is consistent with yield to maturity calculations for other Code §§163(e)(5) and (i) purposes, it is the only sensible approach. In particular, before the 1990 Act, the mandatory redemption rule also applied in determining whether a debenture's yield to maturity exceeded the AFR plus five percentage points and the amount by which yield to maturity exceeded the AFR plus six percentage points. As a result, it was literally impossible to compute yield for these purposes for a debenture that paid interest in stock without a mandatory redemption feature because, under the mandatory redemption rule, such interest literally would be deemed never to be paid. The 1990 Act retroactively amended Code §163(i)(3) to correct this problem, as discussed in ¶1303.3.1.3. A conforming change should be made for significant OID purposes.

Indeed, it is somewhat surprising that Code §163(i) treats interest paid in the form of stock as not having been paid at the time the stock was issued for purposes of the new provision. It treats interest paid in the form of all types of "property" other than Newco's (or a related person's) debentures or stock—e.g., interest paid in cantaloupes, railroad cars, or real estate interests—as paid currently. In the case of interest paid in bunny debentures (i.e., a traditional PIK debenture), the bunny debentures merely evidence the OID accruals and constitute a promise to pay the accrued OID at a specified future date. But in the case of interest paid with common stock (and preferred stock that is not mandatorily redeemable), there is no promise ever to pay the interest in the future; the stock may fluctuate widely in value and be outstanding permanently. For this reason, the regular OID rules treat interest paid in the form of stock as paid currently.[57] By adopting the opposite approach, the new OID/PIK provision opens the troublesome issues discussed immediately above.

Interest paid in stock or debt of a corporation *not* related to the issuer of the underlying debenture *is* treated as paid currently under Code §163(i)(3).

---

[57] See ¶1309.2. See also ¶1303.3.2.3.

EXAMPLE 24

Corporations X and Y are not related to each other. Corporation X issues high yield debentures with semiannual interest payments in cash or, at the issuer's option, in stock (with an FV equal to the interest due) of Corporation Y. Similarly, Corporation Y issues high yield debentures with semiannual interest payable in cash or, at the issuer's option, in stock (with an FV equal to the interest due) of Corporation X. X and Y agree that each will issue to the other, on each semiannual interest payment date, an equal value of their respective common shares in an amount sufficient to fund their respective interest payment obligations. As a result, on each interest payment date, X pays its interest obligation by delivering Y shares, and Y pays its interest obligation by delivering X shares.

Under Code §1032 neither X nor Y is taxed on the receipt of the other corporation's shares in exchange for its own shares. Moreover, under Code §1012 each corporation holds the shares of the other at a cost (FV) basis, so that neither X nor Y is taxed on the delivery of the other's shares in discharge of its interest payment obligation.

Technically, the stock that X and Y distribute on their respective debentures should be treated as interest currently paid for Code §163(i) and (e)(5) purposes, because in each case the stock is stock of a corporation unrelated to the debenture's issuer. Query whether regulations issued under the broad authority of Code §163(i)(5) would alter this result.

Code §163(*l*), enacted in 1997, permanently disallows any deduction for interest paid or accrued (including OID) on debt issued by a corporation if "a substantial amount of the principal or interest" on the debt is payable in, or by reference to the value of, equity of the issuer or a related party (including by reason of a conversion right or similar option exercisable by the issuer or holder). For this purpose, a conversion right or similar option exercisable by the holder is taken into account only if "there is a substantial certainty the option will be exercised." Code §163(*l*) generally applies to debt issued after 6/8/97. To the extent Code §163(*l*) permanently disallows any deduction for interest paid or accrued on debt that pays interest in the form of issuer stock, it is of course irrelevant to the issuer whether Code §163(e)(5) applies. See ¶1306.

¶1303.3.1.7   *Variable Interest Rate*

The 1989 House Report (at 76-77) and the 1989 Senate Report (at 73) contemplate that "[i]n the case of debt instruments providing for a variable rate of interest (within the meaning of [1986] Prop. Reg. §1.1275-5) issued before the issuance of regulations [under section 163(i)], the committee expects that regulations . . . will provide that the determination of whether an obligation is [an AHYDO] will be made by treating the debt instrument as if it provided for a fixed interest rate corresponding to the rate established by the variable rate on the issue date[, and] similar rules would apply where the instrument provides for different variable rates for different accrual periods." 1986 Prop. Reg. §1.1275-5, which generally was authority for debentures issued before 12/22/92, has been superseded by Reg. §1.1275-5, which defines "variable rate debt instrument" somewhat differently.

¶1303.3.1.8   *Contingent Interest*

With respect to a debenture providing for contingent interest, the 1989 House Report (at 77) and the 1989 Senate Report (at 73) state that "the committee expects that the regulations . . . may take into account the *expected amount* of any such contingent payments in determining whether an obligation is [an AHYDO]. Cf. Code §1272(a)(6) [requiring a "prepayment assumption" to be made in the case of debt instruments subject to acceleration]" (emphasis added). Thus, if a Newco debenture with a term exceeding five years provides for both fixed interest and contingent interest (e.g., 25% of the increase over a specified period of time in Newco's value or earnings) payable at maturity, regulations may require the amount of the contingent interest to be estimated at the front end and taken into account over the life of the debenture in determining (1) whether the debenture has significant OID, (2) whether the debenture's yield equals or exceeds the AFR plus five percentage points, and (3) the extent to which the debenture's yield exceeds the AFR plus six points.

Significant original issue discount calculation. IRS has not yet issued regulations addressing the treatment of contingent payments of interest or principal under the AHYDO rules. In the absence of specific regulations, Code §163(i)(2)(A), defining significant OID for AHYDO purposes, looks to "the aggregate amount which would be includible in gross income with respect to [the debenture] before the close of any accrual period."

For debt instruments issued (1) before 8/13/96 or (2) after 8/12/96 in exchange for non-publicly traded property, we do not believe that the "expected amount" of contingent interest should affect the significant OID determination when such contingent interest is required to be paid within the same accrual period in which it ultimately becomes fixed. We reach this conclusion because, under the general accrual method accounting principles applicable to contingent payment debt instruments issued before the 8/13/96 effective date of Reg. §1.1275-4, contingent interest is not includible in the holder's income and deductible by the issuer prior to the taxable year in which the amount of the payment becomes fixed. Likewise, in the case of a contingent payment debt instrument issued on or after the 8/13/96 effective date of Reg. §1.1275-4 in exchange for non-publicly traded property, contingent interest payments are not includible in gross income prior to the taxable year in which the contingent payment becomes fixed.[58] Thus, for these categories

---

[58] Reg. §1.1275-4(c)(4).

of contingent payment debt instruments, we do not believe the quoted 1989 committee report language should be read as requiring contingent interest to be treated as accruing (for purposes of the significant OID measurement) until the amount of the payment becomes fixed.

EXAMPLE 25

On 12/1/93 (before the effective date of Reg. §1.1275-4 and when the AFR is 9%, compounded annually) Newco issues a 10-year $100 face amount debenture for $100 cash. The debenture bears fixed interest at a 15% rate, payable annually in cash on each 12/1. In addition, the debenture requires an additional contingent interest payment at maturity at 12/1/03 equal to 10% of the increase in value of a share of Newco common stock from 12/1/93 to 12/1/03.

On 12/1/93, when the debenture is issued, a reasonable estimate of the amount which will be paid as contingent interest is between $20 and $40, although the various parties to the transaction have widely varying expectations and the amount which will actually be payable is extremely speculative because Newco is in a highly competitive business and its future is uncertain.

The debenture's yield to maturity exceeds the AFR (9%) plus five points even if no contingent interest is ever paid. However, ignoring the contingent interest, the debenture is not an AHYDO, because all interest is paid in cash each year, and hence there is no OID inherent in the debenture. In addition, the contingent interest should not cause the debenture to have significant OID because the contingent interest is payable during the same accrual period (i.e., on 12/1/03) in which it becomes fixed (and hence is required to be included in income) under the general accrual method accounting principles applicable to contingent payment debt instruments issued before the 8/13/96 effective date of Reg. §1.1275-4.

However, in the case of a contingent payment debt instrument issued on or after the 8/13/96 effective date of Reg. §1.1275-4 in exchange for money or publicly traded property, it appears that the "expected amount" of contingent interest, as determined under the rules of Reg. §1.1275-4, does affect the significant OID determination. Under Reg. §1.1275-4, "interest on a [contingent payment debt instrument issued in exchange for money or publicly traded property on or after 8/13/96] must be taken into account whether or not the amount of any payment is fixed or determinable in the taxable year. The amount of the interest that is taken into account for each accrual period is determined by constructing a projected payment schedule for the debt instrument and applying rules similar to those for accruing OID on a non-contingent debt instrument."[59] Because Code §163(i)(2)(A)'s definition of significant OID looks to the "aggregate amount which

---

[59] Reg. §1.1275-4(b)(2).

would be includible in gross income with respect to [the debenture] before the close of any accrual period," contingent interest that is includible in gross income under Reg. §1.1275-4 prior to the time it becomes fixed apparently must be taken into account.

EXAMPLE 26

Same as Example 25, except that the Newco debenture is issued on 12/1/96 (after the effective date of Reg. §1.1275-4) and matures on 12/1/06. Assume that, under Reg. §1.1275-4, the "comparable yield" for the Newco debenture is 16.5% so that the projected contingent interest payment at maturity is $32.78 (i.e., the 15% annual fixed interest payments plus a $32.78 contingent interest payment on 12/1/06 produces a 16.5% yield).

Under Reg. §1.1275-4, the Newco debenture will have a 16.5% yield to maturity and will have $32.78 of OID (in addition to the fixed interest payments), which will accrue on a yield-to-maturity basis over the term of the debenture. Hence, an amount greater than the first year's interest on the $100 debenture (i.e., $16.50) of contingent interest will be includible in the Newco debenture holder's gross income during accrual periods ending before the accrual period in which the 12/1/06 contingent interest payment is to be made. Accordingly, it appears that the Newco debenture in Example 26 would have significant OID and would be an AHYDO.

Applicable federal rate plus five (or six) percentage points calculation. In the absence of AHYDO regulations, it is unclear whether an issuer is required to treat the "expected amount" of contingent interest as influencing whether a debenture's yield equals or exceeds the AFR plus five percentage points (or the extent to which the yield exceeds the AFR plus six points). It strikes us as the most sensible interpretation to apply the same rules as apparently apply for purposes of the significant OID calculation. That is, the "expected amount" of contingent interest should be taken into account only to the extent that the contingent interest is required to be accrued in advance of the time it becomes fixed under the general OID rules (i.e., in the case of a contingent payment debt instrument issued on or after the 8/13/96 effective date of Reg. §1.1275-4 in exchange for money or publicly traded property).

EXAMPLE 27

Just as in Example 25, Newco on 12/1/93 (before the effective date of Reg. §1.1275-4 and when the AFR is 9%, compounded annually) issues a 10-year $100 face amount debenture for $100 cash. However, unlike Example 25, the debenture bears fixed interest at only a 13% rate, and one-half of the interest is payable annually in cash each year while the other half accrues and compounds at a 13% rate to maturity. In addition, the debenture requires an additional contingent interest payment at maturity, just as the debenture in Example 25.

The debenture in Example 25 does not have significant OID if the contingent interest is treated as accruing when fixed (because the fixed interest is payable annually in full, and the contingent interest is payable at the time it accrues). However, the debenture in Example 27 does have significant OID (because one-half of the fixed interest accrues throughout the debenture's 10-year life). However, the Example 27 debenture's 13% yield to maturity (ignoring contingent interest) is less than the AFR (9%) plus five points.

If the contingent interest is taken into account at the front end in computing the debenture's yield to maturity, the characterization of the debenture in Example 27 as an AHYDO will turn on the contingent interest's exact "expected amount": If the estimated amount of contingent interest is sufficient to boost the 13% fixed yield to maturity up to or over 14%, the debenture will be an AHYDO. Because the estimated amount of contingent interest is not required to be determined for purposes of applying the general OID rules, we do not believe it would be sound policy to make a debenture's AHYDO characterization turn on this speculative determination.

In the case of a contingent payment debt instrument issued on or after the 8/13/96 effective date of Reg. §1.1275-4 in exchange for money or publicly traded property, the estimated amount of contingent interest is required to be be determined for purposes of applying the OID rules, and hence we think it likely IRS will require the contingent payment to be taken into account in determining yield for AHYDO purposes.

EXAMPLE 28

Same as Example 27, except that the Newco debenture is issued on 12/1/96 (after the effective date of Reg. §1.1275-4) and matures on 12/1/06. Assume that, under Reg. §1.1275-4, the "comparable yield" for the Newco debenture is 14.5%.

Because the yield on the Newco debenture is treated as 14.5% for purposes of the general OID rules, we think it likely IRS would treat the yield as 14.5% for AHYDO purposes. Under this interpretation, the Newco debenture would be an AHYDO, because 14.5% exceeds the AFR (9%) plus five points.

Post-issuance facts. If the regulations require the "expected amount" of contingent interest to be taken into account in making the front-end AHYDO characterization, but the actual amount of contingent interest (determined many years after the debenture's issuance) turns out to be significantly different than the parties' good faith estimate of the "expected amount" made at the time of issuance, will the regulations require reapplication of Code §163(e)(5) and (i) based on the amounts actually paid, producing retroactive adjustments to the issuer's and (in the case of a corporate holder eligible for the DRD) the holder's taxes? For example, will there be a readjustment where (a) a debenture that was initially treated as an AHYDO would not have been an AHYDO (because the actual contingent interest payment turns out to be *less than* the front-end estimate) *or* (b) a debenture that was initially treated as not an AHYDO would have been an AHYDO (because the actual contingent interest payment turns out to be *more than* the front-end estimate)? Regarding post-issuance conduct, see generally ¶1303.3.3.1.

¶1303.3.1.9　*Corporate Issuer*[60]

Code §163(e)(5) applies only to a debenture "issued by a corporation." There are, however, exceptions and potential exceptions.

First, Code §163(e)(5)(D) exempts from the interest deferral and disallowance rules "any obligation issued by any corporation for any period for which such corporation is an S corporation." The 1989 Conference Report (at 46) states that "[t]he conferees intend that if a C corporation issues an applicable instrument and subsequently converts to S corporation status, previously accrued but deferred interest will be deductible when paid."

Second, effective for partnership transactions occurring on or after 12/29/94, if a partnership issues high yield discount obligations, "each partner [is] treated as issuing its share of the obligations for purposes of determining the deductibility of its distributive share of any interest on the obligations" under Code §163(e)(5) and (i).[61] Therefore, though such an obligation in fact is issued by a partnership and so would appear to avoid the corporate issuer requirement (and hence not be an AHYDO), the obligation is treated as issued by a corporation for Code §163(e)(5) and (i) purposes to the extent any of the partnership's partners are C corporations.

This rule applies even if the transaction has no abusive intent. Indeed, the regulatory example illustrating the rule expressly states that the partnership "for several years has engaged in substantial bona fide business activities" and that the obligation is issued "as part of these business activities" to "an unrelated third party."

Third, Code §163(i)(5) grants the Treasury authority to issue regulations "appropriate to carry out the purposes of this [provision], including . . . regulations to prevent avoidance of the purposes of this [provision] through the use of issuers other than C corporations. . . ." This provision seems intended to target abusive

---

[60] As discussed in ¶1303.2.1.1, the requirement that the issuer be a corporation technically is contained in Code §163(e)(5)'s operative rules rather than in Code §163(i)'s definition of an AHYDO but, for ease of presentation, is treated herein as a fourth AHYDO requirement.

[61] Reg. §§1.701-2(f) example (1), 1.701-2(g). Reg. §1.701-2 generally concerns partnership transactions that are considered abusive.

transactions. Thus, one might expect to see regulations covering a debenture issued by a partnership or other pass-through entity formed by one or more corporations with the intent to avoid Code §163(e)(5) or (i). Presumably, however, such regulations should not cover a debenture issued by a long-standing business partnership (or other pass-through entity) in connection with bona fide business activities.

The suggested limitations on the scope of this regulatory authority are supported by the legislative history. The 1989 House Report (at 77) and the 1989 Senate Report (at 73-74) suggest that regulations cover the following case: Corporation C issues a debenture to Partnership P. C's debenture is not an AHYDO (because it fails at least one of the other three requirements). P then issues a debenture that would constitute an AHYDO if P were a corporation. P's debenture is secured (i.e., collateralized) by C's debenture. The committee reports suggest that the P debenture (although issued by a partnership) will be an AHYDO "at least when the C corporation participates in the collateralization [such as where] the first buyer [here P] engages in collateralization shortly after purchasing the debt instrument [from C]."

The partnership regulation described in *Second* appears to go substantially beyond the scope of the regulatory authority described in *Third* by covering all partnership debt issuances (to the extent the partnership is owned by C corporations), regardless of the intent of the parties. However, when the regulatory authority described in *Third* applies, it may (as illustrated by the example in the Committee report) subject the entire debenture to Code §163(e)(5), even though all or a portion of the issuing entity is not owned by C corporations.

¶1303.3.2   Treatment of Interest on Applicable High Yield Discount Obligations

¶1303.3.2.1   Determining "Disqualified Portion" of Original Issue Discount; Qualified Stated Interest Debentures

(1) Importance of qualified stated interest determination. Because QSI ("qualified stated interest," as described in ¶1303.2.2.3) is not subject to deferral or disallowance, the determination whether interest on a debenture qualifies as QSI can be crucial.[62]

Reg. §1.1273-1(c) defines QSI narrowly as stated interest payments that are unconditionally payable in cash or in property (other than debt of the issuer) at least annually at a single fixed rate (or at a variable rate if certain other requirements are satisfied).[63] Any one of a number of technical footfaults in a debenture's

---

[62] This discussion applies as well to qualified periodic interest payments ("QPIP") under the 1986 proposed OID regulations, which generally are authority for debt instruments issued before 12/22/92. Indeed, the 1989 Conference Report (at 47) expressly refers to QPIP as defined in 1986 Prop. Reg. §1.1273-1(b)(1)(ii)(A).

[63] For debentures issued before 12/22/92, 1986 Prop. Reg. §1.1273-1(b)(1)(ii)(A) defined QPIP, which was similar to QSI, even more narrowly as a series of interest payments based on a fixed interest rate (or a variable rate tied to a single objective index of market interest rates) which is unconditionally

terms can cause the interest payments to fail this narrow QSI definition. For example, if one-half of the interest on a debenture is paid annually and the other half accrues until maturity, but the debenture grants a brief "interest holiday" with respect to the interest due annually (e.g., the first 12 months' interest is not payable until 24 months after issuance) in order to accommodate the issuer's front-end cash flow difficulties, none of the annual fixed interest payments throughout the debenture's entire life would be QSI (because interest is not payable at least annually). If the interest rate is determined by a formula (e.g., 150% of LIBOR), perhaps none of such annual interest payments would be QSI.[64] Payments on a debt instrument that provide for contingent payments (other than contingent payments that are remote or incidental) do not qualify as QSI.[65]

Moreover, because the application of the QSI rules is unclear with respect to many financial products now in use, the parties often may not know with certainty whether a stream of cash interest payments on a debenture represents QSI or OID.

Rev. Rul. 95-70[66] interprets narrowly the already stingy regulatory definition of QSI, increasing the risk that interest on certain debentures will not qualify as QSI and hence will be deferred and/or partially disallowed under Code §163(e)(5). Rev. Rul. 95-70 takes the position that "If the terms of the debt instrument do not provide the holder with the right to compel payment [i.e., the right to accelerate], they must provide for a penalty [1] that inures *directly* to the benefit of the holder and [2] that is large enough to ensure that, at the time the debt instrument is issued, it is *reasonably certain* that, absent insolvency, the issuer will make interest payments when due" (emphasis added).

Rev. Rul. 95-70 then proffers two examples. In the first example, a debt instrument bearing 8% annual interest, payable quarterly, states that (1) interest not paid when due bears additional interest at the coupon rate, (2) if 12 consecutive quarterly payments are missed, the holder can sue for payment, and (3) if past due interest is outstanding, the issuer may not declare or pay any dividends on, or redeem or make any other payments with respect to, its stock. The ruling states that the issuer "has a policy and a long-established history of regularly paying dividends on its stock" so that "any failure . . . to pay regular dividends . . . is reasonably expected to result in a significant decline in the value of its stock." Nevertheless, the ruling concludes that the interest is not QSI, because (a) the debt does not require current payment of interest and (b) the dividend blockage provision does not "inure directly to the benefit of the holder" of the debt.

The second example tracks the first except that, if the issuer fails to pay interest when due, interest accrues on the past due amount at a "penalty rate" of 10% (rather than the 8% coupon rate). The ruling concludes that the interest is not QSI, because the increase in yield is not large enough to ensure with "reasonable certainty" that payments will be made currently absent insolvency. Regarding the second example, the ruling adds: "Depending on the facts and circumstances,

---

payable *at fixed periodic intervals of one year or less* throughout the debenture's life. Hence, in addition to the QSI requirement of annual payment, QPIP was required to be paid at fixed intervals.

[64] See Reg. §1.1275-5(b), (e).

[65] Reg. §1.1275-4(b)(5), (c)(3).

[66] 1995-2 C.B. 124.

however, an increase in yield that is 12 percentage points greater than the stated yield might be sufficient" to ensure reasonable certainty of current payment. Unfortunately, the ruling is (1) silent as to whether an increase of more than 2 points but less than 12 points will suffice and (2) unclear as to whether the additional yield can apply only to the overdue amount or whether the additional yield must, in IRS's view, apply to the entire instrument.

As a result of the narrow QSI concept articulated by the regulations and Rev. Rul. 95-70, minor variations in the terms of a debenture can produce radically different tax consequences, and many types of widely used financial products will not (or may not) qualify for the QSI exception to the new provision, despite payment of substantial amounts of cash at regular intervals.

EXAMPLE 29

Same as Example 13, except that the debenture calls for interest to be paid currently and states a higher penalty rate, but no acceleration, if interest is not paid currently. Thus, at a time when the AFR is 9%, compounded semi-annually, Newco issues for $100 cash a 10-year debenture with a principal amount of $100 bearing 20% annual interest, payable semiannually in cash. The debenture calls for a higher penalty rate for interest not paid semi-annually, but no acceleration.

If the interest qualifies as QSI, there will be no OID on the debenture. Therefore, the debenture will not be an AHYDO and Code §163(e)(5) will not prevent current deductibility of all the coupon interest.

In contrast, if the interest is not QSI (e.g., because there is no immediate acceleration right for non-payment and there is an insufficient penalty rate for late payment—see Rev. Rul. 95-70, described above), it appears that all of Newco's interest deduction will be deferred until the interest is actually paid and a portion will be permanently disallowed under Code §163(e)(5). In particular, because the yield on the debenture (20%) exceeds (by five percentage points) the sum of the AFR plus six points (15%), the debenture's annual "disqualified yield" is 5%. The 5% disqualified yield is 25% of the debenture's total yield (5% ÷ 20%). Hence, it appears that 25% ($5) of the debenture's $20 annual coupon interest is permanently non-deductible by Newco (but includible in the holder's income and eligible for the DRD if the debenture is held by a corporation), even if the interest is paid currently in cash. The remaining 75% ($15) of the $20 annual coupon interest is deductible as paid.[67]

---

[67] This analysis assumes that the scheduled interest payments on the debenture, because they are not QSI, do not constitute "interest to be paid" within the meaning of Code §163(i)(2)(B)(i). If the scheduled payments did count as "interest to be paid," the debenture would have no "significant OID" and therefore would not be an AHYDO. If the concept of "interest to be paid" (which is not defined in the statute) is intended to be identical to QSI, it is unclear why the statute is not more specific on this point.

EXAMPLE 30

The same facts as Example 15, with a minor irregularity in the timing of the third year's interest payment (as described below), so that the annual cash interest payments on the debenture fail to qualify as QSI.

First, let's review Example 15. In that example, at a time when the AFR is 9%, compounded annually, Newco issues for $100 cash a 10-year debenture with a yield to maturity of 20%, consisting of $16 (i.e., 16% on the debenture's original face amount) payable at the end of each year in cash and $4 (i.e., 4% of the debenture's original face amount) that accrues and compounds annually at a 20% rate until maturity. Example 15 concludes that the debenture is an AHYDO and that the yield (20%) exceeds by five percentage points the sum of the AFR plus six points, so that the disqualified yield for the first year is the *lesser of* (a) 25% of the debenture's $20 total return for the first year ($5) or (b) the debenture's OID for the first year ($4). Hence, the first year disqualified yield (i.e., permanently disallowed interest) is $4.

In Example 30, on the other hand, Newco expects heavy capital expenditures in the third year, and hence the debenture permits Newco to elect to defer the 16% interest otherwise payable in cash for the third year until 12 months after it would otherwise have been payable. Because of this brief interest-holiday in the third year, the $16 per year of cash interest is not paid sufficiently regularly to constitute QSI. Thus, all interest on the debenture is OID, including the $16 per year payable in cash.

In contrast to Example 15, where the disallowed portion of the debenture's interest was limited to the accrued OID for the year (e.g., $4 in the first year), in Example 28, 25% of the debenture's total return will be disallowed each year, even if this causes a portion of the annual cash interest payments to be disallowed.

In the first year, for example, $5 (25%) of the $20 interest accruing in that year is disallowed. The logical result would be for this $5 to consist of the $4 of accrued but unpaid interest plus $1 of the cash interest (so that Newco could deduct $15 of the interest actually paid). However, the 1989 Conference Report produces a worse result for Newco. As discussed in ¶1303.2.2.3, according to the 1989 Conference Report's approach, Newco's $16 cash payment in the first year (since it is no longer QSI) is allocated pro rata between the disallowed interest ($5 or 25%) and the potentially deferred interest ($15 or 75%). Thus, 25% of the $16 payment (i.e., $4) is treated as a payment of permanently disallowed interest, and 75% of the $16 payment (i.e., $12) is treated as a payment of potentially deferred interest, so that only $12 of the $16 cash payment is currently deductible.

Thus, in contrast to Example 15, where the $16 first-year cash interest payment is fully deductible currently and the $4 of accrued OID is permanently disallowed, in Example 28 only $12 of the $16 first-year cash interest payment is deductible currently, $5 of interest (consisting of the remaining

$4 of the interest paid in cash plus $1 of the accrued but unpaid interest) is permanently disallowed, and $3 of the accrued but unpaid interest is deferred until subsequently paid. This surprising result is unduly harsh.

Given the inequities of Code §163(e)(5) in respect of debentures that substantially resemble QSI debentures but fail the technical QSI definition, we recommend that regulations (1) relax the QSI definition for purposes of Code §163(e)(5),[68] and (2) adopt an allocation approach more taxpayer-friendly than the 1989 Conference Report's approach in order to avoid the draconian results illustrated in Example 28. For an alternative to the 1989 Conference Report approach, see ¶1303.3.2.2.[69]

(2) Determining disqualified portion of OID on qualified stated interest debentures. Code §163(e)(5) limits the disqualified portion of a QSI debenture's OID to the *lesser of* the debenture's OID or a fraction of its "total return," as discussed in ¶1303.2.2.3. Computation of the disqualified portion of a QSI debenture's OID is unclear in some cases. In particular, the 1989 Conference Report (at 47) states: "If the yield to maturity on the obligation determined by disregarding the OID [i.e., by taking into account only QSI] exceeds the AFR plus six percentage points, then the disqualified portion is the entire amount of the OID." This apparently sensible statement is at odds with the statute's technical operation.

EXAMPLE 31

Same as Example 15, i.e., at a time when the AFR is 9%, compounded annually, Newco issues for $100 cash a 10-year debenture with a yield to maturity of 20%, consisting of $16 (i.e., 16% on the debenture's original face amount) payable at the end of each year as QSI and $4 (i.e., 4% of the debenture's original face amount) that accrues and compounds annually at a 20% rate until maturity. The 16% QSI yield exceeds the AFR plus six percentage points (9% + 6% = 15%). Therefore, under the 1989 Conference Report language quoted above, all OID on the debenture would be disallowed.

The statute, however, does not produce this result. As Example 15 indicates, the disqualified portion of the debenture's OID each year is the *lesser of* (a) the

---

[68] The QSI concept, despite its shortcomings for Code §163(e)(5) purposes, is a substantial improvement over the even narrower QPIP concept of the 1986 proposed OID regulation, which generally is authority for debentures issued before 12/22/92. 1986 Prop. Reg. §1.1273-1(b)(1)(ii)(A) required QPIP to be paid at *fixed periodic intervals* of one year or less (rather than merely at any time annually) through the debenture's term.

[69] For further discussion of "interest-holiday" debentures and other problems raised by the QPIP concept in the context of the 1989 House Bill, see N.Y. St. Bar Assn. Tax Sec., Report on Certain Provisions of the Revenue Reconciliation Act of 1989, 44 Tax Notes 1543, 1544-1550 (1989).

OID accrued during the year or (b) 25% of the debenture's annual "total return" (i.e., accrued OID plus QSI for the year). In the early years, OID on the debenture for a year will be less than 25% of total return for such year, and therefore, all accrued OID for the year will be disallowed, as the 1989 Conference Report contemplates. In the first year, for example, accrued OID is $4, whereas 25% of the debenture's $20 total return would be $5. By year three, however, as a result of compounding on the deferred interest, the debenture's annual OID will exceed 25% of the debenture's total return, and so for that year and subsequent years, the statute would appear to disallow only 25% of the debenture's annual total return, which is less than the debenture's entire OID.[70]

This analysis of Example 29 assumes (as we believe to be the more workable interpretation) that "total return" is an annual concept, not the aggregate of the debenture's lifetime return. An example in the 1989 Conference Report (Example (1) at 47), although it does not involve a QSI debenture, interprets "total return" in this manner. In contrast, the statutory language is rather murky and could be read to define "total return" as the sum of all accrued OID and QSI over the entire life of the debenture. Even applying "total return" as a lifetime concept, however, would not result in disallowance of all OID on the debenture in Example 29. Specifically, the lifetime total return of the debenture in Example 29 is $263.83 ($103.83 lifetime accrued OID plus $160 lifetime QSI). Thus, the disallowed portion of the debenture's lifetime OID would be the *lesser of* (a) the lifetime OID ($103.83) *or* (b) 25% of the $263.83 total return ($65.96). Therefore, the permanently disallowed interest on the debenture would be $65.96, substantially less than the debenture's $103.83 total OID.

We believe that the regulations should follow the clear statutory formula (interpreting "total return" as either annual or lifetime return) rather than the suggestion in the 1989 Conference Report, which would produce excessive OID disallowance.

(3)   "Unconditionally payable." A series of interest payments will not qualify as QSI unless the interest is "unconditionally payable . . . at least annually at a single fixed rate" (or at a variable rate if certain other requirements are satisfied).[71] Where Newco has issued both senior and subordinated debt, Newco is typically prohibited by the subordination agreement from making payments on the subordinated debt if certain events of default have occurred with respect to the senior debt. As discussed below, the risk that Newco may default on its senior debt, and hence be prohibited from continuing to pay interest on its subordinated debenture should not cause interest on the subordinated debt to fail to qualify from the outset as "unconditionally payable" QSI.

Under QSI regulations, interest is "unconditionally payable" only if (i) "late payment (other than a late payment that occurs within a reasonable grace period)

---

[70] For example, in year 3 accrued OID on the debenture's adjusted issue price (i.e., the $100 original purchase amount plus accrued and unpaid OID from the first 2 years) will be $5.76, resulting in a total return of $21.76 ($5.76 OID + $16 QSI). Since 25% of the total return is $5.44, the disqualified portion of the OID would be only $5.44, not the total $5.76 of OID.

[71] Reg. §1.1273-1(c)(1). Similarly, for debentures issued before 12/22/92, 1986 Prop. Reg. §1.1273-1(b)(1)(ii)(A) required that any QPIP be "unconditionally payable . . . at fixed, periodic intervals of one year or less during the entire term of the debt instrument."

or non-payment is expected to be penalized or reasonable remedies exist to compel payment," (ii) either the lending transaction reflects arm's-length dealing or the issuer intends to enforce such remedies, and (iii) the interest is not payable on the occurrence of a contingency such as the existence of profits (for this purpose, the possibility of non-payment due to default, insolvency, or similar circumstances, or due to the exercise of a conversion right, is ignored). Thus, interest on a debenture should qualify as QSI despite the possibility that the issuer will default on the debenture itself. Moreover, debenture interest should so qualify despite the possibility that the issuer will default on a debt which is senior to the debenture. See ¶1303.3.1.2.

See also the discussion of Rev. Rul. 95-70 in ¶1303.3.2.1.

¶1303.3.2.2   *Payments of Original Issue Discount Before Maturity*

As discussed in Example 30 and the accompanying text, the 1989 Conference Report's position regarding allocation of OID payments (i.e., payments other than QSI) made before maturity as between the permanently non-deductible portion of the debenture's OID and the deferred-deduction portion can result in grossly inconsistent treatment of substantially identical debentures, and therefore should be reconsidered. A rule more consistent with the treatment of cash payments on QSI debentures (and therefore, more equitable) would permit a current deduction for such OID payments equal to the *lesser of* (a) the amount paid *or* (b) the deferred-deduction OID that has accrued to the date of the payment.

In Example 30, for instance, under this approach $15 of the first year's $16 cash interest payment would be currently deductible, i.e., the *lesser of* the $16 total cash interest payment *or* the $15 deferred-deduction portion of the first year's accrued OID ($20 total OID less $5 [25%] disqualified portion). This contrasts with the $12 first-year deduction under the 1989 Conference Report approach. This suggested approach would thus reduce the taxpayer-adverse (and illogical) consequences of cash interest failing to qualify as QSI. If the cash interest in Example 28 qualified as QSI, for instance, the first-year interest deduction would have been $16.

¶1303.3.2.3   *"Original Issue Discount" Undefined*

Because Code §163(e)(5) never defines OID, certain ambiguities arise.

First, Code §163(i)(3)(B) generally treats interest paid in stock or bunny debentures as not paid, but specifically states that this rule applies only "[f]or purposes of determining whether a debt instrument is an [AHYDO]." In addition, Code §163(e)(5)(A), as retroactively amended by the 1990 Act, states that "rules similar to [Code §163(i)(3)(B)] shall apply in determining the amount of the original issue discount and when the original issue discount is paid." In contrast, under the regular OID rules, interest paid in stock is treated as currently paid. Moreover, if paid at regular intervals of one year or less, such interest paid in stock is treated as QSI (assuming that the FV of the stock distributed on each interest payment date represents a stream of payments that, if paid in cash, would qualify as QSI). Code §163(e)(5)(A), as retroactively amended, is intended to clarify that interest regularly paid in the form of stock (as well as any other type of PIK interest) should not be regarded as QSI, but rather is treated as OID for Code §163(e)(5) purposes, and thus, is subject to the rules discussed in this ¶1303.

Second, Code §163(e)(5)(B) grants a corporate holder a DRD for "the dividend equivalent portion of any amount includible in gross income of a corporation *under section 1272(a)*" (emphasis added). However, the regular OID rules treat interest paid in *stock* (which constitutes QSI for purposes of the regular OID rules) as paid currently, and hence, the holder's income from receipt of the stock does not result from "section 1272(a)," which deals with OID. Thus, the literal language of Code §163(e)(5)(B) would prevent a corporate holder from obtaining a DRD with respect to interest payable in stock which constitutes QSI under the regular OID rules. Presumably, this result was not intended and should be corrected by technical corrections legislation.

¶1303.3.2.4   Potential Dividend for Dividends-Received Deduction Purposes Only

If a corporate holder owns an AHYDO, Code §163(e)(5)(B) treats the portion of the holder's OID income attributable to the disqualified portion of the debenture's OID as a dividend (the dividend equivalent portion) to the extent of the issuer's E&P "[s]olely for purposes of sections 243, 245, 246, and 246A."

The final statute (unlike the 1989 House Bill) does not, however, treat the debenture as stock for any purpose. Thus, in determining whether a corporate holder is entitled to a 70%, 80%, or 100% DRD (which turns in part on the quantity of the issuer's "stock" owned by the corporate holder), it is reasonably clear that the AHYDO is *not* treated as stock, and hence that the determination turns on the quantity of the issuer's actual stock owned by the corporate holder.

On the other hand, Code §246A cuts back the DRD if "stock" on which a dividend has been paid is debt-financed. It appears that application of Code §246A to dividend-equivalent interest on an AHYDO should turn on how the corporate holder financed its acquisition of the AHYDO (i.e., whether it borrowed to buy the AHYDO).

Similarly, Code §246(c) disallows a DRD where "stock" is not held at risk for a sufficiently long period. Prior to the 1997 Act, a DRD was disallowed under Code §246(c) with respect to a dividend on a share of stock if such share was not held at risk for more than 45 days (90 days in the case of preferred stock) (taking into account all days before the share became ex-dividend and the 45 days (90 days in the case of preferred stock) after the share became ex-dividend). For dividends received or accrued after 9/5/97, the 45/90 day holding period must be satisfied separately with respect to each dividend, taking into account only at-risk holdings during the 45 days before and 45 days after (90 days in the case of preferred stock) the share becomes ex-dividend. It appears that application of Code §246(c) to dividend-equivalent interest on an AHYDO should turn on the corporate holder's at risk holding period for the AHYDO.

These issues as to the interrelation of new Code §163(e)(5) and the DRD provisions should be clarified in the regulations.

Dividend-equivalent interest is treated as a dividend only for purposes of the enumerated DRD provisions. Thus it apparently does not apply for any other purpose, even if DRD-related. For example:

(1) Where interest is paid by a U.S. corporation to a *foreign* corporate holder (or possibly by a *foreign* corporation to a U.S. corporate holder), the rate of tax under the Code and under any applicable treaty is apparently determined by treating the dividend-equivalent interest as an *interest* payment, not a dividend payment.

(2) Code §1059 requires a corporate holder to reduce its basis in stock on which it has received an "extraordinary dividend" by the DRD with respect to the dividend. This basis reduction rule apparently does not apply in the case of dividend-equivalent interest under Code §163(e)(5)(B) because the amount received does not constitute a dividend for purposes of Code §1059 and the AHYDO does not constitute stock for any purpose.

¶1303.3.2.5   Effect on E&P

One apparent effect of the E&P rules described in ¶1303.2.2.5 is that a corporate holder of an AHYDO is entitled to a "priority" allocation of E&P for DRD purposes. Specifically, to the extent the issuer has positive E&P (current or accumulated) after taking into account (1) all AHYDO interest other than the disqualified portion of the OID and (2) all other adjustments except those for distributions on stock, such E&P is allocated on a priority basis to the dividend-equivalent interest paid to corporate holders, even if there is not sufficient E&P to cover distributions to actual shareholders.

EXAMPLE 32

Newco issues an AHYDO to an unrelated corporation ("C"). During the first year, the AHYDO accrues $20 of OID, of which $5 is permanently disallowed and $15 is deferred under Code §163(e)(5). Newco, which is widely held, also pays a $10 cash distribution to its shareholders during the year. Newco has $22 of E&P (current and accumulated) before taking account of either the $20 of accrued OID or the $10 distribution to shareholders.

As illustrated by Example 17, Newco's E&P is reduced for all purposes by the $15 deferred-deduction portion of the OID, i.e., from $22 to $7. Moreover, for all purposes other than determining C's DRD, Newco's E&P is further reduced by the $5 permanently disallowed portion, i.e., from $7 to $2. Thus, in determining whether a distribution to a real shareholder constitutes a dividend, Newco's E&P is only $2. As a result, only $2 of the $10 cash distributed to Newco's shareholders constitutes a dividend. (This is the same amount that would have been a dividend if the Newco debenture were not an AHYDO, since in that case Newco's E&P similarly would have been reduced by the full amount of the debenture's $20 of OID.)

In determining C's DRD with respect to the $5 permanently disallowed portion of the OID, however, such disallowed portion does *not* reduce Newco's E&P.[72] Thus, Newco's E&P is $7 for this purpose, which is sufficient to treat as a dividend the full $5 of permanently disallowed OID, even though $8 of the $10 cash distribution to Newco's actual shareholders was not covered by E&P and hence did not qualify as a dividend.[73]

¶1303.3.3   Other Considerations

¶1303.3.3.1   *Post-issuance Conduct*

It is unclear to what extent post-issuance conduct that is inconsistent with determinations required to be made at the time of a debenture's issuance will result in retroactive adjustments to the treatment of interest on the debenture.

For example, what if Newco's debenture on its face requires Newco to pay interest regularly in cash, so that it is not an AHYDO, but Newco fails to pay the interest as it comes due (either by Newco's unilateral conduct or by subsequent agreement with the holder), and either (1) the interest continues to accrue for a number of years and Newco ultimately pays the interest years later in cash (e.g.) at maturity, so that the debenture in retrospect is like an OID debenture, or (2) Newco later issues (and the holder accepts) bunny debentures or stock in payment of the interest (although no such option was permitted by the debenture)? To what extent will such post-issuance conduct cause the debenture to have significant OID, and hence, be treated as an AHYDO if it fails the other three tests?

See ¶1303.3.1.8 (regarding contingent interest).

¶1303.3.3.2   *Payment of Interest with Borrowed Money*

What if Newco's debenture on its face requires Newco to pay interest periodically in cash (and Newco actually does pay the interest periodically in cash), but

---

[72] Code §163(e)(5)(E).

[73] Cf. Rev. Rul. 69-440, 1969-2 C.B. 46, which establishes that, where total distributions on multiple classes of stock exceed E&P, E&P "must be regarded as having been distributed in accordance with the provisions of the corporate charter giving the prior preferred stockholders the right to dividends before any earnings and profits can be distributed to the other stockholders." Thus, if a corporation has $7 of E&P and pays $5 to its preferred stockholders and $10 to its common stockholders, the preferred stockholders receive dividend treatment on the full $5 distributed to them while the common stockholders receive dividend treatment only on the remaining $2.

Even if Code §163(e)(5)(E) did not make a priority allocation of E&P to AHYDO disqualified interest, it appears that the principle enunciated in Rev. Rul. 69-440 would reach the same result, because the AHYDO holder's right to the disqualified interest is a "prior . . . right . . . before any earnings and profits can be distributed to the other stockholders."

Newco has a separate loan agreement with the debenture holder (the "original lender"), entered into when the debenture is issued, obligating the original lender to make periodic future cash advances to Newco at approximately the same time that interest is due on the debenture? Code §163(i)(5) grants IRS broad authority to promulgate regulations, including "regulations to prevent avoidance of the purposes of this [provision] through the use of . . . agreements to borrow amounts due under the debt instrument." Hence, regulations may well take the position that where Newco has the right to take down future loans from the original lender with which Newco can pay interest on the debenture, Newco is not actually obligated to pay interest on the debenture to the original lender.[74]

However, few factual situations are this clear, so there may be substantial matching or tracing issues. Assume, for example, that a bank or other entity regularly engaged in the lending business enters into three loan agreements with Newco:

(1) a six-year loan to Newco with interest payable in cash each six months (the "debenture"),
(2) a working capital line of credit with Newco, and
(3) a capital expenditure line of credit with Newco.

Assume further that Newco pays the interest on the debenture in cash every six months, but that Newco periodically takes down amounts under (2) to finance inventory and receivables and amounts under (3) to finance plant expansions. How will regulations determine whether the (2) and (3) credit lines were used to pay interest on the debenture so that the (2) and (3) credit lines constitute, with respect to the debenture, "avoidance of the purposes of this [provision] through the use of . . . agreements to borrow amounts due under the [debenture]"? Indeed, how will this determination be made *at the front end when the debenture is issued* (as required by Code §163(i)) rather than later as the lines of credit are actually drawn upon or not?[75]

Presumably, such regulations will not seek to treat a loan agreement permitting Newco to borrow money in the future from a *third party* (i.e., a person not related to the original lender) as allowing Newco not to pay interest on the debenture in cash.[76]

---

[74] The 1989 House Report at 77 and the 1989 Senate Report at 74 add that such regulations "would be retroactive in appropriate circumstances." See also the *Battlestein* case discussed in ¶1303.3.1.2, which involved this issue.

[75] To complicate matters further, if the three loan agreements represent "the same transaction or related transaction," IRS might attempt to treat the loans as a single OID debenture under the aggregation rules of Reg. §1.1275-2(c).

[76] See the *Battlestein* case discussed in ¶1303.3.1.2.

¶1303.3.4 Effective Date and Grandfather Rules

¶1303.3.4.1 *General Effective Date*

Code §163(e)(5) and (i) applies to debentures issued after 7/10/89, with the four exceptions discussed at ¶1303.3.4.2.[77]

The 1989 House Report (at 77) and the 1989 Senate Report (at 74) state that the "assumption by a taxpayer of an instrument issued by another person is treated as a new issuance by the taxpayer for purposes of [the 7/10/89 effective date] rule." This position seems unreasonably harsh and overly broad. It covers, for example, the situation where (1) a target corporation ("T") merges tax free into an acquiring corporation and the acquiring corporation assumes T's debentures, and (2) T sells its assets to an acquiring corporation and the acquiring corporation assumes T's debentures. Indeed, it literally covers even the merger of a holding company into its wholly owned operating subsidiary, or vice versa.

¶1303.3.4.2 *Grandfather Rules*

The four exceptions to the 7/10/89 effective date rule are identical to those appearing in the 1989 Senate Bill, which the 1989 Senate Report discusses in some detail.[78]

(1) Debentures issued as interest. The provision does not apply to any debt instrument "issued pursuant to the terms of a debt instrument" that was either (a) issued on or before 7/10/89 or (b) grandfathered under one of the other exceptions discussed below.[79]

> **EXAMPLE 33**
>
> Newco has a PIK debenture outstanding on 7/10/89 (or issues one thereafter under circumstances satisfying one of the other grandfather rules). Newco bunny debentures issued after 7/10/89 pursuant to the terms of the PIK debenture (i.e., bunny debentures issued on the original debenture as well as bunny debentures issued on the bunny debentures) are grandfathered. Even if Newco merely had the *option* to pay interest on the underlying PIK

---

[77] See 1989 Act §7202(c).

[78] See 1989 Senate Bill §6202(c); 1989 Senate Report at 74-77.

[79] This exception for debentures issued as interest on a grandfathered debenture literally applies only (a) to debentures issued on or before 7/10/89, (b) to grandfathered debentures issued in connection with certain acquisitions (as discussed below), and (c) to grandfathered debentures issued in bankruptcy (as discussed below), but not to grandfathered debentures issued in certain refinancings (as discussed below). However, where a new debenture is issued in a grandfathered refinancing of an old debenture, it appears that each bunny debenture thereafter issued on the grandfathered new debenture would qualify as a grandfathered refinancing of the bunny debenture that would have been issued on the old debenture had it not been refinanced.

debenture in cash or in bunny debentures, any bunny debentures should be grandfathered, because they would be issued "pursuant to the terms" of the grandfathered PIK debenture.

(2) Debentures issued in connection with certain acquisitions. The most elaborate exception is for a debenture issued in connection with an acquisition made or committed to be made on or before 7/10/89. Three requirements must be satisfied.

First, there must have been an "acquisition" made on or before 7/10/89, or for which a written binding contract was in effect on 7/10/89, and at all times thereafter, or for which a tender offer was filed with the SEC on or before 7/10/89. The 1989 Senate Report (at 75) states that an acquisition for this purpose "includes an acquisition of stock (including the stock of the acquiror) or assets." Thus debentures issued in connection with a leveraged recapitalization can satisfy this first requirement.

Second, there must have been a determination on or before 7/10/89 to issue a debenture in connection with the required acquisition. This determination must be evidenced by written documents (a) transmitted on or before such date "between the issuer and any governmental regulatory bodies or prospective parties to the issuance or acquisition" *and* (b) "customarily used for the type of acquisition or financing involved." The documents must specify (a) "the fact that the instrument will be issued with significant OID" (1989 Senate Report at 75), (b) the debenture's maximum term, except that no term need be specified if the debenture ultimately issued has a term not exceeding 10 years (1989 Act §7202(c)(2)(A)(ii)), (c) the maximum proceeds to be raised by the issuance (1989 Act §7202(c)(2)(A)(iii)) or the debenture's issue price (1989 Senate Report at 75), and (d) that the debenture will be used to finance the acquisition (1989 Senate Report at 76). The wording of the 1989 Senate Report suggests that the above list is intended to be exclusive, i.e., that the documents need not specify any other facts relating to the debenture.[80]

The 1989 Senate Report (at 75) states that the required terms are not sufficiently evidenced if the issuer has an option to amend or extend a debenture's required terms or has an option to convert a debenture not subject to Code §§163(e)(5) and (i) to one that is subject to the provision. For example, according to the 1989 Senate Report, if Newco issued (before 7/11/89) preferred stock exchangeable at Newco's option into OID or PIK debentures, the fact that the preferred stock was

---

[80] The 1989 Senate Report (at 75) also states, however, that "the issuer must have made a determination to issue an obligation to which the provision would otherwise apply," which literally would require evidence of a more-than-five-year term and a yield equalling or exceeding the AFR plus five percentage points. Inasmuch as the statute and the 1989 Senate Report specify that the documents need not identify the debenture's term in all instances, it appears that the last quoted statement should not be taken literally. The debenture's yield, in particular, is generally not ascertainable until the debenture is priced shortly before issuance. A conclusion that the yield need not be specified in the pre-7/11/89 documents thus conforms to business reality and is consistent with the 1989 House Bill's grandfather rule, which required the pre-7/11/89 documents to specify the debenture's "significant terms . . . (other than yield)." See 1989 House Bill §11202(d)(2)(A)(ii).

issued before 7/11 does not cause a debenture thereafter exchanged for such stock to be grandfathered.

Third, the debenture actually issued must sufficiently resemble the debenture evidenced by the pre-7/11/89 documents. Specifically:

(a)   The debenture's actual term may not exceed the term specified in the pre-7/11 documents (or not exceed 10 years, if the documents do not specify a term).[81] The 1989 Senate Report (at 76) clarifies that the actual debenture's term may be *less* than that originally specified. Thus, if the pre-7/11 documents call for Newco to issue a 10-year debenture, Newco could ultimately issue a 91/2 year debenture, but not a 101/2 year debenture.

(b)   The statute requires that the debenture's proceeds not exceed the maximum proceeds specified in the pre-7/11/89 documents.[82] The 1989 Senate Report (at 76) cautions that non-compliance will cause the entire issuance to lose the grandfather benefit (rather than just the excess proceeds). The 1989 Senate Report also clarifies that the actual proceeds may be *less* than those originally contemplated.

(c)   The statute otherwise permits the debenture's terms to depart from those originally contemplated, so long as the debenture is actually issued "in connection with [the required] acquisition." The 1989 Senate Report (at 76) states that the "connection" requirement is not met unless the actual debenture has "reasonably the same required terms" (i.e., significant OID, maximum maturity, and issue price or maximum proceeds, as described above) as those evidenced before 7/11/89. Because the statute and the 1989 Senate Report specify the permitted parameters of the actual debenture in respect of term and proceeds, the concept of "reasonably the same required terms" appears to have independent substance (assuming any is intended) only as to the significant OID requirement. According to the 1989 Senate Report (at 75), a debenture will not be grandfathered if the pre-7/11 documents "evidence . . . a determination to issue instruments that provide for the annual payment of at least a portion of the yield and the instruments, as ultimately issued, do not provide for such payments." Beyond this, it is unclear how, if at all, the concept of "reasonably the same required terms" is meant to apply.

For example, suppose the pre-7/11 documents call for interest to be paid in Newco bunny debentures, but the debenture as ultimately issued

---

[81] 1989 Act §7202(c)(2)(A)(ii).

[82] 1989 Act §7202(c)(2)(A)(iii). The 1989 Senate Report at 76 appears to relax this requirement, stating that the proceeds actually raised may not exceed by more than a de minimis amount the amount determined in the pre-7/11 documents. However, this statement in the 1989 Senate Report is identical to its predecessor language in the 1989 House Report (at 80), suggesting that the 1989 Senate Report may have inadvertently (and erroneously) incorporated the 1989 House Report's de minimis concept. In contrast to the 1989 Act (and the 1989 Senate Bill), the proposed statutory effective date rules of the 1989 House Bill did not expressly limit the proceeds actually raised to the amount specified in the pre-7/11/89 documents.

calls for either (i) interest to be paid in stock of Newco or its 100% parent or (ii) no interest to be paid until maturity. On the one hand, the debentures appear to be substantially different. On the other, perhaps there has been no departure at all from the original "required terms," because the only required term here at issue ("the fact that the instrument will be issued with significant OID") is equally well evidenced by both the debenture originally contemplated and the debenture ultimately issued.

(3) Certain refinancings. The provision does not apply to refinancings of grandfathered debentures, provided that the refinancing does not (a) postpone the maturity date or the interest payment dates of the original debenture, (b) result in an issue price above the original debenture's adjusted issue price, (c) increase the stated redemption price at maturity of the original debenture, *or* (d) decrease the interest payments before maturity required under the original debenture. For example, within the above limits, a zero-coupon debenture could be refinanced by a PIK debenture or by a debenture paying some QPIP.

(4) Debentures issued in bankruptcy. The provision does not apply to certain debentures issued pursuant to bankruptcy reorganization plans filed before 7/11/89.

¶1303.4   *Conclusion*

Fundamental aspects of Code §163(e)(5) and (i) are arbitrary, ambiguous, inequitable, and unnecessarily complex.

If a corporate debt instrument fails all four of Code §163(i)'s AHYDO tests (even by a little), it is permanently covered by Code §163(e)(5), with radically different tax consequences to both the issuer (deferral of interest deductions and in some cases partial permanent disallowance) and the holder (if a corporation is eligible for the DRD). If the same debt instrument were restructured prior to issuance so that it barely avoids even one of the four tests (e.g., maturity reduced to exactly five years, or yield reduced to just below AFR plus five percentage points, or all but the first 12 months' yield paid just before the close of each significant OID measurement period), the instrument would not be affected at all by Code §163(e)(5). In addition, application of the AHYDO definition to debentures that are convertible into stock, pay interest in stock, or provide for contingent interest, raises many difficult questions.

Regarding Code §163(e)(5)'s operative provisions, we applaud the 1989 Conference Committee's rejection of the 1989 House Bill's preferred-stock-characterization approach, in light of the profound complexity and inequities inherent in that approach.[83] However, we believe that, in abandoning the 1989

---

[83] See Levin & Gallagher, Proposed Code §386 Treating OID and PIK Debentures as Preferred Stock, 45 Tax Notes 87 (1989).

Senate Bill's straightforward interest deferral rule and instead bifurcating OID into a permanently disallowed portion and a deferred-deduction portion, the 1989 Conference Committee introduced unnecessary complexity and ambiguity.

Moreover, this approach raises to a level of critical importance the often amorphous determination of whether interest payments on a debenture constitute "qualified stated interest." Specifically, the statute treats a series of cash interest payments satisfying the narrow and technical definition of QSI (or, generally for debentures issued before 12/22/92, QPIP) as deductible interest, but treats a series of cash payments failing this definition, even by a little, as OID potentially subject to deferral and permanent disallowance. The substantially disparate treatment of economically similar instruments which results is seriously aggravated by the 1989 Conference Report's position regarding allocation of OID payments made before maturity.

¶1304   CODE §279 LIMITATION ON P's (OR NEWCO's) AND T's DEDUCTION FOR ACQUISITION INTEREST

In a large LBO (or in any other acquisition financed by substantial borrowing), P (or Newco) must be vigilant to assure that some or all of its interest deductions are not disallowed by the peculiar and arbitrary rules of Code §279.

¶1304.1   *Debt to Which Code §279 Applies*

Debt issued by a corporation after 10/9/69 is subject to Code §279 disallowance if *all* the following requirements are met:[1]

(1)   The debt is issued to provide consideration for the acquisition of stock in another corporation (T) or at least two-thirds (by value) of another corporation's (T's) business assets (excluding cash, but including the stock of subsidiaries). This includes (a) debt issued directly in exchange for T's stock or assets, *and* (b) debt issued to raise the money necessary to purchase T's stock or assets, i.e., where P (when it issued the debt) "anticipated the acquisition" of T and the debt "would not have been issued if [P] had not so anticipated such [T] acquisition," *and* (c) debt issued to replace the P working capital spent to acquire T where P (when it used working capital to purchase T) "foresaw or reasonably should have foreseen that it would be required to issue [the debt], which it would not otherwise have been required to issue if the acquisition had not occurred, in order to meet its future economic needs."[2]

¶1304   [1] Code §279(b).
[2] Reg. §1.279-3(b)(2).

(2) The debt is subordinated to "trade creditors" generally *or* is "expressly subordinated" to "any substantial amount" of other unsecured debt (generally 5% or more of the face amount of the indebtedness issued in the acquisition), whether outstanding or subsequently issued.[3]

(3) The debt is convertible "directly or indirectly" into stock of the issuer *or* is part of an investment unit which includes an option to purchase stock of the issuer. Non-convertible debt sold in conjunction with convertible preferred stock or warrants is such an investment unit.[4]

(4) On the last day of the debtor's tax year in which the debt is issued, (a) the debtor's debt to equity ratio ("DER") exceeds two to one, *or* (b) the debtor's average earnings for the past three years do not exceed three times the annual interest to be paid or incurred.

¶1304.2   Effect of Code §279

Code §279 will prevent the debtor from deducting interest paid or incurred during the taxable year on debt described in ¶1304.1 (including OID and other forms of interest), to the extent such interest exceeds:

(1) $5 million *less*

(2) interest paid or incurred during the year on debt that was issued after 12/31/67 to provide consideration directly or indirectly for an acquisition described in ¶1304.1(1) (whether of T or of another corporation) but that fails to satisfy one or more of the other requirements of ¶1304.1 (e.g., bank debt).

Code §279 is cumulative and applies to acquisition debt incurred in multiple acquisitions. Thus, interest on debt arising out of P's (or Newco's) acquisition of T1, which is tainted by Code §279, can be disallowed even where such interest is less than $5 million per year, if interest on other debt (tainted or *not*) arising out of P's (or Newco's) acquisition of T2 pushes the debtor's aggregate interest on debt described in ¶1304.1(1) over $5 million.

EXAMPLE 1

Assume that after 1969 P purchases T1's stock or assets and finances the acquisition through issuance of $40 million of senior bank debt which bears $4 million of interest per year. Assume P thereafter purchases unrelated T2's stock or assets and finances the acquisition with $30 million of convertible debt which also bears interest of $4 million per year and is subordinated to P's trade creditors. Assuming that the T1 acquisition debt is still outstanding

[3] Reg. §1.279-3(c).
[4] Reg. §1.279-3(d).

and that P's DER exceeds 2 to 1 (or P's average annual earnings for the past three years do not exceed three times annual interest) at the relevant times, the convertible subordinated debt is subject to Code §279. In this example, Code §279 would permit P to deduct only $1 million of interest on the convertible subordinated debt (i.e., $5 million statutory amount *less* the $4 million of interest paid on the senior bank debt arising out of P's acquisition of T1).

EXAMPLE 2

P plans to borrow $100 million and use it to purchase all of T's stock or assets. Lender #1 will loan P $50 million unsecured at a 10% interest rate. Lender #2 will loan P $50 million unsecured at a 10% interest rate, subordinated to Lender #1's claim against P (i.e., the loan agreement with Lender #2 will state that in case of P's insolvency, Lender #2 is not entitled to collect on its loan until Lender #1 is fully repaid), and Lender #2 will receive warrants to purchase P common stock.

Assuming that P fails at least one of the required ratios set forth in ¶1304.1(4) above, the $5 million per year of interest payable to Lender #2 is entirely disallowed by Code §279, because the $5 million per year of interest payable to Lender #1 uses up the $5 million statutory deductible.

¶1304.3   *Important Collateral Rules*

Normally, once debt is tainted by Code §279, it is forever so tainted.[5] However, if P's DER and average earnings are such that, for any three consecutive taxable years after issuance, the debt would not have been subject to Code §279 if issued in any of those years, then the Code §279 taint is removed for all taxable years after such three-year period.[6] See ¶1304.8 below for a discussion of refinancing acquisition debt.

Code §279 is applied generally on an affiliated group basis, so that (for example) the ratios discussed in ¶1304.1(4) above are computed based on P's (or Newco's) affiliated group and Code §279 cannot be avoided by having P's subsidiary S borrow to acquire T and having P issue a warrant. For this purpose, affiliated group has the meaning set forth in Code §1504(a) (as discussed in ¶¶211.1, 211.2, and 1205.2.1), except that the Code §1504(b) exclusions are ignored and T is not treated as an includible corporation.[7]

---

[5] Code §279(d)(2).
[6] Code §279(d)(4).
[7] Code §279(g).

Code §279 does not apply to acquisitions of foreign corporations substantially all of whose income for the three-year period ending on the acquisition date was from sources outside the U.S.[8]

If P (or Newco) issues debt to provide consideration for the acquisition of T *stock*, Code §279 will apply to the debt for a taxable year only if, *at any time* after 10/9/69 and before the close of such taxable year, P (or Newco) owns 5% or more of T's voting stock.[9]

¶1304.4   Avoiding Code §279 by Using Common Stock

Code §279 does not apply to an investment unit consisting of P subordinated debt plus P *common stock*. Thus, Code §279 can be avoided by issuing straight debt in conjunction with *non-convertible stock* (thereby avoiding both a conversion feature and warrants).[10]

EXAMPLE 3

Same as Example 2, except that Lender #2 does not receive warrants but rather receives P common stock. Code §279 does not apply, because Lender #2 did not receive any option to purchase P stock or any conversion privilege into P stock.

¶1304.5   Avoiding Code §279 by Subordinating Only to Secured Debt

Code §279 does not apply to the interest on debt which is subordinated *only* to *secured* debt. Hence, if P is incurring two types of acquisition debt, senior debt and subordinated debt, Code §279 can be avoided if the senior debt is secured rather than unsecured and the subordinated debt is subordinated only to the senior secured debt (and not, for example, to P's trade creditors).

EXAMPLE 4

Same as Example 2, except that Lender #1's debt is fully secured by P's assets, including the T stock or assets purchased. Code §279 does not apply because Lender #2 is not subordinated to any *unsecured* debt.

---

[8] Code §279(f).
[9] Code §279(d)(5); Reg. §1.279-4(b).
[10] See IRS Letter Ruling 8810001 (10/1/87).

¶1304.6   *Avoiding Code §279 by Using Holding Company*

One way of subordinating acquisition debt to certain trade debt or to other unsecured debt while attempting to avoid Code §279 is to split P (or Newco) into a holding company parent and a subsidiary. Part of the acquisition debt is then incurred by the parent and part by the subsidiary, and neither the parent's nor the subsidiary's debt is expressly subordinated. In such case, however, with respect to claims against the subsidiary's assets, the parent's debt is implicitly subordinated (by operation of law) to the subsidiary's secured and unsecured debt. The parent's creditors have no claim against the subsidiary's assets and have a claim only against distributions by the subsidiary to the parent, *after the subsidiary has provided for its own debts in full.*

EXAMPLE 5

As in Example 2, P plans to borrow $100 million unsecured ($50 million each from Lender #1 and Lender #2, with Lender #2 also receiving warrants to purchase P common stock) for the purchase of T's stock or assets, and P would like Lender #2's claim to be subordinated to Lender #1's claim. Rather than borrow the money directly, which would trigger Code §279 as illustrated in Example 2, P drops its assets into a newly formed, wholly owned subsidiary S. P borrows $50 million unsecured from Lender #2 with no provision in the documents subordinating Lender #2's claim against P to any indebtedness of P or S. P also issues to Lender #2 warrants to purchase P common stock. P contributes the $50 million to S's capital. S borrows an additional $50 million unsecured from Lender #1. S then uses the $100 million to purchase all of T's stock or assets.

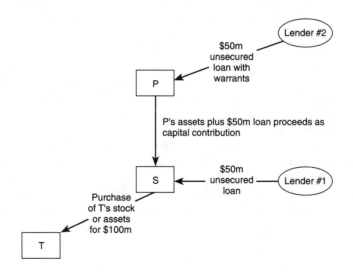

P's debt to Lender #2 is not *expressly* subordinated to any unsecured indebtedness, as it was in Example 2. However, as a practical matter, P's debt to Lender #2 will not be repaid out of S's assets unless S has first repaid Lender #1 in full. This is because Lender #2 has a claim only against P's assets (i.e., the S stock), and P (as S's shareholder) is not entitled to any distributions from S unless S can fully repay its creditors, including Lender #1.

As described below, it is not wholly clear whether Code §279 is avoided in these circumstances.

Code §279(b)(2) states (regarding the subordination requirement described in ¶1304.1(2) above) that the debt must be either:

(A) subordinated to the claims of trade creditors of the [borrower] generally, or

(B) expressly subordinated in right of payment to the payment of any substantial amount of unsecured indebtedness, whether outstanding or subsequently issued, of the [borrower].

In Example 5 P's acquisition debt to Lender #2 is not "expressly subordinated" to any unsecured P indebtedness and is also not "subordinated to the claims of [P's] trade creditors . . . generally." However, Code §279(g) states that Code §279 is generally applied by treating all members of an affiliated group in the aggregate.[11] Thus, although P's debt to Lender #2 is not within (B) above, it is arguably within (A) because it is *subordinated by operation of state law to S's and T's trade creditors* (as well as the trade creditors of any other P subsidiaries).

However, Code §279(g) further states that "affiliated group" has the same meaning as in Code §1504(a) (as discussed in ¶¶211.1 and 1205.2.1), except that the Code §1504(b) exclusions are ignored and, most importantly for the point now being discussed, *the acquired corporation shall not be treated as an includible corporation*"(emphasis added). Thus, at least where P acquires T's stock rather than T's assets, the exclusion of T from P's affiliated group appears to prevent T's trade creditors from being considered and would apparently allow IRS to make this subordination-by-operation-of-law argument only if P subsidiaries *other than T* had trade creditors.

Under this language, if read literally, it may make a difference how P's acquisition of T is effectuated: If S buys T's stock, T's trade creditors are apparently ignored. If S merges into T in a reverse subsidiary merger (treated for tax purposes as if P had purchased T's stock—see ¶202), T's trade creditors are apparently ignored. However, if S purchases T's assets and assumes T's liabilities, T's trade creditors become S's trade creditors and it is not clear that the statutory language

---

[11] See also Reg. §1.279-3(c)(1).

treating T as a non-includible corporation is helpful, so that S's new trade creditors may be counted.

The regulations provide that subordination arising by operation of law is irrelevant in determining *express* subordination.[12] However, the regulations do not specifically exclude subordination by operation of law when subordination to trade creditors is at issue.

IRS has issued private letter rulings taking the position that, in such a case, P's acquisition debt will *not* be regarded as subordinated to its subsidiaries' trade creditors for Code §279 purposes as long as P has incurred a substantial amount of trade debt (apparently at least 6% of the affiliated group's aggregate trade debt).[13] Thus, it appears that P's acquisition debt (which is not expressly subordinated to any unsecured debt) will not be covered by Code §279, even though it is convertible or is issued in conjunction with options, if P has incurred at least 5% of the affiliated group's trade debt.

It is not clear, however, whether IRS would take (or would be successful in taking) the position that P's acquisition debt *is* covered by Code §279 (assuming it is convertible or issued with options) where P has incurred *less* than 6% of the affiliated group's trade debt. If the answer were "yes," many holding companies, formed for legitimate business reasons, which borrowed money without any express subordination to make acquisitions, would probably be surprised at the result.

¶1304.7   Avoiding Code §279 by Redemption

Code §279 applies to debt issued "to provide consideration for the acquisition of . . . stock in an other corporation . . . or . . . assets of another corporation." Where P (or Newco) acquires T's stock and T (rather than P or Newco) ends up liable for all or part of the debt incurred in the transaction, the transaction is treated for tax purposes as a redemption to the extent of the debt for which T (rather than P or Newco) ends up liable. See ¶¶202, 903.2, 1402.1.3, and 1402.1.4. Thus, to the extent of the debt for which T ends up primarily liable, Code §279 would appear not to apply since such debt is incurred to provide consideration for a redemption, rather than "to provide consideration for the acquisition of . . . stock in another corporation."

¶1304.8   Refinancing Code §279 Debt

Code §279(h)(1) provides that "[a]ny extension, renewal, or refinancing of an obligation evidencing a pre-existing indebtedness shall not be deemed to be the issuance of a new obligation." Thus, if the refinanced debt was Code §279-tainted

[12] Reg. §1.279-3(c)(2).
[13] See IRS Letter Ruling 8640073 (7/10/86); IRS Letter Ruling 8336009 (6/9/83).

debt from the outset, the Code §279 taint will *not* be removed by refinancing the original debt with otherwise non-tainted debt. This is true whether or not P or Newco anticipated refinancing the debt from the outset and even where the refinanced debt is not subordinated *and/or* not convertible and not issued with an option to acquire stock.[14]

On the other hand, if the refinanced debt was not Code §279-tainted initially and it is refinanced with debt that would otherwise be Code §279-tainted debt, it is possible that this "new obligation" will *not* be Code §279-tainted. Based on positions taken by IRS in private decisions discussed below, if the refinancing was not anticipated and had a valid business purpose, the new debt will not be Code §279-tainted; however, if P (or Newco) planned from the outset to refinance the original debt with Code §279-tainted debt, the new obligation will be Code §279-tainted.

In IRS Letter Ruling 8712004 (12/11/86) P used money obtained from non-tainted bank debt to finance its acquisitions of T1 and T2. "At the time of the acquisitions, [P] had no intention of issuing any convertible debt[, but d]ue to a large increase in the market price of [P's] stock and a substantial decrease in fixed interest rates, [P] now proposes to issue convertible subordinated debentures and use the proceeds to pay off the bank debt." IRS concluded that the new convertible subordinated debentures were not Code §279-tainted, because P "did not contemplate the proposed refinancing at the time the bank loan was incurred. Rather, the proposed refinancing is clearly in response to an economic opportunity[.]"

In IRS Letter Ruling 8712059 (12/23/86) P used money obtained from non-tainted bank debt to acquire T1. P then issued convertible subordinated debentures to repay the bank loan. Without discussing the reasons for the refinancing, IRS concluded that the convertible subordinated debentures were not Code §279-tainted, because P "has demonstrated that the original . . . bank loan was not a mere sham or conduit to avoid . . . section 279, but was obtained for a valid business purpose."

In Gen. Couns. Mem. 39618 (3/19/87) IRS stated that "if the old . . . debt being refinanced is not [Code §279-tainted], then the obligation issued to refinance it is not [Code §279-tainted] either. . . . Notwithstanding the above, . . . [if] the refinancing is contemplated at the time of the . . . acquisition and [P] is unable to demonstrate that the obligation being refinanced was issued for a valid business purpose, rather than the avoidance of taxes, [IRS] need not honor the original indebtedness, and may determine that the refinancing obligation was issued to provide consideration for the acquisition from the outset."

---

[14] See Reg. §1.279-4(c); Code §279(d)(2).

¶1305 CODE §163(j) LIMITATION ON INTEREST DEDUCTION WHERE DEBT PAYABLE TO OR "GUARANTEED" BY RELATED TAX-EXEMPT ORGANIZATION OR FOREIGN PERSON

The 1989 Act created a new limitation on P's (or Newco's) and T's (the "issuer's") ability to deduct interest paid or accrued (including OID) to a "related" person if the interest is not subject to full U.S. federal income tax, and if certain other conditions are met ("Code §163(j) rule #1"). Thus interest paid to a related tax-exempt U.S. entity or to a related foreign person is often non-deductible under this rule. This "earnings stripping" or "interest stripping" provision limits the possibility of corporate distributions that are tax deductible to the issuer but tax-free or partially tax-free to the ultimate recipient. In 1991 Treasury published extensive proposed regulations under Code §163(j) (the "Proposed Regulations"). Code §163(j) rule #1 is discussed in ¶1305.1.

The 1993 Act substantially expanded Code §163(j) to limit the deductibility of interest paid or accrued on debt *guaranteed* by a tax-exempt organization or foreign person related to the borrower (even though the interest is actually paid to a taxable U.S. lender) if certain other conditions are met. This second limitation—Code §163(j) rule #2—is discussed in ¶1305.2.

¶1305.1 Code §163(j) Rule #1: Debt Payable to Related Tax-Exempt Organization or Foreign Person

¶1305.1.1 In General

Code §163(j) rule #1 prohibits the issuer from deducting interest paid or accrued during the taxable year to the extent that all five of the following requirements are met:

(1) The issuer is a corporation (other than an S corporation, according to the Proposed Regulations[1]). If the issuer is a partnership, each partner is treated (under the Proposed Regulations) as borrowing its allocable portion of the loan to the partnership, so that to the extent the borrowing partnership is owned by C corporations, this test is met.[2]

(2) The issuer's debt-equity ratio on the last day of the taxable year exceeds 1.5:1. See ¶1305.1.3.

(3) No U.S. federal income tax is imposed with respect to the interest. See ¶1305.1.4.

¶1305 [1] Prop. Reg. §1.163(j)-1(a)(1)(i). Under the Proposed Regulations, Code §163(j) applies to a foreign corporation only if the foreign corporation has income effectively connected with a U.S. trade or business, subject to special rules described in Prop. Reg. §1.163(j)-8. Id.

[2] Prop. Reg. §1.163(j)-2(e)(5).

(4) The interest is paid or accrued to a "related person" within the meaning of Code §267(b) or §707(b)(1), which generally requires more than 50% overlapping ownership between the issuer and the interest recipient. See ¶1305.1.5.

(5) The issuer has "excess interest expense" for the year. See ¶1305.1.2.

Interest payments or accruals that satisfy requirements (3) and (4) and are made by an issuer satisfying requirements (1) and (2) ("disqualified interest expense") are non-deductible to the extent the issuer has excess interest expense for the year. Interest so disallowed is carried forward to the following year (and thereafter) and is deductible to the extent described in ¶1305.1.2 (see especially Example 1 below).

The Proposed Regulations contain a general antiabuse rule providing that "[a]rrangements, including the use of partnerships or trusts, entered into with a principal purpose of avoiding the rules of section 163(j) and these regulations shall be disregarded or recharacterized to the extent necessary to carry out the purposes of section 163(j)."[3]

Legislative Update

The American Competitiveness and Corporate Accountability Act of 2002 (H.R. 5095), introduced 7/11/02, includes the following modifications to Code §163(j), generally to be effective in taxable years beginning after 12/31/03:

- Eliminate the current 1.5 to 1 debt-to-equity ratio requirement.
- Eliminate the current 3 year excess limitation carryforward.
- Calculate excess interest expense by reference to 35% (rather than 50%) of the issuer's adjusted taxable income.
- Limit the carryforward of non-deductible disqualified interest expense (currently unlimited) to 5 years.
- Create a complex new formula for an issuer which is part of an affiliated group (as defined in Code §1504(a) without regard to Code §1504(b) (2), (3), and (4)) that includes one or more non-U.S. corporations, Code §801 insurance companies, or Code §936 corporations, under which formula the amount of the issuer's excess interest expense increases if the issuer is more leveraged than such expanded affiliated group as a whole. Since Code §163(j) rule #1 disallows the lesser of issuer's disqualified interest expense or issuer's excess interest expense, such an increase in issuer's excess interest expense may increase issuer's disallowed interest.

---

[3] Prop. Reg. §1.163(j)-1(f).

¶1305.1.2   Disallowance Limited to Excess Interest Expense

As noted, disqualified interest expense is non-deductible to the extent of the issuer's "excess interest expense" for the year.[4] "Excess interest expense" is the excess of (1) the issuer's "net interest expense" for the year over (2) the sum of (a) 50% of the issuer's "adjusted taxable income" for the year plus (b) any "excess limitation" carried forward to that year.[5]

For this purpose, "net interest expense" means interest paid or accrued for the year (other than previously disallowed interest expense that was carried forward to such year under Code §163(j), according to the Proposed Regulations) less interest includible in gross income, with statutory authority for other regulatory adjustments.[6] "Adjusted taxable income" means taxable income computed without regard to net interest expense (or, according to the Proposed Regulations, any carryforward or disallowance under Code §163(j)), NOL carryovers, or depreciation amortization deductions, with statutory authority for other regulatory adjustments.[7]

Disqualified interest expense that is non-deductible in a taxable year under the above rule is carried forward to subsequent taxable years and may be deducted to the extent of any "excess limitation" for the carryforward year.[8] "Excess limitation"

---

[4] Code §163(j)(1)(A); Prop Reg. §1.163(j)-1(a)(2).

[5] Code §163(j)(2)(B); Prop. Reg. §1.163(j)-2(b).

[6] Code §163(j)(6)(B); Prop. Reg. §1.163(j)-2(e)(1). The 1989 Conference Report stated that future regulations could "reduce [or increase] net interest expense where all or a portion of income [or expense] items not denominated as interest are appropriately characterized, in the Treasury's view, as equivalent to interest income [or expense]." H.R. Conf. Rep. No. 386, 101st Cong., 1st Sess. at 66 (1989) (as reprinted in CCH Stand. Fed. Tax Rep. no. 50 (11/22/89)) (hereinafter "1989 Conference Report"). However, the Conference Report contemplated that an income item would not be treated as interest "unless it predominantly reflects the time value of money or is a payment in substance for the use or forbearance of money." The Proposed Regulations define interest income to include original issue discount ("OID") under Code §§1272-1275, acquisition discount under Code §§1281-83, amounts treated as OID under the bond stripping rules of Code §1286, and gain treated as OI on the disposition of a market discount bond under Code §1276(a). They define interest expense to include OID under Code §163(e). Finally, the Proposed Regulations expressly reserve the definition of "interest equivalents." Prop. Reg. §1.163(j)-2(e).

[7] Code §163(j)(6)(A); Prop. Reg. §1.163(j)-2(f)(1). In addition to the items described in text, the Proposed Regulations add back to taxable income (1) any increase between the end of the preceding year and the end of the current year in accounts payable (other than interest payable) and any decrease for such period in accounts receivable (other than interest receivable) that are included in computing taxable income, (2) any tax-exempt interest income, (3) any dividends received deduction, (4) any deduction for capital loss carryovers and carrybacks, and (5) certain other items. Prop. Reg. §1.163(j)-2(f)(2). They deduct from taxable income (1) with respect to any disposition of property, any depreciation or amortization deductions allowed or allowable for taxable years beginning after 7/10/86 with respect to such property, (2) any decrease in accounts payable and any increase in accounts receivable from the prior year end (as described above), (3) any net capital loss, and (4) certain other items. Prop. Reg. §1.163(j)-2(f)(3). The 1989 Conference Report (at 66) expressed the intention that regulations modifying the computation of the issuer's adjusted taxable income "will add back non-cash deductions to earnings generated by operations, but would disregard, e.g., the proceeds of certain capital asset dispositions."

[8] The description in text (including in Example 1) of how disqualified interest expense is treated in subsequent years is based on Prop. Reg. §1.163(j)-1, which differs in technical respects from the statutory treatment but appears to reach the same result.

means the excess, if any, of 50% of the issuer's adjusted taxable income over net interest expense for the year; an excess limitation for a year (after reduction by any disqualified interest expense that was disallowed in a prior year and carried forward to the current year) is carried forward to reduce excess interest expense for up to three succeeding years.[9]

EXAMPLE 1

P issues debt on 1/1/90 to finance its acquisition of T's assets (or for any other purpose). P's net interest expense (as described above), adjusted taxable income (computed without regard to net interest expense, NOLs, depreciation and other appropriate items as described above), and disqualified interest expense (i.e., interest that is paid or accrued to related persons and exempt in whole or part from U.S. tax) for 1990, 1991, and 1992 are as follows:

	Net Interest Expense	100% of Adjusted Taxable Income	50% of Adjusted Taxable Income	Disqualified Interest Expense
1990	$100	$100	$ 50	$70
1991	80	200	100	30
1992	60	50	25	10

Assume that P's DER exceeds 1.5:1 at all relevant times and that P has no excess limitation carryforward to 1990.

For 1990, P's excess interest expense (and hence the maximum amount of disqualified interest expense that will be non-deductible if the other requirements of Code §163(j) are met) is $50 ($100 net interest expense less 50% of $100 adjusted taxable income). Hence, of the $70 of disqualified interest expense that P paid or accrued in 1990 to related tax-exempt persons, $50 is non-deductible under Code §163(j). The remaining $20 of disqualified interest expense is deductible in 1990. The $50 of disallowed disqualified interest expense is carried forward to 1991.

For 1991, P has no excess interest expense, because P's net interest expense ($80) does not exceed 50% of P's adjusted taxable income (50% of $200 = $100). Rather, P has a $20 excess limitation for 1991, because 50% of P's adjusted taxable income exceeds P's net interest expense by $20. Because P

---

[9] Code §163(j)(2)(B)(ii),(iii); Prop. Reg. §1.163(j)-1(d). Prop. Reg. §1.163(j)-10(c) provides that, in computing a corporation's excess limitation carryforwards for its first three taxable years beginning after 7/10/89, the corporation must take into account amounts that would have been treated as excess limitation carryforwards to those years as if Code §163(j) had applied throughout the corporation's taxable years beginning after 7/10/86 (assuming that no excess limitation or disallowed interest expense was carried forward to its first taxable year beginning after 7/10/86).

has no excess interest expense, P may deduct the entire $30 of disqualified interest expense that it paid or accrued during 1991. In addition, because P has a $20 excess limitation for 1991, P may deduct in 1991 $20 of the $50 disqualified interest expense that was disallowed in 1990 and carried forward to 1991, leaving $30 of such disallowed interest to be carried forward to 1992. (Because P's $20 excess limitation for 1991 is used entirely in 1991, there is no excess limitation carryforward to 1992.)

For 1992, P has excess interest expense of $35 ($60 net interest expense less 50% of $50 adjusted taxable income). Because P's excess interest expense for the year ($35) exceeds P's disqualified interest expense paid or accrued to related tax-exempt persons ($10), none of such disqualified interest expense is deductible in 1992. Moreover, since P has no excess limitation for 1992, none of the $30 of disallowed interest carried forward from 1991 to 1992 is deductible in 1992. Therefore, P carries forward to 1993 $40 of previously disallowed disqualified interest expense ($30 from 1990 and $10 from 1992).

The Proposed Regulations impose special limitations on disallowed interest expense carryforwards and excess limitation carryforwards that may apply where an affiliated group of corporations, a Code §381(a) transaction (i.e., certain tax-free reorganizations or a Code §332 tax-free liquidation), or "built-in deductions" are involved.[10] In addition, under the Proposed Regulations, if the issuer has an adjusted taxable *loss* for a taxable year, then (i) its adjusted taxable income is treated as zero, (ii) such loss will reduce the excess limitation carryforward for the purpose of determining whether there is excess interest expense for a taxable year, and (iii) such loss will not affect the determination of the issuer's adjusted taxable income for any other taxable year.[11]

The Proposed Regulations contain rules coordinating Code §163(j) with other provisions affecting the deductibility of interest, such as by permanent disallowance, capitalization or deferral.[12]

¶1305.1.3 Debt-Equity Ratio

Disqualified interest is non-deductible in a taxable year only if the issuer's debt-equity ratio (DER) exceeds 1.5:1 on the last day of such year.[13] For this purpose, the issuer's DER is the ratio of:

(1)   total debt, including accrued OID, but excluding (under the Proposed Regulations) (a) "short-term liabilities" (i.e., accrued operating expenses,

---

[10] See Prop. Reg. §1.163(j)-6.

[11] Prop. Reg. §1.163(j)-2(f)(4).

[12] See Prop. Reg. §1.163(j)-7.

[13] Code §163(j)(2)(A), as retroactively amended by the 1990 Act; Prop. Reg. §1.163(j)-1(b). The statute permits future regulations to identify other DER testing dates. According to the 1989 Conference Report at 67, 1.5:1 exceeded the "median" DER for U.S. corporations at the time Code §163(j) was drafted.

accrued taxes payable, and any account payable for the first 90 days of its existence provided that no interest accrues during such period) and (b) "commercial financing liabilities" (i.e., liabilities incurred under a commercial financing agreement to buy an inventory item that are secured by the inventory item, due on or before the sale of the item and [if between related parties] on arm's length terms), to

(2) net equity, i.e., the excess of total assets (taken into account at their adjusted tax basis, *not* their FV) over such total debt (*including* any short-term liabilities and commercial financing liabilities).[14]

Under the Proposed Regulations, this DER computation is subject to two anti-abuse rules. *First*, an asset is disregarded if "the principal purpose" for acquiring it was to reduce the DER.[15] *Second*, under an "anti-stuffing" rule, any transfer of assets made by a person "related" to the issuer within the meaning of Code §267(b) or §707(b)(1) (as described at ¶1305.1.5) during the last 90 days of its taxable year is disregarded if there is a "a transfer of the same or similar assets" by the issuer to a related person during the first 90 days of the following year, unless there is full consideration for the transfer in money or property.[16]

In determining the deductibility of disqualified interest expense carried forward from a prior taxable year, the requirement of a DER in excess of 1.5:1 is deemed to be satisfied.[17]

EXAMPLE 2

$20 of T's year 1 interest expense is non-deductible under Code §163(j). T carries forward the $20 of year 1 disallowed interest to year 2. In year 2, T has $110 of adjusted taxable income (so that 50% of adjusted taxable income is $55), T has $50 of net interest expense, and T has only a 1:1 DER.

Code §163(j) will not disallow any of T's interest expense actually paid or accrued in year 2, because T's year 2 DER does not exceed 1.5:1.

Notwithstanding T's low DER for year 2, however, only $5 of T's $20 interest expense carried forward from year 1 is deductible in year 2; the other $15 is not. This is because T is treated as having a more than 1.5:1 DER in year 2 for purposes of the year 1 carryforward, so that T's $20 of interest carried forward from year 1 to year 2 is subject to Code §163(j) in year 2, notwithstanding T's actual year 2 DER of only 1:1. Therefore, the year 1 carryforward interest is deductible only to the extent of T's "excess limitation" for year 2, which is $5 (i.e., 50% of T's $110 adjusted taxable income for year 2 [$55] less T's year 2 net interest expense [$50]).[18]

---

[14] Code §163(j)(2)(C); Prop. Reg. §1.163(j)-3.

[15] Prop. Reg. §1.163(j)-3(c)(5)(i).

[16] Prop. Reg. §1.163(j)-3(c)(5)(ii).

[17] Code §163(j)(1)(B), as amended by the Small Business Job Protection Act of 1996 (P.L. 104-188, §1704(f)(2)). The amendment applies retroactively as of the effective date of Code §163(j).

[18] For similar examples, see H.R. Rep. No. 104-586, 104th Cong., 2d Sess. 183 (5/20/96), accompanying the Small Business Job Protection Bill of 1996 (H.R. 3448).

¶1305.1.4 Interest Not Subject to Tax or Subject to Reduced Tax

Code §163(j) applies to interest paid or accrued to a related person only if (1) no U.S. tax is imposed by the income tax provisions of the Code with respect to such interest (e.g., interest paid or accrued to a tax-exempt organization, or interest paid or accrued to a foreign lender fully exempt from U.S. withholding tax under the portfolio interest exception of Code §871(h) or §881(c)) or (2) any treaty reduces the rate of U.S. tax that otherwise would be imposed by the income tax provisions of the Code on such interest (e.g., a treaty reduces the normal 30% withholding tax rate imposed on U.S.-source interest paid or accrued to a foreign person).[19]

The Proposed Regulations clarify that interest paid or accrued to a U.S. taxable person will not be considered subject to no tax or to reduced tax merely because the recipient has an NOL sufficient to shelter all or part of the interest income.[20]

Whether interest paid to a partnership (or other pass-through entity) is subject to tax is determined at the partner level, e.g., if a partnership has three equal partners—a tax-exempt organization, a foreign person with a reduced treaty rate for interest income, and a U.S. taxable person—the provision would apply to interest allocable to the first two.[21]

If a tax treaty reduces the U.S. federal income tax rate applicable to interest paid to a foreign person, a proportionate share of the interest (corresponding to the amount of rate reduction) is treated as not subject to tax.[22]

The Proposed Regulations contain special rules for determining the extent to which interest paid to a controlled foreign corporation, passive foreign investment company, foreign person holding company, or DISC is considered to be subject to U.S. tax.[23]

¶1305.1.5 Related Person

Interest is not disqualified interest unless it is paid to or accrued by a person "related" to the issuer within the meaning of Code §267(b) or §707(b)(1).[24] Those provisions are complex. Stated very generally:

(1) A C corporation issuer ("C1") is related to a C corporation payee ("C2") if (a) either corporation directly or indirectly owns more than 50% of the stock (by vote *or* by value) of the other corporation, (b) a third corporation directly or indirectly owns more than 50% of the stock (by vote *or* by value) of each of C1 and C2, or (c) five or fewer individuals, estates or trusts (including pension trusts) directly or indirectly own more than 50%

---

[19] Code §163(j)(3)(A), (5)(B); Prop. Reg. §1.163(j)-4.
[20] See Prop. Reg. §1.163(j)-4(a).
[21] Code §163(j)(5)(A).
[22] Code §163(j)(5)(B); Prop. Reg. §1.163(j)-4(b).
[23] See Prop. Reg. §1.163(j)-4(d).
[24] Code §163(j)(4); Prop. Reg. §1.163(j)-2(g).

of the stock (by vote *or* by value) of each of C1 and C2.[25] For this purpose, an option to acquire stock is treated as stock (though apparently only to the extent the stock subject to the option is already outstanding).[26] In addition, in determining whether two C corporations are related, non-voting stock that is limited and preferred as to dividends and, in certain cases, stock held by or for employees and certain other stock, is ignored.[27]

(2)   A C corporation issuer is related to another entity or to an individual if that entity or individual owns more than 50% *in value* of the issuer's outstanding stock.

(3)   A C corporation issuer may be related to another entity if the same group of persons owns (a) more than 50% *in value* of the issuer's outstanding stock and (b) more than 50% of the entity.

For purposes of (1), (2) and (3), an individual is treated as owning stock owned by certain family members, and stock owned by a corporation, partnership or other entity generally is treated as owned proportionately by the entity's shareholders, partners or other beneficial owners. For purposes of (2) and (3), an individual (as distinguished from a corporation, partnership, pension trust or other entity) is treated as owning stock owned by co-partners.

The Proposed Regulations provide that related person status is tested with respect to an item of interest expense when such interest expense accrues (assuming daily accrual of interest under principles similar to the OID provisions of Code §1272(a)).[28] In addition, the Proposed Regulations contain an anti-abuse rule providing that "the substance, rather than the form, of ownership" controls the determination whether persons are related. By illustration, they refer expressly to "an arrangement to shift formal voting power or formal ownership of shares away from any person for the purpose of avoiding the application of [Code Sec.] 163(j)."[29]

A special rule applies to partnerships. Any interest paid or accrued to a partnership directly or indirectly by a payor corporation is considered paid or accrued to an unrelated person if less than 10% of the capital and profits interests in the partnership are held by persons not subject to U.S. federal income tax.[30] Where a foreign person is subject to reduced U.S. tax by treaty (e.g., is subject by treaty to less than the normal 30% withholding tax), such person is (for purposes of this exemption for a partnership less than 10% owned by tax-exempt persons) treated as partly a tax-exempt person, depending on the percentage of the tax reduction afforded by such treaty. This 10% exception does not apply to interest allocable to a partner that itself is related to the issuer.

[25] Code §§267(b)(3), 267(f), 1563.
[26] See Reg. §1.1563-3(b)(1).
[27] Code §1563(c).
[28] Prop. Reg. §1.163(j)-2(g)(3).
[29] Prop. Reg. §1.163(j)-2(g)(2), citing the principles of Reg. §1.957-1(b)(2).
[30] Code §163(j)(4)(B); Prop. Reg. §1.163(j)-2(g)(4).

EXAMPLE 3

The capital and profits interests in a partnership ("PS") are owned as follows:

	Percentage
Tax-exempt U.S. entities	12
Foreign persons subject by treaty to tax on U.S. interest income at one-half the normal 30% rate	26
Taxable U.S. persons unrelated to the above owners	62
Total	100

For purposes of the partnership less-than-10% exception, PS is treated as 25% owned by tax-exempt partners:

	Percentage
100% of ownership by tax-exempt entities	12
50% of 26% ownership by foreign persons (because their treaty rate is 50% of the normal 30% tax rate)	13
Total	25

Thus PS does not satisfy the partnership less-than-10% exception.

PS (and possibly others) form Newco to acquire T. PS acquires more than 50% (by value) of Newco's outstanding stock. Newco borrows money from (i.e., issues debt to) PS in 1991 to finance the acquisition.

For as long as Newco has sufficient excess interest expense and a DER exceeding 1.5:1, 25% of the interest Newco pays or accrues to PS (i.e., the portion of such interest allocable to PS's tax-exempt U.S. partners and tax-reduced foreign partners, taking the latter into account only to the extent of their percentage treaty reduction) is not deductible.

EXAMPLE 4

Same as Example 3 except that the tax-exempt U.S. partners and tax-reduced foreign partners own only 9% of PS's capital and profits interests (taking the latter into account only to the extent of their percentage treaty reduction).

None of the interest which Newco pays or accrues to PS will be disallowed by this provision, unless a tax-exempt or tax-reduced partner of PS is itself related to Newco (such as by owning, together with its attributees, more than 50% of Newco's stock directly or indirectly).

EXAMPLE 5

Same as Example 3 except that the tax-exempt and foreign persons, rather than investing in Newco indirectly through PS, directly acquire 38% of Newco's stock and 38% of the newly issued Newco debt (i.e., 12% by the tax-exempt persons and 26% by the foreign persons, as in Example 3). PS, none of whose remaining partners are tax-exempt or foreign persons, acquires the remaining 62% of Newco's stock and debt.

In contrast to Example 3, under the partnership less-than-10% exception, PS is not considered related to Newco, since none of its partners are persons exempt from U.S. tax (or subject to a treaty reduction). Moreover, because the tax-exempt and foreign persons do not own more than 50% of Newco's stock, they will not be deemed related to Newco (unless the substance of the ownership structure differs from its form, so that the anti-abuse rule described above applies). Therefore, subject to the anti-abuse rule, none of the interest paid by PS to the tax-exempt or foreign persons will be subject to disallowance under Code §163(j).[31]

The divergent results in Examples 3 and 5 illustrate the harsh and irrational treatment of partnership arrangements under Code §163(j). That is, the interplay between extending the general 50% relatedness test to a partnership and the low 10% exempt partner threshold effectively penalizes an issuer that sells debt to tax-exempt or foreign investors indirectly through a partnership rather than directly, even though the economic substance of the two transactions is the same. A better approach—one that conforms the tax treatment of the two transactions— would disregard the existence of the partnership for purposes of the 50% relatedness test and consider only whether a single tax-exempt or foreign investor in the partnership indirectly owns more than 50% of the debt issuer.

EXAMPLE 6

Same as Example 3 except that, upon acquiring the Newco debt, PS immediately distributes the debt to its partners.

Subject to the anti-abuse rules described above and in the immediately following paragraph, Code §163(j) will not apply. Although PS is related to Newco, Newco is paying or accruing the interest not to PS but to PS's partners, of which none of the tax-exempt or foreign persons is more-than-50% related to Newco within the meaning of Code §§267(b) or 707(b)(1).

---

[31] See Prop. Reg. §1.163(j)-2(g)(5) example (2).

As noted in ¶1305.1.1, the Proposed Regulations contain a general anti-abuse rule that would "disregard or recharacterize" any "arrangement, including the use of partnerships . . . , entered into with a principal purpose of avoiding the rules of section 163(j)."[32] Treasury provided no guidance as to the types of arrangements it might consider abusive. Given that the partners of PS, in the absence of PS, could have invested *directly* in Newco's stock and debt without triggering Code §163(j), as illustrated in Example 5, it is difficult to see how the arrangement in Example 6 could be regarded as abusive, since it too is a direct investment by PS's partners in Newco debt that essentially was arranged through PS as placement agent.

EXAMPLE 7

Two investment partnerships (PS#1 and PS#2) are formed to coinvest in Newco. PS#1 and PS#2 have a common corporate general partner ("GP") that owns 2% of the capital and profits interest of each of the 2 partnerships. The partners of PS#1 (other than GP) are all tax-exempt organizations ("TEOs"). The partners of PS#2 are all taxable persons who are unrelated (with the exception of GP) to the partners of PS#1. PS#1 and PS#2 each acquire 50% of Newco's stock and certain Newco debt.

Newco and PS#1 are "related" under Code §267(b) because the TEOs and GP collectively own both (a) more than 50% of the capital or profits interest of PS#1 (i.e., they own 100%) and (b) more than 50% in value of Newco's stock (i.e., they indirectly own 51%: 50% of Newco owned directly by PS#1 plus 1% deemed owned by GP indirectly through PS#2). Therefore Code §163(j) will apply to the portion of Newco's interest expense allocable to the TEOs, assuming the other requirements of Code §163(j) are satisfied.

EXAMPLE 8

Same as Example 7 except that PS#1 acquires 48% of Newco's stock (rather than 50% as in Example 7), and PS#2 acquires the remaining 52%.

In contrast to Example 7, if the form of the transaction is respected, then subject to the anti-abuse rules discussed in connection with Examples 5 and 6, Code §163(j) should not apply. The TEOs and GP collectively, though they own 100% of PS#1, do not own more than 50% in value of Newco's stock, but rather they collectively own indirectly only 49.04% of Newco's stock: 48% of Newco owned directly by PS#1 plus 1.04% (i.e., 2% of 52%)

---

[32] Prop. Reg. §1.163(j)-1(f).

deemed owned by GP indirectly through PS#2. Therefore, Newco and PS#1 are not "related" for Code §163(j) purposes.[33]

¶1305.1.6   Back-to-Back Loan and Guarantee

The 1989 committee reports generally contemplate that back-to-back loans will be collapsed. Thus it is intended that future regulations "will treat back-to-back loans through third parties (whether related or unrelated), as well as similar arrangements, like direct loans to related parties" if the ultimate lender is related to the ultimate borrower.[34]

EXAMPLE 9

P, a U.S. corporation, borrows money from a foreign bank that has borrowed money from P's foreign parent. P's interest payments to the foreign bank could be treated as paid to P's foreign parent.

Similarly, regulations "may permit, in appropriate circumstances, interest payments to related parties to be treated as other than disqualified interest where such payments are part of a back-to-back loan from an unrelated lender...."[35]

For the treatment of guarantees and similar arrangements, see ¶1305.2 below, concerning expansive 1993 Act amendments which create Code §163(j) test #2, effective for interest paid or accrued in taxable years beginning after 12/31/93.

Treasury expressly declined to address guarantees and back-to-back loans in the 1991 Proposed Regulations.[36]

In 1993 Congress enacted Code §7701(l) authorizing regulations "recharacterizing any multiple-party financing transaction as a transaction directly among any 2 or more of such parties where [Treasury] determines that such recharacterization is appropriate to prevent avoidance of any tax imposed by this title." This sweeping rule is broad enough

---

[33] Depending on the facts, IRS might seek to treat PS#1 and PS#2 as a single partnership or joint venture for tax purposes, in which case the resulting entity would be "related" to the issuer. Avoiding this result could require being able to establish a sufficient business purpose for two partnerships rather than one, which could be difficult, see, e.g. Gregory v. Helvering, 293 U.S. 465, 35-1 U.S.T.C. ¶9043 (1935); Rev. Rul. 75-19, 1975-1 C.B. 382 (respecting a partnership formed by four C corporations that were owned by one common parent where each subsidiary had "business reasons for existence independent of the business to be performed" by the partnership).

More recently, however, in Rev. Rul. 94-43, 1994-2 C.B. 198, *revoking* Rev. Rul. 77-220, 1977-1 C.B. 263, IRS approved a partnership arrangement involving three S corporations as partners although "the principal purpose" of the arrangement was to avoid the limitation on the permissible number of S corporation shareholders.

[34] H.R. Rep. No. 247, 101st Cong., 1st Sess. at 104 (1989) (as reprinted in CCH Stand. Fed. Tax Rep. no. 40 (9/20/89)) (hereinafter "1989 House Report"). See 1989 Conference Report at 66.

[35] 1989 House Report at 102.

[36] See Prop. Reg. §1.163(j)-9.

to permit regulations that would treat, for Code §163(*l*) purposes, a back-to-back loan through an unrelated third party like a direct loan between the ultimate lender and the ultimate borrower where they are related. However, regulations issued under the authority of Code §7701(*l*) as of the time of this writing do not apply for Code §163(*l*) purposes.

¶1305.1.7 Treatment of Affiliated Group

All members of an affiliated group of corporations (as defined in Code §1504(a)—see ¶1205.2.1 and ¶211.1) generally are treated as one taxpayer for Code §163(j) purposes.[37] Thus, whether the issuer has excess interest expense or a DER exceeding 1.5:1, for example, is determined by taking account of the issuer as well as its affiliates. However, Code §163(j)(7) grants Treasury authority to issue regulations providing any appropriate "adjustments" in the case of affiliated group members. The Proposed Regulations contain elaborate rules regarding the treatment of affiliates.[38] For example, they provide that if 80% of the total voting power and total value of the stock of an "includible corporation" (i.e., a corporation other than a foreign corporation, a tax-exempt corporation, or other excluded corporation described in Code §1504(b)) is owned, directly or indirectly, by another includible corporation, the first corporation generally is treated for Code §163(j) purposes as a member of an affiliated group that includes the other corporation and its affiliates. For this purpose, the attribution rules of Code §318 apply.

EXAMPLE 10

S1 and S2 are wholly owned U.S. subsidiaries of F, a foreign corporation. S1 and S2 are not members of an affiliated group under Code §1504(a), because their foreign parent, F, is not an includible corporation. However, under Code §318(a)(2)(C), because F owns at least 50% of S1, S1 is treated as owning any stock owned by F. Hence, S1 is deemed to own indirectly 100% of S2. Similarly, S2 is treated as owning indirectly 100% of S1. Therefore, S1 and S2 generally are treated as members of an affiliated group for Code §163(j) purposes.[39]

¶1305.1.8 Effective Date

Code §163(j) rule #1 as discussed in this ¶1305.1 applies to interest paid or accrued in taxable years of the issuer beginning after 7/10/89, with two exceptions.

---

[37] Code §163(j)(6)(C); Prop. Reg. §1.163(j)-5(a)(2).

[38] See Prop. Reg. §1.163(j)-5.

[39] See Prop. Reg. §1.163(j)-5(a)(3). This provision addresses a concern expressed in the 1989 House Report (at 106) regarding potential avoidance of the principles of Code §163(j) through the use of intervening foreign entities.

First, interest expense paid or accrued in taxable years beginning before 1/1/94 is not treated as disqualified interest if it is paid or accrued on a *fixed-term* obligation issued on or before 7/10/89 (or issued after that date pursuant to a binding written contract in effect on 7/10/89, and at all times thereafter until issuance).[40] Under the Proposed Regulations, however, such an obligation will be treated as newly issued if, after 7/10/89, either (1) it is "revised (whether by renegotiation, assumption, reissuance, or otherwise) in a manner that would give rise to a deemed exchange of debt instruments by the obligee under [Code Sec.] 1001"[41] or (2) its maturity date is extended (even if this would not cause a deemed Code §1001 exchange).[42] The 1993 Act eliminated this fixed-term loan exception for all interest paid or accrued in taxable years beginning after 12/31/93.[43]

Second, in the case of a *demand loan* (or other loan without a fixed term) outstanding on 7/10/89, interest attributable to pre-9/1/89 periods was not disallowed.[44]

Under the Proposed Regulations, interest expense that is not disallowed under either of the above exceptions is taken into account under Code §163(j) for all other purposes (e.g., "determining whether other interest expense paid or accrued during the taxable year is treated as excess interest expense").[45]

¶1305.2   Code §163(j) Rule #2: Debt "Guaranteed" By Related Tax-Exempt Organization or Foreign Person

¶1305.2.1   In General

Code §163(j) rule #1 as described in ¶1305.1 applies only in certain cases where interest is actually *paid or accrued* (directly or indirectly) to a lender wholly or partially exempt from U.S. tax. The 1993 Act drastically expanded Code §163(j) to limit as well the deductibility of interest paid or accrued on debt *guaranteed* by a tax-exempt organization ("TEO") or foreign person ("FP") "related" to the borrower (even though the interest is actually paid to a taxable U.S. lender) if certain other conditions are met.[46] This second limitation (Code §163(j) rule #2) is effective for interest paid or accrued in taxable years beginning after 12/31/93.

Code §163(j) rule #2 utilizes the mechanics of rule #1 (as described in ¶1305.1) but enacts an alternative for tests (3) and (4) described in ¶1305.1.1. Specifically, Code §163(j) rule #2 applies when *all* seven of the following conditions are satisfied:

---

[40] Code §163(j)(3)(B), before its amendment by the 1993 Act; Prop. Reg. §1.163(j)-10(b)(1).

[41] See, e.g., Rev. Rul. 89-122, 1989-2 C.B. 200 (change in the stated principal amount or the interest rate of a debt instrument is a material modification resulting in a deemed exchange of old bonds for new bonds under Code §1001); Rev. Rul. 87-19, 1987-1 C.B. 249 (waiver by noteholder of right to receive a higher interest rate under an interest adjustment clause is a material change resulting in a deemed exchange under Code §1001).

[42] Prop. Reg. §1.163(j)-10(b)(1)(iii).

[43] See Code §163(j)(3)(B), before and after amendment by the 1993 Act; 1993 Act §13228(d).

[44] 1989 Act §7210(b); Prop. Reg. §1.163(j)-10(b)(2).

[45] Prop. Reg. §§1.163(j)-10(b)(1), (2).

[46] See Code §§163(j)(3) and 163(j)(6)(D) and (E), as amended by the 1993 Act.

(1) The three tests described in ¶¶1305.1.1(1), (2), and (5) are met, i.e., C corporation borrower, borrower debt-to-equity ratio exceeds 1.5:1 and borrower has "excess interest expense."

(2) The borrower's debt to the lender is "guaranteed" by a person more than 50% "related" to the borrower.

   • "Guarantee" is defined extremely broadly as "any arrangement under which a person (directly or indirectly through an entity or otherwise) assures, on a conditional or unconditional basis, the payment of [the borrower's] obligation."[47] According to the legislative history, this includes: "any form of credit support . . . includ[ing] a commitment to make a capital contribution to the debtor or otherwise maintain its financial viability [and] . . . a 'comfort letter,' regardless of whether the arrangement gives rise to a legally enforceable obligation."[48]

   • See ¶1305.1.5 above for the definition of "related"—generally more than 50% by vote or value if the guarantor is a C corporation and more than 50% by value alone if the guarantor is not a C corporation.

(3) Such "related" guarantor is a TEO or an FP, whether or not such FP is entitled to a reduced treaty withholding rate.

   • The statutory language of Code §163(j) rule #2 does not appear to cover the situation where a U.S. partnership with TEO and/or FP ownership of 10% or more (measured by either capital or profits) is "related" to the borrower and such partnership guarantees the borrower's debt even though a direct loan by the partnership would in these circumstances be covered by Code §163(j) rule #1 (see ¶1305.1.5). It is not clear that this difference in scope between rules #1 and #2 was intended. If rule #2 did apply to such a partnership guarantee, the Code §163(j) disallowance rule would presumably apply to the portion of the interest corresponding to the portion of the partnership owned by the TEO-FP persons.

   • Where a partnership is organized under the laws of a foreign country, it appears that a guarantee by such a partnership is treated as a guarantee by an FP, regardless of the nationality of the partners.

   • Because Code §163(j) rule #2 can be triggered by an FP guarantee whether or not FP is entitled to a reduced treaty withholding rate, rule #2 can apply even where interest, had it been payable to FP with respect to a direct loan by FP, would not have been disallowed under Code §163(j) rule #1. See Example 1 below.

(4) The borrowing corporation does not own a controlling interest in the guarantor, i.e., at least 80% by vote and value (80% of capital and profits if guarantor is not a corporation).

(5) The interest is not paid to an FP subject to a 30% U.S. withholding tax on its gross interest income. If the interest is paid to an FP with a treaty-

---

[47] Code §163(j)(6)(D)(iii).

[48] H.R. Rep. No. 111, 103d Cong., 1st Sess. at 249 (Comm. Print 1993) (as reprinted in CCH Stand. Fed. Tax Rep. no. 22 (5/20/93)).

reduced gross withholding rate below 30% a portion of the interest corresponding to the rate reduction is treated as meeting this test.

(6) IRS has authority (by future regulations) to exempt interest which, if paid to the guarantor, would have been subjected to a U.S. net income tax, i.e., where the guarantor is engaged in a U.S. trade or business and the interest could be effectively connected thereto.

(7) The borrower and the lender are not more than 50% "related" (under the rules described in ¶1305.1.5).

Thus, under Code §163(j) rule #2, where a borrower's debt to a taxable U.S. lender is guaranteed by a TEO or an FP (but apparently not by a partnership fund with more than 10% TEO-FP participation), and the other conditions outlined above are satisfied, interest on such debt paid by the borrower to the U.S. lender is treated as "disqualified interest expense" and subjected to the Code §163(j) disallowance rules described in ¶1305.1.2. In that case, the disqualified interest expense under Code §163(j) rules #1 and #2 would be combined and allowed as a deduction only to the extent it exceeds the borrower's "excess interest expense" as described in ¶1305.1.2. Regarding the amount of interest disallowed under Code §163(j) rule #2 where the guarantee is provided by multiple persons, not all of which are TEOs or FPs, see Examples 2 and 3 below.

EXAMPLE 1

A foreign corporation (FC) not engaged in a U.S. trade or business, but subject to full 30% U.S. withholding tax on the receipt of U.S.-source interest income, owns non-voting stock of Newco, a U.S. C corporation. The Newco stock held by FC represents 51% of the total value of Newco's outstanding stock. Newco borrows money from a U.S. bank that is unrelated to Newco or FC. The loan is secured by Newco's assets and is on arm's length terms. FC delivers to the bank a binding or non-binding comfort letter with respect to the loan. Newco's debt-equity ratio exceeds 1.5:1.

Under Code §163(j) rule #2, interest paid or accrued on the bank debt is "disqualified interest expense" which, together with any other disqualified interest expense of Newco, is non-deductible to the extent of Newco's excess interest expense for the year, as described in ¶1305.1.2. This is the case even though the interest, had it been payable to FC rather than to the bank, would have been subject to full 30% U.S. withholding tax and hence fully deductible under Code §163(j) rule #1.

EXAMPLE 2

Same as Example 1 except that all of Newco's shareholders (including FC), rather than FC alone, provide the binding or non-binding comfort letter to the bank.

As in Example 1, Code §163(j) rule #2 applies because the guarantee is made in part by FC, which is more than 50% related to Newco. It is less clear, however, whether the amount of interest disallowed is 100% or only the portion of the interest corresponding to FP's 51% share of the guarantee. Since the bank presumably lent based on the creditworthiness of all Newco's shareholders, arguably FP should be considered to have "guaranteed" only 51% of the loan principal and interest, so that only 51% of Newco's interest expense would be subject to disallowance.

This position is also consistent with Code §163(j) rule #1, which disallows interest expense only *to the extent* it is paid or accrued to a person not wholly subject to tax on the interest income. However, IRS could take the position that all of the interest should be disallowed based on the broad concept of "guarantee," which includes (according to the legislative history) "any form of credit support" by a TEO or FP.

EXAMPLE 3

An investment partnership ("PS") owns 100% of Newco's outstanding stock. One pension fund ("PF") owns a limited partnership interest in PS representing 51% of PS's capital and profits interests. The remaining interests in PS are owned by taxable U.S. partners. Newco borrows money from a U.S. bank that is unrelated to Newco, PS, or the partners of PS. The loan is secured by Newco's assets and is on arm's-length terms. PS delivers to the bank a legally enforceable guarantee with respect to payments on the bank loan. PS's partners are liable severally, but not jointly, with respect to the guarantee (i.e., if PS must make a payment under the guarantee, each partner would be required to fund only its pro rata share of the payment, not the portion of the payment attributable to other partners). Newco's debt-equity ratio exceeds 1.5:1.

Code §163(j) rule #2 arguably applies, because PF is related to Newco (by virtue of PF's 51% ownership in PS which owns 100% of Newco), and PF is providing an indirect guarantee through PS. If rule #2 applies to such an indirect guarantee, it appears that 51% of the interest is subject to disallowance. This is because PF's liability on the guarantee is limited to 51% of any amounts actually payable by PS, so that, in effect, only 51% of the loan amount is subject to PS's indirect guarantee.

EXAMPLE 4

Same as Example 3 except that 2 unrelated pension funds each own 40% of the capital and profits interest of PS, and the remaining 20% of PS is owned by taxable U.S. partners. Based on the law in its current form, Code §163(j) rule #2 apparently does not apply to limit the deductibility of interest paid or accrued by Newco to the bank, because neither pension fund is "related" to Newco.

Legislative Update

Two similar 2002 bills, the International Tax Simplification and Fairness for American Competitiveness Act of 2002 (H.R. 4047) and the Fairness, Simplification and Competitiveness for American Business Act of 2002 (H.R. 4151), propose to amend Code §163(j)(6)(D)(ii) so that a guarantee by a foreign person will not be treated as a "disqualified guarantee" if taxpayer establishes to IRS's satisfaction that it could have borrowed substantially the same principal amount from an unrelated person without a guarantee, applicable to guarantees issued on or after enactment.

¶1305.2.2 Effective Date

Code §163(j) rule #2 applies to interest paid or accrued in the borrower's taxable years beginning after 12/31/93. There is no grandfather rule for old debt and/or old guarantees.

¶1306 CODE §163(l) INTEREST DISALLOWANCE ON DEBT PAYABLE IN, OR BY REFERENCE TO FV OF, ISSUER EQUITY

¶1306.1 In General

Code §163(l), enacted in 1997,[1] permanently disallows any deduction for interest paid or accrued (including original issue discount) on a "disqualified debt instrument" ("*Disqualified Debt*"). "Disqualified Debt" is any debt where all four of the following tests are met:

(1)   The debt is issued by a corporation (see ¶1306.2).
(2)   The debt is payable in, or by reference to the value of, equity (see ¶1306.3).
(3)   The equity described in (2) is equity of the issuer or a person "related" to the issuer under Code §267(b) or §707(b) (see ¶1306.4 and ¶1306.5).[2]
(4)   The debt is issued after 6/8/97, with exceptions for certain issuances then pending (see ¶1306.6).

Code §163(l) does not affect the tax treatment of the holder, who must include in income any interest paid or accrued on Disqualified Debt, nor does it change the treatment of Disqualified Debt as "debt" for tax purposes. Hence,

---

¶1306   [1] 1997 Act sec. 1005.
[2] Code §§163(l)(2), 163(l)(4).

for example, a corporate holder is not entitled to a dividends received deduction for yield on a debt instrument to which Code §163(*l*) applies, and such debt is not treated as equity for purposes of Code §§302, 305, 306, 351 or the reorganization provisions.

Legislative Update

The unenacted Senate version (S. 1054) of the 2003 Act, effective for transactions after 2/13/03, would have expanded the definition of Disqualified Debt to include debt payable in equity held by the issuer (or any related party) in any other person.

An identical provision was reintroduced in the Senate on 6/2/03 as part of the Working Taxpayer Fairness Restoration Act (S. 1162) to be effective for transactions after 2/13/03. An identical provision also appears in the Abusive Tax Shelter Shutdown and Taxpayer Accountability Act of 2003 (H.R. 1555), introduced 4/2/03 and effective for transactions after enactment.

Legislative Update

The Emergency Worker and Investor Protection Act of 2002 (H.R. 3622) introduced 1/24/02 effective for sales or exchanges after the date of enactment would amend Code §163(*l*) to deny a deduction for (1) interest on debt instruments issued by any corporation required to file a certified annual report with SEC or any entity consolidated with the SEC filer for reporting purposes if such indebtedness is not shown as a liability in the certified annual report or (2) interest, to the extent allocable to the SEC filer, on debt instruments issued by an "off-balance sheet entity"—meaning any entity (a) treated as a partnership or trust or disregarded for tax purposes, (b) which is not consolidated for purposes of the certified annual report, and (c) in which the filer holds an ownership interest—if proceeds of such indebtedness are used directly or indirectly to acquire stock of the SEC filer.

¶1306.2   Debt Issued by Corporation

Code §163(*l*) applies only to debt issued by a corporation.[3] However, legislative history indicates that the provision also applies to debt "issued by a partnership to the extent of its corporate partners."[4] Presumably, therefore, interest expense

---

[3] Code §163(*l*)(2).
[4] See H.R. Rep. No. 148, 105th Cong., 1st Sess. 208 (1997) ("*1997 House Report*").

incurred by a partnership on Disqualified Debt is disallowed to a corporate partner to which the interest expense is allocated.[5]

Neither Code §163(*l*) nor the legislative history expressly exempts an S corporation from the interest disallowance rule. As a result, Code §163(*l*) facially would seem to cover S corporation debt as well as C corporation debt. However, Code §1363(b) states that "[t]he taxable income of an S corporation shall be computed in the same manner as in the case of an individual," with limited exceptions not relevant here. This strongly suggests that, for purposes of applying Code §163(*l*), an S corporation should be treated as an individual, not a "corporation," and that Code §163(*l*) therefore should not apply to S corporation debt.[6] In addition to this statutory argument, applying Code §163(*l*) to S corporation debt would make little sense as a policy matter. An S corporation, like a partnership, is a flow-through entity generally not subject to corporate tax (see Chapter 11). Therefore, the issuance of debt by an S corporation does not raise the corporate-tax avoidance concerns Code §163(*l*) is designed to address. Moreover, unlike a partnership, an S corporation is not permitted to have a C corporation shareholder and therefore cannot be used to circumvent Code §163(*l*) by allocating interest expense to a C corporation equity participant. The distinction between S corporation debt and C corporation debt has been acknowledged by the express exclusion of S corporations from the interest deferral/disallowance rules of Code §163(e)(5)[7] and §163(j).[8] We hope Treasury will confirm, by regulation[9] or otherwise, that Code §163(*l*) does not apply to debt issued by an S corporation.

Code §163(*l*) by its terms applies only to interest on "indebtedness" of a corporation.[10] As discussed in ¶606.4.1, where P acquires T's stock or assets in exchange for P shares in a tax-free reorganization, a portion of additional P shares that T's shareholders receive upon the settlement of a contingent stock arrangement (or an escrow arrangement under which T's shareholders are not for tax purposes treated from inception as owning the escrowed P shares) is taxed on receipt as interest income under the Code §483 imputed interest rules. It is not entirely clear whether P's contractual obligation to make future delivery of additional P shares to T's shareholders pursuant to such a contingent stock or escrow arrangement is P "indebtedness" within the meaning of Code §163(*l*), although we fear IRS may some day try for that unfortunate result. If P's contractual obligation is indebtedness, Code §163(*l*) apparently would apply to disallow P's deduction for the corresponding interest expense, because "a substantial amount" (i.e., 100%) of the principal and interest on the debt is paid in P shares (see ¶1306.3.1.1). If P's contractual obligation is not indebtedness, Code §163(*l*) by its terms apparently would not apply. For those of us who would prefer the latter result, a degree of

---

[5] For further discussion of the application of Code §163(*l*) to partnership debt, see ¶1306.5.

[6] This argument may be weakened somewhat by the express statutory exclusion of S corporations from Code §163(e)(5)'s corporate interest deferral/disallowance rules (see Code §163(e)(5)(D)) which could be read as suggesting that Congress may have considered Code §1363(b) insufficient to exclude S corporations from the scope of this provision.

[7] See Code §163(e)(5)(D).

[8] See Prop. Reg. §1.163(j)-1(a)(1)(i).

[9] Code §163(*l*)(5) authorizes regulations "to carry out the purposes" of Code §163(*l*).

[10] Code §163(*l*)(2), defining a "disqualified debt instrument."

comfort resides in the opening sentence of Reg. §1.483-4(b) example (2)(ii): "Section 1274 does not apply to the right to receive the additional shares [in a contingent stock payout reorganization] because *the right is not a debt instrument for federal income tax purposes.*" (Emphasis supplied).

¶1306.3   *Debt Payable in, or by Reference to FV of, Equity*

¶1306.3.1   In General

Debt is Disqualified Debt only if payable in, or by reference to the value of, equity under any of the three tests described in ¶1306.3.1.1, ¶1306.3.1.2 or ¶1306.3.1.3 below ("*equity-linked debt*").[11]

¶1306.3.1.1   *Debt Payable in, or Convertible into, Equity*

Debt is equity-linked debt if "a substantial amount of the principal or interest" on the debt obligation:

(1)   "is required to be paid [in] or converted . . . into . . . equity," *or*

(2)   "at the option of the issuer or a related party is payable in, or convertible into, . . . equity" (regardless of the likelihood the option will be exercised), *or*

(3)   "at the option of the holder or a related party" is payable in, or convertible into, equity, but only if "there is a substantial certainty the option will be exercised"—see ¶1306.3.4.

For this purpose, a person is a "related party" to the issuer or holder if that person and the issuer or holder, as applicable, bear a relationship described in Code §267(b) or §707(b). These provisions generally apply a more-than-50% equity ownership test (e.g., more-than-50% overlapping stock ownership by vote or value in the case of two corporations), as further described in ¶1306.4.

> **EXAMPLE 1.   Debt Convertible at Unrelated Holder's Option, Substantially in the Money**
>
> After the effective date of Code §163(*l*), P, to finance its acquisition of T, issues P debt to unrelated DH (debt holder) for $1,000 cash. The P debt has a 10-year term and bears a fixed, market rate of interest payable annually in cash. When P issues the debt, P's stock has an FV of $10 per share. The $1,000 debt principal is convertible at DH's option into 133 P shares (FV

[11] See Code §163(*l*)(3).

$1,333 on the debt issuance date) (i.e., the conversion feature is 25% in-the-money at the time the debt is issued).

Because a "substantial amount" (here 100%) of the debt principal is convertible at the option of the holder (DH) into P stock, the debt is equity-linked (so that Code §163(*l*) permanently disallows P's interest deductions on the debt) if there is "a substantial certainty" DH will convert the debt. It appears likely that the option would be treated as "substantially certain" to be exercised as a result of the conversion feature being 25% in-the-money at issuance. For a discussion of the "substantial certainty" test, see ¶1306.3.4.

EXAMPLE 2.   Debt Convertible at Unrelated Holder's Option, Substantially Out of the Money

Same as Example 1, except that the $1,000 debt principal is convertible at DH's option into 75 P shares (FV $750) (i.e., the conversion price is 33% out-of-the-money, so that it is not substantially certain DH will convert the debt).

Assuming the likelihood of conversion is tested only at issuance of the debt (see ¶1306.3.4), it is not substantially certain DH will convert the debt. Hence the debt is not equity-linked, and Code §163(*l*) does not apply.

We believe the same conclusion should obtain where the convertible debt is issued at-the-money.

EXAMPLE 3.   Debt Convertible at Issuer's Option

Same as Example 1, except that the debt is convertible at the option of P, the issuer (not DH, the holder). It is unlikely P will exercise this option because the conversion price is significantly in-the-money.

However, a substantial amount of the debt principal (100%) is convertible into P stock at the issuer's option, and the likelihood of conversion at the issuer's option is irrelevant in applying Code §163(*l*). Therefore, the debt is equity-linked, and Code §163(*l*) permanently disallows P's interest deductions on the debt, even if it is unlikely P will ever convert the debt.

Literally applied, the statute appears to take into account any conversion right or similar option exercisable by a debtholder whenever the debtholder is "related" to the issuer, regardless of the likelihood the option will be exercised.

EXAMPLE 4.   Debt Convertible at Related Holder's Option

P acquires 60% of T's stock. The remaining 40% of T's stock continues to be owned by T's historic shareholders, who are unrelated to P. In connection with P's acquisition of T stock, and after the effective date of Code §163(*l*), P purchases from T a 10-year note that bears a market rate of interest and is convertible at P's option into additional T shares at a price which is not in the money.

P is "related" to the issuer (T) because P owns more than 50% of T's stock. Because the conversion right is exercisable by a party (P) related to the issuer (T), the debt appears to be equity-linked debt, and Code §163(*l*), literally read, apparently disallows T's interest deductions on the debt under the test described in ¶1306.3.1.1(2) above, whether or not P is substantially certain to convert the debt.

This unexpected result seems inconsistent with the legislative implication that an option exercisable solely by the debtholder should not be taken into account for Code §163(*l*) purposes unless there is "a substantial certainty the option will be exercised."[12] Although this result appears to follow from a literal reading of Code §163(*l*)(3)(A) and (B), the reference in those provisions to "the issuer or a related party" seems designed to address the issuance of debt to an unrelated holder, where the issuer seeks to circumvent Code §163's expansive rule on issuer options by placing a conversion option with the issuer's affiliate. It does not seem designed to address the case where a bona fide lender in its capacity as debtholder possesses an option not substantially certain to be exercised and the lender happens to be related to the issuer.

As a more extreme example of this problem, Code §163(*l*) literally seems to apply whenever convertible debt is issued by one member of a consolidated group to another, a result that would cause the lender to be taxed on interest income in the consolidated return, while the borrower's equal and offsetting interest deduction is disallowed in the same consolidated return.

EXAMPLE 5.   Debt Convertible at Affiliated Holder's Option

Same as Example 4, except that P buys 100% of T's stock and P and T thereafter file consolidated federal income tax returns. For the reasons described in Example 4, Code §163(*l*), literally read, apparently disallows T's interest deductions.

---

[12] See Code §163(*l*)(3), last sentence.

Even if §163(*l*) is literally interpreted in Example 4, applying Code §163(*l*) to debt issued between consolidated group members makes little sense if the rationale for Code §163(*l*) is to prevent the elimination of corporate tax through the use of debt rather than equity. In the absence of Code §163(*l*), P's interest income on T's debt should precisely offset T's interest deductions, so that on a consolidated basis the P-T group has no income or loss. The result would be the same (i.e., no consolidated income or loss) if P purchased T equity rather than T debt. Applying Code §163(*l*) to T's convertible debt in the above example requires P to include interest income in the consolidated return while disallowing T's interest deduction in the same consolidated return, which is harsh and inconsistent with the consolidated status of P and T. This irrational result should be addressed by regulations or a technical correction treating members of a consolidated group as one taxpayer for Code §163(*l*) purposes.[13]

Finally, Code §163(*l*) appears to cover debt that is equity-linked in a technical statutory sense but whose economics do not really depend on fluctuations in equity value, so that the debt is not participating in any meaningful way.

EXAMPLE 6.   Issuer Option to Pay Interest in Shares

After the effective date of Code §163(*l*), P, a publicly-traded company, issues debt to unrelated DH for $1,000 cash. The P debt has a 10-year term and bears interest of 8% per annum. The interest is payable annually in the form of $80 cash or, at P's option, in such number of P shares (registered with SEC) as have a trading value of $80 at the time of payment.

A "substantial amount" (here 100%) of the interest is payable at the issuer's option in P shares. Therefore, the debt is equity-linked, and Code §163(*l*) permanently disallows P's interest deductions on the debt, regardless of the likelihood that P will elect to pay interest in the form of P shares. This result occurs even though the P debt is not participating in any meaningful sense. That is, any P shares received by DH on an interest payment date are economically equivalent to the $80 cash interest DH would have received had the interest been paid in cash rather than in P shares, because the P shares are worth $80 and readily saleable for $80.

EXAMPLE 7.   Issuer Option to Pay Principal in Shares

Same as Example 6, except that the 8% per annum interest is payable annually in cash, but the $1,000 debt principal is payable at maturity in the form of $1,000 cash or, at P's option, in P shares (registered with SEC) with a trading value of $1,000 at maturity.

A "substantial amount" (here 100%) of the principal is payable at the issuer's (P's) option in P stock. Therefore, the debt is equity-linked, and

---

[13] Code §163(j)(6)(C) adopts this sensible rule for Code §163(j) purposes.

Code §163(*l*) permanently disallows P's interest deductions on the debt, regardless of the likelihood that P will elect to pay principal in the form of P shares. As in Example 6, this result occurs even though the P debt is not participating in any meaningful sense.

¶1306.3.1.2   *Debt Payable by Reference to Equity FV*

Debt is also equity-linked debt if a "substantial amount of the principal or interest" on the debt obligation:

(1)   "is required to be determined . . . by reference to the value of . . . equity," or
(2)   "at the option of the issuer or a related party is determined . . . by reference to the value of . . . equity" (regardless of the likelihood the option will be exercised), or
(3)   "at the option of the issuer or a related party" is determined by reference to the value of equity, but only if "there is a substantial certainty the option will be exercised"—see ¶1306.3.4.

For this purpose, a person is a "related party" to the issuer or holder if that person and the issuer or holder, as applicable, bear a relationship described in Code §267(b) or §707(b). These provisions generally apply a more-than-50% equity ownership test (e.g., more-than-50% overlapping stock ownership by vote or value in the case of two corporations), as further described in ¶1306.4.

EXAMPLE 8.   Mandatory Payment

After the effective date of Code §163(*l*), P, to finance its acquisition of T, issues P debt to unrelated DH for $1,000 cash. The P debt has a 10-year term and bears a fixed, market rate of interest payable annually in cash. When P issues the debt, P's stock has an FV of $10 per share. The debt principal is payable in cash at maturity in an amount equal to the FV of 100 shares of P stock.

The debt is equity-linked, because a substantial amount (here 100%) of debt principal is required to be paid by reference to the FV of P's stock.

¶1306.3.1.3   *Plan or Arrangement*

Debt is equity-linked if it is "part of an arrangement which is reasonably expected to result in a transaction described in" ¶1306.3.1.1 or ¶1306.3.1.2. The 1997 House Report (at 209) identifies as examples of transactions that might be considered part of such an arrangement (1) the issuance of a forward contract in connection with the issuance of debt and (2) the issuance of non-recourse debt secured "principally" by stock.[14] No guidance is provided on how "reasonable expectation" is determined, though presumably all relevant facts and circumstances would be considered.

See the discussion of debt issued in conjunction with warrants at ¶1306.3.5.

¶1306.3.1.4   Contingent Equity Payment or Conversion Features

The treatment under Code §163(*l*) of a debt instrument that is required to be paid in or converted into equity only upon the happening of a contingency is unclear.

> **EXAMPLE 9.   Debt Convertible at Unrelated Holder's Option with Mandatory IPO Conversion**
>
> Same as Example 2, i.e., P issues $1,000 face amount of debt for $1,000 cash, which debt is convertible at DH's option into 75 P common shares with an FV of $10 per share—$750 in the aggregate—so that the conversion price is 33% out-of-the-money at issuance. In addition, upon the occurrence of a "qualified IPO" (defined as an IPO in which the offering price of P common stock exceeds $30 per share), the $1,000 debt principal will be mandatorily converted into 75 P shares.
>
> It is unclear whether interest on the debt is disallowed under Code §163(*l*).

Neither the statute nor the legislative history addresses contingent equity payment or conversion rights and obligations. We think it reasonably clear that the application of Code §163(*l*) can not be delayed or defeated merely by making an otherwise impermissible equity payment or conversion feature contingent upon the passage of time or upon the happening of an event within the control of the issuer or a related party. Where an equity payment or conversion feature is conditioned upon the occurrence of a contingency not within the control of the issuer or a related party, any of three alternative approaches could apply: Under the *first*, most taxpayer-favorable approach, Code §163(*l*)'s application would be determined at the time the debt is issued (see ¶1306.3.4) and, unless it is substantially certain that the contingency will occur, the contingent payment or conversion feature would be disregarded. This approach would treat the contingent payment or conversion feature in the same manner as an equity payment or conversion option exercisable by the holder of the debt instrument.

Under the *second* approach, the contingent payment or conversion feature would be disregarded unless and until the contingency occurs. If the contingency occurs and the debt instrument becomes mandatorily (or at the issuer's option)

---

[14] See 1997 House Report at 209.

payable in or convertible into issuer equity, Code §163(*l*) would disallow deduction for all interest paid or accrued thereafter.[15]

Under the *third* approach, Code §163(*l*)'s application would be determined at the time the debt is issued and the contingent payment or conversion feature would invoke Code §163(*l*) unless the possibility of the contingency occurring is "remote." This third approach would be similar to the treatment of contingent redemption and put rights under Code §351(g) (see ¶604.3.1.2).

Pending issuance of additional guidance on the treatment of contingent payment or conversion features, it should be possible to force a conversion of convertible debt in connection with a "qualified IPO" in a way that does not risk application of Code §163(*l*).

EXAMPLE 10.   Debt Convertible at Unrelated Holder's Option with Conversion Right Terminated Upon IPO

Same as Example 9, except that instead of mandatory conversion upon a qualified IPO, DH's conversion right terminates upon occurrence of a "qualified IPO" (defined as an IPO in which the offering price of P common stock exceeds $30 per share). Hence, upon a qualified IPO DH is faced with the choice of retaining $1,000 principal amount of non-convertible P debt *or* converting the $1,000 of P debt into P stock with a FV of $2,250 (75 shares × $30) or more, and thus would be economically compelled to convert.

Because the conversion option remains merely a holder option, the result should be the same as in Example 2.

¶1306.3.2   "Substantial Amount" of Principal or Interest

As discussed in ¶1306.3.1, Code §163(*l*) applies where a "substantial amount" of debt principal or interest is payable in or by reference to equity. This rule gives rise to two significant points: *First*, neither the statute nor the legislative history furnishes any guidance on what constitutes a "substantial amount" of principal or interest. *Second*, if a substantial amount of principal or interest is payable in, or by reference to, equity so that Code §163(*l*) applies, *all* interest on the debt is non-deductible, not merely the portion of the interest corresponding to the amount of principal or interest payable in equity.

---

[15] Cf. Rev. Rul. 68-601, 1968-2 C.B. 124 and Rev. Rul. 89-64, 1989-1 C.B. 91 (indicating that an option to acquire stock upon the happening of a contingency other than the passage of time is disregarded for Code §318 purposes until the contingency occurs).

EXAMPLE 11.   "Substantial Amount" of Interest

After the effective date of Code §163(*l*), P issues debt to unrelated DH for $1,000 cash. The P debt has a 5-year term and bears 10% per annum interest. Each year's interest ($100) is payable 70% in cash (i.e., $70 annually) and 30% in cash (i.e., $30 annually) or, at P's option, in P shares with a $30 trading value at the time of payment.

Under the test described in ¶1306.3.1.1(3), the debt is equity-linked if a "substantial amount" of the debt principal or interest is payable at P's option in P stock. It is unclear whether 30% represents a "substantial amount" of P interest and therefore unclear whether Code §163(*l*) applies.

If Code §163(*l*) does apply, it will cause *all* interest on the P debt to be non-deductible, not merely the 30% payable in equity at P's option.

EXAMPLE 12.   "Substantial Amount" of Principal

Same as Example 11, except that P's debt has a 20-year maturity. The $600 aggregate interest payable in P equity (at P's option) over the 20-year term of the debt (i.e., $30 annual interest payable (at P's option) in P equity × 20 years) represents 30% of aggregate interest on the debt payable over the 20-year term but 60% of the $1,000 debt principal.

Even if 30% does not constitute "a substantial amount" of the aggregate interest on the debt, the $600 aggregate interest payable in P equity (at P's option) might well be considered "a substantial amount" (i.e., 60%) of debt principal and hence trigger application of Code §163(*l*).

Application of the "substantial amount" concept is complicated further where the amount of principal or interest payable in, or by reference to, issuer equity is not determinable when the debt is issued.

EXAMPLE 13.   Contingent Interest

After the effective date of Code §163(*l*), P issues debt to unrelated DH for $1,000 cash. When P issues the debt, P's stock has an FV of $10 per share. The P debt has a 10-year term and bears interest equal to the sum of (1) 10% ($100) per annum plus (2) a contingent amount equal to the cumulative increase (if any) in value of 10 P shares from issuance to retirement of the debt.

Under the test described in ¶1306.3.1.2(1), the debt is equity-linked if "a substantial amount" of the interest is required to be determined by reference to the value of P's stock. Estimating at issuance the amount (if any) of contingent interest (i.e., interest in excess of the fixed 10% per annum rate) is highly speculative, as is guessing whether such contingent interest will represent "a substantial amount" of total interest or principal.

It is difficult to determine the applicability of Code §163(*l*) to the above example, because there is no guidance (1) when the "substantial amount" determination is made or (2) how the determination is to be made when the amount ultimately payable in or by reference to equity is based on future events. Presumably the determination is made at the time of issuance, not years later when the amount of equity-based principal or interest is ultimately determined and paid. Some front-end determination seems necessary to permit the issuer to file its tax returns and compute estimated taxes. If the determination is made at issuance, is it based on reasonable projections of the amount of principal or interest payable in, or by reference to, equity?[16] Or is it based on a "worst case" approach that assumes the maximum amount payable in equity will be paid.[17] A worst case approach seems unreasonable given the harsh consequences of subjecting debt to Code §163(*l*)—i.e., disallowance of all interest deductions, not merely the equity-linked payments. If the substantial amount test is applied at the front end based on assumptions, presumably the issuer cannot (and is not required to) later amend its original tax return if the assumptions turn out to be inaccurate, though this also is unclear.

Prompt guidance on all these issues, including usable safe harbors as to the meaning of substantial, is needed. One possible safe harbor could treat less than one-third of principal or interest as not "a substantial amount." Such a one-third test seems consistent with the notion of a relatively large amount as implied by the term "substantial." It also conforms to the one-third standard adopted by Proposed Regulations under Code §280G, interpreting two "substantial portion" tests contained in the regulations.[18]

---

[16] Compare the treatment of contingent interest payments under the Code §163(e)(5) AHYDO interest disallowance rules, the legislative history of which states that "regulations . . . may take into account the *expected amount* [as of the time of issuance] of any such contingent payments" for Code §163(e)(5) purposes. See ¶1303.3.1.8.

[17] Cf. Temp. Reg. §15A.453-1(c)(2) (for purposes of applying the installment method to a contingent payment sale, it is assumed that the sale is made at the stated maximum selling price, if any, determinable in the year of sale, subject to later adjustment based on the price ultimately paid).

[18] Specifically, Prop. Reg. §1.280G-1 contains two "substantial portion" tests for determining whether certain provisions of the regulations are applicable. First, Prop. Reg. §1.280G-1, Q&A 6 indicates that, in determining whether a company's stock is publicly traded (and thus ineligible for the "private company" exception—see ¶1505.6(1)), a privately-held company is treated as publicly traded if its stock constitutes a "substantial portion" of the assets of another company, the stock of which is publicly traded. Answer 6 states that a company's stock constitutes a "substantial portion" of another company's assets if the FV of such stock equals or exceeds one-third of the FV of all of the shareholding company's assets. Similarly, under Prop. Reg. §1.280G-1, Q&A 29, a company is treated as undergoing a "change of control" if a "substantial portion" of its assets (again determined as one-third or more, by FV) are transferred to a third party.

Other regulatory interpretations of the term "substantial" have adopted lower thresholds, as low as 20%[19] or even 5%.[20] We believe such lower thresholds are inappropriate for the Code §163(*l*) "substantial amount" test. A more generous threshold such as the one-third standard suggested above should be adopted given the harsh "cliff" effect of Code §163(*l*) whereby all interest deductions on Disqualified Debt are disallowed, rather than merely an amount of the interest corresponding to the portion of interest or principal payable in or by reference to equity.[21]

If future guidance ultimately furnishes a safe harbor, an issuer seeking safe harbor protection could simply cap the contingent payment below the safe harbor threshold.

EXAMPLE 14.   Capped Contingent Interest

Same as Example 13, except that the cumulative yield on the debt (including the 10% fixed cash interest) is capped at 13% per annum, so that there is a 3% cap on the contingent interest.

If a future Code §163(*l*) safe harbor were to permit the payment of up to, for example, one-third of cumulative interest in, or by reference to, equity, capping the contingent interest in this example at 3% should avoid application of Code §163(*l*).

Disallowance of all interest deductions on Disqualified Debt, rather than merely a portion of the interest deductions corresponding to the equity-linked payments on the debt, leads to arbitrary distinctions between similar economic arrangements.

EXAMPLE 15.   Use of Multiple Notes

After the effective date of Code §163(*l*), P issues two 10-year notes to unrelated DH. The first note is sold to DH for $900 cash, has a $900 face

---

[19] Temp. Reg. §15A.453-1(e)(5) states that certain convertible debt otherwise ineligible for installment sale treatment qualifies for such treatment if the debt is convertible only at "a substantial discount." For this purpose, the regulation adopts a safe harbor under which a "substantial discount" is considered to exist if, when the debt is issued, the FV of the stock or security into which the debt is convertible is less than 80% of the FV of the debt.

[20] Under Code §279(b)(2), if acquisition debt is expressly subordinated in right of payment to the payment of "any substantial amount" of unsecured indebtedness of the issuer and its affiliated group, and if certain other conditions are met, interest on the acquisition debt is non-deductible under Code §279 (see ¶1304). Reg. §1.279-3(c)(2) states that, for this purpose, unsecured indebtedness of the issuer and its affiliated group is a "substantial amount" if it constitutes 5% or more of the face amount of the acquisition debt.

[21] The 5% test of Reg. §1.279-3(c) is an inappropriately low benchmark for Code §163(*l*) for another reason. Code §279 tests a single obligation of the issuer by multiplying the 5% threshold by all unsecured indebtedness of the issuer's entire affiliated group. In contrast, a numerical "substantial

amount, and bears 11.1% interest ($100) per annum, payable annually in cash. The second note is sold to DH for $100 cash, has a $100 face amount, and pays annual cash interest equal to the cumulative increase (if any) in the value of 10 P shares. The notes are separately transferable.

Apart from their separate transferability, the two notes taken together are identical economically to the single P note described in Example 13. Nevertheless, assuming the two notes are treated as separate debt instruments for tax purposes, the treatment of the second, equity-linked note as Disqualified Debt will not adversely affect the deductibility of the $100 annual cash interest on the first, fixed-interest note, to which Code §163(*l*) will not apply. This is in contrast to Example 13, where all interest (including the $100 fixed annual cash interest) is non-deductible under Code §163(*l*) if the equity-based interest represents a substantial amount of overall interest on the debt and triggers application of Code §163(*l*).

¶1306.3.3   Payable in, or by Reference to, "Equity"

Code §163(*l*) applies only if debt is payable in, or by reference to, "equity."[22] The concept of "equity" clearly encompasses debt payable in, or by reference to the FV of, the issuer's stock. It is less clear whether "equity" also includes contingent debt payments based on other types of performance measurements relating to the issuer.

EXAMPLE 16.   Interest Contingent on FV of P's Business

After the effective date of Code §163(*l*), P issues debt to unrelated DH for $1,000 cash. The P debt has a 10-year term and bears interest equal to (i) 10% ($100) per annum plus (ii) 2% of the increase in the FV of P's business after issuance of the debt.

Technically, the contingent cash interest on the debt is not computed by reference to the FV of P's "equity" (i.e., FV of P's stock), but rather by reference to the FV of P's business. IRS, however, could well treat the contingent interest as determined by reference to P's equity for Code §163(*l*) purposes, because P's stock FV and the FV of P's business should be equivalent.

---

amount" threshold for Code §163(*l*) would be multiplied only by the principal or interest on the specific obligation of the issuer being tested (rather than on an entire class of debt of the issuer's entire affiliated group)—a potentially much smaller number.

[22] See Code §163(*l*)(2), (3)(A), (3)(B).

EXAMPLE 17.   Interest Contingent on FV of P's Subsidiary

Same as Example 16, except that the contingent interest on the P debt is equal to 2% of the increase in the FV of one of P's consolidated subsidiaries, S, after issuance of the debt.

IRS may treat the contingent interest as determined by reference to S's "equity." If so, because S is more-than-50% "related" to the debt issuer (P), the contingent interest apparently would be treated as paid by reference to "equity of the issuer or a related party" (see ¶1306.4), thus triggering Code §163(l) if the other statutory requirements are met.

EXAMPLE 18.   Interest Contingent on FV of P Divisional Business

Same as Example 16, except that P has three unincorporated operating divisions (Divisions 1, 2 and 3), and the contingent interest on the P debt is equal to 2% of the increase in the FV of Division 1 after issuance of the debt.

In this example, the contingent interest formula is not analogous to a stock-based formula, because fluctuations in P's stock FV turn on the aggregate performance of P's three divisions, which may differ radically from the performance of Division 1. Therefore, in the absence of further guidance, it appears that Code §163(l) does not apply.

EXAMPLE 19.   Interest Contingent on EBITDA Formula

Same as Example 16, except the contingent interest is calculated pursuant to contractual formula based on P's consolidated EBITDA during a specified period (e.g., 2% of [P's EBITDA during the last year the debt is outstanding × 10]).

Absent further guidance, it appears that Code §163(l) does not apply, because such an EBITDA formula may be an indicator of, but does not necessarily track, P's stock FV.

Code §163(l)(5), authorizing "such regulations as may be necessary or appropriate to carry out the purposes" of Code §163(l), provides Treasury with ample authority to address uncertainties regarding the scope of the "equity" concept.

¶1306.3.4   "Substantial Certainty" Holder Will Exercise Conversion Right

As described in ¶1306.3.1, an option exercisable by the debt holder does not invoke Code §163(*l*) unless there is "a substantial certainty" the option will be exercised (subject to the risk identified in Examples 4 and 5 above concerning a holder "related" to the debt issuer). Code §163(*l*) offers no guidance on what constitutes "a substantial certainty" of exercise in the case of a debtholder option. The 1997 House Report (at 209) offers limited comfort: "it is not expected that the provision will affect debt with a conversion feature where the conversion price is *significantly higher* than the market price of the stock on the issue date of the debt" (emphasis added). Unfortunately, there is no statement in the legislative history regarding debt with a conversion price that is only slightly out-of-the money, at-the-money, or slightly in-the-money at issuance.

While the statutory words—"substantial certainty" of exercise—suggest that Code §163(*l*) covers a holder's conversion privilege only if it is significantly in-the-money, the legislative history's favorable reference only to a significantly out-of-the-money conversion privilege creates some ambiguity.

"Substantial certainty" of exercise suggests a high standard that, in other contexts, excludes at-the-money and even slightly in-the-money options. In particular, regulations concerning the treatment of options under the Code §1361 one-class-of-stock requirement, which also adopt a "substantial certainty" of exercise standard, contain a safe harbor for options that are not more than 10% in the money at issuance (and at certain later testing dates).[23] Regulations concerning the treatment of options for Code §1504 affiliation purposes adopt a more lenient "reasonable certainty" standard, yet nevertheless also exclude certain options that are not more than 10% in the money, in addition to providing numerous other safe harbors.[24] Statutory consistency suggests that regulations under new Code §163(*l*) should contain a safe harbor similar to the Code §1361 regulations for less-than-10% in-the-money options.

Another difficulty is Code §163(*l*)'s silence on *when* the substantial certainty test is applied. Certainly the likelihood of exercise would be tested initially at issuance of the debt. However, the statute leaves murky whether an option would be tested only at issuance,[25] or possibly at later dates as well. An annual or other periodic test would seem to make no sense, because it could cause (1) a debt instrument that is outside Code §163(*l*) at issuance to flash in and out of Code §163(*l*) disqualification as P's post debt-issuance stock FV fluctuates or (2) a debt instrument covered by Code §163(*l*) at issuance to flash out and back into Code §163(*l*) disqualification as P's stock FV subsequently fluctuates. The Code §1361 one-class-of-stock regulations and Code §1504 affiliated group regulations, which also address likelihood of option exercise, adopt a more limited approach. Those provisions exempt certain categories of options altogether and, for other options,

---

[23] Reg. §1.1361-1(*l*)(4)(iii)(A), (C). See ¶1102.3.

[24] Reg. §1.1504-4. See ¶211.2.

[25] Cf. Code §163(i) (testing only at issuance whether a debt instrument is an "applicable high yield discount obligation" subject to the interest deferral/disallowance rules of Code §163(e)(5)—see ¶1303).

test likelihood of exercise at issuance and whenever the option is later transferred or materially modified, but at no other time.[26] Future regulations under Code §163(l) should adopt a similar standard, disallowing interest deductions after any testing date on which the option is deemed exercised.

In any event, prompt guidance on the "substantial certainty" of exercise test, including reasonably generous safe harbors, is important to avoid undue disruption of customary business transactions.

¶1306.3.5   Debt Issued with Warrants

Does Code §163(l) apply to debt issued with a warrant to acquire stock of the debt issuer or a related party? The answer is unclear because the tests for equity-linked debt described in ¶1306.3.1 do not apply neatly to an arrangement in which the right to acquire stock is embedded in a security (e.g., a warrant) separate from the debt.

Subject to future regulatory or other guidance, the applicability of Code §163(l) to a debt-and-warrant arrangement apparently depends on the nature of the linkage between the debt and the warrant (e.g., whether the debt and warrant are separately transferable, and whether the warrant is exercisable by delivery of the note, delivery of cash, or both). Of course, even if the debt and warrant are closely linked, Code §163(l) should not apply to the linked arrangement unless the warrant holder is "substantially certain" to exercise the warrant.

EXAMPLE 20.   Closely Linked Debt and Warrant Unit

After the effective date of Code §163(l), P issues to unrelated DH, for $1,000 cash, a P note and a warrant to acquire P shares. The debt has a $1,000 face amount and 10-year term and bears interest of 8% per annum payable annually in cash. The warrant has a 10-year term and is exercisable at any time solely by delivery of the P note. The note and warrant are transferable as a unit but not separately. The warrant is sufficiently in-the-money at issuance that it is substantially certain DH will exercise the warrant.

Code §163(l) seems applicable in this case under either of two theories: (1) the holder's inability to transfer the note and warrant separately likely causes them to constitute for tax purposes a single convertible debt instrument (and hence covered by Code §163(l)(3)(A)—see ¶1306.3.1.1(2)), and (2) because the warrant is exercisable solely by delivery of the note, the debt-warrant arrangement seems "reasonably expected to result in a transaction" in which the note is convertible into or payable in equity (see ¶1306.3.1.3).

[26] See Reg. §1.1361-1(l)(4)(iii)(A); Reg. §1.1504-4(g)(1), -4(c)(4).

EXAMPLE 21.   Debt and Warrant Not Closely Linked

Same as Example 20, except (1) the note and warrant are separately transferable and (2) the warrant is exercisable solely by delivery of cash in the amount of the exercise price.

Code §163(*l*) should not apply in this case, because (1) the separately transferable note and warrant should be treated as separate instruments for tax purposes, (2) the note itself is not payable in, or by reference to, P equity, and (3) the warrant, exercisable solely for cash, is not "part of an arrangement reasonably expected to result in a transaction" in which the note is payable in, or by reference to, P equity (see ¶1306.3.1.3).

EXAMPLE 22.   Intermediate Case

Same as Example 20, except that (1) the note and warrant are separately transferable and (2) the warrant is exercisable, at the holder's option, by delivery of the exercise price in the form of either cash or an equivalent principal amount of the note.

It is unclear whether the holder's mere right to utilize the debt as partial consideration for equity upon exercise of the warrant makes the debt "payable in . . . equity" at the holder's option. Arguably the warrant holder's right to receive P equity is an attribute not of the P debt, but of the P warrant that the tax law views as separate from the debt. On the other hand, the warrant includes a right to "put" the debt to the issuer in exchange for P shares, so that the arrangement is economically similar to convertible debt and hence arguably covered by the "arrangement" test described in ¶1306.3.1.3.[27] The latter approach, however, creates difficult issues where, for example, the holder transfers the warrant or the debt (but not both) to an unrelated third party: Would Code §163(*l*) disallow the issuer's interest deductions before, but not after, the transfer (on the theory that the "put" right is not exercisable by "the [debt]holder or a related party" after the transfer)?[28]

---

[27] Cf. Code §279(b)(3), where the statutory language explicitly treats convertible debt the same as an investment unit consisting of debt and a warrant. See ¶1304.

[28] Cf. Reg. §1.1504-4(d)(2)(vi) (safe harbor for option granted in connection with a loan ceases to apply if option is transferred without a corresponding portion of the loan).

¶1306.4   Related Party Test

Code §163(*l*) applies a "related party" test that is relevant in two ways. *First*, debt is not Disqualified Debt unless a substantial amount of the debt's principal or interest is payable in, or by reference to, equity of the issuer or a person "related" to the issuer.[29] *Second*, a conversion right or similar option potentially causes Code §163(*l*) to apply if the option is exercisable by the issuer, the holder, or a person "related" to the issuer or holder, as applicable.[30]

For both purposes, persons are "related" if they bear a relationship described in Code §267(b) or §707(b).[31] Those provisions are complex. Stated very generally, two persons are "related" if any one of the following, non-exclusive, more-than-50% tests apply:

(1)   One corporation ("C1") is related to another corporation ("C2") if (a) one corporation directly or indirectly owns more than 50% of the stock (by vote *or* by value) of the other corporation, (b) a third corporation directly or indirectly owns more than 50% of the stock (by vote *or* by value) of each of C1 and C2, or (c) five or fewer individuals, estates or trusts (including pension trusts) directly or indirectly own more than 50% of the stock (by vote *or* by value) of each of C1 and C2.[32] For this purpose, an option to acquire stock is treated as stock (though apparently only to the extent the stock subject to the option is already outstanding).[33] In addition, in determining whether two corporations are related, non-voting stock that is limited and preferred as to dividends and, in certain cases, stock held by or for employees and certain other stock, is ignored.[34]

EXAMPLE 23.   Convertible Debt

After the effective date of Code §163(*l*), P issues to corporation DH debt bearing a fixed, market rate of interest payable annually in cash. The debt is convertible at DH's option into newly-issued P shares representing 51% of P's stock on a fully diluted basis. The conversion price is sufficiently out-of-the-money that there is no substantial certainty DH will convert the debt. Beyond DH's right to receive P shares on conversion of the debt, P and DH are unrelated.

DH's conversion right should not cause DH to be related to P for Code §163(*l*) purposes, because the option attribution rule described in text immediately above apparently does not apply to DH's conversion option to acquire unissued P shares. Therefore, Code §163(*l*) should not apply.

---

[29] Code §163(*l*)(2), (3)(A), (3)(B).
[30] Code §163(*l*)(3), as discussed in ¶1306.3.1.
[31] Code §163(*l*)(4).
[32] Code §§267(b)(3), 267(f), 1563.
[33] See Reg. §1.1563-3(b)(1).
[34] Code §1563(c).

(2)   A corporation is related to another entity or to an individual if that entity or individual owns more than 50% *in value* of the corporation's outstanding stock.

(3)   A corporation and a partnership are related if the same persons own (a) more than 50% *in value* of the corporation's outstanding stock and (b) more than 50% of the capital interest, or the profits interest, in the partnership.

(4)   A partnership is related to any person that owns, directly or indirectly, more than 50% of the capital or profits interest in the partnership.

(5)   Two partnerships are related if the same persons own, directly or indirectly, more than 50% of the capital or profits interest of each partnership.

For purposes of the above tests, an individual is treated as owning stock owned by certain family members. In addition, stock owned by a corporation, partnership, or other entity generally is treated as owned proportionately by the entity's shareholders, partners or other beneficial owners. For purposes of tests (2) and (3), an individual (as distinguished from a corporation, partnership, pension trust, or other entity) is treated as owning stock owned by co-partners.

¶1306.5   *Application to Partnership Debt*

As noted in ¶1306.2, while Code §163(*l*) by its terms applies only to debt issued by a corporation, the 1997 House Report (at 208) states that Code §163(*l*) applies to "debt issued by a partnership to the extent of its corporate partners." Moreover, Code §163(*l*)(5) grants Treasury broad regulatory authority, including "preventing the avoidance of [Code §163(*l*)] through the use of an issuer other than a corporation."

In determining whether debt issued by a partnership (or an LLC treated as a partnership for federal income tax purposes) is payable in or by reference to equity "of the issuer or a related party," it is unclear whether the "issuer" is deemed to be the partnership, each corporate partner, or both. If the issuer is deemed to be the partnership, then apparently Code §163(*l*) would disallow interest deductions of the partnership's corporate partners whenever the debt is payable in, or by reference to, equity of the partnership or a person "related" to the partnership under Code §267(b) or §707(b) (see ¶1306.4). If the issuer is deemed to be each corporate partner (as to its pro rata share of the partnership's debt), then Code §163(*l*) apparently would disallow that partner's interest deductions whenever the debt is payable in, or by reference to, equity of the corporate partner or a person "related" to the corporate partner under Code §267(b) or §707(b) (see ¶1306.4). The application of the "issuer" test of Code §163(*l*) at the corporate partner level is supported by the manner in which the 1994 partnership anti-abuse regulations treat corporate partners for purposes of the Code §163(e)(5) AHYDO interest disallowance rules.[35]

IRS could well take the expansive position, in future regulations and/or under the existing partnership anti-abuse regulations, that the partnership and each of its corporate partners is an "issuer" for Code §163(*l*) purposes.

¶1306.6   Effective Date

Code §163(*l*) applies to debt issued after 6/8/97, unless the debt was (1) issued pursuant to a binding written agreement in effect on 6/8/97 and at all times thereafter, (2) described in an IRS ruling request submitted on or before 6/8/97, or (3) described on or before 6/8/97 in a public announcement or SEC filing required solely by reason of the debt's issuance.

¶1307   COSTS OF ISSUING DEBT AND EQUITY INSTRUMENTS

Paragraphs 402.1 and 402.2 discuss the deductibility and/or amortizability of P's or Newco's costs and expenses of issuing debt and equity instruments (1) to raise the money necessary for a taxable acquisition or (2) as consideration for T's assets or stock. Paragraph 613 discusses the slight differences in the applicable rules where the P or Newco instruments are issued to provide the consideration for a tax-free acquisition of T.

¶1308   INTEREST DEDUCTION LIMITATION FOR INDIVIDUAL P (OR NEWCO) SHAREHOLDERS—CODE §§163(d) AND 163(h)

Code §§163(d) (regarding "investment interest") and 163(h) (regarding "personal interest") impose substantial limitations on the interest deduction for an individual who borrows money to buy P (or Newco) stock.

¶1308.1   Basic Investment Interest Limitation

Especially in an LBO where Newco is acquiring T, Newco's shareholders frequently borrow money to purchase Newco common and preferred stock. Where an individual borrows money to purchase Newco stock (either directly or indirectly

---

[35] Code §163(e)(5), like Code §163(*l*), by its terms applies only to "corporate" debt issuers. However, Reg. §1.701-2(f) example (1) states that, in applying Code §163(e)(5) to debt issued by a partnership, each corporate partner of the partnership is treated "as issuing its share of the obligations for purposes of determining the deductibility of its distributive share of any interest on the obligations."

through a flow-through entity such as a partnership or S corporation), as will generally be the case with Mgmt and sometimes also with VCs, Code §163(d) may limit such individual's ability to deduct interest allocable to the purchase of the Newco stock.[1]

Under Code §163(d)(1), an individual may deduct "investment interest" expense only to the extent of the taxpayer's "net investment income" for the taxable year. Investment interest expense not deductible on account of Code §163(d)(1) may be carried forward and treated as investment interest expense in the following year.

"Investment interest" expense generally includes any interest that is paid or accrued on indebtedness properly allocable to property held for investment.[2] "Property held for investment" includes (1) property from which the taxpayer earns interest, dividends, annuities or royalties not derived in the ordinary course of a trade or business of the taxpayer (so-called portfolio income), and (2) any interest in a trade or business in which the taxpayer does not materially participate but that is not a passive activity under Code §469.[3] Investment interest expense does not include interest expense which is taken into account under Code §469 in computing income or loss from a passive activity or which is qualified residence interest (described in ¶1308.2).

For taxable years beginning before 1/1/93, "net investment income" generally included gross income from property held for investment (as described above), as well as CG (short-term or long-term) from disposition of such property, reduced in each case by deductible expenses (other than interest) directly connected with the production of the income.

The 1993 Tax Act revised the definition of "net investment income" to exclude LTCGs, unless the individual taxpayer made a special election as described below. This revision was designed to eliminate the pre-1993 tax rate arbitrage under which an individual taxpayer could deduct against OI (taxed in 1993 at rates up to 39.6% and in 2003 at rates up to 35%) interest expense on debt used to finance investments producing LTCG (taxed in 2003 at a 15% top rate). For taxable years beginning after 12/31/93, "net investment income" generally includes gross income from property held for investment (as described above), *plus short-term* CG from disposition of such property, reduced in each case by deductible expenses (other than interest) directly connected with the production of the income, *plus* such amount of net CG (i.e., the excess of (1) net LTCG over (2) net STCL)[4] and qualified dividend income as the individual taxpayer elects to treat as OI (taxable at rates up to 35% in 2003) rather than as LTCG or qualified dividend income (taxable at rates up to 15% in 2003).[5]

As a result of this change, an individual who has LTCGs and also has investment interest expense in excess of ordinary investment income and short-term CGs will

---

¶1308 [1] See Temp. Reg. §1.163-8T for rules pertaining to allocation of interest expense (generally adopting a tracing approach).

[2] Code §163(d)(3)(A) (as amended by the 1988 Act).

[3] Code §163(d)(5).

[4] See Code §1222(1).

[5] Code §§1(h)(2), 1(h)(11)(D)(i), 163(d)(4).

have to choose between (a) the benefit of the reduced tax rate on LTCGs plus a carryforward of the investment interest expense for possible use in a future year and (b) the benefit of immediate use of the investment interest deduction.

EXAMPLE 1

In year 1, individual A has salary income of $200,000, investment interest income of $50,000, LTCG of $300,000, and investment interest expense (including carryforwards from prior years) of $100,000. A does *not* elect to include any portion of his LTCG in net investment income for purposes of Code §163(d).

A is permitted to deduct only $50,000 of his investment interest expense in year 1 (an amount equal to A's investment income); the remaining $50,000 is carried forward and treated as investment interest expense in year 2 and thereafter. The entire $300,000 of A's LTCG is eligible for the reduced 15% tax rate on LTCGs.

EXAMPLE 2

Same facts as Example 1 except that A elects to include $50,000 of his LTCG in net investment income for purposes of Code §163(d). As a result of making this election, A is permitted to deduct the entire $100,000 of investment interest expense in year 1. However, only $250,000 of A's LTCG is eligible for the reduced 15% tax rate on LTCGs.

¶1308.2   *Qualified Residence Interest*

Mgmt or an individual VC investor may be able to avoid the investment interest limitations by using a principal residence or second home as security for the loan. If the loan qualifies as "home equity indebtedness" as defined in Code §163(h)(3), the deductibility of interest on the loan will not be subject to the investment interest or personal interest limitations. The amount of borrowing which a taxpayer may treat as home equity indebtedness is generally limited to the lesser of $100,000 or the excess of the FV of the principal residence or second home over the amount of any mortgage debt incurred in acquiring, constructing, or substantially improving the home.

¶1308.3   *Employee Holding Stock in Corporate Employer for Business Purpose*

Although the Code §163(d) limitation generally does not apply to interest on indebtedness allocable to a trade or business activity, it will generally not be advantageous for Mgmt to seek to escape Code §163(d) by arguing that Mgmt purchased Newco's stock as part of Mgmt's trade or business of being an employee of Newco.[6] This is because interest on debt incurred in the trade or business of being an employee is treated as "personal interest" under Code §163(h).[7] In contrast to investment interest (deduction of which is limited to net investment income and can be carried forward to later years and deducted subject to the investment income limitation), personal interest is not deductible at all.

¶1308.4 *Active Investor Not Engaged in Business*

An *"investor"* is *not* engaged in a trade or business and hence is subject to the Code §163(d) limitation. However, a *"trader"* is engaged in a business and hence is *not* subject to Code §163(d) or to the personal interest limitations of Code §163(h).

A person is not a trader merely by virtue of actively monitoring personal investments, spending substantial or even full time on investment activities, borrowing very substantial amounts, and engaging in frequent securities purchases and sales. The key characteristic of a trader is that he "derives his profit primarily from frequent exchanges which take advantage of short-term swings in the market rather than from interest, dividends and long-term appreciation. . . . [A]n emphasis on capital growth and an expectation of profit from resale alone [on the other hand] indicate an investment-motivated activity rather than a trade or business. . . . [T]he length of the holding period is a determinative factor. [A person who] held his stocks and bonds for lengthy periods of time anticipating that they would

---

[6] The relevant cases have relied heavily on whether the stock qualified as a capital asset. Compare, e.g., Schanhofer v. Commissioner, 51 T.C.M. 924, T.C. Mem. 1986-166 (1986) (where employee, in order to protect his job, purchased all of employer corporation's stock from its retiring sole shareholder, interest on debt used to purchase the stock was *not* investment interest because employee held stock "predominantly as a means of engaging in the trade or business . . . and not predominantly for the purpose of realizing a gain on its later sale," and employee could satisfy the test set forth in W. W. Windle Co. v. Commissioner, 65 T.C. 694 (1976), *appeal dismissed*, 550 F.2d 43, 77-1 U.S.T.C. ¶9203 (1st Cir.), *cert. denied*, 431 U.S. 966 (1977), for treating stock as other than a capital asset) *with* Gen. Couns. Mem. 39529 (1/8/86) (interest expense incurred by employee in acquiring employer stock was investment interest where stock was purchased with sufficient investment intent to result in capital gain on disposition) Miller v. Commissioner, 70 T.C. 448 (1978) (such interest expense was "investment interest expense" under former Code §57(b)(2)(D) because stock was held with sufficient investment intent to make it a capital asset despite employee's claim that he acquired controlling stock interest to become corporation's president).

The analyses in *Schanhofer*, Gen. Couns. Mem. 39529, and *Miller* rely heavily on the *Corn Products* doctrine. To the extent the scope of *Corn Products* doctrine has been limited by the Supreme Court's decision in Arkansas Best Corp. v. Commissioner, 485 U.S. 212, 88-1 U.S.T.C. ¶9210 (1988), it may be more difficult to avoid the investment interest limitation by arguing that stock was acquired in the ordinary course of, or predominantly as a means of engaging in, a trade or business.

[7] Code §163(h)(2)(A) provides that personal interest excludes "interest paid or accrued on indebtedness properly allocable to a trade or business (other than the trade or business of performing services as an employee)."

appreciate in value" is not a trader, even though he "devoted all his time and attention to the buying and selling of stocks. . . ."[8]

¶1308.5   Debt Incurred to Acquire SCo Stock

Special rules apply to interest on debt incurred, e.g., by Ms. A, to purchase stock in an SCo. For taxable years ending on or before the date a future regulation (or other guidance) is issued, interest expense on debt incurred to finance the purchase of SCo stock is allocated among the assets of the SCo "using any reasonable method," subject, however, to an anti-abuse rule.[9] Consequently, whether such interest (if not considered paid or accrued on home equity indebtedness or in actively carrying on a trade or business) is treated, in whole or in part, as investment interest depends on the assets of the SCo. Hence, if all the assets are business assets, Code §163(d) is inapplicable; if all the assets are investment assets, Code §163(d) is 100% applicable; and if the assets fall into both categories, the interest is allocated between the two.[10]

If Ms. A materially participates in SCo's business for purposes of the Code §469 passive activity loss rules—under Temp. Reg. §1.469-5T where her participation in SCo's business activity, for example as an employee of SCo, exceeds 500 hours during the taxable year—her interest expense reasonably traced to SCo's business assets constitutes trade or business interest deductible by Ms. A "above the line" to arrive at adjusted gross income, and not subject to the passive activity loss rules.[11]

IRS has announced its intention to issue regulations, effective for taxable years ending after the date such regulations are ultimately issued, concerning the allocation of interest expense in connection with a debt-financed purchase of SCo stock, which "regulations may require the allocation of interest expense . . . in a manner different from that provided [for earlier taxable years], without regard to when the debt was incurred."[12] This announcement obviously gives no useful guidance for such future years.

---

[8] Estate of Yeager, 55 T.C.M. 1101, T.C. Mem. 1988-264 (1988), aff'd, rev'd, and remanded, 889 F.2d 29, 89-2 U.S.T.C. ¶9633 (2d Cir. 1989), cert. denied, 495 U.S. 946 (1990). See Levin v. United States, 597 F.2d 760, 79-1 U.S.T.C. ¶9331 (Ct. Cl. 1979) (taxpayer held to be a trader).

[9] IRS Notice 88-20, 1988-1 C.B. 487; IRS Notice 89-35, 1989-1 C.B. 675.

[10] See IRS Notice 88-37, 1988-1 C.B. 522; IRS Notice 89-35, 1989-1 C.B. 675.

[11] See IRS Letter Ruling 9215013 (1/7/92); IRS Letter Ruling 9037027 (6/18/90).

[12] IRS Notice 89-35, 1989-1 C.B. 675.

¶1309   ORIGINAL ISSUE DISCOUNT, IMPUTED INTEREST, AND IMPUTED DIVIDENDS WHEN P (OR NEWCO) ISSUES DEBT OR PREFERRED STOCK—CODE §§1271-1275, 483, AND 305

The following discussion concerns the taxation of debt instruments issued at a discount (¶1309.1), debt instruments that pay interest in the form of other debt instruments or stock of the issuer or a related person (¶1309.2), and preferred stock issued at a discount (¶1309.3).

¶1309.1   *Original Issue Discount Debt Instruments*

If Newco (or P) issues a debt instrument with an issue price below its "stated redemption price at maturity," such as zero-coupon debentures, the difference constitutes original issue discount ("OID"). For this purpose, "stated redemption price at maturity" means the stated amount payable at maturity plus all other payments under the debt instrument other than interest that is (1) based on a fixed rate (or a variable rate tied to a single objective interest rate index such as Prime or LIBOR) *and* (2) unconditionally payable at fixed periodic intervals of one year or less during the entire term of the debt instrument.[1]

OID generally is treated as interest income to the holder (and is deductible by Newco (or P)) on a constant yield-to-maturity basis over the life of the debt instrument.[2] A de minimis exception applies where the amount of OID is less than the product of (1) 1/4% of the debt's stated redemption price at maturity multiplied by (2) the number of complete years to maturity.[3]

The three most common OID situations in an LBO or other acquisition are where Newco (or P) (1) sells a debt instrument for less than its face amount in order to raise money to finance its acquisition of T, thus creating *explicit* OID, (2) sells an investment unit consisting of a debt instrument plus common stock or warrants in order to raise money to finance its acquisition of T, which may create *implicit* OID depending on how the investment unit's purchase price is allocated among the unit's elements,[4] and (3) issues debt instruments to T's shareholders as consideration for their T stock, or to T as consideration for its assets, and the debt instruments issued or the property acquired may be worth less than the debt instrument's face amount.

Code §163(e)(5), as enacted by the 1989 Act, defers and, in some cases, permanently disallows in part the issuer's deduction for OID with respect to certain high yield OID debt instruments. This provision is discussed in detail in ¶1303,

---

¶**1309**   [1] Code §1273(a)(2); Reg. §1.1273-1(b),(c).

[2] Code §1272, 1273, 163(e). See also ¶203.6.

[3] Code §1273(a)(3); see ¶203.6.

[4] For a discussion of the possible charge to Newco's *accounting* net income where it issues a warrant along with a debt instrument, see ¶1705.

and the entire discussion of the issuer's deduction for OID amortization in ¶¶1309.1 and 1309.2 is qualified by ¶1303.

¶1309.1.1   Newco (or P) Debentures Issued for Cash

Where Newco (or P), in order to finance its acquisition of T, issues a debt instrument *for cash*, the excess, if any, of the debt's stated redemption price at maturity (as described above) over its issue price is OID. For this purpose, "issue price" is the amount of cash received or, in the case of publicly offered debt, the initial offering price to the public (excluding bond houses and brokers) at which "a substantial amount" of the debt was sold.[5] Unless the amount of OID is so small that it is disregarded under the de minimis exception discussed in ¶1309.1 above and ¶203.6.5, it will be treated as interest and amortized (as income by the holder and, subject to the limitation discussed in ¶1303, a deduction by Newco or P) on a constant yield-to-maturity basis over the debt instrument's life.

¶1309.1.2   Investment Units Consisting of Newco (or P) Debentures Plus Newco (or P) Common Stock or Warrants Issued for Cash

Assume an investor purchases *for cash* an investment unit consisting of Newco's $1 million face amount 11% debenture, with interest payable semiannually, and 1,000 Newco common shares (or warrants to purchase 1,000 Newco common shares), purportedly paying $1 million for the debenture and $100,000 for the common stock (or warrants).[6] If the debenture's FV may be less than its stated redemption price ($1 million) or the FV of the common shares (or warrants) may be more than their stated purchase price ($100,000), IRS may argue that the debenture's issue price is below its stated redemption price and hence that the debenture has OID.

In determining whether OID exists with respect to a debenture issued as part of an investment unit, the issue price of the unit is allocated between the debenture and the other components of the unit based on their relative FVs.[7] If either the debenture or the stock or warrant component of the investment unit is publicly traded, the issue price of the debenture should equal the debenture's initial trading price (if the debenture is publicly traded) or the excess of the price paid for the investment unit over the initial trading price of the stock or warrant (if the stock or warrant is publicly traded and the debenture is not).

Determining the debenture's issue price is more complex where none of the investment unit's components are publicly traded. Regulations under the old Code §1232 OID provisions (repealed by the 1984 Act and replaced by Code

---

[5] Code §1273(b).

[6] For a discussion of the possible charge to Newco's *accounting* net income where it issues a warrant along with a debt instrument, see ¶1705.

[7] Code §1273(c)(2); Reg. §1.1273-2(h).

§§1271 through 1275) generally allowed OID to be eliminated on privately placed investment units by a written allocation agreement stating that the person acquiring the investment unit was paying face value for the debt instrument. Such an agreement reached after "arm's-length negotiations between parties having adverse interest" would "generally" be accepted, so long as the amount allocated to the debt instrument was not less than its face amount adjusted to a yield one percentage point greater than the debt's stated interest rate.[8]

The proposed OID regulations issued in 1986 and withdrawn in 12/92 also generally allowed OID to be eliminated on investment units (neither component of which was publicly traded) by a written allocation agreement, provided that the agreed-upon yield of the debt instrument (a) was based upon yields of comparable instruments not issued as part of an investment unit and (b) was not less than the applicable federal rate (see ¶203.6.1) on the issue date of the investment unit.

The final OID regulations issued in 2/94 and applicable to debt instruments issued on or after 4/3/94 do not provide any guidance regarding acceptable methods of determining the relative FVs of the components of an investment unit. Instead, the regulations generally require consistency between the issuer and the holder of the investment unit. Specifically, the regulations state that "the issuer's allocation of the issue price of the investment unit is binding on all holders of the investment unit" (but is not binding on IRS), unless the holder discloses on its tax return for the year in which the investment unit is acquired that its allocation is different from the issuer's allocation.[9]

Where a lender purchases an investment unit consisting of debt with warrants, the Ninth Circuit in Custom Chrome held that, in allocating the lender's aggregate purchase price between the debt and warrants, the warrants cannot be assigned zero or nominal value simply because (1) the warrant exercise price is at the money (i.e., the warrant exercise price is equal to the underlying stock's FV at the time of warrant issuance) and (2) the warrants have a highly speculative future value (as held by the Tax Court). Rather, the warrant FV at issuance must be determined using a reasonable method, such as the Black-Scholes warrant valuation model (see discussion at ¶1502.1.7.3) or a calculation of the present value of the additional interest the lender would have charged had it received no warrants.[10]

¶1309.1.3   Issuance of Newco (or P) Notes to T's Shareholders

Newco (or P) may issue Newco (or P) notes to T's former shareholders as all or a portion of the purchase price for their T stock, or to T as all or a portion of the purchase price for T's assets. The OID and Code §483 imputed interest rules applicable where Newco or P issues notes in exchange for T's stock or assets are discussed in detail in ¶¶203.6 and 302.4. Those rules differ significantly from the

[8] Old Reg. §1.1232-3(b)(2)(ii)(b).
[9] Reg. §1.1273-2(h)(2).
[10] Custom Chrome, Inc. v. Commissioner, 217 F.3d 1117, 2000-2 U.S.T.C. ¶50,566 (9th Cir. 2000), aff'g in part and rev'g in part T.C. Memo 1998-317 (1998).

rules applicable where Newco or P issues notes for *cash* (as in ¶¶1309.1.1 and 1309.1.2). Briefly, where Newco or P issues notes in exchange for T's stock or assets, the OID or Code §483 imputed interest rules may apply in *any one* of the following three circumstances:

(1) The Newco (or P) notes are part of a debt issue a portion of which is traded on an "established securities market" (i.e., "publicly traded"), *or* the notes are issued for publicly traded T stock. In either case, if the stated redemption price of the notes exceeds their "issue price" (defined as the FV of the debt if it is publicly traded, and otherwise the FV of the T stock) by more than a statutory de minimis amount, the excess will be OID, which reduces the principal amount of the debt for tax purposes and is amortized (as interest income to the holder and, subject to the limitation discussed in ¶1303, as interest deductions to Newco or P) on a constant yield-to-maturity basis over the debt's life. See generally ¶¶203.6.5 and 302.4.

EXAMPLE 1

Newco buys some T stock from A in exchange for a $3 million face amount Newco note due in three years and bearing 5% stated interest, payable semiannually. The Newco note is not publicly traded, but T's stock is publicly traded. The FV of the T stock purchased from A is $2.7 million. A takes into income (and, subject to the limitation discussed in ¶1303, Newco may deduct) (i) OID of $300,000 (the $3 million face amount of the Newco note minus the $2.7 million FV of the T stock) on a constant yield-to-maturity basis over the term of the Newco note, plus (ii) the 5% stated interest payments.

(2) The notes are not subject to (1) but do not bear interest of at least 100% of the applicable federal rate (the "AFR") as defined in Code §1274, and neither the 1/4% per year statutory de minimis exception nor the 9% safe harbor (where seller financing does not exceed $2.8 million) discussed in ¶203.6.1 is applicable. If stated interest on the notes is determined to be inadequate, interest generally is imputed based on the AFR and, depending on the applicable rules, may be amortized over the life of the notes or reported as principal payments are made (or due) on the notes. See generally ¶¶203.6.1 through 203.6.3.

EXAMPLE 2

Same as Example 1, except that neither Newco's notes nor T's stock is publicly traded. If the AFR is 8%, so that the stated interest rate on the Newco note (5%) is less than the AFR, interest income (OID) is imputed to bring the interest rate up to the AFR. The principal amount of the obligation is reduced (for tax purposes) by the amount of imputed interest, and the imputed interest (OID) is amortized (as income by A and, subject to the limitation discussed in ¶1303, a deduction by Newco) on a constant yield-to-maturity basis over the life of the obligation.

(3) The notes are not subject to (1) and do bear stated interest at a rate equal to or greater than the AFR or other applicable rate so that they are not subject to (2), but the interest is not payable unconditionally at least annually during the entire term of the debt instrument. In such case, the notes will have OID equal to their stated redemption price at maturity (in this case, the sum of all payments due on the notes) less their stated principal amount (i.e., all payments due on the notes excluding any stated interest). See ¶203.6.4.

EXAMPLE 3

Newco buys T stock (not publicly traded) from A on 1/1 year 1 for a $3 million Newco note (not publicly traded) payable in two years and bearing 10% simple stated interest, with the interest payable at the note's maturity in two years (i.e., not payable periodically). Assume the AFR is 8%. Because the 10% stated simple interest exceeds interest computed at the 8% AFR, there is no imputed interest. However, because the stated interest is not unconditionally payable at least annually, the stated interest of $600,000 ($3 million × 10% simple interest × 2 years) is treated as OID and thus amortized (as OI for A and, subject to the limitation discussed in ¶1303, a deduction for Newco) on a constant yield-to-maturity basis over the obligation's 2-year life.

¶1309.2   *Payment-in-Kind Debt Instruments*

Some debt instruments pay (or allow the issuer to pay) interest in the form of (1) additional debt instruments ("bunny" debentures) of the issuer or a related entity (i.e., "PIK" or payment-in-kind debentures) or (2) stock of the issuer or a related entity.

Under the OID regulations, interest paid in the form of bunny debentures is not current "payment" of interest for OID purposes. Rather, the original debenture and the bunny debentures are treated as a single obligation for OID purposes, and therefore all amounts due under the bunny debentures are treated as paid at their maturity, resulting in OID.[11] Accordingly, the holder has PIK interest income, and the issuer deducts PIK interest, in the same manner as interest on an OID debenture, i.e., as interest accrues on the debenture on a constant yield basis (determined by treating all amounts due under the bunny debentures as paid at their maturity).

---

[11] Reg. §1.1275-2(c)(3).

In contrast, if a debenture pays interest in *stock* (common or preferred) rather than in bunny debentures, such interest (whether or not deductible as noted below) is treated as currently paid in an amount equal to the FV of the stock issued. Such interest may be fixed (e.g., stock having an FV equal to a stated amount) or contingent (e.g., a stated number of shares the FV of which is not known at the time the debenture is issued). The application of the OID rules to a debenture paying interest in stock will depend on the terms of the debenture.

In the case of certain high yield debt instruments, Code §163(e)(5) may defer or disallow deductions for interest paid in the form of either bunny debentures or (if otherwise deductible as noted below) stock of the issuer or a related entity. See ¶1303.

Generally applicable to corporate debt issued after 6/8/97, Code §163(*l*) permanently disallows any deduction for interest paid or accrued (including OID) on such debt if "a substantial amount of the principal or interest" on the debt is payable in (or in certain circumstances may be paid in), or by reference to the value of, equity of the issuer or a related party, including by reason of a conversion right, and in some cases a warrant or similar option, exercisable by the issuer (regardless of the likelihood the option will be exercised) or the holder (but only where "there is a substantial certainty the option will be exercised"). See ¶1306.

The holder's obligation to report interest income under its normal accounting method is not affected by deferral or disallowance of the issuer's deduction under Code §163(e)(5) or §163(*l*) (other than the special rule described in ¶1303.2.2.2 entitling a corporate holder to the dividends received deduction for interest permanently disallowed under Code §163(e)(5)).

¶1309.3   *Preferred Stock*

If Newco (or P) issues preferred stock (rather than debt) at a discount, Newco (or P) faces issues similar to those discussed in ¶1309.1.

¶1309.3.1   Problem

(1) Constructive dividend—preferred issued for cash. If Newco (or P) issues preferred stock for a price less than its redemption price, the spread (so-called preferred OID) may be treated under Code §305 as a constructive dividend to the holder taken into account (i.e., amortized into the holder's income) over the term of the preferred stock.[12] This rule would generally apply if Newco (or P) issues preferred stock for cash (to raise money with which to purchase T) and receives less cash for the preferred than the preferred's redemption price.

After 2002, an individual holder is generally taxed on constructive dividend income (as he is taxed on regular dividend income) at a 15% top rate, so long as the dividend is (1) covered by current or accumulated E&P and (2) the stock

---

[12] Code §305(c) and (b)(4); Reg. §1.305-5(b).

satisfies the holding period requirement (more than 60 days during the 120-day period beginning 60 days before the date on which the stock becomes ex-dividend, except in the case of certain preferred stock more than 90 days during the 180 day period beginning 90 days before the ex-dividend date). See Code § 1(h)(11).

(2)   **Preferred issued for cash as part of investment unit.** If VC (or another investor) purchases an investment unit consisting of Newco (or P) preferred stock plus common stock or warrants, IRS may argue that the common stock or warrants are worth more than their stated purchase price, that the preferred stock is worth less than its redemption price, and that the preferred OID so created is a constructive dividend taxable to the holder over the term of the preferred stock.

EXAMPLE 1

VC purchases for $1.1 million an investment unit consisting of $1 million face amount of Newco mandatorily redeemable preferred stock and 1,000 shares of Newco common stock.

IRS argues that the Newco preferred stock purchased by VC is worth $800,000 and the Newco common stock purchased by VC is worth $300,000 when issued. If VC cannot carry its burden of proving that the Newco preferred stock was worth its face of $1 million and the common stock was worth $100,000 on the date of issuance (or proving some other preferred stock value higher than $800,000 and some other common stock value lower than $300,000), the preferred stock will take an initial basis of $800,000 and the common stock an initial basis of $300,000. In such case, there will be $200,000 of preferred OID on VC's preferred stock ($1 million face amount less $800,000 issue price).

(3)   **Preferred issued for property.** Where preferred stock is issued in exchange for property, its issue price is such property's FV, so that if the FV of the property is less than the preferred stock's redemption price, the difference is preferred OID.[13] There is no safe harbor yield in Code §305 for non-traded preferred stock issued in exchange for non-traded property, as there is in Code §1274 (the AFR safe harbor) for non-traded debt issued in exchange for non-traded property. Thus, if Newco (or P) issues preferred stock to T (or T's shareholders) as part of the consideration for T's assets (or T's stock), IRS may argue that the FV of the T assets (or stock) received by Newco (or P) is less than the preferred stock's redemption price, thereby creating preferred OID.

[13] See Rev. Proc. 81-60, §4.02, 1981-2 C.B. 680; Rev. Rul. 75-179, 1975-1 C.B. 103; IRS Letter Ruling 8823113 (3/18/88) (representation (t)); IRS Letter Ruling 8803074 (10/23/87) (representation (q)); IRS TAM 7941009 (undated).

(4) Participating preferred. There is one significant exception to the entire preferred OID concern discussed in this ¶1309.3: Although Code §305(b)(4) purports to apply to "preferred stock," the regulations narrow the statute's sweep to "stock which, in relation to other classes of stock outstanding enjoys certain limited rights and privileges (generally associated with specified dividend and liquidation priorities) *but does not participate in corporate growth to any significant extent.*"[14] Hence, the regulations exclude from the scope of Code §305(b)(4) any preferred stock which "has a real and meaningful probability of actually participating in the earnings and growth of the corporation."[15] Therefore, if a preferred stock has sufficient rights of participation, none of the preferred OID rules discussed in this ¶1309.3 should apply.

However, in one respect (convertible preferred) this regulation takes an unnecessarily narrow view of participation in corporate growth: "The determination of whether stock is preferred for purposes of §305 shall be made without regard to any right to convert such stock into another class of stock of the corporation."[16] Thus, if this form-over-substance sentence in the regulations is valid, non-participating preferred stock would be covered by the preferred OID rules (and would not be treated as participating in corporate growth) even if it is convertible at a reasonable (indeed at an in-the-money) conversion price into a substantial amount of common. Thus, it might be desirable to give convertible preferred some substantial participation features aside from the conversion privilege. One way to give convertible preferred substantial participation features is to allow the preferred to participate in dividends and liquidating distributions on an as-if-converted basis. That is, the holder of the preferred stock is entitled to receive either (1) the dividends and liquidating distributions that a holder of non-convertible preferred would receive or (2) if greater, the dividends and liquidating distributions that would be received if the preferred were converted to common. Because preferred of this type participates in corporate growth without regard to whether it is converted into common, it should qualify as participating preferred.

As a trade-off for obtaining priority over common stock, a preferred stock's participation in corporate growth is typically limited in some fashion. Often, the preferred stock may begin to participate with common stock only after the common has first received a threshold or floor return, with the preferred thereafter having an unlimited participation with common in corporate growth. For this type of preferred stock, whether participation in corporate growth is "significant" depends on whether it is reasonable to anticipate that the threshold to participation will be reached and exceeded.[17]

Alternatively, a preferred stock may be entitled to receive all or substantially all of the issuer's earnings and growth in value, subject, however, to a cap. In at least some situations, this type of capped-participation preferred should also qualify as participating preferred. In IRS Letter Ruling 200116002 (11/29/00)

---

[14] Reg. §1.305-5(a) (emphasis added).
[15] Reg. §1.305-5(a).
[16] Reg. §1.305-5(a).
[17] Compare Reg. §1.305-5(d) example (9) (not reasonable to anticipate participation) and example (10) (reasonable to anticipate participation).

common shareholders of a corporation ("T") with a predictable stream of earnings exchanged most (but not all) of their T common stock for T non-convertible preferred stock bearing no dividend yield but entitled upon T's liquidation (scheduled to occur on a specified date) to receive all of T's assets up to a specified cap. Shortly before T issued the preferred stock, T's "investment advisors estimated that, based upon [T's enterprise value], an unrelated third party purchaser of the [T] preferred stock would require that the preferred stock carry an aggregate liquidation" preference equal to the capped amount. The ruling concluded that the preferred constituted common stock for purposes of Code §305:

> Because the preferred stock liquidation preference is based upon the value of the available [T] assets on [the scheduled liquidation date], up to [the specified cap], we believe the [T] preferred is not limited in its preferences or participation in corporate growth. Furthermore, because the preferred stock liquidation preference exceeds the current value of [T's] assets and the value of all assets [T] is likely to accumulate by [the scheduled liquidation date], the [T] preferred stock significantly, if not entirely, participates in [T's] growth.

A more commonly occurring situation in which capped-participation preferred stock should be treated as significantly participating in corporate growth is where a financially distressed corporation issues preferred stock that is deeply underwater.

EXAMPLE 2

T is a financially distressed corporation with $50 million asset FV and $75 million debt ($45 million senior debt and $30 million subordinated debt). In a restructuring transaction, the subordinated debt holders exchange their $30 million of T subordinated debt for newly issued T preferred stock with a $30 million liquidation value and a 10% fixed annual dividend rate.

The T preferred stock (with a $30 million face amount) has an initial value of approximately $5 million ($50 million T asset FV less $45 million T senior debt) and is entitled to 100% of the increase in T's equity value until T's equity value exceeds $30 million plus accrued preferred yield. The T preferred stock should be treated as participating significantly in corporate growth.

While reasonably clear in the extreme case, it is hard to identify the line at which capped-participation preferred stock should start to be viewed as participating significantly in corporate growth. Some guidance is provided by the legislative history to Code §1504(a)(4)'s rule that ignores, in testing affiliated group status, stock that (among other requirements) is "limited and preferred as to dividends and does not participate in corporate growth to any significant extent." The legislative history states that, for this purpose, "preferred stock carrying a dividend rate materially in excess of a market rate when issued would not be ignored."[18]

---

[18] H.R. Rep. No. 98-861, 98th Cong., 2d Sess. 833 (1984).

We think the market rate to which the legislative history refers is the appropriate market rate on a preferred stock which does not expose the holder to significant entrepreneurial risk with respect to the issuer. Under this view, a preferred stock that, as compensation for common-equity-like risks, offers holders common-equity-like returns (e.g., 20% or higher annual returns)—returns that the issuer is unlikely to be able to pay absent significant growth in equity value—should be viewed as participating significantly in corporate growth.

(5) E&P limitation. Constructive distributions are taxable stock dividends to VC under Code §305(b)(4) only to the extent of Newco's current or accumulated earnings and profits ("E&P"). If the amount of the constructive stock distribution exceeds Newco's E&P, the excess is treated first as a tax-free recovery of basis in the preferred until such basis is reduced to zero, and then as gain from the sale or exchange of the preferred.[19]

(6) Dividends-received deduction for corporate holder. Dividends produced by preferred OID amortization are eligible for the dividends-received deduction ("DRD") if the preferred stock is held by a corporation. Thus, corporate holders of preferred stock (in contrast to most non-corporate holders) may want to amortize preferred OID into income, building up basis at a tax rate reduced by the DRD, rather than recognizing such OID as CG on redemption. But see the discussion in ¶1309.3.4 regarding Code §1059(f).

¶1309.3.2   Preferred Stock Issued Before 10/90

Preferred stock issued before 10/10/90 (or issued thereafter pursuant to one of the grandfather exceptions described below) remains subject to Code §305 and the Code §305 regulations in effect prior to the amendments called for by the 1990 Act ("old Code §305" and the "old Code §305 regulations").

(1) Unreasonable redemption premium. Under the old Code §305 regulations, preferred OID must be taken into income only to the extent that it exceeds a "reasonable" redemption premium. The regulations provide little guidance as to what is reasonable, stating only (i) that "a redemption premium will be considered reasonable if it is in the nature of a penalty for a premature redemption of the preferred stock and if such premium does not exceed the amount the corporation would be required to pay for the right to make such premature redemption under market conditions existing at the time of issuance" and (ii) that there is a safe harbor, under which a redemption premium of up to 10% of the issue price of preferred stock that is not callable for at least five years is considered reasonable.[20]

---

[19] Code §§301(c) and 316(a).

[20] Reg. §1.305-5(b)(2), as then in effect. See also Rev. Rul. 81-190, 1981-2 C.B. 84 (redemption premium exceeding 10% solely as a result of unanticipated market fluctuation affecting stock FV is reasonable); Rev. Rul. 75-468, 1975-2 C.B. 115 (same); Rev. Rul. 75-179, 1975-1 C.B. 103 (on the narrow facts presented, redemption premium equal to 83% of issue price found reasonable).

(2)   Measurement of OID accrual. The statutory language of Code §301 and old Code §305, read together, strongly implied that the amount of a preferred stockholder's taxable income in a year resulting from preferred OID amortization for such year is *the FV of the additional preferred stock the shareholder is deemed to have received* in such year because of the preferred OID amortization, *rather than the face amount thereof.* Obviously the FV of the preferred may be substantially less than its face, because of a lower-than-market dividend rate, the issuer's low credit worthiness, or both. However, the regulations are somewhat less than wholly clear on this point.[21]

---

[21] Code §301(b)(1) states that "the amount of any [corporate] distribution shall be . . . the fair market value of the . . . property received [by the shareholder]." Old Code §§305(b) and (b)(4) stated that where a corporation distributes stock with respect to its preferred stock, the stock so distributed "shall be treated as a distribution of property to which section 301 applies," thus overruling the normal Code §317 directive that for purposes of the dividend rules "property" does not include stock of the distributing corporation. Absent any other statutory or statute-based rule, a corporation's distribution of stock covered by old Code §305(b) should be treated as a distribution equal to such stock's FV.

Old Code §305(c) stated that IRS shall prescribe regulations under which "a difference between redemption price and issue price . . . shall be treated as a distribution." Thus, unless the regulations vary the normal rule stated above, it appears that a difference between a preferred stock's redemption price and its issue price would be treated as a distribution of property pursuant to old Code §305(b) and (b)(4), thus invoking Code §301(b)(1) so that the amount of the distribution looks to "the fair market value of the . . . property."

Old Reg. §1.305-5(b)(1) stated that where "a corporation issues preferred stock which may be redeemed after a specified period of time at a price higher than the issue price, the difference is considered under the authority of section 305(c) to be a distribution of additional stock on preferred stock which is constructively received by the shareholder over [a] period of time." This regulatory language strongly favors the FV result—i.e., the excess of the preferred's redemption price over its issue price is treated as a distribution of additional stock, which is treated as property under old Code §305(b), and, hence, Code §301(b)(1) measures a distribution of property in terms of the property FV.

Old Reg. §1.305-5(d) example (5) dealt with a corporation that issued non-dividend paying preferred stock for $100 per share. The preferred was redeemable after five years for $185. Thereafter the redemption price was scheduled to increase annually by $15. The example stated that a reasonable redemption premium for the preferred is $10; as explained in, under the preferred OID rules applicable when this regulation was promulgated, the constructive dividend was reduced by such a reasonable redemption premium. The example concluded that "the shareholder is deemed under section 305(c) to receive on the last day of each year during the 5-year period a distribution on his preferred stock in an amount equal to 15 percent of the issue price [i.e., $15, equal to ($85 − $10) divided by 5]. Each $15 increase in the redemption price thereafter is considered to be a distribution on the stock at the time such increase becomes effective."

Neither quoted sentence mentions Code §301(b)(1)'s FV prescription. Hence, the two quoted regulatory sentences can be read as implying that the amount of the distribution *for purposes of Code §305(b)* is $15 per year, but that once having determined the amount of the Code §305(b) distribution, the next statutorily mandated step is to determine the FV of the stock deemed distributed, as required by Code §301(b)(1). On the other hand, this murky regulatory language arguably could be read as seeking to leapfrog Code §301(b)(1) altogether by directing that the $15 amount shall be treated as an annual distribution pursuant to both Code §305(b) and Code §301(b)(1). However, it does not seem likely that Treasury by this regulatory example intended to bar the application of Code §301(b)(1)'s FV directive without so much as mentioning the point.

Finally, old Reg. §1.305-7(a) stated that "where a redemption price in excess of a reasonable call premium exists with respect to a class of preferred stock and the other requirements of this section are also met, *the distribution will be deemed made with respect to such preferred stock, in stock of the same class.* Accordingly, the preferred shareholders are considered under sections 305(b)(4) and 305(c) to have *received a distribution of preferred stock to which section 301 applies*" (emphasis added). Thus, this

If the preferred OID exceeds a reasonable redemption premium, the old Code §305 regulations treat the holder as receiving stock distributions equal to only the *excess*, amortized on a *straight-line basis* over the period from issuance to the date the issuer first has the right to call the preferred stock.

EXAMPLE 3

Before 10/10/90, VC purchased for $800,000 Newco preferred stock with a $1 million face amount. The Newco preferred stock is redeemable at Newco's option beginning 5 years after its issuance.

Of the $200,000 of preferred OID, $80,000 (i.e., 10% of the $800,000 issue price) is disregarded as a reasonable redemption premium, unless the facts indicate that a higher premium would be "reasonable." Hence, assuming no such facts are present, VC will be deemed to receive a preferred stock dividend of $24,000 (($200,000 less $80,000) ÷ 5 years) in each of the 5 years during which the preferred stock cannot be called.[22]

(3) **Callable or evergreen preferred.** Prior to the 1990 Act, it was generally possible to avoid amortization of preferred OID by making the preferred stock callable at all times by the issuer, even where the preferred stock was mandatorily redeemable or puttable by the holder at some later date. The old Code §305 regulations appear to require amortization of preferred OID only if there is a "specified period of time" over which the preferred stock cannot be called for redemption. A 1983 published ruling strongly implies that preferred OID will not be amortized if the preferred stock is *immediately* callable at the option of the issuer.[23] The legislative history of the 1990 Act confirms this reading of the old Code §305 regulations.[24]

Preferred OID also was not amortizable if the preferred stock was "evergreen preferred," i.e., never subject to call, mandatory redemption, or a put by the holder. In such case, there is no limited period of time over which to amortize the preferred OID.

---

old Code §305 regulation strongly implies that, after calculating the *amount of stock* the preferred shareholder is deemed to have constructively received for such year as preferred OID under old Code §§305(b) and (c), the holder then applies the Code §301 rules to determine the *amount of his taxable dividend* by looking to the FV of the property (i.e., the preferred stock) deemed distributed.

[22] Reg. §1.305-5(d) example (5), as then in effect. See discussion in item (2) ¶1309.3.2 as to whether VC's taxable dividend is equal to the face or the FV of the preferred stock deemed received.

[23] See Rev. Rul. 83-119, 1983-2 C.B. 57.

[24] H.R. Rep. No. 881, 101st Cong., 2d Sess. at 98 (1990) (as reprinted in CCH Stand. Fed. Tax Rep. no. 46-1 (10/17/90)) (hereinafter "1990 House Report"); see S. 3209, 101st Cong., 2d Sess. at 169 (1990) (as reprinted in CCH Stand. Fed. Tax Rep. no. 46-2 (10/18/90)) (hereinafter "1990 Senate Bill").

¶1309.3.3   Preferred Stock Issued After 10/90

The 1990 Act added new Code §305(c)(1)-(3) directing IRS to amend the Code §305 regulations to change both (1) the determination of whether preferred OID exists and must be amortized and (2) the manner of amortizing preferred OID. The new regulations are intended to broaden the circumstances in which preferred OID must be amortized but will produce slower amortization of preferred OID if amortization is required. New Code §305 regulations were issued in 12/95.

(1)   Determination of preferred OID. New Code §§305(c)(1) and (3) and the 12/95 Code §305 regulations change in two ways the threshold test for determining whether preferred OID must be taken into account.

First, where preferred stock is either mandatorily redeemable "at a specified time" or where the holder has a right to put the stock to the issuer, preferred OID must be amortized into income unless the OID is de minimis. For this purpose, a rule similar to that of Code §1273(a)(3) applies, so that OID on preferred stock is de minimis if it is less than or equals the redemption price of the preferred stock *times* ¼ of 1% *times* the number of *complete* years from issuance to redemption (i.e., fractional years are disregarded).

Under the 12/95 Code §305 regulations, this rule would also apply where a third party, rather than the issuer itself, is obligated to purchase the preferred stock if either (1) the acquisition of the stock by the third party would be treated as a redemption for federal income tax purposes (e.g., under Code §304) *or* (2) the issuer and the third party are members of the same affiliated group of corporations (determined under Code §1504(a), disregarding Code §1504(b)) and a principal purpose of the arrangement is to avoid the Code §305 rules.[25]

Second, if the preferred OID exceeds the applicable threshold (i.e., exceeds a de minimis amount where the preferred is mandatorily redeemable or the holder has a put), the *entire* preferred OID, and not just the excess over the threshold, is amortized.

EXAMPLE 4

On 1/1/96 VC purchases Newco preferred stock which is subject to mandatory redemption by Newco at a redemption price of $800,000 in 4.5 years. If the preferred OID on this stock exceeds $8,000 ($800,000 × ¼ of 1% × 4 complete years)—i.e., if the issue price of the preferred stock is less than $792,000—then the *entire* preferred OID must be amortized into VC's income and taxed after 2002 at a maximum 15% rate if VC is an individual or VC is a flow-through entity with individual owners. See Code §1(h)(11) and ¶108.

---

[25] Reg. §1.305-5(b)(1).

(2) Timing of OID accrual. Once it is determined that preferred OID must be amortized into income, new Code §305(c)(3) and the 12/95 §305 regulations require that the preferred OID be amortized on a yield-to-maturity ("YTM") or economic accrual basis.[26] In contrast to the pre-1990 Act rules, the new rules appear to require accrual of the *face amount* rather than the *FV* of the redemption premium. That is, Code §305(c)(3) and the 12/95 §305 regulations state that the redemption premium shall be "taken into account under principles similar to the principles of section 1272(a)." OID on debt instruments is calculated under Code §§1272 and 1273 based on the difference between the issue price of the debt instrument and the *stated redemption price* of the instrument.[27]

EXAMPLE 5

On 1/1/96 VC purchases for $800,000 Newco preferred stock having a face amount of $1 million. The preferred stock is subject to mandatory redemption by Newco after 5 years at its $1 million face amount. The $200,000 preferred OID produces a 4.564% compound YTM over the 5-year period.[28] Thus, VC will be deemed to receive the following stock dividends:

Year 1: $36,512 ($800,000 issue price × 4.564%)
Year 2: $38,178 ($836,512 adjusted issue price × 4.564%)
Year 3: $39,920 ($874,690 adjusted issue price × 4.564%)
Year 4: $41,742 ($914,610 adjusted issue price × 4.564%)
Year 5: $43,648 ($956,352 adjusted issue price × 4.564%)

As Example 5 illustrates, when compared to the straight-line amortization of the old Code §305 regulations, YTM amortization produces smaller deemed stock dividends in early years and larger deemed stock dividends in later years.

(3) Effective date. The effective date of the above-described changes in the treatment of mandatorily redeemable and puttable preferred stock is somewhat unclear. By their terms, the substantive provisions of the 12/95 regulations apply

[26] While stated dividends on preferred stock can not, under state law, be the equivalent of "qualified periodic interest," it nonetheless appears that any stated dividends on the preferred stock should be ignored in determining the YTM amortization of the preferred OID. However, if, as discussed in ¶1309.3.4(5), IRS adopts regulations to treat stated dividends that cumulate as OID when there is no intention to pay the dividends prior to redemption, it would be appropriate to include such stated dividends in determining the YTM and adjusted issue price.

[27] Examples in the regulations are consistent with this interpretation. See, e.g., Reg. §1.305-5(d) example (5) ("$5 per share, the difference between the redemption price and the issue price, is treated as a constructive distribution received by the holder on an economic accrual basis").

[28] Preferred OID economic accrual over the 5-year period is computed "under principles similar to the principles of [Code§] 1272(a)." Reg §1.305-5(d) example (5)(ii). Code §1272(a) accrual of OID yield on a debt instrument "when expressed as a percentage, must be calculated to at least two decimal places." Reg. §1.1272-1(b)(1)(ii).

only to stock issued on or after 12/20/95.[29] The effective date portion of the regulations states, however, that "the rules of sections 305 (c)(1), (2), and (3) apply to stock described therein issued on or after October 10, 1990" (unless the stock is grandfathered),[30] and the preamble to the 6/94 proposed regulations noted that "the committee reports to the 1990 Act express Congress' intention that the economic accrual and OID de minimis rules generally apply as of the effective date of the 1990 Act without regard to when regulations are amended to reflect such rules." §§305(c)(1), (2), and (3) are not, however, self effectuating. Rather, they merely direct the Treasury to prescribe regulations containing certain provisions.

For taxpayers adversely affected by the changes in the treatment of mandatorily redeemable and puttable preferred stock, it may not be unrealistic to hope that a judge would place more weight on the actual terms of the statute and the regulation than on expressions of intent in committee reports and the regulation preamble, and hence conclude that the changes apply only to stock issued on or after 12/20/95; that is, it is not entirely clear that Treasury has worded the regulations to effectuate Congress' intent that regulations should be issued to make the economic accrual and OID de minimis rules retroactively effective to stock issued on and after 10/10/90.

(4)   Merely callable preferred issued before 1996. The 1990 Act amendments to Code §305(c)(1) were generally aimed at mandatorily redeemable and puttable preferred stock, rather than merely callable preferred. Accordingly, the rules described in ¶1309.3.2 above should generally continue to apply to preferred stock issued before 12/20/95 which is merely callable by the issuer with one exception described in the next paragraph.

The 12/95 §305 regulations, consistent with the legislative history of the 1990 Act, state that, in the case of merely callable stock issued after 10/9/90 which has an unreasonable redemption premium (as described in ¶1309.3.2), the entire redemption premium (rather than only the excess over a reasonable premium) is intended to be accrued under the economic accrual rules (rather than the straight-line amortization rules) over the period during which the preferred stock cannot be called for redemption.[31]

(5)   Merely callable preferred issued after 1995. Although not directed to do so by the 1990 Act amendments to Code §305, the 12/95 §305 regulations treat callable preferred stock in the same manner as mandatorily redeemable and puttable stock if "based on all of the facts and circumstances as of the issue date,

---

[29] Reg. §1.305-5(e).

[30] The 1990 Act grandfathers (i) stock issued pursuant to a binding written contract in effect on or before 10/9/90 (and at all times thereafter and before such issuance), (ii) stock issued pursuant to an offering or registration statement filed with a federal or state securities agency on or before 10/9/90 and issued within 90 days of the date of the filing, and (iii) stock issued pursuant to a bankruptcy reorganization plan filed on or before 10/9/90 in a title 11 (or similar) case.

[31] Reg. §1.305-5(e); H.R. Conf. Rep. No. 964, 101st Cong., 2d Sess. at 94-95 (as reprinted in CCH Stand. Fed. Tax Rep. no. 47 (10/27/90)) (hereinafter "1990 Conference Report"). See 1990 House Report at 100; 1990 Senate Bill at 171.

redemption pursuant to [the issuer's call] right is more likely than not to occur."[32] Thus, in the case of such callable preferred stock, any redemption premium (if greater than the de minimis threshold) would be accrued on a yield-to-maturity basis over the period between the issuance date and the date "redemption is most likely to occur."[33]

The regulations contain a safe harbor under which merely callable preferred stock would not be treated as more likely than not to be called if:

(1) the issuer and the holder are not related within the meaning of Code §267(b) or §707(b) (with these sections modified to apply a "more than 20%" standard of relatedness, rather than a "more than 50%" standard),

(2) there are no arrangements that effectively require or are intended to compel the issuer to redeem the stock (an example of a "bad" arrangement is that the holders of the preferred stock can appoint a majority of the issuer's directors if the stock is not redeemed by a specified date), and

(3) exercise of the call right would not reduce the yield of the stock (a call right would reduce yield if the preferred had an escalating yield or redemption price).[34]

In addition, even if redemption is more likely than not to occur, accrual of the redemption premium would not be required if the premium is "solely in the nature of a penalty for premature redemption," i.e., a premium paid as a result of changes in economic or market conditions over which neither the issuer nor the holder has legal or practical control"[35] (such as, "changes in prevailing dividend rates or in the value of the common stock into which the [preferred] stock is convertible).[36]

Under the regulations, if preferred stock can be redeemed at more than one time (or, presumably, at an indefinite time), "the time and price at which redemption is most likely to occur must be determined based on all of the facts and circumstances as of the issue date." This "most likely" redemption time and price would be used to determine if dividend accrual is required under Code §305 and the regulations. If the preferred stock is not, in fact, redeemed on the "most likely" redemption date, the rules of Code §305 and the regulations would be reapplied as if such date were the issue date and the amount of any additional premium payable on any later redemption date would be treated as a constructive dividend over the period from the missed call or put date to that later date in accordance with the principles stated above.[37]

Under the regulations, the issuer's determination of whether there is a deemed dividend under the Code §305 rules would be binding on all holders of the preferred (but would not be binding on IRS), unless the holder explicitly discloses

[32] Reg. §1.305-5(b)(3).
[33] Reg. §1.305-5(b)(4).
[34] Reg. §§1.305-5(b)(3)(ii) and 5(d) examples (5) and (7).
[35] Reg. §1.305-5(b)(3)(i).
[36] CO-8-91, 1994-2 C.B. 844.
[37] Reg. §1.305-5(b)(4).

on its income tax return for the year that includes the date the holder acquired the stock that it is taking an inconsistent position.[38] This consistency requirement makes it advisable for purchasers of preferred stock to reach agreement with the issuer at the time of purchase regarding (a) the issue price of the stock (e.g., where the stock is issued as part of an investment unit or in exchange for property) and (b) whether callable stock is more likely than not to be called.

(6)   **Accumulating dividends as disguised redemption premium.** The 1990 legislative history states that IRS may provide that disguised preferred OID exists where cumulative preferred stock is issued without a discount, but "at the time of issuance ... there is no intention for dividends to be paid currently...."[39] Although the 12/95 regulations do not address the issue of "disguised" preferred OID, the preamble to the regulations states that "[b]ecause of the complexity of this issue, the final regulations do not provide rules for [unpaid cumulative] dividends. The IRS and Treasury will continue to consider the issue."[40]

It is quite common for highly leveraged or growth-oriented corporations to issue preferred stock where cumulative dividends at a specified rate are payable as declared by the board and the parties anticipate that dividends will not be paid currently for several years until a portion of the issuer's debt is repaid or the issuer's cash flow increases. Any treatment of cumulative dividends on such preferred stock as "disguised" preferred OID would appear to represent a significant and unwarranted change in IRS position.

(7)   **Limits on OID accrual—E&P ceiling, evergreen preferred, and participation in corporate growth.** As is the case under the old §305 regulations, any deemed stock distributions would be taxable stock dividends to VC under Code §305(b)(4) only to the extent of Newco's current or accumulated E&P. If the amount of the constructive distribution exceeds Newco's E&P, the excess is treated first as a tax-free recovery of basis in the preferred until such basis is reduced to zero, and then as gain from the sale or exchange of the preferred.[41]

Even after the effective date of new Code §305(c) and the 12/95 regulations, preferred OID is not amortizable if the preferred stock is "evergreen preferred," i.e., never subject to call, mandatory redemption, or put by the holder. Often, preferred stock is mandatorily redeemable upon the happening of certain events (e.g., an initial public offering or a change in control). Is such stock mandatorily redeemable within the meaning of the 12/95 Code §305 regulations? We think not because, by their terms, the regulations require accrual of preferred OID "if the issuer is required to redeem the stock *at a specified time* or the holder has the option (whether or not currently exercisable) to require the issuer to redeem the stock."[42] The regulations provide further that stock will not be treated as mandatorily redeemable or puttable if the redemption obligation or put right "is subject

---

[38] Reg. §1.305-5(b)(5).
[39] H.R. Rep. No. 881, 101st Cong. 2d Sess. 348 (1990).
[40] T.D. 8643.
[41] Code §§301(c) and 316(a).
[42] Reg. §1.305-5(b)(2).

to a contingency [other than the possibility of default] that is beyond the legal or practical control of either the holder or the holders as a group . . . and that, based on all of the facts and circumstances as of the issued date, renders remote the likelihood of redemption." Where redemption is required upon the happening of a specified *event*, the time of occurrence of which is unknown, the issuer is not required to redeem the stock "at a specified time" and hence no preferred OID accrual should be required.

Surprisingly, however, the preamble to the 12/95 regulations appears to contemplate a different answer, stating:

> The final regulations provide rules for the treatment of mandatory redemption obligations and put options that are subject to contingencies. Generally, premiums on such stock are not subject to constructive distribution treatment if the contingency renders remote the likelihood of redemption. For example, where an issuer issues stock that is mandatorily redeemable in the event of an initial public offering, the regulations require evaluation of the likelihood of the occurrence of the initial public offering.[43]

Under the preamble's interpretation of the 12/95 regulations, which we believe is inconsistent with the regulations' text, accrual of OID on preferred stock that is mandatorily redeemable in the event of a public offering or a change of control would be required unless the likelihood that the specified event will ever occur is "remote." (It would apparently not be sufficient to conclude that the public offering or change of control is less likely than not to occur, because the "more likely than not" hurdle for OID accrual applies only to "merely callable" preferred under the regulations.) Indeed, under the preamble's interpretation of the 12/95 regulations, it can be argued that all preferred stock would be treated as mandatorily redeemable because all preferred stock is mandatorily redeemable in the event of the liquidation of the issuer, and the likelihood that the issuer will at some point be liquidated is more than remote.

Even after the effective date of new Code §305(c) and the 12/95 regulations, preferred OID is not amortizable if the preferred stock has participation rights which give it "a real and meaningful probability of actually participating in the earnings and growth of the corporation" so that it is not treated as preferred stock for Code §305(b)(4) purposes. See ¶1309.3.1.

(8) Dividends-received deduction. Dividends produced by preferred OID amortization are eligible for the DRD if the preferred stock is held by a corporation.

(9) Contingent preferred OID. Finally, what happens and when does it happen if the redemption price is contingent in amount? Compare, with respect to contingent payment debt, Code §1275(d) (grant of regulatory authority). A nice example of the problem is presented in Situation 2 of Rev. Rul. 69-265:[44] S2 preferred stock puttable back to S2, after 5 years, in a Code §302 exchange for shares of P common stock to be contributed to S2 by P, so that the FV of the

---

[43] T.D. 8643.
[44] 1969-1 C.B. 109.

redemption price (i.e., the P common stock) is not determinable at the time the S2 preferred stock is issued.

¶1309.3.4 Code §1059(f) Extraordinary Dividends

The existence of preferred OID which must be amortized, producing a constructive distribution to the holder, may cause adverse tax consequences under Code §1059(f). Code §1059(f) treats all dividends on preferred stock as extraordinary if the stock, when issued, has a dividend rate which declines (or can be reasonably expected to decline) in the future.[45] If a dividend is extraordinary, Code §1059(a) requires a corporate recipient of the dividend to reduce its basis in the underlying stock by the amount of the dividends-received deduction ("DRD") claimed with respect to the dividend. This generally has the effect of taking away the tax benefit of the DRD with respect to the extraordinary dividend as of the time the corporate holder sells the stock. Indeed, as discussed in ¶1402.1.1(3), to the extent the DRD exceeds the corporate holder's basis in the stock, 1997 Act changes to Code §1059(a) eliminated the tax benefit of the DRD by requiring gain recognition in the amount of the excess.

Code §1059(f) was intended to prevent corporate taxpayers from claiming phantom losses on "self-liquidating" preferred stock; as enacted, however, it sweeps much more broadly. Self-liquidating preferred stock is generally preferred stock with an issue price in excess of its redemption or liquidation price where the excess is attributable to unusually high dividends payable over a short period of time. Prior to the adoption of Code §1059(f), the corporate holder used the DRD to offset its income from the high dividends, but was not obliged to reduce its basis in the stock for the "untaxed" portion of the high dividends, which Congress viewed as a recovery of capital. After the high dividends ended, the stock was sold at a CL.

The legislative history of the 1989 Act provides that all distributions, both actual dividends and constructive dividends produced by Code §305, must be considered in determining whether the preferred stock has a dividend rate that declines or is reasonably expected to decline.[46] Where preferred stock has preferred OID that is being amortized into income, the dividend rate on that stock will decline when the amortization period ends if the preferred stock remains outstanding for any period of time thereafter.

---

[45] Code §1059(f) overrides the 2-year exception of Code §1059(a) and the size limitation of Code §1059(c); it is not entirely clear whether it overrides the entire-existence exception of Code §1059(d)(6). See ¶1310.3.2.

[46] The House Report states that "[i]n determining whether a dividend rate declines, or whether the stock would otherwise be subject to the provision, the effect of section 305 or other provisions of law on the timing and amount of the dividend shall be taken into account. For example, if the dividend rate on preferred stock does not decline by its terms, but other provisions of law (such as §305) have the effect of causing the stock to have a declining dividend rate, the provision will apply." H.R. Rep. No. 247, 101st Cong., 1st Sess. at 88 (1989) (as reprinted in CCH Stand. Fed. Tax Rep. no. 40 (9/20/89)); see S. Print No. 56, 101st Cong., 1st Sess. at 87 (1989) (as reprinted in CCH Stand. Fed. Tax Rep. no. 42, pt. II (10/11/89)).

Whether Code §1059(f) applies to preferred stock with preferred OID that is being amortized into income depends in part on the type of preferred stock. If the preferred stock is mandatorily redeemable and the preferred OID is being amortized into the holder's income over the period from issuance to the mandatory redemption date, there should be no period of time when the stock would remain outstanding with a reduced dividend rate. Thus, Code §1059(f) would apparently not apply.

If the preferred stock becomes puttable after a period of time and the preferred OID is being amortized into the holder's income over the period from issuance to the first put date, there is no guarantee that it will be put on the first put date and thus IRS might argue that the dividend rate on the preferred stock is expected to decline and that Code §1059(f) therefore applies. However, looked at from the time of issuance, it may in many cases be more reasonably expected that the holder will put the preferred stock when the put first becomes exercisable, since any yield produced by the preferred OID will be reduced if the holder continues to retain the stock.

Where preferred stock is merely callable at a premium after a period of time and the preferred OID is being amortized into the holder's income over the period from issuance to the first call date, there is a greater risk that Code §1059(f) applies, since the dividend rate on such preferred drops and there is no way for the holder to force the redemption of such stock at the time the rate drops.

While the language and legislative history of Code §1059(f) suggest that it may apply to stock with preferred OID, the application of Code §1059(f) in such a case makes little economic sense. Preferred stock with preferred OID is almost the exact opposite of self-liquidating preferred stock and hence should not be covered by Code §1059(f). The dividends produced by amortizing preferred OID do not in any way liquidate the preferred since they are not paid. In addition, the amortization of preferred OID does not produce a loss when the stock is redeemed for its redemption price.

¶1310   SUBSEQUENT REDEMPTION OF P's (OR NEWCO's) PREFERRED STOCK TREATED AS DIVIDEND

It is not always clear whether a subsequent redemption of non-§306 preferred stock is taxed as a dividend (generally after 2002 at a 15% top individual rate if the more than 60 day holding period requirement (more than 90 days for certain preferred stock) is satisfied but with no basis offset) or as a CG (or CL) transaction (generally for CG after 2002 at a 15% top individual rate if the more than 1 year holding period requirement is satisfied and with full basis offset).[1]

¶1310   [1]This ¶1310 discusses the tax ramifications of preferred stock not covered by Code §306. To the extent the preferred stock is covered by Code §306, additional rules may cause a redemption or sale to be taxed as OI. See Code §306.

¶1310.1   *Preferred Holders' Ownership of Common Stock*

Whenever the holders of Newco's non-§306 preferred stock as a group own a large portion of Newco's common stock, there is a risk that the ultimate redemption of the preferred will be taxed as a dividend to the extent of Newco's E&P (because the redemption is substantially equivalent to a dividend):

Preferred Holders (as a Group) % Ownership of Common	Extent of Dividend Risk
More than 80%	very high risk
60% to 80%	substantial risk
50% to 60%	moderate risk
Less than 50%	slight risk

¶1310.2   *Rev. Rul. 85-106*

However, Rev. Rul. 85-106, 1985-2 C.B. 116, can be interpreted as mandating dividend treatment even where the preferred holders as a group own substantially less than 50% of Newco's common. This 1985 ruling suggests dividend treatment (to the extent of Newco's E&P) where the redeemed preferred holders as a group own only 18% of Newco's common but the preferred holders are part of Newco's control group, so that the redemption of their *non-voting* preferred does not alter their participation in Newco's control.

(1)   If the ruling is interpreted this broadly, it is highly questionable whether the ruling is a valid interpretation of Code §302.

(2)   If the ruling is interpreted this broadly and is valid, the dividend risk can be reduced by making the preferred *voting*, so that the preferred holders' postredemption voting power is significantly less than their preredemption voting power.

(3)   Arguably, the ruling can be read more narrowly. In the ruling the shareholders owned the common and the preferred proportionately (after applying the attribution rules). The redeemed taxpayer thus owned 18% of the common and 18% of the preferred before the redemption. Preferred was redeemed only from the taxpayer; the other 82% of the preferred remained outstanding. Hence, the ruling may turn on the fact that, when the remaining 82% of the preferred is ultimately redeemed, the preferred proceeds (including both the 18% redeemed now and the 82% redeemed later) will have been distributed proportionately to the common shareholders and hence will have been substantially equivalent to a dividend. Accordingly, the ruling arguably applies only where Newco's common and preferred stock are owned proportionately. While the *facts* of the ruling

support this narrower reading, IRS's *reasoning*—which stresses that the redeemed taxpayer (an 18% common shareholder) along with two other shareholders had the ability to control the corporation—supports the broader reading.

¶1310.3   Application to Corporate Shareholder

Dividend treatment for a corporate shareholder is an advantage if the corporate shareholder is entitled to a dividends-received deduction ("DRD"). The DRD advantage will be fully preserved if the Code §1059 extraordinary dividend basis reduction rules do not apply.

¶1310.3.1   Dividends-Received Deduction

Dividend treatment may be an advantage for a preferred (or indeed a common) holder, i.e., a corporation entitled to the 70%, 80%, or 100% (for a corporate SBIC) DRD or a partnership virtually all of whose partners are corporations.

However, Code §1059 could severely limit the benefit of the DRD if the deemed dividend resulting from the redemption of the Newco preferred constitutes an "extraordinary dividend" under that provision. In that case the corporate shareholder's basis in its retained Newco common stock would be reduced by the amount of the DRD. If so, the DRD would be recaptured (presumably as CG) when the shareholder later sold its common stock.[2] See ¶1402.1.1(3) and ¶1310.3.3.

¶1310.3.2   Code §1059 Extraordinary Dividend

In general, an "extraordinary dividend" is defined in terms of the size of the dividend in relation to the shareholder corporation's adjusted basis in its stock.[3] If the dividend is large enough to be extraordinary, Code §1059 generally requires a shareholder to reduce its basis in its common stock *unless* the shareholder has held the common stock *either*:

(1)   "for more than two years before the dividend announcement date,"[4] or

---

[2] Code §1059 literally covers only extraordinary dividends received by a "corporation." Effective for partnership transactions on or after 12/29/94, if an extraordinary dividend is paid with respect to T stock to a partnership that has corporate partners, the basis reduction rule of Code §1059 is applied by treating each partner as owning its pro rata share of the T stock held by the partnership. Hence, the partnership "must make appropriate adjustments to the basis of [its remaining T stock], and the partners must also make adjustments to the basis in their respective interests in [the partnership]." Reg. §1.701-2(e), (f) example (2), (g).

[3] Code §1059(c).

[4] Code §1059(a).

(2)   "during the entire period [the issuing] corporation (and any predecessor corporation) was in existence," so long as this exception's application to the extraordinary dividend "is not inconsistent with the purposes" of Code §1059 (hereinafter referred to as the "entire existence" exception).[5]

Legislative Update

The Abusive Tax Shelter Shutdown and Taxpayer Accountability Act of 2003 (H.R. 1555), introduced 4/2/03 and effective for a dividend after enactment not otherwise covered by Code §1059, would have amended Code §1059 to require a shareholder to reduce its basis in its stock (for purposes of determining loss) by the nontaxed portion (i.e., the DRD amount) of any dividend received on such stock.

¶1310.3.3   Application of Code §1059 to Redemption

(1)   Entire-existence exception. Under Code §1059(e)(1), if a stock redemption is "not pro rata as to all shareholders," then any portion of the redemption proceeds that is treated as a dividend triggers basis reduction *"without regard to the period the taxpayer held such stock"* or the size of the deemed dividend (emphasis added). Prior to the 7/97 issuance of IRS regulations, it was not entirely clear whether this provision was intended to override the entire-existence exception discussed in ¶1310.3.2(2), both of which were also added by the 1986 Act. That is, it was not clear whether the entire-existence exception applied to redemptions which are "deemed" to be extraordinary dividends under Code §1059(e)(1) or only to extraordinary dividends as normally defined.

On the one hand, it can be argued that the phrase "without regard to the period the taxpayer held such stock," together with the statutory requirement that the entire-existence exception apply only to the extent it is consistent with the "purposes" of Code §1059, suggests that the provision deeming redemptions treated as dividends to be extraordinary dividends may override the entire-existence exception. If so, Newco's redemption of its preferred stock triggers a reduction in the basis of the retained common stock if the redemption is (1) treated as a dividend and (2) "not pro rata as to all shareholders."

On the other hand, a substantial amount of legislative history pointed in the opposite direction. The Joint Committee on Taxation's explanation of the 1986 Act (the 1986 Blue Book, at page 285) states that "Congress thus intended the non-taxed portion of any non-pro rata redemption that is treated as a dividend to reduce basis, *without regard to whether the two-year holding period is otherwise satisfied*" (emphasis added), thus implying that the non-pro-rata rule was not meant to override the entire-existence exception. In addition, the Joint Committee

---

[5] Code §1059(d)(6).

on Taxation's explanation of the 1988 Technical Corrections Bill (at page 41) and the House Ways and Means Committee Report on the 1988 Act (at page 40) both state that the Act clarifies that the Code §1059(e)(1) rule deeming that a non-pro-rata distribution or a partial liquidation is treated as a dividend applies *"without regard to whether the two-year holding period requirement has been met"* (emphasis added). This legislative history suggests that the entire-existence exception *can* be invoked to override Code §1059(e)(1).[6]

IRS has resolved this issue in favor of the former—pro IRS—interpretation by 7/97 regulations, which state that the entire-existence exception (as well as another exception under Code §1059(e)(2) for certain dividends paid between members of an affiliated group) does not apply to a distribution treated as an extraordinary dividend under Code §1059(e)(1).[7]

(2) Not pro rata as to all shareholders. In determining whether Code §1059(e)(1) applies to a redemption of preferred stock, query whether the term "not pro rata as to all shareholders" refers only to the shareholders owning the class of preferred stock that is being redeemed or to all shareholders of Newco. In the absence of express guidance, we would have thought it refers only to the shareholders owning the class of preferred stock being redeemed. Code §562(c) (dealing with personal holding companies) and Reg. §1.562-2 state that a preferential distribution with respect to a class of stock is "pro rata" within the meaning of the "preferential dividend" provisions as long as the class is "entitled" to the preference and no "rights to preference inherent in any class of stock are violated."

However, in a 1993 Field Service Advice, IRS took a contrary position. FSA 1998-435 (10/26/93) held that a corporation's redemption of 100% of a class of preferred stock was "not pro rata as to all shareholders" within the meaning of Code §1059(e)(1)(A)(ii) because that phrase "should be applied by looking to all classes of stock of the corporation," rather than only the class of stock redeemed.

Similarly, in Technical Advice Memorandum 200023003 (6/9/00), IRS declared again that for Code §1059(e)(1)(A)(ii) purposes a redemption of all a corporation's preferred stock, not accompanied by a redemption of common stock, is "not pro rata as to all shareholders," although the redemption is pro rata with respect to the class of stock redeemed, i.e., in IRS's view, "all shareholders" refers in the aggregate "to all shareholders of all classes of stock of the corporation."

The TAM declares that IRS's aggregate approach offers a "better interpretation" of Code §1059(e)(1)(A)(ii)'s "all shareholders" than would a class-by-class approach. For that conclusion IRS relies on (1) "literal language," i.e., the statute's use of all shareholders "without limitation," and (2) "legislative history" which, while furnishing no indication how the statute applies to a corporation with multiple classes of stock, indicates the conferees' whipsaw concern that in some redemptions individual distributees claim Code §302(b)(1) sale treatment while

---

[6] The legislative history to the amendments proposed in §11301 of the Revenue Reconciliation Act of 1995 (H.R. 2491) (discussed in ¶1402.1.1(3) and below) sheds no additional light on this particular question.

[7] Reg. §1.1059(e)-1(a). These regulations apply to dividends announced (within the meaning of Code §1059(d)(5)) after 6/16/96. Reg. §1.1059(e)-1(c).

corporate distributees assert Code §302(d) dividend treatment. More precisely, IRS's entire legislative history argument in the TAM runs as follows: (1) Congress, IRS feels sure, intended basis reduction when the risk of shareholder-level whipsaw—i.e., inconsistent Code §302(b)(1) conclusions—is "plausible," (2) in determining dividend equivalence Code §302(b)(1) tests meaningful reduction on an aggregate share ownership basis, thus (3) since meaningful reduction is analyzed using an aggregate approach IRS "find[s] it appropriate to apply section 1059(e) using an aggregate approach."

IRS completed its lean Code §1059(e) analysis by stating that "[a]t first blush, it might appear that the aggregate approach would make every redemption of an entire class of stock an extraordinary dividend." IRS's response in the TAM— that Code §1059 applies only to corporations and Code §1059(e)(1) applies only to redemptions treated as dividends—is surely true but hardly seems material, for it does nothing to dispel the conclusion that IRS's aggregate approach—with which we continue to disagree—makes virtually *every* Code §302(d) redemption treated as a dividend (even a redemption of an entire class of stock) into a non-pro rata extraordinary dividend. We do not think that is what the statute says or means.[8]

Prior to the 1997 Act, the hostile anti-redemption rule of Code §1059(e) on its face applied only to a Code §302(d) redemption dividend and did not apply when the replacement of T stock with cash is by way of a reorganization boot dividend under Code §356(a)(2). However, Code §1059(e)(1)(B), as amended by the 1997 Act, treats Code §356 boot dividends as extraordinary dividends beginning on 5/13/95; although the Conference Report disavows any inference with respect to prior law, the language of the report strongly suggests this amendment constitutes a change in the law.

¶1310.3.4   Conclusion

Depending on whether the redemption of Newco's preferred stock is treated as a dividend and, if so, whether Code §1059 applies, the taxable income to corporate shareholders from (1) the redemption and (2) their later sale of their common stock would be as follows:

---

[8] A review, courtesy of taxpayer's counsel, of its TAM submission to IRS confirms that the taxpayer advanced a number of cogent arguments in addition to over breadth (i.e., under IRS's approach virtually every redemption treated as a dividend becomes an extraordinary dividend). Surprisingly, in the TAM IRS attempted no response and instead simply ignored the taxpayer's arguments. In reading the TAM file we were reminded of Judge Learned Hand's famous admiration of Justice Cardozo: "He never disguised the difficulties, as lazy judges do who win the game by sweeping all the chessmen off the table." See L. Hand, Mr. Justice Cardozo, 52 Harv. L. Rev. 361, 362 (1939).

Treatment of Redemption	Taxable Income to Shareholders from	
	Redemption	Sale of Common
Exchange treatment	Capital gain = redemption price – basis in preferred	Capital gain = sale proceeds – basis of common
Dividend to which Code §1059 applies	Ordinary income = redemption price – DRD	Capital gain = sale proceeds – (combined basis of common and preferred – DRD on preferred redemption)
Dividend to which Code §1059 does not apply	Ordinary income = redemption price – DRD	Capital gain = sale proceeds – combined basis of common and preferred

¶1310.4   Application to Non-Corporate Shareholder

If a preferred holder is not a corporation (or a partnership of corporations), so that it is not entitled to a DRD (including a subchapter S corporation), it may be desirable to give the holder the right to reject a preferred redemption which may be treated as a dividend under ¶¶1310.1 and 1310.2. Such a preferred holder can thus continue to hold his preferred stock until Newco is sold, in order to avoid dividend income (without basis offset).

¶1310.5   Redemption with Dividend in Arrears

Where a redemption of preferred stock is not taxed to the holder as a dividend under the principles discussed in ¶¶1310.1 and 1310.2 above, the portion of the redemption proceeds attributable to accrued but unpaid dividends on the preferred stock may nevertheless be taxed to the holder as a Code §301 dividend— after 2002, taxed to an individual at the 15% top rate if the 61 day holding period requirement (91 days for certain preferred stock) is met—if the accrued but unpaid dividends were "declared" by Newco.

(1)   Dividend Declared. If any accrued but unpaid dividends have previously or contemporaneously been declared by Newco, the portion of the total redemption payment representing the declared dividends is taxed to the holder as a Code §301 dividend distribution to the extent of Newco's E&P. Rev. Rul. 69-130, 1969-1 C.B. 93.[9]

(2)   No Dividend Declared. If the accrued but unpaid dividends have not been declared by Newco, the portion of the total redemption payment representing

---

[9]See ¶1310.3 for a discussion of the possible advantage of dividend treatment to a corporate shareholder.

the undeclared accrued and unpaid dividends is not taxed to the holder as a Code §301 dividend distribution. Rather, the total amount paid in redemption of the preferred stock, including any amount attributable to accrued and unpaid dividends, is taxed to the holder under Code §302. Rev. Rul. 69-131, 1969-1 C.B. 94.[10] Thus, where the redemption meets one of the Code §302(b) tests, the entire amount of the redemption payment (including the amount paid with respect to accrued but unpaid dividends) is taxed to the holder as proceeds from disposition of stock, and hence as CG to the extent such proceeds exceed basis.

¶1311 BASIS SHIFTING STOCK REDEMPTIONS

When a corporation redeems stock, or is treated by Code §304(a) as redeeming stock, surrounding facts direct whether the transaction qualifies as a Code §302(a) exchange (i.e., return of basis and CG/CL treatment)[1] or as a Code §302(d) distribution to which Code §301(c) applies (i.e., generally dividend treatment). This ¶1311 focuses on redemptions treated as Code §302(d)/301(c) distributions.

Under Code §301(c)(1), a distribution is a dividend to the extent of the corporation's current or accumulated E&P. See Code §316(a). A distribution in excess of E&P is, under Code §301(c)(2), applied against and reduces the shareholder's adjusted basis of the stock. Finally, to the extent a distribution exceeds both E&P and the adjusted basis of the stock, the distribution is treated as gain on sale. Code §301(c)(3).

In this ¶1311 we initially concentrate on a distribution treated as a dividend under Code §301(c)(1) with focus on the adjusted basis of the redeemed shares. Later we concentrate on a distribution treated as a return of basis with focus on the adjusted basis of the unredeemed shares.

¶1311.1 Current "Proper Adjustment" Regime

Currently, Reg. §1.302-2(c) announces, as it has for nearly a half century: "In any case in which an amount received in redemption of stock is treated as a distribution of a dividend, *proper adjustment* of the basis of the remaining stock will be made with respect to the stock redeemed" (emphasis added). The regula-

---

[10] Newco cumulative preferred stock on which dividends are regularly payable (e.g., quarterly) ordinarily states that such dividends are to be "declared and paid, or set apart for payment," before any dividends on Newco common stock are declared and paid. If Newco does not formally declare a dividend on the preferred stock, but Newco's board of directors purports to "set apart" the preferred dividend and declares and pays a dividend on common stock, IRS treats as "declared" the full cumulative dividend on preferred stock for the current and all previous dividend periods on the ground that declaring full dividends on the preferred stock was, as a matter of corporate law, prerequisite to declaring a dividend on common stock. Rev. Rul. 75-320, 1975-2 C.B. 105.

¶1311 [1] Code §302(a) exchange treatment obtains where the redemption satisfies the criteria of Code §302(b)(1) (not essentially equivalent to a dividend), §302(b)(2) (substantially disproportionate), or §302(b)(3) (complete termination of interest), taking into account Code §318(a) attribution rules as affected (in the case of a §302(b)(3) redemption) by Code §302(c)(2) attribution cutoff.

tions then illustrate "proper adjustment" in several uncomplicated contexts from which we borrow.

EXAMPLE 1.   Shareholder Actually Owns T Shares Post-Redemption

T's 100 outstanding shares, FV $1,000 per share (total FV $100,000), are owned by A at a basis of $100 per share (total basis $10,000). T's E&P is $85,000. T redeems 40 shares from A for $1,000 per share (total $40,000).

Under Code §301(c)(1) the $40,000 constitutes a dividend to A and A's remaining 60 T shares are awarded an aggregate basis of $10,000—their original $6,000 basis plus $4,000 basis hop over from A's redeemed shares, for a basis of $166.67 per share. See Reg. §1.302-2(c) example (1).

EXAMPLE 2.   Multiple Classes of T Shares

Same as Example 1, except that the 40 T shares redeemed from A are preferred shares, and A continues to hold all 60 of his T common shares.

Same result as Example 1: post-redemption "proper adjustment" of basis contemplates basis reallocation from one class of redeemed shares to another class of shares outstanding after the redemption. See United States v. Davis, 397 U.S. 301 (1970); Rev. Rul. 66-37, 1966-1 C.B. 209.

EXAMPLE 3.   Shareholder Constructively Owns T Shares Post-Redemption

Same as Example 1, except that the 60 T shares outstanding after the 40 share redemption are owned, not by A, but by A's spouse W. Assume A continues as an officer of T and is thus ineligible for Code §302(c)(2) attribution cutoff, so that post-redemption A is deemed under Code §318(a)(1) to own the 60 T shares actually owned by W.

The $40,000 distribution constitutes a Code §301(c)(1) dividend to A. In consequence, immediately after the redemption W holds T's outstanding 60 shares at an aggregate basis of $10,000—their original $6,000 basis plus $4,000 basis hop over from A's 40 redeemed shares, for a basis of $166.67 per share. See Reg. §1.302-2(c) example (2).

EXAMPLE 4.   Code §304 Illustration: A Remains T Shareholder

Same as Example 1, except that A sells 40 T shares, not back to T, but to P, all the stock of which is owned by A's daughter B. P's E&P is $25,000.

Under Code §304(a)(1) P is deemed (1) to issue new P shares to A in a Code §351 exchange and (2) to redeem those shares from A in a transaction governed by §302(d) and §301(c). Under Code §304(b)(2) the $40,000 received by A is a dividend, $25,000 out of P's E&P and $15,000 out of T's E&P.

Because A continues to own T shares after the transaction, the $4,000 basis at which A owned the 40 T shares sold to P is added to A's basis in his 60 retained T shares (making A's aggregate post-sale basis in his 60 remaining T shares $10,000 or $166.67 per T share retained). See Rev. Rul. 71-563, 1971-2 C.B. 175.

EXAMPLE 5.   Code §304 Illustration: A Retains No T Shares

Same as Example 4, except that A sells all 100 T shares to P for $100,000. A continues as a T officer.

The distribution methodology is the same as in Example 4, except that A's Code §301(c)(1) dividend is $100,000, $25,000 out of P's E&P and $75,000 out of T's E&P. Because A owns no T shares and no P shares after the transaction, it is less clear than it ought to be whether, as a "proper adjustment," A's $10,000 basis in the 100 T shares A sold to P is added to the basis at which A's daughter B holds her P shares. Compare Reg. §1.304-2(a) with Rev. Rul. 70-496, 1970-2 C.B. 74.

¶1311.2   IRS Notice 2001-45

In each of the five examples in ¶1311.1, stock basis shift is triggered by a Code §302(d)/301(c)(1) taxable dividend. Emphasis is on the word "taxable"—in each case A was subject to appropriate federal income tax on the dividend he received.

IRS Notice 2001-45[2] addresses recently contrived transactions in which a U.S. taxpayer derived a non-economic tax loss (or reduced tax gain) attributable to stock basis shifted, under the "proper adjustment" regime of Reg. §1.302-2(c), from redeemed shares temporarily held by a tax indifferent party. IRS announced it would attack such transactions, disallowing loss or increasing gain, on various

---

[2] 2001-2 C.B. 129.

grounds including (1) no dividend because Code §302(b) applies to cause the transaction to be taxed as an exchange, (2) basis shift to U.S. taxpayer not a "proper adjustment," and (3) transitory steps disqualify Code §318(a) attribution and basis shift because transaction's only purpose is tax avoidance.

EXAMPLE 6. Transitory Steps

(1) A (a U.S. corporation or individual) purchases an option to buy more than 50% of the stock of X, a Dutch corporation. X in turn purchases at FV 10% of the stock of T, a Dutch bank.

(2) Later (a) T redeems X's 10% of T's stock and (b) A simultaneously purchases at FV stock and warrants in T equal to the number of T shares which T is redeeming from X.

(3) Later still A sells its T stock and warrants at FV.

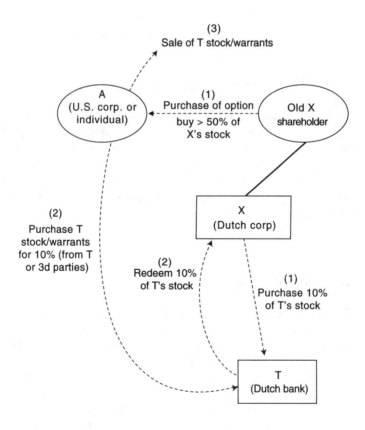

Under Code §318(a)(4), A is deemed to own the more than 50% of X's stock A can acquire by exercise of its option. As a result, under Code §318(a)(3)(C) X is deemed to own any T shares owned by A (or deemed owned by A by virtue of A's warrants to acquire T shares). Thus, when T redeems X's T stock and simultaneously A acquires an equal number of T shares (including T warrants), X's (constructive) interest in T is, on an integrated basis, no less after the redemption than was X's (actual) interest in T before the redemption. In consequence, Code §302(b) does not apply to T's stock redemption from X. Assuming adequate T E&P, X's redemption proceeds constitute a §302(d)/301(c)(1) dividend to X— which is tax indifferent with respect to the Internal Revenue Code—and as a "proper adjustment" X's basis in the redeemed T shares is reallocated to A's new stock/warrant investment in T, resulting in an adjusted basis for A's T stock/warrants far in excess of FV. A's later resale of its T stock/warrants generates a substantial A tax loss. Or so goes the argument.

IRS Notice 2001-45's focused attack on the transitory tax avoidance schemes illustrated in Example 6 seemed to us adequate to punish the miscreants of past transactions and to discourage similar future transactions. We remain of that view.

But there are arrangements, not implicating transitory tax avoidance planning, that are not obviously targeted (or targetable) by Notice 2001-45.

EXAMPLE 7. Non-Transitory Stock Ownership

Foreign Bigco has long owned 100% of each of two subsidiaries: S1 (a U.S. corporation) and S2 (a foreign corporation), and in turn S1 and S2 own 100% of S3 (a foreign corporation), with U.S. S1 owning 49% (49 shares) and foreign S2 owning 51% (51 shares) of S3.[3]

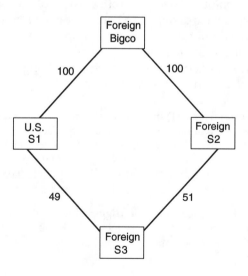

---

[3] Because U.S. S1 owns only 49 of S3's 100 shares (i.e., less than 50%), S3 is not a CFC.

> Bigco makes a business-motivated decision to eliminate foreign S3's bifur-
> cated ownership, which can be implemented either by (1) foreign S3 re-
> deeming U.S. S1's 49 shares of S3 (treated as a taxable Code §302(d)/301(c)(1)
> distribution to U.S. S1) or (2) foreign S3 redeeming foreign S2's 51 shares
> of S3 (not taxed in U.S. and under Reg. §1.302-2(c) facially producing a shift
> of S3 stock basis from foreign S2 to U.S. S1).

Nothing in good sense, established tax law, or IRS Notice 2001-45 requires
Bigco and its subsidiaries to follow taxable plan (1) in preference to non-taxable
plan (2), even though basis shifting is a collateral benefit awarded U.S. S1 in plan
(2) under long-standing regulations.

¶1311.3 *Proposed Anti-Basis Shifting Regulations*

Perhaps less comfortable in Notice 2001-45 than it might have been,[4] IRS/
Treasury in 10/02 published Prop. Reg. §1.302-5 and related proposals designed
to eliminate all basis shifting—without regard to motive however evil or pure—
when a Code §302 stock redemption (or a Code §304(a) stock sale) gives rise to
a dividend. The approach of the proposed anti-basis shifting regulations is to
convert the basis for the redeemed T stock into a suspended (normally capital)
loss that (1) remains with the shareholder from whom the T shares were redeemed
and (2) is allowed to such shareholder on the subsequent final inclusion date
(FID) or, if earlier, on an accelerated loss inclusion date (ALID).

Ordinarily, at this point, we would proffer reams of analysis explaining and
commenting upon the details of so great a departure from more than a half century
of settled tax law. We do not do that in this edition because we are confident it
would waste your time and ours: the 10/02 regulatory proposal is so misguided
as to stand no chance of adoption in anything resembling its 10/02 form.

Our curtailed explanation begins with two new concepts:

FID or final inclusion date is (1) the first date on which the redeemed shareholder
would satisfy the criteria of Code §302(b) if the facts and circumstances that
exist on FID had existed immediately after the redemption (after taking into
account attribution rules) or, if earlier, (2) the date after which there is no
later date on which the redeemed shareholder could take into account the
suspended loss (e.g., the redeemed shareholder's date of death).

ALID or accelerated loss inclusion date triggers loss to the extent the redeemed
shareholder recognizes gain on T stock, whether by sale, taxable exchange,
or Code §301(c)(3) redemption (i.e., distribution in excess of both E&P and
stock basis).

In explanation, we begin by repairing to two earlier examples.

---

[4] See example (7).

EXAMPLE 8. Shareholder Actually Owns T Shares Post-Redemption

Same as Example 1. A's $4,000 basis in 40 redeemed T shares is not added to A's basis in 60 retained T shares. Instead, A recognizes $4,000 as a suspended CL, to be taken into account by A at the later time of an FID or, if earlier, an ALID (i.e., never later than A's death).

If A sells 1 retained T share (basis $100) for its $1,000 FV, the sale is an ALID and A's $900 CG is offset by $900 of A's previously suspended $4,000 of CL, leaving A with $3,100 of suspended CL.

EXAMPLE 9. Shareholder Constructively Owns T Shares Post-Redemption

Same as Example 3. A's $4,000 basis in 40 redeemed T shares is not added to W's basis in T's remaining shares. Instead, A recognizes $4,000 as suspended CL, to be taken into account by A at the later time of an ALID or FID.

EXAMPLE 10. Final Inclusion Date

Same as Example 8, except that A does not sell a T share. Instead, for consideration T issues 61 shares to unrelated B, reducing A's 60 remaining T shares below 50% of T's outstanding stock (60 out of 121 shares). This FID allows A under Prop. Reg. §1.302-5 to deduct his $4,000 suspended CL because, had these facts existed when T redeemed 40 of its shares from A, Code §302(b)(2) would have applied to that redemption.

When Congress in 1997 at the Clinton administration's behest destabilized more than 70 years of settled tax law by inserting in subchapter C part III the hybrid concept of NQ Pfd, we predicted that far from raising revenue as the drafters anticipated, NQ Pfd would, in the hands of ever-inventive subchapter C tax practitioners, prove a grand boon to undeserving but well-advised shareholders and an awesome revenue loser. See ¶604.3.4. We have no doubt our prediction was sound, if perhaps too modest.

We believe the same wisdom applies, a number of times over, to Prop. Reg. §1.302-5. Several hypothetical cases begin to show why.

EXAMPLE 11.   S's Redemption from P

T has long owned S's 100 shares at an aggregate basis of $10,000 ($100 per share). T's FV approximates $13,500 ($135 per share), and T's E&P is $9,000. T and S do not file a consolidated return. S redeems 67 of its 100 shares, distributing to P $9,000. Later, either (1) S liquidates (by merger) into T under Code §332 or (2) T merges downstream into S in a tax-free reorganization.

S's $9,000 redemption distribution is a Code §302(d)()301(c)(1) dividend on which T is not taxed because of Code §243's 100% DRD,[5] and T's $10,000 basis in S's shares is not reduced under Code §1059 by reason of the distribution.[6]

Under Prop. Reg. §1.302-5(a) T's $6,700 basis in redeemed S shares is converted in T's hands into suspended loss. When T and S are later combined on merger date, there is no later date on which the redeemed shareholder (T where S has merged upstream into T *or* S as T's successor where T has merged downstream into S) could take the $6,700 loss into account, because after the merger there is no stock investor separate from the stock investment. Therefore, we believe, under Prop. Reg. §1.302-5(b)(3) the merger constitutes an FID so that the T-S tax-free combination triggers allowance of a $6,700 loss.

Our second illustration, Example 12 below, relies on the demonstrated ingenuity of the Delaware corporate bar and its ability to obtain advantageous amendments to Delaware General Corporation Law. Explicitly, we assume that to generate sufficiently great federal tax benefits, Delaware could and would embrace for public as well as private corporations a concept of proportionately redeemable common stock, it's details as yet unknown, but it's future existence—were Prop. Reg. §1.302-5 adopted—assured.

EXAMPLE 12.   Proportionately Redeemable Common Stock

Public T, a widely held Delaware corporation, has outstanding 10 million shares of proportionately redeemable common stock, FV $100 per share ($1 billion aggregate FV). T's board of directors considers paying a $5 per share ($50 million aggregate) dividend to T's shareholders, but instead votes (1) a $5 per share cash distribution (2) to be paid against the automatic pro rata redemption of 5% of T's outstanding shares. Immediately after the redemption distribution T has outstanding 9.5 million shares, FV $100 per share. Some T shareholders promptly sell a portion of their T shares, thereby decreasing by a tiny amount their percentage ownership of T's stock. Later,

[5] See Code §243(a)(3), (b)(1).
[6] See Code §1059(e)(1), (2)(A).

not pursuant to any obligation or plan so to do, T issues 1,000 T shares to a new investor in a private placement, thereby decreasing by a tiny amount each T shareholder's percentage ownership of T's stock.

If the $50 million redemption is treated as a dividend and Prop. Reg. §1.302-5 were law, the automatic redemption causes 5% of each T shareholder's stock basis to be converted to suspended loss. Then, under Rev. Rul. 76-385[7]—the so-called de minimis shareholder ruling under which each small non-officer-or-director T shareholder qualifies for Code §302(b)(1) CG treatment on a redemption if he suffers even a tiny reduction in his percentage ownership of T's stock—each T shareholder with respect to the suspended loss has enjoyed an FID: if the facts and circumstances that exist at the end of the date on which (1) a T shareholder sells some of his T shares or (2) T later sells 1,000 new T shares had existed immediately after the redemption, Code §302(b)(1) would have applied to the redemption.[8]

Our recommendation to Treasury would be to (1) throw away Prop. Reg. §1.302-5—destabilizing 50 years of settled tax law is risky business—and (2) adopt instead a modified anti-abuse rule for stock redemptions under which stock basis does not shift from a tax indifferent person in any circumstance.[9]

Finally, we turn to Code §302(d) redemption distributions that exceed E&P and therefore implicate Code §301(c)(1) dividend treatment to the extent of E&P and then implicate Code §301(c)(2) stock basis recovery. Most clearly demonstrated in proposed Code §304 regulations that are companion to Prop. Reg. §1.302-5, it is Treasury/IRS's pathbreaking position that a Code §301(c)(2) redemption distribution in excess of E&P applies against and recovers only the basis of the redeemed shares, and not the basis of shares still outstanding at the transaction's close.

EXAMPLE 13.   Code §301(c)(2) Redemption Distribution

T and P each has 100 shares outstanding, all owned by A. A's total basis in T's 100 shares is $100. A's total basis in P's 100 share is $100. T's E&P is $10, and P's E&P is $30. A sells all 100 of his T shares to P for their $250 FV.

---

[7] 1976-2 C.B. 92.

[8] Indeed, if T's issuance of 1,000 additional T shares were viewed as part of the arrangement from inception, step transaction analysis would urge that T's 5% pro rata redemption be treated, not as a Code §302(d)/301(c)(1) dividend followed by FID-triggered CL, but under Code §302(a) and (b) as qualifying for sale (CG) treatment. IRS doubtless would not rush to assert, as it's defense against shareholder basis recovery partly offsetting dividend income, that T's shareholders have no dividend income at all.

[9] The rule we suggest would eliminate the non-abusive example (7) stock basis shift, a result we do not believe achieved by IRS Notice 2001-45.

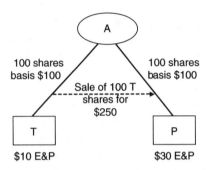

Under Code §304(a)(1) P is deemed (1) first to issue new phantom P shares to A in a Code §351 exchange for A's 100 T shares—with A taking Code §358 substituted basis in the new phantom P shares of $100, same basis as A had in the 100 T shares—and (2) then to redeem those phantom P shares for $250 in a transaction to which Code §301 applies.

Code §304(b)(2) provides for the aggregate application of P's $30 E&P and T's $10 E&P, resulting in $40 Code §302(d)/301(c)(1) dividend to A generally taxed after 2002 at a 15% top individual rate, see Code §1(h)(11) and ¶108. The $210 balance of P's deemed $250 redemption distribution to A is, under Code §301(c)(2), next applied against and recovers the $200 basis of A's P shares (both actual and deemed) with the remaining $10 constituting Code §301(c)(3) CG.

Treasury/IRS in its 10/02 proposed regulations reads Code §301(c)(2) to recover only the $100 basis at which A was deemed to own the redeemed phantom P shares (i.e., the successor to A's T shares). The remaining $110 of P's $250 deemed distribution to A ($250 deemed distribution − $40 dividend and − $100 §301(c)(2) P stock basis recovery) is treated by Treasury/IRS as Code §301(c)(3) CG on A's deemed sale of phantom P shares. Post-transaction, A continues to hold his 100 P shares at a $100 basis.

Example 13 tracks Prop. Reg. §1.304-2(c) example (3) (with simplified numbers) and in its outcome is, we have no doubt, quite wrong. Code §301(c)(2) recovers basis, not merely of P stock redeemed (or treated as redeemed) from A, but also the basis of P shares still held by A after the transaction. Indeed, it was this recover-aggregate-basis rule that required Congress, when in Code §1059 it wished to limit basis recovery only to the basis of shares redeemed, to legislate that limitation explicitly. See Code §1059(e)(1)(A) (final sentence).

Under Code §302(c)(2), the correct answers in Example 13 are that (1) A recovers $200 aggregate basis ($100 basis of A's actual P shares + $100 basis in A's phantom P shares), (2) only the $10 balance of P's $250 deemed distribution to A ($250 deemed distribution − $40 dividend and − $200 Code §302(c)(2) P stock basis recovery) is properly treated by A as Code §301(c)(3) CG, and (3) A's post-transaction basis in his 100 P shares is zero.

CHAPTER 14

Tax Aspects of Structuring LBOs

¶1401 INTRODUCTION

This chapter discusses a number of tax concerns, in addition to those discussed in earlier chapters of this treatise, that arise when P structures a leveraged buyout (an "LBO") of T or when Newco formed to acquire T structures an LBO of T. These tax concerns include:

(1) In an LBO, whether the acquisition should be effectuated (and/or any necessary borrowing be made) by P (or Newco) directly or through a subsidiary (¶1402).

(2) In an LBO in which some of T's old shareholders will own an equity interest in the surviving company, whether this can be accomplished through a tax-free stock rollover (¶1403).

(3) Possible constructive dividend to P (or Newco) from a P (or Newco) foreign subsidiary where P (or Newco) pledges the foreign subsidiary's stock to secure P's debt or the foreign subsidiary guarantees or pledges its assets to secure P's debt (¶1404).

(4) Special tax provisions applicable where an employee stock ownership plan ("ESOP") purchases stock (¶1406).

(5) Possible disallowance of P (or Newco) expenses under the start-up expense doctrine (¶1407).
(6) Application of the special greenmail tax penalty where P (or Newco) first acquires and then sells part of T's stock (¶1408).

As indicated above, where the acquisition is an LBO the acquiring corporation is generally referred to as "Newco" (because it is newly formed for purposes of the LBO) rather than "P," although the operative tax rules are essentially the same. Because many of the following topics are particularly relevant to acquisitions in which substantial debt is incurred, as will be the case in an LBO, the terms "Newco" and "P" generally are used interchangeably.

¶1402   LBO STRUCTURING CONSIDERATIONS

There are several ways to structure an LBO, and many tax and non-tax factors to be taken into account in selecting the proper structure.

¶1402.1   *Alternative Structures*

Discussed below are four alternatives for structuring an LBO and the distinct federal income tax ramifications of each:

(1) a one-corporation approach in which Newco merges directly into T (i.e., a taxable reverse merger) so that T is the only corporation remaining after the merger;
(2) a parent-subsidiary approach with borrowing at the parent level, in which a Newco subsidiary merges into T (i.e., a taxable reverse subsidiary merger), so that after the merger Newco is a holding company owning all of T's stock;
(3) a parent-subsidiary approach, as in (2), but with part of the borrowing at the subsidiary level; and
(4) an approach consisting of part purchase and part redemption, in which Newco purchases part of T's stock directly from T's shareholders and T redeems the rest using borrowed funds.

For a discussion of the Code §302 implications to alternatives (1), (3) and (4) above where the new shareholders acquire preferred stock (rather than common stock) but T's old shareholders retain some common stock in the LBO, see ¶1402.1.5.

For a discussion of the *Danielson* rule under which in some Circuits the taxpayer is bound by the form of the transaction (although IRS can invoke the step-transaction, substance over form, and similar doctrines), see ¶1402.2.

For a discussion of GAAP accounting for the LBO transaction (purchase, part purchase, and recapitalization accounting), see ¶1703. Especially when using alternatives (1) and (4) above, recap accounting may be available if T's old shareholders retain a significant stake in recapitalized T's common equity. See ¶1703.7.

¶1402.1.1   One Corporation Approach

Under the simplest approach, Newco acquires T and after the transaction there is only one corporate entity, T:

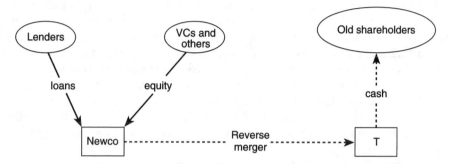

In this structure, Newco is formed and obtains debt and equity financing. Newco then merges into T, with T's old shareholders receiving cash (or cash and T notes) and Newco's shareholders and lenders receiving T stock and T debt instruments. Thus, after the merger only one corporate entity (T) remains.

For tax purposes, Newco is disregarded as a transitory corporation, and in general the transaction is treated as if T had obtained new debt and equity financing and then redeemed all of its old shareholders, who are thus taxed under Code §302.[1]

However, to the extent that T's new shareholders (i.e., the VCs and others buying Newco stock, which is converted in the merger into T stock) have purchased their new stock for cash, T's old shareholders instead may be treated (under a step-transaction analysis) as having sold their stock directly to T's new shareholders; to the extent of such treatment, T's old shareholders would be taxed under Code §1001 rather than under Code §302.[2]

(1)   Code §1001 versus Code §302 treatment. To the extent that an old T shareholder is taxed under Code §1001 on a sale of stock to a new T shareholder,

---

¶1402   [1] Rev. Rul. 78-250, 1978-1 C.B. 83. See ¶¶202 and 903.2 above.

[2] See Rev. Rul. 78-250, 1978-1 C.B. 83; Rev. Rul. 79-273, 1979-2 C.B. 125; Rev. Rul. 73-427, 1973-2 C.B. 301. Under such a Code §1001 analysis, the transaction essentially would be taxed as though (1) Newco had never existed, (2) T had incurred directly the acquisition debt, and (3) T's old shareholders had disposed of their T stock partly by direct sale to VC and the other investors and partly by redemption. A principal reason for not actually structuring the transaction in this manner—which reaches basically the same economic result as the reverse merger structure—is that the reverse merger of Newco into T permits VC and the other investors to cash out old T minority shareholders who would not voluntarily sell their T stock. Compare ¶1702.4 with ¶1702.6. Moreover, a reverse merger of Newco into T is generally preferable to a forward merger of T into Newco because (1) it avoids the need to transfer T's operating assets to a new legal entity, and (2) a forward merger will generally result in corporate-level tax on T as if it had sold its assets to Newco (see ¶¶301 and 405.1.1).

the old T shareholder recognizes CG (or CL) equal to the difference between the sale proceeds and the shareholder's basis in the T stock sold. To the extent that an old T shareholder is taxed under Code §302 on the deemed redemption of his stock by T, he recognizes *either* CG (or CL) equal to the difference between his proceeds and his basis, just as on a sale (generally for post-2002 CG taxed at a 15% top individual rate if the more than 1 year holding period requirement is satisfied), *or* dividend income equal to the full proceeds received (generally for post-2002 dividend income taxed at a 15% top individual rate if the more than 60 day holding period requirement (more than 90 days for certain preferred stock) is satisfied, see Code §1(h)(11) and ¶108, but without reduction for basis) up to the amount of T's E&P. Under the dividend analysis, if the redemption proceeds exceed T's E&P, the excess is treated first as a tax-free recovery of the shareholder's basis in the T stock until such basis is reduced to zero, and then as CG from the sale or exchange of the stock.[3] The type of tax treatment which applies to a Code §302 redemption—a Code §§301-302(d) distribution or CG (or CL) under Code §302(a)—turns on whether the old T shareholder owns any T stock (directly or by attribution under Code §§302(c) and 318[4]) *after* the redemption and, if so, how much.

A corporate holder of T stock (in contrast to most non-corporate holders) may prefer dividend treatment (rather than CG) because of the DRD available to a corporate holder of stock. However, as discussed in (3) below, for a transaction after 5/3/95, the benefit of the DRD to a corporate holder may be either recaptured later or denied at the outset.

However the old T shareholders are taxed on the sale, VC will have a cost tax basis in the Newco stock acquired.

EXAMPLE 1

VC forms Newco and capitalizes it with equity of $1 million. Newco borrows $5 million from various lenders. Newco merges into T, with T's shareholders (who are unrelated to VC) receiving the $6 million of cash for their T stock.

---

[3] Code §§302(d), 301(c).

[4] For example, under Code §318(a)(4) the holder of an option to acquire 100 T shares is considered to own those T shares. IRS applies Code §318(a)(4) to convertible debt, e.g., the holder of T debt convertible into 100 T shares is considered to own those T shares. Rev. Rul. 68-601, 1968-2 C.B. 124.

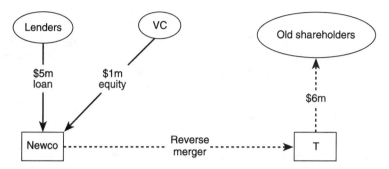

For tax purposes Newco is disregarded as transitory. *Under the redemption-only analysis*, the transaction is treated as if T issued new common stock to VC in exchange for $1 million, borrowed $5 million, and then distributed the $6 million to its historic shareholders in redemption of their T stock. Each old T shareholder has had a complete termination of interest in T under Code §302(b)(3). Therefore, each old T shareholder recognizes CG (or loss) under Code §302 in an amount equal to the difference between the shareholder's T stock basis and the amount of cash received.

Alternatively, under the part sale/part redemption analysis, each of T's historic shareholders is treated as having sold one-sixth of his old T stock to VC ($1 million ÷ $6 million) under Code §1001 and as if the other five-sixths of his stock had been redeemed by T out of borrowed funds ($5 million ÷ $6 million) under Code §302. Each old T shareholder thus recognizes CG (or loss) on one-sixth of his stock under Code §1001 and also recognizes CG (or loss) on the other five-sixths under Code §302(a) because he has had a complete termination of interest in T under Code §302(b)(3).

Under either analysis, VC has a $1 million cost basis in the Newco stock.

(2) Application of Code §302 where old T shareholders invest in Newco. As discussed above, to the extent the acquisition is treated as a redemption, an old T shareholder who completely terminates his equity interest in T will recognize CG (or CL) equal to the difference between the shareholder's basis in the old T shares treated as redeemed and the proceeds received therefor.[5] In such case, the shareholder will be indifferent between Code §302 redemption treatment and Code §1001 sale treatment, because both will result in CG (or CL).

However, in some circumstances an old T shareholder (e.g., Mgmt or Mgmt's relatives) will either purchase Newco stock directly or be treated by the Code §318 attribution rules as owning Newco stock that has been purchased by a related person (such as an immediate family member, a partnership or S corporation in which the old T shareholder is a partner or shareholder, or a C corporation 50% owned by the old T shareholder).[6] If so, after the merger the shareholder (in

---

[5] See Code §§302(b)(3), 302(c)(2).
[6] See Code §302(c).

addition to having received cash in the deemed redemption of the old T stock) will own, directly or by attribution, any T stock received in exchange for the shareholder's or an attributee's Newco stock. In such a case there is not a complete termination of the shareholder's interest in T. Therefore, to the extent a redemption analysis applies, the shareholder recognizes CG (or CL) rather than dividend income with respect to the deemed redemption proceeds *only* by satisfying one or more of the following other Code §302(b) tests:[7]

(a) The redemption is "substantially disproportionate" as to the shareholder; i.e., the shareholder's percentage ownership (actual and by attribution) of each of T's voting stock and T's common stock (the latter measured by FV) immediately after the merger is less than 80% of such percentage ownership immediately before the merger, *and* the shareholder owns less than 50% of T's voting stock immediately after the merger.

(b) There is some reduction in the shareholder's stock interest, and the shareholder is a de minimis shareholder (i.e., a shareholder "whose relative stock interest . . . is minimal and who exercises no control over [T's] affairs").[8] A substantial member of Mgmt or T's control group generally will *not* qualify as a de minimis shareholder.

(c) The transaction is otherwise "not essentially equivalent to a dividend."

If the shareholder does not have a complete termination of interest in T and otherwise fails to qualify for CG (or CL) sale treatment under Code §302(b), the full proceeds received from the deemed redemption *less* the amount reinvested in Newco is taxed (ordinarily at a 15% top individual rate) as a dividend under Code §§302(d), 301, and 1(h)(11) (to the extent of T's E&P), without reduction for the shareholder's basis in the T stock redeemed and with no CL offset allowed. In such case, assuming the shareholder's redemption proceeds exceed the amount of his contribution to Newco, the shareholder's basis in his new T stock (into which his Newco stock is converted in the merger) is the same as the shareholder's old T stock basis, reduced by any amount treated as basis recovery if T's E&P is less than the shareholder's net redemption proceeds. (Any amount the shareholder originally invested in Newco in exchange for Newco stock does not give rise to basis, but instead, as noted, reduces the shareholder's deemed redemption proceeds and hence the amount of the shareholder's dividend.)

Even though the individual post-2002 LTCG and dividend tax rate are the same (15%), the inability to offset basis against a dividend distribution generally makes Code §§301-302(d) distribution treatment less desirable than Code §302(a) or Code §1001 sale treatment, unless the shareholder is a corporation entitled to the DRD.

---

[7] See the discussion at ¶¶801.4 and 805.2.
[8] Rev. Rul. 76-385, 1976-2 C.B. 92.

EXAMPLE 2

VC and A (who is a member of T Mgmt) form Newco. VC contributes $700,000 in exchange for 70% of Newco's common stock, and A contributes $300,000 in exchange for 30% of Newco's common stock. Newco borrows $5 million.

Newco then merges into T, with T's shareholders receiving the $6 million of cash in exchange for their stock. A owned 20% of T's stock prior to the merger, with a basis of $250,000, so that in the merger A receives $1.2 million (20% of $6 million) in exchange for his 20% of T's stock. T's other shareholders are unrelated to VC and A.

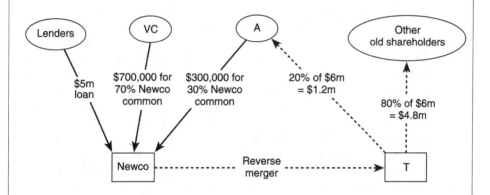

For tax purposes Newco is disregarded as transitory. *Under the redemption-only analysis*, the transaction is treated as if T *issued* new common stock to VC in exchange for $700,000, borrowed $5 million, and then distributed the $5.7 million to T's historic shareholders (including A) in redemption of their T stock, except that A's T stock was only partially redeemed.

Each old T shareholder (other than A) has a complete termination of interest in T. Therefore, each T shareholder other than A recognizes CG (or loss) equal to the difference between the shareholder's T stock basis and the amount of cash received.

However, A's percentage ownership of T stock has increased from 20% before the merger of Newco into T to 30% after the merger (by virtue of A's owning 30% of Newco's stock when Newco merged into T). Accordingly, A's percentage ownership of T has not been substantially reduced (indeed it has increased), and the distribution in redemption of A's T stock therefore will be treated as a Code §§301-302(d) distribution.

Hence, A is viewed as having received a dividend—taxed post-2002 at a 15% top individual rate—of $900,000 ($1.2 million received in the Newco/T merger *less* $300,000 contributed to Newco to purchase 30% of the Newco/T stock), assuming T has at least $900,000 of E&P. If T does not have at least

$900,000 of E&P, A's dividend is equal to T's E&P, and the remaining distribution is treated first as a tax-free recovery of A's $250,000 basis in the old T stock until such basis is reduced to zero, and then as sale CG under Code §301(c)(3).

After the merger, A's new T stock basis is $250,000 (A's historic T stock basis), reduced by any amount treated as a recovery of basis pursuant to the preceding sentence.

Alternatively, under the part sale/part redemption analysis, each old T shareholder is treated as selling some T stock to VC and as having some T stock redeemed by T. The aggregate amount of T stock sold and redeemed is $5.7 million ($4.8 million from T's old shareholders other than A and $900,000 from A), financed $700,000 by VC's equity (12%) and $5 million by T's borrowing (88%).

For T's old shareholders other than A, the tax consequences of the part sale/part redemption analysis are identical to those of the redemption-only analysis: Each of T's old shareholders other than A recognizes CG (or CL) equal to the difference between the shareholder's T stock basis and the amount of cash received. In contrast to the redemption-only analysis, 12% (rather than none) of the CG (or CL) will arise from a Code §1001 sale to VC, and 88% (rather than 100%) will arise from a redemption by T.

For A, the tax consequences of the part sale/part redemption analysis after 2002 are, except for modest basis recovery, essentially unaffected by A's inability to qualify for CG sale treatment with respect to the deemed redemption. A is treated as selling to VC 12% of the $900,000 of T stock that A disposed of. A recognizes a $78,000 CG on this Code §1001 sale (i.e., $108,000 sale proceeds (12% of $900,000) less $30,000 basis (12% of $250,000)). The remaining 88% of A's $900,000 of T stock disposed of is treated as redeemed by T, resulting in a dividend to A of $792,000 (in contrast to a $900,000 dividend under the redemption-only analysis), assuming T has at least $792,000 of E&P, taxed at a 15% top individual rate.

After the merger, A's new T stock basis is $220,000 (88% of A's $250,000 historic T stock basis, i.e., the portion of A's historic basis not offset against the proceeds from selling 12% of his T stock to VC), reduced by any amount treated as a return of basis if T did not have sufficient E&P to cover A's entire $792,000 redemption proceeds.

For a discussion of the Code §302 implications where T's new shareholders (such as VC) acquire T preferred stock (rather than T common stock) in the LBO, see ¶1402.1.5.

(3) Code §1059 limitation on dividends received deduction in redemption from corporate shareholder. As noted above, if the redeemed T shareholder is a corporation entitled to a DRD under Code §243, such a shareholder may well prefer the redemption to be a Code §301-§302(d) distribution rather than a Code §302(a) or Code §1001 sale qualifying for CG.

In fact, corporate shareholders have often attempted to structure redemption transactions to cause the redemption to be treated as a dividend (e.g., by simultaneously acquiring out-of-the-money warrants to repurchase a number of T shares equivalent to those redeemed). In the wake of one such highly publicized transaction—DuPont's early 1995 multi-billion dollar redemption of DuPont stock held by Seagram (coupled with Seagram's acquisition of an out-of-the-money warrant to repurchase DuPont stock)—the chairman and ranking minority member of each of the tax writing committees on 5/3/95 introduced legislation to curtail this strategy.

As originally proposed, this legislation would have mandated Code §302(a) sale treatment in the case of any stock redemption where (a) the stock is redeemed from a corporate shareholder, (b) the redemption is either non-pro rata or is part of a partial liquidation, and (c) treating the redemption as a dividend would entitle the corporate shareholder to a DRD.[9]

In earlier editions of this book we suggested that it was likely that legislation would be enacted, but probably not in the Code §302(b)(5) form proposed on 5/3/95. Instead, we bet on either (1) a limitation on Code §318(a)(4) option attribution or (2) repeal of Code §1059(a)(2)'s gain deferral (similar to an excess loss account) or (3) possibly both. It turned out to be both, in a somewhat strange amalgam.

The legislative solution adopted in the 1997 Act focuses on Code §1059(e)'s "extraordinary dividend" provision, which requires a corporate shareholder receiving an extraordinary dividend to reduce its basis in the distributing corporation's stock by the amount of the holder's DRD.[10] The 1997 Act amends Code §1059 in two significant respects. First, it expands the list of redemptions treated as dividends that are automatically "extraordinary dividends" to include any redemption treated as a dividend by virtue of the option attribution rules of Code §318(a)(4).[11] Second, it requires immediate gain recognition (i) in the case of any redemption treated as an extraordinary dividend by virtue of the option attribution rules (or Code §304(a)), to the extent that the DRD exceeds the basis of the shares redeemed (or deemed redeemed under Code §304(a)) and (ii) in any other case, to the extent that the DRD exceeds the corporate shareholder's basis in the shares with respect to which the extraordinary dividend was received. Previously, where the DRD exceeded the corporate shareholder's basis in the distributing corporation's stock, the shareholder's gain was deferred until the shareholder disposed of the stock, so that a corporate shareholder by retaining indefinitely one share of T stock could postpone indefinitely recognition its negative basis. Taken to-

---

[9] See H.R. 1551 and S. 750 proposing new Code §302(b)(5). The bills granted IRS general authority to provide exceptions from this rule and stated that "[t]o the extent provided in regulations, no loss shall be recognized solely by reason of the application of" the bill.

[10] Code §1059(a)(1).

[11] Code §1059(e)(1)(A)(iii)(I). Previously, only dividends resulting from non-pro rata redemptions or redemptions in partial liquidation were automatically treated as extraordinary dividends by Code §1059.

The expanded list following the 1997 Act also includes amounts treated as dividends under Code §304(a) and certain boot dividends under Code §356.

gether, these amendments have eliminated the perceived (but not as yet confirmed in litigation) tax advantage of using out-of-the-money warrants to create a DRD.

The amendments to Code §1059 are generally effective retroactively to 5/3/95. However, for extraordinary dividends not involving a transaction described in Code §1059(e)(1) (which covers a partial liquidation, non-pro rata redemption, the option attribution rules, a Code §304(a) transaction, and the boot rules of Code §356), the effective date for immediate gain recognition is 9/13/95.

(4)   No Code §338 election. If the LBO is structured with Newco merging into T, as described above, there is no opportunity for a Code §338 election to step up the basis of T's assets, because no corporate buyer has purchased 80% or more of T's stock (except in the unusual situation where 80% or more of Newco is owned by a single corporate entity). See ¶205 for a discussion of Code §338, ¶204 for a discussion of stock acquisitions in which no Code §338 election is made, and ¶¶107.1 and 403.1 for a discussion of the desirability of structuring for an SUB.

¶1402.1.2   Parent-Subsidiary Approach with Borrowing at Parent Level

Under the parent-subsidiary approach to an LBO, Newco acquires T in a taxable reverse subsidiary merger, so that after the transaction Newco is a holding company owning all of T's stock.

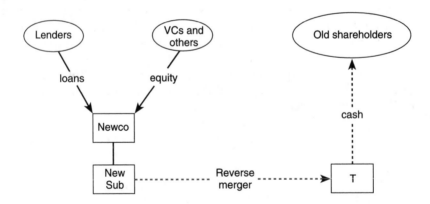

In this structure, Newco is formed and obtains debt and equity financing; Newco forms a subsidiary ("New Sub"); and New Sub then merges into T in a taxable reverse subsidiary merger, with T's old shareholders receiving cash (or cash and Newco notes) and New Sub's sole shareholder (Newco) receiving T stock. Thus, after the merger Newco owns 100% of T's stock.[12]

---

[12] The same economic result (and the same tax result as is described in the text) is achieved if Newco simply buys T's stock from its old shareholders without using New Sub at all. The principal advantage of a taxable reverse subsidiary merger over a direct stock purchase is that often it will

For tax purposes, New Sub is disregarded as a transitory corporation and the transaction is treated as if Newco had obtained new debt and equity financing and then purchased all of T's stock from T's old shareholders.[13] Except as discussed below, T's old shareholders recognize CG or CL under Code §1001 on the deemed sale of their T stock to Newco, and Newco takes a cost basis in the acquired T stock.

(1)   Possible application of Code §304. If Code §304 applies to the transaction, some of T's old shareholders may be treated as receiving a Code §301-302(d) distribution (taxable as a dividend—after 2002 taxed at a 15% top individual rate—to the extent of allocable E&P) unless they satisfy one of the Code §302(b) tests for CG sale treatment discussed in ¶1402.1.1(2).

Code §304 will apply to the transaction if Mgmt and/or other old T shareholders (the "Group") who owned in the aggregate 50% or more (by vote *or* by value) of *T's* stock before the reverse subsidiary merger also own 50% or more of *Newco's* stock after the merger, taking into account direct stock ownership as well as constructive ownership under the Code §318 attribution rules (as expanded by Code §304(c)(3)). To the extent Code §304 applies, cash (or cash and notes) that an old T shareholder receives in the merger is treated as received in *redemption* of *Newco's* stock. In such case the distribution will constitute a Code §301-302(d) distribution to the shareholder unless the shareholder satisfies one of the Code §302(b) tests for CG treatment discussed in ¶1402.1.1(2). To the extent the distribution received by a shareholder is treated as a Code §301-302(d) distribution, the shareholder and Newco are treated as if (a) the shareholder had transferred the T stock to Newco in a transaction to which Code §351 applies in exchange for Newco stock and (b) Newco had then immediately redeemed such stock.[14]

In the context of a Code §304 deemed redemption, the Code §302(b) tests are applied with reference to *T's* stock (not Newco's).[15] As in any redemption, the percentage of T stock owned by the shareholder before the transaction (actually and by attribution) is compared to the percentage of T stock owned (actually and by attribution, including attribution by value through Newco) after the transaction. For this purpose, the Code §318 attribution rules generally apply, except that the 50% stock ownership threshold for corporation-to-shareholder and shareholder-to-corporation attribution of Code §318(a)(2)(C) and (a)(3)(C) is eliminated.[16] Thus, in determining the amount of T stock owned by a Newco shareholder after the

---

enable Newco to cash out old T minority shareholders who would not voluntarily sell their T stock to Newco. Compare ¶1702.4 with ¶1702.6.

Another means of acquiring 100% of T's stock is a 2-step variant of the acquisition structure described in the text: (1) Newco purchases T stock directly (e.g., by tender offer) from those shareholders willing to sell, and (2) T's remaining shareholders are cashed out by a reverse merger of New Sub into T. The tax consequences are the same as those described in the text. This structure is frequently used when T's stock is publicly traded. If Newco acquires sufficient T shares in step (1), the merger of New Sub might be executed through a "short-form merger," which does not require the approval of T's old shareholders. See ¶1702.6.7.

[13] Rev. Rul. 73-427, 1973-2 C.B. 301; Rev. Rul. 79-273, 1979-2 C.B. 125. See ¶¶202 and 903.2.

[14] See Code §304(a)(1) (as amended by the 1997 Act). See also ¶405.1.

[15] Code §304(b)(1).

[16] Code §304(b)(1).

transaction, the shareholder is treated as owning that percentage of Newco's T stock equal to the percentage *by value* (not by vote) of Newco's stock (including both Newco common and Newco preferred stock) owned by such shareholder.

If, for example, Newco owns 100% of T's stock (which often will be the case), a member of the Group who owns 10% of Newco's stock by value will be treated as owning 10% of T's stock in applying the Code §302(b) tests by way of Code §304.

If Code §304 applies (because the Group owns 50% or more of T before and Newco after the merger) and a member of the Group is treated under Code §318 as owning the same or a larger percentage of T's voting stock or T's common stock than he previously owned, he would *not* qualify for Code §302(a) CG treatment under the Code §302(b) tests, but rather his proceeds would be treated as a Code §§301-302(d) distribution taxed, after 2002, at a 15% top individual rate.[17]

If a member of the Group is treated as receiving a Code §301-302(d) distribution, the full proceeds received—probably *less* the amount reinvested in Newco (because, as discussed immediately below, the formation of Newco and the merger of New Sub into T are likely to be treated as integrated steps of a single transaction)—up to Newco's and T's *combined* E&P is taxed as a dividend at a 15% top individual rate, without reduction for his basis in the stock redeemed and without CL offset, see ¶108.[18] Code §301 distribution proceeds in excess of Newco's and T's combined E&P are treated first as a recovery of the shareholder's *Newco* stock basis until such basis is reduced to zero, and then as CG from the sale or exchange of such stock.

After the acquisition, a shareholder's Newco stock basis will vary depending on (1) whether Code §304 applies, (2) whether the shareholder's disposition of T stock gives rise to exchange treatment or a Code §301-302(d) distribution, and (3) whether Newco's Code §351 formation and the shareholder's sale of T stock to Newco are treated as separate transactions or as an integrated transaction. See ¶1402.1.2(2) and (3) below.

Newco's basis in T's stock will equal the purchase price paid by Newco except to the extent the T stock is acquired (1) from a Group member deemed to have received a Code §§301-302(d) distribution or (2) as a Code §351 contribution to Newco's capital. In the latter cases, Newco's basis in T's stock will equal the transferor shareholder's historic T stock basis plus the amount of gain (as distinguished from dividend income) that the shareholder recognizes on the transfer.[19]

See Examples 1 through 3 below.

(2)   Possible application of step-transaction doctrine to Newco's Code §351 formation and Newco's purchase of T's stock. When an old T shareholder (A)

---

[17] For the circumstances under which Code §302(a) CG sale treatment would be available, see ¶¶1402.1.1(2), 801.4, and 805.2, taking into account Code §304's expansion of the Code §318 attribution rules, as discussed above.

[18] The dividend is treated as paid first by Newco to the extent of its E&P and then by T to the extent of its E&P. Code §304(b)(2).

[19] Code §362(a); Reg. §1.304-2(a). It is irrelevant to the basis determination that post-2002 sale CG and qualified dividend income are taxed at the same 15% individual top rate. See generally ¶1402.1.2(2) through (4) below.

purchases Newco stock, so that A both receives cash for his T stock in the merger and contributes cash to Newco in exchange for Newco stock, the two transactions may be treated as integrated steps of a single transaction. *If the two steps are treated as a single transaction,* then A is treated as participating in the Code §351 formation of Newco by contributing T stock to Newco in exchange for both Newco stock and a net amount of cash (i.e., the amount received by A from Newco in exchange for T stock in the merger less the amount contributed by A to Newco for Newco stock).

On the other hand, *if the two steps are treated as separate transactions,* then A is treated as selling his T stock to Newco in the merger for the gross cash he received from Newco in the merger and as separately contributing cash to Newco for Newco stock as part of its Code §351 formation. Resolution of this step transaction issue can affect the amount of A's sale CG or dividend income, A's Newco stock basis, and Newco's basis in the T stock acquired from A, whether or not Code §304 applies to the transaction. Moreover, if Code §304 applies, it can affect whether A is subject to dividend or CG treatment under Code §302, although post-2002 the top tax rate (15% for individuals) is the same. See Examples 1 through 3 below.

It frequently is unclear whether a shareholder's purchase of Newco stock and the shareholder's sale of T stock to Newco will be treated as a single transaction because of the irreconcilable results in the decided cases. *Baker Commodities, Inc. v. Commissioner*[20] dealt with the formation of Newco by a group of ten shareholders, three of whom then purported to sell assets to Newco for a note. Although the Tax Court upheld the note as debt, it treated the "sale" as part of the Code §351 transfer of assets to Newco for a security.

However, *Stevens Pass v. Commissioner,*[21] a virtually indistinguishable case decided by the Tax Court in the same year it decided *Baker Commodities,* reached the opposite conclusion. In *Stevens Pass,* two of T's three shareholders and 10 other persons formed Newco, and Newco then purchased all of T's stock from T's three shareholders for cash and a note. The Tax Court held the transaction to be a "sale," not part of Newco's Code §351 transaction.[22]

Some of the facts relevant in determining whether the formation of Newco and its purchase of T stock are to be stepped together include:

(a)   Whether the price paid by Newco for T's stock in the merger is a fair arm's-length price, separately negotiated from the price to be paid for Newco stock by those subscribing for Newco stock.

(b)   Whether the price paid for Newco stock by those subscribing for Newco stock is a fair arm's-length price, separately negotiated from the price to be paid by Newco for T stock.

---

[20] 48 T.C. 374 (1967), *aff'd,* 415 F.2d 519, 69-2 U.S.T.C. ¶9589 (9th Cir. 1969).

[21] 48 T.C. 532 (1967).

[22] See also LDS, Inc. v. Commissioner, 51 T.C.M. 1433, T.C. Mem. 1986-293 (1986) (sale of real estate was part of Code §351 transaction); Curry v. Commissioner, 43 T.C. 667 (1965) (sale of real estate respected as a sale); Burr Oaks Corp. v. Commissioner, 365 F.2d 24, 66-2 U.S.T.C. ¶9506 (7th Cir. 1966) (sale of real estate for notes treated as part of Code §351 transaction, with the notes treated as equity); Aqualane Shores, Inc. v. Commissioner, 269 F.2d 116, 59-2 U.S.T.C. ¶9632 (5th Cir. 1959) (same as *Burr Oaks*); IRS Letter Ruling 7905011 (10/23/78) (sale treated as contribution).

(c)   The degree of overlap between ownership of T's stock before the transaction and ownership of Newco's stock afterwards.
(d)   Whether the two transactions occur simultaneously or whether there is a more substantial temporal separation between the two transactions.

However, the dichotomy in the cases *cannot* be explained solely on factual grounds such as those enumerated above. At least equally relevant in the decided cases is the particular judge's view of the law—i.e., whether the judge believed that Code §351 permits persons subscribing for Newco stock to separately "sell" assets to Newco or whether the judge took the view that all transfers to Newco by its shareholders are part of the Code §351 process. The majority of the cases (but not all) have taken the step-transaction Code §351 view rather than the separate "sale" approach.

EXAMPLE 1

VC and A, a member of T Mgmt, form Newco. VC contributes $700,000 in exchange for 70% of Newco's stock, and A contributes $300,000 in exchange for 30% of Newco's stock. Newco borrows $5 million with the intent of acquiring all of T's stock for $6 million ($1 million Newco equity and $5 million borrowing).

Before the transaction A holds 20% of T's outstanding stock, with a basis of $250,000. T's other shareholders are unrelated to VC and A.

Newco forms a wholly owned subsidiary S, and capitalizes it with the $6 million. S then merges into T with T's shareholders receiving $6 million cash in exchange for their T shares.

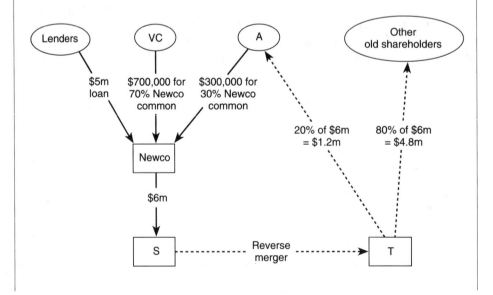

For tax purposes, S is disregarded as transitory, and the transaction is treated as if Newco had purchased T's stock. Code §304 does *not* apply because no group of persons owning 50% or more of T's stock (by vote or value) before the merger owns 50% or more of Newco's stock (by vote or value) after the merger. Because Code §304 does not apply, and because A owns less than 50% of Newco's stock after the merger (so that, for Code §302 purposes, T stock owned by Newco is not attributed to A under Code §318(a)(2)(C)), none of T's shareholders are subject to dividend treatment with respect to cash they receive in the merger.

Accordingly, each T shareholder other than A recognizes CG (or loss) in an amount equal to the difference between the shareholder's T stock basis and the amount of cash received.

As to A, however, there are two possible ways to view the transaction for tax purposes:

First, if A's purchase of 30% of Newco's stock is viewed as separate from Newco's purchase of A's 20% of T's stock, A is treated as having sold his T shares to Newco for $1.2 million (20% × $6 million) and thus recognizes CG of $950,000 ($1.2 million received for T stock *less* $250,000 historic T stock basis).

A takes a $300,000 cost basis in the Newco stock, and Newco takes a $1.2 million cost basis in A's T stock.

The *second* (and more likely) view of the transaction is that A's purchase of 30% of Newco's stock is stepped together with A's sale of 20% of T's stock to Newco. Under this view A is treated as having made a Code §351 contribution of his 20% of T's stock to Newco in exchange for 30% of Newco's stock plus $900,000 net cash. In this case, A *realizes* $950,000 of CG ($1.2 million proceeds, consisting of $300,000 of Newco stock and $900,000 of cash, *less* A's $250,000 historic T stock basis). However, in contrast to the first analysis, A *recognizes* only $900,000 of CG because in a Code §351 transaction the recipient of "boot" (i.e., any property other than Newco stock or securities) recognizes gain equal to the lesser of total realized gain (here, $950,000) and the amount of boot (here, the $900,000 cash).

A's basis in the Newco stock is $250,000 (compared to $300,000 in the first analysis), determined under Code §358(a) as follows: $250,000 historic T stock basis, *less* $900,000 boot received, *plus* $900,000 recognized gain. Newco's basis in the T stock acquired from A is $1,150,000 (compared to $1.2 million in the first analysis), determined under Code §362(a) as follows: A's $250,000 historic T stock basis *plus* A's $900,000 recognized gain on the transfer.

In short, viewing A's purchase of Newco stock and A's sale of T stock to Newco as an integrated Code §351 transaction rather than as separate transactions reduces A's recognized gain (as well as A's basis in his Newco stock and Newco's basis in the T stock acquired from A) by the excess, if any, of A's realized gain in the Code §351 exchange ($950,000) over A's Code §351 boot ($900,000), or by $50,000 in this example. In contrast, if under different facts A's realized gain did not exceed the amount of boot that A received, the CG consequences to A and the basis consequences to A and Newco would be the same under the two views.

For the tax consequences of analogous facts when Newco, rather than acquiring T's stock by reverse subsidiary merger, merges directly into T, see Example 2 in ¶1402.1.1.

(3) Interrelation between Code §§351 and 304. Whether Newco's formation and its purchase of T's stock are treated as integrated or separate transactions, Code §304 will apply if its 50% stock ownership requirements are satisfied. Assume that Newco's formation and its acquisition of T's stock are treated as a single transaction so that A is treated as contributing T stock to Newco in exchange for both Newco stock and a net amount of cash (i.e., the amount that A received from Newco in exchange for T stock in the merger *less* the amount that A contributed to Newco for Newco stock). If the transaction also falls within Code §304 (because a group of persons owns 50% or more of T's stock before and Newco's stock after the merger, measured by vote or by value), then Code §304(b)(3)(A) bifurcates the transaction: Code §351 applies to A's exchange of T stock for Newco stock with an equal FV, and this part of the transaction is tax free under Code §351; and Code §304 applies to A's exchange of T stock for cash, and the cash distribution is *either* a Code §§301-302(d) distribution or a Code §302(a) CG redemption, depending on whether A has met any of the Code §302(b) tests.

This bifurcation will *not* occur if Newco's formation and its purchase of T's stock are viewed separately, because in that case A's disposition of T stock will have been solely for cash and thus governed solely by Code §304.

EXAMPLE 2

In contrast to Example 1, here A and another old T shareholder own sufficient T stock and purchase sufficient Newco stock that Code §304 applies to the transaction. Assume T's stock is owned as follows:

	Percentage	Basis	FV
A	33.3%	$300,000	$2 million
B	33.3	300,000	2 million
C	33.3	300,000	2 million
Total	100.0%	$900,000	$6 million

A, B, and C are not related to each other or to VC. VC forms Newco, along with A and B, each purchasing Newco's stock as follows:

	Percentage	Cash Contributed
VC	49%	$ 490,000
A	41	410,000
B	10	100,000
Total	100%	$1,000,000

T's third shareholder, C, owns no Newco stock.

Newco then borrows $5 million and contributes $6 million to S (Newco's $1 million equity plus its $5 million borrowing). S merges into T with T's shareholders receiving $6 million in exchange for their T shares.

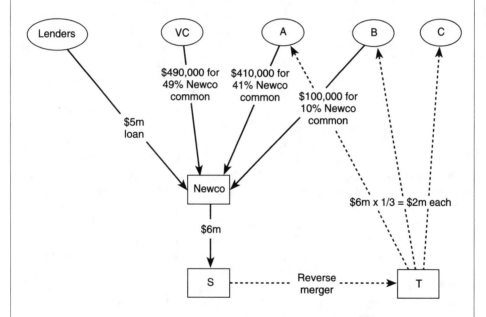

For tax purposes, S is disregarded as transitory. Because A and B, as a group, owned at least 50% of T's stock (by vote or by value) prior to the transaction and also own at least 50% of Newco's stock (by vote or by value) after the transaction, Code §304 applies.

A's Tax Treatment

As to A, the transaction may be viewed in either of two ways for tax purposes. *First*, A's purchase of 41% of Newco's stock for $410,000 may be viewed as separate from Newco's purchase of A's 33.3% of T's stock for $2 million. Because Code §304 applies to the transaction, under this view A is treated as receiving $2 million in redemption of A's *Newco* stock.

In determining whether this deemed redemption gives rise to a Code §§301-302(d) dividend or a Code §302(a) CG sale, the Code §302(b) tests apply with reference to A's ownership of T stock before and after the acquisition. After the acquisition, A is deemed to own 41% of T by virtue of owning 41% (by value) of Newco, T's 100% parent.[23] Because A's percentage interest in T has not declined substantially (and indeed has increased from 33.3% to 41%), the deemed redemption fails the Code §302(b) tests and so is treated as a Code §§301-302(d) distribution.

A is therefore taxed on a $2 million dividend—generally taxed after 2002 at a 15% top individual rate, but without CL offset—except that if Newco and T do not have at least $2 million of combined E&P, the dividend is limited to their combined E&P, and the excess is treated first as a tax-free recovery of A's Newco stock basis (because Code §304 creates a constructive redemption of A's Newco stock, not A's T stock) until such basis is reduced to zero, and then as CG.[24] For this purpose, A's Newco stock basis is $710,000, including both A's $410,000 cash contribution to Newco and A's $300,000 historic basis in the T stock that A is deemed under Code §304(a)(1) to have contributed to Newco in a Code §351 exchange for phantom Newco stock.[25]

After the acquisition, A's Newco stock basis is $710,000 (determined as described above), reduced by any amount treated as return of basis pursuant to the preceding paragraph.[26] Because A is deemed to have contributed his T stock to Newco in a Code §351 exchange, Newco's basis in A's T stock is equal to A's $300,000 historic T stock basis plus (if A's Code §§301-302(d) distribution exceeds Newco's and T's combined E&P and A's Newco stock basis) the amount of Code §301(c)(3) gain recognized by A on the transfer.[27]

The *second* (and more likely) view of the transaction is that A's purchase of 41% of Newco's stock is stepped together with A's sale of 33.3% of T's stock to Newco. Under this view A is treated as having transferred his 33.3% of T's stock plus $410,000 cash to Newco in exchange for 41% of Newco's stock plus $2 million cash. Under such a step-transaction view, A's $410,000 cash

[23] See Code §318(a)(2)(C) and Code §304(b)(1).
[24] On the facts of Example 2 B has sale CG and not dividend income (see text below). Hence all available E&P is allocated entirely to A, since Code §301 includes no "ratable share of E&P" limitation.
[25] See Code §304(a)(1) (as amended by the 1997 Act).
[26] Reg. §1.304-2(a).
[27] Reg. §1.304-2(a); Code §362(a). Although taxed at a 15% top individual rate, qualified dividend income is not "gain" for this purpose.

contribution to Newco would be netted against the $2 million of cash received by A from Newco, so A would be treated as contributing 33.3% of T's stock to Newco in exchange for 41% of Newco's stock plus $1,590,000 net cash.

As described above, Code §304 applies to the transaction. Therefore, under the bifurcation rule of Code §304(b)(3)(A), Code §351 applies to the extent A exchanged T stock for Newco stock of equal value, and Code §304 applies to the extent A exchanged T stock for cash. Thus, A is treated as exchanging T stock with a $410,000 FV tax free for 41% of Newco's stock (FV $410,000) under Code §351; and A is treated as receiving $1,590,000 cash in redemption of part of A's "additional" Newco stock under Code §304.

As discussed above, A's percentage interest in T after the deemed redemption is not substantially lower (and indeed is higher) than before the redemption, and therefore the $1,590,000 cash is taxable as a dividend (post-2002 at a 15% top individual rate) to A to the extent of Newco's and T's combined E&P. If the cash exceeds their combined E&P, the excess is treated first as a tax-free recovery of A's basis in the Newco stock treated as redeemed, until such basis is reduced to zero, and then as sale CG. For this purpose, A's *aggregate* basis in the Newco stock is $300,000, i.e., A's historic basis in the T stock that A is treated as contributing to Newco's capital (partly under Code §351 and partly under Code §304(a)(1)). (A's Newco stock basis does *not* include the $410,000 cash contributed to Newco, because under the integrated transaction view such cash does not give rise to basis, but rather is netted against and thus reduces A's deemed redemption proceeds.) However, it is unclear whether A's entire $300,000 basis is available for recovery against the Code §304 redemption proceeds.[28]

After the acquisition, A's Newco stock basis is $300,000 (determined as described above), in contrast to A's $710,000 basis under the previous analysis, reduced by any amount treated as return of basis pursuant to the preceding paragraph. Because Newco received all of A's stock as a deemed contribution to capital (partly under Code §351 and partly under Code §304(a)(1)), Newco's basis in A's T stock is equal to A's $300,000 historic T stock basis, plus (if A's Code §§301-302(d) distribution exceeds Newco's and T's combined E&P and A's allocable Newco stock basis) the amount of Code §301(c)(3) gain recognized by A on the transfer, as in the previous analysis.

In short, under these facts, where Code §304 results in dividend treatment to A, viewing A's purchase of Newco stock and A's sale of T stock to

---

[28] A's potential basis recovery with respect to the $1,590,000 deemed redemption proceeds may be limited to the portion of A's Newco stock basis arising from the deemed contribution of T stock to Newco under Code §304, or $238,500: 79.5% (i.e., $1,590,000 redemption proceeds divided by $2,000,000 total consideration for A's T stock) of A's $300,000 aggregate Newco stock basis. Compare, e.g., Johnson v. United States, 435 F.2d 1257, 71-1 U.S.T.C. ¶9148 (4th Cir. 1971) (holding, under a "fragmented" basis approach, that a shareholder's basis recovery and capital gain with respect to a Code §301 distribution by a corporation with low E&P are computed by allocating to each share its pro rata portion of the distribution, rather than by aggregating the bases of shares acquired at different costs), with Commissioner v. Fink, 483 U.S. 89, 87-1 U.S.T.C. ¶9373 (1987) (holding, under an "aggregate" basis approach, that a controlling shareholder of T who contributes some of his T stock to T's capital does not incur a deductible loss, but rather must reallocate his basis in the surrendered shares among the T shares retained by him).

Newco as an integrated transaction rather than as separate transactions reduces A's dividend and A's basis in Newco's stock (but *not* Newco's basis in the acquired T stock) by the amount of A's $410,000 cash contribution to Newco.

B's Tax Treatment

The transaction can be viewed in the same two ways for B as for A. However, as described below, B's tax treatment differs from A's under Code §304, because the substantial decline in B's percentage ownership of T results in Code §302(a) CG rather than a Code §§301-302(d) distribution.

First, B's purchase of 10% of Newco's stock for $100,000 may be viewed as separate from Newco's purchase of B's 33.3% of T's stock for $2 million. Because Code §304 applies to the transaction, under this view B is treated as receiving $2 million in redemption of B's Newco stock. However, in contrast to the result for A, the distribution to B is *not* treated as a Code §§301-302(d) distribution. After the transaction, B is treated as owning only 10% of T, because B then owns 10% (by value) of Newco, T's 100% parent.[29] Because B's percentage ownership of T has declined by more than 20% (from 33.3% to 10%—a 70% decline), B's redemption (unlike A's) is substantially disproportionate under Code §302(b)(2) and therefore under Code §302(a) results in CG sale treatment.

B therefore recognizes $1.7 million of CG ($2 million cash proceeds *less* B's $300,000 historic T stock basis). B's basis in his 10% of Newco's stock is $100,000 (the cash that B contributed to Newco to purchase Newco stock). Newco has a cost ($2 million) basis in the T stock acquired from B because, in contrast to the stock acquired from A, Newco is treated as acquiring B's stock by purchase rather than as a Code §351 contribution to capital.

The *second* (and more likely) view of the transaction is that B's purchase of 10% of Newco's stock is stepped together with B's sale of 33.3% of T's stock to Newco. In this case B is treated as having transferred his 33.3% of T's stock plus $100,000 cash to Newco in exchange for 10% of Newco's stock plus $2 million cash. Under such a step-transaction view, B's $100,000 cash contribution to Newco would be netted against the $2 million of cash received by B from Newco, so B would be treated as contributing 33.3% of T's stock to Newco in exchange for 10% of Newco's stock plus $1,900,000 net cash.

As described above, Code §304 applies to the transaction. Therefore, under the bifurcation rule of Code §304(b)(3)(A), Code §351 applies to the extent B exchanged T stock for Newco stock of equal value, and Code §304 applies to the extent B exchanged T stock for cash. Thus, B is treated as exchanging T stock with a $100,000 FV tax free for 10% of Newco's stock (FV $100,000) under Code §351; and B is treated as receiving $1,900,000 cash in a Code §304 redemption. Because B's percentage interest in T has declined by more than 20%, as discussed above, the deemed redemption gives rise to sale CG rather than dividend treatment.

---

[29] Code §§318(a)(2)(C) and 304(b)(1).

B's $300,000 historic T stock basis is allocated $15,000 to the $100,000 FV of T stock exchanged pursuant to Code §351 ($300,000 basis in T stock × $100,000 FV of T stock contributed to Newco ÷ $2 million FV of aggregate T stock) and $285,000 to the $1.9 million FV of T stock redeemed ($300,000 basis in T stock × $1.9 million FV of T stock redeemed ÷ $2 million FV of aggregate T stock).

Hence, B recognizes $1,615,000 of sale CG on the deemed redemption ($1.9 million cash proceeds *less* $285,000 basis allocated to T stock redeemed), and B has a $15,000 basis in his 10% of Newco's stock (B's allocated basis in the T stock covered by Code §351).

Newco's basis in the T stock acquired from B is $1,915,000 (in contrast to $2 million under the separate transaction analysis): $1.9 million cost basis in the T shares acquired by deemed redemption, plus B's $15,000 historic basis in the T shares acquired by Code §351 contribution to capital.

In short, under these facts, where Code §304 results in sale CG and not dividend treatment to B, viewing B's purchase of Newco stock and B's sale of T stock to Newco as an integrated transaction rather than as separate transactions reduces B's CG (as well as B's basis in his Newco stock and Newco's basis in the T stock acquired from B) by the excess of B's cash contribution to Newco ($100,000) over B's historic stock basis in the T stock subject to Code §351 treatment ($15,000), or by $85,000.

C's Tax Treatment

C's tax treatment is different from A's and B's. C owns no Newco stock and therefore is *not* subject to Code §351 or the Code §304 deemed redemption rules. Hence, C recognizes sale CG of $1.7 million ($2 million proceeds *less* $300,000 basis in old T stock) under Code §1001. Newco has a $2 million cost basis in the T stock acquired from C.

EXAMPLE 3

Same as Example 2 except that B does *not* purchase any Newco stock, so that Newco is owned 59% by VC and 41% by A.

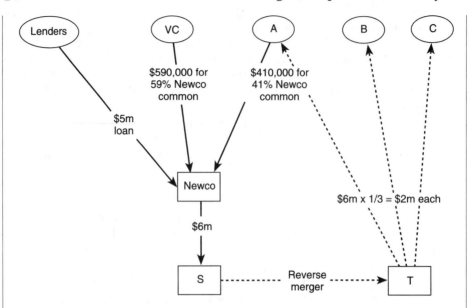

The transaction is *not* covered by Code §304 because A is the only person owning stock of both T and Newco, and A owns only 33.3% of T's stock before the merger and 41% of Newco's stock after the merger.

B and C are each treated as having sold his T shares to Newco for $2 million, and each recognizes $1.7 million of CG under Code §1001.

A's tax treatment can be viewed in either of two ways. *First,* if A's purchase of 41% of Newco's stock is viewed as separate from Newco's purchase of A's 33.3% of T's stock, A is taxed in the same manner as B and C, i.e., A recognizes $1.7 million of CG. In this case A takes a $410,000 cost basis in his 41% of Newco's stock, and Newco takes a $2 million cost basis in the T stock purchased from A.

The *second* (and more likely) view of the transaction is that A's purchase of 41% of Newco's stock is stepped together with A's sale of 33.3% of T's stock to Newco. In this case A is treated as having made a Code §351 contribution of his 33.3% of T's stock (FV $2 million) to Newco in exchange for 41% of Newco's stock (FV $410,000) plus $1,590,000 cash (the $2 million that A received from Newco net of the $410,000 that A contributed to Newco).

Code §304 does *not* apply to the transaction because no group of persons owning 50% or more of T (by vote or value) before the merger owns 50% or more of Newco (by vote or value) after the merger. Thus A realizes $1.7 million of CG under Code §351 (i.e., the excess of A's $2 million proceeds, consisting of $1,590,000 net cash plus $410,000 of Newco stock, over A's historic $300,000 T stock basis), and A *recognizes* this gain to the extent of the $1,590,000 of net cash boot.

In this case A's basis in the Newco stock is $300,000 under Code §358 (i.e., A's $300,000 historic T stock basis, plus A's $1,590,000 recognized gain, less A's $1,590,000 boot received). Newco's basis in the T stock acquired from A is $1,890,000 under Code §362 (i.e., A's $300,000 historic T stock plus A's $1,590,000 recognized gain).

In short, as in Example 1, where Code §304 similarly is inapplicable, viewing A's purchase of Newco stock and A's sale of T stock as an integrated Code §351 transaction rather than as separate transactions reduces A's recognized gain (as well as A's Newco stock basis and Newco's basis in the T stock acquired from A) by the excess, if any, of A's realized gain in the Code §351 exchange (here, $1,700,000) over A's Code §351 boot (here, $1,590,000), or by $110,000. In contrast, if under different facts A's realized gain did *not* exceed the amount of boot (and assuming Code §304 did not apply), the CG consequences to A and the basis consequences to A and Newco would be the same under the two views.

(4)   Possible Code §338 or §338(h)(10) election. Because Newco has acquired T's stock rather than T's assets (in contrast to the one-corporation, LBO structure discussed in ¶1402.1.1 where no one corporate entity purchased 80% or more of T's stock), Newco can make a Code §338 election or, if available (e.g., T is an SCo), a Code §338(h)(10) election to step up the basis of T's assets, unless such a Code §338 or §338(h)(10) election is prevented either by Code §304 or by Code §351. A Code §338 or §338(h)(10) election is permissible only if Newco has made a qualified stock purchase (a "QSP") of T stock; a QSP requires Newco to acquire "by purchase" at least 80% of T's stock (by vote and by value); a "purchase" does *not* include Newco's acquisition of T stock pursuant to Code §304 (to the extent the transferor's proceeds are treated as a Code §§301-302(d) distribution) or pursuant to Code §351.[30] See ¶¶205.3, 206.1.3, and 405.1.

See ¶205 for a discussion of Code §338, ¶206 for a discussion of Code §338(h)(10), ¶204 for a discussion of no Code §338 election, ¶¶107.1 and 403.1 for a discussion of the desirability of structuring for SUB, and (5) and (6) below for the Code §338 implications of T's later liquidation or Newco's later downstream merger into T.

Code §304. As discussed in ¶1402.1.2(1) through (3) immediately above, if T's Management and/or other old T shareholders (the "Group") own in the aggregate 50% or more (by vote or by value) of both T's stock before the acquisition and Newco's stock after the acquisition (taking account of direct stock ownership as well as constructive ownership under the Code §318 attribution rules as expanded by Code §304(c)(3)), then the sale of T stock to Newco constitutes a Code §304 transaction. In this case, any old T shareholder whose proceeds are treated as a Code §301 distribution by virtue of Code §302(d) (rather than as a Code §302(a) CG redemption) is treated (by the last sentence of Code §304(a)(1)) as having transferred his T stock to Newco in exchange for newly-issued Newco shares in

---

[30] Code §§338(a), 338(d)(3), 338(h)(3)(A), 304(a)(1) (last sentence, as amended by the 1997 Act); Reg. §1.338-3(b)(3)(iv) example (1).

a transaction to which Code §351 applies, followed by Newco's redemption of such newly-issued shares. Thus, Newco is treated as *"purchasing"* (for Code §338 or §338(h)(10) purposes) only those T shares (a) acquired by purchase from persons who were *not* members of the Group and (b) acquired by purchase from members of the Group who qualify for Code §302(b) CG treatment.

Hence, Newco can make a Code §338 or §338(h)(10) election with respect to T only if Newco has acquired at least 80% of T's stock (by vote and by value) in the fashion described in (a) and (b) immediately above, i.e., Newco does not qualify for a Code §338 or §338(h)(10) election with respect to T if Newco has acquired more than 20% of T's stock (by vote or by value) in a Code §304(a)(1) deemed Code §351 exchange (or otherwise not as a "purchase").

EXAMPLE 4

Same as Example 2. As discussed in Example 2, if A's and B's purchase of Newco stock is considered to be separate from Newco's acquisition of their T stock, A is treated under Code §304 as receiving a $2 million Code §§301-302(d) distribution. Therefore, $2 million of T's stock is treated as having been contributed to Newco in a Code §351 transaction rather than purchased by Newco. Since the total price for T's stock was $6 million, Newco is treated as having "purchased" only 66.7% ($4 million ÷ $6 million) of T's stock and therefore cannot make a Code §338 or §338(h)(10) election.

Example 2 also concludes that if A's and B's purchase of Newco stock and Newco's acquisition of their T stock are viewed as an integrated transaction, A is treated under Code §304 as receiving a $1,590,000 Code §§301-302(d) distribution. Thus Newco is treated under Code §304 as acquiring 26.5% of T's stock ($1,590,000 ÷ $6 million) in a Code §351 transaction rather than by purchase, so that under this analysis as well Newco has not made a QSP and therefore may not make a Code §338 or §338(h)(10) election. (Moreover, as discussed in Example 2, under the integrated transaction approach, Newco is deemed to receive as a Code §351 capital contribution $410,000 of T stock from A and $100,000 of T stock from B, which increases to 35% (($1,590,000 + $410,000 + $100,000) ÷ $6 million) the amount of T stock that Newco acquired by contribution to capital (i.e., not by "purchase"). See the discussion immediately below.)

For a further discussion, see ¶405.1.2.1.

Code §351. Even where Code §304 does not apply to Newco's acquisition of T's Stock, Code §351 may preclude Newco from making a Code §338 or §338(h)(10) election with respect to T. That is, even if the Group did not own in the aggregate 50% or more (by vote or by value) of both T before and Newco after the transaction, so that Newco's acquisition of T does not fall within the ambit of Code §304, Newco is nevertheless not permitted to make a Code §338 or §338(h)(10) election with respect to T if Newco acquired more than 20% of T's stock (by vote or by value) in a Code §351 transaction, even a Code §351 transaction in which boot was the predominant consideration.

EXAMPLE 5

T's stock is owned as follows:

Shareholder	Number of T Shares	%	FV
A	21 shares	21%	$ 210,000
B	79 shares	79%	790,000
	100 shares	100%	$1,000,000

VC and A form Newco. VC contributes $990,000 cash to Newco in exchange for 99 Newco shares (constituting 99% of Newco's stock). A transfers his 21 T shares (FV $210,000) to Newco for $200,000 cash and 1 share of Newco stock (FV $10,000), constituting 1% of Newco's stock.

B transfer his 79 T shares (FV $790,000) to Newco for $790,000 cash.

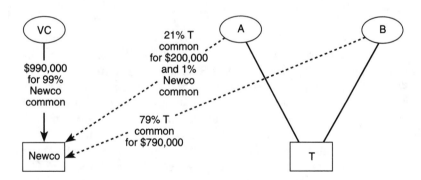

Although Newco's acquisition of T does not fall within Code §304, Newco can *not* make a Code §338 or §338(h)(10) election with respect to T because Newco "purchased" only 79% of T's stock (from B) and received the remaining 21% of T's stock (from A) in a Code §351 transaction, albeit a Code §351 transaction in which the consideration was 95% cash ($200,000 cash out of $210,000 total consideration = 95% cash) and in which A very likely recognized 100% of the gain inherent in his T stock under the Code §351(b) boot rules (unless A's basis in his T stock was less than $10,000).

In Example 5, Newco may be able to qualify for a Code §338 or §338(h)(10) election by restructuring the transaction in one of two ways: *One alternative* is for Newco to purchase 100% of A's T stock for $210,000 cash and, in an apparently separate transaction, for Newco to sell A one share of Newco's stock (constituting 1% of Newco's stock) for cash. If the two transactions are respected as separate, Newco would have "purchased" 100% of T's stock, i.e., 79% from B and 21% from A.

A second alternative is for Newco to purchase (in addition to B's 79 T shares) 20 T shares from A (i.e., 20% of T's stock) for $200,000 cash and, in an apparently separate transaction, for Newco to acquire A's remaining one T share (i.e., 1% of T's stock) in a Code §351 transaction in exchange for one share of Newco's stock (constituting 1% of Newco's stock). If the two transactions are respected as separate, Newco would have "purchased" 99% of T's stock (79% from B and 20% from A) and acquired the remaining 1% from A in a Code §351 transaction.

Whether it is possible to separate the Code §351 aspect from the sale aspect of the transaction by one or both of the alternatives described above is discussed in ¶1402.1.2(2).

The parties might enhance their prospects for making a Code §338 or §338(h)(10) election by other techniques:

(a) **Avoiding Code §351.** Newco could issue convertible debentures to A rather than issuing Newco stock to A, so long as the convertible debentures are treated as debt rather than equity for tax purposes. See ¶¶1302 and 1303. In this manner A will not be a participant in a Code §351 exchange at all.

(b) **Minimizing Code §351 transfer.** Newco's acquisition of T could be carried out in part by Newco and in part by its wholly owned subsidiary S. S could purchase for cash at least 80% (by vote and value) of T's stock. Newco could acquire a lesser portion of T's stock in a Code §351 exchange for Newco stock. Using the facts of Example 5, S could purchase for cash B's 79 T shares and 20 of A's T shares, and *Newco* could acquire A's one remaining T share in exchange for Newco stock (or better yet, for a Newco convertible debenture). Such an arrangement must be carefully structured to minimize the risk that it would be treated as an integrated Code §351 transaction.

For a further discussion of the Code §351 trap and possible solutions, see ¶405.1.2.2 and ¶405.1.2.3.

(5) Possible liquidation of T. If Newco liquidates T (or merges T *upstream* into Newco) after the LBO, the LBO still will be taxed as described in (1) through (4) above unless (a) Newco's acquisition of T's stock is not a QSP and (b) the liquidation (or upstream merger) occurs so quickly after the LBO that Newco is treated as having directly purchased T's assets under the step transaction analysis described in ¶208.3. If Newco's acquisition of T's stock is a QSP, IRS will not apply the step transaction doctrine to T's liquidation. See Rev. Rul. 90-95, 1990-2

C.B. 67, discussed in ¶¶208 and 608.3.6, unless (perhaps) sufficient Newco stock is delivered to T's former shareholders to satisfy COI (generally when at least 40% of the consideration to T's former shareholders is Newco stock—¶610.2) in which event, e.g., T's upstream merger into Newco may be found an integrated "A" reorganization and Newco's "first step" acquisition of T stock disregarded as a QSP. See ¶608.5.2 discussing Rev. Rul. 2001-46, 2001-2 C.B. 321.

Regulatory Update

As this edition went to press, IRS/Treasury commendably announced that for stock acquisitions occurring on or after 7/9/03 in which P's first step acquisition of all or part of T's stock independently viewed constitutes a QSP, a Code §338(h)(10) election trumps a pre-planned second step T-P (or T-S) merger, i.e., when there is a timely Code §338(h)(10) election the first step QSP is not stepped together with the subsequent merger and treated as part of a multi-step integrated acquisitive reorganization. Temp. Reg. §1.338(h)(10)-1T(c), (e) examples (11)-(14) published 7/9/03.

---

(6)   Possible merger of Newco into T. If Newco merges *downstream* into T so quickly after the LBO that the step transaction doctrine may apply, the transaction may be taxed as described in ¶1402.1.1, i.e., as if Newco were a transitory corporation that directly merged into T. Hence, no Code §338 or §338(h)(10) election would be permissible, and T's old shareholders would be tested directly under Code §302 rather than through Code §304 for dividend treatment (after 2002 taxed at a 15% top individual rate, but without basis offset and without CL offset) versus sale CG treatment (with basis offset).

(7)   T assumption of Newco acquisition debt. In some transactions, T may assume some or all of Newco's third-party acquisition debt immediately after Newco's acquisition of T. Alternatively, Newco may pay some of the acquisition price by delivering Newco notes that T assumes and repays with T-level borrowings immediately after Newco acquires T. These arrangements may be used either to give the third-party lenders creditor status directly at the T level and/or to cause T to incur directly the interest expense related to the acquisition debt (which may be important in states that do not permit the filing of a consolidated tax return).

If T's post-acquisition assumption of Newco's acquisition indebtedness is prearranged, then the acquisition proceeds (to the extent T assumes Newco's debt) are likely to be viewed as having been supplied by T, rather than by Newco.[31] Indeed, this view may prevail whenever T assumes Newco acquisition debt shortly after Newco acquires T (even if not pursuant to a prearranged plan to which all the

---

[31] Cf. Waterman Steamship Corp. v. Commissioner, 430 F.2d 1185, 70-2 U.S.T.C. ¶9514 (5th Cir. 1970), *cert. denied*, 401 U.S. 939 (1971).

parties are privy).[32] In any case where T is treated as having supplied the acquisition debt, the T shareholders' tax consequences should be determined under the rules described in ¶1402.1.3, i.e., as if part of the acquisition debt had been incurred at the T level.

¶1402.1.3 Parent-Subsidiary Approach with Part of Borrowing at Subsidiary Level

This approach, like the approach discussed in ¶1402.1.2, uses a taxable reverse subsidiary merger, except that New Sub directly borrows part of the money needed to acquire T:

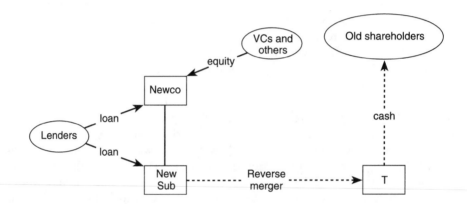

For tax purposes, (1) to the extent New Sub borrows money to pay off T's old shareholders (so that T is liable for the debt after the merger of New Sub into T), the transaction is treated as T's redemption of its stock, and (2) to the extent Newco borrows money (so that T is not liable for the debt after the merger) or Newco raises equity capital to pay off T's old shareholders, the transaction is treated as Newco's acquisition of T stock by purchase or (depending on the application of Code §§304 and 351) by a contribution to Newco's capital.[33]

(1) Application of Code §302 to T's redemption of its stock. To the extent the proceeds are attributable to New Sub's borrowing, the transaction is treated as *T's redemption* of its stock,[34] and Code §302 applies in determining whether T's old shareholders are subject to dividend (after 2002 taxed at a 15% top individual rate, but without basis offset or CL offset) or sale CG treatment with respect to the cash they receive. See ¶1402.1.1. For purposes of Code §302, an old T shareholder is

---

[32] See generally ¶1402.2.

[33] Rev. Rul. 79-273, 1979-2 C.B. 125; Rev. Rul. 78-250, 1978-1 C.B. 83; Rev. Rul. 73-427, 1973-2 C.B. 301. See ¶¶202 and 903.2.

[34] IRS Technical Advice Memorandum 9123002 (holding 1) (2/14/91).

treated as owning a pro rata share of the T stock owned (after the merger) by Newco only if the shareholder and the shareholder's Code §318 attributees own *50% or more* of Newco's stock by value.[35]

(2)   Tax treatment of Newco's acquisition of T stock: Code §§1001, 304, 351. To the extent the proceeds are attributable to Newco's borrowing and equity financing, the transaction is treated as an acquisition of T stock by Newco, and T's old shareholders are treated as having *sold* their T shares to Newco in a Code §1001 exchange (with the shareholders allowed basis offset and recognizing CG and Newco taking a cost basis in the T stock), unless one of the following two exceptions applies:

First, as discussed in ¶1402.1.2(1), Code §304 will apply if Mgmt and/or other old T shareholders (the "Group") who owned in the aggregate 50% or more (by vote or by value) of *T's* stock before the reverse subsidiary merger also own 50% or more (by vote or by value) of *Newco's* stock after the merger, taking into account direct stock ownership as well as constructive ownership under the Code §318 attribution rules (as expanded by Code §304(c)(3)). To the extent Code §304 applies, cash received by an old T shareholder that would otherwise be treated as purchase proceeds from Newco is treated as received in redemption of *Newco's* stock. In determining whether the proceeds attributable to such deemed redemption give rise to a Code §§301-302(d) distribution (after 2002 taxed at a 15% top individual rate, but without basis offset or CL offset) or sale CG, the Code §302(b) tests apply with reference to the shareholder's ownership of *T* stock. For this purpose, Code §304 applies tougher Code §318 attribution rules than those applied in (1) above, including a rule that treats a Newco shareholder as owning that percentage of Newco's T stock equal to the percentage by value of Newco's stock owned by such shareholder (even if the shareholder and the shareholder's Code §318 attributees own less than 50% of Newco's stock).[36] To the extent the distribution received by a shareholder is treated as a Code §§301-302(d) distribution, the shareholder is treated as having transferred its T stock to Newco in a transaction to which Code §351 applies in exchange for newly-issued Newco stock, followed by Newco's redemption of such newly-issued shares.

Second, whether or not Code §304 applies, when an old T shareholder purchases Newco stock, so that the shareholder both receives cash from T in exchange for T stock in the merger and contributes cash to Newco in exchange for Newco stock, the two transactions may be treated as integrated steps of a single Code §351 transaction, with the consequences discussed in ¶¶1402.1.2(2) and 1402.1.2(3).

---

[35] Code §§302(c) and 318(a)(2)(C).
[36] Code §§304(b)(1) and 318(a)(2)(C).

EXAMPLE 1

T's stock is owned as follows:

	Percentage	Basis	FV
A	33.3%	$300,000	$2 million
B	33.3	300,000	2 million
C	33.3	300,000	2 million
Total	100.0%	$900,000	$6 million

A, B and C are not related to each other or to VC. VC forms Newco, along with A and B, each acquiring Newco's stock as follows:

	Percentage	Cash Contributed
VC	49%	$ 490,000
A	41	410,000
B	10	100,000
Total	100%	$1,000,000

So far the facts of this example are the same as Example 2 in ¶1402.1.2(3).

Newco borrows $2 million. Newco forms S and contributes $3 million ($1 million of equity received from VC, A and B *plus* $2 million borrowing) to S in exchange for S's stock. S borrows an additional $3 million.

S merges into T, with T's shareholders receiving $6 million in exchange for their T stock.

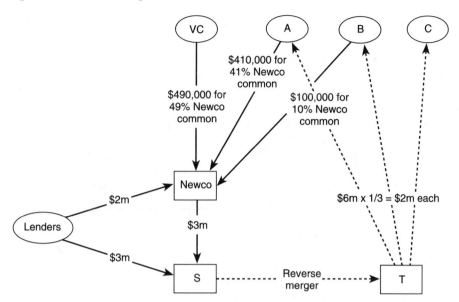

For tax purposes, S is disregarded as transitory. The $3 million borrowed by S is treated as borrowed by T and distributed to its shareholders in redemption of one-half of their T stock, while the $2 million borrowed by Newco plus the $1 million of Newco equity is treated as payment by Newco for one-half of T's stock. Thus, each of T's three shareholders is treated as receiving one-half of his proceeds from T and one-half from Newco.

A's Tax Treatment

As to A, the transaction may be viewed in either of two ways for tax purposes. *First*, A's purchase of 41% of Newco's stock for $410,000 may be viewed as separate from Newco's acquisition of A's 33.3% of T's stock for $2 million. Under this view, A is treated as having received $1 million from T in redemption of one-half of A's T stock under Code §302 and $1 million from Newco to purchase the other one-half of A's T stock.

The tax treatment of the $1 million of redemption proceeds from T is determined under Code §302. Because A owns less than 50% of Newco's stock by value, Newco's ownership of T stock is *not* attributed to A for Code §302 purposes. Hence, A's percentage interest in T was 33.3% before the transaction and zero after the transaction for purposes of Code §302, so that T's redemption of one-half of A's T stock completely terminates A's interest in T under Code §302(b)(3). Thus, A recognizes $850,000 of CG ($1 million proceeds *less* one-half of A's $300,000 T stock basis) rather than a $1 million Code §301-302(d) distribution.

The tax treatment of the $1 million that A received from Newco in exchange for the other one-half of A's T stock is determined under Code §304 (rather than Code §1001), because A and B together owned 50% or more of

T's stock (by vote or by value) before the acquisition and own 50% or more of Newco's stock (by vote or by value) after the acquisition. Thus, A is treated as receiving $1 million in redemption of A's *Newco* stock. In a Code §304 transaction, the Code §302(b) tests apply with reference to A's ownership of T stock before and after the deemed redemption. For this purpose, A is treated as owning 41% of T after the acquisition by virtue of owning 41% (by value) of Newco, T's 100% parent. Because A's percentage interest in T has not declined substantially (and indeed has increased from 33% to 41%), the deemed redemption fails the Code §302(b) tests and so results in a Code §301-302(d) distribution. Thus the $1 million that A is deemed to receive from Newco is taxable after 2002 as dividend income (15% top individual rate, but no basis or CL offset) to the extent of Newco's and T's combined E&P. If the proceeds exceed their combined E&P, the excess is treated first as a tax-free recovery of A's basis in the portion of A's Newco stock subject to the Code §304 redemption, until such basis is reduced to zero, and then as Code §301(c)(3) CG.[37]

After the acquisition, A's basis in his 41% of Newco's stock is $560,000 (i.e., the one-half of A's $300,000 historical basis in T stock not offset against his proceeds *plus* the $410,000 cash that A contributed to Newco), reduced by any amount treated as a return of basis pursuant to the preceding sentence.

Newco's basis in A's T stock is $150,000 (i.e., A's historic basis in the one-half of his T stock treated under Code §304(a) as contributed to Newco's capital in a Code §351 transaction), *plus* (if A's Code §304 redemption proceeds exceed the amount of Newco's and T's combined E&P and A's Newco stock basis allocable to the distribution) the amount of Code §301(c)(3) gain recognized by A on the Code §304 redemption.[38]

The *second* (and more likely) view of the transaction is that A's purchase of 41% of Newco's stock is stepped together with A's sale of 33.3% of T's stock to Newco. In this case A is treated (1) as having one-half of his T stock redeemed by T for $1 million cash under Code §302 and (2) as having transferred the other one-half of his T stock to Newco in exchange for 41% of Newco's stock (FV $410,000) plus $590,000 net cash (i.e., the $1 million cash that A received from Newco less the $410,000 of cash that A contributed to Newco).

This approach does not alter the taxation of the $1 million treated as redemption proceeds from T, which still results in $850,000 of CG to A ($1 million proceeds *less* one-half of A's $300,000 historic T stock basis) under Code §302(a).

However, because Code §304 applies, A's exchange of the other one-half of his T stock for 41% of Newco's stock plus $590,000 cash is bifurcated

---

[37] The amount of A's available Newco stock basis for this purpose is not entirely clear. It appears that A can recover only 50% ($150,000) of his $300,000 historic T stock basis because only 50% of A's T stock is treated under Code §304(a)(1) as contributed to Newco's capital in a Code §351 transaction. But since Code §304 results in a deemed redemption of A's Newco stock, we believe that A's $410,000 capital contribution to Newco can also be recovered in full. Compare the treatment of A in ¶1402.1.2 Example 2.

[38] See Code §362(a).

under Code §304(b)(3)(A). The exchange of T stock with an FV of $410,000 for $410,000 FV of Newco stock is tax free under Code §351. The exchange of $590,000 FV of T stock for $590,000 cash is treated as a Code §304 redemption. As described above, for Code §304 purposes A's proceeds do not qualify for exchange treatment under Code §302. A thus recognizes $590,000 dividend income under Code §§301-302(d), assuming that Newco and T have sufficient combined E&P, taxed post-2002 at a 15% top individual rate, but without basis or CL offset. See Code §1(h)(11) and ¶108.

After the acquisition, A's basis in his 41% of Newco's stock is $150,000 (the one-half of A's $300,000 historical basis in T stock not offset against his proceeds), less any return of basis in the Code §304 redemption (i.e., if Newco and T have insufficient combined E&P).

Newco's basis in A's T stock is again $150,000 (i.e., A's historic basis in the one-half of his T stock treated as contributed to Newco's capital under Code §§351 and 304), *plus* any Code §301(c)(3) gain recognized by A on the Code §304 redemption.

In short, under these facts, when Code §304 results in a dividend to A, viewing A's purchase of Newco stock and A's "sale" of T stock to Newco as an integrated transaction rather than as separate transactions reduces A's dividend and A's basis in Newco's stock (but *not* Newco's basis in the acquired T stock) by the amount of A's cash contribution to Newco (here, $410,000), as in Example 2 in ¶1402.1.2.

B's Tax Treatment

The transaction can be viewed in the same two ways for B as for A. However, as described below, B's tax treatment differs from A's under Code §304, because the substantial decline in B's percentage interest in T results in sale CG rather than a Code §301 dividend.

First, B's purchase of 10% of Newco's stock for $100,000 may be viewed as separate from Newco's purchase of B's 33.3% of T's stock for $2 million. Under this view, B is treated (1) as having received $1 million from T in redemption of one-half of B's T stock under Code §302, resulting in $850,000 of CG for B just as for A, and (2) as having received $1 million from Newco in exchange for the other one-half of B's T stock, the tax treatment of which is determined under Code §304.

However, B (unlike A) has CG sale treatment on this latter $1 million of redemption proceeds deemed received from Newco under Code §304. In applying the Code §302(b) tests for purposes of Code §304, B is treated as owning 10% of T after the transaction, because B then owns 10% (by value) of Newco, T's 100% parent. Because B's percentage ownership of T has declined by more than 20% (from 33.3% to 10%, a 70% decline), B's Code §304 redemption (unlike A's) is substantially disproportionate under Code §302(b)(2). Hence, B recognizes $850,000 of CG on the deemed Code §304 redemption of one-half of B's T stock for $1 million.

B's Newco stock basis is $100,000 (the cash that B contributed to Newco to purchase the stock). Newco's basis in B's T stock is a $1 million cost basis.

The *second* (and more likely) view of the transaction is that B's purchase of 10% of Newco's stock is stepped together with B's sale of 33.3% of T's stock to Newco. In this case B is treated (a) as having one-half of his T stock redeemed by T for $1 million cash, resulting in an $850,000 CG under Code §302(a), and (b) as having transferred the other one-half of his T stock to Newco in exchange for 10% of Newco's stock (FV $100,000) plus $900,000 cash (i.e., the $1 million cash that B received from Newco less the $100,000 cash that B contributed to Newco).

As described above, Code §304(b)(3)(A) bifurcates the portion of the transaction described in (b) immediately above: Code §351 applies to the extent B exchanged T stock for Newco stock of equal value, and Code §304 applies to the extent B exchanged T stock for cash. Thus, B is treated as exchanging T stock with a $100,000 FV tax free for 10% of Newco's stock (FV $100,000) under Code §351; and B is treated as receiving $900,000 cash in a Code §304 redemption with respect to B's remaining T stock. Because B's percentage interest in T has declined by more than 20%, as discussed above, the deemed redemption gives rise to sale CG rather than a Code §§301-302(d) distribution.

B's $150,000 historic basis in the one-half of his T stock covered by this Code §§351-304 transaction is allocated $15,000 to the $100,000 FV of T stock exchanged pursuant to Code §351 ($150,000 historic basis × $100,000 FV of T stock contributed to Newco ÷ $1 million FV of aggregate T stock covered by the Code §§351-304 transaction) and $135,000 to the $900,000 FV of T stock covered by Code §304 ($150,000 historic basis × $900,000 FV of T stock covered by Code §304 ÷ $1 million FV of aggregate T stock covered by the transaction).

Hence, B recognizes $765,000 of CG in respect of the Code §351-304 transaction ($900,000 cash *less* $135,000 basis allocated to T stock covered by Code §304), and B's basis in his 10% of Newco stock is $15,000 (i.e., B's basis allocated to the T stock covered by Code §351).

Newco's basis in B's T stock is $915,000 (i.e., B's $900,000 cost basis in the portion treated as redeemed under Code §304, plus B's $15,000 historic stock basis in the T stock treated as contributed to Newco under Code §351).

In short, under these facts, where Code §304 results in CG sale treatment to B, viewing B's purchase of Newco stock and B's sale of T stock as an integrated transaction rather than as separate transactions reduces B's CG (as well as B's Newco stock basis and Newco's basis in the T stock acquired from B) by the excess of B's cash contribution to Newco ($100,000) over the portion of B's historic T stock basis allocable to the T stock subject to Code §351 treatment ($15,000), or by $85,000, as in Example 2 in ¶1402.1.2.

C's Tax Treatment

C's tax treatment is different from A's and B's. C owns no Newco stock and therefore is *not* subject to Code §351 or the Code §304 deemed redemption rules. Therefore, C recognizes $850,000 of CG under Code §302(a) on the $1 million redemption proceeds from T and $850,000 of CG under Code §1001 on the $1 million sales proceeds from Newco, i.e., total CG of $1.7 million.

Newco's basis in C's T stock is $1 million (i.e., the purchase price Newco paid to C for the one-half of C's T stock treated as purchased by Newco).

EXAMPLE 2

Same as Example 1 except that B does *not* purchase any Newco stock, so that Newco is owned 59% by VC and 41% by A.

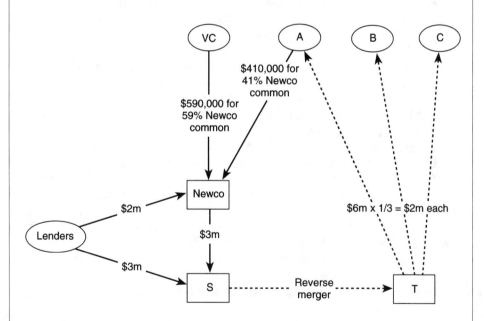

The transaction is not covered by Code §304 because A is the only person owning stock of both T and Newco, and A owned only 33.3% of T's stock before the merger and 41% of Newco's stock after the merger.

B and C are each taxed the same as C is taxed in Example 1, i.e., the one-half of each one's T stock treated as redeemed by T under Code §302 results in $850,000 of Code §302(a) CG, and the other one-half of each one's T stock treated as sold to Newco results in $850,000 of Code §1001 CG.

Newco has an aggregate $2 million cost basis in the T stock acquired from B and C (i.e., Newco's purchase price—$1 million each—for the one-half of B's and C's stock treated as purchased by Newco).

A's tax treatment can be viewed in either of two ways for tax purposes. *First*, if A's purchase of 41% of Newco's stock is viewed as separate from Newco's purchase of A's 33.3% of T's stock, A is taxed the same as B and C, i.e., A recognizes $850,000 of CG on the Code §302 redemption of one-half of A's T stock and $850,000 of CG on the sale to Newco of the other one-half of A's T stock. In this case A takes a $410,000 cost basis in his 41% of Newco's stock, and Newco takes a $1 million cost basis in A's T stock.

The *second* (and more likely) view of the transaction is that A's purchase of 41% of Newco's stock is stepped together with A's sale of T stock to Newco. In this case A is treated (a) as having one-half of his T stock redeemed by T for $1 million cash in a substantially disproportionate redemption under Code §302, again resulting in $850,000 of CG, and (b) as having made a Code §351 contribution of the other one-half of A's T stock to Newco in exchange for 41% of Newco's stock (FV $410,000) and $590,000 cash (i.e., the $1 million cash that A received from Newco less the $410,000 cash that A contributed to Newco). Because Code §304 does not apply, the portion of the transaction described in (b) results in $590,000 of CG under Code §351 (i.e., $850,000 of *realized* gain, *recognized* only to the extent of the $590,000 cash boot).

A's basis in his 41% of Newco's stock would then be $150,000 (A's historic basis in the portion of T's stock subject to Code §351) under Code §358.

Newco takes a $740,000 basis, determined under Code §362(a), in the one-half of A's T stock subject to Code §351 (i.e., A's $150,000 historic basis plus A's $590,000 recognized gain).

As in Examples 1 and 3 in ¶1402.1.2, where Code §304 similarly is inapplicable, viewing A's purchase of Newco stock and A's "sale" of T stock to Newco as an integrated Code §351 transaction rather than as separate transactions reduces A's recognized gain (as well as A's Newco stock basis and Newco's basis in the T stock acquired from A) by the excess, if any, of A's realized gain in the Code §351 exchange (here, $850,000) over A's Code §351 boot (here, $590,000), or by $260,000. In contrast, if under different facts A's realized gain did *not* exceed the amount of boot (and assuming Code §304 did not apply), the CG consequences to A and the basis consequences to A and Newco would be identical under the two views.

See ¶1402.1.5 for a discussion of the Code §302 implications where the new shareholders financing the LBO acquire preferred stock (rather than common stock) but T's old shareholders retain some common stock.

(3) Possible Code §338 or §338(h)(10) election. If the LBO is structured in this manner, Newco can make a Code §338 election or, if available (e.g., T is an SCo), a Code §338(h)(10) election to step up the basis of T's assets, unless such a

Code §338 or §338(h)(10) election is prevented either by Code §304 or by Code §351. See generally ¶¶1402.1.2(4) and 405.1.

(4)   Possible T liquidation or merger. For possible changes in tax treatment if Newco liquidates T (or merges T upstream into Newco) too quickly or if Newco merges downstream into T too quickly, see ¶1402.1.2(5) and (6).

(5)   T assumption of portion of Newco acquisition debt. Where T assumes a portion of Newco's acquisition debt shortly after Newco's acquisition of T, the T shareholders may be taxed under the rules described above. See ¶1402.1.2(7).

¶1402.1.4   Part Purchase/Part Redemption

Under this approach, Newco purchases part of T's stock and T redeems the remainder of its stock.

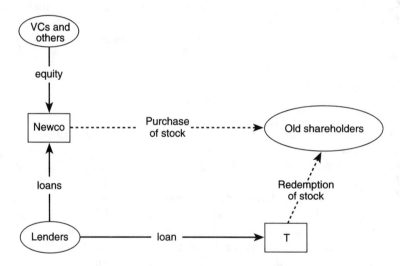

In this structure, Newco is formed and obtains debt and equity financing to purchase part of T's stock and T simultaneously borrows money to redeem the remainder of its stock, so that after the transaction Newco owns all of T's outstanding stock.

For tax purposes, the transaction is treated as if (1) Newco purchased from T's old shareholders the portion of T's stock acquired with money borrowed by Newco and money obtained by Newco as equity and (2) T redeemed the T stock acquired with T's cash on hand and money borrowed by T.[39]

The tax treatment is the same as in ¶1402.1.3.

---

[39] See Zenz v. Quinlivan, 213 F.2d 914, 54-2 U.S.T.C. ¶9445 (6th Cir. 1954).

¶1402.1.5   Use of Preferred Stock in LBOs: Code §302 Implications

In each of the LBO structures described in ¶¶1402.1.1, 1402.1.3 and 1402.1.4, a portion of the cash proceeds received by T's old shareholders was financed with borrowings for which T became liable, and hence was treated for tax purposes as paid to the old T shareholders in redemption of a portion of their T stock. As discussed in ¶1402.1.1(2), where a T shareholder retains an interest in T after VC's investment, in order to obtain CG sale treatment for his redemption proceeds—as distinguished from dividend treatment taxed after 2002 at a 15% top individual rate, but without basis offset or CL offset, see ¶108—the redemption must qualify as (a) a "substantially disproportionate" redemption under Code §302(b)(2) or (b) a redemption that reduces the percentage ownership interest of a de minimis shareholder under Rev. Rul. 76-385 or (c) otherwise "not essentially equivalent to a dividend" under the facts and circumstances test of Code §302(b)(1).

The prior discussion assumes that VC's equity investment is in common stock. Often, however, all or most of VC's equity investment will be in the form of preferred stock (typically, together with warrants or conversion rights to acquire common stock). As discussed below, the form of VC's equity investment may affect the ability of T's old shareholders to obtain CG treatment for their redemption proceeds.

EXAMPLE 1

A owns all of T's stock, FV $6 million. VC invests $1 million in T in exchange for (a) non-participating, non-voting, redeemable T preferred stock with a $1 million liquidation value and (b) a warrant to purchase 80% of T's common stock for $80,000 (which permits VC to surrender $80,000 face amount of T straight preferred stock in payment of the warrant exercise price). T borrows $5 million from lenders. T distributes $5.98 million proceeds from the borrowing and VC's investment to A in redemption of most of A's T shares. Following the redemption, A owns 100% of T's issued and outstanding common shares (but A owns only 20% of the fully diluted common shares, assuming exercise of VC's warrant).

IRS takes the position that VC's warrant is disregarded for purposes of applying Code §302 to A's redemption.[40] Under IRS's position, A would be treated as experiencing no reduction in his percentage ownership of T common stock and as continuing to be entitled to 100% of T's E&P (other than the E&P necessary to pay VC's non-participating preferred dividends). On these facts, IRS will likely assert that A's redemption does not qualify as "substantially disproportionate" under Code §302(b)(2) and that the redemp-

---

[40] Rev. Rul. 68-601, 1968-2 C.B. 124. The Sixth and Tenth Circuits have taken contrary positions regarding whether options held by persons other than the taxpayer should be disregarded under Code §302. Patterson v. U.S., 729 F.2d 1089 (6th Cir. 1984); Sorem v. Commissioner, 334 F.2d 275 (10th Cir. 1964).

tion is "essentially equivalent to a dividend" under Code §302(b)(1), taxed after 2002 at a 15% top individual rate, but without basis offset or CL offset. We believe this likely IRS position wrong, since VC will, in reality, capture most of T's future E&P through VC's ownership of T preferred stock and its future ownership of T common stock upon exercise of the T warrants.

EXAMPLE 2

Same as Example 1, except that VC invests its $1 million in T in exchange for (a) $920,000 liquidation value non-participating, non-voting, redeemable T preferred stock and (b) $80,000 liquidation value T preferred stock convertible into 80% of T's common stock, which votes on an as-if-converted basis but does *not* participate in liquidating and non-liquidating distributions on an as-if-converted basis.

As in Example 1, it appears IRS will assert that the T common stock that may be acquired by VC upon conversion of the T convertible preferred stock is disregarded for purposes of applying Code §302 to A's redemption. Moreover, IRS will likely take the position that the T convertible preferred stock does not, prior to conversion, qualify as common stock for purposes of Code §302.[41] Hence, IRS would treat A as experiencing no reduction in his percentage ownership of T common stock and as continuing to be entitled to 100% of T's E&P (other than the E&P necessary to pay non-participating preferred dividends).

As in Example 1, IRS will likely assert that A's redemption does not qualify as "substantially disproportionate" under Code §302(b)(2) and that the redemption is "essentially equivalent to a dividend" under Code §302(b)(1), taxed after 2002 at a 15% top individual rate, but without basis offset or CL offset. Also as in Example 1, we believe this likely IRS position wrong, since VC will, in reality, capture most of T's future E&P through its ownership of T preferred stock and its future ownership of T common stock upon exercise of its conversion right.

EXAMPLE 3

Same as Example 2, except that VC's T convertible preferred stock *does* participate in liquidating and non-liquidating distributions on an as-if-converted basis. That is, in addition to a fixed annual dividend, the T participating convertible preferred stock is entitled to receive (a) 80% of all residual non-liquidating distributions and (b) upon liquidation, the *greater* of its

---

[41] Cf. Reg. §1.305-5(a) (the determination of whether stock is "common" or "preferred" stock for purposes of Code §305 "shall be made without regard to any right to convert such stock into another class of stock of the corporation.")

liquidation value plus accrued dividends or 80% of all liquidating distributions after repayment of any debt and the non-participating T preferred stock.

We believe IRS should treat the T participating convertible preferred stock as T voting common stock for purposes of applying Code §302 to A's redemption. The character of stock as "preferred" or "common" is relevant in applying Code §§302, 305 and 306, all of which address the issue of whether transactions have the effect of, or create the potential for a future transaction which has the effect of, a dividend. For purposes of Code §305, regulations state that "the distinguishing feature of 'preferred stock' . . . is not its privileged position as such, but that such privileged position is limited and that such stock does not participate in corporate growth to any significant extent."[42] Similarly, several IRS rulings state that participation in corporate growth is the determinative factor in characterizing stock as preferred or common for purposes of Code §306.[43] Finally, the legislative history of Code §302(b)(2) describes a shareholder's common stock interest in a corporation as "his *participating* interest,"[44] suggesting that the participation analysis applied for purposes of Code §§305 and 306 should be applied for purposes of Code §302 as well.[45]

If VC's participating preferred does count as T common stock, A's redemption should qualify under Code §302(b)(2) because (1) his percentage ownership of both T voting and "common" stock after the transaction (20%) is less than 80% of his pre-merger percentage interest in T voting and common stock (100%) and (2) A's percentage ownership (20%) of T's total voting power after the transaction is less than 50%.

¶1402.2   IRS May Recharacterize—But Taxpayer May Be Bound by—Transaction Form

As discussed in ¶1402.1, where there is overlapping ownership between Newco and T, IRS may seek to recharacterize Newco's purchase of T stock as a transaction to which Code §304 or Code §351 applies. While IRS may recharacterize a transaction under the substance-over-form, step-transaction, and similar doctrines, a taxpayer is usually bound by the form of the transaction.

---

[42] See ¶1309.3.1.

[43] See Rev. Rul. 81-91, 1981-1 C.B. 123 (participating preferred stock treated as common stock); Rev. Rul. 79-163, 1979-1 C.B. 131 (non-participating common stock not treated as common stock); Rev. Rul. 76-387, 1976-2 C.B. 96 (non-voting common stock treated as common stock because of participation); Rev. Rul. 75-236, 1975-1 C.B. 106 (non-participating stock not treated as common stock); Gen. Couns. Mem. 37995 (6/29/79) (participating preferred stock treated as common stock).

[44] S. Rep. No. 1622, 83d Cong., 2d Sess. 234 (1954).

[45] See also Rev. Rul. 81-41, 1981-1 C.B. 121 (redemption of preferred stock qualifies under Code §302(b)(2) despite no reduction of percentage ownership in common stock where shareholder owns no common stock) and Gen. Couns. Mem. 38514 (9/26/80), each of which discusses the same Senate Report language. Rev. Rul. 81-41 makes reference to the "bailout" rationale used by the IRS in characterizing stock as preferred or common under Code §306.

Under the *Danielson*[46] rule, which has been adopted by the Third, Fifth, Sixth, Eleventh, Federal, and (by implication in an affirmance of a lower court decision) Second Circuits, a taxpayer may disavow the terms of a contract for tax purposes only by showing proof that would be admissible, in an action between the taxpayer and the other party to the contract, to (1) alter the terms of the agreement or (2) demonstrate that the agreement is unenforceable because of mistake, undue influence, fraud, or duress.[47] The Tax Court applies a somewhat more taxpayer-favorable rule permitting a taxpayer to show by "strong proof" that the form of a transaction should not be controlling for tax purposes. The other circuits have either, like the Tax Court, adopted a more flexible rule than *Danielson* (First, Seventh, and Ninth) or have not addressed the issue (Fourth, Eighth, and Tenth).[48]

In *Insilco*,[49] the Fifth Circuit applied the *Danielson* rule to prevent a corporation from disregarding the form (and the agreed-upon tax characterization) of the following acquisition transaction: Bigco owned 66% of T's stock, with the remaining 34% of T's stock held by the public.

Chart 1: Before transaction began

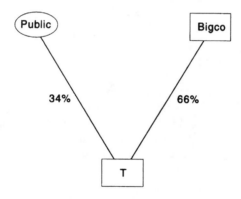

[46] Commissioner v. Danielson, 378 F.2d 771, 67-1 U.S.T.C. ¶9423 (3d Cir.), *cert. denied*, 389 U.S. 858 (1967).

[47] See Spector v. Commissioner, 641 F.2d 376, 81-1 U.S.T.C ¶9308 (5th Cir. 1981), *rev'g* 71 T.C. 1017 (1979); Schatten v. Commissioner, 746 F.2d 319, 84-2 U.S.T.C. ¶9965 (6th Cir. 1984), *aff'g per curiam* 563 F. Supp. 294, 83-1 U.S.T.C. ¶9406 (D.C. Tenn. 1983); Bradley v. United States, 730 F.2d 718, 84-1 U.S.T.C. ¶9413 (11th Cir. 1984), *aff'g unreported District Court case, cert. denied*; Proulx v. United States, 594 F.2d 832, 79-1 U.S.T.C. ¶9218 (Ct. Cl. 1979); In re Tax Refund Litigation, 766 F. Supp. 1248, 91-1 U.S.T.C. ¶50,183 (D.C.N.Y. 1991), *aff'd* 989 F.2d 1290, 93-1 U.S.T.C. ¶50,173 (2d Cir. 1993).

[48] Schmitz v. Commissioner, 51 T.C. 306 (1968), *aff'd sub nom.* Throndson v. Commissioner, 457 F.2d 1022, 72-1 U.S.T.C. ¶9333 (9th Cir. 1972); Harvey Radio Laboratories, Inc. v. Commissioner, 470 F.2d 118, 73-1 U.S.T.C. ¶9121 (1st Cir. 1972); Comdisco, Inc. v. United States, 756 F.2d 569, 85-1 U.S.T.C. ¶9245 (7th Cir. 1985); Cubic Corp. v. United States, 74-2 U.S.T.C. ¶9667 (D.C. Cal. 1974), *aff'd per curiam* 541 F.2d 829, 76-2 U.S.T.C. ¶9642 (9th Cir. 1976).

[49] Insilco Corporation v. United States, 53 F.3d 95, 95-1 U.S.T.C. ¶50,272 (5th Cir. 1995).

In a series of related transactions, Newco was formed, Newco acquired 100% of T's stock, the public shareholders were paid off in cash, partly from T and partly from Newco, and Bigco ended up with $75.1 million of cash and some Newco stock, as follows: First, T made a tender offer to the public to redeem its stock held by the public for $15.25 per share, which closed on 12/26/85.

Chart 2: 12/26/85 T tender offer to public shareholders

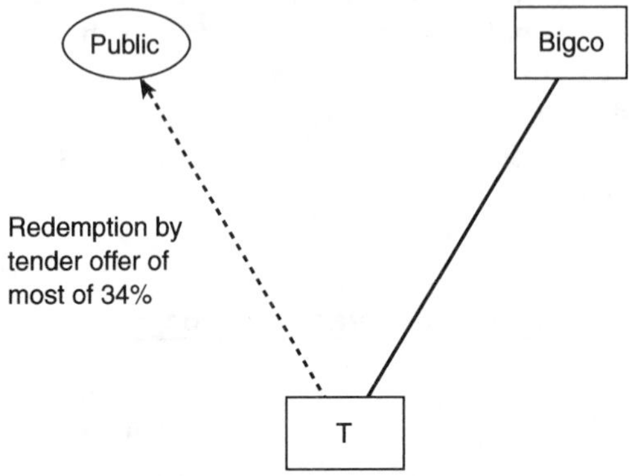

Second, on 12/31/85, several transactions occurred: (1) Bigco sold all of its T stock to Newco for $15.25 per share, a total of $96 million, (2) Newco acquired in a squeeze-out merger (for $15.25 per share) all of the public's remaining T stock not tendered, (3) Bigco purchased $20 million of Newco preferred stock and $900,000 of Newco common stock, which together represented more than 50% by value (but apparently less than 50% by vote) of Newco's outstanding stock, and (4) five other persons purchased the remainder of Newco's common stock for $6.2 million.

Chart 3: 12/31/85 Newco acquisition of T

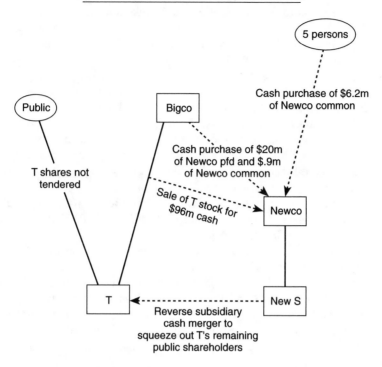

Chart 4: After transaction

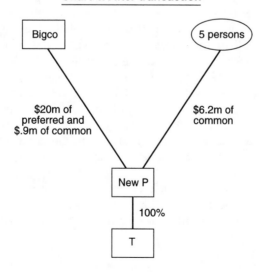

Newco treated its acquisition of T as a qualified stock purchase and made a §338 election. New P and Bigco intended the transaction to be treated as a stock purchase. Bigco was aware that New P planned to, and did, make a Code §338 election. Consistent with the parties' original intent, Bigco initially reported the transactions as a taxable sale of the T stock for cash and a separate purchase of Newco stock for cash. However, after Bigco filed for bankruptcy, Bigco filed an amended tax return unilaterally characterizing the transactions as an exchange of T stock for Newco stock and cash governed by Code §304 and §351.

The court held that Code §304 and §351 would apply only if Bigco were treated for tax purposes as exchanging T stock for Newco stock and that, having agreed to structure the transaction as a separate sale of T stock for cash and purchase of Newco stock for cash, Bigco could not unilaterally recharacterize the transaction as an exchange of T stock for Newco stock and cash.

Of course, the court recognized that IRS, if it had chosen to do so, could have invoked the step-transaction doctrine and applied Code §304 and §351, i.e., that IRS is not bound by the *Danielson* rule.

A taxpayer ("Taxpayer") intending to invoke the step-transaction doctrine can improve its chances of success by insuring that all parties to the transaction report consistently utilizing the step-transaction doctrine. Where none of the parties attempts to whipsaw IRS, IRS and the courts are less likely to invoke the *Insilco* case and more likely to approve Taxpayer's invocation of the step-transaction doctrine. Taxpayer would best protect itself if it binds the other parties to the transaction by contractual covenant to report consistently with Taxpayer's step-transaction approach.

IRS described the circumstances in which it would allow a taxpayer to affirmatively invoke the step-transaction doctrine in a 2002 field service advice.[50] P (a U.S. corporation) loaned funds to a foreign subsidiary (S). Interest on the loan was payable in S stock. P entered into a forward purchase agreement under which it was obligated to purchase S stock upon maturity of the loan for an amount equal to the loan's principal amount. IRS permitted P to disregard the form of the loan and treat the loan and forward purchase agreement for tax purposes as, in substance, an investment in S stock. The FSA lists four principles that must be satisfied by a taxpayer seeking to disavow the form of a transaction: "(1) the taxpayer must not be seeking to disavow its own tax return treatment for the transaction; (2) the taxpayer must show an honest and consistent respect for the substance of the transaction; (3) the taxpayer must not be unilaterally attempting to recast the transaction to obtain tax benefits with the perspective of hindsight; and (4) the taxpayer must not be unjustly enriched by [disavowing] the form of a transaction."[51]

A 1997 TAM provides another taxpayer-favorable example:[52] where IRS allowed Taxpayer to invoke the step-transaction doctrine so that a transaction that was, in form, a cash sale of T stock followed by a reinvestment of the proceeds in New

[50] IRS FSA 200206010 (2/8/02).

[51] FSA 200206010, citing Estate of Durkin v. Commissioner, 99 T.C. 561 (1992), and Taiyo Hawaii Co. v. Commissioner, 108 T.C. 590 (1997).

[52] IRS TAM 9708001 (10/14/96).

T would be treated as a tax-free reorganization. Although IRS did not specifically discuss the issue, it was apparent that none of the parties took an inconsistent position in an attempt to whipsaw IRS. In the 1997 TAM, A owned 50% of T's outstanding stock and wished to purchase the remaining 50% from B. B refused to sell his T stock. Hence, A caused certain investors with whom A was friendly to form New T and T merged into New T. Under the merger agreement, each share of T stock would be converted into the right to receive cash. After the merger agreement was entered into but before it was consummated, A contracted to reinvest in New T all of the cash he was to receive in the merger in exchange for 96% of New T's stock. On the merger date, (1) T merged into New T, (2) B received cash in exchange for his T stock pursuant to the merger agreement, and (3) A assigned to New T his right to receive cash in exchange for 96% of New T's stock.

IRS concluded that the transactions occurring on the merger date should be stepped together in determining whether the continuity of interest requirement for a reorganization was satisfied, because A and New T always intended A to receive New T stock, and the transactions would not have been consummated had A not received New T stock, in exchange for his T stock. Accordingly, IRS treated A as having exchanged his T stock solely for New T stock and held that the transactions qualified as a tax-free reorganization. The 1997 TAM did not discuss the potential application of the *Danielson* or *Insilco* cases.

¶1402.3   Additional Considerations

Described below are some of the additional tax and non-tax considerations that are relevant in choosing between the alternative LBO structures discussed at ¶1402.1 (and other variations).

¶1402.3.1   State Income Tax

In deciding whether the LBO structure should be designed to result in one corporation (as in ¶1402.1.1) or two corporations, i.e., a holding company and an operating company (as in ¶¶1402.1.2 through 1402.1.4), state income tax laws will frequently play a role. For example, in some states a parent and subsidiary are *not* permitted to file a consolidated return or are prevented from so doing if consolidation would achieve a state tax saving. Hence, in such a state, if Newco has borrowed substantial amounts while T earns the group's operating income, Newco's substantial interest expenses may not be offset against T's income for state tax purposes.

One possible partial solution to this problem—if a two corporation structure is desirable although state consolidated returns are prohibited—is for T to pay Newco a reasonable management fee. A second possible solution, where Newco is supplying new capital to T, is for Newco to loan part or all of such new capital to T with T paying reasonable interest to Newco. A third possible solution is for

T to assume a portion of Newco's acquisition debt, so long as Newco does not incur a significant state tax liability from T's assumption of its debt.

¶1402.3.2 T's Taxable Year

The form of the LBO structure may determine whether the acquisition causes T's taxable year to end. The LBO will not affect T's taxable year (i.e., T's taxable year will not end because of the LBO) if (1) the LBO is effectuated by a single corporation structure as in ¶1402.1.1, (2) no corporate shareholder acquires 80% or more of T's stock, and (3) T was not a member of Bigco's consolidated group before the LBO.

However, if a holding company structure is used as in ¶¶1402.1.2 through 1402.1.4, Newco and T typically will file a consolidated federal return. In this event, T will be treated as joining the Newco consolidated group, in which case T's taxable year will end on the acquisition date (see ¶211.2 as to whether it ends at the beginning or the end of the acquisition date) and T will then switch to Newco's taxable year (unless the transaction is a "reverse acquisition"[53]).

If a holding company structure is used as in ¶¶1402.1.2 through 1402.1.4, but Newco and T do not file a consolidated federal return, the LBO will not affect T's taxable year. If a holding company structure is used as in ¶¶1402.1.2 through 1402.1.4, but Newco merges *downstream* into T so quickly after the LBO that Newco is treated as a transitory corporation which merged directly into T (see ¶1402.1.2(6)), the transaction is treated as if a holding company structure had not been used but rather as if the LBO had been effectuated by a single corporation structure (as in ¶1402.1.1), and in that case the LBO would generally not affect T's taxable year, as discussed in the first paragraph of this section.

If T incurs a taxable loss for the period after the LBO, the timing for use of such loss turns on whether T's taxable year ended with the acquisition and whether the CERT rules apply. If T's taxable year was not ended by the acquisition and the CERT rules do not apply, the post-acquisition loss can be used to offset T's taxable income from the pre-acquisition portion of its taxable year and, to the extent an NOL is created, the NOL can be carried back either to T's three previous taxable years (for NOLs arising in taxable years beginning on or before 8/5/97) or to T's two previous years (for NOL's arising in taxable years beginning after 8/5/97). On the other hand, if T's taxable year was ended by the acquisition, the pre-acquisition short taxable year will be the first of the NOL carryback years. Moreover, losses attributable to *Newco* cannot be carried back to T's pre-acquisition years, but can be used only as carryovers to future years of the Newco-T group.[54] See ¶1206 regarding carryback of post-LBO NOLs, including a discussion of how the CERT rules can substantially eliminate the ability to carry back post-acquisition NOLs in the case of LBOs occurring after 8/2/89.

---

[53] If T's former shareholders acquire more than 50% of Newco's stock as a result of owning T's stock, the reverse acquisition rules would treat the T group as continuing, and hence T's taxable year would not end. See, e.g., Reg. §1.1502-75(d)(3) and §1.1502-1(f)(3).

[54] See Rev. Rul. 80-79, 1980-1 C.B. 191.

Frequently T's outstanding stock options are paid off at the time the LBO is consummated, thus creating a substantial tax deduction. Where T's taxable year ends with the LBO, it will often be important whether such stock option cancellation payments are deductible in the pre-acquisition or the post-acquisition taxable year. See the discussion of this subject at ¶1503.1.

EXAMPLE 1

A group of shareholders forms Newco, with no corporate shareholder owning as much as 80% of Newco. T is owned by another group of shareholders, with no corporate shareholder owning as much as 80% of T. On 6/30/90 Newco merges into T, with T's shareholders receiving cash and Newco's shareholders receiving T stock. Before the transaction T was a calendar year taxpayer.

The LBO does not affect T's taxable year, i.e., T will file a single tax return for calendar year 1990.

EXAMPLE 2

Same as Example 1 except that Newco's subsidiary New Sub merges into T, with T's old shareholders receiving cash and Newco receiving T stock so that after the LBO Newco owns 100% of T. Newco is on an 11/30 taxable year and elects to file a consolidated return with T.

The LBO ends T's taxable year on either 6/29 or 6/30/90 (see ¶211.2 as to whether T's year ends on 6/29 or 6/30) and T's taxable income thereafter through 11/30 is included in the Newco-T consolidated return for the year ending on 11/30/90.

EXAMPLE 3

Same as Example 2 except that Newco is a calendar year taxpayer. Same result as Example 2 except that T's taxable income after 6/29 or 6/30, and through 12/31/90, is included in the Newco consolidated return for the year ending on 12/31/90.

EXAMPLE 4

On 6/30/90 T is acquired in an LBO in a fashion that does not cause T's taxable year to end, e.g., in the manner described in Example 1. T's taxable income (loss) is as follows:

1987	$100
1988	$100
1989	$100
1990 pre-acquisition	$ 50
1990 post-acquisition	($400)

Assuming the CERT rules do not apply (see ¶1206), T will have a taxable loss of $350 ($400 less $50) for its 1990 taxable year. $300 of such loss may be carried back against T's taxable income for 1987, 1988, and 1989; the remaining $50 taxable loss may be carried forward. If the CERT rules apply, T might be precluded from carrying back all or part of its 1990 NOL to pre-1990 taxable years.

EXAMPLE 5

Same as Example 4 except that T is acquired in an LBO in a fashion that causes T's taxable year to end and T thereafter to file a consolidated return with Newco, e.g., in the manner described in Example 2.

Assuming that Newco has no taxable income (loss) for 1990, the Newco-T group will have a taxable loss of $400 for its short year from the LBO to 11/30/90 (the end of Newco's first taxable year after the LBO), all of which is attributable to T. Assuming the CERT rules do not apply (see ¶1206), $250 of this loss may be carried back against T's income for its prior three taxable years: 1988 ($100), 1989 ($100), and the short year ending approximately 6/30/90 ($50). Because 1987 is not one of T's prior three taxable years, none of the post-acquisition NOL can be carried back to offset T's 1987 taxable income of $100. The remaining $150 of the Newco-T taxable loss for the consolidated year ending 11/30/90 may be carried forward. If the CERT rules apply, T might be precluded from carrying back all or part of its $400 NOL to its short 1990 taxable year or to prior taxable years.

EXAMPLE 6

Same as Example 5 except that the entire $400 taxable loss for the Newco-T short year ended 11/30/90 is attributable to Newco (e.g., interest on acquisition debt incurred by Newco). None of the taxable loss may be carried back to T's pre-acquisition taxable years; the entire $400 taxable loss may be carried forward.

¶1402.3.3   Relative Priorities Among Creditors

Where a parent (Newco) and a subsidiary (T) each incurs part of the acquisition debt, Newco's debt is implicitly subordinated (by operation of law) to T's debt. Newco's creditors have no direct claim against T's assets. Their rights are limited to the rights they would have if they replaced Newco as T's sole shareholder. Thus Newco's creditors are entitled only to assets of T remaining after T has paid all of its own debts in full. Thus, a two corporation versus a one corporation structure has implications for various lenders as well as trade creditors. Moreover, as discussed in ¶1304, it is sometimes desirable for Code §279 purposes for the acquisition debt to be incurred partly by Newco and partly by T.

¶1402.3.4   Financial Statement Net Worth

It is sometimes desirable for the operating company to have more accounting net worth than Newco will have. By employing a two corporation structure, Newco can use part of its borrowings to make equity contributions to T, so that T's accounting net worth is greater than Newco's.

¶1402.3.5   Fraudulent Conveyance Considerations

As discussed in ¶1706, where Newco and/or T borrows money to pay off old T shareholders, there are sometimes fraudulent conveyance risks. In such a case, if Newco and/or T becomes insolvent, a bankruptcy court may require old T shareholders to return part or all of the consideration received in the LBO, may subordinate the LBO lenders, or may take other steps which defeat the parties' expectations, to the extent necessary to pay creditors with prior claims. The way in which the LBO transaction was structured may influence a court in deciding whether a fraudulent conveyance occurred.

¶1403   USING CODE §351 TO GIVE T SHAREHOLDERS (INCLUDING MGMT) TAX-FREE ROLLOVER OF T STOCK FOR NEWCO STOCK

In an LBO, some of T's shareholders (often Mgmt) frequently use part or all of their proceeds from selling T stock to Newco to make an investment in Newco stock. If these T shareholders first receive the proceeds from their T stock in cash, they must pay tax on their CG, leaving them with less after-tax proceeds to reinvest in Newco stock.

EXAMPLE 1

T's stock is owned as follows:

	Percentage	FV
Mgmt	10%	$ 1 million
Others	90%	9 million
Total	100%	$10 million

Mgmt's basis in their T stock (FV $1 million) is $100,000.

Newco is purchasing T's stock, through a reverse subsidiary merger of Newco's subsidiary (S) into T, for $10 million. Newco will be owned as follows:

	Percentage	Equity Contribution
VC	71%	$2.5 million
Mgmt	29%	1.0 million
Total	100%	$3.5 million

Newco plans to borrow $6.5 million and to use its $10 million ($3.5 million equity contribution plus $6.5 million borrowing) to acquire T.

If Mgmt receives $1 million from Newco as the purchase price for Mgmt's T stock, Mgmt will owe $135,000 of federal income tax (15% LTCG tax rate × ($1 million proceeds *less* $100,000 basis in Mgmt's old T stock)), leaving Mgmt with only $865,000 after tax (rather than $1 million) to invest in Newco.

However, if Mgmt contributes their T stock to Newco in kind, in exchange for Newco stock, the exchange should be tax free to Mgmt under Code §351, so long as (1) Mgmt's contribution of appreciated T stock to Newco (in exchange for Newco stock) is part of the same plan pursuant to which Newco is formed and its other shareholders contribute cash (in exchange for Newco stock), (2) Mgmt's exchange of T stock for Newco stock is properly documented and occurs sufficiently in advance of Newco's cash purchase of the remainder of T's stock, so that Mgmt is not in constructive receipt of the cash they would have received on a sale of their T stock, and (3) the Newco stock received in the exchange is not NQ Pfd.[1] See ¶604.3 for the definition of NQ Pfd and general rules relating thereto. See ¶902 and ¶903 regarding tax-free rollovers for T shareholders, including Mgmt.

¶1403 [1] See Rev. Rul. 84-71, 1984-1 C.B. 106.

EXAMPLE 2

Same as Example 1 except that the contracts executed by T's shareholders and Newco provide for Mgmt to contribute their 10% of T's stock (FV $1 million) to Newco in kind, in exchange for 29% of Newco's common stock the day before Newco is to buy the remaining 90% of T's stock for $9 million in cash. Mgmt's exchange of T stock for Newco common stock is scheduled to take place at approximately the same time as VC contributes $2.5 million cash to Newco in exchange for the other 71% of Newco's common stock and is part of the same Code §351 plan.

Mgmt will owe no tax on its Code §351 swap of appreciated T stock (FV $1 million) for Newco common stock (FV $1 million). Mgmt's basis in the Newco common stock will be $100,000, the same as their basis in the old T stock exchanged.

This Code §351 approach will not reach the desired result if Newco is buying T's *assets* and T is liquidating, since Newco would then recognize gain on T's Code §331 liquidation. Rather, this approach is designed for the situation (discussed above) where Newco is buying T's *stock* (either in a simple stock purchase or by a reverse subsidiary cash merger of Newco's transitory subsidiary into T).

Where Mgmt receives Newco stock subject to an SRF, see ¶604.1.6 as to the desirability of Mgmt filing a Code §83(b) election.

ISO shares. The above discussion of Mgmt's tax treatment assumes that none of Mgmt's T shares contributed to Newco in the Code §351 transaction was received on the exercise of an Incentive Stock Option (ISO) and held less than the requisite time period. As described in ¶1502.2, if an executive exercises an ISO and disposes of the ISO shares *either* less than one year after exercising the ISO *or* less than two years after the ISO grant, the ISO will be disqualified.[2] If the ISO is disqualified, the executive generally recognizes OI equal to the lesser of (1) the spread at exercise *or* (2) the gain realized on disposition of the stock.[3] A Code §351 transfer is a disqualifying disposition.[4]

If the FV of the ISO shares has increased between the ISO exercise and the Code §351 disposition, the executive recognizes OI equal to the spread at exercise (and T is entitled to an equal deduction), but Code §351 prevents recognition of the post-exercise appreciation, i.e., the rise in FV from exercise to the Code §351 exchange.

See the discussion in ¶903 for other qualifications and nuances.

---

[2] Code §422(a)(1).
[3] Code §§421(b) and 422(c)(2).
[4] Code §424(c).

Receipt of Newco preferred stock. Example 2 assumes that the Newco stock received by Mgmt is common stock and hence does not constitute NQ Pfd. Mgmt may, however, receive Newco preferred stock where all or a portion of its stake in T is to be rolled over into a strip of Newco preferred and common stock on the same terms as VC's cash investment. (In such case, Mgmt will often receive additional "incentive" equity in the form of additional Newco common stock (purchased for cash or T stock) and/or options to acquire Newco common stock.) If the Newco stock is NQ Pfd, its receipt by Mgmt will be treated as taxable boot under Code §351(g).

EXAMPLE 3

Executive is a member of T Mgmt and owns 10% of T's common stock (FV $100, basis $10). Executive contributes all of his T common stock to Newco in exchange for $25 of Newco common stock and Newco preferred stock with $75 liquidation preference (FV $75) (i.e., a "strip" of Newco common and preferred in the same 1 to 3 ratio of common to preferred purchased by VC for cash). The Newco preferred stock received by Executive and VC is redeemable on the seventh anniversary of Newco's acquisition of T.

The Newco preferred stock is NQ Pfd because it is mandatorily redeemable within 20 years of issuance. Executive recognizes $75 of gain on the exchange (the lesser of Executive's $90 gain—$100 FV less $10 basis—and the $75 FV of boot received in the form of NQ Pfd). See ¶604.3.2 for the possibility that Executive may report the gain attributable to Newco NQ Pfd on the installment method.

As illustrated by the following examples, Newco preferred stock is not NQ Pfd (and hence may be received by Mgmt tax-free in a Code §351 rollover) in a number of situations, including where:

- the Newco preferred stock is evergreen (i.e., not mandatorily redeemable, puttable, or callable) (see Example 4 below and ¶604.3.1.2);
- the Newco preferred stock participates in corporate growth to a significant extent (see Example 5 below and ¶604.3.1.1);
- the Newco preferred stock is transferred to Mgmt in connection with the performance of services for Newco and is redeemable or puttable only on an individual Mgmt holder's separation from Newco's service (see Example 6 below and ¶604.3.1.2);
- the Newco preferred stock is redeemable only on a Mgmt holder's death, disability, or mental incompetency, so long as neither Newco, T, nor any related corporation has a class of publicly traded stock (or will become publicly traded in a series of transactions) (see Example 7 and 8 below and ¶604.3.1.2 and ¶902.4).

See ¶604.3 for the definition of NQ Pfd and a general discussion of the rules relating thereto. See ¶901 for a general discussion of NQ Pfd and Code ¶351. See ¶902.4 for a general discussion of NQ Pfd in the context of a *National Starch* rollover for non-management T shareholders.

EXAMPLE 4

Same as Example 3, except that the Newco preferred stock received by Executive is evergreen (i.e., not mandatorily redeemable, puttable, or callable).

The Newco preferred stock is not NQ Pfd and Executive recognizes no gain on the exchange.

EXAMPLE 5

Same as Example 3, except that the Newco preferred stock received by Executive is convertible into Newco common stock (with the conversion price equal to the FV of Newco common stock at the time of Newco's acquisition of T) and participates (as if converted) with the Newco common stock in dividends (in excess of its preferred dividend) and liquidation proceeds (in excess of its liquidation preference).

The Newco preferred stock should be deemed to participate in corporate growth to a significant extent. Thus, the Newco preferred stock is not preferred stock for purposes of Code §351(g) and hence does not constitute NQ Pfd. See ¶604.3.1.1 for a discussion of what constitutes significant participation in corporate growth. Executive recognizes no gain on the exchange.

EXAMPLE 6

Same as Example 3, except that the Newco preferred stock is redeemable by Newco and puttable by Executive only on termination of Executive's employment by Newco.

If the Newco preferred stock is received by Executive in connection with Executive's performance of services for Newco in a Code §83 sense, Code §351(g)(2)(C)(i)(II)'s separation-from-service exception should apply and the Newco preferred should not be NQ Pfd. Thus, Executive should receive the Newco preferred tax-free.

There is a risk that Code §351(g)(2)(C)(i)(II)'s exception applies only where the Newco preferred stock "represents reasonable compensation" which will generally not be true where Executive receives Newco preferred stock in exchange for T stock. In such case, while the receipt of Newco preferred stock may be "in connection with the performance of services" by Executive, it will not represent "compensation" because Executive will have paid for the Newco preferred stock by surrendering T stock of equal FV. See ¶604.3.1.2 for a further discussion of the scope of Code §351(g)(2)(C)(i)(II)'s exception.

EXAMPLE 7

Same as Example 3, except that the Newco preferred stock is redeemable by Newco and puttable by Executive only on Executive's death or disability.

If neither Newco nor T nor any corporation related to Newco or T is publicly traded (or will become publicly traded in a series of transactions), the Newco preferred stock is not NQ Pfd and Executive recognizes no gain on the exchange. Code §351(g)(2)(C)(i)(I).

EXAMPLE 8

Same as Example 7, except that VC, a venture capital subsidiary of a publicly traded national bank, owns 51% of Newco.

VC's publicly traded parent is related to Newco and hence Executive may not rely on the Code §351(g)(2)(C)(i)(I)'s death/disability exception to NQ Pfd status.

According to the 1997 Act Bluebook, the treatment of Newco preferred stock that is redeemable on the holder's death but does not qualify for the Code §351(g)(2)(C)(i)(I) death/disability exception (e.g., because Newco's parent is publicly traded) turns on the holder's life expectancy at the time of the exchange.[5]

- If Executive's life expectancy is less than 20 years when the Newco preferred stock is issued, the Newco preferred stock will constitute NQ Pfd and be treated as taxable boot to Executive.
- If Executive's life expectancy is more than 20 years when the Newco preferred stock is issued, the Newco preferred stock apparently will not be NQ Pfd.

See ¶902.4 for a further discussion of the Code §351(g)(2)(C)(i)(I) exception.

---

[5] See 1997 Bluebook 211.

¶1404   CONSTRUCTIVE DIVIDEND RISK WHERE P (OR NEWCO) PLEDGES FOREIGN SUBSIDIARY STOCK OR CAUSES FOREIGN SUBSIDIARY TO GUARANTEE OR ASSUME P (OR NEWCO) DEBT

Where P (or Newco) is borrowing money to purchase T's stock or assets, P's lenders may require P to (1) cause its subsidiaries (including T and its subsidiaries) to guarantee directly, assume or pledge their assets to secure P's acquisition debt (see ¶1706 for a discussion of fraudulent conveyance issues which arise when a subsidiary guarantees a parent's debt) and/or (2) pledge the stock of its subsidiaries (including T and its subsidiaries) to secure such debt. Where P causes a *foreign* subsidiary to guarantee, assume or pledge its assets to secure P debt, or where P pledges its stock in a *foreign* subsidiary to secure P debt, P will (to the extent discussed below) be treated as having received a constructive dividend from the foreign subsidiary.

Code §956 provides that where a foreign subsidiary ("FS") is "a pledgor or guarantor" of an obligation of its U.S. parent, FS's interest in the obligation will be treated as an investment in U.S. property.[1] Any increase in FS's earnings invested in U.S. property is treated as a constructive dividend to the parent to the extent of FS's earnings and profits ("E&P") (except to the extent that such E&P was previously taxed to the parent).[2] Similarly, under general tax principles, FS's assumption of its parent's debt will be treated as a constructive dividend to the parent (to extent of FS's E&P) for U.S. tax purposes.[3]

FS will be treated as a "pledgor or guarantor" of P's debt if FS directly guarantees the debt or pledges its assets to secure the debt. In addition, regulations under Code §956 provide that *the U.S. parent's pledge of FS's stock* as security for a parent debt will be treated as *an indirect pledge of FS's assets* (and therefore subject to the above rules) if the parent pledges (after 9/2/80) two-thirds or more of FS's voting stock *and* enters into one or more negative covenants which effectively restrict FS's ability to dispose of its assets or incur debt outside the ordinary course of business.[4]

¶1404   [1] Code §956(c)(1)(C), (d) (as amended by the 1993 Act).

[2] Code §951(a)(1)(B).

[3] See, e.g., Reg. §1.301-1(m). Code §§951 and 956 will result in the taxation of such constructive dividends to P (or Newco) if and only if FS is a "controlled foreign corporation" ("CFC") in which P owns 10% or more of the voting stock. Code §§951(a), (b). In general, FS will be a CFC if P and other U.S. shareholders (not counting any U.S. shareholder that owns less than 10% of FS's stock by vote) own in the aggregate more than 50% of FS's stock by vote *or* by value. Code §957(a). The inclusion of income under Code §951 may entitle the parent to an indirect foreign tax credit (subject to the general limits on the use of foreign tax credits) for foreign taxes paid on the earnings deemed repatriated. See Code §§902, 904, and 960.

[4] Reg. §1.956-2(c). The Tax Court held in Ludwig v. Commissioner, 68 T.C. 979 (1977), *nonacq.*, 1978-2 C.B. 4, that a pledge of FS's stock did *not* cause FS to be treated as a pledgor or guarantor of its parent's debt. However, at the time of the transaction considered in the *Ludwig* case, the Code §956 regulations did *not* cover this type of "indirect pledge" of FS's assets. The regulations were subsequently amended to provide that a pledge of FS's stock will, in the circumstances described in

If P wishes to avoid constructive dividend income from its foreign subsidiaries under the above rules, it must not allow its foreign subsidiaries to guarantee directly, assume or pledge their assets to secure any P debt. In addition, any pledges of the stock of a foreign subsidiary to secure P debt should either (1) involve less than two-thirds of the subsidiary's voting stock or (2) not contain any negative covenants of the type described above.

¶1405   CARRYBACK OF POST-ACQUISITION NOL AND SURVIVAL OF PRE-ACQUISITION NOL AND OTHER TAX ATTRIBUTES

See ¶1206 for a discussion of the impact of the structure and financing of an LBO on the ability to carry back T's *post*-acquisition NOLs (which may arise from the substantial interest deductions generated by the acquisition debt or from a downturn in business) to recover pre-acquisition taxes paid by T. Where T is acquired after 8/2/89, the CERT limitation of Code §172(b)(1)(E) and (h) (added by the 1989 Act) substantially eliminates Newco's (or P's) ability to carry back a post-acquisition T NOL produced by interest deductions on acquisition debt to T's pre-acquisition years. In addition, the CERT limitation may limit P's ability to carry its post-acquisition NOL to its own pre-acquisition years. See ¶1206.1.

In an LBO or any other acquisition, if T (or P) has a *pre*-acquisition NOL or some other valuable tax attribute (such as a net CL or excess foreign tax credits) that P or Newco wishes to preserve, the creation and restructuring of debt and equity interests in connection with the acquisition should be planned to maximize the future availability of the tax attribute. See generally Chapter 12, including ¶1205.2 (ability to file consolidated returns) and ¶1208.1.1 (interests treated as "stock" for purposes of Code §382).

¶1406   USE OF EMPLOYEE STOCK OWNERSHIP PLAN

There are a number of tax benefits that can be obtained if all or a portion of T's stock is purchased by an employee stock ownership plan (ESOP).

One method for using an ESOP in an LBO of T is for Newco to buy part of T's stock while a newly formed ESOP buys the remainder of T's stock using money borrowed from a bank or other lender. Normally, T will guarantee repayment of the loan and T will make tax-deductible contributions to the ESOP over a series of years, which the ESOP then uses to repay the principal and interest owed to the lender. The interrelationship among T, Newco, the ESOP, VC, and the lender can of course take many more complex forms.

---

the text, cause FS to be treated as a pledgor or guarantor of its parent's debt. Thus, the *Ludwig* case may no longer be good authority.

Chart #1: LBO with ESOP

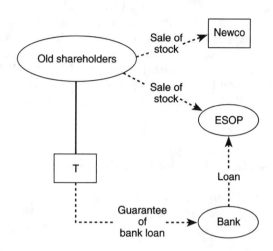

Chart #2: Post-LBO

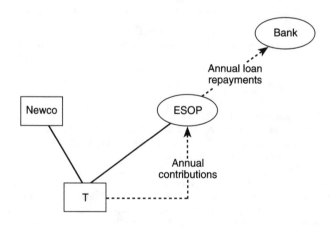

¶1406.1   *Tax Considerations*

Certain of the tax advantages of using an ESOP are set out below.

¶1406.1.1   T's Tax Deduction for Contribution to Employee Stock Ownership Plan

If T is not an SCo, T can generally deduct its contributions to the ESOP to the extent they are used to pay (1) the principal of the ESOP's loan (but such deductions are limited to 25% of the aggregate compensation paid or accrued to the ESOP's participants for the year) and (2) interest on the loan.[1]

If T is an SCo, for years beginning prior to 2002 any contributions made by the SCo to the ESOP are deductible only to the extent that such contributions do not exceed 15% of the aggregate compensation paid or accrued to the ESOP's participants for the year.[2] For years beginning after 2001, the 2001 Act increases the deduction limit applicable to all stock bonus and profit sharing plans (including SCo ESOPs) from 15% to 25% of the aggregate compensation paid or accrued to participants.[3]

¶1406.1.2   T's Tax Deductions for Cash Dividend Paid

T may deduct the amount of cash dividends paid with respect to T's stock held by the ESOP if such dividends are (1) paid in cash to ESOP participants, *or* (2) allocated to the ESOP participants' accounts and then paid in cash to the ESOP participants no later than 90 days after the close of the plan year in which the dividends were paid, *or* (3) used to make principal or interest payments on the ESOP's loan incurred to purchase the stock on which the dividend is paid, *or* (4) at the election of the ESOP participants in taxable years beginning after 12/31/01, either paid in accordance with (1) or (2) or paid to the ESOP and reinvested in T shares (in all cases without regard to the 25% limitation described in ¶1406.1.1).[4]

The Code §404(k) dividends paid deduction is not available to (1) an SCo[5] or (2) any taxpayer if the dividend constitutes, in substance, an avoidance or evasion of taxation.[6]

¶1406   [1] Code §404(a)(9)(A) and (B).

[2] Code §404(a)(9)(C).

[3] Code §404(a)(3) as amended by the 2001 Act.

[4] Code §404(k) as amended by the 2001 Act. IRS Notice 2002-2, 2002-1 C.B. 285, states that dividends subject to the participant election described in (4) above are not deductible under Code §404(k) unless the participant has a reasonable opportunity to make the election before the dividend is paid or distributed and is able to change such election at least annually. In addition, the Notice provides that dividends reinvested in employer securities pursuant to a participant election are deductible in the later of the taxable year of the plan sponsor in which (1) the dividends are actually reinvested in employer securities or (2) the participant's election becomes irrevocable. Dividends paid to participants or paid to the ESOP and distributed to participants within 90 days after the end of a plan year are deductible in the taxable year of the plan sponsor in which the dividends are actually paid or distributed to the participant. See also Code §404(k)(4)(B) as amended by 2002 legislation.

[5] Code §404(k)(1). In addition, Rev. Rul. 2001-6, 2001-1 C.B. 491, takes the position that T is not entitled to a Code §404(k)(1) deduction for a payment (treated as a Code §302 dividend) to an ESOP in redemption of T stock held by the ESOP where such payment is used by the ESOP to make distributions to terminating ESOP participants, on the grounds that (1) Code §162(k) (denying T a deduction for amounts paid in connection with the reacquisition of its stock) bars the deduction and (2) Code §404(k)(1) cannot reasonably be construed to cover a redemption treated as a Code §302 dividend.

[6] Code §404(k)(5)(A) as amended by the 2001 Act. IRS Notice 2002-2, 2002-1 C.B. 285, sets forth at Q&A 11 criteria for determining whether a dividend constitutes avoidance or evasion for Code §404(k) purposes. Specifically, dividends paid on common stock that is primarily and regularly traded on an established securities market are presumed reasonable. However, for a closely held corporation the determination is made by comparing the dividend rate on the stock held by the ESOP with the

¶1406.1.3   Lender's Exclusion for Part of Interest Income—Repealed

Prior to the 1996 repeal of Code §133, banks, insurance companies, regulated investment companies, and corporations actively engaged in the business of lending money ("qualified lenders") could exclude from gross income 50% of interest received on a "securities acquisition loan,"[7] which is generally a loan from a qualified lender to an unrelated corporation or ESOP to the extent that the loan proceeds are used to acquire T employer securities (as defined in Code §409(*l*)) for the ESOP. Code §133 was repealed effective for a loan made after 8/20/96, except for (1) the refinancing of most types of existing Code §133-qualified loans or (2) a loan made pursuant to a binding written contract in effect prior to 6/10/96.

¶1406.1.4   Selling Shareholder's Rollover

A T shareholder (other than a C corporation) who sells T stock to the ESOP may elect under Code §1042 not to pay tax on any LTCG from such sale if all six of the following Code §1042 requirements are met:[8]

(1)   During the period beginning three months before and ending 12 months after the sale, the shareholder reinvests the proceeds in any securities (including stock or debt traded on a stock exchange) issued by a U.S. corporation that is unrelated to T and satisfies certain active business requirements.

(2)   T is a domestic C corporation and, for at least one year before and immediately after the sale, no stock of T or any of its affiliates is readily tradable on an established securities market.

(3)   The ESOP owns, immediately after the sale, at least 30% of:
  (a)   each class of T's outstanding stock (excluding certain non-voting, limited, non-convertible preferred) *or*
  (b)   the total value of all of T's outstanding stock (excluding certain non-voting, limited, non-convertible preferred).

(4)   The T stock sold to the ESOP is either common stock or convertible preferred with certain characteristics.

(5)   The T shareholder held the T securities for at least three years before the sale to the ESOP.[9]

---

dividend rate for common stock of comparable corporations whose stock is publicly traded. Whether a publicly traded corporation is "comparable" to the closely held corporation is determined by comparing "relevant corporate characteristics" such as industry, size of the corporation, earnings, debt-equity structure, and dividend history.

[7] Old Code §133.

[8] Code §1042; Temp. Reg. §1.1042-1T Q&A 1(b); Code §409(*l*).

[9] Code §1042(b)(4). If T is an S corporation and converts to C status, perhaps to enable shareholder A to use Code §1042, A's holding period for Code §1042 purposes will include the time T was an SCo and A held T's stock. See IRS Letter Ruling 200003014 (1/22/00). Where T stock is contributed tax-free to a partnership ("PS") and PS then sells the T stock to the ESOP, PS's holding period for

(6)   The T shareholder timely files the necessary statements with his federal income tax return.[10]

In addition, Code §1042 is not available if the T shareholder received T stock from a qualified retirement plan or pursuant to certain options or other rights to acquire T stock.[11]

The T shareholder's basis in the replacement securities is reduced by the unreported gain.[12] The unreported gain must be recognized whenever the shareholder disposes of the replacement securities, unless the disposition is by reason of a tax-free reorganization, a gift, a death, or another Code §1042 transaction.[13]

If the ESOP disposes of any T stock within three years after a Code §1042 transaction, T may (with certain exceptions) be subject to an excise tax equal to 10% of the amount realized on the disposition.[14] The excise tax would be imposed if the ESOP disposes of any T stock during such three-year period *and either* (1) the total number of T shares held by the ESOP after such disposition is less than the total number of T employer securities held by the ESOP immediately after the Code §1042 transaction *or* (2) the FV of the T stock held by the ESOP after such disposition is less than 30% of the total FV of all T employer securities at such time.

In addition, Code §§409(n), 4975(e)(7), and 4979A impose certain penalties if any T stock acquired by the ESOP in a Code §1042 transaction (or any other ESOP asset attributable to such T stock) accrues or is allocated (1) during a specified 10-year period, for the benefit of any shareholder who made a Code §1042 election or any person related (within the meaning of Code §267(b)) to such shareholder or (2) for the benefit of certain shareholders owning more than 25% of any class of T stock or certain related corporations. Specifically, failure to comply with the above allocation restrictions results in (1) with respect to participants who receive the prohibited allocations, inclusion in income of the FV of their prohibited allocations as of the allocation, (2) an excise tax, imposed directly on *T*, equal to 50% of the amount involved in the prohibited allocation, and (3) failure of the ESOP to be treated as an ESOP, which would preclude use of the tax techniques discussed in this section and may result in imposition of prohibited transaction taxes.

The mechanics of Code §1042 and Code §4978 apparently preclude Newco or T from stepping up the basis of T's assets. Thus, it does not appear possible to both satisfy Code §1042 and avoid the Code §4978 excise tax if Newco either

---

the T stock for purposes of Code §1042 should include the contributor's holding period under the normal tacked holding period rule of Code §1223(2). See IRS Letter Ruling 9846005 (8/6/98).

[10] Code §1042(b)(3); Temp. Reg. §1042-1T Q&A 2 and 3.

[11] Code §1042(c)(1)(B).

[12] Code §1042(d).

[13] Code §1042(e). For example, if the former T shareholder contributes his replacement securities to a partnership ("PS") in an otherwise tax-free exchange under Code §721, IRS takes the position that gain previously deferred under Code §1042 is triggered. Rev. Rul. 2000-18, 2000-1 C.B. 847. However, if the T shareholder had first contributed the T stock to PS, so that PS (rather than the shareholder) sold the T stock to an ESOP and purchased the qualified securities, the unreported gain on the T stock sale would not be triggered. See IRS Letter Ruling 9846005 (8/6/98).

[14] Code §4978.

makes a taxable purchase of T's assets or purchases sufficient T stock to make a Code §338 election.

¶1406.1.5   ESOP Owning SCo Stock

An ESOP constitutes a tax-exempt organization which, under Code §1361(c)(6) as enacted in 1996, is eligible to be an SCo shareholder. The 1996 Act packaged Code §1361(c)(6) with revenue protective Code §512(e) under which the otherwise tax-exempt SCo shareholder must treat the SCo shares as an interest in an unrelated trade or business and must treat as UBTI its Code §1366(a) share of SCo income and deductions as well as its gain or loss on disposition of the SCo shares.

The 1997 Act, however, enacted Code §512(e)(3), repealing in the case of an ESOP shareholder Code §512(e)'s designation of SCo items of income, deduction, gain, or loss as UBTI.

See ¶1102.2.1 for a discussion of (1) several methods for shifting SCo's taxable income away from other owners and to the ESOP (where such income is apparently tax exempt under Code §512(e)(3)) by issuing unvested stock (with no Code §83(b) election) and/or options to other persons intended to own interests in SCo, (2) several issues as to possible interpretations of current Code §512(e)(3), and (3) extremely complex Code §409(p) enacted 6/01 imposing tax penalties where an ESOP owns SCo stock more than a small portion of which is allocated to persons owning substantial amounts of SCo's stock.

¶1406.2   *Non-tax Considerations*

Under the non-discrimination rules applicable to ESOPs, the ESOP generally must be for the benefit of a broad-based group of T's employees. Therefore, in contrast to other forms of equity compensation discussed at ¶1502, it is impossible to confine the beneficial ownership of the ESOP's T stock to T's top management. In addition, since the ESOP is a form of trust, T and/or the ESOP's trustees will have a fiduciary duty with respect to the ESOP's employee-participants.

The principal impediment to having an ESOP invest along with VC in an LBO of T is that the Department of Labor ("DOL") has traditionally required that an ESOP receive an amount of T stock proportionate to its cash contribution. For example, if VC and the ESOP each invests $10 million, each must receive 50% of the stock. From an economic standpoint, it never made sense to insist that the ESOP receive a proportionate amount of stock. This is because VC is supplying $10 million of its own (real) money, while the ESOP is supplying $10 million of borrowed money, repayment of which is normally guaranteed by T. The ESOP's loan is essentially non-recourse to the ESOP because the ESOP has no assets other than the stock it purchased with the borrowed money. Thus, the VC is at risk with respect to its $10 million, whereas the ESOP has no money to lose. Indeed, it is T (in which VC invested) that will have to make good on the guarantee and repay the ESOP's $10 million bank loan if the ESOP cannot.

However, DOL has moved away from its position that the ESOP must receive a proportionate amount of T's stock and instead is insisting on procedural safeguards, such as arm's-length negotiations, independent attorneys, independent financial advisors, independent trustees, and the like. Thus, DOL's position now seems to be that as long as there are procedural safeguards and the negotiation between VC and the ESOP takes place at arm's length with independent advisors, the result reached will be fair. Of course, DOL's position on this matter would not necessarily be binding on the courts if the ESOP participants ultimately brought a lawsuit. Assuming the ESOP receives less than a proportionate amount of T stock, the value of the ESOP's T stock can be boosted (in order to offset its lower share of T's equity) by giving it higher or preferential dividends, a liquidation preference, enhanced voting rights, and other senior stock features.

¶1407   START-UP EXPENSE DISALLOWANCE

Start-up expenses generally are not allowable deductions under the judicially created pre-opening expense doctrine and are confirmed by Code §195.

¶1407.1   *Judicially Created Pre-opening Expense Doctrine*

The judicially created pre-opening expense doctrine prevents Newco from claiming deductions for business expenses incurred prior to beginning business. *Richmond Television Corp.* and *Madison Gas & Electric Co.* exemplify this doctrine, under which Code §162 business deductions are disallowed prior to Newco's beginning business, on the theory that Newco was not yet "carrying on" a trade business.[1]

The precedents (in particular Rev. Rul. 81-150[2]) point toward the commencement of revenue generating operations as the beginning of business. However, in *Blitzer v. United States*, the Court of Claims (in dicta) rejected IRS's contention that no Code §162 expenses are deductible until "revenue producing operations" have begun and stated instead that "normal recurring expenses to maintain any business enterprise ... which are not in the nature of start-up cost nor intended to provide benefits extending beyond the year in question [should be deductible under Code §162] ... although incurred prior to the beginning of actual operations," including "utility bill, rent, stationery and salaries and wages of corporate officers, secretaries and ... those who sweep the floor."[3]

The pre-opening expense doctrine is applied formalistically. For example, if Newco is engaged in a business but establishes a new subsidiary, the subsidiary can be subject to the pre-opening expense doctrine even though the expenses

---

¶1407   [1] Richmond Television Corp. v. United States, 354 F.2d 410, 66-1 U.S.T.C. ¶9133 (4th Cir. 1965); and Madison Gas & Electric Co. v. Commissioner, 633 F.2d 512, 80-2 U.S.T.C. ¶9754 (7th Cir. 1980). See also Rev. Rul. 81-150, 1981-1 C.B. 119.

[2] 1981-1 C.B. 119.

[3] Blitzer v. United States, 684 F.2d 874, 880, 82-2 U.S.T.C. ¶9465 (Cl. Ct. 1982).

would not have been disallowed had Newco expended the funds itself (because it was already engaged in business). In addition, courts also distinguish between expansion of an existing business (expenses deductible) and entering a new business (expenses capitalized).[4]

The doctrine applies only to Code §162 expenses, not to interest (Code §163), taxes (Code §164), or R&D expenses (Code §174) to the extent that such items are deductible without regard to whether they are incurred in "carrying on any trade or business" within the meaning of Code §162. These deductions may have their own peculiar limitations, however. See, e.g., *Malmstedt v. Commissioner*[5] ("preopening" interest deductible only below-the-line); Code §263A (capitalization of production costs, including certain interest and taxes—added by the 1986 Act and generally applicable to costs incurred after 12/31/86); and former Code §189 (capitalization of construction period interest, generally applicable to costs incurred before 1/1/87—repealed by the 1986 Act). In addition, the 1986 Act substantially limited the deductibility of interest and taxes under Code §163 and Code §164. The pre-opening expense doctrine presumably now applies to interest and taxes that are no longer deductible under those provisions and instead are deductible only under Code §162 (and are not covered by new Code §263A).

¶1407.2   Code §195

Code §195 (enacted in 1980 and amended in 1984) confirms the judicially created start-up doctrine by denying any deduction for "start-up expenditures" unless the taxpayer elects to amortize such expenses over a 60-month period beginning in the month business begins.

The 1980 legislative history of Code §195 states that a taxpayer cannot deduct pre-opening expenses as incurred while filing a Code §195 election for 60-month amortization "on a conditional basis."[6]

Legislative Update

The unenacted Senate version (S. 1054) of the 2003 Act, effective for amounts paid or incurred after enactment, would have amended Code §195(b) to allow a taxpayer to deduct start-up expenditures for the taxable year in which the active trade or business begins in an amount equal to the lesser of: (a) the amount of such start-up expenditures and (b) $5,000 reduced (but not below zero) by the amount of such start-up expenditures exceeding $50,000. The remainder of such start-up expenditures would be deducted ratably over 180 months beginning with the month in which the active trade

---

[4] Compare First National Bank of South Carolina v. United States, 558 F.2d 721, 77-2 U.S.T.C. ¶9526 (4th Cir. 1977), with Madison Gas & Electric Company v. Commissioner, 633 F.2d 512, 80-2 U.S.T.C. ¶9754 (7th Cir. 1980).

[5] 578 F.2d 520 (4th Cir. 1978).

[6] S. Rep. No. 1036, 96th Cong., 2d Sess. 14 (1980).

or business begins. If enacted, the amendment would not have applied to taxable years beginning after 12/31/12.

¶1408   CODE §5881 GREENMAIL TAX WHERE P ACQUIRES AND THEN RESELLS PART OF T's STOCK

¶1408.1   1987 Enactment of Code §5881

Under a special tax provision enacted by the 1987 Act, a non-deductible 50% excise tax is imposed on any gain "realized" (even though not "recognized," e.g., because of the reorganization provisions) on the receipt of greenmail. The term "greenmail" means a transaction meeting *all* of the following tests:

(1)   any consideration paid (directly or indirectly) by a corporation to acquire its stock or, according to the Conference Report, by "an entity related to the issuing corporation (e.g., a controlled subsidiary),"[1]

(2)   where the stock is acquired from a shareholder who has held the stock less than two years before agreeing to make the transfer,

(3)   where the stock is acquired from a shareholder who made or threatened to make a public tender offer for stock of such corporation during the two-year period or acted in concert with or was related (within the meaning of Code §267 or Code §707(b)) to a person who made or threatened to make a public tender offer, and

(4)   where the acquisition of stock is pursuant to an offer that was not made on the same terms to all shareholders.[2]

The "consideration" covered by (1) includes any payment in connection with such an acquisition of stock and any payment in a transaction related to such an acquisition of stock, e.g., a standstill payment in connection with a redemption.

The term "public tender offer" is defined as any offer to purchase or otherwise acquire stock or assets in a corporation if the offer was required to be registered with any federal or state agency regulating securities.

¶1408.2   1988 Act's Retroactive Amendment of Code §5881

The 1988 Act (a) retroactively imposed the greenmail tax on any consideration transferred by a corporation, *"or any person acting in concert with such corporation,"* to directly or indirectly acquire stock in the corporation from a shareholder, and (b) clarified that the tax is imposed on any gain realized on the receipt of greenmail,

---

¶1408   [1] 1987 Act Conference Report at A39.
[2] Code §5881.

however characterized (e.g., a payment characterized as a dividend may still be subject to the greenmail excise tax).[3]

¶1408.3   Complex Issues and Traps for Unwary

Although at first reading the greenmail provision appears relatively straightforward and narrow, further study discloses that the provision resembles a form of "verbal vertigo": the more you read Code §5881, the dizzier you get; the dizzier you get, the broader the provision looks. Consider, among others, the following issues.

¶1408.3.1   Meaning of "Made or Threatened to Make Tender Offer"

(1)   P mentioned possible tender offer in its 13D. P buys 20% of T's stock in open market purchases. Because P owns more than 5% of T, P must file a 13D with the SEC, disclosing its intentions with respect to T, among other things. P's 13D states that P has purchased the 20% of T's stock for investment, that P may buy more stock (possibly including additional open market purchases, *a tender offer*, or otherwise), that P may sell all or part of the T stock, and that P is analyzing the possibility of acquiring T and may or may not make an offer for T.

Has P "threatened to make a public tender offer" for T by mentioning in its 13D that a tender offer is one of several or many possibilities? If so, would P owe the Code §5881 tax if it resold its stock to T (or, as discussed at ¶1408.3.2 below, to a white knight) within two years after purchasing it? The answer would appear to be no, i.e., merely mentioning a possible tender offer as one of several or many possibilities would not appear to be a threat of a tender offer.

(2)   P executive mentioned possible tender offer at meeting. Same as (1) above but in addition during meetings between P executives and T executives, the P executives mention a possible tender offer for T. Does their tone of voice or the exact words used determine whether they "*threatened* to make a public tender offer" or merely mentioned it as a possibility? Will oral testimony years later be the only method for determining the tone of voice and exact words used by T executives in the meeting?

(3)   P executive talked to another company threatening tender offer. Same as (1) above except that after P acquired its 20% interest in T, Raiderco also began accumulating T stock. Raiderco then threatened to make a hostile tender offer for T. At one point, Raiderco executives and P executives held several meetings but, in the view of P executives, P never reached any agreement with Raiderco. Did P ever sufficiently "act . . . in concert with" Raiderco so that Code §5881 applies to T?

---

[3] 1988 Act §2004(o)(1)(A) and (B)(i).

(4) Friendly tender offer. P and T are two separate companies with very friendly relationships, i.e., they engage in friendly ordinary course business dealings and their executives have friendly relations. Pursuant to a negotiated agreement between the two companies, P purchases 20% of T's stock in a *friendly* tender offer. Eighteen months later P and T decide that it would be better (perhaps for antitrust reasons, competitive reasons, or because T is then negotiating a possible friendly merger with Bigco) if P were not a 20% shareholder of T. Therefore, T redeems P's 20% interest in T (in a friendly transaction) at a price greater than the price P paid to acquire T's stock 18 months earlier, and T does *not* make a comparable offer to redeem T's 80% public shareholders.

Is Code §5881 applicable because P "*made* [18 months before] . . . a public tender offer for" 20% of T's stock, although P never "*threatened* to make a public tender offer" in any hostile sense?

(5) P proposed purchasing T's assets or merging with T. P buys 20% of T's stock in open market purchases. P then proposes to T that P will purchase all of T's assets in a friendly transaction. Has P "threatened to make a public tender offer" for T by offering to purchase T's assets?

Code §5881 defines the term "public tender offer" to mean "any offer to purchase or otherwise acquire stock or *assets* in a corporation [here T] if such offer was or would be required to be filed or registered with any federal or state agency regulating securities" (emphasis added). If T had accepted P's asset purchase offer, T would have been required to file a proxy statement with the SEC when T's shareholders voted (as required by state law) on the sale of substantially all of T's assets.

If P's friendly asset purchase offer to T constitutes a "threat . . . to make a public tender offer," P would owe the Code §5881 tax if it resold its T stock to P or, as discussed at ¶1408.3.2 below, to a white knight within two years after purchasing it. Is Code §5881 applicable? The answer should certainly be "no," for two reasons: *First*, the traditional meaning of a public tender offer certainly does not encompass an offer by P to buy all of T's assets, which would require the approval of T's board of directors and shareholders; *second*, both the 1987 House Report and the 1987 Conference Report described the proposed Code §5881 tax as applying to a person who has "made or threatened a public tender offer *for stock* in the corporation" (emphasis added).[4]

It is thus hard to believe that Code §5881 was intended to be triggered by a proposed friendly asset purchase, although it is indeed perplexing that Code §5881's statutory definition of "public tender offer" includes an offer to acquire a corporation's assets, which would be required to be filed with a governmental agency regulating securities.

If Code §5881 were interpreted as applying to a proposed asset purchase, would it also apply where P (rather than proposing to purchase T's assets) had proposed that T merge into P or that T merge with P's subsidiary (S) (either forward or

---

[4] H.R. Rep. No. 391, 100th Cong., 1st Sess. 1087 (1987); H.R. Conf. Rep. No. 495, 100th Cong., 1st Sess. 970 (1987).

reverse)? As discussed at ¶301, a merger of T into P or S is treated for tax purposes as an asset acquisition[5] and, as discussed at ¶202, a reverse subsidiary merger of S into T is treated for tax purposes as an acquisition of T's stock.[6] Such a merger transaction would have required T to file with the SEC a proxy statement when T's shareholders voted (as required by state law) on the merger.

Again, the answer should be "no" because a merger is not encompassed within the traditional meaning of a public tender offer. The 1987 legislative history refers to Code §5881 as applying to a person who has "made or threatened to make a public tender offer for *stock*" (emphasis added), and it is hard to believe that Code §5881 was intended to be triggered by a proposed friendly merger between P (or S) and T, although it is indeed perplexing that Code §5881's statutory definition of a public tender offer includes an offer to acquire a corporation's stock or assets, which would be required to be filed with a governmental agency regulating securities.

¶1408.3.2 Application of Code §5881 Where P Sells its T Stock to White Knight

(1) 1987 Act. P purchases 20% of T's stock in open market purchases at an average price of $15 per share, and P then begins a tender offer for the remainder of T's stock at $18 per share. T seeks a white knight, i.e., another friendly company to buy T for a price higher than $18 per share. T reaches agreement with Bigco for Bigco to acquire T at $20 per share. Bigco, in order to avoid a possible fight with P, purchases P's 20% of T for $21 per share (i.e., $1 more per share than Bigco's $20 offer to T's other shareholders). At approximately the same time Bigco acquires the remaining 80% of T for $20 per share.

Code §5881 as enacted in 1987 applied to "consideration transferred by a corporation [here T] to directly or indirectly acquire its stock" and hence appears inapplicable to P's sale of T stock to Bigco. However, the 1987 Conference Report stated that Code §5881 applies to a purchase by "an entity related to the issuing corporation (e.g., a controlled subsidiary)." Was this Conference Report language intended to include Bigco because T became a 100% owned subsidiary of Bigco at approximately the same time as Bigco's purchase of P's 20% interest in T? Would it have mattered if (a) Bigco acquired the 80% of T from the public shortly *before* Bigco's purchase of P's 20% interest in T (so that at the moment Bigco purchased P's 20% interest in T, T was already a Bigco subsidiary) *or* (b) Bigco acquired the 80% of T from the public shortly *after* Bigco's purchase of P's 20% interest in T (so that T was not yet a Bigco subsidiary when Bigco purchased P's 20% interest in T)?

Or was the Conference Report's reference to a related entity intended to refer only to a T subsidiary (notwithstanding the "e.g." preface)? If the Conference Report intended to sweep in Bigco, was it a valid extension of the more limited statutory language?

---

[5] Rev. Rul. 69-6, 1969-1 C.B. 104.
[6] Rev. Rul. 73-427, 1973-2 C.B. 301; Rev. Rul. 67-448, 1967-2 C.B. 144; Rev. Rul. 79-273, 1979-2 C.B. 125.

(2) 1988 Act. The 1988 Act retroactively amended Code §5881 so that it applies to a purchase by the issuer "or any person acting in concert with such corporation." In this case, the surprising result in (1) above would appear to be that Code §5881 does apply to the white knight's (Bigco's) purchase of T stock from P because (at the time Bigco purchased the T stock from P) Bigco had already reached agreement with T, and hence was acting in concert with T.

(3) Surprising tax calculation. Assuming that Code §5881 does apply in (1) and (2) above, how much Code §5881 tax does P owe? The surprising answer is that although P sold its T stock to Bigco for only $1 per share more than the price Bigco paid T's other holders ($21 per share to P and $20 per share to T's other holders), it appears that P owes the 50% greenmail excise tax on its full $6 gain on the sale (P purchased its 20% of T in open market purchases for an average of $15 per share and resold the stock to Bigco for $21 per share).

Hence, P would owe Code §5881 tax of $3 per share ($6 profit × 50% excise tax rate)—leaving P with only $18 per share net proceeds ($21 sale price less $3 greenmail tax)—and P would also owe $2.10 of regular income tax on its $6 gain on the sale unreduced by the $3 non-deductible greenmail excise tax (35% × ($21 selling price less $15 average cost)). This would leave P with net after-tax profit of only $.90 per share:

	Per Share
Selling price	$21.00
Less: greenmail tax ($6 × 50%)	(3.00)
Less: regular income tax ($6 × 35%)	(2.10)
Less: cost of stock	(15.00)
Net after-tax profit	$ .90

By contrast, if P had sold its T stock for $1 per share less, i.e., for the same $20 per share price as was offered to all other T shareholders, P would have avoided the entire $3 per share greenmail excise tax and its net after-tax profit per share would have been *substantially higher,* i.e., P's net after-tax profit would have been $3.25 per T share:

	Per Share
Selling price	$20.00
Less: greenmail tax	0
Less: regular income tax ($5 × 35%)	(1.75)
Less: cost of stock	(15.00)
Net after-tax profit	$ 3.25

Thus, by selling the T stock for $21 rather than $20 per share, P's net after-tax profit *declined* by $2.35 per share (i.e., from $3.35 to $.90).

¶1408.3.3   Possible Application of Code §5881 Where P Does Not Sell T Stock

(1)   Tender offer and squeeze-out merger at different prices. P purchases 80% of T's stock in a tender offer for $15 per share. During the tender offer P announces that it plans a subsequent squeeze-out merger of any non-tendering T shareholders for $14 per share, i.e., $1 less than the $15 tender offer price. P never sells its 80% of T purchased for $15 per share in the tender offer. Rather, P completes its acquisition of 100% of T by merging S (a 100% P subsidiary) into T and giving T's 20% remaining public shareholders $14 cash per share.

Is there any risk that Code §5881 might apply to P on the theory that, in the merger of S into T, P constructively disposed of the 80% of T's stock owned by P "pursuant to an offer which was not made on the same terms to all [T] shareholders"? The answer would seem to be "no", because P did *not* dispose of its 80% of T's stock. Rather P kept the 80% of T purchased in the tender offer and P also acquired the remaining 20% pursuant to the squeeze-out merger of S into T.[7] Thus, the fact that P paid $15 per share for 80% of T's stock in the tender offer and $14 per share for the remaining 20% in the squeeze-out merger should not invoke Code §5881.

(2)   Tender offer and squeeze-out upstream liquidation at different prices. Same as (1) above except that after P first purchases 80% of T's stock for $15 per share in the tender offer, P then squeezes out the 20% T minority shareholders for $14 per share by the following procedure: T merges upstream directly into P with P acquiring all T's assets and T's 20% remaining public shareholders receiving $14 cash per share. For tax purposes, this is a tax-free Code §332 upstream liquidation of T into P.

Is there any possibility that Code §5881 applies to P on the theory that P disposed of its 80% interest in T *in exchange for T's assets* while T's 20% public shareholders were not given the same offer to receive a *pro rata* share of T's assets? On the face of the statute, there appears to be such a risk, although the statutory purpose clearly would not be furthered by such an interpretation. P has not really disposed of its T stock but has merely converted the stock interest into an assets interest.

(3)   Tender offer and squeeze-out upstream liquidation at same price. Same as (2) above, but assume that Code §5881 does apply to the facts set forth in (2) and assume further that, in the squeeze-out upstream merger-liquidation of T into P, the 20% public shareholders received $15 cash per share, i.e., the same amount as P paid the tendering 80% of T's shareholders. Is there any possibility that Code §5881 would apply although all selling T shareholders (both the 80% tendering and the 20% squeeze-out) received $15 per share? The theory for application of Code §5881 is that in the squeeze-out upstream merger-liquidation of T into P, T gave consideration to P (T's assets) in exchange for P's 80% stock interest

---

[7] See, e.g., Rev. Rul. 73-427, 1973-2 C.B. 301; Rev. Rul. 79-273, 1979-2 C.B. 125. See also ¶202.

in T, and the 20% public was not offered an opportunity to sell their stock "on the same terms," i.e., for a pro rata share of T's assets.

If Code §5881 applies in these circumstances, how would P's Code §5881 excise tax be calculated? *First*, assuming that T's net assets (transferred to P in the upstream squeeze-out merger-liquidation) are worth $15 per share, P would apparently owe a Code §5881 excise tax (of 50%) on any T shares P purchased in the past two years for less than $15 per share—e.g., if P had purchased 10% of T's stock in open market purchases at an average price of $12 per share before making the tender offer at $15 per share, which raised P's ownership of T to 80%, P's Code §5881 tax would apparently be $1.50 per T share on the 10% of T's shares purchased by P at $12 per share in the open market purchases (50% tax rate × ($15 per share value of T net assets received by P in the upstream liquidation less $12 cost)).

Second, assuming that T's net assets (transferred to P in the upstream squeeze-out merger-liquidation) are worth $16 per share (i.e., that P has made an advantageous acquisition of T at $15 per share). P's Code §5881 tax would apparently be the sum of:

(a) $2.00 per T share on the 10% of T's shares purchased by P at $12 per share in the open market purchases (50% tax rate × ($16 per share value of T net assets received by P in the upstream liquidation less $12 cost)), and

(b) $.50 per T share on the 70% of T's shares purchased by P at $15 per share in the tender offer (50% tax rate × ($16 per share value of T net assets received by P in the upstream liquidation less $15 cost)).

And this Code §5881 tax would apparently apply even though the upstream merger of T into P was a tax-free Code §332 liquidation, because Code §5881 applies to "realized" gain, not "recognized" gain. Again, on the face of the statute, there appears to be a risk of invoking Code §5881, but the statutory purpose clearly would not be furthered by such interpretation.

¶1408.4   Conclusion

As demonstrated by the discussion in ¶1408.3, the outer limits of the greenmail tax are as yet uncertain, and its proper scope is a subject of speculation and controversy in the investment community. Indeed, it is highly questionable (a) whether tax law (as opposed to corporate or SEC regulatory law) is the appropriate place to deal with issues of the type presented by Code §5881 and, (b) if such issues must be dealt with by tax law, whether such vague language as causes the careful reader to suffer severe "verbal vertigo" is really the proper approach.

CHAPTER 15

Management Compensation

¶1501   INTRODUCTION

This chapter discusses tax, accounting, and certain other issues in compensating P's and T's executives (and Newco's executives where Newco is formed to acquire T in an LBO), including:

- Sales of stock to Mgmt, with and without vesting, including Code §83 issues (¶1502),
- Grants to Mgmt of incentive stock options ("ISOs"), non-qualified stock options ("NQOs"), and stock appreciation rights ("SARs") (¶1503),
- APB 25 and FASB 123 accounting treatment for stock-based Mgmt compensation (¶1502.1.7),
- Handling T's outstanding Mgmt stock options and restricted stock when P (or Newco) acquires T (¶1503), and
- Special golden parachute tax rules applicable to a change in T's control (¶1505).

¶1502   STOCK-BASED COMPENSATION TO MGMT—STOCK SALES OR GRANTS, OPTIONS, AND SARs

Normally in an LBO, Mgmt (1) purchases P (or Newco) common stock *or* (2) receives options to purchase P (or Newco) common stock—either incentive stock options (ISOs) or non-qualified options (NQOs). Frequently Mgmt's purchase price for P (or Newco) common stock (or its exercise price for the options) is relatively low. In order to deter Mgmt from leaving P's (or Newco's) employ, Mgmt's common shares (or options) are generally subject to a vesting schedule based on continued employment, and in order to encourage Mgmt to work hard, Mgmt's common shares (or options) may also be subject to a vesting schedule based on P (or Newco) achieving certain earnings or other performance goals.

The remainder of this section (except ¶1502.3) discusses the tax and accounting ramifications of stock awards, stock sales, and option grants by a corporation in far greater detail.

¶1502.3 discusses certain of these issues in the context of such an award by a partnership or LLC.

¶1502.1   *Purchased Common Stock and Non-Qualified Stock Options—Code §83 and Vesting*

As discussed in greater detail below, the general rule under Code §83(a) in the context of a corporate service recipient is that a service provider receiving P (or Newco) stock in connection with the performance of services (including upon the exercise of an NQO) recognizes OI, either upon receipt of the stock or, if later, when vesting occurs,[1] in an amount equal to the excess of the stock's FV on such recognition date over the amount, if any, that the service provider paid for the stock (the "spread").

Where a service provider receives P (or Newco) stock (including upon exercise of an NQO) and the stock is not vested upon receipt, the service provider can nonetheless elect under Code §83(b) to recognize immediate OI equal to the spread at the time he receives the stock. In that case, there will be no additional OI to the service provider upon vesting, and any future appreciation in the P (or Newco) stock would be taxed as CG upon disposition of the stock.

Subject to certain limitations (discussed below), P (or Newco) generally is entitled to a compensation deduction, at the time the service provider recognizes OI, in an amount equal to the spread.

EXAMPLE

In connection with the performance of services, Newco awards 1,000 shares of Newco common stock to one of its executives (A) for no consideration. The shares, however, do not vest until the end of 3 years following the date Newco grants the shares to A, and then vest only if A remains in Newco's employ throughout the 3-year period, i.e., if A leaves Newco's employ for any reason prior to the third anniversary of grant, A must return the 1,000 shares to Newco. The Newco shares' aggregate FV is $10,000 on the grant date and $40,000 on the third anniversary when they vest.

If A does not make a Code §83(b) election (i.e., A does not elect to be taxed at the time he receives the Newco shares), A recognizes $40,000 OI on the vesting date and, assuming a 35% federal income tax rate, pays $14,000 in federal income tax. Newco generally is entitled to a $40,000 deduction when A recognizes OI, and, assuming Newco's federal income tax rate is 35% (and that Newco can use the deduction), Newco saves $14,000 in federal income tax.

If, on the other hand, A makes a Code §83(b) election promptly upon receiving the shares, A recognizes $10,000 OI upon receipt of the shares and, assuming a 35% federal income tax rate, pays $3,500 in federal income tax. Newco generally is entitled to a $10,000 deduction at the time A recognizes OI, and assuming a 35% federal income tax rate, saves $3,500 in federal income tax.

¶1502 [1]For this purpose, "vesting" occurs when the stock either (a) is no longer subject to a substantial risk of forfeiture ("SRF") or (b) is transferable to a holder free of any SRF. Reg. §1.83-3(b), -3(d).

¶1502.1.1   Purchased Stock

The tax treatment of stock purchased by Mgmt turns on whether the executive pays full value for the stock, whether the stock is fully vested at the time of purchase, whether the executive makes a timely Code §83(b) election, whether the stock certificate contains a legend referring to the vesting provisions, and certain other factors discussed below.

(1)   Immediate taxation of bargain element. The spread between the FV of property (including Newco stock) received in connection with the performance of services and the amount (if any) paid therefor constitutes OI to the service provider on the date he purchases such property and is added to his tax basis in the property.[2] For this purpose, the FV of property is determined without regard to lapse restrictions (i.e., restrictions which lapse with the passage of time or the occurrence of an event). Thus, for example, investment letter restrictions on the Newco stock are ignored.[3] However, "blockage" restrictions (because they do not lapse) *can* be taken into account in determining FV.[4]

EXAMPLE 1

VC forms Newco to acquire T. T Mgmt buys 1,000 shares of Newco common stock, subject to an investment letter restriction (the only restriction), for $1 per share. The Newco stock, if not subject to an investment letter restriction, would have an FV of $10 per share.

Mgmt recognizes $9,000 of taxable income in the year of purchase ($10,000 FV of the Newco stock ignoring the investment letter restriction which will lapse with the passage of time *less* $1,000 paid by Mgmt) and, subject to the qualifications and limitations discussed at ¶1502.1.1(5), Newco is entitled to a $9,000 deduction.

Mgmt recognizes CG or CL when some or all of its Newco common stock is later sold for more or less than $10 per share.

If the service provider is a Newco employee, the amount of the executive's OI upon receipt of the Newco stock is subject to withholding, generally at a 27%

---

[2] Code §83(a); Reg. §1.83-4(b). Code §83 applies to a purchase of Newco shares by T Mgmt only if the stock is issued "in connection with the performance of services." Code §83(a). In determining whether the stock is issued "in connection with the performance of services," the following factors are taken into account: (1) whether the stock is granted at the time the employee becomes employed by the employer, (2) whether any restrictions on the stock are explicitly linked to the employee's tenure with the employer, (3) whether the consideration furnished by the employee in exchange for the stock is services, and (4) the employer's intent in transferring the stock. See Aidoo v. Commissioner, 65 T.C.M. 1798 (1993), and the cases cited therein.

[3] Reg. §1.83-5(c) example (3); Pledger v. Commissioner, 641 F.2d 287, 81-1 U.S.T.C. ¶9314 (5th Cir.), *cert. denied*, 454 U.S. 964 (1981).

[4] Steinberg v. Commissioner, 46 T.C.M. 1238, T.C. Mem. 1983-534 (1983).

federal rate plus any applicable state rate. Thus, Newco is obligated to make a withholding tax payment to the taxing authorities within a few days after selling stock to the executive at a price below FV.

Hence, Newco generally arranges for the executive to pay cash to Newco (over and above the purchase price such executive is paying to Newco for the stock) equal to Newco's withholding obligation. Alternatively, Newco and the executive may agree that Newco will hold back 100% (or some lesser percentage) of the executive's normal salary and bonus until Newco has recouped the full amount of its withholding tax payment. Finally, Newco may agree to pay all or part of the executive's withholding tax as a bonus to the executive, which would, of course, give rise to further withholding tax on the amount of such bonus. In any event, the executive is entitled to credit on his income tax return for the amount of Newco's withholding tax payment to IRS or the applicable state authority.

Legislative Update

The unenacted Senate version (S. 1054) of the 2003 Act, effective for amounts deferred in taxable years beginning after 12/31/03, proposed to amend Code §83 so that assets would be treated as not subject to the claims of creditors in determining whether there has been a transfer of "property" with respect to nonqualified deferred compensation if such assets are located outside the U.S. and are designated or otherwise available for the payment of such nonqualified deferred compensation. The provision carves out property transferred in connection with services performed in the same foreign jurisdiction in which the assets are located, and grants regulatory authority for IRS to exempt other arrangements not resulting in an improper tax deferral where the assets are readily accessible in any insolvency or bankruptcy proceeding.

(2) Delayed taxation if substantial risk of forfeiture. If property (including stock) is subject to a substantial risk of forfeiture ("SRF") (generally referred to as "vesting") when received by the service provider, there is no tax until the SRF lapses. When the SRF lapses, the spread at that time constitutes OI.[5] This is true even if the property's FV at the time the service provider received it did not exceed the amount he paid for it.[6] (As discussed in (3) immediately below, the tax result would be materially different if (a) the service provider made a timely Code §83(b) election, or (b) the service provider has the power to transfer the stock so that the transferee is not subject to the SRF, which may be the case where

---

[5] Code §83(a). Under Code §83(c)(3), if Newco is a public company and the service provider is an "insider" subject to §16(b) of the Securities Exchange Act of 1934, the six-month §16(b) restriction period is an SRF.

[6] Alves v. Commissioner, 79 T.C. 864 (1982), aff'd, 734 F.2d 478, 84-2 U.S.T.C. ¶9546 (9th Cir. 1984).

the stock is evidenced by a stock certificate that does not contain a legend referring to the SRF provisions.)

EXAMPLE 2

Same as Example 1 except that Mgmt's Newco stock is also subject to an SRF which lapses in 5 years (e.g., Newco has an option to repurchase the stock at $1 per share if Mgmt leaves Newco's employ within 5 years after purchasing the stock). When the SRF lapses, Mgmt's Newco common stock has an FV of $100 per share.

Mgmt does not recognize any taxable income at the time of purchasing the Newco stock for less than its FV. Mgmt includes $99,000 in income in the year the SRF lapses ($100,000 FV when SRF lapses minus $1,000 paid by Mgmt for its Newco common), and, subject to the qualifications and limitations discussed at ¶1502.1.1(5), Newco is entitled to a $99,000 deduction.

Mgmt recognizes CG or CL when some or all of its Newco common stock is later sold for more or less than $100 per share.

Property is subject to an SRF where (a) there is a set of circumstances (relating either to the future performance of services or to a purpose of the property transfer) under which the service provider can be required to surrender the property at a forfeiture price, i.e., for less than the property's FV at the time of the surrender and (b) the possibility that such a set of circumstances will occur is substantial. Where, for example, Newco sells stock to a service provider but the service provider is required to sell the stock back to Newco at cost (or at the lower of the stock's cost or its then FV) if the service provider leaves Newco's employ within 5 years, the stock is subject to an SRF. Similarly, stock is subject to an SRF where vesting (i.e., expiration of Newco's buy-back right) turns on Newco reaching a specified earnings or other performance goal (so long as the risk that Newco will fail to achieve such goal is substantial).

However, stock is not subject to an SRF if the event which would allow Newco to repurchase the stock from the service provider at a forfeiture price is deemed highly unlikely to occur, such as commission of a crime. See Reg. §1.83-3(c).

IRS has ruled that where Newco has the right to repurchase stock which fails to vest at a price equal to the stock's "book value" and, during the full period that the stock is repurchasable, the FV of the stock will "substantially exceed its book value," the book-value repurchase price constitutes a forfeiture price.[7] Hence,

---

[7] IRS Letter Ruling 9046030 (8/20/90). In this ruling IRS required the taxpayer to make a factual representation that the FV of the stock substantially exceeded its book value during the full period the stock was repurchasable. In other cases the stock's book value may approximately equal its FV at the time of the issuance with the book and fair values expected later to diverge. In this latter case, we believe a book-value repurchase right should still represent an SRF so long as FV is expected substantially to exceed book value when the repurchase option is triggered since the employer would

in such circumstances Newco's right to repurchase the stock at book value if the service provider's employment terminates within a specified period constitutes an SRF.

Where there are multiple SRFs (i.e., multiple vesting events) with respect to the same stock, the service provider's OI (and hence Newco's deduction) are recognized and measured only upon expiration of the final SRF. This is because Code §83(a)'s statutory language calls for the recognition event to occur "at the first time the rights of the person having the beneficial interest in such property . . . are not subject to a substantial risk of forfeiture."

EXAMPLE 3

VC forms Newco to acquire T. T Mgmt buys 1,000 Newco common shares for $1 per share, subject to the following SRFs:

(1) If Mgmt leaves Newco's employ before the first anniversary of the stock purchase, Newco has an option to repurchase the shares at their cost of $1 per share.

(2) If Mgmt leaves Newco's employ after the first but before the second anniversary of the stock purchase, Newco has an option to repurchase the shares at $1.50 per share (and the stock's FV substantially exceeds $1.50 and is expected to continue substantially to exceed $1.50).[8]

(3) If Mgmt leaves Newco's employ after the second but before the fifth anniversary of the stock purchase, Newco has an option to repurchase the shares at their book value (and the stock's FV "substantially exceeds its book value" and is expected to continue throughout the 5-year SRF period substantially to exceed its book value).[9]

(4) If Mgmt leaves Newco's employ after the fifth anniversary of the stock purchase, Newco has no option to repurchase the shares (or alternatively Newco has an option to repurchase the shares at their then FV).

If Mgmt remains in Newco's employ, Mgmt recognizes OI only at the fifth anniversary of the stock purchase in an amount equal to the FV of the stock at that time minus Mgmt's $1 per share purchase price for the stock. Although Newco's repurchase price moves from $1 per share to $1.50 per

---

not be "required to pay the FV . . . of such property to the employee upon the return of such" as required by Reg. §1.83-3(c)(1) to avoid SRF status.

[8] Cf. IRS Letter Ruling 9046030 (8/20/90) discussed in text and footnote above. While the approach of the letter ruling would require that the stock's FV substantially exceed $1.50 at the time of Newco's original sale to Mgmt, we believe the result would be the same so long as FV is expected substantially to exceed $1.50 when the repurchase option is triggered.

[9] See IRS Letter Ruling 9046030 (8/20/90) discussed in text and footnote above. While the letter ruling would require that the stock's FV substantially exceed its book value at the time of Newco's original sale to Mgmt, we believe the result would be the same so long as FV is expected substantially to exceed book value when the repurchase option is triggered.

share on the first anniversary of the stock purchase and from $1.50 per share to book value on the second anniversary, Mgmt recognizes no income, because the stock remains subject to an SRF until the fifth anniversary, i.e., until then Newco has the right to repurchase the stock at a forfeiture price if Mgmt should leave Newco's employ.

If the service provider is a Newco employee, the amount of the executive's OI when the SRF lapses is subject to withholding, generally at a 27% federal rate plus any applicable state rate, and Newco is obligated to make a withholding payment to the taxing authorities within a few days after the SRF lapses.

Hence, Newco will generally seek to obtain from the executive (at the time the stock subject to the SRF is sold to the executive) a written agreement obligating the executive to make a cash payment to Newco equal to Newco's withholding obligation. Alternatively, the agreement might entitle Newco to hold back 100% (or some lesser percentage) of the executive's post-SRF-lapse salary and bonus until Newco has recouped the full amount of its withholding obligation. As another approach, the agreement might permit the executive to surrender back to Newco a portion of the shares, i.e., Newco shares with an FV equal to the withholding obligation. Finally, the agreement might obligate Newco to pay all or part of the executive's withholding tax as a bonus to the executive, which would, of course, give rise to further withholding tax on the amount of such bonus. In any event, the executive is entitled to credit on his federal income tax return for the amount of Newco's withholding tax payment to IRS or applicable state tax authority.

(3)   Effect of Code §83(b) election or failure to legend certificate.

Timely Code §83(b) election. If the service provider files a Code §83(b) election within 30 days after receipt of the property (including stock) and attaches a copy to his tax return for such year, the spread (if any) at the time of receipt constitutes OI when he receives the property, even though the property is subject to an SRF.[10] The spread is the difference between the property's FV (ignoring the SRF and all other lapse restrictions) and the price he paid for the property. In this case, there is no additional OI when the SRF lapses.

EXAMPLE 4

Same as Example 2 except that each member of Mgmt files a Code §83(b) election.

Even though the Newco common stock is subject to an SRF, Mgmt recognizes income of $9,000 (and Newco is entitled to an equal deduction) in the

---

[10] A Code §83(b) election, once made, may not be revoked without IRS consent. Code §83(b)(2). A revocation request filed within the original 30-day period after acquiring the property normally will be granted. IRS Letter Ruling 200229004 (4/3/02).

year Mgmt acquires the Newco common stock (i.e., the same result as Example 1), and Mgmt does not recognize income (and Newco is not entitled to a deduction) in the year the SRF lapses.

Mgmt recognizes CG or CL when some or all of its Newco common stock is later sold for more or less than $10 per share.

How is the 30-day period for filing a Code §83(b) election measured where the service provider first enters into a binding executory contract to purchase Newco stock in the future and actually does purchase the Newco stock at a subsequent closing? The conventional wisdom long has been that the Code §83(b) 30-day period begins to run when the service provider *receives* the Newco stock at the closing, because (1) the Newco stock is not "transferred" within the meaning of Code §83 until the closing and (2) the service provider's earlier executory contract to purchase the Newco stock is not "property" as defined in the §83 regulations. However, see the discussion in ¶1502.1.1(5), below, for the possibility, under a questionable 5/96 Ninth Circuit decision, that (1) the Code §83(b) 30-day period begins to run when the executory contract is signed (not at the subsequent closing) and (2) the service provider's OI is measured when the executory contract is signed (not at the subsequent closing).

If the service provider is a Newco employee, the amount of the executive's OI upon receipt of the property (covered by the Code §83(b) election) is subject to withholding, generally at a 27% federal rate plus any applicable state rate. As discussed in ¶1502.1.1(1), Newco and the executive should agree in advance of the stock sale on which of several alternative approaches will be used to fund Newco's withholding obligation.

Where the service provider has made a Code §83(b) election and the stock thereafter declines in value, the service provider is entitled to no ordinary deduction for the decline, and if the property is forfeited pursuant to the SRF, the service provider is entitled to a deductible loss only to the extent that the amount paid by the service provider to acquire the property exceeds the amount received upon forfeiture, i.e., the service provider is entitled to no deductible loss with respect to the spread recognized as OI when he received the property.[11]

Failure to legend certificate. Where the service provider does not make a timely Code §83(b) election, there is one other circumstance which nevertheless causes the service provider to be taxed at the time he receives the property. Code §83(a)(1) imposes tax "at the first time the [service provider's] rights . . . in the property are transferable *or* are not subject to a substantial risk of forfeiture" (emphasis added). The meaning of the word "transferable" is contained in Code §83(c)(2), which explains that the service provider's "rights . . . are transferable only if the rights . . . of any transferee are not subject to a substantial risk of forfeiture." The regulations further clarify the meaning of "transferable": "property is transferable if the [service provider] can sell, assign, or pledge (as collateral

---

[11] Code §83(b)(1); Reg. §1.83-2(a).

for a loan . . .) his interest in the property to any person . . . and if the transferee is not required to give up the property or its value in the event the substantial risk of forfeiture materializes."[12]

Where Newco and the service provider have entered into a contractual SRF arrangement with respect to the service provider's Newco stock (e.g., Newco has the option to repurchase the service provider's stock at a forfeiture price under specified circumstances), the arrangement would (under state corporate law—see, e.g., Del. Gen. Corp. Law §202) generally not bind a transferee of the service provider's stock who is ignorant of the arrangement, unless the service provider's stock certificate contains a legend referring to the contractual SRF arrangement. Hence it is typical to place such a legend on the certificate representing SRF shares. Where, however, there is no such legend specifically referring to the SRF (and no other legend which would cause a potential transferee to learn about the SRF), the shares represented by such certificate would appear to be "transferable" within the meaning of Code §83(a) because the service provider has the power under state law to transfer the shares to a purchaser (or pledgee) who "is not required to give up the [shares] or [their] value in the event the substantial risk of forfeiture materializes."

Indeed Code §83's legislative history clearly enunciates this view:

> The House bill requires the recognition of income by an employee on receipt [of property] even though his interest in the property is forfeitable if it is transferable. . . . [A]n interest in property is to be considered to be transferable only if a transferee would not be subject to the forfeitability conditions—for example, where the employee has a forfeitable interest in stock, but *the fact of forfeitability is not indicated on the stock certificate, and a transferee would have no notice of it.*[13]

Notwithstanding this clear language in the Code, regulations, and legislative history, two murky court decisions, dealing with confused facts, might be read as concluding, erroneously in our view, that the absence of a legend does not automatically result in stock being transferable for Code §83(a) purposes.[14] Signifi-

---

[12] Reg. §1.83-3(d).

[13] Senate Report No. 91-552, page 260 (11/21/69) (emphasis added).

[14] In Robinson v. Commissioner, 805 F.2d 38, 86-2 U.S.T.C ¶9790 (1st Cir. 1986), *rev'g* 50 T.C. 89 (1985), a service provider received Newco stock subject to an SRF, but with no legend on the stock certificate referring specifically to the SRF. However, the stock certificate did contain an SEC legend, warning any transferee that the stock could not be transferred without either SEC registration by Newco or an opinion of counsel satisfactory to Newco regarding SEC compliance. In addition, Newco issued a stop-transfer order to its transfer agent and, as is typical, the SRF contract between the service provider and Newco prohibited transfers. Although the certificate lacked a legend referring specifically to the SRF, the court seemed to conclude that any transferee should have learned of the SRF in advance of transfer by virtue of necessary communications with Newco concerning SEC compliance, as required by the certificate's SEC legend. Hence the court could have simply held the SEC legend made the stock non-transferable under the above quoted regulations and legislative history. Nevertheless, using language which could be read either as consistent with this view of the case (i.e., that the SEC legend caused the stock to be non-transferable) or as extending to the situation—not before the court—of a stock certificate with no legend at all, the court held "the stock [to be] non-transferable until the [SRF] lapsed" and stated that "the Tax Court's contrary finding was not based upon evidence of the practical workings of the securities markets, but rather upon a hypothetical, back-door transfer in breach of

cantly, (a) there was actually a legend on the stock certificates in both cases, although in one the legend did not refer specifically to the SRF and in the other the legend had been dropped in the course of a merger, (b) neither of these decisions cited the clearly contrary regulatory definition of transferability or the 1969 legislative history (as quoted above), and (c) the only court carefully to have reviewed the law in this area (the Tax Court in Robinson) clearly held that unlegended certificates are transferable.

(4)   Paying for purchased stock with note. The above-described results would apply even if the service provider paid for the purchased stock with a note, so long as the note bore interest at a rate necessary to avoid the Code §483 and Code §1274 OID and imputed interest rules and the service provider was personally liable on the note.

If the service provider pays for the purchased stock with a non-recourse note secured only by the stock purchased, IRS would undoubtedly take the position that the service provider has not really purchased the stock but merely has an option to purchase the stock, with the tax results described in ¶1502.1.2.[15] However, where the service provider has a substantial amount at risk with respect to stock purchased for a non-recourse note, the arrangement is not the economic equivalent of an option and hence should not be treated as an option for income tax purposes. This is generally the case where:

- the service provider's note is partially recourse to the service provider, or
- the service provider pays a portion of the purchase price in cash and all of the purchased stock (both the stock purchased for cash and the stock purchased for a non-recourse note) secures the non-recourse note, or
- the non-recourse note is secured by property in addition to the stock purchased with the non-recourse note (including other Newco stock owned by the service provider),

so long as the partial recourse features, the cash down payment, or the other property securing the note are "substantial" in relation to the price of the stock.[16]

---

the option agreement. This was error. Transferability under §83(a) depends on standard practices and assumes observance of contracts, not hypothetical *sub rosa* violations."

In McNaughton v. United States, 888 F.2d 418, 89-2 U.S.T.C ¶9599 (6th Cir. 1989), a service provider received Newco stock subject to an SRF with a legend specifically referring to the SRF. Newco subsequently merged into Newco #2 and the Newco #2 certificate issued to the service provider was not legended. Nevertheless a jury concluded that the Newco #2 stock remained non-transferable. The appeals court (in a 2-1 decision), upheld the jury verdict, stating that "a reasonable jury could have concluded" the Newco #2 stock was non-transferable because "transferability under §83 does not require that a written legend appear on the stock certificate" and expressing agreement with the *Robinson* decision.

[15] Reg. §1.83-3(a)(2).

[16] See ¶1502.1.7.5 for a discussion of the possibility that Newco may be forced to apply variable accounting under APB 25 where a service provider purchases Newco stock with a non-recourse or partial recourse note, resulting in increased compensation charges to Newco's income for financial accounting purposes.

If the note did not bear adequate interest, the rules set forth in ¶203.6 would apply, so that the service provider would be treated as buying the stock for a lower price than the face value of the note, the service provider would have an additional interest deduction, and Newco would have additional interest income. The lower purchase price would also increase the income recognized by the service provider and the deduction allowable to Newco under the Code §83 rules.

Legislative Update

The National Employee Savings and Trust Equity Guarantee Act (S. 1971), introduced 2/27/02 and placed on the Senate legislative calendar 8/2/02, would treat certain direct or indirect loans made by a C corporation employer to "applicable employees" (i.e., officer, director, 5% owner (within the meaning of Code §416(i)), or an employee who has outstanding loans from the employer in excess of $1 million) as compensation unless (1) the loan is evidenced by a written instrument, (2) there is adequate collateral for the loan (not taking into account any stock or capital or profits interests in the employer, any option or contract to purchase such stock or interests, any restricted stock or ownership interest, any non-qualified deferred compensation, or any similar asset as provided by Treasury/IRS), and (3) there is a fixed schedule of not longer than 10 years over which the loan is to be repaid in substantially equal installments or in such other form as Treasury/IRS may prescribe. In the case of a person who is an applicable employee solely because of outstanding loans in excess of $1 million, only the loan in excess of $1 million would be subject to this rule.

Loans to an employee for the purchase of a principal residence in connection with an employee relocation would be exempted.

Employees treated as receiving compensation under this provision would be allowed to deduct (and the employer required to include in gross income) repayments of such loans under rules prescribed by Treasury/IRS.

The bill would also modify Code §7872 by using the AFR plus 3 percentage points to determine whether an excessive employee loan (e.g., the portion of any loans made by a C corporation to a "director or employee" that exceed $1 million in principal amount) is a below-market loan.

The proposals would apply to loans made after enactment and refinancings of existing loans after such date.

(5)   Sarbanes-Oxley Act's executive loan prohibition. Sarbanes-Oxley Act of 2002 ("SO") §402 prohibits any company covered by SO's "issuer" definition (generally a company with publicly-issued or publicly-traded securities, as described in more detail below) from:

"directly or indirectly, including through any subsidiary, . . . extend[ing] or maintain[ing] credit, . . . arrang[ing] for the extension of credit, or renew[ing] an extension of credit, in the form of a personal loan to or for any director or executive officer (or equivalent thereof). . . ."[17]

Where a company falling within SO's "issuer" definition sells stock to an executive officer (or director) for a note (or partially for cash and partially for a note), the note likely constitutes an extension of credit in the form of a personal loan and hence falls within SO §402's loan prohibition. This is because (absent favorable, and unlikely, SEC interpretation) the note issued to the company by the executive in exchange for the company's stock (like a personal borrowing of cash) is an obligation of the executive to pay money at maturity, generally with interest.

SO defines "issuer" (i.e., a company subject to SO §402's loan prohibition) as:

(1) a company with a class of equity or debt securities traded on a national securities exchange (a 1934 Act §12(b) company), or

(2) a company with (a) a class of equity securities (or warrants or options) held by 500 or more holders of record and (b) consolidated gross assets of $10 million or more (based on its balance sheet prepared in accordance with GAAP) (a 1934 Act §12(g) company), or

(3) a company which has sold equity or debt securities pursuant to a 1933 Act registration statement and hence is "required to file [10-K, 10-Q, and other] reports [with SEC] under [1934 Act] section 15(d)" (a 1934 Act §15(d) company), except that such a company's status as a §15(d) company (and thus as an "issuer") is automatically suspended for each year (subsequent to the year in which the 1933 Act registration becomes effective) when the company has (on the first day of such subsequent year) fewer than 300 record holders of such 1933 Act registered security, or

(4) a company which has filed with SEC a 1933 Act registration statement covering equity or debt securities that has not yet become effective but has not yet been withdrawn.

If a company falls within any one of these 4 "issuer" definitions, the company is prohibited from making a loan to an executive officer (or director) or continuing a loan previously outstanding (except for such a loan outstanding before SO's 7/30/02 enactment and not thereafter materially modified or renewed). As discussed above, this prohibition likely includes (absent favorable, and unlikely, SEC interpretation) executive's note for the purchase of company stock.

There are several circumstances where a company might become a covered "issuer" (subject to SO §402's loan prohibition) even though the company has no publicly traded equity securities:

(a) Under (2) above, a company with 500 or more record holders of a class of equity securities and $10 million or more of assets is an "issuer" even if there is no public trading in the company's stock.

[17] SO §402 adds this loan prohibition as §13(k) of the Securities Exchange Act of 1934 (the "1934 Act").

(b) Under (4) above, a company which files a 1933 Act registration statement with SEC to sell equity or debt securities (even though the registration statement has never become effective) immediately becomes an "issuer" at the time of filing with SEC, unless or until the 1933 Act registration becomes effective (in which case the company becomes an "issuer" under (3) above) or the company takes affirmative steps to withdraw the not-yet-effective 1933 Act registration statement (so that a company whose 1933 Act registration statement is on hold should generally withdraw the registration statement if the company desires to avoid SO §402's loan prohibition).

For example, a company filing a 1933 Act registration statement for (i) an equity IPO or (ii) an issuance of high-yield bonds—either for cash in the public market or in an A/B exchange for bonds previously issued in a private placement or offshore transaction—is immediately covered at the time of its 1933 Act filing with SEC.

(c) Under (3) above, where a company's 1933 Act registration statement for equity or debt securities (including high-yield bonds) actually becomes effective and the securities are sold, the company is thereafter required to file 1934 Act §15(d) periodic SEC reports and is an "issuer." However, such a §15(d) company—which has not become a §12(b) company (listed on a national securities exchange) or a §12(g) company (with 500 or more record holders of a class of equity securities and $10 million or more of assets)—ceases to be required to file §15(d) SEC reports, and hence ceases to be covered by SO §402, with respect to any year subsequent to the year its 1933 Act registration became effective if, on the first day of such subsequent year, such class of 1933 Act registered securities is held by fewer than 300 record holders.

Thus, where Newco sells stock to an executive officer for a note (or partly for a note) and then acquires T in an LBO financed in part by 1933 Act registered high-yield bonds, Newco (i) becomes an "issuer" under (4) above (so that the executive must pay the note) immediately upon filing with SEC the 1933 Act registration for the high-yield bonds, (ii) continues to be an "issuer" under (3) above once the 1933 Act registered bonds are issued, but (iii) ceases to be an "issuer" once the bonds are (on the first day of a Newco fiscal year subsequent to the year of the bond sale) held by fewer than 300 record holders. The reason Newco ceases to be an issuer once it drops below 300 record holders of the 1933 Act registered bonds is that Newco is no longer "required to file reports under [1934 Act] section 15(d)." However, it is unclear whether Newco continues to be an "issuer" for approximately an additional 3 months, i.e., until Newco files its 10-K report for its last §15(d) year.

EXAMPLE 5

VC-financed (calendar year) Newco files with SEC a 1933 Act registration statement for high-yield bonds on 8/1 year 1. The registration statement becomes effective and the bonds are sold to 20 institutional buyers on 12/1 year 1. Newco has no securities listed on a national securities exchange and no class of equity securities held of record by 500 or more persons. On 1/1 year 2 Newco has fewer than 300 record holders of the bonds.

On 8/1 year 1 when Newco files the 1933 Act registration statement, it becomes an "issuer" under (4) above and hence is covered by SO §402.

On 12/1 year 1 when Newco sells the bonds, it remains an "issuer" under (3) above and hence continues to be covered by SO §402.

However, on 1/1 year 2 Newco (with fewer than 300 record holders of the bonds on the first day of a year subsequent to the year the bonds' 1933 Act registration became effective) automatically ceases to be covered by 1934 Act §15(d) with respect to years subsequent to year 1, i.e., the year in which Newco sold the 1933 Act registered bonds (although SEC requests that Newco file a form 15 notifying SEC that Newco has ceased to be a §15(d) company). Notwithstanding this cessation: (1) Newco is still required to file its 10-K for year 1 with SEC (in approximately March of year 2) and (2) if Newco's 1933 Act registered bonds are ever held by 300 or more record holders in the future, Newco would again be covered by 1934 Act §15(d).

Arguably Newco ceases to be an "issuer" under (3) above—i.e., a company "required to file reports under [1934 Act] section 15(d)"—on 1/1 year 2, since it has only one report (year 1's 10-K) to file with SEC, and is no longer required to file "reports" generally. However, SEC has not yet indicated its view on this timing issue and hence there is risk SEC may take the position that Newco's obligation to file a last 10-K for year 1 (in March of year 2) means that Newco is still required to file "reports" until that final 10-K is actually filed.

Most high-yield indentures for 1933 Act registered bonds require Newco (even after dropping below 300 record holders and thus ceasing to be required by the 1934 Act to file periodic SEC reports) to continue filing with SEC the 1934 Act §15(d) reports which Newco would have been required to file with SEC if Newco still had 300 or more holders of such bonds. This raises the question whether such a "voluntary filer" (i.e., a company required to file 1934 Act reports with SEC by indenture but not by law) is, by virtue of filing SEC reports not required by law, covered by part (3) of the "issuer" definition (i.e., a company "required to file reports under [1934 Act] section 15(d)"). On 11/8/02 SEC announced that "required to file" means required by law, not by contract, so that a voluntary filer is not an "issuer."

Where Newco proposes to issue high-yield bonds to finance its LBO of T, Newco may adopt 3 alternative courses of action to avoid SO §402's loan prohibition:

First, Newco can issue the bonds in the private Rule 144A market (rather than in a 1933 Act registered public offering) without any agreement to effect a subsequent 1933 Act registered A/B exchange of the private bonds for similar SEC registered bonds.

Second, Newco can adopt a two-tier holding company/operating company structure—with 1933 Act registered high-yield bonds issued by operating subsidiary—so that parent holding company, which sells holding company stock to executives, never becomes an SO §402 covered "issuer" at all. Under this approach, holding company must not guarantee operating subsidiary's bonds, because the guarantee is itself a security that must be registered, which would cause holding company to become an "issuer."

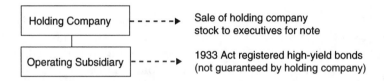

This approach should not violate the spirit of SO §402's loan prohibition, which is designed to prevent a covered "issuer" from risking assets belonging in part to the issuer's public holders by making risky loans to the issuer's executives. However, where only the operating subsidiary has public holders (the high-yield bondholders), the parent holding company's loan to an executive does not put at risk any of the operating subsidiary's assets (just as a loan from a VC investor in holding company to holding company's executives—not guaranteed by operating company—would not put at risk any of operating company's assets).

Because SO §402 also prohibits an "issuer" from "arranging" a loan to an executive officer (or director) of the "issuer," operating subsidiary (which is an "issuer") should not "arrange" for executive's loan from holding company (or from holding company's VC investor). Because holding company and operating subsidiary likely have many overlapping employees, there may be uncertainty on this "arranging" issue where one or more employees of both companies are involved in holding company's sale of stock to a person who is an executive of both. However, it would clearly be helpful if (a) the borrowing executive—although also an operating company executive—has some duties to holding company which make it rational for holding company to extend credit (i.e., engage in a stock sale for a note) to such executive and (b) the holding company officials who approve and document the stock sale for a note are not operating company employees (e.g., the holding company directors who vote for the stock sale and receive the executive's note in exchange are not operating company employees, although they could be employees of the VC investor serving as part-time holding company officials).

Third, Newco's VC investor or some other third party can lend money to the executive (so that the executive can purchase the Newco stock for cash, rather than for a note), with Newco subsequently lending money to executive (so executive can pay off the VC or third party loan) once Newco ceases to be an "issuer""required to file" 1934 Act §15(d) reports (because the bonds are held by fewer than 300 record holders).

An executive officer covered by SO §402's loan prohibition (under 1934 Act Rule 3b-7) is:

- issuer's president
- each of issuer's vice presidents in charge of a principal business unit, division, or function (such as sales, administration, or finance)
- each of issuer's officers performing policy-making functions for issuer
- each executive officer of a subsidiary of issuer performing policy-making functions for issuer

Where Newco is not an "issuer" at the time of Newco's post-7/29/02 stock sale to an executive officer for a note, but becomes an "issuer" subsequently (e.g., because Newco subsequently files a 1933 Act registration statement), the loan becomes a §402 violation as soon as Newco becomes an issuer. Similarly, where Newco is an "issuer" at the time of Newco's post-7/29/02 stock sale to a lower level employee (i.e., not an executive officer) for a note but the lower level employee is subsequently promoted to executive-officer level, the loan becomes a §402 violation as soon as the executive is promoted. Hence any loan documents should require payment of the note immediately before any event that would make the loan illegal under SO §402.

(6)   Executory contract to purchase stock. What are the tax ramifications to a service provider who enters into a binding contract to purchase a specified number of Newco common shares at a specified price on a specified future closing date (or on a closing date to be set in the future by the service provider, which is no later than a specified deadline)? We first review this issue where the Newco shares to be purchased by the service provider are not subject to an SRF but the FV of the Newco shares rises between the contract date and the closing date. We then review this issue where the Newco shares to be purchased by the service provider are subject to an SRF.

Shares not subject to SRF. Where the Newco shares to be purchased by the service provider are not subject to an SRF, is the service provider's Code §83(a) OI measured by the spread (a) at the time the service provider and Newco enter into the executory contract *or* (b) at the time the contract is closed, i.e., when the service provider pays the contract price and receives the Newco shares?

EXAMPLE 6

On 1/1/96 VC forms Newco and executive A enters into a binding executory contract to purchase from Newco 1,000 shares of Newco common stock for $1 per share, closing to take place 5 years later on 1/1/01.

> On 1/1/96 when Newco and A enter into the binding contract, Newco common shares have a $1 per share FV, i.e., an amount equal to the contractual purchase price. Five years later, on 1/1/01, when the sale is closed, Newco common shares have a $100 per share FV.

The conventional wisdom has been that the Code §83(a) event occurs when A closes the sale of the Newco common shares on 1/1/01, so that A at that time recognizes $99,000 of OI (1,000 shares × $99 spread per share at closing), and that A has no taxable event on 1/1/96 when A enters into the executory contract to purchase the 1,000 Newco shares. This conclusion is supported by the following reasoning:

Code §83(a) is triggered only when "property is transferred to [A]." Reg. §1.83-3(a) states that "a transfer of property occurs when a person acquires a beneficial ownership interest in such property." Where A enters into a *binding executory contract* to purchase Newco stock in the future, A does not (until closing) receive the stock, become entitled to dividends on the stock, receive voting rights in the stock, begin to incur interest on the purchase price (where the price will be paid with a note or with borrowed money), or begin to lose interest yield (where the purchase price will be paid out of A's cash on hand). Accordingly, A should not be treated as acquiring beneficial ownership of the Newco stock until closing, and hence the Code §83(a) event with respect to the Newco stock should not occur until closing.

There remains the question whether the binding executory contract itself is property to which Code §83(a) applies. Code §83(e)(3) makes clear that A's receipt of an *option* to purchase Newco shares is not "property" (except in the rare case where the option is treated as having a "readily ascertainable fair market value") so that A's Code §83(a) OI is measured by the FV of the Newco shares (i.e., the property) when A receives the shares on exercise of the option. Although there is one material distinction between an option to purchase stock and an executory contract to purchase stock—with the former A can let the option lapse if the stock's FV declines and in that case A will not be liable for the purchase price—this distinction generally had not been thought to alter the Code §83(a) result.

The regulations have long stated that "property" (the receipt of which triggers Code §83 OI) "includes [1] real and personal property other than . . . an unfunded and unsecured promise to pay money or property in the future . . . and [2] a beneficial interest in assets . . . which are transferred or set aside from the claims of creditors of the transferor, for example, in a trust or escrow account."[18] Under this definition, Newco's promise to pay deferred compensation to A in the future is not taxable until A receives the money (i.e., A receives "property"), unless Newco transfers money or other assets to an escrow or trust account where it is shielded from the claims of Newco's creditors other than A (or Newco otherwise gives A a lien on its assets to secure Newco's deferred compensation obligation so that A's claim against the liened assets is superior to the claims of Newco's unsecured creditors).

---

[18] Reg §1.83-3(e).

Where Newco enters into an executory contract to sell A 1,000 Newco shares (or any other Newco asset) at a future date, it appears that A has not received any "property" (as defined in the §83 regulations) because all of Newco's assets (including the 1,000 Newco shares issuable to A upon closing of A's contract to buy the Newco shares) remain subject to the claims of Newco's unsecured creditors.

However, a 5/96 Ninth Circuit decision (reversing the Tax Court) conflicts with this conventional wisdom.[19] In *Theophilos* the court concluded that:

- In 4/86, A (a Newco executive) entered in a binding executory contract to buy a specified number of Newco shares for $10,000 from Newco's principal shareholder (B).
- Eight months later, in 12/86, A closed the stock purchase, by which time the Newco stock had risen substantially in value to approximately $2.4 million.
- At no time was there an SRF with respect to either A's executory contract to purchase Newco stock or the Newco stock itself.
- "A contractual right to acquire stock is not unsecured or unfunded if it is a binding obligation secured by valuable consideration," and hence "a contractual obligation to acquire stock . . . is 'property' within the meaning of" Code §83 so that A's receipt of "the contractual right to acquire stock is taxable under section 83 [and] the subsequent purchase of the stock [i.e., the closing of the contract] is not."
- On remand the Tax Court should determine the FV of A's "contractual right to acquire Newco stock" when received by A on 4/86 (the date the executory contract was entered into).

Several comments on this surprising Ninth Circuit decision:

First, we do not believe the Ninth Circuit's *Theophilos* decision is a correct interpretation of Code §83, at least in the context of a sale of Newco stock from Newco and to A. Rather we believe that where Newco contracts to sell shares of its stock to A on a deferred closing date, Newco's obligation to deliver its stock to A on the closing date is "an unfunded and unsecured promise to pay money or property [Newco stock] in the future" and that no "beneficial interest in assets [has been] . . . transferred or set aside from the claims of creditors of the transferor." Thus, under the §83 regulations Newco's executory contract to sell Newco stock to A is not "property." We believe the Ninth Circuit was simply wrong when it stated that "a contractual right to acquire stock is not unsecured or unfunded if it is a binding obligation secured by valuable consideration."

The typical promise by Newco to pay deferred compensation to A in cash on a specified future date is (1) a binding obligation (2) secured by valuable consideration, i.e., A's performance of services. Clearly, a service provider is not currently taxable on his employer's binding promise to make a future deferred compensation payment, merely because the service provider supplied valuable consideration (services) in exchange for the employer's binding promise to make the future payment. Otherwise all deferred compensation would be currently taxable.

[19] Theophilos v. Commissioner, 85 F.3d 440, 96-1 U.S.T.C. ¶50,293 (9th Cir. 1996).

Unfortunately, the Ninth Circuit in *Theophilos* confused (1) A's provision of valuable consideration (A's rendering of services to Newco and A's promise to pay $10,000 on the closing date) with (2) the §83 regulations' exclusion from "property" of Newco's "unfunded and unsecured promise to pay money or property [to A] in the future . . . which [property is not] transferred or set aside from the claims of creditors of the transferor. . . ."

Where Newco's principal shareholder, B, rather than Newco itself, has contracted to sell the Newco stock to A, it is possible that the Ninth Circuit's *Theophilos* decision may be correct, because B's promise to deliver Newco stock to A in the future is not subject to the claims of Newco's creditors.[20] Although in fact *Theophilos* involved a sale by shareholder B to executive A, the court's extensive discussion made no particular point of this shareholder-to-executive sale.[21]

In any event, in the context of an executory contract between Newco and executive A, we believe the Ninth Circuit's rationale and conclusion are simply wrong.

Second, if the Ninth Circuit's *Theophilos* decision is correct (i.e., if A's executory contract to purchase Newco stock in the future were "property" for Code §83 purposes), A would recognize OI equal to the FV of the executory contract at the front end when A entered into the executory contract. Normally, A's Code §83(a) OI on a purchase of fully vested Newco stock is the stock's FV on the closing date less the price paid by A. However, in calculating the FV of an executory contract to purchase Newco stock where there is delay between the contract date and the closing date with no escalation of the purchase price for the delay, it appears that, in the absence of other evidence as to the executory contract's FV (e.g., an investment banker's opinion), A's Code §83(a) OI should be calculated by *comparing* (1) the stock FV on the contract date (less the discounted value of dividends and other distributions expected to be paid between the contract date and the closing date, which distributions A will not receive) *to* (2) the purchase price for the stock discounted (presumably at an after-tax market interest rate) from the future closing date back to the contract date. Hence even where the executory contract requires A to pay at closing an amount equal to the stock's FV at the contract date and the stock is not expected to pay dividends, A should

---

[20] Where a shareholder of a corporation transfers property to an employee of the corporation, Reg. §1.83-6(d) treats the corporation (not the shareholder) as the transferor of the property to the employee if the transferee pays less than FV for the property or the property is subject to an SRF. Hence, where a shareholder makes an executory contract to transfer specified assets to an employee, it is arguable that the specified assets are "set aside from the claims of creditors of the transferor."

[21] Indeed, it has long been an unresolved issue in the deferred compensation area whether executive A recognizes OI currently where, in consideration of services rendered by A to his employer, A receives a binding promise from someone other than A's employer to pay future deferred compensation to A. For example, where executive A is employed by Newco and Newco's principal shareholder (or Newco's 100% parent, Bigco) either (a) guarantees Newco's deferred compensation obligation to A *or* (b) is the primary obligor to A from the outset, does A currently recognize OI on the ground that A received more than an unfunded and unsecured promise because the assets which support the shareholder's deferred compensation obligation "are . . . set aside from the claims of [the employer's] creditors"? Is the answer different if Newco arranges for a bank or insurance company to serve as guarantor or primary obligor on Newco's deferred compensation obligation to A?

(absent other evidence as to the contract's value) recognize Code §83(a) OI equal to the discount.[22]

EXAMPLE 7

Same facts as Example 6 and assume further that the Newco shares bear no dividend yield. The present value on 1/1/96 of A's promise to pay $1,000 ($1 per share × 1,000 Newco shares) 5 years later on 1/1/01 is $713 (assuming a fair discount rate of 7% compounded annually). Hence the FV of A's executory contract to purchase 1,000 Newco shares at a price equal to their FV on the contract date but with payment of the purchase price delayed (without interest) for 5 years is apparently $287 (i.e., $1,000 FV of Newco stock less $713 present value of A's promise to pay $1,000 5 years later).

The Ninth Circuit decision did not discuss this issue, but merely stated that "on remand, the Tax Court must make value findings as to the value of [A's] *contractual right* to acquire [Newco] stock as of [the contract date]" (emphasis added).

In a 7/98 decision, *Pahl v. Commissioner,*[23] the Ninth Circuit added to its confused *Theophilos* analysis. In *Pahl*, the Ninth Circuit characterized its *Theophilos* opinion as determining that A "acquired a beneficial interest in the stock not when he paid for the shares, but when the parties executed a shareholder agreement, two employee agreements and other documents," suggesting the Ninth Circuit believes the "property" that was transferred in *Theophilos*, when the parties entered into an executory contract to buy stock, was not the contract right, but rather beneficial ownership of the stock itself.

Shares subject to SRF. If the Ninth Circuit's *Theophilos* decision is correct, what effect does it have on executive A's purchase of Newco stock where (unlike the facts as found by the court in *Theophilos*) the stock is subject to an SRF and A desires to make a Code §83(b) election? A Code §83(b) election must be "made

---

[22] This conclusion is supported by Rev. Rul. 80-186, 1980-2 C.B. 280. In Rev. Rul. 80-186, A granted to A's child B, for nominal consideration, a 2-year binding option to purchase real estate owned by A for 95% of the real estate's FV. IRS concluded that (1) the option was "property" within the meaning of the Code's gift tax provisions (under which "property is used in its broadest and most comprehensive sense"), (2) the gift from A to B was complete on the date A granted the option to B, and (3) the amount of the gift was the FV of the option on the date of the gift less the nominal price B paid A for the option.

We believe that Newco's grant (in the *Theophilos* case) to executive A of an executory contract to purchase Newco stock is not "property" within the meaning of the §83 regulations, but if it were Code §83 property, Rev. Rul. 80-186 supports valuing the executory contract in order to calculate A's OI on the contract date.

See also IRS Letter Ruling 9616035 (1/23/96) (Newco granted executive A an option to buy Newco stock and executive A gifted the option to a family member; held to be a taxable gift in the amount of the FV of the option on the date of the gift).

[23] 150 F.3d 1124, 98-2 U.S.T.C. ¶50,602 (9th Cir. 1998).

not later than 30 days after the date" on which "property is transferred to [A]."[24] Under the Ninth Circuit's rationale,[25] it is arguable that the 30 days would run from the time A entered into the executory contract, not from the closing date when A received the Newco stock, a surprising and highly questionable result.

If the Ninth Circuit's view of Code §83 prevails, we believe that two further conclusions should follow: First, where the Newco stock is subject to an SRF but the binding executory contract itself is not subject to an SRF, no Code §83(b) election would be necessary to trigger Code §83(a) taxation when A and Newco enter into the executory contract. Second, when the contract is closed and the sale is made, A should be treated as transferring the cash purchase price plus the executory contract in exchange for Newco stock which is subject to an SRF. A should then be permitted to make a Code §83(b) election within 30 days of acquiring the property (i.e., the Newco stock) subject to an SRF. Since the sum of the cash purchase price paid by A plus the FV of the executory contract on the closing date should always equal the FV of the Newco stock received by A, A should not recognize OI upon making the Code §83(b) election.[26]

(7)   Newco deduction. Under Code §83(h) the person to whom the services are provided (the service recipient—here, Newco) is entitled to a deduction equal in amount to the income recognized by the service provider under Code §83(a), (b), or (d), subject to (1) the Code §162 reasonable compensation rules, (2) the Code §162(m) $1 million executive-compensation-deduction limitation, and (3) the Code §280G golden parachute strictures. See ¶1506 for a description of Code §162(m) and ¶1505 for a description of Code §280G.

The deduction is included in Newco's taxable year with which or in which the service provider's taxable year ends,[27] except that if Newco transfers fully vested property to the service provider, the timing of Newco's deduction is in accordance with its method of accounting.[28]

According to the §1.83-6 regulations in effect prior to 1/1/95 (the "pre-1995 regulations"), where a service provider was an employee (rather than an independent contractor), the employer forfeited its deduction unless it withheld on the service provider's income so recognized in accordance with Code §3402.[29]

In *Venture Funding*,[30] a 1998 reviewed decision, the Tax Court judges tendered 5 separate and conflicting opinions on the validity of the pre-1995 regulations. A

---

[24] Code §83(b)(2) and (b)(1).

[25] The Ninth Circuit held that "a contractual obligation to acquire stock . . . is "property" within the meaning of" Code §83 so that A's receipt of "the contractual right to acquire stock is taxable under section 83 [and] the subsequent purchase of the stock [i.e., the closing of the contract] is not."

[26] Because closing on an executory contract is not, under general tax principles, a realization event with respect to the executory contract, A likewise should not recognize capital gain on surrender of the appreciated executory contract at closing. Cf. Rev. Rul. 80-244, 1980-2 C.B. 234 (pursuant to Code §1036, employee does not recognize gain on shares used as consideration to exercise a compensatory stock option) and Reg. §1.1001-1(a), -3.

[27] Code §83(h).

[28] Reg. §1.83-6(a)(3).

[29] Reg. §1.83-6(a)(2) (as in effect prior to 1/1/95).

[30] Venture Funding, Ltd. v. Commissioner, 110 T.C. 236 (1998), *aff'd*, 198 F.3d 248, 99-2 U.S.T.C. ¶50,972 (6th Cir. 1999).

bare majority of the Tax Court (9 judges) interpreted (a) Code §83(h) as conditioning the employer's deduction on the employee actually including the Code §83(a) OI in his taxable income and (b) the pre-1995 regulations as granting the employer a safe harbor under which the employer's deduction would be allowed without regard to whether the employee included the Code §83(a) OI if the employer satisfied its withholding requirement. A bare minority of the Tax Court (8 judges) reached a contrary result, (a) 2 judges on the ground that Code §83(h) automatically granted the employer a deduction whenever the Code *required* the employee to recognize Code §83(a) OI so that the pre-1995 regulatory condition to a Code §83(h) deduction (employer withholding) was invalid *and* (b) 6 judges on the alternative grounds that the statute automatically granted the employer a deduction whenever the employee was required to recognize Code §83(a) OI or that the pre-1995 regulations (which these 6 judges read in a strained fashion) did not impose employer withholding as an absolute condition to the employer's Code §83(h) deduction in the case of property that was vested when transferred to the employee.

However, in 7/95 IRS finalized amendments to Reg. §1.83-6 which revise this employer-deduction-forfeiture rule (the "post-1994 regulations").[31] *First*, the post-1994 regulations eliminate the rule that an employer forfeits its Code §83(h) deduction if it fails to withhold on the employee's Code §83 income.

Second, whether the service provider is an employee or an independent contractor, the service recipient is permitted a Code §83(h) deduction only if the Code §83(a) income is "included" in the service provider's gross income, explained in the post-1994 regulatory preamble to mean that the Code §83(a) income is either (1) reported on the service provider's original income tax return or (2) reported on the service provider's amended income tax return or (3) included in the service provider's gross income by IRS on audit.[32]

Third, recognizing that it is generally difficult for the service recipient to ascertain whether a service provider has included an amount in gross income, the post-1994 regulations contain a safe harbor, under which the service provider is "deemed to have included the amount as compensation in gross income if the [service recipient] satisfies in a timely manner all requirements of section 6041 or section 6041A," i.e., timely files form W-2 or form 1099, as applicable, with the service provider and IRS.[33] To meet this rule the service recipient must generally file form W-2 or form 1099, as applicable, with the service provider by 1/31, and with IRS by 2/28, of the year following the year in which the services were performed.[34]

Although form 1099 is not required where the service provider is a corporation, the service recipient can invoke the safe harbor, according to the post-1994 regulatory preamble, for remuneration to a corporation only by filing a voluntary form

---

[31] Reg. §1.83-6(a).

[32] Reg. §1.83-6(a)(1).

[33] Reg. §1.83-6(a)(2).

[34] A special timing rule applies to the safe harbor with respect to a disqualifying disposition of ISO stock, under which the W-2 must be furnished to the service provider and IRS by the time the service recipient files its tax return claiming the deduction.

1099. When the service recipient's gross payments to a service provider fit within a reporting exception (e.g., payments aggregating less than $600 in a taxable year), the service recipient is, according to the regulatory preamble, entitled to rely on the safe harbor without reporting. These safe harbor rules apply equally whether the service provider is an employee or an independent contractor.

If the service recipient has not timely complied with the form W-2 or form 1099 requirements, it is still entitled to a deduction if it can "demonstrate that the [service provider] actually included the amount in income," according to the post-1994 regulatory preamble.

The post-1994 regulations are effective for deductions in taxable years beginning on or after 1/1/95.[35] However, the service recipient is allowed to utilize the post-1994 regulations for any taxable year still open under the statute of limitations. Thus, for example, an employer that failed to withhold, but properly filed a form W-2, for compensation in the form of property to an employee in 1993 forfeits its Code §83(h) deduction (according to the pre-1995 regulations), but under the post-1994 regulations is entitled to the 1993 deduction (by virtue of the timely form W-2 filing and the safe harbor) so long as the claim is not barred by the statute of limitations.

The 9 judges in the Tax Court majority in *Venture Funding, Ltd.*[36] (discussed above) gave every indication that they would read the post-1994 regulations— requiring *either* the service recipient to issue a timely W-2 or 1099 *or* the service provider to include in income the Code §83(a) OI—as a valid condition to the service recipient's Code §83(h) deduction, while the 8 Tax Court judges in the minority would appear likely to apply their dissenting views to the post-1994 regulations.

(8) Mutual cooperation between Mgmt and Newco—formula cash bonus. Through mutual cooperation, Newco and the service provider can often maximize their overall tax position where Newco's stock is expected to rise in value by agreeing that (a) the service provider would not make a Code §83(b) election and (b) Newco would pay the service provider a formula cash bonus, i.e., Newco would pay (to the service provider) a portion of Newco's tax savings on account of its larger deduction at vesting for the appreciated stock value to compensate the service provider for his larger tax cost on the appreciated stock value.

The overall tax advantage to the parties was greater from 1988 through 1992 while the corporate tax rate (and hence the savings rate on the corporation's Code §83(h) deduction) exceeded the individual tax rate. In 2003—when the top marginal income tax rate on OI for individuals (35%) equals the top marginal income tax rate for corporations (35%)—the overall tax advantage of forgoing a Code §83(b) election is reduced.

However, some advantage may still be obtained from forgoing a Code §83(b) election. This is because creating additional OI to the service provider by forgoing a Code §83(b) election increases the service provider's tax rate on post-issuance

---

[35] Reg. §1.83-6(a)(5).
[36] 110 T.C. 236 (1998).

appreciation from the 15% LTCG rate to the 35% OI top rate in 2003, i.e., 20 percentage points greater than for LTCG, while giving the corporation a 35% tax saving on the post-issuance appreciation.

For example, if a service provider receives unvested Newco stock and makes a Code §83(b) election, the service provider recognizes OI equal to the difference between the consideration he paid for the Newco stock and the FV of the stock at the time of issuance, taxed at a marginal rate up to 35% in calendar 2003. At the time of sale, the service provider pays LTCG at 15% on any post-issuance appreciation in value. The corporation is entitled to a deduction at the time of issuance equal to only the amount of the service provider's OI at that time; the corporation is never entitled to a deduction for the post-issuance appreciation.

If, however, the service provider does not make a Code §83(b) election, the service provider recognizes no OI at the time of issuance. He recognizes OI equal to the FV of the Newco stock at time of vesting (less the consideration he paid for the Newco stock), but the corporation is entitled to a deduction equal to the FV of the stock at the time of vesting (less the amount the service provider paid for the stock at issuance). Thus, the service provider pays tax at only an additional 20 percentage points on the post-issuance appreciation (35% in calendar 2003 rather than 15%) while the corporation is entitled to an additional 35 percentage points of tax saving on the post-issuance appreciation (35% rather than zero). Therefore, it may be to the advantage of the corporate employer to agree to some cash bonus (which would also be deductible) to entice the service provider to forgo the Code §83(b) election. However, as described in ¶¶1502.1.7 and 1502.1.8, the accounting rules would cause a reduction in Newco's accounting net income where Newco pays such a tax-offset bonus to the service provider.

Where the service provider forgoes a Code §83(b) election, however, his tax on the post-issuance appreciation is accelerated in time, i.e., he owes the 35% tax on the post-issuance appreciation at the time of vesting, whereas the 15% LTCG tax on the post-issuance appreciation would not have been payable (if he had made a Code §83(b) election) until he sold the stock. On the other hand, the service provider's tax on the pre-issuance appreciation is postponed where he does make a Code §83(b) election, i.e., if the service provider made a Code §83(b) election, he must include, at the time of issuance, OI equal to the difference between the FV of the stock and the consideration (if any) paid for the stock, but if there is no Code §83(b) election, this income is delayed until vesting.

EXAMPLE 8

Same as the example in ¶1502.1, i.e., Newco awards 1,000 shares of Newco common stock (FV $10,000) to executive A for no consideration. The shares will vest three years following grant if A remains in Newco's employ throughout the three-year period. If A leaves Newco's employ for any reason prior to the third anniversary of grant, A must return the 1,000 shares to Newco. The Newco shares are expected to have an aggregate FV of $40,000 at vesting on the third anniversary and A intends to sell those shares promptly after the shares vest. Also assume that A's effective federal income tax rate for LTCG is 15% and for OI is 35% (the top 2003 rates) and that Newco's effective federal income tax rate is 35%.

Code §83(b) Election—A's Taxes

If A were to make a Code §83(b) election upon receipt of the 1,000 Newco shares, A's federal income tax liability in the first year would be $3,500 ($10,000 OI × 35%). If A were to sell the 1,000 shares at the beginning of the fourth year promptly following vesting for $40,000, A would incur additional federal income tax of $4,500 ($30,000 LTCG × 15%). Thus, A would incur total federal income tax of $8,000.

No Code §83(b) Election—A's Taxes

If, instead, A were to make *no* Code §83(b) election, A would incur no tax upon receipt of the 1,000 Newco shares. Upon vesting of the Newco shares at the end of the third year, A would incur a federal income tax liability of $14,000 ($40,000 OI × 35%).[37] Upon sale of Newco shares shortly thereafter for $40,000, A would incur no further federal income tax.

Code §83(b) Election—Newco's Deduction

With regard to Newco, if A makes a Code §83(b) election, Newco is entitled to a $10,000 deduction in the first year and no other deduction (i.e., Newco receives no additional deduction for any future gain recognized by A on the Newco shares). Hence, Newco's tax saving is $3,500 ($10,000 deduction × 35%).

No Code §83(b) Election—Newco's Deduction

If A makes no Code §83(b) election, Newco is entitled to a $40,000 deduction at the end of the third year when the shares vest. Thus, with no Code §83(b) election, Newco saves $14,000 in federal income tax ($40,000 × 35%).

Summary

In summary, A's Code §83(b) election costs Newco $10,500 in federal income tax savings ($14,000 − $3,500) and saves A only $6,000 in federal income taxes.[38]

---

[37] $6,000 difference between A's $14,000 federal income tax with no Code §83(b) election and A's $8,000 federal income tax with a Code §83(b) election represents the lower CG tax rate applicable to the $30,000 postgrant appreciation with a Code §83(b) election, i.e., 20% × $30,000.

[38] Taking the time value of money into account, A's savings would actually be somewhat less than $6,000. With no Code §83(b) election, A would not pay any federal income taxes on receipt of the Newco stock; his $14,000 tax liability upon vesting must therefore be reduced by the after-tax return A would earn on the $3,500 of tax that is deferred from the grant date until the vesting date.

Newco Payment to A

On the facts of this example, Newco's and A's overall tax position is improved if A forgoes the Code §83(b) election. To compensate A for A's additional $6,000 tax liability, Newco could pay a tax-offset bonus to A sufficient to enable A to pay the additional $6,000 of tax, plus the additional tax on the bonus payment, i.e., a $9,231 bonus ($6,000 ÷ .65 = $9,231). Even with this bonus, Newco is in a better tax position than if A makes a Code §83(b) election, i.e., Newco saves $4,500 net ($10,500 additional federal tax saving *less* $6,000 after tax cost of the bonus).[39]

The accounting rules, however, would cause a reduction in Newco's accounting net income equal to Newco's $6,000 after-tax cost of the tax-offset bonus paid to A. And in many circumstances would also transform an arrangement which is "fixed" for APB 25 purposes to "variable." See ¶1502.1.7.9.

See also examples at ¶¶1502.1.6 and 1502.1.8.

(9) Issuance of Newco stock to subsidiary's service provider. Where Newco stock is sold to a person who renders services not to Newco but to Newco's subsidiary (S), (1) S the service recipient (not *Newco* whose stock is being issued) is entitled to the compensation deduction[40] and (2) S recognizes no gain or loss on the delivery of Newco stock, whether Newco issues the stock directly to the S service provider or Newco drops the stock down to S which immediately delivers the stock to the service provider.

From time to time there has been some speculation (with respect to issue (2) above) that S may have a zero basis problem with respect to the Newco stock, i.e., that S may be treated as receiving Newco stock with a zero basis which S then sells to S's service provider. However, in Rev. Rul. 80-76, 1980-1 C.B. 15, without stating any reasoning, IRS stated that "because section 83 applies to the transfer of [Newco] stock [to S's employee], S does not recognize gain or loss on the transfer of the [Newco] stock." In 5/00 IRS issued Reg. §1.1032-3, adopting the cash purchase model—i.e., S is treated as purchasing the Newco stock from Newco for an amount equal to FV and immediately reselling the Newco stock to the service provider—thus confirming, and providing the reasoning behind, the Rev. Rul. 80-76 result.[41] See ¶406. However, if S delivers to an S service provider

---

[39] Newco generally can deduct the $9,231 bonus yielding a tax savings to Newco of $3,231. Thus, Newco's after-tax cost of the bonus is only $6,000 ($9,231 − $3,231).

[40] Reg. §1.83-6(a) (1st sentence) ("a deduction is allowable . . . to the person for whom the services were performed").

[41] The preamble to Reg. §1.1032-3 states that the regulations have made Rev. Rul. 80-76 obsolete. While these regulations, by their terms, apply only to dispositions of P stock or options occurring on or after 5/16/00, the preamble to the regulations states: "IRS will not challenge a taxpayer's position taken in a prior period that is consistent with the requirements set forth in" these regulations.

old and cold Newco shares (i.e., Newco shares that S did not receive immediately before S's transfer of the shares to the service provider), Reg. §1.1032-3 does not protect S from recognizing gain.

¶1502.1.2   Non-Qualified Stock Option

Granting the service provider an NQO to purchase property (except for an option that is actively traded on an established securities market) does not constitute the transfer of property to the service provider until the option is exercised.[42] Hence, a Code §83(b) election cannot be made when the service provider receives the NQO, and the spread at the time the NQO is exercised constitutes OI (except that where the property is subject to a post-exercise SRF and the service provider does not make a Code §83(b) election at exercise, taxation is postponed until the SRF expires and the service provider is then taxed on the FV of the stock at the SRF expiration date less the option price—see ¶1502.1.1(2)).

Legislative Update

The unenacted Senate version (S. 1054) of the 2003 Act, effective for amounts deferred in taxable years beginning after 12/31/03, proposed to amend Code §83 to require a service provider to treat the present value of a right to receive future payments (or such other amount as IRS may by regulations specify) as OI in the taxable year received if such rights are received in exchange for (a) an option to purchase employer securities (as defined in Code §409(*l*)) held by the service provider that is subject to Code §83(a) or that is described in Code §83(e)(3) or (b) any other compensation based on employer securities held by the service provider.

If the service provider is a Newco employee, the amount of the executive's OI at exercise of the NQO (or, where the property is subject to a post-exercise SRF and the executive does not make a timely Code §83(b) election, the amount of OI at the SRF's lapse) is subject to withholding, generally at a 27% federal rate plus any applicable state rate. As discussed at ¶1502.1.1(2), Newco and the executive should generally enter into an agreement at the time the NQO is granted covering which of several alternative approaches will be used to fund Newco's withholding obligation when the NQO is exercised (or when the post-exercise SRF lapses).

Newco is entitled to a deduction equal in amount to the income recognized by the service provider, subject to the qualifications and limitations discussed at ¶1502.1.1(6).

---

[42] Reg. §1.83-7(a).

Legislative Update

The Ending the Double Standard for Stock Options Act (H.R. 626), introduced 2/5/03, would limit Newco's tax deduction attributable to a service provider's NQO exercise to the amount "treated as an expense for the purpose of ascertaining [Newco's] income, profit, or loss in a report or statement to" equity owners, effective for an option exercise on or after enactment, apparently with respect to the stock of either a public or a private company. The same proposal was advanced in two identical 2002 bills introduced in 2/02 (S. 1940) and 3/02 (H.R. 4075) (with Senators Levin and McCain as two of the principal Senate sponsors).

Two later 2003 bills, similar but not identical, introduced as the Broad-Based Stock Option Plan Transparency Act of 2003 in 3/03 (H.R. 1372) and 5/03 (S. 979) would, in general, create a $3\frac{1}{2}$-year moratorium on SEC recognizing as GAAP any new accounting standards related to stock options. See Legislative Update at ¶1502.1.7.3(7) for a detailed discussion.

As discussed in ¶1502.1.7, the GAAP rules which govern the amount treated as compensation expense for accounting purposes are quite complex. If Newco chooses to account for stock-based compensation to its executives under APB 25, the GAAP charge (1) for an option classified by APB 25 as *non-variable* is the spread at the time of grant and (2) for an option classified by APB 25 as *variable* is the spread at the time of exercise (or, if earlier, at time of vesting). Thus, with an APB 25 variable option, where Newco's stock FV increases from grant date to exercise date, Newco's accounting compensation charge also increases, whereas with an APB 25 non-variable option, Newco's accounting charge does not increase.

If instead Newco elects to account for stock-based compensation under newer FASB 123, the GAAP charge in all cases (with no distinction between a variable and a non-variable option) is equal to the FV of the option at time of grant (i.e., the spread at grant plus the FV of the option privilege at grant), generally calculated using a Black-Scholes model, which results in an accounting charge of approximately 20% to 40% of the option stock's grant date FV for an option granted at the money (i.e., where there is no spread at grant). Thus, with an FASB 123 option, Newco's accounting compensation expense does not increase as Newco's stock FV increases from grant to exercise.

If H.R. 626 were enacted, there are many circumstances where Newco's deduction at time of NQO exercise (assuming the Newco stock received upon exercise is not subject to a post-exercise SRF or the service provider then makes a Code §83(b) election) would be reduced below the normal Code §83(h) tax deduction amount (i.e., spread at exercise). For example, if Newco utilizes APB 25, the NQO is classified as non-variable, and the NQO was granted at the money, then Newco's entire Code §83(h) tax deduction would be eliminated by H.R. 626.

If Newco utilizes FASB 123 and the option was granted at the money, so that Newco's FASB 123 charge was approximately 35% of the NQO exercise price, then Newco's normal Code §83(h) tax deduction would be the NQO spread at exercise, but this deduction would be limited by H.R. 626 to 35% of the NQO exercise price (i.e., the FASB 123 charge).

Only where Newco utilizes APB 25 and the NQO is classified as variable, so that the full spread at exercise constitutes an accounting charge, would Newco be assured of its normal Code §83(h) tax deduction if the pending tax bill were enacted.

Exercising NQO with stock in hand. Some NQO plans permit the service provider to pay the option price either (i) in cash or (ii) with previously acquired shares of Newco's stock ("old Newco shares") of the same type as the "new" NQO shares and having an FV on the date of exercise equal to the option price. If the service provider pays the exercise price with old Newco shares, IRS in effect bifurcates the transaction. Specifically, IRS treats the transaction as though (i) the service provider exchanges the old Newco shares for an amount of the new NQO shares having an FV equal to the old Newco shares (a tax-free exchange under Code §1036), and (ii) the service provider receives the remaining new NQO shares as compensation (taxable as described in the preceding paragraph).[43] Basically this means that the service provider (i) will currently recognize OI equal to the amount by which the FV of the new NQO shares exceeds the exercise price of the NQO, (ii) will not currently recognize gain on the appreciation in value of the old Newco shares surrendered, and (iii) will hold part of the new NQO shares at a basis equal to the basis of the old Newco shares (and with a holding period that includes the holding period of the old Newco shares) and will hold the balance of the NQO shares at a basis equal to the OI recognized as a result of the NQO exercise (and with a holding period commencing at that time).

EXAMPLE 1

Individual A, a Newco employee, holds an NQO issued to A by Newco entitling A to purchase 100 Newco common shares at $10 per share (or a total option price of $1,000, i.e., $10 × 100 shares). The NQO states that A can pay the option price either in cash or in shares of Newco common stock having an FV on the date of exercise equal to the option price.

On a date when Newco common stock is trading at $50 per share (so that the FV of A's 100 Newco NQO shares is $5,000), A exercises his NQO by delivering to Newco 20 shares of Newco common stock (the "old Newco shares") in payment of the $1,000 option price (20 old Newco shares × $50

---

[43] See Rev. Rul. 80-244, 1980-2 C.B. 235; Gen. Couns. Mem. 38204 (12/19/79) and Gen. Couns. Mem. 37939 (4/20/79), both underlying Rev. Rul. 80-244.

FV per share = $1,000). A acquired the 20 old Newco shares several years ago at $1 per share.

A is treated as though (i) he exchanged the 20 old Newco shares for 20 of the NQO shares in a tax-free Code §1036 transaction, and (ii) he received the remaining 80 NQO shares as compensation. As a result, (i) A will hold 20 of the NQO shares with a long-term holding period and at a basis of $1 each; (ii) A will have ordinary compensation income of $4,000 (i.e., the FV of the 80 NQO shares A received as compensation), unless the 80 compensation shares are subject to an SRF in which case (absent a Code §83(b) election) A will have ordinary compensation income on the date the SRF expires equal to the FV of the 80 NQO shares on the expiration date; and (iii) A will hold the 80 compensation shares at a basis equal to the amount of A's compensation income.[44]

Excessively low NQO exercise price. If, however, the exercise price of an NQO is excessively low in comparison to the FV of the underlying stock at the time of grant, IRS may take the position that the NQO grant was actually a transfer of the underlying stock rather than a non-taxable NQO grant.[45]

In Rev. Rul. 82-150, 1982-2 C.B. 110, optionee paid 70% of the FV of stock for an option to buy the stock for 30% of FV; IRS ruled that the optionee owned the stock covered by the option as of the date of grant.

In *Morrison v. Commissioner*[46] taxpayer received a compensatory, three-year option to acquire for $1 per share stock worth (at grant) $300 per share. The option was immediately exercisable and transferable; it was not, however, tradable. The court held that the grant of the option was taxable on the ground that the option had a readily ascertainable value at grant under Reg. §1.421-6(c)(3) (which is similar to Reg. §1.83-7(b)(2) and (3)). The court stated, "[t]he option in the instant case, in terms of value, was *the substantial equivalent of the stock itself*. By paying the nominal sum of $1 per share, the petitioner could have received at any time the valuable stock."[47]

---

[44] Suppose the NQO permits A to pay the exercise price in "old" Newco shares that are different in some respect from the NQO shares? For example, suppose the NQO permits A to use old Newco *preferred* shares to pay the exercise price for NQO common shares. Arguably, under the bifurcation approach of Rev. Rul. 80-244, A's exchange of old Newco preferred shares for NQO common shares having an FV equal to the FV of the old Newco preferred shares should qualify as a tax-free recapitalization under Code §368(a)(1)(E), and A should have ordinary compensation income to the extent of the FV of the remaining NQO common shares. It is unclear, however, whether IRS agrees with this conclusion. See Gen. Couns. Mem. 38204 (12/19/79) (IRS position in this General Counsel Memorandum is highly questionable since Code §1036 does not require that the old common stock be of the "same kind" as the new common stock; see, e.g., Reg. §1.1036-1(a); Rev. Rul. 72-199, 1972-1 C.B. 228).

[45] IRS has announced that it is studying the proper year for a service provider to report income from the grant of an option where the option's exercise price is less than the FV of the underlying stock on the date of grant. Rev. Proc. 89-22, 1989-1 C.B. 843, as corrected by IRS Announcement 89-42, 1989-13 I.R.B 53.

[46] 59 T.C. 248 (1972), *acq.*, 1973-2 C.B. 3.

[47] 59 T.C. at 260 (emphasis added).

Although there is little helpful precedent, it appears that where the option price is less than 10% of the option stock's FV at grant, the risk that the option grant will be treated as a transfer of the underlying stock is high; if the option price is between 10% and 25% of FV, the risk appears moderate; and if the option price is 50% or more of FV, the risk appears very low.

If IRS successfully took the position that the NQO grant was actually a transfer of the underlying stock, the "optionee" would immediately be taxed under Code §83(a) on the FV of the stock (less the option price) if there were no SRF. If there were an SRF, the "optionee" would be taxed when the SRF expired on the FV of the stock at the SRF expiration date less the option price.[48]

See also the examples at ¶¶1502.1.6 and 1502.1.8.

Gifting vested NQO. An NQO may by its terms permit the executive to transfer the NQO by gift to the executive's immediate family members or trusts established for their benefit. In a number of private letter rulings,[49] IRS has held that, where the NQO is vested and exercisable at the time of transfer, the gift, estate and income tax consequences of such an NQO transfer, and of the subsequent NQO exercise, are as follows:

(1) For gift tax purposes, the NQO transfer constitutes a completed gift on the transfer date, at the NQO's FV on the transfer date, so long as the transfer is irrevocable and the executive retains no rights or powers associated with the transferred NQO (e.g., the right to determine whether or when to exercise).

(2) For estate tax purposes, the transferred NQO is not included in the executive's estate upon his death, so long as the conditions in (1) above are met.

(3) For income tax purposes, the NQO transfer does not cause the executive to recognize taxable income. However, when the transferee exercises the NQO, the executive recognizes OI under Code §83 equal to the excess of the NQO shares' FV on the exercise date over the NQO exercise price, and the executive's employer (Newco) is entitled to a corresponding deduction under Code §§83(h) and 162 (subject to any applicable limitations, such as the Code §162(m) $1 million deduction limitation on certain executive compensation—see ¶1506).[50]

---

[48] If the "optionee" treated the original grant as the grant of an option rather than as a transfer of stock subject to an SRF, the "optionee" presumably would not have filed a Code §83(b) election. If the "option" grant were later (e.g., on audit) treated as the transfer of the stock, it would be too late to file a timely Code §83(b) election.

[49] See, e.g., IRS Letter Rulings 9616035 (1/23/96), 9722022 (2/27/97), and 199927002 (3/19/99).

[50] In IRS Letter Ruling 9722022 (2/27/97), IRS held that neither (1) amending an existing NQO plan nor (2) amending the terms of previously-granted NQOs, in each case to permit transfers of NQOs to an executive's immediate family members or trusts for their benefit, constituted a "material modification" of the NQO plan or outstanding NQOs for purposes of Reg. §1.162-27(h)(3)(ii)(A). Accordingly, the grandfathered Code §162(m) status of a plan adopted before 2/17/93 should not be lost as a result of amending such plan to permit executives who received or will receive NQOs under the plan to transfer such NQOs to immediate family members or trusts for their benefit. See ¶1506.1.6 for a discussion of the exception to the §162(m) deduction limitation for plans adopted before 2/17/93.

(4) For income tax purposes, the transferee's basis in the NQO shares acquired upon exercise is the FV of such NQO shares at the time of exercise.[51]

In consequence, where the underlying stock is expected to appreciate substantially, an NQO gift to family members immediately or shortly after grant (plus cash to exercise) can result in substantially lower overall gift and estate taxes—with no increase or shift in income tax liability—as compared to a gift of the underlying shares after the NQO exercise.

EXAMPLE 2

Newco grants executive A a vested and exercisable 7-year NQO to purchase 100 Newco common shares at $10 per share (or a total option price of $1,000), at a time when the FV of a Newco common share is $10. A promptly gifts the NQO to family member B, along with $1,000 cash. Assuming A's effective gift tax rate is 50% and the NQO's FV is $300 (i.e., 30% of the underlying stock's FV—see discussion of option valuation techniques below), A owes $650 of gift tax ($1,300 × 50%), of which $150 is attributable to the option. B later exercises the NQO when Newco stock FV is $50 per share. When B exercises the NQO A owes income tax (generally at 35% in calendar 2003) on the $4,000 spread at exercise ($5,000 FV at exercise less $1,000 exercise price).

B's tax basis in the Newco stock should be $5,150 ($1,000 exercise price paid by B, plus $4,000 OI recognized by A, plus $150 gift tax on option transfer by A).

EXAMPLE 3

Same as Example 2, except that A retains the NQO, exercises the NQO when Newco stock FV is $50 per share, and immediately gifts the option shares to B.

A's cash outlays in this Example 3 are the same as in Example 2 ($1,000 NQO exercise price plus OI tax on the $4,000 NQO spread at exercise),

---

[51] Although not addressed in the letter rulings cited above, the transferee's basis in the NQO shares should also include the amount of gift tax paid, if any, with respect to the transferred NQO. See the last sentence of Reg. §1.83-4(b)(1) (basis of non-vested property acquired reflects amount paid for the property, amount of OI recognized, and any Code §§1015 and 1016 adjustments) and Code §1015(d) (adding gift tax to the basis of property transferred). Code §1015(d) states that the basis of gifted property is increased by the gift tax "but not above the fair value of such property at the time of the gift." This limitation should not apply to the gift of an NQO, since the executive generally has a zero basis for the NQO at the time of the gift and the gift tax is a percentage (generally not greater than 55%) of the NQO's FV at the time of the gift. Thus, the basis of the NQO in the transferee's hands immediately after the gift is generally the gift tax paid, which by definition is a percentage (generally not greater than 55%) of the NQO's FV. The Code §1015(d) limitation does not by its terms apply at the later time the NQO is exercised (but only at the time the NQO is gifted).

except that A's gift tax, calculated when A gifts the option shares to B, is $2,500 ($5,000 stock FV × 50%), i.e., $1,850 more than in Example 2 ($2,500 less $650).

B's tax basis in the Newco stock should be $5,000 ($5,000 tax basis of stock in A's hands, not increased by $2,500 gift tax paid by A because of Code §1015(d) limitation).

For gift tax purposes, the FV of a gifted NQO is not simply the spread between the NQO exercise price and FV of the underlying stock at the time of the gift. In Rev. Proc. 98-34,[52] IRS sets forth a safe harbor methodology for valuing a compensatory stock option (either NQOs or ISOs) for gift and estate tax purposes, applicable only to a non-publicly traded option to acquire stock that is traded on an established securities market on the valuation date. Under Rev. Proc. 98-34, a taxpayer may determine the value of a compensatory stock option for gift and estate tax purposes "using a generally recognized option pricing model (for example, the Black-Scholes model or an accepted version of the binomial model)" that takes into account (1) the exercise price of the option, (2) the expected life of the option, (3) the current trading price of the underlying stock, (4) the expected volatility of the underlying stock, (5) the expected dividends on the underlying stock, and (6) the risk-free interest rate over the remaining option term. To determine the expected life of an option, Rev. Proc. 98-34 permits a taxpayer to use either (1) the maximum remaining term of the option on the valuation date or (2) a method set forth in the Revenue Procedure which takes into account the weighted-average expected life of options granted by the taxpayer's employer and disclosed in the employer's financial statements for purposes of complying with FASB 123.[53] In addition, the factors for expected stock volatility and expected dividends must be the same as the expected stock volatility and expected dividends disclosed in the employer's financial statements for the employer's fiscal year that includes the valuation date.

Rev. Proc. 98-34 does not set forth a safe harbor method for valuing an option to acquire non-publicly-traded stock. However, in the absence of additional IRS guidance, taxpayers should be allowed to use good faith efforts to apply the factors set forth in Rev. Proc. 98-34 to value such an option.

Use of the Black-Scholes or similar option pricing model typically produces an option FV (for an option that is at-the-money on the valuation date) equal to 20% to 40% of the underlying stock's FV, depending on such factors as the option's expected life and the price volatility of the underlying stock. Thus, in Example 2 above (where executive A received a 7-year option to purchase 100 Newco common shares at $10 per share, at a time when the FV of a Newco common share was $10), executive A's NQO might be valued at $300 ($1,000 × 30%) at the time of grant. The higher the stock's price volatility and the longer the expected life,

---

[52] 1998-1 C.B. 983.

[53] However, the maximum remaining term of the option must be used if taxpayer's employer "is not required by [FASB] 123 to disclose an expected life of the options granted in the fiscal year of the company that includes the valuation date." See ¶1502.1.7.3 for a discussion of FASB 123.

the higher the value of the option, because of the higher probability of a large option gain. For options that are substantially in-the-money on the valuation date, the option's FV as a percentage of the underlying stock's FV may be significantly greater than 20% to 40%.

Gifting unvested NQO. Is the gift tax result of an NQO gift different where the NQO is not vested and exercisable at the time of the gift, e.g., where the NQO does not become vested and exercisable until executive A subsequently satisfies an employment-related condition, such as A's continued employment for a specified period following grant? Such vesting/exercisability restrictions are a common feature of NQOs. Until early in 1998, there had been hope that IRS would treat a gift of an unvested/unexercisable NQO in the same manner as a gift of a vested and exercisable NQO. However, Rev. Rul. 98-21[54] takes the position that the transfer of an NQO that only becomes vested and exercisable if the executive renders additional services is *not* a completed gift, and therefore is not valued for gift tax purposes, until expiration of such vesting/exercise restrictions.

EXAMPLE 4

Same as Example 2, except that A's NQO is exercisable only if A remains continuously employed by Newco for two years following grant. A immediately gifts this non-vested, non-exercisable NQO to family member B. Two years later the vesting condition is satisfied and the NQO first becomes exercisable, when the FV of the stock underlying the NQO is then $50 per share, or a total of $5,000.

Under Rev. Rul. 98-21, A's NQO gift is treated as complete for gift tax purposes (and the gift is valued) on the second anniversary of grant when the NQO first becomes vested and exercisable.

While Rev. Rul. 98-21 is silent, it is likely that:

- IRS's position would be the same if the option were exercisable from the outset (i.e., from date of grant), but Newco had the right to repurchase the underlying stock at the $10 per share option price should B exercise the option and A then fail to remain a Newco employee until the second anniversary of grant (i.e., where the option is exercisable but the underlying stock is unvested), and
- IRS's position would be the same if there is no option but rather A actually purchases Newco stock for $10 per share (subject to Newco's right to repurchase the stock at $10 per share should A fail to remain a Newco employee until the second anniversary of purchase), whether or not A made a Code §83(b) election, since such an election is relevant only for income (not gift and estate) tax purposes.

[54] 1998-1 C.B. 975.

IRS's position in Rev. Rul. 98-21 appears to be inconsistent with Reg. §25.2511-2(b), stating that a gift is complete when "the donor has so parted with dominion and control over the property transferred as to leave him no power to change its disposition, whether for the donor's own benefit or the benefit of another." Nevertheless, Rev. Rul. 98-21 asserts that an unvested NQO does not constitute an "enforceable property right" for gift tax purposes until the right to exercise the NQO becomes "binding and enforceable," although such an unvested NQO (1) clearly has value and (2) clearly gives the transferee (not the executive) the legal right to exercise the NQO and receive the stock, so long as the condition of the executive's continued employment during the vesting period has been satisfied.[55]

Rev. Rul. 98-21 addresses a vesting/exercise restriction that lapses with the performance of additional services. What about a vesting/exercise restriction that lapses based on the attainment of a pre-determined performance goal regardless of whether the executive renders any additional services? A 3/99 IRS Letter Ruling holds that transfer of an NQO that would become exercisable upon achievement of a pre-determined appreciation target with respect to the underlying stock (without regard to whether additional services are performed by the gifting executive) constitutes a completed gift.[56]

The stated rationale for IRS's letter ruling conclusion suggests that IRS would reach the same result in the case of any purely performance-based vesting/exercise restriction. In this regard, the ruling, after reciting the holding of Rev. Rul. 98-21, continues:

> Although the options . . . are subject to the price appreciation restrictions on exercise, the ability to exercise the options is not conditioned on [A's] continued future employment . . . by the Company.

Hence, assuming this private letter ruling fairly reflects IRS's current view as to the scope of Rev. Rul. 98-21, a completed gift may be made of an NQO that will become vested/exercisable only when, e.g., an as yet unsatisfied earnings-per-share target has been satisfied, so long as vesting/exercise is not also conditioned on the NQO donor's performance of additional services.

Charitable donation of NQO. Less commonly, but more commonly as time goes on, the NQO's terms may permit donation to a charity described in Code §170(c). The generally satisfactory tax consequences of one such arrangement (where donor retained rights causing the donation to be deemed made when the

---

[55] The term "property" has generally been given a broad definition by courts in applying the gift tax. See, e.g., Smith v. Shaughnessy, 318 U.S. 176, 180 (1943) ("the language of the gift tax statute, "property . . . real or personal, tangible or intangible," is broad enough to include property, however conceptual or contingent."); Galt v. Commissioner, 216 F.2d 41, 50 (7th Cir. 1954) (transfer of interest in a percentage of future profits from leased property is a completed gift as of the transfer date even though such future profits were "speculative, uncertain and contingent upon future developments").

[56] IRS Letter Ruling 199927002 (3/19/99). Under the terms of the NQO addressed in the ruling, the share appreciation restriction would lapse prior to expiration of the NQO. However, such pre-expiration lapse does not appear to have been a factor in IRS's analysis.

charity exercised the option)—executive's compensation income at time charity exercises NQO offset by contemporaneous Code §170(a)(1) charitable contribution deduction not subject to reduction under Code §170(e)—are described and explained in IRS Letter Ruling 9737016 (6/13/97).

When the charitable donation is by bequest—i.e., A by will transfers an unexercised NQO to charity C and C thereafter exercises—the generally satisfactory tax consequences are as follows: *First*, the inclusion in A's gross estate of the NQO's FV is offset by a Code §2055(a) estate tax charitable deduction for the NQO's FV. *Second*, if and when C exercises the NQO, the ordinary income (equal to the spread at exercise) is income in respect of a decedent to C under Code §691(a)(1)(C) and not income in respect of a decedent to A's estate (if the estate is still open at the time of exercise) or to A's other devisees (if A's estate is closed at the time of exercise).[57]

Transfer of NQO incident to divorce. Adopting a sensibly expansive approach to the term "property" as used (but not defined) in Code §1041, IRS in 5/02 Rev. Rul. 2002-22[58] announced a follow-the-cash income tax approach: (1) An employee (A) who transfers a vested NQO[59] to a former spouse (B) incident to divorce is not required to include any amount in gross income upon the transfer. (2) When B exercises the transferred NQO, B (and not A) must include the spread (FV in excess of option price) in gross income. IRS explained that "applying the assignment of income doctrine in divorce cases to tax [A] when [B] ultimately receives the income . . . would frustrate the purpose of §1041 . . . and thwart the purpose of allowing divorcing spouses to sever their ownership interests in property with as little tax intrusion as possible."[60]

IRS Notice 2002-31[61] seeks comment on a proposed revenue ruling on the FICA, FUTA, income tax withholding, and other reporting aspects of incident-to-divorce NQO transfer and exercise.

¶1502.1.3 Substantial Risk of Forfeiture Subsequently Imposed on Outstanding Stock

An executive of a newly formed company ("Newco") will often purchase stock (either by outright purchase of stock or exercise of an NQO) which is not subject to an SRF (i.e., unrestricted stock). Later, new investors in Newco (e.g., VCs) may insist that the executive subject his stock to an SRF (e.g., grant Newco or the VCs

[57] IRS Letter Ruling 200012076 (12/23/99), citing Reg. §1.83-1(d); IRS Letter Ruling 200002011 (9/30/99) (same).
[58] 2002-1 C.B. 849.
[59] Rev. Rul. 2002-22 also applies the same tax approach to an incident-to-divorce transfer of a vested non-qualified deferred compensation arrangement that is not an NQO.
[60] Thus, it is not clear why the ruling states that it "does not apply to transfers of [NQOs and non-qualified deferred compensation] to the extent . . . unvested at the time of transfer."
[61] 2002-1 C.B. 908.

an option to purchase the executive's stock at his cost (or at the lower of cost or FV) if he does not meet specified time or performance goals).

It can be argued that (1) the executive's Newco shares were fully vested at the time issued (even without a Code §83(b) election), so that the executive recognizes OI only if (and to the extent) the unrestricted Newco shares were worth more than his cost at the time of Newco's formation and (2) the SRF imposed *after* the executive previously purchased the unrestricted Newco stock does *not* cause Code §83 to apply on the SRF's subsequent lapse. Code §83(a) provides that income (if any) is recognized when the executive's interest in the transferred stock is *first* either transferable or not subject to an SRF. Thus, it can be argued that (1) the executive recognized income under Code §83(a) (if any) when he originally purchased the unrestricted stock (based on FV compared to his cost for such stock at the time of purchase) and (2) Code §83(a) is not applicable on the expiration of an SRF imposed after the executive first held the unrestricted stock for some period.

However, there is risk IRS may reject this approach and argue that the executive (absent a timely §83(b) election) *is* taxable upon the expiration of the subsequently imposed SRF on one (or more) of three grounds:

(1) **Newco a shell company when executive initially purchases stock.** If the executive purchases cheap stock in a shell company (Newco) prior to making arrangements essential to Newco's future operations (such as obtaining commitments for necessary VC financing), IRS might take the position that the initial transfer of the unrestricted cheap stock to the executive should be disregarded as essentially meaningless. If IRS were successful in this position, the transfer of stock to the executive would be deemed to occur at the later date, when the essential business arrangements are settled (e.g., when the VC financing is arranged and the SRF imposed), at which time the stock is subject to an SRF. Thus (absent a timely Code §83(b) election), the executive would recognize OI equal to the spread at the time the SRF expired (i.e., the excess of the stock's FV at SRF expiration over the price paid by the executive).

(2) **SRF imposed shortly after executive's initial stock purchase.** If Newco's subsequent financing is arranged and the SRF imposed shortly after executive's initial purchase of Newco's unrestricted stock, IRS might seek to invoke the step-transaction doctrine to treat the executive's initial stock purchase and the subsequent SRF imposition as a single transaction, especially where Newco is in the process of (or perhaps well along in) negotiating the subsequent financing when executive initially buys the unrestricted Newco stock. If IRS were successfully to assert this position, executive's Newco stock would (absent a timely Code §83(b) election) be treated as subject to an SRF from the outset and executive would recognize OI equal to the spread when the SRF expires (i.e., the excess of the stock's FV at SRF expiration over the price paid by the executive).

(3) **Constructive exchange even where Newco not shell company and SRF not imposed shortly after executive's initial stock purchase.** IRS may

take the position that, although the executive first held unrestricted stock (i.e., from Newco's formation until consummation of the VC financing), he subsequently engaged in a constructive exchange of his unrestricted stock for new stock subject to an SRF. A constructive exchange would create a second transfer of stock (which is subject to an SRF) to the executive. Hence, Code §83 would arguably apply to his receipt of the SRF stock, so that the SRF stock would be taxable when first free of the SRF or transferable. Under this view, the executive would (absent a timely Code §83(b) election) recognize OI when the SRF lapses on the SRF stock equal to the excess of (a) the FV of the SRF stock at SRF expiration over (b) the price the executive paid for the SRF stock (i.e., the FV of the unrestricted stock at the time of the constructive exchange).

To avoid these risks, it appears wise for the executive to make a "protective election" under Code §83(b) within 30 days after SRF imposition. The protective election would take the position that (1) a Code §83(b) election was not necessary because the executive owned fully vested Newco stock from the outset, but that the Code §83 protective election is being made in case IRS seeks to invoke Code §83, and (2) the price paid by the executive for the SRF stock (i.e., the price paid by the executive for the unrestricted stock at the outset in (1) and (2) above and the FV of the unrestricted stock deemed surrendered in the constructive exchange in (3) above) is equal to the FV of the SRF stock received or deemed received (ignoring, as required by Code §83(a), the SRF's effects on FV), so the executive recognizes no OI as a result of the election.[62]

In several private letter rulings and an information letter, beginning 6/00 IRS adopted the pro-taxpayer position that where an executive first receives fully vested stock (or a partnership/LLC interest) and subsequently at the behest of a new financing party agrees to impose an SRF on the stock (or partnership/LLC interest) which was not previously contemplated, "the subsequent imposition of the forfeiture provisions on the founders' [Newco] shares [or partnership/LLC interest] must necessarily have been accomplished in the *absence* of a section 83 transfer (i.e., the shares were *already owned* for section 83 purposes), and that, therefore, these provisions had no effect for section 83 purposes."[63]

While we welcome IRS's conclusion, we are cautious about recommending that executive not file a Code §83(b) election, because, first, private letter rulings and an IRS information letter are not authority on which a taxpayer may legally rely, and second, the private letter rulings and information letter merely indicate IRS would not assert ground 3 (the constructive exchange argument) and do

---

[62] Reg. §1.83-3(g) (1st sentence). The executive should not recognize taxable gain on any appreciation in the unrestricted stock given up in the constructive exchange (i.e., the excess of the FV of the unrestricted stock over its cost). See Code §1036. See ¶604.1.6(2)(c) and ¶604.1.6(1)(d) for a discussion of the risk that a deemed exchange plus Code §83(b) election restarts the executive's holding period for his T stock in whole or in part under a literal reading of Reg. §1.83-4(a).

[63] IRS Letter Ruling 200212005 (11/8/01) (corporate stock), IRS Letter Ruling 200204005 (10/12/01) (LLC interest), IRS Information Letter (6/12/00) from Robert Misner, Assistant Branch Chief, Branch 1, Office of the Division Counsel/Associate Chief Counsel (Tax Exempt and Government Entities).

not address the possibility IRS could, depending on the facts, argue executive recognizes OI on SRF lapse on ground 1 or 2.

For discussion of a T shareholder (owning T vested stock) who receives unvested P stock (subject to an SRF) in a tax-free reorganization, see ¶604.1.6.

¶1502.1.4 Compensating Executive for Taxable Income at NQO Exercise or Lapse of Substantial Risk of Forfeiture Without Code §83(b) Election

Where an executive exercises an NQO (or where purchased stock vests and no Code §83(b) election was made), the executive recognizes OI equal to the spread and Newco is entitled (subject to the qualifications and limitations discussed at ¶1502.1.1(5)) to an equal deduction. In order to compensate the executive for his tax cost, Newco could lend part of its tax saving to the executive to pay his tax at exercise (with the loan due when executive sells the stock, or possibly earlier if his employment ceases), charge interest on such loan at the AFR (in order to avoid the IRS imputed interest rules), and agree to pay an annual bonus to the executive to reimburse him for his interest expense on the loan at the AFR.

Under the 1986 Act, LTCG and OI were taxed at the same unified rates for individuals from 1988 through 1990. However, under the 1990 Act, beginning 1/1/91, for individuals the top rate for LTCG was 3 percentage points lower than the top rate applicable to OI. The rate differential was increased to 11.6% in the 1993 Act, effective 1/1/93, with the top individual OI rate rising to 39.6% but the top CG rate remaining at 28%. The 1997 Act further increased the differential to 19.6% for LTCG (taxed at a maximum rate of 20% for dispositions after 5/6/97), while the 2001 Act reduced the differential to 18.6% by reducing the maximum OI tax rate to 38.6% in calendar 2002. Finally, for the moment, the 2003 Act increased the differential to 20%, 35% OI rate vs. 15% LTCG rate.

Where a preferential LTCG rate applies, Newco could pay the executive a tax-offset bonus equal to part of Newco's tax saving arising out of Newco's deduction for the spread at exercise of the NQO or the spread at vesting for stock purchased without a Code §83(b) election. Newco will still end up with cash in pocket (because its tax saving—which might be delayed if Newco has NOLs—will very likely exceed its bonus to executive). However, generally accepted accounting principles (GAAP) will nevertheless cause a reduction in Newco's accounting net income as described below.

¶1502.1.5 Rescission of Stock Option Exercise

Where stock prices fall sharply after an executive exercises a Newco stock option, the executive may end up holding Newco stock worth less than the taxes triggered by option exercise. In such case, the executive may wish to "unexercise" the option and calculate his taxable income as if the option had never been exercised.

EXAMPLE

In year 1, executive receives a 10-year fixed (i.e., non-variable) option (not an incentive stock option for income tax purposes) to purchase 10,000 Newco shares at $5 per share, the FV of Newco stock at grant. In February year 3, when Newco stock is worth $105 per share, executive exercises the option, paying $50,000 to Newco and receiving 10,000 Newco shares worth $1.05 million, and recognizes $1 million of taxable OI (i.e., the spread in the option at exercise). Executive retains the Newco shares and thereafter their FV falls precipitously to $9 per share in December year 3.

Executive owes $400,000 tax on the option exercise, assuming a 40% effective tax rate, while the Newco shares he holds at year end are worth only $90,000. Executive and Newco agree to "unexercise" the stock option. Prior to the end of year 3, executive returns the 10,000 Newco shares to Newco. Newco returns the $50,000 exercise price to executive and restores the option with its original terms. Executive and Newco both use the calendar year for tax reporting.

In Rev. Rul. 80-58,[64] seller sold land to buyer for cash with the agreement that buyer could reconvey the land to seller if buyer was unable to obtain rezoning. Buyer was ultimately unable to obtain rezoning and, pursuant to their agreement, buyer returned the land to seller and seller returned the purchase price to buyer. IRS ruled that if the rescission occurred not later than the end of the taxable year of the sale, "the original sale is to be disregarded for federal income tax purposes because the rescission extinguished any taxable income for that year with regard to that transaction." In contrast, if seller and buyer had rescinded the sale after the end of the taxable year of sale, IRS ruled that the original sale would be given tax effect (i.e., resulting in gain or loss for seller), because the annual accounting period principle required that taxable income be computed based on facts in existence at year end, in which case the reconveyance would be treated as a separate transaction in the following year.

Although on its facts Rev. Rul. 80-58 involved a situation where there was a pre-existing contractual right to rescind, the ruling is apparently not limited to cases where there is a contractual or other right to rescind. In Rev. Rul. 80-58 IRS stated that "[a] rescission may be effected by mutual agreement of the parties, by one of the parties declaring a rescission of the contract without the consent of the other if sufficient grounds exist, or by applying to a court for a decree of rescission." Rev. Rul. 80-58 also cites Rev. Rul. 74-501[65] where IRS ruled that an investor's purchase of stock pursuant to stock rights received in a corporate distribution would be ignored for tax purposes where the investor and the corpora-

---

[64] 1980-1 C.B. 181.
[65] 1974-2 C.B. 98.

tion voluntarily agreed, after the value of the corporation's stock dropped sharply, to cancel the purchase and refund the taxpayer's purchase price in the same taxable year the rights were issued.

While neither Rev. Rul. 80-58 nor Rev. Rul. 74-501 involves the rescission of a compensatory transaction with a service provider, the same principles should apply where Newco and the executive agree to rescind the executive's exercise of a compensatory stock option. Indeed, a 1990 private ruling applied these principles in disregarding for tax purposes an employee's receipt of restricted stock (and related Code §83(b) election) that was rescinded later in the same year (after discovery that the grant would trigger unanticipated financial accounting charges for the employer).[66] Thus, if the rescission in the Example occurs in the same taxable year as the exercise (i.e., by the end of year 3), the exercise should be ignored for income tax purposes, eliminating executive's $1 million of OI and Newco's $1 million compensation deduction.

Where Newco and executive use different taxable years, it is not entirely clear whether the rescission must occur before the end of the taxable year for both executive and Newco in order to be given tax effect. If, for example, Newco reported its taxable income using a fiscal year ending June 30, the exercise and rescission described in the Example would occur in the same taxable year for executive but in different taxable years for Newco. The annual accounting period principle is the source of Rev. Rul. 80-58's requirement that a rescission must occur in the same taxable year as the transaction in order to eliminate the transaction for income tax purposes. Because executive and Newco file separate tax returns, we believe the annual accounting period principle ought to be applied separately to executive and Newco. Thus, executive ought to be able to treat the rescission as eliminating the exercise of the option, so long as both the exercise and rescission happen within executive's same taxable year, even if they occur in different Newco taxable years. In such case, Newco would presumably be entitled to claim a deduction on exercise of the option,[67] with the deduction recaptured in the following year under the tax benefit rule.

See ¶1502.1.7.10(6) for a discussion of APB 25 rules requiring variable accounting after rescission of a stock option exercise.

¶1502.1.6   Examples

A series of examples illustrates the impact of Code §83 and certain of the other tax principles discussed above in the context of an LBO where Mgmt is to receive Newco common stock.

---

[66] IRS Letter Ruling 9104039 (10/31/90).

[67] Where the stock received by executive on option exercise was fully vested, Newco's deduction would generally be claimed in its year ended June 30 year 3 under its method of accounting. Reg. §1.83-6(a)(3). See ¶1502.1.1(6).

EXAMPLE 1

Assume the parties form Newco with Mgmt purchasing 20% of its common stock for $20 and VC purchasing 80% of Newco's common stock for $1 million. Mgmt's stock is subject to an SRF, e.g., a Mgmt member forfeits his stock to Newco (or Newco has an option to buy his stock at cost) if he ceases to be a full-time Newco employee within 2 years and/or Newco fails to meet specified earnings goals.

A Mgmt member making no Code §83(b) election recognizes OI equal to the FV of the Newco common stock at the time the SRF lapses less the $20 paid for such stock, i.e., on the second anniversary. If the stock is worth $2 million when the SRF lapses, the Mgmt member recognizes $2 million of compensation income (less the $20 cost) and Newco (subject to the qualifications and limitations discussed at ¶1502.1.1(5)) receives an equal deduction.

A Mgmt member making a Code §83(b) election is taxed at the time of purchase on the FV of the stock (presumably approximately $200,000—20% of Newco's $1 million net worth), less the $20 cost, and any later gain (or loss) will be capital in nature. Newco (subject to the qualifications and limitations discussed at ¶1502.1.1(5)) receives a deduction equal to Mgmt's OI. Thus, Mgmt may greatly reduce the amount of OI recognized by making a timely Code §83(b) election.

EXAMPLE 2

Assume that Mgmt purchases 20% of Newco's common stock for $20 (subject to a two-year SRF) and VC purchases (for $1 million) preferred stock with a $1 million liquidation preference, carrying a fair-rate cumulative dividend and convertible into 80% of Newco's common stock. It is still desirable for Mgmt to file a Code §83(b) election, but the fact that VC may choose not to convert its preferred stock into common stock and hence may retain its $1 million prior claim on Newco's assets would reduce (or possibly eliminate) the amount of Mgmt's OI at the time of the Code §83(b) election.

EXAMPLE 3

Assume that Mgmt purchases 20% of Newco's common stock for $20 (subject to a two-year SRF) and VC purchases (for $1 million) non-convertible preferred stock carrying a fair-rate cumulative dividend and with a $1 million liquidation preference, plus 80% of Newco's common stock (for $80). In this case, it is still desirable for Mgmt to make a Code §83(b) election, but the issuance to VC of $1 million of preferred stock even if never converted into common stock reduces (or possibly eliminates) the amount of Mgmt's OI at the time of the Code §83(b) election.

EXAMPLE 4

Assume that Mgmt purchases 20 shares of Newco's common stock for $20 (subject to a two-year SRF) and VC purchases 80 shares of "senior" common stock for $1 million. The terms of the senior common are identical to those of the regular common stock purchased by Mgmt, except that upon Newco's liquidation the senior common receives $1 million *plus* 80% of all Newco assets in excess of $1 million. It is still desirable for Mgmt to make a Code §83(b) election, but the issuance of the senior common stock with a $1 million liquidation priority reduces (or possibly eliminates) the amount of Mgmt's OI at the time of the Code §83(b) election.

EXAMPLE 5

Newco could grant Mgmt an NQO to purchase 20% of Newco's stock. Mgmt cannot make a Code §83(b) election until the NQO is exercised and hence recognizes OI equal to the spread at exercise (assuming that Newco stock is not subject to an SRF at that time *or* that Mgmt files a Code §83(b) election at exercise if such stock is then subject to an SRF).

EXAMPLE 6

Mgmt could purchase shares of "junior" common stock, each of which has the right to (e.g.) $\frac{1}{100}$ of the dividends or liquidating distributions paid to a regular common share, but which becomes convertible share for share into regular common stock upon the occurrence of certain goals (e.g., achievement of a specified earnings goal or a public offering at a specified price or greater). Mgmt should make a timely Code §83(b) election because the achievement of the stated goals appears to be an SRF. Moreover, there is substantial risk that each junior common share is worth much more than $\frac{1}{100}$ of a regular common share, because for Code §83(b) purposes the SRF is ignored.

Therefore, each junior common share would probably be treated as immediately convertible into and hence equal in value to a regular common share. In addition, IRS was at one time considering whether the junior common stock should be treated as if it were in whole or in part an option, so that a Code §83(b) election would not be effective.[68] Finally, the accounting aspects of junior common stock, which are the subject of an FASB interpretation, may be extremely adverse.

¶1502.1.7   Accounting Effect of Stock Sales, Awards, and Options[69]

Under GAAP, Newco's *accounting* net income may be substantially reduced by the sale or award of Newco stock or by the grant of options on Newco stock to Mgmt.[70]

APB 25. For many years prior to 10/95, the governing set of GAAP rules for such stock-based compensation emanated from APB Opinion 25 (published in 1972). APB 25 sharply distinguishes between non-variable (i.e., fixed) and variable compensation, as described in ¶¶1502.1.7.1 and 1502.1.7.2. Under APB 25 (which utilizes the so-called "intrinsic value approach"), the accounting charge for *non-variable* (i.e., *fixed*) compensation turns on the stock FV at the time of the stock sale or award or the option grant (generally charging accounting income for the excess (if any) of the stock's FV at sale or grant over the purchase or option price for the stock), while the accounting charge for *variable* compensation turns on stock FV at the time of vesting (or other specified event) (generally charging accounting income for the excess (if any) of the stock's FV at time of vesting or other specified event over the purchase or option price for the stock). Thus, with variable compensation, where the FV of the stock increases from the time of the stock sale or award or the option grant to the time of vesting, the accounting charge increases, whereas with non-variable compensation the charge does not increase.

FASB 123. In 10/95, after several years of vigorous and heated debate, FASB Statement 123 was published, creating an elective set of alternative GAAP rules in lieu of APB 25. If Newco elects FASB 123 (which utilizes the so-called "fair value approach"), the accounting charge in all cases (both variable and non-variable compensation) is based on the stock's FV at the time of the stock sale or award or the option grant, as discussed in ¶1502.1.7.3. However, under FASB 123, in the case of an option the accounting charge is increased by the estimated FV of the option privilege at the time of the grant. Thus, electing FASB 123 rather than APB 25 increases the accounting charge for a non-variable option (by the estimated FV of the option privilege).

Choosing between APB 25 and FASB 123. If Newco elects to utilize FASB 123, it must account for all of its stock-based compensation under FASB 123 (as de-

---

[68] But see IRS Letter Ruling 8243234 (7/30/82).

[69] We thank Mark V. Sever and James F. Somers of Ernst & Young LLP for their ideas and assistance in the preparation of ¶1502.1.7.

[70] See ¶1502.3 for a discussion of accounting implications of a stock appreciation rights ("SAR") plan.

scribed in ¶1502.1.7.3) and hence cannot utilize APB 25 for any such compensation at any time thereafter.

If instead Newco chooses to continue utilizing APB 25, it must account for all of its stock-based compensation for employees under APB 25 (as described in ¶¶1502.1.7.1 and 1502.1.7.2), in which case (1) Newco is required to disclose prominently in its financial statements the accounting effect if Newco had instead adopted FASB 123, including pro forma net income under FASB 123 and pro forma earnings per share had FASB 123 been adopted and (2) Newco has the choice at any time in the future to switch from APB 25 to FASB 123, in which case it must thereafter account for all of its stock-based compensation under FASB 123.

See ¶1502.1.7.3(8) for discussion of transition rules applicable to companies switching from APB 25 accounting to FASB 123 accounting, including one transition rule available only to companies switching to FASB 123 accounting in an accounting year beginning before 12/16/03.

In the past, most companies continued to account for their stock-based compensation arrangements using APB 25. However, as reaction to the corporate accounting scandals of the early 2000s reached crescendo in mid-2002, there was substantial pressure from Congress and the press to "expense" stock options, and during 2002 a number of large public companies announced plans to adopt FASB 123.

Legislative Update

For legislative proposals which, if enacted, would affect the APB 25-FASB 123 choice, see Legislative Update in ¶1502.1.7.3.

FASB Update

In 3/03, FASB added a new project to re-examine the controversial issue of appropriate accounting for stock-based compensation. One goal is to eliminate companies' current ability to choose between two different sets of accounting rules for stock-based compensation (APB 25's intrinsic value approach and FASB 123's FV approach). FASB stated "an objective of this project is a single, high-quality accounting standard on stock-based compensation" and that "the project should be undertaken in cooperation with the [International Accounting Standard's Board (the "IASB")] in order to achieve maximum convergence to a single, high-quality accounting standard."[71]

---

[71] FASB Action Alert, No. 03-11 (3/19/03); FASB Project Update, Stock-Based Compensation (5/23/03).

One factor causing this reexamination is FASB's 9/02 agreement with the IASB[72] that FASB and IASB will "use their best efforts to (a) make their existing financial reporting standards fully compatible as soon as is practicable and (b) to coordinate their future work programs to ensure that once achieved, compatibility is maintained."[73] As a result of this agreement, FASB has started both short-term and long-term projects intended to lead to "convergence" of U.S. and international accounting standards.

IASB's 11/02 proposal regarding accounting for stock-based compensation is similar to FASB 123, adopting an FV approach to measuring stock-based compensation, but differs in several important ways. For example, the IASB proposal would (1) mandate use of the FASB 123-like FV approach (i.e., bar the use of APB 25's intrinsic value approach), (2) take vesting and forfeiture limits into account in valuing awards and measuring compensation up front, and (3) require non-public entities to estimate stock price volatility in valuing options.[74]

In 11/02, as part of the convergence process, FASB invited interested parties to comment on differences between FASB 123 accounting for stock-based compensation and IASB's pending proposal issued in 11/02.[75] FASB did not, however, seek comments on differences between APB 25 accounting and the IASB proposal, since FASB stated that APB 25 "diverges from the preferable method and from potential international convergence of high-quality accounting standards."[76]

While FASB has not announced a decision requiring all companies to adopt FASB 123, FASB appears to be moving in that direction, with some potentially important modifications. FASB tentatively decided in 4/03 to adopt an FV approach to stock-based compensation transactions, stating:

- "Goods or services received in exchange for stock-based compensation result in a cost that should be recognized in the income statement as an expense."
- "The measurement attribute for an exchange involving stock-based compensation is fair value."
- "With respect to stock-based compensation transactions with employees, . . . [t]he measurement objective for equity-settled awards is to determine the fair value of the goods or services received in the ex-

---

[72] While IASB does not currently set accounting standards for any country, it engages in discussions with the major accounting standards setters around the world to encourage adoption of consistent accounting standards. Certain countries have adopted all or part of the IASB standards as their own. Moreover, the European Union is considering proposals to require companies whose shares are listed in the European Union to follow IASB standards.

[73] Memorandum of Understanding between FASB and IASB (9/18/02).

[74] IASB Proposed International Financial Reporting Standard, *Share-Based Payment* (11/02).

[75] See FASB Invitation to Comment, *Accounting for Stock-Based Compensation: A Comparison of FASB Statement No. 123, Accounting for Stock-Based Compensation, and its Related Interpretations, and IASB Proposed IFRS, Share-based Payment*, p.9 (11/18/02) (the "Invitation to Comment"); IASB Proposed International Financial Reporting Standard, *Share-based Payment* (11/02).

[76] Invitation to Comment, p. 12.

change, which should be based on (1) the fair value of the goods or services received or (2) the grant-date fair value of the stock-based compensation given, whichever is more reliably measurable."[77]

FASB's suggestion that the compensation cost is intended to measure the *value of services received* rather than the *cost of the stock-based compensation granted* is new and has no analogue in APB 25 or FASB 123.[78] It is unclear as of this writing whether this potential change in conceptual focus will result in changes in specific accounting rules for stock-based compensation. In 5/03, FASB further tentatively decided that:

- "Compensation cost would be recognized over the service period."
- "Stock-based compensation awards would be accounted for using the modified grant date approach in FASB Statement No. 123" so that compensation cost would be the FV of awards measured at the grant date, "adjusted to reflect actual forfeitures and outcomes of performance conditions."
- Companies would be required to "base accruals of compensation cost on the best available estimate of the number of equity instruments that are expected to vest and to revise that estimate, if necessary, if subsequent information indicates that actual forfeitures are likely to differ from initial estimates."[79]

In 6/03, FASB decided to explore a potential new conceptual approach to measuring compensation expense, directing the FASB staff to "explore the notion of 'fair value at the date of exchange' as the measurement objective for all stock-based compensation."[80] The "exchange date" is apparently the date on which the parties enter into a firm or enforceable contract to exchange services for stock-based compensation. It is unclear as of this writing whether adoption of the "exchange date" concept would result in a change to any of the tentative decisions described above for employee stock-based compensation. Some FASB members indicated that they felt the exchange date would in most cases involving employees be the same as the grant date, while others speculated that the exchange date approach could lead to the conclusion that the exchange date was the date on which stock-based compensation became vested.[81]

---

[77] FASB Action Alert No. 03-17 (4/30/03); FASB Project Update, Stock-Based Compensation (5/23/03).
[78] Compare FASB Statement 123, ¶¶16 and 17; APB 25 ¶10.
[79] FASB Action Alert No. 03-19 (5/14/03); FASB Project Update, Stock-Based Compensation (5/23/03). This would represent a change from FASB 123, which currently allows, but does not require, companies to base current accruals on estimates of future forfeitures. See FASB Statement 123, ¶28.
[80] FASB Action Alert No. 03-25 (6/25/03).
[81] See Tax Analysts, "FASB Considers Stock-Based Compensation for Nonemployees," 2003 TNT 120-4 (6/20/03).

In light of the controversial nature of accounting for stock-based compensation, these tentative decisions may be revisited. Moreover, many issues have not yet been addressed. FASB's chairman has stated that FASB will hold additional discussions on "measurement methods, option valuation, attribution methods, modification and settlements, income taxes, disclosures, nonpublic enterprises, transition, and effective dates."[82]

FASB plans to issue an exposure draft of its stock-based compensation accounting proposals for public comment by the end of 2003.[83]

It is not clear when or whether such deliberations will ultimately result in changes to U.S. accounting rules for stock-based compensation. Past discussions of potential changes to stock-based compensation accounting were lengthy and highly controversial.[84] However, there currently is additional political pressure for change arising out of the corporate accounting scandals of the early 2000s. See, for example, the legislative proposals discussed in Legislative Update at ¶1502.1.7.3(7). In addition, the Public Company Accounting Oversight Board created by the Sarbanes-Oxley Act of 2002 is empowered to create accounting standards which SEC may adopt for entities reporting under the federal securities laws.[85]

However, there is also political pressure in some quarters in the opposite direction, i.e., to avoid or at least defer mandatory stock option expensing. See Legislative Update at ¶1502.1.7.3(7) for a discussion of H.R. 1372 and S. 979, introduced in 3/03 and 5/03 respectively, which would direct SEC to:

- issue rules requiring increased disclosure regarding stock-based compensation, including the "dilutive effect" of stock options, and
- in the case of the House bill, "not recognize as [GAAP] any new accounting standards related to the treatment of stock options," and in the case of the Senate bill, "not recognize as [GAAP] for purposes of enforcing the securities laws any accounting standards related to the treatment of stock options that [SEC] did not recognize for that purpose before [4/1/03]," in each case during a roughly 3-to-4-year period while SEC adopts the rule requiring more disclosure and studies the "effectiveness" of "enhanced disclosures."

Such legislation, if enacted, would prevent for 3 to 4 years SEC recognizing any new FASB rules requiring the expensing of stock options and is apparently intended to prevent for 3 to 4 years SEC recognizing any FASB requirement to adopt FASB 123 accounting as mandatory (although the legislation,

---

[82] Robert H. Herz, Testimony before House Committee on Financial Services, Subcommittee on Capital Markets, Insurance and Government Sponsored Enterprises (6/3/03) (Herz Testimony).

[83] See Herz Testimony; FASB Project Updates and Technical Plan (5/23/03).

[84] Stock-based compensation accounting is not included on FASB's list of short-term international convergence projects (i.e., those where "convergence around a high-quality solution would appear to be achievable in the short-term, usually by selecting between [IASB's International Financial Reporting Standards] and U.S. GAAP"). FASB Project Update, Short-term International Convergence (6/19/03).

[85] Sarbanes-Oxley Act of 2002, §108(d).

as currently drafted, is somewhat ambiguous here since FASB 123 in its current, non-mandatory form, is not a "new" accounting standard and was "recognized" by SEC prior to 4/1/03).

Scope of APB 25 and FASB 123. APB 25 and FASB 123 generally apply only to (1) a stock sale, award, or option to an employee based on the employer's stock (in our parlance Newco's sale or award of Newco stock or grant of an option thereon to a Newco employee) *or* (2) such a sale, award, or grant by a parent to an employee of a consolidated subsidiary (i.e., a subsidiary which is consolidated with parent for GAAP purposes) (in our parlance Newco's sale or award of Newco stock or an option thereon to the employee of Newco's consolidated subsidiary).[86] Sales, awards, and options based on stock of an unrelated company are not within the scope of either APB 25 or FASB 123, and sales, awards, and options to a non-employee are not within the scope of APB 25 but are covered by FASB 123.[87]

The remainder of this ¶1502.1.7 is organized as follows:

- ¶¶1502.1.7.1 and 1502.1.7.2 explain in more detail the GAAP rules applicable under APB 25 to non-variable and variable stock-based compensation.
- ¶1502.1.7.3 explains in more detail the GAAP rules applicable under FASB 123 to any stock-based compensation (whether non-variable or variable).
- ¶¶1502.1.7.4 through 1502.1.7.16 explain a number of sub rules and nuances applicable to APB 25 and FASB 123.
- ¶1502.1.7.17 discusses the applicability of these accounting rules (1) stock-based compensation to a non-employee and (2) stock-based compensation using stock of an unrelated company.

¶1502.1.7.1   APB 25 Rules for Non-Variable Stock-Based Compensation

If Newco chooses to utilize APB 25 (rather than FASB 123), it must account for each non-variable (i.e., fixed) stock-based arrangement (i.e., each arrangement in which both the number of shares to be received by the executive and the executive's purchase price are known at the date of the stock sale or award or the option grant) as follows:

(1) *Stock sale: where Newco sells stock to Mgmt*, Newco is treated as having compensation expense equal to the excess of the stock's FV (at the time of the sale) over the price paid by Mgmt for Newco's stock (under the so-called "intrinsic value approach"), so that Newco's accounting net income is reduced by this charge, less Newco's expected tax savings, if any,

---

[86] Financial Interpretation No. 44, Accounting for Certain Transactions Involving Stock Compensation, ¶13; FASB 123 ¶¶1 and 6. See also EITF 02-8.

[87] See ¶1502.1.7.17.

from any tax deduction (up to the amount of accounting compensation expense) created by the stock sale.

(2) *Stock award: where Newco issues stock to Mgmt without consideration (a stock award)*, Newco is treated as having compensation expense equal to the stock's FV at the time of such award (under the intrinsic value approach), so that Newco's accounting net income is reduced by this charge, less Newco's expected tax savings from any tax deduction (up to the amount of accounting compensation expense) created by the stock award.

(3) *Stock option: where Newco grants an option to Mgmt*, Newco is treated as having compensation expense equal to the excess of the stock's FV (at the time the option is granted) over the option exercise price (whether the option is an ISO or an NQO for tax purposes) (under the intrinsic value approach), so that Newco's accounting net income is reduced by this charge, less Newco's expected tax savings from any tax deduction (up to the amount of accounting compensation expense) which will be created by the option exercise.

Where the stock purchase price (in (1) above) or the option exercise price (in (3) above) equals or exceeds the stock's FV on the stock purchase date or option grant date, there is no spread (i.e., no excess of stock FV over purchase price or option exercise price) and hence under APB 25 Newco has no compensation expense to reduce its accounting net income.

Under APB 25, the charge to Newco's accounting net income (calculated on the intrinsic value approach as set forth in (1) through (3) above) is accrued (i.e., recognized for accounting purposes) "over the period(s) in which the related employee services are rendered . . . if the award is for future services . . . [which is generally] presumed to be the period from the grant date to the date the award is vested and its exercisability does not depend on continued employment service." Where there is a difference between the length of the executive's employment agreement and the length of the executive's vesting period for the stock-based compensation, APB 25 generally uses the vesting, rather than the employment, period.

Examples 1 through 3 below are all based on the following facts:

Newco stock FV on 1/1 year 1 (date of stock sale or award or option grant)	$11 per share
Stock sale price to executive A or option price to A	$10 per share
Award price to A	0

EXAMPLE 1

On 1/1 year 1, when Newco stock has an FV of $11 per share, Newco sells 100 Newco shares to executive A for $10 each. On such date, the shares are fully vested and there is no other reason for the arrangement to be treated as variable. (See ¶1502.1.7.2 and ¶1502.1.7.4 through ¶1502.1.7.15 for a discussion of the accounting rules for a variable APB 25 stock arrangement.)

Newco recognizes $100 of compensation expense (100 shares × $1 per share), and Newco's accounting net income is reduced by $100 less Newco's expected tax savings from the stock sale.

EXAMPLE 2

Same as Example 1, except Newco awards the 100 Newco shares to A without payment. Same result as Example 1 except that Newco's compensation expense is $1,100 (100 shares × $11 per share).

EXAMPLE 3

Same as Example 1, except that Newco grants A a 10-year option on 100 Newco shares at a $10 exercise price per share. Same result as Example 1, i.e., Newco's compensation expense is $100.

If Newco chooses to continue using APB 25 rather than switching to FASB 123, it must disclose prominently in its financial statements the accounting effect if Newco had instead adopted FASB 123, calculated as described in ¶1502.1.7.3. Specifically, FASB 148[88] requires a company that has any unvested stock options or stock awards outstanding that are accounted for under APB 25 for any period for which an income statement is presented to "disclose prominently," "in the 'Summary of Significant Accounting Policies' or its equivalent" a "tabular presentation" of:

- Net income
- Basic and diluted EPS
- Stock-based employee compensation cost, net of tax effects, included in determining net income
- Stock-based employee compensation cost, net of tax effects, that would have been reported had the company used FASB 123's FV method to value all stock-based compensation granted, modified, or settled in fiscal years beginning after 12/15/94
- Pro forma net income determined as if the company had used FASB 123's FV method to value all stock-based compensation granted, modified, or settled in fiscal years beginning after 12/15/94

[88] FASB Statement 148, Accounting for Stock-Based Compensation-Transition and Disclosure (12/02).

- Pro forma basic and diluted EPS determined as if the company had used FASB 123's FV method to value all stock-based compensation granted, modified, or settled in fiscal years beginning after 12/15/94.[89]

These required disclosures must be made on a quarterly basis.[90]

FASB 148's disclosure rules are effective for financial statements for fiscal years ending after 12/15/02, although earlier adoption is encouraged.[91]

FASB Update

See FASB Update at ¶1502.1.7 for discussion of a current FASB project to reconsider U.S. GAAP accounting rules for stock-based compensation, which may make FASB 123 mandatory.

Legislative Update

For legislative proposals which, if enacted, would affect the APB 25-FASB 123 choice, see Legislative Update in ¶1502.1.7.3.

Where Newco grants an option, sells stock, or awards stock to an executive (a stock-based compensatory transaction) shortly before an IPO of Newco's stock and the IPO offering price substantially exceeds the earlier price utilized in the stock-based compensatory transaction, SEC may (as a part of its review of Newco's IPO filing) seek to increase Newco's accounting charge for the earlier stock-based compensatory transaction. In 1998 and 1999 SEC became more aggressive in challenging such "cheap stock" transactions—seeking an explanation of the difference between the higher IPO price and the lower value utilized by Newco in calculating the accounting charge for the earlier stock-based compensatory transaction. While SEC frequently challenges anything more than a trivial discount off the IPO price where the earlier stock-based compensatory transaction occurred within a year before the IPO, SEC has also sought justification for such pricing differences for stock-based compensatory transactions occurring as much as 9 years before the IPO.

APB 25 generally applies only to stock-based compensation to Newco's employees and to Newco's non-employee directors, not to independent contractors (other than directors). Hence stock-based compensation for Newco's non-employee service providers (other than directors) is generally covered by FASB 123, regardless

---

[89] FASB 123's existing disclosure rules applied to all stock-based compensation granted in fiscal years beginning after 12/15/94, so companies should have data available for these disclosures. See FASB Statement No. 123, ¶¶45 and 53.

[90] FASB 148, ¶2(e) and ¶A23.

[91] FASB 148, ¶4.

of whether Newco uses APB 25 for employee stock-based compensation. See ¶1502.1.7.17.

¶1502.1.7.2   APB 25 Rules for Variable Stock-Based Compensation

If Newco chooses to utilize APB 25 (rather than FASB 123) and the stock sold or awarded or the option granted to Mgmt is pursuant to a variable stock arrangement (i.e., an arrangement where either (or both) the number of shares to be received by Mgmt or Mgmt's purchase price is not known at the outset), the accounting charge to Newco's net income may be substantially increased (over the accounting charge described in ¶1502.1.7.1 for a non-variable arrangement).

Stock-based compensation is variable if the stock or the option is subject to performance vesting (generally based on the achievement of one or more specified goals), because the accounting measurement date for determining Newco's compensation expense is deferred until the performance goals are satisfied, so that the spread at the time of vesting is treated as compensation expense (under the so-called "intrinsic value approach"), as further described in ¶1502.1.7.4. Hence, where the FV of Newco's stock rises between a stock sale or award or an option grant, on the one hand, and vesting on the other, Newco's compensation expense increases.

By contrast, where the stock sold or awarded or the option granted to Mgmt is subject only to time vesting (based on continued employment for a specified period), the accounting measurement date is not postponed, so that the non-variable rules described in ¶1502.1.7.1 apply and only the spread at sale or grant is treated as compensation expense, again as further described in ¶1502.1.7.4.[92]

However, a number of other factors discussed in ¶¶1502.1.7.5 through 1502.1.7.15 below (including Newco's payment of a tax-offset bonus to Mgmt as described in ¶1502.1.7.9 and repricing of a previously granted option as described in ¶1502.1.7.10), when added to a stock sale or award or an option grant, can cause the arrangement to be treated as variable, so that Newco's compensation expense increases as the FV of Newco's stock increases after the stock sale or award or the option grant.

If Newco chooses to utilize APB 25 (rather than FASB 123), a stock appreciation right (an SAR)—under which Mgmt receives either in cash or in Newco stock an amount equal to the spread between the FV of Newco stock at the time the SAR is exercised and the base price established at grant—is also treated as variable compensation. Hence, Newco recognizes compensation expense equal to the amount payable under the SAR, whether payable in cash or Newco stock.

With any variable arrangement, the portion of Newco's compensation expense attributable to pre-sale, pre-award, or pre-grant spread in the stock must be accrued over the service/vesting period as described in ¶1502.1.7.1, and the amount of Newco's compensation expense caused by post-sale, post-award, or

---

[92] As discussed in ¶1502.1.7.4, many of the practical effects of performance vesting can be obtained while achieving the favorable accounting effects of time vesting by use of a TARSAP arrangement.

post-grant changes in stock FV must be accrued quarterly as Newco's stock fluctuates in value, as discussed in ¶1502.1.7.16. Hence, (1) Newco's accounting net income is reduced (over the service/vesting period) by the compensation charge, less Newco's expected tax savings from any tax deduction (up to the amount of such accounting compensation expense), and (2) as Newco's stock fluctuates in value, Newco's accounting net income is reduced (where the stock increases in value) or increased (where the stock declines in value subsequent to an increase in value) each quarter by the compensation charge, as adjusted for changes in Newco's expected tax savings from any tax deduction (up to the amount of accounting compensation expense) created by the variable arrangement.

Examples 4 through 10 below are all based on the following facts:

Same Facts as Examples 1 Through 3
Newco stock FV on 1/1 year 1 (date of stock sale or
    award or option or SAR grant) $11 per share
Stock sale price to executive A or option price to A $10 per share
Award price to A   0

New Facts for Examples 4 Through 10
Newco stock FV on 12/31 year 5 when
    stock or option vests $50 per share

EXAMPLE 4

Same as Example 1, i.e., Newco sells 100 Newco shares to A for $10 each when Newco stock has an FV of $11 per share, except that in this example the 100 Newco shares purchased by A are subject to time vesting, so that shares may not be earned if A leaves Newco's employ within five years. Same result as Example 1, because the shares are not subject to performance vesting, Newco's accounting compensation expense is $100.

EXAMPLE 5

Same as Example 2, i.e., Newco awards 100 Newco shares to A without payment when Newco stock has an FV of $11 per share, except that the 100 Newco shares awarded to A time vest at the end of five years if A is still employed by Newco. Same result as Example 2, i.e., Newco's compensation expense is $1,100.

EXAMPLE 6

Same as Example 3, i.e., Newco grants A a 10-year option on 100 Newco shares at a $10 exercise price per share when Newco stock has an $11 FV per share, except that the 100-share option granted to A time vests at the end of five years if A is still employed by Newco. Same result as Example 3, i.e., Newco's compensation expense is $100.

EXAMPLE 7

Same as Example 1, i.e., Newco sells 100 Newco shares to A for $10 each when Newco stock has an FV of $11 per share, except that the 100 Newco shares vest only if Newco's net income in the fifth year is at least $1,000 and A is still employed by Newco at the end of the fifth year, i.e., performance vesting. In fact, A remains in Newco's employ until the fifth anniversary (at which time Newco's stock FV is $50 per share) and Newco meets the performance goal.

Because this stock purchase arrangement is variable, Newco recognizes aggregate compensation expense of $4,000 ($40 per share spread at vesting × 100 shares). The $100 spread at the time of the stock purchase ($1 per share × 100 shares) is accrued over A's service/vesting period, and the subsequent increases ($3,900) are accrued quarterly as Newco's stock fluctuates in value.

EXAMPLE 8

Same as Example 2, i.e., Newco awards 100 Newco shares to A without payment when Newco stock has an FV of $11 per share, except that (like Example 7) the awarded stock is subject to five-year performance vesting. Because the stock award is variable, Newco recognizes aggregate compensation expense of $5,000 ($50 per share FV at vesting × 100 shares). The $1,100 spread at the time of the stock award ($11 per share × 100 shares) is accrued over A's service/vesting period, and the subsequent increases ($3,900) are accrued quarterly as Newco's stock fluctuates in value.

EXAMPLE 9

Same as Example 3, i.e., Newco grants A a 10-year option on 100 Newco shares at a $10 exercise price per share when Newco stock has an FV of

$11 per share, except that (like Example 7) the option is subject to 5-year performance vesting. Because the option grant is variable, Newco recognizes aggregate compensation expense of $4,000 ($40 per share × 100 shares), accrued as described in Example 7.

EXAMPLE 10

Same as Example 9 except that Newco grants A a 100-share SAR (with a $10 base price per share) when Newco stock has an FV of $11 per share and A exercises the SAR five years later when Newco stock has an FV of $50 per share. Same result as Example 9, whether or not A's SAR is subject to vesting and whether or not the SAR is payable in cash or Newco stock.

If Newco chooses to continue using APB 25 rather than switching to FASB 123, it must disclose prominently in its financial statements the accounting effect if Newco had instead adopted FASB 123, calculated as described in ¶1502.1.7.3. See ¶1502.1.7.1 for a detailed discussion of the disclosure requirements of FASB 148.

FASB Update

See FASB Update at ¶1502.1.7 for discussion of a current FASB project to reconsider U.S. GAAP accounting rules for stock-based compensation.

Legislative Update

For legislative proposals which, if enacted, would affect the APB 25-FASB 123 choice, see Legislative Update in ¶1502.1.7.3.

¶1502.1.7.3   *Elective FASB 123 Rules for Non-Variable and Variable Stock-Based Compensation*

If Newco elects to account for all of its stock-based compensation under FASB 123 rather than continuing under APB 25, Newco will have significantly greater accounting charges for some stock-based arrangements and significantly lower accounting charges for others (as compared to the results under APB 25).

For those electing out of APB 25 or otherwise unable to use APB 25 (e.g., non-employee compensation), FASB 123 abolishes the sharp distinction (created by APB 25's intrinsic value approach) between non-variable compensation and variable compensation (under which the accounting charge for non-variable compensation turns on stock FV at a stock sale or award or an option grant, while the accounting charge for variable compensation turns on stock FV at vesting). Rather, FASB 123 bases the accounting charge on the FV of the stock-based compensation at the date of a stock sale or award or option grant, including in the case of an option grant the FV of the option privilege (under the FV approach).[93] Thereafter, compensation expense is *not* adjusted to reflect changes in the stock FV, whether or not the stock arrangement contains performance vesting, a tax-offset bonus, etc.[94]

FASB Update

See FASB Update at ¶1502.1.7 for discussion of a current FASB project to reconsider U.S. GAAP accounting rules for stock-based compensation, which may make FASB 123 mandatory.

---

(1) FV of stock sale or award. In the case of a stock sale or award, the amount of Newco's compensation expense is equal to the FV of the stock on the sale or award date less the price paid by the executive, so that Newco's accounting net income is reduced by this amount, less Newco's expected tax saving from any tax deduction (up to the amount of accounting compensation expense) created by the stock sale or award.[95]

Under FASB 123 neither a stock sale nor a stock award is an option, so that there is no option value to the executive because he is not deferring payment of the price. Hence, compensation expense for a stock sale or stock award is equal to the stock's spread at the sale or award date, regardless of whether there is performance vesting or a tax-offset bonus.

Where, however, stock is sold to Mgmt for a non-recourse note, the transaction is generally treated as the grant of an option, so that the accounting charge is increased by the value of the option privilege, although any non-refundable inter-

---

[93] Where an option or an award is granted to a non-employee (other than an independent director who would be treated as an employee if APB 25 applied—see ¶1502.1.7.16), FASB 123 generally measures FV on completion of the services or other transaction for which the option or award was granted, rather than at issuance, unless the non-employee has committed to perform the services or engage in the transaction (backed by an economic penalty for non-performance, other than mere forfeiture of the options or award). See EITF 96-18, "Accounting for Equity Instruments that are Issued to Other than Employees for Acquiring, or in Conjunction with Selling, Goods or Services."

[94] FASB 123 does, however, distinguish between variable and fixed options or awards in the case of non-employees. Where the number of shares to which a non-employee (other than an independent director who would be treated as an employee if APB 25 applied—see ¶1502.1.7.16) is entitled can vary (e.g., depending on the outcome of the non-employee's services), FASB 123 generally treats the option or award as modified when there is an increase in the number of shares to which the non-employee is entitled, requiring additional compensation charges. See EITF 96-18.

[95] The tax saving from any tax deduction in excess of the accounting expense is generally credited directly to net worth.

est Mgmt is required to pay on the non-recourse note reduces the value of the option privilege.

(2) FV of stock option. In the case of an option, the amount of Newco's compensation expense is equal to the FV of the option at the grant date, taking into account both (1) the spread (if any) at grant and (2) the value to Mgmt of being able to defer payment of the option price, i.e., the value of the option privilege, so that Newco's accounting net income is reduced by this amount, less Newco's expected tax saving from any tax deduction (up to the amount of accounting compensation expense) created by the option grant and exercise.[96]

FASB 123 states that Newco must use an option-pricing model to estimate the FV of an option (for example Black-Scholes or a binomial model) that takes into account the current price of the underlying stock, the exercise price, the expected option holding period (which FASB calls the "expected life") (i.e., not the stated term of the option but the shorter period Newco expects the option actually to be outstanding before exercise or expiration, but which generally does not take account of the possibility of forfeiture), expected dividends on the stock, the stock's expected volatility, and the risk-free rate of return for the expected life of the option. The most commonly mentioned valuation technique, the Black-Scholes model, typically produces an option FV (for an option that is not significantly in the money at grant) equal to 20% to 40% of the option stock's FV, depending on such factors as the option's expected life and the price volatility of the underlying stock. The higher the stock's price volatility and the longer the expected life, the higher the value of the option, because of the higher probability for a large option gain.

Because a non-public company generally has no information on which to base an estimate of expected future volatility, a non-public company may estimate the value of its options using a method (the minimum-value method) that does not take into account expected volatility. For this purpose, a company is non-public if none of its equity securities (and none of its parent's equity securities) are traded on an exchange or over the counter (including local quotations).

See (3) below for a discussion of the possibility of using actual bid quotations to value an option under FASB 123.

With respect to an option that under APB 25 is *non-variable* (so that the compensation charge is currently the spread at the time of grant), electing FASB 123 would result in a *higher* accounting charge than under current accounting rules. This is because the APB 25 accounting rules for a non-variable option create compensation expense only for the spread at grant, whereas FASB 123 creates compensation expense for the full option FV, taking into account not only the spread at grant but also the value to the option holder of being able to defer payment of the option price, i.e., the value of the option privilege. Moreover, because compensation expense is measured at the grant date under FASB 123, expense is recognized even if the stock price subsequently declines and the option expires unexercised.

---

[96] The tax saving from any tax deduction in excess of the accounting expense is generally credited directly to net worth.

With respect to an option that under APB 25 is *variable* (e.g., because of performance vesting), so that the compensation charge is currently the spread at the time of vesting, FASB 123 results in a *lower* accounting charge, as compared to APB 25, where the FV of the stock increases significantly from grant date to vesting.

Examples 11 and 12 below are both based on the following facts and illustrate the results under FASB 123:

Same Facts as Examples 4 Through 10

Newco stock FV on 1/1 year 1	$11 per share
Option price to executive A	$10 per share
FV of a Newco option, taking into account $1 spread at grant, option term, etc.	$5 per share*
Newco stock FV on 12/31 year 5 when option vests	$50 per share

*This amount is calculated by the Black-Scholes or other option-pricing model.

EXAMPLE 11

On 1/1 year 1 Newco grants a 10-year option to A on 100 Newco shares at a $10 exercise price per share when Newco stock has an FV of $11 per share. The option is non-variable (e.g., there is no performance vesting or tax-offset bonus).

Under APB 25, Newco's aggregate compensation expense is $100 ($1 spread × 100 shares), and Newco's accounting net income is reduced by $100 less Newco's expected tax saving from any expected tax deduction.

If Newco elects FASB 123 (rather than APB 25), Newco's aggregate compensation expense would be $500 ($5 option value × 100 shares), assuming that the options had a value of $5 per share calculated using an option-pricing model at time of grant, and Newco's accounting net income would be reduced by $500 less Newco's expected tax saving from any expected tax deduction (up to $500). Hence, FASB 123 increases the compensation charge for this non-variable option.

EXAMPLE 12

Same as Example 11 except that (a) the option is variable (e.g., performance vesting) and (b) Newco stock has a $50 FV per share when vesting occurs.

Under APB 25, Newco's aggregate compensation expense is $4,000 ($40 spread at vesting × 100 shares).

If Newco elects FASB 123 (rather than APB 25), Newco's aggregate compensation expense would be $500, the same as in Example 11. Hence, FASB 123 reduces the compensation charge for this variable option (as compared to APB 25) where the stock FV increases significantly between grant and vesting.

(3) Using bid quotations to value options under FASB 123. When Coca Cola Company in 7/02 announced adoption of FASB 123, it stated that:

> To determine the fair value of the stock options granted, the company intends to use quotations from independent financial institutions. The option value to be expensed will be based on the average of the firm quotations received from the financial institutions to buy or sell Coca Cola shares under the identical terms of the stock options granted.[97]

Coca Cola's plan was an attempt to determine the FASB 123 FV of stock options without resort to Black-Scholes or other option pricing formulas dependent on variables that can only be estimated, not directly observed, which are, in the view of some critics, open to inconsistent application from company to company.

In 3/03 Coca Cola announced that it would indeed use Black-Scholes to value stock options, abandoning its plans to value stock options using third-party price quotations. According to press reports, Coca Cola executives indicated "the company eventually concluded that current accounting standards wouldn't allow the new approach and instead require companies to perform their own value calculations."[98] Moreover, as it turned out, the "Black-Scholes value [calculated by Coca Cola] was not materially different from the independent quotes,"[99] indicating that investment bankers providing the quotes were also using Black-Scholes.[100]

While it is not clear from published reports exactly why Coca Cola concluded that FASB 123 would not permit the use of independent price quotes to value stock options, we believe (and so stated in editions of this book published before Coca Cola abandoned its original plan) that Coca Cola's original plan raised at least three questions under FASB 123. *First*, does FASB 123 permit options to be valued by a method other than an option pricing model (e.g., quoted market prices)? *Second*, do independent price quotations from financial institutions qualify as quoted market prices? *Third*, if independent quotations are acceptable and financial institutions bid on options with "identical terms" to those options actually granted to employees, what adjustments would be required for FASB 123 purposes?

Read literally, FASB 123 appears to require the use of an option-pricing model to determine a stock option's FV. FASB 123 states that the "fair value of a stock option . . . granted by a public entity *shall* be estimated using an option pricing model (for example, the Black-Scholes or a binomial model)."[101] This language provides no exceptions allowing the use of market prices or negotiated prices, apparently because FASB did not believe that any market or negotiated prices existed that could be used to value stock options.[102]

However, FASB 123 generally expresses a strong preference for the use of quoted market prices in determining FV, stating that FV is:

[97] See Coca Cola Company press release 7/14/02.
[98] Wall Street Journal Online, Coke Plan for Option Valuing Fizzles Out After Few Months (3/7/03).
[99] Coca Cola Proxy Statement (3/5/03).
[100] Wall Street Journal Online, Coke Plan for Option Valuing Fizzles Out After Few Months (3/7/03).
[101] FASB Statement No. 123, ¶19 (emphasis added and deleted).
[102] FASB Statement No. 123, ¶¶161-163.

the amount at which the asset could be bought or sold in a current transaction between willing parties, that is, other than in a forced or liquidation sale. *Quoted market prices in active markets are the best evidence of fair value and shall be used as the basis for the measurement, if available.* If quoted market prices are not available, the estimate of fair value shall be based on the best information available in the circumstances. The estimate of fair value shall consider prices for similar assets and the results of valuation techniques to the extent available in the circumstances. Examples of valuation techniques include the present value of estimated expected future cash flows using a discount rate commensurate with the risks involved, option-pricing models, matrix pricing, option-adjusted spread models, and fundamental analysis.[103]

In addition, FASB's explanation of FASB 123 indicates that use of an option-pricing model was intended to be required only in the absence of quoted market prices:

> It also is conceivable, although unlikely, that options between parties other than employers and employees that are subject to essentially the same restrictions as employee stock options might be developed and traded. For example, a third-party option might in concept be made forfeitable under certain conditions, and the option contract might specify that the options can only be exercised—not transferred to another party. *The provisions of this Statement are not intended to preclude use of quoted market prices to determine the fair values of employee stock options if such prices become available.* However, various implementation questions would need to be considered, such as how to treat options that are forfeited. Because neither quoted nor negotiated market prices existed when the Board developed this Statement, it has not considered those issues. *This Statement specifies the basic method and assumptions to be used in estimating the fair values of employee stock options in the absence of a quoted market price.* Specifically, this Statement requires the use of an option-pricing model, and it also specifies how to reduce the amount resulting from use of a traditional option-pricing model to reflect the unique restrictions inherent in employee stock options.[104]

Thus, it appears reasonably clear that use of an option-pricing model is not required by FASB 123 if quoted market prices are available.

Assuming that quoted market prices are an acceptable method of valuing stock options for FASB 123, do price quotes from independent financial institutions constitute quoted market prices? Because such price quotes do not reflect actual sales of options between the company and the financial institutions, they do not appear to be quoted market prices. However, because a company could accept a bid from a financial institution, either buying or selling an option at the quoted price, a financial institution should have an incentive to set a fair price and its quote would appear to be more than a mere appraisal. Thus, price quotes might reflect good evidence of fair value, even if they do not constitute quoted market prices.

Of course, the use of price quotes could be potentially open to bias, particularly if the company's desire for a low quote is clear and there is an explicit or tacit understanding (perhaps derived from practice) that the company will not actually

---

[103] FASB Statement No. 123, ¶9, quoting FASB Statement No. 121, *Accounting for the Impairment of Long-Lived Assets and for Long-Lived Assets to Be Disposed Of* (emphasis added).

[104] FASB Statement No. 123, ¶163 (emphasis added).

accept the financial institutions' quotes to buy or sell stock options. However, if there were evidence of such circumstances, the price quotes would very likely be disqualified as a measurement of market value.

Assuming that quoted market prices are an acceptable method of valuing stock options for FASB 123 purposes and that price quotes from independent financial institutions on options with identical terms are considered quoted market prices, certain adjustments may be necessary for FASB 123 purposes. For example, FASB 123 does not take into account in measuring FV any restrictions on an option imposed as a result of time or performance vesting, rather FASB 123 accounts for failures to vest by reversing compensation charges previously recognized with respect to an option that ultimately does not vest.[105] Thus, if the terms of the financial institution's stock option bid include vesting restrictions identical to those imposed on the employee options being valued,[106] the bid price (which would undoubtedly take into account the failure-to-vest possibility) should be used as the FV of the compensation without any subsequent adjustment for actual failures to vest.[107]

In applying an option-pricing model, FASB 123 does not take into account the full stated life of an option but rather takes into account the stated life reduced by the likelihood the option may be exercised earlier than its stated expiration date (which FASB calls the "expected life" but we call the "expected option holding period" since it does not take into account any possibility of forfeiture). FASB explains that it so reduces the stated life in order to adjust for the fact that option pricing models are designed to value transferable options while most employee options are non-transferable.[108] If the financial institution's bid is for a non-transferable option, it should be consistent with FASB 123 for the financial institution to bid on options with a term equal to the full stated term of the employee options rather than the shorter expected option holding period, since the financial institution would presumably factor the lack of transferability into its bid.

Alternatively, it might be possible for a company to use price quotes on options that are not identical in all respects to the employee options. For example, a company would appear to obtain an FV consistent with FASB 123's overall scheme if financial institutions bid on options identical to the employee options except that the quoted options (1) were transferable by the financial institution, (2) had a term equal to the shorter expected option holding period (rather than full stated life) of the employee options, and (3) were not subject to vesting. In such case, the company would presumably apply the usual FASB 123 rule reversing prior compensation charges on an actual failure to vest.

---

[105] FASB Statement No. 123, §17. See also ¶1502.1.7.3(4) below.

[106] Where the terms of an option granted to an employee include simple time vesting based on whether the employee remains employed by the company, query whether bidding on options with identical terms might require bidding on a separate option for each employee receiving an option grant. Where the option terms include performance vesting, it might be somewhat easier to include the actual vesting terms (unless performance is personal to a particular employee) in the options to be quoted.

[107] Compare FASB Statement No. 123, ¶162.

[108] FASB Statement No. 123, ¶¶19 and 169-173.

Coca Cola's abandoned plan to expense stock options using independent price quotes is likely to generate substantial discussion on these and other issues. It seems likely that such issues will be further addressed as FASB reconsiders U.S. accounting rules for stock-based compensation. See FASB Update at ¶1502.1.7 for a discussion of FASB's current project to reconsider accounting for stock-based compensation.

(4) Vesting rules. Under FASB 123 (as under APB 25), the charge to Newco's accounting net income (calculated under the FV approach as set forth above) is accrued (i.e., recognized for accounting purposes) over the executive's service/vesting period.

Moreover, under FASB 123 the charge is based on the number of options or shares that actually vest. Newco can calculate this charge based on its best estimate as to the number of options or shares Newco expects will vest, in which case Newco would take additional compensation charges (or credits) in subsequent years as actual vesting experience results in fewer (or greater) forfeitures than originally expected (calculated based on the option value at time of grant date or the stock value at time of sale or award). Alternatively, Newco can calculate the front-end compensation charge on the assumption that all options or shares will vest, in which case Newco would take into account compensation credits as options or shares are forfeited (again calculated based on the option value at time of grant date or the stock value at time of sale or award).

(5) Repurchase rules. If a vested option expires unexercised (e.g., because the option is out of the money), there is no downward adjustment in compensation expense.

Under FASB 123 (unlike APB 25), where Newco is non-public and repurchases a vested option or vested stock at FV on the date of repurchase, there is no additional charge to compensation expense. However, where Newco is public and Mgmt has a right to require Newco to effectuate such repurchase or Newco (although not obligated to do so) has a practice of repurchasing, the transaction is treated as a stock-based compensation arrangement that involves a cash award rather than an equity award and hence results in a compensation charge equal to Newco's net outlay (less any amount previously charged as compensation expense).

For this purpose a company is public if any of its equity securities (or any of its parent's equity securities) are traded on an exchange or over the counter (including local quotations).

(6) SARs. Under FASB 123, an SAR which is payable in cash results in compensation expense equal to the cash payment (accrued as Newco's stock rises in value), just as under APB 25.

However, an SAR payable in Newco stock is treated under FASB 123 similar to an option so that Newco's only compensation expense is the FV of the SAR arrangement at the time of grant, i.e., the amount by which the SAR is in the money at grant (if any) plus the value of the option privilege determined under a Black-Scholes or similar formula (generally 20% to 40% of the stock's FV at grant where the option is at the money).

By contrast, APB 25 treats an SAR payable in Newco stock like an SAR payable in cash.

(7) Choice between FASB 123 and APB 25. In the past, most companies (particularly, those with non-variable arrangements) continued to account for their stock-based compensation arrangements using APB 25. However, as the corporate accounting scandals of the early 2000s reached crescendo in mid-2002, there was substantial pressure from Congress and the press to "expense" stock options, and during 2002, a significant number of companies announced plans to adopt FASB 123, including Coca Cola, General Motors, AT&T, General Electric, Bank One, P&G, AIG, Citigroup and Amazon.com.[109]

If Newco's stock-based compensation arrangements are predominantly variable (e.g., because of performance vesting), election of FASB 123 may well prove advantageous. This is because the compensation charge under APB 25 for a variable arrangement is the spread at the time of vesting, so that FASB 123 (which bases the accounting charge on the spread at grant plus, in the case of an option, the FV of the option privilege) would likely result in a lower accounting charge where the FV of Newco's stock increases significantly from grant date to vesting. Unfortunately FASB 123 does not permit Newco to adopt the rules piecemeal (i.e., Newco cannot adopt FASB 123 for its performance-based compensation but retain APB 25 for its non-variable compensation), and once having adopted FASB 123 Newco cannot subsequently switch back to APB 25.

Legislative Update

Two legislative proposals would, if enacted, have affected Newco's APB 25-FASB 123 choice:

First, in mid-2002 when the Sarbanes-Oxley Act of 2002 was pending in Congress, Senator McCain sought to amend the bill so that "a corporation that grants a stock option to an officer or employee to purchase a publicly traded security in the United States shall record the granting of the option as an expense in that corporation's income statement for the year in which the option is granted." This amendment did not pass.

If enacted, it appears this amendment would have mandated FASB 123 (rather than APB 25) for all publicly traded corporations, but would have required the entire FASB 123 charge to be expensed in the grant year, rather than over the executive's service/vesting period, although the amendment's language is less than a model of clarity on these points.

Second, as discussed in more detail in ¶1502.1.2, pending legislation introduced in early 2003 would, if enacted, limit a company's tax deduction upon an option exercise to the amount "treated as an expense for the purpose of ascertaining [the company's] income, profit, or loss in a report or statement to" equity owners. While this pending legislation would not mandate a change in accounting for options, it would (1) limit Code §83(h)'s tax deduc-

---

[109] See Wall Street Journal Online, *Table of Companies Expensing Stock Options* (11/20/02).

tion to zero for a company using APB 25 which grants an at-the-money option qualifying for non-variable treatment and (2) generally reduce Code §83(h)'s tax deduction for a company using FASB 123 where the stock rises significantly between grant and exercise, as discussed in more detail in ¶1502.1.2.

FASB Update

See FASB Update at ¶1502.1.7 for discussion of a current FASB project to reconsider U.S. GAAP accounting rules for stock-based compensation, which may make FASB 123 mandatory.

Legislative Update

In marked contrast to the FASB proposal which may well make FASB 123 mandatory, two similar 2003 bills introduced as the Broad-Based Stock Option Plan Transparency Act of 2003 in 3/03 (H.R. 1372) and 5/03 (S. 979) would, in general, create a $3\frac{1}{2}$-year moratorium on SEC recognizing as GAAP any new accounting standards related to stock options by:

- Requiring SEC, not later than 180 days after enactment, to promulgate a rule requiring each 1934 Act §13(a) or §15(d) reporting company to include in its periodic reports detailed information regarding stock option plans, stock purchase plans, and other arrangements involving employee acquisition of an equity interest in the company, particularly information on the dilutive effect of stock options.
- Requiring SEC (i) to study the effectiveness of the enhanced disclosures in increasing transparency to investors for the 3-year period after promulgation of the SEC rule and (ii) to report such findings to the House and Senate within 180 days after the end of the 3-year study period.
- Prohibiting SEC, during such $3\frac{1}{2}$-year period (plus 60 days in the case of the Senate bill), from recognizing as GAAP, (i) under the House bill, "any new accounting standards related to the treatment of stock options" and (ii) under the Senate bill, "for purposes of enforcing the securities laws any accounting standards related to the treatment of stock options" not recognized by SEC for that purpose prior to 4/1/03.

(8) Transition Rules. FASB 123 and FASB 148 provide three alternative transition rules for companies switching from APB 25 to FASB 123.

Under the first and original transition rule (the "prospective method") set forth in FASB 123, a company may apply FASB 123 prospectively to all stock sales, awards, and options granted after the beginning of the fiscal year of change (the "change year"), while stock sales, awards, and options granted before the change year continue to be governed by APB 25, unless modified or settled after the beginning of the change year.[110] Use of the prospective method may create a "ramp-up" effect where the company's compensation expense grows for several years after adopting FASB 123 as a larger and larger portion of its outstanding, unvested stock-based compensation is subject to FASB 123. Where this "ramp-up" effect causes transition years not to be representative of future years, the company is required to include an explanatory statement in its financial statements.[111]

FASB 148, issued 12/02, prohibits a company switching from APB 25 to FASB 123 in a year beginning after 12/15/03 from using the prospective method.[112] Instead, such a company must use either the modified prospective method or the retroactive restatement method described below. In some cases, this may create incentive for a company to change from APB 25 to FASB 123 in 2002 or 2003.

Under the first new transition rule (the "modified prospective method"), a company may elect to apply FASB 123 starting with the change year, as if all stock-based compensation granted in fiscal years beginning after 12/15/94 was accounted for under FASB 123. Under this method, the company's financial statements for years prior to the change year are not restated. However, FASB 123 would apply beginning with the change year to all previously granted stock compensation that remain unvested as of the beginning of the change year.

Under the second new transition rule (the "retroactive method"), a company may elect to apply FASB 123 to all years presented for comparison in its financial statements for the change year (and thereafter), as if all stock-based compensation granted in fiscal years beginning after 12/15/94 were accounted for under FASB 123. Under this method, a company is not required (although it is permitted) to restate years prior to those presented for comparison in its change (and subsequent) year financial statements.

The two new transition rules are effective for fiscal years beginning after 12/15/02. However, they may be applied to financial statements for earlier fiscal years if such statements were not issued before FASB 148's 12/02 adoption.[113]

For a company continuing to use APB 25 accounting for a transition period under the prospective method or the modified prospective method, FASB 148 requires prominent, quarterly tabular disclosure in the company's financial statements of the differences between APB 25 and FASB 123 accounting, in a manner similar to the disclosure required of companies continuing to use APB 25 accounting for all employee stock-based compensation.[114] See ¶1502.1.7.1 for a more detailed discussion of the disclosure rules.

---

[110] FASB Statement No. 123, ¶52.
[111] FASB Statement No. 123, ¶54.
[112] FASB Statement 148, ¶2(b).
[113] FASB Statement No. 148, ¶4.
[114] FASB Statement 148, ¶2(e) and ¶A20.

¶1502.1.7.4   APB 25 Rules for Vesting and TARSAP

Under APB 25 (described in ¶¶1502.1.7.1 and 1502.1.7.2), a number of factors affect whether a stock arrangement is variable or non-variable and how the compensation charge is accrued.

(1) When Newco sells or awards stock to Mgmt or grants an option to Mgmt *and* on the sale/award/grant date the option price and the number of shares are fixed (not variable), the arrangement can generally qualify as non-variable and hence receive the generally more favorable accounting treatment described in ¶1502.1.7.1.[115]

(2) The rule set forth in (1) applies even where the arrangement vests over a series of years based on Mgmt's continued employment, i.e., the arrangement is treated as non-variable where it is subject to vesting based only on the executive's continued rendition of services for a specified period.[116]

(3) However, if vesting of the arrangement is based on specified performance goals (e.g., Newco achieving specified earnings levels, stock values, or other goals), the arrangement is treated as variable and hence there will be a charge to Newco's accounting net income equal to the spread in the stock at the time the arrangement vests (i.e., the stock's FV at vesting less the purchase/exercise price) reduced by Newco's tax savings from the stock transaction, i.e., the accounting "measurement date" is deferred until satisfaction of the performance goals, as described in ¶1502.1.7.2.[117]

(4) If the arrangement is variable so that the accounting measurement date is postponed, the charge to Newco's accounting net income must generally be accrued by Newco periodically (e.g., quarterly) as the FV of Newco's stock fluctuates.[118]

(5) However, Newco may be able to obtain the favorable time vesting non-variable accounting treatment (described in (1) and (2) above), while at the same time obtaining some of the practical effects of performance vesting (described in (3) above) by using a time accelerated restricted stock award plan (TARSAP). Under TARSAP (1) the arrangement vests if Mgmt is in Newco's employ (i.e., is still rendering services to Newco) on a specified future date, i.e., solely a time-vesting standard, but (2) if Newco meets specified performance goals while Mgmt is still in Newco's employ, the vesting date is accelerated.

---

[115] APB Opinion No. 25, 10b, states that "The *measurement date* for determining compensation cost in stock option, purchase, and award plans is the first date on which are known both (1) the number of shares that an individual employee is entitled to receive and (2) the option or purchase price, if any" (emphasis in original), so that "a corporation recognizes compensation cost . . . unless the employee pays an amount that is at least equal to the quoted market price of the stock at the measurement date."

[116] APB Opinion No. 25, 11b, provides that the compensation "measurement date is not changed from the grant or award date to a later date *solely by provisions that the termination of employment reduces the number of shares of stock* that may be issued to an employee" (emphasis added).

[117] This position is based on the negative inference from APB Opinion 25, 11b, quoted in the preceding footnote. Cf. APB Opinion No. 25, 30, and FASB Interpretation No. 38 (accounting for junior stock). See also APB Opinion No. 25, 16 and 17 regarding the reduction for Newco's tax saving.

[118] APB Opinion No. 25, 13.

SEC staff has expressed concern over use of a TARSAP arrangement to disguise what is in substance a performance arrangement, and has indicated that (1) the time vesting period for a TARSAP arrangement cannot *significantly* exceed the time vesting period in Newco's other stock-based arrangements (and can in no event exceed 10 years), i.e., if Newco's regular stock-based arrangements have 5-year vesting, TARSAP vesting cannot significantly exceed 5 years (subject to accelerated investing if performance goals are achieved) and (2) to qualify for the TARSAP rule, time vesting must be "more likely than not" even if the performance goals are not achieved.

(6) The rules (set forth in (1) through (5) above) apply whether Newco grants an option to Mgmt subject to vesting *or* Newco sells stock to Mgmt subject to vesting *or* Newco awards stock to Mgmt (i.e., Mgmt's purchase price for the stock is zero) subject to vesting. Hence, for example, if Newco sells stock to Mgmt subject to performance vesting (so that Newco has the right to repurchase the stock if performance targets are not met), Newco's accounting charge is measured as described in (3) and (4) above (generally based on the stock's FV at vesting), unless the TARSAP rules described in (5) above are satisfied.

¶1502.1.7.5   APB 25 Rules for Paying Stock Purchase Price or Option Exercise Price by Note

Where Mgmt uses a note, rather than cash, to purchase Newco stock or to exercise a Newco stock option, a number of additional complex APB 25 rules (which frequently reach results inconsistent with economic reality) come into play as described in (1) through (4) below. These rules often arbitrarily fail to take into account important economic differences with respect to the executive's form of payment for the stock-based compensation (cash, non-recourse note, non-recourse note with recourse interest, or recourse note).

For example, as described in (1)(b) below, an executive who pays for Newco stock with an interest-free non-recourse note is deemed to have paid the same amount for APB 25 purposes as a second executive who buys the same Newco stock with a non-recourse note bearing recourse interest, even though the first executive receives a significantly more attractive economic deal. Similarly, APB 25 takes below-market-interest-rate features into account for recourse loans used to purchase stock or to exercise options (creating variable accounting or other compensation charges) but generally does not take below-market-interest-rate features into account on non-recourse notes used to purchase stock or exercise options, although the below-market-interest-rate feature is an economic benefit in each case. Compare (1) and (2) below with (3) and (4) below.

These inconsistencies between APB 25 accounting and economics are largely attributable to three features of APB 25 accounting: (1) generally under APB 25 a non-recourse note used to purchase stock or to exercise an option is treated as an option, not a loan, (2) APB 25 non-variable accounting (in contrast to FASB 123) has never taken into account option value beyond the current spread (i.e., the value of owning a share of future appreciation without risking current capital) in measuring compensation expense, and (3) APB 25 accounting views non-recourse interest as part of the stock purchase price but recourse interest as not part of the stock purchase price.

As noted below, the accounting consequences of paying for a stock purchase or option exercise with a note turn, in part, on whether the note is recourse or non-recourse. EITF has stated that "the legal form of a recourse note arrangement should be respected . . . unless:"

(i)   the employer "does not intend to seek repayment beyond the shares issued,"
(ii)   the "employer has a history of not demanding repayment of loan amounts in excess of the fair value of shares,"
(iii) the "employee does not have sufficient assets or other means (beyond the shares) to justify the recourse nature of the loan," or
(iv)   the employer has in the past (even if on only one occasion) accepted a recourse note to purchase shares and subsequently converted the note into a non-recourse note.

If any of these four factors is present, the loan is to be treated as non-recourse.

As noted in (iv) above, if Newco forgives all or part of a recourse note or converts a recourse note into a non-recourse note, on even one occasion, EITF applies a one-strike-and-you're-out approach, (a) treating as non-recourse all recourse notes subsequently given by executives to Newco in payment for stock or the exercise price of an option and (b) treating each recourse note previously given by executives in payment for stock or the exercise price of an option as if it were converted into a non-recourse note. See ¶1502.1.7.5(5) for a discussion of the consequences to Newco of converting (or being deemed to convert) a recourse note originally given in connection with an executive's purchase of stock or exercise of an option into a non-recourse note. SEC advances a potentially different view, stating that all facts and circumstances must be considered and noting that if a note is ultimately forgiven, SEC will generally "challenge whether the conclusion that the note was recourse was appropriate."[119]

As discussed in more detail in ¶1502.1.1(5), Sarbanes-Oxley Act of 2002 ("SO") §402 generally prohibits a company with publicly issued or publicly traded securities (an "issuer" as defined by SO) from extending or maintaining credit or arranging for the extension of credit in the form of a personal loan to or for any director or executive officer. Absent a favorable, and unlikely, SEC interpretation, an executive officer's (or director's) note to such a company as the consideration (or as part of the consideration) for such executive's purchase of the company's stock likely constitutes such a prohibited extension of credit in the form of a personal loan.

Discussion in this ¶1502.1.7.5 regarding accounting treatment where a Newco executive pays for his stock purchase from Newco with a note assumes that either

---

[119] See EITF 00-23, ¶151. Although EITF and SEC statements in EITF 00-23 technically refer to whether a note issued in connection with a stock option exercise is considered recourse or non-recourse, the standard should be the same for a note issued in a stock purchase without an option.

Newco is not an "issuer" covered by SO §402 or the executive is not a Newco executive officer or director covered by SO §402, so that paying for the stock with a note is permissible.

(1) Stock purchase by non-recourse note. Where Mgmt purchases Newco stock in exchange for a non-recourse note secured only by the purchased stock, accountants generally take the position that the purchase is, in substance, the issuance of a stock option.[120]

(a) Where interest on the note is non-recourse to Mgmt (as is typically the case with a non-recourse note), accountants treat the interest as part of the purchase price for the stock, in which case accountants further take the position that the award is subject to variable accounting (on the ground that the purchase price is not fixed) where the total amount of interest payable under the note may vary because (1) the note is prepayable at Mgmt's option, or (2) the note is mandatorily prepayable upon the occurrence of specified events (e.g., Newco sale or IPO), or (3) the note bears a floating interest rate.[121]

(b) Fixed, rather than variable, accounting applies, however, notwithstanding the rule set forth in (a), if the award would otherwise qualify as a fixed award apart from the note terms and:

- the interest on the note (although not the principal) is a recourse obligation of Mgmt (because accountants generally do not treat interest which is a recourse obligation as part of the stock purchase price, so that in such case the stock purchase price for accounting purposes is a fixed amount, i.e., the note principal), or
- the interest rate on the note is fixed and the note is not prepayable under any circumstances (so that the total amount of interest payable under the note, and hence in such case the stock purchase price for accounting purposes, is a fixed amount),[122] or
- the note does not bear any stated interest (so that the stock purchase price for accounting purposes is a fixed amount, i.e., the note principal).[123]

With a non-recourse note, even where the interest rate is below market, there is apparently no APB 25 charge for the below market element (as there is with a

---

[120] See ¶1502.1.1(4) for a discussion of the risk IRS will treat the purchase of Newco stock in exchange for a non-recourse loan secured only by the purchased stock as an option for income tax purposes.

[121] EITF 95-16, entitled Accounting for Stock Compensation Arrangements with Employer Loan Features under APB Opinion No. 25.

[122] In some states a clause prohibiting prepayment of Mgmt's note may be unenforceable. To the extent that Mgmt's note is governed by the law of such a state, this technique would probably not avoid variable accounting.

[123] If the note does not bear adequate interest, the tax rules set forth in ¶203.6 would apply, causing Mgmt to be treated for tax purposes as buying the stock for a lower price than the face amount of the note, with the difference treated for tax purposes as additional interest (technically OID), potentially deductible by Mgmt and includable in income by Newco. The lower purchase price for tax purposes would also increase the income recognized by Mgmt under Code §83 and the correlative deduction allowed to Newco. See ¶1502.1.1(4). These tax rules should not affect the accounting conclusions set forth in text above.

recourse note—see (3) and (4) below) because accountants view a stock purchase for a non-recourse note as an option.

(c) If the note is non-recourse but principal and interest are fully secured by property other than Newco stock (in the view of at least some accountants, by property other than Newco securities of any kind), the note should generally be treated the same as a recourse note and should not result in variable accounting if the terms of the stock purchase otherwise qualify as a fixed award. See (3) below dealing with stock purchase with recourse note.

(d) If the note is partially recourse or there are other features (such as a cash down payment or additional property as security for the non-recourse note—including in the view of some accountants other Newco securities owned by Mgmt) so that Mgmt has substantial amounts at risk with respect to the purchased stock,[124] the proper accounting is not clear (unless the note has one or more of the features described in (b) or (c) above so that fixed accounting clearly applies):

- Some accountants take the position—unreasonably harsh in our view—that the entire stock purchase is subject to variable accounting if any portion (however small) of the purchase price is paid with a non-recourse note or a partially non-recourse note.
- Other accountants bifurcate the stock purchase into two pieces, based on the amount Mgmt has at risk with respect to the purchase, so that only a portion of the stock is treated as purchased with a non-recourse note and hence subject to variable accounting.
- Other accountants take the position that no part of the stock purchase should be subject to variable accounting on the ground that the substantial amounts Mgmt has at risk makes the transaction similar in substance to a purchase with a recourse note, although such accountants may take this position only with respect to a privately held company.

In 7/01, EITF apparently adopted the harsher view. EITF 00-23 takes the position that a part-recourse/part-non-recourse note is treated as *entirely* non-recourse, "regardless of the relative percentages of . . . recourse and non-recourse," where the non-recourse portion gives Newco a claim on all of the Newco shares purchased (as is typical in order to avoid unfavorable income tax results) rather than merely a pro rata portion.[125] We believe EITF's position is irrational and ignores the economic substance of part-recourse/part-non-recourse notes.

EXAMPLE 1

Executive A buys Newco stock FV $100 for a $100 note, $99 of which is recourse and only $1 of which is non-recourse. All of the Newco shares are

---

[124] See ¶1502.1.1(4) for a discussion of the tax treatment of such purchases.

[125] EITF 00-23, ¶154. Although this portion of EITF 00-23 explicitly address notes issued in connection with a stock option exercise, the standard should be the same for notes issued in a stock purchase without an option. This portion of EITF 00-23 is effective for a stock option exercised after 7/19/01. For the income tax treatment of a stock purchase for a note, see ¶1502.1.1(4).

pledged to support both the recourse and the non-recourse portions of the note. The pledge agreement states that amounts recovered by Newco are first applied to reduce the non-recourse portion of the note.

Under EITF 00-23's approach, A is treated as purchasing the stock with a 100% non-recourse note, even though the $1 non-recourse portion of the note is collateralized by $100 FV Newco stock. So long as the Newco stock is worth at least $1, Newco can, in case of default, sell the Newco stock, use the proceeds to satisfy the $1 non-recourse portion of the note, apply any additional proceeds to the $99 recourse portion of the note, and sue A, with full personal liability, for any unpaid balance on the $99 recourse portion. Thus, A benefits from the partial non-recourse nature of the note only if the Newco stock falls more than 99% in value. Even if the FV of the Newco stock falls to $0, A is still personally liable to Newco for $99. In light of the economic substance, we believe it irrational to view the note as 100% non-recourse.

EXAMPLE 2

Same as Example 1, except that $50 of the note is recourse and $50 non-recourse and A pledges $50 of U.S. Treasury notes (in addition to the $100 of Newco stock) as collateral.

EITF 00-23 is silent on the impact of additional collateral (i.e., here the Treasury notes). Where the FV of the additional collateral (i.e., property other than Newco stock) is at least equal to the non-recourse portion of the note, and the additional collateral would be applied first to reduce the non-recourse portion of the note, we believe the note should be regarded, in substance, as recourse, for accounting purposes.

If the additional collateral is less than the non-recourse portion of the note, we believe the note should, in substance, continue to be regarded as part-recourse/part-non-recourse (albeit with a smaller non-recourse portion). Thus, if $25 of U.S. Treasury notes are pledged as collateral (in addition to the $100 of Newco stock), the note should be regarded as $25 non-recourse ($50 non-recourse note less $25 of Treasury notes pledged first to the non-recourse note) and $75 recourse.

(2)   Option exercise by non-recourse note. Where Mgmt exercises a stock option and pays the exercise price with a non-recourse note, accountants generally treat Newco as issuing a new stock option to Mgmt—triggering a new measurement date for APB 25 purposes—unless the non-recourse note is viewed as part of the original option because (a) the terms of the original option permitted exercise with a non-recourse note or (b) the non-recourse note is due not later than the expiration of the original option so that the non-recourse note is not viewed as extending the term of the original option.[126]

(a)   Where the original option terms permit exercise of the option for *either* cash or a non-recourse note with non-recourse interest (i.e., so that the interest is considered part of the option price under the rules described in (1)(a) above), the option is considered variable (even if the note is not prepayable) because it is not known until exercise whether the executive will pay with cash or with a non-recourse note reflecting a higher price from an accounting point of view (because the non-recourse interest is treated as part of the exercise price).[127] On the other hand, if the note either does not bear interest or bears recourse interest, fixed accounting applies because the option price (determined under the rules described in (1)(b) above) is the same, whether the executive pays cash or exercises the option using the note.

(b)   Where the original option terms permit exercise of the option only for a non-recourse note (i.e., the option cannot be exercised for cash), the option is subject to variable accounting for the reasons set forth in (1)(a) above, unless the non-recourse note has one or more of the features described in (1)(b) above.

(c)   Where the original option terms do not permit exercise of the option for a non-recourse note, but Newco allows executive to exercise the option for a non-recourse note, the option is subject to variable accounting for the reasons set forth in (1)(a) above, unless the non-recourse note has one or more of the features described in (1)(b) above (except as set forth in (d)). Even if variable accounting does not result, a new measurement date is required where the note term exceeds the option term.

(d)   Where the original option terms do not permit exercise for a non-recourse note, but Newco allows executive to exercise the option for a non-prepayable non-recourse note bearing fixed-rate non-recourse interest, exercise of the option for the note is viewed as an increase in the option exercise price. This is because exercise of the option for the non-recourse note is viewed as either continuing the original option (where the note term does not exceed the original option term) or issuing a new option (where the note term exceeds the original option term) and, in either case, non-recourse interest is part of, and hence an increase to, the option exercise price as described in (1)(a) above. Thus, under EITF 00-23 a new measurement date results and, in addition, the option is forever variable unless facts and circumstances indicate that "future changes to the exercise price . . . will not occur."[128]

Moreover, the original option is apparently considered canceled for purposes of Interpretation 44 and hence can be matched with a new option issuance at a price below the original option price (generally within 6 months before or after the deemed cancellation) to create an indirect option price reduction, triggering variable accounting. See ¶1502.1.7.10(1).

(e)   Where use of a non-recourse note with a below-market interest rate does not cause variable accounting under the rules described in this (2)(a)-(d), there is

---

[126] EITF 95-16.
[127] EITF 95-16.
[128] EITF 95-16 and EITF 00-23.

apparently no APB 25 charge for any below-market element (as there is with a recourse note—see (3) and (4) below) because accountants view option exercise for a non-recourse note as either continuing the original option or as issuing a new option.

(f)   Where the non-recourse note's principal and/or interest is secured as described in (1)(c), the principal and/or interest is regarded as recourse for purposes of applying the rules set forth in (2)(a)-(d) and (3). Where the note is partial recourse and partial non-recourse, the conflicting interpretations described in (1)(d) apply. EITF 00-23 takes the position that a part-recourse/part-non-recourse note is treated as *entirely* non-recourse, "regardless of the relative percentages of the recourse and non-recourse," where the non-recourse portion gives Newco a claim on all of the Newco shares purchased (as is typical for income tax purposes) rather than merely a pro rata portion.[129] As noted in (1)(d) above, we believe this approach ignores the economic substance of part-recourse/part-non-recourse notes.

(3)   Stock purchase by recourse note. Purchase of stock with a full recourse note should not result in variable accounting if the award otherwise qualifies as a fixed award. However, based on the reasoning of EITF 00-23, it is likely that accountants require a compensation charge where Mgmt purchases stock with a recourse note, the face amount of which is equal to the Newco stock's FV, but the note bears interest at a below-market rate, in order to reflect the present value of the below-market interest rate.

(4)   Option exercise by recourse note. Under EITF 00-23, a stock option that permits exercise of the option with a recourse note bearing interest that may not represent a market rate on the *date of exercise* is subject to variable accounting. The EITF treats the exercise price as variable until option exercise because it is not known until exercise whether the executive will pay the exercise price in cash or with a note the FV of which may be less than the option's nominal exercise price due to an interest rate which is below market at time of exercise.

Under EITF 00-23, a stock option that permits exercise with a recourse note bearing interest at a fixed rate specified at grant (even if such interest rate is a market rate at grant) is apparently subject to variable accounting because the interest rate may be below market rate at exercise. On the other hand, if the option allows exercise with a recourse note bearing interest at a market rate to be established *at exercise*, the option is accounted for as fixed (assuming the option otherwise meets the test for a fixed award).

Determining a market interest rate for this purpose apparently requires difficult judgements. EITF 00-23 states that "a statutory rate such as the IRS Applicable Federal Rate does not necessarily represent a market rate" and a market rate "at the date of exercise should consider the credit standing of the [executive] and be determined such that the [executive] would be indifferent as to whether a loan for the exercise price is obtained from [Newco] or from another unrelated lender."

---

[129] EITF 00-23, ¶154. This portion of EITF 00-23 is effective for a stock option exercised after 7/19/01. For the income tax treatment of a stock purchase for a note, see ¶1502.1.1(4).

If a stock option is modified after grant to allow exercise with a recourse note bearing (or which may bear, at exercise) interest at less than a market rate, the modification is generally a repricing which triggers variable accounting. See ¶1502.1.7.10(1).

(5)   Stock purchase or option exercise with recourse note followed by conversion to non-recourse note. Where an executive purchases stock or exercises an option with a note qualifying as recourse for accounting purposes and Newco later converts the recourse note into a non-recourse note (or, as discussed below, Newco is deemed to convert the recourse note into a non-recourse note), EITF 00-23 views Newco as repurchasing the original stock and simultaneously issuing a stock option to the executive in the form of new stock purchased by the executive with a non-recourse note.[130]

Newco is viewed as repurchasing the original stock for an amount equal to the sum of (a) the principal balance of the recourse note, (b) any accrued interest on the recourse note, plus (c) the spread in the new stock option (i.e., the excess of the new stock's FV over the amount of the non-recourse note) at the time the note is converted (or deemed converted) from recourse to non-recourse.

Stock held at least 6 months at conversion. If the conversion from recourse to non-recourse occurs at least 6 months after the executive purchased the stock or exercised the option (so that the executive has held the shares for at least 6 months—see ¶1502.1.7.8), Newco recognizes compensation expense if the repurchase price (as defined above) exceeds the original stock's FV at the time of conversion (i.e., where the stock has declined in FV or failed to rise in FV by the amount of the accrued interest, assuming the executive originally gave a recourse note for the stock's full purchase price and thereafter made no principal payment thereon). Thus, assuming that the amount of the new non-recourse note equals the amount of the old recourse note (including accrued interest), Newco recognizes compensation expense equal to the excess, if any, of the recourse note (including accrued interest) over the original stock's FV at conversion.

Stock held less than 6 months at conversion. If the conversion from recourse to nonrecourse occurs less than 6 months after the executive purchased the stock or exercised the option, the original shares deemed repurchased are considered "immature" and the repurchase transaction is generally integrated with the original purchase or exercise. Newco generally recognizes compensation income equal to the excess, if any, of the purchase price (as defined above) over the sum of (a) the original cost of the stock and (b) the lesser of the spread in the arrangement measured at original grant or measured at conversion (using the original cost of the stock). However, if the purchase price (as defined above) exceeds the stock's FV at conversion, Newco's compensation expense cannot be less than the excess of the purchase price over such FV.

---

[130] Accountants generally treat an executive's acquisition of stock for a non-recourse note as equivalent to the grant of a stock option. See ¶¶1502.1.7.5 and 1502.1.7.5(1).

As a simple illustration, assume that the executive gave a recourse note for the stock's full purchase price and thereafter made no principal payments. If the stock's FV at conversion exceeds the amount owed on the recourse note (including accrued interest) and the new nonrecourse note equals the amount owed on the old recourse note (including accrued interest), Newco recognizes compensation expense equal to the excess of the stock's FV at conversion over the executive's original purchase price for such stock (reduced by any compensation recognized by Newco on the original purchase or option grant). If the amount owed on the recourse note (including accrued interest) exceeds the FV of the stock at conversion, Newco recognizes compensation income equal to the excess of the amount owed on the old recourse note (including accrued interest) over the lesser of (a) the stock's original cost or (b) its FV at conversion.

New option. In either case, the new stock option deemed issued has an exercise price equal to the amount of the non-recourse note. Thus, unless the non-recourse note meets one of the tests outlined in ¶¶1502.1.7.5(1) and (2) above, the new option is subject to variable accounting (because non-recourse interest on the note is treated as part of the option exercise price, making the option exercise price uncertain).

Effect on other notes. Once Newco has converted a recourse note into a non-recourse note (on even one occasion), accountants treat as non-recourse all recourse notes subsequently given by executives to Newco in payment for stock or the exercise price of an option. In addition, if Newco holds other previously issued recourse notes which have not actually been forgiven or converted, EITF treats each such note as if it were deemed converted into a non-recourse note. See ¶1502.1.7.5.

¶1502.1.7.6   *APB 25 Rules for Paying Option Exercise Price with Old Stock or Effecting Cashless Exercise*

(1) If an option holder pays the option exercise price by surrendering some Newco shares he already owns ("old shares") with a value equal to the option exercise price (either because the option permits him to pay the exercise price with old shares *or* because Newco accepts old shares when the option agreement is silent), there is no adverse accounting effect under APB 25 so long as the option holder has held the old shares for at least six months. However, if the option holder pays the exercise price with old shares held for less than six months, the APB 25 option measurement date is postponed until exercise, resulting in a charge to Newco's accounting net income equal to the spread in the option at the time of exercise, reduced by Newco's tax savings from the option exercise and by any prior charge to Newco's earnings at the grant date.[131]

---

[131] Emerging Issues Task Force (EITF) 84-18, entitled Stock Option Pyramiding.

(2) The same result follows under APB 25 if the option holder is permitted to "present" to Newco old shares with a value equal to the option exercise price and Newco then permits him to "retain the [old] shares presented and issues a [new] certificate for the net [option shares]," i.e., Newco issues a new certificate for shares with a value equal to the spread in the option at the time of exercise.[132] If the presented shares have been held for at least six months, there is no adverse accounting effect under APB 25. However, if the presented shares have been held for less than six months, there is an additional compensation charge as described in the prior paragraph.

(3) Under EITF 00-23, old shares are not considered issued until vested in the executive's hands. Thus, the period required before old shares are treated as held for at least six months for purposes of a cashless exercise does not begin to run until the old shares are vested.

(4) Another variation is the so-called cashless (or immaculate) exercise, which encompasses two techniques with dramatically different APB 25 accounting consequences.

(a)   In the first form of cashless exercise, Mgmt exercises the entire option but Newco and Mgmt arrange for an investment banker or broker to sell on the open market the same day or soon thereafter such portion of Mgmt's exercised option shares (the "immediately resold shares") as is necessary to fund the entire option exercise price and Newco then delivers to Mgmt the net number of shares (i.e., the option shares in excess of the immediately resold shares). Often the investment banker or broker funds the option exercise price as a short-term loan to Mgmt and such loan is repaid with the proceeds from the immediately resold shares. In this case, after exercise of the option, all of the original option shares are outstanding—a portion (with an FV equal to the option price) are held by the public and the remainder are held by Mgmt. The APB 25 result is that the option continues to be non-variable and hence Newco has no additional compensation expense, because Newco (and the broker) acted merely as a facilitator assisting Mgmt in funding its obligation to pay Newco the exercise price.[133]

EXAMPLE 13

Newco grants executive A an option on 100 Newco shares with an exercise price of $10 per share. Several years later when Newco's shares are selling

---

[132] EITF 87-6 (pt. D), entitled Phantom Stock-for-Stock Exercise.

[133] See EITF 00-23 confirming this result so long as (1) the executive takes ownership of the option shares prior to the broker's sale and (2) either (a) the broker sells the shares in the open market or (b) the broker sells the shares to a third person other than Newco (not in the open market) or (c) the broker buys the shares for its own account, bears the risk of price fluctuation for a normal settlement period, and then resells to Newco. Moreover, under EITF 00-23 the accounting consequences are the same even where the broker is related to Newco, so long as the broker is a substantive entity with operations distinct from Newco and the broker sells the shares in the open market.

on the open market at $50 per share, executive A borrows $1,000 short-term from broker B, exercises the option, and pays Newco the $1,000 option exercise price ($10 per share option price × 100 shares). Newco and executive A arrange for broker B to sell 20 of A's newly issued Newco shares on the open market for $50 each in order to fund executive A's $1,000 obligation to broker B. Newco delivers 20 Newco shares to broker B for sale on the open market and delivers the remaining 80 Newco shares to executive A. Hence after the option exercise Newco has 100 additional shares outstanding, 80 shares owned by executive A and 20 shares owned by the public.

Under APB 25, the option continues to be non-variable and Newco has no additional compensation expense.

(b) In the second form of cashless exercise, Newco on exercise of the option (i) in effect cancels the option as to a number of Newco shares with an FV equal to the option exercise price and (ii) issues to Mgmt only the net number of shares. Stated differently, Newco cancels the option as to the shares with an aggregate spread (i.e., a FV in excess of option price) equal to the option exercise price for the net shares being issued to Mgmt. In this case, the number of shares to be issued by Newco upon exercise is not known until the exercise date, and the option is thus variable, so that the APB 25 accounting measurement date is postponed. Such a cashless exercise is thus similar to the situation described in ¶1502.1.7.6(1) where the optionholder pays the option exercise price by delivering shares held *less* than six months (here "delivering" shares held no period at all).

EXAMPLE 14

Same as Example 13 except that when executive A exercises the option for 100 Newco shares, Newco issues to A 80 shares and cancels the option on 20 Newco shares with a $1,000 FV ($50 FV per Newco share × 20 shares), that is, Newco cancels the option as to a number of Newco shares with an FV equal to the entire option exercise price. Stated differently, Newco issues to A 80 shares with an $800 total option exercise price (80 shares × $10 per share option exercise price) and cancels the option as to 20 shares with an $800 spread ($50 FV per share *less* $10 option exercise price = $40 spread per share × 20 shares). After exercise, Newco has only 80 additional shares outstanding, not 100 additional shares as in Example 13.

Under APB 25 the option is variable, because the number of shares to be issued by Newco is not known until exercise and executive A has in effect paid the option exercise price with old shares held for less than six months, i.e., with shares held for no period of time.

Newco thus has additional compensation expense of $4,000—100 options × $40 per share spread at exercise—reduced by Newco's tax saving from the option exercise and by any prior charge to Newco's earnings at the grant date (see ¶1502.1.7.4(1)).

¶1502.1.7.7   APB 25 Rules for Paying Withholding Tax with New Shares

(1) As discussed in ¶¶1502.1.1 and 1502.1.2, upon exercise of an NQO, Mgmt recognizes taxable OI equal to the spread (i.e., the stock's FV at exercise less the option exercise price), this OI is subject to income tax withholding, generally at a 27% federal rate plus any applicable state rate and payroll tax withholding, and there are several alternative approaches to funding Newco's withholding obligation.

(2) If Newco holds back a portion of the shares covered by Mgmt's option exercise, sells the held-back shares to a third party, and remits the cash proceeds to IRS and/or other taxing authorities in an amount not exceeding *required* tax withholding (i.e., the minimum federal and state statutory withholding amount, including payroll taxes), there is no APB 25 adverse accounting effect.[134]

(3) If Newco holds back a portion of the shares covered by Mgmt's option exercise, does not sell the held-back shares to a third party, and remits to the taxing authorities an amount of cash out of Newco's treasury equal to the "fair value . . . [of the held-back shares to pay] the *required* tax withholding," there is no APB 25 adverse accounting effect.[135]

(4) The result described in (2) and (3) above would be the same if, instead of Newco holding back shares out of the option being exercised, Mgmt surrendered some old shares with a value equal to the required withholding.

(5) Under FASB Interpretation No. 44, issued 3/31/00, a new measurement date and APB 25 accounting charge is required if shares are withheld in excess of the required tax withholding (i.e., the minimum federal and state statutory withholding amount, including payroll taxes). Where a plan or option permits excess withholding at an executive's election, all awards covered by the plan or option are considered variable. Where a plan or option is silent with respect to tax withholding or permits excess withholding at the employer's discretion, a new measurement date is required with respect to any award where excess withholding actually occurs. If the employer engages in a pattern of consistently approving excess withholding, all awards granted thereafter are considered variable.[136]

[134] APB Opinion No. 25, 11g; FASB Interpretation No. 44, ¶¶75 and 76.
[135] EITF 87-6 (pt. C), entitled Use of Stock Option Shares to Cover Tax Withholding (emphasis in original).
[136] FASB Interpretation No. 44, Accounting for Certain Transactions Involving Stock Compensation, ¶¶75-80.

¶1502.1.7.8   APB 25 Rules for Repurchase of Stock Within Six Months
After Issuance or Repurchase of Option

(1) If Newco repurchases *an option* from Mgmt, there is an APB 25 charge to Newco's accounting net income for the amount paid, reduced by Newco's tax savings from the payment and by any prior charge to Newco's earnings at the grant date.

(2) If Mgmt exercises an option and Newco thereafter repurchases *the stock* from Mgmt "shortly after issuance,"[137] there is an APB 25 charge to Newco's accounting net income for the amount Newco paid to repurchase the stock, reduced by the purchase price paid by Mgmt upon exercise of the option, by Newco's tax savings on the option exercise, and by any prior charge to earnings on account of the grant or exercise of the option.

(3) If Mgmt purchases stock from Newco or receives a stock award from Newco (without the intervention of an option) and Newco thereafter repurchases the stock from Mgmt "shortly after issuance,"[138] there is an APB 25 charge to Newco's accounting net income for the amount Newco paid to repurchase the stock from Mgmt, reduced by the purchase price paid by Mgmt, by Newco's tax savings on the original sale of the stock to Mgmt (if any), and by any prior charge to earnings on account of the original sale of the stock to Mgmt.

(4) The phrase "shortly after issuance" generally has been interpreted to mean less than six months after issuance, by analogy to the accounting rules dealing with a surrender of old shares in payment of the exercise price on an option being exercised, discussed at ¶1502.1.7.6.[139] FASB Interpretation No. 44 clarifies that "shortly after issuance" means less than 6 months.[140] Under EITF 00-23 shares are not issued for this purpose, and hence the 6-month period does not begin to run, until the shares are vested in the executive's hands.

(5) Where a repurchase of stock is pursuant to the terms of the option, purchase, or award and is "expected" to occur within six months after issuance of the stock (even if no actual repurchase occurs within six months), the option, purchase, or award is generally subject to variable accounting. See ¶1502.1.7.14.

(6) If Mgmt purchases stock and pays the purchase price with "a non-recourse note secured by the stock" purchased, the transaction "may be in substance the same as the grant of a stock option and should be accounted for accordingly."[141] Hence, such a purchase would generally not commence the running of the 6-month clock (discussed in (4) above) until the note is paid. On the other hand, if Mgmt pays for purchased stock with a normal recourse note, the 6-month clock should begin to run at purchase. See ¶1502.1.7.5 for a discussion of factors accountants consider in determining whether a loan is recourse or non-recourse.

---

[137] APB Opinion No. 25, 11g.

[138] APB Opinion No. 25, 11g.

[139] See EITF 84-18 and EITF 87-6 (part D) concluding that "a six-month holding period is acceptable to satisfy the holding period requirement" where Mgmt surrenders old shares to pay the option exercise price on an option.

[140] FASB Interpretation No. 44, ¶¶65-69.

[141] APB Opinion No. 25, n.2; FASB Interpretation No. 44, ¶68, n.7.

(7) While the accounting rules discussed in (1) through (6) above are not explicit on this point, we believe (a) the rules set forth in (2) and (3) above assume that the price Newco pays to Mgmt upon repurchase of the stock is the stock's FV, (b) where Newco pays Mgmt a price in excess of the stock's FV, the excess paid over FV constitutes a compensation charge, and (c) the compensation charge described in (b) would apply even if Mgmt had held the stock 6 months or more.

¶1502.1.7.9   APB 25 Rules for Tax-Offset or Other Cash Bonus

(1) FASB Interpretation No. 44, issued 3/31/00, states that "[a] cash bonus and a stock option award shall be accounted for as a combined award if payment . . . of the cash bonus is contingent on the exercise of the option."[142] Where a cash bonus is contingent on exercise of the option and is not fixed in amount (e.g., a tax-offset cash bonus as discussed in (2) and (3) below), the bonus is viewed as causing the exercise price to be variable so that the option is subject to APB 25 variable accounting.

Where a fixed-amount cash bonus established at option grant is contingent on option exercise, the cash bonus is treated as reducing the stated option exercise price (potentially producing additional compensation at grant of the option), but such bonus does not, by itself, cause variable accounting.[143] However, where a cash-bonus feature contingent on option exercise is added after option grant, such bonus would generally constitute a repricing of the option, triggering variable accounting. See ¶1502.1.7.10.

Under EITF 00-23, a cash bonus not contingent on option exercise is not combined with the option award and is instead treated as a separate compensation item. Thus, for example, a cash bonus to be paid only if a stock option (a) vests *and* (b) is in-the-money at vesting is not integrated with the stock option. On the other hand, a cash bonus contingent on sale of stock received on option exercise is integrated with the option and tested as a combined award because the cash bonus is effectively subject to two conditions, one of which is option exercise and the other of which is subsequent sale of the stock.

(2) As discussed in ¶1502.1.2, upon exercise of an NQO, Mgmt recognizes ordinary taxable income equal to the spread (i.e., equal to the stock's FV at exercise less the option exercise price). Thus, the option agreement may call for Newco to pay Mgmt a cash bonus upon exercise equal to the OI tax on the spread (plus the OI tax on the cash bonus), *or* the option agreement may call for Newco to pay Mgmt a smaller bonus equal only to the withholding on the spread (plus the withholding on the bonus).

(3) If Mgmt is entitled to a bonus based on Mgmt's OI tax or withholding tax at exercise (i.e., the "plan . . . contains a tax offset cash bonus"), accounting literature takes the position that the option price was *not fixed* at grant.[144] As a result,

---

[142] Thus, a cash bonus contingent on the vesting of a stock option, rather than its exercise, would not be linked to the stock option for accounting purposes. FASB Interpretation No. 44, ¶94.

[143] FASB Interpretation No. 44, ¶¶90-92.

[144] FASB EITF 87-6 (pt. B), entitled Stock Option Plan with Tax-Offset Cash Bonus.

where Newco is utilizing APB 25, the option is subject to variable accounting and there is a reduction in Newco's accounting net income equal to (i) the spread in the stock at exercise *plus* (ii) the bonus payment (less Newco's tax savings from the stock sale and bonus). This can produce a very substantial reduction in Newco's accounting net income.

(4) If Newco's obligation to pay a tax offset bonus is not contained in the option agreement itself, but is instead contained in a *separate agreement* between Newco and Mgmt which is signed at approximately the same time as the option grant, the APB 25 result is almost certainly the same as in (3) above. Similarly, even if the *separate* tax-offset bonus agreement is signed substantially after the option grant, but pursuant to Newco's and Mgmt's oral understanding reached at approximately the time of the option grant, the APB 25 result is almost certainly the same as in (3) above.

(5) If the parties sign a separate tax-offset bonus agreement substantially after the option grant, and the bonus agreement is not pursuant to any prior oral understanding between Newco and Mgmt (i.e., for a substantial period of time after the option grant, there was no understanding that Mgmt would receive a tax-offset bonus), it was, prior to 3/00, not altogether clear whether accountants would link the two non-contemporaneous agreements (the bonus agreement and the earlier option) to create a variable price option. Under FASB Interpretation No. 44 (issued 3/00), if the bonus is contingent on exercise of the option, it is linked to the option, resulting in a reduction of the option exercise price, triggering variable accounting.[145] See ¶1502.1.7.10.

(6) If there is never any tax-offset bonus agreement at all, but Newco simply pays Mgmt a voluntary, discretionary bonus at or shortly after Mgmt exercises the option, and such bonus is not pursuant to any prior oral understanding that Mgmt would receive a tax-offset bonus (i.e., until the option exercise there was no understanding that Mgmt would receive a tax-offset bonus), it is not clear whether accountants would link the voluntary post-option-exercise bonus with the earlier option to create a variable-price option, although the case for such linking is certainly stronger where the bonus amount correlates with the amount of Mgmt's income tax triggered by the option exercise.

(7) There is no APB 25 adverse accounting effect if Newco agrees to make a normal recourse loan to Mgmt to cover withholding, income taxes, or option exercise price. See ¶1502.1.7.5 for a discussion of factors accountants consider in determining whether a loan is recourse or non-recourse.

(8) In some situations, option awards are coupled with rights to cash payments that vary inversely with the underlying stock price. Such payments may have the effect of guaranteeing that a stock option will have at least a minimum value. For example, Newco may grant an option to an employee with an exercise price equal to $25 per share (the FV of Newco's stock on the grant date) and agree to pay Mgmt a cash bonus equal to the excess (if any) of $50 over Newco's stock trading price per share on the fifth anniversary of option grant. The bonus arrangement effectively guarantees that the option's intrinsic value (in accounting

---

[145] FASB Interpretation No. 44, ¶¶38-39 and 90-91.

parlance) or spread will be at least $25 at the end of five years. EITF 00-23 states that such an award should be accounted for on a combined basis with the underlying option so that Newco recognizes compensation expense equal to the minimum guaranteed amount over the service period.

¶1502.1.7.10   APB 25 and FASB 123 Rules for Option Repricing, Recissions and Other Modifications

(1)   APB 25 repricing rule. Where Newco grants Mgmt an option qualifying as non-variable for APB 25 purposes, but the trading price for Newco's stock thereafter declines, Newco may reprice the option, i.e., reduce the option exercise price to the new lower trading value. Or alternatively Newco may cancel the original option and grant Mgmt a new option at the lower trading value.

The pre-2000 APB 25 accounting rules did not contain a special rule dealing with such option repricing, so that an option qualifying as a non-variable option at grant could continue as a non-variable option for APB 25 purposes after repricing. Thus, if the original non-variable option had an exercise price equal to the Newco stock's FV at grant and the repriced option had an exercise price equal to the Newco stock's lower FV at time of repricing, Newco would generally not record a compensation charge on either the original grant of the option or its repricing.

Under FASB Interpretation No. 44, issued 3/31/00, "[i]f the exercise price of a fixed stock option is reduced, the award shall be accounted for as variable from the date of the modification."[146] The exercise price of an option is considered reduced if "the fair value of the consideration required to be remitted by the grantee upon exercise is less than or potentially less than the fair value of the consideration that was required to be remitted pursuant to the award's original terms." Variable accounting is required even if the reduction is contingent on the occurrence of a future event—whether or not the future event ever occurs.[147]

Variable accounting is also required (even where the stated terms of the option remain unchanged) if Newco "indirectly" reduces the option exercise price, e.g., where:

- Newco grants the executive a cash bonus payable only if the option is exercised or the underlying stock is sold.[148]

---

[146] FASB Interpretation No. 44, Accounting for Certain Transactions Involving Stock Compensation, ¶39. See ¶1502.1.7.10(6) for the effective date of the Interpretation as applied to repricings. Where Newco is an SEC reporting company, SEC applies the APB 25 repricing rules described in text even to Newco options issued by Newco in an acquisition in exchange for old options of the acquired company. EITF had considered requiring only a new measurement date (not continuing variable treatment) for the first post-acquisition modification to such Newco options, to the extent vested at time of modification, but in 4/01 withdrew a tentative decision to that effect. See EITF 00-23, ¶28-33.

[147] FASB Interpretation No. 44, ¶41.

[148] FASB Interpretation No. 44, ¶40, EITF 00-23.

- Newco allows the executive to pay the option exercise price with a recourse note bearing below-market interest.[149]
- Newco cancels (or settles for cash or other consideration) the option and grants a replacement option to the same executive at a lower price, either before or after the cancellation (settlement).[150] A cancellation or settlement is combined with issuance of new option at a lower price to create an indirect option-price reduction where the replacement option is issued within 6 months before or 6 months after the cancellation/settlement, which time period is extended where there is agreement between Newco and executive to compensate the executive for increases in Newco's market price after a cancellation.[151]

Where Newco (and the executive) (1) cancel an outstanding option and (2) agree that Newco will issue the executive a new option more than 6 months later at an exercise price equal to the FV of Newco stock on the reissuance date, the cancellation and reissuance do not result in an indirect repricing, rather the replacement option is "decoupled" from the cancelled option, so long as Newco has not otherwise agreed to compensate the executive for any increase in the FV of Newco stock.[152] Moreover, in such case, the number of at-the-money replacement options Newco can grant to the executive more than 6 months after the cancellation can be greater (or smaller) than the number of options cancelled without causing variable accounting, so long as the number of replacement options is not determined by a formula designed to compensate the executive for any increase in the FV of Newco stock during the more-than-6-month period.

EITF 00-23 states that "grant of an in-the-money option award subsequent to a cancellation of a previous option award creates a presumption that an agreement or implied promise existed to compensate the grantee for increases in the market value of the stock after the cancellation date (even if the market price of the stock has not increased) and, therefore, results in variable accounting for the new award. This presumption may be overcome if the relevant facts and circumstances clearly indicate that the in-the-money option is not related to the prior cancellation."[153]

FASB refused to state a general rule identifying all transactions it will treat as indirect option repricings, stating that "it is not practical to address every potential set of facts or sequence of actions that could cause an effective reduction to the exercise price of a stock option award."

At SEC's request, FASB reviewed the following situation and concluded that it constitutes a repricing triggering variable accounting: Newco grants Mgmt stock options with a $50 exercise price (100% of Newco's stock FV on the option grant date). When Newco's stock subsequently declines in value to $25, Newco grants

---

[149] FASB Interpretation No. 44, ¶40. See ¶1502.1.7.5 for a discussion of the accounting consequences where Newco allows Mgmt to exercise an option with a non-recourse note.

[150] FASB Interpretation No. 44, ¶43.

[151] FASB Interpretation No. 44, ¶¶45 and 47. See also EITF 00-23.

[152] EITF 00-23, ¶¶165-169. However, other option issuances to the executive during the 6-month period following the cancellation could be matched with the cancellation to create an indirect repricing.

[153] See EITF 00-23 for a list of relevant factors to consider.

additional options to Mgmt with a $25 exercise price. The new options expire on the *earlier* of the tenth anniversary of grant *or* 30 days after Newco's stock price reaches $50. According to FASB, "[w]hen and if [Newco's] stock price reaches $50, employees will be economically compelled to exercise the new options, and the old options will continue in place." FASB concluded that an effective repricing has occurred, requiring variable accounting for both the old options and the new options from the grant date of the new options until exercise, forfeiture, or expiration of the old options, on the ground that:

> the new award, through its cancellation provisions, provides an indication of direct linkage to a previously granted out-of-the-money award. . . . [E]conomically, the impact of the above-described sequence of actions is initially similar to a direct reduction to the exercise price of the previously granted stock options.[154]

FASB's focus is apparently on the fact that Mgmt cannot benefit from an option-like privilege—the right to share in stock appreciation without risking a capital investment—on both options (other than for a short 30-day period), since Mgmt must exercise (or lose) the new options once Newco stock reaches $50. Thus, according to FASB, if the new options were exercisable for at least 6 months after Newco's stock price reached $50, the new options would be "uncoupled" from the old options and there would be no indirect repricing.

FASB's conclusion that a repricing has occurred on these facts seems far from compelling, since Mgmt is entitled to retain the old options with their original terms unchanged in all circumstances. Thus, if Newco's stock rises to $75, Mgmt will benefit both from the new options (although forced to exercise the new options within 30 days after Newco's stock reaches $50 in order to retain that benefit) and the old options.

Newco's mere offer to reduce the exercise price of an option or enter into an exchange of options having the effect of a repricing may cause variable accounting for all options eligible for the offer, even options held by executives who do not accept the offer. EITF 00-23 contains two examples where such treatment would apply. In the first example, Newco offers executives a cash bonus conditioned on exercise of their stock options within 2 weeks. After the 2-week period expires, any unexercised options continue in accordance with their original terms. Because the cash bonus is conditioned on option exercise, it is combined with the option and treated as a reduction of the option exercise price. Thus, acceptance of the offer is a repricing (although exercise of the option would cut off variable accounting, limiting the consequences effectively to a new measurement date). However, according to EITF 00-23, "the short-term inducement *potentially* reduces the exercise price . . . under the option (and the grantor can no longer assert that the exercise price . . . [is] fixed and determinable)"[155] (emphasis added). Thus, variable accounting applies to all options subject to the offer, even where the option holder does not accept the offer so the option merely remains outstanding without change after the 2-week offer expires.

---

[154] FASB Staff Announcement, Topic No. D-91 (7/20/00).
[155] EITF 00-23 ¶138.

In the second example, Newco offers executives the ability to exchange out-of-the-money options for options with an exercise price equal to Newco stock's current FV. Because the new options have a longer vesting period, some executives exchange their options for new options and some simply continue to hold their old options. The exchange of new for old options within a 6-month period is an indirect repricing, triggering variable accounting. However, EITF 00-23 states that "the offer introduces variability to the exercise price of the original option award regardless of whether the employee accepts the offer. Therefore, the offer causes variable accounting for the awards subject to the offer."[156]

A modification that increases the option price results in either a new measurement date or variable accounting under EITF 00-23. In addition, under the interpretation, the increase is treated as a cancellation of the original option that may be matched with another option issuance at a lower price than the original option (generally within 6 months before or after the deemed cancellation) to create an indirect option price reduction, triggering variable accounting.[157] Any other modification of an option's terms making it less likely to be exercised is also treated as a cancellation for this purpose.

Under EITF 00-23, "a modification that increases the exercise price or reduces the number of shares under a fixed stock option award should always result in an accounting consequence." If facts and circumstances indicate that "future changes to the exercise price and or number of shares will not occur . . . the award continues to be fixed after the modification . . . [and] the accounting consequence of the modification would be only a new measurement date. In other situations, the nature of the modification and the reasons for it may indicate that there is no practical way to ascertain whether the price is fixed or whether further modifications will occur in the future. In those cases, variable accounting is required for the modified award."[158]

Where Newco settles or replaces a fixed stock option with a stock award, a new measurement date is required. However, variable accounting does not apply to the new replacement stock award, on the ground that the exercise price of the original option has been reduced to zero and no further reductions to the exercise price are possible.[159]

See (6) below for the effective dates for various portions of FASB Interpretation No. 44 relating to option repricing and other modifications.

FASB Interpretation No. 44 is silent on whether repricing a stock sale (as opposed to an option grant) originally accounted for as an APB 25 non-variable transaction might cause the repriced sale to be accounted for as an APB 25 variable transaction, e.g., Newco first sells stock to Mgmt, the stock FV declines, and Newco then reduces the original purchase price by refunding a portion of the cash paid by Mgmt for the stock or canceling a portion of a note given by Mgmt for the stock.

---

[156] EITF 00-23, ¶¶157-164.
[157] FASB Interpretation No. 44, ¶44.
[158] EITF 00-23, ¶114.
[159] FASB Interpretation No. 44, ¶50.

EITF 00-23 notes that a stock award (i.e., a grant of stock where the employee pays no purchase price) "could be considered to be an option with a zero exercise price." Thus, where Newco exchanges new stock options for a previously issued, but unvested, stock award, EITF 00-23 states that the exchange is treated as an "upward repricing" of the stock award, resulting either in a new measurement date or variable accounting under the rules described above for modifications that increase the exercise price of a stock option.[160] While not addressed by EITF 00-23, this position suggests that a similar approach would be taken for repricing an unvested stock purchase.

(2)   APB 25 extension or renewal rule. APB 25 states that a new measurement date (but not full variable treatment) is required if a fixed stock option or purchase right is renewed or extended.[161]

FASB Interpretation No. 44 states that where the terms of an option, purchase, or award are modified to extend the time period beyond the original maximum time period, including a modification contingent on a future separation from service, the modification triggers a new measurement date at the time of the modification.[162] However, if the modification extends the time period, contingent on a future separation from service, but not in excess of the original maximum time period,[163] a new measurement date is triggered at the modification, but additional compensation expense attributable to the new measurement date is ultimately taken into account only if the separation event actually occurs and extends the time period.[164]

A modification that decreases the life of an option does not, by itself, cause variable accounting. However, under the interpretation, the decrease in life is considered a cancellation of the original option that may be matched with another option issuance at a lower price than the original option (generally within 6 months before or after the deemed cancellation) to create an indirect option price reduction, as described above in ¶1502.1.7.9(1), triggering variable accounting.[165]

For a modification that accelerates vesting for a stock option or award, see ¶1502.1.7.11.

(3)   APB 25 change in number of shares rule. FASB Interpretation No. 44 states that where Newco "increases the number of shares to be issued under a fixed stock option award, the award shall be accounted for as variable from the

---

[160] EITF 00-23, ¶¶176-178.

[161] APB Opinion No. 25, ¶11(d). See also EITF 95-16, entitled Accounting for Stock Compensation Arrangements with Employer Loan Features under APB Opinion No. 25.

[162] FASB Interpretation No. 44, ¶34.

[163] This could arise, for example, where the original terms of an option generally provide a maximum 10-year term but require it to be exercised not later than 90 days after a separation from service and the option is amended to allow it to be exercised until the earlier of (1) expiration of the original 10-year term or (2) 2 years after separation from service. In such case, the option has been modified to extend its term, contingent on a separation from service, but not in excess of its original maximum 10-year term.

[164] FASB Interpretation No. 44, ¶¶35, 127, and 164-165.

[165] FASB Interpretation No. 44, ¶44.

date of the modification."[166] Similarly, a fixed stock option is treated as variable from the date of modification if it is modified to grant the executive a new option conditioned on exercise of the old option (a "reload feature").[167]

The interpretation does not generally address the consequences of a decrease to the number of shares issuable under an option, unless the decrease is combined with a grant of a new option that is in substance a repricing of the original option.[168] See ¶1502.1.7.9(1) above. Under EITF 00-23, a modification that decreases the number of shares issuable under an option results in either a new measurement date or variable accounting. See the discussion in (1) above of modifications that increase the exercise price of an option.

Newco's mere offer to increase the number of shares issuable under an option may cause variable accounting for all options eligible for the offer, even options held by executives who do not accept the offer.[169] See (1) above.

(4) APB 25 rules for equity restructuring and certain other transactions. Adjustments to an option's exercise price, number of shares, or both may be made as a result of a stock dividend, spin-off, stock split, rights offering, recapitalization through a large non-recurring dividend, or similar transaction (an "equity restructuring transaction" in accounting parlance) without triggering variable accounting or a new measurement date if:

- the aggregate spread (i.e., the difference between the option exercise price and the FV of the underlying stock) in the option is not increased, and
- the ratio of the exercise price per share to the stock FV per share is not reduced.[170]

In contrast, if a Newco option is exchanged for an option on the stock of another entity with which Newco consolidates for GAAP accounting and the transaction is not an "equity restructuring transaction," either a new measurement date or variable accounting is required:

(1) A new measurement date is required (but not variable accounting) if the two tests set forth above are both met.
(2) Variable accounting is required if either or both of the two tests are not met.[171]

(5) APB 25 rules for other modifications. FASB Interpretation No. 44 states that "[a] modification to a fixed stock option or award that does not affect the

---

[166] FASB Interpretation No. 44, ¶56. Such an increase is, in many cases, also accompanied by a reduction in exercise price.
[167] FASB Interpretation No. 44, ¶58.
[168] FASB Interpretation No. 44, ¶124.
[169] See EITF 00-23, ¶138 and ¶¶157-164.
[170] FASB Interpretation No. 44, ¶53.
[171] EITF 00-23 (7/21/00).

life of the award, the exercise price, or the number of shares to be issued has no accounting consequence."[172]

For example, under EITF 00-23 modifications that eliminate transfer restrictions on stock options do not result in an accounting consequence, so long as such elimination is not intended to circumvent (1) APB 25 cash settlement rules (e.g., by allowing Newco to acquire the option for cash) or (2) rules limiting APB 25 treatment to employees (e.g., by allowing an employee to serve as a conduit for Newco to issue options to a non-employee service provider).

For a modification which accelerates vesting for a stock option or award, see ¶1502.1.7.11.

(6)   APB 25 rules for stock option recission. Where stock prices fall sharply after an executive exercises a Newco stock option, the executive may end up holding Newco stock worth less than the taxes triggered by option exercise. In such case, the executive may wish to "unexercise" the option.

EXAMPLE 15

In year 1, executive receives a 10-year fixed (i.e., non-variable) option (not an incentive stock option for income tax purposes) to purchase 10,000 Newco shares at $5 per share, the FV of Newco stock at grant. In February year 3, when Newco stock is worth $105 per share, executive exercises the option, paying $50,000 to Newco and receiving 10,000 Newco shares worth $1.05 million, and recognizes $1 million of taxable OI (i.e., the spread in the option at exercise). Executive retains the Newco shares and thereafter their FV falls precipitously to $9 per share in December year 3.

Executive owes $400,000 tax on the option exercise, assuming a 40% effective tax rate, while the Newco shares he holds at year end are worth only $90,000. Executive and Newco agree to "unexercise" the stock option. Executive returns the 10,000 Newco shares to Newco. Newco returns the $50,000 exercise price to executive and restores the option with its original terms. Newco and executive both use the calendar year for tax reporting.

For income tax purposes, if executive and Newco "unexercise" the option not later than the end of the taxable year in which the option is exercised (i.e., by the end of year 3), executive and Newco should be treated as if the option had never been exercised, eliminating executive's $1 million OI (and Newco's corresponding $1 million compensation deduction). See ¶1502.1.5.

SEC announced in 1/01 that it would require variable accounting in situations where Newco allows an executive to unexercise or rescind the prior exercise of a stock option.[173] SEC treats the recission as involving two elements: (1) the re-

---

[172] FASB Interpretation No. 44, ¶31.
[173] SEC Staff Announcement, Accounting for the Recission of the Exercise of Employee Stock Options (2001).

purchase of the previously issued stock and (2) the issuance of a new option subject to variable accounting. According to SEC, Newco is required to recognize, on the recission date, compensation expense equal to (a) the cash paid to the executive ($50,000 in Example 15), *plus* (b) the positive spread in the new options deemed issued ($40,000 in Example 15), *plus* (c) the tax benefits lost by Newco ($400,000 in Example 15, assuming Newco's effective tax rate is 40%),[174] *less* (d) the FV of the repurchased shares ($90,000 in Example 15). Thus, in Example 15, Newco recognizes $400,000 of compensation expense on the recission date ($50,000 + $40,000 + $400,000 − $90,000). In addition, the restored option is subject to variable accounting until it is no longer possible to rescind the exercise of the restored option for tax purposes, generally the earlier of expiration or forfeiture of the option or the end of the tax year in which the restored option is exercised.

SEC's rule requiring variable accounting for stock option recissions is effective for recissions after 1/1/01. SEC stated that it would not object to treating recissions occurring before 1/1/01 as "a modification of the original options that result in a new measurement date (rather than variable accounting)." Even where a pre-1/1/01 recission is treated as a modification, Newco would be required to recognize compensation expense on the recission as calculated above.

(7) APB 25 effective date for repricings and other modifications. FASB Interpretation No. 44 is generally effective 7/1/00 and applies prospectively to events on or after that date.

However, the requirement of variable accounting where the exercise price of a fixed stock option is directly or indirectly reduced, discussed in ¶1502.1.7.9(1) above, applies to repricings after 12/15/98 and the requirement of variable accounting where an option is modified to add a "reload feature," discussed in ¶1502.1.7.9(3) above, applies to modifications after 1/12/00. Even in these two situations, no adjustments are required to financial statements for periods prior to 7/1/00 and no expense for additional compensation cost attributable to the interpretation is recognized with respect to periods before 7/1/00.

FASB's conclusion in FASB Staff Announcement, Topic D-91 (7/20/00) discussed in ¶1502.1.7.10(1) above applies only to "indirect repricings through new awards granted after July 20, 2000." The conclusions of EITF 00-23, described in ¶1502.1.7.10(4), with respect to the exchange of a Newco option for an option on the stock of another entity with which Newco consolidates for GAAP accounting, are effective 7/21/00 where the result is a new measurement date and 12/15/98 where the result is variable accounting (on the ground that such exchange results in an indirect repricing).

---

[174] In effect, SEC's formula forces Newco to recapture on recission the tax benefits attributable to the previous option exercise. This seems harsh to us, since in Example 15 (as in many actual option grants) Newco did not receive any benefit on its GAAP income statement for the tax benefits. Because Newco did not record any compensation expense on its GAAP income statement upon issuance or exercise of the option, Newco had no GAAP compensation expense to be reduced to reflect tax benefits; rather the tax benefits were merely recorded for GAAP purposes as an increase in shareholder net worth.

(8)   FASB 123 repricing and other modification rule. Under FASB 123, "[a] modification of the terms of [stock-based compensation] that makes it more valuable shall be treated as an exchange of the original award for a new award. In substance, [Newco] repurchases the original instrument by issuing a new instrument of greater value, incurring additional compensation cost for that incremental value." Thus, where Newco reprices an option (or otherwise modifies an option to increase its value), Newco recognizes additional compensation equal to the excess of (a) the FV of the newly modified option at grant over (b) the FV of the original option (determined immediately before the repricing or modification). In each case, the option FV is determined under the Black-Scholes model or another option-pricing model as discussed in ¶1502.1.7.3. The additional compensation is recognized immediately if the new or modified option is vested and is recognized (together with any unrecognized cost from the original option grant) over the executive's remaining service/vesting period if the new or modified option is subject to further vesting.

A change to an option's terms "in accordance with antidilution provisions that are designed, for example, to equalize an option's value before and after a stock split or a stock dividend" is not considered a modification for this purpose.

¶1502.1.7.11   APB 25 Rules for Accelerated Vesting

When Newco grants Mgmt an option or sells or awards Mgmt stock subject to vesting, the terms of the option or the stock vesting agreement may explicitly provide for accelerated vesting upon occurrence of a specified event, e.g., a change in Newco's control or the executive's death or retirement ("mandatory acceleration"). Even when the option or stock vesting agreement does not explicitly provide for such accelerated vesting, Newco may nevertheless grant the executive accelerated vesting upon the occurrence of such an event ("discretionary acceleration").

The pre-2000 APB 25 accounting rules did not contain a special rule dealing with mandatory or accelerated vesting for options or stock. However, under FASB Interpretation No. 44, issued 3/31/00:

(1)   No new measurement date is required where vesting is accelerated for an option or stock in accordance with the original terms of the option or stock vesting agreement (i.e., mandatory acceleration pursuant to the original agreement).[175]

(2)   A new measurement date occurs (when the option is modified) if acceleration is not pursuant to the original terms of the option or stock vesting agreement (i.e., discretionary acceleration), but only where it ultimately turns out that the acceleration permits the executive to retain stock or exercise an option in circumstances where a forfeiture or expiration would otherwise have occurred according to the original terms. Thus, if vesting

[175] FASB Interpretation No. 44, ¶37.

is accelerated, but the executive continues in Newco's service so that the stock would have vested or the option would have become exercisable under its original vesting provisions, no additional compensation charge is triggered by the acceleration.[176]

(3) Accelerated vesting that the original option or stock vesting agreement permits but does not require is treated in the manner set forth in (2) above, i.e., a new measurement date is required, but only where it ultimately turns out that the acceleration permits the executive to retain stock or exercise an option in circumstances where a forfeiture or expiration would otherwise have occurred according to the original terms.[177]

Where a new measurement date is required, the additional charge to Newco's net income is based upon the FV of Newco's stock on the new measurement date (generally the date Newco agrees to give the executive accelerated vesting), reduced by any prior charge which was measured by the FV of Newco's stock when the option was granted or the stock was sold or awarded to the executive. However, these acceleration rules do not cause the option or stock to become a variable award, i.e., there are no additional charges to Newco's net income for increase in Newco's stock FV subsequent to the new measurement date.

Where Newco modifies an unvested option to allow an executive to exercise such option "early" while it is still unvested (typically for tax reasons, in order to minimize the executive's Code §83 OI), the modification is not treated as an acceleration of vesting and no accounting consequences result if vesting is preserved in the form of a call option in favor of Newco so that Newco can repurchase the shares from the executive at lower of cost or FV (on the call date) where the executive's employment with Newco terminates prior to the time the original option would have vested in accordance with its original terms.[178] An acceleration of vesting occurs only if the executive's employment with Newco terminates but Newco fails to exercise the call option.

Where Newco so modifies an unvested option to allow early exercise, Newco shares received by the executive upon early exercise are generally not considered outstanding for accounting purposes until Newco's call option lapses. Thus, such early-exercise shares are not treated as held for at least 6 months—so that such shares are eligible to be used in a cashless exercise or eligible to be repurchased by Newco in a treasury transaction—until 6 months after lapse of Newco's call option.

¶1502.1.7.12   *APB 25 Rules Where Option Grantor Subsequently Acquired*

FASB Interpretation No. 44, issued 3/31/00, states that for purposes of APB 25, where Newco (the option grantor) is acquired by P:

[176] FASB Interpretation No. 44, ¶¶36 and 126.
[177] FASB Interpretation No. 44, ¶¶36-37.
[178] EITF 00-23, ¶¶143-150.

- No new measurement date is required for an exchange of new P options for old Newco options so long as (1) the P-Newco acquisition qualifies for pooling of interests accounting (see ¶1703.4) and the option exchange is effected at the same exchange ratio as the P-Newco acquisition.[179] However, if old Newco options (whether vested or unvested) are exchanged for new P stock in a pooling of interests transaction, a new measurement date results.[180] Pooling of interests accounting has been eliminated for an acquisition initiated after 6/30/01. See ¶1703.

- If the P-Newco acquisition is accounted for as a purchase (see ¶1703.3), P vested options or stock issued in exchange for Newco options or stock are accounted for as part of the purchase transaction so that the FV of such vested P options or stock is included as part of P's consideration for Newco (thus generally creating additional amortizable goodwill).[181]

    Where non-vested P options or stock issued in exchange for Newco options or stock require the holder to perform services after the transaction in order to vest, the P options or stock are accounted for in part under APB 25 principles and in part as purchase price in the acquisition. A new measurement date is triggered for the new P options or stock on consummation of the transaction; however, only a portion of compensation expense, if any, that would ordinarily result under APB 25 rules on such measurement date—equal to the ratio of the post-transaction service period required to vest the P options or stock to the aggregate service period required under both the P and Newco options or stock—is recognized as compensation expense and taken into account over the post-transaction service period. The excess of the FV of the P options or stock over this compensation expense is taken into account as part of the purchase price paid in the transaction.[182]

    The interpretation is effective for transactions on or after 7/1/00.[183]

¶1502.1.7.13   APB 25 Rules for Formula Option Arrangement

(1) Where Newco grants an option to Mgmt at a price determined by a formula (generally based on book value or earnings) and Mgmt has the right or obligation to resell the option or the stock to be received on exercise of the option back to Newco at a price determined by the same formula upon leaving Newco's employ or at some other time, the option is variable and the APB 25 measurement date is postponed *until Mgmt exercises the option*, so that there is a charge to Newco's

---

[179] FASB Interpretation No. 44, Accounting for Certain Transactions Involving Stock Compensation, ¶82.

[180] EITF 00-23 (7/21/00).

[181] FASB Interpretation No. 44, ¶84.

[182] FASB Interpretation No. 44, ¶85.

[183] FASB Interpretation No. 44, ¶93.

accounting net income for the increases in the formula value of the stock from grant date to exercise, reduced by Newco's tax savings on option exercise.[184]

(2) Where Newco is *privately held after the option has been exercised,* so that Mgmt has "a substantive investment . . . at risk for a reasonable period of time," there is no further APB 25 accounting charge after exercise, except that if Newco repurchases the shares "shortly after exercise," there would be an additional charge to Newco's accounting net income for the cash paid, reduced by the purchase price paid by Mgmt upon exercise of the option, by Newco's tax savings on the option exercise, and by any prior charges to earnings pursuant to (1).[185] "Shortly after exercise" has generally been interpreted to mean less than six months after exercise.

FASB Interpretation No. 44, issued 3/31/00 and generally effective 7/1/00, states that (i) Newco avoids additional compensation charges after exercise if "the employee has made a *substantial investment* and *must* bear risks and rewards normally associated with share ownership for a reasonable period (*at least six months*)"[186] and (ii) an employee is deemed to make a "substantial investment . . . when the employee invests (in a form other than services rendered) an amount equal to 100 percent of the stated share repurchase price calculated at the date of grant."[187] This language can be read as (a) leaving open the possibility that a reasonable period may be more than six months, (b) prohibiting the employee from having a right to sell the stock to Newco during the first six months after exercise, and (c) requiring the employee to pay (or perhaps give a recourse note for) 100% of the purchase price.

EITF 00-23 provides further guidance, stating, "[a]fter a substantial investment . . . has been made, a non-public company would account for the awards as fixed (assuming the awards otherwise qualify for fixed accounting) . . . unless the shares are *expected to be repurchased within six months after the employee makes a substantial investment.*"

EITF 00-23 states that where Newco has a call on shares that "results, or potentially could result, in a repurchase amount that is less than the fair value of the underlying shares . . . there is always an expectation that the repurchase

---

[184] EITF 87-23 (issue 2(b)); EITF Exhibit B 88-6A; APB Opinion No. 25, 16 and 17.

Where Mgmt has the right or obligation to resell the stock or the option at FV (e.g., determined by appraisal or recent actual sales prices) rather than at a formula price, see ¶1502.1.7.14.

If the formula buy-back provisions meet the never-lapse requirements of Code §83(d), the tax ramifications on exercise of the option would be governed by Code §83(d), so that the stock's formula value at any time would generally be treated as the stock's FV for purposes of applying the tax rules discussed in ¶¶1502.1.1 and 1502.1.2. Normally this would be true only if there were no circumstances under which Mgmt could avoid the formula buy-back obligation and realize full FV on the option shares.

[185] EITF 87-23 (issue 2(b)).

[186] FASB Interpretation No. 44, ¶71(b) (emphasis added).

[187] FASB Interpretation No. 44, ¶74. Although a bit unlikely, it may be possible to read this language as a safe harbor—i.e., payment of 100% of the stated share repurchase price is substantial, but a smaller amount might also be substantial.

feature will be exercised."[188] If Newco has a call at a price greater than FV, Newco's stated intention and all other relevant facts and circumstances are to be considered in determining whether the call is expected to be exercised. Where a call is expected to be exercised and Newco is entitled to exercise the call within six months after the employee's substantial investment, variable accounting is required until the earlier of (1) the date the call expires, (2) the date the call is exercised, or (3) six months after the date the employee made a substantial investment in the award. If a Newco call right is subject to a contingency, and the contingency is either in Newco's control or "probable of occurrence," the contingency is ignored and the call tested as described above in this paragraph. If the contingency is outside Newco's control and "not probable of occurrence," the call right is ignored and does not cause variable accounting.

EITF 00-23 states that "the existence of [an employee] put always results in an expectation that the repurchase feature will be exercised." Thus, if the employee is entitled to exercise the put within six months after the time the employee made a substantial investment, variable accounting is required until the earlier of (1) the date the put expires, (2) the date the put is exercised, or (3) six months after the date the employee made a substantial investment in the option shares. There is a special rule for "fixed premium puts" (i.e., a put where the "put price is at a fixed dollar amount greater than the stock price"[189]). Where a fixed premium put is exercisable within six months after option exercise, variable accounting is required until the earlier of (1) expiration of the put, (2) exercise of the put, or (3) six months after option exercise. A fixed premium put not exercisable within six months after the employee's option exercise does not cause variable accounting; instead, the premium is recognized as compensation expense over the service/vesting period. If a put (including a fixed premium put) is subject to a contingency, and the contingency is either within the employee's control or the contingency is probable of occurrence, the put is tested under the rules described above in this paragraph. If the contingency is not within the employee's control and the contingency is "not probable of occurrence," the put is ignored and does not cause variable accounting.

(3) Where Newco is *publicly held,* stock received on exercise of the option has generally been accounted for as a variable award as long as the stock remains subject to formula repurchase rights.[190]

Although not clear, FASB Interpretation No. 44, issued 3/31/00 and generally effective 7/1/00, may change this result. The interpretation first sets forth a *general rule* applicable to publicly held Newco, under which a share repurchase feature causes variable accounting if (i) the shares are expected to be repurchased within six months after option exercise or (ii) the employee has the right to require repurchase within six months after option exercise (regardless of whether the

---

[188] Newco's right to call shares at cost from an employee who fails to perform services for a specified time is considered merely a time-vesting feature and does not trigger variable accounting under these rules.

[189] Presumably the reference to stock price means, in the case of a privately held company, the stock's FV.

[190] EITF 88-6 (issue 1).

employee actually requires Newco to repurchase the shares within six months).[191] The interpretation then explicitly addresses the treatment of formula repurchase features in *two specific situations. First,* variable accounting is required if the "repurchase feature gives the employee the right [after exercise of the option] to sell shares back to [Newco] . . . for a premium (that is not fixed and determinable) over the then-current stock price . . . even if the shares cannot be sold back to [Newco] within six months after option exercise."[192] *Second,* variable accounting is not required (assuming the option otherwise qualifies as fixed) if the "repurchase feature gives the employee the right [after exercise of the option] to sell shares back to [Newco] for a fixed dollar amount over the stock price (but not within six months of issuance of those shares)," in which case the fixed premium is simply recognized as additional compensation expense.[193] The treatment of formula repurchase rights not matching these two specific situations is unclear, including arrangements where (i) the employee has the right to require Newco to repurchase shares at a discount from the then current share price, (ii) there is a mandatory obligation binding on both Newco and the employee to repurchase shares at a formula price, or (iii) Newco has the right to repurchase shares at a formula price. If the interpretation is read as applying the general rule for a publicly held company whenever the two specific situations do not apply, there would be no variable accounting unless (i) the shares are expected to be repurchased within six months after option exercise or (ii) the employee has the right to require repurchase within six months. However, it would be odd if the interpretation resulted in more favorable rules for publicly held companies (as described in this (3)) than for privately held companies (as described in (2) above); thus, many accountants believe the interpretation is intended to retain the prior rule that such features result in variable accounting.

EITF 00-23 attempts to clarify the scope of Interpretation 44. Under EITF 00-23, where Newco is public, a Newco call at other than FV or an employee put feature at other than FV causes variable accounting (until the earlier of the expiration of the call/put or the exercise of the call/put) if the call or put is "expected" to be exercised, *even if shares are not expected to be repurchased within six months after the employee exercises the option.* If a call or put is not "expected" to be exercised, it does not cause variable accounting (i.e., the award is analyzed as if it did not contain the call or put). As described below, a special rule is provided for fixed premium put rights.

EITF 00-23 states that where Newco has a call on shares that "results, or potentially could result, in a repurchase amount that is less than the fair value of the underlying shares . . . there is always an expectation that the repurchase feature will be exercised and variable accounting is required."[194] If Newco has a call at a price greater than FV, Newco's stated intention and all other relevant

---

[191] FASB Interpretation No. 44, ¶68.

[192] FASB Interpretation No. 44, ¶70.

[193] FASB Interpretation No. 44, ¶70.

[194] Newco's right to call shares at cost from an employee who fails to perform services for a specified time is considered merely a time vesting feature and does not trigger variable accounting under these rules.

facts and circumstances are to be considered in determining whether the call is expected to be exercised. If a Newco call right is subject to a contingency, and the contingency is either in Newco's control or "probable of occurrence," the contingency is ignored and the call is tested as described above in this paragraph. If the contingency is outside of Newco's control and "not probable of occurrence," the call right is ignored and does not cause variable accounting.

EITF 00-23 states that "the existence of [an employee] put always results in an expectation that the repurchase feature will be exercised." Thus, variable accounting is required unless the put constitutes a "fixed premium put" (i.e., a put where the "put price is at a fixed dollar amount greater than the stock price"). Where a fixed premium put is exercisable within six months after option exercise, variable accounting is required until the earlier of (1) expiration of the put, (2) exercise of the put, or (3) six months after option exercise. A fixed premium put not exercisable within six months after option exercise does not cause variable accounting; instead, the premium is recognized as a compensation expense over the service/vesting period. If a put (including a fixed premium put) is subject to a contingency, and the contingency is either within the employee's control or the contingency is probable of occurrence, the put is tested under the rules described above in this paragraph. If the contingency is not within the employee's control and the contingency is "not probable of occurrence," the put is ignored and does not cause variable accounting.

(4) See ¶1502.1.7.14(4) defining a company as public if any of its (or its parent's) equity securities are traded.

(5) When a *privately held* Newco has an initial public offering (IPO) and, as part of the IPO, Newco *eliminates or cancels* Mgmt's pre-existing right or obligation to resell to Newco at a formula price an unexercised option or stock covered by such unexercised option, there is an additional APB 25 charge to Newco's accounting net income for the excess of the stock's IPO FV over the formula repurchase price (reduced by Newco's tax saving).[195] Subsequent to the IPO there is no further APB 25 charge to Newco's accounting net income, because the formula buy back no longer exists.[196]

(6) It seems logical that there would also be an APB 25 accounting charge for shares as to which the option had been exercised within one year prior to the IPO, by analogy to formula stock purchase arrangements discussed in ¶1502.1.7.14(5) and (6), although the accounting literature is a tad short of precise on this point.

(7) When a *privately held* Newco has an IPO but *retains* Mgmt's pre-existing right or obligation to resell to Newco at a formula price an unexercised option or stock covered by such unexercised option, there is an APB 25 charge to Newco's accounting net income (i) at the time of the IPO for the increase in the formula price because of the IPO (reduced by Newco's tax savings) and (ii) periodically thereafter for increases in the formula price (reduced by Newco's tax savings).[197] If, as discussed in (2) above, FASB Interpretation No. 44 narrows the circumstances

---

[195] EITF 88-6 (issue 2(a)); EITF Exhibit 88-6A; APB Opinion No. 25, 16 and 17.
[196] EITF 88-6 (issue 2(a)); EITF Exhibit 88-6A.
[197] EITF 88-6 (issue 2(b)); EITF Exhibit 88-6A; APB Opinion No. 25, 16 and 17.

in which a formula option arrangement results in variable accounting for publicly held Newco, it should similarly narrow the circumstances in which variable accounting is required when privately held Newco has an IPO and retains formula repurchase rights after the IPO.

¶1502.1.7.14   *APB 25 Rules for Formula Stock Purchase Arrangement*

(1) Where Newco sells stock to Mgmt at a price determined by a formula (generally based on book value or earnings), Mgmt has the right or obligation to resell the stock back to Newco at a price determined by the same formula upon leaving Newco's employ or at some other time, and Newco is *privately held*, then the APB 25 measurement date is not postponed, so there is no charge to Newco's accounting net earnings.[198] See ¶1502.1.7.14(4) below defining a company as publicly held if any of its (or its parent's) equity securities are traded.

(2) The conclusion described in (1) is premised on the view that "no compensation expense should be recognized for the increase or decrease in [the formula amount] . . . during the employment period if the employee makes a substantive investment that will be at risk for a reasonable period of time."[199] FASB Interpretation No. 44, issued 3/31/00 and generally effective 7/1/00, states that (i) Newco avoids compensation charges if "the employee has made a *substantial investment* and *must* bear risks and rewards normally associated with share ownership for a reasonable period (*at least six months*)"[200] and (ii) an employee is deemed to make a "substantial investment . . . when the employee invests (in a form other than services rendered) an amount equal to 100 percent of the stated share repurchase price calculated at the date of grant."[201] This language can be read as (a) leaving open the possibility that a reasonable period may be more than six months, (b) prohibiting the employee from having a right to sell the stock to Newco during the first six months after issuance, and (c) requiring the employee to pay (or perhaps give a recourse note for) 100% of the purchase price.[202]

---

[198] EITF 87-23 (issues 1 and 2(a)); EITF Exhibit 88-6A.

Where Mgmt has the right or obligation to resell the stock at FV (e.g., determined by appraisal or recent actual sales prices) rather than at a formula price, see ¶1502.1.7.14.

[199] EITF 87-23.

If the formula buy-back provisions meet the never-lapse requirements of Code §83(d), the tax ramifications of Newco's stock sale to Mgmt would be subject to Code §83(d), so that the stock's formula value at any time would generally be treated as the stock's FV for purposes of applying the tax rules discussed in ¶¶1502.1.1 and 1502.1.2. Normally this would be true only if there were no circumstances under which Mgmt could avoid the formula buy-back obligation and realize full FV on the purchased shares.

[200] FASB Interpretation No. 44, ¶71(b) (emphasis added).

[201] FASB Interpretation No. 44, ¶74. Although a bit unlikely, it may be possible to read this language as a safe harbor—i.e., payment of 100% of the stated share repurchase price is substantial, but a smaller amount might also be substantial.

[202] Before the 3/31/00 interpretation, when Newco's original sale of the stock to Mgmt was at a price below the formula price determined at the time of Mgmt's purchase of the stock, there was apparently a charge to Newco's net earnings equal to the amount by which the purchase price paid by Mgmt was below the formula price determined at the time of purchase and there appeared to be no further subsequent charge. This was apparently true even if the purchase price was nominal (or

EITF 00-23 provides further guidance, stating, "[a]fter a substantial investment . . . has been made, a non-public company would account for the awards as fixed (assuming the awards otherwise qualify for fixed accounting) . . . unless the shares are *expected to be repurchased within six months after the employee makes a substantial investment*."

EITF 00-23 states that where Newco has a call on shares that "results, or potentially could result, in a repurchase amount that is less than the fair value of the underlying shares . . . there is always an expectation that the repurchase feature will be exercised."[203] If Newco has a call at a price greater than FV, Newco's stated intention and all other relevant facts and circumstances are to be considered in determining whether the call is expected to be exercised. Where a call is expected to be exercised and Newco is entitled to exercise the call within six months after the employee's substantial investment, variable accounting is required until the earlier of (1) the date the call expires, (2) the date the call is exercised, or (3) six months after the date the employee made a substantial investment in the award. If a Newco call right is subject to a contingency, and the contingency is either in Newco's control or "probable of occurrence" the contingency is ignored and the call is tested as described above in this paragraph. If the contingency is outside Newco's control and "not probable of occurrence" the call right is ignored and does not cause variable accounting.

EITF 00-23 states that "the existence of [an employee] put always results in an expectation that the repurchase feature will be exercised." Thus, if the employee is entitled to exercise the put within six months after the employee made a substantial investment, variable accounting is required until the earlier of (1) the date the put expires, (2) the date the put is exercised, or (3) six months after the date the employee made a substantial investment in the shares. There is a special rule for "fixed premium puts" (i.e., a put where the "put price is at a fixed dollar amount greater than the stock price"[204]). Where a fixed premium put is exercisable within six months after share issuance, variable accounting is required until the earlier of (1) expiration of the put, (2) exercise of the put, or (3) six months after share issuance. A fixed premium put not exercisable within six months of share issuance does not cause variable accounting; instead, the premium is recognized

---

nothing, as is the case with a formula stock award plan). It is arguable that this position was inconsistent with the rule set forth in text because where Mgmt's purchase price was nominal (or nothing), Mgmt had no "substantive investment . . . at risk for a reasonable period of time," and hence there should have been post-purchase charges for increases in the formula buy-back price. On the other hand, it could be argued that Mgmt was at risk because the buy-back price for the stock could decline, in which case Mgmt would lose money compared to the buy-back price at the time Mgmt initially purchased the stock.

A purchase at a price below the formula price determined at the time of purchase would apparently be subject to variable accounting under FASB Interpretation No. 44, unless the interpretation's statement that a substantial investment is made when Mgmt pays 100% of the formula price is merely a safe harbor.

[203] Newco's right to call shares at cost from an employee who fails to perform services for a specified time is considered merely a time-vesting feature and does not trigger variable accounting under these rules.

[204] Presumably the reference to stock price means, in the case of a privately held company, the stock's FV.

as compensation expense over the service/vesting period. If a put (including a fixed premium put) is subject to a contingency, and the contingency is either within the employee's control or the contingency is probable of occurrence, the put is tested under the rules described above in this paragraph. If the contingency is not within the employee's control and the contingency is "not probable of occurrence," the put is ignored and does not cause variable accounting.

However, where Mgmt pays the purchase price by using a non-recourse note secured by the stock purchased, the transaction is generally treated for accounting purposes as an option (rather than a purchase), as described in ¶1502.1.7.5(5), and hence the formula option rules discussed in ¶1502.1.7.13 would generally apply.

If Mgmt has purchased formula shares but Newco thereafter repurchases the shares within six months, there may be an APB 25 charge to Newco's accounting net income, by analogy to the rule discussed in ¶1502.1.7.8(3).

(3) Where Newco is *publicly held*, the APB 25 accounting rule has been considerably different: the measurement date is postponed and hence there are periodic charges to Newco's accounting net income for the increases in the formula value of the stock from sale to Mgmt until repurchase from Mgmt (reduced by Newco's tax savings).[205]

Although not clear, FASB Interpretation No. 44, issued 3/31/00 and generally effective 7/1/00, may change this result. The interpretation first sets forth a *general rule* applicable to publicly held Newco, under which a share repurchase feature causes variable accounting if (i) the shares are expected to be repurchased within six months after issuance or (ii) the employee has the right to require repurchase within six months after issuance (regardless of whether the employee actually requires Newco to repurchase the shares within six months).[206] The interpretation then explicitly addresses the treatment of formula repurchase features in *two specific* situations. *First*, variable accounting is required if the "repurchase feature gives the employee the right [after issuance] to sell shares back to [Newco] . . . for a premium (that is not fixed and determinable) over the then-current stock price . . . even if the shares cannot be sold back to [Newco] within six months after . . . issuance."[207] *Second*, variable accounting is not required (assuming the stock award otherwise qualifies as fixed) if the "repurchase feature gives the employee the right [after issuance] to sell shares back to [Newco] for a fixed dollar amount over the stock price (but not within six months of issuance of those shares)," in which case, the fixed premium is simply recognized as additional compensation expense.[208] The treatment of formula repurchase rights not matching these two specific situations is unclear, including arrangements where (i) the employee has the right to require Newco to repurchase shares at a discount from the then current share price, (ii) there is a mandatory obligation binding on both Newco and the employee to repurchase shares at a formula price, or (iii) Newco has the right to repurchase shares at a formula price. If the interpretation is read as applying the general rule for a publicly held company whenever the two

---

[205] EITF 87-23 and EITF 88-6 (issue 1).
[206] FASB Interpretation No. 44, ¶68.
[207] FASB Interpretation No. 44, ¶70.
[208] FASB Interpretation No. 44, ¶70.

specific situations do not apply, there would be no variable accounting unless (i) shares are expected to be repurchased within six months after issuance or (ii) the employee has the right to require repurchase within six months. However, it would be odd if the interpretation resulted in more favorable rules for publicly held companies (as described in this (3)) than privately held companies (as described in (1) above); thus, many accountants believe the interpretation is intended to retain the prior rule that such features result in variable accounting.

EITF 00-23 attempts to clarify the scope of Interpretation 44. Under EITF 00-23, where Newco is public, a Newco call at other than FV or an employee put feature at other than FV causes variable accounting (until the earlier of the expiration of the call/put or the exercise of the call/put) if the call or put is "expected" to be exercised, *even if shares are not expected to be repurchased within six months after issuance*. If a call or put is not "expected" to be exercised, it does not cause variable accounting (i.e., the award is analyzed as if it did not contain the call or put). As described below, a special rule is provided for fixed premium put rights.

EITF 00-23 states that where Newco has a call on shares that "results, or potentially could result, in a repurchase amount that is less than the fair value of the underlying shares . . . there is always an expectation that the repurchase feature will be exercised and variable accounting is required."[209] If Newco has a call at a price greater than FV, Newco's stated intention and all other relevant facts and circumstances are to be considered in determining whether the call is expected to be exercised. If a Newco call right is subject to a contingency, and the contingency is either in Newco's control or "probable of occurrence," the contingency is ignored and the call is tested as described above in this paragraph. If the contingency is outside of Newco's control and "not probable of occurrence," the call right is ignored and does not cause variable accounting.

EITF 00-23 states that "the existence of [an employee] put always results in an expectation that the repurchase feature will be exercised." Thus, variable accounting is required unless the put constitutes a "fixed premium put" (i.e., a put where the "put price is at a fixed dollar amount greater than the stock price"). Where a fixed premium put is exercisable within six months after share issuance, variable accounting is required until the earlier of (1) expiration of the put, (2) exercise of the put, or (3) six months after share issuance. A fixed premium put not exercisable within six months after share issuance does not cause variable accounting; instead, the premium is recognized as a compensation expense over the service/vesting period. If a put (including a fixed premium put) is subject to a contingency, and the contingency is either within the employee's control or the contingency is probable of occurrence, the put is tested under the rules described above in this paragraph. If the contingency is not within the employee's control and the contingency is "not probable of occurrence," the put is ignored and does not cause variable accounting.

(4) Prior to the release of FASB Interpretation No. 44, a company was publicly held for this purpose if any of its (or its parent's) securities, including debt

---

[209] Newco's right to call shares at cost from an employee who fails to perform services for a specified time is considered merely a time vesting feature and does not trigger variable accounting under these rules.

securities, were traded on an exchange or over the counter (including local quotations).[210]

FASB Interpretation No. 44, issued 3/31/00, states that a company is a public entity if:

- its "securities trade in a public market either on a stock exchange (domestic or foreign) or in an over-the-counter market, including securities quoted only locally or regionally," or
- it "makes a filing with a regulatory agency in preparation for the sale of any class of equity securities in a public market," or
- it is a subsidiary of, or controlled by, an entity that is deemed to be public under either of the preceding paragraphs.

Under the interpretation, "an entity with publicly traded debt but no publicly traded equity securities shall follow the accounting prescribed for a non-public entity."[211]

The interpretation is effective for options granted on or after 7/1/00 and stock purchased on or after 7/1/00 (other than stock purchased pursuant to an option granted before 7/1/00). Although it is generally not effective before 7/1/00, we hope the interpretation will, nonetheless, provide support for treating as private those companies that have registered (or traded) debt but no traded equity.

(5) When a *privately held* Newco has an IPO and, as part of the IPO, Newco *eliminates or cancels* Mgmt's right or obligation to resell to Newco at a formula price stock previously sold by Newco to Mgmt, there is an APB 25 charge to Newco's accounting net income at the time of the IPO if the stock was sold to Mgmt (i) within one year before the IPO or (ii) more than one year before the IPO but "in contemplation of [the IPO]" or (iii) more than one year before the IPO and not in contemplation of the IPO, but at a formula "materially different from the market value [of the stock] at the date of issuance."[212] In these circumstances, the charge to Newco's accounting net income is equal to the stock's estimated FV when sold to Mgmt (taking into account the IPO price and other evidence of FV) reduced by the purchase price paid by Mgmt and by Newco's tax savings.[213] Subsequent to the IPO, there is no further APB 25 charge to Newco's accounting net income, because the formula buy-back no longer exists. There is risk of substantial dispute on the meaning and applicability of exception (iii), but there is little experience with its scope.

(6) When a *privately held* Newco has an IPO but *retains* Mgmt's right or obligation to resell to Newco at a formula price stock previously sold by Newco to Mgmt,

[210] See AICPA Statement of Auditing Standards (SAS) No. 26; EITF 87-23.

[211] FASB Interpretation No. 44, ¶72. The final 3/31/00 interpretation states that the definition of "public entity" is for "purposes of this Interpretation." The earlier draft interpretation's similar definition was "for purposes of applying [APB] Opinion 25." See FAS Proposed Interpretation No. 195-B (3/31/99). It is not clear whether this difference was intended to restrict the scope of the new definition. Because the final interpretation interprets APB 25, we believe that the new definition should apply for all APB 25 purposes.

[212] EITF 88-6 (issue 3(a)); EITF Exhibit 6A.

[213] EITF 88-6 (issue 3(a)); EITF Exhibit Reg. §§88-6A; APB Opinion No. 25, 16, and 17.

there is an APB 25 charge to Newco's accounting net income for shares sold to Mgmt (i) within one year before the IPO, *or* (ii) more than one year before the IPO but in contemplation of the IPO, *or* (iii) more than one year before the IPO and not in contemplation of the IPO, but at a formula "materially different from the market value at the date of issuance."[214] In these circumstances, the charge to Newco's accounting net income is equal to the increase in the formula price from sale to Mgmt until the IPO. After the IPO (because Newco is publicly held and the formula buy-back continues), there are periodic APB 25 charges to Newco's accounting net income for the increases in the formula value of the stock from the IPO until repurchase, reduced by Newco's tax saving.[215] If, as discussed in (3) above, FASB Interpretation No. 44 narrows the circumstances in which a formula stock purchase arrangement results in variable accounting for publicly held Newco, it should similarly narrow the circumstances in which variable accounting is required when privately held Newco has an IPO and retains formula repurchase rights after the IPO.

¶1502.1.7.15   APB 25 Rules for Puts, Calls, and Repurchase Agreements at FV

APB 25 rules relating to stock compensation where there are puts, calls, and rights of first refusal at FV between Mgmt and Newco (e.g., upon exercise of any such put, call, or buy-back, Newco will pay Mgmt an amount equal to the stock's appraised FV or recent sales price) were significantly modified by FASB Interpretation No. 44, issued 3/31/00 and generally effective for options granted and stock purchased on or after 7/1/00.

(1) *Options granted or stock purchased before 7/1/00.* Under APB 25, where Mgmt holds an option granted before 7/1/00 or stock purchased pursuant to an option granted before 7/1/00 or stock purchased without an option before 7/1/00 *and* there are puts, calls, rights of first refusal, or buy-back agreements at FV, APB 25 accounting is generally not affected by the mere existence of an FV put, call, right of first refusal, or buy-back agreement, so long as Newco is *privately held*. However, if Newco actually repurchases the option or actually repurchases the stock within six months after issuance, there will be an APB 25 charge to Newco's accounting net income, as discussed in ¶1502.1.7.7.

Where Newco is *publicly held*, the mere existence of an FV put, call, right of first refusal, or buy-back agreement results in variable accounting and hence creates periodic charges to Newco's accounting net income for the increases in the value of the stock (reduced by any Newco tax savings).

If a privately held Newco becomes public while a FV put, call, or repurchase right remains outstanding, Newco is then required to take an earnings charge that includes past appreciation in the underlying stock or option during the period Newco was private and is thereafter required to take periodic earnings charges

---

[214] EITF 88-6 (issue 3(b)); EITF Exhibit 88-6A.
[215] EITF 88-6 (issue 3(b)); EITF 88-6A; APB Opinion No. 25, 16, and 17.

while publicly held for any additional appreciation in the stock or option. However, if Newco eliminates the FV put, call, or repurchase agreement (either automatically—according to the terms of the relevant plan or the stock/option grant—or by amendment) before or in connection with its IPO, no such earnings charge is required.

Where FASB Interpretation No. 44 does not apply (i.e., in the case of stock purchased before 7/1/00, an option granted before 7/1/00, or stock purchased pursuant to a pre-7/1/00 option), many accountants use the expansive definition of publicly held company set forth in ¶1502.1.7.14(4), i.e., Newco is considered publicly held if it (or its parent) has either publicly traded equity or publicly traded debt. However, that definition seems overly broad when used in this context. The favorable treatment afforded FV puts, calls, and repurchase agreements in the privately held company context is apparently based on the idea that such liquidity devices are needed where there is no market to provide liquidity and hence the rights are not compensatory in nature, reasoning that should apply where Newco has publicly traded debt but no publicly traded equity.

This issue of whether Newco is publicly held may arise where Newco, having no publicly traded equity, issues subordinated debt in a private placement followed by a later exchange of the privately placed notes for identical notes registered with SEC (often called a Rule 144A offering). Although the SEC registered notes are generally not actively traded (either on an exchange or over the counter), they are considered public debt for a number of accounting purposes.[216] Many accountants take the position that such SEC registered debt makes Newco publicly held for purposes of determining the treatment of FV puts, calls, and repurchase agreements.[217] We understand other accountants take the more logical position that such SEC registered debt, even if actively traded, does not by itself make Newco publicly held for this purpose, treating Newco as a private company so long as it has no publicly held equity.[218]

FASB Interpretation No. 44 states that "an entity with publicly traded debt but no publicly traded equity securities shall follow the accounting prescribed for a non-public entity."[219] See ¶1502.1.7.13(4). While the interpretation is generally not effective before 7/1/00, we hope that the interpretation will, nonetheless, provide support for treating as private those companies that have registered (or traded) debt but no traded equity.

(2) *Options granted or stock purchased on or after 7/1/00.* FASB Interpretation No. 44 eliminates the sharp difference in accounting between privately held and

---

[216] For example, SEC registered notes would generally cause Newco to be treated as publicly held for purposes of the recapitalization accounting rules. See ¶1703.7.6.7. See also AICPA Statement of Auditing Standards (SAS) No. 26, which broadly defines a *public entity* as "any entity (a) whose securities trade in a public market either on a stock exchange (domestic or foreign) or in the over-the-counter market, including securities quoted only locally or regionally, (b) that makes a filing with a regulatory agency in preparation for the sale of any class of its securities in a public market, or (c) a subsidiary, corporate joint venture, or other entity controlled by an entity covered by (a) or (b)."

[217] SAS No. 26 is referred to in EITF Issue 87-23, which provides guidance on various stock compensation issues for private companies under the old APB 25 rules.

[218] Indeed, FASB Statement No. 123 specifically adopts a narrower definition of public company, excluding a company with only public debt.

[219] FASB Interpretation No. 44, ¶72.

publicly held companies where stock based compensation is coupled with puts, calls, rights of first refusal, or buy-back agreements at FV, by applying to all companies a modified version of the rule (described in (1) above) previously applicable only to privately held companies. The interpretation, issued 3/31/00, is effective for options granted on or after 7/1/00 and for stock purchased on or after 7/1/00 (other than stock purchased pursuant to an option granted before 7/1/00).

Under the interpretation, variable accounting is not required *unless* (i) the shares are "expected to be repurchased within six months after exercise or share issuance"[220] or (ii) the employee can require Newco to repurchase the shares within six months of option exercise or share issuance.[221] Thus, the interpretation liberalizes the treatment of publicly held companies, allowing them to enter into FV puts, calls, or rights of first refusal without triggering automatic variable accounting.

If the option is actually repurchased by Newco or if the shares are actually repurchased by Newco within six months after option exercise or share issuance (even though such repurchase was not expected), there is an APB 25 accounting charge to Newco's earnings as discussed in ¶1502.1.7.8.

If the shares are not actually repurchased within six months of exercise or purchase, variable accounting required as a result of the expectation that shares would be repurchased within six months continues until the earlier of (1) the date when the expectation no longer exists, (2) the date the put, call or other right expires, or (3) the date shares have been held after option exercise or purchase for more than six months.[222]

¶1502.1.7.16   Timing of Accounting Charges

Whenever there is an APB 25 or FASB 123 charge to Newco's accounting net income under the rules set forth above, Newco must generally accrue it (e.g., quarterly), based on reasonable estimates.

---

[220] In determining whether a repurchase is "expected" to occur within six months, accountants generally review Newco's stated intentions, whether Newco has repurchased shares within six months in the past (and if so, the frequency of, and circumstances surrounding, such repurchases) and whether there are any legal, regulatory or contractual limitations on Newco's ability to repurchase shares. See EITF 00-23.

[221] If the employee's right to put shares to Newco within six months is subject to a contingency outside the employee's control and such contingency is "not probable of occurrence" within six months (e.g., the put right is contingent on the employee's death or disability and the employee is in good health), the contingent put right would not trigger variable accounting. However, if the contingency is either within the employee's control or "probable of occurrence" within six months, variable accounting would be required notwithstanding the contingency. See EITF 00-23.

[222] EITF 00-23.

¶1502.1.7.17   Non-Employee Stock-Based Compensation and
Compensation Based on Unrelated-Company Stock

Prior to 2000 the accounting rules were not wholly clear on the applicability of the principles described in this ¶1502.1.7 where a non-employee receives stock-based compensation for services, i.e., whether the APB 25 principles described above applied, whether the FASB 123 principles described above applied, whether Newco could choose between the two sets of principles but was required to make the same choice it made for employee stock-based compensation, or whether a different set of principles applied. Nor was the meaning of non-employee wholly clear, i.e., while a supplier or vendor was clearly a non-employee, the status of a Newco outside director or independent contractor service provider was unclear.

FASB 123 (issued in 1995) states that:

(1) "[I]n practice, the scope of [APB] 25 has been extended to include many option recipients treated as independent contractors for tax purposes."

(2) *With respect to employees* Newco can elect between FASB 123 and APB 25, *but with respect to non-employees* Newco is required to use FASB 123, even if Newco continues to account for *employee* stock-based compensation under APB 25, so that "except for transactions with *employees* that are within the scope of [APB] 25, all transactions in which goods or services are the consideration received [by Newco] for the issuance [of stock-based compensation] shall be accounted for based on the fair value of the consideration received [by Newco] or the fair value of the [stock-based compensation] issued, whichever is more reliably measured."[223]

A 3/31/00 FASB interpretation states that "[APB] 25 applies only to the accounting by an employer corporation for stock compensation based on the employer's stock granted to individuals who meet the definition of *employee*. . . . [APB] 25 does not apply to stock compensation granted to individuals who are either independent contractors or other service providers who are not employees of the grantor." Whether a service provider is an employee "shall be determined based on common law as illustrated in case law and currently under U.S. Internal Revenue Service Revenue Ruling 87-41."[224]

Although independent directors do not fall within the common law definition of employee, the FASB interpretation requires that stock-based compensation granted to an independent director for services as a director be accounted for under APB 25 (unless Newco has elected to use FASB 123 for stock-based compensation to employees) if (1) the director was elected by shareholders or (2) the director was appointed to a board seat that will be filled by shareholder election on termination of the current term. APB 25 accounting does not apply to stock-based compensation granted to an independent director for services outside his role as a director (e.g., for legal advice).[225]

With respect to stock-based compensation issued to employees of a subsidiary, the FASB interpretation states that parent-company stock issued to an employee

---

[223] FASB 123, ¶8 (emphasis added).
[224] FASB Interpretation No. 44, Accounting for Certain Transactions Involving Stock Compensation, ¶¶3-5. See Rev. Rul. 87-41, 1987-1 C.B. 296.
[225] FASB Interpretation No. 44, ¶8.

of a *consolidated* subsidiary (i.e., a subsidiary which is consolidated with parent for GAAP purposes) is covered by APB 25 (unless Newco has elected to use FASB 123 for stock-based compensation to employees). However, APB 25 does not apply to parent-company stock-based compensation to employees of an *unconsolidated* equity method investee or joint venture.[226]

The FASB interpretation is generally effective 7/1/00 and applies prospectively to events on or after such date. The provisions limiting APB 25 accounting to stock-based compensation granted to employees apply to awards after 12/15/98; however, no adjustments are required to financial statements for periods prior to 7/1/00 and no expense for additional compensation cost attributable to the interpretation is recognized with respect to periods before 7/1/00.[227]

For stock-based compensation to a non-employee (other than an independent director as described above), the FASB 123 accounting charge to earnings is generally measured by the stock's or option's FV on completion of the services or other transaction for which the option or award was granted, rather than at issuance, unless the non-employee has committed to perform the services or engage in the transaction (backed by an economic penalty for non-performance, other than mere forfeiture of the option or award). See EITF 96-18, "Accounting for Equity Instruments that are Issued to Other than Employees for Acquiring, or in Conjunction with Selling, Goods, or Services." In addition, FASB 123 treats an option or award as modified, requiring additional compensation charges, where the number of shares to which the non-employee is entitled can vary (e.g., depending on the outcome of the non-employee's services).[228]

Sales, awards, and options based on stock of an unrelated company are not within the scope of either APB 25 or FASB 123. EITF 02-8 concluded that Newco's grant of an option on stock of an unrelated public company to a Newco employee (giving the employee the right to buy shares of the public company's stock from Newco) should be accounted for as a derivative under FASB Statement 133. Thus, Newco would record compensation expense at grant equal to the option's FV (presumably determined in a manner similar to FASB 123). Subsequent changes in the option's FV would be taken into account in determining Newco's compensation expense and net income during any vesting period. Changes in the option's FV after vesting would continue to be reflected in determining Newco's net income, but would not be required to be shown as compensation expense.

¶1502.1.8   Additional Examples of Tax and Accounting Treatment for NQO

Assume that Newco grants Mgmt an NQO for 1,000 shares of common stock at $100 per share (such stock's FV at grant date), Mgmt exercises the NQO five

---

[226] FASB Interpretation No. 44, ¶¶10-14. See EITF 00-12 for guidance on accounting for parent stock-based compensation issued to employees of an equity method investee.

[227] FASB Interpretation No. 44, ¶¶93-95.

[228] See EITF 96-18, "Accounting for Equity Instruments that are Issued to Other than Employees for Acquiring, or in Conjunction with Selling, Goods or Services." EITF 96-18 should generally not

years later when the stock's FV is $500 per share, and Mgmt sells the stock two years later for $600 per share.

(1) **Tax aspects.**

Mgmt recognizes no OI at grant. At exercise, Mgmt recognizes $400,000 of OI ($400 spread × 1,000 shares), assuming that the stock is then fully vested (or if the stock is then subject to further vesting, that Mgmt makes a timely Code §83(b) election), so that Mgmt owes $140,000 in tax (35% in calendar 2003 × $400,000). Newco is entitled (subject to the qualifications and limitations discussed at ¶1502.1.1(5)) to a $400,000 ordinary deduction, so that it saves $140,000 in tax (35% × $400,000) if it is then in a tax-paying position. When Mgmt sells the stock for $600,000, Mgmt recognizes a further $100,000 LTCG (resulting in $15,000 of tax), and Newco is entitled to no further deduction.

On the other hand, if the stock is subject to post-exercise vesting and Mgmt makes no Code §83(b) election at exercise, Mgmt recognizes no income at exercise but instead recognizes OI at the time of vesting equal to the spread at vesting. Newco has an ordinary deduction at the same time in the same amount. Mgmt's basis for computing CG on a later sale of the stock is the FV at vesting.

(2) **APB 25 GAAP aspects.**

Under APB 25 if the only vesting requirement for the option and the stock is Mgmt's continued employment at Newco for a specified period, there is no reduction in Newco's accounting net income, because the option price was not less than the stock's FV at grant. Newco's tax saving, because of its ordinary deduction for the spread in the stock at exercise (or at vesting), is credited directly to net worth and does not increase its accounting net income (although it increases Newco's net cash flow).

However, if vesting is also dependent on specified performance goals (rather than solely on Mgmt's continued employment for a specified period), Newco's accounting net income under APB 25 will be reduced by the spread at the time of vesting ($400,000 assuming the stock vested at the end of five years when Mgmt exercised the option) less Newco's tax saving of $140,000 ($400,000 × 35%), for a $260,000 net reduction of accounting net income. Newco generally must accrue this charge to net income quarterly as the FV of Newco's stock fluctuates.

Even if there is no performance vesting, if Newco has agreed to pay Mgmt a tax-offset bonus (i.e., to pay the executive all or part of Newco's tax saving to offset the executive's tax on the NQO exercise or vesting), Newco's accounting net income under APB 25 will be reduced by the spread at exercise ($400,000) *plus* the bonus payment to the executive *less*

---

apply to independent directors even where Newco has elected to apply FASB 123 to employees, since FASB Interpretation No. 44 treats independent directors as employees for purposes of APB 25.

Newco's tax saving from deducting the $400,000 and the bonus. Newco generally must accrue this charge to net income quarterly as the FV of Newco's stock fluctuates.

(3)   **FASB 123 GAAP aspects.**

If Newco has chosen to account for stock-based compensation under FASB 123 (rather than APB 25), Newco's accounting net income will be reduced (over Mgmt's service period) by the FV of the option at the grant date—taking into account both (1) the spread at grant (here zero) and (2) the value to Mgmt of being able to defer payment of the option price, i.e., the value of the option privilege—less Newco's expected tax savings for its tax deduction (up to the amount treated as accounting compensation expense) at exercise. The FV of the option, calculated by the Black-Scholes or other appropriate model, will generally be between 20% and 40% of the option price where (as here) there is no spread in the option at grant, depending on the stock's expected future volatility (if Newco is a public company), the expected option life, and other factors, here approximately $20,000 to $40,000 (i.e., $100,000 option exercise price × 20% to 40%). Newco's expected tax saving on exercise of the NQO arising from the tax deduction (up to the amount treated as accounting compensation expense) will be approximately $7,000 to $14,000 ($20,000 to $40,000 × 35%). Hence, Newco's accounting net income will be reduced over Mgmt's service period by approximately $13,000 to $26,000.

This accounting result under FASB 123 is the same whether the option is fully vested from the outset, is subject only to time vesting for Mgmt's continued employment, or is also subject to performance vesting.

¶1502.2   *Incentive Stock Options*

In lieu of (or as a supplement to) selling Mgmt Newco common stock or granting Mgmt NQOs, Newco can grant Mgmt incentive stock options (ISOs) as defined in Code §422.

¶1502.2.1   Taxation of ISO

In general, an executive recognizes no gain or loss upon the grant or exercise of an ISO.[229]

However, the spread between the FV of the stock at the time of exercise and the purchase price is included in alternative minimum taxable income and thus may trigger alternative minimum tax ("AMT").[230]

---

[229] Code §421(a).
[230] Code §56(b)(3).

In addition, a 2001 IRS proposed regulation would treat the spread at exercise as "wages" for employment tax purposes (but not for income tax withholding purposes), thus triggering employment tax withholding (but not income tax withholding).[231] As originally proposed, the regulation would have applied to an ISO issued on or after 1/1/03. In response to complaints that the proposed regulation would impose substantial administrative burdens, IRS in 2002 announced that it would not assess employment tax upon an ISO exercise prior to issuance of further guidance, which it anticipates would not apply to an ISO exercise before January 1 following the second anniversary of such final guidance.[232]

Legislative Update

Two identical bills, nameless H.R. 286 and S. 206, introduced in 1/03, propose to (a) amend Code §§3121 and 3306 to exclude from the definition of "wages" income recognized from the exercise of an ISO or the disposition of ISO stock and (b) add a provision to Code §421(b) stating that no withholding is required on OI recognized as the result of a disqualifying disposition of ISO stock. The proposal would be effective for ISO stock acquired pursuant to an ISO exercised after enactment.

A subsequent disposition of the Newco stock acquired upon exercise of an ISO gives rise to CG or loss (assuming the holding period requirements discussed below are satisfied). However, in determining whether the executive has AMT liability, his basis in the stock is increased by the amount included in AMT income at the time of ISO exercise.[233] Thus, the executive's taxable income for AMT purposes is lower than his regular taxable income. This is because his basis for the ISO stock sold is higher for AMT purposes by the amount of the spread at exercise which was included in AMT income at exercise.

However, if the ISO stock is subject to an SRF (within the meaning of Code §83) at the time of exercise, the AMT income is postponed and measured when the SRF expires. Thus, if the executive expects the value of the unvested ISO stock to rise, he should consider making a Code §83(b) election, discussed at ¶1502.1.1(3), within 30 days after exercise.

Newco receives no deduction at the time of either grant or exercise (assuming the executive satisfies the holding period requirements discussed below).[234]

---

[231] Prop. Reg. §§31.3121(a)-1(k); 31.3306(b)-1(*l*); Notice 2001-14, 2001-1 C.B. 516.
[232] Notice 2002-47, 2002-2 C.B. 97.
[233] Code §56(b)(3).
[234] Code §421(a)(2).

EXAMPLE

On 1/1 year 1 Newco issues an ISO to B, a member of Mgmt, pursuant to which B may buy 100 shares of Newco common stock at any time before 1/1 year 5 for its current FV, $10 per share. On 2/1 year 3 B exercises the ISO, at which time Newco stock's FV is $20 per share. On 3/1 year 5 B sells the stock for $25 per share.

B has no taxable income on grant or exercise of the ISO. However, on 2/1 year 3 when B exercises the ISO, he has an AMT preference item of $1,000 (the spread at exercise). On 3/1 year 5 when B sells the ISO stock, he recognizes $1,500 of LTCG (100 shares × ($25 per share proceeds *less* $10 per share basis)). However, for AMT purposes his taxable income (including the CG) is reduced by $1,000 (i.e., for AMT purposes B has $20 per share basis in the ISO stock, reflecting the spread at exercise already recognized for AMT purposes).

Newco is not entitled to any deductions with respect to the ISO transaction.

¶1502.2.2   Qualification as ISO

Several requirements must be satisfied before an option qualifies as an ISO:

(1) The option must be granted to an individual in connection with his employment by Newco (or a Newco subsidiary).

(2) The option must be granted within 10 years from the earlier of the date the plan was adopted by Newco's board or approved by its shareholders.

(3) The option cannot be exercised after 10 years from the date of grant (or such shorter period as is stated in the ISO grant).

(4) The option price cannot be less than the FV of the stock at the time the option was granted.

(5) The option must be non-transferable (except at death).

(6) The person to whom the option is granted cannot own more than 10% of Newco's (or a Newco subsidiary's) voting stock at the time of grant (unless the optionee satisfies the special rules of Code §422(c)(6)).

(7) The aggregate FV (determined at the time of grant) of stock for which any executive may be granted ISOs from Newco and its affiliated corporations, that are first exercisable during any one calendar year, cannot exceed $100,000. To the extent this $100,000 rule is violated, only the excess options (i.e., stock FV above $100,000) are treated as NQOs, with the attendant tax consequences discussed at ¶1502.1.2. This rule applies to ISOs which first become exercisable during the calendar year in the order granted.

(8)   The option plan must meet technical statutory requirements, including a requirement of timely shareholder approval.[235]

¶1502.2.3   Holding Period Requirement

In order for the executive to qualify for the above described tax benefits, he must continue to own the shares received pursuant to the exercise of the ISO for the *longer* of two years after the ISO was granted and one year after the ISO was exercised.[236] If the executive disposes of the shares prior to satisfying this holding period (a "disqualifying disposition"), the executive would generally recognize OI equal to the *lesser* of (1) the spread at the time the ISO was exercised and (2) the amount of gain recognized upon disposition of the stock.[237] Newco would receive a deduction upon a disqualifying disposition equal to the amount of OI recognized by the executive, in the year such income is recognized.

EXAMPLE

On 1/1 year 1 Newco issues an ISO to B, a member of Mgmt, pursuant to which B may buy 100 shares of Newco common stock at any time before 1/1 year 5 for its current FV, $10 per share. On 2/1 year 2 B exercises the ISO, at which time Newco stock has an FV of $20 per share. On 7/1 year 2 (less than one year after the ISO exercise) B sells the stock for $25 per share.

The $1,000 spread at the time of exercise ($10 spread per share × 100 shares) is treated as OI to B, and Newco is entitled (subject to the qualifications and limitations discussed at ¶1502.1.1(5)) to a $1,000 deduction. B's additional $500 gain recognized on the 7/1 year 2 sale is short-term CG.

Legislative Update

Pending legislation introduced in early 2002 would, if enacted, limit Newco's tax deduction upon an ISO disqualifying disposition (just as the pending legislation would also limit Newco's tax deduction upon an NQO exercise) to the amount "treated as an expense for the purpose of ascertaining [Newco's] income, profit, or loss in a report or statement to" equity owners, as described in more detail in ¶1502.1.2.

The executive's OI, recognized as the result of a disqualifying disposition of ISO shares, is not considered by IRS to constitute "wages" for purposes of Code

---

[235] Code §422(b).
[236] Code §422(a).
[237] Code §422(c)(2) and Code §421(b).

§3401, so that Newco has no income tax or employment tax withholding obligation on such OI.[238] However, such OI must be reported as "other compensation" on Form W-2 (if the executive is a Newco employee during any part of the calendar year in which the disqualifying disposition occurs) or as a payment of compensation on Form 1099 (if the executive is not a Newco employee at any time during the calendar year in which the disqualifying disposition occurs).[239]

¶1502.2.4 Restrictions on Exercise

An employee must exercise the ISO within three months after ceasing to be employed by Newco (or a Newco subsidiary), or one year in the case of cessation caused by permanent disability, and no deadline in the case of cessation as a result of death,[240] or such earlier period as is specified in the option grant.

¶1502.2.5 Use of Cash Bonus

Despite the requirement that an ISO's option price must be set at no less than the stock's FV at the date of grant, Newco can make cash awards to an employee at the time he exercises his ISO.[241] Newco can also grant "tandem" ISO stock appreciation rights in certain situations.[242]

¶1502.2.6 Taxation of CG and OI

After the 2003[243] Act (which reduced the individual top OI tax rate to 35% in calendar 2003 and reduced the top individual normal LTCG tax rate to 15%), there is a 20 percentage point difference between an individual's top OI rate and normal LTCG rate. This preferential LTCG rate makes ISOs significantly more attractive than they were under unified rates in effect from 1988 through 1990 and while there was only a 3 percentage point differential during 1991 and 1992.

---

[238] Notice 2001-72, 2001-2 C.B. 548. As discussed in ¶1502.2.1, IRS has proposed, but indefinitely postponed, regulations that would include the spread at ISO exercise in "wages" for employment tax (but not income tax) purposes, whether or not there is a post-exercise disqualifying disposition.

[239] Notice 2001-72, 2001-2 C.B. 548.

[240] Code §422(a)(2), Code §422(c)(7), and Code §421(c)(1)(A).

[241] Code §422(c)(4)(A).

[242] See Temp. Reg. §14a.422A-1 Q&A 39 (tandem ISOs and non-qualified options are not permitted).

[243] The 2003 Act: (1) reduced the top tax rate for 2003 and later for a calendar year individual from 38.6% to 35%, see Code §1(i)(2), (2) decreased from 20% to 15% the individual top normal LTCG rate, thereby modestly increasing the difference between the top individual OI rate (35%) and LTCG rate (15%) to 20 percentage points, (3) treated qualified dividend income as net CG for purposes of the tax rate (15%) but not for any other purpose, e.g., no CL offset, see Code §1(h)(11), and (4) eliminated a previously enacted special reduction in the top LTCG rate (from 20% to 18%) for property acquired after 2000 and held more than 5 years.

However, the difference between the option price and the FV of the stock on the date of an ISO exercise constitutes an item of tax preference under Code §56(b)(3), and unlike the treatment of an NQO, a corporation that grants an ISO receives no offsetting deduction when the optionee sells the stock after meeting the holding period requirement.

¶1502.3 Stock Appreciation Rights

Newco can also grant Mgmt SARs under which Mgmt receives in cash or Newco stock an amount equal to the spread between the FV of Newco stock at the time the SAR is exercised and the base price established when the SAR was granted. In general, Mgmt will be taxed only at the time the SAR is exercised in an amount equal to the cash or the FV of the Newco stock paid to Mgmt.[244] Newco will receive a corresponding deduction at that time (subject to the qualifications and limitations discussed at ¶1502.1.1(5)). However, if the SAR reaches a ceiling stated in the SAR, so that it cannot grow any larger, Mgmt will be taxed at the time the ceiling is reached (provided the SAR is currently exercisable) regardless of whether the SAR is exercised at that time.[245]

EXAMPLE

Newco issues an SAR to B, a member of Mgmt. B may exercise the SAR at any time during the next five years and receive the spread between the FV of 100 shares of Newco stock on the date of exercise and the FV of such stock at the SAR grant date ($10 per share). Shortly before the fifth anniversary of grant, B exercises the SAR, at which time Newco stock has an FV of $30 per share, so that B receives a payment of $2,000 ($3,000 FV at exercise less $1,000 FV at grant). B recognizes $2,000 of OI at exercise, and Newco is entitled to a corresponding $2,000 deduction.

Under APB 25 (as discussed at ¶1502.1.7.2), an SAR is always treated as a variable plan for accounting purposes and hence Newco suffers a reduction in its accounting net income by the amount payable under an SAR (reduced by Newco's tax savings from the SAR payment), whether the SAR is payable in cash or in stock. Newco must generally accrue this charge to its accounting net income (e.g., quarterly) as the FV of Newco's stock (and hence the amount payable under the SAR) fluctuates.[246]

If Newco has chosen to account for stock-based compensation under FASB 123 (rather than under APB 25), the accounting rules are different:

[244] Rev. Rul. 80-300, 1980-2 C.B. 165.
[245] Rev. Rul. 82-121, 1982-1 C.B. 79.
[246] FASB Interpretation No. 28, entitled Accounting for Stock Appreciation Rights and Other Variable Stock Option or Award Plans.

(1)   Where the SAR is payable in cash or in cash or stock at B's option, the FASB 123 accounting results are substantially the same as under APB 25.

(2)   Where, however, the SAR is payable in stock or in cash or stock at Newco's option, the only FASB 123 compensation expense is the FV of the SAR arrangement at the time of grant, i.e., the amount by which the SAR is in the money at grant (if any) plus the value of the option privilege determined under a Black-Scholes or similar formula (generally 20% to 40% of the stock's FV at grant where the option is at the money). This result is true even if Newco ends up paying the SAR in cash.

(3)   However, where an SAR is nominally payable in stock or in cash or stock at Newco's option (as described in (2) above), but in practice Newco regularly pays cash or regularly pays cash to any employee so requesting, rule (1) rather than rule (2) applies.

¶1502.4   Equity-oriented Mgmt Incentives in Context of Partnership or LLC Service Recipient

Where P (or Newco) is a partnership or LLC, the tax and accounting rules applicable to equity-oriented Mgmt incentives are generally the same as described in ¶1502.1 through ¶1502.3 above, except that (a) the ISO rules (see ¶1502.2) do not apply, so that any option on a partnership or LLC interest falls into the NQO rules (see ¶1502.1.2) and (b) several post-1992 IRS revenue procedures altered the tax rules applicable to the grant or purchase of a partnership or LLC equity interest or exercise of an option on such an interest in a pro-service provider manner. All references in this ¶1502.4 to a partnership includes an LLC taxed as a partnership.

(1) The first question is whether a partnership interest received by a service provider constitutes "property" for Code §83 purposes. If so, (a) a service provider receiving a partnership interest with no SRF (or receiving a partnership interest subject to an SRF with no Code §83(b) election)—including a service provider receiving such a partnership interest upon exercise of an option—would have OI *at the front end* equal to the FV of his interest in the partnership *less* the price paid for such interest and (b) a service provider receiving a partnership interest subject to an SRF with no Code §83(b) election—including a service provider receiving such a partnership interest upon exercise of an option—would have OI *at vesting* equal to the then FV of the interest in the partnership *less* the price paid for such interest, i.e., the same rules as apply to a service provider to a corporation who receives corporate stock (as discussed in ¶1502.1.1 above).

(2) Some pre-1993 cases held that a partnership interest does constitute "property" so that Code §83 applies to a service provider receiving a partnership interest, but most of these cases then valued such interest on a liquidation basis, i.e., at the amount the service partner would have received if the partnership immediately sold its assets at their then FV and distributed the proceeds. When such a liquidation-value ("LV") approach is used with respect to a newly formed partnership, a partnership interest granted to a service provider would generally have

a front-end LV equal to the amount the service provider pays for the interest so that a Code §83(b) election is generally advantageous.

(3) Until 1993 there was some risk that a future court might adopt a speculative-value (rather than an LV) approach and hence impose front-end OI tax on the speculative value of a service provider's right to receive a disproportionately large share of future partnership profits—i.e., a share of future profits disproportionately large in relation to the service provider's capital contribution (generally referred to as a "carried interest"). Such a speculative-value approach might result in very substantial front-end OI where the service provider makes a Code §83(b) election.

(4) In 1993 IRS announced (in Rev. Proc. 93-27[247]) that where "a person receives a profits interest in exchange for providing services to (or for the benefit of) a partnership in a partner capacity (or in anticipation of being a partner), [IRS] will not treat the receipt of such an interest as a taxable event." IRS stated, however, that this taxpayer-favorable rule would not apply in any of the following circumstances:

- Where the service provider receives "a capital interest," defined as "an interest [in the partnership] that would give the [service provider] a share of the proceeds if the partnership's assets were sold at fair market value and then the proceeds were distributed in complete liquidation of the partnership." It is possible (but illogical) to read Rev. Proc. 93-27's words and conclude that IRS intends the taxpayer-favorable LV rule not be available where either (1) the service provider's partnership interest is in the money (even by a small amount) at the time he receives the partnership interest (e.g., the service provider pays $100 for a partnership interest that would yield $101 if the partnership immediately sells its assets and liquidates) or (2) the service provider pays an amount for the partnership interest and, immediately after such purchase, the service provider's partnership interest is worth (on an LV basis) exactly the amount paid for the interest (e.g., the service provider pays $100 for a partnership interest that would yield $100 if the partnership immediately sells its assets and liquidates). However, a far more rational reading is that IRS intends the taxpayer-favorable LV rule not be available only *to the extent* the service provider's partnership interest is in the money at receipt (i.e., $1 in example (1) and zero in example (2) above), so that the taxpayer-favorable LV rule is available for a "profits interest" even if combined with a "capital interest."
- Where "the profits interest relates to a substantially certain and predictable stream of income from partnership assets, such as income from high-quality debt securities or a high-quality net lease."
- Where the service provider "disposes of the profits interest" within 2 years after receipt.
- Where the profits interest is a limited partnership interest in a publicly-traded partnership.

---

[247] 1993-2 C.B. 343.

Hence, in the typical case where (1) a service provider purchases a partnership interest for a nominal amount (or even for a substantial amount) and, at the time of such purchase, the interest is in the money by an amount equal to the price paid by the service provider, (2) the service provider does not dispose of the partnership interest within 2 years, and (3) the service provider makes a timely Code §83(b) election, the service provider should recognize no front-end OI and no back-end OI.

EXAMPLE

Executive A and venture capitalist ("VC") organize a start-up enterprise ("Newco Partnership") in partnership (or LLC) form. Executive A invests $50 and VC invests $950.

Each of Newco Partnership's two partners has the right to receive back (as return of capital) its capital invested in Newco Partnership. Executive A has the right to receive 25% of Newco Partnership's profits (although he invested only 5% of Newco Partnership's capital) and VC has the right to receive the remaining 75% of Newco Partnership's profits.

Executive A's partnership interest vests over 5 years, contingent on A's continued service as a partner. A makes a timely Code §83(b) election.

The *FV* of A's partnership interest in Newco Partnership substantially exceeds A's $50 investment in Newco Partnership, because (1) A has the right to receive back his $50 capital invested in Newco Partnership (constituting 5% of Newco Partnership's capital) and to receive a disproportionately large 25%, rather than merely 5%, of Newco Partnership's future profits and (2) Newco Partnership has the right to receive $950 of funded capital from VC with no interest-like compensation to VC for the use, likely for a number of years, of the $950 of committed capital.

Nonetheless, under Rev. Proc. 93-27 A should recognize no OI upon receipt of the partnership interest. This result follows because if (at the time A receives the partnership interest) Newco Partnership were to sell all its assets (i.e., the $1,000 contributed by A and VC) for FV and liquidate, A and VC as partners would each receive back their contributed capital and there would be no further liquidating distribution to A above his return of capital.

(5) Rev. Proc. 93-27 is not entirely clear on the treatment of a service provider receiving a profits interest subject to vesting who makes no Code §83(b) election. If Code §83 does apply to a profits interest in a partnership or LLC and no Code §83(b) election is made (or deemed made, as described below) the service provider would recognize OI *at vesting*, when the carried interest's value will likely have increased greatly because of appreciation in the partnership's business, so that the service provider's OI will likely be very substantial even if a Rev. Proc. 93-27 LV approach is used at the time of vesting.

(6) In 2001 IRS published Rev. Proc. 2001-43,[248] giving a surprisingly pro-taxpayer answer to the question whether Rev. Proc. 93-27's taxpayer-favorable LV rule applies where the service provider's partnership interest is subject to vesting but the service provider makes no Code §83(b) election. This 2001 Rev. Proc. announces that a service provider "need not file [a Code §83(b)] election" (i.e., IRS will treat the service provider as if he had filed such an election—a deemed election), so that the Rev. Proc. 93-27 "determination . . . whether an interest granted to a service provider is a profits interest is . . . tested at the time the interest is granted, even if, at that time, the interest is substantially non-vested" (i.e., is subject to vesting).

However, Rev. Proc. 2001-43 conditions this *deemed* Code §83(b) election on surmounting several hurdles:

- The *partnership* and *all partners* must consistently report their taxes for all tax periods as if the service provider partner had made a Code §83(b) election. Thus a service provider who relies on a *deemed* Code §83(b) election (i.e., who does not make an *actual* election) is at risk if the partnership or any partner (perhaps a former partner who left the partnership on poor terms but retained a partnership interest) disregards the deemed Code §83(b) election and claims a deduction upon the vesting of the service provider's partnership interest, as is clearly permitted by Code §83 and the regulations.

- The service provider's partnership interest must meet all the requirements of Rev. Proc. 93-27 (discussed in (4) above), some of which (as discussed in (4)) are a bit problematic or cannot be predicted with certainty when the service provider receives the partnership interest (e.g., no disposition within 2 years).

- Because it is often impossible for a service provider to foresee with total clarity (when he receives a partnership interest) whether a deemed Code §83(b) election may later turn out to be unavailable and because the cost of filing an actual Code §83(b) election is low, a service provider receiving a partnership interest subject to vesting should generally file an actual Code §83(b) election. If such an actual election is made, it will be clear that the service provider receives the partnership interest (for tax purposes) at the front end, when it is more likely to constitute a pure interest in future profits, rather than later at vesting when it may have grown into a capital interest. In addition, even if the service provider's equity interest does not qualify for Rev. Proc. 93-27's taxpayer-favorable LV rule (e.g., if the service provider disposes of the interest within 2 years *or* if the interest is in the money to some extent and Rev. Proc. 93-27 is interpreted as not applying to such an interest), it will be clear that the FV of the partnership interest is determined at the front end, rather than later at vesting when the partnership's assets may have appreciated substantially in value.

---

[248] 2001-2 C.B. 191.

(7) The precedents are reasonably clear that where a service provider receives an equity interest for services to be performed as a partner (which equity interest is fully vested or with respect to which a Code §83(b) election is made or deemed made) and the partnership subsequently recognizes OI or CG (e.g., earns profits from its business or sells a partnership asset at a gain), the character of the income in the partnership's hands (OI or CG) passes through to the service provider, i.e., the equity interest holder.

¶1503   HANDLING T's OUTSTANDING MGMT STOCK OPTIONS

When Newco (or P) acquires T's outstanding stock, T executives frequently hold options to purchase additional T shares—either ISOs or NQOs.[1] Often, although not inevitably, these options are "in the money," i.e., they have an exercise price below the price Newco is paying for T's stock. This section discusses the tax ramifications if (1) Newco or T makes a cash payment to a T option holder equal (or approximately equal) to the executive's "spread" (i.e., the excess of Newco's purchase price for the T stock covered by the option over the executive's option price) *or* (2) Newco assumes a T stock option, substituting Newco stock instead of T stock, *or* (3) Newco issues its own stock in cancellation of a T stock option.

Although the discussion in this paragraph is mainly in terms of *Newco* purchasing T's *stock*, the same principles are generally applicable where *P* (rather than Newco) purchases T's stock as well as where P or Newco purchases T's *assets* or acquires T in a *tax-free* transaction.

¶1503.1   *Cash Payment in Cancellation of T's Stock Option*

If Newco or T makes a cash payment to a T option holder equal (or approximately equal) to the executive's spread in his ISO or NQO, such payment constitutes OI to the executive.[2] And properly handled, T (or a T subsidiary) should be entitled to deduct this option cancellation payment (subject to the reasonable

---

¶1503 [1] For a description of the general tax treatment of incentive stock options ("ISOs") and non-qualified stock options ("NQOs"), see ¶¶1502.1 and 1502.2.

[2] See Reg. §1.83-7(a) (third and fourth sentences) ("If section 83(a) does not apply to the grant of . . . an option because the option does not have a readily ascertainable fair market value at the time of grant [and almost no executive option would ever have a 'readily ascertainable' FV—see Reg. §1.83-7], sections 83(a) and 83(b) shall apply at the time the option is . . . disposed of. . . . If the option is sold or otherwise disposed of in an arm's length transaction, sections 83(a) and 83(b) apply to the transfer of money or other property received in the same manner as sections 83(a) and 83(b) would have applied to the transfer of property pursuant to an exercise of the option"); cf. Reg. §1.83-1(b). See also Pagel, Inc. v. Commissioner, 905 F.2d 1190, 90-2 U.S.T.C. ¶50,347 (8th Cir. 1990); Bagley v. Commissioner, 85 T.C. 663, 668-674 (1985), *aff'd*, 806 F.2d 169, 86-2 U.S.T.C. ¶9807 (8th Cir. 1986).

compensation rules, the $1 million executive-compensation-deduction limitation, and the golden parachute rules), although the timing of the deduction is a bit tricky.

The timing of the deduction turns (1) in part on interpretations of confusing language in Code §404(a)(5) and Code §83(h) and the regulations thereunder and (2) where Newco acquires T's stock, in part on whether Newco is filing a consolidated return and acquires sufficient T stock so that T becomes a member of Newco's consolidated group.[3] Except as otherwise stated, this ¶1503 assumes that Newco does file a consolidated return, that Newco acquires sufficient T stock so that T becomes a member of Newco's consolidated group, and that the acquisition was not a reverse acquisition.[4] (If Newco or P purchases T's assets rather than T's stock, the same principles generally apply except that T's year generally does not end at the time of the asset acquisition, as discussed at ¶1503.1.7.)

Timing of the stock option deduction is frequently important, as T may wish to use the deduction to offset taxable income for its current fiscal year (which ends with the acquisition where Newco or P acquires T's stock) or to obtain an immediate refund of income taxes paid by T in the two previous fiscal years.

EXAMPLE

Newco (a calendar-year taxpayer) purchases all of the stock of T (also a calendar-year taxpayer) on 6/30 year 3. Newco is a newly formed corporation and borrows a substantial portion of the purchase price, i.e., the acquisition is an LBO. Beginning on 7/1 year 3, Newco's interest deductions are expected to offset in full T's future taxable income for several years. Newco anticipates filing a consolidated return so that it can offset its interest deductions against T's future taxable income.

On 6/30 year 3, i.e., the day of the acquisition, T's executives receive a $500,000 cash payment equal to the spread on their T stock options. When T enters Newco's consolidated group at the end of the day on 6/30 year 3 (see discussion at ¶1503.1.3.2), T's taxable year closes. If T can deduct the $500,000 in its short taxable year from 1/1 year 3 through 6/30 year 3, it will be able to (1) offset such deduction against T's taxable income for such six-month period and (2) immediately carry back any excess to year 1 and year 2. If, however, the $500,000 deduction is properly taken in the Newco-T consolidated return year beginning on 7/1 year 3, the deduction often will be less useful:

(a) It can be used against the Newco-T taxable income for the last half of year 3, expected to be zero because of Newco's interest deductions.

---

[3] For a discussion of how much T stock P must acquire (generally 80%) in order to include T in P's consolidated group, see ¶¶211.1 and 1205.2.1.

[4] If more than 50% of Newco's stock by value had been acquired by T's old shareholders in the acquisition so that the consolidated return reverse-acquisition rules applied, T's group would have been deemed to continue, and hence its taxable year would not have ended with the acquisition. See, e.g., Reg. §§1.1502-75(d)(3) and 1.1502-1(f)(3).

(b) It can be carried back against T's short year for the first half of year 3 and T's year 2 (but not its year 1) tax year, but only after the Newco-T group files its return through 12/31 year 3. See ¶1206 discussing NOL carrybacks.

(c) It can be carried forward against the Newco-T group's taxable income for future years, but this is expected to be zero for several years because of T's interest deductions.

For a discussion of whether T's payment to the executives is properly taken into account on T's short year return for the first half of year 3 or the Newco-T consolidated return for the last half of year 3, see ¶1503.1.3.2.

¶1503.1.1   Deduction Generally

In general, a cash payment by T equal to the spread inherent in its outstanding stock options, in cancellation of such options, is deductible by T (or by the T subsidiary for which the executive renders services) to the extent such payment (1) constitutes reasonable compensation under Code §162, (2) either does not cause the executive's compensation for T's taxable year to exceed $1 million or qualifies for an exception to the $1 million executive-compensation-deduction limitation discussed at ¶1506, and (3) does not violate the golden parachute rules of Code §280G as discussed at ¶1505.[5]

Where a cash payment is made to the holder of an *unvested* stock option (either because the option provides for special vesting if T is acquired or because Newco or T voluntarily makes a cancellation payment to the holder of an unvested option), at least part and perhaps all of the amount paid may be subject to the $1 million deduction limitation and the golden parachute rules of Code §280G (and Code §4999). See ¶¶1506, 1505.2 and 1505.3 below.

If Newco (rather than T) makes the option cancellation payment, T (or the T subsidiary for which the executive renders services) should nevertheless be entitled to the deduction, on the theory that Newco has made a constructive capital contribution to T (or T's subsidiary) which has in turn made the stock option cancellation payment.[6]

---

[5] See Code §§162 and 83(h); Reg. §§1.83-6 and 1.83-7; Rev. Rul. 73-146, 1973-1 C.B. 61; IRS TAM 9540003 (6/30/97); Venture Funding, Ltd. v. Commissioner, 110 T.C. 236 (1998), *aff'd*, 198 F.3d 248, 99-2 U.S.T.C. ¶50,972 (6th Cir. 1999) (discussed at ¶1502.1.1).

[6] See IRS Letter Ruling 8834051 (5/27/88); Reg. §1.83-6(a)(1) ("In the case of a transfer of property in connection with the performance of services, . . . a deduction is allowable under section 162 or 212, to the person for whom such services were performed" (emphasis added)); Reg. §1.83-6(d)(1) ("if a shareholder of a corporation transfers property to an employee of such corporation . . . in consideration of services performed for the corporation, the transaction shall be considered to be a contribution of such property to the capital of such corporation by the shareholder, and immediately thereafter a transfer of such property by the corporation to the employee. . . ."); Rev. Rul. 84-68, 1984-1 C.B. 31 (P's "payment of cash bonuses to its subsidiary's employees is treated as a contribution to the subsidiary's capital accompanied by a constructive payment by the subsidiary of the cash bonuses

IRS capitalization argument. A 1989 IRS unpublished position (the "1989 LBO ISP")[7] casts somewhat of a cloud on the horizon as to the deductibility of a stock option cancellation payment in the following circumstances:

- T is being acquired by Newco.
- Executive's option on T stock is not yet vested and the option agreement does not provide for special vesting of the option on account of the Newco-T acquisition.
- In anticipation of the Newco-T acquisition, T voluntarily amends the option agreement to provide for a payment to executive equal to the spread in the unvested options.

In a very similar situation,[8] IRS concluded that:

> The additional payments made by [T] to employees . . . as a result of the plan amendments are disallowed [because] the additional cost incurred is originated as a result of a capital transaction rather than . . . pre-existing obligation of a compensatory nature. [Only the payment with respect to options which were] . . . vested prior to the plan amendment is allowable as a compensation deduction. . . .

> If . . . a payment is not pre-existing prior to a capital transaction, . . . such cost should be capitalized. The guidelines discussed in the regulations for IRC Section 280G should be used in making the determination [whether] the payment is a result of a change in control.[9]

---

to its employees, [so] the cash bonuses may be deducted by the subsidiary"); Rev. Rul. 73-13, 1973-1 C.B. 42 (employer corporation paid a fee to a financial consultant who was rendering advice to an executive working for employer; held that executive is treated as receiving compensation equal to the financial counseling fee paid by his employer and executive is also entitled to a Code §212 deduction to the extent that the financial counseling fee falls within Code §212).

[7] LBO Industry Specialization Program, Restricted Stock Purchase in Mergers & Acquisitions, initial draft issue, reprinted 4/24/91, Tax Notes Today (Lexis 91 TNT 90-33).

[8] IRS's 1989 LBO ISP actually dealt with the following facts: Executive held restricted stock of T which was to be forfeited if he left T's employ within five years after grant. Under the restricted stock plan, if T were acquired before expiration of the five-year vesting period, executive would be entitled to retain a percentage of the restricted stock equal to the percentage of the five-year vesting period which had expired prior to the acquisition. Shortly before Newco acquired T in a reverse merger, the restricted stock plan was amended so that, upon consummation of the merger, executive (who was only partly through his five-year vesting period) would receive $36 cash for each and every restricted share he held.

The issue presented by this unvested restricted stock is indistinguishable in law from the issue discussed in text regarding unvested stock options.

Although not explicitly stated in the 1989 LBO ISP, it is reasonably implicit that executive had made no Code §83(b) election when he received the restricted stock.

The 1989 LBO ISP is silent as to whether T's other shareholders received cash or Newco stock in the reverse subsidiary merger and as to whether $36 per share was the FV of the consideration received by T's other shareholders.

The issue presented by this unvested restricted stock is indistinguishable in law from the issue discussed in text regarding unvested stock options.

[9] Query whether the logic of this IRS position could go further and apply to an option that had not yet time vested when Newco acquired T, but that specially vests on account of the Newco-T acquisition by virtue not of an amendment adopted shortly before the acquisition, but rather by virtue of a clause in the original stock option grant providing for special accelerated vesting if T is acquired. While the wording of the LBO ISP would not reach this situation, the logic (although faulty) would apparently do so.

IRS's position in the 1989 LBO ISP seems manifestly wrong. *First*, subject only to *Third* below, T is entitled to deduct any payment to its executives that constitutes reasonable compensation. Nowhere in the 1989 LBO ISP did IRS analyze the services rendered by T's executives or reach a factual conclusion that the payments were unreasonable in light of the executive's past and present services or that the payments were disguised dividends.

Second, it is not unusual for a corporation to pay significant voluntary "good-bye" or "stay-on" bonuses to executives at the time of a merger. These bonuses are deductible (subject to *Third* below) as long as they are reasonable in light of the executives' services (past, present, and future). The fact that T chose to pay these "goodbye" or "stay-on" bonuses by voluntarily vesting executives' previously unvested stock options does not change the deductibility conclusion.

In TAM 9527005, IRS allowed T to deduct voluntary bonuses paid to T executives in connection with Newco's LBO acquisition of T.[10] Certain key T executives held ISOs with respect to T stock which they were forced to exercise prior to the LBO. The T stock received by the executives on exercise of the ISOs was sold to Newco in the LBO and, because the executives had not held the T stock for the requisite holding periods under Code §422(a)(1), the sale of T stock was a disqualifying disposition causing the executives to recognize OI equal to the spread in the ISOs at exercise.

T agreed to pay special bonuses to the key executives to compensate them for the loss of LTCG treatment caused by the disqualifying disposition. The bonuses were voluntary on the part of T since the executives had no pre-existing right to receive the bonuses. The bonuses were also intended, in part, to help the executives pay for Newco stock being purchased as part of the LBO, although there was no requirement that the bonuses be so used. T believed the bonuses would induce the executives to remain with T after the LBO, but each executive was entitled to receive and retain a special bonus whether or not he or she stayed with T after the LBO.

IRS concluded that the bonuses were for "services rendered and/or to be rendered," stating that "although it is clear that the special bonuses made to the managers were coincidental to the buyout and may have been motivated by the desire of all parties concerned that it succeed, the special bonuses have their origin in the longstanding employment relationship with [T] and not the buyout itself." Thus, IRS ruled that the special bonuses were deductible by T.

Since T had no pre-existing obligation to pay the special bonuses, they are analogous to T's voluntary special vesting of options and/or restricted stock discussed above. Such special vesting has its origin in the employment relationship between T and the option holders and compensates them for losing the chance to earn further vesting through continued employment. The 1995 TAM suggests that the 1989 LBO ISP may not represent IRS's current position on whether T may deduct payments with respect to options T voluntarily vests.

Third, precisely because reasonable-in-amount acquisition-triggered "goodbye" and "stay-on" bonuses were deductible (both voluntary bonuses and those paid

---

[10] IRS TAM 9527005 (3/15/95).

pursuant to a previously entered golden parachute or like contract), Congress in 1984 added §280G (the golden parachute provision) to the Code. This section disallows T's deduction for a payment (including a stock option cancellation payment) to an executive where (1) the payment is contingent on a change in T's ownership or effective control and (2) the aggregate of all such payments to the executive exceeds a mathematically defined amount (in general, three times his base compensation). See ¶1505. Code §280G is intended to disallow a payment otherwise deductible as reasonable compensation where the payment is both contingent on a change in control *and* exceeds the statutory formula. If the 1989 LBO ISP were correct (which it is not), there would have been no need for Code §280G, because such payments would have been capitalized rather than deductible (whether they exceeded the §280G statutory formula or not).

Fourth, Code §280G contains a rather murky exception: an otherwise disallowed golden parachute payment is allowed as a deduction to the extent the parties establish *"by clear and convincing evidence"* that the payment is "reasonable compensation for personal services actually rendered before" the change in control,[11] and postenactment legislative history seeks to raise the burden of proof even higher by stating that "only in rare cases, if any, will any portion of a parachute payment be treated as reasonable compensation in response to an argument that the executive was undercompensated [in earlier years]."[12] Thus, Code §280G creates a higher standard (clear and convincing evidence of reasonableness, only in rare cases, if any) for deducting a large change of control payment (i.e., a payment greater than the Code §280G three-times-base-compensation permission). Where, however, the payment does not exceed the Code §280G formula—and there is no suggestion in the LBO ISP that the payments there under review exceeded the formula—it remains deductible under the normal Code §162 reasonable compensation standard.

Surprisingly, IRS in the 1989 LBO ISP referred to the Code §280G regulations for use in determining whether "the payment [in cancellation of the stock option] is a result of a change in control" and hence a non-deductible, capitalized cost. However, IRS ignored the Code §280G statutory formula and made no effort to state a rationale for denying a deduction for a reasonable compensation payment that is not disallowed by the Code §280G formula.

IRS Code §162(k) disallowance argument abandoned. A 1992 IRS field service advice[13] discusses whether T's option cancellation payment should be treated as a payment to redeem T's stock that is non-deductible under Code §162(k), because Code §318(a)(4) treats an option holder as owning the underlying stock for certain purposes. IRS concluded that Code §162(k) does not apply because (1) Code §318(a)(4) does not apply for purposes of Code §162(k) and (2) even if Code §318(a)(4) did apply, the fact that a person is treated as owning the stock underlying an option does not mean that the option itself is treated as stock for tax

---

[11] Code §280G(b)(4)(B) (emphasis added).
[12] 1984 Blue Book at 205.
[13] FSA 1999-896 (11/23/92).

purposes. Hence the FSA declines to apply Code §162(k) principles to the option cancellation payment.

¶1503.1.2   T's Multiple Short Tax Years

¶1503.1.2.1   T's Pre-acquisition Year

T's first short tax year (T's "pre-acquisition year") runs from the beginning of its regular tax year through the date on which Newco purchases T's stock, at the end of which T enters Newco's consolidated group. See ¶1503.1.3.2. Using the facts set forth in the example in ¶1503.1, above, T's pre-acquisition year runs from 1/1/99 through 6/30/99.

If T's $500,000 stock option cancellation payment is properly allocable to the pre-acquisition period (see ¶1503.1.3.2), T can claim the payment as a deduction on its pre-acquisition tax return and, to the extent the deduction creates an NOL, carry the NOL back to T's two previous years, year 1 and year 2 (to the extent not used in year 1) to obtain a refund of income taxes paid in those years. T could fairly quickly (i.e., on filing its tax return for the pre-acquisition year—probably in the late summer or early fall of year 3) obtain a refund of taxes paid during such earlier years.

¶1503.1.2.2   T's Post-acquisition Year

T begins a new taxable year (T's "post-acquisition year") on 7/1 year 3 (the day after the merger). This post-acquisition year is included as a part of Newco's year 3 consolidated return when filed in mid-year 4.

If Newco and its consolidated group (including T) have net taxable income on a consolidated basis (i.e., do not have a consolidated loss) for the year that includes T's post-acquisition year, any T deductions falling into T's post-acquisition year would be used to offset the income of the Newco-T group and would not be part of an NOL that could be carried back.

If, on the other hand, T had a loss for the post-acquisition year and if the Newco group as a whole had an overall consolidated loss, the portion of T's NOL not used by the Newco group could generally be carried back to T's pre-acquisition returns for year 2 and short pre-acquisition year 3 to obtain a refund of taxes paid in such prior years by T. See the discussion of NOL carrybacks at ¶1206. A refund arising out of any such NOL carryback from the post acquisition year would generally be delayed for perhaps a year (i.e., until the post-acquisition year return is filed) when compared to carrybacks from the pre-acquisition year.

¶1503.1.3 Timing of Stock Option Cancellation Deduction (Ignoring Code §§404(a)(5) and 83(h))

The timing of the stock option cancellation payment is important in determining whether T can deduct the payment in its pre-acquisition short year or whether the deduction must be taken in the first (or in a later) Newco-T consolidated return year.

This ¶1503.1.3 discusses this timing issue without regard to Code §§404(a)(5) and 83(h). Then ¶¶1503.1.4 and 1503.1.5 discuss respectively whether Code §404(a)(5) or Code §83(h) changes the conclusions reached in this section.

IRS private rulings indicate that if accrual method T's obligation to make the stock option cancellation payment becomes fixed shortly prior to the date T actually makes the payment, the stock option cancellation payment is deemed to be made and thus gives rise to a deduction when T's obligation to make the payment becomes fixed. For example, in IRS Technical Advice Memorandum 9024002 (2/26/90) the Newco-T merger agreement provided that, upon the merger of T into Newco, the T options were converted into the right to receive cash. Although the cash was not paid to the former option holders until the day after the merger, IRS effectively ruled that the stock option cancellation payment is deemed made and is deductible when the stock options were converted into the right to receive cash.[14] Accordingly, in the discussion that follows, references to "payment" are to the date that the T options are converted into the unconditional right to receive cash promptly.

¶1503.1.3.1 Payment Before Day of Acquisition

If the stock option cancellation payment is made prior to midnight on the day before the day on which the Newco-T stock purchase occurs, it will be deductible in the pre-acquisition year (ignoring, as does this section the provisions of Code §§404(a)(5) and 83(h), which are discussed at ¶¶1503.1.4 and 1503.1.5).

¶1503.1.3.2 Payment on Day of Acquisition—Is Acquisition Date Part of Pre-acquisition or Post-acquisition Year?

If the stock option cancellation payment is made on the day of the Newco-T stock purchase, some care must be exercised to maximize the likelihood that the deduction is includible in T's pre-acquisition year rather than in T's post-acquisition year.

Reg. §1.1502-76(b)(1)(ii)(A), effective for taxable years beginning on or after 1/1/95, states that, "if [T is not an SCo and] becomes . . . a member [of Newco's

---

[14] See IRS Letter Ruling 8834051 (5/27/88) (immediately prior to merger of T into P, T's options were cancelled and converted into the right to receive cash, although cash was not paid to option holders until sometime after the merger; deduction arose at the time the options were converted into the right to receive cash).

consolidated group] during a consolidated return year, it becomes . . . a member at the end of the day on which its status as a member changes, and its tax year ends for all federal income tax purposes at the end of that day." Thus, ordinarily, T's income and expenses for the acquisition date, including T's option cancellation payment, are reported on T's final pre-acquisition return and not on the Newco-T post-acquisition consolidated return.

This general rule is, however, subject to an exception (the so-called next-day rule) in the case of a transaction occurring on the day of Newco's acquisition of T's stock which is "properly allocable to the portion of [T's] day after the [acquisition]."[15] A determination by the parties as to whether a given transaction is properly allocable to the portion of the day after Newco's acquisition of T's stock will be respected if it is "reasonable" and "consistently applied by all affected persons." Although the precise scope of the "next day" rule is unclear, it is doubtful that the rule applies to transactions actually consummated prior to or at the same time as Newco's acquisition of T's stock. See ¶204.3.1.

Prior to the 1/1/95 effective date of Reg. §1.1502-76(b)(1), the precedents were less certain as to the treatment of T's transactions consummated on the day of Newco's acquisition of T's stock:

(1) **Old private rulings re closing acquisition pre-noon and post-noon.** A number of old private letter rulings were consistent with the conclusion that if Newco acquired T's stock *prior to noon*, T's income and expenses for the entire day of the acquisition were on the *Newco-T* post-acquisition consolidated return, but that if the acquisition took place *after noon*, T's income and expenses for the entire day of the acquisition were on *T's* pre-acquisition return.

On the other hand, a number of private rulings, without stating the time at which the closing took place, reached inconsistent results. In a few cases the day on which the acquisition took place was assigned to the T pre-acquisition return; in other cases that day was assigned to the Newco-T post-acquisition return.

(2) **Pre-1995 Code §1502 regulations re closing acquisition at close of business.** Old Reg. §1.1502-76(b)(3) contained two examples both of which stated (emphasis added) that if Newco acquired T's stock *"as of the close of "* a day, T's income and expenses for such day would *not* go on the Newco-T post-acquisition consolidated return (i.e., would be in T's pre-acquisition year). These regulatory examples were wholly consistent with (1) above (i.e., with the view that where the closing was post-noon, the acquisition date was assigned to T's pre-acquisition year).

(3) **Rev. Rul. 80-169 re closing acquisition before start of business.** In Rev. Rul. 80-169, 1980-1 C.B. 188, Newco acquired all of T's stock *"before the start of business"* on a day, and IRS ruled that such day *"is the first day* for which the income of [T] is included in [Newco's] consolidated returns" (emphasis added). This ruling was wholly consistent with (1) above.

---

[15] Reg. §1.1502-76(b)(1)(ii)(B).

¶1503.1.3.3   T Is SCo

Under Reg. §1.1502-76(b)(1)(ii)(A) as applicable to transactions prior to 11/11/99, if Newco acquired T-SCo's stock on, e.g., July 1, no Code §338 or 338(h)(10) election was made with respect to T, and Newco and T thereafter filed a consolidated return, T would undergo three taxable years: (1) T's short SCo year ended the close of June 30, (2) T reported July 1 as a one-day separate C (very short) year, and (3) T entered the Newco consolidated group July 2. See the discussion in ¶¶211.3 and 1109.4.1. Hence a July 1 stock option cancellation payment was unlikely to qualify as optimal tax planning.

Effective for transactions after 11/10/99, Reg. §1.1502-76(b)(1)(ii)(A)(2) eliminated T's one-day C year. T's SCo year, as before, closes June 30, but T now enters Newco's consolidated return group on July 1, i.e., the acquisition date of T-SCo is in the post-acquisition consolidated return year. See Reg. §1.1502-76(b)(5) example (7); ¶1109.4.1.

¶1503.1.3.4   Planning Possibilities

If T is a C corporation[16] and it is desirable for the stock option cancellation payment to be deductible in T's pre-acquisition year, the timing of the payment, *in order of most desirable through least desirable*, would be as follows:

(1)   Make the cancellation payment prior to midnight on the day before consummation of the stock purchase, so that the "next day" rule cannot be invoked.

(2)   Make the cancellation payment on the acquisition date but prior to Newco's purchase of T's stock and contractually bind T and Newco to treat the payment as not allocable to the portion of the day after Newco's acquisition of T's stock. Such an allocation should be respected, because (a) it would appear to be inherently reasonable and (b) it would be consistently applied by the parties.

(3)   Make the cancellation payment at the same time as Newco's purchase of T's stock and contractually bind T and Newco to treat the payment as not allocable to the portion of the day after Newco's acquisition of T's stock. Such an allocation should be respected, as it would appear to be reasonable and as it would be consistently applied by the parties.

It may be desirable for the deduction with respect to T options to arise in a post-acquisition tax year of the Newco-T (or P-T) consolidated group rather than T's pre-acquisition tax year. For example, T may have generated NOLs during the past few years and thus have no use for the deduction, or Newco's (or, more likely, P's) effective federal (and state) tax rate may be higher than T's. If so,

---

[16] If T is an SCo and its stock is acquired after 11/10/99, see Reg. §1.1502-76(b)(2)(v) (income and deductions assigned to each short taxable year under corporation's normal method of accounting).

rather than cashing out the options in the acquisition, either (1) Newco (or P) could exchange its options for T's options (see ¶1503.1), or (2) T could amend the options (assuming the terms of the options permit amendment) to provide that T can satisfy any options that are exercised by delivering to the employee Newco (or P) stock[17] or by paying the employee an amount of cash determined under a formula tied, for example, to post-acquisition performance.[18]

¶1503.1.4   Does Code §404(a)(5) Change Above Conclusions?

(1)   Code §404(a)(5) applies to "compensation . . . paid or accrued on account of any employee under a plan deferring the receipt of such compensation" and postpones the employer's deduction for such deferred compensation until "the taxable year in which an amount attributable to the contribution [i.e., the payment] is includible in the gross income of the employee."

(2)   The regulations elaborate by stating that the deduction will be allowed "only in the taxable year of the employer in which or with which ends the taxable year of an employee in which an amount attributable to such contribution [payment] is includible in his gross income as compensation."[19]

Thus, if a fiscal year employer pays deferred compensation to a calendar-year executive during year 1, the deferred compensation payment would be deductible by the employer in the taxable year which includes 12/31 year 1 (assuming the regulation is valid). For example, if an employer with a fiscal year ending 9/30 year 1 paid deferred compensation on 8/15 year 1 to a calendar-year executive, the employer's deduction would be postponed to 12/31 year 1 and hence would be deductible in the employer's fiscal year ending 9/30 year 2 and *not* in the employer's fiscal year ending 9/30 year 1.

(3)   Using the facts of the above example and assuming that Code §404(a)(5) applies to stock option cancellation payments, T's deduction for the payments made on 6/30 year 1 would be deferred until 12/31 year 1, i.e., the end of the executive's taxable year, and hence would be deductible in the post-acquisition year even if the 6/30 year 1 payment date were included in T's pre-acquisition year.

(4)   Arguably a stock option plan is *not* a deferred compensation plan of the type covered by Code §404(a)(5), on the ground that Code §404(a)(5) was aimed at deferred bonuses and the like, not stock options. Code §404(a)(5)'s

---

[17] The transfer by Newco (or P) of Newco (or P) stock to enable T to satisfy its obligation with respect to any exercised options should not trigger income or gain to T (e.g., on the ground that T holds the Newco (or P) stock at a zero basis). See Reg. §§1.83-6(d) and 1.1032-3. See also ¶406.

[18] The post-acquisition payments by T (i.e., the cash or Newco stock) or by Newco (or P) with respect to the options should not constitute a built-in deduction for purposes of Code §382(h)(6) or Reg. §1.1502-15A(a)(2). See S. Rep. No. 445, 100th Cong., 2d Sess. 48-49 (1988) (providing some insight into Congress's intent with respect to the built-in deduction rules of Code §382(h)(6)).

[19] Reg. §1.404(a)-12(b)(1).

legislative history states that payments of bonuses or other amounts within two and one-half months after the close of the taxable year in which significant services required for payment have been performed is not to be considered a deferred compensation plan. Correctly (as discussed at ¶1503.1.5), Code §83(h) applies to stock options and Code §404(a)(5) does not.

¶1503.1.5 Does Code §83(h) Rather than Code §404(a)(5) Apply to Option Cancellation Payment?

(1) Code §83(e) states that Code §83 does *not* apply to the transfer of a stock option without a readily ascertainable FV, thus inferring that Code §83 *does* apply to the actual exercise of an option which did not have a readily ascertainable FV when granted. Reg. §1.83-7 so provides, stating that:

> If section 83(a) does not apply to the grant of such an option because the option does not have a readily ascertainable fair market value at the time of grant, sections 83(a) and 83(b) shall apply at the time the option is exercised *or otherwise disposed of,* even though the fair market value of such option may have become readily ascertainable before such time. . . . If the option is *sold or otherwise disposed of* in an arm's length transaction, sections 83(a) and 83(b) apply to the transfer of *money* or other property received in the same manner as sections 83(a) and 83(b) would have applied to the transfer of property pursuant to an exercise of the option. [Emphasis added.]

Thus, there appears to be a strong case for the proposition that Code §83 (including Code §83(h) and the regulations thereunder, as described immediately below) applies to a cash payment in cancellation of such an option.

(2) If Code §83(h), rather than Code §404(a)(5), applies, the payment is arguably deductible when paid. Code §83(h) specifically states that the employer's deduction "shall be allowed for the taxable year of such person [i.e., the employer] in which or with which ends the taxable year in which such amount is included in the gross income of the person who performs such services," i.e., the same adverse rule as is contained in the Code §404(a)(5) regulations discussed at ¶1503.1.4. However, Reg. §1.83-6(a)(3) specifically states that "where property is substantially vested upon transfer [as the cash delivered by T to its executives in cancellation of the options will be], the deduction shall be allowed to [the employer] in accordance with his method of accounting," so that T would apparently be entitled to a deduction at the time of payment.

(3) Although Reg. §1.83-3(e) defines "property" as *not* including "money," it is hard to believe that the Code §83 regulations meant to apply a different rule where fully vested *money* is delivered to an executive than where fully vested *other property* is delivered to an executive. Indeed, Reg. §1.83-7 explicitly provides that where an option is sold or otherwise disposed of

in an arm's-length transaction, Code §83(a) and Code §83(b) apply to the
transfer of *money* in the same manner as they would have applied to
the transfer of *property* pursuant to exercise of the option.[20] Under this
regulation, fully vested cash received by an executive as an option cancellation payment should be treated as property subject to Code §83(a). Accordingly, the special rule of Reg. §1.83-6(a)(3) should apply, and the employer
should be entitled to deduct the cash payment in accordance with its
normal method of tax accounting.

(4)   The regulations clearly indicate that Code §83 governs the tax treatment
      of the executive on the cashing out of the T options.[21] Although not explic-
      itly stated in the regulations, there is no rational reason why Code §83
      and the regulations thereunder should not also govern the tax treatment
      of T or Newco.

(5)   In TAM 9024002 (2/6/90) IRS stated that Code §83 in fact applies to the
      cashing out of T's options and that, under Reg. §1.83-6(a)(3), T is entitled
      to an immediate deduction.[22]

¶1503.1.6   Conclusion re Application of Code §§83(h) and 404(a)(5)

If T makes the stock option cancellation payments (1) prior to the acquisition
date—see ¶1503.1.3.1, *or* (2) on the acquisition date (and the transaction is structured so that the acquisition date is included in T's pre-acquisition year—see
¶1503.1.3.2), IRS apparently now agrees that T can deduct such payments in its
pre-acquisition year, notwithstanding Code §404(a)(5) and Code §83(h), on the
ground that Code §404(a)(5) does not apply to a stock option and Code §83(h)
allows an immediate deduction where fully vested money is delivered to the
executive. Further, if T is an accrual method taxpayer, actual cash payment on
or prior to the acquisition date is not necessary. T's binding commitment (entered
into prior to or on the acquisition date but before the merger or other acquisition
event) to make the stock option cancellation payments promptly following the
acquisition transaction will suffice—see ¶1503.1.3.

¶1503.1.7   Applicability to Asset Purchases and Tax-Free Reorganizations

The conclusions discussed above and below in this section—in the context of
Newco's *taxable* purchase of T's *stock*—are also applicable to stock option cancella-

---

[20] See Bagley v. Commissioner, 85 T.C. 663, 673-674 (1985), *aff'd*, 806 F.2d 169, 86-2 U.S.T.C. ¶9807
(8th Cir. 1986). If money were not treated the same as other property, the employer could, of course,
pay the executive in Treasury Notes or Swiss Francs.

[21] See authorities quoted in ¶1503.1 note 2.

[22] See IRS Letter Ruling 8834051 (5/27/88); IRS Letter Ruling 8047123 (8/29/80); IRS Letter Ruling
8230147 (4/30/82). Cf. IRS Letter Ruling 8120103 (2/20/81) (ruling that Code §404(a)(5) governs the
cashing out of options).

tion payments, option assumptions, and cancellations of options in exchange for stock in the context of (1) *P's* taxable purchase of T's stock, (2) Newco's or P's *taxable* purchase of T's *assets*, except that if T sells its assets to Newco or P, T would not enter Newco's or P's consolidated group and hence T's taxable year would not end at the time of the acquisition, and (3) Newco's or P's *tax-free* acquisition of T's *stock or assets*, except that if Newco or P acquires T's assets tax-free, T would not enter Newco's or P's consolidated group and T's taxable year would end on the date of transfer only if the acquisition is a reorganization (as distinguished from a Code §351 transaction) to which Code §381(b)(1) applies.

¶1503.1.8   Deferred Compensation

If T is making any payments to its executives in satisfaction of deferred compensation arrangements (as opposed to stock option cancellation payments discussed above), it appears that Code §404(a)(5) rather than Code §83(h) would apply, so the payments may not be deductible until the last day of the executive's tax year in which the payment was made.

¶1503.2   *Newco Assumes T Stock Option, Substituting Newco Stock Instead of T Stock*

¶1503.2.1   ISO for ISO

If a T executive has an outstanding in-the-money T ISO, Newco can assume the ISO (substituting Newco stock in place of T stock), so that when the executive exercises the ISO, he will receive Newco stock. The substitute Newco option will be an ISO (and hence its exercise will invoke the special ISO tax rules discussed at ¶1502.2 above), so long as the rules of Code §424(a) and (h) are followed.

Generally this means that the terms of the Newco option (expiration date, vesting provisions, etc.) must not be any more favorable to the executive than were the terms of the old T ISO (except that an acceleration in the time when the option may be exercised is permissible), that the spread in the Newco option shares immediately after the assumption must not exceed the spread in the T option shares immediately before the assumption,[23] and that the FV of the Newco option shares immediately after the assumption must not exceed the FV of the T option shares immediately before the assumption.[24]

---

[23] "Spread" means the excess of the option shares' FV over their option price.

[24] Code §424(a) and (h); Reg. §1.425-1(a) and (e). Although Code §424(h)(3)(C)—dealing with ISO modifications—clearly allows amendment of an ISO to accelerate exercisability, Code §424(a)—dealing with ISO assumptions in corporation acquisition—is silent on this point, as are the regulations (which were issued under Code §425 before that provision was redesignated Code §424 in 1990). However, a series of IRS letter rulings confirms that accelerating an ISO's exercisability in connection with a corporate acquisition does not harm the ISO's status. See IRS Letter Rulings 8329029 (4/18/83), 8308062 (11/24/82), 8117198 (1/30/81), 8104057 (10/29/90), 7743055 (7/28/77).

EXAMPLE

On 1/1 year 1 A receives an ISO to purchase 100 T shares at $10 per share, which first becomes exercisable on 1/1 year 3 and which expires on 1/1 year 5.

T shares have an FV of $20 each on 1/1 year 2 at which time Newco purchases all of T's shares and assumes A's option. Newco shares have an FV of $10 each on 1/1 year 2. A's new option is an ISO if:

(1) A's substitute Newco option expires no later than 1/1 year 5.
(2) A's option price for Newco stock is no less than $5 per share—$10 old option price for a T share × 50%, i.e., the ratio which the FV of a Newco share ($10) bears to the FV of a T share ($20).
(3) A's Newco option is for no more than 200 Newco shares, i.e., the $2,000 FV of the T shares subject to A's option (100 T shares × $20)÷ the FV of a Newco share ($10).
(4) The Newco option is not more favorable to A in any other respect than his old T option, except that it is permissible to accelerate the time when A's new option becomes exercisable (e.g., to make the new option immediately exercisable).

Thus, if A receives an option for 200 Newco shares at an option price of $5 per share:

(1) The aggregate spread in A's Newco option is $1,000 (200 Newco shares × ($10 FV per Newco share – $5 option price)), which is the same as the spread in his T option (100 T shares × ($20 FV per T share – $10 option price) = $1,000), and
(2) The aggregate FV of the Newco option shares is $2,000 (200 Newco shares × $10 FV per Newco share), which is the same as the aggregate FV of the T option shares (100 T shares × $20 FV per T share = $2,000).

Legislative Update

The unenacted Senate version (S. 1054) of the 2003 Act, effective for amounts deferred in taxable years beginning after 12/31/03, proposed to amend Code §83 to require a service provider to treat the present value of a right to receive future payments (or such other amount as IRS may by regulations specify) as OI in the taxable year received if such rights are received in exchange for (a) an option to purchase employer securities (as defined in Code §409(*l*)) held by the service provider that is subject to Code

§83(a) or that is described in Code §83(e)(3) or (b) any other compensation based on employer securities held by the service provider.

¶1503.2.2   NQO for ISO

If a T executive has an outstanding T ISO and Newco assumes the T option but the substitute Newco option does not meet the Code §424(a) and (h) rules described at ¶1503.2.1, then the Newco option will be an NQO (rather than an ISO). However, the executive will recognize no taxable income on receipt of an NQO even if the Newco NQO is far more favorable to the executive than the T ISO (except in the extremely unlikely event that the Newco NQO has a "readily ascertainable" FV as defined in Reg. §1.83-7). See ¶1502.1.2 for a risk of immediate taxation if the NQO option price is excessively low.

Thus, where an executive receives a Newco NQO in exchange for a T ISO, he generally recognizes no income until exercise of the NQO, and his OI at exercise of the Newco NQO is governed by the rules described at ¶1502.1.2.

Generally when the executive recognizes OI (at exercise of the Newco NQO or, if the stock is then subject to an SRF and he makes no Code §83(b) election, when the SRF expires—see ¶1502.1), the executive's employer is entitled to an equal deduction under Code §83(h),[25] subject to the reasonable compensation rules, the $1 million executive-compensation-deduction limitation, the golden parachute rules, and the capitalization argument discussed at ¶¶1505 and 1503.1.1. However, IRS may take the position that part of the deduction is lost if (1) the old T option was in-the-money at the time Newco assumed it, and (2) T has gone out of existence and Newco is not its Code §381 successor (i.e., Newco purchased T's stock with a Code §338 election or Newco purchased T's assets). Under the *Pacific Transport* doctrine discussed at ¶304.2, IRS may take the position that the executive's new employer is entitled to deduct only the spread accruing after the acquisition.

Legislative Update

The unenacted Senate version (S. 1054) of the 2003 Act, effective for amounts deferred in taxable years beginning after 12/31/03, proposed to amend Code §83 to require a service provider to treat the present value of a right to receive future payments (or such other amount as IRS may by regulations specify) as OI in the taxable year received if such rights are received in exchange for (a) an option to purchase employer securities (as defined in Code §409(l)) held by the service provider that is subject to Code §83(a) or that is described in Code §83(e)(3) or (b) any other compensation based on employer securities held by the service provider.

---

[25] See Reg. 1.83-6; Venture Funding, Ltd. v. Commissioner, 110 T.C. 236 (1998), *aff'd*, 198 F.3d 248, 99-2 U.S.T.C. ¶50,972 (6th Cir. 1999) (discussed at ¶1502.1.1).

¶1503.2.3 NQO for NQO

If a T executive has an outstanding T NQO and Newco assumes the T option, the executive will generally recognize no taxable income at the time of the assumption even if the Newco NQO is far more favorable to the executive than the T NQO (except in the extremely unlikely event that the Newco NQO has a "readily ascertainable" FV as defined in Reg. §1.83-7).[26] See ¶1502.1.2 for a risk of immediate taxation if the NQO option price is excessively low. The executive's OI and the employer's deduction are governed by the rules described at ¶1402.3.2.

Legislative Update

The unenacted Senate version (S. 1054) of the 2003 Act, effective for amounts deferred in taxable years beginning after 12/31/03, proposed to amend Code §83 to require a service provider to treat the present value of a right to receive future payments (or such other amount as IRS may by regulations specify) as OI in the taxable year received if such rights are received in exchange for (a) an option to purchase employer securities (as defined in Code §409(*l*)) held by the service provider that is subject to Code §83(a) or that is described in Code §83(e)(3) or (b) any other compensation based on employer securities held by the service provider.

¶1503.3 Newco Issues Its Own Stock in Cancellation of T Stock Option

If a T executive has an outstanding T ISO or NQO and Newco issues its stock in cancellation of the T option, the executive will recognize OI equal to the FV of the Newco stock received, unless the Newco stock is subject to an SRF and he makes no Code §83(b) election, in which case the executive's OI is postponed until the SRF expires. See ¶1502.1.

Generally when the executive recognizes OI, the employer is entitled to an equal deduction under Code §83(h),[27] subject to the reasonable compensation rules, the $1 million executive-compensation-deduction limitation, the golden parachute rules and the capitalization argument discussed at ¶¶1505 and 1503.1.1. However, IRS may take the position that a portion of the deduction is lost where (1) the T option was in the money at the time Newco assumed it and (2) T has

---

[26] See, e.g., IRS Letter Ruling 9031009 (5/3/90); IRS Letter Ruling 9023092 (3/15/90); Gen. Couns. Mem. 39399 (4/11/85); Mitchell v. Commissioner, 65 T.C. 1099, 1110 (1976), *aff'd*, 590 F.2d 312, 79-1 U.S.T.C. ¶9235 (9th Cir. 1979).

[27] See Reg. 1.83-6; Venture Funding, Ltd. v. Commissioner, 110 T.C. 236 (1998), *aff'd*, 198 F.3d 248, 99-2 U.S.T.C. ¶50,972 (6th Cir. 1999) (discussed at ¶1502.1.1).

gone out of existence and Newco is not its Code §381 successor (i.e., Newco purchased T's stock with a Code §338 election or Newco purchased T's assets). Under the *Pacific Transport* doctrine discussed at ¶¶304.2 and 1503.2.2, IRS may take the position that the executive's new employer is entitled to deduct only the spread accruing after the acquisition, with the spread at the time of the acquisition being treated as additional purchase price for T's assets.

If Newco issues its stock on the day Newco acquires T's stock, the same timing issue as discussed at ¶1503.1 (where the executive received cash in cancellation of the option) would arise. This timing issue is illustrated by FSA 200206003 (10/22/01), where NQOs held by T executives were exchanged for T stock on a net exercise basis (which T stock was immediately exchanged for P stock pursuant to a T-P merger). The T (and P) stock was subject to an SRF and the T executives made timely Code §83(b) elections. T claimed a deduction for its short taxable year ending on the date of the T-P merger. However, IRS held that because the T shares were subject to an SRF when received by the executives the timing of the deduction was governed by Code §83(h) (deduction generally deferred until end of executive's taxable year, which year ended after the T-P merger) rather than by the special rule of Reg. §1.83-6(a)(3) (deduction allowed under T's normal method of accounting where executive receives property which is "vested upon transfer"), i.e., that the executives' Code §83(b) elections did not cause the T shares to be treated as vested for purposes of the deduction timing rules.

¶1503.4   *Newco or T Issues Deferred Compensation Obligation in Cancellation of T Stock Option*

If a T executive has an outstanding T ISO or NQO and the option is canceled in exchange for Newco's or T's establishment of a deferred compensation account for the executive's benefit (with an initial account balance equal to the option spread and either unfunded or funded through a "rabbi trust"), the executive will generally recognize no taxable income at the time the deferred compensation account is established. Rather, under the general rules for cash method taxpayers, the executive will be taxed only upon the executive's actual or constructive receipt of distributions from the deferred compensation account.[28]

Legislative Update

The unenacted Senate version (S. 1054) of the 2003 Act, effective for amounts deferred in taxable years beginning after 12/31/03, proposed to amend Code §83 to require a service provider to treat the present value of a right to receive future payments (or such other amount as IRS may by regulations specify) as OI in the taxable year received if such rights are received in exchange for (a) an option to purchase employer securities (as

---

[28] See, e.g., IRS Letter Ruling 199901006 (9/28/98).

defined in Code §409(*l*)) held by the service provider that is subject to Code §83(a) or that is described in Code §83(e)(3) or (b) any other compensation based on employer securities held by the service provider.

¶1504   HANDLING T's OUTSTANDING MGMT RESTRICTED STOCK

When Newco (or P) acquires T's outstanding stock (or acquires T's assets by merger), T executives often hold T stock that is subject to a substantial risk of forfeiture (an SRF), e.g., the vesting of the stock is contingent upon continued employment with T for some period of time, and as to which the executives did not make a Code §83(b) election when they acquired it.[1] The same issue is presented if the executive holds publicly traded stock acquired less than six months before, the executive is a person covered by Section 16(b) of the Securities Exchange Act of 1934, and the executive made no Code §83(b) election when he acquired the stock.[2]

As part of the acquisition, T or Newco (or P) might make a cash payment, or Newco (or P) might issue its stock, to the executives in exchange for the restricted T stock. This section discusses tax ramifications of the exchange, incident to the corporate acquisition, of restricted T stock for cash or Newco (or P) stock. Most of the underlying tax rules are detailed in ¶1503; this section contains cross references to the appropriate portions of ¶1503.

¶1504.1   *Cash Payment*

If T or Newco makes a cash payment to a T executive in exchange for his restricted T stock (as to which no timely Code §83(b) election was made), the executive will be taxed on the payment as OI.[3] Properly handled, T should be entitled (subject to the qualifications and limitations discussed at ¶1502.1.1(5)) to deduct this payment (even if Newco makes the payment; see ¶1503.1.1), but the timing of the deduction is somewhat unclear.

The issues surrounding the timing of the deduction basically are the same as those discussed in ¶1503.1 (i.e., interpreting the confusing language of Code §§404(a)(5) and 83(h), and considering whether Newco and T file a consolidated return), with two important differences. *First,* unlike the case of non-statutory stock options, which generally are not subject to Code §83 until exercised or otherwise disposed of, restricted stock is subject to Code §83 upon grant. Therefore, the discussion in ¶¶1503.1.4 and 1503.1.5, regarding whether Code §404(a)(5) or Code §83(h) governs the timing of T's deduction, is not on point in the case of

---

¶1504   [1] See ¶1502 for a discussion of SRFs and Code §83(b) elections.
[2] See Code §83(c)(3).
[3] See Reg. §1.83-1(b)(1).

restricted stock. It ought to be clear that the timing of T's deduction is governed by Code §83(h), although, somewhat surprisingly, the Code §83 regulations are not explicit on this point. Of course, the technical advice memoranda and more recent private letter rulings issued by IRS (discussed in ¶1503.1.5) in the options area, holding that Code §83(h) governs the timing of T's deduction, offer collateral assurance in the case of restricted stock.

Second, assuming Code §83(h) does govern the timing of T's deduction with respect to cashing out restricted stock (as to which no timely Code §83(b) election was made), it seems less clear than in the case of options that T is entitled to an immediate deduction under Reg. §1.83-6(a)(3). As noted above, unlike a non-statutory option, restricted stock is subject to Code §83 upon grant. Because Code §83(a) stock is not "vested" upon grant (see Reg. §1.83-6(a)(1)) an employer can take a deduction with respect to restricted stock only in the employer's taxable year in which or with which ends the taxable year in which the executive takes the restricted stock into income (see ¶1503.1.4 for an example illustrating this principle). When T's restricted stock is cashed out as part of the acquisition of T, IRS could assert that Reg. §1.83-6(a)(1) governs the timing of T's deduction. On the other hand, because the cash the executive receives in exchange for the restricted stock is fully vested upon delivery, it can be argued that the immediate deduction rules of Reg. §1.83-6(a)(3) should apply (see ¶1502.1.1(7)). Currently, the matter appears unresolved.

¶1504.2   *Substituting Newco Stock for T Stock*

If Newco (or P) substitutes its own stock for an executive's Code §83(a) restricted T stock (as to which no timely Code §83(b) election was made), and the Newco (or P) stock is subject to an SRF in the executive's hands, the executive generally will recognize no taxable income at the time of the substitution; rather, the rules of Code §83 will apply to the Newco (or P) stock in the same manner as they applied to the T stock (i.e., the executive will be taxed on the Newco (or P) stock when the SRF lapses).[4] If the Newco (or P) stock the executive receives in exchange for restricted T stock is not subject to an SRF, the executive will be taxed under Code §83 at the time of the substitution.

In either case, Newco (or P) generally should be allowed to deduct the amount the executive takes into income (subject to the reasonable compensation stricture of Code §162, the $1 million executive-compensation-deduction limitation, and the golden parachute rules of Code §280G), with such deduction being available in Newco's (or P's) taxable year in which or with which ends the taxable year in which the executive takes the restricted stock into income. See ¶1503.3 discussing the possibility that a portion of Newco's (or P's) deduction may be disallowed if

---

[4] See IRS Letter Ruling 8720052 (2/18/87). The substitution of Newco (or P) stock for T a restricted stock is not a "transfer of property" for purposes of making a Code §83(b) election. That is, if the 30-day period during which the executive could have made a Code §83(b) election with respect to the restricted T stock lapsed before the substitution of Newco (or P) stock for the T stock, the executive cannot make a Code §83(b) election with respect to the Newco (or P) stock.

T goes out of existence and Newco (or P) is not T's Code §381 successor (e.g., Newco purchases the T stock for cash and makes a Code §338 election or Newco acquires T's assets through a fully taxable merger of T into Newco).

¶1505   TAX PENALTIES FOR GOLDEN PARACHUTE PAYMENT

Code §§280G and 4999 proffer a set of complex tax rules imposing tax penalties for payments to executives (or other service providers) which are connected with a change of control of a corporation (T). Proposed regulations issued in 5/89 and reissued in 2/02 fill many of the statutory gaps. The 2002 proposed regulations apply to payments contingent on a change of control occurring on or after 1/1/04. For payments contingent on a change of control occurring before 1/1/04, taxpayers may rely on either the 1989 or the 2002 proposed regulations.[1]

¶1505.1   *Tax Penalties and Definition of Excess Parachute Payment*

Code §280G disallows a deduction to the payor, and Code §4999 imposes a 20% non-deductible excise tax on the recipient, of any "excess parachute payment."

In general, a person's "excess parachute payment" is the amount of his "parachute payment" described in (1) and (2) below, less the subtraction described in (3) below.

(1) A person's "parachute payment" is any payment (or payments) satisfying *all* of the following requirements:
   (a) a payment "in the nature of compensation" (in cash or property, generally including a stock option and a covenant not to compete payment),[2]
   (b) paid to an executive or other person who is a "disqualified individual" (as described at ¶1505.5.2),
   (c) which is contingent or is presumed to be contingent (as discussed at ¶1505.3) on a change:
      (i) "in the ownership or effective control" of T or
      (ii) in the ownership of "a substantial portion" of T's assets,
   (d) after *reduction by* any portion of the payment either:
      (i) shown by "clear and convincing evidence" to be reasonable compensation for services to be rendered by the person *after* the change, or

---

¶1505   [1] 2002 Prop. Reg. §1.280G-1 Q&A 48.

[2] Staff of Joint Comm. on Taxation, 98th Cong., 2d Sess., Tax Reform Act of 1984: General Explanation of the Revenue Provisions 200, 202, 203 (Comm. Print 1985) (hereinafter "1984 Blue Book"); 1989 and 2002 Prop. Reg. §1.280G-1 Q&A 11 through 13.

        (ii)   to or from a qualified ERISA plan, or

        (iii)   covered by the exceptions for small or privately held companies (as discussed at ¶1505.6.1).

(2)   The amount described in (1) above is a "parachute payment" only if the payments described in (1) above (after reduction by the amount described in (1)(d)) have a present value as of the date of the change equal to or greater than three times the person's average annual compensation from T (or a related or predecessor corporation) includible in his income for the five years ending before the change in control (the person's "base amount").

(3)   An "excess parachute payment" is the excess of the amount described in (1) above (so long as the threshold described in (2) is met) over the *greater of*:

        (a)   the person's base amount or

        (b)   the amount of the payment shown by "clear and convincing evidence" to be reasonable compensation for services rendered by the person *before* the change in control.[3]

EXAMPLE 1

Executive A had $100,000 per year average taxable compensation (i.e., base amount) from T corporation. A receives a $299,000 parachute payment from T (as described in (1) above). The golden parachute provisions do not apply because $299,000 is less than three times A's $100,000 base amount.

EXAMPLE 2

Same as Example 1, except that A receives a $301,000 parachute payment. Because the parachute payment ($301,000) is equal to or more than three times A's $100,000 base amount, the parachute payment ($301,000) less one times A's base amount ($100,000) is an "excess parachute payment" ($201,000) (assuming that the amount set forth in (3)(b) does not exceed the amount set forth in (3)(a)). The golden parachute provisions apply to the $201,000 "excess parachute payment," i.e., $201,000 is non-deductible by T and A pays a 20% non-deductible excise tax on the $201,000 (increasing A's marginal tax rate on such amount by 20 percentage points).

See ¶1503.1.1 for a discussion of other limitations on T's deduction for compensation paid to executives.

---

[3] Code §280G(b).

Legislative Update

The Emergency Worker and Investor Protection Act of 2002 (H.R. 3622) introduced 1/24/02 effective for sales or exchanges after enactment would extend Code §4999's excise tax to any stock sale by a corporate insider (i.e., any individual subject to the requirements of section 16(a) of the 1934 Act) made while the corporation maintains a "transfer-restricted 401(k) plan," i.e., a qualified cash or deferred arrangement (as defined in Code §401(k)(2)) in which a participant cannot freely sell stock of his employer held in such arrangement.

¶1505.2   Definition of Change in Ownership or Control

In order for a payment to be a "parachute payment," the payment must be (or must be presumed to be) contingent on (1) a change in T's "ownership or effective control" or (2) a change "in the ownership of a substantial portion of [T's] assets" (hereinafter a "change").

The proposed regulations define a change in T's *ownership* as occurring on the date that any person (or persons acting as a group) acquires ownership of stock that, together with stock already owned by the person or group, possesses more than 50% of T's total value or voting power.[4]

The proposed regulations state that a change in T's *effective control* is *presumed* to occur on the date that either:

(1)   any person (or persons acting as a group) acquires during a 12-month period stock that possesses 20% or more of T's voting power or
(2)   a majority of the members of T's board of directors is replaced during a 12-month period by persons not endorsed by a majority of the previous board (including a change in directors pursuant to a proxy contest).

This presumption may be rebutted by demonstrating that such event has not transferred the power to control T's management and policies from any one person or group to another.[5] In the absence of either of these two events, a change in effective control is *presumed* not to have occurred.[6]

---

[4] 1989 and 2002 Prop. Reg. §1.280G-1 Q&A 27.

[5] IRS Letter Ruling 200034013 (5/24/00) relied on the following factors to rebut the presumption of a change in effective control where P purchased slightly more than 20% of the stock of public T: (1) T's founders and management continued to hold a substantial stock ownership position in T, (2) P's percentage stock ownership in T was expected to fall below 20% relatively soon as a result of the exercise of management options, (3) none of P's shareholders or executives held management positions with T, and (4) P's acquisition of T stock was consistent with that of an institutional investor.

[6] 1989 and 2002 Prop. Reg. §1.280G-1 Q&A 28.

The proposed regulations state that a change in ownership of *a substantial portion of T's assets* occurs on the date that a person (or persons acting as a group) acquires, within a 12-month period, assets having a total FV equal to one-third or more of T's assets.[7] For this purpose, the following transfers are disregarded: any transfer of T's assets (1) to a shareholder in exchange for or with respect to his T stock *or* (2) to an entity 50% or more of the stock (by vote or value) of which is owned by T or by persons who own 50% or more of T's stock (by vote or value) *or* (3) to a person (or persons acting as a group) who owns 50% or more of T's stock (by vote or value).[8]

In applying these rules:

(1) Persons will not be treated as part of a group merely because they purchase stock at the same time or as part of a single public offering, but will be treated as part of a group if they are owners of an entity that enters into a merger, stock acquisition, or similar transaction with T. The 2002 proposed regulations state that a person who owns stock in both T and P is considered to be acting as a group with respect to the other P shareholders only to the extent of such person's ownership of P stock before the transaction, and not with respect to such person's T ownership.[9]

EXAMPLE 1

T merges into P in a tax-free merger. In the merger, T's shareholders (none of whom previously owned P stock) receive less than 20% of P's stock.

The merger results in a change in ownership of a substantial portion of T's assets. The merger does not result in a change in ownership or control of P.

EXAMPLE 2

Same as Example 1, except that, in the merger, T's shareholders receive 40% of P's stock.

The merger results in a change in ownership of a substantial portion of T's assets. In addition, the merger is *presumed* to result in a change in effective control of P. However, this presumption should be rebutted, so long as T's stock was widely held and, after the merger, the former T shareholders do not act in a concerted way to control P's management and policies.[10]

---

[7] 1989 and 2002 Prop. Reg. §1.280G-1 Q&A 29. The 2002 proposed regulations specify that the "total FV" measure is based on gross FV, rather than FV net of liabilities.

[8] 1989 and 2002 Prop. Reg. §1.280G-1 Q&A 29.

[9] 2002 Prop. Reg. §1.280G-1 Q&A 27(b) and (d) example (4), -1 Q&A 28(d), -1 Q&A 29(d).

[10] IRS Letter Ruling 199905012 (11/4/98); IRS Letter Ruling 200029035 (4/20/00); IRS Letter Ruling 200029042 (4/21/00); IRS Letter Ruling 200041020 (7/13/00); IRS Letter Ruling 200110009 (11/29/00).

EXAMPLE 3

Same as Example 1, except that, in the merger, T's shareholders receive 51% of P's stock.

The merger does *not* result in a change in ownership of a substantial portion of T's assets. The merger *does*, however, result in a change in P's ownership.

A 2002 IRS private letter ruling concluded that T's bankruptcy reorganization did not constitute a change in T's ownership or effective control, notwithstanding that T's creditors acquired most of T's stock in the reorganization (with one creditor receiving more than 20% of T's stock) and entered into a shareholders agreement regarding T's ownership and management, implicitly on the ground that T's creditors would not be treated as a group even though they entered into a shareholders agreement.[11] IRS's rationale for this taxpayer-favorable ruling was that "[t]he passive receipt of stock by a creditor under a bankruptcy plan of reorganization is essentially involuntary in that the creditors . . . typically would prefer that the debt be paid in cash rather than stock of the debtor. The fact that [the] plan of reorganization provides for the creditors to receive stock instead of cash is a function of the financial resources of the [bankrupt's] estate and is not indicative of any intention on the part of the creditors, either singly or acting as a group, to acquire control of the debtor."

(2) If a person or group already has ownership or effective control of T, the acquisition of additional stock or additional control by such person or group is not treated as causing a change in ownership or control.

(3) Where T redeems stock from one or more shareholders, thus increasing the percentage of T's stock owned by T's other shareholders, such increases in T's ownership or control resulting from the redemption are taken into account.

(4) Code §318's attribution rules apply in determining stock ownership.[12] Under Code §318(a)(4) the holder of an option to acquire unissued T stock is generally considered to own that T stock. For this purpose, however, an option is not considered outstanding stock if it is not currently exercisable and will become exercisable only upon the occurrence of a substantial condition precedent.[13]

For purposes of the golden parachute rules, all members of the same affiliated group (as defined in Code §1504(a) but without regard to the Code §1504(b) exceptions)[14] are treated as a single corporation. Accordingly, T and its subsidiary S are treated as a single corporation and a transfer of S's stock is treated as a

---

[11] IRS Letter Ruling 200236006 (5/23/02).

[12] 1989 and 2002 Prop. Reg. §1.280G-1 Q&A 27 through 29.

[13] 2002 Prop. Reg. §1.280G-1 Q&A 17(b) example (1); IRS Letter Ruling 199914032 (1/13/99), citing Rev. Rul. 89-64, 1989-1 C.B. 91.

[14] See ¶¶211.1 and 1205.2.

change in ownership of part of T's *assets*, rather than a change in ownership of S's stock.

EXAMPLE 1

T is the parent of an affiliated group that includes S. T sells all of the stock of S to P. S's assets comprise 20% of the T group's gross assets. For purposes of determining whether a change in ownership or control has occurred, the T group is treated as a single corporation and the sale of S stock is treated as a sale of T group assets.

Since the deemed asset sale constitutes less than one-third of the T group's gross assets, the sale does not result in application of the golden parachute rules to T, S, or any other member of the T group.

EXAMPLE 2

Same as Example 1, except that S's assets comprise 40% of the T group's gross assets. Since the deemed asset sale is of at least one-third of the T group's gross assets, the golden parachute rules are triggered with respect to T, S, and the T group's other members.

EXAMPLE 3

T owns 79% of S's stock and the remainder of S's stock is owned by unrelated persons. The S stock owned by T comprises 20% of the gross assets of the affiliated group of which T is a member. T sells all of its S stock to P.

The sale results in a change in S's ownership, but does not result in a change in ownership of a substantial portion of the T group's assets.

EXAMPLE 4

Same as Example 3, except that the S stock owned by T comprises 40% of the T group's gross assets.

The sale results in a change in S's ownership and also results in a change in ownership of a substantial portion of the T group's assets.

¶1505.3   Definition of Contingent on Change in Ownership or Control

¶1505.3.1   In General

In general, a payment is contingent on a change in ownership or control if the recipient of the payment either (a) acquires a right to receive the payment or (b) receives the payment sooner than he otherwise would have (i) as a result of the change, or (ii) as a result of events that are closely associated with the change, or (iii) (if the taxpayer fails to rebut a presumption) pursuant to a contract entered into or amended within one year before the change.

Under the proposed regulations, when the time of payment of a vested payment right, or the vesting of a payment right that is subject only to time vesting, is accelerated by a change, only a portion of the payment is treated as contingent on the change, as described in ¶¶1505.3.6 and 1505.3.7.

¶1505.3.2   Payment Resulting from Change

A payment generally is treated as contingent on a change "unless it is substantially certain, at the time of the change, that the payment would have been made whether or not the change occurred."[15]

EXAMPLE

On 1/1 year 1 executive A receives T stock subject to a substantial risk of forfeiture (an SRF). The SRF will lapse if A continues to be employed by T through 12/31 year 2 or, if earlier, upon a change in T's ownership. A change in T's ownership occurs on 11/30 year 2 (resulting in the SRF's lapse). A remains employed by T through 12/31 year 2.

Because it was not substantially certain, at the time of the change, that the SRF would lapse had the change not occurred, the vesting of the restricted stock on account of the change is treated as contingent on the change, notwithstanding that A, in fact, remained employed through 12/31 year 2.

See ¶1505.3.7 for discussion of the rule treating only a portion of the "payment" resulting from the vesting of the restricted stock on account of the change as contingent on the change.

---

[15] Staff of the Joint Comm. on Taxation, General Explanation of the Revenue Provision Act of 1984, 98th Cong., 2d Sess. 201 (Comm. Print 1984) (hereinafter "1984 Blue Book"); S. Rep. No. 313, 99th Cong., 2d Sess. 915 (1986) (hereinafter "1986 Senate Report"); 1989 and 2002 Prop. Reg. §1.280G-1 Q&A 22.

¶1505.3.3   **Payment Resulting from Closely Associated Event**

A payment also is generally treated as contingent on a change if:

(1)   the payment is contingent on an event that is closely associated with a change,
(2)   a change actually occurs, and
(3)   the event is materially related to the change.[16]

Under the proposed regulations, an event is treated as closely associated with a change if the event "is of a type often preliminary or subsequent to" a change. A non-exclusive list of "closely associated events" includes the onset of a tender offer, a substantial increase in market price of T's stock within a short period of time before a change, the termination of a person's employment, a significant reduction in the person's job responsibilities, the cessation of the listing of T's stock on an established market, the acquisition of more than 5% of T's stock by a person (or group) not in control of T, and a change in T's control as defined in the person's employment agreement.

IRS has ruled that a parent corporation's sale of a subsidiary was not an event closely associated with the parent's change (and hence payments to the subsidiary's executives triggered by parent's sale of the subsidiary were not contingent on the parent's change) where the parent's decision to sell the subsidiary was made prior to parent's receipt of the unsolicited offer for parent that led to parent's change.[17]

A material relationship is presumed to exist if the event occurs within (and is presumed *not* to exist if it occurs more than) one year before or after the change.[18]

EXAMPLE 1

Under an employment contract with T that was entered into on 1/1 year 1, executive A is entitled to a $500,000 severance payment in the event his employment is terminated. A change in ownership of T occurs on 2/1 year 2. On 4/1 year 2, as a result of differences in management philosophy between A and T's new owner, A's employment is terminated and he receives the severance payment.

The payment will probably be treated as contingent on the change since it is contingent on an event closely associated with a change, the change actually occurred, the termination within one year after the change is presumed to be materially related to the change, and the facts do not support rebuttal of the presumption.

---

[16] 1989 and 2002 Prop. Reg. §1.280G-1 Q&A 22(b).
[17] IRS Letter Ruling 9847011 (8/14/98).
[18] Prop. Reg. §1.280G-1 Q&A 22.

EXAMPLE 2

Same as Example 1, except that A's termination occurs on 9/1 year 2 as a result of unanticipated T losses that are unrelated to the change in ownership.

The payment should *not* be treated as contingent on the change. Although the termination within one year after the change is presumed to be materially related to the change, a showing that the termination resulted from unanticipated losses unrelated to the change should be sufficient to rebut the presumption.

EXAMPLE 3

Same as Example 1, except that the termination of employment occurs on 4/1 year 3.

The payment should *not* be treated as contingent on the change since a termination more than one year after the change is presumed *not* to be materially related to the change.

EXAMPLE 4

Same as Example 3, except that A's employment contract gave A a right to a severance payment only in the event the termination of his employment occurred after a change in ownership.

The payment is treated as contingent on the change under the rule discussed in ¶1505.3.2.

¶1505.3.4   Agreement Within One Year Before Change

Any payment pursuant to an agreement entered into or an amendment made within one year before a change is *presumed* contingent on such change, unless the taxpayer establishes the contrary "by clear and convincing evidence."[19] The 1984 Blue Book states that the presumption is confirmed if, at the time the contract was entered into, the corporation "viewed itself as a likely takeover candidate" or "had been advised by its investment banker that it was a prime takeover candidate."

The proposed regulations state that factors relevant to determining whether the presumption is rebutted include the content of the agreement and the circum-

---

[19] Code §280G(b)(2)(C).

stances surrounding the execution of the agreement, such as whether it was entered into at a time when a takeover attempt had commenced and the degree of likelihood that a change in ownership would actually occur. An example contained in the regulations indicates that the fact that a payment is made before a change occurs does not necessarily rebut the presumption.

The proposed regulations state that the presumption is generally rebutted if the agreement (a) is one of a specified list of non-discriminatory employee benefit programs, or (b) replaces a prior contract that provides no increased payments other than normal increases attributable to additional responsibilities or cost of living adjustments, or (c) provides benefits not significantly different than those provided under contracts with individuals providing similar services (if the other contracts were not themselves entered into in contemplation of the change).[20]

EXAMPLE 5

On 3/1 year 1 T is advised by its investment banker that it is a takeover candidate. On 4/1 year 1 T enters into agreements providing for substantial payments to key executives on 4/1 year 2. On 1/1 year 2 T is acquired by P.

Payments pursuant to this agreement are presumed contingent on a change in control, and under the circumstances it is highly unlikely that T can rebut this presumption.

¶1505.3.5 Agreement After Change in Control

The proposed regulations state that a payment is not treated as contingent on a change if the payment is made pursuant to an agreement entered into *after* the change (and no *legally enforceable* agreement existed before the change).[21]

Two cautionary points: First, where an agreement was negotiated before the change and executed shortly after the change, there is substantial risk IRS will take the position that a legally enforceable agreement existed before the change. Second, if after a change an employee gives up rights to receive a parachute payment in exchange for benefits under a new agreement, the new benefits may constitute parachute payments.

These cautionary points are illustrated by the taxpayer-adverse decision in *Cline v. Commissioner*.[22] In the *Cline* case, T, the target of P's tender offer, entered into written severance agreements with T senior executives. After successful completion of the tender offer, the parties realized that payments under the original severance agreements would run afoul of the golden parachute rules. Thus, T and the executives entered into written amended agreements reducing the amounts payable to less than the three-times-base-amount threshold. In connection with

[20] 1989 and 2002 Prop. Reg. §1.280G-1 Q&A 25 and 26.
[21] 1989 and 2002 Prop. Reg. §1.280G-1 Q&A 23.
[22] 34 F.3d 480, 94-2 U.S.T.C. ¶50,468 (7th Cir. 1994), *aff'g* Balch v. Commissioner, 100 T.C. 331 (1993).

negotiating the reduced payments, P orally assured the executives that P would make a good faith effort to compensate them for the reduction in payments but could make no binding promises. The executives subsequently performed minor consulting and administrative services and received compensation payments closely corresponding to the amounts by which their original severance agreements had been reduced, which appeared to be substantially in excess of reasonable compensation for the services actually rendered.

The Tax Court found that the executives' compensation for post-acquisition services was in excess of reasonable compensation and that P's "best efforts" undertaking to provide such compensation was a legally enforceable agreement entered into before the ownership change. Accordingly, the excessive compensation for post-acquisition services was subject to the golden parachute rules. The court's analysis seems guided by its statement of "concern that other similarly situated disqualified individuals . . . might attempt to avoid [the golden parachute rules] by restructuring the timing and characterization of parachute payments in the future."

On appeal, the Seventh Circuit, relying on the broad language of the statute and legislative history (including an example in the Joint Tax Committee Bluebook characterizing as a parachute payment amounts paid "pursuant to a formal or informal understanding reached before the change occurs") held that the payments would constitute parachute payments even if no legally enforceable agreement existed at the time of the ownership change: "section 280G's applicability is not contingent on the existence of a legally enforceable agreement."

There are at least two possible readings of the Seventh Circuit's *Cline* decision:

Under a *narrow* reading, there was a pre-change agreement (indeed a legally binding written pre-change agreement), i.e., the written severance agreement calling for payments greater than the three-times-base-amount threshold, and hence the later reduction of the amounts to be paid under the severance agreement constituted either a sham or bargained-for consideration for P's promise to pay an amount equal to the reduction. This narrow reading is supported by the *Cline* case's facts (i.e., there was a pre-change binding written agreement) and is consistent with the proposed regulations which state that payments pursuant to an agreement executed after a change in ownership or control are treated as contingent on a change in control only if pursuant to a legally enforceable agreement entered into *before* the change in control.[23]

This narrow reading of the *Cline* case is also supported by one sentence in the appellate court's opinion: "The Tax Court . . . was entitled to conclude the second oral agreement was made simply to circumvent tax restrictions."

The 2002 proposed regulations appear to adopt this narrow reading of *Cline*, stating that "if an individual has a right to receive a parachute payment under an agreement entered into prior to a change . . . and gives up that right as bargained-for consideration for benefits under a post-change agreement, the agreement is treated as a post-change agreement only to the extent the value of the

---

[23] 1989 Prop. Reg. §1.280G-1 Q&A 23.

payments under the agreement exceed the value of the payments under the pre-change agreement."[24]

Under a *broader* (more anti-taxpayer) reading of *Cline*, a payment after the change in control can be contingent on the change in control for §280G purposes even where the payment is unrelated to any binding pre-change agreement to make the payment. This broader reading of the case is far more taxpayer hostile than the proposed regulations (under which a payment is not treated as contingent on a change in control where the payment is made pursuant to an agreement entered into *after* the change and no *legally enforceable* agreement existed before the change in control). However, this broader reading is suggested by the Seventh Circuit's repeated statements, over several pages of the opinion, that no legally enforceable pre-change agreement is necessary:

- "We cannot accept [the executive's] view that a legally enforceable agreement is a necessary predicate to a determination that the payments constitute a golden parachute. . . ."
- The statute "does not require that the payment be made pursuant to a legally enforceable agreement or contract."
- "Section 280G's applicability is not contingent on the existence of a legally enforceable agreement."
- "Whether the oral agreement [to use good faith efforts to pay an amount equal to the reduction in T's written obligation] . . . fails for indefiniteness under Illinois law . . . is of no import."

¶1505.3.6 Accelerated Payment of Vested Benefits

A payment that is accelerated by a change in control, but was (1) "substantially certain" to have been made (under the language of the 1989 proposed regulations) or (2) "vested" (under the language of the 2002 proposed regulations) without regard to the change, is treated as contingent on the change only to the extent the acceleration increases the present value of the payment.[25] In general, a discount rate equal to 120% of the applicable federal rate is used to determine present value.[26]

Where the amount of a payment that is vested without regard to a change in control is not reasonably ascertainable (i.e., the payment, absent the acceleration, is a contingent or fluctuating amount) and the acceleration of the payment does not significantly increase the present value of the payment absent the acceleration, the acceleration is treated as not increasing the present value of the payment at all.[27]

---

[24] 2002 Prop. Reg. §1.280G-1 Q&A 23(a), (b) example (3).

[25] 1989 and 2002 Prop. Reg. §1.280G-1 Q&A 24. The term "vested," as used in 2002 Prop. Reg. §1.280G-1 Q&A 24, apparently means "substantially vested" within the meaning of Reg. §1.83-3(b) and (j). Cf. 2002 Prop. Reg. §1.280G-1 Q&A 12(a). For this purpose, filing a Code §83(b) election does not cause property or a payment which is subject to an SRF to be treated as "vested."

[26] 1989 and 2002 Prop. Reg. §1.280G-1 Q&A 24, 31, and 32.

[27] 1989 and 2002 Prop. Reg. §1.280G-1 Q&A 24(b), 2002 Prop. Reg. §1.280G-1 Q&A 24(f) example (2), 1989 Prop. Reg. §1.280G-1 Q&A 24(e) example (3); IRS Letter Ruling 200110013 (11/30/00).

The 2002 proposed regulations further state that if the acceleration significantly increases the present value of the payment, the future value of such payment is treated as equal to the amount of the accelerated payment (i.e., the recipient is not given credit for any potential increase in the amount of the payment, absent the change-related acceleration).[28]

A 2000 letter ruling applied these concepts to find that executives who, as part of a T-P merger, exchanged T options for P options did not receive a payment contingent on a change notwithstanding that, due to fluctuations in the value of P's stock, the T option holders effectively received higher per share consideration than the T shareholders.[29] In the ruling, public T was acquired by public P in a merger for consideration intended to consist of 2/3 cash and 1/3 P stock. The cash portion of the consideration was a fixed per-share amount, while the stock portion was calculated based on the average trading price (within a specified range) of P's stock for a period prior to the merger (the "valuation period"). As it turned out, the stock exchange ratio did not reflect the full value of P's stock on the merger date, because the market price for P's stock rose during the valuation period so that the stock portion represented more than 1/3 of the actual consideration (based on the actual market price for P's stock on the merger date).

In connection with the merger, vested T options were exchanged for vested P options, based on the stock exchange ratio used in the merger agreement. Because the exchange ratio "undervalued" P shares (in relation to P shares' actual value on the merger date), the exchanging T option holders (who received all P options and no cash consideration) ended up with a somewhat better deal than the T shareholders (who received predominantly cash). Relying on the facts that the determination of the exchange ratio was the subject of arm's-length negotiations between T and P and was not intended to provide any compensatory benefit, IRS ruled that the exchange of vested T options for vested P options was not a payment in the nature of compensation for purposes of Code §280G.

¶1505.3.7   Accelerated Vesting of Unvested Benefits

The proposed regulations also state that only a portion of a previously *unvested* payment will be treated as contingent on the change in control where the vesting of the payment is accelerated by the change, but the payment was (1) substantially certain to have been made without regard to the change "if the individual had continued to perform services for a specified period of time" (under the language of the 1989 proposed regulations) or (2) "contingent only on the continued performance of services . . . for a specified period of time" (under the language of the 2002 proposed regulations). The 2002 proposed regulations add the additional requirement that the payment "is attributable, at least in part, to the performance of services before the date the payment is made or becomes certain to be made." The portion treated as contingent on a change under this taxpayer-favorable rule is equal to the sum of:

[28] 2002 Prop. Reg. §1.280G-1 Q&A 24(b) and 24(f) examples (4), (5), and (6).
[29] IRS Letter Ruling 200032017 (5/9/00).

(1) the increase in the present value of the payment resulting from the acceleration, ignoring the prior SRF, using a discount rate equal to 120% of the AFR to determine the amount of such increase and, subject to the modifications described below, calculated under the rules described in ¶1505.3.6, plus

(2) an amount "reflecting the lapse of the obligation to perform services," which *is* 1% of the accelerated payment per full month under the 2002 proposed regulations (and which under the 1989 proposed regulations had been based on all facts and circumstances, but *at least* 1% of the accelerated payment per full month).[30]

Although the 1989 proposed regulations characterized 1% per month as a minimum amount, it was our experience in practice that the 1% amount was typically used in the case of all accelerated vesting of stock, stock options, and various forms of deferred compensation. A series of identical 2000 IRS rulings seemed to bless this practice.[31] The 2002 proposed regulations simply specify the 1% per month amount.

Under the 1989 proposed regulations, where the future value of the payment is not reasonably ascertainable, the future value is deemed to be equal to the amount of the accelerated payment (i.e., the recipient is not given any credit for any potential increase in the amount of the payment absent the change-related acceleration). This rule applies even if the acceleration is not expected to significantly increase the present value of the payment. Under the 2002 proposed regulations, this variation from the rules described in ¶1505.3.6 applies only to accelerated vesting of stock options or restricted stock and apparently does not apply to accelerated vesting of a stock appreciation right or deferred compensation growing at a market-based rate.[32]

EXAMPLE 6

Executive A holds options to purchase 100,000 T shares at a price of $10 per share. The options are subject to an SRF based on A's continued employment, which will lapse on 12/31 year 1 or, if earlier, upon a change in T's ownership. On 7/15 year 1, when A's options are in the money by $1 million, a change in T's ownership occurs and A receives a $1 million payment in cancellation of the stock options. Assume that the short-term AFR (compounded semiannually) for July of year 1 is 5%.

The portion of the stock option cancellation payment treated as contingent on a change is $76,764: the sum of (a) the increase in the present value

---

[30] 1989 and 2002 Prop. Reg. §1.280G-1 Q&A 24.

[31] IRS Letter Rulings 200046005, 200046006, 200046007 (7/28/00) (applying a 1%-per-month factor without discussion or analysis of factual support for such percentage); cf. IRS Letter Ruling 200110013 (11/30/00) (describing the amount "reflecting the lapse of the obligation to perform services" as "no less than 1%" per month).

[32] 2002 Prop. Reg. §1.280G-1 Q&A 24(c)(3). See also 2002 Prop. Reg. §1.280G-1 Q&A 24(f) examples (4), (5), and (6).

resulting from a five and one half month acceleration of a $1 million payment ($26,764 = $1 million *minus* $973,236 (which is the present value as of 7/15 year 1 of $1 million to be received on 12/31 year 1 using a 6% per annum discount rate—6% being 120% of the 5% AFR)) and (b) 1% of the payment per full month (i.e., ignoring the half month) of acceleration ($50,000 = $1 million × 1% × 5).

This taxpayer-favorable rule treating as contingent on a change only a portion of payments resulting from accelerated vesting of amounts subject to time vesting conflicts in certain circumstances with another rule of the proposed regulations that generally treats the full amount of severance payments triggered by a change as contingent on the change.[33] Severance payments under an employment contract are often measured by reference to the amount of compensation that would have been payable had the employee remained employed for the full term of the contract. Such a severance payment is one that, read literally, is "substantially certain ... to have been made without regard to the change if the disqualified individual had continued to perform services ... for a specified period of time" (under the language of the 1989 proposed regulations) and is "contingent only on the continued performance of services ... for a specified period of time" (under the language of the 2002 proposed regulations) and hence fits within the general language of the taxpayer-favorable rule for accelerated vesting of payments subject to time vesting, a result not intended by IRS/Treasury.

The 2002 proposed regulations attempt to resolve the conflict by imposing the requirement, noted above, that a payment may qualify under the taxpayer-favorable rule for accelerated vesting of payments subject to time vesting only if the payment is attributable, at least in part, to services performed before the date the payment becomes vested.[34] In addition, the 2002 proposed regulations state that the taxpayer-favorable rule does not apply to "the payment of amounts due under an employment agreement on a termination of employment or a change in ownership or control that otherwise would be attributable to the performance of services ... during any period that begins after the date of termination or change in ownership or control, as applicable."[35]

EXAMPLE 7

On 1/1 year 1 executive A enters into a 3-year employment agreement with T. Under the agreement A is entitled to a fixed annual salary of $300,000, a fixed annual minimum bonus of $100,000, and an additional annual bonus based on satisfaction of certain performance goals. The employment agreement states that, in the event of a T ownership change, A will receive a lump sum payment equal to the sum of (1) A's fixed salary multiplied by

[33] 1989 and 2002 Prop. Reg. §1.280G-1 Q&A 44.
[34] 2002 Prop. Reg. §1.280G-1 Q&A 24(a)(1).
[35] 2002 Prop. Reg. §1.280G-1 Q&A 24(d)(2).

the employment agreement's remaining period, plus (2) the highest annual bonus received by A during the preceding 3 years multiplied by the number of remaining years (including fractions of a year) under the employment agreement.

On 1/1 year 2 there is a change in T's ownership. The highest annual bonus received by A during the preceding 3 years was $200,000. Under the change in ownership provision of A's employment agreement, A receives a lump sum payment of $1 million ($300,000 fixed salary × 2-year remaining term, plus $200,000 highest bonus × 2-year remaining term).

Notwithstanding that A's fixed annual salary and minimum annual bonus for years 2 and 3 (aggregating $800,000) were substantially certain to have been made without regard to the change if A had continued to perform services for T through the end of year 3, IRS's position is that the full amount of A's $1 million payment is treated as contingent on T's change in ownership.

This result is achieved under the 2002 proposed regulations on the ground that no portion of A's $1 million payment is attributable to services performed before 1/1 year 2 and the payment is "due under an employment agreement on a termination of employment or a change in ownership or control that otherwise would be attributable to the performance of services . . . during any period that begins after" 1/1 year 2.

A 2001 letter ruling reached the same result under the 1989 proposed regulations, reasoning that the special rule treating only a portion of accelerated time-vesting payments as contingent on a change in ownership "was included in the [1989] proposed regulations to reduce the contingent portion of a non-vested payment that had been partially earned by the taxpayer with services, but had not been paid. This does not occur with amounts paid under an employment agreement because these amounts are paid as they are earned."[36]

Unfortunately, the restrictive language in the 2002 proposed regulations creates its own uncertainty, in part because of the ambiguity of the word "period" in the requirement that the payment must, at least in part, be "attributable to the performance of services . . . during any period that begins after the date of termination or change. . . ."

EXAMPLE 8

On 1/1 year 1 executive A enters into a 3-year employment agreement with T. In addition to normal salary and bonus payments, A is granted options to purchase 300,000 shares of T common stock. The options vest 1/3 on 12/31 year 1, 1/3 on 12/31 year 2, and 1/3 on 12/31 year 3, with vesting

---

[36] IRS Letter Ruling 200110025 (3/9/00). Although not so explained in the letter ruling, this position could be reconciled with the language of 1989 Prop. Reg. §1.280G-1 Q&A 24(c) by viewing the amount "reflecting the lapse of the obligation to perform services" on these facts as equal to the full amount of A's normal salary and bonus payments.

accelerated upon a T change of control. A change of control of T occurs on 1/31 year 2, at which time A receives a payment of $3 million in cancellation of the $300,000 options ($10 per option). On 1/31 year 2 the short-term AFR, compounded semi-annually, is 5%.

The 100,000 options that vested on 12/31 year 1 are potentially treated as contingent on the change only because the change accelerates the time at which a payment ($10 per option) is made to A. Because the value of the payment absent the acceleration is not reasonably ascertainable, and the acceleration does not significantly increase the present value of the payment absent the acceleration, no portion of the $1 million payment for these options is treated as contingent on the change.

The 100,000 options that were scheduled to vest on 12/31 year 2 are potentially treated as contingent on the change because the change accelerates their vesting. These options should qualify for the taxpayer-favorable rule for accelerated vesting of payments subject to time vesting, because vesting of the options was contingent only on A's continued performance of services through 12/31 year 2 and it seems clear that A's receipt on 1/1 year 1 of options vesting on 12/31 year 2 is attributable, at least in part, to services performed before 1/15 year 2. One might be concerned that some portion of the accelerated option vesting could be regarded as "the payment of amounts due under an employment agreement on . . . a change in ownership or control that otherwise would be attributable to the performance of services . . . during any period that begins after the date of . . . change in ownership or control." However, it seems clear that the 2002 proposed regulations do not intend such an interpretation.[37] Because accelerated vesting of a stock option is deemed to significantly increase the present value of the payment, the portion of the payment treated as contingent on the change is $162,806: the sum of (a) the increase in present value resulting from an 11-month acceleration of a $1 million payment ($52,806 = $1 million *minus* $947,194 [which is the present value as of 1/31 year 2 of $1 million to be received on 12/31 year 2 using a 6% per annum discount rate (i.e., 120% of the AFR), compounded semi-annually] and (b) 1% of the payment per 11 full months of acceleration ($110,000 = $1 million x 1% x 11).

The 100,000 options that were scheduled to vest on 12/31 year 3 are also potentially treated as contingent on the change because the change accelerates their vesting. Although we believe these options should qualify for the taxpayer-favorable rule for accelerated vesting of payments subject to time vesting, this result is less clear than in the case of the options scheduled to vest on 12/31 year 2. In the case of the year 3 options, although vesting of the options was contingent only on A's continued performance of services through 12/31 year 3, IRS might argue that A's receipt of the options vesting in year 3 is attributable only to services performed in year 3 (i.e., after 1/15 year 2) and that the accelerated option vesting is "the payment of amounts due under an employment agreement on . . . a change

---

[37] 2002 Prop. Reg. §1.280G-1 Q&A 24(f) example (6).

in ownership or control that otherwise would be attributable to the performance of services . . . during any period that begins after the date of . . . change
in ownership or control." Were such an IRS argument to prevail, the full $1
million payment received by A for the year 3 options would be treated as
contingent on the change.

However, we believe the more reasonable interpretation views the options
issued on 1/1 year 1 and vesting on 12/31 year 3, like the options vesting
on 12/31 year 2, as attributable in part to services performed before the
1/31 year 2 change of control, so that the portion of the payment treated as
contingent on the change is $337,092: the sum of (a) the increase in present
value resulting from a 23-month acceleration of a $1 million payment
($107,092 = $1 million *minus* $892,908 [which is the present value as of 1/31
year 2 of $1 million to be received on 12/31 year 3 using a 6% per annum
discount rate, compounded semi-annually]) and (b) 1% of the payment per
23 full months of acceleration ($230,000 = $1 million x 1% x 11).

The taxpayer-favorable rule for accelerated vesting of payments subject to time
vesting does not apply to accelerated vesting of payments that are subject to
performance or other non-time based vesting contingencies. Where a change in
control triggers accelerated vesting of stock or stock options subject to performance
vesting, the full value of the stock or option is treated as a payment contingent
on the change.[38]

EXAMPLE 9

On 1/1 year 1 executive A enters into a 3-year employment agreement
with T. In addition to normal salary and bonus payments, A participates in
an incentive plan, under which A is entitled to receive, if he continues to
be employed by T at the end of year 3, a formula bonus based on the average
amount of T's earnings per share (if positive) for each of years 1, 2, and 3.
The employment agreement states that, in the event of a change in T's
ownership, A will receive an accelerated payment of amounts under the
incentive plan, with the plan year treated as ending on the date of the
ownership change.

On 9/30 year 3 there is a change in T's ownership. A receives a lump
sum payment based on the average of T's positive earnings per share for
each of year 1, year 2, and the first three-quarters of year 3 ending on 9/30
year 3.

The portion of the payment based on partial year 3 positive earnings
would not qualify for the taxpayer-favorable rule for accelerated time-vesting
payments, because this payment was not subject merely to time vesting
without regard to the change (i.e., absent the change T could have suffered

---

[38] 2002 Prop. Reg. §1.280G-1 Q&A 24(d)(3); IRS Legal Memorandum 200043037 (7/28/00).

losses in the fourth quarter of year 3 which would offset T's positive earnings for the first three-quarters of year 3). However, any losses suffered by T during the fourth quarter of year 3 (even if greater than T's earnings for the first three-quarters of year 3) would not have affected the portion of the bonus calculated by reference to year 1 and year 2 earnings had A continued to perform services for T through the end of year 3 (because A's employment agreement takes into account only a year with positive earnings per share). Thus, the year 1 and year 2 portion of the bonus should qualify for the taxpayer-favorable rule for accelerated time-vesting payments.[39]

As discussed in ¶1502.1.3, IRS has taken the position in several private rulings that where an executive holding fully vested property subsequently agrees to subject that property to vesting restrictions, neither the imposition of such vesting restrictions nor the ultimate lapse of such vesting restrictions results in a "transfer" of property for purposes of Code §83, and hence the executive does not recognize compensation income as a result of the imposition or lapse of such "subsequently imposed" vesting restrictions. A 2001 private ruling applies this reasoning to conclude that where such a "subsequently imposed" vesting restriction lapses upon a change of control, the executive is not deemed to receive any payment in the nature of compensation for purposes of Code §280G.[40]

¶1505.3.8 Agreement Violating Securities Laws

Certain payments that violate a generally enforced federal or state securities law or regulation may be treated as parachute payments without regard to whether the payments are contingent on a change in ownership or control or whether the present value of the payments is at least three times the recipient's base amount. Under the proposed regulations, a violation is presumed not to exist unless the existence of the violation has been determined or admitted in a non-tax civil, criminal, or administrative action. In addition, violations that are merely technical or are not materially prejudicial to shareholders are ignored.[41]

¶1505.3.9 Employment Termination Not Required

A payment "*may*" be covered "even if the employment of the [executive] is not voluntarily or involuntarily terminated." If a contract provides for payments on a change, then "[t]he payments are contingent on the change, even if the [executive] continues in the employ of the corporation."[42]

[39] IRS Letter Ruling 200110013 (11/30/00).
[40] IRS Letter Ruling 200212005 (11/8/01).
[41] 1989 and 2002 Prop. Reg. §1.280G-1 Q&A 37.
[42] H.R. Conf. Rep. No. 861, 100th Cong., 2d Sess. 851 (1984) (hereinafter "1984 Conference Report"); see 1989 and 2002 Prop. Reg. §1.280G-1 Q&A 22(d).

¶1505.4   *Reduction for Reasonable Compensation*

The amount of a "parachute payment" is reduced by the amount that constitutes "reasonable compensation" to the recipient under certain circumstances.

¶1505.4.1   Compensation for Future Services

The amount of a "parachute payment" is reduced by the portion of the payment that the recipient establishes "by clear and convincing evidence" is "reasonable compensation for personal services to be rendered *on or after*" the change in control date.[43]

EXAMPLE 1

Executive A, who is a "disqualified individual," receives a $400,000 payment that is contingent on a change in T's control. A establishes that $150,000 of the payment is reasonable compensation for *future* services. A's base amount is $100,000.

A has received no excess parachute payment because A's $250,000 net parachute payment ($400,000 payment less $150,000 reasonable compensation) is less than three times his $100,000 base amount.

¶1505.4.2   Compensation for Past Services

In computing the amount of an "excess parachute payment," the recipient's parachute payment is reduced by the *greater* of:

(1)   the recipient's base amount,[44] or
(2)   the portion of the parachute payment that the recipient establishes "by clear and convincing evidence" is "reasonable compensation for personal services actually rendered *before*" the change in control date.[45]

EXAMPLE 2

Same as Example 1, except that A establishes that $150,000 of the $400,000 payment is reasonable compensation for *past* rather than *future* services.

---

[43] Code §280G(b)(4)(A) (emphasis added).
[44] Where there are multiple parachute payments (e.g., one at the change and another two years later), the base amount is allocated among the multiple parachute payments based on their relative present values.
[45] Code §280G(b)(4)(B) (emphasis added).

A has received a $250,000 excess parachute payment (rather than $0, as above), because:

(a)   the $400,000 parachute payment (which is *not* reduced by reasonable compensation for *past* services) exceeds three times the executive's $100,000 base amount:

Parachute payment	$400,000
Less: 3 times base amount	(300,000)
Net amount	$100,000

and

(b)   the parachute payment exceeds by $250,000 the greater of the executive's base amount ($100,000) and the portion of the parachute payment attributable to reasonable compensation for past services ($150,000):

Parachute payment	$400,000
Less: greater of base amount or reasonable compensation	(150,000)
Excess parachute payment	$250,000

¶1505.4.3   Determination of Reasonable Compensation

The legislative history, the proposed regulations, and private rulings furnish the following interpretive guidance:

(1)   If parachute payments "are not significantly greater than amounts of compensation . . . paid to the . . . individual in prior years or customarily paid to similarly situated employees by the employer or by comparable employers," these facts will "normally" serve as clear and convincing evidence of reasonable compensation.[46]
(2)   "[O]nly in rare cases, if any, will any portion of a parachute payment be treated as reasonable compensation in response to an argument that the executive was undercompensated [in earlier years]."[47]

[46] 1986 Senate Report at 919-920; 1989 and 2002 Prop. Reg. §1.280G-1 Q&A 42.
[47] 1984 Blue Book at 205.

(3)   Severance payments (and damages for failure to make severance payments) are not treated as reasonable compensation.[48]

(4)   Payments made under certain non-discriminatory employee benefit programs generally are considered to be reasonable compensation.[49]

(5)   An executive's covenant not to compete can constitute personal services actually rendered in an amount equal to the FV of the covenant,[50] so long as the non-compete agreement "substantially constrain[s]" the recipient's ability to perform services and there is a "reasonable likelihood" that the agreement will be enforced.[51]

(6)   T's payments to an executive as damages for breach of an employment contract may be treated as reasonable compensation for future services if:

(a)   the contract was not entered into, amended, or renewed in contemplation of the change,

(b)   compensation under the contract is reasonable,

(c)   the damages do not exceed the present value of the compensation the executive would have received if employment had continued,

(d)   the damages are received because the executive offered to provide services and the employer rejected the offer, and

(e)   the damages are reduced by mitigation (e.g., by the executive's earned income during the remainder of the period the contract would have been in effect).[52]

¶1505.5   Additional Important Definitions and Rules

¶1505.5.1   Identity of Payor

Payments may be treated as parachute payments if paid "directly or indirectly" by the corporation with respect to which a change in ownership has occurred, by the person acquiring ownership of the corporation, or by any person whose relationship to such corporation or other person is such as to require attribution of stock ownership between the parties under Code §318, i.e., generally a 50%-by-value test.

---

[48] 1986 Senate Report at 917; 1989 and 2002 Prop. Reg. §1.280G-1 Q&A 44.

[49] 1989 and 2002 Prop. Reg. §1.280G-1 Q&A 41.

[50] 1984 Blue Book at 204; 2002 Prop. Reg. §1.280G-1 Q&A 42(b); IRS Letter Ruling 200110025 (12/8/00).

[51] 2002 Prop. Reg. §1.280G-1 Q&A 42(b).

[52] 1989 and 2002 Prop. Reg. §1.280G-1 Q&A 42. The preamble to the proposed regulations states that "The proposed regulations do not provide a rule concerning the method of establishing mitigation of damages in other situations, such as where the disqualified individual does not accept alternative employment during the remainder of the contract term or where the individual and the corporation considered mitigation in determining the amount of a lump-sum settlement agreement because IRS is concerned about the administrability of such a rule. Accordingly, IRS solicits comment on how a rule that would allow damages to be treated as mitigated in such cases could be administered." The 2002 proposed regulations provide no additional guidance on this issue.

¶1505.5.2   Persons Covered: Disqualified Individuals

The rules cover payments to (or for the benefit of) any individual (or any personal service corporation or "similar" entity) who is, with respect to T, *both*:

(1)   an employee or independent contractor and
(2)   an officer, shareholder, or highly compensated individual.

For purposes of clause (2), an individual's status as a shareholder is disregarded unless the individual owns (directly or by application of Code §318's constructive ownership rules) more than a threshold amount of T's stock. Under the 1989 proposed regulations, the threshold is stock having a value equal to the *lesser* of $1 million or 1% of the total value of T's stock. Under the 2002 proposed regulations, only the 1% of total value test applies. Accordingly, a T employee who is neither a T officer nor "highly compensated" by T and who owns (directly and by attribution) 1% or less (by value) of T's stock is not treated as a disqualified individual with respect to T.[53] A "highly compensated individual" means someone whose annual compensation equals or exceeds a threshold amount ($75,000 under the 1989 proposed regulations and $90,000, adjusted by an inflation factor for years after 2002, under the 2002 proposed regulations) and who is among:

(1)   the highest-paid 1% of individuals performing services for T's affiliated group, or
(2)   if less, the highest-paid 250 employees of T's affiliated group.[54]

However, the rules do not cover a non-employee of T who performs services in the ordinary course of his business for a significant number of clients unrelated to T, such as brokerage, legal, or investment banking services.[55]

An individual is covered if he has the status of a "disqualified individual" at any time during the "disqualified individual determination period." Under the 1989 proposed regulations, this period is the portion of T's year (either calendar or fiscal at T's election) ending on the date of the change *plus* the immediately preceding twelve-month period. Under the 2002 proposed regulations, the determination period is the twelve-month period ending on the date of the change.[56]

---

[53] Code §280G(c); 1989 and 2002 Prop. Reg. §1.280G-1 Q&A 17. Under Code §318's constructive ownership rules, stock ownership includes ownership through the deemed exercise of a stock option, other than an option the exercisability of which, at the time of the ownership change, remains subject to a substantial condition precedent. 2002 Prop. Reg. §1.280G-1 Q&A 17 example (1); IRS Letter Rulings 200036024-200036027, 200036031, 200036032, 200036037 (6/7/00), citing Rev. Rul. 89-64, 1989-1 C.B. 91.

[54] Code §280G(c) and Code §280G(d)(5); 1989 and 2002 Prop. Reg. §1.280G-1 Q&A 19.

[55] 1989 and 2002 Prop. Reg. §1.280G-1 Q&A 19(b).

[56] 1989 and 2002 Prop. Reg. §1.280G-1 Q&A 20.

¶1505.5.3   Definition of Base Amount

In general, an individual's base amount is the average annual compensation which T paid and the individual included in his gross income (including income from the receipt of (a) property, such as OI recognized on the exercise of a stock option, and (b) payments of previously deferred compensation) for the individual's most recent five taxable years ending before the change. If an individual has been a service provider to T for less than five full years, this calculation is made for the portion of such five-year period during which the individual was an employee of, or independent contractor for, T, with the individual's compensation for any partial year annualized except for a payment, like a sign-on bonus, that will not be regularly repeated.[57]

Thus, an individual's base amount is calculated based on federal income tax principles so that, for example, deferred compensation is included when paid rather than when earned, the income from an NQO is included when the NQO is exercised (where the stock is then vested or, where the stock is subject to an SRF, the individual makes a Code §83(b) election), or when the post-exercise SRF expires (where the stock is subject to a post-exercise SRF and the individual makes no Code §83(b) election), and a payment in property subject to an SRF is included at the time of receipt where the individual makes a Code §83(b) election and at vesting where he makes no Code §83(b) election.

EXAMPLE 1

A change in T's control occurs on 1/15 year 2. T paid a bonus to executive A on 12/15 year 1 in anticipation of the change in control.

This bonus is included in A's year 1 income, and hence increases A's base amount (because A was paid in year 1, i.e., a year ending before the change). Assuming the payment is found to be contingent on a change in T's control, it would presumably be a parachute payment but (a) would be excluded from A's parachute payment amount if A could prove that it was "reasonable compensation" for services to be rendered after the change (see ¶¶1505.1(1)(d)(i) and 1505.4.1) and (b) would be a reasonable compensation subtraction from A's excess parachute payment (if greater than A's base amount) and A could prove that it was "reasonable compensation" for *past* services (see ¶¶1505.1(3)(b) and 1505.4.2).

¶1505.5.4   Deferred Payment

Where some or all of a disqualified individual's parachute payments are to be made after the date of the change in control, the determination whether such

---

[57] 1989 and 2002 Prop. Reg. §1.280G-1 Q&A 34.

individual's aggregate parachute payments equal or exceed three times such individual's base amount is made based on the future payments' present value as of the date of the change. The present value of such future payments is calculated using a discount rate equal to 120% of the AFR in effect as of the date of the change (unless the contract providing for the payment specifies use of the AFR in effect as of the date the contract was entered into). The 2002 proposed regulations also direct use of reasonable actuarial assumptions.[58]

If the present value of an individual's parachute payments equals or exceeds the three-times-base-amount threshold, Code §4999's 20% excise tax applies to the full excess parachute payment (*without* any discounting of the deferred payments). However, the excise tax is payable only as each payment is paid or accrued.

EXAMPLE 2

T enters into an agreement with executive A calling for a parachute payment of $1 million payable three years after any change in T's control. A's base amount is $250,000. A change of T's control occurs on 6/1 year 1, at which time the short-term federal rate is 5% (compounded semiannually). A provides no services to T after the change in control.

The present value on 6/1 year 1 of the $1 million future payment (discounted at 6%—i.e., 5% × 120%, compounded semiannually) is $837,484. The parachute payment's present value exceeds three times A's base amount. Accordingly, an excise tax of $150,000 (($1 million − $250,000) × 20%) is imposed on A for his taxable year ending 12/31 year 4, the year in which the $1 million parachute payment is includible in his income (unless A can establish that more than $250,000 of the parachute payment was reasonable compensation for services rendered before the change).

¶1505.5.5   Definition of Payment: Options and Substantial Risks of Forfeiture

Under the proposed regulations, a parachute payment is generally considered to be made when cash or other property is "transferred" and becomes "substantially vested," as these terms are defined under Reg. §1.83-3. The amount of the payment is generally equal to the FV of the property at the time the property becomes substantially vested over the amount (if any) paid for the property.

The proposed regulations diverge from the normal Code §83 rules in two respects:

---

[58]Code §280G(d)(4); 1989 and 2002 Prop. Reg. §1.280G-1 Q&A 31 and 32. The 2002 proposed regulations state that the present value of an obligation to provide health care over a period of years should be determined in accordance with GAAP and can be measured by projecting the cost of premiums for purchased health care insurance, even if no insurance is actually purchased. 2002 Prop. Reg. §1.280G-1 Q&A 31(b)(2).

First, a stock option is treated as "transferred" not later than the time it becomes substantially vested, provided it has an "ascertainable value" at such time (as opposed to the more narrow "readily ascertainable value" standard contained in the Code §83 rules). It is likely that options will be treated as having an ascertainable value in all but rare cases.[59] (The 1989 proposed regulations reserve on the treatment of incentive stock options (ISOs), but the 2002 proposed regulations sensibly treat ISOs in the same manner as non-qualified stock options.) Thus, where an executive receives a stock option as a parachute payment, the payment is taken into account under the golden parachute rules and its FV is measured when the option vests rather than when it is exercised.

Second, an election made under Code §83(b) is ignored for purposes of the golden parachute rules, and hence where an executive receives property subject to an SRF—either property issued prior to the change in control that vests as a result of the change or property issued as a result of the change that vests based on post-change contingencies—the parachute payment attributable to such property transfer is generally taken into account and is measured when the SRF expires, even if a Code §83(b) election is made.

Since a parachute payment is not deemed to occur until property becomes "substantially vested," if at the time of T's change of control a T executive receives property which would have constituted a parachute payment if vested, but such property is subject to an SRF, the amount of the parachute payment may be substantially increased by post-change appreciation in the property. Under the proposed regulations, post-change appreciation cannot be removed from the parachute calculation by making a Code §83(b) election.

EXAMPLE 3

Contingent on a change in T's ownership, executive A is allowed to purchase for $10 per share 100,000 T shares subject to an SRF. When the time of purchase, the FV of T stock (ignoring the SRF) is $15 per share. When time the SRF lapses several years later, the FV of T stock is $100 per share. At the time the SRF lapses, T is treated as receiving a $9 million parachute payment ($10 million FV of T stock less $1 million purchase price), reduced by the portion of such payment that is established by clear and convincing evidence to constitute reasonable compensation for services rendered by A after the change.

---

[59] Under the proposed regulations, relevant factors in determining the value of an option include (but are not limited to) the spread between the option's exercise price and value of the property, the volatility of the property, and the term of the option. 1989 and 2002 Prop. Reg. §1.280G-1 Q&A 13(a). The 2002 proposed regulations delegate authority to IRS to publish guidance on other methods of valuation. Rev. Proc. 2002-45, 2002-2 C.B. 40 (modifying Rev. Proc. 2002-13, 2002-1 C.B. 637), describes several valuation methods, including a safe harbor approach modeled after the Black-Scholes valuation method, and also approves of any valuation method that is consistent with GAAP and takes into account the factors set forth in the proposed regulations.

¶1505.5.6   Future Uncertain Parachute Payment

If a person receives a payment contingent on a change and also is (or may become) entitled to receive another payment contingent on the same change, the determination of whether or to what extent the first payment is an excess parachute payment will depend on the present value of the second payment. Where the fact, time, or amount of the second payment is uncertain, the present value of the second payment is unknown at the time of the ownership change, and may be difficult to estimate. The 1989 and 2002 proposed regulations differ on how to value future contingent parachute payments (although, as described below, both proposed regulations call for the golden parachute tax calculations to be redone where the actual second payment, when made, differs from the estimate used at the time of the first payment).

The 1989 proposed regulations state that "a reasonable estimate of the time and amount of the future payment shall be made, and the present value of the payment will be determined on the basis of this estimate." For this purpose, "an uncertain future event or condition that may *reduce* the present value of a payment will be taken into account only if the possibility of the occurrence of the event or condition can be determined on the basis of generally accepted actuarial principles or can be otherwise estimated with reasonable accuracy" (emphasis added). Otherwise, the contingency will be ignored and the full amount of the potential future payment will be taken into account (less present value discounting).

Although the language of the 1989 proposed regulations is opaque, it appears that the drafters may have intended to distinguish between (1) conditions precedent to receiving or determining the amount of a payment and (2) conditions subsequent, which might reduce the amount of the payment to which the individual is otherwise entitled. The proposed regulations can be read as applying a reasonable, good-faith valuation standard to the (1) category and a more strict actuarial or reasonable accuracy standard to the (2) category. Thus, an example in the 1989 proposed regulations states that, in the case of a payment that will be made only if the executive's employment is terminated within a specified period (i.e., a (1) category condition precedent), a reasonable estimate should be made of the possibility that the executive's employment will be terminated. The example then states that the reasonable estimate is a 50% probability the executive will be terminated and, accordingly, includes 50% of the potential payment in applying the golden parachute rules. Conversely, another example deals with a payment to which an executive is entitled, but which will be reduced if the executive earns compensation from another employer (i.e., a (2) category condition subsequent) and concludes that inability to determine "with reasonable accuracy" the likelihood that this condition will occur results in the condition being ignored and the full potential payment being taken into account.[60]

The 2002 proposed regulations apply a single more-likely-than-not standard to all parachute payments that are contingent on an uncertain future event or condition. If, based on a reasonable estimate, there is a 50% or greater probability

---

[60] 1989 Prop. Reg. §1.280G-1 Q&A 34(a) and (c) examples (1) and (2).

that the payment will be made, it is assumed that the full amount of the payment will be made and the present value of such assumed full payment is taken into account for purposes of (1) determining whether the individual's aggregate parachute payments reach the three-times-base-amount threshold and (2) allocating the individual's base amount among different parachute payments. On the other hand, if it is reasonably estimated that there is less than a 50% probability that the payment will be made, the payment is disregarded unless and until made.[61] The 2002 proposed regulations do not address how to treat future parachute payments that are contingent in timing or amount. Presumably, a reasonable estimate of the time and amount of payment should be made.

The 1989 and 2002 proposed regulations state that if the actual payments turn out to be different than those estimated, the original parachute calculation must be redone to reflect the actual payments. This will involve a recalculation of the three-times-base-amount threshold and, if the threshold is exceeded, a reallocation of the base amount among the various parachute payments. This recalculation and reallocation may increase or decrease the portion of the earlier payment that is treated as an excess parachute payment, resulting in the need to file an amended return and either pay additional tax or claim a refund for the earlier year (assuming that the statute of limitations has not expired).[62] The 2002 proposed regulations, however, do not require such a recalculation and reallocation if payments to a disqualified individual reached the three-times-base-amount threshold without regard to the contingent future payment and no base amount was previously allocated to such payment.[63]

¶1505.5.7 Withholding

To the extent the 20% excise tax applies to an excess parachute payment which constitutes "wages," the amount required to be withheld is increased by the amount of the 20% excise tax. Code §4999(c)(1).

¶1505.6 Application to Private Company and Friendly Acquisition

¶1505.6.1 Exemption for Small or Privately Held Company

The golden parachute provisions do *not* apply to any payment with respect to a corporation (T) that, immediately before the change, *either*:

---

[61] 2002 Prop. Reg. §1.280G-1 Q&A 33(a) and (c) examples (1) and (2).

[62] 1989 and 2002 Prop. Reg. §1.280G-1 Q&A 33; 1984 Blue Book at 205. For an example of the reallocation of base amount among various parachute payments, see IRS Letter Rulings 200046005, 200046006, 200046007 (7/28/00).

[63] 2002 Prop. Reg. §1.280G-1 Q&A 33(b) and (c) example (3).

(a) could have qualified to be an S corporation (determined without regard to the S corporation prohibition on non-resident alien shareholders), *or*

(b) was not publicly traded, provided (i) the payment was approved by a vote of shareholders who owned, immediately before the change, more than 75% (by voting power) of T's stock and (ii) there was "adequate disclosure to shareholders of all material facts."[64]

EXAMPLE 1

T is a subchapter C corporation with one class of stock outstanding. T's shares are held by 30 individual shareholders, and T meets the other qualifications for electing S status as set forth in Code §1361(d). See ¶1102.

Because T could have qualified as an S corporation, T is exempt from the golden parachute provisions.

EXAMPLE 2

Same as Example 1, except that T's stock is held by 76 unrelated individuals, *or* one of T's shareholders is a partnership or corporation, *or* T has more than one class of stock outstanding, but T's stock is not publicly traded. T, immediately before a change in control, prepares and submits to its shareholders a plan for making payments to its executives contingent upon a change in control. More than 75% of T's shareholders (by vote) approve the plan on the basis of adequate disclosure by T.

T and its executives are exempt from the golden parachute rules even though T could not have qualified as an S corporation.

The 1989 and 2002 proposed regulations state that the "adequate disclosure" must be to "all persons entitled to vote" and that the shareholder vote "must determine the right of the disqualified individual to receive the payment, or in the case of a payment made before the vote, the right of the disqualified individual to retain the payment."[65]

In practice, it may be difficult to take advantage of the shareholder approval exception. A shareholder vote at the time T and its executive enter into a contract to make a payment (which turns out to be a parachute payment) may not qualify for the exception because of changes in the identity of T's shareholders between the time the contract is entered into and the subsequent ownership change, or

---

[64] Code §280G(b)(5). The 2002 proposed regulations specify that, "[f]or each disqualified individual, material facts that must be disclosed include the total amount of payments that would be parachute payments [absent shareholder approval] and a brief description of each payment (e.g., accelerated vesting of options, bonus, or salary)." 2002 Prop. Reg. §1.280G-1 Q&A 7(c).

[65] 1989 and 2002 Prop. Reg. §1.280G-1 Q&A 7.

because subsequent changes in other parachute benefits being provided to executives render the prior disclosure "inadequate." Although these risks could be avoided by holding a shareholder vote at the time of the change, the executive may be unwilling to expose his right to receive or retain the payment to a later shareholder vote.

EXAMPLE 3

On 1/1 year 1, the shareholders of non-publicly traded corporation T unanimously vote to authorize and approve T's entry into an employment contract with A, which contract provides for a $1 million payment to A in the event of a change in T's ownership. The vote occurs after full disclosure of the provisions of A's employment contract. The contract is entered into shortly after the vote.

On 3/1 year 1, several T shareholders sell a total of 30% of T's voting stock. On 6/1 year 1, a change in T's ownership occurs and T makes the payment to A.

The shareholder approval exception does not apply since the vote was not by the persons who owned "immediately before the change" more than 75% of T's voting power.

EXAMPLE 4

Same as Example 3, except that after 1/1 year 1 and before 6/1 year 1 some, but less than 25%, of T's voting shares changed hands.

It appears that the shareholder approval exception applies. There is, however, some risk IRS may take the position that (1) there was not adequate disclosure of all material facts to any of T's shareholders before the 1/1 year 1 vote in that there was no disclosure of the change that would occur on 6/1 year 1 (even though T did not on 1/1 year 1 know that this change would occur) and (2) there was no disclosure to the new T shareholders, and hence there was not adequate disclosure to "all persons entitled to vote," i.e., T's shareholders "immediately before the change."

EXAMPLE 5

Same as Example 4, except that on 5/1 year 1 T, without seeking shareholder approval or making any disclosure to shareholders, agreed to accelerate vesting of a significant number of A's stock options in the event of a change in T's ownership.

It appears that the shareholder approval exception does not apply to either payment to A. With respect to the payment resulting from accelerated vesting of A's stock options, no shareholder approval occurred. With respect to the $1 million original payment, T's failure to disclose the stock option acceleration at the time of the shareholder approval would appear to vitiate the adequate disclosure requirement, even though the stock option cancellation was not agreed upon until four months after the shareholder vote on the $1 million payment.

EXAMPLE 6

Same as Example 5, except that T disclosed to shareholders prior to the 1/1 year 1 shareholder vote that T would accelerate vesting of A's stock options in the event of a change.

It appears that the shareholder approval exception applies with respect to the $1 million original payment. There is, however, some risk IRS may take the position that there was not adequate disclosure because T did not disclose the change that would occur on 6/1 year 1 (even though T did not know on 1/1 year 1 that this change would occur).

EXAMPLE 7

Same as Example 3, except that on 6/1 year 1 T's shareholders voted to approve the payment to A, although A was entitled to receive and retain the payment without regard to the outcome of the vote.

Under the 1989 and 2002 proposed regulations, the result is the same as in Example 3. The second vote does not satisfy the shareholder approval exception since the vote did not determine A's right to receive or retain the payment (i.e., A's right to receive and retain the payment was not contingent on satisfaction of the 75% shareholder vote requirement).

EXAMPLE 8

Same as Example 3, except that A's employment contract states that A will be entitled to the payment only if it is approved by a vote of more than 75% of T's shareholders determined immediately before any change in ownership. In addition, on 1/1 year 1 T's shareholders enter into a voting trust or voting agreement requiring the shareholders and their transferees to vote in favor of the payment to A in any subsequent vote. On 6/1 year 1, immediately before the change in ownership, T's shareholders unanimously vote in favor of making the payment.

We believe the shareholder approval exception should apply, although this conclusion is not free from doubt.

EXAMPLE 9

Same as Example 8, except that prior to the 6/1 year 1 change T issues a class of publicly traded common stock with 24% of T's voting power. Because some T stock is publicly traded immediately before the change, the shareholder approval exception does not apply, even though (1) the payment was unanimously approved by T's shareholders on 1/1 year 1 when no T stock was publicly traded, (2) the approving shareholders continued to own more than 75% of T's voting stock, and (3) on 6/1 year 1, immediately before the change in ownership, more than 75% of T's voting stock voted in favor.

Several other points should be noted in connection with the 75% shareholder vote rule:

(1)   The members of an affiliated group are treated as a single corporation. Accordingly, the exception is not available if the stock of any member of the group is publicly traded. If the exception is available, the 75% approval presumably should be given by the shareholders of the parent corporation. It is unclear, however, how the rules operate where a portion of the stock of one or more of the subsidiary members of the group is owned by unrelated persons.

(2)   In determining whether any T stock is publicly traded, T preferred stock described in Code §1504(a)(4) is ignored, provided that the payment to disqualified individuals "does not adversely affect the redemption and liquidation rights of any shareholder owning such stock."[66]

(3)   Where T stock is owned (directly or indirectly) by a person other than an individual, and the T stock comprises at least one-third (by FV) of such entity shareholder's assets, the vote must be made by more than 75% of voting power of the entity shareholder's owners who are entitled to vote on the entity shareholder's management issues, rather than by the entity shareholder itself, unless the entity shareholder owns 1% or less of T's stock (by value).[67] Moreover, if such an entity shareholder of T is publicly traded, the shareholder approval exception is unavailable to T.

(4)   In applying the 75%-shareholder-approval rule, T stock owned by persons receiving payments that would (but for the shareholder approval rule) be parachute payments (or by certain related persons) is ignored,

---

[66] Code §280G(b)(5)(A).

[67] Several provisions of the 2002 proposed regulations specify that asset FV is measured based on gross FV, rather than FV net of liabilities. The look-through rule for entity shareholders lacks such specification. Presumably, this was an oversight. 2002 Prop. Reg. §1.280G-1 Q&A 7(b)(3); cf. 2002 Prop. Reg. §1.280G-1 Q&A 6(c), 2002 Prop. Reg. §1.280G-1 Q&A 29(a).

unless this rule would have the effect of ignoring all of T's outstanding stock.

(5) If T obtains 75% shareholder approval for a portion of a payment, such portion is exempt from the golden parachute rules. For example, if executive A, with a $300,000 base amount, is to receive $1 million of payments which would (absent 75% shareholder approval) constitute parachute payments, but T obtained 75% shareholder approval for payments aggregating $101,000, the unapproved payments ($899,000) would fall short of the three-times-base-amount threshold and hence the golden parachute sanctions would be avoided.

(6) The 75% shareholder vote can be either a single vote covering the payments to a group of disqualified individuals or a series of separate votes covering payments to each disqualified individual.

(7) The 75% shareholder vote must be separate from any non-tax motivated shareholder vote to approve the transaction which causes the change in T's control. The 2002 proposed regulations state that the 75% shareholder approval exception does not apply "if [any non-tax motivated shareholder] approval of the change in [T's] ownership or control is contingent on [the 75% shareholder] approval of any payment [to a T executive]."[68] Apparently this means that where the non-tax motivated shareholder resolution to approve the merger, sale of assets, or other change of control transaction states that the non-tax motivated shareholder vote approving the change in control transaction will be nullified if there is not also a 75% vote to approve the parachute payment to the T executives, the 75% shareholder vote on the parachute payment does not achieve the desired goal of creating an exemption from the Code §280G rules. Although not wholly clear, it appears the 75% shareholder approval exception should be available if, as is often the case, the documents—e.g., P's tender offer for T's stock or the P-T merger agreement—allow P to decline to complete the transaction if T's shareholders fail to satisfy the 75% shareholder approval exception (e.g., a contractual provision stating that obtaining T shareholder approval of parachute payments is a condition to P's obligation to close on its acquisition of T).

(8) The 2002 proposed regulations grant limited relief from the statutory rule identifying the group of shareholders eligible to vote as those owning T voting stock "immediately before the change." Under the 2002 proposed regulations, the determination of eligible voters may be "based on the shareholders of record at the time of any shareholder vote taken in connection with a transaction or event giving rise to such change in ownership or control and within the three-month period ending on the date of the change in ownership or control, provided the adequate disclosure requirements" are met.[69]

(9) The statute requires approval "by a vote of the persons who owned . . . more than 75% of" T's voting power. Although not explicit, it appears

---

[68] 2002 Prop. Reg. §1.280G-1 Q&A 7(b)(1).
[69] 2002 Prop. Reg. §1.280G-1 Q&A 7(b)(2).

that shareholder action by written consent would satisfy this requirement where, under state law and T's charter, written consent is as effective as a vote, so long as 100% of T's shareholders so consent or, where state law allows action by consent of less than all shareholders, more than 75% consent.

(10) A 2001 private ruling applied the shareholder approval rules to a corporation in bankruptcy, holding that (a) because the corporation's stock (which had traded on a stock exchange) was de-listed after the corporation filed for bankruptcy, the stock was no longer publicly traded and (b) bankruptcy court approval of the reorganization plan (providing for parachute payments) constituted "shareholder" approval "because the creditors' committee and the bankruptcy judge represented the shareholders' interests and the shareholders were not otherwise eligible to approve the payments."[70]

¶1505.6.2 Friendly Acquisition

According to the 1984 Senate Report, the golden parachute provisions were enacted principally to deal with contested takeovers.[71] In such an unfriendly takeover, T may enter into a contract to pay its executives substantial amounts in anticipation of unfriendly P winning control of T. Congress obviously sought to discourage such payments by the golden parachute legislation.

However, the statute as drafted goes further, covering (except to the extent exempted as described in ¶1505.6.1 or treated as reasonable compensation for services rendered after the change in ownership):

(a) Payments arising out of a friendly takeover of T by P in a negotiated transaction where payments to T's executives (by T or P) are contingent on the takeover being consummated.

(b) Payments to T's executives which are not pursuant to pre-existing contracts between T and its executives, but are pursuant to new contracts with T's executives requested by P, entered into before the change in ownership, and designed to encourage T's executives to remain in T's employ after completion of the takeover.

In addition, the 1984 Blue Book states that Congress sought to discourage golden parachute agreements in the context of friendly takeovers because "such arrangements tended to encourage the executives and other key personnel involved to favor a proposed takeover that might not be in the best interests of the shareholders or others."[72]

---

[70] IRS Letter Ruling 200212013 (12/17/01).
[71] S. Rep. No. 169, 98th Cong., 2d Sess. 195 (1984).
[72] 1984 Blue Book at 199.

¶1505.7   *Economic Effect of Code §280G*

Golden parachute contracts may impose a substantial cost (the amount paid to T's executives) on P when P acquires T in an unfriendly or even a friendly takeover. Hence, where P knows about the contracts, P may well pay less to T's shareholders than if there were no golden parachute contracts.

To the extent T makes an "excess parachute payment," Code §280G compounds the problem. By denying T a tax deduction for the payments, T's after-tax cost for the payments is greater, and hence—where P knows about the contracts and their tax effect—P will pay even less to T's shareholders.

On the other hand, if the golden parachute rules actually discourage a generous golden parachute contract (as Congress contemplated they would), and as a result P is willing to pay more for T, T's shareholders benefit.

EXAMPLE 1

T, a publicly held company, is a takeover candidate. T has 1 million shares of stock outstanding, trading at $75.00 a share (aggregate $75 million). T's net assets have an FV of $100 million. T's key officer, B, becomes concerned about his future and demands that T agree to pay him $1 million (grossed-up for the 20% golden parachute excise tax and federal and state income taxes (at an assumed 50% rate) as well as golden parachute excise taxes on the gross-up payment) if T is taken over and B loses his job. B's base amount is $300,000. Accordingly, T and B enter into a golden parachute agreement pursuant to which B is to receive $1,466,667 in the event B loses his job as a result of a takeover. B will thus receive $1,000,000 net of the additional taxes resulting from application of the golden parachute rules [$1,466,667 payment to B − (($1,466,667 payment to B − $300,000 base amount) × 20%) − ($466,667 gross-up payment × 50%) = $1,000,000].

P wishes to acquire 100% of T's stock. P is prepared to pay $100 million ($100 per share), a $25 million premium over the $75 million aggregate price at which T's shares are trading. Upon learning of the golden parachute agreement between T and B, P reduces the amount it is willing to pay by $1,346,667, the after-tax cost to T of a $1,466,667 payment to B under the golden parachute agreement ($1,466,667 payment less $120,000 tax savings (40% × $300,000)). Accordingly, P offers T's shareholders only $98.65 a share (($100 million − $1,346,667) ÷ 1 million shares).

EXAMPLE 2

Same as Example 1, except that T is privately held and more than 75% of T's shareholders (by voting power), after adequate disclosure, approve the parachute agreement with B.

> T can satisfy B's request with an agreement to pay B $1 million rather than $1,466,667 (because B is not subject to a 20% excise tax on such payment). Further, the after-tax cost of the parachute payment to P following a takeover is only $600,000 (assuming no "unreasonable compensation" problem and a 40% federal and state corporate rate), because the $1 million payment would be fully deductible. Accordingly, P is willing to offer each T shareholder $99.40 per share (($100 million − $600,000) ÷ 1 million shares).

As these two examples demonstrate, where the golden parachute tax provisions do not discourage T from adopting a golden parachute for B, the golden parachute tax can have the unfortunate effect of *increasing* the cost to T, and hence *reducing* the yield per share to T's shareholders, i.e., from $99.40 per share in Example 2 (where T was able to opt out of the golden parachute tax) to $98.65 per share in Example 1 (where public T was not allowed to opt out of the tax).

¶1506   CODE §162(m)—$1 MILLION DEDUCTION LIMIT ON EXECUTIVE COMPENSATION

The 1993 Tax Act added to the Code a controversial provision, Code §162(m), disallowing a corporation's federal income tax deduction for compensation to certain executives in excess of $1 million during a corporate taxable year.

On 12/20/93, IRS published Prop. Reg. §1.162-27 interpreting Code §162(m) and adding a number of important transitional rules. IRS clarified many ambiguous and troubling aspects of the 12/20/93 proposed regulations in amendments to the proposed regulations released on 12/2/94. On 12/20/95, IRS issued final Reg. §1.162-27. With the exception of some further clarifications, the final regulations largely adopt the 1993 proposed regulations, as they had been amended in 1994.

The $1 million deduction limit covers all types of compensation, including cash, property, and the spread on the exercise of options. However, there are a series of important exceptions, including:

- compensation paid by a privately held corporation,
- compensation paid by a publicly held corporation under a plan or agreement that existed before the corporation was publicly held,
- compensation paid to an executive other than one of the corporation's top five officers,
- performance-based compensation that is keyed to a pre-established, objective, non-discretionary formula and also meets certain shareholder and outside director approval requirements,
- compensation covered by a pre-2/18/93 binding contract that has not been materially modified, and
- compensation that is not paid for services performed as an employee.

A publicly traded corporation is generally left with two choices. It can either:

- forgo a federal income tax deduction for compensation during a taxable year in excess of $1 million to any one of its top five officers, or
- change its compensation practices so that a covered executive's current salary and discretionary (non-formula) bonuses do not exceed $1 million in any year, and any compensation in excess of $1 million either (1) consists of formula performance-based bonuses, stock appreciation rights ("SARs"), restricted stock, or stock options structured to comply with the requirements of the performance-based compensation exception or (2) is deferred to a time when the recipient is no longer one of the corporation's top five officers.

A publicly held corporation may have to disclose its choice to shareholders; as part of the SEC's 11/29/93 amendments to the proxy disclosure rules,[1] the SEC announced that a corporation must disclose in its proxy statement its "policy with respect to qualifying compensation paid to its executive officers for deductibility under Code §162(m)."[2]

In contrast, a privately held corporation will generally not have to worry about Code §162(m) until it goes public. Compensation deducted while the corporation is private is not subject to the $1 million deduction limit and, under the regulations, compensation subsequently paid pursuant to a plan or agreement adopted when the corporation was private is generally not subject to the $1 million deduction limit even though payable and deductible after the corporation goes public, so long as paid (or, in the case of restricted property or stock-based compensation, granted) within a specified period after the corporation becomes public. See ¶1506.1.3.

¶1506.1 outlines the $1 million deduction limit, the complex statutory and regulatory exceptions to the deduction limit, and a number of uncertainties and pitfalls. ¶1506.2 discusses the important transitional rules under the regulations that postpone the full application of several burdensome aspects of Code §162(m) as interpreted by the regulations. ¶1506.3 discusses certain special issues in the application of Code §162(m) to publicly traded partnerships and the interaction between Code §83(b) and Code §162(m). ¶1506.4 discusses the application of Code §162(m) in the context of a merger or acquisition. ¶1506.5 offers our conclusions.

¶1506.1   Deduction Limit and Exceptions

¶1506.1.1   Basic Deduction Limit

No corporation can deduct more than $1 million per executive per year for compensation to an executive, unless one of the seven exceptions described in

---

¶1506   [1] The amendments were released to the public on 11/22/93 and were published in the Federal Register and made effective on 11/29/93.
[2] 58 Fed. Reg. 63,010, at 63,011 (1993).

¶¶1506.1.2 through 1506.1.8 applies. Code §162(m) does not eliminate the require-ment that, to be deductible, compensation must qualify as "a reasonable allowance for salaries or other compensation for personal services actually rendered."[3] Thus, even if compensation meets one of the exceptions to the $1 million deduction limit, the compensation is still deductible only to the extent "reasonable."

Compensation for this purpose includes all amounts, whether paid in cash, stock options, the corporation's stock, or other property, and is taken into account for purposes of Code §162(m) in the corporation's taxable year in which such compensation would otherwise be deductible.

- The spread on exercise of a non-qualified option ("NQO") is generally taken into account at exercise.
- The spread in an incentive stock option ("ISO") is generally taken into account when (and only if) the executive makes a "disqualifying disposi-tion" of the stock received on exercise of the ISO.
- Deferred compensation is generally taken into account when paid.[4]
- Restricted stock (i.e., stock subject to vesting[5]) is generally taken into account (a) when transferred to the executive (if the executive chooses to be taxed on the receipt of the stock by making a Code §83(b) election) or (b) at vesting (if the executive chooses to be taxed on the stock at vesting by making no Code §83(b) election).
- Phantom stock is generally taken into account when paid (in cash or un-restricted stock).

The $1 million deduction limit does not cover compensation that is in the form of (1) contributions to or payments from qualified retirement plans or (2) non-taxable fringe benefits.[6]

The $1 million deduction limit is reduced by the amount of any non-deductible golden parachute payments the corporation makes to the executive in the same taxable year.[7] This unwarranted statutory provision unfairly penalizes a corpora-tion twice for excess golden parachute payments and, in our opinion, should be

---

[3] Code §162(a)(1).

[4] See Code §404(a)(5). The law is unclear whether payments of interest in connection with deferred compensation are treated as compensation. If such interest payments are not compensation, they would not be subject to the $1 million deduction limit. A deferred compensation plan often provides that deferred compensation accrues "interest" during the period between the time the compensation is earned and the time the compensation is paid. The Ninth Circuit's 12/5/94 opinion in Albertson's, Inc. v. Commissioner, 42 F.3d 537 (9th Cir. 1994), vacated the court's earlier opinion in the same case which had held that "interest" under a deferred compensation plan is deductible interest under the rules of Code §163 and hence not subject to the timing restrictions of Code §404. In its 12/94 opinion, the Ninth Circuit affirmed the Tax Court's position that "interest" on deferred compensation is deductible, under the rules of Code §404, only when paid, but the Ninth Circuit's opinion was ambiguous as to whether the court regarded such additional amount as "compensation" or "interest." Thus, at least in the Ninth Circuit the law remains unclear as to whether the "interest" portion of a deferred compensation payment is compensation subject to Code §162(m).

[5] In tax parlance, stock subject to an SRF. See Code §83.

[6] Code §162(m)(4)(E).

[7] Code §162(m)(4)(F).

repealed. The regulations, however, merely reiterate this statutory rule without explanation or amelioration.[8]

¶1506.1.2   Exception #1: Privately Held Corporation

The $1 million deduction limit does not cover compensation paid by a privately held corporation.[9]

For this purpose, a corporation is privately held if it has no class of "common equity securities" required to be registered under §12 of the Securities Exchange Act of 1934 (the 1934 Act).[10] A corporation thus is privately held as long as it (1) has no class of common equity securities traded on a national securities exchange and (2) does not have both 500 or more holders of a class of common equity securities and $5 million or more of consolidated assets (based on its balance sheet prepared in accordance with GAAP).[11] A corporation is not publicly held if registration of its equity securities is voluntary, e.g., "if a corporation that otherwise is not required to register its equity securities does so in order to take advantage of other procedures with regard to public offerings of debt securities."[12]

The regulations state that whether a corporation is publicly held or privately held is determined solely by its status on the last day of the corporation's taxable year.[13] A publicly held corporation that ceases to be public before the end of a taxable year is not subject to the $1 million deduction limit for any part of the taxable year. Conversely, a corporation that goes public in the middle of a taxable year is treated as publicly held for the entire year and is subject to the $1 million deduction limit for the entire year. However, the effect of this rule is mitigated by Exception #2 for plans or agreements entered into while a corporation was privately held (described immediately below).

¶1506.1.3   Exception #2: Adoption of Plan or Agreement by Privately Held Corporation

Under the regulations, the $1 million deduction limit does not apply to compensation paid under a "plan or agreement" that "existed" while the corporation

---

[8] Reg. §1.162-27(g).

[9] Code §162(m)(1).

[10] Code §162(m)(2). IRS has ruled privately that neither a limited partnership, the limited partner interests in which are required to be registered under §12 of the 1934 Act (but which is not a publicly traded partnership within the meaning of Code §7704), nor a corporate subsidiary of such limited partnership, is a publicly held corporation for purposes of Code §162(m). IRS Letter Ruling 199915036 (4/16/99).

[11] "Publicly held" and "public" are used in ¶1506 to describe a corporation that is required to be registered under §12 of the 1934 Act and that may not, therefore, rely on Exception #1. "Privately held" and "private" are used to describe a corporation that is not required to be registered under §12 of the 1934 Act and that may, therefore, rely on Exception #1.

[12] H.R. Conf. Rep. No. 213, 103d Cong., 1st Sess. 585 (as reprinted in CCH Stand. Fed. Tax Reports No. 33, 8/5/93) (hereinafter "1993 Conference Report"); see Reg. §1.162-27(c)(1)(i).

[13] Reg. §1.162-27(c)(1)(i).

was privately held, even if the compensation is paid and deductible while the corporation is publicly held, so long as paid/deductible (or in the case of restricted property and stock-based compensation, granted) within a specified period (the "reliance period" described below) after the corporation becomes publicly held. Where a corporation becomes publicly held as a result of an initial public offering (an "IPO"), i.e., a primary or secondary sale of the corporation's stock pursuant to a registration statement filed with the SEC, this section applies only if the plan or agreement was disclosed in the corporation's IPO prospectus in accordance with all applicable securities laws. This disclosure requirement does not apply where a corporation becomes publicly held without an IPO.[14]

A corporation may become publicly held without an IPO where (1) the number of shareholders of a privately held corporation with $5 million or more of assets increases to more than 500 as a result of unregistered primary or secondary sales of stock or (2) a privately held corporation (T) is acquired by a publicly held corporation (P) and T thereby becomes publicly held within the meaning of Reg. §1.162-27(c)(1)(ii), because T becomes part of public P's affiliated group. Exception #2 is clearly intended to apply to situation (1). We believe that Exception #2 also applies to situation (2), although (as discussed below) the form of the acquisition (i.e., whether public P acquires T's stock or T's assets) may affect whether Exception #2 applies.[15]

This welcome exception for arrangements in existence while a corporation is privately held is surprisingly broad. It would exempt from the $1 million deduction limit:

- compensation paid under a plan or agreement that is not performance based,
- compensation paid as a result of an award granted by a public corporation under a plan in existence before the corporation became public so long as the award is made (or in certain cases, as described immediately below, the compensation is paid/deductible) within approximately 4 years after the corporation became public as a result of an IPO (but only within approximately 2 years after the corporation became public without an IPO), and
- compensation paid by a public corporation under a plan in existence before the corporation became public even though the corporation is not legally required to make any awards under the plan.

In this latter respect, the exception for arrangements in existence while a corporation is privately held is much broader than the grandfather rule available to public corporations for pre-2/18/93 binding contracts (discussed in ¶1506.1.6).

However, (a) with respect to an award of restricted property subject to vesting or an award of stock-based compensation, this Exception #2 applies to an award *made during the "reliance period"* and (b) with respect to any other type of compensa-

---

[14] Reg. §1.162-27(f)(1).

[15] To the extent that T's executives do not become covered executives with respect to the P affiliated group after P's acquisition of T, as will often be the case, P and T may rely on Exception #3 and will not need Exception #2. See ¶1506.1.4.2.

tion, this exception applies only to an amount which is *paid/deductible during the reliance period*. The reliance period ends at the earliest of (1) the expiration of the plan or agreement, (2) a material modification to the plan or agreement,[16] (3) the issuance of all stock or other property allocated under the plan, or (4) the first meeting of shareholders at which directors are elected occurring after the close of the third calendar year following the calendar year in which the corporation becomes public as a result of an IPO *or* the first calendar year after the year in which the corporation becomes public without an IPO.[17]

This 2-year/4-year reliance period cut-off substantially narrows the temporal sweep of Exception #2 as compared to the scope described in both Code §162(m)'s legislative history and the original 1993 proposed regulations, neither of which contained any such sunset provision. By contrast, the reliance period in the final regulations terminates, so that additional shareholder approval (and compliance with the performance-based compensation rules) is necessary, after the 2-year/4-year cut-off.

The regulations state that Exception #2 applies to "any remuneration paid pursuant to a compensation plan or arrangement that existed" before the corporation became publicly held.[18] The regulations then state that "this section may be relied upon until the earliest of" the four dates described above.[19] Finally, the regulations state that "this section will apply to [restricted property subject to vesting or to stock-based compensation] . . . if the *grant* occurs before the earliest of" the four dates.[20]

The regulations are somewhat ambiguous on what must happen during the reliance period in order for Exception #2 to apply to compensation other than restricted property and stock-based compensation. Commentators had asked IRS to extend Exception #2 as formulated in the 12/94 proposed regulations to cover other compensation "awarded" during the reliance period, in addition to other compensation paid/deductible during the reliance period, in order to conform the treatment of other compensation to the treatment of restricted property and stock-based compensation under Exception #2. IRS refused, stating in the preamble to the final regulations that there was "not adequate justification for a further expansion" of the prior regulatory transition relief without any explanation of why restricted property and stock-based compensation should be treated differently than other compensation under Exception #2.

Literally read, the final regulations are unclear whether compensation (other than restricted property and stock-based compensation) must be *paid* during or must be *deductible* during the reliance period in order to come within Exception #2. The final regulations first state that "a corporation that was not a publicly held corporation and then becomes a publicly held corporation [is not subject to Code §162(m) with respect to] any remuneration *paid* pursuant to a compensation plan or agreement that existed during the period in which the corporation was

---

[16] For a discussion of "materially modified" see ¶1506.1.6.2.
[17] Reg. §1.162-27(f)(2).
[18] Reg. §1.162-27(f)(1).
[19] Reg. §1.162-27(f)(2).
[20] Reg. §1.162-27(f)(3).

not publicly held" [emphasis added] and then state that this rule "may be relied upon until" expiration of the 2-year/4-year reliance period.

Hence the final regulations imply that the event which must take place during the reliance period (with respect to compensation other than restricted property or stock-based compensation) is payment, although this is not clear and hence IRS might argue that the compensation must be deductible during the reliance period. If IRS took this approach, the timing rules of Code §§404(a)(5) and 83(h) would be implicated, i.e., one of these provisions might defer (until after the reliance period has ended) the deduction for an amount paid during the reliance period (see ¶1503.1.4 through ¶1503.1.6). We believe that IRS (1) should amend the regulations so that Exception #2 covers all types of compensation awarded during the reliance period, but (2) if not, should interpret Exception #2 so that it applies to compensation (other than restricted property and stock-based compensation) either paid or deductible during the reliance period.

Compensation in the form of restricted property subject to vesting and stock-based compensation granted during the reliance period are exempt (under Exception #2) from the $1 million deduction limit, without regard to the year in which the corporation is allowed to deduct such compensation.[21] This special rule for compensation in the form of restricted property subject to vesting and stock-based compensation does not extend to other types of deferred compensation awards. Thus, if a privately held corporation (prior to becoming publicly held) grants an executive deferred compensation (other than restricted property subject to vesting or stock-based compensation) that does not qualify for the performance-based compensation exception, and the compensation is paid after the reliance period and while the executive is one of the corporation's top five officers, the compensation is subject to the $1 million deduction limit (notwithstanding the fact that the deferred compensation was awarded during the reliance period). Such deferred compensation paid after the reliance period is subject to the $1 million deduction limit even if such deferred compensation was awarded while the corporation was privately held (and even if disclosed in the IPO prospectus, where the corporation becomes public as a result of an IPO). Code §162(m)'s legislative history, on the other hand, indicates that such deferred compensation would be exempt from the $1 million deduction limit.[22]

It is not entirely clear exactly what constitutes a "plan or agreement" for purposes of applying this exception. The preamble to the 1993 proposed regulations refers to "plans or arrangements" in discussing the exception, suggesting a broad scope.[23] However, the preamble to the final regulations employs the more restrictive phrase "plans and agreements" in its discussion of the IPO disclosure requirements.[24] It may be possible that a "plan or agreement" or "plans or arrangements" could encompass a corporation's consistent practice of paying salaries and bonuses in excess of the $1 million deduction limit and even may extend to

---

[21] Reg. §1.162-27(f)(3).
[22] 1993 Conference Report at 588.
[23] 58 Fed. Reg. 66,310, at 66,311 (1993) (hereinafter "58 Fed. Reg.").
[24] T.D. 8650 (12/20/95).

payments of compensation to the successors of the executives in place at the time the corporation becomes publicly held.

It seems to us clear that Exception #2 applies where public P acquires private T's stock (either by taxable or tax-free stock purchase or by taxable or tax-free reverse subsidiary merger). The regulations state that Exception #2 applies where "a corporation [here T] that was not a publicly held corporation . . . becomes a publicly held corporation." Where public P acquires private T's *stock*, T "becomes a publicly held corporation" as defined by the regulations, which state that a "publicly held corporation includes an affiliated group of corporations, as defined in section 1504 (determined without regard to section 1504(b))," i.e., when T becomes an 80-80 subsidiary of public P, T "becomes [for the first time] a publicly held corporation" entitled to Exception #2, even though the P group may have been public for many years.[25]

The regulations are not wholly clear on the extent to which Exception #2 applies where private T's *assets* are acquired by public P (by taxable or tax-free asset purchase or by taxable or tax-free forward merger) and P assumes T's obligation to pay compensation to covered executives. The regulations state that Exception #2 applies where "a [private] corporation [here T] . . . becomes a publicly held corporation."[26] However, where public P acquires private T's assets, T itself never becomes public and hence there is exposure if IRS takes the position that Exception #2 as written does not apply.[27] This would be an unfortunate result. T's compensation plans and agreements were adopted while T was private and not required to comply with Code §162(m). Hence when public P (or a P 80-80 subsidiary) assumes a private T compensation plan or agreement, the 2-year/4-year transition rule of Exception #2 should apply.[28] See the discussion below of the rationale for Exception #2.

One other factual situation which illustrates this point: where (1) private T recently became publicly held, e.g., because of an IPO, so that it qualified for the 2-year/4-year transition rule, and shortly thereafter (2) public P acquires T's assets

---

[25] Reg. §1.162-27(c)(1)(ii).

[26] Reg. §1.162-27(f)(1).

[27] If T effectuates a tax-free merger or "C" reorganization into P (or its subsidiary, S), so that P (or S) is T's Code §381 successor, it can be argued strongly that T should be treated for §162(m) purposes as having become public. Where T merges into P (or into S), whether such merger is tax-free or not, a similar argument can be made based on state corporate law concepts which treat the surviving corporation in a state law merger as the merged corporation's successor. See Newmarket Manufacturing Co. v. United States, 233 F.2d 493, 499, 56-1 U.S.T.C. ¶9540 (1st Cir. 1956) (a pre-Code §381 decision stating "that the transferee in a statutory merger should be deemed to be continuing in itself the corporate life of the now-defunct component, and that it followed from this conceptual identity that the two corporate entities were to be treated for a substantive purpose in the income tax as the same taxpayer"), citing Helvering v. Metropolitan Edison Co., 306 U.S. 522, 529, 39-1 U.S.T.C. ¶9432 (1939) (concluding similarly where P's acquisition of T was held to constitute a *de facto* merger even though not complying with all the provisions of the state merger law).

[28] IRS Letter Ruling 199915036 (4/16/99) suggests IRS agrees with this conclusion. The ruling concluded that Exception #2 applies to compensation paid by a real estate investment trust (REIT) pursuant to compensation arrangements entered into between certain REIT executives and the REIT's predecessor, a limited partnership that was not a publicly traded partnership within the meaning of Code §7704.

and assumes T's compensation plans and agreements, this asset acquisition should not cut short T's 2-year/4-year reliance period. The correct result is no different where only (2) occurs—i.e., where T did not go public before public P acquired T—since the reason for granting a 2-year/4-year transition period with respect to T's plans and agreements is the same: they were adopted by private T before the obligor on T's plans and agreements was a public corporation.

The rationale for Exception #2 is unclear. However, the exception must be based on more than the mere fact that the new public shareholders may be regarded as having approved the existing arrangements by virtue of purchasing stock in the IPO or other transaction which caused the corporation to become publicly held. If approval by public shareholders alone were enough to justify an exception to Code §162(m), the exception for performance-based compensation (Exception #4) would not be conditioned on meeting other requirements (e.g., a pre-established, objective, formula, performance goal). The rationale for Exception #2 may be that the new public shareholders take the existence of such arrangements into account in determining the amount they are willing to pay for the corporation's stock and that, as a result, the old shareholders (and not the new public shareholders) bear the cost of any excessive compensation arrangements. However, such a rationale would not require a sunset provision. On the other hand, the preamble to the final regulations suggests IRS's and Treasury's rationale for the exception is to avoid creating unnecessary burdens on private corporations, stating that "because there is no requirement for privately held corporations to comply with section 162(m), the IRS and Treasury recognize the need for a transition rule for plans and agreements that are in existence when a privately held corporation becomes public without an IPO." The desire to avoid unnecessary burdens is consistent with a sunset provision.

Because of Exception #2, a privately held corporation will need to worry about the effects of Code §162(m) while it is private only for one of the following two reasons: (1) the corporation desires to adopt one or more plans or agreements before it goes public (either in an IPO, as a result of its acquisition by a publicly held corporation, or otherwise) in order to obtain the benefit of Exception #2 (see ¶1506.1.3.2), or (2) the plans or agreements adopted prior to the date the corporation becomes public will cover compensation extending beyond the reliance period described above.

¶1506.1.3.1   *Subsidiary of Public Company*

Exception #2 generally does not apply to a corporation that was, prior to becoming publicly held, a subsidiary of a publicly held corporation because a "publicly held corporation includes an affiliated group of corporations."[29] The regulations include two rules, however, which may allow certain compensation to qualify for the performance-based compensation exception where the compensation was awarded by a subsidiary (which was itself not publicly held but was a

---

[29] Reg. §1.162-27(c)(1)(ii).

member of a publicly held affiliated group) and the subsidiary thereafter becomes publicly held. Under the first rule, if the compensation met the requirements of the performance-based compensation exception before the subsidiary itself became publicly held (with the shareholders and compensation committee of the parent corporation treated as the shareholders and compensation committee of the subsidiary), such compensation continues to qualify for the performance-based compensation exception after the subsidiary itself becomes public, as long as any required certification that the performance goals were met is made by the compensation committee of the now publicly held subsidiary.[30] The second rule permits compensation to qualify for the performance-based compensation exception without complying with the shareholder disclosure and approval requirements (as long as all other requirements are satisfied) until the first regularly scheduled meeting of the now publicly held subsidiary occurring more than 12 months after the date it went public.[31] For property subject to vesting and stock-based compensation, this transition rule covers such awards "granted" prior to such shareholders' meeting. For other types of compensation, this transition rule applies only if "paid" before such shareholders' meeting.

¶1506.1.3.2 Planning for Initial Public Offering

A corporation planning an IPO should adopt (before the IPO) any compensation plan or agreement the corporation wants to utilize after the IPO so that the plan or agreement can be disclosed in the IPO prospectus and qualify for Exception #2. There appears to be no requirement that any award be made under such a plan or agreement prior to the IPO in order to qualify for Exception #2. However, as discussed in ¶1506.1.3, Exception #2 applies only to amounts which are paid/deductible during the reliance period lasting up to approximately four years after the corporation's IPO, except that with respect to restricted property subject to vesting or stock-based compensation the exception applies to awards granted during the reliance period, regardless of when the corporation's deduction occurs.

¶1506.1.4 Exception #3: Non-Covered Employee

The $1 million deduction limit does not apply to compensation paid to an executive who is not a "covered employee."[32] For this purpose, a "covered employee" means:

- the CEO, "or . . . an individual acting in such a capacity . . . as of the close of the taxable year,"[33] plus

---

[30] Reg. §1.162-27(f)(4)(ii).
[31] Reg. §1.162-27(f)(4)(iii). See IRS Letter Ruling 199950021 (12/17/99) (IPO of up to 20% of S's stock in contemplation of P's later spinoff of balance).
[32] Code §162(m)(1).
[33] Code §162(m)(3)(A).

- the four highest compensated officers (other than the CEO) whose "total compensation . . . for the taxable year is required to be reported to shareholders under the [1934 Act]."[34]

Significantly, the regulations state that a person who is not "the chief executive officer [or acting in such capacity]" or "among the four highest compensated officers" on the last day of the taxable year is not a covered employee.[35] As a result, if an executive ceases to be an officer of the corporation before the last day of the corporation's taxable year (even though continuing to provide services for the corporation, even as an employee), the $1 million deduction limit will not apply to any compensation paid to the executive in such year or in any year thereafter. This is true even if the executive's compensation is disclosed in the proxy statement as compensation paid to a former executive under the broader new SEC disclosure rules described in ¶1506.1.4.1.[36]

¶1506.1.4.1   Coordination with 1934 Securities Exchange Act

In general, Code §162(m)'s reference to compensation "required to be reported to shareholders" under the 1934 Act refers to disclosure in the corporation's annual proxy statement. Registration under the 1934 Act requires a publicly held corporation to disclose the compensation of its CEO and certain other highly paid executive officers in its proxy statement issued to shareholders in connection with the election of directors as well as a vote on certain executive compensation arrangements.[37]

---

[34] Code §162(m)(3)(B). IRS has ruled privately that where two individuals serve as co-CEOs of a publicly held corporation the more-highly compensated of the two co-CEOs is treated as the corporation's CEO for purposes of Code §162(m)(3)(A) and the other co-CEO is a covered employee under Code §162(m)(3)(B) if he is one of the four highest compensated officers (excluding the individual treated as the CEO). IRS Letter Ruling 199921032 (2/25/99).

[35] Reg. §1.162-27(c)(2) and (c)(6) example (1).

[36] IRS Letter Ruling 199910011 (12/4/98).

[37] SEC Schedule 14A, Item 8; SEC Regulation S-K, Item 402(a)(3). Code §162(m) defines "covered employee" by reference to disclosure to shareholders (see Code §162(m)(3)). The legislative history (see 1993 Conference Report at 585) and, in general, the regulations (see Reg. §1.162-27(c)(2)(ii)) and preamble to the 1993 proposed regulations (see 58 Fed. Reg. at 66,311) refer only to a disclosure obligation, without explicitly stating whether disclosure to shareholders or some other disclosure (e.g., disclosure to the SEC) is meant. One example in the regulations implies that shareholder disclosure is required. It reiterates the statutory reference to the 1934 Act shareholder disclosure requirements. See Reg. §1.162-27(c)(6) example (1).

This distinction could prove significant. A publicly held corporation is required to file with the SEC certain forms (e.g., Form 10-K) that do not have to be sent by the corporation to all shareholders. Any disclosure in these forms would arguably not be taken into account for Code §162(m) purposes because such disclosure is not "required to be reported to shareholders."

Where a publicly held corporation files no proxy statement, the SEC requires the summary compensation table to be included in the corporation's Form 10-K filed with the SEC. Query whether disclosure on Form 10-K has the effect of a report to shareholders because the information is made available, although not sent, to them. We do not believe that a disclosure on Form 10-K qualifies as a report to shareholders.

As interpreted by the regulations, Code §162(m)'s definition of covered employee is based on SEC regulations in effect at the time Code §162(m) was enacted (i.e., the SEC regulations in effect before the SEC regulatory amendment described below). Under these "old" SEC regulations, a corporation was required to disclose in its proxy statement the compensation of its CEO and four other highest compensated executive officers as of the end of the last completed fiscal year. Disclosure of an executive's compensation was not required if the executive left the corporation's employ before the end of the last completed fiscal year.[38]

Effective 11/29/93, SEC amended its regulations governing disclosure of executive compensation, broadening the required disclosure to include the compensation of certain executives who left the corporation's employ during the year. Under these "new" SEC regulations, the corporation must disclose the compensation of those executives covered by the "old" SEC regulations plus the compensation of (1) any person who was CEO at any time during the year and (2) up to two executives who would have been among the four highest compensated non-CEO executives but for the fact that they left the corporation's employ prior to the end of the year.[39]

The tax regulations do not utilize the "new" SEC regulations and effectively follow the "old" SEC regulations, stating that a person who is not an officer "employed on the last day of the taxable year" is not a covered employee.[40] Thus, for example, an executive would not be a covered employee if he or she retired or left the corporation's employ before the last day of the year, even if he or she is listed in the corporation's proxy statement under the "new" SEC regulations (because under the "new" SEC regulations he or she would have been among the four highest compensated (non-CEO) officers had he or she not left the corporation's employ). Prior to the issuance of the Code §162(m) regulations, it appeared likely that such an executive would have been a covered employee under Code §162(m) because his or her compensation was required to be reported to shareholders under the 1934 Act.[41]

Where an individual ceases to be an executive officer of the publicly held corporation (i.e., ceases to have policy-making authority within the meaning of the SEC rules[42]) before the last day of the taxable year but remains an employee, IRS has ruled privately that the individual is not a covered employee, even if his or her compensation is disclosed in the publicly held corporation's proxy statement as provided to a former CEO or a former executive officer under the "new" SEC regulations.[43] This ruling is consistent with the tax regulations, which state that a covered employee is "any individual who, *on the last day of the taxable year*," is the CEO or one of the four highest compensated officers whose compensation is

---

[38] SEC Regulation S-K, Item 402(a)(3), as in effect prior to 11/29/93.

[39] See SEC Regulation S-K, Item 402(a)(2), as in effect since 11/29/93.

[40] Reg. §1.162-27(c)(2) and (c)(6) example (1).

[41] See Code §162(m)(3)(B).

[42] See SEC Rule 3b-7.

[43] IRS Letter Ruling 199910011 (12/4/98); IRS Letter Ruling 199928014 (4/13/99); IRS Letter Ruling 199928015 (4/13/99). These rulings were conditioned on the assumption that no intent exists on the part of the corporation or the officers in question "to resume their duties as officers at any time in the foreseeable future."

required to be disclosed to shareholders in the corporation's proxy statement.[44] An individual who is not an officer (within the meaning of the SEC rules) on the last day of the taxable year may be disclosed in the corporation's proxy statement under the "new" SEC regulations as a former CEO or as an individual who would have been one of the four highest compensated officers if he or she were still an officer. But in such case, the disclosure would not be made because the person was the year-end CEO or one of the four highest non-CEO officers on the last day of the taxable year and such individual is therefore not classified as a covered employee under Code §162(m).[45]

In determining the four highest compensated officers at year end as well as the year-end CEO, Code §162(m) and the regulations incorporate SEC reporting principles (not tax principles).[46] Where there are differences between SEC principles and tax principles in terms of timing and amount of compensation (as is frequently the case, for example, with respect to deferred compensation, options, restricted stock, etc.), SEC principles control.[47]

As one illustration of the primacy of SEC principles over tax principles in identifying covered employees, 1999 and 2001 IRS private letter rulings conclude that, where P acquires 100% of T's stock and as a result no compensation information is required to be reported by T in its SEC filings for the year in which such acquisition occurs or any subsequent year, T's officers in the acquisition year are not under Reg. §1.162-27(c)(2), Code §162(m) covered employees.[48]

As a second illustration, a 2000 IRS private letter ruling concludes that where public T changes its fiscal year "for various business reasons unrelated to taxes" and, under SEC rules, is "not . . . required to file any official proxy with . . . SEC . . . for [the resulting] short [fiscal] year" and therefore is not required to report compensation information for its CEO and 4 other highest compensated officers for such a short period, none of T's officers (including its CEO) are "covered employees with respect to the short year," even though T files with SEC "on a voluntary basis . . . information . . . reflect[ing] compensation paid to [T's] top executives for the short year."[49]

---

[44] Reg. §1.162-27(c)(2) (emphasis added).

[45] This conclusion is supported by the preamble to the 1993 proposed regulations which indicated that a covered employee "must be employed as an executive officer on the last day of the taxable year." 58 Fed. Reg. at 66,311.

[46] Code §162(m)(3); Reg. §1.162-27(c)(2)(ii).

[47] Generally, a corporation uses the same year for SEC and financial reporting on the one hand and tax reporting on the other. However, a corporation generally is permitted to use a tax year different from its SEC financial accounting year. Where the corporation's tax year differs from its SEC financial reporting year, the statute is flawed and ambiguous. It states that a covered employee is a person whose "total compensation . . . for the taxable year is required to be reported . . . under the [1934 Act] by reason of . . . being among the four highest compensated officers for the taxable year (other than the [CEO])." Literally read, this requirement will never be met because there is no SEC reporting for the "taxable year." Unfortunately, the regulations provide no clarification of this issue.

[48] IRS Letter Ruling 200152003 (9/14/01); IRS Letter Ruling 199928015 (4/13/99).

[49] IRS Letter Ruling 200044007 (7/26/00).

¶1506.1.4.2   Employee of Subsidiary

Under SEC rules, compensation paid to an employee of a privately held subsidiary is clearly required to be disclosed in the publicly held parent's proxy statement where (1) the employee would, if he or she were an employee of the parent, be among the four highest compensated non-CEO officers, and (2) the employee is an officer of the subsidiary, and (3) the employee exercises policy-making authority with respect to the parent's business.[50] For SEC purposes, it appears that a subsidiary is any corporation controlled by the parent (in general, this would normally mean a corporation of which 50% or more of the voting power is owned by the parent, although in some cases control could exist where the parent owns less than 50% of the subsidiary by vote).

In contrast, the statutory language of Code §162(m) seems expressly to limit the application of Code §162(m) to employees of the publicly held parent (not including employees of subsidiaries, even 100% subsidiaries). The statutory definition of covered employee refers to "any employee of the taxpayer"[51] and "the taxpayer" clearly refers back to the publicly held corporation mentioned in Code §162(m)(1).[52] In spite of this statutory language, the regulations announce that a publicly held corporation includes not only the corporation that is publicly held but also all members of its affiliated group as defined in Code §1504(a) (without regard to Code §1504(b)),[53] regardless of whether a consolidated return is filed.

Thus, where a publicly held corporation owns sufficient stock of a privately held subsidiary to satisfy both the 80%-by-value and the 80%-by-vote requirements of Code §1504(a), the regulations would treat an executive of the subsidiary as a covered employee if the executive's compensation is required to be disclosed in the publicly held parent's proxy statement for SEC purposes (generally where the subsidiary executive exercises policy-making authority with respect to the parent's business and the executive is one of the four highest compensated year-end non-CEO officers so disclosed in the parent's proxy statement).

Where the publicly held parent's stock ownership in the privately held subsidiary does not meet both the 80%-by-value and 80%-by-vote tests, the non-80-80 subsidiary will not be treated as part of the publicly held corporation under the regulations and hence an executive of the non-80-80 subsidiary would not be a covered employee. Even in that case, however, it is possible that the subsidiary executive's compensation could be disclosed in the parent's proxy statement because, as discussed above, the SEC does not limit subsidiaries to those that meet Code §1504's 80-80 test. However, Code §162(m) would not apply to the non-80-80 subsidiary's executive compensation.

The regulations limit the definition of publicly held corporation so that, for purposes of Code §162(m), an affiliated group which would otherwise be treated

---

[50] SEC Regulation S-K, Instruction 2 to Item 402(a)(3); SEC Rule 3b-7.

[51] Code §162(m)(3).

[52] In contrast, under the golden parachute rules of Code §280G, the statute explicitly treats the members of an affiliated group as a single corporation and any officer of a member of the group as an officer of that single corporation. See Code §280G(d)(5).

[53] Reg. §1.162-27(c)(1)(ii).

as a single publicly held corporation does not include any subsidiary that is itself publicly held (as well as any subsidiary of such publicly held subsidiary).[54] Such a publicly held subsidiary and its subsidiaries are treated as separately subject to Code §162(m). However, a transition rule limits the application of this definition of affiliated group to periods commencing with the first regularly scheduled shareholders' meeting occurring more than 12 months after 12/2/94, unless the taxpayer elects retroactive application.[55]

¶1506.1.4.3   Payment After Status Change

Where compensation is earned by an executive while he or she is a covered employee but is not deductible until after he or she ceases to be a covered employee, the $1 million deduction limit does not apply. Conversely, where compensation is earned by an executive before he or she becomes a covered employee but becomes deductible while he or she is a covered employee, the $1 million deduction limit does apply.

This rule is particularly important for compensation that is deductible one or more years after grant, when the executive's status may have changed, such as:

- Deferred compensation which is generally deductible when paid.
- An NQO which is generally deductible when exercised.
- Restricted stock (i.e., stock subject to vesting) which is generally deductible at vesting (where the executive makes no Code §83(b) election at grant).
- Phantom stock which is generally deductible when paid (in cash or unrestricted stock).

Thus, where compensation otherwise payable to a covered executive exceeds the $1 million deduction limit, the corporation may want to grant all or a portion of the compensation in the form of deferred compensation which is payable after the covered executive's retirement. Alternatively, the corporation may want to grant NQOs, restricted stock, or phantom stock that will generate a deduction after the covered executive's retirement.[56]

Conversely, a corporation may also find it desirable to structure compensation arrangements to fit the performance-based compensation exception (Exception #4 below), even where the executive is not a covered employee when the arrangement is entered into, if there is any possibility that the executive may subsequently be a covered employee when the compensation becomes deductible.

---

[54] Reg. §1.162-27(c)(1)(ii).

[55] Reg. §1.162-27(j)(2)(ii).

[56] As noted above, the regulations state that an executive is a covered employee only if employed as the corporation's CEO or as one of the corporation's four highest compensated officers (other than the CEO) on the last day of the corporation's taxable year. Reg. §1.162-27(c)(2) and (c)(6) example (1). As a result, if an executive retires or otherwise leaves the corporation's employ before the last day of the corporation's taxable year, the $1 million deduction limit will not apply to any compensation paid to the executive in that or a subsequent year.

¶1506.1.4.4   Management Corporation or Partnership

The definition of covered employee may leave some opportunities for aggressive taxpayers.[57] For example, an executive could set up a wholly owned corporation which would employ the executive to perform services for the publicly held corporation. The publicly held corporation would pay compensation to the executive's corporation (but not to the executive). If the arrangement is respected, the publicly held corporation may be able to deduct the compensation without regard to the $1 million deduction limit on the ground that the executive's personal service corporation is not a covered employee, and the executive's corporation could deduct compensation it pays to the executive because it is not a publicly held corporation subject to Code §162(m).[58]

In this situation, there are at least three alternatives as to whom the corporation would disclose in its directors' proxy statement as one of its most highly compensated officers: the executive's personal service corporation, the executive, or a third person (i.e., a different executive). The executive's personal service corporation cannot be a covered employee because it is not an individual.[59] Thus, if the publicly held corporation treats either the personal service corporation or a third person as the officer whose compensation was required to be disclosed in the proxy statement for SEC purposes,[60] neither the executive nor his personal service corporation would be a covered employee and hence the technique should work if the arrangement is respected.

---

[57] The techniques suggested in ¶1506.1.4.4 may raise collateral issues, e.g., an executive's eligibility for benefit plans may turn on whether the executive is an employee. These collateral issues should be examined if a corporation is contemplating the use of one or more of these techniques.

[58] Code §269 would not apply to this situation, because it applies only where a "person [here the executive] . . . acquire[s] . . . control of a corporation [here his or her personal service corporation] . . . and the principal purpose . . . is avoidance of federal income tax by securing the benefit of a deduction . . . *which such person [here the executive] or corporation [here his or her personal service corporation]* would not otherwise enjoy" (emphasis added). In this case, the deduction is enjoyed by the publicly held corporation.

Personal service corporations have sometimes been upheld as separate entities for tax purposes and in other cases disregarded. Compare, e.g., Sargent v. Commissioner, 929 F.2d 1252 (1991) with Johnson v. Commissioner, 78 T.C. 882 (1982), *aff'd without opinion*, 734 F.2d 20 (9th Cir.), *cert. denied*, 469 U.S. 857 (1984).

However, recent developments with respect to personal service corporations tend to focus on eliminating the tax benefits to the owners of the personal service corporation. See, e.g., Code §269A (eliminating some benefits obtained by owners of a personal service corporation); Sargent v. Commissioner, 929 F.2d 1252 (1991); Johnson v. Commissioner, 78 T.C. 882 (1982), *aff'd without opinion*, 734 F.2d 20 (9th Cir.), *cert. denied*, 469 U.S. 857 (1984). In contrast, under Code §162(m), the benefits described in the text would flow to the publicly held corporation rather than to the executive-owner of the personal service corporation.

Although a payment to a personal service corporation is treated as a payment to an individual for purposes of the golden parachute rules, this treatment is based on a specific statutory provision in Code §280G. See Code §280G(d)(5); Prop. Reg. §1.280G-1 Q&A 16. The lack of any similar statutory provision in Code §162(m) may suggest that payments to a personal service corporation would be respected for purposes of Code §162(m).

[59] See Reg. §1.162-27(c)(2)(i).

[60] It seems unlikely, however, that the SEC rules would require, or even allow, a corporation to be treated as an officer in the proxy statement.

If the corporation treats the executive as an officer whose compensation was subject to disclosure in the proxy statement, the result is somewhat less clear. While the executive would be a covered employee, the compensation paid by the publicly held corporation would not be paid to the covered employee. Thus, if the arrangement were respected, the technique might still avoid the $1 million deduction limit.

Under a second potential technique, a publicly held corporation could establish a 79%-owned subsidiary (i.e., a subsidiary that is not part of the publicly held parent's affiliated group) to employ and compensate top executives who would otherwise be covered employees of the publicly held parent.[61] The publicly held parent would make payments to the subsidiary for the management services of the top executives and the privately held subsidiary would pay a similar amount of compensation to the top executives. If this arrangement is respected, the subsidiary would not be treated as part of the publicly held parent under the regulations (because it does not meet Code §1504's 80-80 test) and, as a result, the executives would not be covered employees of the publicly held parent. The publicly held parent's payments to the subsidiary (and the subsidiary's payments to the executives) would apparently be deductible without regard to Code §162(m). Because the privately held 79%-owned subsidiary would be controlled by the publicly held parent under SEC standards, the subsidiary officers would be listed in the parent's proxy statement (assuming they performed policy-making roles with respect to the parent's business). See ¶1506.1.4.2.

A third potential technique involves the creation of a partnership owned largely by the publicly held corporation that would employ one or more executives who would otherwise be covered employees if they were employed directly by the publicly held corporation.[62] As in the case of the 79% subsidiary, the partnership would not be part of the publicly held corporation's affiliated group for tax purposes and hence would not be treated as part of the publicly held corporation under the regulations. By contrast, when (as is likely with a 79%-owned partnership) the partnership is controlled by the publicly held corporation under SEC standards, the partnership's policy-makers would likely be listed as officers in the publicly held corporation's proxy statement. This arrangement is more risky from the tax standpoint than the use of a 79% subsidiary since the partnership's deductions for compensation paid to the executives would flow through onto the publicly held corporation's tax return with its character determined "as if such item were . . . incurred [by the publicly held corporation] in the same manner as incurred by the partnership."[63]

---

[61] Unlike the first potential technique discussed above and the third potential technique discussed below, this second potential technique risks attack under Code §269.

[62] Unlike the other two potential techniques discussed above, this third potential technique risks attack under Reg. §1.701-2, the partnership anti-abuse proposal.

[63] Code §702(b).

¶1506.1.5 Exception #4: Performance-Based Compensation

The $1 million deduction limit does not apply to compensation where all four of the following tests are met:

- The compensation is payable solely on account of attaining one or more pre-established, non-discretionary, objective, performance goals.
- The performance goal is determined by a compensation committee of the board of directors comprised solely of two or more outside directors.
- The material terms under which the compensation is to be paid (including the performance goals) are disclosed to shareholders and approved by a separate majority shareholder vote.
- Before the compensation is paid, the compensation committee certifies that the performance goals and any other material terms were satisfied.

¶1506.1.5.1 through ¶1506.1.5.4 discuss each of these requirements in greater detail.

¶1506.1.5.1   Non-Discretionary Performance Goal

(1)   Objective formula. The first requirement of the performance-based compensation exception is that the compensation be payable solely on account of attaining one or more pre-established non-discretionary objective performance goals.[64] According to the regulations, a "pre-established performance goal must state, in terms of an objective formula or standard, the method for computing the amount of compensation payable to the employee if the goal is attained."[65] For this purpose, a formula or standard is objective "if a third party having knowledge of the relevant performance results could calculate the amount to be paid to the employee."[66]

Performance goals may be "based on one or more business criteria that apply to the individual, a business unit, or the corporation as a whole . . . includ[ing], for example, stock price, market share, sales, earnings per share, return on equity, or costs."[67] A formula goal will not qualify if it relates solely to (a) an outside standard (e.g., the S&P 500 Index reaching a specified level)[68] or (b) the executive's continued employment (e.g., requiring at least five years of continuous employment).[69]

---

[64] Code §162(m)(4)(C). See also Reg. §1.162-27(e)(2).

[65] Reg. §1.162-27(e)(2)(ii). See also 1993 Conference Report at 586.

[66] Reg. §1.162-27(e)(2)(ii).

[67] Reg. §1.162-27(e)(2)(i).

[68] The corporation's own performance on a particular business criterion can, of course, be measured against an outside standard. For example, a performance goal could state that a bonus would be paid to executives if the total shareholder return on the corporation's stock exceeded the total return on the S&P 500 index.

[69] Reg. §1.162-27(e)(2)(i).

The regulations clarify that a "performance goal need not . . . be based upon an increase or positive result under a business criterion and could include, for example, maintaining the status quo or limiting economic losses (measured, in each case, by reference to a specific business criteria)."[70]

The performance goals, however, need not be connected to any minimum length of *service* by the executive, as long as the goal itself is performance-related. Thus, an award may be performance-based even if an executive who retires before the goal is either met or not (e.g., an executive who retires in the second year of a three-year incentive bonus program) is entitled to receive compensation if the goal is satisfied after his retirement. One day of service by the executive may be enough to allow an award based on multiple years of profits or stock appreciation to qualify as performance-based.

(2)   Substantially uncertain and pre-established. The regulations require that a goal relating to a period of service must satisfy the following requirements:

- the compensation committee establishes the goal in writing within "90 days after the commencement of the period of service to which the performance goal relates,"
- no more than "25% of the period of service (as scheduled in good faith at the time the goal is established [by the compensation committee]) has elapsed," and
- "the outcome [of the goal] is substantially uncertain at the time the compensation committee actually establishes the goal."[71]

Although the regulations do not specifically define "period of service to which the performance goal relates," it appears that the phrase means the period during which the performance goal is to be measured. Hence if a corporation which normally pays a bonus shortly after the end of each calendar year establishes a performance goal on 3/15 of a year (i.e., 2 ½ months into the calendar year), it can establish as a goal certain performance criteria for the entire calendar year. However, if it does not establish the performance goal until 6/15 of the year, it cannot use as a goal performance criteria for the entire calendar year (because it is more than 90 days and more than 25% into the period of service, i.e., the calendar year), but such corporation could establish as a goal for the bonus to be paid shortly after the end of the calendar year certain performance criteria for the last half of the calendar year (because it is less than 90 days and less than 25% into the period of service, i.e., the last half of the calendar year).

Examples in the regulations clarify that (1) a formula based on a percentage of profits is substantially uncertain, regardless of the corporation's historic profitability (apparently on the theory that it is always substantially uncertain whether a corporation engaged in business in the U.S. today will have profits for its coming year) and (2) a performance goal based on a percentage of sales (with no minimum

---

[70] Reg. §1.162-27(e)(2)(i).
[71] Reg. §1.162-27(e)(2)(i).

threshold) is not substantially uncertain because a corporation is virtually certain to have some sales during the year.[72] The regulations contain another example illustrating a purported performance goal which was not substantially uncertain when established: an executive was granted compensation contingent on settlement of certain litigation, but, at the time of the grant, the other party to the litigation had already "informally indicated . . . a willingness to settle" on the terms set forth in the grant.[73]

There is some risk that this substantially uncertain standard (as applied to a test not based on profits) may invite IRS agents to assert, with the benefit of 20-20 hindsight, that a performance goal was, when set, too easy to attain and hence was not substantially uncertain. We hope that IRS agents, and ultimately the courts, will give substantial credence to the compensation committee's implicit determination that the goal it set was substantially uncertain at the time the committee set such goal.

(3)   Discretion. The legislative history states that the goal(s) must be a "pre-established objective performance formula or standard that precludes discretion [so that] . . . a third party with knowledge of the relevant performance results could calculate the amount to be paid to the executive."[74] The regulations confirm that there must be no discretionary right to *increase* compensation[75] but permit the compensation committee to retain unfettered discretion to *reduce or eliminate* the amount payable upon attainment of the goal.[76]

An objective formula based on a percentage of salary or base pay will not be viewed as giving the corporation discretion to increase the award if the dollar amount of salary or base pay is fixed at the time the performance goal is established.[77] However, if the dollar amount of salary or base pay is not fixed at the time the performance goal is established, then the absolute maximum dollar amount that may be awarded must be fixed at that time in order for an objective formula based on a percentage of salary or base pay to be considered non-discretionary.[78]

The regulations indicate that an increase in deferred compensation based on either (i) a reasonable interest rate or (ii) one or more predetermined actual investments (as long as adjustments include any decreases in the value of the

---

[72] Reg. §1.162-27(e)(2)(vii) examples (2) and (3).

[73] Reg. §1.162-27(e)(2)(vii) example (4).

[74] 1993 Conference Report at 586. See also Reg. §1.162-27(e)(2)(ii).

[75] Indeed, the language of the regulation could be read to suggest that the grant must explicitly preclude any discretion to increase the compensation. See Reg. §1.162-27(e)(2)(iii)(A). In our view, it should be sufficient that the formula results in an objective amount without any resort to discretion. There should be no further need to state explicitly that there is no discretion to increase the amount.

[76] Under the regulations, it is apparently only the compensation committee that can have the discretion to reduce awards. See Reg. §1.162-27(e)(2)(iii)(A). Thus, such discretion could not be given to the board of directors as a whole or to the CEO.

[77] Reg. §1.162-27(e)(2)(iii)(A).

[78] Reg. §1.162-27(e)(2)(iii)(A).

investments) does not constitute discretion to increase the amount of the award.[79] Although the amount of the award need not be actually invested, this adjustment *must* be based on actual investments (e.g., an existing mutual fund) and *cannot* be based merely on a broad-based market index (e.g., the Standard & Poor's 500).[80] However, an existing mutual fund that tracks the Standard & Poor's 500 (or any other broad-based market index) qualifies as an actual investment.

The discretion to reduce may in fact be the practical equivalent of discretion to increase. For example, assume that a publicly held corporation (through its compensation committee) grants an employee the right to receive a $1 million bonus if a performance goal is met but also authorizes the compensation committee to reduce the bonus to an amount not less than $500,000. The arrangement resembles the grant of an award entitling the employee to receive a $500,000 bonus if the goal is attained, coupled with the prohibited discretion to increase the bonus. While such an arrangement is permitted by the literal words of the regulations, query whether there are circumstances in which IRS might seek to treat the discretion to reduce as a prohibited discretion to increase (e.g., where the corporation had stated that it intended to exercise its discretion to reduce the award to $500,000 unless the executive's performance was particularly deserving in the committee's discretion). Moreover, a publicly held corporation may in fact be reluctant to use the "discretion-to-reduce" technique because the corporation must disclose the high potential bonus number to shareholders (under the shareholder approval requirements described in ¶1506.1.5.3).

There are often "subjective" determinations which must be made in the calculation of a business criterion used to set a performance goal. For example, where a corporation grants a performance-based award to a covered employee based on achieving an earnings per share ("EPS") goal, the corporation's management makes and its auditors certify a number of "subjective" judgments in applying generally accepted accounting principles ("GAAP") to determine EPS. In general, such subjective judgments in the calculation of business criteria used in setting a performance goal should not be viewed as a prohibited discretion to increase an award where such criteria are determined for substantial non-compensatory business purposes (e.g., for reports to shareholders, lenders, securities analysts, etc.), and we believe that the final regulations should not be read to preclude such types of subjective determinations even though this principle is not explicitly stated therein.

A more serious issue regarding discretion arises where a publicly held corporation wishes to eliminate the effect of unexpected events on the determination of a business criterion. For example, the corporation may wish to calculate EPS for purposes of an incentive plan without regard to the effects of material unexpected events. Where the potential unexpected events are of a type specified with particularity in advance (e.g., a casualty loss arising out of an act of God with damage in excess of $1 million or a product liability judgment in excess of $1 million),

---

[79] Reg. §1.162-27(e)(2)(iii)(B). These deferred compensation rules also apply to compensation payable under the transition rule for compensation payable under a written binding contract in effect on 2/17/93 (see ¶1506.1.6). Reg. §1.162-27(h)(1)(iii)(B).

[80] Reg. §1.162-27(e)(2)(vii) example (16).

there should generally be no problem. The exclusion of specified, unexpected events is merely an additional objective element in an overall objective formula (a third party with the relevant information would be able to do the calculation) and does not give rise to any prohibited discretion.[81] When the corporation wishes, however, to exclude the effect of unexpected events without specifying the types of events in advance (or wishes to retain *discretion* to exclude or not exclude specified events), there is a strong risk that the corporation will be found to have retained discretion, hence barring reliance on the performance-based compensation exception (whether or not such an unexpected event occurs).

A formula should not be disqualified where discretion is retained to adjust the formula if the result will be a reduction of the award. Similarly, we believe that a formula should not be disqualified if the formula mandates the exclusion of "extraordinary items" as determined under GAAP since the use of professional judgment in applying GAAP should not be viewed as the equivalent of discretion.

The compensation committee may adjust previously granted stock-based compensation (including stock options and stock appreciation rights) without violating the prohibition against discretion if such adjustment "is made to reflect a change in corporate capitalization, such as a stock split or stock dividend, or a corporate transaction, such as any merger . . . , any consolidation . . . , any separation . . . (including a spinoff or other distribution of stock or property . . .), any reorganization . . . , or any partial or complete liquidation."[82] In a 2000 private letter ruling where the plan gave the compensation committee power to adjust the terms of outstanding options if certain events occurred,[83] IRS held that this regulation applies to unusual cash distributions, although not rising to the level of a spinoff or a partial liquidation.

This letter ruling does not address whether the plan under which performance-based compensation is granted must specifically permit post-grant adjustments (as did the plan in the 2000 private ruling) in order for such adjustments to come within the regulation. The answer should be "no," since the regulation itself contains no such requirement. However, Reg. §1.162-27(e)(2)(vii) example (13) (not cited in the 2000 ruling) implies that performance target adjustments to take into account unanticipated events, such as a change in accounting rules, constitute the exercise of impermissible discretion unless "made pursuant to the plan provisions." Since the 2000 letter ruling does not explicitly address this point, cautious taxpayers may want to include in their performance-based compensation plans

---

[81] See Reg. §1.162-27(e)(2)(vii) example (13) (adjustment to reported EPS to factor out a change in accounting standards not considered an exercise of impermissible discretion where made pursuant to a provision of the plan that established the EPS performance goal); IRS Letter Ruling 9827021 (4/3/98) (company's plan provides that, unless otherwise determined by the compensation committee by the 90th day of the company's fiscal year, the net income for such year is adjusted to factor out extraordinary items (determined in accordance with GAAP); held, such adjustment is not an exercise of impermissible discretion where made pursuant to a provision of the plan establishing the net income performance goal).

[82] Reg. §1.162-27(e)(2)(iii)(C).

[83] IRS Letter Ruling 200051018 (9/18/00).

a provision permitting or requiring the compensation committee to adjust stock-based compensation for events covered by Reg. §1.162-27(e)(2)(iii)(C).[84]

(4)   Aggregation rules. The regulations clarify when two awards will be aggregated, stating that (1) the grant-by-grant approach is the general rule and (2) "all plans, arrangements, and agreements" are considered together only to test "whether the employee would receive all or a part of the compensation regardless of whether the performance goal is attained," so that where payment of a bonus under a non-performance-based arrangement is contingent on failure to attain the performance goal under a qualified performance-based arrangement, both plans are disqualified.[85] The regulatory preamble to the 1994 proposed regulations states:

> [T]he grant-by-grant rule is the general rule under which compensation arrangements are tested for purposes of determining whether they are performance-based. Thus, whether a compensation arrangement is performance-based is generally determined without regard to other compensation arrangements. The change makes clear that the aggregation rule requiring all plans, arrangements, and agreements providing compensation to an employee to be taken into account is a limited exception to the general grant-by-grant rule, and applied only for the purpose of determining whether the employee would receive, regardless of whether the performance is attained, compensation that purports to be performance-based. Thus, for example, if payment under a non-performance-based compensation arrangement is contingent upon the failure to attain a performance goal under an otherwise performance-based arrangement, neither arrangement provides for compensation that is performance-based.

If an executive receives a tandem award (i.e., an arrangement allowing the executive to choose one, but only one, of two alternative awards), both alternative awards must qualify for the performance-based compensation exception if either is to qualify. For example, assume that a corporation grants an executive the right to receive one, but not both, of the following: (1) a $2 million bonus in any event or (2) 100,000 shares of the corporation's stock if an objective performance goal is met and the executive so elects.

Such an arrangement should be treated as one award for purposes of the $1 million deduction limit. Because it is in-the-money at grant (i.e., because the executive is guaranteed at least $2 million), the entire award should fail to qualify for the performance-based compensation exception even if the executive meets the objective performance goal and chooses to receive the 100,000 shares of stock.

(5)   Change-in-control, death, or disability feature. Many compensation plans contain "change in control" features that may cause options, SARs, restricted

---

[84] See the more extensive discussion of this 2000 private letter ruling under "Stock option or stock appreciation rights" below.

[85] Reg. §1.162-27(e)(2)(iv), (e)(2)(v).

stock, and phantom stock to vest and/or be cashed out on a "change in control."[86] A similar provision may accelerate vesting in the case of death or disability.

The statutory language of Code §162(m) originally caused concern that a change-in-control, death, or disability feature in an award (even one that was never used) would prevent the award from qualifying as performance-based because such a feature would mean that the executive had some chance of receiving the compensation under the award even though the performance goals were not met. The regulations eliminate this concern, stating that compensation "does not fail to be qualified performance-based compensation merely because the plan allows the compensation to be payable upon death, disability, or change of ownership or control."[87] Some risk exists, however, that IRS would challenge a plan that defined disability or change of ownership or control too broadly, e.g., whatever the compensation committee deems in its sole, unfettered discretion to be a disability or change of ownership or control, as a "sham" and consider such a provision merely the retention by the compensation committee of discretion to grant the award even if the performance goals are not met.

The regulations go on to state that "compensation paid on account of [death, disability, or change of control] prior to the attainment of the performance goal would not satisfy the requirements of [the performance-based compensation exception]."[88] If, however, the employee ceases to be employed by the corporation prior to the last day of the deduction year (whether as a result of death, disability, a change of control, or otherwise), such compensation will nonetheless be exempt from the $1 million deduction limit on the ground that the executive is not a covered employee.[89] See ¶1506.1.4.

(6)   **Cash bonus.** For a cash bonus payable to a covered employee to be exempted from the $1 million deduction limit, the amount of the bonus must be based on a pre-established, objective, performance formula that precludes discretion and

---

[86] Change-in-control features come in many varieties, sometimes encompassing only hostile changes in control and sometimes both hostile and friendly.

[87] Reg. §1.162-27(e)(2)(v). A feature that allowed compensation to be paid on any other event but attainment of the performance goal would disqualify the award as performance-based. For example, an award that was payable on the executive's retirement or termination without cause would fail to qualify as performance-based (even if the executive did not retire and was not fired without cause). The corporation could, however, allow an executive to retain the award in this case without causing the award to fail as performance-based if the award remained subject to the subsequent attainment of the performance goal.

[88] Reg. §1.162-27(e)(2)(v).

[89] An individual may continue to be a covered employee, however, if he or she ceases to be employed by the corporation on the last day of the corporation's taxable year because, in that case, he or she is an employee on the last day of the taxable year. In such case, a corporation may wish to defer payment of compensation that would otherwise be subject to the $1 million deduction limit to the following year, in order to shift the deduction to a year in which the executive is not a covered employee. Where compensation is already deferred compensation subject to Code §404(a)(5), the corporation may need to defer payment only to the first day of the next year. On the other hand, compensation which is not already deferred compensation (such as an annual bonus) may have to be deferred more than two and one-half months into the following year in order to defer the deduction to the following year.

meets the other tests described in this ¶1506.1.5. Many traditional features of corporate incentive bonus arrangements raise issues under the performance-based compensation exception.

Many corporations have traditionally created a formula bonus pool for top executives where the amount of the available pool is contingent on the attainment of one or more performance goals. Frequently, however, the corporation does not specify in advance each executive's share of the pool (i.e., the corporation determines each executive's share of the pool at some later time). In such case, the bonus arrangement will not qualify for the performance-based compensation exception because a third party could not calculate each executive's bonus.[90]

As discussed above, a cash bonus payable in accordance with an objective formula based on a percentage of salary or base pay can qualify for the performance-based compensation exception if either (1) the dollar amount of salary or base pay is fixed at the time the performance goal is established or (2) the absolute maximum dollar amount that may be awarded is fixed at the time the performance goal is established.

Because of this limitation on the structure of a bonus plan intended to qualify for the performance-based compensation exception, a corporation may wish to establish one arrangement for top executives who are covered employees (or likely to be covered employees) meeting all the requirements of the performance-based compensation exception and another, more discretionary, arrangement for executives unlikely to be covered employees that does not meet the requirements of the performance-based compensation exception.[91] This could be accomplished either with two separate plans or with one plan offering two different types of awards.

(7) Stock option or stock appreciation right.[92] The legislative history of Code §162(m) states that a stock option or SAR is automatically treated as meeting the performance goal requirement "because the amount of compensation attributable to the options or [SARs] received by the executive would be based solely on an increase in the corporation's stock price."[93] In short, share appreciation is treated by the new rules as an objective performance goal. However, if the option or SAR is in-the-money at grant, so that "the executive would have the right to receive compensation on the exercise . . . even if the stock price decreases or stays the same," the legislative history takes the position that such option or SAR does

---

[90] See Reg. §1.162-27(e)(2)(vii) example (7).

[91] Determining those executives likely to be covered employees will generally not be difficult for plans covering a short period of time (e.g., an annual incentive plan). However, where the plan covers a longer time period, it may be difficult to predict the identity of covered employees when compensation under the plan becomes deductible.

[92] Code §162(m) will be most relevant for NQOs. Where a corporation issues ISOs under Code §422, it is not allowed any deduction unless the employee makes a disqualifying disposition of the ISO stock. However, because of possible disqualifying dispositions (and the fact that the ISO requirements are generally consistent with the requirements of the performance-based compensation exception), a corporation should generally qualify its ISO plan for the performance-based compensation exception.

[93] 1993 Conference Report at 587.

"not meet the requirements for performance-based compensation" unless the vesting or exercisability of the award is conditioned on the attainment of a performance goal.[94]

The regulations follow the legislative history in this respect.[95] An option or an SAR granted with an exercise price equal to (or greater than) the fair market value of the underlying stock on the grant date will meet the performance goal requirement. On the other hand, an option or SAR that is even a small amount in-the-money at grant will not meet the performance goal requirement, even as to postgrant appreciation (unless the option or SAR is subject to vesting or restrictions on exercise based on a separate performance goal[96]).

However, it can be argued that an in-the-money option or SAR that is not immediately exercisable meets the performance goal requirement, notwithstanding that it is in-the-money at grant and has no separate performance goal for vesting. This is because the delayed exercisability of an in-the-money option or SAR is the practical equivalent of a goal that the corporation's stock not decline in value more than the in-the-money element over the period that the option or SAR cannot be exercised. Where this would otherwise be a valid performance goal, the option or SAR should not be disqualified by its in-the-money exercise price.

A more sensible regulatory approach to an immediately exercisable in-the-money option or SAR would have been to bifurcate the option or SAR so that the amount the option or SAR is in the money at grant does not qualify for the performance-based compensation exception (and hence is subject to the $1 million deduction limit), while any spread attributable to post-grant appreciation in the stock is treated as performance-based.

In light of the harsh approach of the regulations—that an option or SAR that is only slightly in-the-money does not qualify for the performance-based compensation exception—it is unfortunate that the regulations give no guidance on how to determine the FV of stock on the grant date. We believe that any reasonable method of determining FV should be acceptable, following the rule in the Code §421 regulations.[97] Moreover, we hope that a good faith effort to value stock for this purpose will be respected by IRS agents.[98] However, cautious taxpayers are likely to adopt conservative valuation methods to avoid the potential disqualification of an entire grant of options or SARs.

---

[94] 1993 Conference Report at 587.

[95] Reg. §1.162-27(e)(2)(v) and (vi).

[96] For example, the exercise of the option or SAR with an in-the-money exercise price at grant could be conditioned on a further rise in the value of the underlying stock over the FV at grant. In this case, the requirement of a further rise in value should generally be a valid performance goal.

[97] See Reg. §1.421-7(e)(2) and Prop. Reg. §§1.421-1(e) and 1.422-2(e).

[98] Compare Code §422(c)(1), providing a "good faith" rule for valuing stock subject to an incentive stock option. See also Temp. Reg. §14a.422A-1 Q&A 2(c)(4) and Prop. Reg. §1.422-2(e)(2).

EXAMPLE 1

Corporation P grants 1,000 options to acquire P stock to individual A who is a "covered employee" for purposes of Code §162(m). The stock of P trades on the New York Stock Exchange. On the grant date, P stock opened at $45.25 and closed at $45.75. Its high for the day was $46.00 and its low was $44.50. P intends the options granted to A to qualify as performance based. Possible methods for determining the FV of P stock as of the grant date for this purpose include:

- the closing price on the grant date ($45.75)
- the average of the high and low selling prices for the grant date (($46.00 + $44.50)/2 = $45.25)
- the average of the opening and closing prices on the grant date (($45.25 + $45.75)/2 = $45.50)
- the lowest selling price on the grant date ($44.50)
- the highest selling price on the grant date ($46.00)

The lowest selling price is risky and the highest selling price appears unnecessarily conservative, but each of the first three approaches is commonly used in corporate stock option plans and any one of them should be an acceptable method of determining the FV of stock for purposes of qualifying a stock option under Exception #2.[99] It would be nice, however, if IRS gave guidance, in the form of a regulatory amendment or published ruling, as to one or more specific acceptable methods.[100] In the absence of such guidance, query whether other methods would be acceptable, e.g., multi-day trading averages where the corporation's stock is thinly traded.[101]

Where the recipient of a stock option is also granted the right to receive dividend equivalent payments without regard to whether the stock option is ever exercised,

---

[99] The average of the highest and lowest selling prices is treated as a reasonable method by the Code §421 regulations. See Reg. §§1.421-7(e)(2) and 20.2031-2(a) and (b)(1).

[100] Although no published guidance has yet been forthcoming, IRS Letter Ruling 200016024 (1/19/00) concludes that establishing an exercise price equal to the closing price of the underlying shares on the last business day preceding the grant date satisfies the requirement that exercise price be at least equal to the underlying shares' FV on the grant date, and IRS Letter Ruling 199942012 (7/20/99) concludes that the following two methods for establishing exercise price satisfy the requirement that exercise price be at least equal to the underlying shares' FV on the grant date: (1) average of the high and low trading price for the stock on the grant date and (2) in the case of a "reload option" (i.e., a new NQO issued to an executive when he exercises an existing NQO) issued in connection with the executive's cashless exercise of an old NQO, the actual stock price utilized in determining the number of options shares the executive must surrender to "pay" the old NQO's exercise price.

[101] See Reg. §20.2031-2(a) and (b)(1).

the regulations treat the right to receive the dividend payments separately from the stock option for Code §162(m) purposes. Hence, such a dividend equivalent will not cause the stock option to fail to qualify as performance based,[102] but the dividend equivalent payments will be subject to the $1 million deduction limit (unless the dividend equivalent is also subject to a performance test).[103]

If payment of a dividend equivalent with respect to a stock option is contingent on the exercise of such option, the regulations treat such dividend equivalent payment as a reduction in the exercise price for the stock option. According to the preamble to the final regulations, this rule causes an option with a dividend equivalent payment contingent on exercise to "be non-performance based upon its exercise,"[104] presumably because the resulting reduction in the option's deemed exercise price causes the option to be in-the-money on its grant date. However, where an option is significantly out-of-the-money at grant or it is not certain the corporation will pay any dividends, this rule raises two difficult questions, neither of which is answered by the regulations or the preamble:

- If the dividend equivalent payment is contingent on option exercise, is the option automatically non-performance based, or is it only non-performance based if the amount of the dividend equivalent payments exceeds (or is expected to exceed—see next question) an amount which would reduce the deemed exercise price sufficiently to cause the option to be in-the-money at grant?
- Is the determination whether such an option is non-performance based made on the grant date (by estimating the future dividend equivalent payments with respect to the option to arrive at an estimated net exercise price) or is a "wait-and-see" approach appropriate in which the option remains performance based as long as the aggregate dividend equivalent payments with respect to the option do not actually exceed the amount by which the option was out-of-the-money at grant?

Even accepting the argument that dividends payable only on option exercise should be viewed as a reduction in the option exercise price, we believe that the final regulations are wrong as a matter of economic analysis in taking the position (as they appear to do) that such a dividend payment right with respect to an option on *common stock* granted at the money automatically produces an in-the-money option (and therefore one not performance-based). IRS's analysis ignores the fact that payment of a dividend contingent on option exercise reduces the FV of the underlying common stock by an amount equal to the dividend. Thus, payment of a dividend reduces (by an exactly equal amount) both the option exercise price and underlying stock FV, so that (1) the net effect is not the same as an "in-the-money" option and (2) the executive will not find it advantageous to exercise the option and receive the dividends unless changes in the stock's FV

---

[102] Reg. §1.162-27(e)(2)(vi)(A). The regulations apply a similar rule to dividend equivalent payments with respect to restricted stock. See ¶1506.1.5.1.

[103] Compare Reg. §1.162-27(e)(2)(iv).

[104] T.D. 8650 (12/20/95).

plus dividends have, overall, produced a positive return since grant date. We believe that this situation should still be treated as performance-based.[105]

EXAMPLE 2

A corporation's common stock has an FV of $50 per share. The corporation grants executive an option on common stock with a $50 per share exercise price. The option entitles the executive to receive dividends paid on the underlying common stock, but only if the executive exercises the option.

The FV of corporation's common stock increases to $75 per share. The corporation declares a $26 dividend. Assuming that the FV of the corporation's common stock does not change further as a result of factors other than the dividend, the FV of the corporation's common stock will fall to $49 ($75 less $26) when the stock becomes ex-dividend.

If the executive exercises the option before the dividend record date, the executive receives stock worth $75. If the executive exercises the option after the dividend (which the executive will find it advantageous to do even though the FV of the common stock is now $49), the executive will receive stock worth $49 plus $26 in cash attributable to the dividend, the same $75 of total value. The executive's compensation attributable to the option is the same either way.

EXAMPLE 3

Same as Example 2, except that the FV of the corporation's common stock prior to the dividend has remained at $50 (i.e., the stock has not appreciated in value).

Assuming that the FV of the corporation's common stock does not change as a result of factors other than the dividend, the FV of the corporation's stock common will fall to $24 ($50 less $26) when the stock goes ex-dividend.

The executive will presumably not exercise the option, because the property the executive would receive on exercise is equal to (i.e., does not exceed) the exercise price. If the executive exercises the option before the dividend record date, the executive will receive common stock worth $50. If the executive exercises the option after the dividend, the executive will receive stock worth $24 and $26 of cash attributable to the dividend, the same $50 of total value.

---

[105] We recognize that an option with rights to dividends on exercise is more valuable than one without such dividend rights and will be exercised in some cases where the option without dividend rights will not be exercised. Nonetheless, as set forth in the text and examples, we believe that the return on an option (with an exercise price equal to FV on the date of grant) is still performance-based even if dividends are paid only where the option is exercised, and the option does not have any of the characteristics of an in-the-money option.

Example 3 illustrates that, notwithstanding the executive's right on exercise to the $26 dividend payment, the executive has not received the equivalent of a discount option with a $24 exercise price. The executive in Example 3 receives no compensation benefit unless the common stock FV increases before (or after) the dividend. In contrast, an executive who had received a discount option with an exercise price equal to $24 (i.e., an option with a $24 exercise price on common stock with a $50 FV) would exercise under the facts of Example 3 (either before or after the dividend) and receive $26 in compensation based on the discount in the exercise price even though the value of the common stock had not increased.

Although Examples 2 and 3 deal with extraordinary dividends, we believe that the conclusion is equally true with respect to ordinary course dividends on common stock. The distribution of corporate assets in the form of a dividend reduces the FV of the corporation's assets and hence reduces the FV of its common stock unless earnings from the corporation's business or an increase in the value of its assets offsets the effect of the dividend payment.

EXAMPLE 4

Same as Example 2, except that the corporation pays a $.50 dividend each quarter on its common stock. Thus, if the executive exercised the option after five years, the executive would receive a share of stock plus $10 in cash reflecting the quarterly dividends paid over the five years.

The executive will not exercise the option unless the common stock FV is more than $40, so that the FV of the stock received on exercise plus the $10 in cash is greater than the $50 option exercise price. The common stock will be worth more than $40 only if the corporation has had earnings or an increase in value of its assets over the 5-year period to offset the $10 reduction in the corporation's assets from the dividends.

As illustrated by Example 4, an option granted at FV under which the holder receives dividends on the underlying common stock if the option is exercised will be exercised only if the corporation's earnings plus changes in the FV of its assets exceed the dividends paid on the stock between grant date and exercise date.[106] Equivalently, the executive will not exercise the option unless the corporation's stock generates a positive total return, measured by changes in common stock FV plus dividends from the grant date to the exercise date. We believe that this is an adequate performance standard and that the regulations should be amended to allow options on common stock to qualify for the performance-based compensation standard even if the holders receive dividends paid on the common stock only upon option exercise.[107]

---

[106] Where a corporation does not pay dividends, this merely illustrates that an option will be exercised only if the FV of the company's common stock increases.

[107] While the conclusions set forth above are valid for options on ordinary common stock, they may not be valid for options on debt-like preferred stock and certain forms of alphabet stock, where

In the absence of further guidance, it would be safest not to grant dividend equivalents contingent on option exercise.

However, a 2000 private letter ruling suggests an alternative approach which would afford option holders the economic equivalent of exercise-contingent dividends without violating the performance-based rules, at least in the case of unusual dividends.[108] Under this alternative approach, the option could not *require* the corporation to pay dividends with respect to the option shares contingent upon option exercise, but rather could grant the compensation committee the right to adjust the option exercise price (if it wished to do so) by deciding (after an unusual dividend has been paid) to adjust the option by agreeing to pay the unusual dividend upon exercise of the option.

In the 2000 ruling, T made two unusual cash distributions to its parent corporation prior to the parent's sale of T stock in an IPO. Under T's stock option plan, the compensation committee could adjust the terms of an outstanding stock option (including paying cash compensation to reflect lost value) if certain events occurred for the purpose of making such option economically equivalent to the option prior to such event. As a result of T's unusual cash distributions, the compensation committee granted each option holder a right to receive a cash payment, generally at the time the holder exercises the option, apparently equal to the unusual cash dividends (although the ruling's language is confusingly unclear on the exact calculation of such payment). Relying on a surprisingly broad reading of Reg. §1.162-27(e)(2)(iii)(C), IRS ruled that such cash payment to the exercising option holder did not cause the option to cease to qualify as performance-based so long as the option would otherwise so qualify.

Reg. §1.162-27(e)(2)(iii)(C) states that a change to the terms of stock-based compensation does not cause such compensation to fail to satisfy the performance-based requirements if made to reflect a "change in corporate capitalization, such as a stock split or stock dividend, or a corporate transaction, such as any merger . . . , any consolidation . . . , any separation . . . (including a spinoff or other distribution of stock or property . . .), any reorganization . . . , or any partial or complete liquidation." In the letter ruling, IRS (quoting only a portion of the above quoted regulatory language) obviously concluded that this regulation covers cash or property distributions, although not rising to the level of a spinoff or a partial liquidation.[109]

This letter ruling leaves unanswered at least two questions regarding the scope of Reg. §1.162-27(e)(2)(iii)(C). First, must the plan under which stock-based compensation is granted specifically permit post-grant adjustments (as did the plan in the 2000 private ruling) in order for such adjustments to come within the regulation? The answer should be "no," since the regulation itself contains no such requirement. However, Reg. §1.162-27(e)(2)(vii) example 13 (not cited in the

---

the relationship between the stock FV, the company's earnings and assets, and the payment of dividends is different.

[108] IRS Letter Ruling 200051018 (9/18/00).

[109] IRS ruled that the compensation "attributable to the options exercised by covered employees" satisfies the performance-based exception, which apparently covers the cash payments as well as the spread at exercise.

2000 ruling) implies that performance target adjustments to take into account unanticipated events, such as a change in accounting rules, constitute the exercise of impermissible discretion unless "made pursuant to the plan provisions." Since the 2000 letter ruling does not explicitly address this point, cautious taxpayers may want to include in their stock incentive plans a provision permitting or requiring the compensation committee to adjust stock- based compensation for events covered by Reg. §1.162-27(e)(2)(iii)(C).

The second unanswered question is whether Reg. §1.162-27(e)(2)(iii)(C) covers adjustments to stock-based compensation to reflect regular, periodic dividends in addition to the unusual dividends covered by the 2000 private ruling. The answer is likely "no," since such a result would effectively negate the Reg. §1.162-27(e)(2)(vi)(A) rule discussed above (as interpreted by the preamble to the final regulations) that dividends contingent on the exercise of an option are treated as a reduction in the exercise price of the option that causes the option to fail the performance-based standard. It is also reasonable to read Reg. §1.162-27(e)(2)(iii)(C) as applying to unusual dividends but not regular dividends since the transactions described in that regulation all fall into the category of unusual corporate transactions.

The regulations contain one additional requirement that must be met if a stock option or SAR plan is to qualify for the performance-based compensation exception. Under the regulations, a stock option or SAR plan must include the maximum number of shares with respect to which any one employee could receive an award during a specified period.[110] The mere fact that a plan contains an aggregate limit on the number of shares that may be issued to all employees under the plan does not meet this requirement. Furthermore, the language of the regulations does not permit a plan to satisfy this requirement by setting the maximum number of shares per employee as a percentage of outstanding shares.

The regulations contained a special transitional rule for plans or agreements approved by shareholders before 12/20/93, which generally waived compliance with the per employee maximum until the corporation's first election of directors after 12/31/96, so long as the plan stated the maximum number of shares in the aggregate that could be issued to all employees and the plan was not materially modified. To have qualified for this transitional relief, the regulations required that the "directors administering the plan or agreement [were] disinterested directors" within the meaning of SEC Rule 16b-3 under the 1934 Act and that the plan was approved by shareholders "in a manner consistent with" such SEC rule.[111] See ¶1506.2.1.

(8) Restricted stock. The legislative history states that a grant of restricted stock does not qualify for the performance-based compensation exception (where the stock is worth more than the executive pays for it, if anything) because the executive can profit even if the stock value stays the same or declines after grant,

---

[110] Reg. §1.162-27(e)(2)(vi)(A). The legislative history of Code §162(m) was ambiguous on this point. See 1993 Conference Report at 587.

[111] Reg. §1.162-27(h)(3)(iii).

unless "the grant or vesting of the restricted stock is based upon the attainment of a performance goal."[112]

Thus, for a grant of restricted stock (subject to vesting) to qualify for the performance-based compensation exception, the grant must either:

- be received as a result of the attainment of one or more pre-established objective performance goals (i.e., similar to the cash bonus rules discussed above), or
- be received subject to a vesting restriction that will allow the executive to retain the restricted stock only if one or more objective performance goals are met.[113]

When restricted stock is granted subject to a vesting restriction that allows the executive to retain the stock only if one or more objective performance goals are met, the corporation should consider whether to require its executives to forgo a Code §83(b) election to be taxed on the receipt of restricted stock, so that the restricted stock will qualify for the performance-based compensation exception. This is because a Code §83(b) election would cause the corporation's deduction to occur before the performance goals can be met and hence might be viewed as preventing compliance with the first and fourth requirements of the performance-based compensation exception.[114] See ¶1506.3.2 for a further discussion of this issue.

Dividends that are payable on restricted stock that has not yet vested and are payable without regard to whether the restricted stock ever vests do not affect the determination of whether such restricted stock qualifies for the performance-based compensation exception.[115] Thus, such a dividend payment on unvested stock is compensation subject to the $1 million deduction limit (along with all of the executive's other non-performance based compensation), unless the dividend equivalent payment is subject to a vesting test which separately satisfies the performance based exception,[116] but the executive's receipt of such a dividend does not "taint" the performance-based nature of the restricted stock.

[112] 1993 Conference Report at 587.

[113] As discussed above, a mere time-based vesting relating to the executive's continued employment would not qualify as a performance goal.

[114] The executive should not object to forgoing a Code §83(b) election, at least where the executive pays nothing for the restricted stock. In those circumstances, a Code §83(b) election would trigger ordinary income for the executive on receipt of the restricted stock equal to the stock's then value, determined without regard to the restrictions, and the executive would be entitled to no offsetting tax deduction if the restricted stock were later forfeited. Hence, an executive who receives free restricted stock is not likely to make a Code §83(b) election, unless the corporation defrays at least part of the tax burden (e.g., through a cash bonus which would further increase the executive's gross income).

[115] Reg. §1.162-27(e)(2)(iv).

[116] If the executive makes a Code §83(b) election on the restricted stock, the dividend does not qualify as compensation and the corporation does not receive a deduction for the dividend, without regard to Code §162(m).

¶1506.1.5.2   Goal Set by Compensation Committee

The second requirement of the performance-based compensation exception is that the performance goal be determined by a compensation committee comprised solely of two or more outside directors.[117] The statute states merely that the compensation committee must be composed solely of two or more "outside" directors and does not define "outside" director. The compensation committee would be tainted if even one member fails the test as an "outside" director.

(1)   Outside director. The legislative history of Code §162(m) states that a person is an "outside" director only if such person:

- is not a current employee of the corporation or a "related" entity,[118]
- was not an officer of the corporation or a "related" entity at any time,
- is not a former employee of the corporation or a "related" entity currently receiving compensation for prior services (other than from a tax-qualified pension plan), and
- is not currently receiving compensation for "personal services" in any capacity other than as a director (e.g., as a consultant).[119]

The regulations greatly expand on this fourth disqualification from outside director status, dropping the requirement that the services furnished be "personal" and adding a prohibition on remuneration for furnishing "goods" as well as services,[120] although the underpinning for this drastic expansion by IRS is not at all obvious.

Further, the regulations add two sets of indirect compensation rules where individual A (a P director) owns a part of, or works for, XCo which receives remuneration from P for goods or services. Under the first set of rules—contained in regulatory examples—A is treated as receiving indirect remuneration from P if A's employer XCo *either* (a) pays a commission to A based on A's sales of XCo goods or services to P *or* (b) calculates A's compensation by treating XCo sales of goods or services to P (whether or not by A) more favorably than XCo sales to other customers.[121] These examples suggest that P can treat A as a qualifying outside director if (a) P obtains representations that A does not receive such indirect compensation from P through XCo and (b) P has no reason to believe the representation false.[122]

Under the second set of indirect compensation rules, an amount paid by P to XCo (where XCo is owned in whole or in part by individual A or where A works for XCo) is treated as paid by P indirectly to its director A if:

---

[117] Code §162(m)(4)(C)(i).

[118] The legislative history is wholly silent on the meaning of "related."

[119] 1993 Conference Report at 587. The legislative history is wholly silent on whether the payor of this prohibited compensation is only the corporation or may also be a "related" entity.

[120] Reg. §1.162-27(e)(3)(i)(D).

[121] Reg. §1.162-27(e)(3)(ix) examples (3) and (4).

[122] Reg. §1.162-27(e)(3)(ix) examples (3) and (4).

(a) A has a beneficial ownership interest of more than 50% in XCo, so that *any* remuneration (no matter how small) from P to an entity (XCo) in which A has a more than 50% ownership interest prevents A from qualifying as an outside P director, *or*

(b) A has a beneficial ownership interest in XCo of at least 5% (but not more than 50%) and the remuneration from P to XCo for goods or services exceeds the lesser of $60,000 or 5% of XCo gross revenue,[123] *or*

(c) A "is employed or self-employed other than as a director" by XCo (even though A has no ownership in XCo) and the remuneration from P to XCo exceeds 5% of XCo's gross revenues,[124] except that if the remuneration from P to XCo is for personal services (e.g., legal, accounting, investment banking, or management consulting services) rendered by XCo to P (but not including services incidental to P's purchase of goods or to P's purchase of services which are not personal services), then the remuneration from P to XCo cannot exceed the lesser of $60,000 or 5% of XCo's gross revenues.[125]

For these rules, remuneration is taken into account when actually paid by P or, if earlier, when P becomes liable to pay, except that for (a) above remuneration is taken into account when paid and, if earlier, throughout the period when a contract to pay is outstanding.[126]

The approach taken in these regulations is surprisingly inconsistent: dramatically overbroad in excluding certain directors from the definition of "outside" director and curiously permissive in several other important respects. For example, as discussed above, the regulations limit the definition of outside director based on whether P *purchases* goods or services from the director or from the director's employer XCo, but neither the statute nor the regulations impose a similar limitation based on goods or services *sold* by P to the director or to the director's employer XCo. Thus, where P sells substantial manufactured goods to the phone company, an employee of the phone company may still qualify as a P outside director. Similarly, each of the following would appear eligible to be an outside director (assuming the candidate meets the other tests):

(a) the CEO's spouse or other family member,

(b) the CEO's personal (as opposed to P's) lawyer, accountant, or financial advisor, and

(c) the CEO's (as opposed to P's) full-time employee.

The regulations depart from legislative history in one other respect. In determining who is an outside director, the regulations disregard congressional references to related entities. It at first appeared that the regulations had substituted "affiliated" corporations (in Code §1504's 80-80 sense) for "related entities," since a

---

[123] This 5% test measures P's payments to XCo during P's preceding taxable year against XCo's gross revenue for XCo's taxable year ending with or within P's preceding taxable year.

[124] See preceding footnote.

[125] Reg. §1.162-27(e)(3)(ii).

[126] Reg. §1.162-27(e)(3)(ii).

publicly held corporation includes the members of its affiliated group.[127] However, IRS Letter Ruling 199950021 (12/17/99) reveals that even an 80-80 corporate parent can furnish Code §162(m) outside directors to its not-wholly owned subsidiary, at least where the subsidiary's minority interest is publicly held:

> "The employees and officers of [P] may serve as 'outside directors' of [S] on the [S] compensation committee so long as the remuneration paid by [S] to [P] does not exceed more than 5 percent of [P's] gross revenues."

(2) Transitional rules. In an implicit recognition of the surprisingly harsh approach of the regulations on the meaning of "outside director," the regulations contained an important ameliorating transitional rule treating as a qualified outside director until the corporation's first election of directors that occurred on or after 1/1/96, any person who was a "disinterested director" for SEC purposes under SEC Rule 16b-3(c)(2)(i) as in effect prior to 8/96 ("pre-8/96 SEC §16(b) Rules") or under SEC Rule 16b-3(d)(3) as it was in effect on 4/30/91 ("1991 SEC §16(b) Rules").[128]

For a discussion of another special transitional rule that applied to certain plans or agreements approved by shareholders before 12/20/93, see ¶1506.2.1. This other special transitional rule waived compliance with the regulation's stringent standards for determining outside directors in connection with such a pre-existing plan. This waiver generally lasted until the corporation's first election of directors after 12/31/96. To have qualified for this transitional relief, the regulations required that the "directors administering the plan or agreement [were] disinterested directors" within the meaning of the pre-8/96 or 1991 SEC §16(b) Rules and that the plan was approved by shareholders "in a manner consistent with" such SEC rules (see the discussion of the role of the compensation committee immediately below).[129]

---

[127] Reg. §1.162-27(e)(3) and (c)(1)(ii).

[128] Reg. §1.162-27(h)(2). See IRS Letter Ruling 9601032 (10/2/95) (confirming, under the proposed regulations, that if the SEC permits a corporation to elect to use either the pre-8/96 SEC §16(b) Rules or the 1991 SEC §16(b) Rules, then either may also be used for purposes of the Code §162(m) transition rule). Pursuant to amendments effective 8/96, the term "disinterested director" has been replaced in the SEC §16b-3 Rules with the term "non-employee director." SEC Rule 16b-3(b)(3)(i). In general, the definition of "non-employee" director contained in the current SEC §16b-3 Rules is somewhat more restrictive than the definition of "disinterested director" in the pre-8/96 SEC §16(b) Rules. However, notwithstanding this amendment, a director that meets the definition of "disinterested director" under either the pre-8/96 SEC §16(b) Rules or the 1991 SEC §16(b) rules continued to qualify after 8/96 as an "outside director" for purposes of the special transition rules (but only until such special transition rules expired) for outside directors and for certain plans or agreements approved by shareholders before 12/20/93 (see ¶1506.2.1). In this regard, Reg. §1.162-27(h)(2) states that: "A director *who is a disinterested director* is treated as satisfying the requirements of an outside director under paragraph (e)(3) of this section until the first meeting of shareholders at which directors are to be elected that occurs on or after January 1, 1996. For purposes of this paragraph (h)(2) and paragraph (h)(3) of this section, *a director is a disinterested director* if the director is disinterested within the meaning of Rule 16b-3(c)(2)(i), 17 CFR 240.16b-3(c)(2)(i), under the Exchange Act (including the provisions of Rule 16b-3(d)(3), as in effect on April 30, 1991)" (emphasis added).

[129] Reg. §1.162-27(h)(3)(iii).

(3) Compensation committee role. The regulations state that the compensation committee is "the committee of directors (including any subcommittee of directors) . . . that has the authority to establish and administer performance goals."[130] The regulations allow the compensation committee to be a subcommittee of another board of directors committee and allow the decisions of the compensation committee to be subject to ratification by another board of directors committee (containing non-outside directors) or the entire board of directors (containing non-outside directors).[131]

The regulations apparently require the compensation committee to make all grants and awards intended to qualify for the performance-based compensation exception.[132] The regulations state that the committee must "establish and administer performance goals" and, in discussing the particular requirements of option or SAR plans, state that the compensation committee must approve each grant or award.[133]

¶1506.1.5.3   Shareholder Disclosure and Vote

The third requirement of the performance-based compensation exception is that the material terms under which the compensation is to be paid (including performance goals) be disclosed to shareholders and approved by a separate majority shareholder vote.[134] The legislative history states that the executive's right to receive the compensation must be contingent on a separate shareholder approval.[135] Thus, where shareholder approval will be sought after the grant to, or agreement with, the executive, the documents evidencing the grant or agreement should state that if majority shareholder approval is not subsequently obtained, the grant or agreement is void and the executive forfeits the right to receive the compensation.[136]

---

[130] Reg. §1.162-27(c)(4).

[131] Reg. §1.162-27(c)(4).

[132] Where an 80%-or-greater subsidiary is a member of a publicly held corporation's affiliated group (but the subsidiary is not itself publicly held without regard to Code §1504), the parent's compensation committee (and not the subsidiary's compensation committee) should approve a grant or award to the subsidiary's employee if the grant or award is intended to qualify for the performance-based compensation exception. Under the regulations, the publicly held parent corporation is treated as including its affiliated subsidiary. See Reg. §1.162-27(c)(1)(ii).

Where the affiliated subsidiary is itself publicly held (i.e., publicly held without regard to Code §1504), the subsidiary's (and not the parent's) compensation committee must make grants or awards of the parent's stock to a covered employee of the subsidiary (who is not independently a covered employee of the parent) because such a publicly held subsidiary is not included in the affiliated group of its parent for purposes of Code §162(m) (see ¶1506.1.4.2).

[133] Reg. §1.162-27(e)(2)(i) and (vi).

[134] Code §162(m)(4)(C)(ii).

[135] 1993 Conference Report at 587. If this were not the case, the shareholders would merely be voting on whether the corporation would receive a deduction. Compare Prop. Reg. §1.280G-1 Q&A 7 (requiring that compensation to an executive be at risk in a shareholder vote that is a condition to a safe harbor under the golden parachute rules).

[136] In IRS Letter Ruling 200027012 (3/31/00), a corporation granted an option to acquire shares of its stock to a covered employee in an amount which exceeded the number of shares authorized

Shareholder approval must be obtained prior to the time when the compensation is paid by the corporation.[137] Because the shareholder vote must be determinative of whether the executive may retain the compensation, the parties will generally find it desirable to obtain shareholder approval as early as possible, i.e., before the arrangements are substantially in the money so that they may appear unfairly generous from the shareholders' standpoint.

Shareholder approval means the approval by a majority of the votes cast, not by a majority of all the outstanding shares.[138] Neither the legislative history nor the regulations suggests that the majority vote must be calculated by excluding any particular shares, such as those owned by the covered executive.[139]

Disclosure. The regulations clarify the information a publicly held corporation must disclose to shareholders to obtain shareholder approval of performance-based compensation. Under the regulations, a corporation must generally disclose each of the following:

- The individuals eligible to receive the compensation (who may be identified by name, by title, or by class of executive). The regulations make clear that a reference to "all salaried employees," to "all executive officers," or to "all key employees" is adequate.[140]
- A description of the "business criteria on which the performance goal is based," which "need not include [(a)] the specific targets . . . under the

---

under the corporation's incentive stock plan at the time of grant. In order to qualify the grant as performance-based for purposes of Code §162(m), the terms of the grant conditioned exercise on subsequent shareholder approval of the grant. IRS ruled that (i) the option qualifies as performance-based where shareholder approval is subsequently obtained and (ii) for purposes of determining whether the option satisfies the requirement that it not be in-the-money on its grant date (see ¶1506.1.5.1), the grant date is the actual grant date (as opposed to the subsequent shareholder approval date).

[137] Reg. §1.162-27(e)(4)(i). Where an 80%-or-greater subsidiary is a member of a publicly held corporation's affiliated group (but the subsidiary is not itself publicly held without regard to Code §1504), the parent's shareholders (and not the shareholders of the subsidiary which is 80%-or-more owned by the parent) should approve a grant or award (or a plan providing for such grant or award) to the subsidiary's employee if the grant or award is intended to qualify for the performance-based compensation exception. Under the regulations, the publicly held parent corporation is treated as including its affiliated subsidiary. See Reg. §1.162-27(c)(1)(ii); IRS Letter Ruling 199950021 (12/17/99).

Where the affiliated subsidiary is itself publicly held (i.e., publicly held without regard to Code §1504), the subsidiary's (and not the parent's) shareholders must approve grants or awards of the parent's stock to a covered employee of the subsidiary (who is not independently a covered employee of the parent) because such a publicly held subsidiary is not included in the affiliated group of its parent for purposes of Code §162(m) (see ¶1506.1.4.2).

[138] Code §162(m)(4)(C)(ii); Reg. §1.162-27(e)(4)(vii); 1993 Conference Report at 587. Compare Rev. Rul. 75-256, 1975-2 C.B. 194 (shareholder approval of qualified stock option plan required approval of majority of outstanding shares) with Reg. §1.422-5 and Prop. Reg. §1.422-2(b)(2) (shareholder approval of an ISO plan requires only a majority of the shares voting unless state law or corporate charter or bylaws establish a different method).

[139] In contrast, the legislative history and proposed regulations under the golden parachute compensation-disallowance rules (Code §280G) do contain such an exclusion. See H.R. Rep. No. 426, 99th Cong., 1st Sess. 902 (1985); Prop. Reg. §1.280G-1 Q&A 7.

[140] Reg. §1.162-27(e)(4)(i) and (ii).

performance goal" or (b) any information determined by the compensation committee to be "confidential commercial or business information the disclosure of which would have an adverse effect" on the corporation (e.g., a schedule for developing a new product), so long as the disclosure to shareholders states that such information has been omitted as confidential information.[141]

- Either (a) "the maximum amount of compensation that is payable to an individual" or (b) sufficient information "so that shareholders can determine the maximum amount of compensation that could be paid to any employee" or (c) "the formula used to calculate the amount of compensation."[142] However, in the case of a formula based at least in part on salary or base pay, the maximum dollar amount of compensation that could be paid to the employee must be disclosed to the shareholders (apparently even if the dollar amount of salary or base pay is fixed at the time the performance goal is established under corrections to T.D. 8650 issued 2/5/96).[143]

Where the regulations do not provide specific guidance, SEC principles govern whether disclosure is adequate.[144]

The regulations allow a publicly held corporation to obtain shareholder approval once for a multi-year plan so long as the compensation committee does not, after such approval, change the material terms of the performance goal(s) disclosed to shareholders. However, if the plan allows the compensation committee to change the targets under a performance goal (e.g., by setting a new annual target each year), shareholder approval is good for only five years and the plan must be reapproved by shareholders after five years.[145]

Hence, where the plan (and shareholder disclosure) states that the business criteria are sales, EBIT, EPS, share price, and/or return on equity and that the compensation committee will from time to time set specific targets based on these business criteria, the plan (1) must be approved by shareholders, (2) must be reapproved if the business criteria are materially changed, and (3) in any event must be reapproved by shareholders after five years.

Transitional rule. The regulations state a special transitional rule that applies to certain plans or agreements approved by shareholders before 12/20/93. See ¶1506.2.1. This special transitional rule waives compliance with the regulations' stringent shareholder disclosure and approval requirements in connection with such a pre-existing plan. This waiver generally lasts until the corporation's first

---

[141] Reg. §1.162-27(e)(4)(i) and (iii). The regulations use the following terms: (1) "business criterion" or "business criteria" means the general category or categories used to define a goal (e.g., EBIT, EPS, share price, return on equity, etc.), (2) "specific target" or "target" means the specific numerical amount which must be equalled or exceeded in order for a performance goal to be attained, and (3) "performance goal" or "goal" means the combination of a business criterion, a formula, and a specific target.

[142] Reg. §1.162-27(e)(4)(i) and (iv).

[143] Reg. §1.162-27(e)(4)(i). Under a transitional rule adopted by the final regulations, this disclosure requirement does not apply to plans approved by shareholders before 5/1/95. Reg. §1.162-27(j)(2)(v).

[144] Reg. §1.162-27(e)(4)(v).

[145] Reg. §1.162-27(e)(4)(vi).

election of directors after 12/31/96. To qualify for this transitional relief, the regulations require that the "directors administering the plan or agreement are disinterested directors" within the meaning of either pre-8/96 or 1991 SEC §16(b) Rules[146] and that the plan be approved by shareholders "in a manner consistent with" either pre-8/96 or 1991 SEC §16(b) Rules.[147]

¶1506.1.5.4   Compensation Committee Certification

The fourth requirement of the performance-based compensation exception is that before the compensation is paid, the compensation committee certify that the performance goals and any other material terms were satisfied.[148] The legislative history states that the executive's right to receive the compensation must be contingent on certification. However, according to the legislative history and the regulations, certification is not required in the case of a stock option or SAR otherwise meeting the first three requirements.[149]

Although the regulations require the compensation committee to certify that the "performance goals and any other material terms were in fact satisfied," Treasury personnel have informally stated that the reference to "other material terms" was not intended to create an additional substantive requirement for the performance-based compensation exception. Thus, for example, a corporation should be entitled to waive a vesting restriction that requires the executive's continued employment with the corporation without fear that the waiver would cause the loss of the performance-based compensation exception (by preventing the compensation committee from certifying that the other material terms of the award have been met).[150] It is unfortunate that the final regulations do not clarify that the compensation committee need only certify that the performance goals were met and need not certify that other conditions to the award that are not performance goals were met. In short, we believe that as the regulations are now drafted, the "other material terms" are the non-performance-based terms in effect, as modified, on the date of payment.

¶1506.1.6   Exception #5: Pre-2/93 Grandfathered Arrangement

The $1 million deduction limit does not apply to compensation payable under "a written binding contract that was in effect on February 17, 1993" and not

---

[146] See the discussion of transitional rules in ¶1506.1.5.2.

[147] Reg. §1.162-27(h)(3)(iii).

[148] Code §162(m)(4)(C)(iii).

[149] 1993 Conference Report at 587; Reg. §1.162-27(e)(5).

[150] Reg. §1.162-27(e)(2)(iii)(B) indicates that, where a transfer of stock is subject to the attainment of both a performance goal and a vesting schedule, the corporation may "change" the vesting schedule to defer or accelerate the transfer of stock without being treated as increasing the compensation under the award. This provision of the regulations would be superfluous if a change to the vesting schedule were viewed as a change to the material terms of the award, thus preventing compensation committee certification. See also IRS Letter Ruling 9649014 (8/10/96) (voluntary acceleration of time-vesting options in connection with corporation's change in ownership does not cause loss of the performance-

modified thereafter in any material respect.[151] This grandfather rule protects the deduction for future payouts on written contracts entered into on or before 2/17/93 and written awards made on or before 2/17/93, so long as the corporation's obligation under the old contract or award is not subject to discretion, i.e., the corporation is obligated to make the payment.

¶1506.1.6.1   Binding Contract in Effect in 2/93

Under the regulations, a written contract is binding where "under applicable state law, the corporation is obligated to pay the compensation if the employee performs services."[152] Where the contract is "terminable or cancelable by the corporation after February 17, 1993, without the employee's consent, [the contract] is treated as a new contract as of the date that any such termination or cancellation, if made, would be effective" and ceases to be grandfathered thereafter.[153] Similarly, a contract that is renewed after 2/17/93 is treated as a new contract that was not binding on 2/17/93, and hence does not qualify for the grandfather rule.[154]

Plan or arrangement. A mere plan which permits the corporation to make a future discretionary award or a future contract would generally appear not to be a binding contract because the corporation is not "obligated to pay the compensation if the employee performs the services." Thus, the grandfather rule would appear not to protect a post-2/17/93 award or contract merely because it is made pursuant to a pre-2/18/93 plan.

The regulations indicate that a "plan or arrangement" may in some cases be a "written binding contract" for purposes of the grandfather rule.[155] Thus, for example, a bonus plan adopted by a corporation prior to 2/18/93 that provided for a specific award to eligible executives would qualify for the grandfather rule if the plan creates a binding legal obligation on the part of the corporation to pay the compensation.

However, the grandfather rule for pre-2/18/93 plans and arrangements may be broader. The regulations also state that where a plan or arrangement is a written binding contract, the grandfather rule applies "even though the employee was not eligible to participate in the plan as of February 17, 1993," so long as "the employee was employed [by the corporation] on February 17, 1993 . . . or the employee had the right to participate in the plan or arrangement under a written binding contract as of that date."[156] Thus, at least in the case of an employee who was not eligible to participate in a plan on 2/17/93 but who later becomes

---

based compensation exception because the accelerated vesting does not increase the compensation payable upon attainment of the Code §162(m) performance goal, i.e., the appreciation in value of the underlying stock).

[151] Code §162(m)(4)(D).
[152] Reg. §1.162-27(h)(1)(i).
[153] Reg. §1.162-27(h)(1)(i).
[154] Reg. §1.162-27(h)(1)(i).
[155] Reg. §1.162-27(h)(1)(ii).
[156] §1.162-27(h)(1)(ii).

eligible, the grandfather rule applies to a benefit under a plan that the corporation was not legally bound to pay by contract on 2/17/93, and only became bound to pay based on subsequent events that were presumably at least partly in the corporation's control (e.g., the executive's promotion).

Thus, it is not wholly clear whether the grandfather rule would apply where the corporation had, before 2/18/93, adopted a binding plan calling for a bonus (each year through 2000) to corporate officers equal, in the aggregate, to 3% of the corporation's net income, granting the board of directors or a committee discretion to allocate this amount among the corporate officers.[157] It is possible that the discretionary allocation right would destroy grandfathering. However, we believe that such a plan should be covered by the grandfather rule because the corporation is required to pay the compensation in the aggregate, even though no one executive is entitled to a specific amount. If the grandfather rule applies, it appears that a bonus to a particular officer would be grandfathered only if he or she (1) were eligible to participate in the plan on 2/17/93 or (2) were employed by the corporation on 2/17/93 (even if not yet an officer on 2/17/93), or (3) had a contract on 2/17/93, giving him or her the right to participate when he or she became an employee. However, the regulations, as described above, are unclear and to some extent contradictory on the extent to which a plan or arrangement may be covered by the grandfather rule.

Discretionary payments. The regulations do not specifically state that the grandfather rule is inapplicable to discretionary benefits under a pre-2/18/93 plan or arrangement. However, the regulations do state, with respect to a contract, that the compensation must be "payable under a written binding contract that was in effect on 2/17/93," and that "under applicable state law, the corporation [must have been] obligated to pay the compensation if the employee performs services."[158] Hence, with respect to a grandfathered contract, it appears that a payment permitted but not required under the contract is not grandfathered.

Thus, where a corporation agreed under a pre-2/18/93 contract to pay an executive a fixed salary, a minimum bonus, and a discretionary bonus in excess of the minimum bonus, the discretionary bonus, if paid, appears not to qualify for the grandfather rule. However, as discussed below, the payment (or non-payment) of the discretionary bonus should not constitute a material modification of the contract and hence should not adversely affect the ability of the fixed salary and fixed bonus to qualify for the grandfather rule.

¶1506.1.6.2   *Material Modification*

Because a material modification of an old (pre-2/18/93) contract or award will result in loss of grandfather protection, a publicly held corporation and its

---

[157] Although the liability to any one officer may be contingent since the officer may forfeit his or her rights to a bonus by leaving the corporation's employ, the corporation may accrue the deduction once the amount owed to the group is fixed under the "all events" test. See Washington Post Co. v. United States, 405 F.2d 1279, 69-1 U.S.T.C. ¶9192 (Cl. Ct. 1969).

[158] Reg. §1.162-27(h)(1)(i).

executives should be careful about making any changes to old compensation arrangements. The regulations state that a material modification of a grandfathered contract occurs "when the contract is amended to increase the amount of compensation payable to the employee" (except an increase not exceeding a reasonable cost-of-living increase, as described below).[159] Thus, it appears that an amendment which causes any increase in excess of a reasonable cost-of-living increase (as described below) will destroy grandfathering. However, it also appears that an amendment which does not increase the amount of the employee's compensation does not destroy grandfathering.[160]

Acceleration of a payment is a material modification unless the payment "is discounted to reasonably reflect the time value of money."[161] If a payment is deferred, the amount paid may be increased without causing a material modification where the increase "is based on either a reasonable rate of interest or one or more predetermined actual investments."[162]

Moreover, IRS has ruled privately that a voluntary acceleration of time-vesting options in connection with a corporation's change in ownership does not destroy grandfathering under Exception #2 discussed in ¶1506.1.3 (plan or agreement adopted prior to corporation's IPO), because the accelerated vesting does not increase the compensation payable upon attainment of the Code §162(m) performance goal, i.e., the appreciation in value of the underlying stock.[163]

The regulations further state:

> The adoption of a supplemental contract or agreement that provides for increased compensation, or the payment of additional compensation, is a material modification of a binding, written contract where the facts and circumstances show that the additional compensation is paid on the basis of substantially the same elements or conditions as the compensation that is otherwise paid under the written binding contract.[164]

It appears, under the quoted language, that a supplemental contract or even the mere payment of additional compensation without a supplemental contract may be integrated with a grandfathered contract and hence may destroy grandfathering. In this respect, the material modification test for a grandfathered contract apparently incorporates an approach similar to the aggregation rule discussed in ¶1506.1.5.1, leaving the scope of the material modification rule unclear.

---

[159] Reg. §1.162-27(h)(1)(iii).

[160] See IRS Letter Ruling 9551024 (9/22/95) (amendment to a stock option plan giving participants the right to transfer stock options to family members and certain family trusts is not a material modification for purposes of the transitional rule of Reg. §1.162-27(h)(3) on the ground that "the amendment does not effect [sic] either the timing or the amount of income recognition to the participants").

[161] Reg. §1.162-27(h)(1)(iii)(B). See IRS Letter Ruling 199920011 (2/10/99) (no material modification where accelerated payment amount based on reasonable estimate of future payments (which were uncertain in amount), discounted at an interest rate "similar to" the applicable federal rate).

[162] Reg. §1.162-27(h)(1)(iii)(B).

[163] IRS Letter Ruling 9649014 (8/10/96).

[164] Reg. §1.162-27(h)(1)(iii)(C).

The regulations create an exception from this general rule under which a material modification is not triggered by (1) "a supplemental payment that is equal to or less than a reasonable cost-of-living increase" or (2) a payment that qualifies for the performance-based compensation exception.[165]

It is not clear when "additional compensation is paid on the basis of substantially the same elements or conditions as the compensation that is otherwise paid under the written binding contract."[166] One example makes clear that a restricted stock grant which does not qualify for the performance-based compensation exception is nonetheless sufficiently different from salary paid pursuant to a grandfathered contract because the restricted stock grant is "based . . . on the stock price."[167] Another example strongly implies that any salary increase or salary payment is integrated with the contractual salary payments.[168] However, additional salary should be sufficiently separate if the additional salary is for additional duties or additional services.

Moreover, we believe that grandfathering should not be lost for contractually fixed payments of salary and bonus where the contract also (1) permits the corporation to pay a completely discretionary bonus and the corporation does so or (2) requires the corporation to pay a bonus between two specified amounts and the corporation pays a greater bonus than the contractual minimum. While such discretionary bonus payments appear not to qualify for the grandfather rule, their payment should not be viewed as a material modification of the contract. As long as the payment of a discretionary bonus amount is within the terms of the pre-2/18/93 contract, the payment of the discretionary bonus is not a modification at all. Query whether grandfather protection for a pre-2/18/93 salary contract will be lost if the corporation pays the executive an additional discretionary bonus not mentioned at all in the contract.

¶1506.1.6.3   *Assumption of Grandfathered Obligation*

Special problems arise when one corporation ("P") acquires the stock or assets of another corporation ("T"). Where P assumes a T grandfathered compensation arrangement (i.e., a written binding T contract entered into on or before 2/17/93 and not materially modified thereafter) in an acquisition, qualification for continuing grandfather protection after the acquisition will be lost if the assumption involves a material modification.[169] Such an assumption should not be treated as a material modification unless the terms of the compensation agreement (other than the identity of the party obligated to pay the compensation) are materially modified in connection with the assumption. In short, where there is a mere

---

[165] Reg. §1.162-27(h)(1)(iii)(C).
[166] Reg. §1.162-27(h)(1)(iii)(C).
[167] Reg. §1.162-27(h)(1)(iv) example (3).
[168] Reg. §1.162-27(h)(1)(iv) example (2).
[169] This discussion assumes that the T executive, whose compensation arrangement is being assumed by P, is a covered employee of P after the acquisition.

substitution of parties, the result is not an increase in compensation, and there should be no material modification.[170]

A question also arises as to whether the substitution of a P stock option for a grandfathered T stock option would be considered a material modification. We believe that the standards of Code §424(a) and (h) should be applied in determining whether a material modification has occurred (e.g., there should be no modification if the substituted P option had a spread that was not greater than the assumed T option and the executive was given no new benefits under the P option). The regulations do not address this issue, and specific guidance in this area would be desirable.[171]

¶1506.1.7   Exception #6: Compensation Not Paid for Services as Employee

By its terms, the Code §162(m) deduction limit applies only to compensation for services performed by an *employee*.[172] It follows that payments made to an individual other than for services performed *as an employee* are not subject to the $1 million deduction limit, even where such payments are made to the individual at a time when the individual is an employee of the corporation making the payment. This exception was confirmed in IRS Letter Ruling 9745002 (7/25/97), where a public corporation's CEO retired and became a consultant, but then, later in the same year in which he retired, returned as CEO. The corporation represented that the relationship under the consulting agreement was not an employer-employee relationship. Based on this representation, IRS ruled that the consulting fees paid by the corporation to the service provider as a consultant during the period when he was not an employee were not applicable employee remuneration within the meaning of Section 162(m)(4).[173]

This ruling is predicated upon the taxpayer's representation that the consulting fees at issue were not consideration for services performed as an employee. In

---

[170] See discussion of IRS Letter Ruling 9801043 at ¶1506.4, which tends to support this position.

[171] There are greater technical problems where an old T option is not grandfathered but, when issued by T, such option qualified for the performance-based compensation exception. In such case the question is not whether a grandfathered arrangement has been materially modified but rather whether the new option qualifies for the performance-based compensation exception because the old option so qualified. This issue is relevant where the new P option would not by itself qualify for the performance-based compensation exception because (as is likely) the P option is in the money at the time of the assumption or because the P option may not have been approved by P shareholders.

Again, we believe that IRS should allow a P option issued by P in an assumption of a T option to continue to qualify for the performance-based compensation exception (on the technical ground that there is no new issuance) if (1) the T option qualified for such exception when issued and (2) the assumption would qualify under the principles of Code §§424(a) and (h).

[172] Code §162(m)(4)(A) (defining "applicable employee remuneration" as "remuneration for services performed by [a covered] employee"); Reg. §1.162-27(c)(3)(i) ($1 million deduction limit applies only to "remuneration for services performed by a covered employee").

[173] IRS also ruled that directors' fees paid to the individual during the interim period in which he was not an employee were not "applicable employee remuneration" within the meaning of Code §162(m)(4) (the corporation paid directors' fees only to non-employee directors; hence, the individual received such fees only during the period of time he was not an employee).

any given situation, the issue of whether a payment is made as consideration for services performed in an individual's capacity as an employee (as opposed to as an independent contractor) is factual in nature.

Similarly, we believe that payment of a signing bonus or hello bonus by a corporation to an executive in connection with the commencement of such executive's employment by the corporation should not constitute "applicable employee remuneration" within the meaning of Code §162(m)(4) so long as the receipt and retention of such bonus by the executive is not conditioned on the performance of services as an employee.[174] Thus, for example, a bonus should not be subject to the $1 million deduction limit where it is paid under the following circumstances:

- A corporation pays a signing bonus to an executive prior to the date the executive becomes an employee of the corporation, so long as such executive has no obligation to repay the bonus if he never commences employment with the corporation.
- A corporation enters into an employment contract with an executive granting such executive a signing bonus on a specified date (which may be after the date the executive commences employment with the corporation), so long as the corporation is legally bound to pay the signing bonus to the executive (or his or her heirs or assignees) without regard to whether the executive commences employment with the corporation.
- A corporation enters into an employment contract with an executive granting such executive a hello bonus at the time the executive arrives at work on the first day his or her employment commences with the corporation, and the corporation is legally bound to pay the hello bonus if (and only if) the executive arrives at work on such date but without regard to whether the executive actually performs any services as an employee.

However, where an executive must perform at least some services in his or her capacity as an employee in order to either receive or (if the bonus is paid before employment commences) retain a signing or hello bonus, the bonus will likely be regarded as compensation for services performed as an employee and therefore subject to the $1 million deduction limit.[175]

---

[174] Cf. Rev. Rul. 58-145, 1958-1 C.B. 360 (a bonus payment made by a baseball club to a new ballplayer solely for signing a contract with the baseball club, without any requirement of performing services for the baseball club, does not constitute "wages" subject to income tax withholding under Code §3402. "Wages" are defined in Code §3401(a) as "all remuneration (other than fees paid to a public official) for services performed by an employee for his employer."

[175] Rev. Rul. 58-145, 1958-1 C.B. 360 (signing bonus paid to a new baseball player constitutes "wages" for income tax withholding purposes to the extent the bonus is paid only if services are actually performed by the ballplayer or the baseball club retains the ballplayer after a specified date).

¶1506.1.8   Exception #7: Commissions

The $1 million deduction limit does not apply to compensation "payable on a commission basis solely on account of income generated directly by the individual performance of the [executive] to whom such [compensation] is payable."[176]

The good news is that this exception does not require a compensation committee and/or shareholder vote, as does the performance-based compensation exception. The bad news is that this exception will almost never be of use with regard to a key corporate executive.

Compensation based solely on a percentage of sales made by the executive would qualify for this exception. However, compensation based on a broader performance standard (such as the income or sales produced by the entire corporation or by a business unit) would not qualify for this exception because it would not be based "solely" on sales generated directly by the executive.[177] Hence, this is an extremely narrow exception that is unlikely to apply to compensation earned by the top five officers of a publicly held corporation.

¶1506.2   Transitional Rules

¶1506.2.1   Pre-12/93 Plan

There were several liberalizing transitional rules for any plan or agreement approved by shareholders prior to 12/20/93. Such a plan was treated as satisfying both (1) the shareholder disclosure and approval requirements discussed in ¶1506.1.5.3 (even though the prior shareholder disclosure and approval did not meet all the technical requirements of the regulations) and (2) the compensation committee requirements discussed in ¶1506.1.5.2 (even though the composition of the compensation committee does not meet all the technical requirements of the regulations).

In addition, where this transitional rule applied to a plan covering stock options and/or SARs, the transitional rule also waived compliance with the requirement (discussed in ¶1506.1.5.1) that such a stock-based plan state the maximum number of shares with respect to which an option or SAR may be granted to an employee, so long as the plan stated an aggregate limit on the number of shares with respect to which awards may be made under the plan.[178]

---

[176] Code §162(m)(4)(B).

[177] Reg. §1.162-27(d).

[178] Reg. §1.162-27(h)(3)(i). The regulations, which refer to pre-8/15/96 SEC Rule 16-3(b), appear to allow the aggregate limit for this purpose to be expressed as a percentage of outstanding shares. The reference in the regulations to pre-8/15/96 SEC Rule 16-3(b) is apparently in error; pre-8/15/96 Rule 16b-3(b) contains no reference to the maximum number of shares to be awarded under an employee benefit plan. We think that the regulations are meant to reference pre-8/15/96 SEC Rule 16(a)(1), which requires that an employee benefit plan set forth either a maximum number or a determinable amount of shares to be awarded. The SEC requirement is satisfied if the plan expresses that amount as a percentage of the company's outstanding shares. See Kathleen A. Weigand, SEC No-Action Letter, [1991 Transfer Binder] Fed. Sec. L. Rep. (CCH) ¶79,764.

This transitional rule was available where the following conditions were met:

- "[T]he plan was approved by shareholders [prior to 12/20/93] in a manner consistent with" SEC principles (i.e., under pre-8/96 or 1991 SEC §16(b) Rules).[179]
- "[T]he directors administering the plan or agreement [were] disinterested directors" within the meaning of the pre-8/96 or 1991 SEC §16(b) Rules.[180]

Generally, a public corporation would have obtained shareholder approval for a plan or agreement only if it was stock based so that SEC Rule Reg. §16b-3 would (if complied with) provide certain exemptions from the short-swing profit rules of §16(b). In some cases cash arrangements may have been approved by shareholders if the arrangements were included in a larger plan that also included stock-based awards.

This liberalizing transitional relief expired (and hence, the plan must have been approved by shareholders in compliance with all the technical requirements of the regulations and the compensation committee must comply with all the technical requirements of the IRS regulations) at the time of the corporation's first election of directors after 12/31/96 (or if earlier, the date on which the plan expired or was materially modified or, for a stock-based plan, the date on which all of the stock authorized under the plan had been issued, if earlier). Compensation in the form of restricted property subject to vesting or stock-based compensation is exempt under this transitional rule if the award was made during this transitional

---

[179] See the discussion of transitional rules and the definition of pre-8/96 or 1991 SEC §16(b) Rules in ¶1506.1.5.2.

[180] Reg. §1.162-27(h)(3)(iii). The pre-8/96 SEC §16(b) Rules provide the following definition of "disinterested director":

> a director who is not, during the one year prior to service as an administrator of a plan, or during such service, granted or awarded equity securities pursuant to the plan or any other plan of the issuer or any of its affiliates, except that: (A) participation in a formula plan . . . shall not disqualify a director from being a disinterested person; (B) participation in an ongoing securities acquisition plan . . . shall not disqualify a director from being a disinterested person; (C) an election to receive an annual retainer fee in either cash or an equivalent amount of securities, or partly in cash and partly in securities, shall not disqualify a director from being a disinterested person; and (D) participation in a plan shall not disqualify a director from being a disinterested person for the purpose of administering another plan that does not permit participation by directors.

SEC Rule 16b-3(c)(2)(i), as in effect prior to 8/96. 1991 SEC §16(b) Rules provide the following definition of "disinterested director":

> an administrator of a plan who is not at the time he [or she] exercises discretion in administering the plan eligible and has not at any time within one year prior thereto been eligible for selection as a person to whom stock may be allocated or to whom stock options or [SARs] may be granted pursuant to the plan or any other plan of the issuer or any of its affiliates entitling the participants therein to acquire stock, stock options or [SARs] of the issuer or any of its affiliates.

SEC Rule 16b-3(d)(3), as in effect on 4/30/91.

period, without regard to the year in which the corporation's deduction arises.[181] However, other types of deferred compensation are exempt under this transitional rule only if *paid* during the transitional period (without regard to when the deferred compensation is *awarded*). For a discussion of "materially modified," see ¶1506.1.6.2.[182]

¶1506.2.2 Postponement of Outside Director Definition

The regulations state an important transitional rule that treated as a qualified "outside director" any person who was a "disinterested director" for SEC purposes (under the pre-8/96 or 1991 SEC §16(b) Rules) until the corporation's first election of directors that occurred on or after 1/1/96.[183] An action performed by disinterested directors during this transitional period (e.g., establishing a performance goal) qualified as an action by outside directors within the meaning of Code §162(m) even after the transitional period expired, without regard to whether such directors continued to qualify as outside directors. This relief allowed a corporation to establish plans or set performance goals in compliance with the performance-based compensation exception at a time when the corporation did not have a compensation committee composed solely of outside directors within the meaning of Code §162(m).[184]

¶1506.3   Other Issues

¶1506.3.1 Application to Publicly Traded Partnership

Code §7704(a) generally causes a "publicly traded partnership" (PTP) to be treated as a corporation "for purposes of this title." Certain PTPs in existence when Code §7704 was adopted by the 1987 Tax Act and which do not otherwise qualify for the Code §7704(c) exception were grandfathered for 10 years until their first taxable year beginning after 12/31/97.[185]

It is not entirely clear whether Code §162(m) will apply to a PTP that is treated as a corporation under Code §7704 (a "PTP corporation"). It would appear that a PTP corporation would be covered by Code §162(m) because (1) Code §7704 states that a PTP corporation is a corporation "for purposes of this title" and this

---

[181] Reg. §1.162-27(h)(3)(iii).

[182] See IRS Letter Ruling 9551024 (9/22/95) (amendment to a stock option plan giving participants the right to transfer stock options to family members and certain family trusts is not a material modification for purposes of the transitional rule of Reg. §1.162-27(h)(3) on the ground that "the amendment does not effect [sic] either the timing or the amount of income recognition to the participants").

[183] Reg. §1.162-27(h)(2). The definition of "disinterested director" for SEC purposes is described in *supra* note 180. See ¶1506.1.5.2 for the definition of pre-8/96 and 1991 SEC §16(b) Rules.

[184] See Reg. §1.162-27(e)(3).

[185] 1987 Tax Act, Pub. L. No. 100-203, §10211(c), as amended by Pub. L. No. 100-647, §2004(f)(2).

title includes Code §162(m),[186] and (2) a PTP is required to register its common equity securities under §12 of the 1934 Act.

However, the preamble to the 1993 proposed regulations states:

> Questions have arisen as to the application of Code §162(m) to certain master limited partnerships whose equity interests are required to be registered under the [1934 Act] and that, beginning in 1997, may be treated as corporations for Federal income tax purposes. Whether these partnerships would be publicly held corporations within the meaning of Code §162(m) and, if so, the manner in which they would satisfy the exception for performance-based compensation is currently under study and is not addressed in these proposed regulations.[187]

Unfortunately, the final regulations also do not address the application of Code §162(m) to such master limited partnerships.

If PTP corporations were to be treated as publicly held corporations for purposes of Code §162(m), it is unclear how various provisions of the regulations would apply.

- Who are a PTP corporation's covered employees? An executive who acts solely as a general partner would generally not be an employee at all. Moreover, a PTP corporation may not file a proxy statement disclosing executive compensation (given that it may not need to seek the approval of its public limited partners for such compensation).[188]
- What would constitute shareholder approval of a plan for purposes of the performance-based compensation exception (see ¶1506.1.5.3) since a PTP has no shareholders and its public partners generally are limited partners?
- How would a compensation committee be formed since a partnership need not have a board of directors?
- Could Exception #2 for pre-IPO plans and agreements apply since the exception literally applies only to a "*corporation* that was not publicly held" (emphasis added)?[189] Literally read, Exception #2 would not apply to a plan or agreement adopted by a partnership prior to becoming a PTP corporation because such a partnership (which becomes a PTP corporation) is not a "corporation" at the time it adopts the pre-IPO plan or agreement.

Moreover, where a PTP begins to be taxed as a corporation as a result of the expiration of Code §7704's 10-year grandfather rule, the PTP corporation will

---

[186] The golden parachute regulations state that, for purposes of Code §280G, a corporation shall include a corporation as defined in Code §7701(a)(3) (i.e., an association taxable as a corporation) and a PTP treated as a corporation under Code §7704(a). Prop. Reg. §1.280G-1, Q&A 45.

[187] 58 Fed. Reg. at 66,311.

[188] If a PTP corporation does not file a proxy statement, it is required to include a summary compensation table disclosing executive compensation as part of its Form 10-K filed with the SEC (and available to the public). As noted in ¶1506.1.4.1, it is not clear whether disclosure in a Form 10-K is sufficient to make a person a covered employee (on the ground that the Form 10-K is not mailed directly to shareholders, and hence the contents may not be "reported to shareholders").

[189] Reg. §1.162-27(f).

generally not need to issue a prospectus to its shareholders (since it will not be issuing new securities to its shareholders). Thus, there will be no prospectus in which to make the disclosure necessary to satisfy Exception #2.

We regret that the final regulations did not expand Exception #2 to exempt compensation arrangements entered into by any entity (whether or not it is then treated for tax purposes as a corporation) prior to its becoming a publicly held corporation even though such a partnership (which becomes a PTP corporation) is not a "corporation" at the time it adopts the pre-IPO plan or agreement.

¶1506.3.2 Code §83(b) Election

There may be a technical problem under the performance-based compensation exception where (1) an executive of a publicly held corporation receives a grant of restricted stock, (2) the restrictions on the stock require that the executive attain an objective pre-established performance goal in order to retain the stock, and (3) the executive makes a Code §83(b) election to be taxed on the receipt of the stock rather than on its vesting.[190] In such case, the executive immediately recognizes ordinary compensation income equal to the difference between the FV of the stock at the time of grant and the amount paid for the stock, and the corporation would normally receive a corresponding deduction. However, by accelerating both the executive's income and the corporation's deduction, the Code §83(b) election causes the corporation's deduction to occur before the performance goals can be met (and hence also before the compensation committee can certify that they are met). See ¶¶1506.1.5.1 and 1506.1.5.4. Thus, it is not clear whether the corporation can rely on the performance-based compensation exception in such case even if the performance goals are ultimately met.

The preamble to the 1993 proposed regulations states that the "proposed regulations do not address this issue and comments are specifically requested."[191] We believe that IRS should clarify by regulatory amendment or published ruling that, assuming the award would otherwise qualify for the performance-based compensation exception, a Code §83(b) election does not prevent reliance on such exception.[192]

The statute (and regulations) require that the compensation committee certify that the performance goals are met before the payment of the compensation.[193]

---

[190] In many cases, the executive will not want to make a Code §83(b) election. If the executive pays nothing for the restricted stock, a Code §83(b) election would trigger ordinary income for the executive on receipt equal to the value of the stock, determined without regard to the restrictions, and the executive would be entitled to no offsetting tax deduction if the restricted stock were later forfeited. Hence, an executive who receives restricted stock without payment is not likely to make a Code §83(b) election unless the corporation defrays at least part of the tax burden (e.g., through a cash bonus, which would further increase the executive's gross income).

[191] 58 Fed. Reg. at 66,313.

[192] Compare the Code §280G proposed regulations that ignore the Code §83(b) election in determining the timing of compensation for purposes of the golden parachute rules. Prop. Reg. §1.280G-1 Q&A 12(b).

[193] See Code §162(m)(4)(C)(iii); Reg. §1.162-27(e)(5).

Although a Code §83(b) election alters the timing of the employee's income and the corporation's deduction, the election does not alter the economic reality of when the employee receives payment. Even if an employee makes a Code §83(b) election, the stock is still subject to a substantial risk of forfeiture until the performance goal is attained. Thus, in an economic sense, payment does not occur until the performance goal is met and the stock vests. While the corporation may take the deduction before the compensation committee's certification, the payment of compensation would not occur until after certification and vesting.

This result is consistent with the Code §83 rule that if an employee later forfeits restricted stock, the employer must include in income for the forfeiture year the amount the employer previously deducted as compensation in the grant year.[194] Thus, if the employee fails to satisfy the objective performance goals, the employer loses the economic benefit of the deduction under both Code §83 and Code §162(m) because the employer must take into income in the forfeiture year an amount equal to the employer's deduction in the grant year.

Of course, if the corporation allowed the employee to retain the stock although the performance goals were not met, the employer should similarly lose the economic benefit of the deduction under Code §162(m), even though not required by Code §83. This logical result could be achieved by requiring the employer to report income in the year the performance goal was failed equal to its grant year deduction (just as the Code §83 regulations would require when the property is forfeited). The alternative approach of requiring the employer to amend its grant year return to eliminate the deduction (rather than reporting income in the later year equal to the earlier deduction) is a far less desirable approach due to its administrative and practical difficulties (e.g., statute of limitations).

¶1506.3.3   Relinquishment of Discretionary Power

As discussed in ¶1506.2.1, the regulations provide a transitional rule for plans that were approved by shareholders prior to 12/20/93. This transitional rule relaxes the outside director requirement (see ¶1506.1.5.2) and shareholder approval requirement (see ¶1506.1.5.3) but still maintains the non-discretionary performance goal requirement (see ¶1506.1.5.1). Therefore, many plans that otherwise would qualify under the transitional rule will not qualify because the compensation committee and/or board of directors have the discretionary power to increase awards under the plan.

¶1506.4   *Application to Merger or Acquisition*

The application of the $1 million deduction limit when a purchaser ("P") acquires a target ("T") raises a number of issues, several of the more interesting of which are discussed in ¶¶1506.1 through 1506.3:

---

[194] Reg. §1.83-6(c).

- Exception #2 applies for approximately two years after a corporation becomes public without an IPO (i.e., until the first election of directors after the close of the first calendar year after the calendar year in which T becomes public). If T becomes publicly held under Reg. §1.162-27(c)(1)(ii) as a result of its acquisition by publicly held P, we believe Exception #2 should apply until the first election of directors after the calendar year following the calendar year in which the acquisition occurs. Unfortunately, the regulations do not make entirely clear whether the applicable election is the election of T's directors (suggested by the fact that in other circumstances the reliance period for application of Exception #2 generally turns on the election of T's directors) or the election of P's directors (suggested by the fact that P's affiliated group is generally treated as the publicly held corporation).

- Where public P acquires private T's *stock* (either by taxable stock purchase or by taxable or tax-free reverse merger), Exception #2 should apply on the ground that after the acquisition the T corporate entity is publicly held within the meaning of Reg. §1.162-27(c)(1)(ii), albeit as part of the P affiliated group. Where public P acquires T's *assets* (by taxable purchase or by taxable or tax-free forward merger) and assumes T's obligation to pay compensation to covered executives, Exception #2 should also apply because the T compensation plans and agreements were adopted while T was private and not required to comply with Code §162(m). However, there is a risk that IRS may argue (incorrectly, in our view) that Exception #2 does not apply on the ground that the T corporate entity did not become public even under Reg. §1.162-27(c)(1)(ii). See ¶1506.1.3.

- When public P acquires T, a T employee may be treated as a P covered employee if the individual has policy-making authority over P's business and either acts as P's CEO or is one of P's four most highly compensated non-CEO officers at the end of P's taxable year. See ¶1506.1.4.2.

- Under the proposed regulations the mere existence of a change-in-control feature which would accelerate the vesting of T's options, SARs, restricted stock, and phantom stock does not preclude use of the performance-based compensation exception (Exception #3 above). See ¶1506.1.5.1. If vesting actually occurs because of a change in T's control (i.e., where P actually acquires T before the performance goal has been met), Exception #3 ceases to apply; but, if at year's end the executive is no longer a T-covered employee, the Code §162(m) limit would not apply.

- Where P acquires T's stock or assets and assumes T's employment contracts, T's pre-2/18/93 contracts should still qualify for grandfather protection (Exception #5 above). See ¶1506.1.6.3. (Whether an assumed T employment contract that qualified for the performance-based compensation exception prior to its assumption may continue to qualify for the performance-based compensation exception after its assumption by P is discussed in a footnote in ¶1506.1.6.3.).

Issues are also raised where, prior to being acquired by (public) P, T adopts a performance-based compensation plan for which it obtains shareholder approval meeting the requirements of Reg. §1.162-27(e)(4)(i). In particular, such a circumstance raises the question whether awards granted under T's plan qualify for the performance-based exception where either (1) such awards are granted before but are paid (in the case of cash-based awards) or are deductible (in the case of stock-based awards) after such acquisition or (2) such awards are granted after the acquisition. In a pleasantly surprising 1997 private letter ruling (discussed below), IRS opted for a "yes" answer to both questions.

In IRS Letter Ruling 9801043,[195] T adopted an incentive plan authorizing a variety of stock-based awards, and obtained approval from its shareholders, prior to merging into P with P surviving. Interestingly, the letter ruling does not state the form of the merger consideration or whether the merger was tax-free or taxable, which suggests that such facts were not considered relevant to the analysis. The merger was approved by both P's and T's shareholders, but there is no indication that separate approval of T's incentive plan was requested from P's shareholders in connection with the merger. Following the merger, the only adjustments made to T's incentive plan were to replace references to T with references to P and to change the number of shares issuable under the plan (presumably to reflect the difference in per share values between P's stock and T's stock as of the merger date).

With minimal explanation, IRS ruled that following the T-P merger (1) T's incentive plan continues to meet the shareholder approval requirement of Reg. §1.162-27(e)(4)(i) (and hence approval of the plan by P's shareholders is not required) and (2) the eligibility criteria of the plan will not be considered to have been modified if awards are made under the plan to employees of pre-merger P subsidiaries.[196]Although we applaud this result slightly ameliorating the unnecessary and deplorable administrative burdens imposed by §162(m), we must admit that it represents a pleasantly surprising interpretation of the regulations. Under the facts stated in the letter ruling, it appears that P's shareholders were not asked to approve, in a separate vote, T's incentive plan which P assumed as a result of the merger. The regulations could be read strictly to require that *P's shareholders* must *approve* the plan under which performance-based awards are to be granted

---

[195] IRS Letter Ruling 9801043 (10/2/97).

[196] Other than a recitation of the relevant statutory and regulatory provisions, the analysis contained in the ruling is confined to the following statement: "The regulations underlying section 162(m)(4)(C) of the Code contain no provision requiring that, in a case such as this, a performance based plan adopted by a target corporation must be resubmitted to the shareholders of the surviving corporation after the merger at any time prior to the time that target corporation would have been required to resubmit the plan under section 1.162-27(e)(4)(vi) of the regulations. In this regard, compare regulation section 1.162-27(f)(4)(ii) [addressing spin-offs; see discussion at ¶1506.1.3.1]."

It appears that eligibility to participate in T's plan was described in general terms, e.g., "all executive officers and key employees of T." Following the merger of T into P, the plan was amended by replacing references to T with references to P; as a result, the eligibility requirement would have been amended to read, e.g., "all executive officers and key employees of P." Apparently, T did not have subsidiaries, and therefore P requested a ruling that the eligibility criteria of the plan, as so amended, could be interpreted to encompass employees of P's subsidiaries as well as employees of P itself. Such a ruling is sensible because the regulations treat all members of an affiliated group as a single corporation. Reg. §1.162-27(c)(1)(ii).

because P will be claiming the deductions arising from such awards.[197] However, in IRS Letter Ruling 9801043, IRS concludes that approval by the shareholders of the corporation that initially adopted the plan (here T) is sufficient to satisfy the requirements of Reg. §1.162-27(e)(4)(i). In other words, shareholder approval attaches to the plan itself and continues to be an attribute of the plan even where the rights and obligations associated with the plan are transferred to another corporation (here P) in connection with P's acquisition of T, the corporation that adopted the plan.

Does the favorable result reached in IRS Letter Ruling 9801043 depend upon there having been a disclosure of the material terms of T's incentive plan to P's shareholders in connection with their approval of the merger?[198] Requiring such disclosure without requiring a separate approval vote by P's shareholders would seem illogical because Reg. §1.162-27(e)(4)(i) requires *both* disclosure *and* approval. The text of the ruling supports this view, i.e., that no disclosure of the material terms of T's incentive plan to P's shareholders is required so long as approval of the incentive plan by T's shareholders had been obtained in accordance with the requirements of Reg. §1.162-27(e)(4)(i).

The favorable result reached in IRS Letter Ruling 9801043, we believe, should apply equally where P acquires by deed (rather than by state law merger) substantially all of T's assets and employees, and assumes all the rights and obligations of T's pre-existing performance-based plan in connection with such acquisition. The only potentially relevant difference between a non-merger asset acquisition and a merger is that, in the former case, T's plan is assumed by P pursuant to contract, while in the latter case, T's plan is assumed by P by operation of state merger law. If the principle underlying IRS Letter Ruling 9801043 is as stated above (i.e., that shareholder approval—by T's shareholders—becomes an attribute of the plan), the legal mechanism by which P assumes T's plan should not matter.

¶1506.5 Conclusion

We think Code §162(m) is an unwise exercise in political and social engineering and an embodiment of manifestly unsound tax policy. As such, Code §162(m) deserves the quick repeal which, unfortunately, it did not receive.

First, Code §162(m) makes an irrational distinction—imposing the compensation-deduction limit on remuneration to a corporate executive of a publicly held corporation but not (e.g.) to an athlete or a thespian.

Second, there is no more rational tax-policy reason for imposing a deduction limit on executive compensation than on advertising, research, marketing, or other expenditures.

[197] In this regard, the regulations state that "[t]he material terms of the performance goal under which the compensation is to be paid must be disclosed to *and subsequently approved by* the shareholders of *the* publicly held corporation before the compensation is paid." Reg. §1.162-27(e)(4)(i) (emphasis added).

[198] In this regard, the facts given in IRS Letter Ruling 9801043 indicate that the merger was approved by both T's and P's shareholders, but do not indicate whether P disclosed the material terms of T's incentive plan in P's proxy statement requesting approval of the merger from P's shareholders.

Third, even more important, Code §162(m) has imposed a tremendous, and senseless, time burden on U.S. publicly held companies. As amply demonstrated in the discussion in ¶¶1506.1 through 1506.3 above, the Code §162(m) rules (even had they contained no ambiguities) would place a substantial and unnecessary burden on publicly held corporations (e.g., creating and administering complex and formulistic compensation plans, obtaining legal advice on whether particular plans comply with Code §162(m), and ascertaining which old plans are grandfathered).

Moreover, the Code §162(m) rules are hardly free from ambiguity. Hence, a significant (and expanding) amount of time is being spent by lawyers, accountants, compensation consultants, and busy executives debating the obscure and unproductive, but tax-important, nuances of Code §162(m). This burgeoning time and cost drain on U.S. industry is directly counter to our important national goal of increasing productivity and competitiveness.

Finally, by forcing much of U.S. industry to adopt rigid and unalterable bonus formulas at least nine months in advance, Code §162(m) will inevitably cause some executives to receive unduly generous compensation while others receive inappropriately smaller compensation when the corporation's financial results take an unexpected turn.

Although the regulations take a reasonable (and occasionally even a pro-taxpayer) position on many issues, there are several key points where the regulations are terribly ambiguous, harsh, or unworkable.

In light of the above, it is not clear whether many corporations will consider it worthwhile to change compensation practices in order to preserve the compensation deduction for amounts paid to their top five executives in excess of $1 million per executive per year. However, an 11/93 SEC policy requires that the compensation committee's report disclose how Code §162(m) will be taken into account in setting executive compensation. Thus, even where the value of the lost deductions is not material to the corporation's finances, a public corporation may find it unpleasant to report that the compensation to be paid one or more of its top executives will not be deductible in full.

CHAPTER 16

Evolving Acquisition Techniques Using Partnership or LLC

¶1601 INTRODUCTION

Although statutory changes and regulatory exegesis in recent years have curtailed some of the more extreme opportunities afforded in the past, a partnership continues to offer patient taxpayers special advantages in acquiring or disposing of corporate assets and in bringing to a corporate acquisition investors of disparate economic and tax status:

(1) A partnership (unlike a C corporation) is a flow-through, not a taxable, entity; hence, each partner separately takes into account his distributive share of the partnership's income, deductions, and other tax items.[1]

(2) In order to qualify for flow-through tax treatment, a partnership must not be a publicly traded partnership taxed as a corporation under Code §7704.

(3) If appreciated property contributed by Partner A to the partnership later is distributed back to Partner A by the partnership, no gain is recognized to the partnership, to Partner A, or to any other partner.[2] This rule of non-recognition is not time sensitive; it applies whether the time elapsed between contribution and distribution does or does not exceed five years (or, indeed, five weeks).

(4) Moreover, when a partnership distributes appreciated property to a partner other than Partner A (who earlier contributed that property), and that property is not marketable securities and was not contributed to the partnership within five years of the distribution, then ordinarily no gain is recognized to the partnership, to the distributee partner, or to any other partner (including Partner A).[3] By contrast, a corporation (including an S corporation on a pass-through basis) recognizes gain on a distribution of appreciated property to a shareholder, with only the rarest of exceptions.[4] This is the case because the 1986 *GU* repeal, which had so material an impact in the corporate tax arena (see ¶107.1), is not a relevant concern in partnership taxation.

(5) When a partnership distributes appreciated property to a partner other than Partner A (who earlier contributed that property), and that property was contributed to the partnership within seven years of the distribution,

---

¶1601 [1] Code §§701 and 702. A partner's distributive share of partnership items is determined under the partnership agreement and the complex "substantial economic effect" regulations promulgated under Code §704(b). See Reg. §1.704-1(b). If a partner contributes appreciated or depreciated property to a partnership, the income, deductions, etc. with respect to such property are shared among the partners in accordance with Code §704(c).

[2] See Code §§704(c)(1)(B), 707(a)(2)(B), 731(c), 737(b)(1), and 751(b)(2)(A).

[3] If cash is distributed to a partner in excess of his basis in his partnership interest, the distributee partner recognizes gain to that extent. Code §731(a)(1). In addition, under the extraordinarily complex rules of Code §751(b), on a distribution to a partner of more or less than his proportionate share of the partnership's "hot assets"—essentially unrealized accounts receivable, recapture items, and certain inventory gains—either the partnership (i.e., the other partners) or the distributee partner or both will recognize gain and asset basis will be concomitantly increased. With respect to marketable securities the non-pro-rata distribution of which generally is treated by the recipient partner as a distribution of cash, see ¶1604.2.

[4] Gain recognition is required by Code §§311(b), 336, 351(f), 355(c), and 361(c). An exception is provided by Code §337 for a distribution in complete liquidation to an 80% controlling parent corporation.

gain may be recognized to the distributee (Partner B),[5] to the contributor (Partner A),[6] and quite probably to both partners.[7]

(6)   Finally, if (after considering the recognition rules referred to in the preceding items (3) and (4)) a partnership's distribution of assets (in liquidation of a partner's interest or in liquidation of the partnership itself) does not trigger gain recognition to any party, the distributee takes a basis in the distributed property equal to the adjusted basis at which he held his partnership interest, reduced by any money distributed in the same transaction.[8]

¶1601.1   Limited Liability Company

In recent years, all 50 states and the District of Columbia have enacted statutes allowing the formation of a new type of entity called a limited liability company ("LLC").[9] This entity is frequently a good alternative to a partnership, since, like a corporation, its owners are not automatically liable for the entity's debts, i.e., the owners have the shield of limited liability. However, like a partnership, the entity's basic documents can allocate gains, losses, distributions, etc., in a very flexible fashion.

Moreover, an LLC is generally treated like a partnership (if it has two or more equity owners and is not publicly traded) or is disregarded (if it has only one equity owner) for federal (and usually for state—see ¶1601.3) income tax purposes, so that the LLC is not subject to entity-level federal (or generally state) income tax. Rather, each of the LLC's equity owners, generally called "members" under a typical LLC statute, reports his share of the LLC's profits and losses on his tax returns. More generally, the rules set forth in ¶1601 immediately above will apply.

Throughout this chapter (and this treatise), any reference to a partnership is understood to include a reference to an LLC taxed for federal income tax purposes as a partnership.

¶1601.2   IRS Entity Classification Rules

Prior to 1/1/97, an LLC with two or more equity owners or partnership was entitled to flow-through tax status (i.e., was treated as a partnership rather than

---

[5] Code §737.

[6] Code §704(c)(1).

[7] In addition to the simultaneous application of Code §§737 and 704(c)(1), if contribution and distribution (of property or property and money) are within two years (and in extreme cases more than two years), the disguised sale rules of Code §707(a)(2)(B) and Reg. §1.707-3 may come into play. See ¶1604.

[8] Code §732(b). The partner's aggregate basis (reduced by any money distributed or deemed distributed under Code §752(b)) is first allocated to "hot assets" up to but not in excess of the basis at which the partnership held those assets; remaining aggregate basis is allocated to all other distributed properties (except money) in proportion to their adjusted bases to the partnership. Code §732(c).

[9] The last two states to adopt LLC statutes were Vermont and Hawaii. Vermont's LLC statute took effect 7/1/96 and Hawaii's 4/1/97.

as an "association" taxable as a corporation) for federal income tax purposes only if it met several strange tests set forth in IRS regulations (the "old *Kintner* regulations"), as supplemented by subsequent IRS interpretations. In 12/96 IRS repealed the old *Kintner* regulations effective 1/1/97 and dramatically simplified the procedure by which an unincorporated organization, such as an LLC or partnership, achieves flow-through (i.e., partnership) status for tax purposes. Under the 12/96 regulations, a domestic non-corporate entity (as well as many types of foreign entities) with two or more equity owners can simply choose (i.e., "check-the-box") whether to be taxed as a partnership (so long as the entity is not a publicly traded partnership taxed as a corporation under Code §7704) or as a corporation.[10]

In general, a domestic LLC with two or more equity owners is taxed as a partnership absent an affirmative election to be taxed as a corporation.[11] A foreign unincorporated entity with two or more equity owners is generally (1) taxed as a partnership for U.S. federal income tax purposes (absent an affirmative election to be taxed as a corporation) where at least one of its members has personal liability for some or all of the debts of the entity by reason of being a member and (2) taxed as a corporation (absent an affirmative election to be taxed as a partnership) where none of its members has such personal liability.[12]

IRS had long taken the position that an LLC could qualify as a partnership for federal income tax purposes only if it had two or more members, so that it was unclear whether a single-member LLC would be treated for federal income tax purposes as a corporation (subject to entity-level tax) or as a sole proprietorship or division (disregarded for tax purposes). The 12/96 check-the-box regulations generally treat a single-member domestic unincorporated entity as a sole proprietorship or division (disregarded for tax purposes) unless it affirmatively elects to be taxed as a corporation.[13] A single-member foreign unincorporated entity is generally (1) taxed as a sole proprietorship or division for U.S. federal income tax purposes (absent an affirmative election to be taxed as a corporation) where the member has personal liability for some or all of the debts of the entity by reason of being a member and (2) taxed as a corporation (absent an affirmative election to be taxed as a sole proprietorship or division) where the member does not have such personal liability.[14]

The check-the-box regulations are effective 1/1/97 and apply to existing LLCs and other unincorporated entities regardless of when the entity was formed. In the case of an entity in existence before 1/1/97, the entity's pre-1/1/97 claimed classification will be respected by IRS for all pre-1/1/97 periods if (1) the entity had a reasonable basis for its claimed classification, (2) the entity and all of its members recognized the federal tax consequences of any change in the entity's classification within 60 months prior to 1/1/97 (e.g., treated a change during such 60-month period from corporate to partnership tax classification as a taxable

---

[10] Reg. §301.7701-2, -3.
[11] Reg. §301.7701-3(b)(1).
[12] Reg. §301.7701-3(b)(2).
[13] Reg. §301.7701-3(b)(1).
[14] Reg. §301.7701-3(b)(2).

corporate liquidation), and (3) neither the entity nor any of its members had been notified in writing before 5/9/96 that its classification was under examination.[15]

The check-the-box regulations do not address the issue of when an owner of an interest in a partnership "will be respected as a bona fide [partner] for federal tax purposes" (rather than treated as a mere service provider to the partnership). Rather, the preamble to the regulations indicates that resolution of this issue "is based on all the facts and circumstances" of each case. Hence, even with the check-the-box regime, there is some possibility IRS may take the position (at least for ruling purposes) that for a service provider to be treated as a partner entitled to flow-through treatment, such service provider must have *either* (1) a substantial investment in the limited partnership *or* (2) an obligation to make up a substantial portion of any deficit in the service provider's capital account at the conclusion of the partnership. Only if the service provider is treated as a partner would its share of the partnership's LTCG qualify for flow-through LTCG treatment on its tax return; conversely if it were treated merely as a service provider to (and not a partner in) the partnership, its share of the partnership's LTCG would constitute OI (i.e., a fee for services rendered) on its tax return.

¶1601.3   *State and Foreign Entity Classification*

The check-the-box regulations apply only for *federal* income tax purposes. Although most states automatically follow the *federal* classification of an entity for *state* income tax purposes, not all do so. Indeed a few state and local jurisdictions impose a full or partial entity-level tax on both a partnership's and an LLC's income. And some jurisdictions treat an LLC more harshly for local tax purposes than they treat a partnership. For example, Texas treats an LLC (but not a partnership) as a corporation for state tax purposes, as does Canada for Canadian tax purposes. Similarly, Pennsylvania subjects an LLC (but not a partnership) to the Pennsylvania Capital Stock and Foreign Franchise Tax if the LLC does business within Pennsylvania.[16]

Similarly, foreign jurisdictions may classify a U.S. partnership or LLC in a manner different from the U.S. federal income tax classification. For example, Canada treats an LLC as a corporation for Canadian income tax purposes. The potential "hybrid" classification of an entity as a partnership in the U.S. and as

---

[15] Reg. §301.7701-3(f). If a pre-1/1/97 entity previously classified as a corporation makes a check-the-box election to be taxed as a partnership, the election will generally cause a deemed liquidation of the corporation and deemed formation of a new partnership, resulting in double tax (i.e., an entity-level tax on the asset built-in gain at the time of the deemed corporate liquidation and a member-level tax on the deemed receipt of the corporate assets to the extent their FV exceeds the members' tax bases in their ownership interests).

[16] Although Florida treated an LLC (but not a partnership) as a corporation for state tax purposes for tax years ending prior to 7/1/98, for tax years ending on or after such date an LLC classified as a partnership for federal income tax purposes is not subject to the Florida corporate income tax.

While California announced (shortly after adoption of the federal check-the-box regulations) that the old *Kintner* regulations remained the law for California, subsequent legislation has adopted check-the-box for tax years beginning after 1996.

a corporation in a foreign country led to certain abuses that caused enactment of Code §894(c) as part of the 1997 Act. Effective 8/5/97, Code §894(c) denies U.S. tax treaty benefits with respect to certain payments made to foreign persons through "hybrid" entities. This anti-abuse provision was intended to target the following type of transaction utilizing a Canadian corporation and U.S. LLC:

EXAMPLE

A Canadian corporation ("CanCo") forms a U.S. corporate subsidiary ("USSub") and a U.S. LLC ("USLLC"). USLLC makes a loan to USSub. USSub pays interest to USLLC, which distributes the interest payments to CanCo.

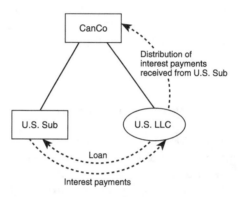

USLLC is treated as a corporation for Canadian tax purposes. Hence, for Canadian tax purposes, (1) CanCo is not taxable on USLLC's undistributed earnings, and (2) USLLC's distribution of its earnings is treated as a dividend excluded from CanCo's income. On the U.S. side, (1) USSub's interest expense on the loan is deductible (assuming neither Code §163(j)—see ¶1305— nor other interest deduction limitations apply), and (2) before the 1997 Act, USSub's interest payments to USLLC were subject to a reduced 10% withholding rate under the U.S.-Canada treaty (rather than the normal 30% statutory withholding rate of Code §871 and §881).[17] The result was avoidance of both U.S. and Canadian tax.

Code §894(c) addresses the above arrangement by providing that a foreign person (here, CanCo) is not entitled to reduced withholding under a U.S. treaty on "an item of income derived through an entity [here, USLLC] which is treated as a partnership (or is otherwise treated as fiscally transparent)" for U.S. tax purposes if (1) the foreign country does not include the item in the foreign person's

---

[17] In this example, the interest payments would not qualify as exempt portfolio interest because the payments are treated as made to a 10% shareholder of USSub. See §881(c)(3)(B).

income, (2) the treaty does not contain a provision addressing the applicability of the treaty to income derived through a partnership, and (3) the foreign country does not impose tax on an actual distribution of the income item from the fiscally transparent entity to the foreign person. Under Code §894(c), in the above arrangement USSub's payments of interest to USLLC are subject to the maximum statutory withholding rate of 30%, rather than the reduced treaty rate of 10%.

¶1602   PURCHASE OF T ASSETS BY PARTNERSHIP OR LLC

If P proposes to acquire T in concert with other investors—in particular, in concert with a venture capitalist ("VC") or with the key executives who will continue to manage the acquired business ("Mgmt")—it may make sense for P to establish a partnership ("PS") to undertake the acquisition of T's assets and to operate the T business. After *GU* repeal an asset acquisition by PS is not always feasible from a tax standpoint. Nonetheless, in at least five circumstances, despite *GU* repeal, P (wishing to acquire T) can feasibly structure the transaction as a purchase of T's assets (rather than a purchase of T's stock):[1]

(1)   Bigco (which has several divisions and/or subsidiaries) is selling T, which is a division or subsidiary.
(2)   T has a substantial NOL (and/or a CL carryover) with which to offset, largely or entirely, the gain to be recognized on the asset sale.
(3)   T is an S corporation and is not subject to the penalty tax of Code §1374 or, if subject to Code §1374, is permitted under particular circumstances to avoid a dramatic tax bite. See ¶¶1103.7.4 through 1103.7.6.
(4)   T is a partnership or proprietorship.
(5)   The FV of T's assets does not exceed, or does not dramatically exceed, the basis of those assets.

EXAMPLE 1

Bigco proposes to sell its X Division, consisting of assets worth $5 million and liabilities of $3 million, for a cash purchase price of $2 million. PS, a general partnership, is organized by P corporation, VC (which may be an individual, a partnership, or a corporation), and Mgmt (four individuals).

PS obtains a substantial part of the $2 million cash purchase price as a loan from Bank. PS obtains the balance as equity capital from P and VC, in different amounts, with Mgmt investing a relatively modest amount of capital. In a fashion that observes the "substantial economic effect" directive of the Code §704(b) regulations and perhaps takes advantage of the Code

---

¶1602   [1] See ¶¶107.2 and 403.1, discussing the desirability of structuring the acquisition for SUB (and taxation to T on the gain inherent in its assets) rather than COB (and no tax on T's inherent gain).

§707(c) guaranteed payment provision,[2] each investor shares in the income and deductions generated by the acquired business in a way that is advantageous to each.

No tax is imposed at the PS level on PS's income from the acquired business. PS can allocate to Mgmt income and cash flow substantially greater than a proportionate return on Mgmt's modest capital investment (i.e., PS can give Mgmt a carried interest) and, because PS is not a taxable entity, the income allocated to Mgmt is taxed at a maximum rate of 35% in calendar 2003.

Similarly, the income allocated to P is taxed only once, at the P level, even if P owns less than 80% of T and hence could not have filed a consolidated return with PS if it were a corporation. And the income allocated to VC (regardless of whether it is a corporation, individual or partnership) will be taxed only once.

Abundant variations, significant and minor, can be worked on the basic plan. PS may be a limited partnership rather than a general partnership, with investors who will not be active in the business and seek limited liability by acquiring PS's limited partnership interests. If PS may be subject to the law of a state in which Mgmt's participation in PS's control may preclude Mgmt from limiting its liability, Mgmt or each member of Mgmt separately can acquire its, his, or her partnership interest through an S corporation, thereby limiting liability without adverse tax consequence.

If, however, one of the partners (e.g., P) has an NOL, a disproportionate allocation of partnership income to P must survive the substantial economic effect test of the Code §704(b) partnership regulations.[3] Further, even if the Code §704(b) requirements are met, regulations that may be promulgated under Code §382(m)(3) with retroactive effect[4] may eliminate almost completely any tax advantage that might otherwise accrue from a special income allocation. See the discussion of these so-called Goldome arrangements at ¶1205.3.

¶1603   POST-ACQUISITION DROP DOWN TO PARTNERSHIP OR LLC

P corporation, or its controlled subsidiary S, after purchasing T's assets or controlling stock, may create a partnership with Mgmt and perhaps others (VC) through which to conduct part or all of the former T business.

---

[2] Under Code §707(c) a partner may receive payments from the partnership either for services or for the use of capital—in economic effect a loan to the partnership that is not treated (under Code §707(a)) as a loan but rather as a special form of investment in the partnership—and such payments, if "determined without regard to the income of the partnership" and not required to be capitalized under standard capitalization rules, will be deductible by the partnership and in any event will be income to the recipient, although not part of his "distributive share" of partnership income.

[3] See Reg. §1.704-1(b)(5) example (8).

[4] See H.R. Rep. No. 841, 99th Cong., 2d Sess. II, at 194 (1986).

EXAMPLE 2

P, common parent corporation of an affiliated group that files or will file a consolidated return, purchases all of T's stock for $2 million. P makes no Code §338 election.

One of T's businesses, worth $1 million (net of liabilities), is successfully operated by Mgmt, which seeks a sizable equity position in the business. Desirable expansion of the business requires the infusion of substantial additional capital.

T (now a 100% P subsidiary) transfers the $1 million business (along with its liabilities) to a partnership (PS) jointly organized by T, VC, and Mgmt. VC invests $250,000 of cash (for expansion), and Mgmt invests nominal cash of $10,000 in PS. Although Mgmt's initial capital interest in PS is small, the partnership agreement grants Mgmt a significantly higher percentage of PS's profits (i.e., a carried interest).

PS, as a partnership, is not a taxable entity. T, as a wholly owned P subsidiary, is included in P's consolidated return. Thus, T's partnership share of PS's income will be reflected on P's consolidated return and will be subjected to no federal tax burden other than P's consolidated return liability.

Similarly, VC's and Mgmt's shares of Ps's income will be reflected on their tax returns and will not be subjected to tax at the PS level.

Additions and variations to the basic plan are, of course, available. A portion of P's investment, or VC's, in PS may be evidenced by a senior partnership interest that calls for an annual, interest-like return payable without regard to PS's income or lack thereof.

EXAMPLE 3

Same facts as Example 2 except that P, in exchange for the business transferred to PS, receives, in addition to its regular partnership interest in PS, a senior preferred partnership interest, capital value $500,000, calling for an annual guaranteed payment to P of $50,000 so long as the senior preferred partnership interest remains outstanding (without regard to the amount of PS's income).

If PS is on the accrual method, it will each year deduct $50,000 of "guaranteed payment" whether or not the payment is in fact made that year (or is accrued but postponed to a later time). Concomitantly, if PS is on the accrual method, P (whether on the cash or accrual method) each year will take into income its $50,000 guaranteed payment whether or not payment is in fact made. See Code §707(c).[1]

¶1604 ACQUISITION THROUGH DEFERRED EXCHANGE MIXING-BOWL PARTNERSHIP OR LLC

Generally speaking—subject to exceptions discussed below that can often be avoided with sufficient patience and planning—neither the liquidation of a partnership nor the liquidation of a partner's interest in a continuing partnership is a taxable event.[1] Specifically, if partnership PS distributes property to partner A (other than cash or in certain cases marketable securities in excess of A's basis in PS) in liquidation of PS or in liquidation of A's interest in PS, neither PS, A, nor any other partner in PS recognizes any gain or loss on the distribution, so long as A receives no more or less than his proportionate share of any "hot assets" (i.e., unrealized receivables, "recapture amounts," and substantially appreciated inventory) owned by PS.[2] A holds the distributed property at a basis equal to his basis in his partnership interest minus any cash distributed to him in the liquidation.

With some skill and, as discussed below, seven years of patience, taxpayers may well be able to take advantage of the partnership rules and, through a "mixing bowl" partnership, exchange appreciated assets without recognizing gain.[3]

¶1603 [1] The deduction disallowance rule that ordinarily applies to unpaid expenditures from an accrual method partnership to a cash method partner (see Code §267(a)(2) and (e)) does not apply to a guaranteed payment under Code §707(c). See Code §267(e)(4).

¶1604 [1] Code §§731 and 732 and exception identified in ¶1601.

[2] If partner A's interest in the partnership is liquidated but the partnership is not, the payment of a premium to A (i.e., payment in excess of the value of A's share of partnership assets and/or for goodwill of the partnership when the partnership agreement does not provide for a payment with respect to goodwill) is OI to A and deductible to the partnership under Code §736(a) if, but only if, capital is not a material income-producing factor for the partnership *and* A was a general partner. See Code §736(b)(3), generally effective for partners retiring or dying after 1/5/93.

[3] However, effective in general for partnerships distributing after 7/14/99 (after 6/30/01 if the distributee corporation was a partner as of 7/14/99) Code §732(f) states that where (1) PS makes a distribution to a corporate partner (T) consisting of stock in another corporation (X) so that T—or the consolidated group of which T is a member (see below)—is then or thereafter in 80-80 control of X and (2) T's basis in the distributed X stock is less than the basis at which PS held that X stock (the amount by which PS's pre-distribution basis in the X stock exceeds T's post-distribution basis being the "stock basis stepdown"), then (3) X (and any 80-80 X subsidiaries) must (a) reduce asset basis by an amount equal to the stock basis stepdown but (b) not below T's basis in X's stock (the "floor limit"), and (4) if the stock basis stepdown would otherwise reduce T's basis in the X stock below the floor limit, T recognizes immediate LTCG (and steps up X's stock basis) by such amount. In Sec. 311(c) of the 2000 Act Congress with retroactive effect instructed that when T is a member of an affiliated group filing a consolidated return, the X stock ownership of all T group members shall be aggregated under Reg. §1.1502-34 to determine whether T is in 80-80 control of X for purposes of applying Code §732(f), and in 6/01 Reg. §1.1502-34 was retroactively amended and conforming Reg. §1.732-3 was added to reflect the 2000 Act's clarification.

EXAMPLE 4

T holds its X division at a basis of $200,000 and would like to sell that division for $1 million (the FV of the division). P would like to buy the division, using appreciated Y stock which has a basis in P's hands of $300,000 and an FV of $1 million (or, alternatively, P would like to buy the X division for $1 million cash). T agrees to the exchange, but T and P desire to effect the exchange without triggering any gain.

To achieve their objectives, T and P form partnership PS. T transfers its X division, and P transfers the Y stock (or cash), to PS in return for partnership interests.

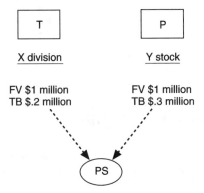

There is no express agreement to liquidate PS after a set period of time, nor is there an express agreement identifying the particular properties that may be distributed to each partner were PS liquidated. Additionally, the PS partnership agreement provides for straight-up allocation of income and loss of PS (other than Code §704(c) gain or loss, i.e., subsequently recognized (by PS) built-in appreciation or depreciation in the value of property contributed to PS, which is allocated to the contributing partner).

For a period of at least seven years, PS operates the X division and manages its investment in the Y stock (or uses the P cash to operate the X division or invests the cash). Sometime thereafter, PS liquidates. Pursuant to negotiations first entertained at that time, T receives the Y stock (or cash) and P receives the X division.

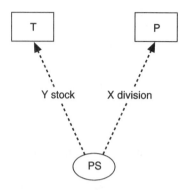

If this transaction is successful, T and P have in effect exchanged appreciated assets without recognizing gain, and each holds the asset received in liquidation at a basis equal to its basis in PS. As we shall see, after 12/94 the arrangement may succeed for P but (if PS distributed to T Y stock that is a "marketable security") not for T.

¶1604.1   General Anti-Abuse Regulation

After trying to attack abusive uses of partnerships in a piecemeal manner through legislation, regulations, and notices,[4] IRS and Treasury in 5/94 proposed a comprehensive approach. Specifically, IRS issued Prop. Reg. §1.701-2,[5] announcing that

(1)   "[t]he intent of the partnership provisions in subchapter K is to permit taxpayers to conduct business for joint economic profit through a flexible arrangement that accurately reflects the partners' economic agreement without incurring an entity-level tax"; and

(2)   "[i]f a partnership is formed or availed of in connection with a transaction or series of related transactions (individually or collectively, the transaction) with a principal purpose of substantially reducing the present value of the partners' aggregate federal tax liability in a manner that is inconsistent with the intent of subchapter K, the Commissioner can disregard the form of the transaction."[6]

The proposed regulation attracted much comment. A good deal of that comment was hostile and focused on a perceived compounding of uncertainty of tax

[4] The more recent attempts by IRS are discussed in ¶¶1604.2 through 1604.4; see IRS Notice 94-48, 1994-1 C.B. 357. But cf. Rev. Rul. 94-43, 1994-2 C.B. 198. (discussed at ¶1104.2.3).

[5] PS-27-94, 1994-1 C.B. 832.

[6] The regulation was proposed to be effective "for all transactions relating to a partnership" occurring on and after 5/12/94.

treatment likely to result if the proposed regulation were enacted. Other comment, avoiding or downplaying the Chicken Little approach, suggested it was about time Treasury regulated comprehensively but urged that more attention be paid to the details of the proposal.

Final Reg. §1.701-2 was promulgated in 12/94, effective in most respects for transactions occurring on or after 5/12/94 and in all other respects on or after 12/29/94.[7] The rhetoric of the 5/94 proposal quoted above has been toned down, and some of the proposal's more encompassing pronouncements implementing that rhetoric have disappeared, in the final regulation. As adopted, Reg. §1.701-2's "subchapter K anti-abuse rules" couple broad administrative authority with a narrowed focus. IRS is given broad powers to ensure that (1) a partnership transaction is entered into for a substantial business purpose, (2) its form is entitled to respect under substance-over-form principles, and (3) except as subchapter K otherwise clearly contemplates, its intended tax consequences properly reflect the economic agreement and income of the partners.[8] Examples in the regulation make clear the narrowed range in which it is designed to operate. In our view, a not-aggressive mixing-bowl partnership of the sort illustrated in Example 4 does not fall within the prohibition of Reg. §1.701-2.

¶1604.2   Partner Gain on Distribution of Marketable Securities

While the transaction described in Example 4 may fall outside the ambit of Reg. §1.701-2, another 1994 pronouncement—part of the GATT implementing legislation enacted in 12/94—has a direct and adverse impact on T in that example. Effective 12/8/94, Code §731(c) generally treats marketable securities (expansively defined) like cash for purposes of determining gain recognized by the distributee partner(s). There are exceptions, e.g., pro rata distribution to all partners and a distribution of securities back to the partner who initially contributed them to the partnership, but a mixing-bowl partnership fits none of these exceptions. Thus, after 12/94 the arrangement described in Example 4 may work for partner P, but not for partner T if T receives a distribution consisting of marketable securities.

¶1604.3   Code §707(a)(2)(B) Disguised Sale

There is a risk that Code §707(a)(2)(B) may apply to this transaction,[9] thereby causing the transaction to be treated as though either (1) T sold its X division,

---

[7] See Reg. §1.701-2(g).

[8] Reg. §1.701-2(a).

[9] In Otey v. Commissioner, 70 T.C. 312 (1978), aff'd per curiam, 634 F.2d 1046, 80-2 U.S.T.C. ¶9817 (6th Cir. 1980), decided before the enactment of Code §707(a)(2)(B), A and B formed a partnership (PS), to which A "contributed" real estate (FV $65,000) and B contributed no property. Pursuant to the agreement between the parties, PS "distributed" $65,000 to partner A as soon as it took down a loan, half within a month and the other half within a few months, and A and B thereafter shared profits equally. Regulations stated that a transfer of property by a partner to a partnership followed

and P sold its Y stock, to PS in a fully taxable transaction, or (2) T and P exchanged between themselves the X division and the Y stock in a fully taxable transaction.[10] However, given that both T and P are at economic risk for at least seven years with respect to all the assets held by PS, and that any subsequent distribution of the Y stock to T and the X division to P arguably is dependent upon the "entrepreneurial risks" of PS's operations (i.e., at the time T and P form PS, it is not substantially certain that T will receive the Y stock and P will receive the X division), a strong argument can be made that Code §707(a)(2)(B) should not apply to the transaction.[11] The risk that Code §707(a)(2)(B) may apply would increase if (1) P contributes cash (rather than Y stock) and PS invests that cash in relatively safe investments, and/or (2) the PS partnership agreement in fact or in effect allocates a disproportionate amount of the income from the X division to P and from the Y stock to T.[12]

---

within a short period by a distribution of money by the partnership to the partner would be treated according to its substance as a sale. However, Code §707(a)(2)(B) had not yet been enacted. The courts held the *Otey* transaction to be a contribution of property and a subsequent distribution of money rather than a sale, so A was entitled to receive the $65,000 tax free to the extent of its basis in the partnership interest. In so holding, the Tax Court stated that "the form of the transaction was a contribution to capital rather than a sale," that "there are no elements of artificiality in the form selected," that contractual "provisions for preferential distributions out of borrowed funds to restore capital accounts to equality after non-pro rata partnership contributions do not necessarily demonstrate that the contributions were really sales," and that "the payment by the partnership to . . . partner [A] is at the risk of the economic fortunes of the partnership [i.e., its ability to borrow]." The Sixth Circuit affirmed *per curiam*. Congress then enacted Code §707(a)(2).

[10] The regulations implementing Code §707(a)(2)(B) announce that if Code §707(a)(2)(B) applies, (1) T and P will be treated as having sold the X division and the Y stock to PS in exchange for PS's obligation to transfer the Y stock to T and the X division to P, if in fact T and P have formed a partnership between themselves for tax purposes, and (2) T and P will be treated as having exchanged directly between themselves the X division and the Y stock, if it is determined that no partnership exists between T and P. See Reg. §1.707-3(a)(1) to (3). The regulations also indicate that, in the circumstances of Example 4, T and P will be deemed to have formed a partnership between themselves for tax purposes. See Reg. §1.707-3(f) example (8).

[11] See Reg. §1.707-3(b). Because the liquidation of PS occurs more than two years after T and P contributed the X division and Y stock to PS, there is a presumption that a deemed sale did not occur at the time T and P formed PS. See Reg. §1.707-3(d).

Note that none of the factors listed in Reg. §1.707-3(b)(2) indicating the existence of a deemed sale applies to the partnership arrangement between T and P described in Example 4. Additionally, the partnership between T and P (i.e., PS) differs from partnership IJK in Reg. §1.707-3(f) example (8) in that (1) unlike in the case of partnership IJK, neither P nor T is contributing safe investment securities to PS, (2) unlike the IJK partnership agreement, which largely shifted the benefits and burdens of ownership through disproportionate allocations, the PS partnership agreement provides for straight-up allocations, and (3) from the onset, the partners in the IJK partnership intended to liquidate I's interest for an amount equal to the FV of the building at the time of the liquidation and did in fact liquidate I's interest for that amount, whereas the relative FVs of the X division and the Y stock at the time PS liquidates may, but probably will not, be equal.

[12] See Reg. §1.707-3(b)(2)(vii) and (viii), (f) example (8). For example, the transaction might be suspect under Code §707(a)(2)(B) if the partnership agreement allocated the first $120,000 of partnership income to T, the next $200,000 to P, and any balance 99% to P and 1% to T.

¶1604.4   Code §§704(c) and 737 Seven-Year Requirement

The requirement that T and P wait at least seven years before liquidating PS derives from (1) amendments made to Code §704(c) by the 1989 Act, (2) the 1992 enactment of Code §737,[13] and (3) the 1997 Act's amendment of Code §§704(c)(1)(B) and 737(b)(1) to substitute seven years for what previously had been a delay period of five years.[14]

Under amended Code §704(c)—enacted by Congress out of concern that *GU* repeal significantly increased the attractiveness of mixing-bowl partnership—a partner ("Partner A") who contributes appreciated (or depreciated) property to a partnership must recognize the precontribution gain (or loss) if the partnership distributes the property to another partner ("Partner B") during the (now) seven-year period following the contribution. Specifically, if the partnership distributes the contributed property to Partner B during the postcontribution seven-year period, contributing Partner A is deemed to recognize the gain (or loss) that he would have been required to take into account under Code §704(c) had the partnership instead sold the property at FV.[15]

While 1989's Code §704(c)(1) concentrates on Partner A, the contributor of the appreciated property, 1992's Code §737 focuses on Partner B, the appreciated property's distributee. Partner B must recognize gain (that would not otherwise have been recognized on the distribution) equal to the lesser of (1) the excess of (a) the FV of the property (other than money) distributed to B over (b) B's adjusted basis in her partnership interest (reduced by any money distributed to her) measured immediately before the property distribution, or (2) Partner B's "net precontribution gain." Net precontribution gain, as defined in Code §737(b), is the net gain Partner B would have recognized under Code §704(c)(1)(B) if all property contributed to the partnership by Partner B during the preceding seven years (and still held by the partnership) had been distributed by the partnership to another partner. Thus, Code §737 cannot trigger any gain to Partner B, when property is distributed to her by the partnership, unless she earlier (within the preceding seven years) contributed other property to the partnership and that other property was worth in excess of its basis at the time of contribution.

Thus, deferred exchanges through mixing-bowl partnerships retain (1) full vitality only if the parties are willing to wait at least seven years (five years if the property was contributed (1) prior to 6/8/97 or (2) on or after that date but pursuant to a contract binding on 6/8/97) before distributing contributed property and have not precommitted to that transaction; and (2) circumscribed vitality that is limited to property contributed to a partnership prior to 10/4/89 and, with respect to property contributed on or after that date, to the extent of the postcontribution appreciation of that property.

---

[13] Code §737 was added to the Code by the Energy Policy Act of 1992 (H.R. 776), Pub. L. No. 102-486, §1937 (10/24/92). Code §737 applies to partnership distributions on or after 6/25/92.

[14] The seven year requirement was inserted by the Taxpayer Relief Act of 1997 (Pub. L. 105-34), effective in general with respect to property contributed to the partnership after 6/8/97.

[15] For a discussion of the operation of amended Code §704(c), see S. Rep. No. 56, 101st Cong., 1st Sess. 195 (1989). Amended Code §704(c) applies to contributions after 10/3/89, but with a five-year fuse for contributions prior to 6/8/97.

Taxpayers contemplating a mixing-bowl partnership should bear in mind that unlike, for example, the two-year waiting period of old Code §334(b)(2), the seven-year waiting periods of Code §704(c) and Code §737 are not safe harbors, i.e., waiting more than seven years to liquidate the partnership will not preclude the application of Code §707(a)(2)(B) to the transaction. In other words, the Code §707(a)(2)(B) risk (discussed above) associated with mixing-bowl partnerships remains after the 1989 amendments to Code §704(c) and the 1992 enactment of Code §737, and the 1997 amendments to both.

¶1604.5   Unsuccessful Variation of Mixing-Bowl Partnerships

Finally, one variation of mixing-bowl partnerships deserves special attention—when one partner contributes stock of another partner to the partnership in return for an interest in the partnership (or when one partner contributes cash which the partnership uses to purchase from a third party or on the market stock of another partner).

EXAMPLE 5

Same facts as in Example 4 except that, instead of Y stock, P contributes T stock to PS. (Alternatively, P contributes cash to PS which PS immediately uses to purchase T stock.) More than five years later, PS is liquidated and T receives those T shares.

Assuming that, through a combination of patience, skill, and good fortune, this arrangement escapes disadvantageous recharacterization under Code §707(a)(2)(B), under regulations proposed in late 1992 T will nonetheless recognize gain on both the contribution of the X division to PS and upon the liquidation of PS.[16] Specifically, upon the contribution of the X division to PS (or, if later, PS's acquisition of T stock), T will be deemed to have exchanged 50% of the X division for 50% of PS's T stock (assuming PS is a 50/50 partnership).[17] As a result, (1) T will recognize a $400,000 gain, (2) T will hold its interest in PS at a basis of $600,000, and (3) PS will hold the X division at a basis of $600,000.[18] Upon the liquidation of PS, T will be deemed to have redeemed all the T shares held by

[16] See Prop. Reg. §1.337(d)-3 (PS-91-90), 1993-1 C.B. 919, applicable (when finalized) to transactions and distributions occurring after 3/9/89, i.e., the date IRS issued Notice 89-37, 1989-1 C.B. 679, which announced IRS's intent to issue regulations attacking transactions such as that in Example 5 above.

[17] See Prop. Reg. §1.337(d)-3(d), (h) examples (1) and (2).

[18] See Prop. Reg. §1.337(d)-3(d), (h) examples (1) and (2). T's gain equals the excess of (a) $500,000 (i.e., 50% of the FV of the T shares held by PS), over (b) $100,000 (i.e., 50% of T's basis in the X division). T's basis in its interest in PS, and PS's basis in the X division, is increased by T's gain (i.e., $400,000).

PS in exchange for T's interest in PS.[19] Accordingly, T will recognize gain equal to the excess of the FV of the T shares over T's basis in its interest in PS. Apparently, neither PS nor P will recognize any gain or loss under the proposed regulations upon the contributions to PS or the liquidating distributions by PS.

¶1605   IN-HOUSE PARTNERSHIP OR LLC TO FACILITATE DISPOSITIONS

The plan described below was aggressively marketed through the spring of 1989 by various tax professionals. We know of no case (although there may have been one or even many) in which a corporate group actually adopted and implemented the plan. That is fortunate since IRS, on 6/19/89, announced its extreme hostility in a distinctly plausible way. Here, unadorned, is an illustration of the plan.

EXAMPLE

Among its many subsidiaries with which T files a consolidated return, three—T1, T2, and T3—own real property (land and factory building) having, in each case, an FV of $12 million and an adjusted basis of $2 million. T1, T2, and T3 each transfers its real property to new partnership PS with each receiving in exchange a one-third interest in partnership capital and profits. PS files an election under Code §754. T1 sells its partnership interest to S, another P subsidiary, for $12 million. Subsequently, PS sells to an unrelated buyer for $12 million the real estate that had been contributed by T1. S maintains its one-third partnership interest and PS invests the $12 million cash in useful business activity.

Under the deferred intercompany transaction rules of the consolidated return regulations in effect at that time, T1 initially deferred its $10 million gain on the sale of its PS partnership interest to S.[1] T1's deferred gain was triggered as and when S enjoyed tax benefits, through depreciation or on resale, from its stepped-up purchase price basis.[2] But in the immediately preceding example the property that is subject to an allowance for depreciation, and that is later sold to the unrelated buyer, is not the partnership interest purchased by S from T1, but rather is the real property contributed to PS by T1. By virtue of the Code §754 election filed by PS, under Code §743(b) the basis of the T1-contributed real estate is stepped up, for the benefit of partner S, to $12 million.[3] Thus, when PS sold the

---

[19] See Prop. Reg. §1.337(d)-3(e), (h) examples (1) and (4).

¶1605   [1] Reg. §1.1502-13(c)(1)(i), as then in effect.

[2] Reg. §1.1502-13(d)(1), (f)(1), as then in effect.

[3] See Reg. §1.743-1(d)(3) example (2); 1954 Act Conference Report at 63-64.

real estate to the unrelated buyer for that sum, no gain was recognized and allocated to partner S.

Central to the plan was this further conclusion: Since S retained the PS partnership interest purchased from T1, neither disposing of it nor receiving any distribution of real estate sale proceeds with respect to it, T1's intercompany gain of $10 million should continue deferred into the dim future.

Applying an aggregate approach to at least this segment of partnership taxation, IRS quite reasonably reached a contrary conclusion, holding that T1's deferred gain must be restored to income as and when partner S claims cost recovery deductions or eliminates resale gain attributable to PS's basis adjustment under Code §743(b).[4]

Effective, in general, for taxable years beginning after 12/31/88 (years for which the due date of the tax return is after 3/14/90), Temp. Reg. §1.1502-13T(*l*)(1) and (2) example (1) adopted a "follow the stepped-up asset basis" approach and confirmed that T1's deferred gain must indeed be restored to income as and when partner S claims cost recovery deductions or eliminates resale gain attributable to PS's basis adjustment under Code §743(b). The same result is achieved under the consolidated return regulations in effect for years beginning on or after 7/12/95.[5]

[4] Rev. Rul. 89-85, 1989-2 C.B. 218.
[5] Reg. §1.1502-13(c)(2)(ii).

CHAPTER 17

Corporate and Securities Law, Accounting, Fraudulent Conveyance, Antitrust Reporting, and Other Non-Tax Considerations in Taxable and Tax-Free Acquisitions

Chapter 17. Non-Tax Considerations

¶1701 INTRODUCTION

This chapter provides an overview of the more important non-tax considerations in structuring and effectuating a merger, acquisition, or leveraged buyout ("LBO").

¶1702 focuses on the general non-tax considerations applicable to P's acquisition of T and reviews P's acquisition of T's stock, P's acquisition of T's assets, a merger of T with P or a P subsidiary, and a squeeze out of T's minority shareholders. Some of the legal issues reviewed include acquisition of less than 100% of T, liability for T's indebtedness, mechanical problems of transferring T's assets, transfer taxes, use of non-pro-rata consideration, dissenters' rights, shareholder votes, proxy rules, SEC registration obligations under the Securities Act of 1933, and SEC regulation of tender offers.

These issues are discussed in ¶1702 in the context of (1) a privately held T or (2) a publicly held T when the acquisition is not (and is not expected to be) hostile or contested.

¶1703 deals with accounting considerations in a merger, acquisition, or LBO, including purchase accounting, pooling of interests accounting (only for a transaction initiated before 7/1/01), and (for an LBO) special no purchase, part-purchase, and recapitalization accounting.

¶1704 and ¶1705 discuss accounting considerations for stock-based compensation to management and for stock-based kickers to lenders.

¶1706 discusses LBO structures that prejudice T's creditors and reviews the application of the fraudulent conveyance doctrine to void payments to T's shareholders, impair notes and asset liens given to the LBO lenders, and otherwise defeat the expectations of the LBO participants.

¶1707 deals with P's and T's obligations to file with the Federal Trade Commission (in advance of consummating an acquisition, including tender offers and even purchases of minority blocks of T's stock) under the Hart-Scott-Rodino Antitrust Improvements Act, if the transaction meets certain size tests.

¶1702 NON-TAX CONSIDERATIONS APPLICABLE TO ACQUISITIONS IN GENERAL

¶1702.1 *Evaluation of T*

In addition to the usual economic and business considerations, there are a number of principal factors P will normally evaluate in determining whether to acquire T, in identifying possible obstacles to such an acquisition, and in formulating an acceptable structure for the transaction. These factors are discussed below.

¶1702.1.1 Shareholder Profile

T's shareholder profile will frequently influence P's approach to and structuring of the acquisition. If T is closely held, P may be able to negotiate directly with all of T's shareholders to acquire 100% of T's stock. If T is publicly held (or privately held by a large, diverse group of shareholders), this would be virtually impossible, necessitating a different approach than a direct purchase of T's stock if P intends to acquire 100% of T (for example, a merger with T, a purchase of T's assets, or a two-step acquisition, i.e., as a purchase of controlling blocks of T stock or a tender offer for T stock followed by a "squeeze-out" merger).

¶1702.1.2 Asset Profile

T's asset profile will also frequently influence P's approach to and structuring of the acquisition. If T has difficult-to-transfer assets (such as hundreds of parcels of real estate, hundreds of vehicles, or important contracts, leases, licenses, and the like that prohibit assignment), P's purchase of T's stock or a reverse merger of a P subsidiary ("S") into T will normally obviate the need for such asset transfers. On the other hand, some agreements or licenses are specifically drafted to require the other party's approval for even a change in control of T (i.e., a sale of a controlling interest in T's stock) or a merger involving T.

¶1702.1.3 Other Practical Considerations

Despite T's favorable business and economic characteristics, a number of other factors may either discourage P from acquiring T or influence P's structuring of the acquisition. These include:

(1) significant T contingent liabilities, such as environmental clean-up responsibilities, product liabilities, employee discrimination claims, antitrust claims, asserted tax deficiencies, or other threatened or pending lawsuits;

(2) T "hidden" liabilities, such as underfunded pension plans, burdensome long-term debt covenants, or labor problems;

(3) T loan agreements with acceleration provisions triggered by a change in T's control, or restrictive debt covenants that would be breached by a leveraged acquisition of T;

(4) risk of antitrust challenge to the P-T combination;

(5) necessity for state or federal regulatory approval of a change in T's control, applicable if T is, for example, a bank, insurance company, common carrier, defense contractor, broadcaster, or other regulated entity;

(6) existence of T foreign branches or subsidiaries requiring foreign governmental approval for a change in T's control;

(7) adequacy of T's intellectual property protection (e.g., patents, trademarks, copyrights, secrecy agreements, covenants not to compete);

(8) T anti-takeover measures or "shark repellents," such as defensive charter or bylaw provisions, outstanding "poison pills," and existing "golden parachute" or severance agreements.

¶1702.2 General Structuring Considerations

¶1702.2.1 Acquiring Less Than 100% of T

¶1702.2.1.1 Acquisition of Stock

When P acquires T's stock in a voluntary stock-for-stock, cash-for-stock, or notes-for-stock transaction (including a tender offer or exchange offer), each T shareholder decides whether to sell his T stock. Hence, P may end up owning less than 100% of T's stock. See ¶1702.2.7.1 regarding application of SEC's tender offer rules to P's acquisition of public T's stock.

If P becomes T's controlling (but not 100%) shareholder, P has all the concerns associated with the presence of T minority shareholders, such as possible P liability (as T's controlling shareholder) for breach of fiduciary duties in its dealings with T or T's minority shareholders. Difficult fairness and "going private" issues may be raised if P later decides to acquire the T minority interest (i.e., "squeeze out" the minority shareholders) through merger or otherwise. See ¶1702.7.

¶1702.2.1.2 Merger or Acquisition of Assets

If P acquires T in a merger (either T into P, T into S, or S into T) or P acquires all or substantially all of T's assets, P will not be left to deal with any T minority shareholders following the transaction. If the requisite vote of T's shareholders is obtained for a merger or sale of assets, all of T's shareholders are required to give up their T stock in exchange for the acquisition consideration specified in the merger agreement, unless they dissent and seek appraisal rights, in which case they will receive cash. See ¶1702.2.7 regarding shareholder votes and ¶1702.2.6 regarding dissenters' rights.

¶1702.2.2   Liability for T's Indebtedness

¶1702.2.2.1   *Acquisition of Stock*

Generally, if P acquires T's stock, T's creditors can reach only T's assets and not P's assets.

¶1702.2.2.2   *Merger*

If T and P merge or T and S merge, most state corporation laws allow T's creditors to reach both T's and P's assets (if T and P merge) or both T's and S's assets (if T and S merge in a reverse or forward subsidiary merger).

¶1702.2.2.3   *Acquisition of Assets*

If P acquires T's assets, the bulk sales provisions of the Uniform Commercial Code (UCC Article 6) generally permit T's creditors to sue P (at least up to the FV of T's assets acquired by P) for six months (or as adopted in some states, 12 months) after the acquisition, unless notice was given to all of T's creditors (in some states by registered mail and in other states by publication) and other specified procedures were followed. The UCC bulk sales provisions generally apply regardless of any contract provision between P and T to the contrary if T transfers the major part of the inventory of an enterprise whose principal business is the sale of merchandise from inventory. Although almost all states at one time had the UCC bulk sales provisions (or some variation thereof), approximately half the states have repealed their bulk sales provisions.

In addition, even if the parties have complied with the notice and other requirements of the bulk sales law or the relevant state laws do not contain the bulk sales law (so that UCC Article 6 does *not* make P liable for T's debts), courts increasingly have held P responsible for some or all of T's debts and contingent liabilities (especially tort liabilities for defective products) under the common law doctrines of "*de facto* merger" and "successor liability." This can occur when T's business has been transferred to P as a going concern and T goes out of existence (especially, but not exclusively, when T's shareholders receive an equity interest in P).

If S (rather than P) acquires T's assets, the bulk sales law and the common law doctrines of *de facto* merger and successor liability may apply to make S liable for T's debts and contingent liabilities (but generally not P unless P has done something to permit a creditor to pierce the corporate veil).

¶1702.2.2.4   *Taxes*

When P acquires T's assets or P and T merge (or when S acquires T's assets or S and T merge), P (or S in a subsidiary acquisition) may have transferee liability for T's federal income tax obligations (Code §6901) and for certain of T's state and local taxes under special state transferee liability statutes. Frequently state law provides that P (or S in a subsidiary acquisition) will not inherit T's state and local tax obligations if it complies with certain notice and delay procedures.

¶1702.2.3   Mechanical Problems of Transferring T's Assets

¶1702.2.3.1   Acquisition of Assets

When P (or S) purchases T's assets for cash, notes, or P stock, substantial paperwork can be required (including recording of real estate, vehicle, patent, trademark, and airplane transfers) and difficult problems can arise in transferring thousands of assets. In addition, significant loan agreements, leases, licenses, and other contracts may prohibit assignment, in which case consent must be obtained from the other party to the contract or license, who may attempt to exact some consideration for granting consent.

¶1702.2.3.2   Acquisition of Stock

When P acquires T's stock so that T's assets are not transferred, the difficulties described at ¶1702.2.3.1 are generally not encountered. However, certain types of agreements to which T may be a party (e.g., loan agreements and leases) and certain types of licenses may explicitly require the consent of the other party to the agreement or the issuer of the license in the event of a change in T's control, i.e., a sale of a controlling interest in T's stock.

¶1702.2.3.3   Merger

A forward merger in which T merges into P (or S) may avoid the asset transfer problems described at ¶1702.2.3.1 because a merger transfers T's assets by operation of law. However, some leases, loan agreements, licenses, and other contracts expressly require consent of the other party even for transfers by operation of law.

A contractual provision that generally requires the other party's consent to assignment, but does not expressly address a merger or transfer by operation of law, may or may not be interpreted to prohibit a transfer by forward merger. In the absence of such an express prohibition, the court in *Brunswick Corp. v. St. Paul Fire & Marine Insurance Co.*, 509 F. Supp. 750 (E.D. Pa. 1981), held that the effect of a "no assignment" clause on a merger is governed by state corporation law. The *Brunswick* court held that all of T's rights and benefits under an insurance contract were vested in P upon T's forward merger into P, despite a provision in the contract prohibiting assignments by T generally.

However, the court in *PPG Industries, Inc. v. Guardian Industrial Corp.*, 597 F.2d 1090 (6th Cir.), *cert. denied*, 444 U.S. 930 (1979), reached a different result. In

PPG Industries T held a license to use certain patents, which was by its terms "non-transferable . . . for the use and benefit" of T, the licensee. The license did not specifically require consent to (or otherwise mention) a merger of T into another corporation. T merged into P. The court held that federal law, not state corporation law, governs the transfer of a patent license in a merger. The court concluded that the merger of T into P did not effectively transfer the license to P even though T's assets were otherwise transferred to P by operation of law. In so holding, the court emphasized the "personal" nature of patent licenses generally and the courts' historical reluctance to recognize a transfer of a license that is not expressly assignable.

A reverse subsidiary merger of S into T will normally avoid the asset transfer problems described at ¶1702.2.3.1 because T's assets are not being transferred. However, a particular agreement or license may explicitly require consent to a change in T's control or may require consent to a merger, even when T is the surviving entity.

¶1702.2.4 Transfer, Sales and Use Taxes

Most states impose transfer taxes on the sale of real property (real estate transfer taxes) and on the sale of tangible personal property not for resale (sales and use taxes).

Some state sales and use taxes exempt the transfer of tangible personal property in an isolated sale or a sale not in the ordinary course of business. In these states, T's sale of its assets and business to P would not be subject to sales and use taxes.

However, some other states, such as California, do not provide such an exemption and hence impose a sales tax on T's sale of its assets and business to P. Nevertheless, even in states that tax an isolated sale, T's sale of inventory to P would almost always be exempt because the inventory would be for subsequent resale by P (so sales tax will be payable when P resells such inventory). In such states, T's sale of its machinery and equipment, furniture, tools and dies, etc., to P would be subjected to sales tax. State law varies on whether less tangible property (such as computer software) is considered tangible personal property subject to sales tax.

In order to avoid sales and use taxes, it may be advantageous (depending on state law) to structure the acquisition as either (1) P's purchase of T's stock (possibly followed by liquidation or upstream merger of T into P) or (2) a merger between T and either P or S.

However, some states impose a stock transfer and/or stock issuance tax, which could apply to an acquisition structured as a sale of T stock or to P's issuance of its stock in a merger.

¶1702.2.5 Non-Pro-Rata Consideration

¶1702.2.5.1 *Acquisition of Stock*

In an acquisition of T stock (not constituting a public tender offer) in which P deals separately with each T shareholder, P may give different amounts or types of consideration to different T shareholders (subject to state corporate law—see ¶1702.2.5.3—and full disclosure under SEC Rule 10b-5). For example, P can pay $10 per share to some T shareholders and $9 per share to others. Or P can pay some T shareholders with cash, others with P notes, and still others with P stock.

In a public tender offer, however, all of T's tendering shareholders must receive the same consideration. See ¶1702.2.7.1.

¶1702.2.5.2 *Merger or Acquisition of Assets*

In a merger, most (but not all) states allow cash, property, securities, or a combination thereof to be used as consideration. In a sale of assets, any consideration agreed upon by the parties may be used.

However, there is some question whether a merger agreement (or a liquidation following a sale of assets) can (without the consent of 100% of T's shareholders) provide for some T common shareholders to receive different amounts or different types of consideration than other holders of identical stock. If not, the same practical result can be achieved if P acquires some T stock for one amount or type of consideration and immediately thereafter follows with a merger (or acquisition of assets followed by T's liquidation), with the remaining T shareholders receiving another amount or type of consideration in the merger (or liquidation).

This technique is frequently used in an LBO in which T's management is swapping its T stock for P stock in a tax-free Code §351 transaction and T's other shareholders will receive cash (or cash and P notes) in a reverse subsidiary merger of S into T immediately after the Code §351 transaction. See ¶1403.

¶1702.2.5.3 *Legality of Premium for Control*

Regarding the legality of paying a premium price for a control block of shares, compare, e.g., *Perlman v. Feldmann*, 219 F.2d 173 (2d Cir.) (control shareholders liable to other shareholders for the premium), *cert. denied*, 349 U.S. 952 (1955), with, e.g., *Essex Universal Corp. v. Yates*, 305 F.2d 572 (2d Cir. 1962) (control shareholders not liable).

¶1702.2.6 Dissenters' Rights

¶1702.2.6.1 *Acquisition of Stock*

Because of the voluntary nature of a stock acquisition (i.e., a T shareholder is not compelled to sell his T shares to P), statutory dissenters' or appraisal rights entitling a T shareholder to sue to recover the FV of his T stock do not apply.

¶1702.2.6.2   *Acquisition of Assets*

The laws of many jurisdictions permit a T shareholder who dissents from the sale, lease, exchange, or other disposition of all or substantially all of T's assets to receive in cash the appraised FV of his T stock, as determined by a court. Delaware, however, is an exception, as it allows no dissenters' or appraisal rights to a T shareholder when T sells all or substantially all of its assets unless T's charter otherwise provides.[1]

¶1702.2.6.3   *Merger*

If T and P merge, the laws of most jurisdictions allow a T or P shareholder who dissents to receive in cash the appraised FV of his shares, as determined by a court.

Delaware, however, denies appraisal rights to a T shareholder involved in a merger if (1) the class of shares he held before the transaction is listed on a national securities exchange or is held by at least 2,000 shareholders and (2) he receives either (a) shares of the surviving corporation, (b) shares of another corporation (e.g., the surviving corporation's parent) that are listed on a national securities exchange, traded on the Nasdaq National Market ("Nasdaq NM"), or held by at least 2,000 shareholders, (c) cash in lieu of fractional shares, or (d) any combination of the foregoing.[2]

Delaware also denies appraisal rights to a P shareholder if the class of shares he held before the merger is listed on a national securities exchange, or traded on the Nasdaq NM, or held by at least 2,000 shareholders.[3] Moreover, if P's shareholders are not required to vote on the merger, either because of the Delaware "small merger" provision (the amount of P stock to be issued in the merger is relatively small compared to P's outstanding stock) or because of the Delaware "short-form merger" provision (T is a 90% or greater P subsidiary), both discussed at ¶1702.2.7.3, P's shareholders are denied appraisal rights.[4]

If T and S merge (in a forward or reverse subsidiary merger), P's shareholders are not entitled to appraisal rights (because P is not a party to the merger).[5] This is true even if P's shareholders vote in connection with the T acquisition for one or more of the reasons set forth in ¶1702.2.7.3.

However, a Delaware corporation may in its certificate of incorporation provide additional appraisal rights not otherwise required by law.[6]

¶1702   [1] Delaware General Corporation Law (hereinafter "Del. GCL") §262.
[2] Del. GCL §262(b).
[3] Del. GCL §262(b)(1).
[4] Del. GCL §262(b).
[5] See Del. GCL §262.
[6] Del. GCL §262(c).

¶1702.2.7   Shareholder Vote, SEC Proxy Rules, SEC Tender Offer Rules, and SEC Stock Ownership Disclosure Rules

¶1702.2.7.1   Acquisition of Stock

No vote of T's, P's, or S's shareholders is necessary when P (or S) acquires T's stock, unless one of the following applies:

(1)   P's charter explicitly requires the approval of P's shareholders.
(2)   P is issuing stock to T's shareholders in excess of P's authorized shares (so a vote of P's shareholders is necessary to amend P's charter to authorize the stock).
(3)   P's stock is listed on the New York Stock Exchange ("NYSE"), the American Stock Exchange ("AMEX"), the Nasdaq NM, or certain regional exchanges which would de-list P's stock if it effectuated the transaction without a shareholder vote. Each of the NYSE, AMEX, and Nasdaq NM rules has slightly different substantive provisions and somewhat different wording.

The NYSE rules require a shareholder vote when:
(a)   P is issuing 20% (in voting power or in number of shares) or more of its common stock (or equivalent such as warrants or convertibles), or
(b)   the acquisition is from a director, officer, or substantial shareholder of P (or of a P subsidiary, affiliate, or other closely related person), or from any company or party in which one of such persons has a substantial direct or indirect interest, and P is issuing 1% (in voting power or in number of shares) or more of its common stock (or equivalent such as warrants or convertibles), or
(c)   the issuance will result in a change of control of P.

The AMEX rules require a shareholder vote when:
(a)   P is issuing or potentially issuing (e.g., through the issuance of warrants or options) common stock or securities convertible into its common stock which could result in an increase in its outstanding common stock of 20% or more, or
(b)   any director, officer, or substantial shareholder of P has a 5% or greater interest (or such persons collectively have a 10% or greater interest), directly or indirectly, in the company or assets to be acquired or otherwise has such an interest in the consideration to be paid in the transaction and the present or potential issuance of P's common stock, or securities convertible into P's common stock, could result in an increase in outstanding P common stock of 5% or more, or
(c)   P is issuing or selling its common stock (or securities convertible into its common stock) (and, although the rule is silent, apparently also warrants to acquire common stock) at a price below the greater of book or market value and such issuance or sale (together with any sales by P's directors, officers, or substantial shareholders) equals 20% or more of P's presently outstanding common stock.

The Nasdaq NM rules require a P shareholder vote when:

    (a)   P is issuing 20% (in voting power or in number of shares) or more of its common stock (or equivalent such as warrants or convertibles), or

    (b)   P is issuing or selling its common stock (or equivalent such as warrants or convertibles) at a price below the greater of book or market value, and such issuance or sale (together with any sales by P's directors, officers, and substantial shareholders) represents 20% or more in voting power or in number of common shares, or

    (c)   any director, officer, or substantial shareholder of P has a 5% or greater interest (or such persons collectively have a 10% or greater interest), directly or indirectly, in the company or assets to be acquired or otherwise has an interest in the consideration to be paid, and P is issuing 5% (in voting power or in number of shares) or more of its common stock (or equivalent such as warrants or convertibles), or

    (d)   the issuance will result in a change of control of P.[7]

See ¶1702.2.7.6 for a description of SEC's proxy rules applicable where a publicly held company holds a shareholder vote.

Where T's stock is publicly held and P is purchasing T stock from a number of holders, P must comply with the 1934 Act's tender offer provisions (also known as the Williams Act) and SEC's tender offer rules, governing timing and disclosure of tender offers. All tender offers, whether the consideration offered by P consists of cash or stock, must be made on SEC schedule TO, with substantive disclosure as required by SEC reg. M-A.

    (1)   After P has publicly announced its intention to make a tender offer for T stock, P must file a schedule TO with SEC describing the tender offer and must deliver a copy to T.

    (2)   There is no time limit on the period P can wait after announcing its intention to tender for T stock before "commencing" its tender offer, but P must send T's shareholders the information required by SEC schedule TO and SEC reg. M-A no later than the time P sends to T's shareholders a letter of transmittal to be used by them in tendering their T stock to P.

    (3)   T must file a schedule 14D-9 with SEC within 10 business days after P commences its tender offer for T stock containing T's recommendation to its shareholders regarding acceptance of, rejection of or, no position on P's tender offer.

    (4)   P's tender offer must remain open for at least 20 business days.

    (5)   P's tender offer must be open to all T shareholders and must offer each T shareholder the highest consideration P paid to any other T shareholder during such tender offer.

---

[7] Under the NYSE and NASD rules, these percentage tests are calculated using (a) *as the numerator*, the voting power, or the number of shares, of common stock that will be issued or sold in the transaction (assuming exercise of any warrants and conversion of convertibles that will be issued or sold in the transaction), and (b) *as the denominator*, the voting power of all voting securities (i.e., not merely common stock), or the number of shares of common stock, actually outstanding immediately before the proposed

(6)   P can first begin purchasing T shares 20 business days after commencing its tender offer and can not purchase (or agree to purchase) T shares outside the tender offer once it has commenced.

(7)   If P's tender offer is not for "any and all" T shares, P must purchase T shares on a pro rata basis from all T tendering shareholders.

  • If P seeks (e.g.) 51% of T's stock, P cannot accept the first 51% tendered and reject the excess. Rather, where more than 51% of T's stock is tendered during the tender offer and P chooses to buy only 51%, P must buy a pro-rated portion from each tendering T shareholder.

(8)   A T tendering shareholder may withdraw any tendered T shares prior to expiration of the tender offer.

(9)   If P makes a material change in the terms of its tender offer (e.g., a change in the percentage of T shares sought or the amount of consideration to be paid), the tender offer must remain open for at least 10 business days thereafter.

(10) P must announce any extension of the tender offer's expiration date by 9:00 a.m. EST on the day following scheduled expiration.

(11) P must pay the consideration offered or return the T shares tendered promptly after consummation, termination, or withdrawal of P's tender offer.

(12) P (after consummating its initial tender offer which was for any and all T shares) may elect to make a second tender offer at the same price as the initial tender offer without a 20 business day waiting period and without allowing tendering T shareholders any withdrawal rights. This second tender offer must be open at least 3 business days and no more than 20 business days. P must immediately accept and promptly pay for T shares as tendered during the second tender offer.

(13) The rules are somewhat different for a tender offer by T for its own stock (a "self tender"). See SEC Rule 13e-4.

Where P is purchasing publicly held T shares that are registered under 1934 Act §12 (see ¶1702.2.7.6 below), SEC's 13D disclosure rules are applicable, so that, in general, P is required to file schedule 13D with SEC once P has purchased more than 5% of such class of T's publicly held voting shares (or P's ownership of such T shares when aggregated with other T shareholders with whom P is acting in concert exceeds 5%). More specifically:

(1)   Any person (a "5% shareholder") who acquires beneficial ownership of more than 5% of a class of publicly held voting equity securities generally must file with SEC a schedule 13D or, in certain cases, a less burdensome schedule 13G. The 5% shareholder's intent, characteristics and percentage ownership determine the type of filing required (e.g., schedule 13D or 13G) and the timing of the filing, as discussed below.

---

issuance or sale (this time without assuming exercise of any warrants or conversion of any convertibles, whether those outstanding or those being issued or sold in the transaction).

(2)   Multiple persons acting in concert are treated as a "group" and the holdings of each member of the group are aggregated in calculating percentage ownership. Beneficial ownership is defined broadly to include the right to acquire stock, and thus the holder of a currently exercisable option would generally be treated as beneficially owning the shares which can be acquired upon exercise.

(3)   The filing must disclose the 5% shareholder's intent with respect to T and, for a schedule 13D, substantial additional information, including the source and the amount of the 5% shareholder's financing, the 5% shareholder's contacts with the issuer, and a detailed explanation of any proposed acquisition.

(4)   Each 5% shareholder is required to file schedule 13D, except (a) certain institutional investors (e.g., insurance companies, registered investment companies, registered broker dealers, employee benefit plans) (an "Institutional Investor") acquiring securities in the ordinary course of business and with no purpose or intent of changing or influencing control of the issuer are permitted to file schedule 13G and (b) any investor (other than an Institutional Investor) beneficially owning less than 20% of a class of voting securities is permitted to file schedule 13G if such investor does not intend to change or influence control of the issuer (a "Passive Investor").

(5)   Under SEC Rule 13d-1, a schedule 13D, or a Passive Investor's schedule 13G, must be filed within 10 days after the person or group acquires beneficial ownership of more than 5% of the outstanding class of publicly held voting securities. Any changes in ownership or purpose following an initial schedule 13D filing must be promptly reported on a supplemental 13D. An Institutional Investor's schedule 13G must be filed within 45 days following the end of the year in which the investment occurred, unless such investor has acquired more than 10% of the outstanding class of publicly held voting securities, in which case the filing is due within 10 days following the end of the month in which that threshold was crossed. A Passive Investor that changes its investment intent or crosses the 20% threshold is required to file a schedule 13D within 10 days after the event, and is subject to a 10-day cooling off period during which such investor is prohibited from voting its securities and acquiring additional securities.

¶1702.2.7.2   Acquisition of Assets

If P (or S) acquires all or substantially all of T's assets, state law generally requires the approval of T's shareholders, with the necessary percentage for approval varying according to the law of T's jurisdiction of incorporation and the specific provisions of T's charter (which generally may require a higher percentage than applicable state law).

In Delaware, for example, the sale of all or substantially all of T's assets requires approval of a majority of T's outstanding voting stock, subject to higher requirements in T's charter.[8] Many other states require a higher percentage (frequently two-thirds) for approval.

States differ in their interpretation of "substantially all" of a corporation's assets, with some cases indicating that over 50% may be "substantially all."

No vote of P's shareholders is necessary in an acquisition of T's assets unless one of the following applies:

(1) P's charter explicitly requires the approval of P's shareholders.

(2) P is issuing stock to T's shareholders in excess of P's authorized shares (so a vote of P's shareholders is necessary to amend P's charter to authorize the stock).

(3) P's stock is listed on the NYSE, the AMEX, or the Nasdaq NM, which would de-list P's stock if it effectuated the transaction without a shareholder vote. As discussed at ¶1702.2.7.1 above, each of the NYSE, AMEX, and Nasdaq NM rules has slightly different substantive provisions and somewhat different wording.

¶1702.2.7.3 Merger

A merger of T into P or a merger of P into T will require the approval of both T's shareholders and P's shareholders with a very few exceptions, as discussed below. The necessary percentage for approval varies from state to state and generally may be increased by a corporation's charter.

In Delaware, for example, except as discussed below, a merger requires approval of a majority of T's and P's outstanding voting stock, subject to higher requirements in their respective charters.[9] Many other states require a higher percentage (frequently two-thirds) for approval.

When T and S merge (in a forward or reverse subsidiary merger), approval is generally necessary only from T's and S's shareholders. Since P is usually S's only shareholder, P can consent on behalf of S. Normally no approval of P's shareholders is necessary unless one of the following applies:

(1) P's charter explicitly requires the approval of P's shareholders.

(2) P is issuing stock to T's shareholders in excess of P's authorized shares (so a vote of P's shareholders is necessary to amend P's charter to authorize the stock).

(3) P's stock is listed on the NYSE, the AMEX, or the Nasdaq NM, which would de-list P's stock if it effectuated the transaction without a shareholder vote. As discussed at ¶1702.2.7.1 above, each of the NYSE, AMEX, and Nasdaq NM rules has slightly different substantive provisions and somewhat different wording.

---

[8] Del. GCL §271(a).
[9] Del. GCL §251(c).

Most states provide for a so-called short-form merger—without any shareholder vote—between a parent corporation ("P") and one of its subsidiaries ("T"), with T's minority shareholders receiving P stock, cash, or other consideration as specified in the short-form merger agreement. The precise percentage of ownership that P must have in T to carry out a short-form merger varies from state to state (90% being required in Delaware—Del. GCL §253(a)). Thus, once P has acquired the requisite stock ownership in T by purchasing T stock (e.g., 90% in Delaware) in a tender offer or negotiated stock purchase, P can (if such a short-form merger statute is applicable) merge with T without a T or P shareholder vote.[10] Care should be taken to assure that the relevant state statute permits the merger in the direction desired (T into P versus P into T). Delaware, for example, allows a short-form merger to be either upstream or downstream.[11]

Delaware also provides an exception (the "small merger" exception) from the usual P-shareholder voting requirement if T merges into P (even though P may own no T stock), the amount of P stock to be issued is relatively small compared to P's outstanding stock, and P is a Delaware corporation. Under this provision, no vote of P's shareholders is required if the merger does not involve (1) a change in P's charter, (2) a change in the stock held by P's shareholders, or (3) the issuance of P common stock (or securities convertible into P common stock) exceeding in the aggregate 20% of P's outstanding common stock immediately prior to the merger.[12] However, the laws of T's state of incorporation may require the vote of both T's and P's shareholders, thus nullifying the Delaware exception. In addition, P's charter or a stock exchange rule (such as the NYSE 20% rule) may require a vote of P's shareholders.

¶1702.2.7.4   Notice Period

When a vote of P's or T's shareholders is necessary, state law generally requires that written notice of a shareholders' meeting be sent to all shareholders (in some states, whether or not entitled to vote) a specified number of days in advance of the meeting, unless there is attendance at the meeting or a waiver of notice (generally by 100% of the shareholders).

In Delaware, for example, 10 days' advance notice is required for most shareholders' meetings, but 20 days is required for a shareholder vote on a merger or sale of assets.[13] A corporation's charter or bylaws may provide for a longer notice period. A shareholder generally may waive notice in writing.[14]

---

[10] Of course, a vote of P's shareholders would be necessary if explicitly required by P's charter *or* if P stock is being issued and either (1) P does not have sufficient authorized stock or (2) a listing or trading rule (such as the NYSE or NASD 20% rule) requires a P shareholder vote.

[11] Del. GCL §253(a).

[12] Del. GCL §251(f).

[13] Del. GCL §§222(b), 251(c), and 271(a).

[14] Del. GCL §229.

¶1702.2.7.5 *Action by Consent*

Most states permit a corporation, if authorized by its charter or bylaws (or in some states, if not expressly prohibited in the charter or bylaws), to obtain shareholder approval by written consent, obviating the need for a formal shareholders' meeting. Under Delaware law (unless prohibited by charter), action may be taken by shareholder consent if written consent is obtained from the number of shareholders whose votes would have been sufficient to take such action at a shareholders' meeting (generally a majority for a merger or sale of assets), followed by "prompt" notice to the non-consenting shareholders.[15] Some other states require unanimous shareholder consent in lieu of a meeting, without regard to the percentage that would have been sufficient to take action at a meeting.

¶1702.2.7.6 *SEC Proxy Rules*

If T is publicly held and proxies are solicited from T's shareholders regarding approval of a merger or sale of all or substantially all of T's assets, or if P is publicly held and proxies are solicited from P's shareholders in connection with a merger or acquisition of assets or an amendment to P's charter to authorize additional stock in a stock-for-stock or stock-for-assets transaction or otherwise, such proxies must be solicited pursuant to a proxy statement prepared, filed, and distributed to shareholders in accordance with §14(a) of the Securities Exchange Act of 1934 (the "1934 Act") and SEC Regulation 14A thereunder. Matters required to be disclosed in the proxy statement include:

(1) information concerning P and T, their businesses, principal security holders, executive officers, and directors;

(2) a summary of material features of the acquisition; and

(3) historical and pro forma financial statements and information.

In the event that approval from the shareholders of a publicly held T or P is to be obtained either by written consent in lieu of a shareholders' meeting or at a shareholders' meeting without the solicitation of proxies, an information statement containing substantially the information required by SEC proxy rules must be distributed to non-consenting shareholders, pursuant to §14(c) of the 1934 Act and SEC Regulation 14C thereunder, not less than 20 days prior to the date when action may be taken by written consent or the date of such meeting.

Any proxy statement (pursuant to Reg. 14A) or information statement (pursuant to Reg. 14C) must be filed with SEC at least 10 days before mailing to shareholders. Frequently SEC review takes longer than 10 days.

Hence if P or T is publicly held and a vote by shareholders is necessary for an acquisition, there is often a substantial delay between the time P and T reach

---

[15] Del. GCL §228(a) and (d).

agreement and consummation of the acquisition, in order to accommodate the following procedures:

- preparation and filing with SEC of a lengthy proxy statement or information statement describing P and T and the transaction
- SEC review period of at least 10 days and frequently substantially longer
- mailing of the proxy statement or information statement to shareholders
- 20 days' wait before holding a shareholders' meeting (under most state laws) or 20 days' wait before action may be taken by written consent (under Reg. 14C).

For purposes of SEC's proxy and information statement rules, a company is *publicly held* (and hence subject to the requirements described) if it has an equity security registered pursuant to §12 of the 1934 Act. Generally this means a company that has *either:*

(1)   as of the last day of its fiscal year, consolidated assets of $10 million or more (based on its balance sheet prepared in accordance with GAAP) and 500 or more holders of such equity security (although the company may de-register the security if, as of the end of a fiscal year, it is held by less than 300 persons or less than 500 persons if the company's consolidated assets have been less than $10 million at the end of each of its last three fiscal years); or

(2)   an equity security listed on a national securities exchange.

¶1702.2.7.7   State Disclosure Obligations

If T is a private company asking its stockholders to take action by written consent or to submit proxies for a meeting of T's shareholders, some states impose disclosure obligations on T. For example, Delaware cases indicate that T has an affirmative duty of "complete candor" to disclose material facts to stockholders (at least those stockholders who are not already fully familiar with the facts, e.g., through service as a T officer or T director or close relationship to a T officer or T director) when seeking action by written consent or submission of a proxy.

Applicability of affirmative state disclosure obligations in the context of a meeting of a private company's stockholders without solicitation of shareholder consents or proxies is unclear under Delaware law, although T is under an obligation to truthfully answer any questions asked by T stockholders.

Where T is a private company, a proxy statement meeting SEC requirements would undoubtedly satisfy any state disclosure laws, but such an extensive disclosure document may well not be necessary. Rather, T (and its directors) would likely be well protected by preparing a slimmed down version of an SEC proxy statement containing all material facts about the transaction, i.e., a mini-proxy statement, for distribution to T's shareholders without filing with SEC or any other government agency.

¶1702.2.8 Application of 1933 Act When P (or S) Issues Stock or Notes to T or Its Shareholders

An acquisition of T in which part or all of the consideration is stock or debt instruments (i.e., "securities" within the meaning of the Securities Act of 1933) of P (or S) will necessitate compliance with the Securities Act of 1933 (the "1933 Act"). The 1933 Act prohibits the sale of securities unless (1) such sale is registered with SEC and certain other requirements are satisfied or (2) an exemption from registration applies, e.g., the private placement, Rule 701, or intrastate exemption.

¶1702.2.8.1 *Public Offering*

If T's shareholder group is of any significant size, P will generally not be able to qualify for an exemption and will be required to register under the 1933 Act the issuance for T of the P stock or notes. This process is likely to require at least several weeks, and more likely several months.

SEC form S-4 may be utilized for the registration of securities issued in business combinations and exchange offers, whether or not P and/or T is already a reporting company. Form S-4 is generally advantageous when P and/or T is a reporting company under the 1934 Act, because certain financial and other information regarding such company may be incorporated by reference from 1934 Act reports filed by such company.[16] Alternatively, a long-form S-1 could be utilized for the registration of such securities.

If T is a public company subject to SEC's proxy rules, and the acquisition requires a vote of T's shareholders (so T has distributed a 1934 Act proxy statement to its shareholders), this 1934 Act proxy statement can (with modifications) be used as the 1933 Act registration statement.

¶1702.2.8.2 *Private Placement*

Section 4(2) of the 1933 Act exempts P (or S) from the requirement to register the issuance of its stock or debt securities if the issuance does not involve a public offering (i.e., the offering constitutes a private placement)—including the issuance of P (or S) stock or debt securities to a reasonably small group of T shareholders in exchange for T's stock or assets.

SEC Regulation D (Rules 501 through 508 under the 1933 Act) provides a safe harbor for certain private placements. If an offering does not comply with Reg. D, it may still fall within §4(2). However, the parameters of §4(2) outside the Reg. D safe harbor are vague and determinable only by reference to case law, which

---

[16] A short-form primary registration on form S-3 (discussed in ¶1702.2.8.5(3)) is limited to a cash sale of P securities and hence cannot be used when P is issuing its stock and/or notes to acquire T assets or stock. A short-form primary registration on form S-2 cannot be used when P is issuing its stock and/or notes in an "exchange offer," hence it appears that an S-2 cannot be used to acquire T stock but can be used to acquire T assets.

is often fact specific and provides no easily discernible bright lines to distinguish a public from a private offering.

Reg. D contains three operative exemptions: Rule 504 is applicable to a small offering, Rule 505 to a somewhat larger offering, and Rule 506 to an offering of P (or S) securities of any size.

Rule 504. This rule:

(1)   Exempts the offer and sale of up to $1 million of P securities less sales during the 12 months before the start of the Rule 504 offering (and during the Rule 504 offering) that are:
   (a)   pursuant to any exemption under §3(b) of the 1933 Act (other than Rule 701), including Rules 504 and 505 and Reg. A, or
   (b)   in violation of the 1933 Act.

(2)   Imposes no limitation on the number of purchasers and no requirement that they be sophisticated investors.

(3)   Imposes no express informational requirement (i.e., no formal private offering memorandum is required), but information sufficient to satisfy the general anti-fraud provisions of the federal securities laws (i.e., all "material" information) must be made available to purchasers and any offering materials must neither misstate a material fact nor omit a material fact necessary to prevent the offering materials or any other statements from being misleading.

(4)   Is not available if P is either a reporting company under the 1934 Act, an investment company, or a so-called blank check company.
   A 1934 Act reporting company is generally one that either:
   (a)   has consolidated gross assets of $10 million or more (based on its balance sheet prepared inTo accordance with GAAP) and 500 or more holders of a class of equity securities (although a reporting company can de-register if it is subsequently held by less than 300 persons or less than 500 persons if the company's gross assets have not exceeded $10 million on the last day of each of its three most recently ended fiscal years), or
   (b)   has a security (debt or equity) listed on a national securities exchange, or
   (c)   has made a 1933 Act registered public offering (although such a reporting company can, after the first fiscal year as a reporting company, de-register if it is held by less than 300 persons or less than 500 persons if the company's gross assets have not exceeded $10 million for a three-year period).

(5)   Prohibits general solicitation of, and general advertising for, potential purchasers unless the offering is (a) solely to "accredited investors" (as defined below) pursuant to state securities law exemptions permitting general solicitation and advertising so long as sales are made only to "accredited investors" (and at least 30 states have such exemptions) *or* (b) registered pursuant to each applicable state securities law requiring public

filing and delivery to investors of a pre-sale public disclosure document, the offering is so registered in at least one state, and such registration document is delivered to purchasers in all states (including those states that do not require such registration). Hence, for an offering meeting the requirements of (a) or (b) above, there is no prohibition on seminars or meetings with potential purchasers who are invited by general solicitation or advertising.

(6) Causes the securities issued thereunder to be restricted securities (see ¶1702.2.8.5(3) regarding resales of restricted securities) unless the offering is (a) solely to "accredited investors" (as defined below) pursuant to state securities law exemptions permitting general solicitation and advertising so long as sales are made only to "accredited investors" (and at least 30 states have such exemptions) *or* (b) registered pursuant to each applicable state securities law requiring public filing and delivery to investors of a pre-sale public disclosure document, the offering is so registered in at least one state, and such registration document is delivered to purchasers in all states (including those states that do not require such registration). For an offering meeting the requirements of (a) or (b) above, the securities are not restricted and generally can be freely resold by the holder. See ¶1702.2.8.5(3) regarding resales of unrestricted securities by P affiliates (i.e., members of P's control group).

Rule 505. This rule:

(1) Exempts the offer and sale of up to $5 million per year of P securities less sales during the 12 months before the start of the Rule 505 offering (and during the Rule 505 offering) that are:
   (a) pursuant to any exemption under §3(b) of the 1933 Act (other than Rule 701), including Rules 504 and 505 and Regulation A, or
   (b) in violation of the 1933 Act;
(2) Allows an unlimited number of "accredited investors" (as defined below), plus up to 35 additional investors;
   • In determining whether there are more than 35 non-accredited investors, (a) all relatives of a purchaser with the same principal residence as the purchaser are ignored, (b) a trust or estate in which a purchaser and his or her relatives with the same principal residence own in the aggregate more than 50% of the beneficial interest is ignored, and (c) any entity in which a purchaser and his or her relatives with the same principal residence own in the aggregate more than 50% of the equity securities is ignored.
(3) Imposes no sophistication requirement;
(4) Requires that for any purchaser who is not an accredited investor, a substantial disclosure document (i.e., a private offering memorandum) be delivered to such non-accredited investor;
(5) Prohibits general solicitation of, and general advertising for, potential purchasers. Hence, no seminars or meetings with potential purchasers

who are invited by general solicitation or advertising are allowed. While nothing has been heard from SEC since 6/95, SEC had then announced that it was considering revising or eliminating the prohibition on general solicitation;

(6)   Causes securities issued thereunder to be restricted securities. See ¶1702.2.8.5(3) regarding resales of restricted securities.

Rule 506. This rule:

(1)   Imposes no limitation on the dollar size of the offering.
(2)   Allows an unlimited number of "accredited investors" (as defined below), plus up to 35 additional investors (defined and counted as described in the Rule 505 discussion above);
(3)   Requires each non-accredited investor to be sophisticated (alone or along with a purchaser representative not affiliated with P);
(4)   Requires that for any purchaser who is not an accredited investor, a substantial disclosure document (i.e., a private offering memorandum) must be delivered to such non-accredited investor;
(5)   Prohibits general solicitation of, and general advertising for, potential purchasers. Hence, no seminars or meetings with potential purchasers who are invited by general solicitation or advertising are allowed. While nothing has been heard from SEC since 6/95, SEC had then announced that it was considering revising or eliminating the prohibition on general solicitation;
(6)   Causes securities issued thereunder to be restricted securities. See ¶1702.2.8.5(3) regarding resales of restricted securities.

Accredited investor. This term refers to:

(1)   Certain institutional investors, i.e., a bank, a savings and loan, or a similar financial institution (whether acting in an individual or fiduciary capacity), an insurance company, an SBIC, a registered investment company, a business development company or a private business development company, or a registered broker-dealer;
(2)   A plan established and maintained by a state (or any of its political subdivisions, agencies, instrumentalities, etc.) for the benefit of its employees, if such plan has total assets in excess of $5 million;
(3)   An ERISA plan (a) with a fiduciary that is a bank, savings and loan, insurance company, or registered investment advisor, or (b) with total assets in excess of $5 million, or (c) that is a self-directed plan with investment decisions made solely by accredited investors;
(4)   A corporation, partnership, business trust, or Code §501(c)(3) charitable organization, in each case with total assets in excess of $5 million and not formed for the specific purpose of acquiring the securities offered. SEC

takes the perfectly logical interpretative position that, while not specifically enumerated in Reg. D's list of entities, an LLC may be treated as an "accredited investor" as long as it meets the other requirements, i.e., total assets in excess of $5 million and not formed for the specific purpose of acquiring the securities;

(5) A trust with total assets in excess of $5 million and not formed for the specific purpose of acquiring the securities offered, whose purchase is directed by a "sophisticated person" (i.e., a person who either alone or with his purchaser representative(s) has such knowledge and experience in financial and business matters that he is capable of evaluating the merits and risks of the prospective investment);

(6) A director or executive officer of P (or if P is a partnership, a general partner of P or a director, executive officer, or general partner of P's general partner);

(7) An individual with more than $1 million net worth or $1 million joint net worth with the individual's spouse;

(8) An individual with more than $200,000 of "income" in each of the two most recent years, or joint income with such individual's spouse in excess of $300,000 during such periods, who reasonably expects income in excess of such amount in the current year. In general, "income" means adjusted gross income for tax purposes before any deduction for depletion or partnership losses allocated to a limited partner (or under prior tax law, any deduction for LTCG), plus tax-exempt interest income.

(9) An entity in which all of the equity owners are accredited investors.

Other Reg. D provisions. Except as described below, SEC's normal factually based integration doctrine (which applies to all securities offerings) is applicable in determining whether P's offering qualifies under Reg. D. Under the integration doctrine, the following factors are considered in determining whether one sale of securities by P will be integrated with (i.e., treated as part of the same offering as) a prior or subsequent offer or sale of P securities:

- whether the sales are part of a single plan of financing
- whether the sales involve issuance of the same class of securities
- whether the sales occur at or about the same time
- whether the same type of consideration is received
- whether the sales are for the same general purpose.

Reg. D sets forth a safe harbor exception to SEC's normal integration doctrine: Sales of P securities more than six months before the beginning of the Reg. D offering or more than six months after the completion of the Reg. D offering will not be integrated with the Reg. D offering if during those six-month periods P makes no offers or sales of the same or a similar class of securities as those sold in the Reg. D offering.

In some cases, P may begin a private offering and subsequently determine that a registered public offering would be a better alternative. Conversely, P may begin a registered public offering and subsequently determine that a private offering would be a better alternative (e.g., because of insufficient public interest). SEC Rule 155 sets forth conditions that must be met in order to allow P to convert a private offering into a public offering, or a public offering into a private offering, without risk the offerings will be integrated and violate the 1933 Act. In the case of a private offering converted into a public offering: no securities may be sold in the private offering, the private offering must be terminated and all selling activities terminated, there must be a 30-day waiting period prior to filing the registration statement (unless the securities in the private offering were offered only to accredited and sophisticated persons), and the public offering prospectus must disclose certain information about the abandoned private offering. In the case of a public offering converted into a private offering: no securities may be sold in the public offering, the registration statement must be withdrawn, there must be a 30-day waiting period prior to commencement of the private offering, certain information about the abandoned public offering must be provided to each offeree in the private offering, and the private offering memorandum must contain current information about P.

Three additional types of sales are never integrated with a Reg. D offering:

(1)   sales pursuant to SEC Rule 701 (discussed below)
(2)   sales pursuant to Reg. A that are consummated subsequent to the Reg. D offering or that are consummated more than six months prior to the Reg. D offering
(3)   sales to foreign persons made outside the U.S. in compliance with SEC Reg. S, i.e., in an "offshore transaction" where there have not been any "directed selling efforts" into the U.S. market with respect to such securities and the securities are restricted from resale to a U.S. person for a specified period, one year in the case of P equity securities and 40 days for P debt securities.

P is required to file a Reg. D notification with SEC within 15 days after the first sale of securities, but failure to file does not destroy prior exempt issuances of securities pursuant to Reg. D.

¶1702.2.8.3   SEC Rule 701

If an offering of P securities to P employees, directors, officers, consultants, and advisors (or those of its majority-owned subsidiaries) does not qualify as a private placement under either Reg. D or 1933 Act §4(2), such offering will still be exempt from registration under the 1933 Act if it fits within the Rule 701 safe harbor. Rule 701 exempts offers and sales of P securities in compensatory circumstances to such employees, directors, officers, consultants, and advisors, as discussed below:

The securities must be issued in compensatory circumstances, not to raise capital, and must be issued pursuant to a written compensatory benefit plan or a written compensatory contract. Each purchaser must receive a copy of the written plan or contract.

Rule 701 is not available if P is a reporting company under the 1934 Act (as described at ¶1702.2.8.2) or an investment company.

Although there are no specific disclosure requirements (i.e., no formal private offering memorandum is required), information adequate to satisfy the general anti-fraud provisions of the federal securities laws (i.e., all "material" information) must be made available to purchasers and any offering materials must neither misstate a material fact nor omit a material fact necessary to prevent the offering materials or any other statements from being misleading. In addition, if P sells more than $5 million of securities in reliance on this exemption in any 12-month period, or believes that its sales will exceed $5 million in a 12-month period, P must deliver to purchasers a written disclosure of risks associated with an investment in the P securities, a summary of material terms of the compensatory plan, and certain P financial statements. For an option, such disclosure is required a reasonable period before option exercise.

The amount of securities sold under Rule 701 (less sales during the prior 12 months in reliance on Rule 701) may not exceed the greater of:

(1) $1 million, or
(2) 15% of P's total assets measured at its most recent balance sheet date, or
(3) 15% of P's outstanding securities of the class being issued (including securities issuable under currently exercisable or convertible warrants, options, rights, or other securities not originally issued pursuant to Rule 701) at its most recent balance sheet date.

For purposes of calculating whether P's Rule 701 sales are within this maximum amount, options are treated as securities sold by P on the date of grant and at the exercise price, without regard to whether the option is then vested or exercisable.

Rule 701 contains no limitation on the type of distribution that may be engaged in, the number of offerees or purchasers, or the sophistication of the offerees or purchasers. However, each purchaser must be a P employee, director, officer, consultant, or advisor or (in certain cases such as an option exercise) a person who formerly held such a position or a family member of such a person.

Offerings under Rule 701 are not integrated with any other offering or sale of securities, whether or not registered under the 1933 Act. In addition, a Rule 701 offering is not subtracted in determining the permissible amount of sales under other SEC rules adopted pursuant to 1933 Act §3(b), such as Rules 504 and 505.

Securities received in a Rule 701 offering are "restricted securities" that cannot be resold without 1933 Act registration or an exemption. See ¶1702.2.8.5(3) regarding resales of restricted securities. However, ninety days after P becomes a 1934 Act reporting company securities issued by P under Rule 701 (unlike other restricted securities) will be free of most of the requirements of SEC Rule 144, as discussed in ¶1702.2.8.5(3)(b). If an offering fails the safe harbors of both Reg. D and Rule 701, it may still fall within §4(2) of the 1933 Act. However, the parameters of §4(2) outside the two safe harbors are vague and determinable only by reference to case law, which is often fact specific and provides no bright lines to distinguish a public from a private offering.

¶1702.2.8.4 Intrastate Offering

Section 3(a)(11) of the 1933 Act exempts intrastate offerings. SEC Rule 147 provides a safe harbor for certain intrastate offerings. An offering that does not comply with Rule 147 nevertheless may fall within §3(a)(11). To be exempt under Rule 147, the offering must meet the following requirements:

(1) P must be incorporated in the state in which the P stock is to be sold, must derive 80% of its revenues from such state, must have at least 80% of its assets located within such state, must intend to and actually use at least 80% of the net proceeds within such state, and must have its principal office within such state.

(2) All the offerees and purchasers of the P stock must be residents of such state.

(3) The P stock must "come to rest" in such state, i.e., there may be no out-of-state resales of the stock during the offering or for a period of nine months following the date of the last sale by P. Sales may be integrated with other non-intrastate sales so as to make the exemption unavailable.

¶1702.2.8.5 Restrictions on Resale of P Securities

When P (or S) has issued stock or debt securities to T or T's shareholders in exchange for T's stock or assets, there are frequently SEC restrictions on resale of the P stock or debt securities (unless P files an effective 1933 Act registration statement covering such resale). The exact nature of the restrictions turns on (1) whether the P securities were registered under the 1933 Act when they were issued to T or T's shareholders, (2) whether the transaction was structured (a) as a voluntary acquisition of T stock in which each T shareholder had the right to decide whether to retain his T stock or to swap his T stock for P securities (an "exchange offer") or (b) as an acquisition of T's assets or a merger in which T shareholder approval by a prescribed majority was binding on all T shareholders (other than dissenters), (3) the status of the particular T shareholder who desires to sell, and (4) the status of the particular purchaser.

(1) P (or S) acquires T's stock in voluntary exchange offer for P securities registered under 1933 Act. If P (or S) acquires T's stock in an exchange offer in which each T shareholder had the right to retain his T stock or exchange it for consideration consisting (in whole or in part) of P stock or debt securities, and the P securities issued to T's shareholders are registered pursuant to the 1933 Act (because the transaction does not qualify for exemption as a private placement, intrastate offering, or otherwise), the exchanging T shareholders are generally free to resell their P securities publicly without any SEC restriction.

However, a T shareholder who is or becomes a P "affiliate" (i.e., a member of P's control group) is limited (so long as he remains a P affiliate) by the restrictions of SEC Rule 144 as to the amount of P securities he may sell publicly and the manner of sale, except that he is not subject to Rule 144's one-year holding period. See the discussion of Rule 144 in (3) below. Of course, this restriction does not apply if P files an effective 1933 Act registration statement covering a resale.

(2)   P (or S) acquires T's assets or merges with T in exchange for P securities registered under 1933 Act—Rule 145. SEC Rule 145 applies when P (or S) acquires T's assets or merges with T (so T shareholder approval is binding on all T shareholders except dissenters), T's shareholders receive P stock or debt securities (in whole or in part) as the consideration (directly in a merger or on T's liquidation in an asset sale), and the P securities are registered under the 1933 Act (because the transaction does not qualify as a private placement, intrastate offering, or otherwise).

After such a registered Rule 145 transaction, all of T's former shareholders (other than those who were T affiliates—i.e., members of T's control group) are free to sell the P securities publicly without SEC restriction. However, a person who was a T affiliate at the time of the acquisition is subject to restrictions on public sale of the P securities (unless at the time of such resale P files an effective 1933 Act registration statement covering such resale). These restrictions are discussed in (a) through (c) below.

(a) During the one year following the transaction, he can sell the P securities publicly only pursuant to Rule 144 (discussed in (3) below), except that he is not subject to Rule 144's one-year holding period requirement or to Rule 144's notice requirement (whether he becomes a member of P's control group or not).

(b) One year after the acquisition, he will be subject to a less restrictive rule than rule (a) if he is not a member of P's control group at the time of sale, i.e., he may sell his P securities publicly beginning one year after the acquisition without limitation so long as P is filing periodic reports with SEC as required by Rule 144's information requirements.

(c) Two years after the acquisition, he will no longer be subject to either rule (a) or rule (b) so long as he is not a member of P's control group at the time of sale or during the three months before, i.e., he may sell his P securities publicly beginning two years after the acquisition without any restriction.

(d) If a T shareholder who was not a T affiliate at the time of the acquisition is then or thereafter becomes a P affiliate, he will be subject to the restrictions of Rule 144 (so long as he remains a P affiliate) except that he is not subject to Rule 144's one-year holding period.

(e) While nothing has been heard from SEC since 2/97, SEC had then announced that it was considering eliminating the restrictions described in (a) through (c) on a former T shareholder who was a T affiliate immediately before P's acquisition of T.

(3)   P (or S) acquires T's stock in voluntary exchange offer for P securities not registered under 1933 Act—contractual registration rights, Rule 144, and Rule 144A. If P (or S) acquires T's stock in an exchange offer in which each T shareholder had the right to retain his T stock or exchange it for consideration consisting (in whole or in part) of P stock or debt securities, and the P securities issued to T's shareholders are not registered pursuant to the 1933 Act (because the transaction qualifies for exemption as a private placement, intrastate offering, or otherwise), a former T shareholder is subject to significant SEC restrictions on resale of the "restricted" P securities. He may resell them (a) in a private placement in which the buyer becomes subject to the Rule 144 restrictions described below, (b) in a public offering if P files a registration statement under the 1933 Act covering such resale (hence, T's shareholders may want to seek—as a part of the P-T acquisition agreement—contractual registration rights), (c) in public resales pursuant to SEC Rule 144, or (d) in resales to qualified institutional buyers pursuant to SEC Rule 144A.

(a)   Contractual registration rights. A T shareholder acquiring new restricted stock in exchange for his old T stock would be wise to obtain from P (at the time he acquires the T stock) contractual SEC registration rights, obligating P to register the holder's resale of the restricted P securities either at the holder's demand (a "demand registration right") or as an add-on to another SEC registration statement being filed by P (a "piggyback registration right").

(i)   **P resistance.** An SEC registration statement for a secondary offering of restricted P stock must be effective when the holder actually sells the P stock to the public. Because an SEC registration statement is generally time-consuming and expensive, P may resist granting contractual SEC registration rights to an old T shareholder unless the SEC registration rights are limited as to the number of SEC registrations, the timing, etc. In addition, P may seek to limit such rights to the less expensive short-form registration formats described below.

(ii)   **Piggyback.** A piggyback SEC registration is, of course, not as expensive as a demand registration because P is registering the holder's resale of P restricted stock only as an add-on to an SEC registration being filed by P for other primary or secondary securities. However, a piggyback registration right does not give the holder flexibility to choose the timing for the registration.

(iii)   **Short-form S-2 or S-3.** If P is a 1934 Act reporting company and meets certain other requirements, P can use a short-form registration statement to register with SEC the holder's resale of P stock: form S-3 incorporates most information by merely referring to P's periodic 1934 Act filings while form S-2 requires that certain of P's periodic 1934 Act filings actually be delivered to buyers.

To qualify for form S-3, P must:

(A)   have been a 1934 Act reporting company (as described in ¶1702.2.8.2) for 12 months and have filed all required material,

(B)   have made all filings for the prior 12 months on a timely basis,

(C)   not have failed to make preferred dividend or sinking fund pay-
      ments and not have defaulted on repayment of borrowings or
      long-term lease rental payments for approximately a year,

(D)   for a primary or secondary offering, have aggregate market value
      of stock held by P non-affiliates (i.e., persons not in P's control
      group) of at least $75 million (calculated as of any date within 60
      days of the filing), and

(E)   alternatively, for a secondary offering by P shareholders, have secu-
      rities of the same class registered on a national securities exchange
      or quoted on Nasdaq NM, in which case it need not meet the $75
      million public float test.

To qualify for form S-2, P must:

(A)   have been a 1934 Act reporting company (as described in
      ¶1702.2.8.2) for 36 months and have filed all required material,

(B)   have made all filings for the prior 12 months on a timely basis, and

(C)   have made preferred dividend or sinking fund payments and have
      not defaulted on repayment of borrowings or long-term lease rental
      payments since the end of its last fiscal year for which certified
      financial statements were included in a 1934 Act filed report.

(b)   **Rule 144.** Under the safe harbor provisions of SEC Rule 144, such restricted
or unregistered P stock may be sold publicly without registration if all of the
following conditions are satisfied:

(i)   **Current public information.** Certain public information about P must
       be available. Generally this requirement is satisfied if P has been a 1934
       Act reporting company (as described in ¶1702.2.8.2) for at least 90 days
       and has been current in its 1934 Act filings for the past 12 months
       (or such shorter period as it may have been subject to the reporting
       requirements, but not less than 90 days).

(ii)   **One-year holding period.** As a general rule, a minimum of one year
       must have elapsed since the *later* of (A) the original issuance of the
       restricted security by P *or* (B) the most recent sale (if any) of the restricted
       security by an affiliate of P (i.e., a member of P's control group). Hence,
       if a purchaser (whether or not a P affiliate) buys a restricted security
       from a seller that is neither P nor a P affiliate, the purchaser inherits the
       accumulated holding period of the seller and all previous holders (i.e.,
       the holding period will "tack") except that if any prior holder was a P
       affiliate, the holding period of such affiliate and holders prior to such
       affiliate will not tack but will commence on the date of the purchase.
       While nothing has been heard from SEC since 2/97, SEC had then an-
       nounced that it was considering reducing this one-year holding period
       to as short as six months. SEC was also considering how to address
       hedging transactions involving restricted securities and may reinstate

the concept of tolling the holding period where the holder engages in puts, short sales, or other options to sell securities.

With a convertible debenture or convertible preferred, the Rule 144 holding period for the debenture or preferred tacks to the common stock into which the debenture or preferred is converted.

With a warrant, a new Rule 144 holding period starts at exercise, except that if the warrant exercise price is paid solely by surrender of other securities of the same company (debenture, preferred, common), the holding period of the surrendered security tacks to the new common. If the warrant is surrendered for common stock with an FV equal to the warrant spread (i.e., no warrant exercise price is paid), the holding period of the warrant tacks to the holding period of the new common.

If the holder purchased the securities from P or a P affiliate, the holding period generally does not begin until the full purchase price has been paid, although a full recourse note (secured by assets (other than the P securities being purchased) with an FV at least equal to the note) from the purchaser will also generally start the holding period, so long as such note is paid before resale of the securities.

No holding period is required, however, if the seller is the estate of a deceased shareholder (or a beneficiary thereof) unless the estate (or beneficiary thereof) is itself a P affiliate.

There are also certain tacking provisions concerning stock dividends, stock splits, recapitalizations, contingent stock issuances, pledges, trusts, estates, and Rule 145(a) transactions.

Possible delay in SEC holding period for unvested stock issued to executive. Where a P executive receives restricted P stock subject to vesting, there is a question whether the P executive's SEC holding period begins at the time the P restricted shares are issued to him or only when the P stock ultimately vests. In 1979, SEC published its position that where restricted securities are issued pursuant to "an employee benefit plan which requires the plan participants to remain as employees for a specified period of time before the securities ... vest ... [, the SEC] holding period ... will commence when the securities are allocated to the account of an individual plan participant [and the] fact that the securities may not vest until some later date does not alter the result." It has long been widely believed that this salutary rule applies to all securities granted or sold to employees pursuant to a formal or informal plan.

However, SEC staff created uncertainty in an early 1994 no-action letter where P granted stock to a number of executives pursuant to substantially similar individual contracts approved by the board (under which the stock would vest pro rata over 5 years, based on continued employment). The staff stated that "if the restricted securities are not issued pursuant to an employee benefit plan, the holding period does not begin to run until the date of vesting," and the staff then declined to determine whether the contracts constituted an employee benefit plan.

SEC rules define "employee benefit plan" extremely broadly, as including a "contract, authorization or arrangement, whether or not set forth in any formal documents, . . . [even if] applicable to one person." Hence, there is no rational reason for SEC to distinguish between a formal employee benefit plan and one or a set of individual contracts intended to incent one or more employees.

Discussions with SEC staff indicate that this early 1994 no-action letter was meant merely to restate SEC's long-standing policy that it would not comment on whether a particular employment agreement constitutes an employee benefit plan. SEC staff takes the position that such a determination must be made by the issuer and its counsel based on the facts and circumstances of each case. Hence, it appears that SEC meant no inference in the no-action letter that the situation then presented fell short of constituting an employee benefit plan.[17]

(iii) **Volume limitation.** After the one-year holding period has run, a shareholder may sell only a limited amount of P securities in any three-month period (generally the *greater* of 1% of the class outstanding or the average weekly trading volume over the four-week period prior to notice of the sale) unless the exception set forth in (vi) below applies. While nothing has been heard from SEC since 2/97, SEC had then announced that it was considering eliminating the four-week average trading volume test, so that the permitted volume would simply be 1% of the class outstanding.

Under certain circumstances, public sales by more than one person are aggregated for purposes of this volume limitation (e.g., persons acting in concert in the sale of P securities, a donor and donee, a deceased person and the estate). Securities sold pursuant to an effective 1933 Act registration statement are not counted against the volume limitation.

(iv) **Manner of sale.** Sales may be made only directly with a market maker or in brokers' transactions involving no more than the customary broker's commission and no solicitation of buyers, except in the case of an estate or a beneficiary thereof that is not a P affiliate or when the exception set forth in (vi) below applies. While nothing has been heard from SEC since 2/97, SEC had then announced that it was considering eliminating these requirements.

(v) **Notice.** A form 144 must be filed with SEC when sales in a three-month period will exceed, in the aggregate, either 500 shares or units or $10,000. Notice must also be given to the principal exchange on which the security

---

[17] If P's original issuance of the stock to the executives qualified under SEC Rule 701, the stock can be sold free of most Rule 144 restrictions once P has been a 1934 Act reporting company for at least 90 days. Hence, when Rule 701 covered P's original issuance of the executive's stock and P has been a reporting company for at least 90 days, the Rule 144 issue as to when the executive's SEC holding period commences is not even relevant.

is listed at the time sale commences. While nothing has been heard from SEC since 2/97, SEC had then announced that it was considering raising the reported thresholds to 1,000 shares or $40,000.

(vi)   **Sales by P non-affiliate after two-year holding period.** A person who is not (and has not been during the last three months) a P affiliate and who holds restricted P securities for at least a two year SEC holding period (calculated as described in (ii) above) may under Rule 144(k) sell such securities without any limitation on volume or manner of sale, without being required to file a form 144 with SEC, and without any requirement that there be current public information available about P. While nothing has been heard from SEC since 2/97, SEC had then announced that it was considering how to address hedging transactions involving restricted securities and may reinstate the concept of tolling the holding period where the holder engages in puts, short sales, or other options to sell securities. A P affiliate (i.e., a member of P's control group), however, does not qualify for this special rule and hence remains subject to all of the requirements of Rule 144, until such person has not been a P affiliate for at least three months.

(vii) **Rule 701 stock.** If the holder originally acquired the restricted P securities from P pursuant to Rule 701, the holder is generally free (once P has been a 1934 Act reporting company for at least 90 days) to resell the restricted securities under Rule 144 without complying with any of the Rule 144 requirements except manner of sale. However, if the holder is a P affiliate (i.e., a member of P's control group), he must also comply with the volume limitation and SEC notification requirements.

Rule 144 is a safe harbor for resales of restricted securities and (as discussed below) sales of unrestricted securities by affiliates of the issuer. It may be possible for such persons to sell publicly without complying with Rule 144, but they would have the burden of establishing that they were not "underwriters" of the securities on behalf of the issuer.

(c)   Resale of P unrestricted securities by P affiliates.

(i)   Even when a holder's P securities are not restricted, if the holder is a P affiliate (i.e., a member of P's control group), his resale of such unrestricted P securities must meet all the Rule 144 requirements (as set forth in (b)(i) through (v) above) except for the one-year holding period, which does not apply.

(ii)   In applying (c)(i), all sales of both restricted and unrestricted P securities by the P affiliate (and anyone acting in concert with him in selling P securities) are taken into account in applying the volume limitation (described in (b)(iii)).

(iii) A person who is not a P affiliate can generally resell unrestricted P securities freely.

(d)   Rule 144A. Under the safe harbor provisions of SEC Rule 144A, restricted or unregistered stock may be resold to certain qualified institutional buyers if all of the following conditions are satisfied:

(i)   **Qualified institutional buyer.** The securities must be offered or sold only to a "qualified institutional buyer" or to an offeree or purchaser that the seller and any person acting on behalf of the seller reasonably believe is a qualified institutional buyer. For purposes of Rule 144A, a "qualified institutional buyer" means:

(A)   an "institutional investor" acting for its own account or the accounts of other qualified institutional buyers, that in the aggregate owns and invests on a discretionary basis at least $100 million in securities of issuers that are not affiliated with such entity.

An *"institutional investor"* is a corporation (other than a bank, savings and loan, or similar institution), a partnership, an insurance company (including an insurance company's unregistered separate accounts), a registered investment company, a business development company, an SBIC, a business trust, a collective or master trust (a legal form commonly used for the collective investment of pension and other employee benefit plan funds), a registered investment advisor, a Code §501(c)(3) charitable organization, an ERISA plan, or a plan established and maintained by a state (or any of its political subdivisions, agencies, or instrumentalities) for the benefit of its employees.

(B)   any registered dealer, acting for its own account or the accounts of other qualified institutional buyers, that in the aggregate owns and invests on a discretionary basis at least $10 million in securities of issuers that are not affiliated with the dealer.

(C)   any registered dealer acting in a riskless principal transaction on behalf of a qualified institutional buyer.

(D)   any registered investment company, acting for its own account or the accounts of other qualified institutional buyers, that is part of a family of investment companies owning in the aggregate at least $100 million in securities of issuers that are not affiliated with the family of investment companies.

(E)   any bank, savings and loan, or similar institution, acting for its own account or the accounts of other qualified institutional buyers, that in the aggregate owns and invests on a discretionary basis at least $100 million in securities of issuers that are not affiliated with it, and that has an audited net worth of at least $25 million.

(F)   any entity, all of the equity owners of which are qualified institutional buyers, acting for its own account or the accounts of other qualified institutional buyers.

(ii)   **Inform purchaser of reliance on Rule 144A.** The seller and any person acting on its behalf must take reasonable steps to ensure that the purchaser is aware the seller may rely on the Rule 144A exemption from registration.

(iii) **Securities not of class publicly traded.** The securities offered or sold (A) must not, when issued, have been of the same class as securities listed on a national securities exchange or quoted in a domestic automated interdealer quotation system (e.g., Nasdaq) and (B) must not be securities of a registered investment company or similar entity.

(iv) **Availability of reasonably current information.** In the case of securities of an issuer that is not a reporting company under the 1934 Act, the holder and a prospective purchaser designated by the holder have the right to receive from the issuer, upon request of the holder, and the prospective purchaser must have received, at or prior to the time of sale, upon such prospective purchaser's request, the following reasonably current information:

(A) a very brief statement of the nature of the issuer's business and its products and services and

(B) the issuer's most recent balance sheet and profit and loss and retained earnings statements, and similar financial statements for such part of the two preceding fiscal years as the issuer has been in operation (audited to the extent reasonably available).

Securities acquired in a Rule 144A transaction are "restricted securities" for purposes of Rule 144.

Offers and sales of securities pursuant to Rule 144A will not affect the availability of any exemption or safe harbor relating to any previous or subsequent offer or sale of such securities by the issuer or any prior or subsequent holder thereof.

(4) P (or S) acquires T's assets or merges with T in exchange for P securities that are not registered under the 1933 Act. If P (or S) acquires T's assets or merges with T (so T shareholder approval is binding on all T shareholders except dissenters), and T or T's shareholders receive (as all or part of the consideration) P stock or debt securities that are not registered under the 1933 Act (because the transaction qualifies for exemption as a private placement, intrastate offering, or otherwise), T or T's shareholders may resell the P securities under the same conditions set forth in (3) above.

¶1702.2.8.6 Compliance with State Securities Laws

An offering of P securities must also comply with each applicable state securities (blue sky) law. This includes a primary issuance by P, as well as a secondary resale of P securities by an old T shareholder to third parties.

While many state securities laws contain exemptions from registration similar to the federal exemptions already described, additional conditions are often imposed. Also, many states do not recognize Rule 504 or Rule 701 and object to recent

SEC liberalizations allowing general solicitation of, and general advertising for, potential purchasers in offerings not exceeding $1 million.

In addition, while federal securities laws focus on disclosure of information about Newco and the manner of sale, some state securities laws go further and seek to regulate the substantive fairness of the offering.

However, under federal legislation (1) where Newco issues securities pursuant to SEC Rule 506, no state may impose merit review or require any filing other than a filing substantially similar to that required by SEC Rule 503 and (2) where Newco or a Newco shareholder sells securities to be traded on the NYSE, AMEX, or Nasdaq National Market, no state may impose merit review or require any filing. The legislation does not affect any required state broker-dealer filings.

¶1702.2.9   Other Considerations

¶1702.2.9.1   *Accounting Rules*

Under GAAP, whether P's acquisition of T is accounted for as a purchase, a part purchase, or a recapitalization can have a material effect on P's post-acquisition accounting net income, balance sheet, and other accounting results. These issues are discussed in detail at ¶1703.

¶1702.2.9.2   *Fraudulent Conveyance Considerations*

Some LBO structures prejudice T's creditors and hence might cause payments, transfers, liens, and obligations arising out of the LBO to be voided under fraudulent conveyance law. These issues are discussed in detail at ¶1706.

¶1702.2.9.3   *Hart-Scott-Rodino Act*

The Hart-Scott-Rodino Antitrust Improvements Act of 1976, and the rules and regulations promulgated by the Federal Trade Commission thereunder, prohibit P from acquiring more than a certain percentage or dollar amount of voting securities or assets of T unless (1) P and T complied with the reporting and waiting periods of the Act, (2) the size of P and T falls below the size-of-person criteria, (3) the size of the transaction falls below the size-of-transaction criteria, or (4) a specific exemption applies. The statute and rules apply to acquisitions of stock, acquisitions of assets, and mergers alike (with minor timing variations for tender offers). These issues are discussed in detail at ¶1707.

¶1702.2.9.4   Lock-Up Agreements

In 2003, the Delaware Supreme Court, in its 3-2 *Omnicare* decision,[18] invalidated deal protection mechanisms adopted by T's board and controlling stockholders. In *Omnicare*, T, after conducting a full auction, entered into a merger agreement with P, containing a "force the vote" provision allowed under Delaware law, but no "fiduciary out." At the same time, the controlling shareholders, holding a majority of T's voting power, entered into "lock-up" agreements with P that did not contain any "fiduciary out." The court determined that the combination of the merger agreement and stock "lock-ups" was both preclusive and coercive, and invalidated the merger agreement and the stock "lock-ups."

¶1702.3   *Drafting Acquisition Agreements*

¶1702.3.1   Representations and Warranties

Some of the key non-tax aspects in drafting an acquisition agreement (and frequently the most disputed) are (1) the extent of the representations and warranties P obtains from seller or sellers (T in a sale of assets or merger, T's shareholders in a sale of stock), (2) the extent of sellers' liability for breach of those representations and warranties (e.g., the time period within which P must make a claim, whether there is a limitation based on sellers' knowledge, the threshold amount, the ceiling amount), and (3) P's method for recovering from sellers—T in a sale of assets or T's shareholders in a sale of stock or merger (e.g., escrow, note offset, lawsuit).

*¶1702.3.1.1   Sellers' Contractual Asset Representations and
           Warranties*

One issue is the extent to which sellers give P contractual representations and warranties regarding T's assets and business, including real estate and personal property with good title and in good operating condition, inventory saleable, receivables collectable, no material adverse change in, or material adverse effect on, business, and correct historical financial statements.

¶1702.3.1.2   Sellers' Liability Representations and Warranties

Another issue is the extent to which P on the one hand or T's old shareholders on the other bear the burden of T's liabilities and obligations. The transaction could be structured and the documents drafted so that P bears the burden of all T's liabilities and obligations, including those for environmental clean-up,

---

[18] Omnicare v. NCS Healthcare, 818 A.2d 914 (Del. 2003).

employment discrimination, antitrust violations, patent and trademark infringe-ments, product liability, product warranty, prior years' tax deficiencies, current year's taxes, unfunded pensions, and other claims and lawsuits, even if not known at the time the contract is signed and the acquisition closed.

Alternatively, the transaction could be structured and the documents drafted so that P bears the burden of only specified T liabilities and obligations, such as those shown on the latest T balance sheet available before the signing of the acquisition documents plus those arising in the ordinary course of business there-after (but not including lawsuits, disputed claims, and the like). If this latter approach is adopted, the documents contain extensive representations, warranties, and indemnifications running from the sellers to P.

¶1702.3.1.3   Qualifying Representations and Warranties by Knowledge and/or Materiality

For sellers' representations and warranties discussed at ¶¶1702.3.1.1 and 1702.3.1.2, the contract may make the allocation of risk between P and sellers turn on whether the particular fact represented (e.g., the existence of a T liability or a defect in a T asset) is "known" or is "material." If so, the contract should specify the person(s) whose knowledge is relevant (e.g., all T officers, directors, and employees versus specified high-level T executives). In addition, it may be desir-able for the contract to define "knowledge" (e.g., whether it implies a duty to investigate and whether it includes "should have known") and "materiality" (e.g., more than $50,000).

¶1702.3.1.4   Survival

P will desire sellers' representations and warranties to survive the closing of the acquisition for a long time, if not indefinitely, so P can recover for breaches that do not become known until substantially after the closing (unless, as discussed at ¶1702.3.1.7, T is publicly held and P is acquiring all of T).

On the other hand, sellers will generally want the representations and warrant-ies to terminate at the closing (i.e., not to survive the closing, so that they merely function as closing conditions) or, if they survive the closing, to survive only if P makes a claim within a specified short period of time.

Often the parties will agree on some arbitrary period of survival, perhaps with a longer period for third party claims (such as environmental cleanup or IRS claims).

¶1702.3.1.5   Deductible Threshold, and/or Ceiling

Another issue is whether there is a deductible (e.g., sellers are liable only if and only to the extent damages from breaches of representation and warranty exceed $100,000) or a minimum (e.g., if damages from breaches of representation and warranty exceed $100,000, sellers are liable for the entire amount), and whether there will be a ceiling (e.g., sellers' liability for breaches will not exceed $1 million).

¶1702.3.1.6   *Escrow, Set-off, Security Interest, Etc.*

There is generally vigorous discussion as to the method for protecting P against breaches of sellers' representations and warranties, including P's right to recover back a portion of the purchase price by lawsuit (or mandatory arbitration if the acquisition agreement so specifies) against T (or in a sale of stock, in a sale of assets if T is liquidating, or in a merger, against T's shareholders), an escrow of a portion of the purchase price to secure against claims for breach of representation and warranty, P's right to set off against any P notes issued to sellers, and/or a P security interest in specific assets of sellers.

¶1702.3.1.7   *Public T*

If all of publicly held T is being acquired by P, T's representations and warranties generally do not survive the closing of the acquisition, i.e., P is generally not entitled to recover any of the purchase price from sellers, for two reasons. *First*, P will have the comfort of the substantial public information about T available in T's SEC filings, and hence the risk of material undisclosed liabilities or other breaches of representations and warranties are reduced. *Second,* as soon as the acquisition is closed, the purchase price is generally disbursed to T's public shareholders, so that collection on P's indemnification clauses would be difficult. Although an escrow for a portion of the purchase price is feasible, it is almost never used.

¶1702.3.2   Covenants

P generally seeks a contract provision requiring T to operate its business in the ordinary course and in accordance with past custom and practice pending the closing of the acquisition and, consequently, may seek clauses prohibiting T activities that would materially diminish the value of T's business or assets (such as large capital expenditures, dividends, issuance or redemption of T securities, the ability to enter into new material contracts, bonus payments, and salary increases).

¶1702.3.3   Closing Conditions

P generally seeks closing conditions, the failure of which allow P to refuse to consummate the acquisition (after the agreement is signed and before the closing) in case of certain events, such as (a) material breach of T's representations, warranties, and covenants, (b) litigation challenging the transaction, (c) material adverse change ("MAC") in, or material adverse effect ("MAE") on, T's business, (d) P's inability to consummate its financing necessary for the acquisition, and (e) less often P's dissatisfaction with the results of its continuing due diligence investigation of T.

T generally objects to closing conditions which give P a virtual option to terminate the transaction, such as (e) and to some extent (d).

In the 2001 *IBP* decision the Delaware Chancery Court (1) rejected a claim by P (Tyson Foods) that an MAE had occurred, allowing P to terminate its merger agreement with T (IBP) and (2) granted T the remedy of specific performance, requiring P to consummate the merger.[19]

In the IBP case, the merger agreement defined MAE broadly as "any event, occurrence, or development of a state of circumstances or facts which has had or reasonably could be expected to have a Material Adverse Effect on the condition (financial or otherwise), business, assets, liabilities or results of operations of [T] and [its] Subsidiaries taken as a whole."[20] P argued that recent T financial declines and an impairment charge to one of T's smaller subsidiaries due to accounting irregularities constituted such an MAE. The court determined that under New York law, a buyer:

> ought to have to make a strong showing to invoke a Material Adverse Effect exception to its obligations to close. . . . [E]ven where a Material Adverse Effect condition is as broadly written as the one in the merger agreement, that provision is best read as a backstop protecting the acquiror from the occurrence of unknown events that substantially threaten the overall earnings potential of the target in a durationally-significant manner. A short-term hiccup in earnings should not suffice; rather the Material Adverse Effect should be material when viewed from the longer-term perspective of a reasonable acquiror.[21]

The court found it significant that (1) P was aware before the merger agreement was signed that fluctuations in T's performance were part of its business reality and (2) P's investment banker concluded just prior to P's termination of the merger agreement that the purchase price for T established in the merger agreement was still within the range of fairness and a great long term value for P.

As *IBP* illustrates and other case law confirms, a court determination of whether an MAE exists is very fact-specific. Under *IBP* P can maximize legal enforceability by drafting a highly specific MAE provision, but an overly specific MAE provision may inadvertently exclude unanticipated risks not specifically described. Hence in the MAE clause P may seek to address specific matters and also may seek broad coverage (as in the MAE clause in sample acquisition agreement 2002.1 (the *pro-buyer* stock purchase agreement)) to cover an unanticipated adverse event.

---

[19] In re IBP, Inc. Shareholders Litigation 789 A.2d 14 (Del. Ch. 2001).

[20] 789 A.2d at 65.

[21] 789 A.2d at 68. In the relevant agreement the parties (both Delaware corporations) had chosen New York law.

¶1702.3.4   Sample Acquisition Agreements

A companion volume contains sample acquisition agreements suitable for taxable stock purchases, taxable asset purchases, taxable reverse subsidiary mergers, and tax-free mergers. With respect to most such transactions, the companion volume contains pro-buyer, pro-seller, and neutral samples.

¶1702.4   Stock Acquisition

Some of the key considerations when P is purchasing T's stock (rather than acquiring T's assets or merging with T) are described below.

¶1702.4.1   Acquiring Less than 100% of T

When the acquisition is structured as P's voluntary acquisition of T's stock, each T shareholder has the right to retain his T stock or sell it to P. In the case of a closely held T, it may be possible to negotiate the acquisition of 100% of T's stock. This is much less likely in the case of a widely or publicly held T. In this situation, P may end up owning less than 100% of T's outstanding stock, in which case P has all the concerns associated with the presence of T minority shareholders, such as possible P liability (as T's controlling shareholder) for breach of fiduciary duties in its dealings with T or its minority shareholders. Moreover, difficult fairness and "going private" issues will generally be raised if P later determines to acquire the T minority interest (i.e., "squeeze out" the minority shareholders) through merger or otherwise, as discussed at ¶1702.7.

¶1702.4.2   Liability for T's Indebtedness

Generally if P acquires T's stock, T's creditors can reach only T's assets and not P's assets.

¶1702.4.3   Mechanical Problems in Transferring T's Assets

When P acquires T's stock so that T's assets are not transferred, the difficulties involved in actually conveying title to numerous parcels of real estate, motor vehicles, or the like are generally not encountered. However, certain types of agreements to which T may be a party (e.g., loan agreements and leases) and certain types of licenses may explicitly require the consent of the other party to the agreement or the issuer of the license in the event of a change in T's control, i.e., a sale of a controlling interest in T's stock.

¶1702.4.4   Transfer, Sales and Use Taxes

There is generally no transfer or sales and use tax on P's purchase of T's stock. However, some states impose a stock transfer tax. There may be transfer taxes on a subsequent merger between P and its subsidiary T or on a subsequent liquidation of T, depending upon the laws of the particular state involved.

¶1702.4.5   Non-Pro-Rata Consideration

In an acquisition of T stock (not constituting a public tender offer) in which P deals separately with each T shareholder, P may give different amounts or types of consideration to different T shareholders (subject to state corporate law and full disclosure under SEC Rule 10b-5). For example, P can pay $10 per share to some T shareholders and $9 per share to others. Or P can pay some T shareholders with cash, others with notes, and still others with P stock.

In a public tender offer, however, all of T's tendering shareholders must either receive the same consideration or have the option to receive the same consideration in a cash-option offer. See ¶805.

¶1702.4.6   Dissenters' Rights

Because of the voluntary nature of a stock acquisition (i.e., a T shareholder is not compelled to sell his T stock to P), statutory dissenters' or appraisal rights entitling a T shareholder to sue to recover the FV of his T stock do not apply.

¶1702.4.7   Shareholder Vote

Because of the voluntary nature of a stock acquisition from the perspective of T's shareholders, no vote of T's shareholders is required if P is acquiring T's stock. Approval by P's shareholders will be required only if one of the following applies:

(1) P's charter explicitly requires the approval of P's shareholders.
(2) P is issuing stock to T's shareholders in excess of P's authorized shares (so a vote of P's shareholders is necessary to amend P's charter to authorize the stock).
(3) P's stock is listed on the NYSE, the AMEX, the Nasdaq NM, or certain regional exchanges which would de-list P's stock if it effectuated the transaction without a shareholder vote. As discussed at ¶1702.2.7.1 above, each of the NYSE, AMEX, and Nasdaq NM rules has slightly different substantive provisions and somewhat different wording.

If P is publicly held and a vote of its shareholders is necessary, P must comply with SEC's proxy rules, as described at ¶1702.2.7.6.

¶1702.4.8   Application of 1933 Act

Acquisitions of stock are generally effected for cash, other securities (including P debt and/or equity securities), or some combination thereof. Whenever part or all of the consideration is P (or S) securities, P (or S) must comply with the 1933 Act, which prohibits the sale of securities unless (1) such securities are registered with SEC and certain other requirements are satisfied or (2) there is an applicable exemption from registration, e.g., the private placement or intrastate exemption.

¶1702.4.8.1   Public Offering

If T's shareholder group is of any significant size, P will generally not be able to qualify for an exemption and will be required to register under the 1933 Act the P stock or notes being issued for T stock. This process is likely to require at least several weeks and more likely several months.

SEC form S-4 may be utilized for the registration of securities issued in business combinations and exchange offers, whether or not P and/or T is already a reporting company. Form S-4 is generally advantageous when P and/or T is a reporting company under the 1934 Act, because certain financial and other information regarding such company may be incorporated by reference from 1934 Act reports filed by such company.

¶1702.4.8.2   Private Placement

Section 4(2) of the 1933 Act exempts P (or S) from the requirement to register its stock or debt securities if the issuance does not involve a public offering (i.e., the offering constitutes a private placement)—including the issuance of P (or S) stock or debt securities to a reasonably small group of T shareholders in exchange for T stock. SEC Regulation D (Rules 501 through 508 under the 1933 Act) and SEC Rule 701 each provide a safe harbor for certain private placements. If an offering does not comply with Reg. D or Rule 701, it may still fall within §4(2). However, the boundaries of §4(2) outside the Reg. D and Rule 701 safe harbors are vague and determinable only by reference to case law, which is often fact specific and provides no easily discernible bright lines to distinguish a public from a private offering. Reg. D and Rule 701 are discussed in detail at ¶¶1702.2.8.2 and 1702.2.8.3.

¶1702.4.8.3   Intrastate Offering

Section 3(a)(11) of the 1933 Act exempts intrastate offerings. SEC Rule 147 provides a safe harbor for certain intrastate offerings. Rule 147 is discussed in detail at ¶1702.2.8.4.

¶1702.4.8.4   Resale Restrictions

When P issues its securities to T's shareholders in exchange for T's stock, significant restrictions upon the subsequent resale of such P securities by T's shareholders may apply (especially if P's issuance of its securities in exchange for T's stock was not registered under the 1933 Act). Such resale restrictions are covered in detail at ¶1702.2.8.5.

¶1702.4.9   Other Considerations

¶1702.4.9.1   Existing Buy-Sell Agreements and Rights of First Refusal

Care should be taken, particularly in the case of a closely held T, to insure that P's purchase of T's stock is carried out in compliance with any restrictions in T's charter or bylaws or any agreement among T's shareholders restricting the free sale of T stock to P.

¶1702.4.9.2   Plan of Exchange

Although not commonly used, some state corporation statutes authorize the shareholders of two corporations, by requisite vote of their shareholders, to adopt a "plan of exchange" that forces all T shareholders to exchange their T securities for P securities or other consideration. This sort of acquisition requires compliance with (1) the 1934 Act's proxy requirements if the shareholders of publicly held T or P are voting on the transaction (see ¶1702.2.7.6) and (2) the 1933 Act's registration requirements if P securities are being issued to a group of T shareholders of any significant size (see ¶1702.2.8).

¶1702.4.9.3   Tender Offer Rules

If T's stock is widely held, any effort by P to acquire T stock from a significant number of T shareholders on any systematic basis (other than through open-market purchases and privately negotiated purchases, generally including street sweeps) would necessitate compliance with tender offer disclosure requirements of the 1934 Act. See ¶1702.2.7.1.

¶1702.4.9.4   SEC Stock Ownership Reporting

Where P is purchasing publicly held T shares, SEC's 13D disclosure rules are applicable, so that, in general, P is required to file schedule 13D with SEC once P has purchased more than 5% of a class of T's publicly held shares (or P's ownership of T's stock when aggregated with other T shareholders with whom P is acting in concert exceeds 5%). See ¶1702.2.7.1.

¶1702.4.9.5   Sample Acquisition Agreements

A companion volume contains several sample acquisition agreements for P's purchase of T's stock: (1) pro-buyer terms (see ¶2201), (2) pro-seller terms (see ¶2202), (3) neutral (i.e., neither pro-buyer nor pro-seller) terms (see ¶2203), (4) additional provisions when T is a subsidiary of another corporation before the acquisition (see ¶2204), and (5) additional provisions when there is to be a purchase price adjustment based on T's closing date balance sheet (see ¶2205).

¶1702.5   Asset Acquisition

Some of the key considerations when P is purchasing some or all of T's assets (and assuming some or all of T's liabilities), leaving T and the balance of its assets and liabilities, if any, as a separate non-controlled company, are described below.

¶1702.5.1   Acquiring Less Than 100% of T

If P acquires all or substantially all of T's assets, P will not be left to deal with any T minority shareholders following the transaction (as P may when it buys T's stock). If the requisite vote of T's shareholders is obtained for a sale of assets, the sale takes place notwithstanding dissenting shareholders.

¶1702.5.2   Liability for T's Indebtedness

If P acquires T's assets, the bulk sales provisions of the Uniform Commercial Code (UCC Article 6) generally permit T's creditors to sue P (at least up to the FV of T's assets acquired by P) for six months after the acquisition, unless notice was given to all of T's creditors (in some states by registered mail and in other states by publication) and other specified procedures were followed. The UCC bulk sales provisions generally apply regardless of any contract provision between P and T to the contrary if T transfers the major part of the inventory of an enterprise whose principal business is the sale of merchandise from inventory.

In addition, even if the parties have complied with the notice and other requirements of the bulk sales law (so that UCC Article 6 does not make P liable for T's debts), courts have increasingly held P responsible for some or all of T's debts and contingent liabilities (especially tort liabilities for defective products) under the common law doctrines of "*de facto* merger" and "successor liability." This can occur when T's business has been transferred to P as a going concern and T goes out of existence (especially, but not exclusively, when T's shareholders receive an equity interest in P).

If S (rather than P) acquires T's assets, the bulk sales law and the common law doctrines may apply to make S liable for T's debts and contingent liabilities (but generally not P unless P has done something to permit a plaintiff to pierce the corporate veil).

¶1702.5.3 Mechanical Problems in Transferring T's Assets

When P purchases T's assets for cash, notes, or stock, substantial paperwork can be required (including recording of real estate, vehicle, patent, trademark, and airplane transfers) and difficult problems can arise in transferring thousands of assets. In addition, significant loan agreements, leases, licenses, and other contracts may prohibit assignment, in which case consent must be obtained from the other party to the agreement, who may seek to exact some consideration for granting consent.

¶1702.5.4 Transfer, Sales and Use Taxes

Most states impose transfer taxes on the sale of real property (real estate transfer taxes) and on the sale of tangible personal property not for resale (sales and use taxes). Some state sales and use taxes exempt the transfer of tangible personal property in an isolated sale or a sale not in the ordinary course of business. In these states, T's sale of its assets and business to P would not be subject to sales and use taxes.

Some states, such as California, do not provide such an exemption and hence impose a sales tax on T's sale of its assets and business to P. Nevertheless, even in states that tax an isolated sale, T's sale of inventory to P would almost always be exempt because the inventory would be for subsequent resale by P (so sales tax will be payable when P resells such inventory). In such states, T's sale of its machinery and equipment, furniture, tools and dies, etc., to P would be subjected to sales tax. State law varies on whether less tangible property (e.g., computer software) is considered tangible personal property subject to sales tax.

¶1702.5.5 Non-Pro-Rata Consideration

Most states do not allow the consideration received by T in a sale of assets to be distributed in liquidation so that some T common shareholders receive different amounts or different types of consideration than other holders of identical stock (without the consent of 100% of T's shareholders). However, the same practical result can be achieved if P acquires some T stock for one amount or type of consideration and immediately thereafter follows with a purchase of assets, with the remaining T shareholders receiving another amount or type of consideration in T's liquidation.

¶1702.5.6 Dissenters' Rights

The laws of many jurisdictions permit a T shareholder who dissents from the sale, lease, exchange, or other disposition of all or substantially all of T's assets to receive in cash the appraised FV of his T stock, as determined by a court. Delaware, however, is an exception, as it allows no dissenters' or appraisal rights to a T shareholder when T sells all or substantially all of its assets unless T's charter otherwise provides.[22]

¶1702.5.7 Shareholder Vote and Proxy Rules

When P acquires all or substantially all of T's assets, state law generally requires the approval of T's shareholders, with the necessary percentage for approval varying according to the law of T's jurisdiction of incorporation and the specific provisions of T's charter (which generally may require a higher percentage than applicable state law).

In Delaware, for example, the sale of all or substantially all of T's assets requires approval of a majority of T's outstanding voting stock, subject to higher requirements in T's charter.[23] Many other states require a higher percentage (frequently two-thirds) for approval.

States differ in their interpretation of "substantially all" of a corporation's assets, with some cases indicating that over 50% may be "substantially all."

No vote of *P's* shareholders is necessary in an acquisition of T's assets unless one of the following applies:

(1) P's charter explicitly requires the approval of P's shareholders.

(2) P is issuing stock to T's shareholders in excess of P's authorized shares (so a vote of P's shareholders is necessary to amend P's charter to authorize the stock).

(3) P's stock is listed on the NYSE, the AMEX, the Nasdaq NM, or certain regional exchanges which would de-list P's stock if it effectuated the transaction without a shareholder vote. As discussed at ¶1702.2.7.1 above, each of the NYSE, AMEX, and Nasdaq NM rules has slightly different substantive provisions and somewhat different wording.

If a vote of P's or T's shareholders is necessary, as in the case of an acquisition of all or substantially all of T's assets, state law generally requires that written notice of a shareholders' meeting be sent to all shareholders (in some states,

---

[22] Del. GCL §262.
[23] Del. GCL §271(a).

whether or not entitled to vote) a specified number of days in advance of the meeting, unless there is attendance at the meeting or a waiver of notice (generally by 100% of the shareholders).

In Delaware, for example, 10 days' advance notice is required for most shareholders' meetings, but 20 days is required for a shareholder vote on a sale of assets.[24] A corporation's charter may provide for a longer notice period. A shareholder generally may waive notice in writing.[25]

Most states permit a corporation, if authorized by the corporation's charter or bylaws (or, in some states, if not expressly prohibited in the charter or bylaws), to obtain shareholder approval by written consent, obviating the need for a formal shareholders' meeting. Under Delaware law (unless prohibited by charter), action may be taken by shareholder consent if written consent is obtained from the number of shareholders whose votes would have been sufficient to take such action at a shareholders' meeting (generally a majority for a sale of assets), followed by "prompt" notice to the non-consenting shareholders.[26] Some other states require unanimous shareholder consent in lieu of a meeting, without regard to the percentage that would have been sufficient to take action at a meeting.

If T is publicly held and proxies are solicited from T's shareholders regarding approval of a sale of all or substantially all of T's assets, or if P is publicly held and proxies are solicited from P's shareholders in connection with an acquisition of assets or an amendment to P's charter to authorize additional stock in a stock-for-assets transaction or otherwise, such proxies must be solicited pursuant to a proxy statement prepared, filed, and distributed to shareholders in accordance with §14(a) of the 1934 Act and SEC Regulation 14A thereunder. The proxy rules are discussed in greater detail at ¶1702.2.7.6.

¶1702.5.8 Application of 1933 Act

If part or all of the consideration to T in an acquisition constitutes stock or debt instruments of P, P will be required to comply with the 1933 Act, which prohibits the sale of securities unless (1) such securities are registered with SEC and certain other requirements are satisfied or (2) an exemption from registration applies, e.g., the private placement or intrastate exemption. If T intends to hold such P securities without further distribution to T's shareholders or resale to the public and T does not plan to dissolve, P may be able to rely on a private placement exemption under the 1933 Act. Otherwise, registration of such securities may be required, depending on the number and nature of T's shareholders. When P issues its securities to T or its shareholders in exchange for T's assets, significant restrictions upon the subsequent resale of such P securities by T's shareholders may apply (especially if P's issuance of its securities in exchange for T's assets was not registered under the 1933 Act). See ¶1702.2.8 for a more complete discussion of the securities registration and resale issues.

[24] Del. GCL §§222(b) and 271(a).
[25] Del. GCL §229.
[26] Del. GCL §228(a).

¶1702.5.9   Sample Acquisition Agreements

A companion volume contains several sample acquisition agreements for P's purchase of part or all of T's assets: (1) pro-buyer, pro-seller, and neutral (i.e., neither pro-buyer nor pro-seller) versions when P is purchasing all of T's assets (see ¶¶2301, 2302, and 2303), (2) pro-buyer, pro-seller, and neutral versions when P is purchasing a T divisional business (see ¶¶2401, 2402, and 2403), and (3) additional provisions when there is to be a purchase price adjustment based on T's closing date balance sheet (see ¶2205).

¶1702.6   Merger

A merger is negotiated by the constituent corporations and effectuated pursuant to state corporation statutes by one or more filings with state officials. Absent an applicable "short form" merger procedure or other exception, a merger must be approved by shareholders of both corporations. If approved by the requisite shareholder votes, the conversion of T's securities pursuant to the terms of the merger agreement is mandatory with respect to all T shareholders, except dissenters who (depending on state law) may be entitled to receive cash equal to the FV of their T stock.

The consideration offered pursuant to a merger may (if allowed by state law) be cash, P securities, or any other property. If the principal consideration is P stock, the merger may be structured as a tax-free reorganization. See Chapters 6 through 8. The issuance of T securities pursuant to the merger will require compliance with the 1933 Act's registration provisions or an applicable exemption therefrom.

The mechanics of a merger are, of course, governed by the corporation laws of the states in which the constituent corporations are incorporated and by the charters, bylaws, and other governing documents of such corporations.

¶1702.6.1   Acquiring Less Than 100% of T

If P and T merge or S and T merge, P will not be left to deal with any T minority shareholders following the transaction (as P may when it buys T's stock). If the requisite vote of T's shareholders is obtained for the merger, the transaction takes place notwithstanding dissenting shareholders.

¶1702.6.2   Liability for T's Indebtedness

If T and P merge or T and S merge, most corporation laws allow T's creditors to reach both T's and P's assets (if T and P merge) or T's and S's assets (if T and S merge in a reverse or forward subsidiary merger).

¶1702.6.3   Mechanical Problems of Transferring T's Assets

A forward merger in which T merges into P (or S) may avoid the asset transfer problems encountered in a sale of assets because a merger transfers T's assets by operation of law. However, some leases, loan agreements, licenses, and other contracts specifically require consent of the other party even for transfers by operation of law. Moreover, some courts have interpreted contracts, licenses, and the like (in light of ambiguous contract and/or ambiguous local law) to require consent to the transfer of assets pursuant to a forward merger even in the absence of specific contractual language. See, e.g., *PPG Industries, Inc. v. Guardian Industrial Corp.*, 597 F.2d 1090 (6th Cir.), *cert. denied*, 444 U.S. 930 (1979), discussed at ¶1702.2.3.3.

A reverse subsidiary merger of S into T will normally avoid asset transfer problems because T's assets are not being transferred. However, a particular agreement or license may explicitly require consent for a change in T's control or may require consent for a merger, even if T is the survivor, under certain circumstances (e.g., T's net worth after the merger is lower than before, as is frequently the case in an LBO when S borrows, and hence T becomes liable for, part of the money being paid to T's shareholders).

¶1702.6.4   Transfer, Sales and Use Taxes

Most states do not impose sales and use taxes generally with respect to a merger, although a particular state's law may differ on this point. Nevertheless, the formal transfers of certain assets in the merger (particularly titled assets, e.g., motor vehicles, aircraft) may give rise to a specific transfer tax. In addition, some states impose a stock transfer and/or issuance tax, which may apply if P issues its stock in a merger.

¶1702.6.5   Non-Pro-Rata Consideration

In a merger, most (but not all) states allow cash, property, securities, or a combination thereof to be used as consideration. However, there is some question whether a merger agreement can (without the consent of 100% of T's shareholders) provide for some T common shareholders to receive different amounts or different types of consideration than other holders of identical stock. If not, the same practical result can be achieved if P acquires some T stock for one amount or type of consideration and immediately thereafter follows with a merger, with the remaining T shareholders receiving another amount or type of consideration in the merger.

This technique is frequently used in an LBO in which T's management is swapping its T stock for P stock in a tax-free Code §351 transaction and T's other shareholders are receiving cash (or cash and P notes) in a reverse subsidiary merger of S into T immediately after the Code §351 transaction. See ¶1403.

¶1702.6.6   Dissenters' Rights

When T and P merge, the laws of most jurisdictions allow a dissenting T or P shareholder to receive in cash the appraised FV of his shares, as determined by a court. Delaware, however, denies appraisal rights to a T shareholder involved in a merger if (1) the class of shares he held before the transaction is listed on a national securities exchange or held by at least 2,000 shareholders and (2) he receives either (a) shares of the surviving corporation, (b) shares of another corporation (e.g., the surviving corporation's parent) that are listed on a national securities exchange or held by at least 2,000 shareholders, (c) cash in lieu of fractional shares, or (d) any combination of the foregoing.[27]

Delaware also denies appraisal rights to a P shareholder if the class of shares he held before the merger is listed on a national securities exchange or held by at least 2,000 shareholders.[28] Moreover, if P's shareholders are not required to vote on the merger, either because of the "small merger" provision (the amount of P stock to be issued in the merger is relatively small compared to P's outstanding stock) or because of the "short-form merger" provision (T is a 90% or greater subsidiary), P's shareholders are denied appraisal rights.[29]

When T and S merge (in a forward or reverse subsidiary merger), P's shareholders are not entitled to appraisal rights (because P is not a party to the merger).[30] This is true even if P's shareholders vote in connection with the T acquisition for one or more of the reasons set forth in ¶1702.6.7. However, a Delaware corporation may in its certificate of incorporation provide additional appraisal rights not otherwise required by law.[31]

¶1702.6.7   Shareholder Vote and Proxy Rules

A merger of T into P or a merger of P into T will generally require the approval of both T's shareholders and P's shareholders. The necessary percentage for approval varies from state to state and generally may be increased by a corporation's charter.

In Delaware, for example, a merger requires approval of a majority of T's and P's outstanding voting stock, subject to higher requirements in the respective charters.[32] Many other states require a higher percentage (frequently two-thirds) for approval.

When T and S merge (in a forward or reverse subsidiary merger), approval is generally necessary only from T's and S's shareholders. Since P is normally S's only shareholder, P can consent on behalf of S. Usually no approval of P's shareholders is necessary, unless one of the following applies:

---

[27] Del. GCL §262(b).
[28] Del. GCL §262(b)(1).
[29] Del. GCL §262(b).
[30] Del. GCL §262.
[31] Del. GCL §262(c).
[32] Del. GCL §251(c).

(1) P's charter explicitly requires the approval of P's shareholders;

(2) P is issuing stock to T's shareholders in excess of P's authorized shares (so a vote of P's shareholders is necessary to amend P's charter to authorize the stock);

(3) P's stock is listed on the NYSE, the AMEX, the Nasdaq NM, or certain regional exchanges which would de-list P's stock if it effectuated the transaction without a shareholder vote. As discussed at ¶1702.2.7.1 above, each of the NYSE, AMEX, and Nasdaq NM rules has slightly different substantive provisions and somewhat different wording.

Most states provide for a so-called short-form merger—without any shareholder vote—between a parent corporation ("P") and one of its subsidiaries ("T"), with T's minority shareholders receiving P stock, cash, or other consideration as specified in the short-form merger agreement. The precise percentage of ownership that P must have in T in order to carry out a short-form merger varies from state to state (90% being required in Delaware[33]). Thus, once P has acquired the requisite stock ownership in T by purchasing T stock (e.g., 90% in Delaware) in a tender offer or negotiated stock purchase, P can (if such a short-form merger statute is applicable) merge with T without a T or P shareholder vote.[34] Care should be taken to assure that the relevant state statute permits the merger in the direction desired (T into P versus P into T). Delaware, for example, allows a short-form merger to be either upstream or downstream.[35]

Delaware also provides an exception (the "small merger" exception) from the usual P-shareholder voting requirement if T merges into P (even though P may own no T stock), the amount of P stock to be issued is relatively small compared to P's outstanding stock, and P is a Delaware corporation. Under this provision, no vote of P's shareholders is required if the merger does not involve (1) a change in P's charter, (2) a change in the stock held by P's shareholders, or (3) the issuance of P common stock (or securities convertible into P common stock) exceeding in the aggregate 20% of P's outstanding common stock immediately prior to the merger.[36] However, the laws of T's state of incorporation may require the vote of both T's and P's shareholders, thus nullifying the Delaware exception. Or P's charter or a stock exchange rule (such as the NYSE 20% rule) may require a vote of P's shareholders.

When a vote of P's or T's shareholders is necessary, state law generally requires written notice of a shareholders' meeting to be sent to all shareholders (in some states, whether or not entitled to vote) a specified number of days in advance of the meeting, unless there is attendance at the meeting or a waiver of notice (generally by 100% of the shareholders).

---

[33] Del. GCL §253(a).

[34] Of course, a vote of P's shareholders would be necessary if explicitly required by P's charter *or* if P stock is being issued and either (1) P does not have sufficient authorized stock or (2) a listing or trading rule (such as the NYSE or Nasdaq NM 20% rule) requires a P shareholder vote.

[35] Del. GCL §253(a).

[36] Del. GCL §251(f).

In Delaware, for example, 10 days' advance notice is required for most shareholders' meetings, but 20 days is required for a shareholder vote on a merger.[37] A corporation's charter or bylaws may provide for a longer notice period. A shareholder generally may waive notice in writing.[38]

Most states permit a corporation, if authorized by the corporation's charter (or in some states, if not expressly prohibited in the charter) to obtain shareholder approval by written consents, obviating the need for a formal shareholders' meeting. Under Delaware law (unless prohibited by charter), action may be taken by shareholder consent if written consent is obtained from the number of shareholders whose votes would have been sufficient to take such action at a shareholders' meeting (generally a majority for a merger), followed by "prompt" notice to the non-consenting shareholders.[39] Some other states require unanimous shareholder consent in lieu of a meeting, without regard to the percentage that would have been sufficient to take action at a meeting.

If T is publicly held and proxies are solicited from T's shareholders regarding approval of a merger, or if P is publicly held and proxies are solicited from P's shareholders in connection with a merger or an amendment to P's charter to authorize additional stock for issuance in the merger or otherwise, such proxies must be solicited pursuant to a proxy statement prepared, filed, and distributed to shareholders in accordance with §14(a) of the 1934 Act and SEC Regulation 14A thereunder. The proxy rules are discussed in greater detail at ¶1702.2.7.6.

¶1702.6.8   Application of 1933 Act

A merger between P (or S) and T in which part or all of the consideration to be received by T shareholders in the merger is stock or debt instruments (i.e., "securities" within the meaning of the 1933 Act) of P (or S) will necessitate compliance with the 1933 Act. The 1933 Act prohibits the sale of securities unless (1) such securities are registered with SEC and certain other requirements are satisfied or (2) there is an applicable exemption from registration, e.g., the private placement or intrastate exemption. When P issues its securities to T's shareholders in a merger, significant restrictions upon the subsequent resale of such P securities by T's shareholders may apply (especially if P's issuance of its securities was not registered under the 1933 Act). For a more complete discussion of the 1933 Act in this context, see ¶1702.2.8.

¶1702.6.9   Sample Acquisition Agreements

A companion volume contains sample acquisition agreements for P's acquisition of T through a merger, including (1) a taxable reverse subsidiary merger of P's transitory subsidiary into T for cash and notes (see ¶2500), (2) a tax-free merger

---

[37] Del. GCL §§222(b) and 251(c).
[38] Del. GCL §229.
[39] Del. GCL §228(a).

of T into P for P stock (see ¶2600), (3) examples of types of representations, warranties, and other terms that would be appropriate for either (1) or (2) if T were not publicly held and the parties agreed upon pro-buyer terms (see ¶2201 and ¶2301), pro-seller terms (see ¶2202 and ¶2302), or neutral (i.e., neither pro-buyer nor pro-seller) terms (see ¶¶2203 and 2303), and (4) additional provisions for when there is to be a purchase price adjustment based on T's closing date balance sheet (see ¶2205).

¶1702.7 *Acquisition of Minority Interest*

¶1702.7.1 Acquisition Techniques

If P has purchased part (but not all) of T's stock, P may wish to "squeeze out" T's minority shareholders. Depending upon P's percentage ownership of T's voting securities, P may be able to effect a short-form merger without a vote of T's shareholders. See, e.g., Del. GCL §253 (authorizing short-form merger with a 90% subsidiary), as discussed at ¶1702.2.7.3. Otherwise, effectuation of a "cleanup" transaction will require a T shareholder vote (and if T remains a publicly held company, compliance with Rule 13e-3 and Regulation 14A or 14C under the 1934 Act). Finally, if P securities are to be issued, compliance with the registration provisions of the 1933 Act (or an exemption therefrom) will be required. See ¶1702.2.8.

¶1702.7.2 State Law Fairness Requirements

In a "squeeze-out" merger, the interests of T's minority shareholders are likely to conflict with the interests of P as majority shareholder (and also, in an LBO, with those of T's management who are (or are becoming) P shareholders). As a general matter, state law rather than federal securities law will be applied in assessing the merits of fairness claims by T's minority shareholders in such cases, and the only federal issue arises if P has not made full disclosure in any required proxy material or registration statement.[40] Typically, such fairness claims are resolved through the application of fiduciary duty standards to T's directors and controlling shareholder.

¶1702.7.2.1 Weinberger

Prior to 1983 Delaware law prohibited a merger effected solely for the purpose of eliminating minority shareholders, in the absence of a valid business purpose.[41] In 1983 the Delaware Supreme Court abandoned the "business purpose" require-

---

[40] See Santa Fe Indus., Inc. v. Green, 430 U.S. 462 (1977).
[41] See Singer v. Magnavox Co., 380 A.2d 969 (Del. 1977).

ment and articulated a standard of "entire fairness" by which parent-subsidiary squeeze-out mergers are judged.[42] As described by the court, the "entire fairness" standard incorporates concepts of "fair dealing" and "fair price." The "fair dealing" concept encompasses issues of timing and structure of a transaction as well as disclosure.[43]

When, however, the only disputed matter is adequacy of price (without allegations of facts tending to support a finding of unfair dealing), *Weinberger* makes statutory appraisal rights the minority shareholders' exclusive remedy. The *Weinberger* court redefined substantially the evidentiary standards applicable to appraisal proceedings to permit "proof of values by any techniques or methods which are generally considered acceptable in the financial community and otherwise admissible in court," as opposed to the weighted average formula based on market price, earnings, and asset values theretofore employed in such proceedings.

¶1702.7.2.2 *Impact of* Weinberger

Under *Weinberger*, the approval of a squeeze-out merger by the vote of a fully informed minority shifts to the plaintiff shareholder the burden of establishing that the transaction is unfair. The evidentiary burden in the absence of minority approval is unclear. The effect of *Weinberger* is that, absent fraud or breach of fiduciary duty, complaining shareholders must rely on the appraisal remedy rather than resort to class actions to block squeeze-out mergers. The practical impact of the decision is that the risk of a squeeze-out merger being enjoined is substantially reduced.

Moreover, when appraisal is the exclusive remedy, fewer T shareholders generally seek relief than in a class action, because appraisal rights apply only to a shareholder who "opts in" while a class action proceeds on behalf of all class members unless they "opt out." Traditionally, very few shareholders have taken either of these affirmative steps.

¶1702.7.2.3 *Post-*Weinberger *Decisions*

In *Patents Management Corp. v. O'Connor*,[44] the Delaware Court of Chancery ruled that, absent unusual circumstances, the appraisal remedy is exclusive. The court stated that, in order to avoid an appraisal proceeding, "not only must a [minority shareholder] allege specific acts demonstrating the unfairness of the merger terms to the minority, but also its allegations must demonstrate that an appraisal would not adequately remedy that misconduct."[45]

---

[42] Weinberger v. UOP, Inc., 457 A.2d 701 (Del. 1983).

[43] See generally Sterling v. Mayflower Hotel Corp., 93 A.2d 107 (Del. 1952).

[44] 11 Del. J. Corp. Law 693, 1985.

[45] See Sealy Mattress Co. of N.J., Inc. v. Sealy, Inc., 532 A.2d 1324 (Del. Ch. 1987) (where court found that appraisal would not constitute an adequate remedy).

In *Glassman v. Unocal Exploration Corporation*,[46] P owned 96% of T's outstanding common stock and acquired the remaining 4% through a short-form squeeze-out merger, although T established no special committee to protect the 4% minority shareholders' rights. The Delaware Supreme Court held that, absent fraud or illegality, the minority shareholders were entitled only to an appraisal remedy where the controlling parent owns over 90% of T's outstanding common stock and acquires the balance through a short form merger, although P has a duty of full disclosure to the minority shareholders.

Rabkin v. Philip A. Hunt Chemical Corp.,[47] provides an example of the type of "unfair dealing" by a controlling shareholder that enables a minority shareholder to avoid relegation to an appraisal remedy (P) in connection with a squeeze-out merger (of T's minority shareholders). The T-P merger was allegedly structured to avoid the provisions of a stock purchase agreement pursuant to which P, T's controlling shareholder, had acquired its interest in T. The stock purchase agreement provided that if P acquired the minority interest in T within one year after purchasing the controlling interest, P was required to pay the same price per share as P paid in acquiring the controlling interest. The minority shareholder alleged that, although P always intended to acquire the entire equity interest in T, P delayed the merger until after the one-year period had expired so P could avoid its obligation under the stock purchase agreement and pay a lower price in the merger. In refusing to dismiss the minority shareholder's suit, the court stated that "unfair dealing" under *Weinberger* does not turn solely on issues of deception but rather embraces questions of the timing and structure of a transaction.

¶1702.7.2.4   Tender Offer by Controlling Shareholder

In contrast to a squeeze-out merger, a tender offer by a controlling shareholder does not involve issues of fair price under *Weinberger* inasmuch as the minority shareholder is free to accept or reject the offer. The controlling shareholder does, however, have a duty of "complete candor" under Delaware law.[48] See ¶1702.2.7.1 for a discussion of SEC's tender offer rules.

¶1702.7.2.5   Other States

The courts in a number of other states have adopted the *Weinberger* "entire fairness" standard.[49]

[46] 777 A.2d 242 (Del. 2001).

[47] 498 A.2d 1099 (Del. 1985)

[48] See Lynch v. Vickers Energy Corp., 429 A.2d 497 (Del. 1981); Lewis v. LFC Holding Corp., 11 Del. J. Corp. Law 254, 1985 WL 11554 (1985); Joseph v. Shell Oil Co., 482 A.2d 335 (Del. Ch. 1984); In Re Siliconix,CA No. 18700 (Del. Ch. 6/19/01).

[49] See, e.g., Perl v. IU International Corp., 607 P.2d 1036 (Haw. 1980); Linge v. Ralston Purina Co., 293 N.W.2d 191 (Iowa 1980).

¶1703 ACCOUNTING FOR THE ACQUISITION[1]

The accounting treatment for P's acquisition of T is important if for example:

(1) P's stock is publicly traded, so its accounting results (e.g., its earnings per share) affect the trading market for its stock,

(2) P's debt instruments are publicly traded, so its accounting results (e.g., its earnings as a percentage of its fixed charges) affect the trading market for its debt instruments,

(3) although P's stock and debt are not publicly traded, P's bankers or other creditors are influenced (e.g., in their willingness to increase or continue P's credit lines or their inclination to raise or lower the interest rate) by P's financial statements,

(4) although no P shareholders or creditors are currently influenced by P's accounting results, P's shareholders anticipate a future sale of P in which the selling price the buyer is willing to pay will be influenced by P's accounting net income or other accounting results,

(5) P's debt agreements contain financial covenants (e.g., a minimum net worth requirement, an earnings requirement, a maximum debt-equity ratio).

Under GAAP, whether P's acquisition of T is accounted for as a purchase, a part purchase, a recapitalization, or (for transactions initiated before 7/1/01) a pooling of interests can have a material effect on P's post-acquisition accounting net income, balance sheet, and other accounting results.

FASB adopted two significant changes to acquisition accounting in 7/01. *First*, FASB Statement 141 eliminated pooling of interests accounting for transactions initiated after 6/30/01.[2] Thus, all transactions initiated after 6/30/01 must use purchase accounting, unless they qualify for part-purchase or recapitalization (i.e., no purchase) accounting. *Second*, FASB Statement 142 eliminated amortization of purchased goodwill, substituting a non-amortization approach under which goodwill is periodically written off (or down) only to the extent "impaired."[3]

This ¶1703 is organized as follows:

- ¶1703.1 discusses the relationship of GAAP accounting rules to the form of the transaction, the form of the entities involved, SEC reporting rules, and the tax rules applicable to acquisitions.

- ¶1703.2 discusses purchase accounting, including the treatment of purchased goodwill.

¶1703 [1] We thank James F. Somers of Ernst & Young LLP's Transaction Support Group for his ideas and assistance in the preparation of ¶1703.

[2] FASB Statement of Financial Accounting No. 141, *Business Combinations*.

[3] FASB Statement of Financial Accounting No. 142, *Goodwill and Other Intangible Assets*.

- ¶1703.3 discusses the part-purchase and recapitalization (or no-purchase) accounting rules applicable to an LBO with overlapping shareholders (i.e., where pre-LBO shareholders continue to own stock in the post-LBO company).
- ¶1703.3.7 and ¶1703.3.8 discuss recapitalization (i.e., no purchase) accounting where there are no overlapping shareholders (i.e., where no pre-LBO T shareholders continue to own stock in the post-LBO company—¶1703.3.7 where T has publicly held pre-LBO debt or preferred stock that remains outstanding after the LBO and ¶1703.3.8 where at least one of the new investors purchasing a stake in T as part of the LBO is independent of the investors sponsoring the LBO.
- ¶1703.3.9 discusses circumstances in which it may be possible to acquire a Bigco division in an LBO structured for recapitalization (i.e., no purchase) accounting where Bigco retains a significant equity stake in the division after the LBO.
- ¶1703.4 discusses pooling of interest accounting for transactions initiated prior to 7/01/01.

FASB Update

FASB Statement 141 (eliminating pooling of interests accounting) issued in 7/01 generally restated and "carried forward without reconsideration the guidance in [APB] Opinion 16 and certain of its amendments and interpretations related to the application of purchase accounting," but in 10/01 FASB began a project to reconsider purchase accounting procedures, including the APB Opinion 16 rules carried forward in Statement 141. As part of their 10/02 agreement to work together to promote convergence of international accounting standards, FASB and the International Accounting Standards Board ("IASB") agreed to conduct the purchase accounting procedures review as a joint project. (See FASB Update at ¶1502.1.7 for further discussion of FASB's and IASB's agreement to work toward convergence of international accounting standards.)

FASB expects to issue an Exposure Draft containing proposed purchase accounting revisions in third quarter 2003. See ¶1703.2.1 FASB Update and ¶1703.2.1.2 FASB Update for discussion of FASB's tentative decisions regarding purchase accounting revisions.

Although FASB Statement 141 and FASB Statement 142 (eliminating amortization of goodwill and substituting an impairment approach) do not address recapitalization accounting, FASB previously stated that it would review recapitalization accounting during a second phase of its business combinations project. During 2000 FASB identified areas to be reviewed in the second phase of its business combinations project and stated that the first issues to be addressed would be "new basis issues," including push-down accounting. FASB began its deliberations on "new basis issues" in 9/00 and announced on 9/13/00 a tentative principle to "be used in deciding whether recognizing a new basis of accounting is appropriate":

> "The transfer or loss of control by an entity over net assets is an economic event that results in their carrying values no longer being relevant. The users of financial statements, as of the date of the transfer or loss, in which these assets and financial performance are reported rely on their fair values to evaluate performance, stewardship, and accountability. Accordingly, a new basis of accounting, using fair values as of the date of transfer or loss of control, should be recognized when control is transferred:
>
> (1)   to another entity or entities that acquire control by purchase or otherwise;
> (2)   to an arrangement in which control is shared by others; or
> (3)   to the governing board or management of an entity, for example, a former subsidiary that obtains control."

It is unclear whether this murky tentative principle has anything to do with recapitalization accounting, since in a recap accounting transaction the entity owning the assets does not change. On the other hand, a recap accounting transaction typically involves a change in control of the recapitalized entity and if FASB adopts an approach to new basis that turns on whether there is a change of control, changes to the push-down accounting rules could follow.

As part of their 10/02 agreement to work together to promote convergence of international accounting standards, FASB and the IASB have also agreed to conduct their review of new basis issues as a joint project. However, the new basis issues project was placed on hold in 2002 "[b]ecause of the pressures of other priorities."

Thus, the long-term viability of recapitalization accounting may be in some doubt. By analogy to FASB's decision in Statement 141 to abolish pooling prospectively, we believe that any change to current recap accounting rules should apply only to transactions occurring after final FASB rules are published. Because any changes to recap accounting rules, as well as related changes to joint venture and other accounting rules to be addressed by FASB in phase two of the business combinations project, are likely to involve extensive debate and considerable controversy, it is impossible to predict at this time either the likely outcome or the timing of any final proposals.

¶1703.1   Relationship of GAAP Acquisition Accounting Rules to Form of Transaction, Form of Entity, SEC Reporting Rules, and Tax Rules for Acquisitions

The purchase accounting rules (as well as the pre-7/01 pooling of interests accounting rules) generally apply to P's acquisition of T regardless of the mechanical form the transaction takes, including:

(1)   a forward merger of T into P or one of P's subsidiaries ("S"),
(2)   a reverse merger of S into T, with T becoming a P subsidiary,
(3)   an acquisition of T's stock by P (or S), whether T is thereafter held as a P (or S) subsidiary or whether T is thereafter liquidated into P (or S), or
(4)   an acquisition of all or substantially all of T's assets by P (or S).[4]

In contrast, recapitalization accounting rules are sensitive to the legal form of the acquisition. See ¶1703.3.6.

The GAAP acquisition accounting rules generally treat corporations, partnerships, and LLCs alike. Thus, the acquisition accounting rules discussed in this ¶1703 also generally apply where (1) one of P or T is a partnership or LLC, rather than a corporation, and the other is a corporate entity *or* (2) both P and T are partnerships or LLCs. In applying the accounting rules to such a transaction, references to P or T voting common stock should be read as referring to P or T voting common partnership or LLC interests.

Public company financial statements must generally be filed with SEC and are subject to SEC reporting rules which may supplement and in some cases override FASB and other GAAP rules.[5] In addition, SEC accounting staff may review a public company's financial statements (e.g., in the context of a company's IPO or other securities offering) and object to the manner in which a public company has applied GAAP rules, including GAAP acquisition accounting rules.

The GAAP acquisition accounting rules are not the same as the tax rules and the tax treatment of an acquisition is generally irrelevant in determining the proper accounting treatment. Thus, after the 7/01 elimination of pooling of interests accounting, unless an acquisition qualifies for part-purchase accounting or for recapitalization accounting, P's acquisition of T is generally accounted for as a purchase, resulting in a full step-up (or down) in accounting book values, regardless of whether the acquisition results in (1) tax basis step up (or down) for T's

---

[4] See FASB Statement 141, ¶10.

[5] Generally, a company's financial statements must be filed periodically with SEC if (1) the company has a class of securities (debt or equity) registered under 1934 Act §12 (either under 1934 Act §12(b), which requires a class of debt or equity securities to be registered under the 1934 Act if such securities are traded on a national securities exchange, or under Act 1934 §12(g), which requires a class of equity securities to be registered under the 1934 Act if such class is held by 500 or more record holders and the company has total assets of $10 million or more) or (2) the company has filed a registration statement that has become effective under the 1933 Act. See 1934 Act §§12(b), 12(g), 13(a), and 15(d); SEC Rule 12g-1 under the 1934 Act.

assets (where P acquires T's assets in a taxable transaction or P acquires T's stock in a taxable transaction with a Code §338 or §338(h)(10) election) *or* (2) carryover tax basis for T's assets (where P acquires T's stock without a Code §338 or §338(h)(10) election or where P acquires T's assets in a tax-free reorganization).

Similarly, prior to the 7/01 elimination of pooling accounting, a transaction structured as a tax-free reorganization for IRS purposes (so that T's asset basis carried over to P) might have failed the rigorous GAAP pooling requirements and hence have been accounted for as a purchase. Conversely, a transaction that was taxable for IRS purposes (resulting in either a stepped up or carryover T asset tax basis, depending on structure) might have constituted a pooling for accounting purposes.

¶1703.2   Purchase Accounting

¶1703.2.1   Effect of Purchase Accounting

After 7/01 P's acquisition of T is accounted for as a purchase, unless the transaction qualifies as (1) a part-purchase or a recapitalization as a result of overlapping shareholders, i.e., T's pre-acquisition shareholders own P stock after the transaction or (2) as a recapitalization as a result of independent T shareholders or certain pre-acquisition publicly traded T preferred stock or debt that remains outstanding. See ¶1703.3 for a discussion of part-purchase and recapitalization accounting. Where P's acquisition of T is a purchase and P acquires 100% of T, T's assets are restated for GAAP purposes to reflect their cost to P.

Thus, when purchase accounting applies, T's old accounting book values are not relevant. T's asset book values are generally stepped up (or down) to their current FV (resulting in higher (or lower) post-acquisition depreciation, amortization, and cost of goods sold), and goodwill is created for any excess of P's cost for T over the FV of T's assets (including identifiable intangible assets).

Unless otherwise stated, we assume throughout that P acquires 100% of T. If P acquires less than 100% of T's stock, purchase accounting applies to the percentage of T's assets corresponding to the percentage of T's stock acquired by P, and carryover book value applies to the percentage of T's assets corresponding to the percentage of T's stock remaining in the hands of minority shareholders.

Where purchase accounting applies and P's cost for T exceeds T's old carrying value for T's assets, the result is that (1) P's new accounting carrying value for T's assets (including identifiable intangible assets but excluding goodwill) is increased and (2) a new asset (purchased goodwill) is created on P's accounting books for the excess of P's cost for T over the FV of T's identifiable assets. Both of these results are generally desirable from a balance sheet standpoint, because they increase P's assets. However, both of these results are generally undesirable from the standpoint of P's future income statements, because P's increased accounting carrying value for T's assets (other than goodwill) must generally be written off over a series of years, and P's newly created goodwill is potentially required to be written off in the future if, and to the extent that, it becomes "impaired" (see ¶1703.2.1.3 below), in each case reducing P's accounting earnings below the amount P would have reported if there had been no purchase accounting for P's acquisition of T.

FASB Update

FASB Statement 141 (eliminating pooling of interests accounting) issued in 7/01 generally restated and "carried forward without reconsideration the guidance in [APB] Opinion 16 and certain of its amendments and interpretations related to the application of purchase accounting," but in 10/01 FASB began a project to reconsider purchase accounting procedures, including the APB Opinion 16 rules carried forward in Statement 141. As part of this project, FASB tentatively decided in 10/01 that:

> In the acquisition of less than 100 percent of the acquired entity, the identifiable assets and liabilities of the acquired entity should be recorded at full fair value. The current practice of considering the subsidiaries' carryover basis to the extent of the non-controlling interest should be eliminated.

In 10/02, FASB also tentatively decided, and in 6/03 reaffirmed, that 100% of the acquired entity's goodwill would be recorded at full FV.[6]

This tentative decision would require that T's assets be written up (or down) to 100% of FV where P acquires less than 100% of T (but enough of T so that push down accounting applies to T's financial statements). It is not clear whether such decision will be adopted as final and, if it is, what the effective date and transitional rules will be. The tentative decision does not appear to address part-purchase accounting for LBOs under EITF 88-16 or recapitalization accounting, both of which are expected to be addressed in the future as part of the next phase of FASB's business combinations project. See ¶1703.3.

As part of their 10/02 agreement to work together to promote convergence of international accounting standards, FASB and IASB agreed to conduct the purchase accounting procedures review as a joint project. (See FASB Update at ¶1502.1.7 for further discussion of FASB's and IASB's agreement to work toward convergence of international accounting standards.) FASB expects to issue an Exposure Draft containing proposed purchase accounting revisions in third quarter 2003. See ¶1703.2.1.2 FASB Update for discussion of other FASB tentative decisions regarding purchase accounting revisions.

See ¶1703 FASB Update for a discussion of FASB's continuing business combinations project.

---

[6] FASB Action Alert No. 02-42 (11/6/02); FASB Action Alert No. 03-23 (6/11/03).

¶1703.2.1.1   Acquiring Company

Because purchase accounting is imposed only on the acquired company (T in our parlance) and not for the acquiring company (P or Newco in our parlance), FASB Statement 141 contains rules for determining which of the entities involved in an acquisition is to be regarded as the acquiring company. In many situations, the identity of the acquiring company is clear. Where the consideration for the acquisition is solely cash, assets (other than equity in the combined entity), or the incurrence of liabilities, the entity that distributes the cash or other assets, or incurs the liabilities, is generally the acquiring company.[7]

In other circumstances, identifying the acquiring company is more complex. The form of the transaction and relative size of P and T do not necessarily dictate the identity of the acquiring company. Where an acquisition includes the exchange of equity interests, "all pertinent facts and circumstances [are] considered"[8] in identifying the acquiring company, including:

- **Relative voting rights in combined entity.** All other factors being equal, the acquiring company is the company whose "owners as a group retained or received the larger portion of the voting rights in the combined entity." In making this determination, "the existence of any unusual or special voting arrangements and options, warrants, or convertible securities" is considered.[9]
- **Large minority voting block.** If "no other owner or organized group of owners has a significant voting interest," all other factors being equal, the acquiring company is the company "whose single owner or organized group of owners holds the large [significant] minority voting interest in the combined entity."[10]
- **Board composition.** All other factors being equal, the acquiring company is the company "whose owners or governing body has the ability to elect or appoint a voting majority of the governing body of the combined entity."[11]
- **Senior management composition.** All other factors being equal, the acquiring company is the company "whose senior management dominates that of the combined entity."[12]
- **Market premium.** Where the P and T securities exchanged in the acquisition are publicly traded, all other factors being equal, the acquiring company is the company "that pays a premium over the market value of the equity securities of the other" company.[13]

---

[7] FASB Statement 141, ¶16.
[8] FASB Statement 141, ¶17.
[9] FASB Statement 141, ¶17a.
[10] FASB Statement 141, ¶17b.
[11] FASB Statement 141, ¶17c.
[12] FASB Statement 141, ¶17d.
[13] FASB Statement 141, ¶17e.

¶1703.2.1.2   Aggregate Cost and Allocation to T's Assets

P's aggregate cost for T is whichever of the following is more readily ascertainable:

(1)   the FV of the consideration given by P (P stock and securities, cash, and other consideration) plus the present value of T's liabilities transferred to P (or to a P subsidiary, including T if it becomes a P subsidiary) plus the costs of the acquisition (e.g., legal and accounting fees and expenses), or

(2)   the FV of T's gross assets (including goodwill and identifiable intangibles).

If P pays for T with cash, debt instruments, and other readily valued consideration, the consideration given by P ((1) above) will normally be more readily ascertainable. If P pays for T with P stock or securities, the FV of the P stock and securities takes account of such factors as blockage and SEC restrictions on resale.

P is required to identify all T assets acquired and T liabilities assumed, including any intangible assets acquired that are required to be recognized separate and apart from goodwill. P's aggregate cost for T is allocated to T's assets (other than goodwill) "based on their estimated FV at the acquisition date."[14] To the extent that P's cost exceeds the FV of T's assets (including identifiable intangible assets other than goodwill), the excess is treated as goodwill.[15]

FASB's 7/01 pronouncements contain specific rules identifying intangibles that must be recognized separately from goodwill. These rules require separate recognition of certain intangibles that have often previously been lumped together with goodwill.

An intangible asset is recognized as separate from goodwill if:

(1)   the asset "arises from contractual or other legal rights (regardless of whether those rights are transferrable or separable from the acquired entity or from other rights and obligations)," or

(2)   the asset "is separable, that is . . . capable of being separated or divided from the acquired entity and sold, transferred, licensed, rented, or exchanged (regardless of whether there is an intent to do so)," and for this purpose "an intangible asset that cannot be sold, transferred, licensed, rented, or exchanged individually is considered separable if it can be sold, transferred, licensed, rented, or exchanged in combination with a related contract, asset, or liability."[16]

Once an asset is recognized as separate from goodwill, all "[a]ssumptions" (e.g., potential future contract renewals) that would be considered by "marketplace

---

[14] FASB Statement 141, ¶35. See FASB Statement 141, ¶37 for general rules to be followed in allocating purchase price to specific assets.

[15] FASB Statement 141, ¶43. See FASB Statement 141, ¶44-46 for a discussion of the rules applicable to "negative goodwill" (i.e., where the FV of T's assets—other than goodwill—exceeds P's cost).

[16] FASB Statement 141, ¶39. See FASB Statement 141, ¶¶A10-A28 for examples of assets recognized separately from goodwill. See also EITF 02-17, Recognition of Customer Relationship Intangible Assets Acquired in a Business Combination.

participants" must be taken into account in determining the asset's FV, even if those assumptions would not themselves meet the contractual-legal or separability tests.[17]

Based on these tests, assets such as favorable leases, government licenses, and patents are recognized separately from goodwill because they arise from contractual or legal rights (and in some cases may also be capable of separate transfer).[18] Customer lists and subscriber lists are recognized separately from goodwill because they meet the separability criterion (i.e., such assets are often licensed or transferred, even though they generally do not arise from contractual or legal rights).[19] Bank depositor relationships are also considered separable—and hence must be recognized separately from goodwill—because they are transferred in connection with the transfer of deposit liabilities.[20]

FASB adopted a per se rule under which the value of T's assembled workforce is treated as part of T's goodwill, i.e., is not recognized separately from goodwill, because "techniques to measure the value of an assemble workforce and the related intellectual capital with sufficient reliability are not currently available."[21]

FASB Update

In 10/01 FASB began a project to reconsider purchase accounting rules and procedures, including APB 16 rules carried forward as part of FASB Statement 141 (see ¶1703.2.1 FASB Update). As part of their 10/02 agreement to work together to promote convergence of international accounting standards, FASB and IASB agreed to conduct the purchase accounting procedures review as a joint project. (See FASB Update at ¶1502.1.7 for further discussion of FASB's and IASB's agreement to work toward convergence of international accounting standards.) FASB expects to issue an Exposure Draft containing proposed purchase accounting revisions in third quarter 2003. During 2002 and 2003 FASB announced several tentative decisions (apparently effective for years beginning after 12/15/04, with early adoption encouraged, but retroactive application not allowed[22]), including:

(1)   The acquisition date (the date P's cost to acquire T is measured) is the date P "gains control over" T.

(2)   P's cost to acquire T is the "fair value of the acquired business . . . represented by the exchange price agreed between the buyer and the seller. Acquisition-related costs paid to third parties are not part of the exchange and should be expensed as incurred."

---

[17] EITF 02-17.
[18] FASB Statement 141, ¶A10.
[19] FASB Statement 141, ¶A11.
[20] FASB Statement 141, ¶A13.
[21] FASB Statement 141, ¶39 and ¶B169.
[22] FASB Action Alert No. 03-22 (6/4/03).

(3) P stock issued in the acquisition must be valued as of the acquisition date, although FASB has deferred decision on whether blockage factors are taken into account in valuing P stock.

(4) Where P agrees to pay contingent consideration as part of its acquisition of T, the contingent consideration must be measured at FV, as of the acquisition date. To the extent P's obligation to pay contingent consideration is regarded as equity under GAAP rules, P's obligation to pay contingent consideration is not thereafter remeasured. To the extent that P's obligation to pay contingent consideration is treated as a liability, it must be remeasured after the acquisition date as contingencies are resolved, with any change in the amount of liability recorded on P's income statement but not altering P's purchase price for T.

(5) T's preacquisition contingent assets and liabilities must be reflected in purchase accounting at FV as of the acquisition date.

(6) P's costs to (a) terminate a T activity, (b) terminate T employees, or (c) relocate T employees, are not treated as assumed liabilities unless T's obligations with respect to such costs meet GAAP liability recognition rules (as modified by FASB's project on obligations associated with disposal activities) prior to the acquisition date. In addition, in some cases, an amount resulting from a contractual agreement that is "triggered" by the acquisition (e.g., a payment due as a result of a change-in-control provision in an employment agreement) may be treated by P as an assumed liability. Where a payment has a "double trigger" (e.g., where a payment is conditioned on a change of control *plus* a post-change event, such as termination of employment), it appears likely that P is not entitled to treat the amount as an assumed liability.

(7) P is no longer required (or presumably allowed) to expense T's in-process R&D. Rather, P recognizes T's in-process R&D as acquired assets measured at FV (subject to post-acquisition review for impairment). Post-acquisition expenditures with respect to such R&D are expensed under normal R&D rules. See FASB Update at ¶1703.2.1.5 for further discussion of the treatment of in-process R&D.

¶1703.2.1.3 *Goodwill Impairment, Not Amortization*

Under FASB Statement 142, goodwill acquired in an acquisition is not amortized. Instead, P must periodically review T's goodwill for "impairment" and record an expense against earnings in any period when T's goodwill is found to be impaired, i.e., when "the carrying amount of goodwill exceeds its implied fair value."[23]

Statement 142 represents a sharp break from the prior accounting treatment for goodwill. Under APB Opinion 17, in effect prior to Statement 142, goodwill was required to be amortized over its useful life, not to exceed 40 years.

Because goodwill is no longer amortizable, P generally has an incentive to maximize the allocation to T's goodwill, since depreciation and amortization charges for all of T's other assets (i.e., both tangible assets and identifiable intangible assets other than goodwill), including the effect of any purchase accounting step-up, continue to be subtracted from income over the life of the asset. However, FASB Statement 141 rules requiring separate recognition of intangibles meeting certain tests (see ¶1703.2.1.2) limit P's ability to do so.

FASB's 7/01 adoption of the goodwill impairment approach—adopted just as the 2001-2002 recession was reaching full bloom—came just in time for a huge number of telecom, internet, technology, and other companies, which had made high-priced acquisitions during the late 1990s boom years, to write off huge amounts of purchased goodwill quickly, thus avoiding the risk of future damage to their earnings. As one example, AOL-Time Warner in 3/02 announced a $54 billion write-off of goodwill resulting from the AOL acquisition.

The determination of whether T's goodwill is impaired is a complex process and requires a number of difficult and subjective judgements to be made by P and its auditors. P must initially allocate T's goodwill, determined as set forth in ¶1703.2.1.2, to one or more "reporting units" of the combined P-T company.[24]

Reporting units are generally the same as the "operating segments" for which a public company must provide segmented financial information under FASB Statement 131.[25] However, private companies must identify reporting units for purposes of measuring goodwill impairment even if not otherwise subject to FASB Statement 131 segment reporting.[26] An operating segment may be broken up into more than one reporting unit if the operating segment consists of economically distinct components, each constituting a business for which discrete financial information is available and regularly reviewed by segment management. Economically similar components of an operating segment may, however, be combined into a single reporting unit.[27]

Once allocated to reporting units, goodwill is reviewed for impairment at the reporting unit level in a two-step process. Under the *first step*, P must determine the FV of each reporting unit[28] and compare "the fair value of [the] reporting unit with its carrying amount, including goodwill. . . . If the fair value of the reporting unit exceeds its carrying amount, goodwill of the reporting unit is considered not impaired [and] the second step of the impairment test is unnecessary."[29]

---

[23] FASB Statement 142, ¶18.

[24] FASB Statement 142, ¶34.

[25] FASB Statement 142, ¶30.

[26] FASB Statement 142, ¶31.

[27] FASB Statement 142, ¶30. See also FASB Staff Announcement, "Clarification of Reporting Unit Guidance in Paragraph 30 of FASB Statement No. 142" (11/01).

[28] See FASB Statement 142, ¶¶23-25 for guidance on determining the fair value of a reporting unit.

[29] FASB Statement 142, ¶19.

Under the *second step*, P must determine the "implied fair value of reporting unit goodwill" by applying the purchase accounting rules outlined in ¶1703.2.1.2 (including identifying any intangible asset required to be recognized separately from goodwill that has not previously been reflected on P-T's books) to the reporting unit as if it had been purchased for the FV determined in step one.[30] P must recognize an impairment loss if "the carrying amount of reporting unit goodwill exceeds the implied fair value of that goodwill, . . . equal to that excess."[31] Once a goodwill impairment loss is recognized, it cannot later be reversed, even if the FV of the reporting unit increases.

P must test for goodwill impairment at least annually,[32] with two exceptions. *First*, P must test for impairment between annual tests "if an event occurs or circumstances change that would more likely than not reduce the fair value of a reporting unit below its carrying amount." For example, such an interim test might be required as a result of "[a] significant adverse change in legal factors or in the business climate," adverse regulatory actions, unanticipated competition, or a loss of key personnel.[33]

Second, where P makes a "detailed determination of the fair value of a reporting unit" in one year, P is not required to retest the value of the reporting unit (i.e., is not required to reapply step one of the impairment test) in a subsequent year if:

- "The assets and liabilities that make up the reporting unit have not changed significantly since the most recent fair value determination,"
- "The most recent fair value determination resulted in an amount that exceeded the carrying amount of the reporting unit by a substantial margin," and
- "Based on an analysis of events that have occurred and circumstances that have changed since the most recent fair value determination, the likelihood that a current fair value determination would be less than the current carrying amount of the reporting unit is remote."[34]

Goodwill impairment losses are reported on a separate line item as part of operating income and reduce earnings per share. FASB Statement 142 did not adopt a 9/99 proposal to allow companies to report, in addition to regular earnings per share, earnings per share computed without goodwill amortization and impairment charges. Goodwill impairment losses associated with a discontinued operation are generally reported as part of the results of discontinued operations.

---

[30] FASB Statement 142, ¶21. Application of purchase accounting rules in step two is solely for purposes of identifying and quantifying any goodwill impairment. No other assets are written up (or down) or recognized on P-T's books as a result of step two. Of course, other reporting unit assets may be subject to impairment loss rules under standards other than FASB Statement 142.

[31] FASB Statement 142, ¶20.

[32] FASB Statement 142, ¶26.

[33] FASB Statement 142, ¶28.

[34] FASB Statement 142, ¶27.

¶1703.2.1.4   Treatment of Intangibles Other than Goodwill

Purchase price allocated to a separately recognized intangible is amortized over the intangible's useful life, unless that life is "indefinite."[35] Amortizable intangibles are periodically reviewed for impairment, albeit under a less rigorous standard than that applied to goodwill. P must record an impairment loss for an amortizable intangible if "the carrying amount of [such] intangible asset is not recoverable and its carrying amount exceeds its fair value."[36]

Where a separately recognized intangible has an indefinite life, the intangible "shall not be amortized until its useful life is determined to be no longer indefinite."[37] Non-amortizable intangibles are reviewed for impairment at least annually on an asset-by-asset basis (i.e., without regard to the reporting unit(s) used to determine whether goodwill is impaired). P must record an impairment loss for a non-amortizable intangible if its "carrying amount . . . exceeds its fair value."[38] Non-amortizable intangible assets (other than goodwill) "whether acquired or internally developed, should be combined into a single unit of accounting for purposes of testing impairment if they are operated as a single asset and, as such, are essentially inseparable from one another."[39]

FASB Statement 142's recognition of non-amortizable intangibles is a significant change from APB Opinion 17, as in effect prior to Statement 142's 7/01 publication. Under APB Opinion 17, all intangibles were presumed to have a useful life not in excess of 40 years and were amortized accordingly.

¶1703.2.1.5   In-Process R&D

To the extent T's assets consist of either (1) assets used in a T R&D project (e.g., R&D supplies and equipment) or (2) a T R&D project in process (e.g., a new product in the development stage or another R&D project which has not yet reached marketability), P can (and indeed must) write off the amounts allocated to such in process R&D assets immediately after P consummates its purchase accounting acquisition[40] of T (just as accounting rules require P to write off its internal R&D costs as incurred).

Indeed, in several large purchase accounting acquisitions of software companies during the 1990s, the acquirors (according to published reports) used this approach, by immediately writing off significant portions of the purchase price as R&D, thereby (1) reducing the amount of purchase accounting goodwill or asset carrying values to be amortized in future years and hence (2) increasing P's future accounting earnings. Examples include IBM's acquisition of Lotus, Computer Associate's acquisition of Legent, Novell's acquisitions of Unix System Labora-

---

[35] FASB Statement 142, ¶12.
[36] FASB Statement 142, ¶15. See also FASB Statement 144.
[37] FASB Statement 142, ¶16.
[38] FASB Statement 142, ¶17.
[39] EITF 02-7.
[40] FASB Interpretation No. 4 (2/75); ETIF 86-14.

tories and Quattro Pro, and Lotus' acquisition of Samna. Between 1/1/90 and early 1999 a total of approximately 400 companies reportedly wrote-off a substantial portion of an acquisition purchase price, with the average write-off being 72% of purchase price.

However, starting in 1998 SEC began to scrutinize numerous acquisitions—by, e.g., MCI WorldCom, Lemont & Hauspie, Cendant, America Online, Sunbeam, and Network Associates—on the ground that the R&D write-off exceeded the portion of the purchase price properly allocable to T's in-process R&D (i.e., generally the FV of such in-process R&D at the time of the acquisition), and in response many of the companies challenged by SEC drastically scaled back their proposed in-process R&D write-offs.

FASB Update

FASB tentatively decided in 2/03 that P is no longer required (or presumably allowed) to expense T's in-process R&D (apparently effective for years beginning after 12/15/04, with early adoption encouraged, but retroactive application not allowed).[41] Rather, P recognizes T's in-process R&D as acquired assets measured at FV (subject to post-acquisition review for impairment). Post-acquisition expenditures with respect to such R&D are expensed under normal R&D rules. While FASB had previously decided to exclude treatment of in-process R&D from the business combinations project, FASB reversed this decision in light of its goal of promoting convergence between the IASB's International Financial Reporting Standards and U.S. GAAP. See FASB Update at ¶1502.1.7 for a discussion of FASB's 9/02 agreement with IASB to promote convergence between U.S. and international accounting standards. See FASB Updates at ¶1703 and ¶1703.2.1.2 for a discussion of FASB's purchase accounting procedures project.

¶1703.2.1.6 *Effective Dates and Transition Rules*

FASB Statement 141's repeal of pooling of interests accounting is effective for transactions "initiated" after 6/30/01.[42] FASB Statement 141's other provisions, including the requirement that P identify intangible assets separately recognized from goodwill, apply to all transactions for which "the date of acquisition" (i.e., ordinarily the closing date) is after 6/30/01.[43]

Where P acquired T prior to 7/1/01 in a transaction accounted for as a purchase, P must reclassify as goodwill any T assets previously recognized that do not meet the FASB Statement 141 criteria for recognition apart from goodwill. P is generally not otherwise required (or permitted) to restate the goodwill resulting from the

---

[41] FASB Action Alert No. 03-06 (2/12/03), FASB Action Alert No. 03-22 (6/4/03).
[42] See ¶1703.4 for the definition of "initiated."
[43] FASB Statement 141, ¶59 and ¶48.

acquisition of T (i.e., P is not required or permitted to determine whether there were any T assets included as part of goodwill that would have been recognized apart from goodwill under FASB Statement 141 if it had applied to the acquisition). However, P must restate an amount reported as goodwill (or as goodwill and other intangible assets) in P's external financial statements with respect to a prior acquisition if (1) the amount relates to an asset that meets Statement 141's standard for recognition separate from goodwill, (2) the asset was separately valued at the time of the acquisition, *and* (3) P has maintained separate internal accounting records for the asset (including calculation of separate amortization and impairment charges) since the acquisition.[44]

FASB Statement 142's adoption of a non-amortization approach to goodwill is generally effective for accounting years beginning after 12/15/01. Adoption of the non-amortization approach is permitted only at the beginning of an accounting year and may not be done retroactively.[45] Where P acquired T prior to 6/30/01, the balance of any remaining goodwill is subject to the non-amortization approach beginning with the year in which P adopts FASB Statement 142. However, where P acquired T in a purchase accounting transaction after 6/30/01, any goodwill created is not amortized, even prior to P's adoption of FASB Statement 142.[46]

P is required to allocate all goodwill created before its adoption of FASB Statement 142 to reporting units and perform a transitional goodwill impairment test during the year it adopts Statement 142. Any impairment loss recognized as a result of this transitional test is generally treated as a change in accounting principle.[47]

On adoption of FASB Statement 142, P must reassess the useful life of previously recognized intangible assets (other than goodwill) and adjust the remaining amortization periods accordingly. Any assets determined to have an indefinite life would cease to be amortized.[48]

---

[44] FASB Statement 141, ¶61 and FASB Staff Announcement, "Clarification of Paragraph 61(b) of FASB Statement No. 141 and Paragraph 49(b) of FASB Statement No. 142" (11/01).

[45] FASB Statement 142, ¶48. Early adoption was permitted for companies with a fiscal year beginning after 3/15/01, so long as the company had not previously reported interim financial statements for the first quarter of such year under APB Opinion 17.

[46] FASB Statement 142, ¶50.

[47] FASB Statement 142, ¶¶54-58.

[48] FASB Statement 142, ¶53.

¶1703.2.1.7   Example of Purchase Accounting

EXAMPLE

P acquires T on 1/1 year 2 in a transaction initiated after 6/30/01. Immediately before the acquisition, T's GAAP balance sheet is as follows:

Assets		Liabilities and Net Worth	
Cash	$ 100	Liabilities	$ 200
Receivables	100	Net worth (100 shares of voting	
Inventory	100	common stock)	800
PP&E	700		
Total	$1,000		$1,000

T's GAAP income statement for year 1 (the year before the acquisition) is as follows:

Sales	$2,000
Cost of goods sold and other expenses	1,167
Income before income tax	833
Income tax (at an assumed federal-state 40% rate)	333
Net income	$ 500

When P acquires T on 1/1 year 2, P issues either P voting common stock with an FV of $5,000 to T's common shareholders or pays $5,000 in cash to T's common shareholders or a combination thereof. The transaction is accounted for as a purchase.

T's assets take on a new BV of $5,200 (i.e., $5,000 of P stock and/or cash that P paid for T plus $200 transferred T liabilities) plus any costs of the acquisition (assumed for simplicity to be zero). This amount is allocated among the acquired assets (including identifiable intangible assets but not goodwill) according to their FVs, with the excess (i.e., the residual) allocated to goodwill:

	Old BV of T's Assets	FV of T's Assets
Cash	$ 100	$ 100
Receivables	100	100
Inventory	100	550
PP&E	700	2,000
Identifiable intangible assets, such as patents, know-how, and customer lists	0	500
Subtotal	1,000	3,250
Residual goodwill	0	1,950
Total	$1,000	$5,200

Each T asset goes on P's GAAP balance sheet at its FV as allocated above, i.e., P's assets increase by $4,200, consisting of a $1,750 increase in cash, receivables, inventory, and PP&E, a $500 increase in identifiable intangible assets, and a $1,950 increase in goodwill. P's GAAP liabilities increase by $200. P's GAAP net worth is not affected at all by the acquisition. The old BV of T's assets are ignored.

If the T business performs in year 2 (the year of the acquisition) the same as in year 1, P's GAAP net income from the T business will be substantially less than $500 (T's year 1 GAAP net income). This is the case because the T business's accounting depreciation, amortization, cost of goods sold, etc., are all increased by the GAAP write-up in the T assets. For example:

(1) If T and P account for inventory on a FIFO basis and T's 12/31 year 1 inventory on hand is sold in year 2, the T business will have a year 2 cost of goods sold of $550 (under the purchase method of accounting) rather than $100 (T's old FIFO book value for its inventory). (If P accounted for the purchased T inventory on a LIFO basis and did not reduce the quantity of inventory on hand, the $450 step-up would probably be locked into P's LIFO layers and would not affect P's post-acquisition GAAP net income until P invaded the LIFO layers.)

(2) If the T business's PP&E is depreciated (for accounting purposes) over an average of 10 years, the T business's year 2 accounting depreciation will be $200 ($2,000 new purchase book value for T's PP&E divided by 10 years) rather than $70 ($700 old book value for T's PP&E divided by 10 years).

(3) If the T business's identifiable intangible assets (e.g., patents, know-how, and customer lists) are amortized (for accounting purposes)

over an average of 10 years, the T business's year 2 accounting amortization will be $50 ($500 new purchase BV for identifiable intangible assets divided by 10 years) rather than zero (the old BV for T's identifiable intangible assets).

Hence, the T business's year 2 GAAP before-tax income (on P's GAAP consolidated income statement) would be $630 less than for year 1 (on T's GAAP income statement) because of purchase accounting:

Increase in cost of goods sold	$450
Increase in PP&E depreciation	130
Intangible assets amortization	50
Total reduction in the T business's year 2 GAAP before-tax income because of purchase accounting	$630

Thus, if the T business performs the same in year 2 as it did in year 1, its year 1 GAAP before-tax income of $833 would decline to $203 in year 2 because of purchase accounting:

T's year 1 GAAP income before income tax	$833
T's year 2 purchase accounting reduction in income before income tax	630
T's year 2 GAAP income before income tax	$203

T's $1,950 of goodwill is not amortized; rather it is periodically reviewed for impairment. See ¶1703.2.1.3. Prior to the issuance of FASB Statement 142, T's $1,950 of goodwill would have been amortized over a period not exceeding 40 years.

Calculation of the T business's after-tax net income is more complicated, since it depends on (a) whether the P-T acquisition results in a carryover tax basis for T's assets or a stepped-up tax basis for T's assets and (b) certain complex accounting rules for establishing a deferred tax liability reserve when there is a differential between the GAAP BV and the tax basis for acquired assets and liabilities.

¶1703.2.2 Which Entities' Financial Statements Affected By Purchase Accounting

When P's acquisition of T is accounted for under purchase accounting, both P's and T's subsequent financial statements may be impacted.

Where P (or P's subsidiary S) has purchased T's *assets*, purchase accounting applies to P's (or S's) subsequent financial statements which include T's old business and assets (now owned by P (or S)). For example, where S has purchased T's assets, purchase accounting affects S's financial statements and, where S is included in P's consolidated financial statements, affects P's consolidated financial statements.

Where P (or P's subsidiary S) has purchased T's *stock* and P thereafter includes T in P's subsequent consolidated financial statements (generally where P owns more than 50% of T's voting power), purchase accounting applies to P's subsequent consolidated financial statements which include T.

Where P (or P's consolidated subsidiary S) has purchased T's *stock* but T is not included in P's consolidated financial statements (generally because P does not own more than 50% of T's voting power), P generally accounts for T on the equity method of accounting where P owns 20% or more, but not more than 50%, of T's voting power. In this case, purchase accounting applies to P's financial statements, i.e., in calculating P's share of T's accounting net income on the equity method, P must take into account any changes to its share of T's income produced by application of purchase accounting to its share of T's assets (whether or not purchase accounting is actually applied by T on its own financial statements, see ¶1703.2.3).

EXAMPLE

T has an FV of $1,000, but a GAAP net book value of $800 (i.e., T's GAAP assets exceed T's GAAP liabilities by $800). P purchases 40% of T's stock for $400 (i.e., 40% of T's $1,000 FV).

P accounts for its 40% ownership in T on the equity method, because P owns 20% or more, but not more than 50%, of T's voting power. P's 40% share of T's GAAP net book value is $320. P's purchase price for 40% of T's stock ($400) exceeds P's 40% share of T's GAAP net book value by $80. P must account for the $80 excess on the purchase method of accounting. Assuming that this $80 is allocable to amortizable intangibles (i.e., not goodwill) which are amortizable over 20 years, the GAAP impact is a $4 per year charge for intangible amortization on P's financial statements.

In year 1 after the acquisition, T's GAAP net income is $100. Under the equity method of accounting P picks up on its financial statements $40 of T's net income (40% × $100) less $4 of P-level intangible amortization, or a net $36 addition to P's year 1 GAAP net income (reduced by a GAAP accrual for P's deferred income taxes which will be due when P subsequently recognizes this amount as taxable income, e.g., as P receives dividends or sells the T stock).

After P has acquired T's stock in a transaction treated as a purchase on P's financial statements, *T* may prepare *separate* financial statements for some purposes. Whether P's purchase accounting acquisition of T stock affects T's separate financial statements is dealt with in ¶1703.2.3 immediately below.

¶1703.2.3   "Push-Down" Purchase Accounting

Where P has acquired T's stock in a transaction treated as a purchase, does P's purchase accounting for T affect T's subsequent separate financial statements, or does T simply continue to use its old accounting book values for its separate financial statements? In accounting parlance, the question is whether P's new purchase price for T's stock is "pushed down" to T's separate financial statements.

The answer to this question turns on whether or not T's separate financial statements are included in an SEC filing. The two principal reasons that T's separate financial statements may be included in an SEC filing are, *first*, P is subject to periodic SEC reporting of its financial statements under the 1934 Act (or P is filing a registration statement for a public offering under the 1933 Act) and T's separate post-acquisition financial statements are being included in P's financials as supplemental data, or *second*, after the P-T acquisition T is subject to SEC reporting of its separate financial statements under the 1934 Act because T still has public securities outstanding.[49]

When T's separate financial statements are included in an SEC filing after P has acquired T's stock in a purchase transaction, SEC requires P to use push-down purchase accounting for T's separate financial statements if P wholly or substantially wholly owns T. SEC has stated that when P's form of ownership of T is within P's control, push-down purchase accounting must be used so that the basis of accounting for the purchased assets and liabilities (i.e., T's assets and liabilities) will be the same regardless of whether T continues to exist as a separate entity or is merged into P. SEC recognizes, however, that the existence of outstanding T public debt, preferred stock, or a significant minority common stock interest might impact P's ability to control the form of its ownership of T. As a result, although encouraging the use of push-down purchase accounting, SEC generally does not insist on its application in these three circumstances.[50]

The test used by SEC to determine whether T can avoid push-down purchase accounting is the same as the guidelines used to determine whether T qualifies for recap accounting discussed at ¶1703.3.6, i.e., where minority shareholders (other than P) own more than 20% of T's common equity, push-down accounting is not required; where minority shareholders own 5% or less push-down account-

---

[49] Generally, a company's financial statements must be filed periodically with SEC if the company (1) has a class of securities (debt or equity) registered under 1934 Act §12(b), which covers a class of debt or equity securities traded on a national securities exchange, or (2) has a class of equity securities registered under 1934 Act §12(g), which covers a class of equity securities held by 500 or more record holders where the company has total assets of $10 million or more, or (3) the company has filed a registration statement that has become effective under the 1933 Act. See 1934 Act §§12(b), 12(g), 13(a), and 15(d); SEC Rule 12g-1 under the 1934 Act.

[50] SEC Staff Accounting Bulletins, Topic 5: Miscellaneous Accounting, Section J, Push Down Basis of Accounting Required in Certain Limited Circumstances, CCH Fed. Sec. L. Rep. ¶75,721 (1994).

ing is required; where minority shareholders own between 5% and 20%, the transaction is in a gray zone.

If T's separate financial statements are not included in an SEC filing after P has acquired T's stock in a purchase transaction, the use of push-down purchase accounting for T's separate financial statements is optional.

One other point: When T's separate financial statements are included in an SEC filing after P has acquired T's stock in a purchase transaction, SEC also requires that P's debt, interest expense, and debt issuance costs incurred in connection with or otherwise related to the acquisition of T be pushed down to T's financial statements if (1) T is to assume P's debt, either presently or in a planned transaction in the future, (2) the proceeds of a T debt or equity offering will be used to retire all or part of P's debt, or (3) T guarantees or pledges its assets as collateral for P's debt.[51]

¶1703.3 Accounting for Leveraged Buyouts—No Purchase, Part Purchase, and Recapitalization Accounting for Overlapping Shareholders

If a newly formed acquiror ("Newco") with no substantive business operations acquires T in an LBO and there is overlapping ownership between T and Newco (i.e., some of T's shareholders own part of Newco's stock), the 100% purchase accounting rules described in ¶1703.2 may not apply to the transaction. Rather, in these circumstances EITF 88-16 may require *"no purchase" accounting* (where there is no change in control of T as described in ¶1703.3.1 below) or *"part purchase"* accounting instead of 100% purchase accounting (where there is a change in T's control as described in ¶1703.3.1 through ¶1703.3.5 below).[52]

The very complex conclusions set forth in EITF 88-16 have been the subject of substantial debate among SEC, the FASB and its staff, the FASB's EITF, and the accounting and legal communities. This debate is ongoing.

Moreover, even where T has a change in control, *"recapitalization" accounting* (i.e., no purchase accounting) may apply on T's separate financial statements where (1) T survives and (2) T's old shareholders continue to own a "significant" stake in recapitalized T's common equity. Generally, where T's old shareholders as a group own more than 20% of recapitalized T's common equity, the significant continuing stake test is satisfied; where they own 5% or less, the test is not satisfied (so that purchase accounting applies to T's financial statements); and where they own between 5% and 20%, the transaction is in the gray zone, so that the result depends on factors such as the number and type of old T shareholders with a continuing interest in T's common equity. See ¶1703.3.6.

Although T must generally survive as a legal entity to qualify the transaction for recapitalization accounting, in some circumstances it may be possible to struc-

---

[51] SEC Staff Accounting Bulletins, Topic 5: Miscellaneous Accounting, Section J, Push Down Basis of Accounting Required in Certain Limited Circumstances, CCH Fed. Sec. L. Rep. ¶75,721 (1994).

[52] EITF 88-16, Basis in Leveraged Buyout Transactions (5/18/89), *superseding* EITF 86-16 (7/9/87).

ture the acquisition of a Bigco division to obtain recapitalization accounting where Bigco retains a significant continuing equity interest in the division. See ¶1703.3.9.

Recapitalization accounting may also apply in two circumstances where T's old shareholders do not retain a significant (or indeed any) continuing interest in recapitalized T's common equity. *First*, recapitalization accounting generally applies where T has publicly held debt or publicly held preferred stock outstanding prior to and independent of the recapitalization and such public debt or preferred stock remains outstanding after the recapitalization. See ¶1703.3.7. *Second*, SEC has approved recap accounting where at least one of the new investors purchasing a significant stake in T's recapitalized equity as part of the LBO is "independent" of the investors sponsoring the recapitalization transaction. See ¶1703.3.8.

Even where T qualifies for recapitalization (no purchase) accounting on its own financial statements, purchase accounting is nevertheless required on the financial statements of any new T shareholder (P or Newco) which acquires sufficient T stock to use the equity method of accounting for T (generally 20% or more of T's voting power) or the consolidated method of accounting for T (generally more than 50% of T's voting power). See ¶1703.2.2 and ¶1703.3.6.5.

As described below, where an LBO qualifies for part-purchase accounting, T's or Newco's asset book value increases (from T's pre-LBO book net worth) by only a fraction of the increase required in a 100% purchase accounting transaction, i.e., T's old asset book value carries over for a percentage of each asset (generally corresponding to the post-LBO percentage ownership by T's old shareholders) and T's asset book value is stepped up to FV for the remaining percentage of each asset (generally corresponding to the post-LBO percentage ownership by T's new shareholders). Hence T's or Newco's book net worth (1) increases (from T's pre-LBO net worth) by both the new equity money raised and the asset write up, but (2) declines by the amount paid out to T's old shareholders. These adjustments frequently produce a book net worth substantially less than the book net worth determined under 100% purchase accounting, and more than occasionally produce a negative net worth. See ¶1703.3.5 below. While a lower T or Newco book net worth may be disadvantageous, the future book earnings of T or Newco will be higher than under 100% purchase accounting as a result of reduced future depreciation and amortization charges.

Also as described below, where an LBO qualifies for recapitalization accounting (i.e., no purchase accounting), (1) T's asset book value is the same both before and after the transaction and (2) T's book net worth (a) increases (from T's pre-LBO book net worth) by the new equity money raised, but (b) declines by the amount paid out to T's old shareholders (frequently producing a negative net worth). See ¶1703.3.6 below.

Thus, recapitalization accounting impacts in the same way on T's book earnings (although not in the same way on T's book net worth) as pooling accounting. Where, for example, T's new owners plan to take T public, qualifying for recapitalization accounting and avoiding full or partial purchase accounting may yield substantial benefits. Because T's assets are not written up in connection with a recapitalization LBO, T's future depreciation and amortization charges will be lower, and hence T's future book earnings higher, than if purchase accounting had applied. Because the price of T's shares in a public offering is often based on a multiple of T's per share earnings, the use of recapitalization accounting may allow T's new owners to realize greater proceeds in a future public offering of T's shares.

FASB Statement 142, issued 7/01, eliminated amortization of purchased goodwill, substituting a non-amortization approach under which goodwill is periodically written off (or down) only to the extent "impaired." See ¶1703.2.1.3. The elimination of goodwill amortization reduces (but does not eliminate) the desirability of recapitalization accounting. First, under a non-amortization/impairment approach, goodwill created by purchase accounting does not reduce earnings unless and until that goodwill's FV is subsequently impaired. Thus, using recapitalization accounting to avoid goodwill creation eliminates the possibility of an earnings reduction in the future should goodwill become impaired. Second, recapitalization accounting also avoids an accounting basis step-up for both tangible assets and intangible assets other than goodwill and hence avoids an earnings reduction due to increased depreciation and amortization charges for these assets.

For a discussion of some tax and structuring issues in an LBO, see ¶1402.1, and for an LBO structured as a recapitalization, see ¶1402.1 (1) and (4) and ¶1703.3.6.10.

FASB Update

FASB Statement 141 (eliminating pooling of interests accounting) issued in 7/01 generally restated and "carried forward without reconsideration the guidance in [APB] Opinion 16 and certain of its amendments and interpretations related to the application of purchase accounting," but in 10/01 FASB began a project to reconsider purchase accounting procedures, including the APB Opinion 16 rules carried forward in Statement 141. As part of this project, FASB tentatively decided in 10/01 that:

> In the acquisition of less than 100 percent of the acquired entity, the identifiable assets and liabilities of the acquired entity should be recorded at full fair value. The current practice of considering the subsidiaries' carryover basis to the extent of the non-controlling interest should be eliminated.

In 10/02, FASB also tentatively decided, and in 6/03 reaffirmed, that 100% of the acquired entity's goodwill would be recorded at full FV.[53]

This tentative decision would require that T's assets be written up (or down) to 100% of FV where P acquires less than 100% of T (but enough of T so that push down accounting applies to T's financial statements). It is not clear whether such decision will be adopted as final and, if it is, what the effective date and transitional rules will be. The tentative decision does not appear to address part-purchase accounting for LBOs under EITF 88-16

---

[53] FASB Action Alert No. 02-42 (11/6/02); FASB Action Alert No. 03-23 (6/11/03).

or recapitalization accounting, both of which are expected to be addressed in the future as part of the next phase of FASB's business combinations project.

As part of their 10/02 agreement to work together to promote convergence of international accounting standards, FASB and IASB agreed to conduct the purchase accounting procedures review as a joint project. (See FASB Update at ¶1502.1.7 for further discussion of FASB's and IASB's agreement to work toward convergence of international accounting standards.) FASB expects to issue an Exposure Draft containing proposed purchase accounting revisions in third quarter 2003. See ¶1703.2.1.2 FASB Update for discussion of other FASB tentative decisions regarding purchase accounting revisions.

See ¶1703 FASB Update for a discussion of FASB's continuing business combinations project.

¶1703.3.1　No Purchase Accounting at All Unless Change of T's Control

Purchase accounting will apply to an LBO only if there is a change in T's voting control such that an investor or group of investors (the "Newco control group") who did not have voting control of T before the LBO transaction has voting control of Newco after the transaction.

If purchase accounting does not apply, the transaction will be treated similarly to a recapitalization or restructuring, i.e., the old GAAP book value of T's assets will carry over to Newco for accounting purposes. Because Newco will generally borrow substantial amounts to pay off T's shareholders, Newco's GAAP book net worth will generally be negative after such a transaction, i.e., Newco's GAAP net worth will generally be equal to:

(1)　T's old GAAP book net worth,

(2)　*less* the amount paid to T's shareholders,

(3)　*less* the costs of the transaction, such as legal and accounting fees and expenses (other than those costs attributable to Newco's borrowings that are capitalized and amortized over the life of the borrowings),

(4)　*plus* the net proceeds from the issuance of Newco's equity securities.

This GAAP result is the same as if there had been no Newco and T had repurchased its old stock and sold new T stock (i.e., a recapitalization or restructuring).

(1)　Voting control measured by majority of voting power. In determining whether there has been a change in T's voting control (i.e., whether an investor or group of investors who did not have voting control of T before the LBO has voting control of Newco after the LBO), voting control is generally measured by a majority of voting power.

(2) Mgmt as part of Newco control group. There is a rebuttable (but not easily rebutted) presumption that Mgmt is part of Newco's control group if Mgmt owns any Newco residual equity or other Newco securities exercisable/convertible into Newco's residual equity securities. See ¶1703.3.3.

(3) Non-Mgmt investor as part of Newco control group. A Newco investor, other than a member of Mgmt, is automatically considered a member of Newco's control group if:

(a) the investor has a greater residual common equity interest in Newco than he had in T, and such investor's residual common equity interest in Newco is 5% or more, or

(b) the investor has the same or a lesser residual common equity interest in Newco than he had in T and such investor's fully diluted voting interest or capital at risk (at any risk level) is 20% or more of Newco's fully diluted voting interest or capital at risk.

(4) Non-Mgmt investor not part of Newco control group. A Newco investor, other than a member of Mgmt, is automatically excluded from the Newco control group if:

(a) the investor has a greater residual common equity interest in Newco than he had in T and such investor's residual common equity interest in Newco is less than 5%, or

(b) the investor has the same or a lesser residual common equity interest in Newco than he had in T and neither such investor's fully diluted voting interest nor such investor's capital at risk (at any risk level) is 20% or more of Newco's fully diluted voting interest or capital at risk.

(5) Determining change in control. Typically, a change in T's voting control is deemed to have occurred if:

(a) a single investor (whether or not he owned any T stock, including a member of Mgmt) obtains control of Newco and that investor did not control T, or

(b) a group of new investors (i.e., investors who owned no residual common equity interest in T, which may include Mgmt if they owned no T residual common equity) obtains control of Newco, or

(c) a group of investors that includes one or more old T shareholders obtains control of Newco and no subset of such Newco control group previously controlled T.

EXAMPLE 1

Before and after Newco purchases T, T's and Newco's voting and residual common equity interests are owned as follows (and T and Newco have no dilutive securities outstanding):

	Before	After
A (T's and then Newco's president)	20%	60%
VC #1	40%	40%
VC #2	40%	—
Total	100%	100%

The transaction qualifies as a change in control because a single shareholder (A), who did not previously control T, has obtained unilateral voting control of Newco. See (5)(a) above.

EXAMPLE 2

Before and after Newco purchases T, T's and Newco's voting and residual common equity interests are owned as follows (and T and Newco have no dilutive securities outstanding):

	Before	After
A (T's and then Newco's president)	20%	30%
VC #1	40%	10%
VC #2	40%	—
VC #3	—	30%
VC #4	—	30%
Total	100%	100%

The transaction qualifies as a change in control because VC #3 and VC #4, who had no prior interest in T, obtained voting control of Newco. See (4)(b) above.

EXAMPLE 3

Before and after Newco purchases T, T's and Newco's voting and residual common equity interests are owned as follows (and T and Newco have no dilutive securities outstanding):

	Before	After
A (T's and then Newco's president)	20%	—
VC #1	40%	45%
VC #2	40%	15%
VC #3	—	20%
VC #4	—	20%
Total	100%	100%

In addition, VC #2 has no capital at risk in Newco other than its 15% common equity interest. Hence VC #2 is not part of Newco's control group because (i) VC #2's residual common equity interest in Newco is less than its residual common equity interest was in T, so it does not fit the first category of control group member other than Mgmt described in (3)(a) above, and (ii) VC #2's voting interest and capital at risk in Newco is less than 20%, so it does not fit the second category described in (3)(b) above.

Thus, Newco's control group consists of VC #1 (an old T shareholder) and VC #3 and VC #4 (who were not old T shareholders). The transaction qualifies as a change in control because no subset of the Newco control group (VC #1, VC #3, and/or VC #4) controlled T. See (5)(c) above.

EXAMPLE 4

Before and after Newco purchases T, T's and Newco's voting and residual common equity interests are owned as follows (and T and Newco have no dilutive securities outstanding):

	Before	After
A (T's and then Newco's president)	20%	40%
VC #1	40%	20%
VC #2	40%	—
VC #3	—	20%
VC #4	—	20%
Total	100%	100%

All four of Newco's shareholders are included in Newco's control group. Because A is a part of Newco's management, there is a strong presumption that he is part of Newco's control group. See (2) above. Because VC #1 has 20% of Newco's voting interest and/or capital at risk, it is part of Newco's control group even though its residual common equity interest declined. See (3)(b) above. Because VC #3 and VC #4 each has a 5% or greater residual common equity interest in Newco, and each also has a greater residual common equity interest in Newco (20% each) than in T (0% each), each is a part of Newco's control group. See (3)(a) above.

Thus, the transaction does not qualify as a change in control because a subset of Newco's control group (A and VC #1) controlled T. See (5)(c) above.

(6)   Rules for determining members of control group. In determining membership in Newco's control group:

(a)   Related parties (other than those related only because of ownership of T) are aggregated and considered a single investor.

(b)   Members of Mgmt who receive any Newco residual common equity are generally treated as a single investor, except that for purposes of (5)(a) above members of Mgmt can also be considered individually.

(c)   For purposes of (2), (3)(a), and 4(a) and (b) above, an investor's residual common equity interest is computed by treating him as having exercised or converted all dilutive securities. Dilutive securities not held by the investor are treated as exercised or converted to the extent that the terms of those dilutive securities are no less favorable than the terms of the dilutive securities held by the overlapping investor. However, the effect of including the dilutive securities not held by the overlapping investor may not reduce the overlapping investor's residual common equity interest below his undiluted residual common equity interest.

(d)   For purposes of (3)(b) and 4(b) above, an investor's fully diluted voting interest is determined by treating him as having exercised or converted all dilutive securities. Dilutive securities not held by the investor are treated as exercised or converted to the extent that the terms of those dilutive securities are no less favorable than the terms of the dilutive securities held by the overlapping investor. However, the effect of including the dilutive securities not held by the overlapping investor may not reduce the overlapping investor's voting interest below his undiluted voting interest.

(e)   For purposes of (3)(b) and 4(b) above, in determining whether an investor has 20% or more of Newco's cumulative capital at risk at any risk level, the calculation of the investor's capital at risk is made first at the common stock level, i.e., the Newco security with the lowest priority in liquidation, and continues cumulatively to the security with the highest priority in liquidation (i.e., senior debt), based on each investor's ownership of Newco equity and debt securities plus the maximum amount of any direct or indirect guarantees made by the investor for Newco or its other investors. The maximum amount of any guarantees should be included in the capital-at-risk test at the risk level of the security guaranteed. Capital at risk includes all debt and equity securities, including short and long-term debt, notes payable, and capital lease obligations.

(7)   Change in control must be more than temporary. To qualify as a change in control, the change in T's voting control (i.e., the acquisition of voting control of Newco by the Newco control group) must be substantive, genuine, and not temporary. If a new investor or group of investors has acquired voting control of Newco, but persons other than the Newco control group hold Newco convertibles, options, and warrants to acquire Newco voting securities, the Newco control group may be treated as holding only temporary control of Newco (so that there has been no substantive change in T's control). This is the result if (a) the Newco convertibles, options, and warrants held by third parties are "substantially equivalent" to the underlying Newco voting securities so that they are treated like the underlying Newco voting securities into which they convert or exercise and (b) once the third parties are treated as owning those additional Newco voting securities, the Newco control group falls below a majority of Newco's voting securities.

Factors to be considered in determining whether convertibles, options, and warrants held by third parties are "substantially equivalent" to the underlying voting securities into which they convert/exercise include the delay until conversion/exercise, remoteness of triggering events or vesting events, relationship between conversion/exercise price and FV (after taking into account the volatility of leveraged securities), and any requirement that public sale follow conversion/exercise.

(8)   Effect of change in control. If the LBO qualifies as a change in control, there will be 100% purchase accounting unless one of the exceptions discussed in ¶¶1703.3.2 through 1703.3.4 applies or recapitalization accounting discussed in ¶1703.3.6 applies.

¶1703.3.2   Part-Purchase Accounting When Newco Acquires Less Than 100% of T

If Newco acquires less than 100% of T's residual common equity securities, there is purchase accounting only for the percentage of T acquired by Newco, and T's old book value carries over for the percentage of T's residual common equity securities remaining in the hands of minority shareholders (i.e., anyone other than Newco).

For example, if Newco acquires 85% of T's residual common equity, and the remaining 15% of T's residual common equity continues to be held by minority shareholders, then Newco accounts for 85% of T's assets on a "purchase basis" in Newco's consolidated financial statements and 15% as a carryover of T's old asset book value (i.e., a part-purchase acquisition). On the right side of Newco's balance sheet, it reports (below liabilities and above net worth) a liability-like "minority-interest-in-subsidiary" item equal to the 15% of T's carryover book value assets (net of 15% of T's carryover book value liabilities).

If the transaction qualifies for recapitalization accounting at the T level, the transaction will not affect T's asset book value. See ¶1703.3.6 for a discussion of recapitalization accounting. If the transaction does not qualify for recapitalization accounting at the T level, Newco's part-purchase accounting will be "pushed down" to T and a percentage of T's assets equal to the percentage of T residual common equity acquired by Newco will be accounted for on a "purchase basis."

See ¶1703.3 Update for discussion of (1) an FASB project considering purchase accounting procedures in light of the 7/01 issuance of FASB Statements 141 (eliminating pooling of interests accounting) and 142 (eliminating goodwill amortization and substituting an impairment approach for goodwill) and (2) FASB's 10/01 and 10/02 tentative decision to eliminate part-purchase accounting, which does not appear to address part-purchase accounting for LBOs under EITF 88-16 or recapitalization accounting, both of which are expected to be addressed as part of the next phase of FASB's business combinations project.

¶1703.3.3 Part-Purchase Accounting When Member of Newco's Control Group (Including T's Mgmt) Owned a Residual Common Equity Interest in Pre-LBO T

If an LBO transaction results in a change in T's control but a member of Newco's control group owned a residual common equity interest in T before the LBO, purchase accounting does not apply to the lesser of that investor's residual common equity interest in T or Newco. Instead, "predecessor basis" accounting applies with respect to this overlapping interest.

Under predecessor basis accounting, an overlapping shareholder's adjusted cost for the lesser of his residual common equity interest in T or Newco is carried over to Newco's financial statements (in lieu of purchase accounting) for the portion of T's net assets corresponding to the lesser of such shareholder's percentage residual common equity interest in T or Newco. Such an overlapping shareholder's adjusted cost for his T interest is determined as follows:

(1) overlapping shareholder's original cost for his T interest,
(2) plus his share of T's earnings while he held the interest,
(3) less dividends paid to him,
(4) less any payment or other distribution received from Newco for his T stock.

The result of this type of accounting is to use newly calculated purchase accounting for the portion of T's assets not treated as owned by the overlapping shareholder and to use old purchase accounting (i.e., purchase accounting based on the overlapping shareholder's adjusted cost) for the portion of T's assets treated as owned by the overlapping shareholder.

EXAMPLE 1

Before and after Newco purchases T, T's and Newco's voting and residual common equity securities are owned as follows:

	T *Before LBO*	Newco *After LBO*
VC	—	70%
Mgmt	20%	30%
Various Persons (or the public)	80%	—
Total	100%	100%

Newco acquires 100% of T's stock in an LBO.

The acquisition is accounted for 80% as a purchase and 20% at predecessor basis, using Mgmt's adjusted cost for its 20% interest in T, even though VC owned no T stock before the LBO and by itself controlled Newco after the transaction.

In determining the extent to which Newco's net assets are valued at predecessor basis, (1) members of Mgmt are considered individually and (2) related parties are aggregated and considered a single investor.

An overlapping investor's residual common equity interest is computed by treating him as having exercised or converted dilutive securities in the same fashion as described in ¶1703.3.1(6)(c).

The predecessor-basis rule applies regardless of whether (1) the T shareholder swaps his T stock for Newco stock or (2) the T shareholder sells his T stock to Newco and buys Newco stock in a purportedly separate transaction.

Where an LBO is accounted for partially at predecessor basis, each of T's assets (both tangible and goodwill) is stepped-down proportionally from the amount of such asset's carrying value if 100% new purchase accounting had applied.

EXAMPLE 2

Same as Example 1. In addition, (1) if 100% purchase accounting had applied to the LBO, T's assets would have taken a new carrying value of $5,000 but (2) because of the 20% overlapping ownership, T's assets take a carrying value of $4,500 (deriving 80% from the $5,000 new purchase accounting amount and 20% from $2,500 predecessor basis accounting).

> Each of T's assets (tangible and goodwill) take a new carrying value equal to 90% ($4,500÷$5,000) of such asset's carrying value if the LBO had been accounted for as a 100% purchase.

See ¶1703.3 FASB Update for discussion of (1) an FASB project considering purchase accounting procedures in light of the 7/01 issuance of FASB Statements 141 (eliminating pooling of interests accounting) and 142 (eliminating goodwill amortization and substituting an impairment approach for goodwill) and (2) FASB's 10/01 and 10/02 tentative decision to eliminate part-purchase accounting, which does not appear to address part-purchase accounting for LBOs under EITF 88-16 or recapitalization accounting, both of which are expected to be addressed as part of the next phase of FASB's business combinations project.

¶1703.3.4 Part-Purchase Accounting When T Shareholders Not Part of Newco's Control Group Receive Some Newco Equity Securities

Predecessor basis accounting (as described in ¶1703.3.3) also applies to the residual common equity interest in Newco held by two or more investors (a) each of which owned a residual common equity interest in T, (b) each of which has a residual common equity interest in Newco of at least 5%, (c) none of which is a member of Newco's control group (i.e., because none of such investors, individually, has a greater equity interest in Newco than in T or has a fully diluted voting interest or capital at risk of 20% or more in Newco), and (d) all of which, in the aggregate, have a 20% or more residual common equity interest in Newco.

Finally, if equity interests in Newco (other than mandatorily redeemable preferred) constitute 20% or more of the total consideration paid to the T shareholders for their shares, predecessor basis accounting (as described in ¶1703.3.3) applies with respect to *all* of the T shareholders who acquire residual common equity interests in Newco (whether or not such shareholders are members of Newco's control group or are described in the preceding paragraph).

Thus, where T shareholders receive some Newco equity securities in an LBO, 100% purchase accounting applies only where (a) the LBO results in a change in T's control, and (b) no T shareholders are included in Newco's control group, and (c) the cash/notes/debt-like preferred received by T shareholders from Newco constitutes more than 80% of the total consideration received by the T shareholders, and (d) less than 20% of Newco's residual common equity is owned, in the aggregate, by T shareholders who own 5% or more of Newco's residual common equity.

See ¶1703.3 FASB Update for discussion of (1) an FASB project considering purchase accounting procedures in light of the 7/01 issuance of FASB Statements 141 (eliminating pooling of interests accounting) and 142 (eliminating goodwill amortization and substituting an impairment approach for goodwill) and (2) FASB's 10/01 and 10/02 tentative decision to eliminate part-purchase accounting, which does not appear to address part-purchase accounting for LBOs under EITF 88-16 or recapitalization accounting, both of which are expected to be addressed as part of the next phase of FASB's business combinations project.

¶1703.3.5   LBO Part-Purchase Accounting's Drastic Effect on Newco's Net Worth

If an LBO qualifies as a change in T's control (so that purchase accounting applies as described in ¶1703.3.1) but the LBO does not qualify for 100% purchase accounting for one or more of the reasons described in ¶¶1703.3.2 through 1703.3.4, a relatively small reduction in the carrying value for Newco's assets below 100% purchase accounting can cause a very substantial reduction in Newco's net worth (or even create negative Newco net worth).

EXAMPLE 1.   100% Purchase Accounting

Before Newco acquires T, T's GAAP balance sheet (and the FV of T's assets) are as follows:

	T's Old BV	FV
Assets	$1,000	$5,000
Liabilities	100	100
Net worth	$ 900	$4,900

Newco acquires T (by purchasing 100% of T's stock, or by purchasing all of T's assets subject to its liabilities, or by merger) for $4,900 in cash, which Newco obtains as follows:

Equity contribution by Newco's shareholders	$ 500
Borrowing from bank or other third-party lender	4,400
Total	$4,900

Where 100% purchase accounting applies, Newco's GAAP balance sheet will be as follows:

Assets ($4,900 purchase price + $100 transferred liabilities)	$5,000
Liabilities ($100 of liabilities transferred from T + $4,400 new borrowing)	4,500
Net worth	$ 500

Hence, with 100% purchase accounting, Newco's GAAP net worth is equal to the full $500 contributed by its shareholders.

EXAMPLE 2.   Part-Purchase Accounting

Same as Example 1 except that T's Mgmt (1) owned 30% of T's residual common equity securities before the acquisition, (2) owns 40% of Newco's residual common equity securities after the acquisition, and (3) had predecessor basis for such T securities (immediately before the LBO) of $270 (30% of T's pre-LBO net worth of $900).

Newco qualifies for purchase accounting with respect to 70% of T but must use predecessor-basis accounting for 30% of T. Thus, under part-purchase accounting, Newco's GAAP balance sheet will be as follows:

Assets:

70% purchase: ($4,900 purchase price + $100 transferred liability) × 70%	$3,500
30% predecessor basis: $1,000 T old asset book value × 30%	300
Total Newco assets	$3,800
Liabilities:	
Transferred from T	100
Borrowed by Newco	4,400
Total Newco liabilities	$4,500
Newco negative net worth	$ (700)

Stated differently, Newco's net worth is $500 (i.e., the amount of equity contributed by its shareholders) less a $1,200 reduction from 100% purchase accounting (because Mgmt's 30% of Newco's assets using full purchase accounting would be $1,500 ($5,000 × 30%) as compared to $300 using predecessor-basis accounting ($1,000 × 30%)).

One other way to calculate this $1,200 reduction from 100% purchase accounting (by using the formula defining predecessor-basis accounting set forth in ¶1703.3.3(1) through (4)): Mgmt's $270 predecessor basis for its T securities (immediately before the LBO) reduced by the $1,470 cash Newco paid to Mgmt for Mgmt's T securities ($4,900 purchase price for 100% of T's stock × 30%), i.e., a $1,200 negative amount.

Hence, part-purchase accounting causes a $1,200 reduction in Newco's assets from $5,000 to $3,800 and an equal $1,200 reduction in Newco's net worth from $500 to negative $700.

¶1703.3.6   Recapitalization (Rather than Purchase) Accounting Where T's Old Shareholders Have Significant Continuing Ownership in Recapitalized T

Where T's new owners plan to take T public, avoiding full or partial purchase accounting by qualifying for recapitalization accounting may yield substantial benefits.

FASB Statement 142, issued 7/01, eliminated amortization of purchased goodwill, substituting a non-amortization approach under which goodwill is periodically written off (or down) only to the extent "impaired." See ¶1703.2.1.3. The elimination of goodwill amortization reduces (but does not eliminate) the desirability of recapitalization accounting. First, under a non-amortization/impairment approach, goodwill created by purchase accounting does not reduce earnings unless and until that goodwill's FV is subsequently impaired. Thus, using recapitalization accounting to avoid goodwill creation merely eliminates the possibility of an earnings reduction in the future should goodwill become impaired. Second, recapitalization accounting also avoids an accounting basis step-up for both tangible assets and intangible assets other than goodwill and hence avoids an earnings reduction due to increased depreciation and amortization charges for these assets.

See ¶1703 FASB Update for a discussion of FASB's continuing business combinations project which is reconsidering, in a second, post-7/01 phase, various aspects of accounting for business combinations, including recapitalization accounting. See ¶1703.3 Update for a discussion of (1) an FASB project considering purchase accounting procedures in light of the 7/01 issuance of FASB Statements 141 and 142 and (2) FASB's 10/01 and 10/02 tentative decision to eliminate part-purchase accounting, which does not appear to address part-purchase accounting for LBOs under EITF 88-16 or recapitalization accounting, both of which are expected to be addressed as part of the next phase of FASB's business combinations project.

¶1703.3.6.1   *Recap Accounting General Description*

Where recap accounting applies so that T's assets are not written up in connection with an LBO, T's future depreciation and amortization charges will be lower, and hence T's future accounting earnings will be higher, than if purchase accounting had applied. Because the price of T's shares in a public offering typically is based on a multiple of T's per share earnings, the use of recapitalization accounting may allow T's new owners to realize greater proceeds in a future public offering of T's shares.

Even where an LBO results in a change of control for T, recapitalization accounting—and not purchase accounting—will generally apply to T so long as (1) T survives and (2) T's old shareholders continue to own a "significant" stake in recapitalized T's common equity. Generally, where T's old shareholders as a group own more than 20% of recapitalized T's common equity, the significant continuing stake test is satisfied. Where this group owns 5% or less, the test is not satisfied, so that purchase accounting applies. Where this group owns more than 5% but not more than 20%, the transaction is in the gray zone, so that the result turns on factors such as the number and type of old T shareholders with a continuing interest in T's common equity.

- In the event that the continuing interest in T's stock held by old T shareholders is "widely-held," accounting firms and SEC appear to be comfortable with continuing ownership as low as 5.5% to 7%.
- Where the continuing interest in T's stock held by old T shareholders is not "widely-held," but the continuing old T shareholders are not part of T's post-transaction management, at least some accounting firms appear to be comfortable with continuing ownership as low as 5.5% to 7%.
- However, where the only continuing old T shareholders are part of T's post-transaction management, 7% to 10% continuing ownership appears to be the minimum, since management is viewed as being less independent of the new investors due to their employment relationship (and in certain cases, accounting firms have sought a somewhat larger continuing stake).

See ¶1703.3.6.4 below for (1) further discussion of the continuing interest in T which must be retained by old T shareholders and (2) discussion of SEC Staff's 4/01 announcement that, effective for transactions initiated after 4/19/01, stock retained by an old T shareholder counts toward the significant retained interest requirement only if such old T shareholder is not part of a "collaborative group" with T's new investors.

The typical transaction which qualifies for recap accounting because of overlapping shareholders is where (1) a group of new shareholders invests new money in T for new stock (common and/or preferred) without forming a new holding corporation for T, (2) T borrows additional money, (3) T uses its new equity money and its new debt financing to redeem a portion of its outstanding stock, and (4) after the transaction T's old shareholders continue to own a significant stake in recapitalized T's common equity.

EXAMPLE 1

T's outstanding stock (aggregate FV $100) consists of 100 common shares, each with a $1 FV, all of which are owned by individual A. Venture capitalist ("VC") proposes a recapitalization transaction in which:

(a) Bank loans $70 to T,
(b) VC invests $20 in T in exchange for $20 liquidation value of T's non-convertible preferred stock,
(c) VC invests an additional $8 in T in exchange for 8 new shares of T common stock (80% of T's post-recap common shares),

(d) T redeems 98 T common shares from A, and

(e) A retains 2 T common shares (20% of T's post-recap common shares).

This LBO qualifies for recap accounting because after the transaction T's old shareholders own 20% of (i.e., a significant stake in) T's common equity.

However, it is not essential that the new shareholders invest their new money in T. The transaction can qualify for recap accounting where the new shareholders pay their new money directly to T's old shareholders to purchase previously outstanding T stock, so long as after the transaction T's old shareholders continue to own a significant stake in T's common equity.

Where T qualifies for recap accounting, the book value of T's assets does not change at all (i.e., there is no purchase accounting or partial purchase accounting) and T's book net worth changes only to reflect (a) the increase for the new equity investment and (b) the decrease for the amounts paid out in the redemption. Hence T's book net worth generally declines by the excess of (i) the amount T paid out in the redemption of T's old stock over (ii) the amount T received for new T stock. This may, in some cases, cause T to have a negative book net worth to an even greater degree than described in ¶1703.3.5 because with recap accounting there is no partial asset write-up as there is with part-purchase accounting. Recap accounting's impact on T's book net worth should be considered in negotiating the financial covenants in T's new debt agreements.

By contrast, under the rules discussed in ¶¶1703.3.1 through 1703.3.5, T would have been subjected to part-purchase accounting. However, where the test for recap accounting is satisfied, the part-purchase rules are not applicable.

Once T has engaged in a recap accounting transaction (which involves redemption of T stock), T would generally not thereafter qualify for pooling accounting treatment (either as a target or as an acquiring corporation) for at least two years, because of the pooling prohibition on a prior redemption.

There are two additional circumstances (discussed in ¶1703.3.7 and ¶1703.3.8) where recapitalization accounting may apply although T's old shareholders do not retain a significant (or indeed any) continuing interest in recapitalized T's common equity: *First*, recap accounting generally applies where T has publicly held debt or publicly held preferred stock outstanding prior to and independent of the recapitalization and such public debt or preferred stock remains outstanding after the recapitalization. *Second*, SEC has approved recap accounting where at least one of the new investors purchasing a significant stake in T's recapitalized equity as part of the LBO is "independent" of the investors sponsoring the recap transaction.

¶1703.3.6.2 *Use of Transitory MergerCo*

In some LBOs the new shareholders form a transitory new entity ("Transitory MergerCo" or "TMC") for purposes of merging Transitory MergerCo into T and forcing T's shareholders to accept the consideration specified in the merger agreement in exchange for their T stock.

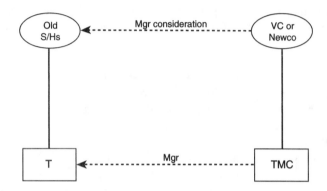

Despite the formation of Transitory MergerCo, the transaction can still qualify for recap accounting, although for some extremely murky reasons some accountants apparently take the position that recap accounting will not apply if the amount of money flowing through Transitory MergerCo to T's old shareholders is more than 50% of T's pre-merger stock FV, i.e., where, in accounting parlance, the merger transaction results in a change of T's control.

Thus, recap accounting (1) is apparently precluded in the view of some accountants where a substantial portion of the money flowing to T's old shareholders (more than 50% of T's pre-merger stock FV) is funded into Transitory MergerCo (by the new shareholders and lenders), but (2) is apparently not precluded in such accountants' view where all or a sufficient portion of the money for T's old shareholders is funded directly into T (by the new shareholders and lenders), i.e., not funded through Transitory MergerCo, so that the cash they receive from Transitory MergerCo constitutes 50% or less of their pre-merger T stock FV. In the latter situation, returning once again to accounting parlance, the merger transaction (meaning the money flowing through Transitory MergerCo) did not result in a change of T's control, rather the money funded directly into T (without passing through Transitory MergerCo) caused the change in T's control.

A second group of accountants takes the view that use of Transitory MergerCo does not preclude recap accounting, even where more than 50% (or even all) of the transaction consideration flows through Transitory MergerCo. These accountants adopt a position similar to the income tax law and ignore the existence of Transitory MergerCo because it is transitory and used merely as a mechanism to effect the T recapitalization.

A third group of accountants takes the view that use of Transitory MergerCo does not preclude recap accounting so long as (1) Transitory MergerCo is used solely as a mechanism to force, through a state law merger, all of T's shareholders to participate in the recapitalization transaction and (2) Transitory MergerCo serves no other business purpose. These accountants generally allow the new shareholders' equity money to flow through Transitory MergerCo, but believe that recap accounting is precluded if Transitory MergerCo borrows any of the debt financing required in the recapitalization.

In 4/00, SEC staff informally enunciated a view resembling that of the third group of accountants—i.e., that use of a Transitory MergerCo in a recap transaction is permissible only if the Transitory MergerCo lacks "substance" and that "substance" is generally present—thus precluding recap accounting—if Transitory MergerCo borrows a portion of the acquisition debt. SEC's position may be evolving and hence some accountants now advise it is desirable for Transitory MergerCo to incur no debt and receive only a nominal amount of the equity financing.

EXAMPLE 2

Same as Example 1, except that (1) T's 100 common shares are owned by 10 persons (individuals A through J), not all of whom will voluntarily participate in the redemption (step d in Example 1), and (2) VC forms Transitory MergerCo to force all 10 old T shareholders to participate, by undertaking the following steps:

(a) VC forms Transitory MergerCo and invests $28 in Transitory MergerCo in exchange for Transitory MergerCo stock,

(b) Bank lends $70 to Transitory MergerCo,

(c) Transitory MergerCo merges into T.

Pursuant to the merger terms, 98% of each old T share is converted into cash, so that T's 10 old shareholders end up receiving $98 cash (previously held by Transitory MergerCo) and continuing to own 2 T shares (20% of T's post-recap shares). Pursuant to the merger terms, VC's stock in Transitory MergerCo is converted into $20 liquidation value of T's non-convertible preferred and 8 new shares of T common stock (80% of T's post-recap common shares).

Although the transaction described in this Example 2 reaches the same economic result as the transaction described in Example 1, one group of accountants takes the position that this Example 2 transaction does not qualify for recap accounting because (1) the parties used a Transitory MergerCo *and* (2) the amount of money flowing through Transitory MergerCo to T's old shareholders is more than 50% (here 98%) of T's pre-merger stock FV. A second group of accountants ignores Transitory MergerCo's existence and supports recap accounting on these facts. A third group of accountants (and possibly SEC) takes the position that recap accounting is unavailable on these facts because Transitory MergerCo borrowed a portion of the debt financing used in the transaction.

EXAMPLE 3

Same as Example 2, except that only a portion of the $98 of new debt and equity financing flows through Transitory MergerCo (amounting to 50% or less of T's pre-merger stock by FV) and the remainder flows directly into T, in particular:

(a) VC forms Transitory MergerCo and invests $28 in Transitory MergerCo in exchange for Transitory MergerCo stock,
(b) Bank lends $20 to Transitory MergerCo,
(c) Bank lends $50 directly to T,
(d) Transitory MergerCo merges into T.

Pursuant to the merger terms 98% of each old T share is converted into cash, so that T's 10 old shareholders end up (1) receiving $98 cash ($48 funded through Transitory MergerCo and $50 funded directly into T) and (2) continuing to own 2 shares (20% of T's post-recap shares).

Although the transaction described in this Example 3 reaches the same economic result as the transaction described in Example 2, the first group of accountants who rejected recap accounting for the transaction described in Example 2 (because more than 50% of the money flowed through Transitory MergerCo) generally advises that this LBO transaction should qualify for recap accounting (because the money flowing through Transitory MergerCo to T's old shareholders does not exceed 50% of T's pre-merger stock FV). The second group of accountants (that ignores Transitory MergerCo and supports recap accounting in Example 2) also ignores Transitory MergerCo in Example 3 and supports recap accounting. The third group of accountants (and possibly SEC) takes the position that recap accounting is unavailable on these facts because Transitory MergerCo borrowed a portion of the debt financing used in the transaction. This group of accountants would support recap accounting on these facts if all $70 of bank financing were borrowed by T and only the new equity flowed through Transitory MergerCo.

¶1703.3.6.3   Use of Newco to Acquire T

(1) Partnership or LLC Newco. A transaction may qualify for recap accounting even where the new shareholders form a permanent new entity ("Newco") to hold their T stock. If such a Newco is formed, it will frequently be a partnership or LLC (i.e., a flow-through entity for tax purposes) so that (1) Newco can be dissolved tax free or (2) if Newco has not previously dissolved, there will be no federal income tax at the Newco level when Newco sells its T stock.

Newco should in most cases not be formed as a corporation because (i) Newco will be subject to corporate-level tax on its gain from selling T stock (e.g.) to the public and (ii) a sale of Newco stock to the public (which would avoid Newco corporate-level tax on Newco's gain in its T stock) would not benefit from recap accounting because Newco is required to use purchase accounting at the Newco level for its interest in T.

(2) Subsequent elimination of corporate Newco. Where there are reasons to form Newco as a corporation (e.g., if T's new shareholders wish to acquire T and make a Code §338(h)(10) election to obtain tax SUB in T's assets—see ¶1703.3.6.10), the question arises whether Newco can later be eliminated in a tax-free transaction, avoiding corporate-level tax on Newco's gain in its T stock, with T retaining its recap accounting.

(3) Newco-Target merger. A simple upstream or downstream merger of Newco and T some time after T's recap would eliminate Newco corporate-level tax on Newco's gain in its T stock. However, such a merger would (in the view of the accounting profession) eliminate the benefits of recap accounting (even where such merger occurs after T goes public), because where Newco owns more than 50% of T's common stock when Newco and T merge (either upstream or downstream), Newco would be viewed as the surviving entity for accounting purposes, regardless of the legal form of the merger (i.e., even if T was the surviving entity). Accordingly, Newco's higher accounting basis in its percentage interest in T would survive, effectively forcing push-down purchase accounting on T.[54]

(4) Corporate downstream "C" or "D." In contrast, if Newco is formed as a corporation and is later eliminated in a downstream "C" or "D" reorganization (not carried out under a state law merger statute), T should continue to qualify for recap accounting because accountants generally view a downstream "C" or "D" reorganization as a mere dissolution of Newco (since Newco corporation is dissolved for state corporate law purposes after exchanging its assets (i.e., the T stock owned by Newco) for new T stock, even though for income tax purposes, a downstream "C" or "D" reorganization is treated as a tax-free combination of T and Newco).

(5) LLC downstream "C" or "D." We understand SEC has informally stated it would allow recap accounting for a transaction using a variation of the corporate downstream "C" or "D" structure described above. Under this variation, Newco is formed as an LLC but elects to be taxed as a corporation under IRS's check-the-box regulations (generally so that Newco can make a Code §338(h)(10) election with respect to its acquisition of T). After a sufficient wait, Newco exchanges its old T stock for new T shares and Newco "unchecks" the box, i.e., elects to be taxed as a partnership. Newco treats its transformation for tax purposes from a corporation to a partnership (i.e., the deemed liquidiation for tax purposes of Newco

---

[54] Furthermore, it is possible that the interest formerly held by T's minority shareholders would be revalued using purchase accounting rules at the time of the merger (i.e., treated as if the minority interest were purchased by Newco).

"corporation" into Newco partnership) and Newco's exchange of old T stock for new T stock as a downstream "C" or "D" reorganization of Newco "corporation" into T. After this deemed liquidation of Newco "corporation," Newco is a partnership for tax purposes and can sell T stock in a public offering without corporate-level tax.

Many accountants believe this LLC downstream "C" or "D" variation is more desirable from an accounting standpoint than the corporate downstream "C" or "D" approach described above (where Newco is actually a corporation liquidated as part of a downstream "C" or "D" reorganization). This is because some accountants believe that where Newco is a corporation, there is risk SEC might view Newco corporation's actual liquidation during the non-merger downstream "C" or "D" reorganization as the equivalent of a Newco-T combination (resulting in loss of T's recap accounting) rather than as a mere Newco dissolution. In contrast, where Newco is an LLC which unchecks the box (so that it continues to exist as an LLC without change for state law purposes), there should be little or no SEC/accounting issue.

¶1703.3.6.4   *Nature of Old T Shareholder Retained Equity Interest*

As described in ¶1703.3.6.1 above, recap accounting may apply even if T's old shareholders do not own (after the LBO) more than 20% of T's common equity, but rather in some cases may apply even if they own slightly more than 5%, with qualification for recap accounting where the old T shareholders' ownership is in the gray zone (more than 5% but not more than 20%) presenting a factual issue.[55]

(1)   Old T shareholders not part of collaborative group with new T investors. A 4/01 SEC Staff Announcement stated that "it is appropriate to aggregate the holdings of those investors who *both* 'mutually promote' the acquisition and 'collaborate' on the subsequent control of the investee company (the collaborative group)."[56] Under this standard, "a member of a collaborative group would be any investor that helps to consummate the acquisition and works or cooperates with the subsequent control of the acquired company." The Announcement also adopts "a rebuttable presumption . . . that any investor investing at the same time as or in reasonable proximity to the time others invest in the investee is part of the collaborative group with the other investor(s)."

---

[55] Recapitalization accounting may also apply in two circumstances where T's old shareholders do not retain a significant (or indeed any) continuing interest in recapitalized T's common equity. *First*, recapitalization accounting generally applies where T has publicly held debt or publicly held preferred stock outstanding prior to and independent of the recapitalization and such public debt or preferred stock remains outstanding after the recapitalization. See ¶1703.3.7. *Second*, SEC has approved recap accounting where at least one of the new investors purchasing a significant stake in T's recapitalized equity as part of the LBO is "independent" of the investors sponsoring the recap transaction. See ¶1703.3.8.

[56] SEC Staff Announcement, Topic D-97—Push Down Accounting (2001). Emphasis in original.

Although the Announcement focuses primarily on the circumstances in which recap accounting is permissible after a 100% change in T's stock ownership,[57] it also states "[p]reexisting, or rollover, investors should be evaluated for inclusion in the collaborative group on the same basis as new investors." Thus, if old T shareholders are viewed as part of a "collaborative group" with new T investors, their retained T equity will apparently not be counted toward the significant retained interest test.

The 4/01 Staff Announcement contains a detailed (although non-exhaustive) list of factors SEC reviews in determining whether an investor is viewed as part of a collaborative group, divided into four categories: whether the investor is independent of the other investors, whether the investor shares the risks and rewards of ownership on the same basis as other investors, whether the investor is involved in promoting the investment to other parties, and whether the investor collaborates in T's post-recap control.

It is not clear how SEC will apply the definition of "collaborative group" to old T shareholders rolling over (i.e., retaining) part (or all) of their T common stock. Because old T shareholders made their investment in T prior to the recapitalization, old T shareholders are, by definition, more independent than new investors. Moreover, for the same reason, old T continuing shareholders should escape the "rebuttable presumption" (persons investing in reasonable proximity to each other presumably are a collaborative group) discussed above. However, even without the presumption, old T continuing shareholders are subjected to the mutually-promote and the collaborate-on-control tests. The 4/01 Staff Announcement's concept of "collaborative group" appears to be very broad and its application to old T shareholders may narrow significantly T's ability to obtain recap accounting.

The 4/01 Staff Announcement "should be applied prospectively to transactions initiated after April 19, 2001."

(2) T voting common stock. In determining whether T's old shareholders have retained the requisite continuing common equity in T (i.e., in applying the more than 5% to 20% continuing common equity test), the principal measurement is the percentage of T's post-recapitalization voting common equity owned by T's old shareholders on account of their ownership of T's pre-recapitalization common equity.

Although the written rules are silent, other types of voting stock with common-like features retained by T's old shareholders logically should count toward the requisite retained equity interest, for example, voting participating preferred stock with common-like participation features (particularly where preferred and common stock have been amalgamated into one instrument). Voting convertible preferred stock may also count. However, there is little indication of SEC's view on these types of stock. See ¶1703.3.6.4(8) below for a discussion of the possibility that the FV of the old T shareholder retained equity interest must also constitute

---

[57] See ¶1703.3.8 for a discussion of the 4/01 SEC Staff Announcement where the recapitalization involves a 100% change in T's equity ownership.

more than 5% of the aggregate FV of Target's post-recap common and preferred stock equity.

(3) T stock options. The treatment of unexercised vested options held by old T shareholders—both pre-recapitalization and post-recapitalization—is unclear, i.e., it is not clear whether unexercised vested options held by old T shareholders before the recapitalization *or* held by old T shareholders after the recapitalization *or* held at both times can be counted to create the more than 5% to 20% requisite continuing common equity.

However, if old T shareholders exercise their previously held vested options before the recapitalization transaction, the stock they receive on exercise can be counted toward the requisite continuing common equity if it is retained as T stub common stock. However, accountants believe it unlikely that newly purchased T common stock (retained as T stub common stock) may be counted if it is purchased pursuant to unvested options that are vested in anticipation of the transaction or pursuant to new options granted in anticipation of the transaction.

(4) Newly purchased T stock. Additional T shares purchased as part of the recapitalization transaction by an old T shareholder may constitute a favorable factor for determining qualification for recapitalization accounting where the level of continuing common ownership is in the more than 5% to 20% gray zone. Most accountants, however, recommend against relying on such purchased equity in order to reach the desired threshold of retained ownership.

EXAMPLE 4

A owns 4,950 shares of T common stock (FV $4,950) and B owns 50 shares (FV $50). In the recap transaction, VC purchases 425 shares of T common stock for $425, together with $1,000 of T debt-like preferred stock. B retains his 50 T shares and purchases an additional 25 shares for $25. T borrows $3,500 from an unrelated bank. T redeems all of A's T stock for $4,950.

B is only a 10% continuing shareholder for recap accounting purposes, but the additional 5% of T's shares purchased by B in the recapitalization transaction may be a favorable factor in determining whether the transaction qualifies for recap accounting.

Where an old T common shareholder is paid in cash for his old T stock but as part of the recap transaction reinvests all or a portion of the proceeds in new T shares, logic would suggest that such new T shares (up to the percentage of T's post-recap common shares such old T shareholder would have retained if his old T common shares had not been paid off in cash in the recapitalization) should be counted as continuing common equity. However, it is not clear whether this result will be accepted by accountants and SEC, since the reinvestment by an old T common shareholder may be viewed as a separate investment decision rather than as a continuing common equity interest, thereby precluding recap accounting treatment.

EXAMPLE 5

Same as Example 4, except that (1) in the recapitalization transaction B is paid in cash for his 50 old T common shares (which constituted 1% of T's pre-recap common shares), (2) as part of the recapitalization transaction B reinvests all of the proceeds to purchase new T common shares, and (3) B does not purchase any additional shares, so that after the recapitalization transaction B owns 10% of T's outstanding common stock, the same percent of T's post-recap common shares as B would have held if B had not been paid off in cash for his 50 old T shares.

It is not clear whether B is a 10% continuing shareholder for recap accounting purposes.

However, newly purchased T shares would appear to fall within the rebuttable presumption discussed in (1) above.

(5)   Restrictions on retained equity interest. If the old T shareholders' continuing equity interest in T is subject to significant restrictions (e.g., imposed under a shareholders' agreement, call option, etc.) which tend to eliminate the old T shareholders' ability either to control their continuing stake or to realize the economic benefits and burdens of its ownership, it is possible that the old T shareholders' retained equity will not count toward the continuing common ownership threshold needed for recap accounting. A 4/01 SEC Staff Announcement, effective for transactions initiated after 4/19/01, states that old T shareholders rolling over equity in the recapitalization of T must be tested to determine whether they are part of a "collaborative group" with T's new investors.[58] If an old T shareholder is part of the "collaborative group," that shareholder's retained T stock cannot be counted toward the significant retained interest required for recap accounting.

Voting agreements. As discussed above, the old T shareholders' continuing interest in T must carry the right to vote in order to constitute a significant retained equity stake in T. Any agreement requiring the old T shareholders to vote their post-recap T stock as directed by T's new investors would likely disqualify the old T shareholders' retained stock so that it would not count toward recap accounting.

In contrast, there should be no adverse impact on recap accounting if T's new investors merely agree to vote for a specified number of nominees to T's board selected by the old T shareholders, without placing any restrictions on the old T shareholders' right to vote their own stock. Such an agreement would strengthen the voting power of the old T shareholders' stock, not reduce or eliminate it.

---

[58] SEC Staff Announcement, Topic D-97—Push Down Accounting (2001). See ¶1703.3.6.4(1) and ¶1703.3.8 for a detailed discussion of the 4/01 Staff Announcement.

Most accountants believe that a mutual voting agreement requiring T's new investors and the old T shareholders to vote for a specified number of each other's board nominees should not adversely affect T's recap accounting, so long as old T's shareholders are entitled to select a percentage of the board nominees approximately equal to their percentage ownership of T stock. Such an agreement merely insures that the old T shareholders' ownership of voting stock translates into board representation. The agreement of old T shareholders to vote for the new investors' board nominees constitutes a quid pro quo for the new investors' promise to vote for the old T shareholders' nominees and hence should not be viewed as a limitation that reduces the old T shareholders' voting power. Some accountants, however, have expressed concern (misplaced in our view) that any limitation on the right of old T shareholders freely to vote their stock—even a limitation established by a mutual voting agreement—creates risk such stock may be viewed as non-voting for recap accounting purposes.

The 4/01 SEC Staff Announcement states that the following factors (among many others) would be favorable factors in showing that an investor is not part of a collaborative group:

- "The investor is free to exercise its voting rights in any and all share-holder votes."
- "The investor does not have disproportionate or special rights that other investors do not have, such as a guaranteed seat(s) on the investee's board, required supermajority voting rights for major or significant corporate decisions, guaranteed consent rights over corporate actions, . . . and so forth."

These two favorable factors suggest that (1) an arrangement guaranteeing old T shareholders a board seat (or similar rights) or (2) a mutual voting agreement would be viewed as a negative factor at least suggesting the old T shareholder was part of a collaborative group with new T investors.

Drag-along and tag-along rights. T's new investors often desire an agreement from old T shareholders (and from any other T shareholders) to sell their T stock when the new investors sell their T stock (on the same terms and conditions as the new investors' sale). Most accountants believe a reasonable "drag-along" obligation should not prevent recap accounting.

Some accountants, however, are concerned that a drag-along obligation (particularly when coupled with transfer restrictions preventing old T shareholders from selling their stock in other circumstances) may reduce the ability of old T shareholders to control their retained stock and/or realize its economic benefits sufficiently so that the underlying stock may not count toward recap accounting. For these accountants, the form of the drag-along agreement may be important, so that an agreement obligating all shareholders to participate in a sale approved by a specified majority of shareholders as a group (with each shareholder retaining the right to vote for or against the sale) may be less troublesome than an agreement obligating the old T shareholders simply to follow the new investors' decision on whether to sell or not.

Tag-along rights, giving old T shareholders the right (but not the obligation) to participate in a sale of T stock arranged by T's new investors, enhance the rights of old T shareholders and should generally not create any recap accounting problems.

The 4/01 SEC Staff Announcement states "[p]ut options, call options, tag-along rights, and drag-along rights should be carefully evaluated. They may act to limit an investor's risk and rewards of ownership, effective voting rights, or ability to sell its investee shares." Drag-along rights may force old T rollover shareholders to sell, cutting off their ownership rights, and, depending on how the drag-along rights are drafted, could prevent old T shareholders from voting against a sale of T advocated by new investors. SEC's interest in tag-along rights is less clear, although SEC may be concerned that tag-along rights could limit an old T continuing shareholder's ability to sell its retained T shares, by allowing new investors to tag along on the old T shareholder's sale. Of course, both tag-along rights and drag-along rights represent some degree of cooperation and coordination between old and new T shareholders.

In discussing transfer restrictions in general, the 4/01 Staff Announcement states that transfer restrictions "provided by securities laws or by what is reasonable and customary in individually negotiated investment transactions for closely held companies (for example, a right of first refusal held by the investee on the investor's shares in the event of a bona fide offer from a third party)" are not to be considered a factor suggesting collaborative group membership. Thus, because drag-along and tag-along rights are customary features for investments in closely held companies, they should not cause a problem if properly drafted and of normal scope.

Transfer restrictions. Some accountants believe extensive transfer restrictions on old T shareholders' retained stock (e.g., a blanket prohibition on sales by old T shareholders other than in connection with a sale of T by all shareholders) may prevent their stock from counting toward recap accounting. Accountants who take this view generally suggest that old T shareholders must, at a minimum, have the right to sell their retained T stock with T's or the new investors' consent which will not be unreasonably withheld.

The 4/01 SEC Staff Announcement states as a factor supporting the view that an investor is not part of a collaborative group that "[t]he investor's ability to sell its investee shares is not restricted, except as provided by securities laws or by what is reasonable and customary in individually negotiated investment transactions for closely held companies (for example, a right of first refusal held by the investee on the investor's shares in the event of a bona fide offer from a third party)."

(6)   Value of retained equity interest. If the value of recapitalized T's common stock is reduced by leverage (i.e., where T issues T debt or T debt-like preferred stock to fund redemptions of T stock), old T shareholders who retain a stub percentage of common equity in T do not have to leave behind a similar percentage of their pre-recap T equity value. Thus, for example, a 1% or 2% stake in pre-recap T could be worth 10% - 15% of post-recap T.

As an economic matter, however, new investors may insist that old T shareholders retain a strip of T securities, including both less desirable (i.e., lower potential return) subordinated debt or debt-like preferred stock and more desirable (i.e., higher potential return) "cheap" common stock.

Receipt of subordinated debt by old T shareholders in a Code §368(a)(1)(E) recapitalization exchange for old T common stock is taxable boot. See ¶1703.3.6.10 below for a discussion of the possibility that the receipt of T preferred stock (constituting NQ Pfd) in an exchange is taxable boot.

EXAMPLE 6

A owns all 5,000 shares of T's outstanding common stock (aggregate FV $5,000). T engages in a recapitalization transaction as follows: T borrows $3,500 from an unrelated bank. VC purchases 395 shares of T common stock for $395 and $1,000 of T debt-like preferred stock. T redeems 4,895 shares of T stock from A for $4,895. A retains 105 shares of T common stock (FV $105).

The transaction should qualify for recap accounting. A has retained 21% of T's post-recap common stock (105 out of 500 post-recap shares), even though this stock has a $105 FV or approximately 2% of the FV of T's pre-recap common stock.

EXAMPLE 7

Same as Example 6, except that (1) before the recapitalization A owns 4,950 shares of T stock (FV $4,950) and B owns 50 shares (FV $50), (2) in the recap transaction VC purchases 450 newly issued T common shares for $450, together with $1,000 of T debt-like preferred stock, and T redeems all of A's T stock for $4,950, while B retains his 50 T shares.

B's 50 T shares represented 1% of T's pre-recap common stock and represent 10% of T's post-recap common stock. The transaction falls in the gray zone and qualification for recap accounting is a factual question. However, as noted above, as of this writing, accounting firms will in many cases support recap accounting where T's old shareholders retain a 10% post-recap stake.

EXAMPLE 8

Same as Example 6, except that (1) VC insists that A exchange a portion of his 5,000 T common stock for T preferred stock so that, after the recap, A holds a "strip" of T common and preferred in the same proportions (here a 1 to 2 ratio of common to preferred) as VC, (2) VC purchases 395 shares of T common stock for $395 and $790 of T debt-like preferred stock, (3) A exchanges 210 T common shares for $210 of new T debt-like preferred,[59] A retains 105 T common shares, and T redeems 4,685 T common shares from A for cash.

A holds 21% of the T common stock after the recap (105 shares out of 500) and the transaction should qualify for recap accounting. A's post-recap T common and preferred stock has an FV of $315 ($105 of T common stock and $210 of T preferred stock) or 6.3% of the value of A's pre-recap T common stock.

See ¶1703.3.6.4(8) for a discussion of the possibility that the FV of the old T shareholders' retained equity interest must constitute more than 5% of the aggregate FV of T's post-recap common and preferred stock equity. If there is such a requirement, it may not be satisfied where T's new investors purchase newly-issued T common stock and preferred stock while old T shareholders retain or acquire less than a pro rata portion of T's post-recap preferred stock.

(7) New investors' ownership of T warrants or convertibles. Whether T's old shareholders retain a sufficiently large percentage of T's post-recap common equity is generally determined on a fully diluted basis, so that the test is failed where the new T shareholders (or certain persons considered to be closely associated with T or T's new shareholders) receive warrants or convertibles, either at the time of the recap transaction or later (but prior to T's becoming a public company), which would, if exercised, dilute T's old shareholders below the level of a significant stake.

(8) New investors' ownership of T preferred stock. Whether T's old shareholders retain a sufficiently large equity stake in T is generally determined based on their percentage ownership of T's post-recap voting common stock. However, if T's new investors purchase T preferred stock with voting rights or conversion or other participation features (including a coupon rate significantly exceeding market rate), such T preferred stock is generally taken into account in measuring the size of the old T shareholders' retained interest.

Where T's new investors purchase newly issued T common and debt-like preferred stock (i.e., preferred stock that is non-voting, non-convertible, and non-participating), some accountants take the position that the FV of T stub common stock retained by old T shareholders (together with the FV of any T preferred stock retained by old T shareholders or acquired by them in the recapitalization in exchange for pre-recap T common stock) must exceed 5% of recapitalized T's aggregate common and preferred stock FV.[60] This additional requirement—if

---

[59] If the T preferred stock is T NQ Pfd, A will recognize gain on the exchange of T common stock for T preferred stock. See ¶1703.3.6.10 for a discussion of this risk. See ¶604.3 for a general discussion of NQ Pfd.

[60] Accountants taking this view may be willing to ignore debt-like preferred stock issued to a new investor who does not participate in controlling T, e.g., an unrelated mezzanine investor purchasing preferred stock in the recapitalization.

actually part of recap accounting standards—is generally satisfied if old T share-holders retain or acquire a pro rata portion of T's preferred stock along with their retained T stub common stock, but may not be met if old T shareholders retain or acquire less than a pro rata portion of T's preferred stock.

Other accountants believe that where the FV of recapitalized T's common stock in the aggregate is significant in relation to the FV of recapitalized T's debt-like preferred stock, the new investors' preferred stock need not be taken into account in measuring the old T shareholders' retained interest.

¶1703.3.6.5   Effect on P's or Newco's Financial Statements

Where a change in T's stock ownership qualifies for recap accounting but one of T's new shareholders (P or Newco) is an entity owning sufficient T stock so that P or Newco must account for its T stock investment on the equity method of accounting (generally where P or Newco owns 20% or more of T's voting power) or on the consolidated method of accounting (generally where P or Newco owns more than 50% of T's voting power), P (or Newco) must use purchase accounting principles in preparing its financial statements, even though T can use recap accounting in preparing its separate financial statements.

Thus, even where T qualifies for the recap method and hence no goodwill or other accounting basis step-up is reflected on T's financial statements, P (or Newco) (which owns 20% or more of T's voting power and hence utilizes either the equity or consolidated method of accounting for T) must, in calculating P's (or Newco's) net income (1) depreciate or amortize P's (or Newco's) share of the P-level (or Newco-level) accounting basis step-up in T's tangible assets and intangible assets other than goodwill and (2) write off (or down) P's (or Newco's) share of the P-level (or Newco-level) accounting basis step-up in T's goodwill that becomes "impaired." See ¶1703.2.2 for an example of the manner by which P (or Newco) calculates its net income where it accounts for its investment in T on the equity method.

¶1703.3.6.6   Recap Accounting Uncertainties

The guidelines used to determine whether T qualifies for recap accounting are the same as the test used by SEC to determine whether T can avoid push-down purchase accounting discussed at ¶1703.2.3, i.e., where a recapitalization of T results in such a substantial change in T's ownership that push-down purchase accounting would apply to T, recap accounting generally will not apply to T.

Determining whether a transaction qualifies for recap accounting is not without complexities. Recap accounting rules are not extensively—in truth, are only mini-mally—spelled out in SEC staff rules. Thus, application to varying circumstances is necessarily subject to substantial judgment and accounting firms at times dis-agree on the rules' application to specific circumstances. SEC staff generally dis-likes recap accounting. Hence, SEC staff will generally examine T's recap accounting when T goes public and may challenge T's recap accounting if it disagrees with T's use of recap accounting.

Moreover, there is risk SEC might in the future limit or eliminate recap accounting altogether. Such a change could be effective for a T that was not public at the time of the change, even though a previous acquisition of T (completed before the change) was structured to obtain recap accounting.

Although not entirely clear, it is likely that T's public offering of debt will "lock-in" T's recap accounting so that a later change in SEC policy should not require T to use purchase accounting for its earlier LBO, even if T has not yet had a public stock offering.

FASB Update

FASB has stated that it will review recap accounting as part of its ongoing project regarding accounting for business combinations, creating additional uncertainty regarding the future of recap accounting. By analogy to FASB's 7/01 decision in FASB Statement 141 to abolish pooling of interests accounting prospectively, we believe that any change to current recap accounting rules should apply only to transactions occurring after final FASB rules are published. See ¶1703 Update for a discussion of the FASB business combinations project. See ¶¶1703.2 and 1703.4 for a discussion of 7/01 FASB Statement 141.

¶1703.3.6.7 Effect of Post-LBO Events on Recap Accounting

If, after an LBO of T structured to achieve recap accounting but before recapitalized T becomes public, T or the new investors purchase all or part of the old T shareholders' continuing equity stake in recapitalized T, so that the old T shareholders cease to have a significant continuing equity stake in recapitalized T, T will be required to use purchase accounting, i.e., T's earlier recap will be disqualified. This is true even if the purchase from the old T shareholders occurs a number of years after the LBO and is not part of a plan in existence at the time of the LBO.

In contrast, purchase accounting should not be required if the old T shareholders sell all or a portion of their continuing T equity stake to buyers other than T or the new investors who led the LBO (or to certain persons considered to be closely associated with T or the new investors).

If, after the LBO but before recapitalized T becomes public, T issues additional stock or options that dilute the old T shareholders' continuing equity stake so that it is no longer significant, T may be required to use purchase accounting if the additional stock or options are issued to the new investors that led the LBO (or to certain persons closely associated with T or the new investors).

Once T becomes public (with either publicly traded equity or publicly traded debt), subsequent events should not eliminate T's ability to use recap accounting for the LBO.

¶1703.3.6.8   *Structuring for Recap Accounting Where T's*
              Shareholders Numerous or Recalcitrant

Where T's shareholders are numerous or recalcitrant so that a redemption of
T shares can not be accomplished consensually, a transaction qualifying for recap
accounting can nevertheless be structured as outlined below.

Pro-rata recap by forced merger. Where T's shareholders are numerous or recalcitrant and all of T's shareholders are to be treated identically, a recapitalization
can still be accomplished through a merger of Transitory MergerCo into T, in which
the consideration to T's shareholders is cash and stub shares in recapitalized T.

As an alternative, the old T shareholders can be given the option to elect to
take stub shares in recapitalized T or to take cash. However, if an insufficient
number of old T shareholders elect to take stub shares, other T shareholders must
take stub shares in recapitalized T in the amount necessary to qualify for recap
accounting treatment. And if too many old T shareholders elect to take T stub
shares, a proration mechanism must be in place to apportion the T stub shares
among the old T shareholders electing continuing T stock.

Non-Pro-Rata Recap. In many circumstances, VC (or other new investor) desires
only certain old T shareholders to continue as shareholders of recapitalized T
(e.g., members of T's management). In the event that this cannot be accomplished
by a consensual non-pro-rata redemption, there are alternative methods to accomplish this objective.

Alternative #1—Front-end T recapitalization. T's shareholders vote to authorize
a new class of equity securities (the "New Class") which are issued in a voluntary
stock swap to those old T shareholders (in exchange for a portion of their old T
common stock) who are to retain T stub common shares. Immediately thereafter,
Transitory MergerCo merges into T, with the holders of the New Class receiving
T stub common stock and the remaining old T shareholders receiving cash. An
old T shareholder who is to receive part cash and part T stub common stock
exchanges only a portion of his old T common stock for the New Class (i.e., makes
such exchange only to the extent he is to receive T stub common stock).

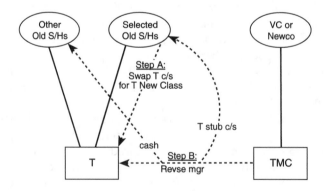

Alternative #2—Front-end TMC swap. An old T shareholder who is to retain T stub common shares contributes T common shares to Transitory MergerCo in exchange for stock in Transitory MergerCo. Transitory MergerCo then merges into T, with Transitory MergerCo stock being exchanged for T stub common stock and the remaining T stock not held by Transitory MergerCo being redeemed for cash. An old T shareholder who is to receive part cash and part T stub common stock exchanges only a portion of his old T common stock for Transitory MergerCo stock (i.e., makes such exchange only to the extent he is to receive T stub common stock).

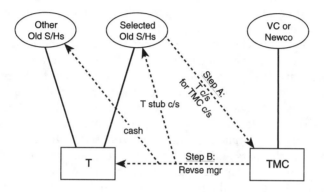

Currently, some accounting firms are more comfortable with Alternative #1 and others with Alternative #2.

Alternative #3—Merger with different consideration for different T common stockholders. The merger agreement between T and Transitory MergerCo may simply state that one group of old T shareholders is to receive cash in the merger in exchange for their T shares (generally all T shareholders other than those named in the exhibit to the merger agreement), while a second group of old T shareholders (generally those T shareholders named in an exhibit to the merger agreement), is to retain their T stub common stock (or retain their T stub common stock and also receive some cash).

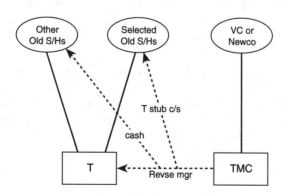

Most accounting firms are more comfortable with Alternative #3 as a method of achieving recapitalization accounting than either Alternative #1 or #2, since in Alternative #3 the old T shareholders with a continuing interest in T stub common stock simply retain their T stock and do not swap their T shares either for a new class of T stock (as in Alternative #1) or for Transitory MergerCo stock (as in Alternative #2). The concern expressed by certain accountants appears to be that if the continuing old T shareholders swap their old T stock as required under Alternative #1 or #2, they may be viewed as participating in the change of control transaction and thus aggregated with the new investors for purposes of determining whether T qualifies for recap accounting.

While Alternative #3 may have this advantage from an accounting standpoint, it may raise issues under state corporation law. Many state corporation laws traditionally have been viewed as requiring that all shareholders holding the same class of T stock must receive identical consideration in a merger. However, under Delaware law, it appears likely, although not certain, that a merger agreement, approved by the requisite majority of T's board and the requisite majority of T's shareholders, may specify that different groups of T shareholders holding the same class of T stock prior to the merger receive different consideration in the merger, so long as *inter alia* the board has exercised in good faith its fiduciary duty to all the shareholders and the merger is fair to all shareholders (generally, the shareholders in one group are receiving consideration with roughly the same FV per share as the shareholders in the other group). See Delaware General Corporation Law §251.

Where only large shareholders of T are to retain equity in recapitalized T, two additional alternatives are available.

- *Alternative #4—Front-end reverse stock split*. T does a reverse stock split (e.g., each 1,000 old T common shares are transformed into 1 new T common share), transforming each smaller shareholder's stock into a fractional share which is cashed out, thus eliminating smaller shareholders immediately before the recapitalization.
- *Alternative #5—Fractional merger exchange ratio*. Transitory MergerCo merges into T with consideration to the old T stockholders consisting of cash and a fractional share of T stub common stock (e.g., for each old T share an old T shareholder receives a specified amount of cash plus 1/1,000 of a T stub share), so that each small T stockholder receives a fractional T stub common share which is cashed out, again eliminating smaller shareholders.

In any non-pro-rata transaction, T's board of directors must ensure that the transaction is fair to all shareholders. This may require creation of a special independent committee of the board to negotiate and approve the transaction on behalf of minority shareholders and may require the retention of a financial advisor to advise the board or the special committee on the economic fairness of the transaction to all shareholders.

¶1703.3.6.9   Recap Accounting Where T Is Partnership or LLC

Recap accounting may be obtained, under the rules outlined above, where T is a partnership or LLC, if T's pre-recap equity owners (i.e., its partners or members) retain a significant continuing equity stake in T (generally by owning voting common partnership or LLC interests) after the recapitalization.

¶1703.3.6.10   Recap Accounting Tax Issues

A recap structure raises several tax issues for old T shareholders, T, and new investors.

(1)   Taxation of continuing old T shareholders. Where an old T shareholder retains a portion of his T stock and the balance is redeemed by T, the old T shareholder is entitled to CG sale treatment on the redemption only to the extent the redemption qualifies as an exchange under Code §302(a). This will generally be the case where the shareholder's percentage interest (both by vote and value) in T declines after the recapitalization. However, if an old T shareholder's percentage interest in T stays the same or increases (e.g., because the shareholder receives new equity in recapitalized T as part of its management group), such shareholder's redemption will generally not qualify under Code §302(a) for CG sale treatment and will instead be treated under Code §302(d) as a dividend to the extent of T's E&P, taxed after 2002 at a 15% top individual rate, but without basis offset or CL offset.

In contrast, Code §302 does not apply to stock sold to a person other than T or, through Code §304, a T subsidiary. Thus, if the recapitalization can be structured so that the continuing shareholder sells T stock to the new investors, such old T shareholder should be entitled to CG sale treatment, even where his continuing percentage interest in T stays the same or increases. So long as old T shareholders as a group retain the requisite amount of T stock, the sale of stock from old T shareholders to the new investors should not impact adversely on T's ability to use recap accounting. See ¶1703.3.6.1.

Where the new investors wish to hold a strip of securities different than those purchased from old T investors, the new investors may engage in a swap with T, surrendering all or a portion of the T stock purchased from old T shareholders for a different class or classes of T stock. If the swap produces Code §306 stock for the new investors, they may in some circumstances recognize on ultimate redemption or sale of the Code §306 stock dividend income taxed after 2002 at a 15% top individual rate. Such a swap may also create risk IRS could recharacterize the old T shareholder's sale to the new investors as a redemption, although post-2002 IRS's incentive so to do is limited, i.e., same 15% individual top rate for dividend or CG, but no basis or CL offset for dividend. See ¶108.

Where a continuing old T shareholder has a portion of his T stock redeemed for cash and exchanges the balance of his old shares for shares of one or more new classes of T stock, there is risk IRS could treat the cash redemption and the stock-for-stock exchange as one transaction, in which case the old T shareholder would recognize (under Code §356) all of the inherent gain in his stock (both the stock redeemed and the stock exchanged) up to the amount of the cash received, generally resulting in the recognition of more gain than if the redemption and exchange were treated as separate transactions. This risk is minimized where the recapitalization is structured so that the old T shareholders merely retain a portion of their T stock without exchanging for a new class of T stock. If the recapitalization can be structured so that the old T shareholder sells his T stock to the new investors, as described above, this Code §356 risk should generally be eliminated.

The 1997 Act treats NQ Pfd (i.e., most redeemable debt-like preferred stocks) as boot in otherwise tax-free exchanges. Where new investors want old T shareholders to roll their continuing equity stake into a "strip" of T common stock and debt-like preferred stock which constitutes NQ Pfd, the T NQ Pfd is taxable boot, triggering gain. See Example 8 in ¶1703.3.6.4. See ¶604.3 for a general discussion of NQ Pfd. This adverse tax result can be avoided in three ways:

- The T preferred stock is redesigned so that it has a significant stake in corporate growth (e.g., by amalgamating T preferred stock and T common stock together into a single instrument) and hence will not be NQ Pfd. See ¶604.3.1.1. As noted in ¶1703.3.6.4 above, this type of stock, if voting, should count toward a significant retained equity stake for recap accounting purposes, although the GAAP rules are not wholly clear.
- The T preferred stock may be re-designated so that it is evergreen (i.e., not mandatorily redeemable, puttable, or callable) and hence will not be NQ Pfd. See ¶604.3.1.2.
- The redemption, put, or call features with respect to the T preferred stock may be limited to ones which qualify for Code §351(g)(2)(C)(i)(I)'s death or disability exception or Code §351(g)(2)(C)(i)(II)'s issued-in-connection-with-services exception, so that in either case the T preferred stock will not be NQ Pfd. See ¶604.3.1.2 and ¶1403.

See ¶604.3.2 for the possibility that old T shareholders can report gain attributable to the receipt of T NQ Pfd on the installment method.

Where an old T shareholder holding vested T shares not subject to an SRF ends up holding after the recap *unvested* T shares subject to an SRF, see ¶604.1.6 for a discussion of (1) possible Code §83 OI and (2) the advisability of making a Code §83(b) election within 30 days after the recap exchange.

(2)   Tax SUB for T's assets. Recap accounting requires T to survive with T's old shareholders retaining a significant stake in recapitalized T's common equity, thereby precluding an asset purchase as a means to achieve asset SUB. Asset SUB for tax purposes can be achieved where a single corporate entity ("Newco") purchases an 80-80 amount of T's stock (i.e., a QSP) so that Newco can make a Code §338 or Code §338(h)(10) election for T (see ¶205 and ¶206), while still leaving T's old shareholders with a sufficiently significant stake in T to qualify for recap accounting.

In most cases, an asset SUB will be tax-efficient only if T is an S corporation or a subsidiary of Bigco so that a Code §338(h)(10) election can be made with a single level of tax. However, a Code §338(h)(10) election triggers gain in all of T's assets, so that (1) where T is an S corporation, old T shareholders who retain target stock will nonetheless be taxed on their full share of the gain in T's assets and (2) where T is a Bigco subsidiary, Bigco will be taxed on all of the gain in T's assets although Bigco retains some T stock.

Use of a corporate Newco to purchase T's stock—so that a Code §338(h)(10) election can be made to step up the tax basis of T's assets in a transaction structured for recap accounting—is attractive only if there is a way subsequently to eliminate Newco in a tax-free manner without forcing purchase accounting on T. As discussed in ¶1703.3.6.3 above, if Newco corporation were to remain a T shareholder (i) an unwanted corporate-level tax would be imposed on Newco when Newco sells its T stock to the public (resulting in double tax) and (ii) should Newco itself go public (owning T's stock), Newco is not entitled to recap accounting.

Eliminating corporate Newco. There are several methods for eliminating Newco corporation tax free after a sufficient wait so that Newco corporation's elimination does not jeopardize the Code §338(h)(10) election by causing Newco to be disregarded as the QSP purchaser of T's stock.

Corporate downstream "C" or "D." Eliminating of Newco corporation after a sufficient wait by a non-merger downstream "C" or "D" reorganization should accomplish this goal.

While eliminating Newco corporation by a upstream or downstream merger of Newco and T would also accomplish this tax goal, such a Newco-T merger would have the adverse result of eliminating the benefits of recap accounting (even when such merger occurs after T goes public). If Newco owns more than 50% of T's common stock and Newco and T subsequently merge (either upstream or downstream), after the merger Newco would be viewed for accounting purposes as the surviving entity so that Newco/T would generally be required to use purchase or partial purchase accounting.

Eliminating Newco corporation by a non-merger downstream "C" or "D" reorganization, on the other hand, should be treated by accountants as a mere dissolution of Newco corporation (since Newco is dissolved for state law purposes after exchanging its assets (i.e., the old T stock owned by Newco) for new T stock).

LLC downstream "C" or "D." We understand SEC has informally stated it would allow recap accounting for a transaction using a variation of the corporate downstream "C" or "D" structure described above. Under this variation, Newco is formed as an LLC but elects to be taxed as a corporation under IRS's check-the-box regulations so that it can make a Code §338(h)(10) election with respect to the Newco-T acquisition. After a sufficient wait, Newco exchanges its T stock for new T shares and Newco "unchecks" the box, i.e., elects to be taxed as a partnership. Newco and its owners treat Newco's transformation for tax purposes from a corporation to a partnership (i.e., the deemed liquidation for tax purposes of

Newco "corporation" into Newco partnership) and Newco's exchange of old T stock for new T stock as a downstream "C" or "D" reorganization of Newco "corporation" into T. After this deemed liquidation of Newco "corporation," Newco is a partnership for tax purposes and can sell T stock in a public offering without corporate-level tax.

Many accountants believe this LLC downstream "C" or "D" variation is more desirable from an accounting standpoint than the corporate downstream "C" or "D" approach described above (where Newco is actually a corporation eliminated in a downstream "C" or "D" reorganization) because Newco continues to exist, minimizing risk SEC might argue there was a Newco-T combination that would eliminate T's recap accounting. See ¶1703.3.6.3.

T partnership or LLC. Where T is a partnership or LLC, it should be possible to obtain asset SUB without double tax and without forming a corporate Newco (i) for the new investors' share of T's assets, where the new investors purchase partnership or LLC interests from T's equity owners (see Code §§754 and 743) and (ii) for gain recognized by old T equity owners on redemption of their interests (see Code §§754 and 734).

(3) Taxation of new investors. New investors in T will generally not qualify for Code §1202's 14% LTCG rate because of the substantial redemptions of T stock that take place in the recapitalization transaction.

¶1703.3.7 Recapitalization (Rather than Purchase) Accounting Where T Publicly Held Pre-Recapitalization Debt or Preferred Stock Remains Outstanding after Recapitalization

Recapitalization accounting also generally applies to the acquisition of T where (1) T continues to exist after the recapitalization *and* (2) T has publicly held debt or publicly held preferred stock outstanding prior to and independent of the recapitalization that remains outstanding after the recapitalization,[61] even if T's old shareholders do not retain a significant (or indeed any) continuing interest in recapitalized T's common equity.[62] According to SEC, the existence of T continuing, pre-recapitalization publicly held debt or preferred stock "might impact the parent's ability to control the form of [its] ownership [of T]" and hence SEC allows

---

[61] See SEC Staff Accounting Bulletin No. 54; EITF 85-21.

[62] See ¶1703.3.6 for a general discussion of (i) recap accounting for T's acquisition and (ii) qualifying for recap accounting where T's old shareholders continue to own a significant stake in T's common equity after the recapitalization. See ¶1703.3.8 for a general discussion of the possibility that T may qualify for recap accounting where at least one new independent T shareholder, not part of T's control group, acquires a significant stake in T's post-recapitalization common equity, even though there are no continuing old T shareholders and T has no pre-recapitalization publicly held debt or preferred stock that remains outstanding.

recap accounting and "generally does not insist on ... [purchase] push-down accounting in these circumstances."[63]

However, recap accounting is not supported where T's publicly held debt or preferred stock arises (1) as part of the recapitalization transaction (e.g., to finance the redemption of T common stock) or (2) only after T's recapitalization so that, for a period of time, T has no outstanding publicly held debt or preferred stock.

Although SEC accounting bulletins do not explicitly impose any such requirement, an SEC staff member stated in a 12/99 speech that SEC would support recap accounting based on T's pre-recap public debt only if the pre-recap public debt is "significant." According to the staff member, SEC applied this test to deny recap accounting in a transaction where T's pre-recap debt was not significant in either a "quantitative" sense or a "qualitative" sense:

- T's pre-recap public debt was not considered *quantitatively* significant because it "amounted to approximately 5 percent of [T's] net book value and less than 1 percent of [T's] fair value" and would have converted into approximately 1% of T's stock.
- T's pre-recap public debt was not considered *qualitatively* significant because "the debt holders had virtually no ability to control or influence the form of [P's] ownership of [T], nor did the debtholders have any consent rights regarding the buying out of the existing minority interests, issuing [T] equity, or [T] paying dividends."

It is unclear whether SEC will require that T pre-recap public debt be significant in *both* a quantitative *and* a qualitative sense or merely in *either* a quantitative *or* a qualitative sense. Although preferred stock was not mentioned by the SEC staff member, presumably the same significance requirement will apply to T's pre-recap public preferred stock.

EXAMPLE

T has 100 shares of common stock outstanding (aggregate FV $100). T also has outstanding publicly held debt issued several years ago in an unrelated financing with a remaining maturity of 3 years. VC invests $30 in T in exchange for T common stock and T issues an additional $70 of subordinated debt or preferred stock to a mezzanine fund. T uses the entire $100 cash to redeem all of the T common shares outstanding other than those shares purchased by VC in the transaction. T's publicly held debt remains outstanding.

T may use recap (rather than purchase) accounting so long as the pre-recapitalization public debt is "significant" and remains outstanding.

---

[63] SEC Staff Accounting Bulletin No. 54.

The usefulness of T pre-recapitalization public debt or preferred stock as a route to recap accounting may be limited in some instances by restrictive covenants in the public debt or preferred stock which may limit T's ability to do an LBO recapitalization while the public debt or preferred stock remains outstanding. In such case, T may need to negotiate a modification to the terms of the publicly held debt or preferred and/or a waiver of applicable debt or preferred covenants to permit the recapitalization and the holders may demand a fee for consenting to such modification or waiver. If the modification or waiver, including any consent fee paid to holders, results in a deemed extinguishment of the old debt or preferred and the deemed reissuance of new debt or preferred for GAAP purposes, the "new" publicly held debt or preferred would be considered issued in connection with the recapitalization and would therefore not support recap accounting. A 1996 FASB pronouncement in an analogous area (dealing with debt) suggests that there would be a deemed extinguishment and reissuance if, in general, the modification or waiver, including any consent fees, results in a 10% or greater change in the PV of the payments due under the instrument.[64] Even where a modification or waiver does not result in a deemed extinguishment and reissuance, there may be risk (depending on the nature of the modification or waiver) SEC could take the position that the modification or waiver taints the publicly held debt or preferred (causing it to be viewed as related to the recapitalization transaction or causing the holders to be treated as acting in concert with T or the new investors).

T will generally cease to qualify for recap accounting and be forced to apply purchase accounting if T's publicly held debt or preferred stock is repaid or redeemed after the recapitalization but before T has a common stock IPO (assuming that there is no other basis to support recap accounting). However, while not entirely clear, T's recap accounting should not be affected if T merely refinances its pre-recapitalization public debt or preferred stock with new public debt or preferred stock so that T continuously maintains either public debt or public preferred stock at all times after the recapitalization and before its common stock IPO. It is desirable that such refinancing not occur too soon after the recapitalization or SEC might assert that the refinancing was part of the recapitalization plan and force purchase accounting. Of course, T can also avoid purchase accounting on a repayment/redemption of public debt or preferred stock if T also has either (i) a sufficient pre-recapitalization-T-shareholder continuing equity interest (see ¶1703.3.6) or (ii) a new independent T shareholder (based on an SEC view outlined in ¶1703.3.8), so that T's recapitalization accounting is not dependent on the publicly held debt or preferred stock.

See ¶1703 Update for a discussion of an FASB project which is reconsidering various aspects of purchase and recapitalization accounting.

[64] See EITF 96-19, Debtor's Accounting for a Modification or Exchange of Debt Instruments.

¶1703.3.8 Recapitalization (Rather than Purchase) Accounting Where T Has Significant New Shareholder Independent of Investors Sponsoring Recap Transaction

In 1998, SEC pre-approved recapitalization accounting for a transaction in which there was a 100% change in T's equity ownership (so that there was no continuing equity interest on the part of old T shareholders) and no pre-recapitalization public debt or preferred stock remained outstanding after the recapitalization. In this transaction, as we understand it, two investors each acquired approximately 47% of T's common stock, while a third investor who was considered independent of the first two investors acquired the remaining 6% of T's common stock.

SEC did not require that the two new investors' purchase accounting be pushed down to T, because even though SEC aggregated the interests of the first two investors, they held in the aggregate only 94% of T, just short of the 95% threshold for mandatory pushdown purchase accounting. In SEC's view, the key fact was that the third investor was independent of the first two investors and thus not part of their "collaborative group." In effect, SEC focused more on whether one person or a group of persons properly aggregated flunked the 95% test for mandatory pushdown accounting than on the identity of the owner of T minority stake. See ¶1703.3.6.6 and ¶1703.2.3. Had the third investor been aggregated with the first two, T's new control group would have held 100% of T's equity and pushdown purchase accounting would have been required for T.[65]

EXAMPLE 1

VC1 and VC2 each acquire 47% of T's common equity. VC3 acquires 6% of T's common equity. VC3 is unrelated to VC1 and VC2 and does not constitute a part of VC1's and VC2's collaborative group.

Assuming VC3 is independent of VC1 and VC2, T should qualify for recap accounting under SEC's 1998 position.

EXAMPLE 2

VC acquires 94% of T's common equity. At the same time, a second investor, A, acquires the remaining 6% of T's common equity. Under SEC's reasoning described above, if A is independent of VC (i.e., not part of a

---

[65] It is also important that the independent shareholder invest in T not later than simultaneously with the new investors sponsoring the recapitalization. If the independent investor invests later than the other investors, there is a moment in time during which the other investors own 100% of T and SEC requires pushdown purchase accounting. See SEC Staff Announcement, Topic D-97—Push Down Accounting (2001).

> collaborative group with VC), T should qualify for recap accounting so long as A holds a significant stake in T's post-recapitalization equity. The rules outlined above in ¶1703.3.6.1 and ¶1703.3.6.4 should apply in determining whether A's stake is significant.

The scope of SEC's approach is not entirely clear. For example, it is not clear what factors SEC will consider in determining whether an investor is not part of a collaborative group with the new investors or instead must be aggregated with the new investors sponsoring the recapitalization.

Because the scope of this SEC approach is unclear, some accountants are advising that it is safer to base recap accounting on old T shareholders who retain a continuing equity stake in post-recapitalization T. Even under SEC's 1998 approach, a continuing interest on the part of old T shareholders may be preferable to a stake held by a new investor because it may be easier to demonstrate the required independence in the case of the old T shareholder—who acquired a T equity stake in a transaction unrelated to the recapitalization—than in the case of a new investor who invests in T at the same time as the claimed recapitalization.

During 1999 and 2000, SEC reconsidered its position on whether recap accounting is appropriate where old T's shareholders do not continue to own a significant stake in T's stock after the recapitalization. A 4/01 SEC Staff Announcement states that "it is appropriate to aggregate the holdings of those investors who *both* 'mutually promote' the acquisition and 'collaborate' on the subsequent control of the investee company (the collaborative group)."[66] Under this standard, "a member of a collaborative group would be any investor that helps to consummate the acquisition and works or cooperates with the subsequent control of the acquired company." The Announcement also adopts "a rebuttable presumption . . . that any investor investing at the same time as or in reasonable proximity to the time others invest in the investee is part of the collaborative group with the other investor(s)."

The 4/01 Staff Announcement contains a detailed (although non-exhaustive) list of factors SEC reviews in determining whether an investor is viewed as part of a collaborative group, divided into four categories: whether the investor is independent of the other investors, whether the investor shares the risks and rewards of ownership on the same basis as other investors, whether the investor is involved in promoting the investment to other parties, and whether the investor collaborates in T's post-recap control.

The 4/01 Staff Announcement considers an example in which a financial investor C formulates a plan to acquire and consolidate companies in a fragmented industry. C approaches financial investors A and B who agree to invest in C's plan. A, B, and C are substantive entities with no employee overlap. A, B, and C have previously participated in joint investments and have other material business relationships with each other. A, B, and C acquire T for cash and, after the recapitalization, T's stock is held 40% each by A and B and 20% by C. A and B

---

[66] SEC Staff Announcement, Topic D-97—Push Down Accounting (2001). Emphasis in original.

provide a "limited first-loss guarantee" to C with respect to C's investment. T's bylaws are revised so that (1) A, B, and C receive equal representation on T's board of directors (along with T's CEO and two independent directors) and (2) any significant corporate action requires unanimous approval of all investors. A, B, and C agree not to transfer their shares for 5 years; thereafter, the shares are subject to a right of first refusal in favor of the other investors and each investor holds tag-a-long rights in the event of a sale by the others.

SEC concluded that A, B, and C are a collaborative group which acquired 100% of T, so that pushdown purchase accounting is required. SEC cited the following factors as important in concluding A, B, and C are part of a single collaborative group:

- A, B, and C "acted in concert to negotiate their concurrent investments in [T], which were made pursuant to the same contract."
- The investments in T were "made in connection with a broader strategic initiative [A, B, and C] were pursuing."
- "There were a number of prior business relationships between [A, B, and C] that were material to" them.
- A and B provided a "limited first-loss guarantee" of C's investment.
- By virtue of bylaw provisions requiring unanimous investor approval of significant corporate actions, "A, B, and C were compelled to collaborate on the subsequent control of [T]."
- There are restrictions on A, B, and C's ability to transfer their shares.

By taking an expansive view of the collaborative group, the 4/01 Staff Announcement appears to narrow significantly T's ability to obtain recap accounting where there is a 100% change in T's equity ownership.[67] The 4/01 Staff Announcement "should be applied prospectively to transactions initiated after April 19, 2001."

See ¶1703 Update for a discussion of an FASB project which is reconsidering various aspects of purchase and recapitalization accounting.

¶1703.3.9   Recap of Bigco Division

As described above, T must generally survive as a legal entity to qualify the transaction for recap accounting. Thus, where the business to be acquired is a division of Bigco, rather than a Bigco corporate or LLC subsidiary, recap accounting does not apply if the new investors form Newco (whether Newco is a corpora-

---

[67] The SEC announcement may also narrow availability of recap accounting where T rollover shareholders hold a significant stake in post-recap T, since the announcement states that pre-existing T shareholders who roll over their investment in T as part of the recapitalization are to be tested to determine whether they are part of the collaborative group under the same standard applied to new investors (although rollover old T shareholders should escape the rebuttable presumption (person investing in reasonable proximity to each other presumably are a collaborative group), unless perhaps they invest new money in addition to rolling over all or a portion of their pre-existing T stake). See ¶1703.3.6.4.

tion, partnership, or LLC) to purchase Bigco's divisional assets, even where Bigco obtains a significant continuing stake in Newco.

There are, however, three possible routes to recap accounting where the target business is a Bigco division:

Route #1. If Bigco transfers the divisional assets to a newly formed subsidiary (NewSub) before beginning the sale process, Bigco and the new investors could later engage in a recap transaction in which NewSub (formerly a 100% Bigco subsidiary) survives as a legal entity. Bigco's transfer of divisional assets to New-Sub—whether a corporation, LLC, or partnership—causes no change to the accounting basis of the divisional assets and creates no goodwill, and the subsequent recapitalization of NewSub can qualify for recap accounting so long as (1) NewSub is formed before Bigco has any substantive discussions with the new investors or other potential NewSub investors and (2) the transaction meets the other requirements set forth in ¶1703.3.6 or ¶1703.3.8 (or possibly ¶1703.3.7).

On the other hand, if NewSub is formed only after Bigco has begun discussions with the new investors, most accountants take the position that recap accounting is not available on the ground that the transaction is equivalent to a sale of assets by Bigco to Newco formed by the new investors.

Route #2. If Bigco has an existing subsidiary (OldSub), not formed in connection with any discussions or transaction with the new investors, to which the assets of the target division can be transferred prior to the recap, it may be possible to structure a recapitalization of OldSub (which owns the target Bigco division) to qualify for recap accounting, even where the drop down to OldSub takes place after Bigco and the new investors begin discussing a possible transaction. Most accountants take the view that a transfer of divisional assets to OldSub (rather than to NewSub), followed by OldSub's recapitalization by the new investors, is not the equivalent of an asset sale by Bigco to a Newco established by the new investors, so that recap accounting applies if the transaction meets the other requirements set forth in ¶1703.3.6 or ¶1703.3.8 (or possibly ¶1703.3.7).

Two possible transactional complexities may arise where OldSub has preexisting assets and liabilities:

First, where OldSub is a corporation with preexisting assets not wanted by the new investors, Bigco's extraction of such unwanted OldSub assets (generally at the same time as Bigco drops down the target division to OldSub) generally triggers any inherent gain in such unwanted assets into Bigco's taxable income (as discussed further below).

Second, the new investors generally seek assurances from Bigco (in the form of representations, warranties, and indemnification) that OldSub does not have contingent liabilities from prior activities or transactions.

Route #3. If the target business is a division of an existing Bigco subsidiary (rather than a direct division of Bigco itself), an additional route to recap accounting may be available. Bigco can remove the "unwanted assets"—the assets other than the target division—from the existing subsidiary, the new investors can then acquire an interest in the existing subsidiary (which by then owns only the target division) in a traditional recapitalization described in ¶1703.3.6 or ¶1703.3.8 (or possibly ¶1703.3.7).

Unfortunately, Bigco's extraction of the unwanted assets from the existing subsidiary generally triggers any inherent gain in such unwanted assets into Bigco's taxable income when the existing subsidiary leaves Bigco's consolidated group as part of the recapitalization. However, if the recapitalization transaction is structured for tax purposes so that a Code §338(h)(10) election is made to treat the sale of the existing subsidiary's stock as a sale of its assets followed by a tax-free deemed Code §332 liquidation of the existing subsidiary into Bigco, distribution of the unwanted assets from the existing subsidiary to Bigco would generally be part of the existing subsidiary's Code §332 liquidation so that no taxable gain is recognized with respect to the unwanted assets. See ¶1703.3.6.10 for a discussion of structuring the recap of a Bigco subsidiary so that a Code §338(h)(10) election can be made.

See ¶1703 Update for a discussion of an FASB project which is reconsidering various aspects of purchase and recapitalization accounting.

¶1703.4   Pooling of Interests Accounting for Transactions Initiated Before 7/1/01

FASB Statement 141, issued in 7/01, eliminates pooling of interest accounting for transactions initiated after 6/30/01.[68] Thus, all acquisitions initiated after 6/30/01 are accounted for as purchases, unless the transaction qualifies for part-purchase accounting or recapitalization (i.e., no-purchase) accounting. See ¶1703.2 and ¶1703.3 above.

For transactions initiated prior to 7/1/01, if the combination qualifies for pooling of interests accounting treatment, P generally picks up T's assets, liabilities, and net worth at the same book values as those items had on T's financial statements, without regard to the current FV of T's assets or liabilities or the FV of the consideration P issued in exchange for T's net assets. Thus, in a pooling no new accounting goodwill is created; the accounting book value of T's property, plant, and equipment ("PP&E"), and identifiable intangibles (and thus its post-acquisition depreciation and amortization) carries over without change; and the accounting book value of T's inventory (and thus its post-acquisition cost of goods sold) carries over without change.

Moreover, in a pooling, because T's old accounting book values carry over to P without change, the costs of the acquisition (e.g., legal and accounting fees and expenses) are generally expensed in the first combined P-T post-acquisition income statement.

In addition, in a pooling P picks up T's earnings from the beginning of the year of acquisition, and if P reports its prior years' earnings and balance sheets for comparative historical purposes, P picks up T's prior years' earnings and

---

[68] FASB Statement of Financial Accounting No. 141, *Business Combinations*, ¶59(a).

balance sheet numbers. For an example of the operation of pooling accounting, see ¶1703.4.15, Example 1.

A transaction is considered "initiated" for these purposes:

> on the earlier of (1) the date that the major terms of the plan, including the ratio of exchange of stock, are announced publicly or otherwise formally made known to the stockholders of any one of the combining companies or (2) the date that stockholders of a combining company are notified in writing of an exchange offer.[69]

Thus, a transaction need not be closed, or even approved by shareholders, prior to 7/1/01 in order to be "initiated" prior to 7/1/01. However, "[a]ny alteration in the terms of the exchange in the plan of combination [after 6/30/01] constitutes initiation of a new plan of combination" and requires the use of purchase accounting.[70]

To qualify for pooling accounting treatment, an acquisition must meet, *inter alia*, all the requirements discussed below.[71]

¶1703.4.1   P Voting Stock as Principal Consideration

T's voting common shareholders must all be offered and receive only P voting common stock in exchange for their T voting common stock, except as set forth below.

(a) If P has multiple classes of common stock outstanding, T's voting common shareholders must receive P common stock with rights identical to those of the majority of P's outstanding voting common stock (i.e., the class of voting common stock that controls P).

(b) A holder of a T security that is convertible into T voting common stock and that is sufficiently in the money is treated as holding equivalent T voting common stock. A holder of a T warrant or option that is exercisable into T voting common stock is treated as holding equivalent T voting common stock, regardless of whether such warrant or option is in or out of the money. In such case, pooling rules require that the T security holder must receive either (i) P voting common stock with rights identical to those of the majority of P's outstanding voting common stock or (ii) a P security equivalent to his T security (i.e., a P warrant for a T warrant, a P option for a T option, or a P convertible for a T convertible, in each case that is exercisable/convertible into P voting common stock with rights identical to those of the majority of P's outstanding voting common stock and terms equivalent to the T security surrendered in the exchange).

---

[69] FASB Statement 141, ¶59, adopting the definition of initiated contained in APB Opinion 16, ¶46.

[70] FASB Statement 141, ¶59.

[71] See APB Opinion No. 16, ¶¶46–48; SEC Staff Accounting Bulletins 65 and 76; SEC Accounting Series Releases 130, 135, 146, and 146A; FASB Emerging Issues Task Force ("EITF"), Issues 86-10, 87-15, 87-16, 87-27, 88-26, and 90-10.

(c) There is an important exception to the requirement that P voting common stock be the sole consideration to T's voting common shareholders (and equivalents): P may pay cash or other consideration for less than 10% of T's voting common stock (or equivalents) so long as such consideration is used only (i) to pay for fractional shares and/or (ii) to purchase all the voting common stock (and equivalents) held by one or more T shareholders who do not wish to receive P stock. Thus, P voting common stock must be the principal consideration issued for T's voting common stock (and equivalents) in a pooling; cash, P debentures, P preferred stock (whether or not convertible), and other P securities (e.g., non-voting P common or P common with voting rights different from the controlling class) can be issued in exchange for only a small fraction of T's voting common stock (and equivalents) in a pooling. For a sample computation of the "10% basket," see ¶1703.4.15, Example 5.

(d) The less-than-10%-cash-and-other-consideration basket (the "10% basket") described in (c) above is reduced to the extent (i) either P or T holds "tainted treasury stock" (as described in ¶1703.4.3 below), (ii) either P or T holds any intercompany investment in the other (as described in ¶1703.4.8 below), and/or (iii) any T voting common stock remains outstanding as a minority interest (as described in (e) immediately below). For a sample computation of the "10% basket," see ¶1703.4.15, Example 5.

(e) It is permissible for a few T voting common shareholders to remain outstanding as minority interests so long as these minority interests plus the other items described in (c) and (d) do not exceed the 10% basket.

(f) A holder of T *non-voting* common stock must receive P voting common stock, although the exchange ratio for T non-voting common can be lower than the comparable exchange ratio for T voting common to take cognizance of the potentially lower value of the T non-voting common. Similarly, a holder of a T security that is convertible/exercisable into T non-voting common stock and under the rules described in (b) is treated as holding equivalent T non-voting common stock must receive either (i) P voting common stock or (ii) a P security equivalent to his T security but convertible/exercisable into P voting common stock with rights identical to those of the majority of P's outstanding voting common.

(g) A holder of T preferred stock, debentures, and the like (which are not treated as T voting common stock equivalents under the standard described in (b)) can receive cash or other consideration without disrupting pooling accounting.

There are two exceptions to this favorable rule:

First, if T's preferred stock or debt securities were issued in exchange for its voting common stock during a two-year period preceding the initiation of the business combination, P may issue only voting common stock to the holder of those securities, using the exchange ratio based on its former holding of T voting common stock.

Second, where (i) there is significant overlap between the holders of T preferred stock or debentures on the one hand and the holders of T common stock on the other, (ii) most of the holders of T preferred or debentures also own T common stock, and (iii) the holders of T preferred or debentures received such preferred or debentures in the same transaction in which they received their T common stock (or at about the same time), there is risk SEC may take the position (under a facts and circumstances test) that P issue P voting common stock (see (b)(iii) above) for the T preferred or debentures in order to preserve pooling.

(h) In the unusual situation when T is controlled not by its common stock but rather by voting preferred stock, pooling is permitted only if T's voting preferred (as well as T's common) is exchanged for P voting common. Similarly, if P is controlled not by its common stock but rather by its voting preferred, pooling is permitted only if a sufficient number of P's voting preferred shares are exchanged for P voting common shares as to cause P's common stock to control P prior to or at the date of the P-T combination.[72]

¶1703.4.2 P and T as Autonomous Entities

(1) General autonomy rule. P and T must each be autonomous and neither P nor T can have been a subsidiary or division of another entity within two years before initiation of the plan of combination. This rule is violated (hence, pooling is precluded) in each of the following cases:

(a) P is currently a subsidiary of another company ("Bigco") and P acquires T in exchange for P stock (rather than Bigco stock).

(b) P is not a Bigco subsidiary, but P was formerly a Bigco subsidiary (or division), Bigco had sold more than 50% of P's stock to the public less than two years before, and P is acquiring T in exchange for P stock.

(c) At the time P acquires T for P stock, T is a subsidiary or division of Bigco.

(d) At the time P acquires T, T is not a subsidiary or division of Bigco, but T was formerly a Bigco subsidiary or division and Bigco had sold more than 50% of T's stock to the public less than two years before.

If T was a Bigco subsidiary (or division), Newco acquired T in a transaction treated as a purchase, and Newco is autonomous (i.e., is not a subsidiary of another entity), then Newco-T is immediately poolable. That is, if P thereafter acquires Newco-T (in a transaction otherwise qualifying for pooling), the autonomous requirement will not preclude pooling because Newco's acquisition of T in a "purchase" wipes out T's former history as a Bigco subsidiary.

(2) Acquiring T through P subsidiary. The autonomous requirement also is not violated when P's subsidiary S acquires T voting common stock for P voting common stock. In this case *P* is viewed as the "acquiring" company, and so long as neither P nor T has been a subsidiary or division of another company (Bigco)

---

[72] EITF 87-27.

for at least two years (and all the other pooling requirements are met, so that P's acquisition of T would have qualified as a pooling), P can acquire T (through S) in a pooling.

(3)   **T as subsidiary of conglomerate or personal holding company or under common control with another company.** If a conglomerate (Bigco) controls several subsidiaries (including T), P's acquisition of T cannot qualify for pooling even if T was not engaged in the same business as Bigco's other subsidiaries. FASB has justified this result on the theory that a conglomerate typically plays an active role in all aspects of the strategic and day-to-day operations of its subsidiaries and manages them with the objective of maximizing overall shareholder return for the parent.

However, in Interpretation 28 (12/71), FASB's predecessor concluded that P's acquisition of a subsidiary of a personal holding company owned by a single individual (a "PHC") could qualify for pooling (i.e., the PHC could be "ignored" and the subsidiary treated as autonomous) as long as the PHC "is a convenience established for federal income tax reasons" and the PHC's owners operate the subsidiary companies "as if the [PHC] did not exist."

In Interpretation 27 (12/71), FASB's predecessor permitted pooling when P acquired an entity controlled by one or a few individuals (without the intervention of a holding company) who also controlled several other entities not being acquired by P. FASB's predecessor stated that "the relationship between the . . . businesses [under common control] is more important than the fact that each business is theoretically a subsidiary, because [the pooling rules] preclude fragmenting a business and pooling only a part of the business." If the person or group controls two entities in the same business, which are "presumably part of a single kind of business," but P acquires only one of the entities, the transaction does not qualify for pooling. But if the person or group controls "two unrelated businesses," P's acquisition of one entity could qualify for pooling. Thus, "considerable judgment" will be required in such cases.

(4)   **T controlled by venture capital company.** In 1990 and 1991 FASB's Emerging Issues Task Force ("EITF") grappled with the question whether P's acquisition of T qualifies for pooling when (before the acquisition) "a venture capital company [had] a greater-than-fifty-percent ownership interest in an investor [i.e., T or P]."[73] EITF considered identifying "criteria that distinguish (1) an entity that functions solely as an investment conduit from an operating entity and (2) an investee [i.e., a T] that is autonomous from one that is a fragment of another entity." However, in 5/91, "the FASB staff expressed the view that a majority-owned investee would generally be a subsidiary and ineligible for pooling . . . , except in the limited circumstances addressed in Interpretations 27 and 28 [which], in limited circumstances, might be applicable to this situation [depending upon] the specific facts and circumstances of each transaction."[74]

---

[73] EITF 90-10.
[74] EITF 90-10.

With respect to this conclusion,

> The SEC Observer [to the EITF] stated that a business combination involving a majority-owned investee of a venture capital company, including turnaround funds, typically involves elements of control that are inconsistent with [autonomy] and Interpretations 27 and 28. The SEC staff position is consistent with the views of the FASB staff. The SEC staff will consider the accounting for such transactions based on the specific facts and circumstances of each transaction.[75]

Hence, under EITF 90-10, if a venture capital company (that controls multiple entities) also controls T or P, T or P generally would be considered a subsidiary of the venture capital company and ineligible for pooling. For purposes of EITF 90-10, control apparently means either (a) ownership of more than 50% of T's or P's voting stock, including in some cases not yet fully defined (to the extent owned by the venture capital company) rights to acquire voting shares (whether in or out of the money) or (b) the right to elect a majority of T's or P's board of directors (whether by voting agreement or otherwise), including stock, rights to acquire stock, and contractual rights held by parties related to the venture capital company. Control does not include ownership of 50% or less of T's or P's voting stock (without any contractual control rights over other voting shares) even if, as a practical matter, such less-than-50%-control of T's or P's voting shares allows the venture capital company to elect a majority of T's or P's directors because other T or P shareholders do not vote.

This is an evolving area: SEC and FASB are dealing with cases on their specific facts as they arise. However, the philosophical underpinning of EITF 90-10 does not seem wholly consistent with that of Interpretations 27 and 28. The 1990 venture capital interpretation focuses on control versus autonomy, while the 1971 interpretations focus principally on the interrelationship between concededly commonly controlled entities. This philosophical divergence is, of course, masked in part by EITF 90-10's reference to the 1971 interpretations as possible exceptions to EITF 90-10's anti-pooling approach "in limited circumstances [depending upon] the specific facts and circumstances," but the difference in philosophical approach is nonetheless reasonably manifest.

¶1703.4.3　P or T Redemptions

Neither P nor T can have reacquired shares of its voting common stock within two years before initiation of the P-T plan of combination or between the initiation date and consummation (i.e., "tainted treasury stock"). There are several narrow exceptions to this rule, including the use of all or a portion of the 10% basket described in ¶¶1703.4.1(c) and (d) and 1703.4.15, Example 5 to cover a small amount of tainted P and/or T treasury stock, the purging of tainted P and/or T treasury stock by certain types of reissuances, and purchases of P and/or T treasury stock pursuant to a regular systematic plan.

---

[75] EITF 90-10.

In addition, SEC has taken the position that a P plan (at the time of the acquisition) to reacquire shares of P voting common stock after consummation of a combination to be accounted for as a pooling will generally preclude the pooling (if the reacquisition does not fit within an exception such as the 10% basket).[76]

¶1703.4.4 P or T Spin-Offs or Other Changes in Capital Structure

Neither P nor T can have made certain other types of changes in its voting common stock equity interests during such period, e.g., (a) a spin-off or other abnormal distribution or (b) an accelerated vesting of unvested Mgmt options or other Mgmt stock-based compensation not contractually provided for in the option or other arrangement at least two years prior to the initiation of the transaction, with a possible exception when the parties can demonstrate that such accelerated vesting was not in contemplation of the P-T acquisition. Changes of this type cannot be covered by the 10% basket described in ¶1703.4.1(c) and (d).

¶1703.4.5 No Earnout and Limited Other Contingencies in Consideration Being Paid for T

The consideration must be completely resolved at the consummation of the transaction, i.e., there can be no earnout, whether structured as contingent or escrowed stock, and there can be only limited liability of T or its shareholders to P for breaches of contractual representations and warranties.

(a) Pooling is not precluded if T or its shareholders put in escrow (i) not more than 10% of the P stock received for a period not exceeding one year (or if shorter, until completion of the first post-acquisition audit) to secure their liability to P for breach of general representations and warranties in the acquisition agreement relating to pre-acquisition facts and claims (but not to predictions of future earnings or other future events) and/or (ii) a reasonable amount of P stock to secure P against specifically identified T contingencies (e.g., a tax dispute, lawsuit, or other claim existing at the consummation of the acquisition), but not relating to predictions of future earnings or other future events, for a period that is reasonable in light of the specific contingencies so identified, so long as any P stock ultimately returned to P on account of liability for breach of representation and warranties is valued at the time the P-T acquisition was consummated, i.e., any post-acquisition fluctuation in the value of the P stock is ignored.

(b) Pooling is also not precluded if T or its shareholders do not put P stock in escrow but agree to return P stock to P in circumstances and amounts permitted by (a).

---

[76] SEC Staff Accounting Bulletin 96.

(c) Pooling is also not precluded if the acquisition agreement obligates T or its shareholders to pay money damages to P for breach of representations and warranties so long as (i) the circumstances when T or its shareholders will be liable to P and the amount of the liability do not exceed those permitted by (a) and (b) and (ii) T and its shareholders will owe money (rather than P shares) to P only when the P shares that would have been returned to P under (a) and (b) have been sold.

(d) Pooling is generally precluded if the acquisition agreement makes T's shareholders liable to deliver any stock, property, or cash to P for breach of a contractual representation or warranty, other than as permitted by (a) through (c). There may be circumstances, other than those described in (a) through (c), in which pooling is permitted even though T or its shareholders are obligated to pay money damages to P for breach of representations and warranties. However, because this is an area that is facts and circumstances intensive, accountants have not provided any general guidance.

¶1703.4.6   Prohibition on Resales of Stock by P and T Affiliates

P's and T's affiliates (generally their officers, directors, 10% shareholders, and any other members of their control groups) generally may not dispose of any P or T voting common stock (or their equivalents), or otherwise reduce their risk of holding such securities, for a period beginning 30 days before consummation of the P-T acquisition and lasting until public issuance of financial results covering at least 30 days of post-acquisition P-T combined operations, subject to a de minimis exception.

Pooling requires that the combination result in the sharing of risk equally among P and T shareholders. SEC will generally conclude that risk sharing has been achieved if P's and T's affiliates have not sold or otherwise reduced their risk during the restricted period. Therefore, pooling treatment is generally precluded where an affiliate enters into a contract to sell, put, or other risk-minimization hedge during the restricted period or uses shares as collateral for a non-recourse loan secured only by the shares (subject to the de minimis exception).

¶1703.4.7   No Restrictions on P or T Shareholders' Post-acquisition Ability to Vote or Sell Their Shares

P may not place any restrictions on the right of T's shareholders or on the right of P's shareholders to vote or sell their P shares after the transaction has been consummated.

¶1703.4.8   Intercorporate Ownership Between P and T

Prior to the combination, intercorporate investments between P and T cannot exceed 10% of outstanding voting common stock, and any such intercorporate investments reduce the 10% basket described in ¶1703.4.1(c) and (d). For a sample computation of the 10% basket, see ¶1703.4.15, Example 5.

¶1703.4.9 Financial Arrangements Between T's Shareholders and P

P may not agree to reacquire any of the common stock issued to T's former shareholders, nor may P enter into other financial arrangements for the benefit of T's former shareholders.

¶1703.4.10 Intended Asset Dispositions

P must not intend to dispose of any significant portion of P's or T's assets within two years, other than in the ordinary course of business or to eliminate duplicate facilities or excess capacity. Although not addressed by the FASB or its predecessor, SEC has taken the view that sale of significant assets by P or T during the two-year period *before* consummation would preclude pooling. "Significant" for this purpose generally means a reportable business segment under FASB Statement No. 14, *Financial Reporting for Segments of a Business*. Therefore, dispositions of assets representing more than 10% of operating profits, assets (on either a book basis or FV basis), or revenues would be deemed significant.

¶1703.4.11 Executive Compensation Arrangements

Pooling is generally not precluded if P enters into employment or consulting contracts with and/or grants options or other stock-based compensation to T ex-shareholders who become P employees or consultants.

If, however, such an employment or consulting contract grants a T ex-shareholder unreasonably large compensation in light of the services actually to be provided to P, such payment maybe treated as disguised purchase price for T shares and hence preclude pooling. Similarly, if options granted to a T ex-shareholder constitute unreasonably large compensation in light of the services actually to be provided to P or are in substance a contingent earnout for T shares, pooling would be precluded.

¶1703.4.12 Anti-Takeover Issues

T's agreement to pay P a break-up fee should T withdraw from the proposed P-T combination does not preclude pooling so long as the P-T acquisition is consummated and the break-up fee expires unexercised. When T actually pays a break-up fee to P1 (on T's withdrawal from a proposed P1-T combination) and T is then acquired by unrelated P2, the break-up fee paid to P1 often precludes pooling for the P2-T combination, i.e., pooling for the P2-T combination is permitted only if (i) the P1 break-up fee is reasonable in amount, (ii) P1 was not a T shareholder, (iii) the P1 breakup fee agreement was entered into in the normal course of negotiating the P1-T combination, and (iv) the triggering of the P1 breakup fee was not in contemplation of the subsequent P2-T combination. SEC generally presumes that the triggering of the P1 breakup fee payment is in contemplation of the subsequent P2-T combination and, therefore, precludes pooling for the combination. SEC's presumption seems most likely to be correct where the P1 breakup fee is payable only on T's combination with an entity other than P1 (here P2) or the P1 breakup fee is calculated by reference to the consideration paid by P2 (i.e., where the payment is a "topping fee"). However, where the P1 breakup fee is payable without regard to whether there is a P2-T combination (e.g., where T agrees to pay P1's expenses of a failed P1-T combination regardless of whether there is a P2-T combination), the presumption seems incorrect, and it may be possible to persuade SEC to accept pooling for the P2-T combination, notwithstanding the P1 breakup fee, at least where there is some period of time between the payment of the P1 break up fee and the P2-T combination.

T's grant of an option to P, entitling P to buy, for example, 19.9% of T's stock will not preclude pooling for the P-T combination so long as P gave no specific consideration for the option, P's option was exercisable only on occurrence of a triggering event (e.g., a third-party offer for T), and P's option is not exercised prior to consummation of the P-T acquisition. The same approach applies when T grants P an option to acquire specified T assets.

When T enters into a standstill agreement with Bigco (a T shareholder) that extends beyond consummation of the P-T combination[77] pooling is not precluded if the standstill agreement was not made in contemplation of the P-T combination. However, pooling is precluded if the standstill agreement was made in contemplation of the P-T combination and binds a more than 10% shareholder. Finally, if the standstill agreement was made in contemplation of the P-T combination but binds a less-than-10% shareholder, such shareholder's shares are treated as tainted for purposes of the 10% basket described in ¶1703.4.1(c) and (d).

¶1703.4.13 Other Pooling Requirements

There are a number of other highly technical and arbitrary rules that apply, including retroactive invalidation of pooling if, shortly after a pooling acquisition, P takes an action that would have precluded pooling if undertaken before the acquisition. See, e.g., the precedents cited in the footnote at the beginning of this section.

---

[77] EITF 87-15.

¶1703.4.14   Pooling for Transactions Involving Partnerships or LLCs

The GAAP rules generally treat corporations, partnerships, and LLCs alike for purchase and pooling accounting. Thus, the pooling rules outlined above also apply where either P or T is a partnership or LLC, rather than a corporation, and the other is a corporate entity *or* where both P and T are partnerships or LLCs. In applying the pooling rules to such a transaction, references to P or T voting common stock should be read as referring to P or T voting common partnership or LLC interests.

Where a partnership (or LLC) is controlled by a sole general partner (or managing member) that is an entity, there is risk SEC may take the position the partnership (or LLC) is not autonomous and hence is ineligible for pooling—i.e., that the partnership (or LLC) is in effect a subsidiary of the general partner (or managing member) entity. See ¶1703.4.2. The partnership (or LLC) should not, however, fail the autonomy test in these circumstances, where the limited partners (or non-managing members) have a general right to remove the general partner (or managing member) or have significant veto or other voting rights with respect to day-to-day operations.

¶1703.4.15   Examples

EXAMPLE 1.   Pooling Accounting

P acquires T on 1/1 year 2, in a transaction initiated before the 7/1/01 repeal of pooling accounting. Immediately before the acquisition, T's GAAP balance sheet is as follows:

Assets		*Liabilities and Net Worth*	
Cash	$ 100	Liabilities	$ 200
Receivables	100	Net worth (100 shares of voting	
Inventory	100	common stock)	800
PP&E	700		
Total	$1,000		$1,000

T's GAAP income statement for year 1 (the year before the acquisition) is as follows:

Sales	$2,000
Cost of goods sold and other expenses	1,167
Income before income tax	833
Income tax (at an assumed federal-state 40% rate)	333
Net income	$ 500

When P acquires T on 1/1 year 2, P issues P voting common stock with an FV of $5,000 to T's common shareholders. The transaction qualifies as a pooling of interests because the sole consideration issued to T's common shareholders is P voting common stock and the other requisites for pooling accounting are also satisfied.

Each T asset and liability goes onto P's GAAP balance sheet at its old book value ("BV") on T's books, i.e., P's assets increase by $1,000, P's liabilities increase by $200, and P's net worth increases by $800. The FV of the consideration issued by P ($5,000 FV of P stock) over (a) the old BV of T's assets ($1,000) and (b) the old BV of T's net worth ($800) is ignored.

P's and T's costs of the acquisition (e.g., legal and accounting fees and expenses) are expensed in year 2 as part of the first P-T combined post-acquisition income statement.

If the T business performs in year 2 (the year of the acquisition) the same as in year 1, P's GAAP net income from the T business will be $500, the same as T's year 1 GAAP net income (i.e., there is no increase in T's depreciation, amortization, cost of goods sold, etc., from the acquisition) reduced by the costs of the acquisition.[78]

EXAMPLE 2.   Purchase Accounting—Purchase Price Paid in Cash

Same as Example 1, except that T's common shareholders receive $5,000 cash (rather than $5,000 FV of P voting common stock). The transaction does not qualify as a pooling of interests because the consideration is not predominantly (i.e., 90% or more) P voting common stock. Hence, the transaction is accounted for as a purchase.

---

[78] This example also assumes that P's acquisition of T is either a tax-free reorganization (with T's tax basis for its assets carrying over to P) *or* a taxable acquisition of T's stock with no Code §338 or §338(h)(10) election (so T's tax basis for its assets is not affected by the transaction). In this case, the T business's year 2 income taxes would be the same as in year 1.

EXAMPLE 3. Purchase Accounting—Purchase Price Paid Partly in Common and Partly in Preferred Stock

Same as Examples 1 and 2, i.e., P acquires T on 1/1 year 2, in a transaction initiated before the 7/1/01 repeal of pooling accounting, for $5,000 of consideration (P voting common stock in Example 1 and cash in Example 2), except that in this Example 3, T's common shareholders receive P voting common stock with an FV of $2,500 and P preferred stock with an FV of $2,500.

Same result as Example 2, i.e., purchase accounting, because the consideration is not predominantly (i.e., 90% or more) P voting common stock.

EXAMPLE 4. Purchase Accounting—Technical Pooling Requirement Breached

Same as Example 1, i.e., P acquires T on 1/1 year 2, in a transaction initiated before the 7/1/01 repeal of pooling accounting, for $5,000 of P voting common stock, except that one of the other pooling requirements set forth in ¶1703.5 is not met (e.g., T was a subsidiary or division of Bigco within two years before initiation of the P-T plan of combination, or P or T redeemed some of its voting common stock or made other prohibited changes in its capital structure during such period).

Same result as Example 2, i.e., purchase accounting, because the transaction does not qualify for pooling of interests treatment.

The result reached in each of the four examples above is the same regardless of the mechanical form of the transaction. Thus, in Example 1, the transaction is a pooling whether structured as a merger of P into T for P voting common stock, as a merger between S and T for P voting common stock, as P or S acquiring T's stock for P voting common stock, or as P or S acquiring T's assets and liabilities for P voting common stock. In Example 2, the transaction is a purchase whether it is structured as P or S purchasing T's stock or assets for $5,000 cash, as T merging into P for $5,000 cash, or as a merger between T and S for $5,000 cash.

EXAMPLE 5. Pooling Accounting—Illustration of 10% Basket

P is acquiring T in a combination initiated before the 7/1/01 repeal of pooling accounting, which the parties intend to qualify for pooling treatment. On the date the plan of combination is initiated, P and T have the following number of shares (all voting common) issued and outstanding, respectively:

	P	T
Number of shares issued	1,000	500
Number of treasury shares—all tainted[79]	(10)	(8)
Number of shares outstanding	9,990	492

In the combination, P is issuing one P voting common share for each T share. At the date the plan of combination is initiated, P and T each own the following number of shares in the other:

Number of P shares owned by T   14
Number of T shares owned by P   12

Several T shareholders owning in the aggregate five T shares dissent from the combination (as permitted by state law) and claim appraisal rights. P pays such T dissenting shareholders in cash for their five T shares.

The following computation is used to determine whether the 10% basket test is satisfied:

	Equivalent No. of P Shares
Number of P shares which would be issued in exchange for 100% of T's outstanding shares (492 T shares issued × 1-for-1 exchange ratio)	492
Number of tainted P treasury shares	10
Number of P shares owned by T	14
Number of P shares that would be issued in exchange for T shares owned by P	12
Number of P shares that would be issued in exchange for tainted T treasury shares	8
Number of P shares that would be issued in exchange for T shares owned by dissenters	5
Total bad shares	49
10% of the number of P shares that would be issued in exchange for 100% of T's outstanding shares	49.2

The 10% basket test is satisfied because the number of bad shares is less than the 10% limit (49.2).

[79] For the definition of "tainted treasury stock," see ¶1703.4.3.

¶1704   ACCOUNTING FOR STOCK-BASED COMPENSATION TO MANAGEMENT

The accounting treatment for stock-based compensation to P's (or Newco's) management—principally stock options (both ISOs and NQOs), stock awards, and stock sales—is discussed extensively in ¶¶1502.1.7, 1502.1.8, and 1502.3.

¶1705   ACCOUNTING FOR STOCK-BASED KICKER TO LENDERS[1]

When Newco (or P) borrows money to finance an LBO, Newco must frequently grant warrants (or a similar stock-based kicker to its lenders), most frequently to its subordinated lenders. Such kicker warrants will frequently result in a reduction of (i.e., a charge to) Newco's accounting net income.

(1)   Pre-12/95 accounting rule. Prior to the 12/15/95 effective date of FASB 123, the applicable accounting rule was as follows:

First, Newco's aggregate proceeds from sale of a debenture (or other debt instrument) plus warrants were allocated between the debenture and the warrants "based on the relative fair values of the debt security without the warrants and of the warrants themselves at the time of issuance."[2] If the lender paid less than FV for the warrants, this generally resulted in a portion of the price that the lender paid for the debenture being reallocated to the warrants, so the debenture was treated as "issue[d] . . . at a discount."[3]

The amount of this original issue discount ("OID") on the debenture was then "amortized as interest expense . . . over the life of the note in such a way as to result in a constant rate of interest when applied to the amount outstanding at the beginning of any given period."[4] This OID amortization resulted in an annual reduction of (i.e., an annual charge to) Newco's accounting net income.[5]

Second, if the warrant issued by Newco had more debt characteristics than equity characteristics (e.g., the lender had a put right to require Newco to re-purchase either the warrant or the underlying stock at a price that substantially exceeds the warrant's or the stock's FV at the time the warrant was issued), there

---

¶1705   [1] We thank Mark V. Sever of Ernst & Young LLP for his ideas and assistance in the preparation of ¶1705.

[2] APB Opinion No. 14, ¶15. See also EITF 86-35 and EITF 88-9.

[3] APB Opinion No. 14, ¶15. See also EITF 86-35 and EITF 88-9.

[4] APB Opinion No. 21, ¶15.

[5] However, when Newco issued a convertible debenture (rather than a straight debenture with warrants), "no portion of the proceeds from the issuance . . . should be accounted for as attributable to the conversion feature, [because of] the inseparability of the debt and the conversion option." APB Opinion No. 14, ¶12. When Newco issued a straight debenture with warrants that "are not detachable from the debt and the debt security must be surrendered in order to exercise the warrant, the two securities taken together are substantially equivalent to convertible debt and the [same] accounting . . . should apply," i.e., no debenture OID is created by allocating purchase price to the non-detachable warrant. APB Opinion No. 14, ¶16.

was another charge to Newco's accounting net income. In such case, the warrant "should be characterized as a debt instrument," so that the excess of the put price over the value assigned to the warrant at issuance (by allocation as described above) was treated as OID on a second debt instrument, i.e., the warrant.[6] Such OID was thus amortized as interest expense "from the date of issuance to the earliest put date of the warrants," thus resulting in a reduction of (i.e., a charge to) Newco's accounting net income, and if the put price increased, the amount of such increase similarly resulted in a further charge to Newco's accounting net income.[7]

EXAMPLE 1

Newco issued a subordinated note to Lender along with a detachable warrant entitling Lender to purchase 6,250 Newco shares for $75 per share and to put the warrant (or the shares) back to Newco for at least $2,010 per share seven years later. These are the facts of EITF 86-35, as supplemented by EITF 88-9. The EITFs conclude that, because "the put price is substantially higher than the value of the warrant exclusive of the put at the time of issuance," the accounting results are as follows:

(1) Newco's proceeds from the subordinated note and warrant are allocated between the two instruments.

(2) This allocation creates OID on the subordinated note, which is amortized "as interest expense" over the subordinated note's life, thus creating a charge to Newco's accounting net income.

(3) The put warrant is also "characterized as debt," so the excess of the put price over the amount allocated to the warrant at issuance constitutes OID, which is amortized "as interest expense" over the put period, creating a further charge to Newco's accounting net income.

---

(2) Post-12/95 accounting rule. At first blush, it appears that FASB 123 (effective 12/15/95) supersedes the accounting treatment described above. FASB 123 states that "Except for transactions with employees that are within the scope of [APB] 25, all transactions in which goods or services are the consideration received [by Newco] for the issuance of equity instruments shall be accounted for based on the fair value of the consideration received [by Newco] or the fair value of the equity instruments issued, whichever is more reliably measurable." It appears that Newco's receipt of money from the lender (i.e., the loan proceeds) in exchange for a note and an equity kicker is covered by this language.

[6] EITF 86-35.
[7] EITF 88-9.

Thus, if this reading of FASB 123 is correct, it appears that for a transaction after 12/15/95 Newco recognizes an FASB 123 charge to its accounting net income (accrued over the life of the loan) equal to the FV of the stock-based kicker (at either the grant date or the vesting date[8]), reduced by any tax savings arising out of the equity kicker. Where the equity kicker is an option to purchase Newco stock, the FV of the option takes into account both (1) the amount by which the option is in the money at grant and (2) the value of the option privilege. Moreover, where Newco is obligated to repurchase the equity kicker at a future time, or to repurchase it at the lender's option, Newco also recognizes future quarterly charges to its accounting net income as the repurchase price increases over the equity kicker's original FV. For a more complete discussion of FASB 123, see ¶1502.1.7.3.

However, two statements in FASB 123 can be read as saying that the FASB 123 accounting rule for an equity kicker issued to a lender is, in effect, the same relative-value approach as the pre-12/95 rule described above. First, in a paragraph dealing with other issues, FASB 123 states that: "Equity instruments other than employee stock options and the consideration received for them are recognized at their fair values on the dates the instruments are issued. For example, the initial recognition of debt issued with detachable stock purchase warrants is based on *the relative fair values of the debt and the warrants at the date of issuance . . .*" (emphasis added).

Second, in discussing the 12/15/95 effective date for the new rules, FASB 123 states that for the issuance of an equity instrument to acquire goods or non-employee services, FASB 123 "essentially codifies current best practice," thus implying that the pre-12/95 relative-value approach described above has not been altered.

Hence there is at present some uncertainty as to the proper accounting treatment of a lender equity kicker.

¶1706   FRAUDULENT CONVEYANCE AND RELATED RISKS

The essence of an LBO transaction is the use of T's "value" (real value of assets less liabilities) to finance the acquisition of T or its assets. While an LBO can take many forms, LBO structures can be categorized in two groupings from the standpoint of T's creditors.

(1)   No impact on T's creditors. T's assets are left in a separate corporation (generally T) that does not assume any liability for the newly created LBO debt. Rather, the LBO debt is the obligation of a separate entity, usually Newco (or P), the entity that acquired T's stock. T's pre-acquisition creditors have not been disadvantaged by this LBO because the assets available for satisfaction of the

---

[8] FASB 123 does not specify whether the grant or the vesting date is the applicable measurement time, although in practice a lender's equity kicker will normally be vested when granted.

creditors' claims (T's pre-acquisition assets) have not been diminished and the liabilities that are a claim against such assets (T's pre-acquisition liabilities) have not been increased.

(2)   Adverse impact on T's creditors. All or part of the newly created acquisition debt is inserted into T (or its successor), so that T (or its successor) ends up liable for the acquisition debt, and T (or its successor) usually pledges its assets to secure the acquisition debt. Consequently, the claims of T's pre-acquisition creditors end up either subordinate to the newly created acquisition debt (if such debt is secured) or *pari passu* with the acquisition debt (if such debt is unsecured). Since the cash proceeds of the acquisition debt have been paid out to T's shareholders, T's pre-acquisition creditors are adversely impacted by this structure.

When an LBO structure prejudices T's pre-acquisition creditors (by inserting new acquisition debt into T or its successor) and T is or thereby becomes insolvent (or, depending on which of the four statutory schemes discussed herein is applicable, T suffers certain other "badges of fraud"), the fraudulent conveyance laws may well apply.

These laws permit a prejudiced creditor or a trustee in bankruptcy to avoid obligations incurred or transfers of property or interests in property (including liens), for the benefit of unpaid creditors who have been disadvantaged by the new obligation or the transfer, if other factors (discussed below) are present. Moreover, T's board of directors may be held liable to T's creditors for breach of fiduciary duty and/or an illegal dividend or redemption distribution by acquiescing in an LBO in which T's shareholders receive money while the acquisition debt burden is placed on T (or its successor) and T (or its successor) is or thereby becomes insolvent.

Fraudulent conveyance laws derive from the sixteenth-century English Statute of Elizabeth,[1] which was designed to cover simple transactions between human beings (e.g., a gift by an insolvent debtor of all or a substantial portion of his assets to his spouse or his sibling) rather than modern, complex business transactions like LBOs. There are now four statutory schemes under which fraudulent conveyance risks may arise:

(1)   the Bankruptcy Code, which has national application;
(2)   modern versions of the old Statute of Elizabeth;
(3)   the Uniform Fraudulent Conveyance Act ("UFCA");
(4)   the Uniform Fraudulent Transfer Act ("UFTA").

All states have adopted one of the uniform acts or some form of the Statute of Elizabeth. Each of the four statutory schemes, discussed at length below, permits the avoidance of a transfer made, or obligation incurred, with actual intent to hinder, delay, or defraud creditors. However, because of the difficulty of proving actual intent, courts operating under the Statute of Elizabeth developed "badges of fraud" from which a court may infer an intent to hinder, delay, or defraud creditors.

¶1706 [1] 13 Eliz., ch. 5 (1570).

The Bankruptcy Code and the two uniform acts have each codified these "badges of fraud" into statutory constructive fraud provisions permitting the avoidance of a transfer made, or obligation incurred, if (1) the consideration for the transfer was inadequate *and* (2) either the transfer rendered the transferor insolvent or undercapitalized or the debtor intended or believed that it would be unable to pay its obligations as they mature.

All the statutes generally immunize a transferee to the extent such transferee gave real consideration in good faith and without knowledge (or reason to have knowledge) of the voidability of the transfer. Moreover, in a few Statute of Elizabeth states that use as the test for a valid transaction whether the transferee gave "consideration deemed valuable in law," the whole transaction is apparently immunized if any value went to T. However, as discussed below, courts will sometimes apply a step-transaction doctrine under which consideration given by a transferee in one step of a multistep transaction (e.g., a lender into an LBO who receives a note and a lien on T's assets) is ignored (i.e., all the steps of the transaction are collapsed) if the loan proceeds are immediately disbursed to T's shareholders.

These statutes have increasingly been applied to LBO transactions. Because of the archaic origins of the statutes, because the fraudulent conveyance doctrine was designed to cover simple transactions between individuals rather than complex business transactions, because LBO transactions are often very complex both legally and factually, and because there are nuances of difference between the various statutory schemes, the decided cases in this area are inconsistent and often vague as to their reasoning.

This section approaches fraudulent conveyance law as follows:

- ¶1706.1 describes a number of LBO structures and identifies those that do or do not prejudice T's creditors.
- ¶1706.2 identifies the participants in an LBO transaction who may be exposed to a loss if a fraudulent conveyance attack is successful.
- ¶1706.3 reviews the principal defenses to a fraudulent conveyance claim.
- ¶1706.4 discusses each of the four applicable statutory schemes—the Bankruptcy Code, the Statute of Elizabeth, the UFCA, and the UFTA—and reviews the often subtle differences between them.
- ¶1706.5 discusses how directors and other persons who acquiesced or assisted in the LBO transaction may be viewed as liable to T's creditors for (1) breach of fiduciary duty or (2) permitting T to make an illegal dividend distribution to T's equity holders.
- ¶1706.6 reviews each of the principal decided cases dealing with LBO fraudulent conveyance actions to illustrate how the courts have applied the often ill-suited statutory framework to complex LBO transactions.

¶1706.1   *LBO Structure Creating Fraudulent Conveyance Risk by Prejudicing T's Creditors*

When the LBO is structured so that T (or its successor) ends up liable for the newly-created acquisition debt in a way that disadvantages or prejudices T's pre-acquisition creditors (as illustrated at ¶¶1706.1.2 through 1706.1.7), there will generally be a fraudulent conveyance risk unless one or more of the defenses described in ¶1706.3 is met. Conversely, there is generally no fraudulent conveyance risk when T's pre-acquisition creditors are not prejudiced. For example, if the LBO is structured so that a separate entity, usually T's parent (Newco), and not T (or its successor), is liable for the acquisition debt (as illustrated at ¶1706.1.1), there is generally no fraudulent conveyance risk.

¶1706.1.1   Newco Purchases T's Stock

VC forms Newco by contributing $1 million of equity capital. Newco borrows $9 million and uses the $10 million ($1 million of Newco equity plus $9 million of Newco acquisition borrowings) to buy 100% of T's stock. T's assets have an FV of $12 million (including intangibles and goodwill), and T has $2 million of existing unsecured liabilities (e.g., trade payables and working capital loans). T remains a separate subsidiary of Newco following the transaction and does not guarantee (or otherwise become liable for) Newco's $9 million acquisition debt.

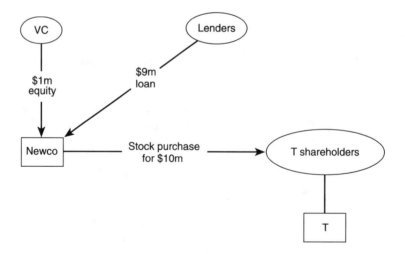

No fraudulent conveyance risk arises under this scenario because T's old creditors have not been disadvantaged. After the transaction is consummated, T has assets with a $12 million FV and only $2 million of liabilities, just as before the transaction. T's pre-acquisition creditors would not be disadvantaged even if Newco pledged T's stock to secure Newco's $9 million acquisition debt, because

T's assets are still subject only to the same $2 million of debts after the stock pledge, as before.

¶1706.1.2   Newco Purchases T's Stock and T Guarantees Newco's Acquisition Debt

As in ¶1706.1.1, VC forms Newco by contributing $1 million of equity capital, Newco borrows $9 million, and Newco buys T's stock for $10 million. In this scenario, however, T (which became a Newco subsidiary), guarantees Newco's $9 million acquisition debt.

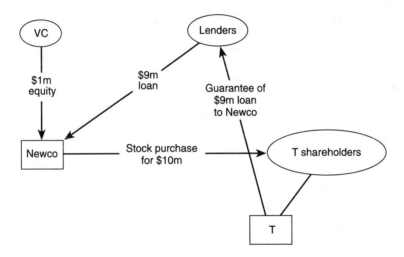

This scenario presents a fraudulent conveyance risk *if* a "badge of fraud" is present, e.g., T becomes insolvent as a result of the LBO transaction, because T's creditors have been disadvantaged. Although T still has assets with a $12-million FV, T now has $11 million of liabilities ($2 million of old T unsecured liabilities plus the $9 million guarantee of Newco's acquisition debt incurred to pay T's shareholders). T (as opposed to Newco) received no consideration for the new $9 million of debt.[2]

If T grants a lien on its assets to Lender to secure the $9 million guarantee, the prejudice to T's old creditors is exacerbated. If T encounters financial difficulties, the $9 million guarantee would take priority over the old $2 million of unsecured claims held by T's pre-acquisition creditors.[3]

---

[2] See *Gleneagles* (discussed at ¶1706.6.1), *Moody* (discussed at ¶1706.6.9), and *O'Day* (discussed at ¶1706.6.10).

[3] See *Gleneagles* (discussed at ¶1706.6.1) and *O'Day* (discussed at ¶1706.6.10).

¶1706.1.3   Newco Buys T's Stock with Money Borrowed by T and Reloaned to Newco

As in ¶1706.1.1, VC forms Newco by contributing $1 million of equity capital, but in this case T (rather than Newco) borrows the $9 million and then reloans it to Newco in return for a Newco note. Newco then buys T's stock for $10 million ($1 million of Newco equity plus $9 million borrowed from T).

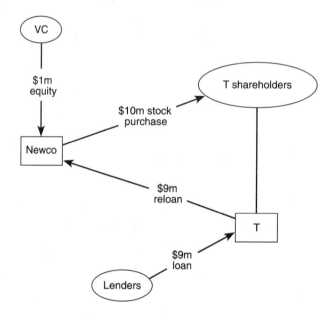

A fraudulent conveyance risk also arises under this scenario because T's creditors have been disadvantaged. After the LBO, T still has assets with a $12 million FV, just as in prior scenarios. However, T now has a new asset, a $9 million note receivable from Newco. Newco, however, has no assets out of which to repay the note other than the T stock. Consequently, unless T is successful (so that it can pay dividends to Newco or Newco can sell the T stock at an advantageous price), Newco will not be able to service its $9 million note to T. T (which still owes its pre-acquisition creditors $2 million) now has $11 million of liabilities ($2 million of old T unsecured liabilities plus the $9 million acquisition debt). The prejudice to T's old creditors is exacerbated if T's $9 million acquisition debt is secured by a lien on T's assets. In case of T's financial difficulty, the $9 million acquisition debt would take priority over the old $2 million of unsecured claims held by T's pre-acquisition creditors.[4]

---

[4]See *Gleneagles* (discussed at ¶1706.6.1), *O'Day* (discussed at ¶1706.6.10), and *Richmond Produce* (discussed at ¶1706.6.11).

¶1706.1.4   Newco Purchases T's Stock and Newco and T
             Combine

As in ¶1706.1.1, VC forms Newco by contributing $1 million of equity capital.
Newco borrows $9 million, and Newco buys T's stock for $10 million. In this
scenario, however, Newco and T are combined immediately after Newco purchases T's stock, either through a liquidation of T into Newco, an upstream merger
of T into Newco, or a downstream merger of Newco into T.

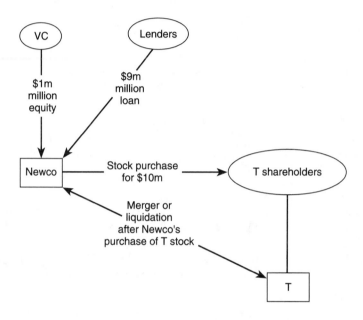

This scenario presents a fraudulent conveyance risk because T's creditors again
have been disadvantaged. After the transaction, the surviving entity (T or Newco)
has assets with a $12 million FV, the same as T had before the transaction.
However, the surviving entity, which owes T's old unsecured creditors $2 million,
now has $11 million of liabilities ($2 million of old T unsecured liabilities plus the
$9 million acquisition debt). The adverse effect on T's old creditors is exacerbated if
the new $9 million of acquisition debt is secured by a lien on T's old assets,
because in case of the surviving entity's financial difficulties, the acquisition debt
would take priority over T's old $2 million of pre-acquisition unsecured liabilities.[5]

¶1706.1.5   Newco Purchases T's Assets or T and Newco Merge

VC forms Newco by contributing $1 million of equity capital, and Newco
borrows $9 million. In this case, however, instead of Newco buying T's stock

---

[5] See *Kupetz* (discussed at ¶1706.6.5) and *Ohio Corrugating* (discussed at ¶1706.6.6).

from T's shareholders, either (1) Newco purchases T's assets for $10 million and assumes T's $2 million of unsecured liabilities, and T then liquidates, distributing the $10 million to its shareholders, or (2) T merges with Newco (with either T or Newco surviving the merger), and T's shareholders receive $10 million pursuant to the asset purchase or plan of merger.

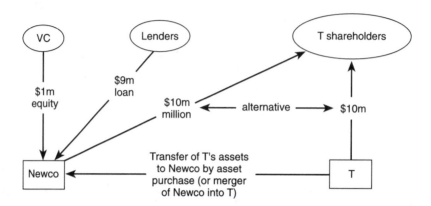

Again there is a fraudulent conveyance risk because T's creditors have been disadvantaged. T's creditors previously had $2 million in claims covered by $12 million FV of assets. However, after the LBO, there is a new $9 million claim—the acquisition debt—to be covered by the same $12 million FV of assets. The prejudice to T's old creditors is exacerbated if the new acquisition debt is secured by a lien on T's old assets.

¶1706.1.6   Newco Purchases Part of T's Stock and T Borrows to Redeem Remainder

As in the preceding scenarios, VC forms Newco by contributing $1 million of equity capital. Newco then uses its $1 million of equity to purchase 10% of T's stock from T's old shareholders. Simultaneously, T borrows $9 million, which T uses to redeem the remaining 90% of its stock from its old shareholders.

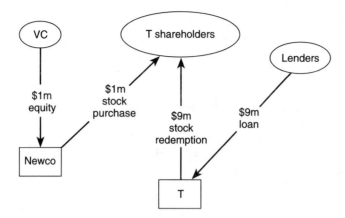

T's creditors have been disadvantaged in the same fashion as described at ¶¶1706.1.2 through 1706.1.5.

¶1706.1.7   Newco Acquires T by Forward or Reverse Subsidiary Merger

As in the prior scenarios, VC forms Newco by contributing $1 million of equity capital. In this scenario, Newco then contributes the $1 million to its wholly owned subsidiary, S. S borrows $9 million. S then merges into T (in a reverse subsidiary merger) or T merges into S (in a forward subsidiary merger), with T's shareholders receiving $10 million pursuant to the plan of merger (the $1 million of equity plus the $9 million of S acquisition debt).

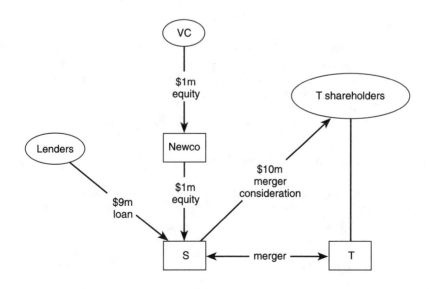

There is a fraudulent conveyance risk for the same reasons described at ¶¶1706.1.2 through 1706.1.6.

¶1706.2 Parties Exposed to Loss in Fraudulent Conveyance LBO

Fraudulent conveyance exposure can, at least theoretically, run to many of the parties involved in an LBO.

¶1706.2.1 Lender

The acquisition lender may find its liens avoided and/or its loans subordinated to the claims of other creditors, unless the acquisition lender did not know (and had no reason to know) that the loan proceeds would be paid out to T's old shareholders while the acquisition debt would be imposed on T's assets.

¶1706.2.2 Bridge Lender

An LBO bridge lender may be required to refund loan repayments received on the bridge loan long after it has been repaid out of permanent acquisition debt, unless the bridge lender did not know (and had no reason to know) that the loan proceeds of the bridge loan would be paid out to T's old shareholders while the acquisition debt would be imposed on T's assets.

¶1706.2.3 T's Selling Shareholders

Those of T's selling shareholders who knew (or should have known) that the LBO was being structured so that T's pre-acquisition creditors would be prejudiced (i.e., T's old shareholders were being paid out of borrowed money, the debt for which was being imposed on T's assets) may be required to refund the purchase price received for their T stock.[6]

¶1706.2.4 Newco and Its Shareholders

Newco (or possibly even Newco's shareholders) may be liable for the amount of the fraudulent conveyance, (a) as transferees of T's assets, (b) on the ground

---

[6] See O'Donnell v. Royal Business Group, Inc. (In re Oxford Homes, Inc.), 180 B.R. 1 (Bankr. D. Me. 1995), where the court enjoined a selling shareholder from transferring the cash proceeds received in an LBO on the ground that the LBO may have been a fraudulent transfer under the UFTA.

that the payment to T's selling shareholders was made for Newco's (or its shareholders') benefit, or (c) as aiders and abettors of a breach of fiduciary duty by T's directors.[7]

¶1706.2.5   T's (or Its Successor's) Directors

T's (or its successor's) directors may be liable for a breach of duty to creditors.[8]

¶1706.2.6   T's and Newco's Professionals

The professionals (e.g., investment bankers, accountants, and attorneys) who assisted in the LBO arrangements may be required to refund their fees. They may also find themselves sued on grounds of negligence or even culpability for damages to T and its creditors arising out of the transaction (including a claim by T's directors for indemnification for damages for which they have been held liable).

¶1706.2.7   Guarantors of LBO Acquisition Debt

If VC or other Newco shareholders guarantee the acquisition debt incurred by Newco or T to effectuate the LBO, and the LBO acquisition debt is later impaired by the fraudulent conveyance doctrine (e.g., the lien on T's assets is voided and/or the acquisition debt is subordinated to other T creditors), the guarantor may find itself the sole remaining obligor on the acquisition debt.

¶1706.2.8   Guarantors of T's Pre-acquisition Debts

If some of T's pre-acquisition indebtedness (e.g., T's old working capital line) is paid off as a part of the LBO, and such old T indebtedness was guaranteed by an old T shareholder or other person, the guarantor would normally be released when the old T debt was paid as part of the LBO. However, if the fraudulent conveyance doctrine is applied to the LBO, the old guarantor may be required to reimburse T for the amount paid to the old T creditor in the LBO on the ground that the payment releasing the guarantee was a fraudulent conveyance (or preference) for the benefit of the guarantor.

---

[7] See *HealthCo* (discussed at ¶1706.6.17).
[8] See *HealthCo* (discussed at ¶1706.6.17).

¶1706.3   Principal Defenses to Fraudulent Conveyance Claim

Participants in an LBO (e.g., T's selling shareholders, the acquisition lenders, Newco, and Newco's shareholders including VC) generally have five possible defenses to a fraudulent conveyance claim.[9]

(1)   No prejudice to creditors. T's pre-acquisition creditors were not prejudiced by the LBO (nor were its post-acquisition creditors) because T's assets were not burdened by the acquisition debt. For example, Newco (not T) borrowed the money for the LBO and Newco purchased T's stock, T did not guarantee Newco's acquisition debt, and T was thereafter a separate Newco subsidiary.

(2)   No badge of constructive fraud. Even though T (or its successor) was burdened (in whole or in part) with the acquisition debt so that T's pre-acquisition creditors were prejudiced, nevertheless T (or its successor) after the LBO was (a) solvent, (b) had adequate capital, and (c) was expected to be able to pay its obligations as they mature, i.e., none of the "badges of constructive fraud" enumerated in the various fraudulent conveyance statutes was present, and indeed the subsequent financial distress suffered by T (or its successor) was caused by events that could not have been reasonably anticipated at the time of the LBO. It is helpful to VC in establishing this defense that substantial time passed between the LBO and T's bankruptcy and that T was able to meet its obligations as a going concern during this period.[10]

(3)   Adequate consideration. T (or its successor) received adequate consideration for incurring the acquisition debt, even after application of the step-transaction doctrine, which would collapse the transaction vis-a-vis a transferee (e.g., an old T shareholder receiving sales proceeds or an acquisition lender receiving a note and asset lien) who knew (or had reason to know) that T's creditors were being prejudiced by the LBO, i.e., that the borrowed money was being paid out to T's old shareholders while the acquisition debt was being imposed on T's (or its successor's) assets to the detriment of T's creditors.

(4)   Good faith. The LBO participant under attack neither knew nor had reason to know that the LBO would result in T's insolvency, undercapitalization, or inability to pay debts as they mature. In making this determination, either such participant was not required to make a due diligence investigation or such participant's due diligence investigation (if made or if required) reasonably supported the conclusion that none of such badges of constructive fraud was present.

---

[9] This section assumes that the LBO was not effectuated with actual intent to hinder, delay, or defraud T's (or its successor's) present or future creditors.

[10] Thus, a 1998 Ninth Circuit case upheld a jury verdict for VC where VC produced evidence at trial that T's trade creditors were paid in full for three years following T's LBO and T's insolvency was caused by post-LBO increased competition in the home building industry. Pay 'n Pak Stores, Inc. (In re PNP Holdings, Corp.), 141 F.3d 1178 (Table Disposition) (9th Cir. 1998).

(5)   No standing. At the time of T's (or its successor's) financial collapse, there were no remaining creditors with standing to complain about the LBO—i.e., there were no pre-acquisition creditors and (if the LBO resulted in undercapitalization or inability to pay debts as they mature) no post-LBO creditors (other than those who assumed the risk by intentionally extending credit to a highly leveraged entity) if, as certain cases suggest, this developing defense is accepted.

The exact wording of a particular defense may vary depending upon whether the fraudulent conveyance claim turns on Bankruptcy Code §548, the UFCA, the UFTA, a modernized version of the Statute of Elizabeth, or Bankruptcy Code §544(b)'s incorporation of state law.

Moreover, these defenses are not mutually exclusive. Indeed, as applied by the courts, they often tend to merge and overlap based on the particular facts of the case.

Reviewing these defenses is useful in identifying evolving trends in LBO fraudulent conveyance law, which should be considered in structuring LBOs.

¶1706.3.1   No Prejudice to Creditors

¶1706.1.1 illustrates a structure in which none of T's creditors (neither pre-acquisition nor post-acquisition creditors) as prejudiced by the LBO because T assumed no obligations and granted no asset liens in connection with the transaction. Should T ultimately suffer financial collapse, the problem necessarily results from events unrelated to the LBO and related financing.

¶1706.3.2   No Badge of Constructive Fraud

Under this defense, T (or its successor) after the LBO did not suffer any of the three badges of constructive fraud enumerated in the various fraudulent conveyance statutes (discussed in ¶1706.4.1). That is, T (1) was solvent, (2) had adequate capital, and (3) was reasonably expected to be able to pay its obligations as they mature. This defense applies even if T was adversely affected by the LBO financing in that T (or its successor) incurred or guaranteed the LBO debt or granted an asset lien to secure the LBO debt. However, because the LBO did not create any of the three "badges of constructive fraud," the various fraudulent conveyance statutes do not apply, even if T (or its successor) ultimately suffers financial collapse and, as a result of the LBO debt, T's other creditors suffer diminished recovery.

Thus, for example, the district court in *Moody* (discussed at ¶1706.6.9), after finding that the LBO did not create any of the three badges of constructive fraud, denied the fraudulent conveyance claim on the following ground: "The law, as it now stands, does not require participants in a leveraged buyout to become insurers of the company's ultimate success."[11]

---

[11] See *Moody* (discussed at ¶1706.6.9).

(1)   Insolvent. While the various fraudulent conveyance statutes define solvency differently, the courts have been generally consistent in assessing whether particular facts should give rise to a finding of solvency or insolvency. Generally, if the court finds that T (or its successor) was left as a viable and strong enterprise immediately after the LBO, it will value T's assets as a going concern.[12] If, however, the court concludes that T was not a viable enterprise immediately after the LBO, it will value T's assets at their liquidation value.[13]

(2)   Adequate capitalization. The courts have also emphasized T's viability as a going concern in determining whether T was left with adequate capital after the LBO. Factors such as conservative operating projections,[14] access to new lines of credit after the LBO,[15] and post-LBO refinancing[16] have served as the basis for findings of adequate capitalization.[17]

(3)   Contemporaneous evidence. Two items of factual proof regarding the parties' pre-LBO planning have been persuasive to courts. *First*, it is helpful to show that the parties engaged in reasonable pre-LBO due diligence procedures to ascertain and evaluate all of the economic risks that T (or its successor) would face after the LBO, and that the ultimate financial collapse of T (or its successor) was attributable to an unanticipated (and not anticipatable) event, i.e., an independent, intervening event that was not reasonably predictable at the time of the LBO.

Second, it is helpful to show that the parties' reasonable pre-LBO due diligence included (1) the preparation of reasonable asset appraisals and reasonable liability analyses (including reasonable estimates of contingent and unliquidated claims), which demonstrated that T (or its successor) would be solvent (i.e., asset FV in excess of reasonably anticipated liabilities) after the LBO[18] and (2) the preparation of reasonable cash flow projections (based on reasonable assumptions as to such issues as sales levels, expense levels, obsolescence of technology, success of re-

---

[12] See *Mellon* (discussed at ¶1706.6.8), *Moody* (discussed at ¶1706.6.9), and *Morse Tool* (discussed at ¶1706.6.12).

[13] See *O'Day* (discussed at ¶1706.6.10) and *Gleneagles* (discussed at ¶1706.6.1). In *Mellon* (discussed at ¶1706.6.8), in which T and Newco's parent had each guaranteed the acquisition debt incurred by Newco, the court declined to treat T as liable for the entire acquisition debt in assessing T's solvency, because Newco's parent was a viable guarantor.

[14] See *Moody* (discussed at ¶1706.6.9) and compare *O'Day* (discussed at ¶1706.6.10) and *Morse Tool* (discussed at ¶1706.6.12).

[15] See *Mellon* (discussed at ¶1706.6.8).

[16] See *Mellon* (discussed at ¶1706.6.8).

[17] In *HealthCo* (discussed at ¶1706.6.17) the court explained that unreasonably small capital "connotes a condition of financial debility short of insolvency . . . but which makes insolvency reasonably foreseeable." Brandt v. Hicks, Muse & Co., Inc. (In re HealthCo Int'l, Inc.), 208 B.R. 288, 302 (Bankr. D. Mass. 1997).

[18] However, if T has significant unliquidated claims at the time of the LBO (e.g., alleged asbestos liability), one court concluded that Bankruptcy Code §548 and the Uniform Fraudulent Transfer Act require the court, for purposes of an insolvency analysis, to make its own "objective" determination during a fraudulent conveyance trial of the amount of the liability as such liability existed at the time of the transfer, and T's contemporaneous estimate at the time of LBO consummation has no bearing on the court's later valuation of the liability for purposes of the solvency analysis. Committee of Asbestos Personal Injury Claimants, et. al. v. Sealed Air Corp. (In re W.R. Grace & Co.), 281 B.R. 852, 857 (Bankr. D. Del. 2002) .

search and development efforts, interest rates, ability to renew or extend the acquisition debt, ability to weather reasonably foreseeable economic downturns, ability to borrow additional working capital, ability to sell extraneous assets (and use the sales proceeds therefrom), recession versus boom, etc.), which demonstrated that T (or its successor) would be expected to be able to meet its debts as they mature.[19]

¶1706.3.3   Adequate Consideration

To assert this defense successfully, an LBO participant generally must be able to show that T (or its successor) received adequate consideration for incurring LBO obligations. Several important aspects of this defense are discussed below.

(1)   Amount of consideration required. The Bankruptcy Code, the UFTA, and the UFCA all require that T (or its successor) receive consideration reasonably equivalent to the amount of liability T incurred in the LBO. However, a few Statute of Elizabeth states, such as Virginia, apparently allow substantially smaller consideration. Thus, in the C-T case,[20] T assumed $27 million of LBO debt but received only $4 million of new equity investment plus new management. The court upheld these two elements of value as satisfying Virginia's version of the Statute of Elizabeth, which required that T receive "consideration deemed valuable in law."

(2)   Step-transaction doctrine. The step-transaction doctrine (discussed at ¶¶1706.4.2 through 1706.4.5) is generally applied in the context of the adequate-consideration defense. A court is likely to find that T received inadequate consideration for incurring the LBO debt if loan proceeds were paid out to T's selling shareholders. For example, in *Gleneagles* (discussed at ¶1706.6.1), Lender made a loan to T in exchange for T's note and mortgage. T reloaned the proceeds to Newco, which used the proceeds to purchase T's stock. The court held that T transferred the note and mortgage to Lender and received nothing in return. However, in *Morse Tool* (discussed at ¶1706.6.12), the court used the step-transaction doctrine to find that there was adequate consideration, reasoning after collapsing the LBO steps that T purchased its predecessor's assets having a value of $13 million for a purchase price of $10.4 million.

Whether a court will apply the step-transaction doctrine to a particular LBO participant (e.g., an LBO lender receiving a note and asset lien or an old T shareholder receiving sales proceeds) generally turns on the degree of such participant's knowledge of, and participation in, the LBO transaction. If such LBO participant knows (or has reason to know) that the LBO was structured so that borrowed

---

[19] In *HealthCo* (discussed at ¶1706.6.17), where T was acquired in an LBO that rendered T undercapitalized, the court held that T's directors had a duty to carefully consider the consequences of the LBO to T's creditors, and were negligent in failing to consider whether VC's projections of T's post-LBO performance were credible.

[20] C-T of Va., Inc. v. Euroshoe Assocs., 762 F. Supp. 675 (W.D. Va. 1991), *aff'd*, 953 F.2d 637 (4th Cir. 1992).

money was being paid out to T's old shareholders while the acquisition debt was being imposed on T's (or its successor's) assets to the detriment of T's creditors, and the participant assists in implementing the LBO, a court will likely collapse the transaction as to such participant.[21]

(3) Direct and indirect consideration. Obviously, if T receives and retains cash or assets in the LBO transaction, T is receiving consideration. For example, in *Morse Tool* (discussed at ¶1706.6.12), the court found that the spin-off of certain assets to T in the LBO was analogous to an asset sale in which T received its predecessor's assets, which, on a going concern basis, were found to be worth more than the price T paid for those assets in connection with the LBO. Courts have also recognized certain kinds of indirect consideration. In *Mellon* (discussed at ¶1706.6.8), the court concluded that business synergies between T and Newco constituted consideration to T and that T's increased borrowing ability arising out of the LBO constituted consideration to T. However, in *O'Day* (discussed at ¶1706.6.10), the court refused to find that T's access to new lines of credit as a consequence of the LBO constituted consideration to T. While these decisions at first blush appear inconsistent, this may be explained by the fact that in *Mellon* T was a viable entity after the LBO, while in *O'Day* T was insolvent after the LBO and hence presumably unable to use its new lines of credit.[22]

¶1706.3.4 Good Faith

Good faith is both an affirmative requirement of certain statutes (the UFCA requires a finding of "good faith" to establish that "fair consideration" was given)

---

[21] See *O'Day* (discussed at ¶1706.6.10), *Moody* (discussed at ¶1706.6.9), *Gleneagles* (discussed at ¶1706.6.1), *Wieboldt Stores* (discussed at ¶1706.6.7), and *Bay Plastics* (discussed at ¶1706.6.15). The step-transaction doctrine has also been used with increasing frequency to collapse multistep transactions outside the LBO context. For example, the Bankruptcy Court for the Southern District of New York, citing *Gleneagles* and *Wieboldt Stores*, applied the step-transaction doctrine to find that certain leases were, in substance, loans. See In re Best Prods. Co., 157 B.R. 222, 229 (Bankr. S.D.N.Y. 1993). Similarly, the Second Circuit Court of Appeals has upheld the use of the step-transaction doctrine to void a mortgage when the lender knew that the borrower had received the mortgaged property in a potentially fraudulent conveyance. See Orr v. Kinderhill Corp., 991 F.2d 31 (2d Cir. 1993) (applying N.Y. Debt. & Cred. Law §273-a (McKinney 1966 & Supp. 1993)). In 1995, a federal district court invoked the step-transaction doctrine (although rejecting the fraudulent transfer attack) with respect to a multistep transaction in which VC paid T $200 million for (1) $125 million of T's common stock and (2) T's agreement to use $75 million of the $200 million to repurchase T shares from its existing shareholders in a tender offer. The court, citing *Gleneagles*, held that the two transactions must be collapsed to assess their impact upon T (which was by then in bankruptcy). After collapsing the transaction, the court concluded that T received FV for the $75 million of its own shares which it purchased in the tender offer because the money to fund that redemption came from VC. See Official Committee of Unsecured Creditors of Phar-Mor, Inc. v. Action Indus., Inc. (In re Phar-Mor Sec. Litigation), 185 B.R. 497, 503 (W.D. Pa. 1995).

[22] A 1998 Ninth Circuit case upheld a jury verdict for VC where VC produced evidence at trial that T received value from the LBO because T was saved from being taken over by a corporate raider and T's pre-LBO management was preserved, as a consequence of which alleged benefits T was enabled to survive as a going concern for three years after the LBO. Pay 'n Pak Stores, Inc. (In re PNP Holdings, Corp.), 141 F.3d 1178 (Table Disposition) (9th Cir. 1998).

and a defense in others (the Bankruptcy Code and the UFTA permit a transferee who gave "value" in "good faith" to retain a lien for value actually given). Certain elements of the good-faith defense appear to be consistently applied:

(1)   Step-transaction doctrine. Courts have directly linked the application of the step-transaction doctrine and a participant's good faith. If the participant—particularly an LBO lender or a selling T shareholder—knew (or should have known) that LBO loan proceeds were being paid to T's old shareholders while T's assets were being burdened by the acquisition loan, the courts have held that such participant did not act in good faith and have collapsed the various steps of the LBO to find the participant liable for a fraudulent conveyance. In *Gleneagles* (discussed at ¶1706.6.1), the court applied the step-transaction doctrine against Lender, who knew that T would obtain no ultimate benefit from the LBO loan and would be left insolvent after the LBO. Even more dramatically, in *Wieboldt Stores* (discussed at ¶1706.6.7), the court applied the step-transaction doctrine against T's selling shareholders who actively participated in structuring the LBO (i.e., shareholders who were T officers, directors, or control persons) but refused to apply the doctrine to public selling T shareholders who were passive participants in Newco's tender offer for T's stock.

(2)   Due diligence. If an LBO participant engaged in reasonable due diligence and thereafter reasonably believed (or had reason to believe) that T (or its successor) was receiving fair value, such participant generally has been found to have acted in good faith and hence has been absolved of responsibility for T's demise.[23] It would appear, however, that not all LBO participants are held to the same standard of due diligence. In *Kupetz* and *Wieboldt Stores*[24] the courts held that certain old T selling shareholders, who did not participate in structuring the LBO, did not have exposure despite the fact that they did not perform any due diligence investigations.[25] On the other hand, in *Gleneagles* and *O'Day*[26] the courts refused to absolve lenders who claimed no knowledge of the facts that led to T's bankruptcy, on the ground that those lenders knew enough to require an investigation of the facts.

These cases may well be reconcilable on the ground that the amount of required due diligence by a participant should vary depending upon the nature of the participant.[27] A professional lender, for example, should be required to make the type of investigation normally made by a professional lender, while a public

---

[23] See *Moody* (discussed at ¶1706.6.9).

[24] Discussed at ¶1706.6.5 and ¶1706.6.7, respectively.

[25] See *HealthCo* (discussed at ¶1706.6.17).

[26] Discussed at ¶1706.6.1 and ¶1706.6.10, respectively.

[27] See generally Sherwin, Creditors' Rights Against Participants in a Leveraged Buyout, 72 Minn. L. Rev. 449, 509-520 (1988): "Rather than selecting one degree of *scienter* to determine the good faith of all transferees, courts should develop a set of principles defining how the *scienter* standard should vary in different contexts." Id. at 512. See also Fogelson, Toward a Rational Treatment of Fraudulent Conveyance Cases Involving Leveraged Buyouts, 68 N.Y.U. L. Rev. 552, 553 (1993): The absence of a clear standard for determining whether to step transactions together "undermines the ability of LBO lenders to assess the possibility of liability before extending LBO loans. . . ."

shareholder (or a private non-control, non-officer, non-director shareholder) should not be expected to conduct nearly as thorough an examination, at least in the absence of facts putting the shareholder on notice as to the potential for a fraudulent conveyance.

¶1706.3.5   No Standing

(1)   Statute of Elizabeth states. In an action under state law when a version of the Statute of Elizabeth applies, the challenging creditor, to have standing to assert the claim, must generally have been a pre-LBO T creditor or his status as a creditor must have been reasonably foreseeable (e.g., an ongoing supplier). Moreover, as discussed at ¶1706.4.2, successful assertion of a fraudulent conveyance claim in a state law action by such a creditor benefits only creditors with such standing to assert the claim.

(2)   UFCA and UFTA states. In an action under state law when the UFCA or the UFTA applies, only an existing T creditor at the time of the LBO has standing if the fraudulent conveyance results from T's (or its successor's) insolvency as a result of the LBO.[28] However, if the fraudulent conveyance results from T's (or its successor's) unreasonably small capital as a result of the LBO or the expectation that T (or its successor) would incur debts which are beyond T's (or its successor's) ability to pay as they mature, not only do T's creditors at the time of the LBO have standing, but so do future creditors of T (or its successor).

It would be logical to deny standing to a post-LBO creditor who intentionally extended credit to T (or its successor) knowing about the company's highly leveraged condition. Although the statutes do not suggest that such a defense exists, the decision in *Ohio Corrugating II* (discussed at ¶1706.6.6) and certain Ninth Circuit cases seem to adopt such a position.

In *Ohio Corrugating II* the court commented that "subsequent creditors are in a substantially different position from existing creditors" because they "willingly extend ... credit to the Debtor after the buyout in reliance on the performance of the 'new' company," and there is "no basis ... for holding that the constructive fraud provisions of [Bankruptcy Code] §548 [which permits the trustee to avoid a transfer for the benefit of subsequent creditors] may be utilized as a form of insurance for creditors whose claims matured after the buyout."[29] By a parity of reasoning, the same conclusion should apply under the UFCA and the UFTA. Indeed, courts in the Ninth Circuit have stated in several decisions that "in the context of LBOs, future creditors' right to sue [under the UFCA] must be limited to cases where there is actual intent to defraud or to conceal the transaction from

---

[28] In *Morse Tool* (discussed at ¶1706.6.12), T had no separate corporate existence prior to the LBO; the court found that T could not have had pre-LBO creditors, and therefore neither an alleged pre-LBO T creditor nor Newco-T's trustee would have standing to sue under the UFCA on the ground that the transaction rendered Newco-T insolvent.

[29] See *Ohio Corrugating II* (discussed at ¶1706.6.6).

public scrutiny."[30] These courts reason that fraudulent conveyance statutes were designed to protect creditors from secret transactions by debtors, and therefore post-LBO creditors should not be able to avoid as a fraudulent conveyance an LBO when such creditors "knew or could easily have found out about the transaction."[31]

By contrast, a district court in Rhode Island has held that the Ninth Circuit's application of California law is incorrect and that under California's version of the UFTA, a creditor whose claim arose after a well-publicized LBO would be permitted to challenge the LBO as a fraudulent transfer.[32]

Whether the Ninth Circuit's judicial exception to the application of fraudulent conveyance laws to LBO transactions marks the beginning of a trend to protect LBOs against subsequent creditors who intentionally extended credit to the post-LBO entity, knowing that it was highly leveraged, is not yet clear.

Successful assertion of a fraudulent conveyance claim in a state law action (i.e., a case pending either in state court or in a federal court pursuant to diversity jurisdiction) by a creditor with standing under the UFCA and the UFTA benefits only that creditor and other creditors with standing.

(3)   Bankruptcy Code §548. In an action under Bankruptcy Code §548 (which can be asserted only if the LBO occurred within one year before filing of the bankruptcy petition), it is not necessary for any creditor to have standing to assert the fraudulent conveyance claim, since the trustee has power to assert the claim. In *Ohio Corrugating II* (discussed immediately above), however, the court did dismiss a §548 case on the ground that the statute's constructive fraud provision cannot be applied to benefit post-LBO creditors who knowingly dealt with the highly leveraged debtor. Similarly, certain Ninth Circuit cases have noted in dicta that transfers attacked under Bankruptcy Code §548(a)(2)(B) (the Bankruptcy Code's constructive fraud provisions) may not be avoided unless there are pre-LBO creditors with claims against T's bankruptcy estate.[33] It is not clear whether these precedents mark the beginning of a trend to protect LBOs against subsequent creditors who intentionally extended credit to the post-LBO entity, knowing of its highly leveraged status.

Unless the standing rule in *Ohio Corrugating II* and the Ninth Circuit cases applies, successful assertion of a fraudulent conveyance claim under Bankruptcy Code §548 by the trustee would avoid the LBO transfer for the benefit of all unpaid creditors, not merely those (if any) who can demonstrate actual harm caused by the LBO.

---

[30] Lippi v. City Bank, 955 F.2d 599, 606 (9th Cir. 1992), (citing *Credit Managers*, discussed at ¶1706.6.3, and *Kupetz*, discussed at ¶1706.6.5). But see *Yucaipa* (discussed at ¶1706.6.18).

[31] See *Kupetz* (discussed at ¶1706.6.5). See also Lippi v. City Bank, 955 F.2d 599, 606 (9th Cir. 1992), and *Credit Managers* (discussed at ¶1706.6.3).

[32] See *Yucaipa* (discussed at ¶1706.6.18).

[33] See *Richmond Produce*, discussed at ¶1706.6.11 (citing *Kupetz*, discussed at ¶1706.6.5). See also Lippi v. City Bank, 955 F.2d 599, 606 (9th Cir. 1992), and *Credit Managers* (discussed at ¶1706.6.3). But see *Yucaipa* (discussed at ¶1706.6.18) where the court concluded that cases in the Ninth Circuit were wrong in holding that the UFTA may not be used to attack well-publicized, above board LBOs.

(4) Bankruptcy Code §544(b) state law claim. If the LBO occurred earlier than the one-year period of Bankruptcy Code §548, an action nevertheless can be brought by the trustee under Bankruptcy Code §544(b), based on the applicable state law fraudulent conveyance statute, so long as the LBO occurred within four (or six) years (or whatever limitation period is specified by the applicable state law) before the date of the bankruptcy petition and so long as the trustee commenced the action within the applicable period permitted by the Bankruptcy Code (generally two years after the trustee's appointment).[34] In a §544(b) case, the trustee can assert the claim only if there is at least one creditor with standing under state law (as described above) to assert such state fraudulent conveyance claim. As a practical matter, a debtor is highly likely to have at least one pre-acquisition creditor with such standing (as discussed in ¶1706.4.5) and even if it does not, post-LBO creditors frequently have standing under state law (as discussed above in this ¶1706.3.5) to assert state fraudulent conveyance claims, unless the courts engraft onto state law standing or onto §544(b) actions a limitation like the one imposed by *Ohio Corrugating II* and the Ninth Circuit cases (excluding subsequent creditors who willingly extended credit after the LBO in reliance on Newco's performance). Unless the standing rule in *Ohio Corrugating II* and the Ninth Circuit cases applies, successful assertion of a fraudulent conveyance claim under Bankruptcy Code §544(b) by the trustee would avoid the LBO transfer for the benefit of all unpaid creditors, not merely the one (or more) with state law standing.

¶1706.3.6 Examples

The examples below illustrate how the authors believe a court might handle a fraudulent conveyance attack on an LBO.

EXAMPLE 1. No One Knew the Problem

T is a computer manufacturer with leading-edge technology that causes its computers to be in hot demand and gives it strong cash flow.

Newco is formed by VC for the purpose of buying T. Newco receives $1 million from VC as equity, borrows $9 million from Lender, purchases T's assets for $10 million, and assumes T's pre-acquisition debt (or otherwise structures its acquisition of T so as to impose the $9 million acquisition debt on T's assets).

Everyone in the industry believes that T's technology will not be rendered obsolete for at least five years, so T's strong cash flow over the next five years will allow it to pay off the full $9 million acquisition debt and provide VC with a large profit. All the LBO participants (Lender, Newco, VC, and

---

[34] 11 U.S.C. §546(a)(1)(A). See Murphy v. Meritor Sav. Bank (In re O'Day Corp.), 126 B.R. 370, 391-392 (Bankr. D. Mass. 1991), discussed at ¶1706.6.10.

T's old shareholders) perform a reasonable due diligence investigation that confirms these facts, and indeed, even T's principal competitor ("CompetitorCo") does not expect to develop new technology that would render obsolete T's leading-edge technology for at least five years. Based on these facts, Lender, Newco, VC, and T's old shareholders (1) obtain appraisals and solvency opinions showing Newco to be solvent and adequately capitalized immediately after the LBO and (2) prepare cash flow projections showing Newco to be able to pay its debts as they mature after the LBO.

Shortly after the Newco/T LBO, CompetitorCo makes a startling and unanticipated breakthrough discovery that causes T's technology and products to be rendered obsolete only one year after the LBO, leaving Newco unable to pay Newco's acquisition or T's pre-acquisition liabilities.

T's pre-acquisition creditors claim a fraudulent conveyance against Lender, T's old shareholders, and VC.

It appears that all the parties should be able to defend the case successfully on the ground that Newco (immediately after the LBO) was solvent, was adequately capitalized, and was expected to be able to pay its debts as they mature, and that T's financial troubles are due to an unanticipated intervening event.

EXAMPLE 2.   Third Party to Whom LBO Participants Had No Access Knew the Problem Before the LBO

Same facts as Example 1 except that an engineer who worked for CompetitorCo knew shortly *before* the LBO that he was in the process of developing new technology that would render obsolete T's technology and products. The engineer, however, maintained this information in strict confidence for CompetitorCo's benefit until after the LBO. Thus, everyone else in the industry (including all of Newco's and T's employees) believed (at the time of the Newco/T LBO) that T's technology would remain on leading edge for five years.

It appears that Lender, T's old shareholders, and VC should successfully defend the fraudulent conveyance claim on the ground that all of the LBO participants (after performing adequate due diligence) reasonably believed that Newco (immediately after the LBO) was solvent, was adequately capitalized, and was expected to be able to pay its debts as they mature, and that Newco's subsequent financial troubles are due to an intervening act that they could not have anticipated at the time of the LBO. Although CompetitorCo's engineer was aware (at the time of the LBO) of the financial troubles that would befall Newco, he was an employee of T's principal competitor (with fiduciary duties to CompetitorCo to maintain the technology breakthrough in strict confidence for CompetitorCo's benefit), and hence, no amount of reasonable due diligence investigation would have uncovered this information for the participants in the Newco/T LBO.

EXAMPLE 3. The Problem Was Generally Known Before LBO, but LBO Participants Did Not Discover It

Same facts as Example 2 except that (1) it was widely rumored in the industry that CompetitorCo was in the process of developing technology that would render obsolete T's technology and hence its computers, although no hard facts were available, and (2) the participants in the Newco/T LBO did no due diligence investigation and hence failed to discover the widely rumored problem.

A court might well uphold a fraudulent conveyance charge against a participant in the Newco/T LBO if the court concluded that both (a) and (b) below were true.

(a) Such LBO participant had a duty to perform a due diligence investigation. A court is most likely to so hold with respect to a professional lender, for whom a due diligence investigation is routine. A court is also likely to so hold with respect to T's control shareholders (i.e., T shareholders who, before the LBO, were T officers or directors or who held controlling blocks of T stock), who thus are actively participating in the LBO transaction for T. A court may also so hold with respect to VC, who is actively engaged in structuring the LBO transaction for Newco. Whether a court would so hold with respect to minority T shareholders probably turns on whether they knew (or should have known) of the rumors that CompetitorCo was developing technology that would render obsolete T's technology and hence its computers, and whether they knew (or should have known) that they were being paid with borrowed money, the debt for which was being imposed on T's assets to the detriment of T's pre-acquisition creditors.

(b) The rumors, if known to a party to the Newco/T LBO, would have been sufficiently credible as to cause it reasonably to change its belief as to Newco's financial condition immediately after the LBO, i.e., its solvency, capital adequacy, and/or expected ability to pay debts as they mature.

EXAMPLE 4. The Problem Was Actually Known to LBO Participant Before LBO

Same facts as Example 3 except that a particular participant in the Newco/T LBO actually knew of the rumors that CompetitorCo was in the process of developing technology that would render obsolete T's technology and hence its computers, but ignored this information in concluding that Newco (immediately after the LBO) would be solvent, adequately capitalized, and expected to be able to pay debts as they mature. A court might well uphold a fraudulent conveyance charge against this participant if the court concluded that this participant's knowledge should reasonably have caused it to change its belief as to Newco's solvency, capital adequacy, and/or expected ability to pay debts (viewed immediately after the LBO).

EXAMPLE 5.   LBO Participant Did Not Actually Know of the Problem but Should Have Known

Same facts as Example 4 except that a particular LBO participant, although not actually learning of the rumors, did know of some facts indicating that such rumors existed. For example, several industry members told the LBO participant that odd information was surfacing regarding T's technology and that the LBO participant should check it out carefully, but the LBO participant failed to do so.

The answer would be similar to Examples 3 and 4, i.e., a court might well uphold a fraudulent conveyance charge against the LBO participant if the court concluded that (a) the LBO participant had a duty to perform a further due diligence investigation, (b) the LBO participant would have learned of the rumors if it had properly carried out any investigation it had a duty to perform, and (c) the rumors, if the LBO participant had learned of them, would have been sufficiently credible as to cause it to change its belief as to Newco's solvency, capital adequacy, and/or expected ability to pay debts (viewed immediately after the LBO).

Hence, when an LBO participant has a duty to perform a due diligence investigation, there is generally a duty to pursue reasonable leads generated by the due diligence investigation. Indeed, even if an LBO participant does not have such a duty to perform an investigation, once the participant has actual knowledge of adverse information of the type that would cause a reasonable person to look further into the facts, the LBO participant may well have a duty to do so.

¶1706.4   Sources of Fraudulent Conveyance Law

¶1706.4.1   General Considerations

(1)   **Time period.** Fraudulent conveyances made within one year before commencement of a bankruptcy case are voidable under the Bankruptcy Code, whether or not there is an actual unpaid creditor who was harmed by the transac-

tion, because the trustee can assert the claim.[35] However, in bankruptcy, the trustee can rely on state law if it provides a longer limitation period (which will be extended by the Bankruptcy Code, as discussed below) and if there is at least one creditor with standing to assert the claim.[36] The applicable statutes of limitation for state fraudulent conveyance actions vary. In some states, the time period may be as long as six years.[37] In states that have adopted the UFTA, however, the time period is four years unless modified by state law.[38]

(2) Choice-of-law issues. Choice of state law, frequently a difficult issue, turns on such factors as the debtor's state of incorporation, its principal place of business, the state in which the transfers took place, and the states in which the creditors are located. Because a fraudulent conveyance action by a creditor or the trustee in bankruptcy is not an action on a contract, choice-of-law clauses in contracts do not bind the creditors or the trustee.[39]

¶1706.4.2 Statute of Elizabeth States

(1) Generally. As of 6/1/03, 6 states (mainly in the South) and Puerto Rico still operated under somewhat modernized versions of the 1570 English Statute of Elizabeth:[40]

Alaska	Puerto Rico
Kentucky	South Carolina
Louisiana	Virginia
Mississippi	

These laws generally void transfers made with an intent to hinder, delay, or defraud creditors. Because it is difficult to prove actual intent, certain circumstances (known as "badges of fraud") are presumptive of intent to hinder, delay, or defraud creditors. The most significant "badge of fraud" is the giving of "inadequate consideration" at a time when the transferor was "insolvent" in the sense that either it had liabilities greater than assets or it was unable to pay its debts as they mature.

(2) Standing. Generally, the challenging creditor must have been an actual creditor at the time of the transfer, or his status as a creditor thereafter must have

---

[35] Bankruptcy Code §548.

[36] Bankruptcy Code §544(b).

[37] Indeed, a bankruptcy court applying Massachusetts' (now superceded) UFCA has held that the statute of limitations for a fraudulent conveyance challenge to an LBO was as long as 20 years, as an action on a contract under seal. Stevens Linen Assocs. v. Crawford (In re Stevens Linen Assocs.), 156 B.R. 718, 721 (Bankr. D. Mass. 1993).

[38] UFTA §9, 7A U.L.A. 665 (West 1985).

[39] See O'Day (discussed at ¶1706.6.10).

[40] See UFTA, Prefatory Note, 7A, Part II U.L.A. 268 (West 1999).

been reasonably foreseeable (e.g., an ongoing supplier). In Statute of Elizabeth states, successful assertion of a fraudulent conveyance claim benefits only those plaintiff creditors with standing to assert the claim[41] (whereas the rule under federal bankruptcy law may be far more draconian because, on the face of the statute and unless limited by judicial rulings such as *Ohio Corrugating II* and certain Ninth Circuit cases, the trustee is permitted both to challenge the transaction even when there is no remaining creditor who was harmed by the transaction and to avoid the transaction for the benefit of all unpaid creditors—see ¶1706.4.5).

(3) **Inadequate consideration.** The law is unclear on the meaning of adequate consideration. While precedent is skimpy, most courts would probably require at least some reasonable equivalence between the value of the property transferred by the debtor and the value received by the debtor in exchange. One LBO was upheld, although the value given was far less than the property transferred: the case arose under Virginia law, which requires only "consideration deemed valuable in law."[42] In that case T provided $27 million to redeem its old shares at the same time as Newco merged into T, bringing T "an investment of new capital [in the amount of $4 million] as well as new management. . . . Although [T] may have given up more than it received, it gained something and that is enough to prevent avoidance of the transaction" under Virginia law.[43]

(4) **Insolvent.** It is likely that a court in a Statute of Elizabeth state will analyze issues regarding valuation of the debtor's assets and timing of its liabilities in the same fashion as courts dealing with the UFCA, the UFTA, and the Bankruptcy Code. For a discussion of the going concern versus the liquidation-value test, see ¶¶1706.4.3 through 1706.4.5.

(5) **Step-transaction doctrine.** The courts in Statute of Elizabeth states are likely to find that, if an LBO is structured so the newly-created acquisition debt (incurred to pay T's shareholders) becomes a claim against T's (or its successor's) assets, the LBO steps should be collapsed and viewed as if T received inadequate consideration for incurring obligations to the lenders, because the amount supplied by the lenders as consideration for such obligations was paid to T's shareholders rather than adding to T's assets. *Wieboldt Stores* (discussed at ¶1706.6.7) so held in applying Illinois's (now superseded) version of the Statute of Elizabeth, but only vis-a-vis a transferee who knew or should have known that T was being burdened by debt while not receiving and retaining adequate consideration therefor.

---

[41] See, e.g., Va. Code Ann. §55-81 (Michie 1991).
[42] C-T of Va., Inc. v. Euroshoe Assocs., 762 F. Supp. 675 (W.D. Va. 1991), aff'd, 953 F.2d 637 (4th Cir. 1992).
[43] 762 F. Supp. at 678.

¶1706.4.3   Uniform Fraudulent Conveyance Act

(1)   Generally. The UFCA was drafted by the National Conference of Commissioners on Uniform State Laws in 1918 in an effort to bring uniformity to the law of fraudulent conveyances. As of 6/1/03, 3 states (including New York), plus the Virgin Islands, operated under the UFCA:

Maryland	Virgin Islands
New York	Wyoming

To constitute a fraudulent conveyance under the UFCA, a conveyance must be made either (1) with actual intent to hinder, delay, or defraud present or future creditors *or* (2) for something less than "fair consideration" (to constitute "fair consideration" a conveyance must be made in "good faith" and for a "fair equivalence") *and* either (a) the transferor must be insolvent (present fair saleable value of its assets less than the amount required to pay probable liability on existing debts as they become absolute and mature) at the time of the transfer or rendered insolvent thereby, *or* (b) the transferor's property remaining after the transfer must be an unreasonably small capital for the business in which the transferor is engaged, *or* (c) the transferor must intend to, or believe that it will, incur debts beyond its ability to pay as the debts mature.[44]

(2)   Standing. Under the UFCA, a present or future creditor may challenge a conveyance as fraudulent if the challenge is based upon actual intent, unreasonably small capital, or the expected incurring of debts beyond the debtor's ability to pay as the debts mature—(1), (2)(b), and (2)(c) above. Ninth Circuit cases, however, suggest that "in the context of LBOs, future creditors' right to sue [under the UFCA] must be limited to cases where there is actual intent to defraud or to conceal the transaction from public scrutiny."[45]

Only creditors with existing claims (or a bankruptcy trustee on their behalf) may challenge a fraudulent conveyance on the basis of insolvency—(2)(a) above.[46] In UFCA states, successful assertion of a fraudulent conveyance claim benefits

---

[44] Unlike the UFTA and the Bankruptcy Code (discussed at ¶1706.4.4 and ¶1706.4.5) under which a transferee can assert "good faith" as an affirmative defense to a fraudulent transfer charge "to the extent of the value given" by such transferee, under the UFCA "good faith" is not a separate defense but is a part of the definition of "fair consideration."

[45] Lippi v. City Bank, 955 F.2d 599, 606 (9th Cir. 1992) (*citing Credit Managers*, discussed at ¶1706.6.3, and *Kupetz*, discussed at ¶1706.6.5).

[46] In *Morse Tool* (discussed at ¶1706.6.12), T had no separate corporate existence prior to the LBO; the court found that T could not have had pre-LBO creditors, and therefore neither an alleged pre-LBO T creditor nor Newco-T's trustee would have standing to sue under the UFCA's insolvency test. But see SPC Plastics Corporation v. Griffith (In re Structurlite Plastics Corp.), 193 B.R. 451, 457-458 (Bankr. S.D. Ohio 1995), where the court held that if a trade creditor that maintained a continuing commercial relationship with T had unpaid invoices both at the time of the LBO and when the Chapter 11 case commenced, the requirement of (2)(a) was satisfied even though the actual invoices at each point in time were different.

only those plaintiff creditors with standing to assert the claim (whereas the rule under federal bankruptcy law may be far more draconian because, on the face of the statute and unless limited by judicial rulings such as *Ohio Corrugating II* and certain Ninth Circuit cases, the trustee is permitted both to challenge the transaction even when there is no creditor who was harmed by the transaction and to avoid the transaction for the benefit of all unpaid creditors—see ¶1706.4.5).

(3)   Insolvent. Under the UFCA, a transferor is insolvent when the present fair saleable value of its assets is less than the amount required to pay its probable liability on its existing debts as they become absolute and mature. This requires a court to determine the value of the transferor's assets and the time when its liabilities will be due (and the amount thereof). Courts applying the UFCA are divided over whether to use a going concern or liquidation-value test to determine the value of the transferor's assets and the timing of its liabilities. As discussed in ¶1706.4.5, a court is more likely to use a going concern valuation if T's business at the conclusion of the LBO was strong and viable,[47] but a liquidation-value approach if the viability of T's business was then in doubt.[48]

(4)   Unreasonably small capital. Although the UFCA does not define "unreasonably small capital," *Moody* (discussed at ¶1706.6.9) held that it "refer[s] to the inability to generate sufficient profits to sustain operations." To determine whether the LBO left T with an unreasonably small capital, the *Moody* court looked to financial projections—including a month-by-month analysis of T's balance sheet and analyses of T's income statement and credit availability—showing that T could continue in business after the LBO. It held these projections "reasonable" and therefore held that the LBO did not leave T with an unreasonably small capital. By contrast, in *Morse Tool* (discussed at ¶1706.6.12), the court found that VC's projections, which were based on unduly optimistic and erroneous assumptions, were unreasonable and that the LBO therefore left Newco-T with an unreasonably small capital.[49]

(5)   Limitation on extent of avoidability. If the transferee paid less than a "fair consideration" but did not know (or have reason to know) that the transaction violated the UFCA, the transferee may retain the assets transferred to it as security for repayment of the fair consideration paid by it in the transaction.

---

[47] See, e.g., *Moody* (discussed at ¶1706.6.9) and *Mellon* (discussed at ¶1706.6.8).

[48] See, e.g., *Gleneagles* (discussed at ¶1706.6.1) and *O'Day* (discussed at ¶1706.6.10).

[49] In *HealthCo* (discussed at ¶1706.6.17) in the context of denying motions to dismiss breach of fiduciary duty claims against directors for approving an LBO that allegedly left T with unreasonably small capital, the court explained that the term unreasonably small capital "connotes a condition of financial debility short of insolvency . . . but which makes insolvency reasonably foreseeable." Brandt v. Hicks, Muse & Co., Inc. (In re HealthCo Int'l, Inc.), 208 B.R. 288, 302 (Bankr. D. Mass. 1997).

(6)   Step-transaction doctrine. As discussed in ¶1706.4.2, courts are likely to collapse multistep LBOs in evaluating whether T received fair consideration for the debts incurred in the LBO, at least vis-a-vis a transferee who knew or should have known that T was being burdened by debt without receiving and retaining fairly equivalent consideration therefor.[50]

For example, in *Gleneagles* (discussed at ¶1706.6.1), Lender made a loan to T in return for T's note and mortgage approximately equal to the value of the loan. T then reloaned the proceeds to Newco, which used them to purchase T's stock. Under the step-transaction approach adopted in *Gleneagles*, the loan from Lender to T was stepped together with the reloan from T to Newco. Also, although the court did not discuss this point, it appears that it would have collapsed Newco's purchase of T's stock from T's shareholders into the loan and reloan transaction. Once the transactional formalities were stepped together, T was held, in essence, to have transferred a valuable note and mortgage while receiving nothing of value in return. Consequently, Lender's lien was avoided. However, in *Morse Tool* (discussed at ¶1706.6.12), the court used the step-transaction doctrine to find that there was adequate consideration, reasoning after collapsing the LBO steps that T received its predecessor's assets valued at $13 million in exchange for a purchase price of $10.4 million.

¶1706.4.4   Uniform Fraudulent Transfer Act

(1)   Generally. The UFTA was drafted in 1984 by the National Conference of Commissioners on Uniform State Laws. As of 6/1/03 it has been adopted by 41 states and the District of Columbia:

---

[50] Similarly, in a case that did not involve an LBO, the Second Circuit Court of Appeals upheld the use of the step-transaction doctrine to void a mortgage when the lender knew that the borrower had received the mortgaged property in a potentially fraudulent conveyance. See Orr v. Kinderhill Corp., 991 F.2d 31 (2d Cir. 1993) (applying N.Y. Debt. & Cred. Law §273-a (McKinney 1966 & Supp. 1993)).

Alabama	Montana
Arizona	Nebraska
Arkansas	Nevada
California	New Hampshire
Colorado	New Jersey
Connecticut	New Mexico
Delaware	North Carolina
District of Columbia	North Dakota
Florida	Ohio
Georgia	Oklahoma
Hawaii	Oregon
Idaho	Pennsylvania
Illinois	Rhode Island
Indiana	South Dakota
Iowa	Tennessee
Kansas	Texas
Maine	Utah
Massachusetts	Vermont
Michigan	Washington
Minnesota	West Virginia
Missouri	Wisconsin

The UFTA is substantially similar to the fraudulent transfer provisions of the Bankruptcy Code, discussed at ¶1706.4.5. Four LBO fraudulent transfer cases have been decided under the UFTA.[51]

To constitute a fraudulent transfer under the UFTA, a transfer must be made (1) with actual intent to hinder, delay, or defraud a creditor of the debtor *or* (2) without receiving a "reasonably equivalent value" *and either* (a) the transferor was insolvent or became insolvent as a result of the transfer, *or* (b) the transferor was engaged, or was about to engage, in a business or transaction for which the remaining assets were unreasonably small in relation to the business or transaction, *or* (c) the transferor intended to incur, or believed or reasonably should have believed that it would incur, debts beyond its ability to pay them as they became due.

(2)   Standing. Under the UFTA, a present or future creditor may challenge a transfer if the challenge is based upon actual intent, or if the debtor was engaged in a business for which its remaining assets were unreasonably small, or if the debtor believed it would incur debts beyond its ability to pay—(1), (2)(b), and (2)(c) above. However, only a creditor whose claim arose before the transfer may challenge a transfer that is fraudulent because of the transferor's insolvency—(2)(a) above.

---

[51] See *Richmond Produce* (discussed at ¶1706.6.11), O'Donnell v. Royal Business Group, Inc. (In re Oxford Homes, Inc.), 180 B.R. 1 (Bankr. D. Me. 1995), *Bay Plastics* (discussed at ¶1706.6.15), and *Yucaipa* (discussed at ¶1706.6.18).

In UFTA states, successful assertion of a fraudulent conveyance claim benefits only those plaintiff creditors with standing to assert the claim (whereas the rule under federal bankruptcy law may be far more draconian because, on the face of the statute and unless limited by judicial rulings such as *Ohio Corrugating II* and certain Ninth Circuit cases, the trustee is permitted both to challenge the transaction even when there is no remaining creditor who was harmed by the transaction and to avoid the transaction for the benefit of all unpaid creditors— see ¶1706.4.5).

(3) Insolvent. Under the UFTA, a transferor is insolvent if its assets (valued at FV) are less than its debts. A debtor who is not paying its debts as they become due is presumed to be insolvent.

Courts applying the UFTA will likely apply a going-concern-value approach for T's assets if T's business at the conclusion of the LBO was strong and viable, but a liquidation-value approach if the viability of T's business was then in doubt.

There is risk that a court will use hindsight in valuing the assets of a failed enterprise, so goodwill and other intangible assets, while theoretically valid assets for purposes of the insolvency test, may be given little value as a practical matter if the business has failed soon after the LBO. This should not, however, be the result if T's business was strong and viable at consummation of the LBO.[52]

(4) Unreasonably small assets. A court applying the UFTA would likely consider (1) how the debtor's remaining assets compare with those of other companies in a similar line of business, (2) the debtor's ability to pay its debts as they become due, and (3) whether the debtor's failure to pay its debts as they mature was affected by events unforeseeable at the time of the LBO.[53]

(5) Step-transaction doctrine. As discussed in ¶¶1706.4.2 and 1706.4.3, a court applying the UFTA will likely collapse multistep LBOs in evaluating whether T received fair consideration for the debts incurred in the LBO, at least vis-a-vis a transferee who knew or should have known that T was being burdened by debt without receiving and retaining fair equivalent consideration therefor.[54]

---

[52] However, one court concluded that even where T's business is strong at LBO consummation unliquidated claims existing at such time which had not yet been asserted (e.g., for alleged asbestos liability) must, for purposes of a solvency analysis, be valued by the court at the time of a fraudulent conveyance trial, and T's contemporaneous estimate at the time of the LBO consummation has no bearing on a court's later valuation of the liability for purposes of the solvency analysis. Committee of Asbestos Personal Injury Claimants, et. al. v. Sealed Air Corp. (In re W.R. Grace & Co.), 281 B.R. 852, 857 (Bankr. D. Del. 2002).

[53] For a discussion of "unreasonably small capital" under the UFCA, see the discussion of *Moody* at ¶1706.4.3.

[54] See *Richmond Produce* (discussed at ¶1706.6.11) and *Bay Plastics* (discussed at ¶1706.6.15), which applied the step-transaction doctrine to collapse an LBO where T's shareholders knew the LBO nature of the transaction, but went further, stating that the court would have collapsed the LBO steps even if T's pre-LBO shareholders lacked knowledge of the LBO nature of the transaction, since ". . . knowledge of the LBO feature of the transaction . . . is material to whether the transaction's various parts should be collapsed only when challenged by post-transaction creditors." TI Bay Plastics, Inc. v. BT Commercial Corp. (In re Bay Plastics, Inc.), 187 B.R. 315, 329 (Bankr. C.D. Cal. 1995).

(6)   Good faith. Under the UFTA, a transferee who gave the debtor "value" in "good faith" generally may, to the extent value was given, retain the property such transferee received or a lien thereon. However, under the step-transaction doctrine a court may collapse a multistep LBO so that T (or its successor) is treated as not having received the loan proceeds supplied by the LBO lender if they were in turn distributed to T's old shareholders. In this case, the LBO lender may be treated as not giving "value" in exchange for T's promissory note (and/or lien on T's (or its successor's) assets) and may also be treated as not acting in "good faith," if the LBO lender knew or should have known that T's (or its successor's) assets were being burdened by the LBO debt while the proceeds were being distributed to T's old shareholders.

¶1706.4.5   U.S. Bankruptcy Code

(1)   §548. Bankruptcy Code §548 permits a bankruptcy trustee, debtor-in-possession, or court-authorized creditor or creditors' committee standing in the shoes of a trustee to avoid a transfer of property or an interest in property under two circumstances: (1) a debtor transfers property with actual intent to hinder, delay, or defraud creditors *or* (2) a debtor transfers property, regardless of actual intent, and receives less than a "reasonably equivalent value" in return for the transfer, *and* the debtor either

(a)   was insolvent (asset FV less than liabilities) at the time of the transfer or became insolvent as a result of the transfer, or

(b)   was engaged, or was about to engage, in a business or a transaction for which remaining property was "an unreasonably small capital," or

(c)   intended to, or believed that it would, incur debts beyond its ability to pay as the debts mature.

(2)   Time period and standing. A transfer is subject to attack under §548 of the Bankruptcy Code if it occurred within one year before the filing of the bankruptcy petition. The trustee can assert such claim whether or not there is an actual unpaid creditor who has standing to challenge (i.e., who was harmed by) the transaction. When the trustee successfully avoids a transfer under §548, there is a draconian result: The transfer is avoided for the benefit of all unpaid creditors, including those who did not have standing to complain in that they were not harmed by the transaction.[55] It would, however, be logical to deny benefit to a post-LBO creditor who intentionally extended credit to T (or its successor) knowing about the company's highly leveraged condition. Although the Bankruptcy Code does not suggest that such a defense exists, *Ohio Corrugating II* (discussed at ¶1706.6.6) seems to adopt such a position. The court commented that "subsequent creditors are in a substantially different position from existing creditors" because they

---

[55] Bankruptcy Code §548 and §550; Moore v. Bay, 284 U.S. 4 (1931).

"willingly extend ... credit to the Debtor after the buyout in reliance on the performance of the 'new' company," and there is "no basis ... for holding that the constructive fraud provisions of [Bankruptcy Code] §548 may be utilized as a form of insurance for creditors whose claims matured after the buyout."[56] Whether the *Ohio Corrugating II* decision marks the beginning of a trend to protect LBO transferees against subsequent creditors who intentionally extended credit to the post-LBO entity, knowing that it was highly leveraged, is not yet clear.

A transfer occurring earlier than one year before bankruptcy may nevertheless be challenged by a bankruptcy trustee (or someone acting with the trustee's powers) under Bankruptcy Code §544(b), which permits the trustee to avoid a transfer under applicable state law if (1) there is in existence, on the date the bankruptcy petition is filed, at least one creditor who has standing to assert such a state law claim, (2) the applicable state statute of limitations (generally four or six years) has not expired as of the petition date, and (3) the trustee (or someone acting with the trustee's powers) asserts the claim within the additional two-year extended limitation period provided under the Bankruptcy Code.[57] Thus, the effect of §544(b) is effectively to extend the exposure period for an LBO far longer than the period provided by the Bankruptcy Code. And when an LBO transfer is avoided under §544(b) by use of the state fraudulent conveyance law, the result is equally as draconian as avoidance under §548 by use of the federal fraudulent conveyance law, as explained below.

If the LBO took place less than four (or six) years prior to filing of the bankruptcy petition, so the applicable state limitation period is still open, there will generally be at least one creditor with state law standing to challenge the LBO as a fraudulent conveyance, for two reasons. *First*, under the UFTA and the UFCA, post-LBO creditors have such standing if the LBO left T (or its successor) with an unreasonably small capital or if at the time of the LBO the parties believed that T (or its successor) would not be able to pay its debts as they mature.[58]

Second, under the UFTA and the UFCA, only pre-LBO creditors have such standing if the LBO left T (or its successor) insolvent (but did not violate the unreasonably-small-capital and the unable-to-pay-debts tests). While many pre-LBO creditors are paid off relatively quickly after an LBO (e.g., trade creditors, utilities, employee claims), at least a few pre-LBO creditors generally retain such claims for many years (e.g., retired employee claims for continuing payment of health and life insurance premiums, industrial revenue bondholders, environmental cleanup claims, pre-LBO public debentures).

Hence, if bankruptcy occurs within four (or six) years after the LBO, at least one creditor with standing to challenge the LBO as a fraudulent conveyance under state law will still generally be unpaid.

When there is at least one creditor with such state law standing, the trustee's successful assertion of a §544(b) fraudulent conveyance claim would generally

---

[56] Ohio Corrugating Co. v. DPAC, Inc. (In re Ohio Corrugating Co.), 91 B.R. 430, 435 (Bankr. N.D. Ohio 1988).

[57] See Bankruptcy Code §546(a)(1)(A).

[58] See ¶¶1706.4.3 and 1706.4.4.

benefit all of T's (or its successor's) creditors, even those without standing.[59] For example, (1) a lender into the LBO (who knew or should have known that the loan proceeds were going to old T shareholders and that the loan was structured so as to prejudice T's pre-acquisition creditors) may lose its lien on T's (or its successor's) assets and be subordinated to other creditors of T (or its successor), and (2) an old T shareholder (who knew or should have known at the time of the LBO that his stock sale proceeds were being paid with debt incurred in a fashion that prejudiced T's pre-acquisition creditors) may have to return his stock sale proceeds. Only a portion of the recovery from such lender or such old T shareholder (the lender's avoided lien and subordinated claim, the cash received from the old T shareholder) will actually go to creditors with state law standing; the remainder will go to creditors without such standing.

It is not yet clear whether *Ohio Corrugating II* discussed above marks the beginning of a trend to protect LBO transferees against subsequent creditors who intentionally extended credit to the post-LBO entity, knowing of its highly leveraged status.

(3)   Reasonably equivalent value. Although the term "reasonably equivalent value" is not defined by the Bankruptcy Code, the word "value" is defined in relevant part to mean "property, or satisfaction or securing of a present or antecedent debt of the debtor."[60] Consequently, in an LBO transaction, if a debtor gives a note and a security interest in its property to a lender in return for a loan, the lender has given "value."

The Supreme Court's *BFP* opinion gave some guidance on the meaning of "reasonably equivalent value." There the Court held (in a non-LBO context) that "the price in fact" received at a non-collusive foreclosure sale is "reasonably equivalent value" for purposes of Bankruptcy Code §548(a)(2) "so long as all the requirements of the State's foreclosure law have been complied with."[61]

The *BFP* decision effectively overruled a number of cases that had allowed a bankruptcy trustee to challenge the price actually received at a non-collusive foreclosure sale on reasonably-equivalent-value grounds, even when all requirements of a state's foreclosure law had otherwise been satisfied.[62]

(4)   Step-transaction doctrine. As discussed in ¶¶1706.4.2, 1706.4.3, and 1706.4.4, courts are likely to collapse multistep LBOs in evaluating whether T received reasonably equivalent value for the debts incurred in the LBO, at least vis-a-vis a transferee who knew or should have known that T was being burdened by debt without receiving and retaining reasonably equivalent value therefor.

---

[59] See Bankruptcy Code §544(b); see also Moore v. Bay, 284 U.S. 4 (1931).

[60] Bankruptcy Code §548(d)(2)(A).

[61] BFP v. Resolution Trust Corp., 511 U.S. 531, 544 (1994).

[62] Bundles v. Baker (In re Bundles), 856 F.2d 815, 824 (7th Cir. 1988) (reasonably equivalent value rebuttably presumed to be price received at non-collusive foreclosure sale, but court must analyze all facts and circumstances); Durrett v. Washington Natl. Ins. Co., 621 F.2d 201, 204 (5th Cir. 1980) (non-collusive foreclosure sale yielding 57% of property's FV could be set aside on reasonably-equivalent-value grounds).

(5)   Insolvent. A debtor is insolvent under the Bankruptcy Code if its assets (valued at FV) are less than its debts (also fairly valued). It may be necessary to include contingent and unliquidated liabilities (e.g., environmental cleanup obligations, pending claims and lawsuits, potential multi-employer pension plan withdrawal liabilities) along with the debtor's non-contingent and liquidated liabilities in the insolvency analysis. Such contingent and unliquidated liabilities are to be valued on the basis of potential exposure at the time of the transaction.[63]

Balance sheet book values for T's assets are not determinative.[64] Courts are likely to use a going-concern-value approach for T's assets if T's business at the conclusion of the LBO was strong and viable, but a liquidation-value approach if the viability of T's business was in doubt at the conclusion of the LBO.[65]

There is, of course, the risk that a court might use hindsight in valuing the assets of a failed enterprise, so goodwill and other intangible assets, while theoretically valid assets for purposes of the insolvency test, may be given little value as a practical matter if the debtor's business has failed soon after the LBO, unless the failure was due to events unforeseeable at the time of the LBO (e.g., a fire or unexpected strike).[66] One court, however, has suggested that a "presumptive validity" ought to be assigned "to the treatment of assets and liabilities according to GAAP." See *Ohio Corrugating II* (discussed at ¶1706.6.6).[67]

Contemporaneous evidence of value and of going concern viability (e.g., independent appraisals and projections prepared during the LBO planning or immediately after the closing) is important in establishing T's solvency immediately after the LBO.

(6)   Unreasonably small capital. In determining whether a debtor has been left with "unreasonably small capital," the courts generally consider (1) how the debtor's capitalization compares with that of other companies in a similar line of business, (2) the debtor's ability to pay its debts as they become due, and (3) whether the debtor's failure to pay its debts as they mature was affected by events unforeseeable at the time of the LBO.[68]

---

[63] Covey v. Commercial Natl. Bank, 960 F.2d 657, 660-661 (7th Cir. 1992).

[64] See O'Donnell v. Royal Business Group, Inc. (In re Oxford Homes, Inc.), 180 B.R. 1 (Bankr. D. Me. 1995), which found under the UFTA that a debtor could be solvent in a balance sheet sense, but nonetheless equitably insolvent (i.e., unable to pay debts as they become due) and undercapitalized.

[65] Compare *Mellon* (discussed at ¶1706.6.8) with *O'Day* (discussed at ¶1706.6.10).

[66] See *Bay Plastics* (discussed at ¶1706.6.15), holding that intangible assets such as goodwill must be disregarded in a liquidation of T.

[67] Compare *Richmond Produce* (discussed at ¶1706.6.11), which found that T could be insolvent under the UFTA even though solvent under GAAP.

[68] See also the discussion of *Moody* at ¶1706.4.3 and O'Donnell v. Royal Business Group, Inc. (In re Oxford Homes, Inc.), 180 B.R. 1 (Bankr. D. Me. 1995), which found that a debtor could be solvent in a balance sheet sense but nonetheless undercapitalized where, by virtue of the LBO, its cash flow was "strained to the breaking point." Similarly, in *HealthCo* (discussed at ¶1706.6.17) the court explained that the term unreasonably small capital "connotes a condition of financial debility short of insolvency . . . but which makes insolvency reasonably foreseeable." Brandt v. Hicks, Muse & Co., Inc. (In re HealthCo Int'l, Inc.), 208 B.R. 288, 302 (Bankr. D. Mass. 1997).

(7)   Ability to pay debts as they mature. The test of whether the parties believed at the time the LBO was consummated that T (or its successor) would not be able to pay its post-LBO debts as they mature turns in part on the objective facts and in part on the parties' subjective beliefs at the time the LBO was consummated. The same issue is also relevant to the insolvency test (i.e., courts will generally value T's (or its successor's) assets as a going concern only if T's business was strong and viable at the conclusion of the LBO) and to the unreasonably-small-capital test as well. Hence, the parties planning the LBO generally prepare cash flow projections contemporaneously with the LBO to demonstrate their good faith belief that T (or its successor) will be able to pay its post-LBO debts as they mature.

The results of such cash flow projections will frequently turn significantly on subjective business issues, such as whether T's technology will remain state of the art or will be rendered obsolete by new developments, whether T's research and development will bear fruit, whether the future portends recession or boom, etc. Such projections also may be significantly influenced by even more subjective financing issues, such as whether T (or its successor) will be able to borrow working capital after the LBO, whether maturing debt-for-borrowed-money can be refinanced, whether T (or its successor) can sell certain divisions or subsidiaries (and if so, at what price). In general, for cash flow projections to influence a court, the parties must be reasonable in making the assumptions on which such projections are based.

(8)   Good faith. Under the Bankruptcy Code, even when the transaction constitutes a fraudulent conveyance, a transferee who gave the transferor "value" in "good faith" generally may retain a lien on the property or interest received by the transferee to the extent of the value given. However, under the step-transaction doctrine a court may collapse a multistep LBO so that T (or its successor) is treated as not having received the loan proceeds supplied by the LBO lender because they were in turn distributed to T's old shareholders.[69] In this case, the LBO lender may be treated as not giving "value" in exchange for T's (or its successor's) promissory note (and/or asset lien) and may also be treated as not acting in "good faith," if the LBO lender knew or should have known that T's (or its successor's) assets were being burdened by the LBO debt while the proceeds were being distributed to old T shareholders.

¶1706.5   LBO Risks for T's Directors and Professionals

¶1706.5.1   Directors

Wieboldt Stores (discussed at ¶1706.6.7) illustrates the risk to T's directors for acquiescing in or supporting an LBO that renders T insolvent. In that case, the bankruptcy trustee asserted claims against T's directors based on alleged breach

---

[69] See *Richmond Produce* (discussed at ¶1706.6.11) and *Bay Plastics* (discussed at ¶1706.6.15).

of a state law fiduciary duty to T's creditors and on alleged violation of Illinois corporate law prohibiting distributions to T's shareholders when there is not adequate surplus and solvency. The *Wieboldt Stores* court rejected a motion to dismiss by T's directors and held that they could be sued on both grounds under Illinois law.

First, the directors could be held liable for breaching their state law fiduciary duty of good faith, care, and loyalty to T. T's directors argued that *Revlon, Inc. v. MacAndrews & Forbes Holdings*[70] precluded recovery from them because "their duty was to the shareholders alone and not to the corporation and the creditors."[71] The *Wieboldt Stores* court held that the directors' reliance on *Revlon* was misplaced because, while in *Revlon* "it [was] *inevitable* that the company [would] be sold to one of the bidders competing to acquire it," in *Wieboldt Stores* there was no bidding contest and it was not inevitable that T would be sold.[72] Consequently, the board had an affirmative duty to determine if the LBO was in the best interests of T as well as T's shareholders. The court held that the complaint alleged sufficient facts to support a cause of action against the directors for breach of fiduciary duty because "the directors acted in their own interests [as T shareholders] in approving the tender offer notwithstanding the fact that the LBO would result in harm to" T.[73]

Second, the *Wieboldt Stores* court held that the directors could be sued under Illinois corporate law for paying an illegal distribution to shareholders, i.e., a distribution prohibited by Illinois corporate law, which caused or exacerbated T's insolvency or reduced its net assets below zero. The directors argued that T paid no distribution because T's pledge of its assets in connection with the LBO was a different transaction from Newco's purchase of T's stock in a tender offer. The court, applying the step-transaction doctrine, rejected this argument, concluding that the term "distribution" in state corporate law was sufficiently broad to include "indirect transfers such as the exchange of cash and shares [in the LBO] between" Newco and T's old shareholders when, in a related transaction, T pledged its assets to enable Newco to obtain the acquisition loan.[74]

---

[70] 506 A.2d 173, 179-180 (Del. 1986).

[71] Weiboldt Stores, Inc. v. Schottenstein, 94 B.R. 488, 510 (Bankr. N.D. Ill. 1988).

[72] Weiboldt Stores, Inc. v. Schottenstein, 94 B.R. 488, 510 (Bankr. N.D. Ill. 1988) (emphasis in original).

[73] Weiboldt Stores, Inc. v. Schottenstein, 94 B.R. 488, 510 (Bankr. N.D. Ill. 1988).

[74] Weiboldt Stores, Inc. v. Schottenstein, 94 B.R. 488, 512 (Bankr. N.D. Ill. 1988). See also *Buckhead America* (discussed in more detail at ¶1706.6.14), where in step 1 a subsidiary ("T") financed a going private transaction by its 100% corporate parent ("ParentCo"), as follows: ParentCo was owned 50.5% by public and other shareholders and 49.5% by a partnership ("Control Shareholder"). T borrowed $57 million and dividended such amount to ParentCo at a time when T was allegedly insolvent and had inadequate surplus under Delaware corporate law. ParentCo used the $57 million to redeem the 50.5% of its stock owned by the public and other shareholders, so that Control Shareholder then became ParentCo's 100% shareholder.

A year later, in step 2, Control Shareholder sold 100% of ParentCo's stock to Newco, and T paid (partly in cash and partly by delivering a T note) all of the purchase price for ParentCo's stock owed by Newco to the Control Shareholder. In a subsequent bankruptcy case, the court concluded that if T's financial condition was as alleged, both transactions would be illegal *dividends* by T under Delaware corporate law. However, the court concluded that neither transaction was an illegal *redemption* by T under Delaware corporate law because T's money (in step 2, T's money and notes) was used to purchase ParentCo shares rather than T shares.

Generally, under most states' corporate laws, T's directors owe no fiduciary duty to the corporation's creditors.[75] For instance, the Delaware courts have stated that "a debenture holder has no independent right to maintain a claim for breach of fiduciary duty [against the debtor's directors] and in the absence of fraud, insolvency or statutory violations, a debenture holder's rights are defined by the terms of the indenture."[76]

However, a long-recognized exception to this rule holds that T's directors owe a fiduciary duty to creditors once the company is insolvent. This exception was established before 1900 and was predicated upon a trust fund theory: The condition of insolvency puts the assets of a company in trust, first for the creditors and then for the shareholders of the company.[77] In the 1991 *Credit Lyonnais Bank Nederland, N.V. v. Pathe Communications Corp.* case,[78] the Delaware Chancery Court appears to have found director duties to creditors even broader than the trust fund theory. *Credit Lyonnais* involved Newco's purchase through an LBO of T's stock. Although the narrow issue before the court was the proper membership of T's board (Lender claiming that it had succeeded to certain governance rights by virtue of T's payment defaults), the court also considered the duties of T's board generally, given that T was "in the vicinity of insolvency." The court reasoned:

> At least where a corporation is operating in the vicinity of insolvency, a board of directors is not merely the agent of the residue risk bearers, but owes its duty to the corporate enterprise.[79]
>
> In managing the business affairs of a corporation in the vicinity of insolvency (both the efficient and the fair) course to follow for the corporation may diverge from the choice that the stockholders (or the creditors, or the employees, or any single group interested in the corporation) would make if given the opportunity to act.[80]

In 1992, the Delaware Chancery Court, in *Geyer v. Ingersoll Publications Co.*,[81] held that a director's fiduciary duty "arise[s] at the moment of insolvency in fact" and that insolvency for this purpose included not only a balance sheet test (asset FV less than liabilities) but also a test focusing on the debtor's ability to pay its debts as they become due.[82] The court so held because, among other reasons, the "existence of the fiduciary duty at the moment of insolvency may cause directors to choose a course of action that best serves the entire corporate enterprise rather

[75] See, e.g., Katz v. Oak Indus., 508 A.2d 873, 878-879 (Del. Ch. 1986). However, some states including Connecticut and New Jersey, have statutorily created corporate fiduciary duties to creditors. See, e.g., Conn. Gen. Stat. Ann. §33-321(b) (West 1992); N.J. Stat. Ann. §14A:6-12 (West 1991).

[76] Continental Ill. Natl. Bank & Trust Co. v. Hunt Intl. Resources Corp., 1987 WL 55826, No. C.A. 7888 (Del. Ch. 2/27/87).

[77] See, e.g., Hollins v. Brierfield Coal & Iron Co., 170 U.S. 371, 382 (1893); Wood v. Dummer, 30 F. Cas. 435, 436 (C.C.D. Me. 1824) (No. 17944).

[78] 1991 WL 277613 (Del. Ch. 12/30/91).

[79] 1991 WL 277613 at *34 (Del. Ch. 12/30/91).

[80] 1991 WL 277613 at n.55 (Del. Ch. 12/30/91).

[81] 621 A.2d 784 (Del. Ch. 1992).

[82] 621 A.2d at 788-789.

than any single group ... at a point in time when shareholders' wishes should not be the directors' only concern."[83]

In the *HealthCo* case (discussed at ¶1706.6.17) Massachusetts' U.S. District Court, applying Delaware law, clarified that in the context of an LBO, a director's duty to protect the interests of creditors arises at the time the LBO is being considered by the board, even if T is solvent at that time. Thus, in denying motions of T's directors to dismiss a bankruptcy trustee's breach of fiduciary duty claims against the directors in connection with approving a failed LBO, the court reasoned "[w]hen a transaction renders a corporation insolvent, or brings it to the brink of insolvency, the rights of creditors become paramount."[84] The court held that T's trustee could establish that the director's duty to creditors was breached either by showing at trial that T was (i) rendered insolvent (in either the "bankruptcy sense" (excess of liabilities over assets) or the "equity sense" (inability to pay debts as they mature)) or (ii) undercapitalized, which the court characterized as subject to "an unreasonable risk of insolvency."[85] The court also held that the business judgment rule afforded the directors no protection, because approval of their decision to cause the LBO was predicated solely on a finding that the LBO was in the best interests of T's shareholders, rather than T itself; and was made with inadequate information because the directors failed to consider projections of T's economic performance after the LBO.

Taken together, *Wieboldt Stores, Geyer, Credit Lyonnais*, and *HealthCo* serve as clear warning to T's directors that any LBO structure they approve should not cause reasonably anticipated harm to T's present and future creditors.

¶1706.5.2　Professionals

Professionals who advise LBO participants are generally vulnerable in one of two ways: (1) The payment for professional services rendered in connection with the LBO may itself be found to constitute a fraudulent conveyance and (2) professionals may be accused of negligence or culpability in connection with the LBO transaction. In addition, as discussed below, professionals that represented VC, Newco, and, after the LBO, Newco-T, in connection with the LBO may be disqualified from representing Newco-T in bankruptcy if T's LBO appears susceptible to a fraudulent conveyance attack.

When T pays a professional for services in connection with an LBO transaction, and the LBO is subsequently unwound as a fraudulent conveyance, professionals whose services actually benefited Newco are vulnerable because T received no benefit from those services. This was the holding in *C-T*,[86] in which Newco had retained an investment banker to advise it in connection with Newco's proposed

---

[83] 621 A.2d at 789.

[84] Brandt v. Hicks, Muse & Co., Inc. (In re HealthCo Int'l, Inc.), 208 B.R. 288, 300 (Bankr. D. Mass. 1997) (citations omitted).

[85] 208 B.R. at 301-302.

[86] C-T of Va., Inc. v. Paine Webber, Inc., 124 B.R. 700, 701 (Bankr. W.D. Va. 1990), *aff'd*, 940 F.2d 651 (4th Cir. 1991).

LBO of T. At the time the LBO transaction was closed, Newco lacked sufficient funds to pay the investment banker's fee. Therefore, the parties agreed that T would pay the fee after the LBO was consummated. T paid only part of the fee after the LBO, and the investment banker filed a claim in T's bankruptcy for the unpaid portion of its fee. The court held that T paid the investment banker for services rendered to Newco, not to T, and therefore T received no consideration for paying the investment banker's fee.[87]

Professionals involved in LBO transactions may also be vulnerable for professional malpractice claims alleging negligence and, even more seriously, culpability. In *Wieboldt Stores* (discussed at ¶1706.6.7), the court permitted lawsuits to proceed against accountants and attorneys for T alleging that these professionals negligently advised T's board in considering whether to consummate the LBO. T's former directors (themselves subject to suits for breach of fiduciary duties, among other things) sued (1) T's accountants for negligent misrepresentations as to T's projected solvency after the LBO and (2) T's attorneys for negligence in (among other things) failing to inform T's board about *Gleneagles*.[88] Although these lawsuits ultimately settled before trial, the district court held that such professionals could be sued for negligence in connection with the failed LBO.

Similarly, in *Interco* a bankruptcy examiner concluded that certain professionals were vulnerable to actions for professional malpractice.[89] In particular, the examiner noted that T's appraiser failed to meet the standard of care required of appraisers by failing, among other things, to consider T's historical performance or corporate overhead and to provide for taxes or other contingent liabilities. In addition, the *Interco* bankruptcy examiner scrutinized the services of Newco's financial advisors, questioning the merits of analyses performed by the advisors that failed to challenge management's assumptions. Claims against the financial advisors were settled in 6/92.

In *Wieboldt Stores* and *Interco*, T's lawyers were accused of aiding and abetting the LBO when they knew that the LBO (1) constituted a fraudulent conveyance, (2) was illegal under applicable state corporate law, (3) constituted an affirmative breach of the board's fiduciary duties, or (4) was done without appropriate investigation. In *Wieboldt Stores*, these claims for compensatory damages from T's attorneys settled before trial.

Finally, a law firm that represented VC, Newco, and, after the LBO, Newco-T in connection with the LBO may be disqualified from representing Newco-T in bankruptcy if T's financial problems result from the LBO. This was the holding in *Envirodyne Industries*,[90] in which a law firm represented VC and Newco in Newco's LBO of T and thereafter represented both VC and Newco-T in various capacities, including in the merger of Newco into T and in VC's underwriting of

---

[87] Similarly, a bankruptcy examiner's report in In re Revco D.S., Inc., also concluded that payments by T for professional services that did not benefit T may be recoverable as fraudulent conveyances. Barry L. Zaretsky et al., Final Report of Examiner Professor Barry Lewis Zaretsky, In re Revco D.S., Inc., et al., at 239 (12/17/90).

[88] For a discussion of *Gleneagles*, see ¶1706.6.1.

[89] Sandra E. Mayerson et al., Report of Examiner Sandra E. Mayerson, In re Interco Inc. et al. (10/23/91).

[90] In re Envirodyne Indus., Inc., 170 B.R. 1008, 1021-1022 (Bankr. N.D. Ill. 1993).

certain of Newco-T's debt securities. VC held a controlling interest in Newco-T, was a "substantial creditor" of Newco-T, and was also a "significant client" of the law firm in matters unrelated to Newco-T.[91] When certain of Newco-T's creditors forced Newco-T into bankruptcy, Newco-T sought to retain the law firm as general bankruptcy counsel, and the law firm advised VC to retain independent counsel in connection with Newco-T's bankruptcy.

Despite the fact that VC retained independent bankruptcy counsel in connection with Newco-T's bankruptcy, the bankruptcy court refused to permit Newco-T to retain the law firm. The court found that the law firm's "significant" relationship with VC gave the law firm "an important economic interest in maintaining good relations with [VC]."[92] The court reasoned that this economic interest would prevent the law firm from vigorously investigating or litigating a fraudulent conveyance challenge to the LBO and would therefore prejudice the bankruptcy process.

¶1706.6   Principal Decided Cases in Which LBO Attacked as Fraudulent Conveyance

The following reviews significant cases dealing with LBO transactions challenged as fraudulent conveyances.[93]

¶1706.6.1   *Gleneagles* Case[94]

Newco was formed to acquire the stock of T, a producer of anthracite coal and the owner of substantial coal reserves. Newco was secretly owned 50% by James R. Hoffa, Jr., but Newco's original equity capital is not stated. T borrowed from Lender $8.5 million ($7 million in cash and a $1.5 million interest reserve withheld by the Lender) in return for a note and a mortgage on T's assets. T then reloaned $4.1 million of the borrowed money on an unsecured basis to Newco. Newco used this $4.1 million, plus $2.1 million out of $3.5 million borrowed from other sources, plus a $500,000 note to purchase T's stock for $6.7 million.

---

[91] 170 B.R. at 1013-1014, 1019.

[92] 170 B.R. at 1016, 1021-1022.

[93] Because the discussion of these cases is designed to illustrate basic principles of fraudulent conveyance law, many factual details have been simplified or omitted. As with all litigated cases, there is thus the possibility that courts may subsequently distinguish these cases on grounds not discussed herein.

[94] United States v. Gleneagles Inv. Co., 565 F. Supp. 556 (M.D. Pa. 1983), *aff'd sub nom.* United States v. Tabor Court Realty Corp., 803 F.2d 1288 (3d Cir. 1986), *cert. denied sub nom.* McClellan Realty Co. v. United States, 483 U.S. 1005 (1987).

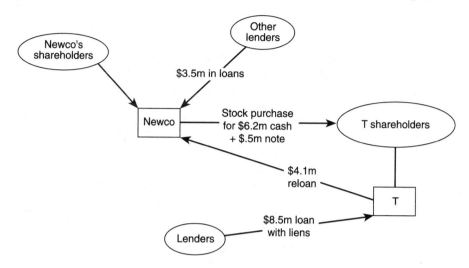

Seven years after the LBO, the United States, asserting tax claims both predating and postdating the LBO, successfully brought an action under Pennsylvania's (now superseded) version of the UFCA to avoid T's obligation on the note and liens to Lender. The district court concluded that (1) Lender knew how its loan proceeds would be used when it loaned them to T, (2) all parties knew Newco could not repay the loan from T absent receipt of funds from T, (3) T would be rendered unable to pay its debts as they matured after the transaction and thus was rendered insolvent under the UFCA, and (4) Lender "knew or strongly suspected" that the loan would "probably" have the effect described in (3).

The district court held that the transaction between Lender and T violated the UFCA, and this was affirmed on appeal to the Third Circuit Court of Appeals. Both courts held that although T received money from Lender in exchange for the note and mortgage, the loan was not given in "good faith" and T did not receive fair consideration because Lender was aware that the loan proceeds would immediately be reloaned to Newco and then paid to T's old shareholders and that Newco could not repay T.

The *Gleneagles* courts also found that Lender and other parties to the transaction, including T's selling shareholders, violated the UFCA rule against transfers with actual intent to hinder, delay, or defraud creditors. The district court stated that the intent to hinder, delay, or defraud creditors can be inferred where both "the transferor and transferee have knowledge of the claims of creditors and know that the creditors cannot be paid and where consideration is lacking for the transfer."[95] Furthermore, the court said that even if the parties did not have actual intent to hinder or delay creditors, "[i]f the parties could have foreseen the effect on creditors resulting [from the transaction,] the parties must be deemed to have intended the same."[96]

---

[95] 565 F. Supp. at 581.
[96] 565 F. Supp. at 581.

¶1706.6.2   *Greenbrook Carpet Co.* Case[97]

Although this case did not involve a typical LBO in which Newco acquires T, the facts and the court's decision appear relevant to the LBO area. Oldco's principal shareholders ("Owners") sought a bank loan to finance their personal purchase of a controlling block of T stock. Lender refused to make the loan to the Owners because their collateral was inadequate. Lender, however, agreed to lend $350,000 to Oldco (the stock of which was owned by the Owners) in return for an Oldco note and a security interest in Oldco's inventory. Oldco then reloaned the proceeds to the Owners in return for their non-recourse note and a security interest in the purchased T stock. Lender was aware of the use to which Oldco and the Owners would put the loan.

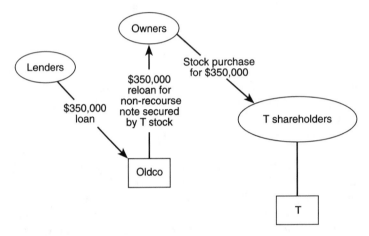

Thereafter Oldco filed a chapter 11 petition, and the bankruptcy trustee argued that Oldco's note and lien to Lender constituted a fraudulent transfer. The court held that the transaction was not a fraudulent transfer under the Bankruptcy Code. The court rejected an argument that the transfers should be characterized as a loan directly from Lender to the Owners so that Oldco was not liable to Lender. The court concluded that although Lender

> knew the intended use of the funds, this [knowledge] does not necessarily render the transfers invalid under [the Bankruptcy Code. Lender] could properly loan [Oldco] funds knowing [it] would use the funds for a speculative venture. The issue under [the statute] is whether [Lender] received more consideration than it was due; if the transaction between [Oldco] and the [Owners] constituted a fraudulent transfer, the trustee may sue the [Owners, who were not parties to the case].[98]

---

[97] Jones v. National City Bank of Rome (In re Greenbrook Carpet Co.), 722 F.2d 659 (11th Cir. 1984).
[98] Jones v. National City Bank of Rome (In re Greenbrook Carpet Co.), 722 F.2d 659, 661 (11th Cir. 1984).

¶1706.6.3   *Credit Managers Association* **Case**[99]

T's management formed Newco with $450,000 equity to purchase T. Newco then purchased T's stock for $236,000 in cash and a $1.2 million note executed by both Newco and T, secured by a lien on T's assets.

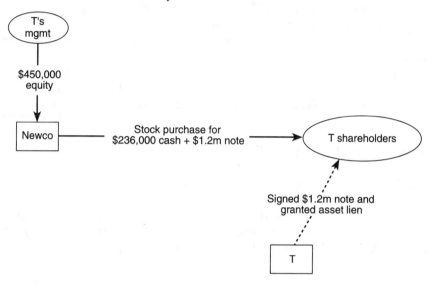

About one-and-a-half years later, T made an assignment for the benefit of its creditors. The assignee for the benefit of creditors sued to recover from T's old shareholders the proceeds from their sale of T's stock. The assignee sued only under the provision of California's (now superseded) UFCA that permits avoidance of transactions for less than fair consideration if the effect of the transaction is to leave the transferor with "unreasonably small capital."[100] On its face, this provision of the UFCA gives a T creditor with claims arising after the LBO transaction standing to sue under the UFCA.

The court first considered whether, in view of the fact that T's LBO was well publicized, it should limit the right of an assignee on behalf of T's creditors whose claims arose after the LBO to bring such a suit. It noted that "when the California legislature passed this provision in 1939, it clearly did not intend to cover leveraged buyouts which are very public events."[101] The court reasoned that because T's creditors waited two years to challenge the buyout, the defense of laches "might be appropriate to limit fraudulent conveyance actions so that they would not be brought each and every time a leveraged buyout failed."[102] The court did not resolve this issue because it first found that T was not left with an unreasonably small capital.

---

[99] Credit Managers Assn. v. Federal Co., 629 F. Supp. 175 (C.D. Cal. 1985).
[100] See UFCA §5, 7A U.L.A. 504 (West 1985).
[101] 629 F. Supp. at 181.
[102] 629 F. Supp. at 181.

Although the court concluded that T received nothing of value when it signed the $1.2 million note to T's selling shareholders, the court nevertheless held that the transaction did not leave T with an unreasonably small capital.

In determining that T was not left with an unreasonably small capital at the time of the LBO, the court focused primarily on a cash flow projection prepared by Lender at the time of the LBO. The court concluded that the projections of T's future sales, gross profit margin, and inventory turnover were "reasonable and prudent" at the time prepared but that the projected accounts receivable collection period was not. However, any problem caused by the imprudent receivable collection projection was overcome because, two months subsequent to the LBO, Lender prepared another cash flow projection for T, using a lower sales projection and a longer receivable collection period, and decided to increase T's line of credit.

¶1706.6.4   *Anderson Industries* Case[103]

Newco was organized to purchase T's stock from T's shareholders for $5.7 million. Newco was capitalized through a sale of stock and subordinated notes for $1.7 million. For the remainder of the money needed to purchase T's stock, T borrowed $4.6 million from Lender and then reloaned that money to Newco. Newco purchased T's stock, and T was then merged upstream into Newco.

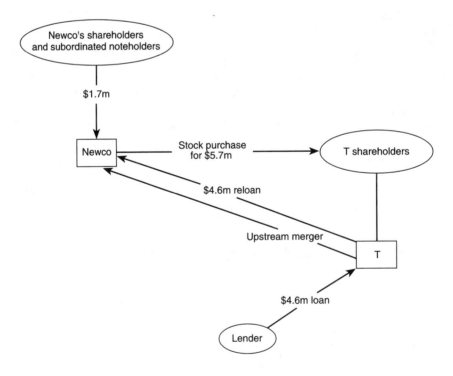

---

[103] Anderson Indus., Inc. v. Anderson (In re Anderson Indus., Inc.), 55 B.R. 922 (Bankr. W.D. Mich. 1985).

Approximately four years later, Newco filed a chapter 11 petition. Newco's creditors sued T's old shareholders, alleging that the stock sale violated the UFCA. T's old shareholders requested summary judgment.

According to the court, the fair consideration determination is to be made from the "creditors' standpoint and depends upon whether the conveyance renders [Newco] execution proof."[104] After comparing the consideration Newco gave to T's old shareholders and the consideration T's old shareholders gave to Newco, the court stated that if these facts were established at trial, it "could reasonably conclude that [T's old shareholders] gave a fair equivalent of what they received."[105] According to the court, this had been a "bargained for exchange reached through arms length negotiations."[106]

However, the court denied summary judgment because it believed there was a disputed issue of fact as to whether T's old shareholders had given fair consideration.

¶1706.6.5   *Kupetz* Case[107]

Newco was capitalized by VC with $100 of equity, and Newco borrowed $1.1 million from Lender. Newco then purchased T's stock, paying $1.1 million in cash and issuing a $1.9 million note backed by Lender's letter of credit in favor of the selling shareholders. After purchasing T's stock, Newco merged downstream into T, with T surviving. T then pledged its assets to secure the $1.1 million loan from Lender and the $1.9 million letter of credit issued by Lender.

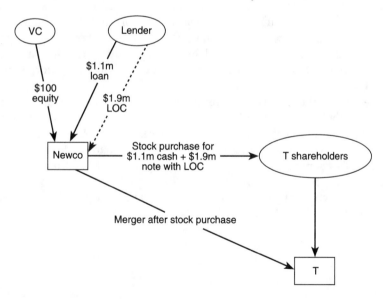

---

[104] 55 B.R. at 927.

[105] Anderson Indus., Inc. v. Anderson (In re Anderson Indus., Inc.), 55 B.R. 922, 927 (Bankr. W.D. Mich. 1985).

[106] 55 B.R. at 927.

[107] Kupetz v. Wolf, 845 F.2d 842 (9th Cir. 1988), *aff'g* Kupetz v. Continental Ill. Natl. Bank & Trust Co., 77 B.R. 754 (Bankr. C.D. Cal. 1987).

Approximately two-and-a-half years later, T filed a chapter 11 petition and the trustee then brought a fraudulent conveyance action under California's (now superseded) UFCA against VC, Lender, and T's selling shareholders. The court did not decide whether VC and Lender were liable for a fraudulent conveyance, as these parties settled with the trustee. The court, however, did hold that the selling T shareholders were not liable under a fraudulent conveyance theory.

According to the court, if an LBO is intentionally designed to defraud creditors, courts have little difficulty in holding the transaction fraudulent. However, "those transactions in which all was 'above board' to begin with have been 'ratified' by the courts even though the creditors may have suffered in the end."[108]

The court cited the following factors as supporting its conclusion that the selling T shareholders in *Kupetz* should not be held to have received a fraudulent conveyance on account of the LBO transaction involved in that case:

(1) There was no evidence that the selling T shareholders intended to defraud T's creditors. The court did not believe that it was "appropriate to utilize constructive intent to brand most, if not all, LBOs as illegitimate."[109]

(2) The selling T shareholders neither knew nor had reason to know that VC intended to finance the purchase through an LBO. The court found that the T shareholders had been fairly careful in selecting a purchaser.

(3) There were no unpaid creditors whose claims arose prior to the LBO. Citing the *Credit Managers* decision (discussed at ¶1706.6.3), the court reasoned that all existing claims at the time of the chapter 11 petition arose after the LBO, and therefore the creditors had the opportunity to evaluate T prior to extending credit. The court stated that "[i]n the context of this well-publicized LBO, this court will not permit later-arising creditors to attack an LBO purchase transaction as a fraudulent conveyance under section five of the UFCA."[110]

(4) The form of the LBO transaction reflected a sale by the T shareholders to an entity other than T. The LBO "transaction bore the indicia of a 'straight' sale [to Newco] rather than the marks of a serial redemption by [T] of its own stock."[111] According to the court, the selling T shareholders should not be Newco's guarantor. The court, however, said that the bankruptcy trustee's case would have been stronger if the T shareholders had "known, or should have known, that their stock was being paid for by [a T] asset depleting transfer."[112]

---

[108] 845 F.2d at 847.

[109] 845 F.2d at 848.

[110] 845 F.2d at 849-850 n.16.

[111] 845 F.2d at 850.

[112] 845 F.2d at 850. Compare *Yucaipa* (discussed at ¶1706.6.18) in which the court disagreed with the holding in *Kupetz*, that California's fraudulent transfer statute may not be used to attack well-publicized, above board LBOs.

¶1706.6.6   *Ohio Corrugating* Case[113]

The essence of this complex LBO transaction was that Newco (the initial equity capital of which is not stated) borrowed $1.3 million from Lender to purchase T's stock. Both Newco and T signed the loan agreement with Lender, and T pledged its assets to secure the loan to Newco. After this loan transaction, a holding company ("ParentCo") was formed to own all of Newco's stock. Newco then merged downstream into T, with T as the surviving company.

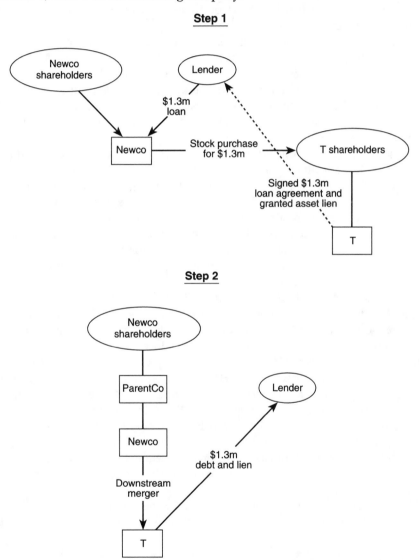

Step 1

Step 2

---

[113] Ohio Corrugating Co. v. Security Pac. Business Credit, Inc. (In re Ohio Corrugating Co.), 70 B.R. 920 (Bankr. N.D. Ohio 1987) (hereinafter *Ohio Corrugating I*), and Ohio Corrugating Co. v. DPAC Inc. (In re Ohio Corrugating Co.), 91 B.R. 430 (Bankr. N.D. Ohio 1988) (hereinafter *Ohio Corrugating II*).

T filed a chapter 11 petition within one year after this transaction. T's unsecured creditors brought a fraudulent conveyance action against Lender, T, ParentCo, and ParentCo's shareholders to recover the loan proceeds under Ohio's (now superseded) UFCA and the Bankruptcy Code.

ParentCo (which was not in existence at the time of the LBO) and ParentCo's shareholders sought summary judgment dismissal of the case against them. In *Ohio Corrugating I* the court held that if there were a fraudulent conveyance, T's creditors would be permitted to recoup the transfer from "any entity for whose benefit the transfer was made. The [Bankruptcy] Code does not restrict recovery to those persons or entities receiving the property."[114]

The court did not address (1) whether a fraudulent transfer occurred or (2) whether it was done for the benefit of ParentCo and/or ParentCo's shareholders.

In *Ohio Corrugating II*,[115] after a trial, the court held that the transfers involved in the LBO were not susceptible to avoidance under either Bankruptcy Code §548 or Ohio UFCA §4 dealing with insolvency, because (1) no creditors with matured claims were in existence at the time of the alleged fraudulent transfer and (2) T was not insolvent or rendered insolvent by the transfer.

The court held that creditors whose claims arise subsequent to the alleged fraudulent transfer cannot attack the transfer, because they do not need the protection afforded by the fraudulent conveyance laws. According to the court (which relied on *Credit Managers*, discussed at ¶1706.6.3), "subsequent creditors are in a substantially different position from existing creditors" because they "willingly extend . . . credit to the Debtor after the buyout in reliance on the performance of the 'new' company."[116] Moreover, the court said that "[w]e see no basis here for holding that the constructive fraud provisions of . . . §548 may be utilized as a form of insurance for creditors whose claims matured after the buyout."[117]

Under the analysis of *Ohio Corrugating II*, an LBO cannot be challenged as an alleged fraudulent transfer under any of the Bankruptcy Code's constructive fraud provisions if all creditors' claims at the time of the chapter 11 filing arose after the LBO and were willing extensions of credit in reliance on Newco's performance. This holding limits the effect of the plain language of all three subparts of Bankruptcy Code §548 and also the effect of the UFCA subparts dealing with undercapitalization and expected inability to pay debts as they mature (which two UFCA provisions were not at issue in *Ohio Corrugating* because the claim related only to an insolvency assertion), under which provisions a trustee or subsequent creditor is permitted to challenge the transfer. Whether the *Ohio Corrugating II* decision marks the beginning of a trend to protect LBO transferees against subsequent creditors who intentionally extended credit to the post-LBO entity, knowing that it was highly leveraged, is not yet clear.

In *Ohio Corrugating II*'s insolvency analysis, the court strongly emphasized a balance sheet approach toward measuring insolvency. The court suggested that a

---

[114] *Ohio Corrugating I*, 70 B.R. at 924.

[115] *Ohio Corrugating II*, 91 B.R. 430.

[116] 91 B.R. at 435.

[117] 91 B.R. at 435. But see *Yucaipa* (discussed at ¶1706.6.18) where the court concluded that cases in the Ninth Circuit, including *Credit Managers*, were wrong in holding that the UFTA may not be used to attack well-publicized, above board LBOs.

"presumptive validity" ought to be assigned "to the treatment of assets and liabilities according to GAAP."[118] The court refused to require the potential claim of an unfunded benefits plan to be treated as a future liability. In making this determination, the court considered the fact that "Announcement 36 from the Financial Accounting Standards Board (FASB 36) only requires footnote disclosure of unfunded defined benefit plan obligations; it requires inclusion neither on the balance sheet nor in a court's solvency analysis."[119] The court concluded that failure to accord this presumptive validity to balance sheets prepared in accordance with GAAP "would unfairly penalize the LBO participants who reasonably relied on GAAP in assessing the solvency of the Debtor prior to the buyout."[120] Moreover, the court said, "if insolvency is clearly demonstrated according to a balance sheet determination, the Debtor's ability to pay its debts as they mature is irrelevant."[121]

¶1706.6.7   *Wieboldt Stores* Case[122]

Newco was organized to purchase T's stock from T's pre-acquisition shareholders for $38.5 million through a public tender offer. Newco's capitalization consisted of a $38.5 million loan, from third-party Lenders, collateralized by a pledge of T's assets; i.e., although Newco purchased T's stock with money loaned to Newco by Lenders, T, for no consideration, granted liens on T's assets to Lenders. (The opinion makes no reference to any capital infusion to Newco by VC.)

In the tender offer, Newco purchased 99% of T's stock for $38.5 million. Subsequent to the LBO, T gave Lenders a T note for the outstanding principal balance of the acquisition loan collateralized by the pledge of T's assets.

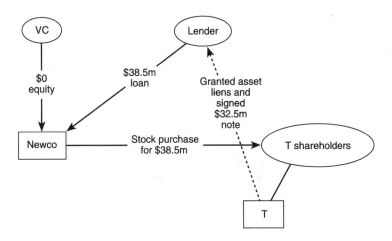

[118] 91 B.R. at 438.

[119] *Ohio Corrugating II*, 91 B.R. 430, 438.

[120] 91 B.R. at 439.

[121] 91 B.R. at 439.

[122] Wieboldt Stores, Inc. v. Schottenstein, 94 B.R. 488 (Bankr. N.D. Ill. 1988). See also Wieboldt Stores, Inc. v. Schottenstein, 111 B.R. 162 (Bankr. N.D. Ill. 1990); Wieboldt Stores, Inc. v. Schottenstein, 131 B.R. 655 (Bankr. N.D. Ill. 1991).

Approximately nine months after completion of the LBO, T entered chapter 11 and then commenced an action in the bankruptcy court based on the LBO. In that action, T asserted, among other things, claims under Illinois's now superseded version of the Statute of Elizabeth and the Bankruptcy Code against (1) T's controlling shareholders, officers, and directors (the "Controlling Shareholders"), (2) T's other shareholders who sold in the tender offer (the "Public Shareholders"), and (3) Lenders. All defendants moved to dismiss.

The Controlling Shareholders argued that T failed to state a claim under either federal or state fraudulent conveyance laws, because the "tender offer and LBO were composed of a series of interrelated but independent transactions" and thus T's shareholders did not receive T's "property [when they sold their T shares to Newco] during the tender offer but rather received [Newco's] property in exchange for their [T] shares."[123] The court rejected this argument and, in effect, applied a step-transaction analysis.[124]

According to the court, the focus for analyzing an LBO transaction should not be "on the formal structure of the transaction but rather on the knowledge or intent of the parties involved in the transaction."[125] Applying this standard, the court concluded (assuming, as it must in a motion to dismiss, that the plaintiff's allegations were true): "[I]t is clear that, at least as regards the liability of the controlling share-holders [and] the Lenders, . . . the LBO transfers must be collapsed into one transaction."[126] According to the court, these parties "knew that [Newco] intended to finance its acquisition of [T] through an LBO and not with any of its own [i.e., Newco's] funds. They knew that [T] was insolvent before the LBO and the LBO would result in further encumbrance of [T's] already encumbered assets."[127]

The court concluded that under the step-transaction doctrine, T cannot be said to have received any benefit from the transfers because all the money went to consummate the tender offer. The court treated the LBO as if T "granted a security interest in [its] assets to [Lenders] and received from [T's old] shareholders in return 99% of its outstanding shares of stock. . . . This stock was virtually worthless to [T]."[128]

Although the *Wieboldt Stores* court *denied* the Controlling Shareholders' and Lenders' motion to dismiss, it *granted* the Public Shareholders' motion to dismiss. The court refused to apply the step-transaction doctrine to the Public Shareholders because T had not alleged that the Public Shareholders were aware or had reason to be aware that Newco's "acquisition encumbered virtually all of [T's] assets."[129] Nor had T alleged "that these shareholders were aware that the consideration they received for their tendered shares was [T's] property."[130] Rather, the Public Shareholders were merely "innocent pawns in the scheme. They were aware only that [Newco] made a public tender offer for shares of [T's] stock."[131] The court concluded that because

---

[123] 94 B.R. at 500.
[124] 94 B.R. at 502.
[125] 94 B.R. at 502.
[126] 94 B.R. at 502.
[127] 94 B.R. at 502.
[128] 94 B.R. at 505.
[129] 94 B.R. at 503.
[130] 94 B.R. at 503.
[131] 94 B.R. at 503.

it would not collapse the transaction as to the Public Shareholders who received money from Newco rather than T, these defendants were not transferees of T's property who could be sued under federal or state fraudulent conveyance laws.[132]

With regard to the structuring of an LBO, the *Wieboldt Stores* court stated:

> In sum, the formal structure of the transaction alone cannot shield the LBO lenders or the controlling and insider shareholders from [T's] fraudulent conveyance claims. These parties were aware that the consideration they received from their financing commitments or in exchange for their shares consisted of [T's] assets and not the assets of [Newco] or any other financial intermediary. The [Public Shareholders], on the other hand, apparently unaware of the financing transactions, participated only to the extent that they exchanged their shares for funds from [Newco].[133]

For a discussion of additional *Wieboldt Stores* issues relating to T's directors, accountants, and attorneys, see the discussion at ¶1706.5.

¶1706.6.8   *Mellon* Case[134]

Newco was organized to purchase T's stock from T's old shareholders for $1.85 million. Newco borrowed $1.85 million from Lender, guaranteed by T. Newco's equity capital is not stated. Newco's stock was 100% owned by ParentCo.

ParentCo owned several other businesses. Shortly after Newco purchased T's stock, ParentCo began operating several of its businesses in a fashion complementary to T's business, which benefitted T by taking advantage of a "synergy of complementary services."[135] At the time of and shortly after the LBO, Lender extended $4.55 million of credit to T, approximately half at the time of the LBO and the other half five months later.

T granted liens on its assets to Lender to secure both its guarantee of Newco's $1.85 million acquisition loan to purchase T's stock and T's $4.55 million of borrowings. ParentCo also guaranteed Lender's $1.85 million loan to Newco and Lender's $4.55 million of loans to T.

Approximately one year after the LBO, T filed a bankruptcy petition under chapter 11 because of an unpredicted and adverse antitrust decision.

---

[132] The court did not address disclosures in the tender offer documents concerning the consequences of the LBO. It is not clear whether the tender offer disclosure revealed the adverse impact of the transaction on T's shareholders or, if it did and the court had focused on that fact, whether the Public Shareholders would have been treated differently.

[133] 94 B.R. at 503.

[134] Mellon Bank, N.A. v. Metro Communications, Inc. (In re Metro Communications, Inc.), 945 F.2d 635 (3d Cir. 1991) (*rev'g* 95 B.R. 921 (Bankr. W.D. Pa. 1991)), *cert. denied*, 503 U.S. 937 (1992).

[135] 945 F.2d at 647.

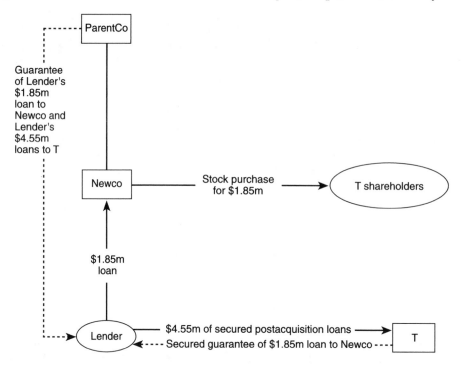

The Third Circuit Court of Appeals applied Pennsylvania's (now superseded) UFCA to determine whether T received reasonably equivalent value for incurring the liens on its assets. The court reasoned that T had received reasonably equivalent value because

- T benefited from the "synergy" of ParentCo's businesses, and
- the $4.55 million of new loans from Lender to T was obtainable through ParentCo's guarantee.

The court also considered whether the acquisition caused T to become insolvent or inadequately capitalized. In pursuing this inquiry, the court declined to treat T's full $1.85 million guarantee of Newco's debt as a T liability (and hence as a reduction of T's solvency and capitalization) because ParentCo (which was solvent at the time of the LBO) had also guaranteed the $1.85 million debt. Indeed, the court acknowledged that T's ultimate insolvency resulted from the unpredicted and adverse antitrust decision several months after the LBO.

The plaintiff strenuously argued that because T ended up liable on the $1.85 million loan, which was equal to the full purchase price for T's stock, the LBO had caused T to be insolvent and/or undercapitalized. The court rejected this argument, stating that "when the debtor is a going concern and its realizable going concern value after the transaction is equal to or exceeds its going concern value before the transaction, reasonably equivalent value has been received."[136] By this the court probably meant that the synergistic addition to T's value exceeded the portion of the acquisition debt that T could (at the time of the LBO) have expected to pay (after taking into account ParentCo's guarantee of the same acquisition debt), although the court is not at all clear on this point.

Hence, the court held that the LBO was not a fraudulent conveyance.

¶1706.6.9   *Moody* Case[137]

Newco was organized to purchase T's stock from T's old shareholders for $12.1 million. Newco's capitalization consisted of a $200,000 equity contribution from VC, a $200,000 subordinated loan from VC, and an $11.7 million cash transfer from T (which in turn borrowed the $11.7 million from Lender, giving Lender a lien on T's assets). Whether the cash transfer from T to Newco was a dividend or a loan is unclear.[138]

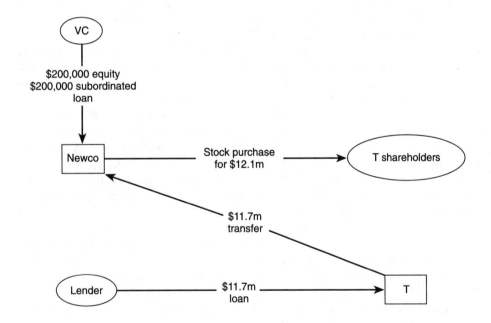

---

[136] 945 F.2d at 646.

[137] Moody v. Security Pac. Business Credit, Inc., 127 B.R. 958 (Bankr. W.D. Pa. 1991), aff'd, 971 F.2d 1056 (3d Cir. 1992).

[138] In fact, Lender made two loans. First, Lender loaned $12.1 million to Newco (due on demand), which Newco used to purchase T's stock for $12.1 million. Immediately thereafter, Lender loaned $11.7 million to T, the proceeds of which T transferred to Newco. Newco then used the $11.7 million from T along with the $400,000 received from VC to pay off the first loan of $12.1 million from Lender to Newco.

Fifteen months after the LBO, an involuntary bankruptcy petition was filed against T.

The United States District Court for the District of Pennsylvania, applying Pennsylvania's (now superseded) UFCA, found (after applying the step-transaction doctrine) that although T did not receive fair consideration for the encumbrance of its assets, T was not rendered insolvent by the LBO or left with an unreasonably small capital. The Third Circuit Court of Appeals affirmed.

On the solvency issue, the district court had reasoned:

> In considering the "present" fair salable value of [T's] assets . . . we hold that we must value them on a going concern basis. Several courts which have considered fraudulent conveyance suits have held that courts should use going concern values rather than liquidation values, unless the company's failure is clearly imminent. [T] was not a company whose failure was clearly imminent [at the time of the acquisition because T's business as a going concern] had substantial value.[139]

The court of appeals affirmed on this point: "Where bankruptcy is not 'clearly imminent' on the date of the challenged conveyance, the weight of authority holds that assets should be valued on a going concern basis."[140] T's bankruptcy was not "clearly imminent" at the time of the LBO because, among other reasons, T then had a positive cash flow and the year prior to the LBO T's business had improved.

The court of appeals also held that the LBO did not leave T with an unreasonably small capital. The court looked to financial projections—including month-by-month analysis of T's balance sheet and analyses of T's income statement and credit availability—showing that T could continue in business after the LBO. It held these projections to be "reasonable."[141] Although the court acknowledged that the projections used were "not entirely on the mark," the reasonableness of such projections was "bolstered by the fact that during the five months following the [LBO, T's] cash flow tracked the projections contained in [T's] business plan."[142] The court therefore distinguished the projections in *Moody* from those found unreasonable in *O'Day* (see ¶1706.6.10), in which "the parties' worst case scenario exceeded the company's best financial performance in the preceding years."[143]

T's downfall, the court further noted, was due not to the LBO but to a "dramatic" unanticipated downturn in orders and sales caused by increased competition.[144] The court of appeals thus affirmed the district court's view that "the fraudulent conveyance laws were not designed to insure creditors against all possible consequences of a company's post-leveraged buyout errors in judgment or poor business practices. . . . [LBO participants] do . . . not . . . become insurers of [T's] ultimate success."[145]

The court, therefore, held that the LBO was not a fraudulent conveyance.

---

[139] 127 B.R. at 995.
[140] 971 F.2d at 1067.
[141] 971 F.2d at 1071.
[142] 971 F.2d at 1073-1074.
[143] 971 F.2d at 1074.
[144] 971 F.2d at 1074.
[145] 127 B.R. at 989-1000.

¶1706.6.10   *O'Day* Case[146]

The essence of this complex LBO transaction was that Newco (the initial equity capital of which was approximately $2.5 million) was created to acquire T's stock for approximately $12.1 million. Newco borrowed approximately $9.6 million from Lender, secured by T's assets. Newco used the $9.6 million loan and the $2.5 million equity to pay the $12.1 million purchase price for T's stock.[147]

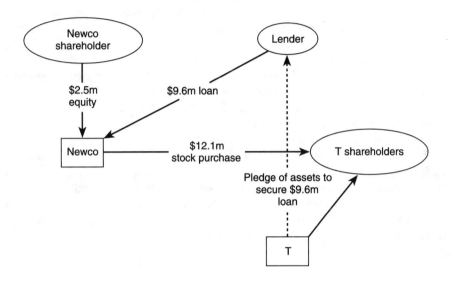

Before the merger, three analyses of T were performed to determine the effect of the LBO on T: (1) A financial advisor to Newco prepared an offering memo that noted "softness" in T's industry and certain other problems facing T,[148] (2) Lender prepared a credit memo remarking that "[T's] industry has hit bottom and should remain stable over the foreseeable future,"[149] and (3) Newco projected that sales following the LBO would be sufficient to permit T to repay the LBO loan.

Twenty-two months after the LBO, T's trade creditors filed an involuntary bankruptcy petition against Newco.

To determine whether T received fair consideration, the court, using the Massachusetts UFCA, collapsed the LBO under the step-transaction doctrine, reasoning that "all parties, including [Lender] were aware of the structure of the transaction and participated in implementing it."[150]

---

[146] Murphy v. Meritor Sav. Bank (In re O'Day Corp.), 126 B.R. 370 (Bankr. D. Mass. 1991).
[147] T received $235,000 of the purchase price and used approximately $233,000 of that amount to pay LBO transaction fees.
[148] 126 B.R. at 375.
[149] 126 B.R. at 376.
[150] 126 B.R. at 394.

The court found that T received inadequate consideration for pledging its assets to secure Newco's acquisition loan. In particular, the court found that Lender's agreement to make additional loans to T was not adequate consideration.[151]

In determining whether T was solvent, the court used a liquidation analysis because "the post-LBO losses demonstrate that the transaction placed [T] on the brink of collapse."[152] (It is unclear why post-LBO losses should have been considered in determining whether T was a going concern at the time of the LBO.)

The court also considered whether the LBO left T inadequately capitalized and, relying on *Credit Managers* (discussed at ¶1706.6.3), reasoned that to determine the adequacy of working capital, it was necessary to examine whether the projections used prior to the LBO were prudent. The court found that Newco's projections were "totally inconsistent" with both historical figures in Newco's financial advisor's memo and the relevant fiscal data available to them.[153] "The projections prepared by [Lender] had no cushion, no room for error. Nevertheless, [Lender] approved the loan facilities ... despite a collateral shortfall."[154] Newco's projections were, therefore, "imprudent" and left T with an unreasonably small capital.

The court accordingly found that the LBO was a fraudulent conveyance. It ordered the subordination of Lender's lien on T's assets to the claims of T's prejudiced creditors under the equitable subordination doctrine. The court reasoned that Lender should be equitably subordinated because Lender's "post-LBO conduct was tantamount to overreaching [and Lender and Newco] suffered from an overweening optimism about [T's] financial abilities, and their own, which addled their ability to evaluate the company in light of its financial condition in the months prior to the LBO...."[155]

¶1706.6.11 *Richmond Produce* Case[156]

In 8/87 the shareholders of T, a closely held corporation, sold their T stock to individual A[157] for $3 million, which was paid $1.5 million in cash and $1.5 million by A's promissory note backed by a $1.5 million letter of credit (the "LOC") issued

---

[151] Interestingly, the *O'Day* court relied on the bankruptcy court opinion in *Mellon*, discussed at ¶1706.6.8. In *Mellon*, the bankruptcy court was reversed on this issue by the Third Circuit Court of Appeals, which found that a new line of credit *could* be fair consideration. Compare the *Bay Plastics* case (discussed at ¶1706.6.15), in which the court, in finding that T did not receive reasonably equivalent value, ignored the value to T of a revolving credit facility obtained by T in connection with T's LBO, where there was no evidence that advances under the credit facility were actually made.

[152] 126 B.R. at 399.

[153] 126 B.R. at 404.

[154] 126 B.R. at 411.

[155] 126 B.R. at 411.

[156] Kendall v. Sorani (In re Richmond Produce Co.), 151 B.R. 1012 (Bankr. N.D. Cal. 1993), *aff'd*, 195 B.R. 455 (N.D. Cal. 1996).

[157] The opinion states that T's shareholders sold "most" of their T stock to A. In the interest of simplifying the complicated facts of the case, this analysis assumes that T's shareholders sold all of their stock to A.

by Lender #2.[158] In order to obtain the LOC, A took control of T before the closing of the sale of T's stock to A, and A arranged for the following to occur:

- Lender #1 loaned $1.5 million to T, secured by T's assets.
- T paid the $1.5 million proceeds of this loan to Lender #2, in consideration for which Lender #2 issued a $1.5 million certificate of deposit (the "CD") in A's (not T's) name.
- Lender #2 retained the $1.5 million CD as security for the $1.5 million LOC, which Lender #2 issued to T's shareholders to back A's $1.5 million note to T's shareholders.
- A agreed that if Lender #2 were ultimately liable on the $1.5 million LOC, A would indemnify Lender #2, and A pledged personal assets (which the court ultimately held were worthless) to secure that indemnity.

Chart #1: Simple depiction

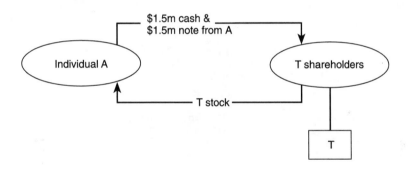

---

[158] The opinion initially states that A purchased T's stock for $4 million. The transactions, as described in the opinion, however, show that A actually purchased T's stock for $3 million, consisting of $1.5 million in cash and A's $1.5 million promissory note payable to T's former shareholders.

Chart #2: More complete depiction

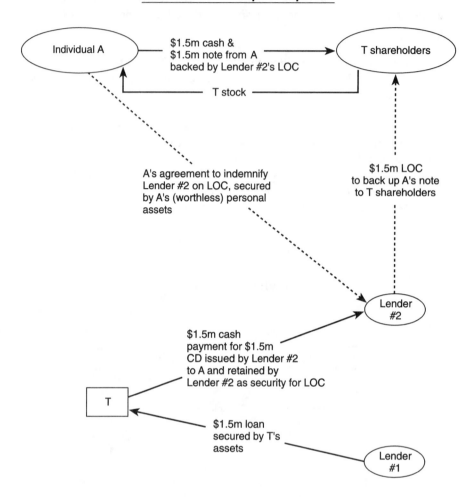

Before issuing the LOC, a loan officer of Lender #2 expressed concern about the enforceability of the LOC transaction. In particular, Lender #2's loan officer was concerned that T was providing the $1.5 million of security for the LOC, but T did not appear to obtain any benefit from the LOC. Lender #2 sought legal advice about the enforceability of the LOC transaction and received a letter from A's counsel (which it apparently relied upon as an opinion letter) stating that the LOC transaction was not vulnerable to attack as a fraudulent transfer.

T began to experience financial difficulties shortly after A took control of T, due primarily to A's inability to manage T's cash flow. Approximately one year after A's purchase of T's stock, A defaulted on his $1.5 million note to T's former shareholders, who made demand on Lender #2 as issuer of the LOC. Lender #2 paid the LOC and thereafter foreclosed on the $1.5 million CD that A had pledged to secure the LOC (but for which T had paid the purchase price).

T's trustee in bankruptcy contended that T's $1.5 million payment to Lender #2 as the purchase price of the CD was a fraudulent transfer under §548 of the Bankruptcy Code and/or under the UFTA as adopted in California because T received less than reasonably equivalent value for making the $1.5 million payment at a time when T was insolvent and/or undercapitalized or was thereby rendered insolvent and/or undercapitalized.

First, the court found that T did not receive reasonably equivalent value for making the $1.5 million payment to Lender #2 for A's purchase of the CD because (1) the CD was issued to A (not to T) and was ultimately used to satisfy A's (not T's) obligations to T's former shareholders, (2) A's agreement to indemnify Lender #2 for the $1.5 million LOC and A's pledge of personal assets were worthless, and (3) A's managerial skills did not constitute consideration for T's $1.5 million payment for the CD because A was being paid $20,000 a month to run T and "[g]iven the rapid demise of [T] after the sale, it is difficult to argue that the value of [A's] services exceeded this amount."[159]

Second, the court found that although T was not insolvent at the time the LOC transaction occurred, this transaction did render T insolvent because the purchase of the LOC should be treated as a $1.5 million reduction in T's shareholder equity. In reaching this conclusion, the court looked particularly to A's ability to repay the obligation backed by the LOC. It concluded that although there were several ways of treating the transaction under GAAP (including carrying the CD that secured the LOC as a T asset), treating the transaction as a reduction in T's shareholder equity "more fairly reflects the actual financial condition of [T] after the transfer from a creditor's point of view," in light of the fact that A was in a position neither to pay A's $1.5 million note to T's former shareholders nor to honor his indemnity to Lender #2 for making payment on the $1.5 million LOC.[160]

The court held that T's bankruptcy trustee could recover the amount of the $1.5 million CD (plus prejudgment interest) from Lender #2. Lender #2 had argued that T's trustee should not recover this amount from Lender #2 because Lender #2 was entitled to the defense, under Bankruptcy Code §550, that Lender #2 gave value for the transfer in good faith and without knowledge of the voidability of the transfer. The court found that while Lender #2 gave value and may have acted in good faith, Lender #2 had sufficient knowledge of the voidability of the LOC transaction to lose on this defense. The court explained:

> [Lender #2] knew the details of [A's purchase of T's stock] and the fact that [A] intended to heavily leverage his purchase of [T's] stock. This was sufficient to put [Lender #2] on notice that the proposed [LOC transaction] would render [T] insolvent and/or undercapitalized. Had [Lender #2] investigated further the effect of the transaction on [T's] financial condition, the Court is satisfied that it would have discovered that [the LOC transaction] rendered [T] insolvent.[161]

The court also noted that Lender #2 was on "inquiry notice" as to the voidability of the LOC transaction because, instead of performing its own due diligence, Lender

---

[159] 151 B.R. at 1018.
[160] 151 B.R. at 1019.
[161] 151 B.R. at 1022.

#2 relied on the "vague assurances" of A's (not its own) counsel that the LOC transaction would not be avoidable.

The court also rejected Lender #2's defense "that the transfer may not be avoided because there is no bona fide claim against [T's bankruptcy] estate that existed at the time of the transfer."[162] The court agreed that this defense reflected the requirements of the UFTA when the allegation is that the debtor was (or was rendered by the transaction) insolvent, and also agreed that this defense was consistent with the law of the Ninth Circuit in constructive fraudulent transfer cases brought under Bankruptcy Code §548(a)(2)(B). The court concluded however, that T's bankruptcy trustee "proved to the Court's satisfaction that there was a bona fide claim against the estate that existed prior to the [LOC transaction]."[163]

¶1706.6.12 *Morse Tool* Case[164]

In 8/84 Newco purchased T's stock from Oldco in a four-step LBO, described below.

Step one. Individual A created Newco with equity of $100,000 and became the sole member of Newco's board of directors.

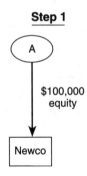

162 151 B.R. at 1016 n.5.
163 151 B.R. at 1016 n.5.
164 Ferrari v. Barclay's Business Credit, Inc. (In re Morse Tool, Inc.), 148 B.R. 97 (Bankr. D. Mass. 1992).

Step two. Oldco created T, a shell corporation with no assets or liabilities, and transferred to T the assets (subject to liabilities) of two of Oldco's unincorporated divisions (the "Divisions"), in exchange for which T issued to Oldco all of T's stock. Importantly, there was no novation and therefore Oldco also remained legally liable on the transferred liabilities.[165]

Step 2

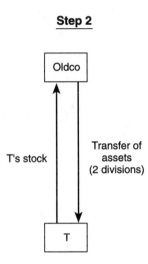

Step three. Newco purchased all of T's stock from Oldco for $10.4 million, which Newco paid with a $6.6 million promissory note (guaranteed by A and secured by T's machinery, equipment, and slow-moving inventory) and cash of $3.8 million. Newco paid the $3.8 million in cash with the proceeds of a $3.8 million loan from Lender to T, which loan was secured by a lien on T's accounts receivable and inventory and was guaranteed by A and Newco. The court did not indicate whether T's $3.8 million in cash was transferred to Newco as a dividend, a loan, or otherwise.

---

[165] As part of Oldco's sale of T stock to Newco, Newco and T also agreed to be contingently liable to Oldco for potential pension liabilities of up to $2.1 million. Because the contingencies could not have occurred at the time of the LBO, the court subsequently valued this contingent liability at zero as of the time of the LBO.

Step 3

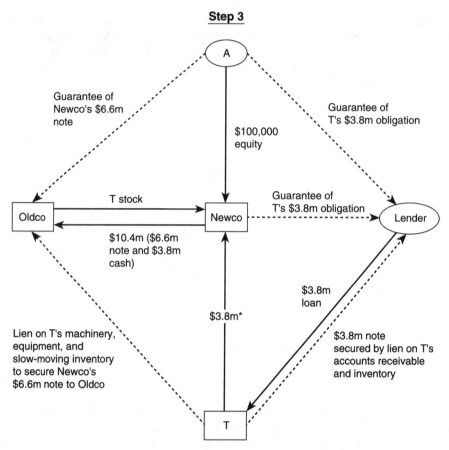

*The court did not indicate whether T's $3.8m cash was transferred to Newco as a dividend, a loan, or otherwise.

Step four. Approximately one month after Newco purchased T's stock, Newco merged downstream into T, with T as the surviving entity.

Step 4

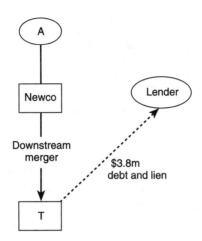

Prior to the LBO, A had performed an analysis of Newco-T's likely post-LBO performance based on the unfounded assumption that Newco-T could raise prices and reduce certain costs. In fact, market conditions after the LBO prohibited Newco-T from raising prices, and Newco-T was unable to reduce costs. In 1/87, after operating at a loss for more than two years following the LBO, Newco-T filed bankruptcy and ultimately a chapter 7 trustee was appointed.

Shortly after his appointment, Newco-T's trustee (along with Newco-T's creditors' committee) objected to the payment of Lender's claim on the ground that Newco-T's $3.8 million cash payment to Oldco (made with the proceeds of Lender's loan to T) was a fraudulent conveyance because made without fair consideration and while T was insolvent and/or undercapitalized.[166]

The court first considered whether Newco-T's trustee had standing to sue Lender under the UFCA's insolvency provisions. The court found that only a creditor (or trustee on such creditor's behalf) with a claim that actually existed prior to the LBO had standing to sue under the UFCA's insolvency test. The court therefore distinguished the standing provided under the UFCA's insolvency test from the standing provided under the UFCA's other fraudulent conveyance tests based on the plain language of the UFCA, which gives post-LBO creditors standing to sue on the grounds of unreasonably small capital and no reasonable expectation of the ability to pay obligations as they mature.[167] The court then found that although

[166] Newco-T's trustee also alleged that Lender participated in the LBO with actual intent to hinder, delay, and defraud T's creditors. Because the court ultimately found that the LBO was supported by adequate consideration (and was therefore not a constructive fraudulent conveyance), it also found that the trustee's intentional fraud claim was barred. 148 B.R. at 139.

[167] But see *Credit Managers* (discussed at ¶1706.6.3), *Kupetz* (discussed at ¶1706.6.5), and *Ohio Corrugating* (discussed at ¶1706.6.6), all of which deny post-LBO creditors standing to sue on grounds of unreasonably small capital and/or no reasonable expectation of ability to pay obligations as they mature, despite the plain language of the UFCA, on the ground that the UFCA may not be used to attack well publicized,

certain claims may have existed against Oldco's two transferred Divisions before the LBO, these claims failed to confer standing to sue on the basis of insolvency:

> Prior to the [LBO] the obligor on each of these claims was [Oldco,] which remained obligated on the claims (and solvent) after the [LBO]. As to [Newco-T], these were not pre-existing claims. [Newco-T] had no debts before the [LBO]; it could not have had any because it was created only at the [LBO]. . . . The [LBO] did not weaken the obligor on these claims [Oldco]; rather it gave the claimants a second obligor to look to for satisfaction of their claims.[168]

The court next considered whether Newco-T's trustee could avoid the LBO on unreasonably-small-capital grounds. The court found that Newco-T's trustee had standing to sue on unreasonably-small-capital grounds because the UFCA's unreasonably-small-capital test expressly "extend[s] standing to [sue to] 'future creditors.'"[169] The court adopted the reasoning of the *Moody* court, stating that "unreasonably small capital denotes a level of capitalization that renders a debtor unable to generate sufficient profits, or at least cash flow, to sustain operations."[170] The *Morse Tool* court determined that the LBO *did* render Newco-T undercapitalized because:

> [A's] projections were unreasonable and imprudent; this was discernible from information available before the [LBO]; and both [A] and [Lender] had reason to be skeptical and to inquire into the assumptions that rendered the projections so unreasonable. Even if the assumptions on which the projections were based had been sound, the projections themselves still provided only a small margin of error. . . . But the projections were not sound. They relied heavily on a price increase that never occurred, on cost-saving measures that were untested, and on sales and market performance that were significantly better than existed at the time of the [LBO]. . . . They demonstrated . . . that [Newco-T], as capitalized after the [LBO], could survive only under the most favorable and improbable of conditions.[171]

However, the court did not avoid the LBO as a fraudulent conveyance because it found that T *did* receive fair consideration for the obligations it incurred in borrowing and securing the $3.8 million cash payment Newco made as part of the $10.4 million purchase price payment to Oldco. Newco-T's trustee had urged the court to focus only on the second step of the LBO and to find that the LBO should be characterized as a form of stock redemption in which T received no consideration other than its own stock. The court rejected the trustee's argument and, citing *Gleneagles*,[172] used the step-transaction doctrine to collapse all four steps of the LBO. On this collapsed basis, the LBO was:

---

above board LBOs on behalf of post-LBO creditors. Compare *Yucaipa* (discussed at ¶1706.6.18) in which the court, in the context of the UFCA, found these cases wrongly decided.

[168] 148 B.R. at 131. As discussed below, the court apparently also believed that the LBO did not weaken T because Newco-T received assets worth a net consideration of $13 million for a purchase price of $10.4 million. Interestingly, the court failed to explain how T could have had no pre-LBO liabilities since the sale of the two Divisions to T was made subject to the Divisions' liabilities.

[169] 148 B.R. at 131.

[170] 148 B.R. at 132 (citing Moody v. Security Pac. Business Credit, Inc., 971 F.2d at 1070). For a discussion of *Moody*, see ¶1706.6.9.

[171] 148 B.R. at 133.

[172] For a discussion of *Gleneagles*, see ¶1706.6.1.

in essence . . . a purchase of assets and liabilities from [Oldco]. . . . It was not a stock sale because [T] had no separate corporate existence prior to the [LBO]. [T] consisted of [the Divisions], which were assets of [Oldco]. It is true that these assets were spun-off into [T] before they were sold to [Newco], but this amounted to mere packaging. . . .[173]

The court valued the Divisions on a going concern (not a liquidation) basis because Newco-T remained in business for more than two years after the LBO, and therefore Newco-T's bankruptcy was not "'clearly imminent'" at the time of the LBO.[174] The court concluded that the going concern value of the Divisions was $19.6 million, while the liabilities assumed by Newco-T did not exceed $6.6 million, for a net consideration of $13 million. Such value was found to be more than adequate consideration for the $10.4 million purchase price (consisting of the $6.6 million note and the $3.8 million cash payment to Oldco).

¶1706.6.13 *Best Products* Case[175]

In the first step of this LBO, VC created Newco in 10/88 to make a tender offer for the outstanding shares of common stock of T, a public company. Newco's capitalization consisted of $50 million of equity contribution from VC and $679 million in short-term debt (the "Short-Term Debt") from third-party lenders, all of which Newco used to purchase 97% of T's shares in the tender offer at $27.50 per T share.

Step 1 (10/88)

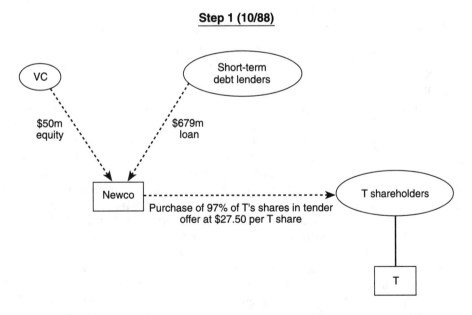

---

[173] 148 B.R. at 134.

[174] 148 B.R. at 136 (quoting *Moody*). For a discussion of *Moody*, see ¶1706.6.9.

[175] In re Best Prods. Co., 168 B.R. 35 (Bankr. S.D.N.Y. 1994), *aff'd sub nom.* Resolution Trust Corp. v. Best Prods. Co. (In re Best Prods. Co.), 177 B.R. 791 (S.D.N.Y. 1995).

In the second step, Newco was merged with and into T in 3/89, with T the surviving entity. At this time VC made an additional equity infusion into T of $35 million, and T borrowed approximately $872 million in partially secured long-term debt (the "Long-Term Debt"), part of the proceeds of which T used to retire the Short-Term Debt and to operate T.[176]

Step 2 (3/89)

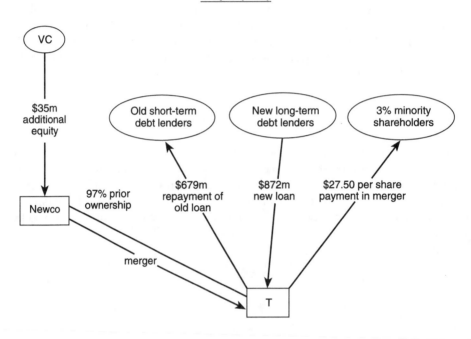

Shortly after the Newco-into-T merger, T began to experience financial trouble, including a loss of trade credit. After suffering significant losses in 1990, T found itself unable to pay the Long-Term Debt and filed bankruptcy in 1/91.

After T's bankruptcy filing, the court appointed an examiner (the "Examiner"), who concluded that T had meritorious fraudulent conveyance causes of action against (1) the Long-Term Debt lenders to the extent they received liens in exchange for money used to finance the LBO (but not for liens in exchange for money used to operate T), (2) T's pre-LBO shareholders who tendered more than 1,000 T shares or received more than $27,500 for T shares, and (3) VC for fees T paid to VC in connection with arranging the LBO.

After a year of litigation and negotiation, the parties entered into a court-approved global settlement of T's fraudulent conveyance causes of action. Pursuant to this settlement, (1) the Long-Term Debt lenders gave T creditors allegedly harmed by the LBO approximately $30 million in value (composed of cash and shares of reorga-

---

[176] The Short-Term Debt and the Long-Term Debt each actually consisted of multiple debt tranches. For simplicity, this analysis treats these multiple tranches as if each were a single tranche.

nized T) and released liens on approximately $45 million of T's cash, (2) T's pre-LBO shareholders who tendered more than 1,000 T shares or received more than $27,500 for their T shares paid T $600,000, and (3) VC paid T $2 million.

In approving the settlement as "reasonable," the court first considered which state's law governed the LBO action, New York's UFCA or Virginia's Statute of Elizabeth. The court viewed choice of law as "critical" because, citing *C-T*,[177] Virginia's Statute of Elizabeth validates transfers made even for "slight consideration" rather than "fair consideration" as required by New York's UFCA.[178] The court agreed with the Examiner's analysis that "the case for the application of New York law was the stronger"[179] because, among other reasons, the LBO documents referenced New York law and the LBO was negotiated and consummated in New York.

Assuming that New York law applied, the court next considered whether, under the UFCA, T was (or was rendered by the LBO) insolvent and/or undercapitalized. The court reviewed the many solvency analyses performed by the litigants and the Examiner. The Examiner performed five alternative solvency tests, finding that T was solvent under two of the tests (a reconstituted balance sheet test and a comparable LBO multiplier test) but insolvent under three other tests (a liquidation analysis, a comparable public trading multiplier analysis, and a discounted cash flow analysis). The court therefore concluded that "there would be potentially credible evidence on both sides of the issue of solvency with the result that 'this would be a very, very hard case to predict.'"[180]

The court stated that pre-LBO reports upon which VC relied were "overly optimistic"[181] and that T would have "an easier time"[182] of demonstrating undercapitalization than insolvency. The court concluded that the settlement was appropriate because "the evidence at trial probably could be viewed either favorably or unfavorably toward [T]."[183]

On the question of fair consideration, the court noted that if it used the step-transaction doctrine to collapse the multiple steps of the LBO, it could find that the consideration for the Long-Term Debt actually went to T's selling shareholders and not to T. Citing an earlier decision in T's bankruptcy case, the court suggested that it would collapse the LBO steps, noting that "'collapsing transactions is little more than an effort . . . to focus not on the formal structure of a transaction, but rather on the knowledge or intent of the parties.'"[184]

---

[177] C-T of Va., Inc. v. Euroshoe Assocs., 762 F. Supp. 675 (W.D. Va. 1991), *aff'd*, 953 F.2d 637 (4th Cir. 1992), discussed at ¶1706.4.2.

[178] In re Best Prods. Co., 168 B.R. at 52 (Bankr. S.D.N.Y. 1994).

[179] 168 B.R. at 53 (footnote omitted).

[180] 168 B.R. at 54.

[181] 168 B.R. at 40.

[182] 168 B.R. at 56.

[183] 168 B.R. at 56.

[184] 168 B.R. at 56. For a discussion of the earlier *Best Products* decision, In re Best Prods. Co., 157 B.R. 222 (Bankr. S.D.N.Y. 1993), see ¶1706.3.3.

¶1706.6.14   *Buckhead America* Case[185]

As step 1, T in 1988 borrowed $57 million and dividended this amount to its 100% parent, ParentCo.[186] ParentCo used this $57 million to fund a going private transaction in which ParentCo purchased the 50.5% of its stock owned by certain public shareholders and insider shareholders, so that the partnership which owned 49.5% of ParentCo's stock immediately prior to the transaction ("Control Shareholder") became ParentCo's 100% shareholder.[187]

Step 1 (1988)

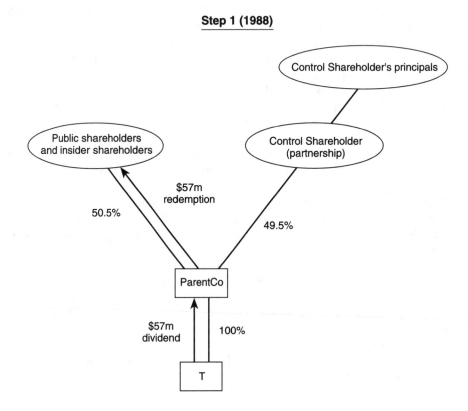

In 11/89 Control Shareholder sold 100% of ParentCo's stock to Newco for $83 million (the "step 2 transaction"). Apparently Newco made no payment to Control

---

[185] Official Committee of Unsecured Creditors of Buckhead America Corp. v. Reliance Capital Group, Inc. (In re Buckhead America Corp., f/k/a Days Inn of America), 178 B.R. 956 (D. Del. 1994).

[186] Although the opinion is silent on the mechanism used to transfer the $57 million from T to ParentCo, it appears to have been a dividend from T to ParentCo.

[187] The court did not explain the mechanism ParentCo used to effect the going private transaction, i.e., to buy out all 50.5% of the public and insider shareholders. Because a public tender offer generally does not result in the purchase of 100% of publicly owned shares, it is likely that some other mechanism, such as a "squeeze-out" merger, was used.

Shareholder, but rather T paid $38 million cash to Control Shareholder and T issued its $45 million note to Control Shareholder.

Step 2 (11/89)

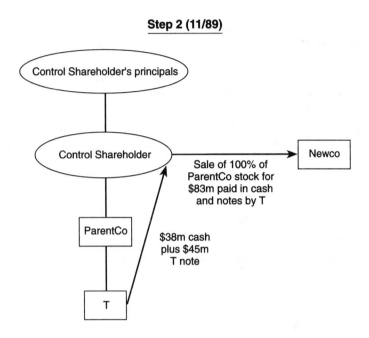

In 1991 T filed bankruptcy and its unsecured creditors' committee sued Control Shareholder and Control Shareholder's principals (the "Principals"), alleging among other things that the step 1 transaction and the step 2 transaction were both fraudulent conveyances because in each (1) T received no consideration, (2) T's net assets were diminished (by $57 million in step 1 and by $83 million in step 2), and (3) T was insolvent, undercapitalized, and unable to pay its debts. Subsequently, Control Shareholder was dropped from the case because of a prior release. However, the case continued against the Principals.

Plaintiffs alleged that the fraudulent conveyances could be recovered from the Principals under §550(a)(1) of the Bankruptcy Code which permits the recovery of a fraudulent transfer from "the initial transferee of such transfer *or the entity for whose benefit such transfer was made*" (emphasis added). The defendant Principals moved to dismiss these counts on the ground that the complaint was "legally insufficient because none of the defendants are alleged to be parties whom the debtor *intended* to benefit by making the transfer at issue."

In the step 1 transaction, T's transfer of $57 million in cash went to the public shareholders and insider shareholders (not to the Principals), and in the step 2 transaction, T's transfer of the $83 million in cash and notes went to Control Shareholder (not the Principals). In both cases the benefit to the Principals was incidental.

The court held that the §550(a)(1) claim was legally sufficient where the Principals were alleged to have used their control over T to cause improper transfers and were thereby enriched (because Control Shareholder became ParentCo's 100% owner in step 1 and received $83 million of proceeds (cash and notes) in step 2), regardless of whether the defendant Principals received any of those funds.[188]

¶1706.6.15   *Bay Plastics* Case[189]

Newco was organized by ParentCo to purchase T's stock from T's three pre-acquisition shareholders for $5.3 million. T borrowed $4 million from Lender in return for a note and a mortgage on T's assets. ParentCo "then caused [T] to direct that $3.5 million of the loan be disbursed to" Newco.[190] Newco used this $3.5 million cash plus a $1.8 million Newco note to purchase T's stock from T's three pre-acquisition shareholders for $5.3 million.

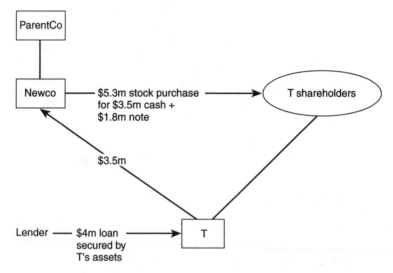

T filed a chapter 11 petition 15 months after the LBO transaction and made a fraudulent transfer claim against Lender and T's old shareholders to recover $3.5 million of the loan proceeds under California's UFTA. Specifically, T alleged that the LBO was a fraudulent transfer because T incurred $3.5 million in debt to Lender secured by T's assets without receiving reasonably equivalent value and was thereby rendered insolvent. Lender settled, leaving T's three old shareholders as the only defendants.

---

[188] The court also refused to dismiss numerous other counts in the complaint alleging other theories of liability against the defendants including that certain of the defendants, who were T directors, approved illegal dividends by T in connection with both the step 1 and step 2 transactions. The court's ruling on this matter is discussed at ¶1706.5.1.

[189] TI Bay Plastics, Inc. v. BT Commercial Corp. (In re Bay Plastics, Inc.), 187 B.R. 315 (Bankr. C.D. Cal. 1995).

[190] The opinion does not state whether T's transfer of the $3.5 million to Newco was a loan, a dividend, or otherwise; it merely states that ParentCo "caused [T] to direct that $3.5 million of the loan [from Lender to T] be disbursed to" Newco.

The court first reviewed prior Ninth Circuit cases applying fraudulent transfer principles to LBOs and concluded, relying principally on *Kupetz*, that:

> First, subsequent [i.e., post LBO] creditors (and a bankruptcy trustee standing in the shoes of subsequent creditors) lack standing to challenge an LBO if it has been widely publicized at the time, absent actual intent to defraud. . . . Second, an LBO transaction should not be collapsed [in order to make T's pre-acquisition stockholders liable] for the benefit of subsequent creditors, . . . if the following four factors are present: (a) there is no evidence that the selling shareholders intended to defraud creditors; (b) the selling shareholders did not know that the purchaser intended to finance the purchase through an LBO; (c) there were no pre-transaction creditors; (d) the form of the transaction reflects a sale to an entity other than the issuer of the stock.[191]

The Court then observed that in the present case, T's trustee stands in the shoes of at least one pretransaction creditor so that the transaction is a fraudulent transfer under §5 of California's UFTA where:

> the debtor (1) made a transfer or incurred an obligation, (2) without receiving a reasonably equivalent value in exchange, (3) which rendered the debtor insolvent (or the debtor was already insolvent), and (4) which is attacked by a pre-transaction creditor.[192]

The court next held that T did not receive reasonably equivalent value for the loan from Lender because it is "appropriate to collapse the various pieces of this transaction into one integral transaction,"[193] so that "in substance $3.5 million of the funds that [T] borrowed from [Lender] went to pay for the stock of the selling shareholders, rather than to [T]".[194] The court believed this to be an appropriate result for each of two reasons: *first*, because T's pre-acquisition shareholders knew of the LBO nature of the transaction,[195] and *second*, because the knowledge of the pre-acquisition shareholders is not relevant where there existed pre-LBO T creditors when the chapter 11 was ultimately filed. According to the court, "knowledge of the LBO feature of the transaction by the selling shareholders . . . is material to whether the transaction's various parts should be collapsed only when challenged by post-transaction creditors."[196]

The court next considered whether the transaction left T insolvent. The court noted that the UFTA, like the Bankruptcy Code, employs a balance sheet test for insolvency, whereby a debtor is insolvent if the sum of the debtor's debts is greater than the sum of the debtor's assets.[197] According to T's post-acquisition balance sheet,

---

[191] 187 B.R. at 326-327.

[192] 187 B.R. at 328.

[193] 187 B.R. at 329.

[194] 187 B.R. at 328.

[195] The court noted that the knowledge of T's shareholders distinguished the *Bay Plastics* case from *Kupetz*, where selling shareholders did not know or have reason to know of the LBO nature of the transaction and there were no pre-LBO creditors, and made the *Bay Plastics* case more like *Richmond Produce*, *Wieboldt*, and *Gleneagles*, where the LBO was collapsed (and the selling shareholders held liable) because the selling shareholders knew of the LBO nature of the transaction. 187 B.R. at 329.

[196] 187 B.R. at 329.

[197] See UFTA §2(a), 7A U.L.A. 648 (West 1985 & Supp. 1995).

the transaction left T with $250,000 in equity. However, this included $2.26 million of goodwill on the asset side of T's post-acquisition GAAP balance sheet created by applying purchase accounting principles to the LBO transaction (see ¶1703.3 for a discussion of purchase accounting). Prior to the transaction, T had never carried any goodwill on its balance sheets. The court held that because T was in a liquidating bankruptcy, and because goodwill could not be sold to satisfy a creditor's claim, goodwill was not properly includable as a T asset, so that T was left with a $2 million negative net worth and thus was rendered insolvent by the transaction.

Next the court discussed whether fraudulent conveyance principles render all LBOs invalid. In the court's view, there are two scenarios in which an LBO should legitimately escape fraudulent transfer attack:

> First, in a legitimate LBO, in which the assets mortgaged by a corporation to support an LBO do not exceed the net equity of the business (after appropriate adjustments), the transaction will not make the corporation insolvent, at least according to the balance sheet test. If in addition it has sufficient projected cash flow to pay its debts as they come due, the cash flow solvency test is met, also. This leaves an LBO exposed to fraudulent transfer attack only if the margin of equity is too thin to support the corporation's business [and thus the corporation is rendered undercapitalized].
>
> A second kind of LBO also escapes fraudulent transfer attack, even though it leaves the subject corporation insolvent. If the cash flow is sufficient to make the debt payments, the transaction also is unassailable. This ordinarily turns on two factors: the degree of risk of default undertaken in the first instance, and the degree to which projected economic developments impacting the business are not overly optimistic. These LBOs escape fraudulent transfer attack either because of good financial projections or because of good luck: either factor is sufficient.[198]

Finally, the court concluded that applying fraudulent conveyance principles to LBOs is an appropriate policy:

> The Court's view of the proper application of fraudulent transfer law to LBO's does not make the selling shareholders the guarantors of the success of the LBO. A legitimate LBO . . . shifts the risk of failure off [the selling shareholders] . . . shoulders. As to subsequent creditors, . . . [the selling shareholders] should not be required to shoulder the risk if the failure is caused by outside forces not reasonably foreseeable at the time of the transaction.
>
> However, an LBO that is leveraged beyond the net worth of the business is a gamble. A highly leveraged business is much less able to weather temporary financial storms, because debt demands are less flexible than equity interest. The risks of this gamble should rest on the shoulders of the shareholders (old and new), not those of the creditors: the shareholders enjoy the benefits if the gamble is successful, and they should bear the burdens if it is not. This, after all, is the role of equity owners of a corporation. The application of fraudulent transfer law to LBOs shifts the risks of an LBO transaction from the creditors, who are not parties to the transaction, back to the old and new shareholders who bring about such transactions.[199]

---

[198] 187 B.R. at 334.
[199] 187 B.R. at 334-335.

Based on the foregoing analysis the court granted T's motion for summary judgment finding the LBO was a voidable fraudulent transfer.

¶1706.6.16   *Munford* Case[200]

In this case VC formed a wholly owned subsidiary, Parentco, and a second tier subsidiary, Newco, to acquire T in an LBO. The transaction was effected through a merger of Newco into T under Georgia's merger statute, with T as the surviving company. In the LBO transaction, the court stated that T received $90.6 million: $54 million as a loan from Lender to T, secured by T's assets, and some of the remaining $36.6 million as an equity contribution from VC, although the court did not make clear the amount of VC's equity consideration. In the LBO transaction T paid approximately $62 million to redeem T's shares (at $17 per share) and $1.556 million to pay certain pre-LBO creditors.

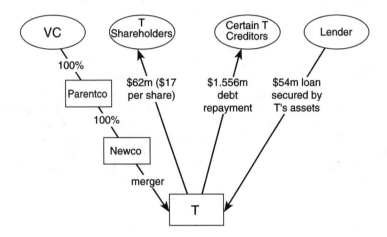

T filed a chapter 11 case thirteen months after the LBO closed and thereafter commenced a lawsuit to recover the redemption payments from T's directors, among others. The complaint against T's directors was based on two theories. First, T asserted that the directors were liable for the redemption payments under Georgia's then-existing stock distribution and repurchase statutes, which prohibit such transactions when "the corporation is insolvent or when such distribution would render the corporation insolvent."[201] The directors moved for summary judgment on the ground that because the LBO was structured as a merger, only Georgia's merger statute applied, and that statute did not make T's solvency an issue.

---

[200] Munford v. Valuation Research Corporation (In re Munford, Inc.), 97 F.3d 456 (11th Cir. 1996) (dealing with the directors' liability for illegal distribution and redemption) and 98 F.3d 604 (11th Cir. 1996) (dealing with the directors' alleged breach of fiduciary duty).

[201] O.C.G.A. §14-2-91 (1988) and O.C.G.A. §14-2-92(3)(1988).

The court of appeals denied the directors' motion on the ground that the essence of the transaction was a repurchase of T's shares from T's then existing shareholders, rather than a traditional merger. The court explained:

> We note that the LBO transaction in this case did not merge two separate operating companies into one combined entity. Instead, the LBO transaction represented a "paper merger" of [T] and [Newco], a shell corporation with very little assets of its own. To hold that Georgia's distribution and repurchase statutes did not apply to LBO mergers such as this, while nothing in these statutes precludes such a result, would frustrate the restrictions imposed upon directors who authorize a corporation to distribute its assets or to repurchase shares from stockholders when such transactions would render the corporation insolvent.[202]

On the other hand, the court of appeals affirmed the lower courts' granting of summary judgment in favor of the directors on T's second theory, that in approving the LBO, T's directors had breached their fiduciary duty to T and engaged in negligence, mismanagement and waste of corporate assets. The court observed that "the Georgia Code requires directors and officers of companies to discharge their duties in good faith and with the care of an ordinary prudent person."[203] The court then explained:

> In determining whether directors and officers have satisfied their statutory duty, Georgia courts apply the business judgment rule. . . . The business judgment rule protects directors and officers from liability when they make good faith business decisions in an informed and deliberate manner. In this case, the record is replete with evidence that the directors and officers consulted legal and financial experts throughout the solicitation and negotiation for a purchaser for [T]. Applying the business judgment rule, we conclude that the directors and officers satisfied their duties under [the Georgia Code].[204]

¶1706.6.17   *HealthCo* Case[205]

This two-step LBO was accomplished by (1) AcquisitionCo's cash tender offer (the "Tender Offer") for 100% of T's stock at $15 per share (in which AcquisitionCo actually purchased approximately 90% of T's stock), followed by (2) AcquisitionCo's cash-out merger (the "Merger") into T (in which the remaining approximately 10% of T's shareholders were paid $15 per share).

Both before and after the transaction, AcquisitionCo was 100% owned by HoldingCo which, in turn, was 100% owned by VC.

---

[202] 97 F.3d 456, 564 (11th Cir. 1996). In so holding the court of appeals expressly rejected the decision in C-T of Virginia, Inc. v. Barrett, 958 F.2d 606 (4th Cir. 1992), where the court, on similar facts "refused to apply Virginia's corporate distribution statute to recapture payments made to shareholders pursuant to an LBO merger." 97 F.3d at 563-564.

[203] 98 F.3d 604, 610.

[204] Id. at 611.

[205] Brandt v. Hicks, Muse & Co., Inc. (In re HealthCo Int'l, Inc.), 208 B.R. 288, 300 (Bankr. D. Mass. 1997).

AcquisitionCo's aggregate price paid for T ($15 per share, partly paid in the Tender Offer and partly paid in the Merger) of approximately $142 million, plus related professional expenses, was financed as follows:

- VC made a $55 million capital investment into HoldingCo (in exchange for 100% of HoldingCo's preferred and common stock) and HoldingCo in turn downstreamed this amount to AcquisitionCo,
- AcquisitionCo received $45 million in exchange for debentures sold to third parties, and
- AcquisitionCo received $50 million from several banks (the "Banks") as a loan secured (prior to the Merger) by a first lien on T's stock and (after the Merger) by a lien on T's assets.

As a consequence of this two-step LBO, T took on $95 million of additional debt ($45 million of debentures and $50 million of bank debt), the proceeds of which (along with VC's capital contribution) were paid to T's shareholders.

STEP 1: The Tender Offer

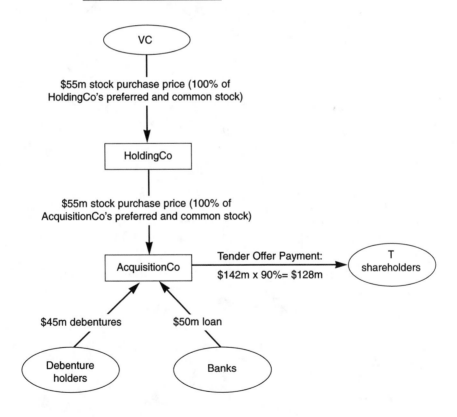

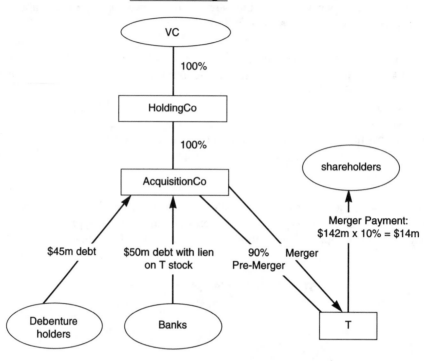

STEP 2: The Merger

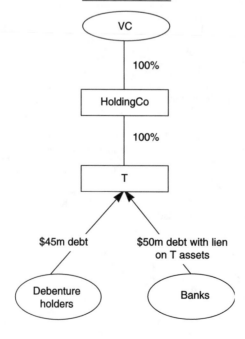

STEP 3: Post LBO

Both before and after consummating the Merger, T suffered significant operating losses. As a consequence of these operating losses VC had abandoned a prior proposed LBO of T which contemplated a tender offer at $19.25 per share.

Approximately two years after consummating the Merger, following continued operating losses, T filed for bankruptcy. T's chapter 7 trustee (the "Trustee") sued "virtually everyone" who participated in the LBO alleging, among other things, that the LBO constituted a fraudulent conveyance, that certain T directors breached fiduciary duties of loyalty and care to T, and that VC and certain T shareholders aided and abetted this breach of duty.

The bankruptcy court denied defendants' motion for summary judgment on the breach of fiduciary duty counts. The bankruptcy court's analysis was based on the basic proposition that directors of a Delaware corporation owe fiduciary duties of care and loyalty to the corporation, rather than to any particular constituency. While, in some contexts, the interests of shareholders may be the primary interest that directors must protect in exercising their fiduciary duties, "[w]hen a transaction renders a corporation insolvent or brings it to the brink of insolvency, the rights of creditors become paramount."[206] Thus, the bankruptcy court applied customary Delaware director fiduciary duty rules to assess whether T's directors could be sued because, as a consequence of the LBO, T's creditors went unpaid. The bankruptcy court held that the directors would be liable if they breached their duties of care or loyalty to the corporation and, as a result of the LBO, T was (i) rendered insolvent (in either the "bankruptcy sense" (excess of liabilities over assets) or the "equity sense" (inability to pay debts as they mature)) or (ii) undercapitalized, which the court characterized as subject to "an unreasonable risk of insolvency."[207]

The bankruptcy court found that three of T's directors were interested in the transaction (one director owned 25% of a partnership that was a significant T shareholder and the other two directors were put on T's board by a significant T shareholder to protect shareholder interests). Accordingly, the bankruptcy court held that the three interested directors would not be permitted to assert the business judgment rule as a defense to the claim that they breached their duty of care because that defense applies only to disinterested directors. Rather, their care in approving the LBO would be judged on a negligence standard. In addition, the bankruptcy court held that because the LBO was not approved by a majority of disinterested directors (the four disinterested directors voted two for and two against the LBO), the three interested directors would be required to show that the LBO was fair to T in order to establish that they had not breached their duty of loyalty to T.

T's four independent directors also did not qualify for the business judgment rule defense to the claim that they breached their duty of care because (1) their articulated objective in approving the LBO was to protect the interests of shareholders, rather than T, and (2) they negligently failed to analyze the consequences of the LBO to determine whether it would leave T insolvent or undercapitalized. However, these directors were protected from personal liability for breach of their duty of care as a

---

[206] 208 B.R. at 300.
[207] 208 B.R. at 302.

consequence of provisions in T's charter, permitted by Delaware law, exonerating them from such personal liability.[208]

The bankruptcy court also held that VC, T's old shareholders who controlled the LBO, and financial advisors to T's board could be held liable for aiding and abetting the directors' breach of fiduciary duty.

Subsequently, the liability issues were tried to a jury in the United States District Court, which exonerated all the defendants.[209] The district court's jury instructions differed in key respects from the bankruptcy court's analysis of Delaware law.[210] In particular, while the bankruptcy court found that three of T's directors were interested in the transaction (either because of their ownership of an interest in a partnership that was a significant T shareholder or because they were placed on T's board by that shareholder to protect its interests), the district court instructed the jury that "merely owning stock in a company does not make a director self-interested . . . even if a director defendant was a substantial [T] stockholder."[211] The district court further instructed the jury that "the fact that a particular director defendant was appointed to the board of directors by a particular group of stockholders does not necessarily constitute self-interest."[212]

Finally, the district court instructed the jury that "[u]nless you find at least four of the director defendants [out of the seven directors on T's board] breached any of one of his fiduciary duties . . . then you must find that the board as a whole satisfied its fiduciary duties."[213] These instructions opened the door for the jury to exonerate the board as a whole.

Because of the bankruptcy court's holding that T's charter exonerated directors from personal liability for breach of their duty of care, the Trustee withdrew his claims based on aiding and abetting this breach of duty which had been asserted against VC, T's controlling shareholders, and T's financial advisors. Thus, this issue never reached the jury.

---

[208] The bankruptcy court noted that the directors would not be protected from personal liability for breach of their duty of loyalty by such charter provisions.

[209] Although T's financial advisor had waived its right to a jury trial, so the jury verdict as to it was advisory, the district court accepted the jury's advisory verdict. See Brandt v. Hicks, Muse & Co., Inc., 213 B.R. 784 (D. Mass. 1997), aff'd sub nom. Brandt v. Wand Partners, 242 F.3d 6 (1st Cir. 2001).

[210] While the district court's jury instructions are not reported, a discussion of the district court proceedings may be found in John J. Rapisardi & Jacqueline B. Stuart, LBO Jury Verdict in HealthCo Bankruptcy Case, N.Y.L.J., 8/21/97, at 5, and in Dennis J. Block & Stephen A. Radin, The Standards by Which a Board of Directors' Conduct is Measured When a Leveraged Buyout Fails were the Subject of a Unique Case in Massachusetts, Nat'l L.J., 8/18/97, at B4.

[211] John H. Rapisardi & Jacqueline B. Stuart, LBO Jury Verdict in HealthCo Bankruptcy Case, N.Y.L.J., 8/21/97, at 5.

[212] John H. Rapisardi & Jacqueline B. Stuart, LBO Jury Verdict in HealthCo Bankruptcy Case, N.Y.L.J., 8/21/97, at 5.

[213] Dennis J. Block & Stephen A. Radin, The Standards by Which a Board of Directors' Conduct is Measured When a Leveraged Buyout Fails were the Subject of a Unique Case in Massachusetts, Nat'l L.J., 8/18/97, at B4.

¶1706.6.18   *Yucaipa* Case[214]

Acquisition Co. purchased all of T's stock from T's former shareholders for a $63 million note. T then borrowed approximately $94 million from a bank syndicate ("Lenders"), pledging all of its assets and paid a $44 million dividend to Acquisition Co., Acquisition Co. then used the distributed funds, along with $19 million of its own money, to repay the $63 million note held by T's old shareholders.

STEP 1:

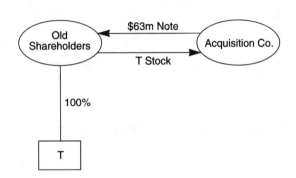

STEP 2:

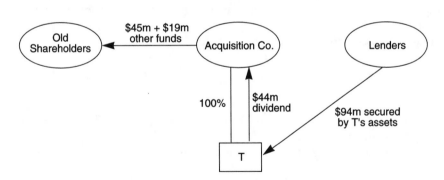

Approximately two years after the LBO, T filed a chapter 11 petition and a trustee was appointed, among other reasons, to bring a fraudulent transfer action against T's former shareholders, Acquisition Co., and Lenders.

The fraudulent transfer action was brought under Rhode Island's version of the UFTA. The defendants moved to dismiss the complaint arguing, among other things, that because the LBO occurred principally in California, that state's version of the

[214] Zahn v. Yucaipa Capital Fund (In re Almac's, Inc.), 202 B.R. 648 (D.R.I. 1996), and Zahn v. Yucaipa Capital Fund, 218 B.R. 656 (D.R.I. 1998).

UFTA should apply, and under California law, pursuant to the *Kupetz* case and other Ninth Circuit authority,[215] the UFTA:

> does not apply to LBOs that are 'above board' or not otherwise intentionally fraudulent and . . . a creditor whose claim arises after the consummation of an LBO may not bring a constructive fraudulent transfer claim under [the California UFTA] where the LBO was highly publicized and was not actually fraudulently concealed.[216]

The *Yucaipa* court rejected this argument and denied the motion to dismiss, concluding that the Ninth Circuit's analysis of California's fraudulent transfer law is an improper judicial limitation on the scope of the UFTA which California state courts would not follow. In the view of the *Yucaipa* court, even if California law applied to the transaction, that law required the court to follow the plain language of the UFTA, pursuant to which LBOs may be subject to attack even if they are above board, well publicized, and being attacked for the benefit of post-LBO creditors.

¶1707   FTC PRE-MERGER NOTIFICATION RULES—HART-SCOTT-RODINO ACT

The Federal Trade Commission ("FTC") Pre-merger Notification Rules (the "HSR Rules") were promulgated pursuant to the Hart-Scott-Rodino Antitrust Improvements Act of 1976 (as amended, the "HSR Act"), which added new §7A to the Clayton Act.[1] (The HSR Act and HSR Rules are collectively referred to as "HSR.") HSR potentially covers any type of transaction that results in one entity (including a natural person) acquiring the voting securities or assets of another entity, through any direct or indirect means.

Transactions treated as *voting security acquisitions* include:

- a purchase of stock,
- a merger,
- an exercise of warrants or options,
- a conversion from one class of security to another that increases the holder's voting power,
- an acquisition of a 100% interest in a partnership or LLC that holds voting securities,
- a distribution of voting securities from a partnership or LLC to a partner or member (either a controlling or a non-controlling partner or member),
- some recapitalizations or redemptions funded by an existing shareholder,
- formation of a new corporation, and
- a contribution of voting securities to an LLC controlled by another person that combines two previously separate businesses.

---

[215] See *Kupetz* (discussed at ¶1706.6.5); *Credit Managers* (discussed at ¶1706.6.3); and Lippi v. City Bank, 955 F.2d 599 (9th Cir. 1992).

[216] 218 B.R. at 666.

¶1707   [1] 15 U.S.C. §18A.

Transactions treated as *asset acquisitions* include:

- a purchase of tangible or intangible assets (including the transfer of an existing leasehold, distributorship, license, or other existing contractual right),
- entering into a new license granting exclusive rights even within a limited field of use or territory,
- an acquisition of a 100% interest in a partnership or LLC that holds assets,
- a distribution of assets from a partnership or LLC to a partner or member (either a controlling or a non-controlling partner or member),
- a merger or other transfer of control of an entity that does not have voting securities (such as a non-profit hospital), and
- a contribution of assets to an LLC controlled by another person that combines two previously separate businesses.

Entering into a newly created lease, franchise, or other newly created contract is not covered by HSR unless the contract also transfers other tangible or intangible assets (although, as described above, entering into a newly created exclusive license or transferring an existing contract does constitute an asset transfer for HSR purposes).

For a discussion of FTC's rather strange position on application of the HSR rules to a partnership or LLC (rather than a corporation), see ¶1707.2.1.

For purposes of several exemptions discussed below making a distinction between United States and foreign transactions, the term United States includes the United States' territories, possessions, and commonwealths.

¶1707 is organized as follows:

- ¶1707.1 describes the general application of HSR to most acquisitions by corporate, partnership, or LLC P of corporate, partnership, or LLC T voting securities or assets.
- ¶1707.2 describes the special application of HSR to the formation of a new corporation, partnership, or LLC.
- ¶1707.3 describes the special application of HSR to acquisitions of T's voting securities or assets by a newly formed corporate, partnership, or LLC acquisition vehicle.
- ¶1707.4 describes the nature of the reporting requirements imposed by HSR.
- ¶1707.5 describes the waiting periods that apply to a reportable transaction.
- ¶1707.6 describes the penalties for non-compliance with the applicable requirements.

¶1707.1   Corporate, Partnership, or LLC P Acquires Corporate, Partnership, or LLC T's Stock (i.e., Ownership Interests) or Assets

HSR requires P and T to comply with reporting and waiting period requirements, prior to P acquiring voting securities or assets of T, if:

(1) the transaction meets the $200 million size-of-transaction test (described at ¶1707.1.1), *or*

(2) the transaction meets the $50 million size-of-transaction test (described at ¶1707.1.1) and P and T both meet the dollar criteria of the size-of-person test (described at ¶1707.1.2),

(3) unless the transaction is covered by a specific exemption (described at ¶1707.1.4).

For purposes of this ¶1707.1, HSR generally applies (1) whether P is a corporation, partnership, or LLC and (2) whether T is a corporation, partnership, or LLC, except as set forth below.

T as partnership or LLC. Where T is a partnership or an LLC, FTC takes the position that T's ownership interests constitute *neither* voting securities *nor* assets, so that where P acquires ownership interests in T partnership or T LLC, P has not acquired T voting securities or T assets (subject to further qualification below) for HSR purposes.

However, where P acquires 100% of T partnership's or T LLC's ownership interests, P is treated as acquiring T's *assets*. As a result, when T partnership's or T LLC's assets consist of (or include) voting securities (i.e., voting corporate stock) in another entity (S corporation) and P acquires 100% of T's ownership interests, P is treated as acquiring 100% of the S voting securities owned by T.

Moreover, where P acquires less than 100% of T partnership's or T LLC's ownership interests, P is not viewed for HSR purposes as acquiring T voting securities or T assets (including S corporation stock owned by T), and in such circumstances P has no HSR reporting or waiting period requirements.[2] If, however, T partnership or T LLC is newly formed or receives a new contribution of assets, see the HSR rules described in ¶1707.2.1 and ¶1707.2.2.

¶1707.1.1 Size-of-Transaction Test

If the $200 million size-of-transaction test is met, P and T must comply with the HSR reporting and waiting period requirements. If the $200 million size-of-transaction test is not met but the $50 million size-of-transaction test is met, P and T must comply with the HSR reporting and waiting period requirements only if the size-of-person test described at ¶1707.1.2 is met.

The $50 million or $200 million size-of-transaction test is met if P, after the acquisition, will hold at least one of the following:

(1) T *voting securities* with an "HSR value" exceeding the specified $50 million or $200 million threshold (including all T voting securities being acquired or then owned by P, P's ultimate parent entity, and all of their controlled entities). (The definition of "HSR value" for voting securities is described at ¶¶1707.1.1.1, 1707.1.1.2, and 1707.1.1.5. The definitions of "ultimate parent

---

[2] See, however, ¶1707.1.3 discussing employment of a device for the purpose of avoiding HSR reporting.

entity" and "control" for the size-of-transaction test are the same as for the size-of-person test as described at ¶1707.1.2.)

As described at ¶1707.1.4.1, there is an exemption if P, its ultimate parent entity, and their controlled entities hold 10% or less of T's voting power and have no intention to participate in T's basic business decisions.

(2) T *assets* with an "HSR value" exceeding the specified $50 million or $200 million threshold, including any assets acquired within 180 days before the current acquisition agreement or letter of intent was executed (and including all assets acquired by P, P's ultimate parent, and their controlled entities, from T, T's ultimate parent, and their controlled entities). (The definition of "HSR value" for assets is described at ¶¶1707.1.1.3 and 1707.1.1.4.)

(3) any combination of (1) and (2) with an aggregate HSR value exceeding the specified $50 million or $200 million threshold.

Application of this test is described at ¶1707.1.1.1 through ¶1707.1.1.9.

¶1707.1.1.1 HSR Value of Publicly Traded Securities

The HSR value of T's publicly traded voting securities *being acquired* in the present transaction is the greater of their acquisition price or their "market price." The HSR value of T's publicly traded voting securities *previously acquired* by P, P's ultimate parent, and their controlled entities is their "market price."

"Market price" for HSR purposes is the lowest closing quotation or lowest closing bid price within 45 calendar days prior to consummation of the acquisition (without taking into account any day earlier than the day prior to the execution of the contract, letter of intent, or agreement in principle regarding the acquisition). However, in the case of a tender offer, open-market purchase, or similar transaction, the period for determining "market price" is 45 days prior to (1) closing of such purchase if it need not be reported or (2) receipt by T of P's notification that P is filing a report with FTC regarding the acquisition (P being required to notify T where such an acquisition is reportable).

EXAMPLE 1

T voting stock is traded on the NYSE. The lowest closing quotation in the last 45 calendar days is $10. P already holds 4.9 million shares of T common stock (representing 2% of T's outstanding voting power). T wishes to acquire additional voting common shares today at their current market price of $12. P has made no HSR filing. P and T satisfy the size-of-person test.

P's existing block of T common shares is valued for HSR purposes at $49 million (4.9 million shares × $10 lowest closing quotation in past 45 calendar days), and its purchases today will be valued for HSR purposes at $12 per share (greater of acquisition price or lowest quotation during the past 45 calendar days).

Because P and T satisfy the size-of-person test, the HSR value of P's T voting securities may not exceed $50 million without HSR compliance. Thus, P may purchase no more than 83,333 T shares today (83,333 × $12 = $999,996, and $999,996 + $49 million = $49,999,996).

EXAMPLE 2

Same as Example 1, except that after purchasing 83,333 shares of T voting common stock today, P wishes to purchase additional T shares tomorrow.

In this case, beginning tomorrow the T shares purchased by P today will be revalued for HSR purposes from $12 per share (their acquisition price) to their "market price" (i.e., $10 per share if that is still the lowest closing quotation in the prior 45 calendar days), so the old 4.9 million shares plus the 83,333 shares purchased today will have an HSR value of $49,833,330.

P can thus purchase up to an additional 13,889 T common shares tomorrow if the acquisition price is still $12 as it is today (13,889 shares × $12 = $166,668, and $166,668 + $49,833,330 = $49,999,998).

¶1707.1.1.2   HSR Value of Nonpublicly Traded Securities

The HSR value of a T voting security that is not publicly traded is its acquisition price unless none is determined (e.g., because the acquisition of T voting securities is part of a larger transaction in which the purchase price is not allocated, the purchase price is contingent on future revenues or profits, or for some other reason the total consideration to be paid is not reduced to a dollar figure by the time of closing). If the acquisition price of a non-publicly traded T voting security is not determined, the HSR value is the security's FV.

¶1707.1.1.3   Acquired Assets

The HSR value of acquired assets is their FV unless their acquisition price has been determined and is greater. The assets to be valued include both tangible and intangible property of any description, including leaseholds and other contractual rights such as distributorships and license agreements.

¶1707.1.1.4   Determining Fair Value

FV is determined in good faith by the board of directors (or equivalent) of P's ultimate parent entity or by a person delegated that function by such board. Such determination is to be made as of a date within 60 days prior to (1) closing (if no report is required) or (2) reporting.

¶1707.1.1.5   Acquisition Price

Acquisition price includes all consideration paid for T assets or voting securities.

Liabilities assumed by P are generally added to the acquisition price in an *asset* acquisition.

In an acquisition of T *stock*, however, T's liabilities are generally not added to the acquisition price of the T stock purchased by P, although FTC staff has taken the position in some transactions that T's liabilities are added to the acquisition price of T stock if the purchase agreement specifies that P will pay the T liabilities.

¶1707.1.1.6   No Present Voting Rights

P need not report the acquisition of T options, warrants, or convertible securities with no present right to vote for T directors. When P exercises/converts to voting securities, the rules for reporting P's acquisition of T voting securities are applied at that time.

¶1707.1.1.7   Secondary Acquisitions

When P acquires control over T, P also acquires the voting securities of any other entity (e.g., S) of which T is the beneficial owner. If T does not control S, then P's "secondary" acquisition of S voting securities is separately subject to HSR in the same manner as any other acquisition of S voting securities. (If T controls S, then S is considered part of T for HSR purposes as described at ¶¶1707.1.2.1 and 1707.1.2.2.)

¶1707.1.1.8   Recapitalizations and Redemptions

T need not report the acquisition of its own voting securities in a recapitalization or redemption. However, where P owns some T stock and a T recapitalization or redemption causes P's percentage ownership of T voting securities to increase, T's acquisition of stock from its other shareholders (in the recapitalization or redemption) may be attributed to P, and P may be subject to HSR reporting and waiting period requirements, if P is "instrumental" in providing the capital used to carry out the recapitalization or redemption. FTC has not defined "instrumental" for this purpose but has taken the position that P's arranging for financing does not subject P to HSR if the financing comes from a bona fide third party.

¶1707.1.1.9   Beneficial Ownership

P is treated for HSR purposes as acquiring T voting securities or T assets, and the size of the transaction is measured, when P becomes the beneficial owner of the T voting securities or assets, whether directly or indirectly through fiduciaries, agents, controlled entities, or other means. Beneficial ownership is determined by reference to the following indicia:

- right to vote or determine who may vote
- right to receive dividends
- right to dispose
- risk of loss or benefit of gain
- investment discretion.

FTC has left unclear how these indicia are balanced in determining beneficial ownership.

EXAMPLE 1

P acquires T voting securities valued at $49.9 million for HSR purposes. P then enters into an arrangement whereby an investment banker or broker ("IB") buys T voting securities valued at $1 million for HSR purposes and simultaneously sells P an option to purchase the T voting securities once P has complied with HSR. P agrees to indemnify IB if P fails to exercise the option and IB sells the T shares at a loss. If the option-indemnification arrangement makes P the beneficial owner of the T voting securities held by IB and subject to P's option, P would (because of the other T voting shares already owned by P) be required to file an HSR report with FTC and observe the waiting period before becoming the beneficial owner of the securities.

FTC has initiated enforcement actions against P in several such situations when P did not report and observe the waiting period prior to entering into the option-indemnification agreement with IB (frequently referred to as a parking arrangement). To date, all such enforcement actions have been settled by consent decree.

Because the actions were not litigated and FTC has not disclosed all the facts (or alleged facts) in these cases, it is unclear in precisely what factual situations FTC would bring an enforcement action. (Such an arrangement may also be considered a device for avoidance, described at ¶1707.1.3.)

EXAMPLE 2

P enters into a contract to acquire T's assets. Pursuant to the contract P immediately makes a non-refundable payment to T equal to the entire purchase price. P agrees to cover any liabilities from continuing operations while T operates the business pursuant to its existing business plan, and P is entitled to the benefit of any cash flow between contract signing and closing.

On such facts, FTC took the position that P acquired beneficial ownership of T's business, so P and T were obligated to file an HSR report and observe the waiting period before P paid T.

EXAMPLE 3

P enters into a contract to acquire T from T's shareholder. Pursuant to the contract, P makes a non-refundable payment to T's shareholder in excess of $50 million and T's shareholder places 100% of T's stock into an irrevocable trust for P's benefit, with a financial institution as trustee.

When the trustee had the sole power to vote T's stock, but all other indicia of beneficial ownership in T passed immediately to P, FTC took the position that P and T were obligated to file an HSR report and observe the waiting period before P paid T.

EXAMPLE 4

P and T each own a radio station. P and T simultaneously enter into (1) a merger agreement (or an agreement for P to acquire all of T's assets) and (2) a marketing and programming agreement under which (pending FCC approval of the transaction) P will supply programming to T and P will market all of T's advertising time.

FTC took the position that such an agreement entered into in connection with a pending P-T acquisition transfers beneficial ownership of T to P, so that the agreement cannot take effect until after HSR filing and waiting period requirements have been satisfied.

The additional examples at ¶1707.1.5 also illustrate the size-of-transaction test.

¶1707.1.2   Size-of-Person Test

If the size-of-person test is met, P and T must comply with the HSR reporting and waiting period requirements where the transaction meets the $50 million size-of-transaction test (even though the $200 million size-of-transaction test is not met).

The size-of-person test is satisfied if at least one of the following size criteria is met:

(1) T is engaged in manufacturing and has annual net sales or total assets of at least $10 million, and P has annual net sales or total assets of at least $100 million.

(2) T is not engaged in manufacturing and has total assets of at least $10 million, and P has annual net sales or total assets of at least $100 million.

(3) T (regardless of its business) has annual net sales or total assets of at least $100 million, and P has annual net sales or total assets of at least $10 million.

Application of these criteria is described in ¶¶1707.1.2.1 through 1707.1.2.6.

¶1707.1.2.1   *Annual Net Sales and Total Assets*

"Annual net sales" and "total assets" are measured at the level of P's or T's "ultimate parent entity" (i.e., an entity that is not "controlled" by any other entity), to which is added the assets and sales of any controlled entity.

¶1707.1.2.2   *Control*

"Control" means (1) beneficial ownership of securities with 50% or more of an entity's voting power or contractual power to designate 50% or more of the entity's directors (or individuals exercising similar functions in an unincorporated entity, e.g., trustees) or (2) in the case of an entity that FTC believes has no voting securities (e.g., a partnership or U.S. LLC), the right to receive 50% or more of the profits of the entity (or of its assets on dissolution).

In applying (1), FTC has taken the position that where P1 holds (e.g.) 90% of S's voting securities but P1 contractually agrees (in a voting agreement) to permit P2 (who holds the remaining 10% of S's voting securities) to designate 3 of S's 5 directors, both P1 and P2 control S.

EXAMPLE 1

P controls both S1 (which in turn controls S2) and S3 (which in turn controls S4). If S4 is making an acquisition, the size-of-person test for the acquiring entity takes into account the sales and assets of P, S1, S2, S3, and S4.

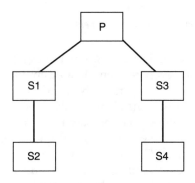

EXAMPLE 2

Same as Example 1, except that P also has an interest in a partnership (or LLC) ("Partnership #1"), which gives P the right to 50% or more of Partnership #1's profits, and Partnership #1 controls S5. In such case, P is also the ultimate parent of both Partnership #1 and S5, and P must take their sales and assets into account (in measuring the size of the acquiring entity for any acquisition by P, S1, S2, S3, S4, Partnership #1, or S5).

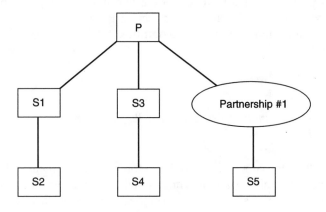

EXAMPLE 3

Same as Example 2, except that no entity (including P) has the right to receive 50% or more of the profits (or the assets on dissolution) of Partnership #1, and S5 is making an acquisition. In such case, the size of the acquiring entity is determined by taking into account only the sales and assets of Partnership #1 and S5.

¶1707.1.2.3   Measurement of Sales and Assets

Sales are generally measured based on the net sales stated in the ultimate parent entity's most recent regularly prepared consolidated annual income statement. Assets are generally measured based on total assets stated in the ultimate parent entity's most recent regularly prepared consolidated balance sheet (whether or not a year end balance sheet). Such statements are prepared in accordance with the accounting principles normally used by the entity *and* as of a date not more than 15 months prior to the date of (1) filing or (2) consummation (if no filing is required).

If an entity controlled by the ultimate parent entity is not included in such statements, the ultimate parent's net sales and total assets must be recomputed to include the non-duplicative net sales and total assets of such unconsolidated controlled entity.

EXAMPLE

P controls S1, S2, and S3. S3's total assets are not included in P's most recent regularly prepared consolidated balance sheet. P's total assets on its most recent regularly prepared consolidated balance sheet are $90 million, including S1 and S2 on a consolidated basis and a $10 million investment in S3. S3's total assets on its most recent regularly prepared balance sheet are $50 million.

For HSR purposes, P's total assets ($90 million) are recomputed by adding S3's total assets of $50 million and subtracting P's $10 million investment in S3 (which is duplicative), so that P's recomputed total assets for HSR purposes are $130 million.

¶1707.1.2.4   Measurement of Assets Without Regularly Prepared
Balance Sheet

If T (or its ultimate parent) does not have the regularly prepared balance sheet described immediately above, and it is not a newly formed corporation as described in ¶1707.2, then a balance sheet must be prepared (in accordance with T's normal accounting principles) that includes all the assets of T, its ultimate parent entity, and their controlled entities.

If P (or its ultimate parent) does not have the regularly prepared balance sheet described, then P's total assets are determined as follows:

(1) all assets held by P at the time of the acquisition, including all cash provided by lenders or equity investors,

(2) less all cash used as consideration for T or for incidental expenses in connection with the acquisition of T,

(3) less all T securities held by P.

¶1707.1.2.5   Determining Size of Natural Person

A natural person may control but may never be controlled by other entities, and the net sales and total assets of all controlled entities must be consolidated with those of a controlling natural person. The following two special rules apply only to a natural person:

(1) A natural person is always deemed to include his or her spouse and minor children.

(2) A natural person's assets are deemed to include only investment assets (consisting of cash, deposits in financial institutions, other money market instruments, and instruments evidencing government obligations), voting securities, and other income-producing property. Hence, a natural person's other assets (e.g., home, boat, jewelry, car) are ignored.

EXAMPLE

Individual A controls P1 and P2. The size-of-person test is applied to A, P1, and P2 by considering their sales and assets together.

¶1707.1.2.6   Determining Control over Trust

A trust is generally considered to be controlled by a person with the contractual power to designate 50% or more of its trustees in the event that all current trustees were to be replaced for any reason. In addition, assets and voting securities constituting the corpus of a trust are considered to be held by the settlor of a revocable trust and of an irrevocable trust in which the settlor retains a reversionary interest.

The examples at ¶1707.1.5 also illustrate the size-of-person test.

¶1707.1.3   Device for Avoidance

Any transaction or other device employed by P for the purpose of avoiding the obligation to report and wait before acquiring T voting securities or assets is disregarded, and the obligation to report and wait is determined by applying HSR to the substance of the transaction. Thus, if the parking arrangement between P and IB described in ¶1707.1.1.9 Example 1 were considered to be a device for avoidance, P's obligation to report and wait would be determined as if P were acquiring the T shares that are the subject of the option-indemnification arrangement between P and IB.

¶1707.1.4   Principal Exemptions

Even though a transaction meets (1) the $200 million size-of-transaction test or (2) the $50 million size-of-transaction test plus the size-of-person test described in ¶¶1707.1.1 and 1707.1.2 above, the transaction is nevertheless exempt from HSR reporting and waiting period requirements if covered by one of the exemptions described in this ¶1707.1.4 (or other more specialized HSR exemptions not described herein).

¶1707.1.4.1   10% or Less Voting Power Acquisition Solely for Investment Purpose

P's acquisition of T voting stock is exempt if it results in voting securities with 10% or less of T's voting power being held by P, P's ultimate parent entity, and their controlled entities, regardless of the dollar value of the T securities, so long as P and its ultimate parent entity have "no intention of participating in the formulation, determination or the direction of [T's] basic business decisions."

Where P has the intention, or obtains the right, to designate one or more of T's directors, this exemption is not available. FTC has informally indicated that this exemption is also not available where P has a board observer who is expected to contribute to board deliberations, but this exemption may be available if the observer is not expected to contribute to board deliberations and P's intentions are otherwise passive.

¶1707.1.4.2   Ordinary Course of Business Acquisition

P's acquisition of goods or realty in the ordinary course of business is exempt from reporting. P's acquisition of T voting securities, when T's assets consist solely of real property and assets incidental to the ownership of real property (e.g., cash and rental receivables), is deemed an acquisition of realty. In all other cases, an acquisition is not "in the ordinary course of business" if, as a result, P will hold all or substantially all of the assets of T or a T operating unit.

This exemption includes acquisitions of the following, except in connection with the acquisition of substantially all the assets of a business unit:

(1)   new goods produced by T for sale to others or held by T solely for resale to others,

(2)   non-durable goods (i.e., goods other than those designed to be used repeatedly with a useful life greater than one year) that are (a) acquired for the purpose of resale by P (e.g., inventory), (b) for consumption in P's business (e.g., office supplies), or (c) to be incorporated in P's final product (e.g., raw materials),

(3)   used durable goods (i.e., goods designed to be used repeatedly with a useful life greater than one year) that (a) are acquired and held by P solely for

resale, (b) were acquired and held by T solely for resale, (c) have been replaced (or contracted to be replaced) by T, or (d) have been used in an auxiliary function (e.g., accounting, data processing) by T where T has contracted to have the same or similar function performed by other means,

(4)   unproductive real property that has not generated total revenues in excess of $5 million during the 36 months preceding the acquisition, such as (a) raw land, (b) structures or other improvements (but not equipment and not manufacturing and non-manufacturing facilities that have not yet begun operation or that began operation within the 12 months preceding the acquisition) and (c) natural resources,

(5)   retail rental space (e.g., shopping centers, strip malls) or warehouses except when the retail rental space or warehouse is to be acquired in an acquisition of a business conducted on the property,

(6)   new facilities that have not produced income and were constructed or held (at all times) by T for sale to another party,

(7)   office and residential property used primarily for office and residential purposes,

(8)   hotels and motels, except a hotel or motel that includes a casino or that is being acquired as part of the acquisition of a ski resort,

(9)   agricultural property and associated assets that primarily generate revenues from the production of crops, fruits, vegetables, livestock, poultry, milk, and eggs (but processing facilities, assets, and real property adjacent to and/or used in conjunction with processing facilities on the agricultural property are not exempt),

(10)   carbon-based mineral reserves (oil, natural gas, coal, shale, or tar sands) or rights to carbon-based mineral reserves and associated exploration or production assets if the value of the assets to be held as a result of the acquisition does not exceed $500 million (but pipelines or processing facilities are not exempt), and

(11)   investment rental property acquired by institutional investors or any other person whose sole business is the acquisition or management of investment rental property assets if (a) the property will be held solely for rental or investment purposes and (b) will be rented only to entities not included in the P ultimate parent entity.

¶1707.1.4.3   *Foreign Asset Acquisition*

P's acquisition of T assets located outside the United States is exempt unless T's net sales in or into the United States attributable to such foreign assets being acquired by P exceeded $50 million during T's most recent fiscal year.[3]

Where U.S. sales attributable to T's foreign assets being acquired by P exceed the $50 million threshold, P's acquisition is nevertheless exempt if:

---

[3] For purposes of the entire HSR discussion in this ¶1707, the term United States includes the United States' territories, possessions, and commonwealths.

(1)   the ultimate parent entities of both P and T are foreign,
(2)   the aggregate sales in or into the United States of P and T, together with their ultimate parent entities and any other controlled entities, are less than $110 million in their most recent fiscal years,
(3)   the aggregate total assets located in the United States (other than investment assets and securities) of P and T, together with their ultimate parent entities and any other controlled entities, are less than $110 million, and
(4)   the transaction does not exceed the $200 million size-of-transaction threshold.

For purposes of this ¶1707.1.4.3, an entity is foreign if it is not incorporated or organized in the United States and the entity's principal office is not in the United States, and a natural person is foreign if he is neither a United States citizen nor resident.

¶1707.1.4.4   *Foreign Voting Securities Acquisition*

Where T or its ultimate parent entity is foreign, there are a series of possible exemptions as described below.
     P's acquisition of foreign T voting securities is exempt unless:

(1)   foreign T and controlled entities hold assets (other than investment assets and securities) located in the United States with an aggregate value exceeding $50 million, or
(2)   foreign T and controlled entities made aggregate sales in or into the United States exceeding $50 million in the most recent fiscal year.

If P acquires securities of multiple foreign issuers from T's ultimate parent entity, assets located in the United States and sales in or into the United States must be aggregated to determine whether either of the $50 million thresholds is exceeded.
     Even if foreign T exceeds one or both of the above $50 million thresholds, P's acquisition of foreign T voting securities is exempt where:

(1)   P's ultimate parent entity is foreign, and
(2)   P will not control T.

Even if none of the previous exemptions is applicable, P's acquisition of T's voting securities is exempt where:

(1)   the ultimate parent entities of both P and T are foreign,
(2)   the aggregate sales in or into the United States of P and T, together with their ultimate parent entities and any other controlled entities, are less than $110 million in their most recent fiscal years,
(3)   the aggregate total assets located in the United States (other than investment assets and securities) of P and T, together with their ultimate parent entities and any other controlled entities, are less than $110 million, and

(4)   the transaction does not exceed the $200 million size-of-transaction threshold.

For purposes of the several exemptions discussed in this ¶1707.1.4.4, an entity is foreign if it is not incorporated or organized in the United States and the entity's principal office is not in the United States, and a natural person is foreign if he is neither a United States citizen nor resident.

¶1707.1.5   Examples of P Acquisition of T Voting Securities or Assets

These examples assume that, unless otherwise indicated, P and T are not controlled by any other entity, do not control any other entity, and are incorporated or have their principal offices in the United States.

EXAMPLE 1

P buys T assets worth $201 million (or any combination of T assets and T voting securities worth $201 million). The $200 million size-of-transaction test is satisfied. No specific exemption applies.

P and T are obligated to comply with HSR reporting and waiting period requirements.

EXAMPLE 2

P is buying $51 million worth of T voting securities or assets. The $50 million size-of-transaction and size-of-person tests are both satisfied. No specific exemption applies.

P and T are obligated to comply with HSR reporting and waiting period requirements.

EXAMPLE 3

Same as Example 2, except that the size-of-person test is not met because T's annual net sales and total assets are less than $10 million.

No HSR reporting or waiting period requirements apply.

EXAMPLE 4

Same as Example 2, except that P's annual net sales and total assets are each $99 million, and T's annual net sales and total assets are each $99 million. Because neither P nor T meets the $100 million criterion of the size-of-person test, no HSR reporting or waiting period requirements apply.

EXAMPLE 5

Same as Example 2, except that P's annual net sales or total assets are $100 million or more, T is not engaged in manufacturing, T's annual net sales are more than $10 million but less than $100 million, and T's total assets are less than $10 million.

Because T does not satisfy the size-of-person test for a non-manufacturer, no HSR reporting or waiting period requirements apply.

EXAMPLE 6

Same as Example 5, except that T is engaged in manufacturing.

The size-of-person test is satisfied because T's annual net sales are $10 million or more and P's annual net sales or total assets are $100 million or more.

P and T are obligated to comply with HSR reporting and waiting period requirements.

EXAMPLE 7

Same as Example 6, except that while P's annual net sales are $100 million or more, its total assets are very small (e.g., $5 million).

The size-of-person test is still satisfied because it is sufficient that *either* P's annual net sales or P's total assets are $100 million or more.

EXAMPLE 8

P buys T voting securities (with 9% of T's voting power) worth $51 million, thus satisfying the $50 million size-of-transaction test. The size-of-person test is also satisfied. No specific exemption applies.

HSR reporting and waiting period requirements apply.

However, if P has no intention to participate in T's basic business decisions, the transaction is exempt from HSR reporting and waiting period requirements because P holds 10% or less of T's voting power (even though P holds T voting securities with an HSR value exceeding $50 million).

EXAMPLE 9

Same as Example 8, except that the $51 million of T voting securities purchased by P constitutes more than 10% of T's voting power.

Even if P has no intention of participating in T's basic business decisions, the transaction is not exempt from HSR reporting and waiting period requirements because P holds more than 10% of T's voting power.

EXAMPLE 10

P pays $47 million cash for T's assets and assumes $4 million of T's liabilities, making the acquisition price for HSR purposes $51 million. The $50 million size-of-transaction test is satisfied.

EXAMPLE 11

Same as Example 10, except that instead of buying T's assets and assuming T's liabilities, P buys T's stock, paying $47 million in cash for 100% of T's stock. T remains liable for its $4 million of liabilities and intends to pay or refinance them in the ordinary course of its business. P makes no commitment to pay T's $4 million of liabilities. P's acquisition price (for HSR purposes) for 100% of T's stock is $47 million.

The $50 million size-of-transaction test is not satisfied.

EXAMPLE 12

P purchases T assets for $47 million cash plus a percentage of the T business's future revenues. The acquisition price is not determined for HSR purposes. P's board of directors determines in good faith that the acquired assets have an FV of $49 million as of a date 30 days before closing.

The $50 million size-of-transaction test is not satisfied.

¶1707.2   P1, P2, and P3 Form New Corporation, Partnership, or LLC

This section assumes for illustrative purposes that three persons (P1, P2, and P3) form a corporate Newco to acquire T. However, HSR applies in the same fashion where only two persons or more than three persons form corporate Newco.

¶1707.2.1   Partnership as New Entity

FTC takes the position that the formation of a partnership or the transfer of partnership interests is not the acquisition of a voting security or an asset. Therefore, such a transaction is generally not reportable, as it would be in the case of a corporate Newco.

Nevertheless, FTC has taken the position that a contribution of assets or voting securities to a new partnership ("New PS") in exchange for a partnership interest plus cash may, in some circumstances, be HSR reportable on the ground that in substance there has been a sale to New PS. FTC took this position in one transaction where (1) the contributing person received a minority interest in New PS (less than 10% interest in New PS in the particular transaction) and substantial cash consideration (equal to more than 90% of the contributed business in the particular transaction) and (2) the partnership structure may have been used for the purpose of avoiding HSR reporting.

The transfer of a partnership interest (even to a person who was not previously a partner) is a reportable event only if as a result of such transfer a single person obtains a 100% interest in the partnership, in which case the transaction is treated as an acquisition of the partnership's assets (including any voting securities in other entities owned by the partnership).

The distribution of assets (including voting securities in other entities) from a partnership to its partners, upon dissolution or otherwise, is covered by HSR as an acquisition by the partner from the partnership (or from the partnership's control person).

See ¶1707.3 for a description of the reporting obligations where a newly-created entity (whether corporate, partnership, or LLC) acquires T voting securities or T assets from a third person, i.e., from a person other than one of the newly created entity's owners.

¶1707.2.2   LLC as New Entity

The rules for a U.S. LLC are the same as set forth in ¶1707.2.1 for a partnership, except as follows:

The formation of a new U.S. LLC ("New LLC") and the contribution of voting securities or assets to New LLC by a member in exchange for a membership interest in New LLC are covered under HSR where:

(1) two or more separately controlled businesses are being contributed to New LLC, *and*

(2) New LLC is controlled after the transaction by at least one member, *and*

(3) the $200 million size-of-transaction test is met *or* both the $50 million size-of-transaction test and the size-of-person test are met.

In applying this rule:

- Control means the right to receive either 50% of LLC profits or 50% of LLC assets in the event of dissolution.
- The control member is treated as acquiring assets or voting securities contributed to the LLC by the other members (or, where there are two 50% control members, each is treated as acquiring the assets or voting securities contributed to the LLC by the other) for purposes of the size-of-person and size-of-transaction tests.

  This same rule applies where a business is contributed to a previously existing LLC. Where a new contribution is made to a previously existing LLC, the LLC is treated as if it were newly formed, so that a member who controls the LLC after the new contribution is treated as acquiring the voting securities or assets that it did not previously control.

Hence, New LLC's control person(s) must observe HSR reporting and waiting requirements where such person(s) is treated as acquiring (a) New LLC's assets or (b) voting securities in other entities contributed by other LLC members in an HSR reportable transaction.

¶1707.2.3   Corporation as New Entity

HSR applies to the formation of a new corporation ("NewCorp") by two or more persons (e.g., P1, P2, and P3) that do not have the same ultimate parent entity. When P1, P2, and P3 acquire NewCorp voting securities (upon NewCorp's formation), HSR reporting and waiting obligations for each of P1, P2, and P3 are determined separately. NewCorp itself never reports its own formation (but may report its acquisition of voting securities or assets from T as described at ¶1707.3).

For illustrative purposes, this section discusses only the HSR reporting obligation and waiting period of P1 (unless otherwise stated), but HSR is applied in the same fashion to P2 and P3.

HSR prohibits P1 from participating in the NewCorp formation, unless P1 has complied with reporting and waiting period requirements, if:

(1) P1's acquisition of NewCorp voting securities meets the $200 million size-of-transaction test (described at ¶1707.1.1 and applied to the formation of NewCorp at ¶1707.2.3), *or*

(2) P1's acquisition of NewCorp voting securities meets the $50 million size-of-transaction test (described at ¶1707.1.1 and applied to the formation of NewC-

orp at ¶1707.2.3.1) and P1, NewCorp, and *either* P2 *or* P3 meet the dollar criteria of the special "formation" size-of-transaction test (described at ¶1707.2.3.2),

(3) unless the transaction is covered by a specific exemption (described at ¶1707.1.4 and applied to the formation of NewCorp at ¶1707.2.3.1).

¶1707.2.3.1   Size-of-Transaction Test Applied to Formation of NewCorp

If P1's acquisition of NewCorp voting securities meets the $200 million size-of-transaction test, P1 must comply with the HSR reporting and waiting period requirements. If P1's acquisition of NewCorp voting securities does not meet the $200 million size-of-transaction test but meets the $50 million size-of-transaction test and P1, NewCorp, and *either* P2 or P3 meet the dollar criteria of the special "formation" size-of-person test, P1 must comply with HSR reporting and waiting period requirements.

The $50 million or $200 million size-of-transaction test is met by P1 if, after the acquisition, P1 will hold NewCorp voting securities with an HSR value exceeding the specified $50 million or $200 million threshold (including all NewCorp voting securities being acquired by P1, P1's ultimate parent entity, and all of their controlled entities). (The definitions of "ultimate parent entity" and "control" for the size-of-transaction test are the same as for the size-of-person test as described at ¶1707.1.2.)

As described at ¶1707.2.6, there is an exemption if P1, its ultimate parent entity, and their controlled entities hold 10% or less of NewCorp's voting power and have no intention of participating in NewCorp's basic business decisions.

Application of this test is described in ¶1707.1.1.

¶1707.2.3.2   Special Size-of-Person Test for Formation of NewCorp

If the special-formation size-of-person test is met, P1 must comply with the HSR reporting and waiting period requirements where the transaction meets the $50 million size-of-transaction test (even though the $200 million size-of-transaction test is not met).

The special-formation size-of-person test is met by P1 if at least *one* of the following size criteria is satisfied:

(1) NewCorp will have assets of $10 million or more, P1 has annual net sales or total assets of $100 million or more, and at least one of P2 or P3 has annual net sales or total assets of $10 million or more, or

(2) NewCorp will have assets of $100 million or more, P1 has annual net sales or total assets of $10 million or more, and at least one of P2 or P3 has annual net sales or total assets of $10 million or more.

In determining whether NewCorp will have total assets of $10 million or more or $100 million or more, NewCorp is treated as having received (1) all assets that

P1, P2, and P3 are contractually committed to contribute to NewCorp (even though the commitment provides for the transfer to take place in the future) and (2) all amounts that are borrowed by NewCorp if the borrowings are to be provided by or guaranteed by P1, P2, or P3 (but NewCorp borrowings are not counted if they are not made by or guaranteed by P1, P2, or P3).

Application of these criteria is described in ¶1707.1.2.

¶1707.2.4   Device for Avoidance

Any transaction or other device employed by P1 for the purpose of avoiding the obligation to report and wait before acquiring NewCorp voting securities is disregarded, and the obligation to report and wait is determined by applying HSR to the substance of the transaction.

¶1707.2.5   Waiting Period Start

If P1 and one or both of P2 or P3 are required to file in connection with NewCorp's formation, P1's waiting period does not begin to run until all those who are required to file have complied with HSR reporting requirements.

¶1707.2.6   Principal Exemptions

Even though a transaction is required to be reported under the tests described above in this ¶1707.2, the transaction is nevertheless exempt from HSR reporting and waiting if covered by one of the exemptions described at ¶1707.1.4.

¶1707.2.7   Examples of NewCorp Formation

EXAMPLE 1

P1 agrees to contribute $55 million cash and P2 and P3 each agrees to contribute $10 million cash to the formation of NewCorp in return for NewCorp voting securities which give each of P1, P2, and P3 one-third of NewCorp's voting power. In such case, P1 satisfies the $50 million size-of-transaction test because P1 is paying in excess of $50 million for NewCorp voting securities. For HSR purposes, NewCorp has total assets of $75 million (the total of all promised contributions to NewCorp, whether the actual contribution is made immediately or is deferred).

Further assume that P1's annual net sales or total assets are $100 million, P2's annual net sales or total assets are $10 million, and P3's annual net sales and total assets are less than $10 million. In such case, P1 satisfies the size-of-person and the size-of-transaction tests and must comply with HSR reporting and waiting requirements. P2 and P3 need not report or wait. NewCorp never needs to report its own formation.

EXAMPLE 2

Same as Example 1, except that P2 agrees to contribute $55 million and P1 and P3 each agrees to contribute $25 million to NewCorp. NewCorp has $105 million in total assets for HSR purposes. P2 satisfies the size-of-person criterion (i.e., annual net sales or total assets of $10 million when NewCorp has total assets of $100 million and another contributor has annual net sales or total assets of $10 million). P2 must report and wait.

P1 would have to report and wait if it contributed $50 million or more. P3 would not have to report and wait if it contributed $50 million or more, because P3 does not meet the size-of-person test.

EXAMPLE 3

Same as Example 1, except that P1 agrees to contribute to NewCorp $5 million, P2 agrees to contribute $55 million, and P3 agrees to contribute all the voting securities of S1, a corporation with total assets of $50 million. NewCorp has total assets of $110 million for HSR purposes (S1's assets plus the $60 million in cash from P1 and P2). P2 meets the size-of-person and $50 million size-of-transaction tests and must report and wait.

P1 does not satisfy the size-of-transaction test. P3 does not satisfy the size-of-person test.

EXAMPLE 4

NewCorp is formed by P1, P2, P3, and T's management for the purpose of acquiring T from T's sole shareholder, Bigco. No entity, together with its ultimate parent entity and their controlled entities, will acquire more than $50 million in "value" of NewCorp voting securities. No entity will satisfy the size-of-transaction test. The formation of Newco need not be reported and no waiting period applies. Newco's acquisition of T must be separately analyzed as described at ¶1707.3.

EXAMPLE 5

Same as Example 4, except that P1 pays in excess of $50 million for NewCorp voting securities. P1 meets the size-of-transaction test and must report and wait if the size-of-person test is also met by P1 and the transaction is not otherwise exempt.

¶1707.3 Newly Formed Corporate, Partnership, or LLC Acquisition Vehicle Acquires T Voting Securities or Assets

¶1707.3.1 Entity Controls New V

When an entity ("P") controls a newly formed corporate, partnership, or LLC acquisition vehicle ("New V"), any acquisition of voting securities or assets by New V is an acquisition by P and HSR applies as described at ¶1707.1 (except that where New V is a partnership or LLC, a contribution of voting securities or assets to New V by a New V partner or member is not an acquisition by New V—see ¶1707.2.1 and ¶1707.2.2).

¶1707.3.2 No Entity Controls New V

When New V is not controlled by another entity, HSR prohibits New V from acquiring T voting securities or assets, unless New V and T have complied with HSR reporting and waiting period requirements, if:

(1) the transaction meets the $200 million size-of-transaction test (described at ¶1707.3.3), or

(2) the transaction meets the $50 million size-of-transaction test (described at ¶1707.3.3) and New V and T both meet the dollar criteria of the size-of-person test (described at ¶1707.3.4),

(3) unless the transaction is covered by a specific exemption (described at ¶1707.3.6).

¶1707.3.3 Size-of-Transaction Test

If the $200 million size-of-transaction test is met, New V and T must comply with the HSR reporting and waiting period requirements. If the $200 million size-of-transaction test is not met but the $50 million size-of-transaction test is met, New V and T must comply with the HSR reporting and waiting period requirements only if the size-of-person test described at ¶1707.3.4 is met.

The $50 million or $200 million size-of-transaction test is met for purposes of ¶1707.3.2 if New V (including any entity controlled by New V) after the acquisition will hold at least one of the following:

(1) T *voting securities* with an "HSR value" exceeding the specified $50 million or $200 million threshold (including all T voting securities being acquired or then owned by New V). (The definition of "HSR value" for voting securities is described at ¶¶1707.1.1.1, 1707.1.1.2, and 1707.1.1.5.)

As described at ¶1707.3.5, there is an exemption if New V holds 10% or less of T's voting power and has no intention of participating in T's basic business decisions.

(2) T *assets* with an "HSR value" exceeding the specified $50 million or $200 million threshold, including any assets acquired within 180 days before the current acquisition agreement or letter of intent was executed. (The definition of "HSR value" for assets is described at ¶1707.1.1.3.)

(3) any combination of (1) and (2) with an aggregate HSR value exceeding the specified $50 million or $200 million threshold.

This test does not refer to a New V ultimate parent entity because the entire discussion in ¶1707.3.2 and this ¶1707.3.3 assumes a New V that is not controlled by any other entity. See ¶1707.3.1 where New V is controlled by another entity.

Application of these criteria is described in ¶1707.1.1.

¶1707.3.4 Size-of-Person Test

If the size-of-person test is met, New V and T must comply with the HSR reporting and waiting period requirements where the transaction meets the $50 million size-of-transaction test (even though the $200 million size-of-transaction test is not met).

The size-of-person test is satisfied for purposes of ¶1707.3.2 if at least *one* of the following size criteria is met:

(1) T or its ultimate parent is engaged in manufacturing and has annual net sales or total assets of at least $10 million, and New V has total assets of at least $100 million.

(2) T or its ultimate parent is not engaged in manufacturing and has total assets of at least $10 million, and New V has total assets of at least $100 million.

(3) T or its ultimate parent (regardless of its business) has annual net sales or total assets of at least $100 million, and New V has total assets of at least $10 million.

The test described in this ¶1707.3.4 does not refer to a New V ultimate parent entity because the entire discussion in ¶¶1707.3.2 and 1707.3.4 assumes a New V that is *not* controlled by any other entity. If New V were controlled by another entity (e.g., P1), P1 would be treated as the acquiring entity (as described in ¶1707.3.1) and ¶1707.1 would apply to P1 (rather than the test described in this ¶1707.3.4 applying to New V).

Application of these criteria is described in ¶1707.1.2.

If (as is generally the case) New V is newly formed with no regularly prepared balance sheet when it acquires T, New V's total assets for HSR purposes are determined as follows:

(1)   all assets held by New V (including any entity controlled by New V) at the time of the acquisition, including all cash provided by lenders or equity investors,
(2)   less all cash used as consideration or for incidental expenses in connection with New V's acquisition of T,
(3)   less all T securities held by New V.

¶1707.3.5   Device for Avoidance

Any transaction or other device employed by New V for the purpose of avoiding the obligation to report and wait before acquiring T voting securities or assets is disregarded, and the obligation to report and wait is determined by applying HSR to the substance of the transaction.

¶1707.3.6   Principal Exemptions

New V's acquisition of T voting stock or assets is exempt for purposes of ¶1707.3.2 if the acquisition meets one of the exemptions described at ¶1707.1.4.

¶1707.3.7   Examples of Acquisitions by New V

EXAMPLE 1

New V is a new corporation formed for the purpose of acquiring T from Bigco for $170 million, using $70 million of equity capital contributed by P1, P2, and P3 plus $94 million of borrowings.

Before the acquisition Bigco satisfies the $100 million size-of-person criteria. New V is not controlled by any other entity, has no sales, and has no regularly prepared balance sheet. At the time New V purchases T from Bigco, New V has $70 million of equity capital and $94 million of borrowings. New V uses $170 million to acquire T from Bigco, pays $5 million incidental expenses related thereto, and has $9 million left over.

For HSR purposes, New V has $9 million in assets at closing ($164 million less $170 million and $5 million), does not meet the size-of-person test, and need not report the acquisition of T or comply with any waiting period.

EXAMPLE 2

Same as Example 1, except that one of the contributors to the New V formation has transferred to New V a $2 million factory, which New V will transfer to Bigco as part of the acquisition price for T. The $2 million factory cannot be subtracted from New V's assets, and New V therefore has total assets of $11 million for HSR purposes ($9 million in equity and borrowings not expended to acquire T or pay incidental expenses related thereto plus the $2 million factory).

Since New V has more than $10 million in HSR assets (while T's ultimate parent Bigco meets the $100 million size criteria), New V and Bigco must report the acquisition of T from Bigco and comply with the waiting period requirement.

EXAMPLE 3

Same as Example 1, except that New V also has arranged a separate loan to provide working capital after the acquisition. If New V borrows (i.e., takes down) $2 million on this loan at or prior to closing, such $2 million is an asset of New V for HSR purposes, New V has excess cash totaling $11 million at closing, and New V satisfies the $10 million size-of-person test. New V and Bigco must report the acquisition of T from Bigco and comply with the waiting period requirement.

The result would be the same if New V's additional loan (on which New V borrowed (i.e., took down) $2 million at or prior to closing the T acquisition) was for the purpose of refinancing T's debt, which was not part of the consideration for New V's acquisition of T voting securities or assets.

If New V does not borrow (i.e., take down) any amount on this separate loan facility until after the closing of the T acquisition, the result would be the same as Example 1, i.e., no reporting and no waiting.

¶1707.4   *Reporting Obligations*

(1) The HSR report form must be filed with FTC and Department of Justice ("DOJ") on behalf of the "ultimate parent entities" of both P and T. (If New V is the acquiring entity, "P" means New V for purposes of this section. If P1, P2, and

P3 are forming NewCorp, "P" means P1, P2, or P3 for purposes of this section.) If T voting securities are being acquired from a non-controlling T shareholder, it is T and not the shareholder that must report.

(2) P must pay a filing fee for each reportable acquisition:

Fee	Transaction value
$ 45,000	less than $100 million
$125,000	at least $100 million but less than $500 million
$280,000	$500 million or more

(3) Both P and T must submit an affidavit stating that a contract, letter of intent, or agreement in principle has been executed (a copy of which must also be included) and stating their good faith intention to close, except if P is acquiring voting securities from a non-controlling T shareholder.

(4) If P is acquiring T voting securities from a non-controlling T shareholder (e.g., tender offers and open-market purchases, including such purchases after which P ends up in control of T), P must submit an affidavit stating, among other things, (a) that P has a good faith intention to acquire sufficient T voting securities to satisfy the size-of-transaction test and (b) that P has given T notice of P's intention.

(5) P also must state on the form (and notify T if voting securities are being purchased from a non-controlling T shareholder) whether P is acquiring more than $50 million, $100 million or more, $500 million or more, 25% if greater than $1 billion, or 50% of T's voting securities and assets. P then may make acquisitions exceeding the reported threshold (but less than the next higher threshold) for one year from the expiration of the waiting period (described in ¶1707.5). If the reported threshold is to be crossed after one year has elapsed, or if a threshold higher than that initially reported is to be crossed, a new filing is required and a new waiting period must be observed.

(6) The HSR report form requires the submission of substantial data regarding the transaction, the identity and business structure of both P and T, the lines of business of P and T, and any competitive overlaps, including the following:

(a)   a description of the acquisition, the parties, and the assets or securities to be acquired;

(b)   subject to certain dollar and percentage thresholds, identification of all entities controlled by P's and T's ultimate parent entities, identification of minority shareholders of P, T, and controlled entities, and identification of the shareholdings of the reporting entities in companies that are not controlled (all of which must be furnished for both foreign and domestic entities);

(c)   copies of acquisition agreements, SEC filings, and annual reports of the reporting company and unconsolidated controlled entities;

(d)   revenue data by North American Industry Classification System ("NAICS") classification for all of P's lines of business and for the lines of business to be acquired from T;

(e)   with respect to any NAICS classification in which revenues are derived *both* by T's acquired lines of business and by P, P's ultimate parent or any entity controlled by P's ultimate parent, additional geographic information (including, for manufactured products, identification of states where the products were resold by the reporting person's customers);

(f)   data on P's domestic acquisitions in the last five years in those NAICS classifications from which both T and P, P's ultimate parent, or any entity controlled by P's ultimate parent derived revenues (subject to certain dollar and percentage thresholds); and

(g)   copies of all studies, surveys, analyses, and reports that were (i) prepared by or for any officer or director (or person exercising similar functions in an unincorporated entity) of either party to the transaction, including any controlling parent or other controlled entity, (ii) prepared for the purpose of evaluating the transaction, and (iii) addressing market shares, competition, competitors, markets, and potential for sales growth or expansion (either geographic or with new products).

With respect to item (g) above, FTC takes the expansive position that an "analysis" includes any interoffice memorandum, handwritten note, correspondence, computer file, slide presentation, or board minutes, if such document contains even a brief evaluation or analysis of the acquisition's competitive advantages, even where such document contains substantial other information not responsive to item (g). FTC further takes the position that failure to include any such analysis as part of the HSR report renders the filing deficient. As a result, the HSR waiting period restarts when the omitted analysis is subsequently submitted, unless FTC in its discretion waives a restart. Moreover, in 1996, 1999, and 2001 cases FTC—signaling its intent to enforce vigorously the obligation to submit all such analyses—imposed approximately $3 million to $4 million civil penalties in each case when FTC subsequently discovered (after consummation of the P-T acquisition) that P had failed to submit several analyses, even though in one of the cases P's failure apparently was the result of a careless internal search and not a deliberate decision to disregard HSR Rules.[4]

Once the filing is made, it need not be updated (e.g., for a market study or new agreement prepared thereafter), but additional information may be requested by FTC or DOJ.

(7) Even when T is not a party to the transaction (e.g., when P is acquiring a non-controlling or controlling block of T stock, including a tender offer, whether or not hostile), T (or its ultimate parent entity) is required to file the necessary information.

¶1707.5   Waiting Period

(1) For cash tender offers, the waiting period expires at 11:59 p.m. Eastern time) 15 days after FTC and DOJ receive completed report forms from the acquiring person (along with the required fee).

---

[4] The 1996 case dealt with Automatic Data Processing, Inc.'s acquisition of AutoInfo, Inc., the 1999 case dealt with Blackstone Capital Partners' acquisition of Prime Succession, Inc., and the 2001 case dealt with Hearst Corporation's acquisition of Medi-Span, Inc.

(2) For all other types of acquisitions, the waiting period expires at 11:59 p.m. Eastern time) 30 days after FTC and DOJ receive completed report forms from all parties required to report (along with the required fee).

(3) If FTC or DOJ requests additional data with which to investigate potential substantive antitrust concerns, the waiting period is extended until 11:59 p.m. Eastern time) 10 days (in the case of a cash tender offer) or 30 days (in the case of another type of acquisition) after the additional data is supplied.

(4) If the waiting period expires on a weekend or holiday, the waiting period is extended to the following business day.

(5) Early termination of the waiting period may be requested, and is normally granted, if requested by either P or T in the absence of any substantive antitrust issue. The fact that early termination has been granted is published in the Federal Register and listed on the FTC Internet website.

¶1707.6   Noncompliance Penalties

A party failing to comply with the HSR reporting and waiting period requirements is subject to a civil penalty of up to $11,000 per day during the period of non-compliance.

Table of Internal Revenue Code Sections

References are to sections.

Table of Internal Revenue Code Sections

Table of Internal Revenue Code Sections

Table of Internal Revenue Code Sections

Table of Internal Revenue Code Sections

Table of Internal Revenue Code Sections

Table of Internal Revenue Code Sections

Table of Internal Revenue Code Sections

Table of Internal Revenue Code Sections

Table of Internal Revenue Code Sections

Table of Treasury Regulations

Table of Treasury Regulations

Table of Treasury Regulations

Table of Treasury Regulations

Table of Treasury Regulations

Table of Treasury Regulations

Table of Treasury Regulations

Table of Treasury Regulations

Table of Treasury Regulations

Table of Treasury Rulings

References are to sections.

Table of Treasury Rulings

Table of Treasury Rulings

Table of Treasury Rulings

GENERAL COUNSEL'S MEMORANDA

Table of Treasury Rulings

Table of Treasury Rulings

Table of Treasury Rulings

Table of Securities Laws

References are to sections.

Table of Cases

Table of Cases

Table of Cases

Table of Cases

Table of Cases

Index

References are to sections.

A, 101
A reorganizations
  additional requirements, 801.3
  attribution rules, 801.4.4
  drop down, 801.1
  flexibility, 801.2
  shareholder receiving only boot, 801.4.2
  shareholder receiving only P stock,
    801.4.1
  shareholder receiving only stock/boot,
    801.4.3
  step-transaction doctrine, 801.4.5
  T-into-P merger, 801.5
  tax rates, 801.4.6
  treatment of T's shareholders, 801.4
Accelerated gain recognition, 203.7
Accounting
  APB 25. *See* APB Opinion 25
  FASB 123. *See* FASB 123
  generally, 1703
  pooling. *See* Pooling of interest
    accounting
  purchase. *See* Purchase accounting
  recap, 1703.7.6
  stock-based kicker to lenders, for, 1705
  stock-based management compensation,
    for, 1704
  tax rates, contrasted, 1703.1
Accredited investor, 1702.2.8.2
Accumulated adjustments account (AAA),
  1103.8
Acquisition agreements
  closing conditions, 1702.3.3
  covenants, 1702.3.2
  deductible/threshold/ceiling, 1702.3.1.5
  escrow/set-off/security interest,
    1702.3.1.6
  knowledge/materiality, 1702.3.1.3
  public T, 1702.3.1.7
  representations/warranties, 1702.3.1
  sample agreements
    asset acquisition, 1702.5.9
    generally, 1702.3.4
    merger, 1702.6.9
    stock acquisition, 1702.4.9.5
Acquisition expenses. *See* Expenses of

taxable acquisitions
Active trade or business, 1004.1, 1004.5
Adequate consideration defense, 1706.3,
  1706.3.3
Adjusted grossed-up basis (AGUB), 205.7
ADSP formula, 205.5
  MADSP formula and, 206.1.6
Advertising expenses, 402.16.1
Advisory fee, 402.5.3, 402.10.1
Affiliated group, 1205.2.1
Affiliated group definition, 211.1
Affiliated group exception, 1206.1.2.1
AFR, 101
Aggregation rules
  disqualified distributions, 1009.5
  5% shareholders, 1208.1.7.2
  $1 million executive compensation
    deduction limit, 1506.1.5.1
AGUB, 205.7
AHYDO
  allocation of OID made before
    maturity, 1303.3.2.2
  conclusion, 1303.4
  contingent interest, 1303.3.1.8
  corporate issuer, 1303.3.1.9
  disqualified portion of OID, 1303.2.2.3,
    1303.3.2.1
  DRD for corporate holder, 1303.2.2.4,
    1303.2.2.5, 1303.3.2.4
  E&P rules, 1303.2.2.5, 1303.3.2.5
  effective date, 1303.3.4.1
  four-factor test, 1303.2.1.1
  grandfather rules, 1303.3.4.2
  issues/problems, 1303.3.1
  more than five year term, 1303.3.1.2
  not limited to LBOs/subordinated
    debentures, 1303.3.1.1
  OID, undefined, 1303.3.2.3
  payment of interest with borrowed
    money, 1303.3.3.2
  PIK interest treated as OID, 1303.2.1.2,
    1303.3.1.6
  post-issuance conduct, 1303.3.3.1
  QSI, 1303.2.2.3, 1303.3.2.1
  significant OID, 1303.2.1.3, 1303.3.1.5
  treatment of holder, 1303.2.2.2

Index

Index

Index

Index

Index

Index

Index

Index

Index

Index